Exchange 2000 Server: The Complete Reference

About theAuthors

Scott Schnoll (MCSE, MCT) is the Product Support Manager for TNT Software, developers of monitoring and management applications for Windows NT and Windows 2000. Scott is a regular contributor to *Exchange & Outlook Magazine*, and an active participant in a variety of Windows and Exchange-related communities. He has received Microsoft's Most Valuable Professional (MVP) award for the last three years in a row.

Bill English (MCSE, MCT, CTT) is the Senior Exchange Technologist for MindSharp Learning Center in Minneapolis, where he provides training on Exchange 2000 Server. He is the author of *Exchange 2000 Server Administration: A Beginner's Guide* and has worked as a System Administrator and consultant for some of Minnesota's leading companies. He is a contributor to several magazines and is a regular speaker at conferences.

Nick Cavalancia (MCSE, MCT, MCNE, MCNI) is Director of Training and Consulting for Comsphere (www.comsphere.com), where he specializes in high-end Exchange 2000 and Windows 2000 infrastructure designs. Nick has worked as a Microsoft and Novell trainer, and a consultant for large scale Exchange 5.x and Exchange 2000 projects supporting 2,000 to 150,000 users. He is an editor of and contributor to numerous books, and also speaks regularly at conferences including the Microsoft Exchange Conference 2000. He is the coauthor of *Exchange 2000 Server Administration: A Beginner's Guide.*

Exchange 2000 Server: The Complete Reference

Scott Schnoll,
Bill English &
Nick Cavalancia

Osborne/**McGraw-Hill**
New York Chicago San Francisco
Lisbon London Madrid Mexico City
Milan New Delhi San Juan
Seoul Singapore Sydney Toronto

Osborne/**McGraw-Hill**
2600 Tenth Street
Berkeley, California 94710
U.S.A.

To arrange bulk purchase discounts for sales promotions, premiums, or fund-raisers, please contact Osborne/**McGraw-Hill** at the above address. For information on translations or book distributors outside the U.S.A., please see the International Contact Information page immediately following the index of this book.

Exchange 2000 Server: The Complete Reference

1234567890 CUS CUS 01987654321

ISBN 0-07-212739-2

Publisher
Brandon A. Nordin

Vice President & Associate Publisher
Scott Rogers

Senior Acquisitions Editor
Jane Brownlow

Project Editor
Lisa Wolters-Broder

Acquisitions Coordinator
Ross Doll

Technical Editors
Andy Webb, Missy Koslosky, Ed Woodrick, Wesley Peace, Ed Crowley

Copy Editors
Lunaea Weatherstone, Sudha Putnam, Carl Wikander

Proofreaders
Sally Englefried, Susie Elkind, Cheryl Abel

Indexer
Rebecca Plunkett

Computer Designers
Carie Abrew, Michelle Galicia

Illustrator
Alex Putney

Series Deign
Peter F. Hancik

This book was composed with Corel VENTURA™ Publisher.

For Karen, Devon, and Ava - SS

To Kathy, my lovely wife. You are simply the best. - BE

To Jenay-my wife, my confidant, and my best friend. - NC

Table of Contents

Acknowledgements xvii
Introduction xxi

Part I
Exchange 2000 Server Basics

1 Exchange 2000 Server Summary 3
Introduction to Microsoft Exchange 2000 Server 4
Exchange 2000 Flavors and Features 5
Administration and Management of Exchange 2000 12
User Management Concepts 18
Exchange 2000 Clients and Client Support 21
Summary 25

2 Active Directory Summary 27
Overview of Active Directory 28
What Is Active Directory? 29
Understanding Active Directory 30
The Active Directory Structure 37
Active Directory Security 50
Summary 53

3 Exchange 2000 Directory 55
The New Exchange Directory 56
Exchange Directory Objects 58
Global Address List 67
Exchange 2000 Directory Data 67
Replicating Additional Attributes to the Global Catalog 76
Address List Services 80
Offline Address Lists 84
Exchange 2000 and Active Directory Security 86
Summary 89

4 Exchange 2000 Architecture 91
Overview of the Exchange 2000 Architecture 92
Message Flow in Exchange 2000 97
The Web Storage System 110
Exchange 2000 Event Sinks 113
Administration and Routing Models 114
Summary 120

5 Exchange 2000 Public Folders 121
Introduction to Exchange 2000 Server Public Folders 122
Public Folder Architecture 124
Creating Public Folders 129
Public Folder Replication 140
Public Folder Referrals 144
Public Folder Security 146
Public Folder Store Policies 151
Internet Newsgroups 154
Summary 160

Part II

Administering Exchange 2000 Server

6 Installing Exchange 2000 Server 163
Installation Requirements 164
Hardware 164
Software 168
Windows 2000 and Active Directory Considerations 168
Installation Considerations 169
Exchange 2000 Installation Types 171
Changes Made by Setup 189
Summary 194

7 Upgrading and Co-existing with Exchange 5.5 195
Planning and Design 197
Network Considerations 197

Windows 2000 Considerations 202
Active Directory Considerations 203
Active Directory Connector 204
Legacy Exchange Pre-Installation Requirements 224
Choosing an Upgrade Path 230
Performing an In-Place Upgrade (Step-by-Step) 237
Upgrading an Exchange 5.5 Cluster 244
Mixed Mode vs. Native Mode 246
Summary 251

8 Administering Recipients 253
Preliminary Administration Steps 254
Exchange System Manager 254
ADSI Edit 254
Active Directory Administration Tool 255
Active Directory Schema 255
Installing Administrative Tools 256
Active Directory Users and Computers 256
Types of Recipients 256
Using the Exchange Tasks Wizard 257
Creating Mailbox-Enabled Users 257
Creating Mail-Enabled Users 259
Creating Mail-Enabled Contacts 260
Creating Mail-Enabled Groups 260
Creating a Mail-Enabled Public Folder 262
Administering Mail-Enabled Accounts 263
Mailbox-Enabled Users 263
Mail-Enabled Users 266
Mail-Enabled Contacts 267
Mail-Enabled Groups 268
Mail-Enabled Public Folders 269
Making Bulk Changes to the Directory 270
LDIFDE 270
CSVDE 277
Windows Script Host 278
Recovering a Mailbox 280
Configuring Deleted Mailbox Retention Times 280
Summary 281

9 Managing Servers 283
Using Exchange System Manager 284
Working with Administrative Views 286
Creating New Consoles from the ESM Snap-In 287
Administrative Groups 288
Planning for Administrative Groups 288
Creating Administrative Groups 290
Assigning Permissions to Administrative Groups 292

Routing Groups 296
Planning for Routing Groups 297
Connecting Routing Groups 299
Link State 313
Link State Architecture 314
Routing Group Master 314
Viewing Link State Information 315
Routing Messages in Exchange 2000 315
Routing and Selection Process 316
Working with a Failed Link 318
Address Lists 320
Default Address Lists in Exchange 2000 Server 320
Custom Address Lists 320
Offline Address Lists 320
Creating Address Lists 321
Securing Address Lists for Hosting 324
The Recipient Update Service 325
Creating and Managing Recipient Policies 326
Creating a Recipient Policy 326
System Policies 327
Summary 330

10 Managing Protocols 331
Exchange 2000 Protocol Management 332
Management Permissions 332
Protocol Virtual Servers 332
Starting, Stopping, and Pausing 335
Virtual Servers 335
Managing SMTP 336
General 336
Messages 338
Delivery 340
Managing SMTP Queues 343
Managing Current SMTP Sessions 345
Securing SMTP 345
Access Control 346
Secure Communications 346
Certificate 346
Communication 346
Connection Control 347
Relay Restrictions 347
Managing POP3 347
General 348
Message Format 348
Managing Current POP3 Sessions 350
Securing POP3 350
Access Control 350
Secure Communications 350
Connection Control 351

Managing IMAP4 351
General 352
Message Format 353
Managing Current IMAP4 Sessions 353
Securing IMAP4 353
Access 353
Managing HTTP 353
Securing HTTP 354
Anonymous Access and Authentication Control 355
IP Address and Domain Name Restrictions 356
Secure Communications 356
Managing NNTP 357
General 358
Settings 358
Managing Newsgroups 360
Managing Feeds 361
Managing Expiration Policies 361
Managing NNTP Virtual Directories 362
Managing Current NNTP Sessions 363
Securing NNTP 363
Securing an NNTP Virtual Server 363
Securing a Newsgroup 363
Securing a Virtual Directory 364
Summary 364

11 The Exchange 2000 Store 365
Exchange 2000 Storage Architecture 366
Multiple Stores and Storage Groups 367
Store Databases 368
Transaction Logging 372
The Exchange Installable File System 376
Full-Text Indexing 378
Web Store Events 382
Managing Exchange 2000 Storage 383
Creating Storage Groups 383
Creating Stores 385
Moving Stores and Transaction Logs 394
Deleting Stores and Storage Groups 396
Summary 398

12 Backup, Restore, and Disaster Recovery 399
Where Exchange 2000 Keeps Data 400
Active Directory 400
Databases and Transaction Logs 401
IIS Metabase 402
Exchange Software 403
IM, SRS, and KMS Database Files 404
Third-Party Applications 404

Types of Backups ... 404
Offline Backups ... 405
Online Backups ... 407
Mailbox-Level Backups ... 410
Backup Strategies ... 411
Restoring Exchange 2000 ... 412
Restore Strategies ... 412
Offline Restores ... 413
Online Restores ... 413
Restoring to an Alternate Server ... 416
Restoring a Single Mailbox ... 417
Backup Applications ... 419
Windows 2000 Backup ... 419
Third-Party Backup Applications ... 425
Disaster Recovery ... 426
Pre-Flight Checklist ... 426
Installing Windows 2000 ... 427
Restoring the System Drive ... 428
Restoring the System State ... 428
Installing Exchange 2000 in Disaster Recovery Mode ... 428
Restoring Service Databases ... 428
Best Practices ... 429
Summary ... 430

Part III

Exchange 2000 Server Collaboration

13 Exchange 2000 Clients ... 433
Legacy Clients ... 434
Exchange Client ... 434
Outlook 97 ... 435
Outlook 98 ... 435
Existing Client: Outlook 2000 ... 436
Outlook 2000 Functionality ... 436
Configuring Outlook for Exchange 2000 ... 437
Future Clients: Outlook 2002 ... 443
Messaging Enhancements ... 443
Calendaring and Scheduling Enhancements ... 446
Security Enhancements ... 448
Mailbox Cleanup ... 449
Internet Clients ... 450
Outlook Express ... 450
Outlook Web Access ... 451
Unix-Based Clients ... 452
Macintosh Clients ... 453
Choosing the Right Client ... 453
Summary ... 454

14 Outlook Web Access 455
Introducing Outlook Web Access 2000 456
New Architecture 459
Installing and Configuring Outlook Web Access 462
Virtual Servers 465
Deploying Outlook Web Access 470
Outlook Web Access Security 473
Customizing Outlook Web Access 480
Ongoing Maintenance 482
Summary 483

15 Exchange 2000 Conferencing Server 485
Introduction to Exchange 2000 Conferencing Server 486
Conferencing Server Architecture 487
Conference Management Service 487
Data Conferencing Provider 488
Video Conferencing Provider 488
Conference Calendar Mailboxes 488
Conferencing Standards 489
Planning for Exchange 2000 Conferencing Services 495
Software Planning 496
Hardware Planning 496
Conferencing Server Placement 497
Planning for the Multipoint Control Unit (MCU) 499
Planning for the Conference Calendar Mailbox 499
Planning for Conferencing Resources 499
Planning for Multicasting and Routers 500
Naming Conventions 501
Conferencing across a firewall 501
Best Practices in planning for ECS 501
Installing and Configuring Exchange Conferencing Services 502
Installing Exchange 2000 Conferencing 502
Troubleshooting Failed Installations 504
Configuring Exchange 2000 Conferencing Server 505
Configuring Technology Providers 509
Configuring the T.120 MCU 511
Adding a Resource 512
Client Configuration 515
Configuring Internet-Based Clients 517
Scheduling a Conference 517
Joining a Conference 518
Working with the Conferencing Client 520
Sharing Applications 522
Summary 523

16 Exchange 2000 Instant Messaging 525
What Is Instant Messaging? 526
Exchange 2000 Instant Messaging Services 527

Planning Your Instant Messaging Infrastructure 534
Windows 2000 Considerations 535
Managing Instant Messaging Services 540
Instant Messaging Security 546
Monitoring Instant Messaging Servers 550
Future of Instant Messaging 551
Summary 552

17 Chat Services 553
Introduction to Chat Services 554
Chat Service Architecture 554
Chat Commands 555
Chat Servers 564
Chat Clients 564
Operators 564
Channels 565
Installing Chat Service (Step-by-Step) 566
Administering Chat Service 566
Managing Communities 568
Managing Channels 571
User Bans 580
Network Security 584
Upgrading Exchange 5.5 Chat Service 584
Managing Chat Clients 585

Part IV

Exchange 2000 Server Security

18 Securing Exchange 2000 Server 593
Internal Security 594
Domain Security 594
Exchange 2000 Shared Folders 595
Mailbox Access 595
Protocol Access 602
Administrative Access 604
External Security 606
Securing Protocol Access 607
Anti-Virus Software 610
Firewalls 614
Putting It All Together 620
Summary 622

19 Public Key Infrastructure Services 623
PKI Security 624
Message Encryption 625
Digital Signatures 626

Certificates and Certification Authorities 626
CA Hierarchies 626
Windows 2000 Certificate Services 627
Certificate Services CA Types 628
Installing Certificate Services 629
Managing Certificates 633
Key Management Service 633
Pre-Installation Issues 634
Installing KMS 634
KMS Management 639
Enrolling Users 641
Completing the Enrollment 645
Using E-mail Security 649
Recovering and Revoking Keys 650
Summary 650

Part V

Exchange 2000 Server Scalability and Reliability

20 Clustering Exchange 2000 655
What Is a Cluster? 656
High Availability 657
Fault Tolerance 657
What Problems Does Clustering Solve? 659
Cluster Terminology 660
Windows 2000 Clustering 662
Cluster-Aware vs. Cluster-Unaware 665
Exchange 2000 Support for Windows 2000 Clustering 667
Installing Exchange 2000 in a Cluster 669
Installing the Second Server in the Cluster 672
Installing and Configuring Exchange 2000 in a Cluster 673
Creating an Exchange 2000 Virtual Server in a Cluster 676
Administering an Exchange 2000 Virtual Server 681
Configuring Resources 682
Configuring Resource Groups 683
Cluster.exe 683
Network Load Balancing 687
How NLB Works 687
Configuring NLB 689
Front-End/Back-End Configuration 692
Clustering Caveats 695
Clustering in Mixed-Mode Environments 695
Configuration Issues 695
Exchange Cluster Administration 697
Managing Services in a Cluster 697

Exchange Cluster Recovery 698
Recovering a Single Cluster Node 698
Recovering an Entire Exchange 2000 Cluster 698
Summary 699

21 Performance Tuning and Monitoring 701
Tuning Exchange 2000 702
Self-Tuning Enhancements 702
Hardware Selection and Tuning 703
Processors 704
Memory 705
Network Interface 705
Disk Subsystem 705
Tuning Exchange 2000 Components 706
Exchange 2000 ESE Stores and Transaction Logs 707
Message Transfer Agent 713
Active Directory and Optimization 716
Active Directory Connector 718
Monitoring Exchange 2000 Health and Performance 719
Proactive Monitoring Techniques 719
Server Monitor Tools in Exchange 2000 727
Logging Diagnostic Data 732
Enabling Protocol Logging 733

Part VII
Appendixes

A Technology Primer—What Is WebDAV? 739
Technology Primer: What Is WebDAV? 740
Overview of WebDAV Functions 741
Extending HTTP 1.1 743
The Future of WebDAV 748
Summary 748

B Knowledge Management 751
Overview of Knowledge Management 752
Information as an Asset 752
What Is Information? 753
What Is Knowledge? 755
Knowledge Management Systems 757
Workflow 760
Customer Relationship Management 764
Microsoft Knowledge Management Offerings 765
Summary 770

Index 771

Acknowledgments

Writing any book is a challenge, especially a book on a complex piece of software like Exchange 2000. Many more people than the three of us whose names are on the cover of this book were involved in its production.

I would like to thank all of the folks at Osborne/McGraw-Hill (OMH) who worked long hours for more than a year to produce this book. This book would not be here without the steadfast efforts of Jane Brownlow, Senior Acquisitions Editior for OMH. Despite constant setbacks, Jane persevered to see this project through to the end. So Jane, now that this is over, what's our next book? <g> I'd also like to thank Lisa Wolters-Broder, the Project Editor on this book, and Tara Davis and Ross Doll, Acquisitions Coordinators at OMH, and Copy Editors Lunaea Weatherstone, Sudha Putnam, and Carl Wikander.

Special thanks goes to the great technical editors on this book, fellow Microsoft MVPs Andy Webb, Ed Woodrick, Wesley Peace, Ed Crowley, and Missy Koslosky. Their depth of knowledge, technical acumen, and real-world experiences helped shape and guide this book into reality.

I'm deeply in debt to my fellow authors, Bill English and Nick Cavalancia, who stepped up to their respective plates in more ways than one. Bill and Nick both signed on late in this project, and despite looming deadlines, they jumped in without fear and did a stellar job. Gentlemen, it has been an honor to have written with you. I hope I haven't put you off with my zeal for perfection, as I would welcome the opportunity to write with you both again.

On a more personal note, I would like to thank some friends who, whether they realize it or not, contributed to the making of this book. First, I would like to thank my MVP Buddy and friend, John Eddy, a Product Support Engineer at Microsoft. John, you happily researched even my dumbest questions (Do you really need to restart ESM after turning admin groups on and off? <g>). Thank you for your professional assistance and your friendship. I would also like to thank Janni Clark, Program Manager for the MVP Program at Microsoft. Janni, this book would not be here without your unrelenting encouragement and steadfast belief in me. You are an amazing friend! Thank you for your kindness, generosity, and support.

Finally, I'd like to thank my family. My wife, Karen, endured countless hours of watching me in front of a bunch of computers, building them up, tearing them down, configuring them, taking screen captures, and then writing it all down. Honey, thank you for your patience, your support, and your constant (and sometimes successful) efforts to get me out of my chair and into the real world. ILY! I'd also like to thank my stepdaughter, Devon, the other writer in our family, for thinking it's really cool that my name is on this book. Sorry for all of the missed soccer games, Devon! Lastly, I'd like to thank my daughter, Ava, for making me the happiest, most proudest dad in the world!

Scott Schnoll
Portland, Oregon

I would like to acknowledge the outstanding job my two coauthors, Scott and Nick, did on this book. Both of you have a depth of understanding of the Exchange 2000 Server platform that is more than impressive. My only hope is to try to keep up with you two!

I'd also like to thank Neil Salkind, my agent at Studio B. As always, Neil, you demonstrated professionalism and service that is unmatched in the publishing industry. Every time we work out a new book contract, I'm impressed with how you get it done.

Here in Minnesota, I'd like to thank Dave Fletcher and Mary Texer at MindSharp Learning Center for giving me some time off from the training classroom to help write this book. You two, along with Jim Ginther, have helped create one of the best CTECs I've ever worked for. Thanks for having me on the MindSharp team.

Finally, I'd like to thank Jesus Christ, who gave me the talent and opportunity to coauthor this book and without whom I would be lost forever.

Bill English
Maple Grove, Minnesota

I want to thank my coauthor Scott, who spent so much time conversing with me in helping to make my contribution to this book even better. Additional thanks to my other coauthor, Bill, who acted as my sounding board when writing on various topics. Without the two of you, my contribution to this book would not have been what it is. Thanks so much!

I also want to thank my family, who were a major source of encouragement throughout the writing process. You are my cheering section - thanks so much for that. To my son Colin, who begged to go to Chuck E. Cheese's all throughout my work on this book (and we did go the week I finished!): thank you for keeping my eyes fixed on the important things in life. You are my personal "Daddy, you're working too much" alarm!

To my friends at the Monroe County School District who love to have "author signing" parties for me - your friendship is a treasure (and I expect apple-filled donuts this time! <g>).

And last but certainly not least, I want to thank God, who gave me the opportunity, desire, and ability to work on this book.

Nick Cavalancia
Plantation, Florida

Introduction

At 9:19 A.M. on August 31, 2000, the next generation of Microsoft Exchange—Exchange 2000 Server—was released to manufacturing. This was a watershed event for Microsoft. Exchange 2000 is one of the most powerful messaging and collaboration systems in the world, and it helps run some of the biggest companies in the world. It is a core component of Microsoft's .NET Server Platform, and one of the first applications to leverage the Windows 2000 directory service known as Active Directory.

Exchange 2000 represents a radical departure from Exchange 5.5. After incorporating more than two years' worth of customer feedback into Exchange 2000, Microsoft has released a messaging and collaboration platform capable of scaling to millions of users per organization, and a comprehensive communications platform that can communicate with a wide variety of messaging and personal digital devices.

Exchange 2000 boasts an impressive set of new features that will be compelling for all organizations, and not just those currently running a prior version of Exchange. There's something in there for everyone, whether you are upgrading to Exchange, migrating to Exchange, or installing Exchange as your first messaging system.

Businesses will enjoy the cost savings that result from the server consolidations made possible by Exchange 2000's scalability. And because Exchange 2000 leverages an organization's existing investment in Active Directory, deployment costs are reduced because the directory and directory service infrastructure is already in place.

Administrators will love the architectural enhancements in Exchange 2000, such as support for multiple databases, two-node and four-node Active/Active clustering, fault-tolerant SMTP routing, and a much improved Outlook Web Access. Integrated tools that support the Microsoft Management Console framework are also a much-needed and welcome addition.

Knowledge workers and end-users will enjoy the beefed-up, full-text indexing and the real-time collaboration features. Features such as instant messaging, chat services, and data and video conferencing will make them more productive and enhance their working relationships.

Programmers and independent software vendors will undoubtedly appreciate the development opportunities presented by Exchange 2000. Exchange 2000 has many significant improvements over prior versions, such as support for Extensible Markup Language, Collaboration Data Objects 3.0, OLE DB, Active X Data Objects, and Web Distributed Authoring and Versioning.

This book was more than a year in the making. It is based on the personal and professional experiences, knowledge, and skills of three highly-respected authors and Exchange experts. If you would like to ask a question of or provide feedback to the authors directly, you may do so by contacting Bill English at benglish@networknowledge.com, Nick Cavalancia at nickc@comsphere.com, or Scott Schnoll at scott_schnoll@msn.com.

Who Should Read This Book?

Exchange 2000 is radically different from its predecessors. It boasts a wide variety of new features and benefits, but in doing so it adds to the complexity of the product. This book provides details on designing and implementing an Exchange 2000 infrastructure and step-by-step instructions for Exchange 2000 administrators. If you are responsible for deploying Exchange 2000 in your company, you should read this book cover-to-cover prior to deploying any servers.

This book is written from the perspective that you are new to Exchange 2000, but that you have some Exchange 5.5 experience. Even if you have been working with Exchange 2000 for some time and consider yourself an experienced administrator, you will still find this book useful. This book builds on the earlier Osborne book, *Exchange 2000 Server Administration: A Beginner's Guide*, by providing you with detailed technical information on the inner workings of Exchange 2000 and a wealth of experience and know-how from seasoned Exchange 2000 administrators.

What's in This Book

Exchange 2000 Server: The Complete Reference is organized into six parts.

Part I, "Exchange 2000 Server Basics," provides an in-depth look at Exchange 2000 and its new architecture. Chapter 1 begins the introduction with a summary of Exchange 2000's features and benefits. It discusses the various editions of Exchange 2000, as well as the new features present in each of the three editions: Exchange 2000 Server, Exchange 2000 Enterprise Server, and Exchange 2000 Conferencing Server. Chapter 2 provides an overview of Active Directory, the Windows 2000 directory, and directory service required by Exchange 2000. A variety of Active Directory concepts and terms are presented along with an in-depth look at the physical and logical makeup of Active Directory.

Chapter 3 builds on Chapter 2 by discussing Exchange 2000's integration with Active Directory. Readers will also be exposed to Active Directory objects and their relation to Exchange 2000. Chapter 4 presents a high-level overview of Exchange 2000's new architecture. This "under-the-hood" discussion is intended to provide you with details on how Exchange 2000 works. Exchange 2000 public folders and the public folder hierarchy are the focus of Chapter 5. Administrators will learn how public folders work and how to leverage them as a collaborative resource.

Part II, "Administering Exchange 2000 Server," covers a wide variety of administrative tasks. Chapter 6 discusses the various installation options, and walks you through various installation procedures with detailed, step-by-step instructions for installing Exchange 2000. Chapter 7 focuses on upgrading from and co-existing with Exchange 5.5. The differences between Mixed mode and Native mode are discussed along with the various options for upgrading or migrating to Exchange 2000.

Chapter 8 covers recipient administration. Readers will learn how to create and administer mail-enabled Active Directory objects using various methods and tools. Chapter 9 provides you with the knowledge and skills necessary to manage Exchange 2000 servers. It also discusses Exchange's new routing architecture, address lists, and recipient policies. In Chapter 10, you will learn how to manage the Internet protocol supported by Exchange 2000: SMTP, POP3, HTTP, IMAP4, and NNTP.

Chapter 11 covers the Exchange information store and the Web Storage System. It also includes an overview of full-text indexing and store event sinks. Chapter 12 concludes this section with a discussion of the issues related to backup, restore, and disaster recovery. It ends with several best practices for implementing good backup and recovery procedures, and implementing policies that can obviate the need to restore data.

Part III, "Exchange 2000 Server Collaboration," includes a discussion of the various clients for Exchange along with in-depth information on the real-time collaboration features in Exchange 2000: conferencing services, instant messaging, and chat services. Chapter 13 begins this section by covering the available Exchange clients, including Outlook 2002. Chapter 14 continues this discussion with a detailed look at Outlook Web Access.

Chapter 15 introduces Exchange 2000 Conferencing Server, a version of Exchange 2000 that provides real-time data and video conferencing services. Readers are provided with step-by-step instructions for installing, implementing, and maintaining Exchange 2000 conferencing services. Chapter 16 contains everything you need to know about instant messaging, including step-by-step instructions for installing, implementing, and maintaining Exchange 2000 Instant Messaging services. Chapter 17 discusses Exchange 2000 Chat services. Included with the discussion of the Chat service architecture are step-by-step instructions for installing, implementing, and managing Exchange 2000 chat communities.

Part IV, "Exchange 2000 Server Security," shows you how to secure your Exchange infrastructure from internal and external attacks or abuses, and how to secure your electronic messages. You'll find everything you need to know for deploying a secure Exchange 2000 environment in Chapter 18. This chapter covers protocol security, certificates, anti-virus software, and firewalls, and gives you real-world advice on protecting your servers. Chapter 19 covers the basics of the Public Key Infrastructure services. This chapter also discusses how to install and use Certificate Server, and how to obtain certificates from an authorized Certificate Authority.

Some advanced aspects of Exchange 2000 are presented in Part V, "Exchange 2000 Server Scalability and Reliability." This section begins with Chapter 20, which covers clustering Exchange 2000. This chapter includes step-by-step instructions for building two-node Exchange 2000 clusters from scratch, and tells you how to perform disaster recovery of an Exchange cluster. This chapter also covers Network Load Balancing and the Front-End/Back-End configuration model. In Chapter 21, you'll learn how to how to tune Exchange servers on a variety of levels. This chapter also include details on monitoring an Exchange infrastructure for health and performance issues.

The last section of this book is Part VI, "Appendixes." In it, you'll find a technology primer on Web Distributed Authoring and Versioning (WebDAV), and a summary of knowledge management and Microsoft's knowledge management offerings. Appendix A provides an overview of what WebDAV is and how it works. WebDAV is an integral component in many of Microsoft's core products, including Exchange 2000 and Outlook, and it may radically change the way applications and messaging works in the near future.

In Appendix B, you'll be introduced to the concepts of knowledge management, workflow, and customer relationship management. You learn how information is an important asset of your organization and how you can use Microsoft's various knowledge management offerings to enable your company's knowledge workers to collaborate more effectively.

Part I

Exchange 2000 Server Basics

Chapter 1

Exchange 2000 Server Summary

Introduction to Microsoft Exchange 2000 Server

Though they might not realize it, the success of many companies is closely tied to their information technology infrastructure and how they use it. In business today, information is everything. It needs to flow to the right people at the right time, often so that it can be acted upon quickly. Most corporate information can be divided into two categories: information that is used to further the business, such as sales, marketing, and market research data, and information that is used to support the business's own internal processes, such as human resources, payroll, and accounting data. Much of this data is shared between users through electronic mail systems. Since the 1980s, the number of companies deploying and using electronic mail systems has skyrocketed, and an ever-increasing amount of corporate information now flows through corporate e-mail systems and the Internet. In addition, personal use of electronic mail is at an all-time high. Despite the proliferation of the World Wide Web, e-mail is still the most widely used Internet application.

In early 1996, Microsoft released Exchange Server 4.0, the successor to Microsoft Mail. Exchange Server 4.0 ushered in a new era of client/server electronic messaging for business users. Client/server messaging systems are distinguished from post office e-mail systems in that they provide a server-based message store for users. Exchange Server provides two primary types of stores: private information stores, which contain individual mailboxes, and public information stores, which contain a shared public folder hierarchy.

Yet another new era was realized a year later with the release of Exchange Server 5.0. Version 5.0 represented a significant improvement over the prior version, due in large part to the integration of Internet standards into the product. In late 1997, Microsoft released Exchange Server 5.5, which further integrated Internet standards, increased scalability by removing size limitations on the database, and positioned Exchange Server as a viable application platform for three-tier workflow and collaborative applications.

At 9:19 A.M. on August 31, 2000, the next generation of Microsoft Exchange—Exchange 2000 Server—was released to manufacturing. When Microsoft began work on Exchange 2000 Server, then code-named "Platinum," they had three primary design goals. First, it would be designed with reliability, scalability, and manageability in mind. Second, it needed to provide a solid platform for applications that support business logic and business processes, as well as synchronous and asynchronous collaboration. Third, it needed to provide fast and easy access to people and information at any time and from any place.

The creation of this next-generation version of Exchange Server resulted in major architectural and design changes. Indeed, despite its name, Exchange 2000 Server bears little resemblance to its predecessors. Far more than an electronic mail system, it provides corporations a backbone for communication, collaboration, and information sharing. With the addition of Windows 2000's Active Directory, Internet Information services, instant messaging, data, audio, and video conferencing, chat services, and more, it also adds new levels of complexity for administrators moving from prior versions of Exchange. These days, most messaging systems typically provide multiple functions: electronic mail, groupware, electronic forms, workflow, and document and information exchange. Exchange 2000 provides all of this and much more.

Exchange 2000 Flavors and Features

Exchange 2000 comes in three different editions:

- **Exchange 2000 Server** This is the successor to the Standard Edition of Exchange 5.5. Exchange 2000 Server is designed for small- to medium-sized businesses, and remote or branch offices of larger businesses.
- **Exchange 2000 Enterprise Server** This replaces the Enterprise Edition of Exchange 5.5, and like its predecessor, it supports unlimited growth of the information store databases and clustering.
- **Exchange 2000 Conferencing Server** This is a brand new flavor of Exchange that provides audio, video, and data conferencing and conference management.

Exchange 2000 Server and Enterprise Server both support the following new or improved features:

- Integration with Windows 2000 and Active Directory
- Integration with Internet Information Server
- Fault-tolerant SMTP routing
- Indexing and searching
- Enhanced development platform

Integration with Windows 2000 and Active Directory

Exchange 2000 is deeply integrated with Windows 2000 and the Windows 2000 directory and directory service known as Active Directory. A directory acts as the central clearinghouse for objects on the network, such as servers, users, printers, and the like. Directory services publish these objects so that users and applications can locate these resourses and use them.

Exchange 2000 relies on Windows 2000 and Active Directory for three critical functions: directory services, name resolution, and transport. As a result, Exchange 2000 can only be installed in a Windows 2000 network containing an Active Directory.

Directory Services Prior versions of Exchange Server did not deeply integrate into the directory services provided by Windows NT 4.0. Earlier versions used integrated Windows NT security for Exchange Server operations and client mailbox access, but instead of leveraging the NT accounts database, Exchange Server used its own separate directory and directory services. This meant that administrators had to configure, manage, replicate, and maintain separate directories for their accounts database and their mail system. For small- and medium-sized companies, this added to the administrative burden of what is typically a small pool of administrators. For larger organizations, this design impacted the scalability and manageability of Exchange Server, and in some cases, negatively impacted the total cost of ownership of the product.

Certainly, the next generation of Exchange Server needed to be more scalable, more reliable, and more manageable than ever. It had to be capable of supporting millions of users. To accomplish this, Microsoft has integrated Exchange 2000 with Windows 2000 and, more importantly, Windows 2000 Active Directory. Unlike its predecessors, Exchange 2000 does not have its own directory service. It uses Active Directory, the directory services included in Windows 2000. Exchange 2000 stores recipient information, distribution lists, contact (formerly custom recipient) information, and system configuration information in Active Directory. Instead of separate Exchange and NT domain directories, administrators can now create a single enterprise directory for managing all users, groups, permissions, shares, and more. In Chapter 3, we'll delve into exactly how Exchange 2000 stores data in Active Directory and how it leverages objects in the Windows 2000 environment.

Name Resolution Name resolution in the context of Exchange refers to the client's and server's ability to perform address book lookups and resolve recipient names. Since the directory information is now stored with Active Directory, Exchange 2000 will use this directory service for recipient resolution, distribution list processing, and address book lookups.

Name resolution in the general sense refers to one computer's ability to translate another computer's name into an IP address. Like all TCP/IP-based applications, Exchange 2000 is entirely dependent upon the underlying network layers that provide connectivity with other systems. This includes the physical network components, the proper operation of the network protocol, and name resolution. As a Winsock-based application, both Exchange and Outlook use the Domain Name System (DNS) for name resolution.

Transport Exchange 2000 also integrates tightly with Internet Information Services (IIS), the next-generation Internet server built into Windows 2000. Every Windows 2000 computer provides native support for a variety of Internet services (in this context, also called transport stacks), such as the Simple Mail Transport Protocol (SMTP) and the Network News Transport Protocol (NNTP). Exchange 2000 installs a set of sinks that register with each protocol and extend these transport stacks. In Exchange 2000, the preferred method of transport is SMTP, which is now a full peer to X.400, the transport of choice between Exchange Sites in earlier versions of Exchange. We'll get into this more in Chapter 4, where we discuss the architecture of Exchange 2000.

Fault-Tolerant SMTP Routing

Servers running prior versions of Exchange natively use Remote Procedure Calls (RPCs) to communicate with one another. Exchange 2000 Servers use RPCs to communicate with an Exchange 5.5 Server and with clients, such as Microsoft Outlook, that support the messaging application programming interface (MAPI). But when communicating with another Exchange 2000 Server, it uses SMTP. This increases performance and robustness, especially for Internet messaging traffic.

In addition to using SMTP as the native transport protocol, Exchange 2000 has a new routing engine that uses a *link state algorithm* (LSA) to provide efficient routing of messages based on the current network conditions. Previous versions of Exchange routed messages based on network conditions at the point of routing. Exchange 2000 uses link state information to maintain information about the condition of the network and servers with other Exchange 2000 Servers so that routing paths can be determined at the source of the message. More on this in Chapters 4 and 9.

Indexing and Searching

Exchange 2000 also includes Microsoft Search, a built-in content indexing engine that enables users to quickly locate data in the Exchange store. Microsoft Search uses the same indexing mechanism found in Internet Information Services and SQL Server 7.0. Users can query Exchange 2000 for e-mail messages, Office documents (such as Word, Excel, and PowerPoint files), Web content (including HTML and ASP files), and application and workflow data. Prior versions of Exchange relied on additional components, such as Microsoft Site Server, or Exchange clients, such as Microsoft Outlook, to provide indexing and search capabilities. By using the Microsoft Search engine natively, content indexing is enabled directly at the Exchange Server level, which makes indexing efficient, and searching astonishingly fast. Searches that took as long as a minute to complete now only take a couple seconds.

Because Office documents are included in the search index, advanced searches are possible using the property promotion feature of the Exchange *Web Store*. This enables users to locate documents based on document properties such as Author, Manager, and so on. Full-text indexing consumes server resources, such as disk space, memory, and CPU time, but when configured properly, it can increase productivity for knowledge workers by significantly reducing the time it takes to locate information. We'll discuss indexing in greater detail in Chapter 11.

Enhanced Development Platform

From a development perspective, Exchange 2000 has many significant benefits over prior versions of Exchange. Among them are support for Extensible Markup Language (XML), Collaboration Data Objects 3.0 (CDO), OLE DB, Active X Data Objects (ADO), HTTP Distributed Authoring and Versioning (WebDAV), server events, and Web forms.

Extensible Markup Language Extensible Markup Language (XML) is a text-based development language that enables the description and exchange of structured data between applications and servers. XML facilitates the identification and processing of data in a manner that is mutually understood by the servers and applications that are exchanging the data.

Collaboration Data Objects 3.0 Collaboration Data Objects 3.0 (CDO) supports Internet messaging (MIME, LDAP, and so on) and access to Exchange 2000's information stores and messaging services, as well as Active Directory. CDO is a scripting-object library that can be used to design collaborative applications in a client/server environment. It can be used to streamline workflow applications, client and Web applications, and Exchange applications such as server-event scripts and mailbox agents. CDO, which is built on top of OLE DB, uses ADO to access the raw data in the information store. CDO 3.0 is both an API specification and object library. CDO 3.0 is has a very different object model from CDO 1.2, which represents a significant improvement over the basic application services for messaging and calendaring provided by CDO 1.2 and Exchange 5.5.

OLE DB OLE DB is a low-level, object-based interface designed to provide "universal" data access. OLE DB defines interfaces that can be used by applications and database providers for accessing and manipulating data. Exchange 2000 includes two OLE DB providers: a local provider used internally by the Exchange Server for functions such as workflow and virus scanning, and a remote provider used by clients, such as Microsoft Office applications (including Outlook).

ActiveX Data Objects ActiveX Data Objects (ADO) is an object-based interface to OLE DB. The primary benefits of ADO are ease of use, speed, and small memory and disk footprint. ADO is an object model that exposes data raised by an underlying OLE DB provider. The most commonly used OLE DB provider is the OLE DB provider for ODBC drivers, which exposes ODBC data sources to ADO.

WebDAV WebDAV, as defined by RFC 2518, is an extension to the HTTP 1.1 protocol. It provides a way to store and retrieve document object properties, such as author, title, publication date, and so on. In addition, it allows users to manage Web items as if they were file system items. Under the WebDAV model, items stored in the Web Store are addressable using a human-readable URL, making the Web Store user- and application-friendly.

Server Events Exchange 2000 includes a server event model that provides two types of events: transport events and Web storage system events. As the name implies, *transport* events are used for transports, namely SMTP and NNTP. They are used to track and customize server operations during the processing of SMTP and NNTP requests.

Web storage system events, which are based on OLE DB events, occur when Exchange processes content in the Web storage system, when the information store starts or stops, and when a specific amount of time has elapsed. They can be synchronous or asynchronous. Synchronous events, which are new to Exchange 2000, occur before the change is committed to the store. During a synchronous event, Exchange suspends processing on items until the event is executed. Asynchronous events are notifications that occur after an item is saved or deleted.

All of these concepts will be discussed in greater detail later on, and Appendix A covers WebDAV in depth.

Exchange 2000 Server

Exchange 2000 Server is Microsoft's messaging platform for small- to medium-sized businesses or branch offices. It provides basic messaging and groupware capabilities but does not contain many of the new advanced features that are found in the Enterprise edition, such as multiple message databases, clustering in any form, deployment in a front-end/back-end configuration, or chat services. An Exchange 2000 Server's public or private mail store is limited to 16GB.

Exchange 2000 Enterprise Server includes support for advanced features, such as:

- Unlimited growth of information store databases
- Multiple public and private information stores per server
- Two-node and four-node active/active clustering
- Distributed (partitioned) services
- Instant messaging, chat, and collaboration services

Multiple Database Support

Exchange Server stores its data in databases. Prior versions of Exchange only provided administrators with two Extensible Storage Engine (ESE) databases per server: a private store database containing mailbox data and a public store database containing the shared public folder contents. Exchange 2000 provides enhanced database support by enabling you to create multiple public and private store databases per server. This provides administrators with entirely new architectural options, which we'll discuss in Chapter 4. One of the benefits of multiple databases is that recovery can be accomplished in a shorter period of time and with less impact to the greater user community. The ability to perform backup and restore operations on individual databases means that one database can be restored from backup while other databases are still serving users.

The enhanced database support also provides new opportunities for application development. Developers can leverage the multidatabase architecture to create scenarios for specific data storage. For instance, public folder databases can be created for workgroups or departments, enabling solutions that are both group-specific and contained from other applications. In Chapter 4, we'll examine this new architecture in detail.

Two-Node and Four-Node Active/Active Clustering

Exchange 2000 was designed for increased reliability. Exchange Server 5.5 provides support for clustering using Microsoft Cluster Server (MSCS) in an active/passive manner. The Windows NT 4.0 implementation of MSCS provides support for two-node clusters. A *cluster* is a group of independent computers working together as a single system to ensure that mission-critical applications and resources are as highly available as possible. An active/passive cluster in MSCS is one where the clustered application runs on one node at a time—the active node. If a hardware failure occurs on the active node, the cluster software triggers a failover, moving the application and its resources (network name, IP address, shared storage, and so on) from the active node to the passive node, which then becomes the active node.

Windows 2000 Advanced Server provides native support for clustering of two nodes. Windows 2000 Datacenter Server enhances native clustering by providing support for four-node clusters. Exchange 2000 fully supports twonode active/active clustering. This means that Exchange 2000 can simultaneously run on both nodes within a single cluster, with each node providing failover for the other nodes in case of a hardware failure. Support for four-node clustering will arrive after the release of Exchange 2000 Service Pack 1. Exchange 2000 also supports network load balancing for its IP-based services, such as Outlook Web Access. The ability to use all of the servers in a cluster reduces system costs and increases reliability. We'll explore clustering and load balancing in Exchange 2000 in Chapter 20.

Distributed (Partitioned) Services

In order for Exchange 2000—or really any application—to scale to millions of users, you must be able to distribute its services. Exchange 2000 lets you distribute protocol services, information store services, and directory services across multiple servers. System architects can configure Exchange 2000 servers as *front-end* servers or *back-end* servers, separating the access protocols from the physical databases.

In prior versions of Exchange, the STORE.EXE process managed both the databases and the Internet access protocols (for example, HTTP, IMAP4, and POP3). In Exchange 2000, the protocols are now managed by Internet Information Services. A front-end/back-end architecture enables system architects to configure the access protocols on servers without any information store databases. Front-end servers request information from back-end servers on behalf of clients using the client's access protocol. For example, if an IMAP4 client connects to a front-end server, the front-end server uses IMAP4 when communicating with the back-end server.

When you combine load-balanced front-end servers with clustered back-end servers, you have a highly scalable and reliable infrastructure. We'll cover this in more depth in Chapter 20.

Instant Messaging, Chat, and Collaboration Services

Collaborative environments can eliminate the boundaries of organizational structure and geographic location. The most successful collaborative environments typically use workflow applications to streamline processes or interaction among team members by enabling them to locate data, share information, create or review documents together, and publish information.

Instant messaging and chat services enable users to communicate with one another in real time over TCP/IP networks. Instant messaging allow users to know immediately which of their business contacts (or friends) are online and to contact them for private keyboard chats. In a business context, instant messaging and chat services enable collaboration in new and exciting ways. Instant messaging works on the concept of *presence information*, that is, the determination of whether or not someone is online. This presence information can be leveraged by knowledge workers and applications, providing businesses with information that can be used to streamline workflow and other business processes.

The combination of Exchange 2000, Office 2000, NetMeeting, and Instant Messenger provide an enterprise-class collaboration environment that enables knowledge workers to be highly productive. It also gives developers a mechanism for integrating presence information with workflow applications. If an application needs to flow critical information to an individual who is currently offline, it can be programmed to reroute the information to someone else with the authority to act upon the information who is online. You'll learn more about these exciting technologies in Chapters 15 and 16 and find out how you can plan, design, and implement them in your environment.

Exchange 2000 Conferencing Server

Exchange 2000 Conferencing Server is a special edition of Exchange that provides both unicast and multicast video and phone conferencing. It enables knowledge workers to hold online meetings, or as Microsoft puts it, "meetings without walls." Instead of using physical conference rooms, participants use virtual meeting rooms. Exchange 2000 Conferencing Server includes several components, such as the Conference Management Service, data and video conferencing providers, multipoint control units (MCUs), and Conference Access Pages.

Online conferences can be scheduled through Outlook or Outlook Web Access. These conferences can be either public or private, and unlike a standalone NetMeeting conference, they can accommodate more than two attendees. Exchange 2000 Conferencing Server provides a central reservation system that lets knowledge workers schedule and join conferences from their Outlook calendars. Conferences can also be joined by opening the conference location URL in Internet Explorer.

Conference Management Service As its name implies, the *Conference Management Service* is used for conference management functions, such as the reservation of virtual conference rooms and other conferencing resources, the storage of all scheduled conferences, controlling access to and auditing of conferences, and providing support for conference technology providers. Online conferences include resources, which are mailbox-enabled objects in Active Directory. The availability of these resources is published by the Conference Management Service via the Exchange 2000 Server Free/Busy data.

The Conference Management Service provides access to online conferences using IIS. When a conference is scheduled, the Conference Management Service creates a unique URL that can be used to join the conference. Links to scheduled conferences that are public are listed on a conference access page; knowledge workers can browse the available conferences and participate in conferences of their choice. If a conference is marked as private, participants must have the exact conference URL in order to join the conference.

Data Conferencing Provider A *data conferencing provider* is a conference technology provider that enables application and desktop sharing, group electronic whiteboards, document and file transfer, and real-time keyboard chatting. Any application that supports the ITU's T.120 network communications standard (such as Microsoft NetMeeting), can be used with Exchange 2000's data conferencing provider. Data conferences use MCUs to interconnect conference participants and synchronize the conference data between them.

Video Conferencing Provider A video conference is when two or more people in different locations exchange audio and video in real time. Prior to Exchange 2000 Conferencing Server, Microsoft NetMeeting could be used to establish peer-to-peer video conferences using the ITU H.323 unicast standard. The *video conferencing provider* is a conferencing technology provider in Exchange 2000 that enables multiparty audio and video conferencing over multicast-enabled IP networks. The technology is based on the Internet Engineering Task Force (IETF) IP multicast standards.

Exchange 2000 conferences can also include clients with H.323 capabilities over an IP multicast/H.323 unicast bridge. This provides greater efficiency on multicast-enabled networks and wider accessibility and support for lower bandwidth on non-multicast networks, such as the Internet.

For more information on Exchange 2000 Conferencing Server, see Chapter 15.

Administration and Management of Exchange 2000

Certainly all these new features mean added complexity to Exchange 2000. For this reason, one of Microsoft's primary design goals for Exchange 2000 was manageability. Among the challenges of administrating Windows NT, BackOffice applications, and third-party server-based applications is the sheer number of administrative tools required to perform the wide variety of administrative tasks. Often, these tools were specialized to specific functionality, and due to their different interfaces, they increased the learning curve for using them.

To overcome this tools deluge, Microsoft created the Microsoft Management Console (MMC), shown in Figure 1-1.

The MMC provides a framework, or console, for administration tools. The console hosts programs, which are called snap-ins. In addition, the MMC helps administrators create customized consoles for different individuals with different levels of authority and responsibility. By using a standard framework for administration tools, the

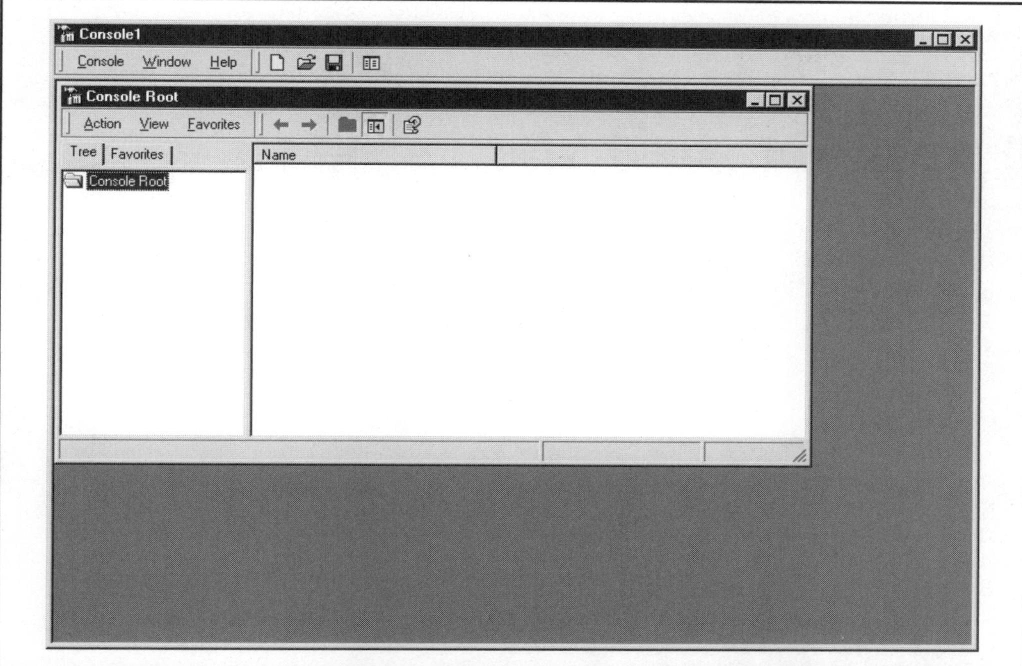

Figure 1-1. *The Microsoft Management Console is the universal tool used to manage Windows 2000 and BackOffice 2000 applications, such as Exchange 2000 and SQL Server 2000.*

learning curve for new tools is significantly reduced; therefore, so is the total cost of ownership.

Exchange System Manager

Prior versions of Exchange used the Exchange Administrator application to manage Exchange Servers. In Exchange 2000, an MMC snap-in called the Exchange System Manager is the administrative tool used to manage objects such as recipient policies and address lists, routing groups and storage groups, and chat communities and public folders. Like the Exchange Administrator application, System Manager displays the Exchange components in a hierarchical, dual-pane view (see Figure 1-2). As a bonus, and unlike the older Exchange Administrator application, System Manager supports the right mouse click and context-sensitive menus.

In addition to the System Manager, other MMC snap-ins are needed to manage mailboxes, configure Internet services, analyze and implement security, and troubleshoot problems. For example, the Active Directory Users and Computers snap-in uses the

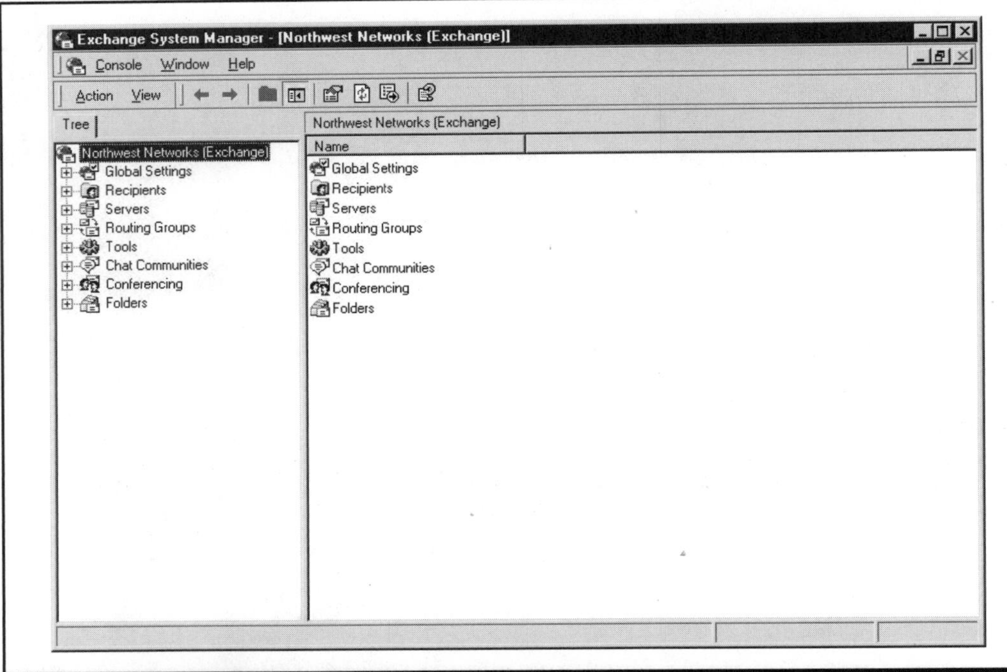

Figure 1-2. *The Exchange System Manager is one of several MMC snap-ins used to manage an Exchange 2000 infrastructure.*

Exchange Task Wizard to create and delete mailboxes, enable and disable conferencing services, move mailboxes, and perform other Exchange-related tasks. The Internet Information Services snap-in is used to manage Internet protocols, the Telephony snap-in is used to manage TAPI services, the Exchange Advanced Security snap-in is used to manage message encryption settings, and so forth.

Regardless of what snap-in you need to use, the MMC provides the capability to use a single container to hold them all. At a basic level, most of the tools used to administrate an Exchange 2000 infrastructure are performing the same function: the modification of objects in Active Directory. You can create a "master" console containing a variety of snap-ins, making you a click away from all of your management tools (see Figure 1-3).

Administrative Groups

Exchange 5.5 and earlier used the concept of a site to represent the routing and administrative topologies of the Exchange infrastructure. In Exchange 2000, the site concept is divided into two distinct components, *administrative groups* and *routing groups*. In Exchange 2000, an administrative group is a group of Exchange servers that

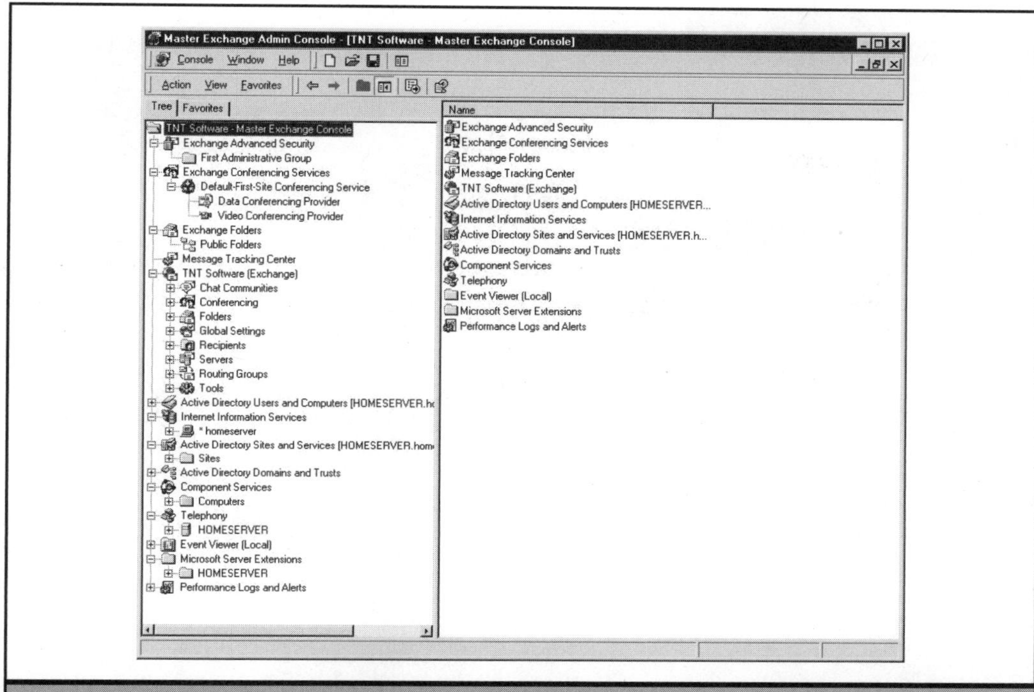

Figure 1-3. *The MMC framework provides a flexible and familiar console for your favorite management tools.*

are managed as a single unit. Administrative groups can contain a variety of Active Directory objects, such as servers, public folder trees, chat networks, conferencing services, and monitors. They group objects together for permissions management and enable administrators to define units of access control. This approach makes administrating Exchange 2000 much easier in larger organizations where different responsibilities are distributed among a larger pool of support individuals.

Once you've created administrative groups, you can use the Exchange Delegation Wizard to delegate control of Exchange Active Directory objects to other users (see Figure 1-4).

In addition to the above-mentioned objects, administrative groups can also contain routing groups and policies.

Routing Groups

Whereas administrative groups map to the administrative topology of an Exchange infrastructure, routing groups map to an organization's routing topology. In Exchange 2000,

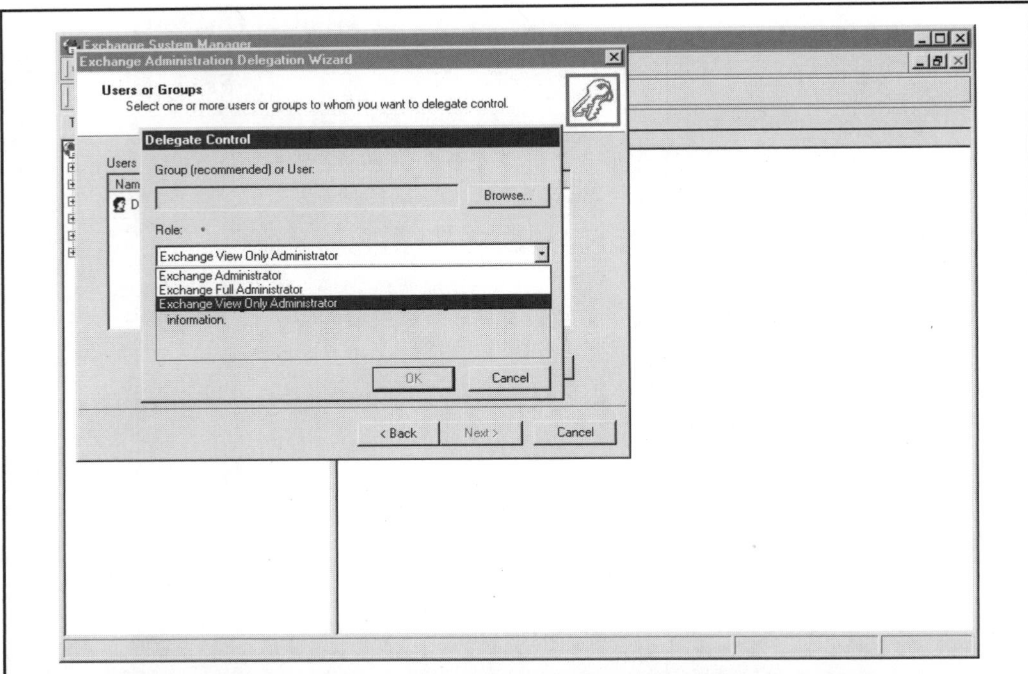

Figure 1-4. *The Exchange Delegation Wizard allows you to grant one of four predefined administrator roles to other individuals in your organization.*

a routing group is a connection of servers connected by fast, reliable links. Servers in the same routing group are assumed to have a mesh topology and persistent, 24x7 connectivity. Servers separated by slow links should be put into separate routing groups.

The primary reason to create a routing group is to define single-hop routing in your Exchange organization; however, you might also create routing groups to manage and control the flow of messages across administrative boundaries. If you have a small number of servers in the same location that are connected with a full-time, reliable network, you don't need to create routing groups. In fact, until you enable and create routing groups, the Routing Groups container will not appear in System Manager.

The transfer point between routing groups is called a *bridgehead* server. All message traffic coming into a routing group enters through a bridgehead server. Multiple servers in a single routing group can be defined as a bridgehead server. Multiple bridgehead servers in a routing group provide fault tolerance for communication between routing groups. Routing groups are connected using routing group connectors. While the routing group connector is the preferred connector between routing groups, you also have the choice of using an SMTP connector or an X.400 connector. Routing groups are discussed in much greater detail in Chapter 9.

Policies

Another way Exchange 2000 is more manageable is through the addition of policy-based administration. Prior versions of Exchange required you to configure server settings independently. Although some settings could be applied to an entire Exchange site, there was no way to apply these settings to some or all of the servers in all of the sites. Exchange 2000 Server includes a policy-based administration model that enables the configuration of options across a group of objects, such as mailboxes, public folders, and servers, in a single operation. A *policy* is a collection of configuration settings that apply to one or more Exchange 2000 configuration objects. System policies can be defined across hundreds of objects, and recipient policies can be defined across hundreds of thousands of users, groups, and contacts in the Active Directory using the LDAP query interface.

Exchange 2000 supports policies for four types of objects: mailboxes, public folders, servers, and address generation. You can apply policies to each object, and you must have sufficient rights to objects in order to apply policies to them. Policies are created with the System Manager MMC snap-in (see Figure 1-5).

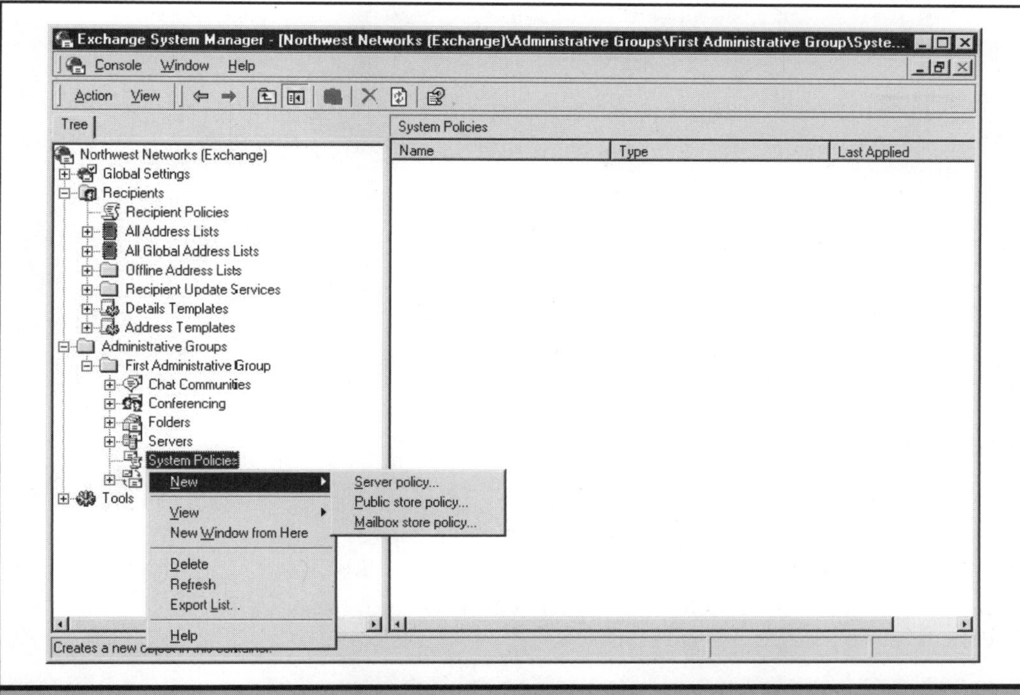

Figure 1-5. *Once the System Manager has been configured to display administrative groups, you can create mailbox, public folder, and server-based policies.*

Server policies let you control settings at the server level, such as subject logging and display, message tracking, and message tracking log file removal. Public folder and mailbox policies include database maintenance, replication, and store limit policies. Address generation policies—called *recipient policies*—define what addresses will be used for those users to whom the policy is applied, enabling administrators to define proxy addresses based on fields in Active Directory. We'll discuss policies and the rights needed to apply them in Chapter 9.

User Management Concepts

The first Exchange 2000 Server installed in an Active Directory forest modifies the existing schema and adds context menu items to user objects in Active Directory. Thereafter, all user mailboxes are created using Active Directory Users and Computers MMC snap-in. In previous versions of Exchange, administrators used the Exchange Administrator application to create mailboxes and assign e-mail addresses. A mailbox was associated with a specific user by assigning a primary Windows NT account to the mailbox. If the Exchange Administrator application was installed on an administrator's NT machine, a user mailbox could also be created through User Manager for Domains.

There are three types of Exchange 2000 users. Users with mailboxes and e-mail addresses are referred to as *mailbox-enabled users*. These users are security principals in Active Directory who can send and receive messages and who are identified by one or more SMTP addresses. Administrators have the option of creating an Exchange mailbox at the same time the user account is created. If the administrator needs to mailbox-enable an existing user, they can do so by using the Exchange Task Wizard (see Figure 1-6).

The second type of user is a *mail-enabled* user. These are users with a valid Windows 2000 account and an SMTP address, but no mailbox. By definition, a mailbox-enabled user is also a mail-enabled user, but not vice versa.

The remaining type of user is a *mail-enabled contact*. This is a user who does not have either a mailbox or a Windows 2000 user account, but who does have an SMTP address associated with him. Prior versions of Exchange could contain objects known as *custom recipients*, which were foreign e-mail addresses that did not have a mailbox associated with them. In Exchange 2000, these objects are called mail-enabled contacts. Mail-enabled contacts are typically created for distribution list purposes, although they may also include recipients from outside the organization who frequently receive mail from many users in the organization.

Once a user object has been mailbox-enabled, mail-enabled, or designated a mail-enabled contact, a number of new property pages are added to enable configuration of the user. Figure 1-7 illustrates the difference between a user account that is an Exchange 2000 user and one that is not.

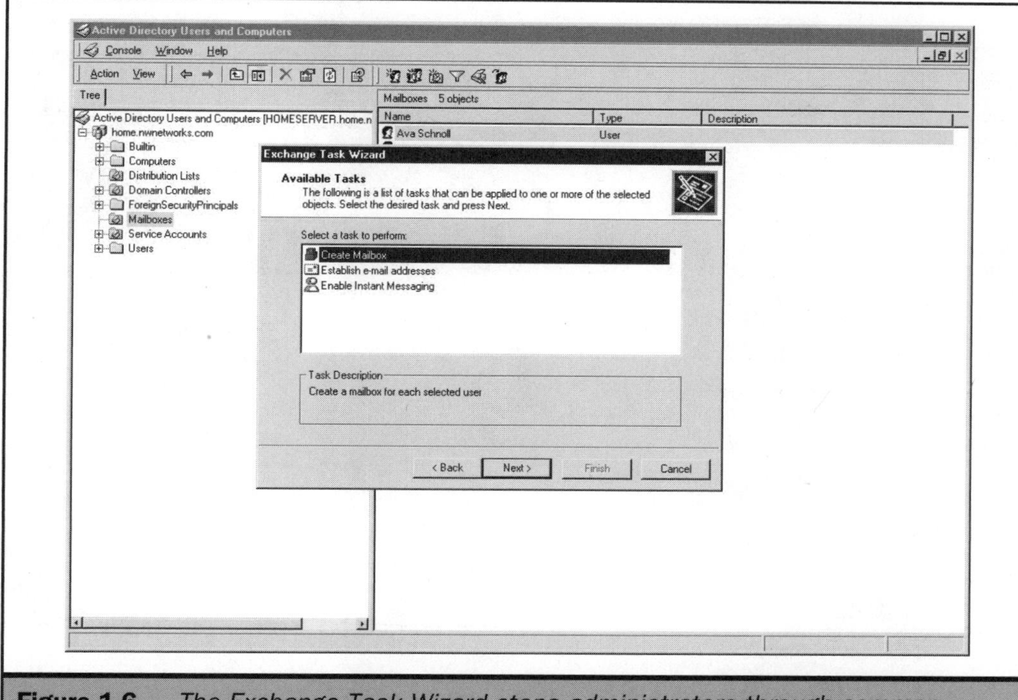

Figure 1-6. *The Exchange Task Wizard steps administrators through common Exchange tasks, such as creating and deleting mailboxes, moving mailboxes, and enabling or disabling instant messaging.*

Distribution Group

A Windows 2000 group is roughly the equivalent of a distribution list in earlier versions of Exchange. Groups are collections of users, groups, and contacts. There are two types of groups in Active Directory. One is a security principal defining a collection of users and groups used to allow or deny access to resources. The other is a simple distribution list (not a security principal). Groups can have e-mail addresses and Exchange mailboxes. When a Windows 2000 group is mail-enabled, it becomes a *distribution group*. Any group—security or distribution; local, global, or universal—can be mail-enabled and turned into a distribution list. This eliminates the need to create multiple duplicate groups in the same organization, as was the case with prior versions of Exchange and Windows NT.

Ultimately, the groups you'll create depend on your business and user requirements. Regardless of whether you create security principals or distribution lists, Microsoft

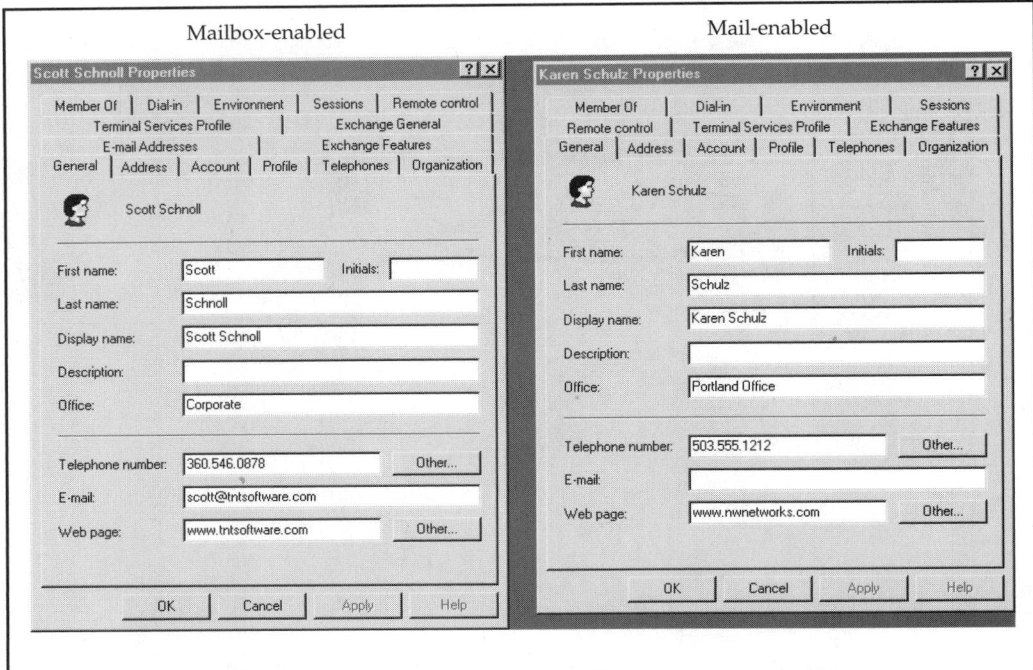

Figure 1-7. *Mailbox-enabled users and mail-enabled users and contacts have additional property pages that can be configured by an administrator.*

recommends that you limit group membership to fewer than 5,000. If you expect group membership to exceed this amount, you should consider nesting groups—that is, creating groups within groups. For efficiency and scalability, Microsoft further recommends that nested groups contain no more than 500 members.

A special kind of distribution list, called a *dynamic distribution list*, can also be created, although not through any available user interface. Instead, an LDAP query with a custom expression can be used to construct a set of users which can then be sent e-mail.

Address List Services

Like its forebears, the directory in Exchange 2000 comprises the *Global Address List* (GAL). Windows 2000 provides address list services for the GAL, as well as for address book views and offline address books. When Exchange users want to locate someone else in their organization, they would normally conduct a search of GAL. In Exchange 2000, search results are retrieved from Global Catalog servers in the Active Directory.

The concept of address book views was introduced with Exchange 5.0. This enabled administrators to create views of the GAL that were based on field groupings. In Exchange 2000, address book views have been replaced with *address lists*. Address lists, which are created using the Exchange System Manager, are formed by using rules that use LDAP search filters. Figure 1-8 depicts an address list for an accounting department using a filter of "Department = Accounting."

In its continued support of mobile users, Exchange 2000 supports the concept of *offline address books*. Offline address books allow users to copy server-based address lists to their local hard disk for use while disconnected. Offline address lists are created through the Exchange System snap-in. Administrators can make any existing address list available offline. A default offline address book exists in the Exchange organization.

Exchange 2000 Clients and Client Support

Exchange 2000 supports a wide variety of clients, including all versions of Microsoft Outlook, Outlook Express, standards-based e-mail clients (such as Pine, Eudora, and Netscape Messenger), and Web browsers (such as Internet Explorer and Netscape Navigator). Microsoft has stated that Outlook 2000 is the client of choice for Exchange 2000, although that will change when the next version of Outlook, code-named Outlook 10, is released.

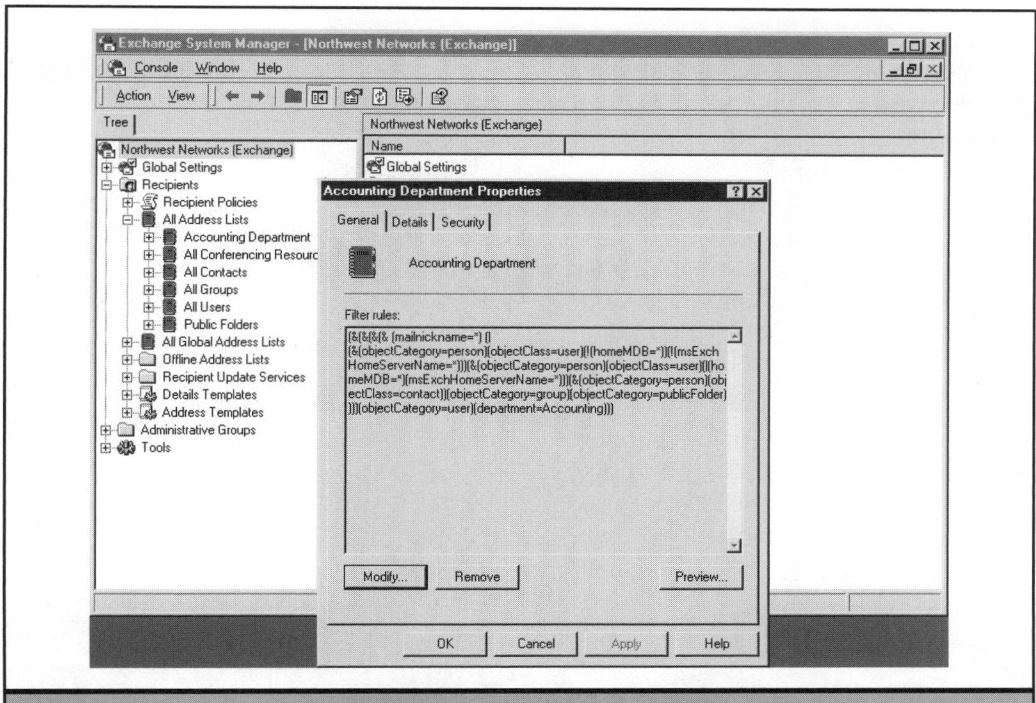

Figure 1-8. *Address lists are easy to create using the Exchange System Manager.*

Exchange 2000 also supports a wide variety of client access, e-mail, and other protocols. The available protocols and the clients that use them are listed in Table 1-1.

Protocol	Description	Microsoft Clients Supporting	Some Non-Microsoft Clients Supporting
Simple Mail Transport Protocol (SMTP)	Transport mechanism used for sending messages	Outlook 98, Outlook 2000, Outlook Express, Entourage, and Outlook 10	Netscape Messenger, Eudora, and Pine
Post Office Protocol v. 3 (POP3)	Transport mechanism used for receiving messages	Outlook 98, Outlook 2000, Outlook Express, Entourage, and Outlook 10	Netscape Messenger, Eudora, and Pine
Internet Message Access Protocol v. 4 (IMAP4)	Internet standard used to access and store e-mail in one or more folders on mail servers	Outlook 98, Outlook 2000, Outlook Express, Entourage, and Outlook 10	Netscape Messenger, Eudora, and Pine
Messaging Application Programming Interface (MAPI)	An API used to access multiple resources, such as e-mail, calendaring, task information, and so on, from a single client	Outlook 97, Outlook 98, Outlook 2000, and Outlook 10	None
Multipurpose Internet Mail Extensions (MIME)	Provides support for transmitting binary messages without loss of format	Outlook 98, Outlook 2000, Outlook Express, Entourage, Outlook 10, and Outlook Web Access	Netscape Messenger, Eudora, and Pine

Table 1-1. *Supported Protocols. Exchange 2000 supports several Internet standards, allowing you to choose from a variety of Microsoft and non-Microsoft clients.*

Protocol	Description	Microsoft Clients Supporting	Some Non-Microsoft Clients Supporting
Secure MIME (S/MIME)	Allows for digital signing and encryption of messages	Outlook 98, Outlook 2000, and Outlook 10	Netscape Messenger
Hypertext Transport Protocol (HTTP)	The client/server protocol used to access information through a Web server	Outlook Web Access	Netscape Navigator
Web-distributed authoring and versioning (WebDAV)	An extension to the HTTP protocol that provides authoring support for Web sites	Outlook Web Access (using IE5 or greater), Outlook Express 5 or greater, Outlook 2000, and Outlook 10	None
Hypertext Markup Language (HTML)	Enables users to exchange e-mail in HTML format	Outlook 98, Outlook 2000, Outlook Web Access, Entourage, and Outlook 10	Netscape Messenger, Netscape Navigator
Network News Transport Protocol (NNTP)	Used to post and retrieve messages in newsgroup forums and bulletin boards	Outlook Express	Netscape Messenger, Gravity, and Free Agent
Lightweight Directory Access Protocol (LDAP)	Enables users to perform searches against LDAP directories	Outlook 97 (with third-party add-on), Outlook 98, Outlook 2000, Outlook Express, Entourage, and Outlook 10.	Netscape Messenger

Table 1-1. *Supported Protocols. Exchange 2000 supports several Internet standards, allowing you to choose from a variety of Microsoft and non-Microsoft clients.* (continued)

Protocol	Description	Microsoft Clients Supporting	Some Non-Microsoft Clients Supporting
vCARD (virtual card)	Enables the exchange of electronic business cards	Outlook 97 (with Microsoft add-on), Outlook 98, Outlook 2000, Outlook Express, Entourage, and Outlook 10	Novell Groupwise, Calypso E-mail, FoneSync, Gnome Office, Goldmine, Lotus Organizer, Netscape Communicator, Palm III, Sidekick 98, TeamWARE, and Zoomit VIA
vCalendar (virtual calendar)	Internet standard that enables the exchange of calendaring and scheduling information	Outlook 98, Outlook 2000, Entourage and Outlook 10	Appointments Plus, CalenGo, EPOC PIM, Gnome Office, Lotus Organizer, Netscape Communicator, Sidekick 98, Softimage Events Calendar, Nokia 9110 Communicator
iCalendar (Internet calendar)	Emerging standard described in RFC 2445 for the format and storage of schedule information	Outlook 98, Outlook 2000, Entourage, and Outlook 10	Lotus Organizer, Netscape Communicator

Table 1-1. *Supported Protocols. Exchange 2000 supports several Internet standards, allowing you to choose from a variety of Microsoft and non-Microsoft clients.* (continued)

Chapter 13 will discuss in great detail the numerous choices for Exchange 2000 clients available to administrators and end-users.

Summary

Exchange 2000 Server is a major product release for Microsoft, and it should provide increased value for companies and their end-users. It is tightly integrated with Windows 2000 and Active Directory and is designed to meet the messaging and collaboration needs for businesses of all sizes. While the critical success factors for each business are unique, this book provides a complete reference for deploying Exchange 2000 in your organization.

Exchange 2000 is radically different from its predecessors. While it boasts a wide variety of new features and benefits, it does so by adding a substantial amount of complexity. As a result, careful planning should be performed prior to deploying Exchange 2000 in your organization. This book provides detailed planning and implementation information and instructions for administrators using Exchange 2000. If you are responsible for deploying Exchange 2000 in your company, you should read this book cover to cover prior to deploying any servers. Even if you've already deployed Exchange 20000, you'll find this book to be a valuable reference for maintaining your Exchange infrasructure.

Chapter 2

Active Directory Summary

Prior versions of Microsoft Exchange contained their own directory and directory service, which were managed and replicated separately from the accounts database directory in Windows NT domain. Exchange 2000 does away with a separate directory, relying instead on the directory and directory services built into Windows 2000—Active Directory. You cannot understand or manage Exchange 2000 without a solid understanding of Active Directory. However, if you already understand the Exchange 5.5 directory and directory service, you are well on your way to understanding Active Directory.

This chapter provides an introduction to Windows 2000 Active Directory and describes the key concepts and terms you will need to properly design, deploy, and manage an Exchange 2000 infrastructure. Standards, such as the Domain Name System (DNS) and the Lightweight Directory Access Protocol (LDAP), will be discussed as they relate to Active Directory and therefore to Exchange 2000. Finally, we will discuss the physical and logical structure of Active Directory, as well as Active Directory security.

Active Directory is a topic that can, and does, fill entire books, so we won't cover it in its entirety here; however, because Active Directory replaces the Exchange directory services, a review of the basic structure and elements of Active Directory is necessary.

Overview of Active Directory

For businesses to remain competitive, networked computing is a must. Networks are growing ever larger and more complex, making information and resources difficult, if not impossible, to find. Public and private networks typically contain many interesting objects, such as users, file servers, printers, fax servers, applications, and databases. Even on the smallest networks, important data and shared resources can be hard to locate and manage. Users want to find and use these objects, and administrators need to manage these objects.

To overcome these challenges, many companies have deployed multiple directories that contain published information about some of the objects available on the network. An electronic mail system, a corporate telephone book, and a Windows NT accounts database are all examples of directories that are used by companies today. These directory services attempt to offer organized approaches to managing the data contained in the directory. Unfortunately, as is almost always the case when a single organization deploys multiple directories, usability, data integrity, and cost-of-ownership issues will arise. Microsoft created Active Directory to address these issues. Active Directory is the name of the directory and directory service in Windows 2000, the next-generation network operating system for business users. Active Directory is also the replacement for the Exchange Server directory services in Exchange Server 2000.

Imagine that you are giving a presentation on your company's latest product offering to the sales staff in one of your remote offices. For some reason, you weren't able to print out enough color handouts for all of the attendees, but you aren't worried because you know there's a color printer somewhere in this remote office. But when you get to the remote office, you can't locate the color printer. Perhaps you might even locate it physically, but unfortunately, you're not able to determine what server the printer is connected to or what its share name is, so you can't use it. Wouldn't it be great if the printer were published in a readily accessible directory and easily located? An ideal directory would allow you to locate the printer using natural language queries, such as "all color printers in E-wing," or "color printers that duplex in Tallahassee." With Windows 2000 and Active Directory services, you *can* locate resources this way.

What Is Active Directory?

If you've administered previous versions of Exchange Server, you already have experience managing a directory and a directory service. In general terms, a directory contains information about network objects, such as applications, files, printers, and people. It also provides a consistent way to name, describe, locate, access, manage, and secure information about these individual resources. Active Directory is the central authority in Windows 2000 networks that manages identities and relationships between distributed resources, enabling the resources to work together. Because Active Directory performs essentially network operating system functions, it is tightly coupled with Windows 2000 and its security subsystem to ensure the integrity and privacy of the network. Active Directory also plays a crucial role in an organization's ability to manage its network infrastructure, administer its systems, and control the overall user experience of accessing the organization's information systems.

Active Directory is a significant enhancement over the directory services provided in prior versions of Windows NT. Prior versions of Windows NT include services such as the Windows Browser Service and the Windows Internet Name Service to help users and administrators find and manage network resources. While these services had a solid conceptual foundation, the interfaces used to present them were neither intuitive nor uniform. Users were stuck with the Network Neighborhood, the clumsy, network counterpart to My Computer, that only made locating information easy if you knew exactly where it was located. Moreover, even though their managed objects resided in the same container—an NT domain—administrators were forced to use individual tools, such as User Manager for Domains, Server Manager, and many others, instead of a single management console. For these reasons, Windows NT domains really worked best in small- to medium-sized businesses. Due to limitations on the size of the Windows NT domain database, larger companies typically needed to use the master or multimaster domain models, which made locating information and managing domain objects even more difficult.

The Windows 2000 Active Directory replaces the functionality of the Windows NT domain. Active Directory stores information about organizations, users, and shares, and just about any other network object. It uses a structured data store as the basis for a logical, hierarchical organization of directory information. This data store, also known as the directory, stores information about directory objects, such as servers, files, printers, and the user and computer accounts. A set of rules, called the schema, defines the classes of objects and attributes contained in the directory, the constraints and limits on instances of these objects, and the format of their names.

Active Directory uses a Global Catalog that contains information about all objects in the directory. This Global Catalog allows users and administrators to find information regardless of its location. It features an indexing mechanism, enabling users and network applications to easily locate stored and published information. Active Directory also includes a replication service that distributes directory data across a network. Any change to directory data is replicated to all domain controllers in the domain, and each domain controller contains a complete copy of all directory information for its domain.

Because it contains the published information, Active Directory also acts as the central authority for network security, allowing the operating system to readily verify a user's identity and control his or her access to network resources. Active Directory is integrated with the Windows 2000 security subsystem, allowing for a single, secure logon process, as well as access control for data queries and data modifications. This integration is mainly through logon authentication and access control to objects in the directory. With this single network logon, administrators can manage data located anywhere on the network, and authorized users can access resources from anywhere on the network.

Understanding Active Directory

Understanding Active Directory is an important step toward understanding Windows 2000 and Exchange 2000. As part of their goal to immerse Windows 2000 in the Internet, Microsoft built Active Directory on two Internet standards: DNS, a standard for naming and locating domain names on the Internet, and LDAP Version 3, an Internet Engineering Task Force standard for exchanging directory information with clients and other directories.

The Active Directory database is built on the Extensible Storage Engine (ESE), the same database engine that was introduced with Exchange Server 5.5. This database allows you to create up to a 16-terabyte database that can theoretically contain 40 million objects per domain. Table 2-1 illustrates the differences between the Exchange directory service and the Active Directory directory service.

Another benefit of using ESE is that Active Directory was built for speed, availability, and reliability. It is capable of performing lookups in a database with more than a million objects in mere seconds. This is due in part to a new, separate index file called the Global Catalog, which is replicated to all Active Directory servers. Because Active Directory uses ESE, its store architecture looks similar to Exchange 5.5. Figure 2-1 illustrates the structure of Active Directory.

In the broadest context, Active Directory is a namespace that is integrated with DNS. The Active Directory directory service is an object-oriented X.500-compliant database, which organizes resources available on your network in a hierarchical,

Active Directory Directory Services	Exchange Server Directory Services
Attribute-based replication	Object-based replication
Flexible/powerful access control	Limited access control
Multimaster in domain	Multimaster in site
Full schema extensibility	Limited schema "extensibility"
Rename-safe objects	Objects not rename-safe
ADSI and LDAP v3+ extensions	ADSI and LDAP v3 support

Table 2-1. *Comparison of Active Directory and Exchange Server Directory Services*

tree-like structure. However, Active Directory is not an X.500 directory; instead, it uses LDAP as an access protocol, and it supports the X.500 information model without requiring systems to host the entire X.500 overhead.

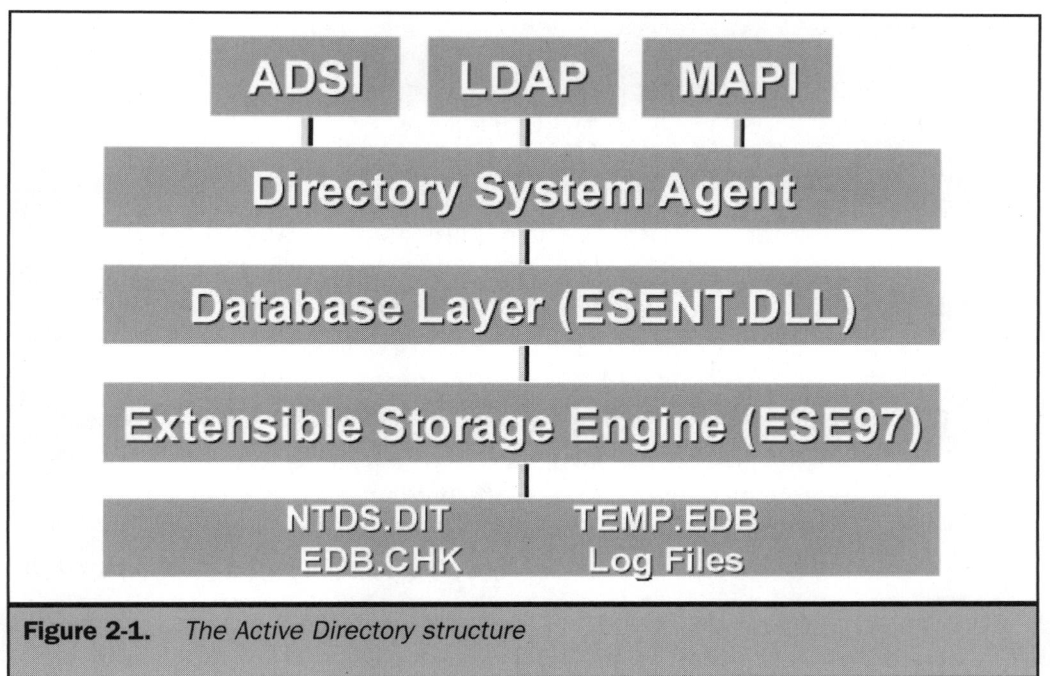

Figure 2-1. *The Active Directory structure*

X.500 is the most widely used protocol for directory management. Currently there are two different standards, one from 1988 and one from 1993, with the 1993 standard providing a number of advances over the older standard. The Active Directory directory services are derived from the 1993 X.500 standard.

Technically, DNS and Active Directory are both namespaces. A namespace is an area in which a name is resolved through a process known as *name resolution*. Names are great for use by people, but by themselves, names don't contain enough information to be useful to computers. Name resolution is used so that computers have a mechanism for associating a name with the object or information it represents. It is the process of translating a friendly name into an identifier that can be utilized by a computer. This is a very common process that occurs on public and private networks millions of times every day. Each time you visit a Web site, the site's name, or uniform resource locator (URL) is *resolved* to its TCP/IP address. This resolution is done through a DNS lookup. Each time you log on to a Windows NT system, your username is resolved to a security ID (SID).

Overview of Domain Name Service

Before you can fully understand Active Directory, it is helpful to review the basics of DNS and its relationship to TCP/IP and to the Internet. As previously mentioned, Active Directory combines the best of DNS as a locator service with X.500 naming standards and LDAP as its core protocol. DNS is the most widely used locator service in the world. A locator service is used to translate a name—for example, www.tntsoftware.com—into a TCP/IP address. DNS is designed to scale to very large systems; it supports the Internet, the world's largest network. Yet, it remains lightweight enough for use in a network that has just a few computers.

DNS Windows 2000 domains rely on DNS for resource naming. DNS is a name service standard of the Internet Engineering Task Force (IETF), whose Web site is found at http://www.ietf.org/. DNS locates TCP/IP computers and devices by resolving *host* names—the names understood by users—to IP addresses, a special number that computers understand. Internet IP addresses are managed by a globally distributed DNS database, and DNS is often implemented in private TCP/IP networks. DNS is comprised of three main components:

- The DNS namespace, a distributed database containing the name-related information
- Name servers, which contain a physical representation of the namespace and resource records (RR), and which replicate information to other name servers
- Resolvers, which contact and query name servers for name resolution purposes

Note *DNS is defined by RFC 1034, which can be found at http://www.ietf.org/rfc/rfc1034.txt. This RFC has been updated by RFCs 1101, 1183, 1348, 1876, 1982, 2065, 2181, 2308, and 2535.*

DNS is organized into a hierarchy of domains, making the Internet a single namespace. DNS is also used in private companies to construct custom namespaces. DNS starts with a root domain that has a null label (in other words, is unnamed) and has several top-level domains subdivided into second-level domains. Figure 2-2 details the structure of the Internet DNS namespace.

The Internet Domain Namespace The root of the Internet domain namespace is managed by an Internet authority (currently, the Internet Corporation for Assigned Names and Numbers, or ICANN). This authority is responsible for delegating administrative responsibility for the top-level domains of the DNS namespace and for registering second-level domain names. The top-level domains are the familiar domain categories: commercial (.com), educational (.edu), governmental (.gov), and so forth. Outside the United States, two-letter country codes are used, such as .au for Australia. The United States also has a country code of .us assigned to it, but it is used

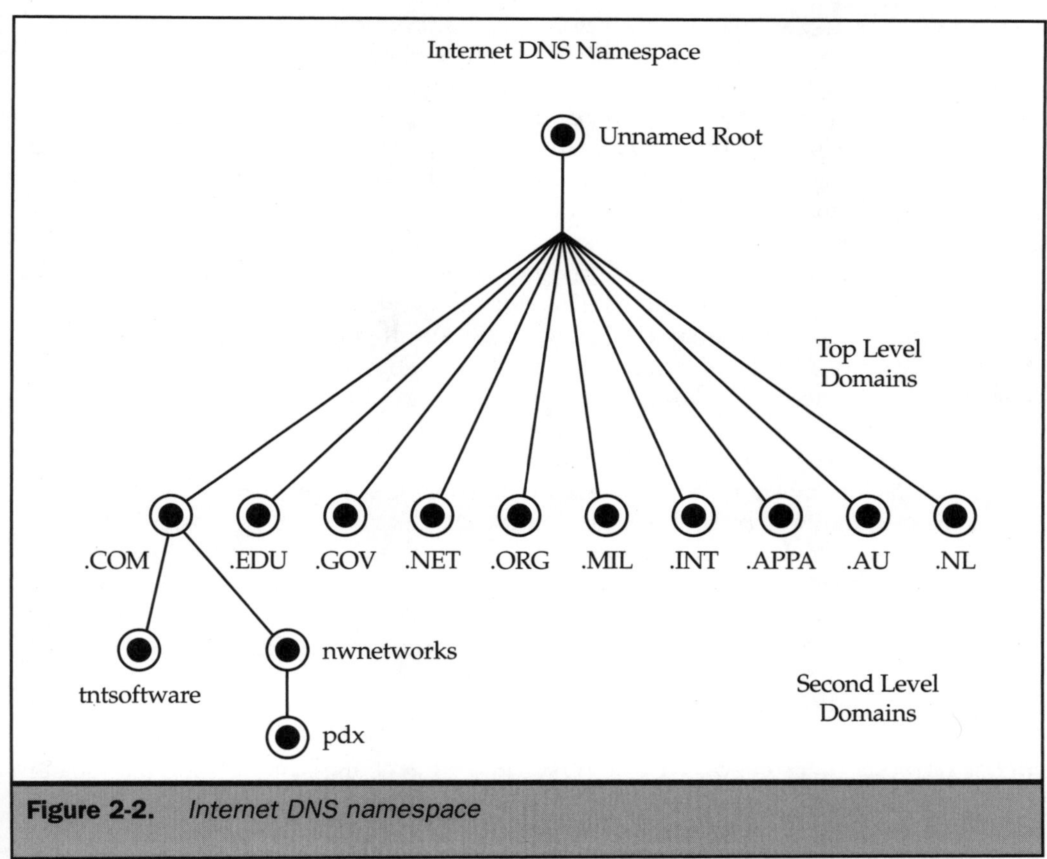

Figure 2-2. *Internet DNS namespace*

infrequently. Second-level domains, such as tntsoftware.com and nwnetworks.com, represent namespaces that are formally registered to institutions and individuals.

ICANN is a nonprofit corporation that has assumed responsibility for coordinating certain Internet technical functions, including the management of Internet domain name system. To learn more about ICANN, visit http://www.icann.org/.

DNS databases can be partitioned into multiple *zones*. Zones are portions of the database containing resource records with the owner names that belong to the contiguous portion of the DNS namespace. A single DNS server can be configured to host none, one, or multiple zones. Each zone is anchored to a specific domain name, which is referred to as the zone's *root domain*. Zones contain information about all names that end with the zone's root domain name. A DNS server is considered authoritative for a name if it loads the zone containing that name. The first record in any zone file is a Start of Authority resource record (SOA RR). The SOA RR identifies a primary DNS name server for the zone as the best source of information for the data in that zone and as an entity processing the updates for the zone.

As previously mentioned, you can have multiple zones representing the same portion of the namespace. There are two types of zones in standard DNS: primary and secondary. A primary zone is where all updates for the zone records are made. A secondary zone is represented by a read-only copy of the primary zone. The changes made to the primary zone file are then replicated to the secondary zone file. A single DNS server can contain both types of zones. It can be primary for one zone (that is, it has the master copy of the zone file) and secondary for a different zone (it has a read-only copy of the zone file). In addition to these zones, Windows 2000 also includes *Active Directory Integrated DNS*. Active Directory Integrated DNS uses the directory for the storage and replication of DNS zone databases. If you decide to use Active Directory Integrated DNS, DNS runs on one or more domain controllers (and only on Windows 2000 domain controllers) and you do not need to set up a separate DNS replication topology. During directory replication, the zone information is distributed to all the other DNS servers in your domain.

The process of replicating a zone file to multiple name servers is called *zone transfer*. Zone transfer is achieved by copying the zone file information from the master server to the secondary server. A master server is the source of the zone information. The master server can be primary or secondary. If the master is primary, the zone transfer comes directly from the source. If the master server is secondary, the file received from the master server by means of a zone transfer is a copy of the read-only zone file.

Dynamic DNS Windows 2000's DNS service supports Dynamic DNS (DDNS)—also known as dynamic host updates—as covered in RFC 2136. This RFC introduces a new opcode or message format called UPDATE. The UPDATE message can add and delete resource records from a specified zone and test for prerequisite conditions. UPDATE is atomic—that is, all prerequisites must be satisfied or no update operation will take place. By default, every Windows 2000 computer attempts to register its own A (forward), PTR (reverse), and SRV (service) records. If desired, this behavior can be disabled by following the step-by-step instructions in Microsoft Knowledge Base article Q246804 (http://support.microsoft.com/support/kb/articles/Q246/8/04.asp).

The DHCP client service is responsible for generating these updates. As a result, this service runs on every Windows 2000 computer regardless of whether it is configured as a DHCP client. The algorithm for the dynamic updates differs for the three different types of clients: those with static IP addresses, those using DHCP, and those accessing the network via Remote Access Services.

Note *RFC 2136 can be read in its entirety at http://www.ietf.org/rfc/rfc2136.txt.*

Active Directory Integration with DNS

In Active Directory, Windows 2000 domain names are DNS namespaces called zones. The same naming convention used on the Internet is also used in Active Directory. Itntsoftware.com can be both a DNS domain (an area of addressing) and a Windows 2000 domain. In Windows 2000, JohnDoe@tntsoftware.com.com is both an Internet e-mail address and a user name in the tntsoftware.com domain. This also means that Windows 2000 domains need to be located using DNS.

Windows NT computers that are members of a domain participate in domain security. To do this, these computers require accounts in the accounts database of the is domain to which they belong. When a computer is running Windows NT, its net logon service attempts to locate a domain controller in its domain. The process of locating an NT domain controller is typically handled by NetBIOS name resolution of the domain's <1C> record. This process returns the IP addresses of the primary domain controller and all backup domain controllers.

The general process is the same in Windows 2000, except that DNS is used instead of NetBIOS name resolution. In order for a Windows 2000 computer to log on and perform Active Directory queries, it must locate a domain controller or a Global Catalog server that can process the requests. This is done by a DNS lookup. The DNS database contains information about which servers contain the physical components of Active Directory—in other words, which servers are the domain controllers.

The integration of DNS and Active Directory is at the core of Windows 2000. Keep in mind, though, that DNS domains and Active Directory domains use the same domain names for *different* namespaces. Even though both namespaces share an identical domain structure, they are not the same namespace. Each namespace stores different data and manages different objects. DNS stores zones and resource records; Active Directory stores domains and domain objects.

Active Directory domain names are based on the DNS hierarchical naming structure, with an inverted tree structure. It is a single root domain, underneath which can be parent and child domains, which are called branches and leaves. A Windows 2000 domain name such as *exchange.pdx.tntsoftware.com* identifies a domain named *exchange*, which is a child domain of the domain named *pdx*, itself a child of the domain *tntsoftware.com*. Each computer in a DNS domain is uniquely identified by its fully qualified domain name (FQDN). The FQDN of a computer located in the *exchange* domain is *server1.exchange.pdx.tntsoftware.com*.

Every Windows 2000 domain and every Windows 2000 computer has a DNS name. As such, they are represented both as Active Directory objects and as nodes in the DNS hierarchy.

Note *While Microsoft recommends that you use the DNS included with Windows 2000, it is not a requirement. You can use any version of DNS you prefer, provided that it supports SRV RR records (as defined in RFC 2782, formerly 2052) and the dynamic update protocol (as defined in RFC 2136). BIND version 8.1.2 and later supports both SRV RR records and dynamic updates (version 8.1.1 also supports dynamic updates, but it has bugs that were corrected in version 8.1.2).*

Lightweight Directory Access Protocol

As the name implies, the Lightweight Directory Access Protocol (LDAP) is an IETF standard for locating and accessing information stored on directory servers over TCP/IP connections. LDAP is mainly used as a means of accessing X.500—and more recently, non-X.500—directory systems. LDAP has strong industry support, and it is widely expected to become an industry standard for directory services. Active Directory supports LDAP 3.0, as defined by RFC 2251, and LDAP 2.0, as defined by RFC 1777.

Note *For a listing of and links to common LDAP RFCs, see Microsoft Knowledge Base article Q221606 (http://support.microsoft.com/support/kb/articles/Q221/6/06.asp).*

Directory services depend on namespaces, which provide for the efficient referencing and retrieval of collections of related information, such as a person's name, organization, physical address, and e-mail address. Like X.500, LDAP bases its directory model on entries, where the distinguishing name is used to refer to an entry without ambiguity. But rather than use the highly structured X.500 data encodings, LDAP adopts a simple, string-based approach for representing directory entries, which simplifies an application's requirement for processing directory entries.

The LDAP information model is based on the *entry*, which contains information about some object. Entries are composed of attributes, which have a type and one or move values. Each attribute has a syntax that determines what kind of values are allowed in the attribute and how those values behave during directory operations.

Active Directory also uses LDAP for interoperability with other LDAP-compatible client applications. With the appropriate permissions, you can use any LDAP-compatible client application to browse, query, add, modify, or delete information in Active Directory. The physical directory information that is stored on the hard disk is called the *store*. Access to the store is provided by a component known as the *directory system agent*

(DSA). Windows 2000 and Windows 9x clients that have the Active Directory client components installed use LDAP 3.0 to connect to the DSA. Windows NT 4.0 computers and earlier connect to the DSA using the Security Account Manager (SAM) interface.

The Active Directory Structure

The following concepts are the foundation upon which Active Directory and (by proxy) Exchange are based. Active Directory can be thought of as two structures: the physical structure you use to configure and manage your network and the logical structure you use to organize your network resources. These structures are independent of one another, which means there is no correlation between your domain structure and your physical structure.

The logical structure of Active Directory enables organizations to define and group resources so they can be easily located, regardless of the resource's physical location.The physical structure of Active Directory is based on *domain controllers* and sites. While this separation of structures provides flexibility in the design of a directory structure, it also requires careful planning.

The Logical Structure of Active Directory

In Active Directory, resources are organized in a logical structure. By grouping resources logically, you are able to easily locate them regardless of their physical location. There are several logical structure elements, beginning with the most basic unit of Active Directory, the *object*.

Objects Objects in Active Directory must be unique. Active Directory uses naming conventions to ensure that the names of objects are only resolvable to the objects they represent. Objects are distinct, named sets of *attributes* that represent something concrete, such as file shares, users, or computers, that can be organized by classes. Attributes—also referred to as properties—are categories of information that define the characteristics of all objects. All objects of a given type have the same attributes. It is the value of these attributes that make each object unique. For example, John Smith is an object. Its attributes include the first name of John and the last name of Smith.

Schema Object classes are the definitions of the types of objects that can be created. These definitions are stored in a logical construct known as the *schema*. The schema is stored in Active Directory. Schema definitions are themselves also stored as objects—Class Schema objects and Attribute Schema objects. This allows Active Directory to manage Class and Attribute objects in the same way it manages other directory objects. The schema contains the definitions for objects stored in the directory, and it enforces the rules that govern the structure and content of the directory. The schema consists of a set of *classes*, *attributes*, and *syntaxes* that represent an instance of one or more classes in the schema. Classes are categories of objects that share a set of characteristics. They are formal descriptions of discrete, identifiable types of objects that are stored in the directory.

Each object in the directory is an instance of one or more classes in the schema. Attributes describe the characteristics of an object. They define the types of information an object can hold. For each class, the schema specifies the mandatory and optional attributes that constitute the set of shared characteristics of the class. The values assigned to attributes define specific characteristics. A *syntax* is the data type of a particular attribute. It determines what data type an attribute can have.

Active Directory uses a set of predefined syntaxes, and you cannot add new syntaxes. However, the schema is extensible, which means that new definitions of object classes and attributes can be added. Changes to the schema are updated dynamically, which means that newly added items can be used immediately. When Exchange Server 2000 is installed, it modifies and extends the existing Active Directory schema. More on this in Chapter 6.

The Active Directory Hierarchy

Objects in Active Directory are represented in a hierarchical structure. There are four basic components that make up the logical structure of Active Directory: *forests*, *trees*, *domains*, and *organizational units*. Whether you are planning, implementing, managing, or troubleshooting Active Directory, understanding these components and their purposes is very important.

Domains The core storage unit of Active Directory is the *domain*. A domain is a logical container of objects (users, computers, and so on) that share a common security boundary. All Windows 2000 domains in an Active Directory forest trust one another using transitive trusts. However, the existence of these trusts does not convey any rights or privileges to administrators in individual domains. Unless rights have been explicitly granted in another domain, domain administrators only have administrative rights and permissions in their domain. All Windows 2000 domains in the same forest share the following traits:

- A common schema
- A common Global Catalog
- Common configuration information
- Transitive trust relationships between domains
- Transitive trust relationships between domain trees

All network objects must exist in a domain. Like their Windows NT predecessors, Windows 2000 domains can span geographic locations. Every domain has a domain partition that contains all of the objects in the directory for that domain. These domain partitions replicate between domain controllers in that domain. The domain partitions do not replicate between domain controllers across domains.

Also like their Windows NT predecessors, replication units that represent the domain (the domain accounts database) are stored on domain controllers. But unlike prior versions of Windows NT, Windows 2000 does away with the concept of primary and backup domain controllers in favor of multimaster replication and flexible single-master operations (FSMO) or operations masters. This role means that changes are implemented on one controller and pushed to all other controllers in the forest.

Organizational Units In prior versions of Windows NT, delegation of administration in a domain was limited to the use of built-in local groups. These groups had predefined capabilities, but in many cases these capabilities did not fit the needs of a particular situation. As a result, there were many situations where granting administrators Domain Administrator rights was the only solution. In Windows 2000, delegation of administration is very granular. Administration can be delegated arbitrarily by granting a set of users the ability to create specific classes of objects or to modify specific attributes on specific classes of objects.

For these administrative purposes, Windows 2000 domains can be subdivided into organizational units (OUs). An OU is a container object used to organize objects in a domain into logical administrative subgroups. For all intents and purposes, OUs replace Windows NT domains. They are much easier to create, delete, move, and modify than domains, and they are better suited to the delegation role. OUs can also be nested; they can contain child OUs, enabling you to create a hierarchical tree structure inside a domain. Using a combination of nested OUs and access control lists, you can get very granular in your delegation of the administration of objects in the directory. For these reasons, Microsoft strongly recommends that administrators use OUs for creating security boundaries instead of domains.

OUs can be used to group objects according to geographical boundaries, internal administrative models, or any other hierarchy that works for your organization. Delegating administration in your organization has several benefits. Delegating specific rights enables you to minimize the number of users who have high levels of access. When accidents or mistakes are made by an administrator with restricted capability, only their area of responsibility will be impacted. In addition, in many organizations, it is common for non-IT groups to submit change requests to high-level administrators, who make the changes on their behalf. With delegation of administration, this responsibility can be granted to the individual groups in your organization, reducing your company's costs by eliminating the overhead of sending requests to administrators.

Tip *The OU used to hold users or computers in a domain has no effect on Exchange 2000. In addition, your OU hierarchy doesn't need to resemble your business hierarchy. In fact, it might be a good idea if it didn't. Although OUs are easily restructured, you will still save yourself a lot of work if your company ever goes through a reorganization.*

Forests and Trees The moment you create your first Windows 2000 domain, you're creating two Active Directory structures: a *forest* and *tree*. The forest is the boundary for Active Directory; all objects in an Active Directory are contained in a single forest. Forests consist of one or more domains, each of which provides a security context for the forest.

The very first domain in an Active Directory forest is especially important. The first domain in your organization is known as the *root domain*. The root domain holds the configuration and schema for the forest. In addition, its DNS name forms the basis for the forest's name and namespace. As a result, the first domain cannot be removed from the forest.

The first domain in a forest is also the first domain in a domain tree. Keep this in mind when deciding what DNS name you'll be using for your forest's first domain. Because it is the first domain in a domain tree, other domains cannot be represented above it. For example, if you name your forest's first domain *us.mycompany.com*, you won't be able to create *mycompany.com* in the same forest.

Depending on your naming conventions, additional domains are added to either the tree structure or the forest structure. Although a single Windows 2000 domain can contain millions of objects in its directory, there are a few reasons why you might want to create additional domains—for example, if you need to decentralize network administration, or if you have separate business entities under your control that require separate security boundaries.

Note *As previously mentioned, Microsoft recommends that administrators use OUs to create additional administrative boundaries. Therefore, you should only create additional domains when absolutely necessary.*

A tree is a hierarchical arrangement of domains with a single root name, such as tntsoftware.com. The domain tree is the key to scalability of Active Directory. In addition to sharing a common root domain name, all domains share a common schema, a common configuration, and a common Global Catalog. They also share information through automatic, two-way transitive Kerberos v5 trust relationships. This is a substantial departure from prior versions of Windows NT, which used point-to-point, nontransitive trusts. This is illustrated in Figure 2-3.

Continuing the tree metaphor, a forest is one or more domain trees that are not part of the same namespace but that share a common schema, configuration, and Global Catalog. This sharing of common schema and configuration data, in addition to trust relationships between their roots, is what distinguishes a forest from a set of unrelated trees. All trees in a forest trust each other, so if security permits it, all objects in these trees are available to all users. Unlike a tree, a forest does not need a distinct name. As you might have guessed, the first tree in a forest is the root tree. The name of this root tree is used to refer to the forest. Every tree in a forest has its own namespace. A single domain constitutes a tree of one domain, and a single tree constitutes a forest of one tree. A forest exists as a set of cross-referenced objects and Kerberos trust relationships known to the member trees.

The tree structures for an entire forest are stored in Active Directory in the form of parent/child and tree/root relationships. For each domain in a forest, information about its connection to a parent domain or to another tree root domain is added to the

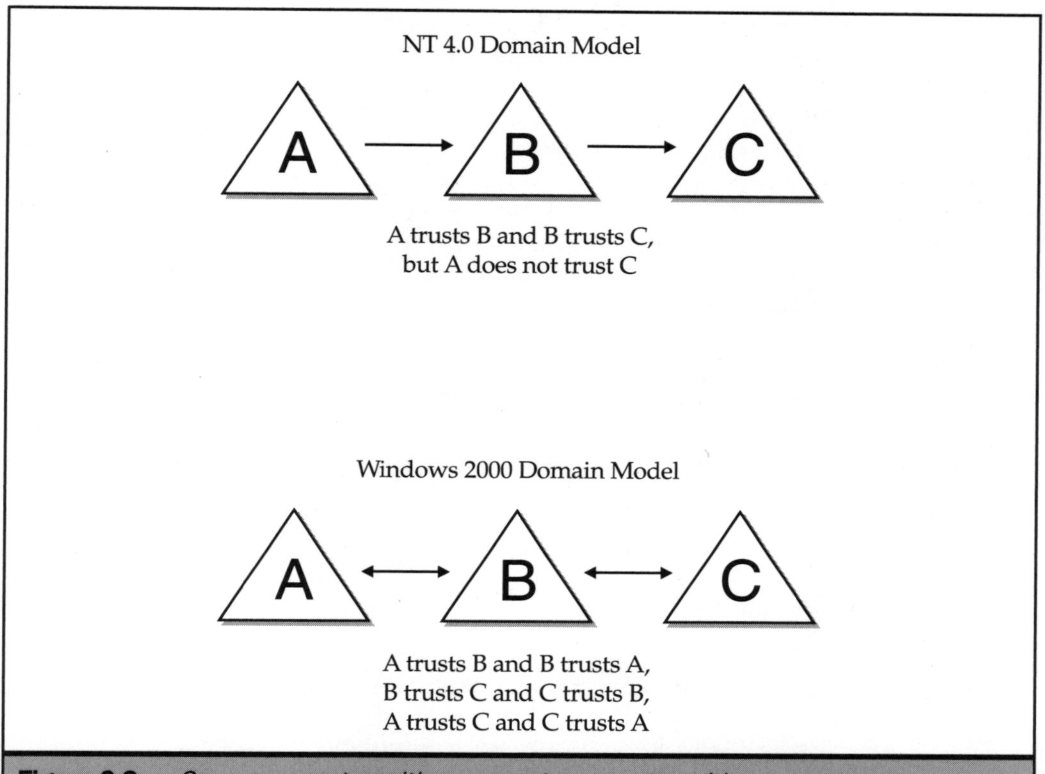

Figure 2-3. *One-way, non-transitive versus two-way, transitive trusts*

configuration data that is replicated throughout the forest. Therefore, every domain controller in a forest has knowledge of the tree structure for the entire forest, including knowledge of the links between trees.

An Active Directory stores data for the entire forest. "Active Directory" and "forest" can be considered synonymous. Although there is a single directory, data storage is distributed among one or more domains while consistent data for all domains is maintained throughout the forest. Moreover, the forest is the boundary for an Exchange 2000 organization.

Global Catalog Servers A Global Catalog (GC) server holds a complete replica of the configuration and schema naming contexts for the forest, a complete replica of the domain naming context in which the server is installed, and a partial replica of all other domains in the forest. These servers have knowledge about every object in the entire forest; however, they may not know about all attributes for objects in other domains. In Exchange Server 2000, all of the information about users and mailboxes resides on GC servers.

A GC server is both a physical storage location and a service. Therefore, it is part of both the physical and logical structure of Active Directory. The purpose of a GC server is to provide a central location for all directory objects. The first domain controller installed in a forest is automatically selected to be a GC server, although GC servers can be domain controllers from any domain.

A Global Catalog server is queried each time a message needs to be routed and each time an address book lookup is performed. According to Microsoft's published guidelines, you should deploy at least one GC server for every four Exchange 2000 Servers. I recommend deploying at least two for every four Exchange 2000 Servers.

GC servers replicate a copy of all objects from every domain in the forest, but they themselves only contain a subset of each object's attributes. The attributes that are replicated are typically those that will be those used in most common queries (name, city, state, and so on). They can also be manually assigned by using the Active Directory Schema MMC snap-in (see Figure 2-4). The Active Directory Schema Manager snap-in is not installed by default; it is installed manually as part of the Windows 2000 Administration Tools package. To install the snap-in:

1. Log on as Administrator.
2. Navigate to the System32 folder.
3. Double-click Adminpak.MSI. This will launch the Windows 2000 Administration Tools Setup Wizard and install the tools.
4. Next, start a new MMC console. Click Start, and then click Run. Enter **MMC /a**, and click OK. Alternatively, open the console to which you'd like to add the snap-in.
5. From the Console menu, click Add/Remove Snap-in, and then click Add.
6. Under Snap-in, double-click Active Directory Schema, and then click Close.
7. If you don't have any more snap-ins to add to the console, click OK.
8. To save this console, on the Console menu, click Save.

The first domain controller is the only server that is automatically designated a GC server. Additional GC servers need to be created manually using the Active Directory Sites and Services MMC snap-in (see Figure 2-5).

A GC server also contains *binding information*—data that is used to locate the actual object. Binding information is used by a client to connect (or bind) to a service on a network. Binding information encompasses a wide range of possible types of data, such as file services, Web services, and RPC server services. A UNC path for a share, a URL, and a DNS name are all examples of binding information. It is this binding information that allows both users and administrators to locate objects regardless of their physical location.

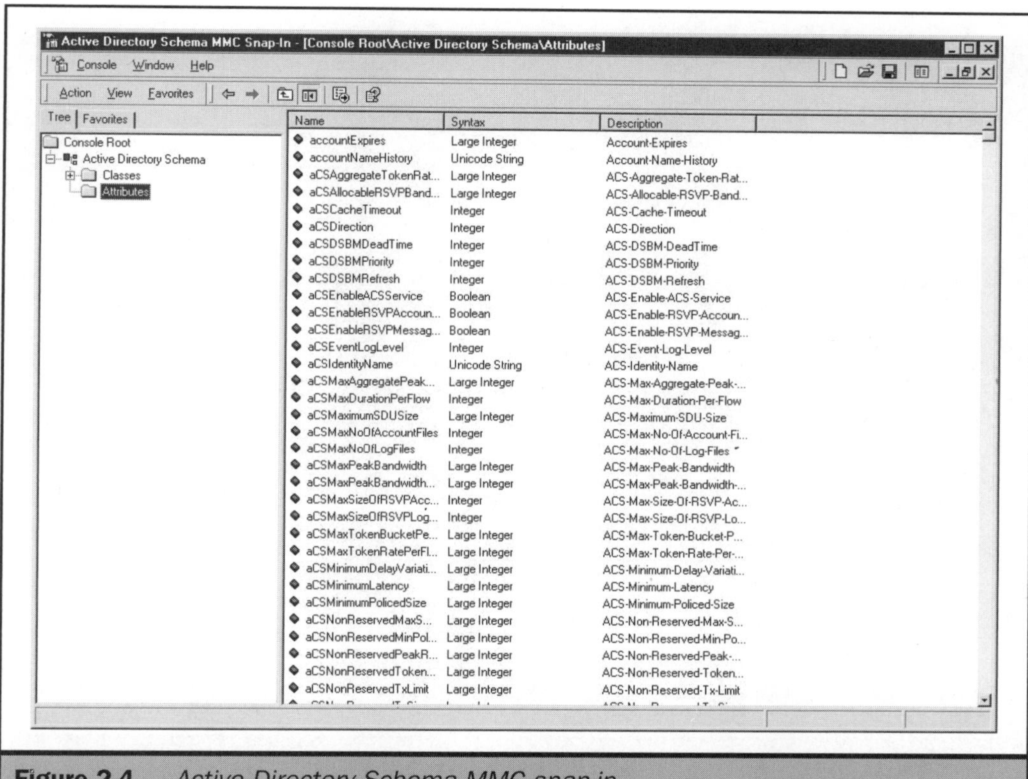

Figure 2-4. *Active Directory Schema MMC snap-in*

Partitioning In addition to being replicated, Active Directory is also *partitioned*. To support tens of millions of objects and provide support for hundreds of thousands of clients, the Active Directory directory tree is partitioned into logical segments. Each logical partition replicates its changes separately among those domain controllers in the forest that store replicas of the same directory partitions.

Some partitions store forest-wide configuration and schema information; others store information specific to individual domains. Domain-specific data is stored in a *domain directory partition*. Forest-wide data is stored in two directory partitions, the *configuration directory partition* and the *schema directory partition*.

Directory partitions that store domain information are replicated to domain controllers in that domain only; however, directory partitions that store configuration and schema information are replicated to domain controllers in all domains. Because all domain controllers store forest-wide configuration and schema information, a domain controller in one domain can reference a domain controller in any other domain if the information being sought is not stored locally. In addition, domain controllers that are Global Catalog

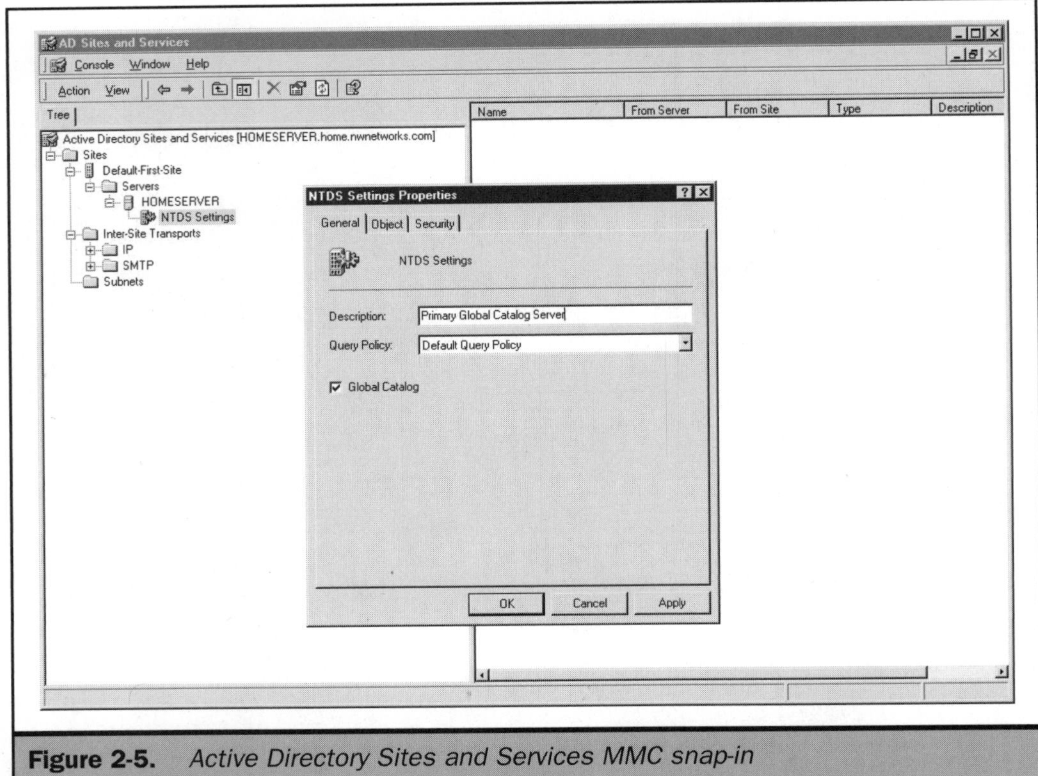

Figure 2-5. *Active Directory Sites and Services MMC snap-in*

servers contain a full replica of one domain directory partition plus a partial replica of every other domain in the forest. Thus, a domain controller that is a Global Catalog server can be queried to find any object in the entire forest.

The Physical Structure of Active Directory

Physically, Active Directory is an ESE database called NTDS.DIT. This database lives on an NTFS partition on every Windows 2000 domain controller. The physical structure of Active Directory is comprised of *domain controllers* and *sites*. Domain controllers in the same domain may reside in several different sites, and a site may contain domain controllers from several different domains. Sites, however, are not part of the namespace. The site topology information is stored in a separate part of the directory.

Domain Controllers Like its Windows NT counterpart, a Windows 2000 domain controller is a server that manages user authentication and logon and access to shared resources. But unlike prior versions of Windows NT, all Windows 2000 domain controllers contain a writable copy of the domain's directory. Active Directory must reside on a domain controller. Domain controllers store a complete copy of all Active Directory information for that domain. They also manage changes to that information and replicate changes to other domain controllers.

Tip *To eliminate single points of failure, Microsoft recommends a minimum of two domain controllers for every Active Directory domain in your organization. In addition, there are other factors, such as location of user base, available bandwidth, and network reliability, that could also create the need for additional domain controllers.*

In Windows NT 4.0 and earlier, the primary domain controller is the only domain controller that has a writable copy of the Security Accounts Manager (SAM) database. Backup domain controllers have read-only copies of the SAM database. This is referred to as a master/slave model. Active Directory uses a multimaster model. Any server with Active Directory installed is a domain controller, with each having a writable copy of the directory database. This means that, generally speaking, all domain controllers are equal.

However, as George Orwell might put it, some domain controllers are more equal than others. Even if a domain controller is disconnected from the network, changes can be made to its copy of the directory. When the domain controller is reconnected, these changes, like changes made at online domain controllers, are automatically replicated to all of the other domain controllers in the domain. Multimaster replication raises several issues avoided by the master/slave model, such as conflicting updates. If two people simultaneously make conflicting updates, each set of updates is replicated. However, even in the presence of conflicting updates, all domain controllers eventually converge to the same value through a process called conflict resolution.

Active Directory deals with conflicting updates by using a conflict resolution algorithm that handles discrepancies in values by determining which changes were written last. The last writer wins, and the conflicting changes are discarded. This resolution method may be acceptable in some cases, but there are times when this approach is insufficient for resolving conflicts. Even with this process, it is sometimes better to prevent conflicts than to resolve them after the fact. For example, if different domain controllers have conflicting versions of the directory schema, the situation could be resolved using the normal conflict resolution methods. However, because the schema is updated infrequently and because the consistency of the schema is very important, conflict prevention is better than relying on normal conflict resolution methods.

To prevent conflicts, Active Directory performs schema updates in a single master fashion. Only the domain controller holding the schema master role can accept updates to schema objects. The schema master role can be assigned to any domain controller, as the need arises, but at any given moment, only one domain controller holds this role. The schema master role is one example of a flexible single-master operation role, also called an operations master role, or an FSMO (often pronounced "fizz-mo") role. Other operations master roles are a part of Windows 2000 Server, and each role controls a specific set of directory changes. For each role, only the domain controller holding that role can make the associated directory changes. If the domain controller holding this role is taken offline or is otherwise unreachable, the schema cannot be updated.

Note *Although the FSMO for schema operations is the only domain controller that can perform schema modifications, you don't need to connect directly to it when making modifications. The domain controller you connect to will generate a referral to the current FSMO during processing of the modifications.*

In Windows 2000, there are five FSMO roles: schema master, domain naming master, RID master, PDC emulator, and infrastructure daemon. These roles can all be held by a single domain controller or by multiple domain controllers. The schema master FSMO role holder is the domain controller responsible for performing updates to the directory schema. The domain naming master FSMO role holder is the domain controller responsible for making changes to the domain namespace of the directory. The RID master FSMO role holder is the domain controller responsible for processing relative ID pool requests from all domain controllers in the domain. The PDC emulator FSMO role holder is a domain controller that advertises itself as the primary domain controller to down-level clients, such as Windows NT and Windows 9x computers. Finally, the infrastructure FSMO role holder is the domain controller responsible for updating an object's security ID and distinguished name in a cross-domain object reference.

By default, the first domain controller you install becomes the schema master. The "flexible" in FSMO means you can reassign this role to another domain controller. This can be done through the Active Directory Schema MMC snap-in or through a command-line utility called NTDSUTIL.

To change the current schema master using the Active Directory Schema MMC snap-in:

1. Go to Start | Run and enter **MMC /a**. This will launch an empty MMC console in Author Mode.
2. Click on Console | Add/Remove Snap-in and add the Active Directory Schema snap-in.
3. In the left pane, right-click on Active Directory schema, and then select Operations Master from the menu. The Change Schema Master dialog box will be displayed (see Figure 2-6). This will display the current schema master.
4. Click the Change button to select another domain controller.

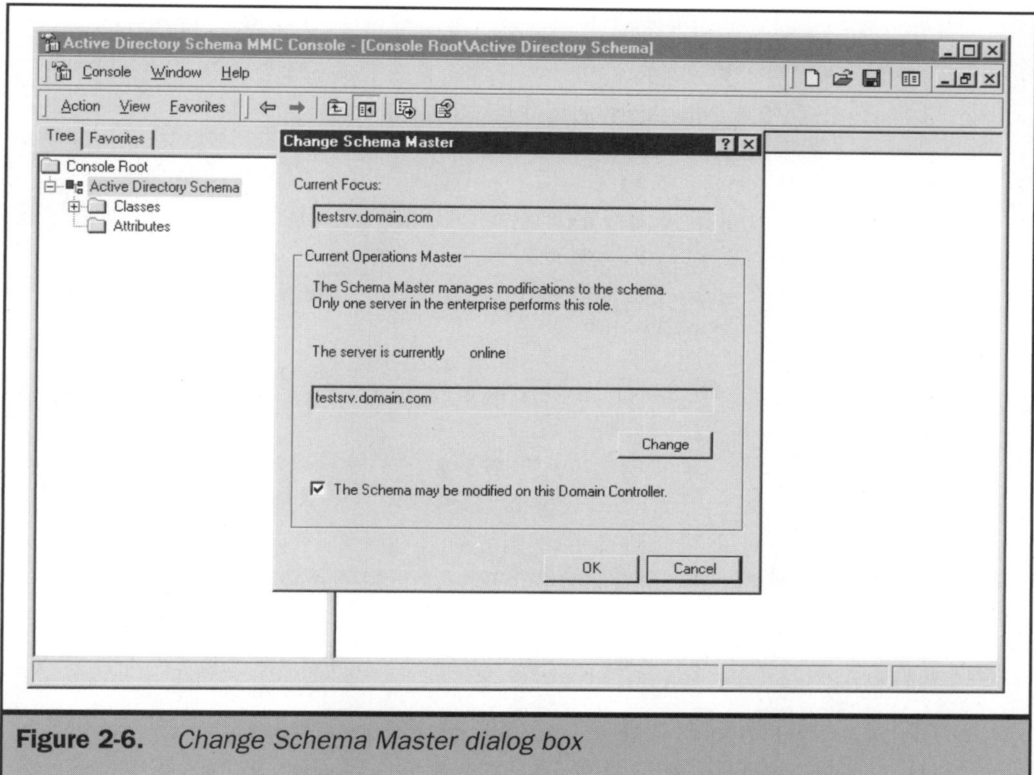

Figure 2-6. *Change Schema Master dialog box*

Note *You must first connect to the domain controller to which you want to assign the FSMO role. You cannot use one domain controller to designate another domain controller as the FSMO master.*

NTDSUTIL is a command-line utility included in Windows 2000 that can be used to manage an Active Directory. It can be run interactively or through an automated script. To change the current schema master using NTDSUTIL, with the original role owner online:

1. Log on locally on the domain controller you want to become the schema master.
2. Go to a command prompt and type **NTDSUTIL**. The ntdsutil: command line will appear.

3. Type **roles** and press ENTER. The fsmo maintenance: prompt will appear.
4. Type **connections** and press ENTER. The server connections: prompt will appear.
5. Type **connect to server <*name*>** (without the <> and where ***name*** is the name of the local server). NTDSUTIL will bind to the local server using your credentials.
6. Type **quit,** then press ENTER to return to the fsmo maintenance: prompt.
7. Type **transfer schema master** and press ENTER. The Role Transfer Confirmation dialog box will appear (see Figure 2-7).
8. Click the Yes button to transfer the schema master role. The role transfer will be verified in the command window.

To change the current schema master using NTDSUTIL, with the original role owner offline:

1. Log on locally on the domain controller you want to become the schema master.
2. Go to a command prompt and type **NTDSUTIL**. The ntdsutil: command line will appear.
3. Type **roles** and press ENTER. The fsmo maintenance: prompt will appear.
4. Type **connections** and press ENTER. The server connections: prompt will appear.
5. Type **connect to server <*name*>** (without the <> and where ***name*** is the name of the local server). NTDSUTIL will bind to the local server using your credentials.
6. Type **quit,** then press ENTER to return to the fsmo maintenance: prompt.
7. Type **seize schema master** and press ENTER. The Role Seizure Confirmation dialog box will appear (shown in Figure 2-8). You should verify the information on this dialog box before seizing the schema master role.
8. Once you have verified the information in the Role Seizure Confirmation dialog box, click Yes to seize the schema master role. The role seizure will be verified in the command window.

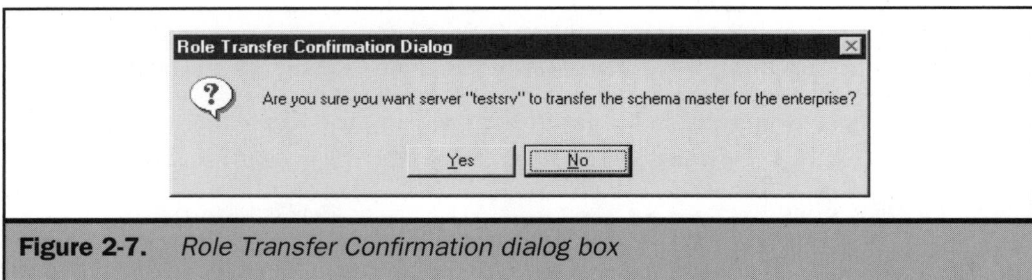

Figure 2-7. *Role Transfer Confirmation dialog box*

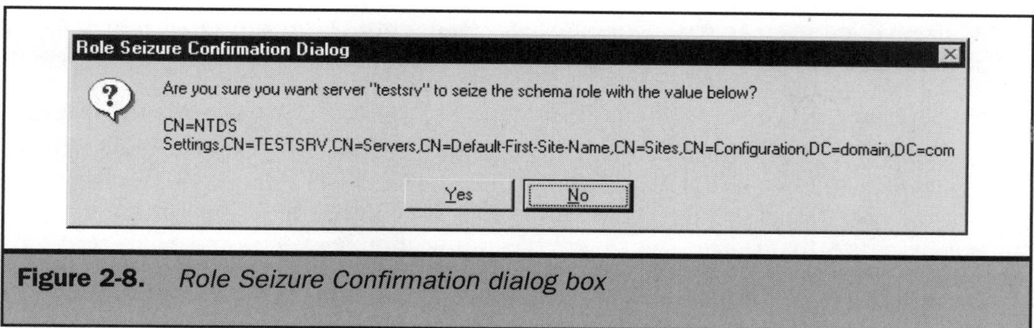

Figure 2-8. *Role Seizure Confirmation dialog box*

Domain Modes An Active Directory domain can exist in one of two modes: *mixed* mode or *native* mode. A mixed mode Active Directory domain contains both Active Directory domain controllers and Windows NT 4.0 backup domain controllers. In this mode, an Active Directory domain controller acts like an NT 4.0 primary domain controller. It holds the only writable copy of the accounts database, and it authenticates users. Because it contains Windows NT 4.0 BDCs, the scalability of an Active Directory domain in mixed mode is bound by the limitations of an NT 4.0 domain. This means a practical limit of about 40,000 objects.

In a native mode Active Directory domain, there are no Windows NT 4.0 backup domain controllers; all domain controllers are Windows 2000 Active Directory domain controllers. As a result, the limitations imposed by Windows NT 4.0 domains are removed, and the domain is capable of containing more than a million objects. The change from mixed mode to native mode is irreversible. Once your domain is in native mode, you cannot revert back to mixed mode, nor can you introduce any Windows NT 4.0 domain controllers. However, you can have NT 4.0 member servers and workstations as members of a native mode Active Directory domain.

Note *An Exchange 2000 organization can also exist in mixed mode or native mode; however, that mode refers to Exchange 2000 only, and it is independent of your Active Directory domain mode.*

Sites A Windows 2000 site is a different from the concept of site in prior versions of Exchange. Both concepts include permanent high-bandwidth connectivity, but unlike Exchange sites, Windows 2000 sites do not depend on namespaces or domains. In a Windows 2000 network, a site is an area (or collection of subnets) with good TCP/IP connectivity, such as a LAN, a high-speed backbone, or some other network connection faster than 10Mbps. Windows 2000 sites allow you to correlate replication traffic to your physical infrastructure. In a single site, replicas of a given domain replicate among each other. Servers are designated in each site to replicate changes to partners in other sites.

Whereas domains map to the logical structure of your organization, sites map to the physical structure of your network. Sites allow you to maximize network efficiency and provide fault tolerance. Mapping sites to IP subnets allows administrators to configure the topology of Active Directory to match the physical network. When a user logs on from an Active Directory client, the client looks for Active Directory servers that are in the same site as the user. Determining the local site at logon time is easy because the user's workstation already knows what TCP/IP subnet it is on, and the subnets map directly to sites. This makes communication between Active Directory clients and servers fast, efficient, and reliable.

Because Active Directory clients look to their own sites for authentication, access, and GC lookups, you should have at least one Global Catalog server and one DNS server in each Windows 2000 site. Two or more GC servers per site is even better.

Active Directory Security

Strong and consistent security is essential to the health of corporate networks and corporate knowledge. In order for Active Directory to be successful, it has to be secure, especially since it is actually part of the Windows 2000 security subsystem. This subsystem has four primary functions:

- It is a directory service store for account information and security policies.
- It stores trust information for Active Directory.
- It implements security models for all directory objects.
- It authenticates Active Directory access.

The primary component of the Windows 2000 security subsystem is the Local Security Authority (LSA). Like prior versions of Windows NT, this protected subsystem maintains the security for the local computer. The LSA is responsible for managing the local audit and security policies, as well as authenticating users and generating access tokens. The LSA is comprised of several system DLL files. These files and their purposes are detailed in Table 2-2.

Active Directory itself is stored in the LSA's *directory service* module. This module is comprised of three parts: the DSA, a database layer, and the physical ESE database. As previously mentioned, users and applications use LDAP to access the DSA. The DSA is responsible for processing transactions, propagating security descriptors, and enforcing the schema and directory service semantics. It also provides GC server access and supports replication. Active Directory DSAs periodically connect to each other to perform replication using a proprietary remote procedure call interface. In addition, MAPI clients can connect to the DSA using the MAPI remote procedure call interface.

All objects in Active Directory are physically stored in an ESE database. This database has been tested with directories as large as 40 million objects per domain. ESE is well suited to Active Directory. It supports indexing and multivalue attributes, as well as

DLL File	Purpose
KDCSVC.DLL	Kerberos KDC Service: Generates tickets to clients
KERBEROS.DLL	Kerberos v5 protocol
LSASRV.DLL	LSA Server: Enforces security policy
MSV1_0.DLL	NTLM authentication protocol
NETLOGON.DLL	Maintains secure channels
NTDSA.DLL	Provides LDAP support and manages data partitions
SAMSRV.DLL	Security Accounts Manager: Enforces policies and provides support for legacy APIs
SCHANNEL.DLL	Secure Sockets Layer authentication
SECUR32.DLL	Ties all of the above components together as a multiple authentication providers

Table 2-2. *The Components of the Local Security Authority*

transaction rollback. In addition, backups of ESE databases can be taken while the servers that use them are online. The database layer, ESENT.DLL, lies between the DSA and the ESE database. This layer implements the search and retrieval functionality of the underlying database.

Active Directory objects have security descriptors called *discretionary access control lists* (DACLs). DACLs are responsible for granting or denying access to objects. DACLs contain items called *access control entries* (ACEs), which have a SID and a set of access rights.

In Active Directory, users, groups, computers, and services are known as *security principals*. All security principals have accounts. Local accounts are managed by the local SAM manager, and domain accounts are managed by Active Directory. Every security principal is identified by a SID. In Windows 2000, all activities take place in a *security context*. A security context is information that describes a security principal's identity and rights. The Windows 2000 security subsystem uses a security context to determine what can be done to objects on the computer and what kind of auditing is to occur.

Authentication

Windows 2000 supports a number of authentication methods, such as Kerberos 5, X.509 certificates, and smart cards. It also includes protocols for authenticating dial-up connections and for users who access the network over the Internet. But there are only two choices for network authentication in Windows 2000 domains: the NT LAN Manager protocol (NTLM) or security principal, which is the default authentication in Windows 2000.

Kerberos and NTLM Kerberos is a protocol that originated at MIT more than a decade ago. Kerberos provides a mechanism for mutual authentication between a client and a server, or between servers, before a network connection is opened between them. This protocol is secure because it works on the simple yet effective premise that if a secret is only known to two entities, they can verify each other's identity by confirming that the other entity knows the secret. The protocol also assumes that, at least initially, transactions between entities take place in an unsecured manner—for example, on an open network whose computers are not physically secure and whose network traffic can be monitored and modified at will. The implementation of the protocol in Windows 2000 closely follows Internet RFC 1510. In addition, the mechanism and format for passing security tokens in Kerberos messages follows the specification defined in Internet RFC 1964.

NTLM is a network protocol designed for Windows NT. Windows 2000 retains NTLM compatibility for downlevel client support and to authenticate logons to standalone Windows 2000 computers. Windows 3.11, Windows 9x, and Windows NT use the NTLM protocol for network authentication in Windows 2000 domains. Windows 2000 computers also use NTLM when authenticating to Windows NT servers or accessing resources in Windows NT domains.

One of the primary design goals of Windows 2000 is to allow administrators to turn off NTLM authentication once all of the network clients support Kerberos authentication. Kerberos has several advantages over NTLM: speed, interoperability, and simplified trust management, to name a few. But what really makes Kerberos ideal is its support for delegated and mutual authentication.

NTLM allows servers to verify the identities of their clients. It does not allow clients to verify a server's identity or one server to verify the identity of another. NTLM authentication was designed for environments in which servers were assumed to be genuine. Kerberos makes no such assumption. Parties at both ends of a Kerberos connection know that the party on the other end is who it claims to be. Moreover, Windows services use *impersonation* when accessing resources on behalf of a client. Often, services can complete the work for the client by using resources on the local computer, although some distributed applications use front-end services that must impersonate clients when connecting to back-end services on other computers. Both NTLM and Kerberos provide the information that a service needs to impersonate its client locally. But only Kerberos has a mechanism that allows a service to impersonate its client when connecting to other services. NTLM has no such mechanism.

Summary

Active Directory is a directory and directory service that stores and provides information about organizations, users, and shares, and other network objects. It uses a structured data store that stores information about directory objects, such as servers, files, printers, and the user and computer accounts. These objects are represented in an X.500-compatible manner and are locatable using industry standard LDAP queries.

Active Directory is also a namespace that integrates with and relies on the Domain Name System. In fact, the integration of Active Directory and DNS is the very core of Windows 2000. Planning for Active Directory is no small task. Many companies will spend upwards of a year just in the planning stages alone. The larger your network, the more planning you will need to do. The overall quality of your Active Directory design will determine the success of your company's Windows 2000 deployment. In Chapter 3, we'll discuss how Exchange 2000 impacts the design of your Active Directory.

The Complete Reference

Chapter 3

Exchange 2000 Directory

Gaining an understanding of the Windows 2000 Active Directory is the first step toward understanding how Exchange 2000 Server functions and what it can do to help you meet your enterprise goals. The unification of the previously separate domain and Exchange directories provides significant advantages over the previous architecture, but it also makes things more complex.

In Chapter 2, we introduced Active Directory and brought forth several key concepts. In this chapter, we will discuss how Exchange 2000 integrates with Active Directory. We'll talk about the benefits of a single directory and directory service and provide an overview of Exchange-specific directory objects. We'll also discuss how information is stored, retrieved, and replicated across domain controllers and what that means to your Exchange infrastructure. Finally, we'll look at the integration of Exchange 2000 and Active Directory from a security perspective.

The New Exchange Directory

Prior versions of Exchange include an integrated directory comprised of two components: the directory database and the directory service. The directory database contains all of the Exchange directory objects, such as mailboxes, distribution lists, site connectors, custom recipients, and other Exchange data. Once directory replication connectors are properly configured, the directory is replicated to other servers in the Exchange organization, ensuring that all users have access to consistent and up-to-date information. The directory service is responsible for providing the Global Address List and the address book views, transmitting and processing replication notifications, and enforcing the rules governing the structure of the directory database.

The integration of Exchange and Active Directory provides several benefits over earlier designs, which used separate directories for Exchange mailboxes and security principals. In Exchange 2000, all directory information—mailboxes, distributions lists, servers, and so on—is stored in Active Directory. This provides a variety of benefits, such as:

- **Single-seat administration** Using Microsoft Management Console snap-ins, administrators have a single tool (or *single seat*) through which all directory objects can be managed.
- **Integrated security** Exchange 2000 uses native Windows 2000 access control lists. This means you can use the available Windows 2000 Server security options to protect your Exchange infrastructure. Previous versions of Exchange integrated with Windows NT security. Access control in Windows NT is at the object level, whereas Active Directory supports object- and attribute-level security. This gives administrators very granular control over their Exchange infrastructure.

- **Elimination of redundancy** Prior versions of Exchange and Windows NT used separate directory replication and separate group management. The supplanting of the separate Exchange directory in favor of Active Directory eliminates this redundancy and the additional overhead it consumed.

While Active Directory provides the infrastructure for Exchange 2000, a messaging system like Exchange requires several more properties on the objects, including e-mail addresses, home server values, and others. Exchange 2000 takes advantage of the extensibility of the Active Directory schema by adding Exchange-specific objects and attributes. During setup, Exchange 2000 makes permanent, irrevocable changes to the schema of the Active Directory forest in which it is installed. Although changes to the schema cannot be reversed, they can be disabled if Exchange is removed from the forest. The Active Directory schema is extended with new classes and attributes, as shown in Figure 3-1. You can use this MMC snap-in to view and modify these new objects.

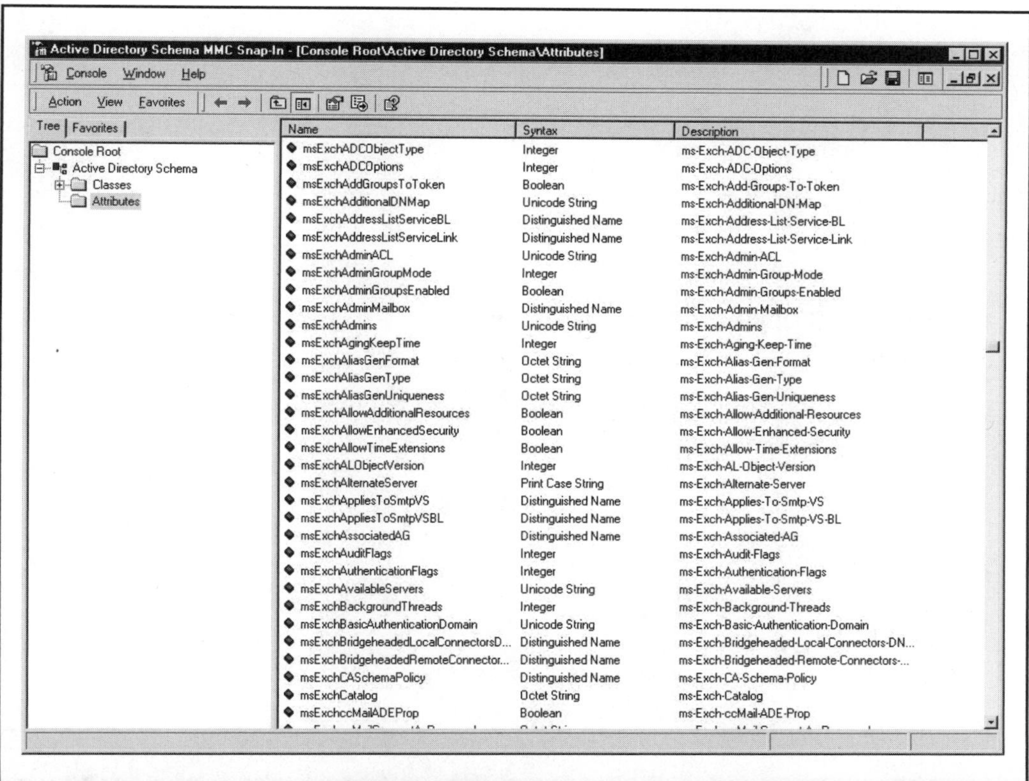

Figure 3-1. *Active Directory Schema snap-in. The newly created Exchange classes and attributes begin with "msExch."*

For some organizations, it may be advantageous to effect the Exchange 2000 schema changes before Active Directory grows too large. The schema changes made by Exchange are replicated to all domain controllers in every domain in the forest. If you have a large number of domain controllers, replication traffic can have a heavy impact on your network. You can extend the Active Directory schema without actually installing Exchange by using the /forestprep setup option. See Chapter 6 for more information on /forestprep installation.

An Exchange 2000 installation will affect your Active Directory and your network. As previously mentioned, Exchange 2000 extends the existing Active Directory schema. In addition, Exchange 2000 also promotes a large number of properties to the Global Catalog. Depending on your Exchange Server's hardware resources, as well as the size of your Active Directory, this process could take a while. Once this process has completed, the schema modifications need to replicate to all of the Active Directory controllers and Global Catalog servers in the forest. Depending on the number of servers involved in replication and the network links between them, this could have a substantial impact on your network. For these reasons, you may find it beneficial to perform a /forestprep installation as soon as your first Active Directory controller has been created.

Exchange Directory Objects

The marriage of the Exchange and Windows directories creates offspring in the form of new directory objects. Each of these objects is described in Table 3-1.

Exchange 5.5 Object	Active Directory Object	Description
Mailbox	Mailbox-enabled and mail-enabled	These are user accounts that can send and receive e-mail. They have mailboxes and unique SMTP addresses assigned to them.
Distribution list	Mail-enabled group	These can be *mail-enabled security groups* or *mail-enabled distribution groups* (see below).

Table 3-1. *Exchange 5.5 and Active Directory Objects. The terminology used to describe objects in Exchange 2000 Server is now the same as that used to describe objects in Active Directory.*

Exchange 5.5 Object	Active Directory Object	Description
Custom recipient	Mail-enabled contact	This is an object in Active Directory that has an assigned SMTP address but no user account or mailbox.
No corresponding object	Mail-enabled user	This is a security principal in Active Directory that has an e-mail address but no mailbox.

Table 3-1. *Exchange 5.5 and Active Directory Objects. The terminology used to describe objects in Exchange 2000 Server is now the same as that used to describe objects in Active Directory.* (continued)

See Microsoft Knowledge Base article Q252370 for a semi-graphical representation of how Exchange 2000 configuration information is stored in Active Directory.

Users

A *user* is an Active Directory security principal object that contains a logon password, belongs to one or more groups, and has rights, privileges, and permissions that are used to access network resources. User objects are referenced in the directory by their *distinguished name.* An object's distinguished name indicates where the object is located within the directory hierarchy. For example, the distinguished name cn=jannic,cn=pss,cn=users,dc=redmond,dc=microsoft,dc=com identifies the *jannic* object in the *redmond.microsoft.com* domain.

Because distinguished names can be both long and difficult to remember, user objects can also be referenced by a *relative distinguished name.* An object's relative distinguished name, also known as an object's friendly name, is an attribute of the distinguished name. In the preceding example, the relative distinguished name of the user object is *jannic* and the relative distinguished name of the parent object is *users.*

Another name, called the *user principal name* is also generated for each user object in Active Directory. This name takes the form of *username@domainname* and can be used to log on to the network. Because this name can be used to log on, it must be unique throughout the forest. Active Directory will not allow you to create multiple users with the same user principal name.

Windows 2000 user objects can also be mailbox-enabled, which establishes an Exchange 2000 Server mailbox in a message store. Once this is done, the user object represents a single point of administration (also known as *single-seat administration*) for both Windows 2000–specific and Exchange activities.

In prior versions of Exchange, the Exchange Administrator program could be installed on a Windows NT computer that was not running Exchange. This enabled Exchange to be managed remotely by an administrator from his Windows NT workstation. Installing the Exchange Administrator program added some extensions to User Manager for Domains in an attempt to integrate the management functionality of the separate directories. For example, when creating a new account, User Manager was capable of displaying the new mailbox dialog box, enabling the administrator to create a mailbox for the new user without having to switch to Exchange Administrator.

This concept has been carried forward with Exchange 2000 and Windows 2000. When you install System Manager on the computer running Windows 2000, a set of extensions is added to the standard console that enables administrators to create an Exchange Mailbox when creating a new user. This functionality can be found in the Active Directory Users and Computers snap-in. Because the management tools for Active Directory are a part of Windows 2000, you must also install the Windows 2000 Server Administrator tools in order to manage Exchange. The properties of a Windows 2000 user are shown in Figure 3-2.

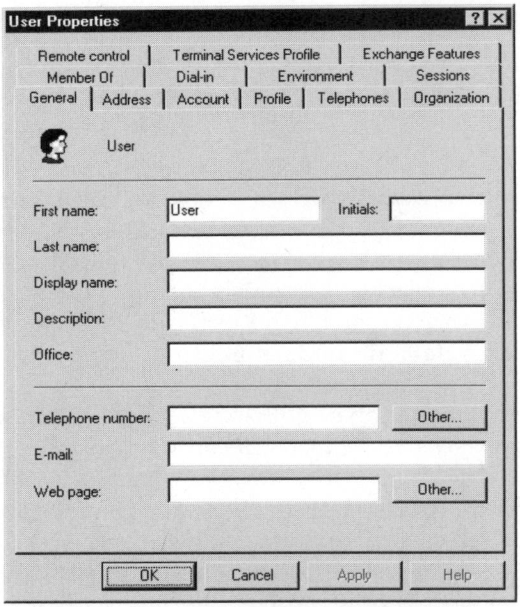

Figure 3-2. *A Windows 2000 user. This user has not yet been mailbox-enabled.*

The Active Directory Users and Computers snap-in shortcut in the Microsoft Exchange program group is a modified version of the identically named snap-in in the Windows 2000 Administrative Tools program group. It includes Exchange-specific columns and views that make administering users, contacts, and groups a bit easier.

Groups

A *group* is roughly the equivalent of an Exchange 5.5 distribution list. There are two types of groups: security groups and distribution groups. Security groups are security principals that define a collection of users and groups. These groups are used in access control lists (ACLs) to grant or deny access to resources. Distribution groups are distribution lists that aren't security principals. Both types of groups can be mail-enabled and used for delivering mail to their membership. Security and distribution groups are scoped into one of three boundaries: domain local, global, or universal.

Groups help alleviate the administration burden by reducing the number of objects that require direct administration. Generally speaking, you should not grant or deny object privileges to individual users. This concept has been carried forward from Windows NT; users are added to groups, which can be added into other groups, enabling bulk administration for tasks such as assigning permissions, and so on. Exchange 2000 also uses the concept of bulk administration and permission assignment, but it allows groups to be used as distribution lists.

Domain Local Groups Domain local groups are similar to local groups in a Windows NT 4.0 domain. These groups can contain members from other domains, but they can only be used for setting ACLs on objects in the domain containing them. In a native mode Active Directory, domain local groups can be used to grant access rights to resources on any computer in the domain. In a mixed mode Active Directory, where Windows NT 4.0 domain controllers are still present, domain local groups can only be created on domain controllers.

Global Groups Global groups, which are also similar to Windows NT 4.0 global groups, can be used for setting ACLs on any object in the forest. However, like their predecessor, a global group can only contain members from its own domain. Global groups are typically used for groups whose membership changes frequently. In a native mode Active Directory, global groups can contain both user accounts and other global groups (that is, they can be nested). However, in a mixed-mode Active Directory, global groups can only contain user accounts.

Outlook users are only able to view membership for domain local groups and global groups in their own domain. If an Outlook client attempts to view membership of a domain local group or a global group from a remote domain in the same forest, the action will fail and membership will not be displayed.

Universal Groups Universal groups are groups without the restrictions imposed on domain local or global groups. Universal groups can contain members from any domain in the forest and can be used to set ACLs on any object in the forest. In addition to overcoming their limitations, universal groups also have a replication advantage over domain local and global groups. While membership of a domain local or global group is only replicated to domain controllers in the domain containing the group, universal group membership is replicated to all Global Catalog servers in the forest.

Exchange 2000 uses groups in two ways. The first way is through the traditional granting of privileges and rights to certain configuration and server objects in Exchange. Because public folders are objects in Active Directory, permissions to public folders can be granted to security groups. The second way is by using groups as distribution lists. Figures 3-3 and 3-4 show a distribution group and a security group, respectively. Neither of these groups is mail-enabled.

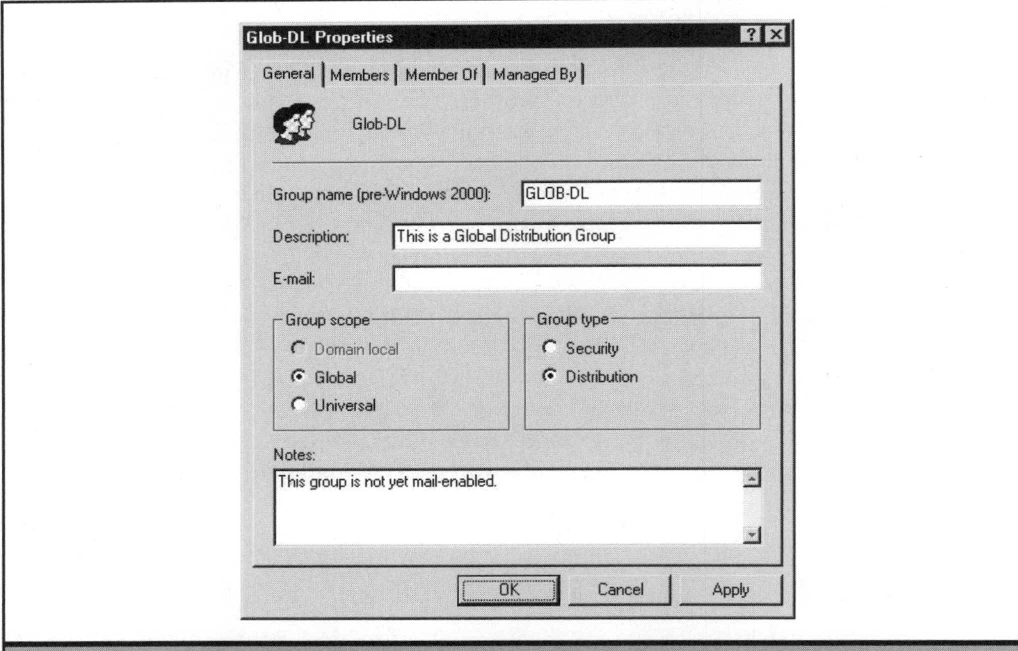

Figure 3-3. *A global distribution group. Once this group has been mail-enabled, Exchange 2000 users can use it as a distribution list.*

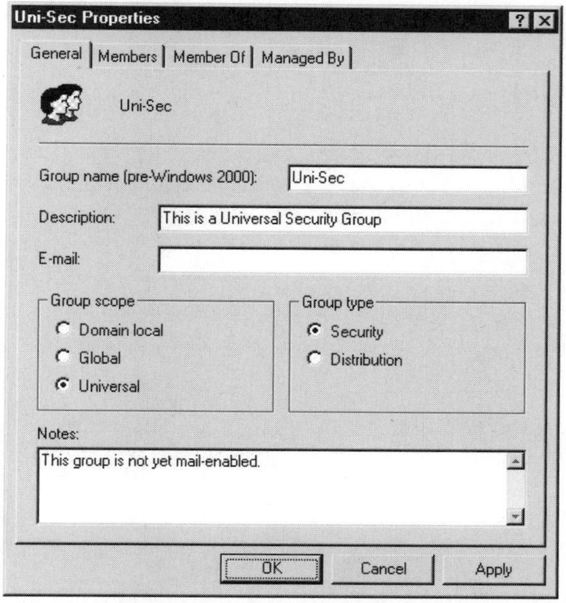

Figure 3-4. *A universal security group. You can add this group to ACLs, and once it is mail-enabled, it can also be used a distribution list by Exchange 2000 users.*

Mail-Enabled Objects

A mail-enabled object is a Windows 2000 Active Directory user or group that has at least one e-mail address associated with it. A mail-enabled user has an e-mail address but does not have an Exchange mailbox. If the mail-enabled object is a user, they can receive e-mail, but they can't send mail via Exchange. Figure 3-5 shows the properties for a mail-enabled group.

Some consideration needs to be given to the type and scope of the groups used in Exchange 2000. Microsoft recommends using universal security groups once the Windows 2000 domain containing your Exchange servers has been converted from mixed mode (Windows 2000 and Windows NT domain controllers) to native mode (Windows 2000 domain controllers only). As previously mentioned, universal groups are advantageous over global groups because global groups don't have their membership published in the Global Catalog; this means that Outlook clients cannot view global group membership at the recipient level.

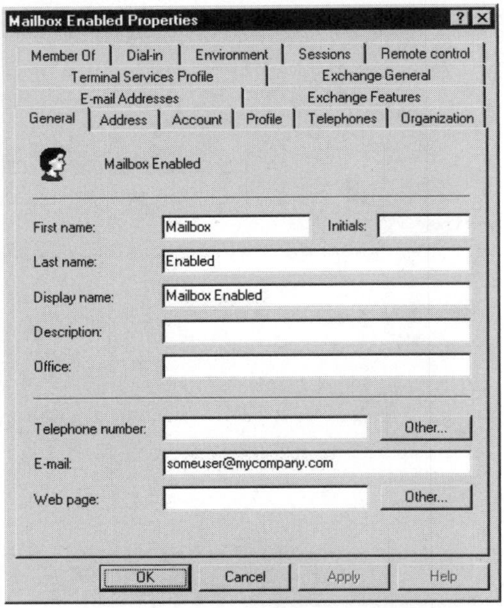

Figure 3-5. Exchange General and e-mail addresses

If you do decide to primarily use universal groups, keep in mind that group membership changes result in replication traffic. This is because group membership information is contained in a multivalued property on the group object. Therefore, the larger the group, the greater the replication traffic that is generated when a change is made. To mitigate this overhead, Microsoft recommends placing user objects into multiple universal groups and nesting these groups under a master universal group. This way, when group membership is changed, the master universal group object is not changed and no replication traffic is created.

Tip *Microsoft recommends that group membership not exceed 5,000 for performance reasons. If you are planning on groups that have a large number of members (5,000 or more), you should use nested groups instead. For ease of administration and reduced replication traffic, you should consider nesting groups well before they get too large.*

Groups are also used for determining public folder access. Unlike Exchange 5.5, the Exchange 2000 information store no longer needs to expand a group when a user accesses a public folder. Public folder ACLs are held in Active Directory, and group membership information is contained in the access token provided to the user, which is presented to Exchange upon connection to the public folder.

Mailbox-Enabled User

A mailbox-enabled user is a Windows 2000 user that has an Exchange mailbox associated with it, enabling the user to send and receive messages, as well as access other mailbox-related features. By definition, a user that is mailbox-enabled is also mail-enabled. Figure 3-6 shows a mailbox-enabled user.

Mail-Enabled Contact

A *contact* is a Windows 2000 Active Directory user object that is not a security principal. Contacts have one or more e-mail addresses associated with them, but they do not have a mailbox or a Windows 2000 user account. Figure 3-7 shows a Windows 2000 contact.

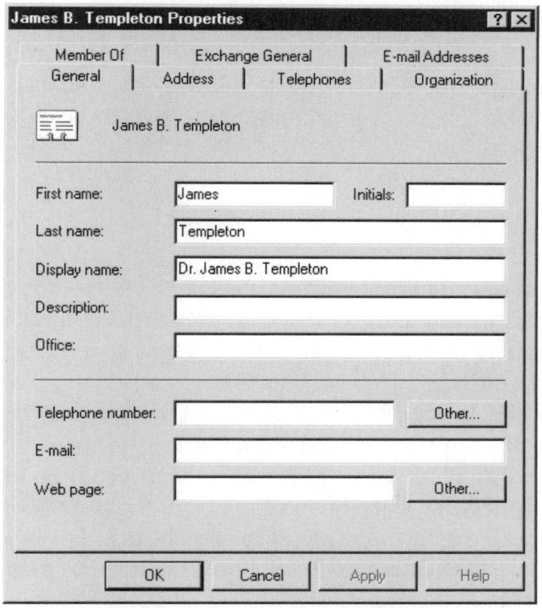

Figure 3-6. *Exchange General and e-mail addresses*

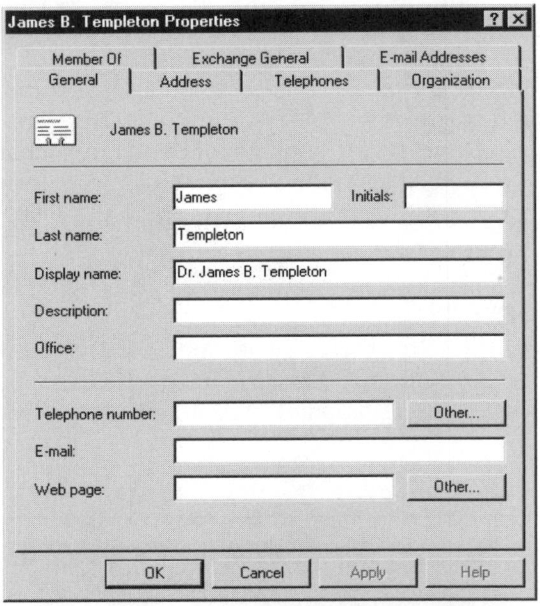

Figure 3-7. *A Windows 2000 contact. Although contacts do not have mailboxes, you can specify message size restrictions and delivery options.*

Mailboxes

In Exchange 5.5 and earlier, mailboxes were objects in the Exchange directory. That is no longer the case with Exchange 2000. Mailboxes are not Active Directory objects; instead, they are attributes of a directory object, such as a user. As a result, mailboxes are much easier to manage.

With prior versions of Exchange, it was difficult to associate mailboxes with more than one user. One such example is when someone leaves the company and another individual needs to assume his or her mailbox. You could change the primary Windows NT account that was associated with the mailbox from the old user to the new user, but that doesn't completely change ownership at the attribute level—specifically, the *legacy distinguished name* (legacy DN) attribute level. It is this attribute that links an Exchange 5.5 mailbox to a Windows NT 4.0 user account.

Each Exchange mailbox now has a globally unique identifier (GUID) that is used to connect a mailbox to an Active Directory user. Each mailbox-enabled Active Directory user has the GUID of the mailbox it owns. This enables you to delete a user account without affecting the mailbox, which can be reconnected to a different user.

Global Address List

Previous versions of Exchange include a feature called the *Global Address List* (GAL). The GAL is a list of all of the recipients in an Exchange organization. This includes mailboxes, distribution lists, custom recipients, and public folders. The GAL was part of, and created from, the directory information contained in Exchange. The GAL still exists for Exchange 2000, but because all Exchange directory information is now in Active Directory, that information is elsewhere. In Exchange 2000, the GAL is located in the Active Directory Global Catalog servers. The GAL is an Active Directory object that is derived from an LDAP query on a subset of Active Directory objects.

One of the primary features of the Global Catalog is its enhanced search capabilities. Users (and applications) can find objects in Active Directory if they know one or more attributes of the object being sought. To make things easier, the Global Catalog is prepopulated with the most commonly searched attributes—such as a user's name or department—along with attributes that are used to locate a full replica of the object. You can augment the default set of properties contained in the Global Catalog by adding properties that are specific to your organization.

The Active Directory replication mechanism handles Global Catalog replication and is responsible for generating the replication topology. This eliminates the need to perform independent directory replication in Exchange. Changes made to an Exchange user's profile are automatically replicated to all the domain controllers in the forest to update the Global Catalogs.

Exchange 2000 Directory Data

Exchange 2000 stores all of its configuration, schema, and domain-naming context data in Active Directory. As a result, both Exchange servers and Exchange clients need to query Active Directory—and more specifically, domain controllers and Global Catalog servers—when any of this data is sought.

DSAccess

Because it no longer has its own directory, Exchange 2000 must look to Active Directory to store and retrieve its configuration information. The Active Directory site coverage algorithm is one way access to Global Catalog data is optimized. To further reduce the burden on Global Catalog servers, various Exchange 2000 components use a shared API called *DSAccess*. Except for address book lookups from MAPI clients and certain types of SMTP routing, all directory access occurs through the DSAccess cache. DSAccess provides a number of benefits, such as load balancing and failover support, a common connection pool, and a reduced burden on both the network and the Global Catalog servers.

The configuration information stored by Exchange 2000 in Active Directory consists of its schema-naming context, which is used for identifying schema extensions; its configuration-naming context, which includes the organization name and the breakdown of administrative and routing groups; and the domain-naming context, which includes user object extension attributes.

Exchange makes extensive use of Active Directory domain controllers and Global Catalog servers. When the System Attendant Service starts, it does a lookup using the DSGetDCName API to locate up to ten domain controllers and Global Catalog servers in its Windows 2000 site. It uses this list to fill three roles that it requires for its operation:

- **Configuration domain controller** This is the domain controller in the Exchange server's domain that will be used for writing all of the configuration-naming context data, such as the organization name, administrative groups, routing groups, and so on. Exchange will connect to port 389 on the configuration domain controller to retrieve this information.
- **Working domain controller lookup list** This is a cached list of active domain controllers (up to ten) in the Exchange server's Windows 2000 site. Exchange 2000 uses a round-robin mechanism to load balance its reading of local domain information.
- **Working Global Catalog lookup list** Similar to the working domain controller list, this is a cached list of active Global Catalog servers (up to ten) in the Exchange server's Windows 2000 site. Exchange 2000 uses a round-robin mechanism to load balance its reading of user-based data from anywhere in the forest.

The detection algorithm used by DSAccess depends on whether a domain controller or a Global Catalog server is being sought. It also depends on the locality of the Exchange server. After examining the registry for hard-coded entries (see below), DSAccess issues a DsBind to any domain controller in the Exchange server's domain. It then issues a Win32 API call to DsListServersForDomainInSite() to the domain controller to which it binds. This call returns a list of all domain controllers in the Exchange server's domain and site. DSAccess then saves up to ten domain controllers in a cached list, and then uses a round-robin mechanism to load balance requests across them.

The algorithm for Global Catalog server detection is slightly different. Using the existing LDAP connection to the domain controller it bound to when dynamically detecting domain controllers, DSAccess reads the Options attribute for the NTDS Settings object for each domain controller returned. If the Options attribute exists, and if it has the GC flag set, it is a Global Catalog server. DSAccess will cache up to ten Global Catalog servers.

If DSAccess can't find any Global Catalog servers in its site, it calls the Win32 API DsGetDCName() and looks for any available Global Catalog server. DSAccess will only use one Global Catalog server from outside its site because it assumes that, as per the definition of a Windows 2000 site, all Global Catalog servers outside its site are likely connected via a slow link.

The Exchange System Manager can be used to view the current configuration domain controller. Right-click on any Exchange server in System Manager and select Properties. The current configuration domain controller is displayed on the General tab (see Figure 3-8).

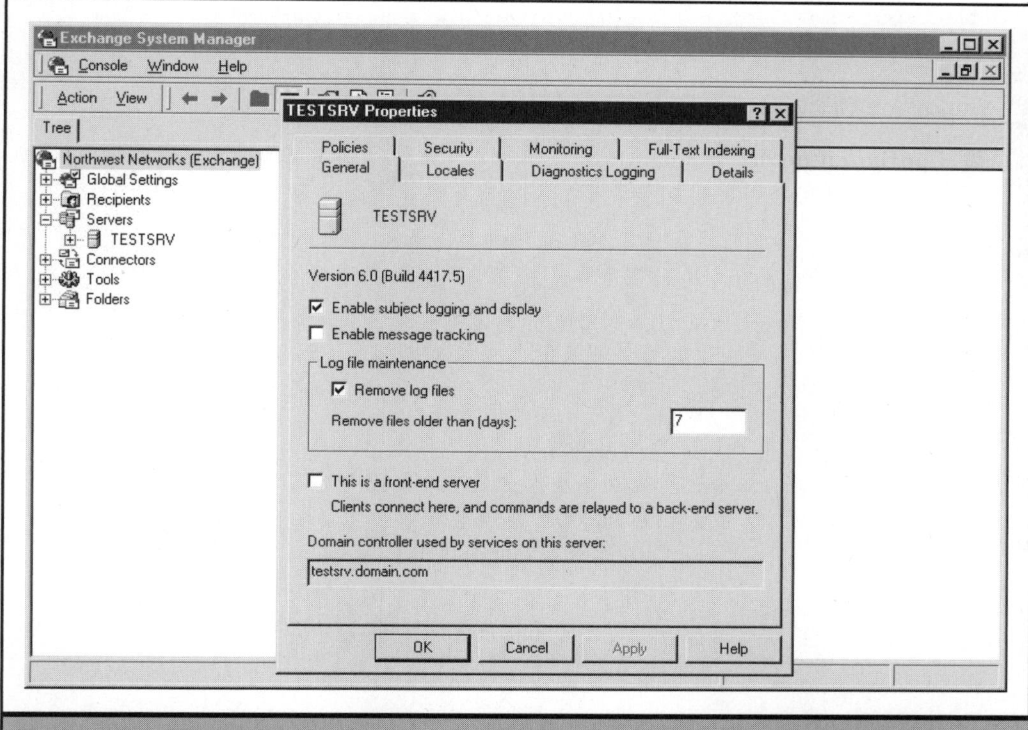

Figure 3-8. *The General tab on a server's properties dialog box. The "Domain controller used by services on this server" field indicates the current configuration domain controller.*

DSADIAG You can use dsadiag.exe, a free utility from Microsoft, to view the cache lists of domain controllers and Global Catalog servers, as well as the current configuration domain controller. You can download dsadiag from http://www.ExInternals.com/, an Exchange 2000–related Web site run by Paul Bowden, a program manager in Microsoft's Exchange Product Unit.

Dsadiag should be placed in your program files\exchsrvr\bin folder (or wherever dsaccess.dll is located). Its usage is:

```
DSADIAG 1
or
DSADIAG 2
```

where:

1 = List domain controllers and Global Catalog servers

2 = Force rediscovery of topology

The output should look similar to the following:

```
Working DCs:
UP FAST DOWN InSync     Name

X   X          X         testsrv.domain.com
X   X          X         testsvr.domain.com
X   X          X         corpdc1.domain.com
X   X          X         corpdc2.domain.com

Working GCs:
UP FAST DOWN InSync     Name

X   X          X         testsrv.domain.com
X   X          X         testsvr.domain.com
X   X          X         gengc1.domain.com
X   X          X         gengc2.domain.com

Config DC:
                          testsrv.domain.com

Done
```

The System Attendant uses the DSGetDCName API to monitor for new Global Catalog servers, and it will adjust its working list of Global Catalog servers as necessary. In addition, the working lists are freshly recreated whenever the IIS Admin Service (InetInfo) is restarted and when the server's Kerberos ticket expires (every ten hours). You can also use DSADIAG to perform a manual rediscovery of active domain controllers and active Global Catalog servers. This is particularly useful if you've just brought a production Global Catalog server back online and you want to have it utilized by Exchange right away.

Manually Adjusting the DSAccess Cache Parameters

By default, DSAccess caches up to 4MB of directory data for up to five minutes. The size of the cache and the cache TTL are both configurable through the registry. Before doing so, you should monitor the performance of the cache using Performance Monitor or some other tool that is capable of collecting performance data. There are several DSAccess performance counter objects available for monitoring. Figure 3-9 shows a few of the DSAccess counters that are available.

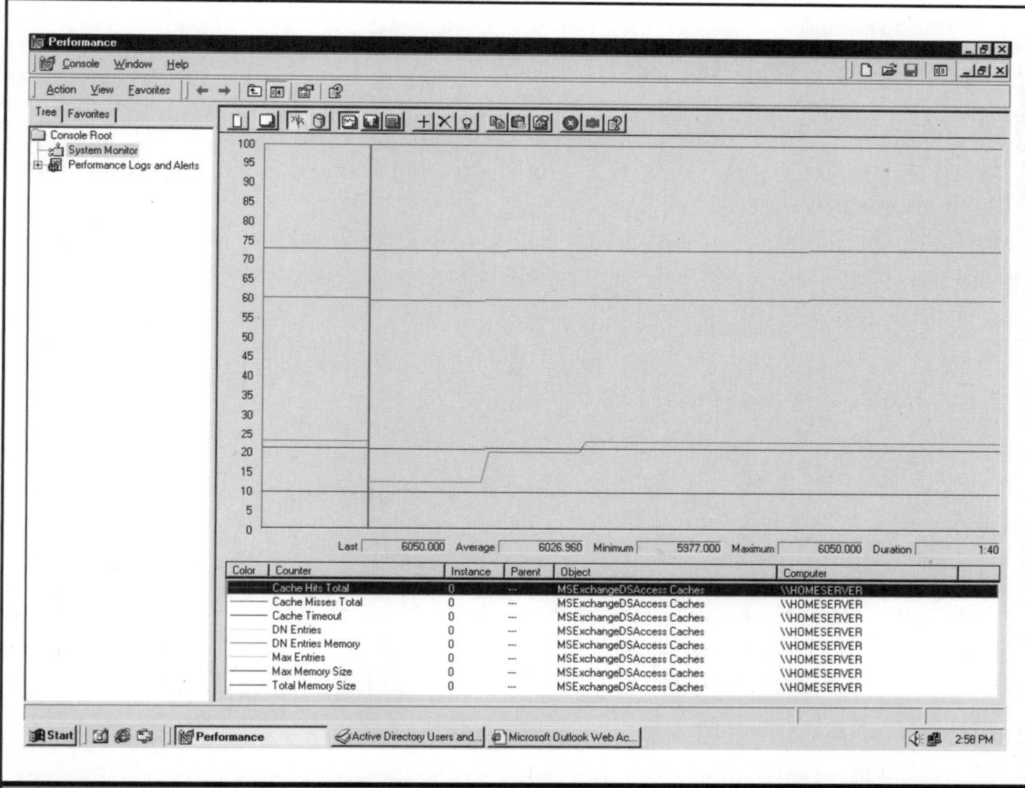

Figure 3-9. *System Monitor/Performance Logs and Alerts. You can use System Monitor or Performance Logs and Alerts to collect and view DSAccess performance counters. Regularly monitoring these counters will help you determine if your DSAccess cache is tuned properly.*

Although the DSAccess cache is turned on by default, it can be disabled by adding or modifying the following registry value:

```
HKEY_LOCAL_MACHINE\System\CurrentControlSet\Services\MSExchangeDSAccess
    Value name: CachingEnabled
    Value type: REG_DWORD
```

```
    Value data: 0x1 (Enabled - Default)
                0x2 (Disabled)
```

You can adjust the time to live (TTL) for cached entries by adding or modifying the following registry value:

```
HKEY_LOCAL_MACHINE\System\CurrentControlSet\Services\MSExchangeDSAccess\Instance0

    Value name: CacheTTL
    Value type: REG_DWORD
    Value data: 0x600 (seconds)
```

You can control the size of the cache in two ways. You can limit the number of entries that can be cached, or you can limit the amount of memory allocated to the cache. The cache process itself consumes 2.5MB of memory, and each cached entry uses another 3.6KB.

Tip *You can monitor DSAccess performance using Performance Monitor or any other tool that can collect performance counter data. See Microsoft Knowledge Base article Q246271 for details on the DSAccess performance counters that can be collected.*

The 4MB default cache size, which can hold a maximum of 416 entries, should be sufficient for most organizations, although larger organizations will need to increase its size. However, tuning these parameters may be required to meet specific service needs. You can set the cache size by adding or modifying the following registry parameters:

```
HKEY_LOCAL_MACHINE\System\CurrentControlSet\Services\MSExchangeDSAccess\Instance0

    Value name: MaxMemory
    Value type: REG_DWORD
    Value data: 0x0 (value in KB; default is 4096KB)
```

```
Value name: MaxEntries
Value type: REG_DWORD
Value data: 0x0 (default is 0 (unlimited))
```

Hard-coding the DSAccess Cache You can hard-code the DSAccess cache to point to a specified set of domain controllers or Global Catalog servers by modifying the registry. When initialized, DSAccess reads the registry first to determine if any domain controllers or Global Catalog servers have been hard-coded. If no hard-coded entries are found in the registry, it begins the dynamic topology detection process to look for directory service servers in its Windows 2000 site. If it finds hard-coded entries, it will not perform dynamic topology detection.

Caution *The DSAccess process does not validate hard-coded entries. This means it will not recognize typos, misspellings, or other mistakes in the entries. In addition, when the DSAccess cache has been hard-coded, it will never use any other directory service server that would have been dynamically detected. As a result, if all the hard-coded directory service servers are down or otherwise unavailable, all DSAccess operations will fail.*

The registry keys used to hard-code entries in the DSAccess cache need to be manually created. The directory service servers used for user-context requests are profile-dependent. As a result, the registry settings are located under the Profiles\Default subkey. The following registry keys are hard-coding the list of domain controllers and Global Catalog servers for use by DSAccess processes:

```
HKLM\System\CurrentControlSet\Services\MSExchangeDSAccess\Profiles\Default\UserDC1
(UserDC2, and so on)
IsGC = REG_DWORD 0x0
HostName = REG_SZ <DC's Fully-Qualified Domain Name>
PortNumber = REG_DWORD (0x185 by default or 0x27C for SSL)

HKLM\System\CurrentControlSet\Services\MSExchangeDSAccess\Profiles\Default\UserGC1
(UserGC2 and so on)
IsGC = REG_DWORD 0x1
HostName = REG_SZ <GC's Fully-Qualified Domain Name>
PortNumber = REG_DWORD (0xCC4 by default or 0xCC5 for SSL)
```

The configuration domain controller is shared among all profiles and is located under the \Instance0 subkey in the registry:

```
HKLM\CurrentControlSet\Services\MSExchangeDSAccess\Instance0
ConfigDCHostName = REG_SZ <Config DC's Fully-Qualified Domain Name>
ConfigDCPortNumber = REG_DWORD (0x185 by default or 0x27C for SSL)
```

You can't really hard-code the configuration domain controller for DSAccess per se. Even if you create this registry entry and add the name of a the domain controller you want used as the configuration domain controller, DSAccess may use another domain controller for the Config DC. Any entry you place here is treated by DSAccess as a suggestion. DSAccess initially uses the hard-coded domain controller for configuration context requests; however, if it becomes unavailable, DSAccess will attempt to dynamically detect other active domain controllers.

DSProxy

Exchange 2000 performs two types of Active Directory lookups: address book lookups and configuration lookups. An address book lookup is performed whenever a user or application needs to resolve a name in the directory. When performing an address book lookup, Exchange 2000 will contact the Global Catalog servers that are closest to it. A configuration lookup is performed whenever routing or other configuration information needs to be determined. For these queries, Exchange 2000 can contact any domain controller in the domain to locate the information.

When an Exchange client requests recipient name resolution, the process used depends on the version of the Exchange client. Older Exchange clients, such as Outlook 9x, perform directory service requests using MAPI. Backward-compatibility code in Exchange 2000 proxies these requests to a Global Catalog server using a process called the *DSProxy*.

The DSProxy process enables Exchange clients to access data in Active Directory by performing two functions. First, it's a name service provider interface (NSPI) that proxies pre-Outlook 2000 client requests to Active Directory. Second, it is a referral service that refers Outlook 2000 and newer clients directly to Active Directory. When the Exchange System Attendant initializes, the DSAccess process locates directory service servers and passes the list of Global Catalog servers to the DSProxy process (dsproxy.dll). The DSProxy process filters out Global Catalog servers that aren't in its domain and uses the remaining list to perform directory lookups on behalf of clients and for referral purposes. You can find out which domain controller is being used by the DSProxy by viewing the General tab on the Exchange server's Properties dialog box in System Manager. The field used for the configuration domain controller is the same domain controller being used by DSProxy.

When a pre-Outlook 2000 client requests a directory lookup, the Exchange 2000 Server hashes out its IP address and proxies the request to the closest Global Catalog server (closest to the server, not the client). The Global Catalog server returns the results to Exchange, which in turn sends the data to the client. The Exchange client sends an acknowledgement to the Exchange server, which proxies it along to the Global Catalog server. This entire process is completely hidden from the Exchange client (and end-user), and consists of six frames being sent over the wire.

Outlook 2000 uses a slightly different, and more efficient, process for directory service requests. Outlook 2000 uses the DSProxy process for only its first session. After the initial request has been made, the DSProxy process sends back a referral to Outlook, indicating that future requests should be sent directly to the Global Catalog server. DSProxy makes these referrals on a round-robin basis so as not to overload a single directory service server. Outlook then stores the name of the Global Catalog server in its MAPI profile settings in the registry, and begins sending directory requests directly to the Global Catalog server.

Tip *If you are running Outlook 98, applying the latest Service Pack enables Outlook 98 to take advantage of DSProxy referral mechanism.*

This process offloads directory requests from the Exchange server to the Global Catalog server. If the Global Catalog server being used for Outlook 2000 referrals goes down or becomes otherwise unavailable to the client, Outlook directory requests that are not in the *directory access cache* will fail until Outlook is restarted. Upon restarting, Outlook will be referred to a different Global Catalog server and recipient resolution should resume normally.

Should the need arise, you can configure Outlook 2000 clients to use the DSProxy process for all requests instead of being referred to a Global Catalog server. For example, if the Outlook 2000 client is accessing directory data over a very slow link, such as a dial-in connection, or if a firewall sits in between the Global Catalog server and the client. You can disable the referral mechanism by modifying the following registry entry on the Exchange server and restarting the System Attendant Service:

```
HKEY_LOCAL_MACHINE\System\CurrentControlSet\Services\MSExchangeSA\Parameters
    Value name: No RFR Service
```

```
Value type: DWORD
Value data: 0x1
```

Keep in mind that this is a server-wide setting. All Outlook 2000 clients connecting to this Exchange server will use the DSProxy process for all directory requests.

Replicating Additional Attributes to the Global Catalog

As mentioned in Chapter 2, Exchange requires access to a complete listing of the objects in the entire Active Directory. For this access, Exchange turns to its forest's Global Catalog servers. Global Catalog servers contain a complete read/write replica of the domain to which they belong and a partial read-only replica of each domain in the forest. A partial replica is one where every domain object is represented in the Global Catalog, but only a limited number of attributes for that object are replicated. In addition to extending the Active Directory schema, Exchange 2000 also takes existing Active Directory attributes and adds them to the Global Catalog. Table 3-2 lists the attributes that are added to the Global Catalog once Exchange is installed. You can manually remove these attributes from the Global Catalog or add additional attributes to the Global Catalog to meet your company's specific business needs.

The number and placement of Global Catalog servers in your organization will directly impact your Exchange infrastructure. For example, the more Global Catalog servers you have, the greater the replication traffic. However, by providing additional Global Catalog servers, you can provide quicker responses to queries.

By default, the Global Catalog only shows objects in the forest containing the Global Catalog. This means that a single Exchange organization is contained in a single Windows 2000 forest. This is a departure from previous versions of Windows NT and Exchange, where an Exchange 5.5 organization could be deployed across multiple domains. Because Exchange 2000 uses the Windows 2000 security subsystem, Exchange 2000 organizations cannot span multiple Windows 2000 forests. Of course, like earlier versions of Exchange, organizations can span multiple domains.

Microsoft recommends at least two Global Catalog servers per Active Directory site. In addition, Microsoft recommends one Global Catalog server for every four Exchange 2000 servers. This will provide scalability and reliability. Exchange 2000 is capable of load-balancing requests between multiple Global Catalog servers, and if one of the two Global Catalog servers goes down, clients won't experience any degradation in performance or interruption in service. For those sites that span multiple domains, Microsoft recommends creating a Global Catalog server in each domain containing Exchange 2000 servers and/or clients.

Attribute	LDAP Attribute Name	In GC Pre-Exchange 2000	In GC Post-Exchange 2000
First name	givenName	No	Yes
Last name	Sn	No	Yes
Display name	displayName	No	Yes
Alias	mailNickname	N/A	Yes
City	L	No	Yes
State	St	No	Yes
Country	C	No	Yes
Job title	Title	No	Yes
Company	company	No	Yes
Office	physicalDeliveryOffice Name	No	Yes
Telephone	telephoneNumber	No	Yes
Manager	manager	Yes	Yes
SMTP address	Mail	No	Yes

Table 3-2. *Global Catalog Attributes Added by Exchange*

Large organizations may not be able to host two Global Catalog servers in every site, and some organizations may not be able to host a Global Catalog server in all of their locations. Using a mechanism called the *site coverage algorithm*, Active Directory automatically compensates for Global Catalog server deployments that are less than optimal. The site coverage algorithm is calculated using the least cost defined in the site link topology, thereby allowing Active Directory to associate Global Catalog servers with sites that don't have any. This algorithm is not necessary for Outlook 2000 clients, as they are redirected to Global Catalog servers when they first connect to Exchange 2000.

As illustrated in Figure 3-10, Global Catalog servers are represented with service record (SRV) entries in DNS.

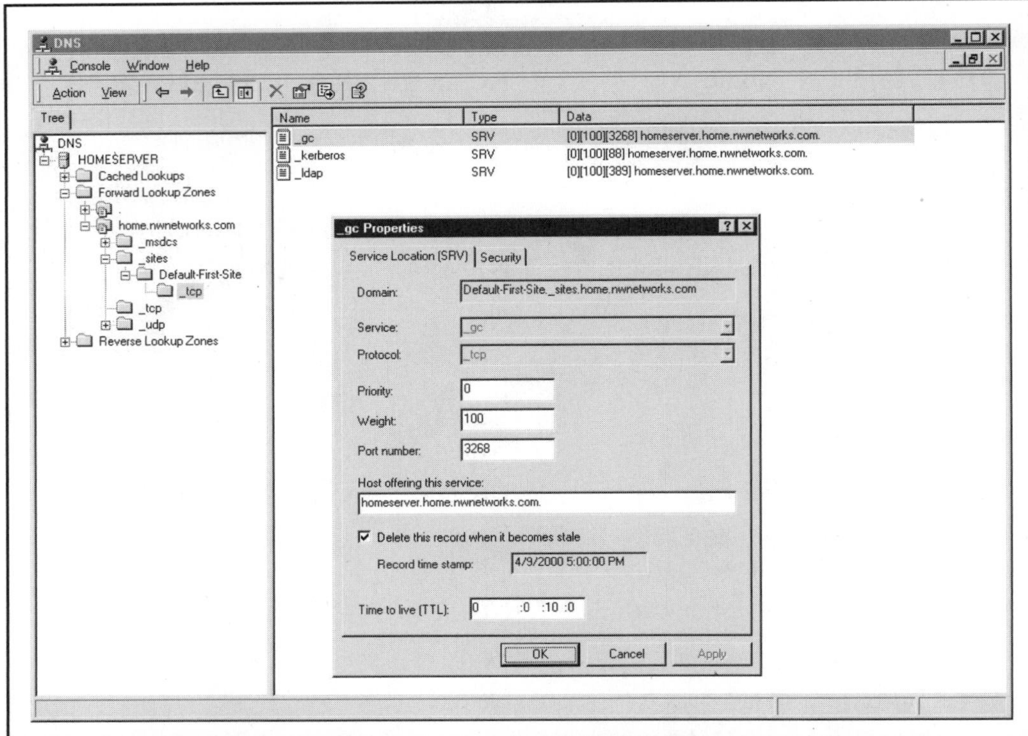

Figure 3-10. *DNS entry for Global Catalog server. Global Catalog servers are located through DNS queries.*

Generally, most queries against domain controllers are LDAP requests that enter through port 389 on Active Directory domain controllers. The Global Catalog listens on port 3268 for Global Catalog–specific requests. Global Catalog servers return different attributes depending on which TCP port is used for the query. Queries sent to port 389 enable clients to locate objects only in the home domain of the Global Catalog. Queries sent to port 3268 enable clients to locate objects throughout the entire forest. Exchange 2000 and other Active Directory–aware applications query the Global Catalog through port 3268.

You can specify which attributes are included in the Global Catalog and replicated throughout your forest. Before doing so, you should consider the additional network traffic that will occur as a result of the additional information that needs to be replicated. Adding an attribute to the Global Catalog will cause all Global Catalog servers to set their update sequence numbers (USNs) to 0. As a result, all objects—not just the modified property—must be replicated to each Global Catalog server. This replication represents a very large amount of network data, and it could represent a significant problem, particularly if some of your Global Catalog servers are connected via slow links.

Ultimately, however, this will still translate into less network traffic than what you would find in a comparable Exchange 5.5 organization. If you make a change to a directory object in Exchange 5.5, the *entire* object is replicated throughout the organization to all other Exchange servers. If you make a change to an Exchange 2000 directory object, only the changed attributes are replicated and only to domain controllers in the local domain and Global Catalog servers. This per-property replication—and replicating only to specific computers—means the amount of data that traverses the wire is much smaller.

Additional attributes can be tagged for inclusion in the Global Catalog by using the Active Directory Schema snap-in. You can use this snap-in to add attributes to or remove attributes from the Global Catalog. To do this:

1. Launch an empty MMC console.
2. Press CTRL-M to add a snap-in.
3. Click Add.
4. Select Active Directory Schema and click Add. If this snap-in is not available, you can use the step-by-step instructions from the section on Global Catalog servers in Chapter 2 to add it to your system.
5. Click Close.
6. Click OK.
7. In the left pane, expand the Active Directory Schema object.
8. Select Attributes.
9. In the right pane, locate the attribute you want to modify. Double-click the attribute to view its properties.
10. As appropriate, check or uncheck the Replicate This Attribute to the Global Catalog checkbox.
11. Click OK to save the change.
12. Repeat this process for each attribute you want to modify.
13. Close the MMC console when finished. You will be prompted to save the console. Saving the console eliminates the need to perform steps 1-6 later on.

Figure 3-11 displays an Exchange attribute with the Global Catalog replication checkbox unchecked.

Address List Services

In Exchange Server 5.0, Microsoft introduced the concept of *address book views*. Address book views let administrators organize GAL entries into groups, providing different views to Exchange clients. For example, you could create views that organized GAL recipients by department, city, or state. Although address book views work well, they do have their limitations and typically are not flexible enough for larger organizations.

In Exchange 2000, this functionality has been replaced with *address lists*. Address lists are containers that have a rule in the form of an LDAP query associated with it (see Figure 3-12).

All address lists, including the GAL, are created this way. As you can see from Figure 3-13, the rule used to create the default GAL cannot be modified. However, you can delete the default GAL or create custom address lists.

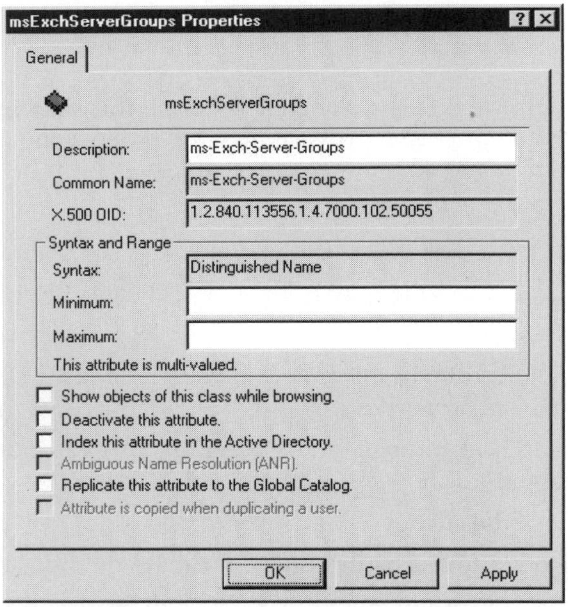

Figure 3-11. *Properties of an attribute. Use the Active Directory Schema snap-in to add or remove attributes to or from the Global Catalog.*

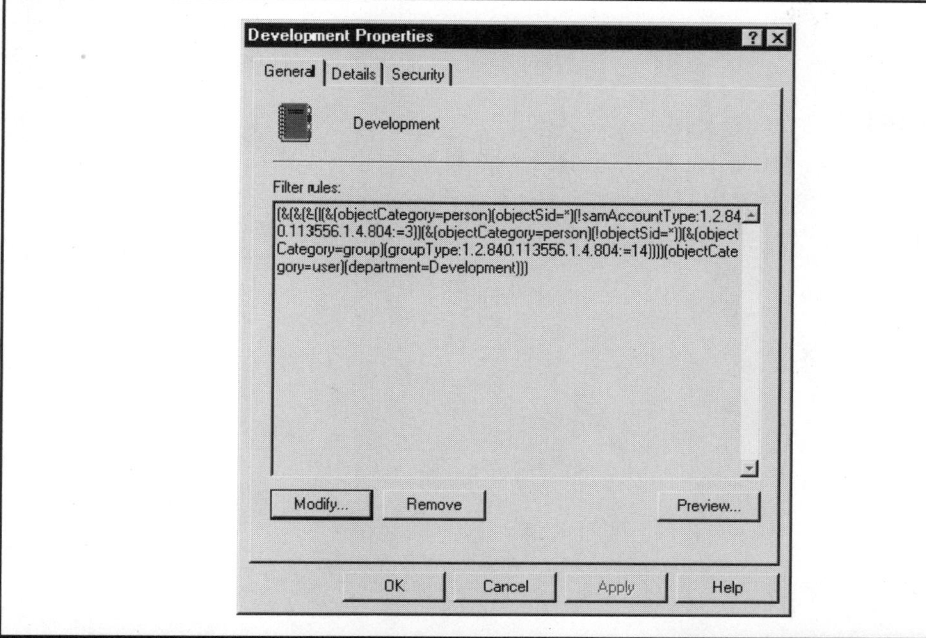

Figure 3-12. *Properties of a custom address list. This particular address list includes all users, groups, and contacts whose department attribute equals "Development."*

Some of these LDAP queries can be quite complex. Fortunately, you do not need to create them by hand. The System Manager contains a wizard-like applet that steps you through creating address lists. Using an intuitive Find dialog box, you can create address lists based on any number of user, group, contact, and public folder attributes (see Figure 3-14).

Each address list is updated periodically by the System Attendant; however, at any given time, only one Exchange server is actually performing this function. At the specified interval—which is configurable—the Address List Service, through the System Attendant, contacts a domain controller and updates the address lists accordingly.

Note *If you are running a mixed mode Exchange organization, keep in mind that address list updates and new address lists do not get replicated back to the Exchange 5.5 directory.*

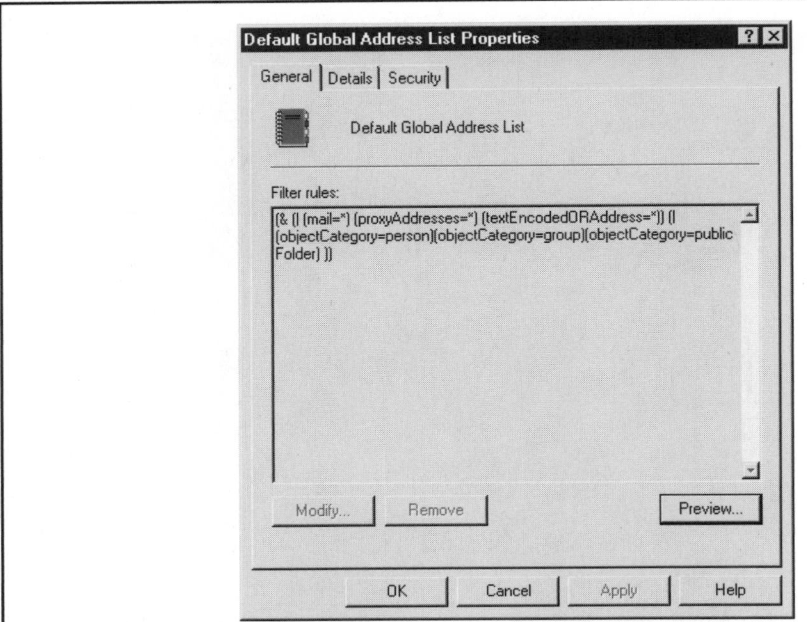

Figure 3-13. *The default GAL. Although you cannot modify the default GAL, you can delete it.*

Exchange 2000 creates several default address lists. These default address lists and the LDAP search filters used to create them are listed in Table 3-3.

Address List Views	LDAP Filter (RFC 2254)
Default Global Address List	(&(|(mail=*)(proxyAddresses=*)(textEncodedORAddress=*)) (|(objectCategory=person)(objectCategory=group)(objectCategory=publicFolder)))
All Users	(&(|(mail=*)(proxyAddresses=*)(textEncodedORAddress=*)) (|(&(objectCategory=person)(objectClass=user))))
All Groups	(&(|(mail=*)(proxyAddresses=*)(textEncodedORAddress=*)) (|(objectCategory=group)))

Table 3-3. *Default Address Lists in Exchange 2000 and the LDAP Filters Used to Create Them*

Address List Views	LDAP Filter (RFC 2254)
All Contacts	(&(|(mail=*)(proxyAddresses=*)(textEncodedORAddress=*))(|(&(objectCategory=person)(objectClass=contact))))
Public Folders	(&(|(mail=*)(proxyAddresses=*)(textEncodedORAddress=*)) (|(objectCategory=publicFolder)))
All Conferencing Resources	(msExchResourceGUID=*)

Table 3-3. *Default Address Lists in Exchange 2000 and the LDAP Filters Used to Create Them* (continued)

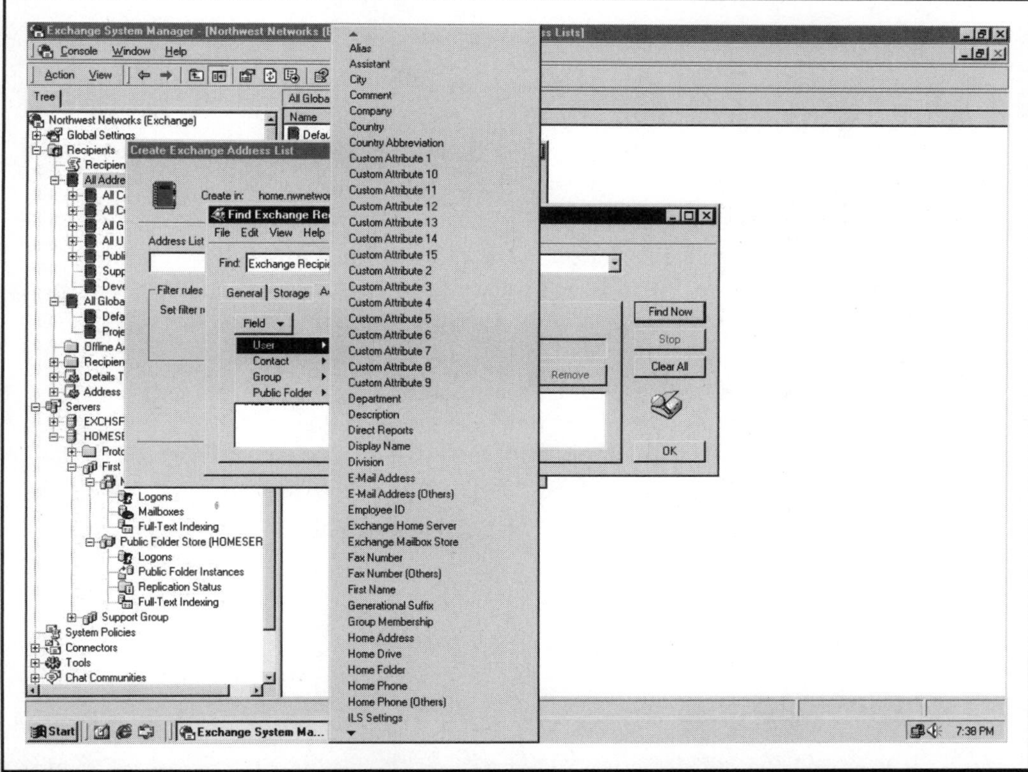

Figure 3-14. *Find Exchange Recipient dialog box. You can specify one or more attribute expressions in your query and use wildcard expressions, such as "starts with..." and "ends with..."*

Offline Address Lists

Like its predecessors, Exchange 2000 provides *offline address list* services in support of mobile users (see Figure 3-16). Although the GAL is typically selected as the default offline address book, Exchange 2000 allows any address list to be made available to offline users. Exchange 2000 uses Active Directory to provide the offline address list services previously provided by the Exchange directory.

When an offline address list is generated, the individual address lists that comprise it are converted to a data file and stored in a hidden public folder. This information is downloaded by users and stored as an offline address book file (.OAB file) on the user's PC. Keep in mind that downloading the whole address book over a slow link can be very time consuming.

Offline address lists are configured and managed using the System Manager. An address list must exist before it can be made available offline. To make an address available offline:

1. Open System Manager.
2. Expand Recipients.
3. As illustrated in Figure 3-15, right-click on Offline Address Lists and select New | Offline Address List.
4. The New Object – Offline Address List dialog box will appear. Provide a name for the offline address list, then click the Browse button to select an offline address list server. Click Next to continue.
5. The default GAL will be included in the new offline address list. If you do not want it included, select it and click the Remove button. Click the Add button to select which address list(s) you want to make available offline. Click Next to continue.
6. A warning message will appear indicating that the public folder containing the new offline address list object will be created at the next store maintenance interval and will not be available until then. Click Next to continue.
7. The final confirmation dialog box will be displayed. When you click the Finish button, the new offline address list object will be created.

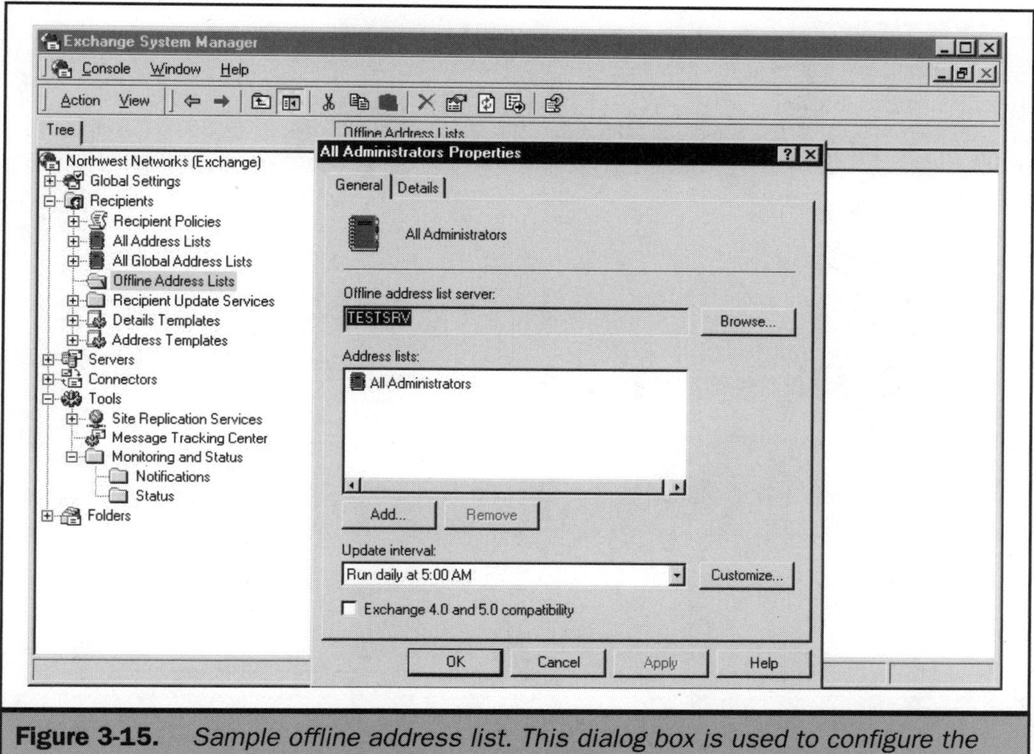

Figure 3-15. *Sample offline address list. This dialog box is used to configure the offline address list.*

To modify an Offline address list, right-click on the offline address list and select Properties. Its Properties sheet will be displayed.

You can select another offline address list server for this list, add and remove address lists, and change the update interval for list generation.

If you have Exchange 4.0 or 5.0 servers in your Exchange organization, you must select the Exchange 4.0 and 5.0 compatibility checkbox. For performance reasons, this checkbox is unchecked by default.

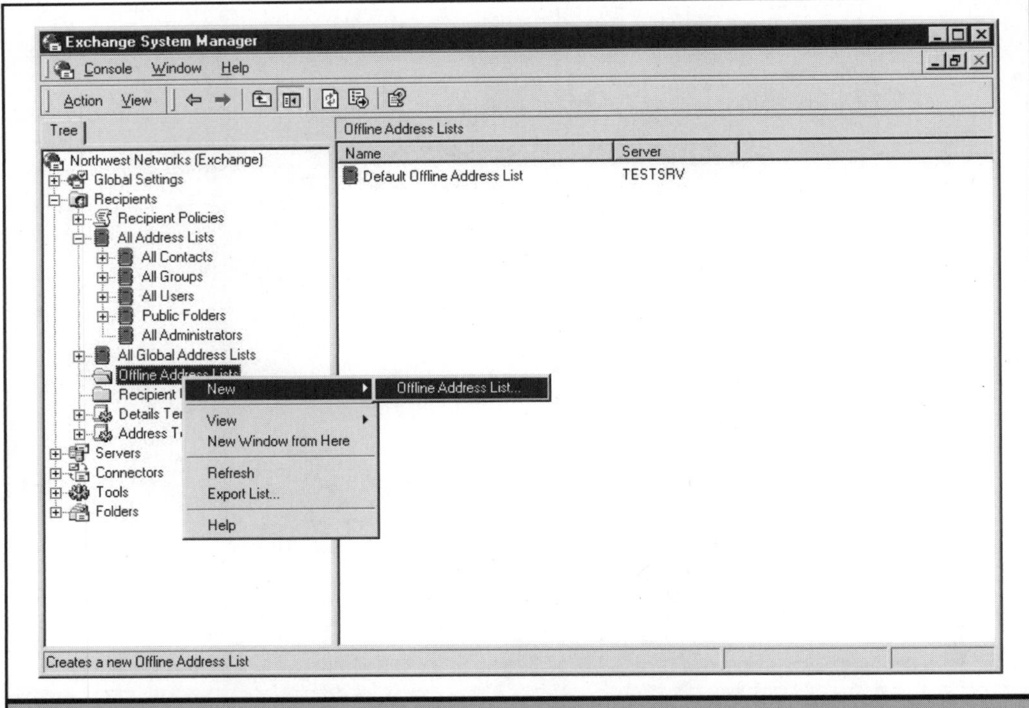

Figure 3-16. *New offline address list. Offline address lists are created using a wizard-like interface in System Manager.*

Exchange 2000 and Active Directory Security

In addition to being a directory service, Active Directory is also a component of the Windows 2000 security subsystem. Security identifiers (SIDs) are used to link Windows 2000 Active Directory objects with Exchange 2000. From a security standpoint, Exchange 2000 leverages Active Directory in several ways: for client authentication, Exchange service authentication, delegation, access control, and certificates. The following sections discuss Exchange 2000 integration with Windows 2000 security.

Authentication

A user is authenticated with each logon. If the logon is successful, the system generates a security access token. The access token includes security information that identifies the user, as well as the groups to which the user belongs. The token also includes a list of the privileges held by the user and the groups to which the user belongs. Every process executed by or on behalf of the user has a copy of their access token. The system uses this token to identify the associated user when a process tries to access a securable object or perform a system administration task that requires privileges.

Exchange 2000 includes two major changes in its authentication routines from prior versions. First, Exchange no longer uses a service account. Instead, it runs under the LocalSystem account and uses its credentials whenever authentication is required. Second, all Exchange 2000 services use the Kerberos security protocol for authentication. Prior versions of Exchange used a service account for the Exchange services. In native mode, Exchange 2000 eliminates the dependency on this service account and uses the LocalSystem account instead. The LocalSystem account uses a secret password that is automatically changed by Windows 2000 every seven days, making it significantly more secure than an Exchange 5.5 service account. Kerberos is used by Exchange when performing service logons through the LocalSystem account.

Kerberos Kerberos is another subject that can, and does, fill entire books itself, so we won't duplicate those efforts here. However, a basic review of Kerberos is in order. Kerberos V5 is a new native security protocol integrated into the administrative and security model of Windows 2000. When a user logs on to the network, Kerberos authenticates the user to the *key distribution center* (KDC). The KDC issues a *ticket-granting ticket* (TGT), which the client uses to access a service, such as Exchange. The complete process looks like this:

1. A user on a client system that supports Kerberos authenticates to the KDC.
2. The KDC issues a TGT to the client, which uses it to access the ticket-granting service (TGS) on a domain controller.
3. The TGS issues a service ticket to the client, which the client then presents to the requested network service. This ticket proves identity in both directions.
4. The user then authenticates with the requested network service.

Note *Exchange 2000 is considered a network service with respect to Kerberos. Before a Kerberos-capable client can access an Exchange server or the first time, it must request and obtain an Exchange service ticket from the Kerberos service. Thereafter, the client uses this service ticket for each subsequent access.*

Both Active Directory accounts and Windows 2000 computers can be trusted for Kerberos delegation. A computer that is trusted for delegation can forward credentials to any other computers. This is especially helpful in a front-end/back-end configuration, where clients access resources through one or more front-end systems, and the front-end system authenticates to the back-end system on behalf of the client. In this case, the Outlook Web Access server and the Exchange 2000 server are separate computers. The client identifies itself to the KDC and, using a flag on the ticket, the client is authenticated through delegation. Delegation can be performed two different ways:

- The client can obtain a proxy ticket for the back-end server and give it to the front-end server

- The client can give the front-end server a TGT, which can be used by the front-end server to request session tickets for back-end servers. These tickets are called forwarded tickets.

Windows 2000 computers are the only operating systems in the Windows family that natively support Kerberos. There are Kerberos add-ons for the Windows 9x platform, but not for Windows NT 4.0. When a user first accesses Exchange, their computer (if it supports Kerberos) requests an Exchange service ticket from a KDC on an Active Directory controller. This ticket is then used for authentication with the Exchange 2000 Server. Each subsequent authentication occurs much faster because the client computer already has the Kerberos ticket.

You can find more information on Kerberos by reading RFC 1510, which you can find at http://www.ietf.org/rfc/rfc1510.txt.

Access Control

All Active Directory objects are protected by *discretionary access control lists* (DACLs). When a user or an application attempts to access an object or attribute, the attempt is validated against the DACL by access validation routines. The access control model used in Exchange 2000 offers more granularity than the one used in Exchange 5.5. In Exchange 5.5, access control is at the container level. In Exchange 2000, access privileges can be set at the container, item, and property levels.

Windows 2000 implements access control by assigning security descriptors to Active Directory objects. These security descriptors are lists that contain the users and groups that are granted access to an object, the permissions assigned to them, and the access events that get audited. When a user is authenticated, they are assigned an access token that contains their security identity. This access token contains a user SID, the user's group SIDs, their privilege information, and other access rights.

When a user launches an application, it runs in that security context. Each thread spawned by the application receives a copy of the user's access token. When one of the application's threads needs to access an object, it identifies itself as the user's agent by presenting the user's access token. Before allowing the thread access to an object, Windows 2000 performs an access control check to determine whether the security principal associated with the thread is allowed access.

Here's how it works. First, the security subsystem reads the object's DACL, looking for access control entries (ACEs) that apply to the user and group SIDs contained in the user's access token. Each ACE is examined until one is found that either allows or denies access to either the user or one of the user's groups, or until all ACEs have been checked. If no ACE explicitly allows or denies access to the object, the security subsystem will deny access to the object.

Exchange 2000 Key Management Service

The Microsoft Certificate Service is a certificate authority mechanism that is integrated with Active Directory. The Exchange 2000 Key Management Service (KMS) uses these certificate services to provide application-layer security. The KMS produces X.509v3 user certificates that are used for digital signatures and encryption. Implementing security enhancements at the application layer ensures that only authorized users can gain access to application data.

Previous versions of the KMS restricted it to a single site. In Exchange 2000, the KMS organizational unit becomes the admin group. Each new admin group that is created allows the KMS to be pointed to an existing KMS. This means that administrators no longer need to decrypt existing messages when moving mailboxes. This was because the old keys could not be recovered when a user was moved to a new mailbox. Exchange 2000 allows users to be exported from one KMS to another.

See Chapters 18 and 19 for complete details on the Exchange 2000 Key Management Service and using certificates.

Summary

Exchange 2000 is deeply integrated with the Windows 2000 Active Directory. This deep integration provides organizations of all sizes with an easier administration model, more granular security control, and enhanced scalability. But this integration also comes with a price: added complexity that raises the learning curve. Ultimately, the success of your Exchange 2000 deployment will depend in large part on the integrity and success of your Active Directory deployment.

After reading this chapter, you should have a good understanding of how Exchange integrates with Active Directory. You should feel comfortable creating and configuring Exchange directory objects and querying Active Directory for Exchange-related data. You should understand how directory access caching works, how to replicate additional attributes to the Global Catalog, and how Exchange leverages Kerberos security.

As the primary focus of this book is Exchange 2000, you'll definitely want to look elsewhere for additional information on Active Directory. Some excellent sources of information include *Windows 2000 Active Directory* by Joe Casad and *Windows 2000: The Complete Reference* by Kathy Ivens and Kenton Gardinier.

The Complete Reference

Chapter 4

Exchange 2000 Architecture

Since the initial release of Exchange, Microsoft has continuously reworked and improved upon its core architecture. Microsoft had three specific design goals in mind when creating Exchange 2000. First, create a reliable and scalable platform. Second, create new ways for knowledge workers to collaborate. And third, provide an infrastructure that's available from any device and anywhere. To meet these goals, Microsoft made some major changes to Exchange's architecture.

A good portion of Exchange's functionality has been farmed out to several Windows 2000 components. Exchange 2000 boasts a new architecture that requires several external components, such as Active Directory and Internet Information Services. Microsoft also made changes to the underlying database component of Exchange 2000, the Extensible Storage Engine 98 (ESE98), and added a new store type for native Internet content.

In Chapters 2 and 3 we discussed how Exchange 2000 leverages and relies on Windows 2000, Active Directory, and DNS. This chapter covers the new Exchange 2000 architecture as it relates to the changes to the information store and the integration with Internet Information Services—specifically, SMTP and NNTP.

Overview of the Exchange 2000 Architecture

While its functionality remains the same, albeit substantially enhanced, the core components of Exchange 2000 differ greatly from their ancestors. The most substantial changes are in the areas of:

- **Directory services.** Exchange 2000 eliminates its own directory in favor of the Windows 2000 Active Directory. This provides enhanced scalability and added security while simultaneously reducing administrative costs and eliminating directory redundancy. Active Directory enables administrators to get very granular when delegating permissions to directory objects and network resources. Exchange 2000 leverages this granularity for applying permissions to Exchange objects, items, and attributes. Active Directory groups are also used as distribution lists by Exchange 2000, which simplifies administration. Exchange 2000 also takes advantage of Kerberos, the security protocol in Windows 2000. Exchange 2000, and Exchange clients that support Kerberos use secure service tickets for logon and access.
- **Information store.** The information store still exists, but it has been augmented in several respects. First, the Internet protocols have been removed from the store and offloaded to Internet Information Services. Second, Exchange 2000 supports multiple public and private databases on the same server, as well as the ability to put databases into storage groups. Third, the information store now includes an addressable URL namespace and supports

file system access. This combination of features, dubbed the Web Storage System, provides an entirely new development and collaboration platform. Finally, the information store also includes a new streaming database store (STM files), which contains native MIME and Internet content.

- **Integration with Internet Information Services.** By offloading Internet protocol support such as HTTP, SMTP, POP, and NNTP to Internet Information Services, and allowing these services to be distributed across load-balanced front-end servers, Exchange 2000 is able to scale much higher than before.

As you can see from Table 4-1, Exchange 2000 Server has an architecture that is radically different from its predecessors. Some of these components have been replaced with Windows 2000 components; others remain and are relatively unchanged in terms of functionality.

In addition to having its own directory service, Exchange 5.5 also supports Internet protocols such as POP3 and IMAPv4r1 that are integrated into the information store. Figure 4-1 illustrates the component architecture of Exchange 5.5.

Component	Exchange 5.5 Function	Exchange 2000 Replacement
Exchange Directory and Directory Service	Responsible for creating and managing the storage of all information regarding Exchange objects, such as mailboxes, distributions lists, public folders, custom recipients, and so on. The dsamain.exe process is responsible for directory replication, global and offline address list generation, and management of the physical directory database, an Extensible Storage Engine 97 (ESE97) database (DIR.EDB). ESE97 is a transactional database with rollback capabilities.	Windows 2000 Active Directory. This is an ESE97 database file and directory service that completely replaces the Exchange 5.5 directory and directory service. See Chapters 2 and 3 for more information on Active Directory and how Exchange 2000 integrates with it.

Table 4-1. *Exchange 2000 Components and Their Exchange 5.5 Counterparts.*

Component	Exchange 5.5 Function	Exchange 2000 Replacement
Information Store (Private and Public)	Provides individual mailboxes and a shared environment that can be used for document exchange, workflow, and applications. These are ESE97 databases housing the private mailboxes (priv.edb) and public folders (pub.edb). The store.exe process is responsible for data storage and management, as well as public folder replication. Supports one mailbox store and public folder store per server.	Information store, also known as the Web Storage System. The public and private information stores are ESE98 databases, and now include a streaming store (STM file) for native MIME and Internet content, such as audio and video multimedia. Multiple databases can be created within storage groups on each server. You can have a maximum of four storage groups per server, and each storage group can contain up to 5 databases for a total of 20 individual databases on each server.
Message Transfer Agent	The MTA manages the routing of messages between servers in an Exchange site, between servers in different sites, and between Exchange and some foreign e-mail systems. The emsmta.exe process performs these functions.	The MTA is still present for connectivity with foreign and legacy system (cc:Mail, MS Mail, and X.400 systems); however, the primary transport between Exchange 2000 servers is now SMTP.
System Attendant	Manages Exchange by verifying directory replication, writing the message tracking logs, building the routing tables for the MTA, and monitoring other servers through link monitors and server monitors. The mad.exe process performs these functions.	Still present and relatively unchanged, except that instead of building a routing table, it now maintains link state information.
Internet Mail Service	Provides SMTP functionality, allowing Exchange to send and receive Internet e-mail.	Replaced with the Windows 2000 SMTP service, which provides the same functionality. When installed, Exchange adds Transport sinks to the SMTP service in order to enhance its capabilities.

Table 4-1. *Exchange 2000 components and their Exchange 5.5 counterparts.* (continued)

Component	Exchange 5.5 Function	Exchange 2000 Replacement
Internet News Service	Provides NNTP functionality, allowing Exchange to host newsgroups.	Replaced with the Windows 2000 NNTP service, which provides the same functionality.
Connectors	Provide message exchange and directory synchronization with certain foreign mail systems: MS Mail Connector Schedule+ Free/Busy Connectivity Lotus cc:Mail Connector Lotus Notes Connector IBM Office Vision/VM	Some connectors are gone (for example, IBM Office and Vision/VM). Others remain (cc:Mail, Schedule+, Lotus Notes, and MS Mail). Novell GroupWise connector has been added.
Key Management Server	Provides enhanced security features, such as digital signatures and encryption.	Still present and relatively unchanged. See Chapters 18 and 19 for more information on Exchange 2000 security.
Outlook Web Access	Limited-functionality Web-based interface to Exchange. Outlook Web Access runs under Internet Information Server, and it is implemented as a set of Active Server Pages that use MAPI and CDO to communicate with the information store.	Still present but significantly overhauled to provide substantial performance gains and additional usability. See Chapter 14 for more information on Outlook Web Access.
Data and Video Conferencing	Internet Locator Service servers could be publisher for Exchange 5.5 users, enabling them to set up online meetings.	Exchange 2000 Conferencing Server provides support for T.120 clients, such as Microsoft NetMeeting, and multicast and H.323 clients. Chapter 15 covers Exchange 2000 Conferencing Server in depth.
Chat Service	Provides chat and Internet Relay Chat through Exchange, allowing for real-time, keyboard-based conversation.	Still present and relatively unchanged. See Chapter 17 for complete details.

Table 4-1. *Exchange 2000 components and their Exchange 5.5 counterparts.* (continued)

Component	Exchange 5.5 Function	Exchange 2000 Replacement
Scripting Agent	Provides basic workflow functionality for the public folders through Visual Basic and JScript.	Replaced with the Windows 2000 event model, an architecture that supports transport and protocol event sinks. Also augmented with event sinks that can run within the information store.
Instant Messaging	No Exchange 5.5 counterpart.	The Microsoft Exchange Instant Messaging Service provides real-time ad hoc communications, as well as online presence information.
Exchange Administrator Application	Used to manage the Exchange directory and information store.	Split into multiple MMC snap-ins, such as the Exchange System Manager, Active Directory Users and Computers, Internet Information Services and DNS, among others.

Table 4-1. *Exchange 2000 components and their Exchange 5.5 counterparts.* (continued)

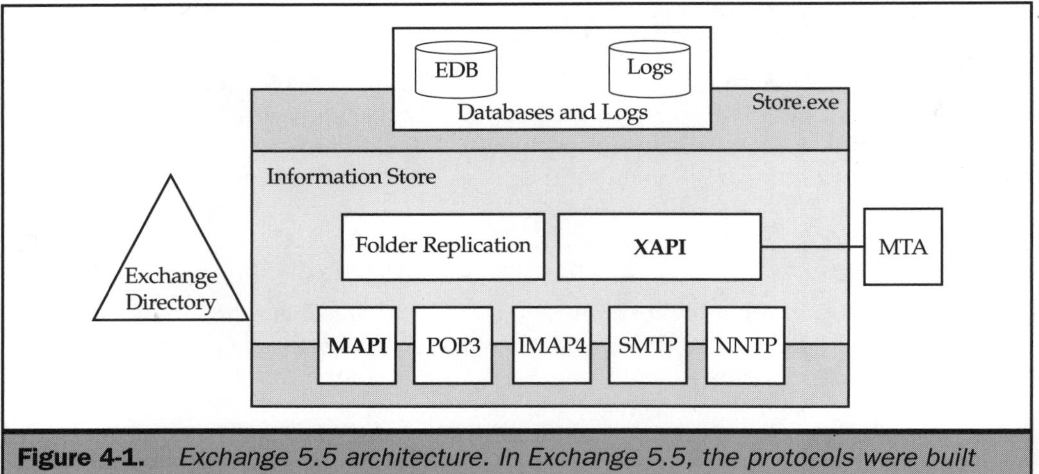

Figure 4-1. *Exchange 5.5 architecture. In Exchange 5.5, the protocols were built into the information store.*

Message Flow in Exchange 2000

Understanding this new architecture is best understood by examining how messages flow through Exchange 2000. Messages can enter an Exchange server in a number of ways. They can come from an Exchange 2000 mailbox, from other Exchange servers, or foreign mail systems. Exchange 2000 relies on Windows 2000 Active Directory and Internet Information Services for message flow. As shown in Figure 4-2, several Exchange 2000 and Windows 2000 components work together to route messages throughout a system.

The Information Store

Within an Exchange environment, messages flow in and out of the information store. It is the starting point for messages composed by an Outlook client and the end point for messages sent to a mailbox-enabled user. The information store is both a service and a database within Exchange. As a database, it is primarily responsible for creating and managing the Exchange databases files containing the private and public information stores. These stores contain user mailboxes and the public folder hierarchy, respectively. As a service, it processes server-side rules, delivers messages between users on the same server, and notifies users of new mail.

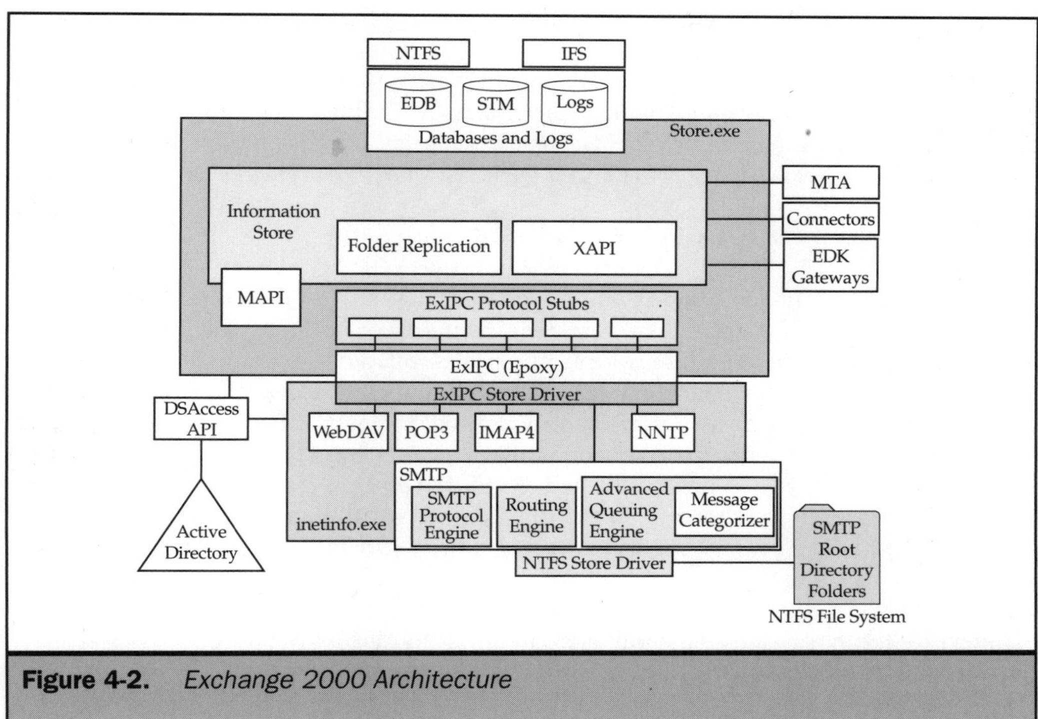

Figure 4-2. *Exchange 2000 Architecture*

Exchange's information store has had a rapid evolution over the last several years, much of which was the result of customer feedback. It uses an embedded database engine—called the Extensible Storage Engine 98 (ESE98)—that lays out the structure of data on the disk and manages memory. The engine caches database information by swapping chunks of data called pages in and out of memory. The database files (.edb files) are made up of 4Kb pages. This process is referred to as *paging*. When database requests occur, the database engine uses memory instead of disk, which is much slower than memory I/O operations. It loads the requests into memory and the pages are marked as *dirty*. Dirty pages are pages in memory that contain written data that will need to be written, or flushed, to disk.

Checksumming Checksumming refers to the creation of a string of 4-byte bits that is calculated and added to every page in the database. The integrity of pages in memory is verified through checksumming a 4-byte page number in the header of the database page. This header contains flags that indicate the type of page and what data the page contains. Each time store.exe reads pages out of a database, the pages are checksummed to ensure that the data in the page is undamaged.

Exchange 2000 performs checksumming on all information store files, including .edb, .stm, .log, and .pat files. This process is designed to inform an administrator immediately after a database becomes damaged. If any of the files become corrupt or damaged, the database engine will dismount the database and return an error. In addition, the application event log will contain an event that includes recommended repair actions.

Tip *Esefile, which can be found in the Support folder on the Exchange 2000 CD, can be used to verify the checksum integrity of all database, log and checkpoint files. See Microsoft Knowledge Base articles Q248406 and Q253325 for more information on using Esefile.*

Table 4-2 lists the various checksum errors that can occur.

The ACID Test The ESE database is designed to pass the ACID test (atomic, consistent, isolated, and durable). Atomic means it's all or nothing. The transaction is either committed to the database completely, or it's rolled back completely. As with most relational databases, Exchange uses transaction logs to accomplish atomicity —transaction log files improve performance and data integrity. Changes are recorded sequentially in one or more transaction log files before being committed to the database file. If the server crashes or an unexpected shutdown occurs, the data is still held in the transaction logs and is recoverable up to the last successfully written transaction. This helps prevent the data from becoming inconsistent or corrupted.

As transactions in the log files are committed to the database, a checkpoint file is written and updated. This file keeps track of which transactions are outstanding by using a pointer to the last successful transaction. If the system does crash, this file tells the database engine where to start its transaction log processing.

Error No.	ESE98 Error Message	Description
-612	JET_errLogReadVerifyFailure	Checksum error in LOG file during backup
-613	JET_errSLVReadVerifyFailure	Checksum error in SLV file during backup
-1018	JET_errReadVerifyFailure	Checksum error on a database page
-2210	JET_errSLVHeaderBadChecksum	SLV file header failed checksum verification
-2240	JET_errSLVInvalidSpaceMapChecksum	Checksum in SpaceMap is invalid
-6000	JET_errSFSReadVerifyFailure	Checksum error while verifying an SFS cluster
-7504	JET_errSFSFileShadowDataCorrupt	Checksum failed on the file's shadowed data

Table 4-2. *List of ESE98 Error Messages*

By being atomic, the database is also going to be consistent. Consistent means that the database is transformed from one valid and correct state to another. Consistent also means that a transaction never leaves the system in an unrecoverable state if it fails to write to the database.

In an isolated database, transactions are written serially, and changes are not visible until the transaction has been fully committed. When a database is handling multiple simultaneous transactions, the results of a single transaction should be the same as if it were the only transaction occurring. Simultaneous user operations should not conflict in any way that could jeopardize the integrity of the database.

Durable speaks to the database's ability to survive a system crash and retain committed transactions. When the system restarts, transactions that have not been committed to the database are either played back, rolled forward and committed, or rolled back completely.

Single-Instance Storage Single-instance message storage is where messages sent to multiple mailboxes on the same database are only stored once. All versions of Exchange support single-instance storage for recipients that reside in the same database. If a message is sent to one recipient and copied to other recipients, Exchange maintains a single copy of the message in its database and uses pointers that point to the single message. When recipients are located in different databases, the message is copied once to each database. If the databases are also in different storage groups, the message is added to each database and each transaction log set.

Single-instance storage is also maintained when a mailbox is moved to a different database, even if the database is on a different server. During the mailbox move process, Exchange checks the user's messages against the internally assigned message IDs. If Exchange determines that a message is a duplicate, it creates a pointer in the user's mailbox that points to the message.

Transaction Logs ESE databases use transaction logging to ensure data integrity and consistency in the event of a system crash. Transactions are written to both memory and the transaction log files before they are committed to the database. ESE uses transaction logs to "replay" transactions that haven't been written to the database, up to the moment of server failure. Each ESE transaction log is exactly 5MB (5120K) in size. Unless *circular logging* has been enabled, when the current log file reaches 5MB, the file is closed and a new transaction log file is created.

Circular logging is a holdover from the days when disk storage was at a premium. Circular logging refers to a process that overwrites and reuses transaction log files after the data in them has been committed to the database. This prevents the continuous buildup of transaction log files. The amount of disk space required for transaction log files can range anywhere from 20MB to 5GB, or more.

When developing a disaster recovery plan, you should consider the implications of enabling circular logging. Circular logging still writes log files, but once a checkpoint has been advanced, the inactive portion of the log file, which usually represents the majority of the transaction data, is discarded. Since transaction log history is cyclical, this data cannot be restored. In fact, when using circular logging, you can restore data only up to the last backup, and not to the point of failure, because the required log files may have been overwritten. As a result, if you enable circular logging, you can only perform full backups. With circular logging disabled, you can perform full, incremental, and differential backups of your databases. As its name implies, a full backup is a complete backup of the database, after which the log files are flushed (deleted). An incremental backup provides a backup of the data that has been changed or added since the last incremental backup. Once an incremental backup is complete, the transaction logs are flushed. A differential backup provides a backup of data that has been changed or added since the last full backup was taken. Unlike the full and incremental backups, a differential backup does not flush the transaction logs.

Tip *By default, circular logging is disabled in Exchange 2000. Because of the effect it can have on recovery, and because disk space is substantially less expensive than it used to be, most companies should choose to keep circular logging disabled. You should only consider enabling circular logging when absolutely necessary and only for servers that do not contain critical data (such as a bridgehead server, a public folder replica server, test servers, or any other Exchange server that contains disposable data).*

IMail Prior versions of Exchange stored messages in the database in a format called Message Database Encapsulated Format (MDBEF). If a message does not leave the Exchange server or is transported using intra-site RPCs, a site connector, a dynamic RAS connector, or an X.400 connector, it remains in MDBEF format. When it leaves the Exchange organization, or if it is requested by a non-MAPI client, it is converted to the Multipurpose Internet Mail Extensions (MIME) format, which the receiving computer can understand. MIME, which is detailed in RFC 1521, is a protocol used to include binary data that cannot be represented in ASCII text in e-mail messages.

The information store process called IMAIL handles the message conversion. IMAIL converts messages delivered via SMTP or NNTP to MDBEF before they are stored in the public or private information store. When messages are transported across the Internet Mail Connector, they are converted to an encoding format called Transport Neutral Encapsulation Format (TNEF). TNEF transported messages separate the message from the rich text formatting that may be in the message text. When a message arrives at the intended recipient, the mail client reassembles the message in to a richtext format. If the recipient client doesn't understand TNEF, the richtext formatting is delivered as an attachment to the message. This is often confusing to the recipient because the attachment is marked as an unknown type and disappointing to the sender because the richtext used in the message does not display in the message for the recipient.

The content conversion processes enables users to exchange e-mail with users on a wide variety of mail servers and client. However, the conversion process adds a few seconds to message processing and consumes a small amount of additional system resources. With Internet applications more ubiquitous than ever, more and more people and companies are turning to non-MAPI clients and using SMTP, POP3, IMAP4, HTTP, and NNTP for their messaging needs.

Information Store Types

To reduce the need for message format conversion, and to provide robust support for native Internet messages, the information store within Exchange 2000 has been augmented to provide two separate databases, each of which stores its content in a different format.

MAPI Store This store—a descendent from prior versions of Exchange—contains messages from MAPI clients, such as Microsoft Outlook. This type of store will always be beneficial for organizations that standardize on the Outlook 2000 client because no message conversion is required if both the sender and recipient are using MAPI clients. For those messages sent by Outlook users that are transported via an Internet protocol, the IMAIL process still converts the message into the appropriate format. In addition, all richtext information continues to be sent in TNEF format. The richtext store is still contained in .edb files.

Native Content Store Today's e-mail messages range from simple text messages to large multimedia messages containing audio and/or video. Exchange 2000 provides native support for these messages by storing their content in their native format. To do this, Exchange 2000 includes a new type of store—the streaming store. Along with the .edb files that house the private and public information stores, .stm files are used to store native MIME content, which can include audio, video, voice, or other multimedia formats as streams of MIME data. Like the MAPI store, the native content store also uses 4Kb pages and performs automatic online defragmentation and compaction.

By storing the content in its native format, the IMAIL conversion process is not needed when data is requested by a non-MAPI based client. If Outlook 2000—or any other MAPI client—requests this data, it is converted from MIME to MAPI and sent to the client. This conversion, which is only performed when necessary, is known as deferred content conversion. If conversion does take place, it takes place entirely in memory, and no content is moved from one database to another unless the content is changed by the MAPI client. If changes are saved by a MAPI client, the changed version is stored in the richtext store, and the original version remains in the streaming store.

Storage Groups and Multiple Databases

Exchange 5.5 and earlier versions store mailboxes and public folders in two databases: priv.edb for mailboxes and pub.edb for public folders. Exchange 2000 provides support for multiple databases contained in *storage groups*. A storage group is a virtual container for multiple databases that share a common set of transaction logs. Each storage group is managed in memory by the store.exe process, which runs as a single instance. Storage groups can contain as many as five databases, and each server can hold as many as four storage groups (a fifth storage group is reserved for recovery). Each server can therefore have a maximum of 20 databases.

Note *The 20 database limit will be increased in the 64-bit versions of Windows 2000 and Exchange 2000.*

Multiple databases can be used to increase the number of simultaneous users on a server while reducing the impact of a damaged database. Moreover, using multiple databases decreases the size of each database making backup and recovery much faster.

Multiple database support also helps to improve disaster recovery procedures by enabling a server to remain online while its databases are being restored. In previous versions, the server had to be taken offline in order to restore data from backup. The only alternative was to dedicate a recovery server to the process, which resulted in the need to perform lengthy data exports and imports in order to recover the data.

For organizations that require absolutely minimal downtime, the restoration process was a constant point of contention. Some addressed this issue by limiting the number of users per server and by limiting the allotment of storage to each user. Others used leading and bleeding-edge storage technologies, such as very fast SCSI and fibre channel disks or large capacity optical media for storage. Both solutions consumed expensive resources.

Storage groups are an attempt to address these issues. Databases in a storage group can be backed-up or restored individually or together, easing the burden for administrators who must meet their service level agreements. If one database goes offline, other databases can be online and servicing users while restoring the downed database from backup.

Deploying Multiple Databases and Storage Groups Before deploying multiple storage groups, you should consider that each database consumes 10MB of memory and an absolute minimum of 10MB of disk space for log files. The 10MB of memory is above and beyond the memory used by the store.exe process to manage the information stores. It is important to understand the implications of using multiple databases and multiple storage groups. There are some definite business advantages to both methodologies. The most common scenarios are described below.

- **Better backup, recovery, and maintenance**. By using many small databases instead of fewer large ones, the backup and restore windows are shorter. Even though backups occur while the server is online, a performance hit is taken during the backup. By reducing the amount of time it takes to back up a database, you reduce the impact on performance. In addition, smaller databases take less time to restore. Finally, database maintenance, such as offline defragmentation, will take less time to perform, thus reducing your maintenance window.
- **VIP Mailboxes**. These are mailboxes belonging to the most important executives in the organization. These mailboxes can also be indexed separately from other databases in the same storage group.
- **Large public folder applications**. This isolates the application from other server use, allowing you to more accurately gauge its performance.
- **Multiple company support**. This feature is most attractive to Internet service providers and application service providers who need to host multiple companies on the same server. Each company can have its own separate partition or disk, databases, logs, public folders, and so forth.

Internet Information Services Components

Exchange 5.5 provided support for Internet protocols through the information store. In Exchange 2000, these protocols have been offloaded to Internet Information Services (IIS), which is now fully integrated into the operating system. IIS runs as a process called inetinfo.exe. Offloading these services to IIS provides many advantages over previous designs, but the most compelling advantage is the ability to scale an Exchange infrastructure. In addition, offloading protocol support to IIS enables administrators to dedicate servers to deploy Exchange in a front-end-protocol-server /back-end-mailbox-server configuration. By servicing Internet protocols through the IIS process, system architects can distribute Exchange 2000 protocol, storage, and directory services across multiple servers for improved scalability.

SMTP Once installed, Exchange 2000 extends the SMTP protocol stack in Windows 2000 by adding additional command verbs and advanced routing components. Exchange 2000 extends the Windows 2000 SMTP Service, enhancing its delivery functions without compromising compatibility with other messaging systems that support SMTP. SMTP is also used as the primary message transport protocol in Exchange 2000. Prior versions of Exchange used RPC, MAPI, and a Message Transfer Agent based on the X.400 standard to transfer messages. Due to their synchronous nature, RPCs and MAPI do not perform well over networks with high latency or limited bandwidth. As a result, administrators typically designed their Exchange infrastructure around their network topology, as opposed to primarily addressing their administrative needs. Because Exchange 2000 uses SMTP instead of RPC for basic communication, architects can design an infrastructure that is better aligned with an organization's administrative needs. In addition, SMTP provides added flexibility when designing a message routing architecture.

Windows 2000's SMTP services are extended by Exchange 2000 through the use of transport and protocol event sinks. These sinks add new command verbs which support link state information. The specific additions to the SMTP Service are described below.

Advanced Queuing Engine The Advanced Queuing Engine is a primary component within the SMTP transport. All messages submitted to Exchange pass through this engine. There are two differences in the way messages are handled in Exchange 2000. First, all messages are sent to the transport mechanism, even when the sender and recipients are on the same server. This is necessary to allow event sinks to operate in a single-server environment. Second, the Advanced Queuing Engine reads the message data directly out of the information store through a file handle. This is much faster than the older MTA process, which copied the data out of the information store before transporting it.

There are two types of queues managed by the Advanced Queuing engine:

- Domain queues, which provide views of all messages that are destined for the foreign domains.
- Link queues, which provide a view—by logical link—of all messages that have the same next-hop in the routing infrastructure.

The Advanced Queuing Engine receives messages from SMTP and passes them to the Message Categorizer, which determines the message's destination. Once the destination has been determined, the Message Categorizer returns the message to the Advanced Queuing, which delivers the message to its destination via a local store driver or the SMTP stack.

Message Categorizer The Windows 2000 SMTP service includes a basic message categorization called cat.dll, which is turned off by default. Exchange 2000 upgrades and activates this component with an agent—called phatcat.dll—that can read Exchange-specific attributes from Active Directory. The message categorizer agent is a collection of event sinks that perform address resolution for all messages traveling through the Advanced Queuing Engine. In addition, the Message Categorizer checks message size limits and restrictions in Active Directory, handles group expansion, and if necessary performs *bifurcation*. Bifurcation is the process of creating separating content for RTF and MIME recipients. Once a message has been categorized, it is transferred into a domain-specific queue within the Advanced Queuing Engine.

Routing Engine The routing engine, or router, determines the best route for each message. This engine uses link-state routing to provide next-hop information to the Advanced Queuing Engine. Because the routing engine uses link state information, fewer mail loops occur.

The routing engine uses a sophisticated algorithm similar to the OSPF (Open Shortest Path First) algorithm used by many TCP/IP routers. This algorithm is responsible for propagating the state of the messaging system in near real-time to all of the other servers in the organization.

Note *The algorithm used is a variation of Dijkstra's Single Source Shortest Path algorithm, which dates back to 1959. This algorithm, which was invented by Edsger Wybe Dijkstra, solves routing problems by finding the shortest paths from an originating point to all destination points at the same time.*

Store Driver Exchange 2000 installs two DLLs—called store drivers—that enable the SMTP Service to read to and write from the information store and the NTFS file system. The database store driver (drviis.dll) is responsible for interfacing with the Exchange Interprocess Communication (ExIPC) layer, which saves messages to the information store. It also delivers inbound messages from the Advanced Queuing Engine to the information store for local delivery. For nonlocal delivery, NTFS store driver (ntfsdrv.dll) submits messages from the information store to the file system, where they are passed off to the Advanced Queuing Engine for delivery to other gateways.

SMTP Protocol Engine This component, which is implemented in smtpsvc.dll, is responsible for answering inbound connections and initiating outbound connections. It also issues and processes all protocol commands.

Exchange Interprocess Communication Layer Offloading protocol services to IIS increases scalability, but without a fast mechanism for exchanging data between IIS and the information store, bottlenecks will result. To address this issue, Exchange 2000 has a high-performance queuing layer called the *Exchange Interprocess Communication* layer (ExIPC) that allows IIS and the information store to quickly exchange data. As the name implies, an interprocess communication mechanism enables different processes—even those on different computers—to connect over a secure, reliable communication channel and exchange data. Figure 4-3 illustrates the relationship between the Exchange protocol DLLs and their IIS counterparts.

ExIPC has two primary parts: a binding facility and protocol stubs. The binding facility handles the creation of and connection through queues between the IIS and the information store. The binding facility contains a Central Queue Manager, which manages the various queues each process uses for communication. The binding facility also handles unbinding and cleanup when any one of the processes fails. Before binding occurs, the ExIPC DLL and the appropriate protocol DLL load into memory. ExIPC is loaded first, followed by the protocol DLL. Each protocol has an ExIPC interface to the information store. These components exchange data between the information store and the ExIPC interface in IIS. The protocols and their corresponding DLLs are listed in Table 4-3.

Now that we have described the components involved in the flow of messages, let's examine the flow of messages in different scenarios.

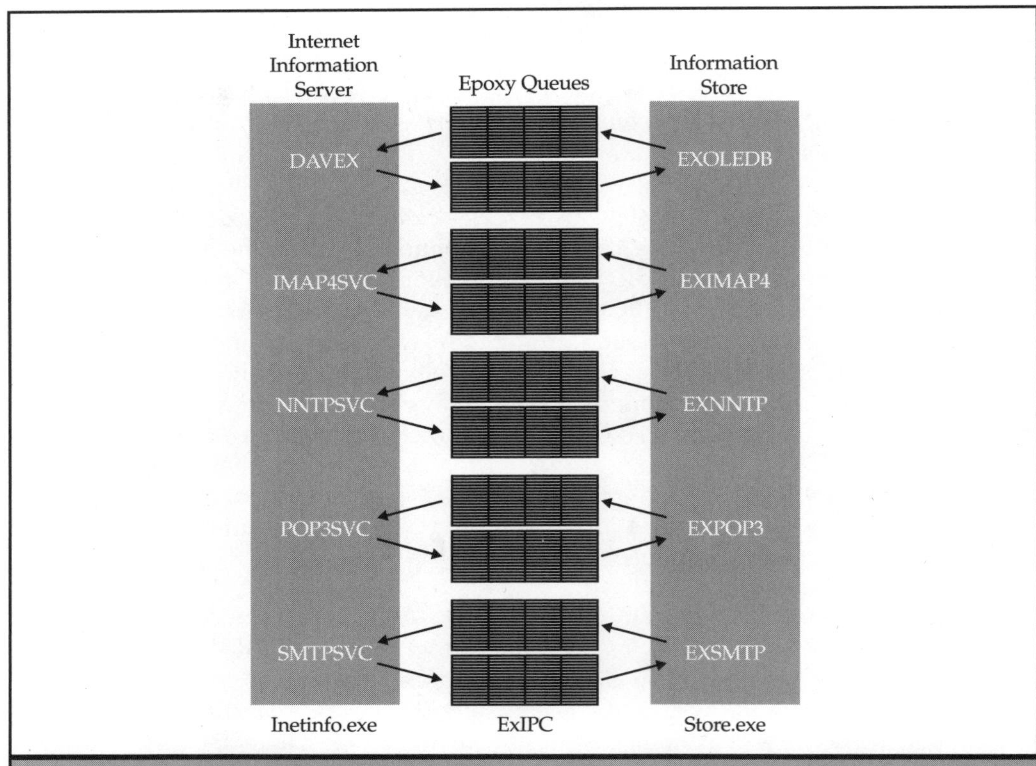

Figure 4-3. *ExIPC relationships between IIS (inetinfo.exe) and the Information Store (store.exe).*

Protocol	DLL
IMAP	ExIMAP4.dll
NNTP	ExNNTP.dll
POP3	ExPOP3.dll
SMTP	ExSMTP.dll
HTTP (WebDAV)	ExOLEDB.dll

Table 4-3. *Protocol Stubs for the ExIPC Facility*

Scenario 1 – Message Between Outlook Users on the Same Server

Even when users have mailboxes located on the server messages between them still flow through IIS. A message from one user to another user on the same server flows as follows:

1. The user clicks the Send button in Outlook and the information store receives the message.
2. A MailMsg object known as Imailmsg is passed to the Advanced Queuing Engine, which places this object in the precategorizer queue.
3. The Message Categorizer retrieves the Imailmsg object from this queue and, because the recipient is local, it places the message in the local delivery queue.
4. The information store receives the message and the store driver then creates and associates a pointer from the message to the recipient's mailbox.

Scenario 2 – Message from Outlook User to Internet Recipient

When an Outlook user sends a message to an Internet recipient, the initial flow of messages is similar to that described in Scenario 1 above. The following steps describe this process:

1. The user clicks the Send button in Outlook and the information store receives the message.
2. The information store uses the DSAccess API to check size limits for outbound messages.
3. The information store places the message in a SendQ folder and generates an event that notifies the store driver of the new message.

4. The store driver receives the event, collects the message, and creates an Imailmsg object.
5. The store driver passes the Imailmsg to the Advanced Queuing Engine, which places this object in the precategorizer queue.
6. The Message Categorizer retrieves the Imailmsg object from this queue and, if necessary, bifurcates the message. When necessary, the Message Categorizer also expands groups, checks message size limits, and sets the appropriate content type for each recipient.
7. The Advanced Queuing Engine passes the message destination(s) to the routing engine, which returns the SMTP host(s) to which the message(s) should be sent.
8. The Imailmsg object(s) is(are) passed to an outbound domain queue in the Advanced Queuing Engine.
9. The SMTP protocol engine connects to port 25 on the destination SMTP host(s) returned and establishes an SMTP session.
10. The store driver retrieves the body of the message from the information store to the SMTP protocol engine, converting it to the proper format as needed.
11. The SMTP protocol engine streams the message to the destination SMTP host and closes the SMTP session when finished.

Scenario 3 – Inbound Messages from the Internet to an Outlook User

Messages to Outlook users from the Internet are also processed via IIS prior to being received by the information store. The following steps describe this process:

1. A remote SMTP host connects to port 25 on an Exchange server in the Outlook user's organization (the local SMTP host).
2. The two hosts establish an SMTP session, exchanging commands regarding the message.
3. The remote host streams the message to the local SMTP host's protocol engine.
4. The local SMTP service raises a store driver event, causing the store driver to create an Imailmsg object.
5. The local SMTP service stores the envelope properties within the Imailmsg object, and then begins to receive the remaining data from the remote SMTP host.
6. The store driver returns a file system pointer to the message body, and then stores the pointer within the Imailmsg object.
7. The store driver writes the message body to the Queue folder.
8. The SMTP service requests a *commit,* which guarantees that both the envelope data and the message data have been successfully written to the file system.

9. The Advanced Queuing Engine retrieves the Imailmsg object from the Queue directory and places it in the precategorizer queue.
10. The Message Categorizer retrieves the Imailmsg object from this queue and, if necessary, *bifurcates* the message by creating separate Imailmsg objects for RTF and MIME recipients. When necessary, the Message Categorizer also expands groups, checks message size limits, and sets the appropriate content type for each recipient.
11. The Advanced Queuing Engine passes the destination(s) to the Routing Engine, which returns the next-hop routing information for each recipient.
12. If the recipient's mailbox is on a different server, the Message Categorizer then places the Imailmsg object in a domain queue in the Advanced Queuing Engine. If the recipient is local to this server, it places the Imailmsg object in the local delivery queue.
13. If the message is being routed to another server, the routing engine creates a next-hop identifier for its destination. Otherwise, the local delivery queue passes the message to information store.
14. The store driver creates and associates a pointer from the message to the recipient's mailbox.

Other Internet Protocol Support

POP3 client support remains relatively unchanged from Exchange 5.5. Although it performs faster and is more robust than its predecessor, there is no additional functionality within Exchange 2000's POP3 implementation. IMAP4 and NNTP support have been enhanced to provide enhanced additional functionality. These enhancements are briefly described below.

IMAP4 Support Exchange 2000 enhances IMAP4 support in several respects. Exchange 2000 implements IMAP4 support for RFC 2359. This provides access to public folders and enables users to delegate permissions to others for their mailbox. IMAP4 is more flexible than POP3 because it enables users to download message headers and read messages individually. In addition, Administrators can enable anonymous access to specific IMAP4 accounts. All IMAP4 messages are stored in the .stm store as native MIME content.

NNTP Support Exchange 2000 also extends the Windows 2000 NNTP Service. MAPI and NNTP clients can post or read newsgroup messages through the information store. The Windows 2000 NNTP service is intended as a standalone newsgroup server. When Exchange 2000 is installed, the NNTP protocol stack is extended. This enables the replication of newsgroups to Usenet host computers through newsfeeds.

Exchange 2000 also enhances the usability of newsgroups by indexing their contents. Content indexing provides the ability to use full-text searches against the newsgroups.

The Web Storage System

Exchange 2000 includes enhancements to the information store that expand the ways it can be accessed. Microsoft has combined the URL addressability of the Web, the familiarity and functionality of a file system, and a collaboration tool in a single repository for information access, storage, and management. This repository, called the Web Storage System—or the Web Store for short—enables users to work with e-mail messages, documents, and other files stored within the information store as if the information store was a file system. The Web Store provides three primary services:

- **File system services.** The Exchange Installable File System (IFS) provides support for Win32 file system services, enabling administrators to create network shares to information store data.
- **Database services.** The Web Store enables different types of information to be stored in a single repository. This can include data from OLE DB and ADO recordsets, XML data, and MIME messages.
- **Collaboration services.** The Web Store provides integration for common collaborative items—messages, contacts, calendar information, and workflow applications—by providing an object model for developers.

Installable File System

The Exchange databases found in most companies contain much more data than just electronic mail and calendar and task information. The average content ranges from Office documents to Internet documents, from images to application binaries, and from off-the-shelf workflow applications to custom, in-house applications. Just like a file system or network share, the information store is capable of storing many different types of data.

Microsoft added extensions to Exchange 2000 that enable administrators to share folders in Exchange as if they were network shares. The Installable File System (IFS) allows a folder or object to be exposed to network client redirectors as if it were a file share. This means that drives can be mapped using the Windows Explorer or the net use command. The IFS enables other familiar features, such as drag-and-drop file management and programmatic access through Win32 file system APIs.

Drive M on the Exchange server is exposed as a hidden share called BackOfficeStorage. You can create visible and accessible shares by sharing out the M drive the same way you would with any other drive on your server. You can also access the IFS by programmatically mapping to *server*\BackOfficeStorage, where *server* is the name of the Exchange server.

Note *If the M drive is already assigned to another storage device, Exchange will use the next available drive letter.*

The IFS hierarchy has two root folders: the MBX folders and the public folders.

- The MBX folder is the root of all mailboxes. All folder names under the MBX root are invisible; however, clients with the appropriate permissions can navigate by using explicit folder names that equate to mailbox alias names.
- The public folders folder is the root of all public folders. This enables you to access data within the public folders to which you have been given permissions.

Objects in folders from both stores can be enumerated using the dir command, and they can be manipulated using other file system commands such as copy and delete. As illustrated in Figure 4-4, message contents can also be viewed by using the type command.

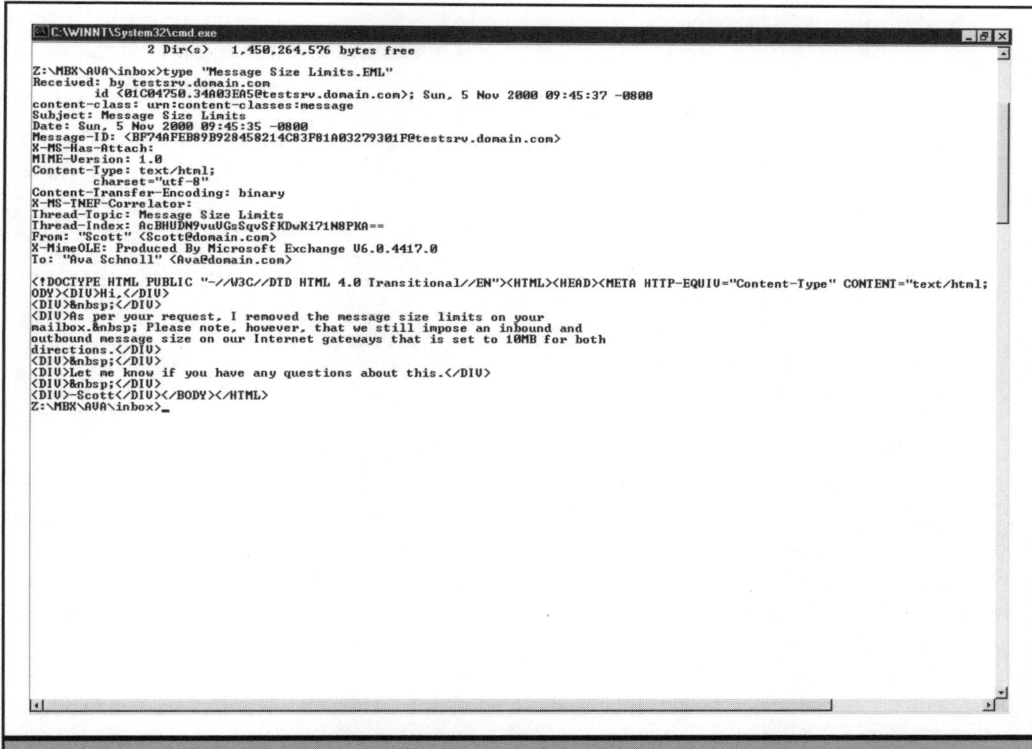

Figure 4-4. *Accessing a message via the type command.*

Property Promotion Microsoft Office documents can contain custom document properties that provide information about the document, such as author, date/time last saved, keywords, and so on. Users can locate documents using one or more of these properties in their search criteria. When these documents are stored in Exchange, the Web Store stores the custom properties in its database. Once the document properties have been promoted to the Web Store database, Outlook users can use the document properties to quickly locate documents across all of their folders. This makes accessing information easy and efficient by eliminating the need to switch applications or use separate search features.

WebDAV Support

Microsoft added HTTP support in Exchange Server 5.0. This version included a new component called Outlook Web Access that enabled users to access their mailbox and public folders using a web browser. Exchange 2000 has a completely redesigned Outlook Web Access component, which is detailed in Chapter 14. Exchange 2000 also includes additional HTTP support through Web Distributed Authoring and Versioning (WebDAV). WebDAV is defined in RFC 2518 as a set of extensions to the HTTP 1.1 protocol. Appendix A covers WebDAV in more detail.

WebDAV has three primary features. First, it provides a means of storing and retrieving metadata—the information that is known about a document—such as the author, title, publication date, etc. Second, it provides a mechanism for namespace management, allowing users to manage Web-based items as if they were stored within the file system. Third, it allows users to edit documents without overwriting one another's changes by implementing file locking.

Note *The versioning feature of the WebDAV protocol has not yet been implemented in Exchange 2000.*

Under the WebDAV model, each item and folder has a human-readable URL associated with it, such as http://mailserver/exchange/mailboxname/inbox. When IIS receives a request for such a URL, it passes the request to an ISAPI application (davex.dll) that communicates with the Exchange store through the ExIPC and the information store driver, exoledb.dll. The application parses the request for specific information. Next, the item type is determined (e.g., mail message, contact, Microsoft Office document), and the appropriate form is selected by the ISAPI application. Finally, the information store returns the requested data and davex.dll renders an HTML view of each item using view-specific properties. This process is illustrated in Figure 4-5.

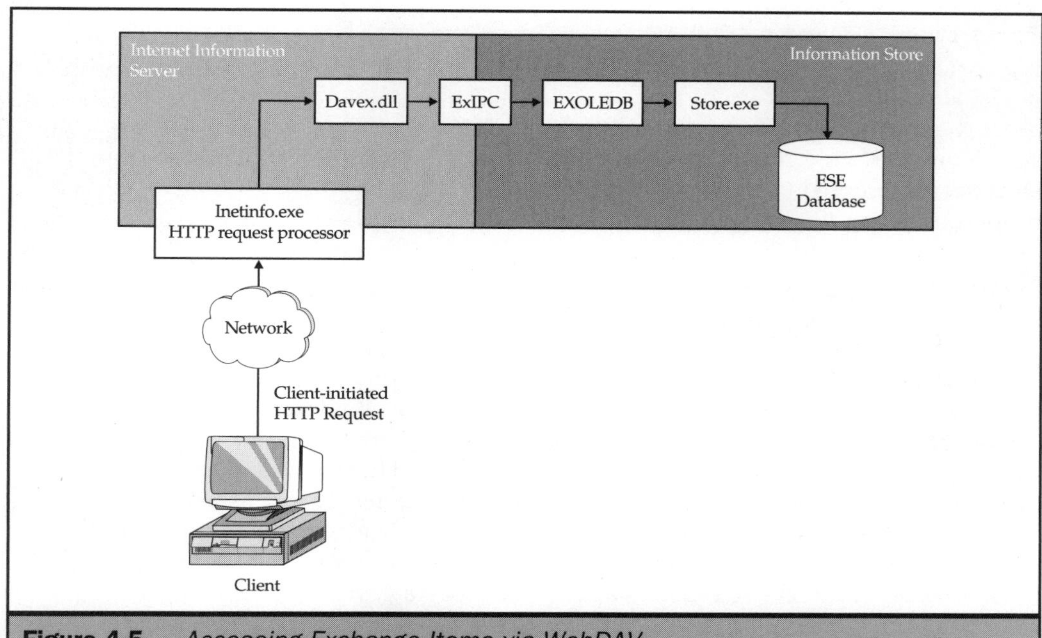

Figure 4-5. *Accessing Exchange Items via WebDAV*

Exchange 2000 Event Sinks

Exchange 2000 enables developers and administrators to write code that acts upon an event—such as the arrival of a new message—and performs some task. This code is known as an *event sink*. An event sink is a piece of code that is activated by a predefined trigger called an "event." Scanning new messages for viruses as they arrive, adding a company disclaimer to all outgoing messages, or initiating a workflow process when data changes are all functions that can be performed by event sinks. Event sinks can be synchronous or asynchronous. Synchronous sinks execute when the event occurs, and asynchronous sinks execute after the event has occurred. Both types enable you to specify what folders and subfolders are available to an event sink.

Event sinks are implemented as COM objects and can therefore be written in any language that supports COM, such as C++, Visual Basic, VBScript and JScript. In addition, Exchange 2000 provides support for CDO, ADO, and ATL.

There are three types of events: transport events, protocol events, and Web Store events. These are described below. For more information on event sinks or using Exchange as a development platform, see Chapter 23.

Transport Events

Transport events are used to send messages through a custom process before they are stored or relayed. They occur as a message moves through the SMTP or NNTP transport. Adding a company disclaimer to outgoing messages is an example of a transport event.

Protocol Events

Protocol events are used to extend the SMTP command verbs. They occur when a client connects to the server and issues one or more commands, such as EHLO or DATA. You can use them to add your own protocol commands or to modify how existing protocol commands are processed.

Web Store Events

Developers can use OLE DB to create events—known as Web Store events—that extend the functionality of the information store. Web Store events fire exclusively through the Exchange OLE DB provider. Web Store event sinks are bound to store events by registering them in the IIS metabase through Server Extension Objects (SEOs). The ExOLEDB provider reads the metabase data and translates the event's binding information into store restrictions. If a store restriction is met, the ExOLEDB provider triggers an event and activates the appropriate sink(s).

Administration and Routing Models

In Exchange 5.5 and earlier, the routing and administration models were inseparable. Exchange 2000 redefines its routing and administrative boundaries in ways that more accurately reflect real-world Exchange deployments. The end result is that administrators can separate their administrative and routing topologies. Exchange 2000 administration can be separated into two categories: server administration and recipient administration. Server administration refers to the management of system policies, public folder trees, services such as chat and conferencing, and so forth. Recipient administration, which is covered in Chapter 8, refers to the management of mailboxes, mailbox- and mail-enabled contacts, users and groups, and recipient policies. The next few sections briefly discuss Exchange's new architecture as it relates to managing servers. Chapter 9 discusses server administration in more depth.

Server Administration

Managing an Exchange 2000 server is quite different from managing an Exchange 5.5 or earlier server. Like many other Windows 2000–based applications and services, Exchange 2000 servers are managed using one or Microsoft Management Console (MMC) snap-ins. The primary snap-in used to manage Exchange 2000 servers is called the System Manager. System Manager is used to view, create, and modify administrative groups and routing groups.

Administrative Groups An administrative group is a collection of Exchange 2000 objects that are grouped for administrative purposes. Objects within the same administrative group share a security context. Any server that needs to be administered by a specific set of administrators can be placed in its own administrative group. Only authorized administrators can make changes to the configuration of that server. Configuration data for administrative groups is held within the configuration naming context of Active Directory. Because this data is replicated throughout the organization, a single administrative group is not bound by the underlying network or domain structure. This means that these groups can be created based upon business requirements.

Exchange 2000 servers can be managed using one of three administration models:

- Centralized administration model, where all servers are in the same administrative group, regardless of their physical location.
- Distributed administration model, where servers are placed in the administrative groups that correspond to their physical location.
- Mixed administration model, where servers are placed in the administrative groups that correspond to their services or user base.

As illustrated by Figure 4-6, in the centralized administration model, Exchange 2000 servers are managed from a central location, such as a corporate headquarters. Because

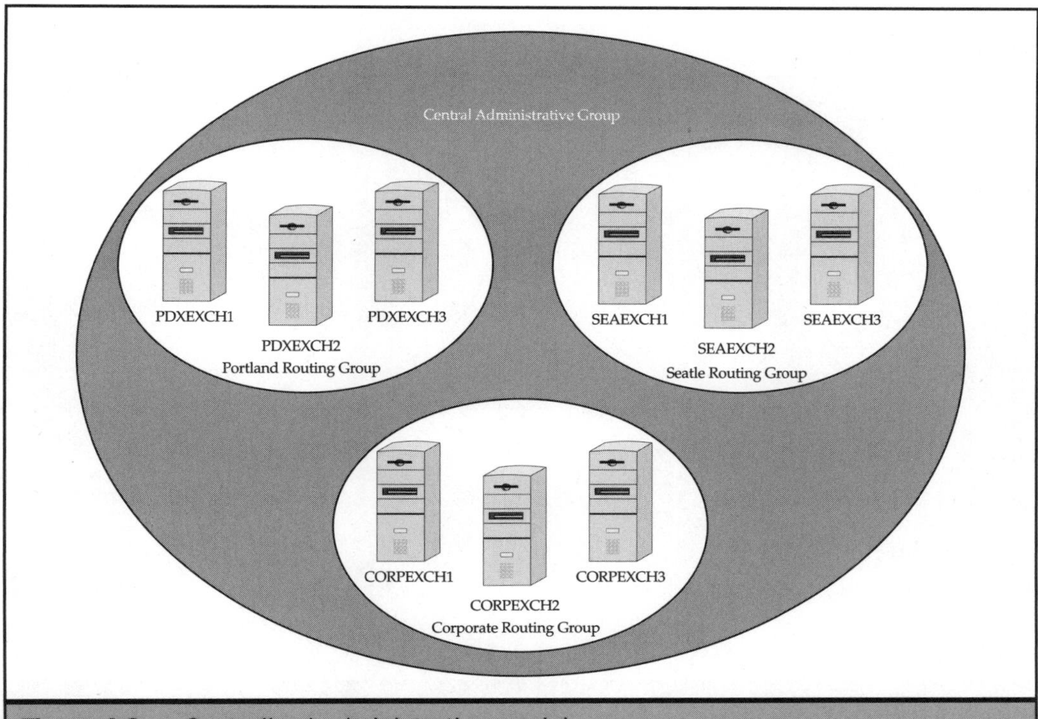

Figure 4-6. *Centralized administration model*

administrative groups and routing groups are separate topologies, you can simplify your administrative group architecture by placing all of your Exchange 2000 servers within a single administrative group. This is typically the best approach because a single administrative group can contain multiple routing groups.

Exchange 2000 also supports a distributed administration model in which you use administrative groups that match your organization's administrative divisions. For example, all servers within a single remote or branch office can be placed into a single administrative group that is managed by the remote office's local IT staff as shown in Figure 4-7.

Within the mixed administration, model, multiple, administrative groups are used to manage message routing. For examplė, you can use administrative groups to separate management of system policies, routing groups, public folders trees, conferencing servers, or chat communities. Figure 4-8 depicts an example of a mixed administration model.

Administrative groups also make mailbox management significantly easier. In prior versions of Exchange, the organization was a collection of one or more sites containing one or more well-connected servers. Well-connected generally means that the servers in a site have dedicated reliable connections of at least 512Kbps between them. Servers within these sites shared a common namespace and were administered as a single unit. As a result, administrators could move mailboxes between servers in the same site, but not

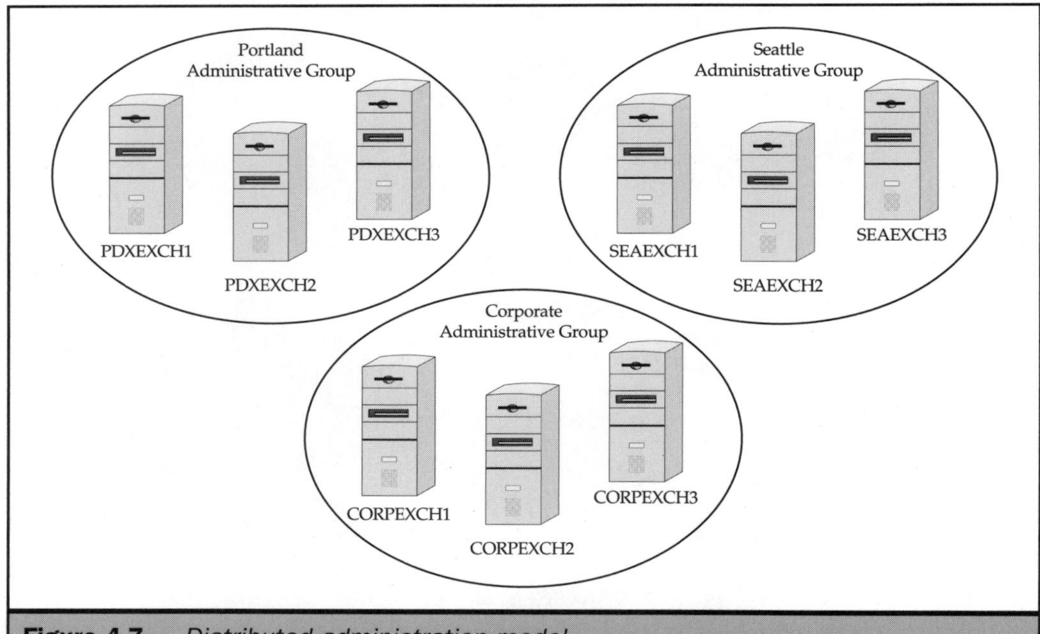

Figure 4-7. *Distributed administration model*

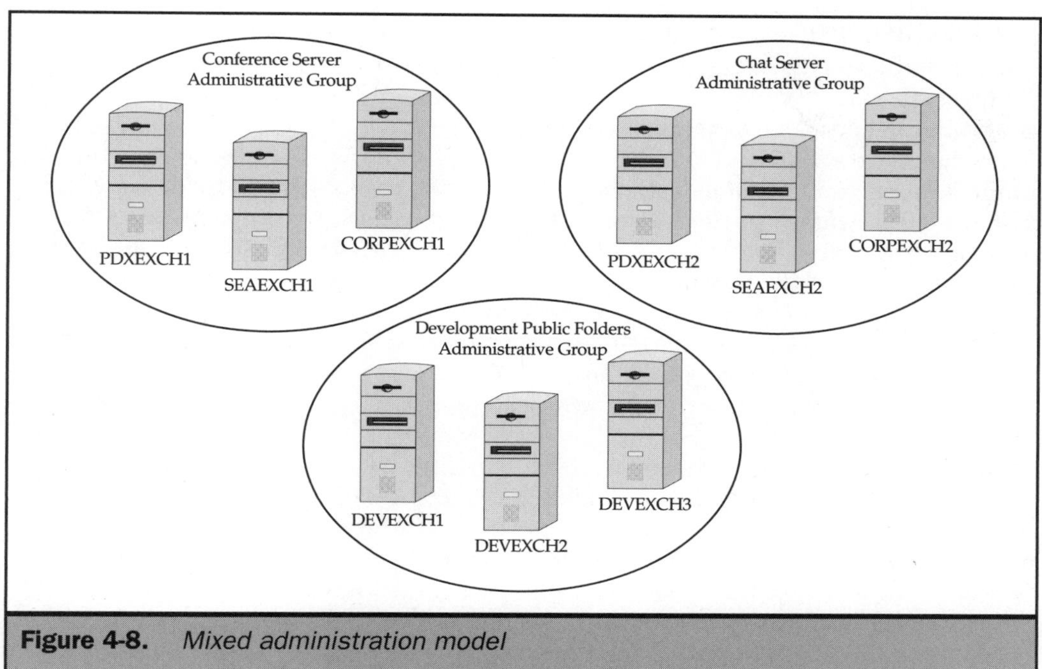

Figure 4-8. *Mixed administration model*

between sites. In Exchange 2000, administrative groups are used to overcome this limitation, enabling administrators to move a mailbox between any two servers within the Exchange organization.

Routing Groups

A routing group is a collection of servers that constantly share information with each other over a reliable LAN (or with adequate links, a reliable WAN). These servers communicate using *routing group connectors*. These are SMTP-based connectors that are similar in nature to the Exchange 5.5 Site Connector. A routing group belongs to an administrative group, but it can be one outside of the server's administrative group.

Note *When an Exchange 2000 server communicates with an Exchange 5.5 server over a routing group connector, communication uses RPCs instead of SMTP.*

Routing groups also host connectors to other routing groups, or to foreign messaging systems. For example, you can use an SMTP connector to connect a routing group to a foreign SMTP mail system. You can also use an X.400 connector to connect a routing group to an X.400 messaging system.

Routing groups overcome link failures that cause message routing problems by continuously sharing link state information with each other. In addition to automatic replication of link state information within a routing group, link state information is also passed between routing group connectors. This enables a server to be aware of and therefore circumvent physical link failures and to restore logical links once the failed physical links become available again.

Note *If Exchange 2000 is running in mixed mode, it continues to support the Exchange 5.5 administrative model. In this case, you can only create one routing group per administrative group. As a result, before you can add additional routing groups, you must define additional administrative groups. Once these have been defined, you can configure routing group connectors between them. Once Exchange is converted to native mode, you can separate your routing groups and administrative groups. This is an important milestone in your Exchange 2000 deployment, because it means you can create administrative groups that align with your support infrastructure.*

When the sender and recipient are located in different routing groups, messages between them are transferred via a routing group connector. Each server maintains a link state table that identifies which servers are routing servers and which connectors are active and available. If both servers are also routing servers, they can open a direct connection to exchange the message. If only the sender's server is a routing server, it will open a connection to a routing server in the recipient's routing group and relay the message through it. Once this routing server has the message it will query Active Directory for the recipient and transmit the message to the recipient's server via SMTP.

If the recipient is located on a foreign mail system, the message will travel over the appropriate connector. This can be an SMTP connector, an X.400 connector, a Lotus Notes connector, etc. Once it leaves the Exchange infrastructure, it can travel over a multitude of other routes and connectors until it reaches its intended destination.

Link State

Previous versions of Exchange supported routing on a "least cost" basis. Ideally, a message would get routed using the shortest route and least amount of bandwidth possible. Servers maintained a gateway address resolution table (GWART) that contained the routing information for the Exchange organization. This method worked wonderfully when all of the routes are up and available. However, if a connection was lost, the servers had no way of intelligently rerouting the message. Instead, a message would bounce from server to server until either the routes were restored or it was marked as undeliverable.

Every Exchange 2000 server maintains a dynamic link state table that replaces the Exchange 5.5 GWART and serves as a map of the entire messaging topology. Exchange 2000 still supports least-cost routing, but it also uses a link state algorithm to determine the status of links. The link state algorithm is similar to and, in part, based on the Open Shortest Path First (OSPF) protocol used in many networks today. A link can have a status of up or down. This status is collected by each routing group through its *routing group master*. A routing group master handles the collection and dissemination of link state information.

All link state information is held in memory within a link state table. In addition to containing link state information, the in-memory link state table also includes routing group, connector and bridgehead GUIDs, costs and address spaces, and the link state itself. At any given moment, each Exchange server knows the best route to take for message delivery. This means that if routing information changes before a message has reached its intended recipient, Exchange can intelligently reroute the message using the next least cost route.

Tip *You can use WinRoute from the Exchange 2000 Resource Kit to view a server's link-state table.*

The size of the link state table—and therefore the amount of memory that will be consumed by each server maintaining the table—depends on the number of servers, connectors and routing groups within your Exchange organization. Each of these objects will consume 32 bytes of memory. Therefore, if you have 100 servers, 200 routing groups, and 100 connectors, the link state table will consume approximately 12.5Kb of memory.

The way link state data is propagated depends on whether it is being exchanged with servers within the same routing group or between routing groups. Link state data that travels between routing groups is relayed via SMTP on port 25. Updated link state data is sent any time a link state change occurs. Link state data that travels within a routing group occurs via TCP on port 691.

Note *TCP port 691 was registered by Microsoft with the Internet Assigned Number Authority (IANA) specifically for this purpose.*

Servers in different routing groups communicate using a link state algorithm that is an extension to SMTP. When one server sees that another server is advertising a change in routing information, it connects to that server and attempts to exchange routing information. Routing information is only exchanged between the two servers if (1) they are in the same organization, and (2) they have different routing information.

Note *If you connect routing groups using an X.400 connector, routing information is exchanged as dummy messages that contain the link state information.*

Whenever a nonrouting group master receives updated link state information, it transfers it to the routing master, which in turn immediately notifies the other servers.

If a link is marked as down, the server so designating it as down notifies the routing group master. The server then tries every 60 seconds to connect to port 25 on the unreachable server. Once the link is re-established, the server aborts its connection attempts and notifies its routing group master that the link is up.

Summary

Exchange 2000 has a brand new architecture that is integrated with Windows 2000, Active Directory, and Internet Information Services. This new architecture represents some major differences from—and improvements over—previous versions of Exchange.

The Exchange 2000 information store uses a database architecture that is more robust and manageable that its predecessors. Exchange 2000 also supports new features such as storage groups and multiple stores per server. A server can contain as many as four storage groups, and each storage group can contain as many as 5 databases. Each server can therefore have a maximum of 20 databases. The information store also contains a new database file for storing native Internet content. The information store has also been enhanced to support item URL-addressability and access via the file system. This combination of features, dubbed the Web Storage System, provides an entirely new development and collaboration platform.

Exchange 2000 leverages the Internet protocol support within Internet Information Services. By offloading Internet protocol support to IIS, Exchange 2000 is able to scale much higher than before and leverage new technologies, such as a distributed architecture and event sinks. Exchange 2000 also redefines its routing and administrative boundaries in ways that more accurately reflect real-world Exchange deployments, enabling administrators to separate their administrative and routing topologies.

Finally, Exchange 2000 is more resilient in its message routing capabilities. Exchange 2000 servers can be grouped into routing groups, which automatically share link state information between them. As a result, each Exchange server always knows the best route to take to deliver a message. In addition, if routing information changes before a message has reached its intended recipient, Exchange can intelligently re-route the message using the next least-cost route.

Chapter 5

Exchange 2000 Public Folders

The most obvious use for Exchange is e-mail; however, Exchange also provides other collaborative features that enable knowledge workers to be more productive than ever before. In any company of any size in any industry, collaboration between employees is essential. E-mail works well if there are fewer than four people involved, but when there are more, e-mail can get confusing and difficult to manage, especially when documents are being exchanged.

Exchange 2000 Server provides knowledge workers with two general functions: the ability to send and receive information and the ability to share information. Exchange 2000 includes a public information store that enables knowledge workers to share messages, files, calendar data, contacts, journal items, notes, and tasks. This public information store—which contains public folders—can also act as a repository or container for workflow applications, digital dashboards, team projects, and other collaborative solutions.

In this chapter, we provide an overview of the public folders in Exchange 2000. We will cover what public folders are and how they can be used, as well as how to manage them.

Introduction to Exchange 2000 Server Public Folders

Public folders can be used to share a wide variety of information, such as documents and files, project information, discussions, and Internet content. Public folders can also host custom forms and collaborative applications, enabling organizations to leverage their investment in Exchange by providing knowledge workers with information tools they can use in a familiar environment. The Exchange public folder hierarchy represents a core component of Microsoft's knowledge management strategy. The key to knowledge creation is bringing people and information together. Sometimes collaborators on a project may not be close to each other, so tools need to enable collaboration across distance and time.

Public folders are a hierarchical storage area in the information store. Public folders are also referred to as the public information store or simply the public store. They are, at a very basic level, similar in nature to the NTFS file system. Messages and documents are stored in one or more folders. Granular security permissions enable administrators to control access to specific items and item properties. And public folders can be shared out over the network and made available to users and applications.

However, that is where the similarities end. Because public folders are more easily replicated to other servers, and because searching and indexing is server-based and extremely fast, you and your users may find public folders even easier to use than the traditional file system. The folders are organized in a tree-like structure, much like a directory structure. Granular security permissions can be applied to individual folders—and to a certain extent to items in folders—much like directory and file ACLs. Folders can store files of any type and their contents can be replicated to other Exchange servers.

Public folders are what make Exchange a viable platform for knowledge sharing and collaborative applications. Public folders can be leveraged a number of ways:

- **Workflow applications** *Workflow* can be defined as a mechanized management of a defined business process. There are many processes in every business that either are or should be explicit. At each stage of a given process, business rules need to be applied and actions need to be taken. Workflow applications that automate the processes can live in the public folder system, even if some of the data used to execute the business process is external to Exchange.
- **Web Storage System applications** The Web Storage System—or simply, the "Web Store"—is a development platform for collaborative applications that can use a variety of technologies, such as ADO, OLE DB, and CDO. With the Web Store, Exchange derives a number of benefits, including the ability to host Web sites from within the public information store. With the enhanced, installable file system and everything being URL-addressable, you can access just about anything in the store from just about anywhere.
- **Digital dashboards** Digital dashboard solutions can integrate a wide variety of information, including personal, team or project, corporate, or external data in the familiar public folder environment. The Outlook Today page is a first-generation digital dashboard, displaying information nuggets, such as your calendar and your task list. Second-generation digital dashboards can be created by Web authors and developers using the Digital Dashboard Resource Kit and SDK tools. XML editors, such as Visual Interdev and Microsoft FrontPage, can be used to create Web pages containing reusable Web parts.
- **Team Centers** Team Centers are sets of applications that leverage the Web Storage System to provide the most common collaborative functions. Each application has a series of Web pages that are stored in a set of public folders. Microsoft has many sample applications, such as Team Projects, Calendaring, Discussion Forums, Frequently Asked Questions, Document Management, Team Tasks, and Shared Contacts. Because these applications exist in the public information store, they are automatically shared among users in a workgroup or department, or throughout the enterprise.
- **Outlook forms** Outlook forms add application-like functionality to public forms. Forms can be based on existing forms (appointment, message, post, and so on), or you can create forms from scratch. You can modify the default form used to post to folders. You can also create full applications that perform database lookups, route messages, or perform some other function.
- **Discussion groups** These enable users to conduct online discussions through standard public folders or through Internet newsgroups. Users communicate asynchronously by posting articles. Discussion group applications serve as the foundation for creating threaded conversations in views, so users can view the history of responses to a particular item. This is analogous to posting messages

and replies on a public corkboard, except that it is electronic. This means that the messages can also be organized in a variety of ways and searched through using full-text searches.

Tip *For more information on applications that leverage the new capabilities of the Web Store, visit http://msdn.microsoft.com/exchange.*

Exchange 2000 provides the native content store for MIME content, enabling you to host HTML or Active Server Pages in public folders. In fact, you can house entire Web sites in the public folder hierarchy and replicate the Web sites to other Exchange servers. This provides a compelling alternative to Web sites—or Web applications—that are hosted in a file system. In fact, Microsoft's internal testing has shown that pages are served up faster from public folders than they are from the file system.

Public Folder Architecture

Exchange public folders are comprised of two parts, the *top-level hierarchy* (TLH) and *public folder trees*. The TLH is the root of a public folder tree. The hierarchy of the public folder environment is what your users see when they expand the All Public Folders tree in their Exchange client. Prior versions of Exchange supported only one TLH. Exchange 2000 supports multiple top-level hierarchies. The default public folder TLH is known as the MAPI TLH. Any additional top-level hierarchies that are created are referred to general purpose top-level hierarchies or application top-level hierarchies.

Note *An Exchange organization can contain only one MAPI TLH.*

To access public folders, users can use a MAPI client, a newsreader, an IMAP4 client, Outlook Web Access, a WebDAV browser, or Windows Explorer. Each private information store has a default public folder store that is associated with it. Users see the tree in the public folder store that is associated with their mailbox. As shown in Figure 5-1, the hierarchy is called the public folder tree due to its treelike structure.

At the top level of this hierarchy is an object called Public Folders, which is automatically created at install time. Prior versions of Exchange only supported one public folder tree per server. Exchange 2000 supports multiple public information stores, enabling you to create multiple public folder trees in your organization. However, MAPI and IMAP4 clients can only access the default All Public Folders tree. As a result, the default All Public Folders tree is often referred to as the MAPI hierarchy.

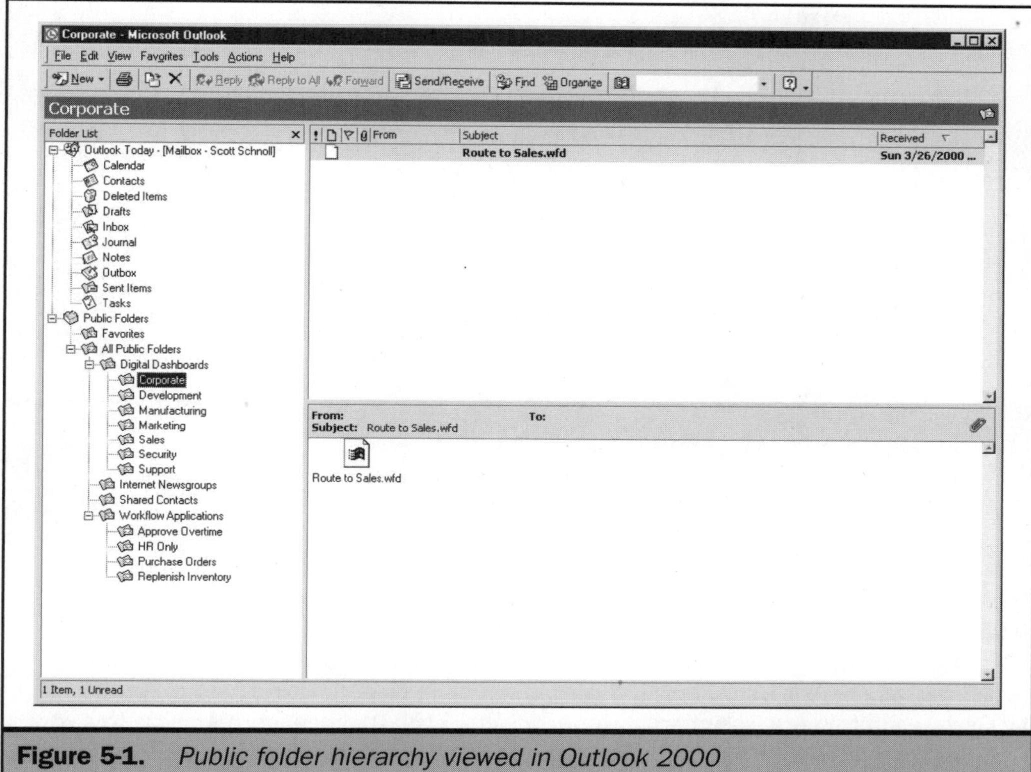

Figure 5-1. *Public folder hierarchy viewed in Outlook 2000*

Any additional public folder trees you create will only be visible through a Web client or as a file share, and Internet newsgroups are only available through an NNTP client. These trees are known as alternate hierarchies.

Note

The first public folder tree is the default MAPI public folder tree, and it cannot be deleted. Therefore, regardless of what mailbox store holds a user's mailbox, MAPI and IMAP4 clients will only see the default MAPI public folder tree. In fact, the only public folder store you can associate with a mailbox is the default public folder store.

Table 5-1 lists the various Exchange clients and the top-level hierarchies they can access.

TLH	Accessible By
MAPI TLH	MAPI clients (such as Outlook) IMAP4 clients Outlook Web Access (requires browser that supports WebDAV) Windows Explorer via IFS
General Purpose TLH	Outlook Web Access (requires browser that supports WebDAV) Windows Explorer via IFS

Table 5-1. *List of TLHs and Client Access Methods*

Public Folder Databases

Public folders and their contents are stored in a public information store—an ESE98 database that is similar to the private information store, except that it contains public folder data instead of mailbox data. The MAPI TLH is stored in the pub*X*.edb and pub*X*.stm, where *X* is a number that is automatically created during setup. In the database, each folder is assigned a unique *folder ID* (FID), which corresponds to a row in the Folders table in the store. Internally, the information store process refers to and addresses folders by their FIDs. Messages in folders are referenced by their unique *message ID* (MID), which corresponds to a row in the MsgFolder table in the store.

Subtrees The public folder database is split into two trees: the IPM_Subtree and the non-IPM Subtree. The IPM_Subtree contains public folders that are visible to users. These folders can be created, deleted, renamed, searched, and used as storage containers by Exchange clients, such as Outlook. The non-IPM_Subtree contains system folders that are not directly accessible by users. These include folders that contain free and busy data, offline address lists, views, and MAPI forms.

Multiple Public Folder Trees

Prior versions of Exchange supported a single public folder hierarchy that was replicated to every server in the organization. This wasn't so much a bad design, it just didn't scale well. Like most tree-structured directories, each time new branches in the hierarchy were created, it became more difficult for administrators to manage and for users to navigate. The Favorites feature in the Public Folder view in Outlook attempts to overcome this problem, but like the problem it attempts to solve, it too only scales to a certain point.

Because Exchange 2000 supports multiple databases, it can also support multiple public folder trees. Each tree replicates to one public information store per server; however, you can replicate individual folders in the tree to any server that has a public folder store associated with that public folder tree. This provides a finer level of control over public folder replication and network bandwidth consumption. Replication is still possible across all servers, but folders can now be dedicated to remote users by locating them on the server closest to them. This also helps reduce the size of each user's public folder tree, making the trees easier to navigate.

Each public store you create contains a single public folder tree, and public folder trees cannot span multiple public stores. Therefore, if you plan on creating additional public folder trees, you'll also need to create additional public stores to contain them. The public store hierarchy, shown in Figure 5-2, is managed using System Manager.

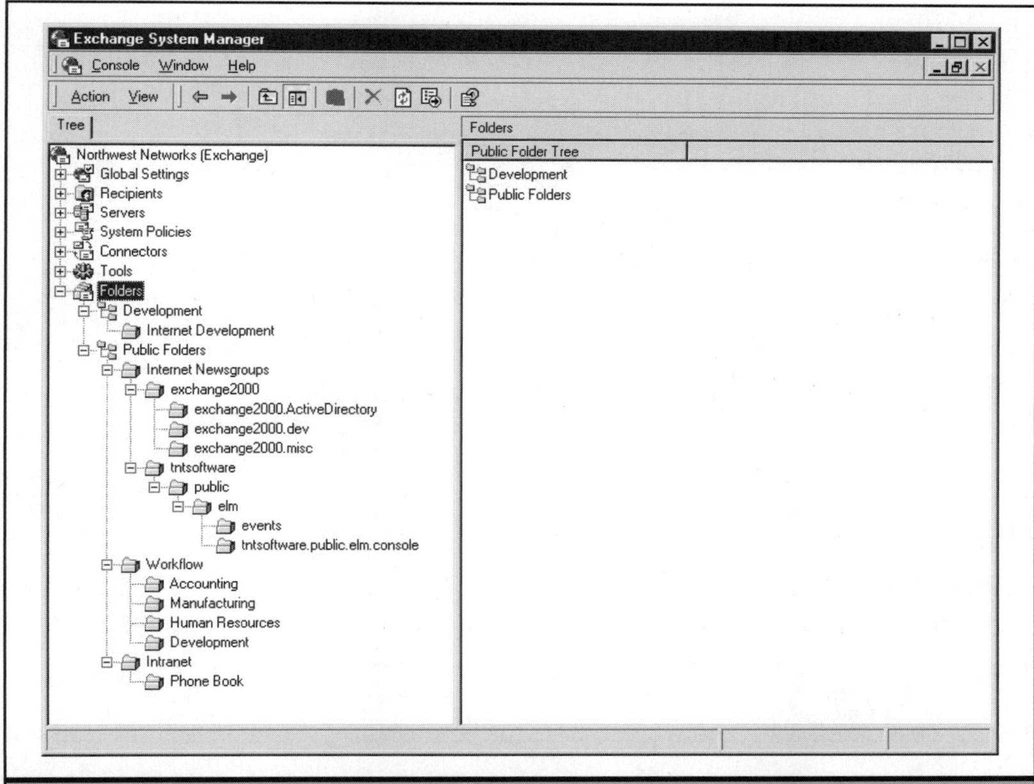

Figure 5-2. *Public store hierarchy as displayed in System Manager*

System Manager is also used to create additional public folder trees and public information stores. Each public store has several subcontainers which can be used to view information pertaining to the public folder store. These containers are:

- **Logons** By default, this container displays the currently connected users, the date and time they logged on, and version information about the Exchange client they are using. As you can see from Figure 5-3, there are several additional columns that can be added to this container view to provide additional information about the currently logged-on user.

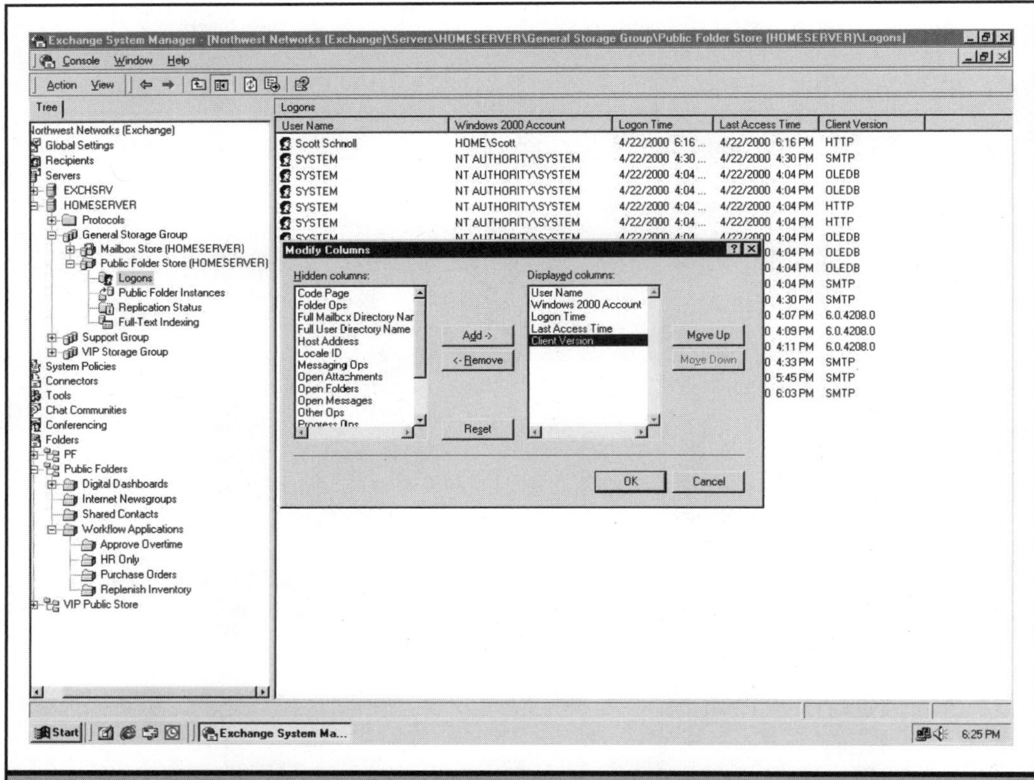

Figure 5-3. *Modify Columns dialog box. Only a few columns are displayed in the initial view of the Logons container.*

- **Public folder instances** This displays the folder name, display name, size, and folder path for folders stored in the public folder store. There is also a column called Removed Older Than which will indicate the enforcement of age limits.
- **Replication status** This container displays information about folders that are replicated to other servers, such as the folder name, the number of replicas, the status of replication, and the date and time replication last occurred.
- **Full-text indexing** If a full-text index hasn't been created for the public store, this container is neither interesting nor useful. When a full-text index has been created and populated, this container will display information about the full-text index. This will include the location and size of the index, the status of indexing, the date and time indexing last occurred, and the number of documents that were indexed.

Creating Public Folders

Both the Exchange System Manager and Outlook can be used to create public folders. Each application provides a different set of configuration options. Being able to create and manage public folders is a big improvement that eliminates the need to defer to an Exchange client each time a new folder needed to be created. Moreover, administrators may assign privileges at a very granular level, enabling them to safely and securely delegate responsibility for folders to end-users.

Creating Public Folders using Outlook 2000

Creating public folders using Outlook 2000 is a relatively straightforward process. The highest level at which you can create new public folders is the All Public Folders container. Folders created at this level are called *top-level folders* because they are at the highest level on the tree. All folders created by an Outlook client exist in the IPM_Subtree.

Before you can create a folder at this level, you must have both Create Public Folder and Create Top Level Public Folder permissions. As shown in Figure 5-4, these permissions are assigned using System Manager.

To create a new top-level public folder using Outlook 2000:

1. Expand Public Folders, and then expand All Public Folders.
2. Right-click on All Public Folders and select New Folder. The Create New Folder dialog box will appear (shown in Figure 5-5).

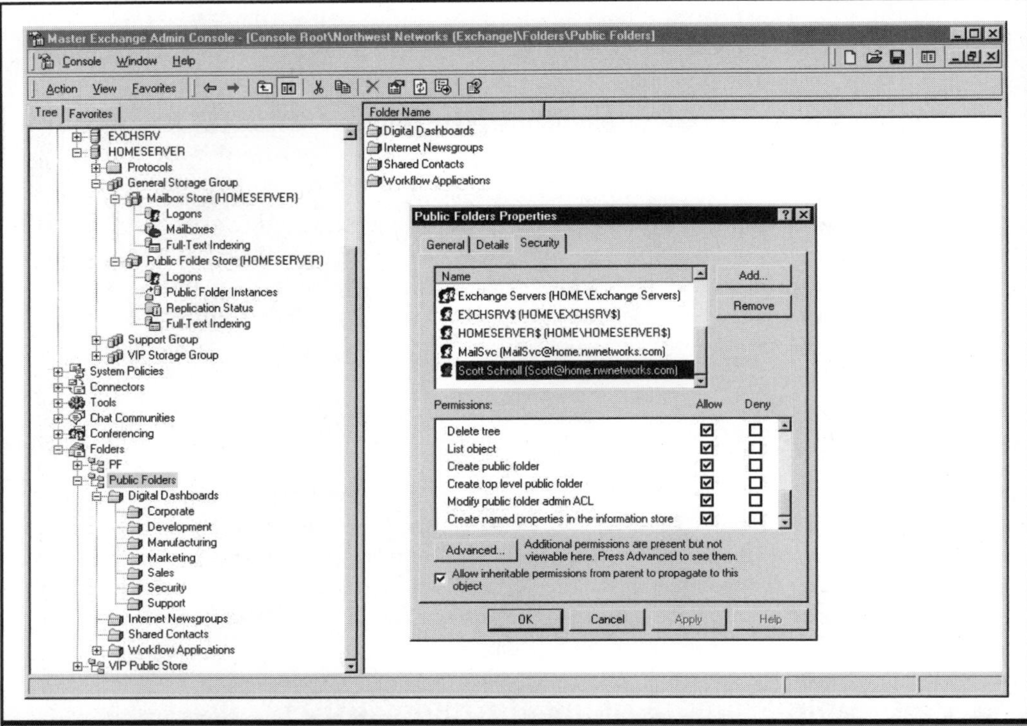

Figure 5-4. *Security permissions for default public folder tree*

Tip

Shorter names are better due to the way the Outlook client displays the folder pane.

4. In the Folder Contains field, select the type of content this folder will contain. Your choices are appointment, contact, journal, mail, note, and task items.
5. In the Select Where to Place the Folder field, expand Public Folders. Then select the parent folder in which you want to create your new folder. For example, if you wanted to create a top-level folder, you would select All Public Folders. If you wanted to create a subfolder of a top-level folder, you would select the appropriate top-level folder.
6. Click OK to create the new folder.

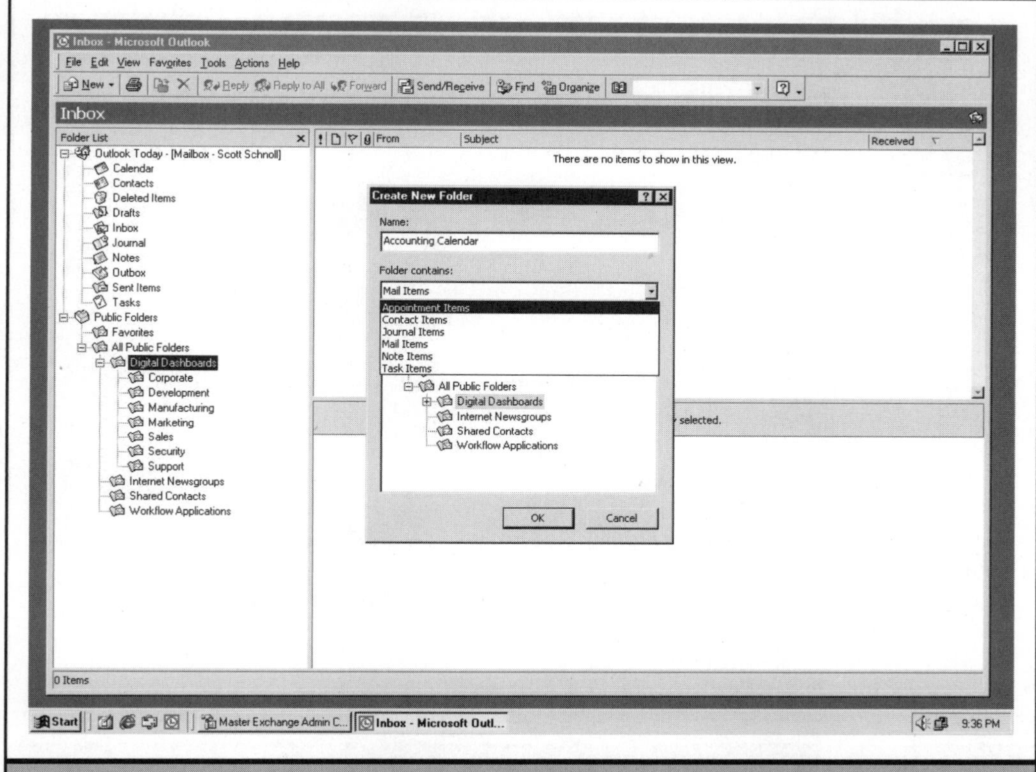

Figure 5-5. *Create New Folder dialog box. In the Name field, enter a name for the public folder. The name can be up to 256 characters long.*

Creating Public Folders Using System Manager

Although public folders can be created in a MAPI client, such as Outlook 2000, Exchange administrators will likely prefer to create and manage them using the Microsoft Management Console (MMC). Unlike their Exchange 5.5 predecessors, Exchange 2000 public folders can be managed through System Manager or through any MMC console containing the Exchange Folders snap-in.

To create a new top-level folder using the Exchange System Manager:

1. Launch the System Manager.
2. Expand the Organization container, and then expand the Folders container.
3. Right-click on Public Folders and select New | Public Folder. A properties dialog box for the new folder will appear, as shown in Figure 5-6.

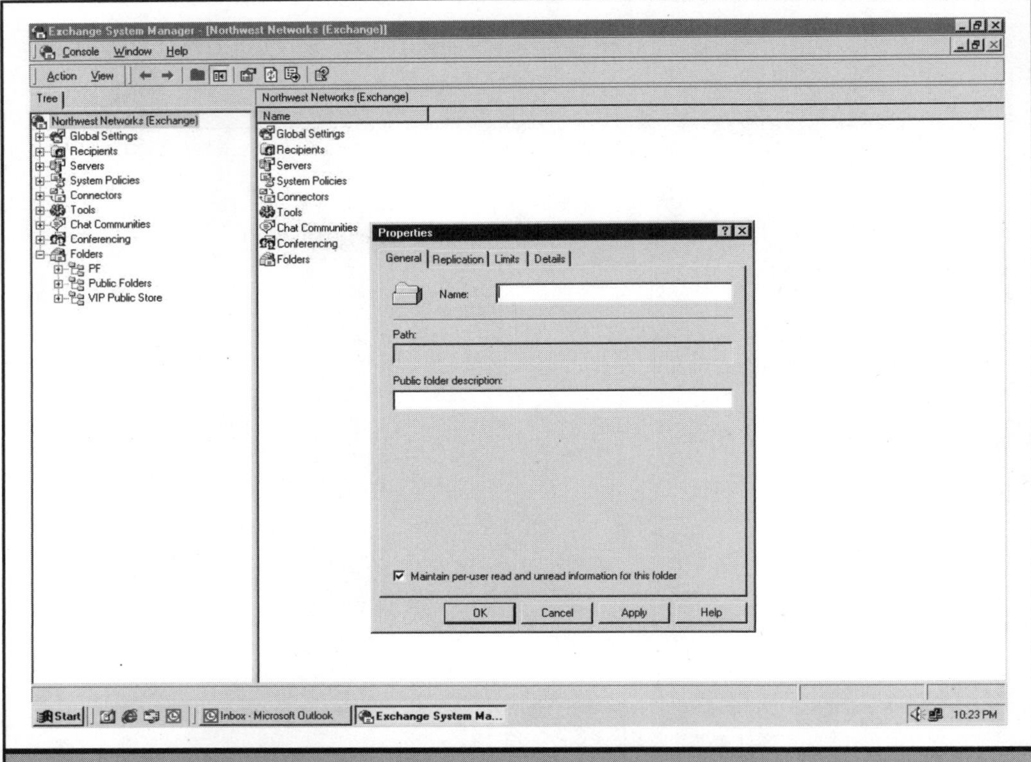

Figure 5-6. *Properties dialog box for the new public folder. The General tab is displayed by default.*

4. By default, the General tab is displayed. In the Name field, enter a name for the public folder. The name can be up to 256 characters long, but again, shorter names work best.
5. Enter an optional description in the Public Folder Description field.
6. Select the Replication tab (see Figure 5-7).
7. Click the Add button to select the server(s) to which you want to replicate this folder.

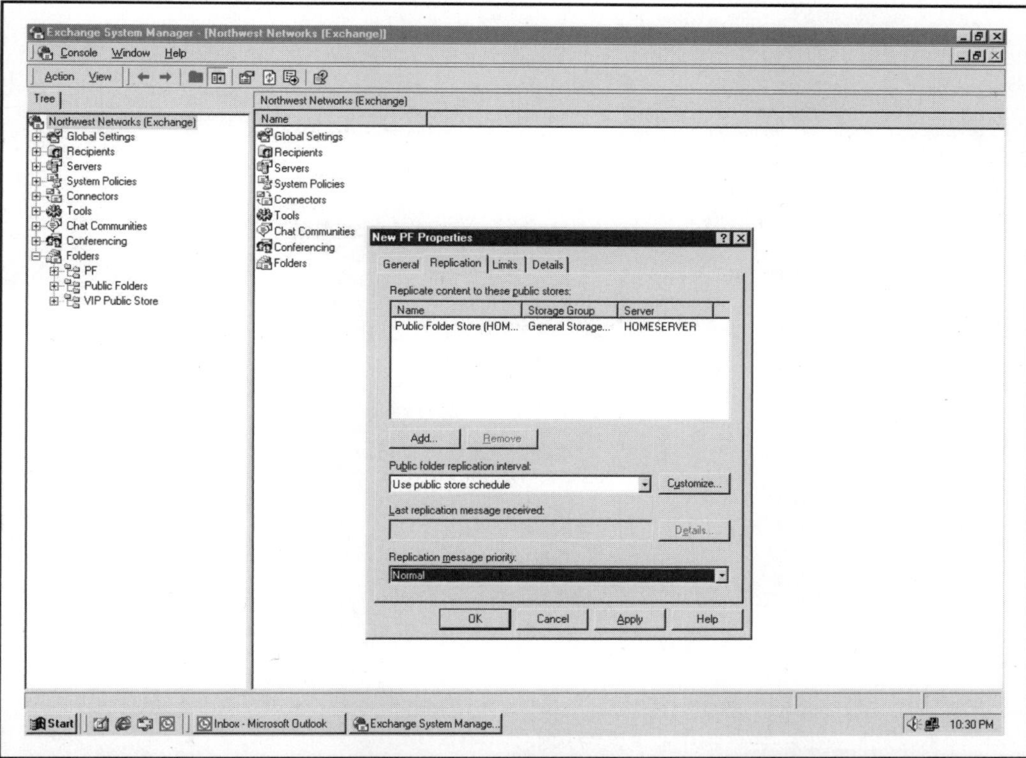

Figure 5-7. *The Replication tab is used to specify what servers the folder will replicate to, as well as the replication schedule and priority.*

8. In the Public Folder Replication Interval field, select a predefined replication schedule, or click the Customize button to create a custom replication schedule.
9. Select the desired priority from the Replication Message Priority field.
10. Next, select the Limits tab, shown in Figure 5-8.
11. In the Storage Limits area, configure any desired storage warnings or limits. You can also inherit the public store limitations by checking the Use Public Store Defaults checkbox.

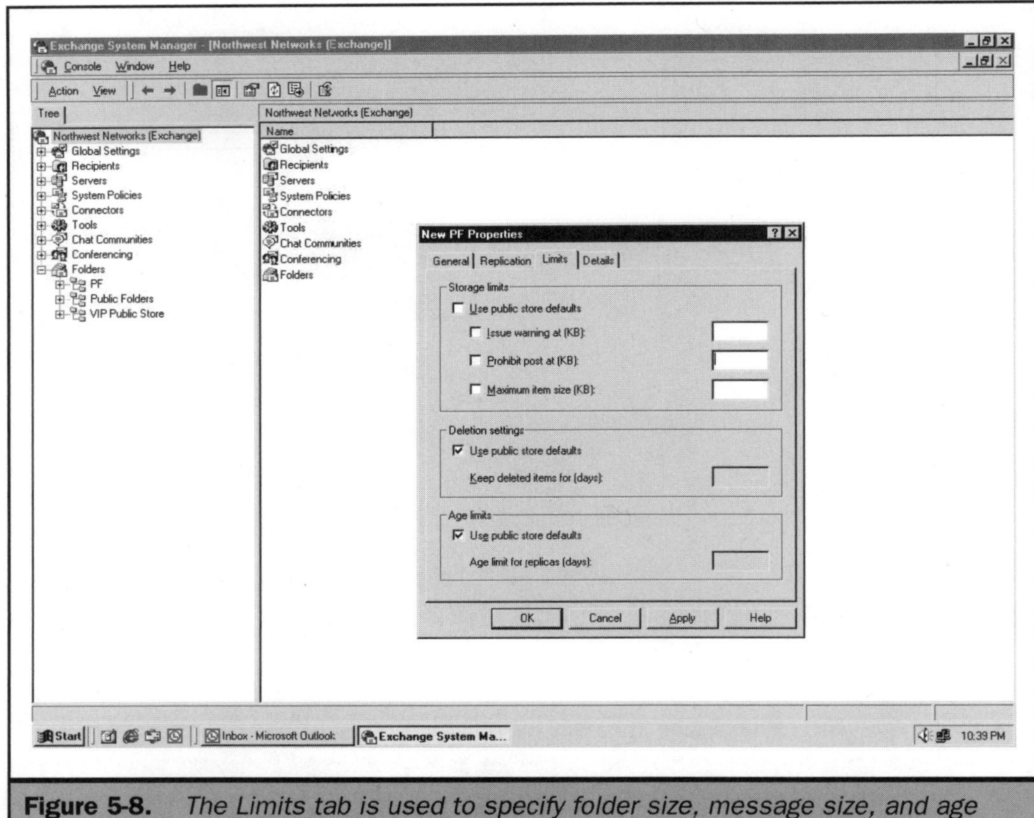

Figure 5-8. *The Limits tab is used to specify folder size, message size, and age limits.*

12. In the Deletion Settings area, you can configure a folder-specific deleted item retention period or inherit the public store defaults by checking the Use Public Store Defaults checkbox.
13. In the Age Limits area, you can configure folder-specific age limits or inherit the public store defaults by checking the Use Public Store Defaults checkbox.
14. Select the Details tab (see Figure 5-9). This tab is used to enter optional administrative notes. In addition, it displays the creation date and last modification date of the selected public folder.

Once a public folder has been created, permissions to the folder can be configured using System Manager. Each folder has several property sheets—such as the previously described General, Replication, Limits, and Details tabs—which control various aspects

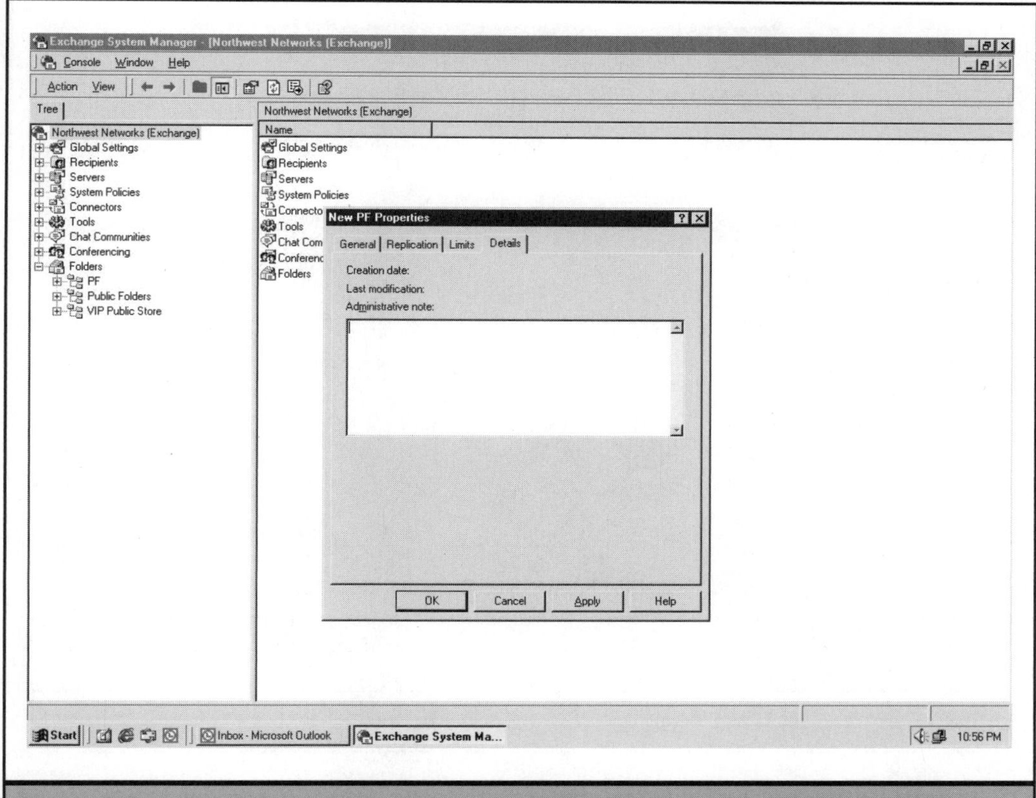

Figure 5-9. *The Details tab allows you to enter administrative comments about the public folder. In addition, it also displays the date the folder was created and last modified.*

of the folder. In addition to these tabs, there is a Permissions tab (see Figure 5-10) which can be used to control who can access the public folder, who can access the object representing the public folder in Active Directory, and who can administer the public folder.

Propagating Properties to Subfolders If you plan on creating subfolders, and you want them—or certain aspects of them—configured identically, you can propagate configuration settings from a parent folder to its subfolders. You cannot do this with every property. For example, administrative notes from the Details tab cannot be propagated to subfolders. Table 5-2 lists the configuration options (by property sheet)

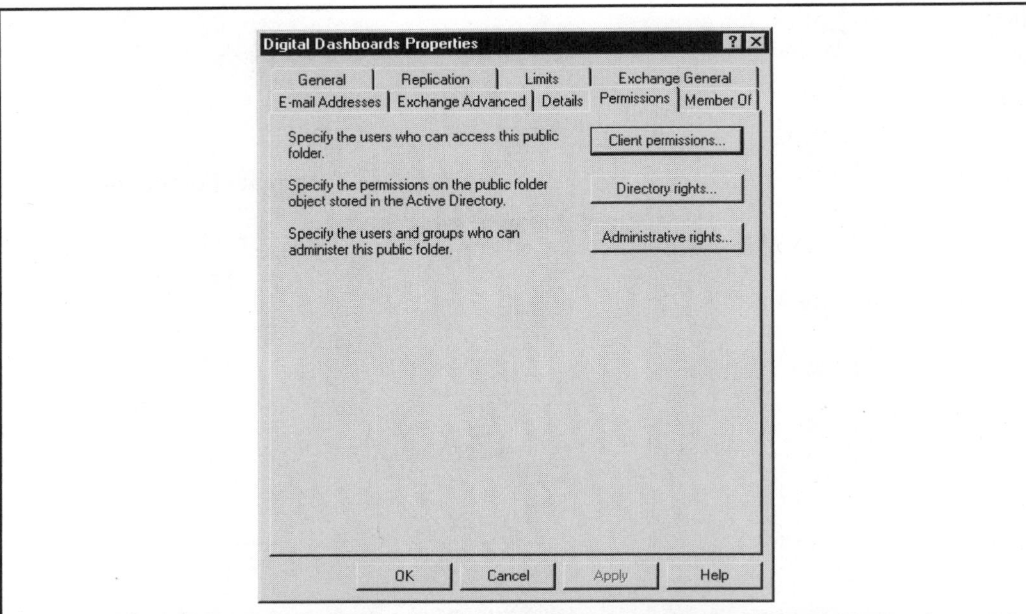

Figure 5-10. *Permissions tab. You can configure client permissions, directory rights (if the folder is mail-enabled), and administrative rights.*

Property Sheet	Settings
General	Maintain per-user read and unread information for this folder
Replication	Replication content to these public stores Public folder replication interval Replication message priority
Limits	Storage limits Deletion settings Age limits
Details	*Cannot be propagated to subfolders*
Permissions	Client permissions Administrative rights

Table 5-2. *Some Folder Property Settings Can Be Propagated to Subfolders*

that can be propagated to subfolders. In addition, you can also propagate mail-enabled status to all subfolders.

To propagate parent folder properties to all subfolders:

1. Right-click on the desired folder.
2. Select All Tasks, and then Propagate Settings. The Propagate Folder Settings dialog box will appear, as shown in Figure 5-11.
3. Select the properties you want to propagate and click OK.

Depending on the number of properties you selected and the number of subfolders, this process could take a while. Don't forget: not everything can be propagated; some things may need to be done manually. Consider the following:

Example: You have a parent folder with 20 subfolders. You want all subfolders to use the same replication and limits settings. The parent folder is mail-enabled, but none of the subfolders are. You want all subfolders to be mail-enabled.

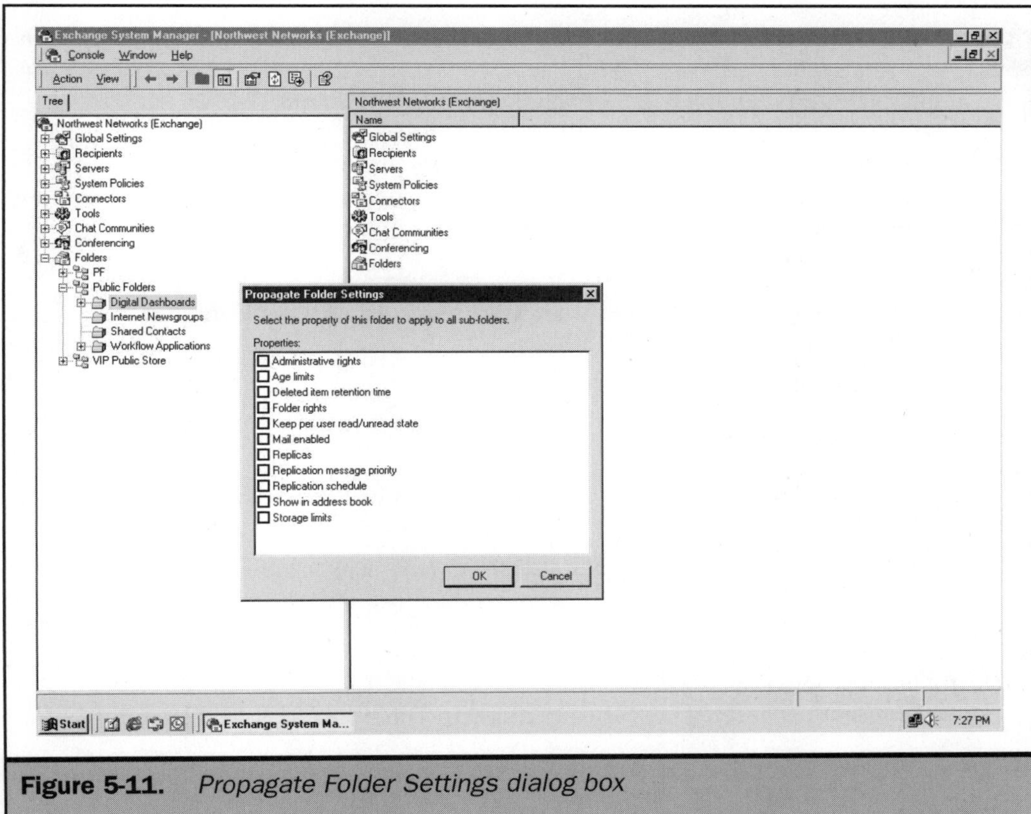

Figure 5-11. *Propagate Folder Settings dialog box*

Solution: Propagate only the replication and limits settings and do not propagate mail-enabled settings. You can mail-enable any public folder with a click of the right mouse button. When you do this, the folder will be assigned one or more e-mail addresses based on the name of the folder. This is far easier than manually editing 20 folders individually to assign e-mail addresses.

Mail-Enabling Public Folders As was the case with prior versions of Exchange, public folders can be assigned e-mail addresses. This allows them to be published in Active Directory and, if desired, the Global Address List. Public folders can then receive e-mail like any other mail-enabled recipient.

A public folder's default mail-enabled status depends on whether Exchange is running in mixed mode or in native mode. If Exchange 2000 is running in mixed mode, public folders in the MAPI hierarchy are automatically mail-enabled and hidden in the Global Address List. In mixed mode, you cannot mail-disable a MAPI public folder. Public folders in the alternate hierarchy are mail-disabled, although they can be mail-enabled. Once mail-enabled, they are automatically published to the Global Address List.

Note *For backward compatibility, MAPI public folders are always mail-enabled and cannot be mail-disabled in mixed mode. This is because Exchange 5.5 public folders were stored in the directory by default but not displayed in the Global Address List.*

When Exchange is in native mode, new public folders in both hierarchies need to be mail-enabled manually. After a public folder is mail-enabled in native mode, it will be automatically published to the Global Address List.

To mail-enable a public folder:

1. Launch the System Manager (or an MMC console with the Exchange Folders snap-in).
2. Right-click on the desired folder and select All Tasks | Mail Enable.

To mail-disable a public folder:

1. Launch the System Manager (or an MMC console with the Exchange Folders snap-in).
2. Right-click on the desired folder and select All Tasks | Mail Disable.

Once a public folder has been mail-enabled, additional property sheets are available for further configuration. Figures 5-12 and 5-13 show a mail-enabled and mail-disabled public folder, respectively.

The additional property sheets are explained in Table 5-3.

Figure 5-12. *Mail-enabled public folder. Note the additional property sheets that are available.*

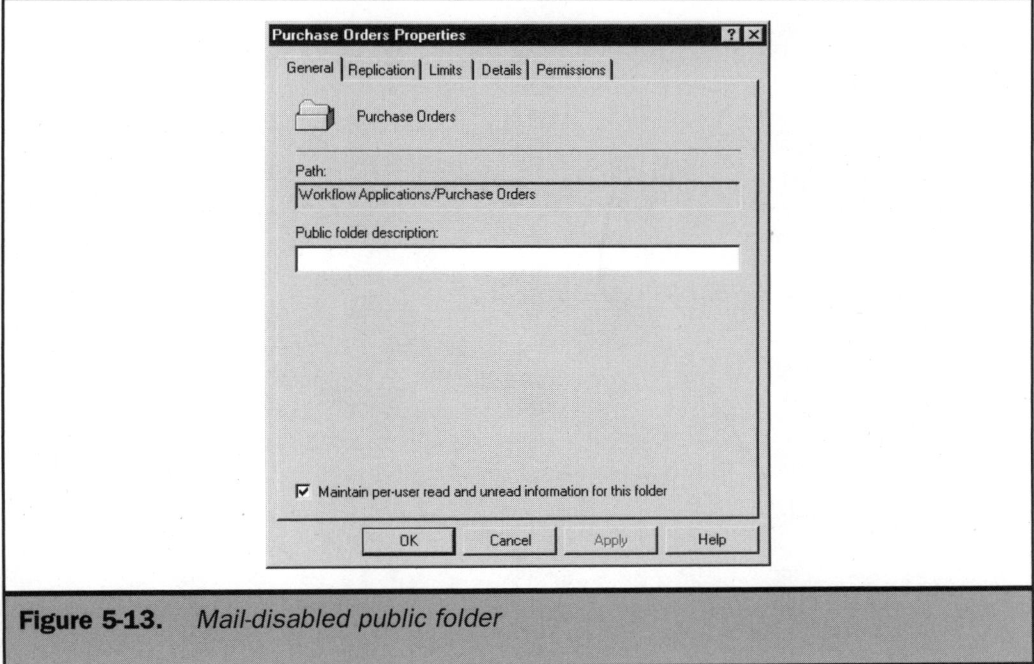

Figure 5-13. *Mail-disabled public folder*

Public Folder Replication

When a public folder is first created, it initially exists as a single instance in the organization. This instance—despite its singularity—is known as a *replica*. Any public folder can exist as one or more replica. Additional replicas are created through the process of *replication*. No matter how many replicas you create, all replicas of a public folder are equal; there is no master replica. Replication is the process of copying data in public folders between stores in the same TLH. During this process, the folder hierarchy is replicated via hierarchy replication messages, and the contents are replicated via content replication messages. In addition to these messages, there are Backfill Replication messages, Status messages, and Status Request messages, which keep replication between stores synchronized. Public folder replication provides three primary benefits:

- **Fault-tolerance** By having copies of public folders stored on more than one server, the data is able to survive the loss of a server.
- **Load balancing** This helps to prevent any one server from getting bogged down because all of the requests are being sent to it.
- **Optimized access for remote users** It is a considerable savings of bandwidth for clients to be able to connect to local servers instead of servers across the WAN.

Property Sheet	Settings
E-mail Addresses	This sheet is used to create, edit, or delete e-mail addresses for the selected folder.
Exchange Advanced	This sheet is used to provide an optional display alias for the folder, to hide or unhide the folder from address lists, and to view and modify custom attributes assigned to the folder.
Exchange General	This sheet is used to view the public folder tree containing the folder, to specify an alias for the folder, and to specify delivery options and restrictions, such as message size limits or send-on-behalf rights.

Table 5-3. *Description of Additional Property Sheets for Mail-Enabled Folders*

Tip *Like its predecessors, Exchange 2000 can only natively replicate folders in the same Exchange organization. To replicate folders between Exchange organizations, you can use the InterOrg Replication Connector (Exchsync), which can be found on the Exchange 2000 Server CD.*

Replication occurs at specific time intervals. A thread called the *public folder replication agent* (PFRA) runs in the store.exe process that polls for replication events. When it's time for replication to occur, the PFRA spawns a new thread that performs the actual replication process. Exchange 2000 sets default intervals for replication:

- Hierarchy replication: Every 5 minutes
- Content replication: Every 15 minutes
- Status replication: Every 24 hours

Public folder replication occurs via SMTP. Replication messages are actually e-mail messages that are sent between the public stores in each TLH. Public folder data is inserted into replication messages by means of a process called *packing*. The process of retrieving the public folder data from a replication message is called *unpacking*. There are five types of replication messages:

- **Hierarchy replication messages** These are messages between servers in the same TLH. Creating, deleting, and modifying a folder in some respect will cause a hierarchy replication message to be generated.
- **Content replication messages** These messages replicate public folder contents between replicas of individual folders. Adding, deleting, or modifying the contents of a public folder will cause content replication messages to be generated.
- **Backfill messages** These can be Backfill Request or Backfill Response messages. These messages are used to request or provide missing data. These messages are generated when a public folder store determines that it is not synchronized with other stores that contain a replica of the data.
- **Status messages** These messages are used by public folder stores to determine whether they are synchronized with one another. If the stores are out of sync, Status Request and Backfill messages will be generated.
- **Status Request messages** These are messages that are sent by one public folder store to another public folder store to trigger the replication of missing data. These are typically generated by the addition of a new public folder store or a new public folder replica.

You can cause public folder messages to log to the Windows 2000 application log by configuring Replication Incoming and Replication Outgoing to maximum logging under MSExchange IS\Public Folders on the Diagnostics Logging tab of the server's Properties dialog box.

Backfilling

Any time an update is made to a public folder, a *change number* (CN) is assigned to the folder, which is used by the replication engine to keep track of folder updates. A set of CNs is called a CNSet. Each time a server sends an update to another server, it includes the CNs. The receiving server reads the CNs to determine if this is a new change and if the receiving server is missing any data. Backfilling provides a recovery mechanism when replication messages have been lost, when a public folder store has been restored from a backup, and when a public folder store has been offline for some time.

Backfilling is used by public folder stores to determine if they are missing data. If a public folder store detects a gap or missing sequence in any folder's CNSet, it will issue a Backfill Request message. The server to whom the Backfill Request is directed will then issue a Backfill Response message that contains the missing data. A server can issue a Backfill Request for missing hierarchy or missing content data.

In order to keep track of pending Backfill Request messages, Exchange 2000 uses *backfill arrays*. Backfill arrays are lists of requests that are stored in memory until the timeout interval expires, at which point a replacement Backfill Request message is generated. The default timeout intervals are listed in Table 5-4. These timeouts are used to track Backfill Request messages and to prevent unnecessary backfilling.

Configuring Public Folder Replication

Public folder replication is configured from within System Manager or through an MMC console containing the Exchange Folders snap-in. As mentioned previously, you can configure replication settings for one folder and then propagate those settings down to all subfolders below it.

Request	Intersite Timeout	Intrasite Timeout
Initial backfill	12 hours	6 hours
First backfill retry	24 hours	12 hours
Subsequent backfill retries	48 hours	24 hours

Table 5-4. *Backfill Request Timeouts*

To configure replication for a public folder:

1. Right-click on the desired folder and select Properties.
2. Select the Replication tab.
3. Click the Add button to select the server(s) to which you want to replicate this folder.
4. In the Public Folder Replication Interval field, select a predefined replication schedule, or click the Customize button to create a custom replication schedule.
5. Select the desired priority in the Replication Message Priority field.

To propagate the replication settings to all subfolders below this folder:

1. Right-click on the folder and select Propagate Settings.
2. Select one or more replication settings (Replicas, Replication Message Important, and/or Replication Schedule).
3. Click OK to propagate the settings.

To verify that replication is occurring as expected, you can view the current replication status from a couple of different places:

- Replication Status object under the Public Folder store
- Details button on the Replication tab of the Folder Properties dialog box

Tip *If you suspect replication problems, use System Manager to see if folders have replicated. Don't rely on an Exchange client's view of the public folders to determine if replication has occurred successfully. The problem might be related to permissions and not replication itself.*

Public Folder Content Conflicts

Because public folders and their contents are replicated to multiple servers, content conflicts can and will occur from time to time. The most common scenario is when one user edits content on his server, and another user edits the replica of that item on another server before the first changes have been replicated to all of the replicas. There are two types of conflicts: folder edit conflicts and message edit conflicts.

Folder Edit Conflicts A folder edit conflict occurs when two or more users modify the design of a public folder at the same time. Whenever a folder edit conflict occurs, the last modification is saved, which overwrites all previous changes. In addition, a Design Conflict message is sent to all public folder contacts, or if there are no contacts, to the public folder owners.

The only exception to this is when an administrator makes a change to the replica list. In this event, the replica lists of the public folder stores are merged.

Message Edit Conflicts A message edit conflict occurs when two or more users modify a message or item contained in a public folder. Whenever this occurs, a Conflict Resolution message that contains the conflicting messages is sent to the public folder contacts, or if there are no contacts, to the public folder owners. The user receiving the message can then select which changes to keep and which changes to discard.

Public Folder Referrals

The larger your Exchange infrastructure grows, the more important replicas become. Understanding why this is so requires an understanding of what happens when you access a public folder. Each time a client accesses a public folder, a connection is made to a server containing a replica of the data. Clients are capable of connecting to any server containing a replica of the folder they're accessing, but there is some logic built in to this process that attempts to make the most efficient connection available.

Prior versions of Exchange used the concepts of location and affinity to determine which public folder server provided the most efficient connection for the client. These provided cost-like functionality, where the client was connected using the least cost route. This method certainly worked, but it did require some administrative effort to configure the affinity and location settings. Public folder affinities in earlier versions of Exchange were nontransitive. Exchange 2000 uses transitive affinities known as *referrals* between routing groups.

Note

Microsoft's IMAP4 clients do not support referrals.

Referrals, like affinities, enable a user on a remote server to access files on a local server. The difference is that Exchange 2000 uses routing information and not affinity cost to determine the proper server to which a client should be referred. To illustrate this, let's examine a typical public folder architecture. In Figure 5-14, we have five sites, A through E.

The client is located in Site B, and as you might expect, it first looks to its default public information store for the information. If its default public store is unavailable or does not contain the replica being sought, the client is sent a list containing the names of servers that do have a replica. The client examines its current connections, and if it has a connection to one of the servers on the list, it uses that connection and accesses the replica.

If the client does not have a connection to a server on the list, it then determines which servers are in the same routing group as the client's public information store.

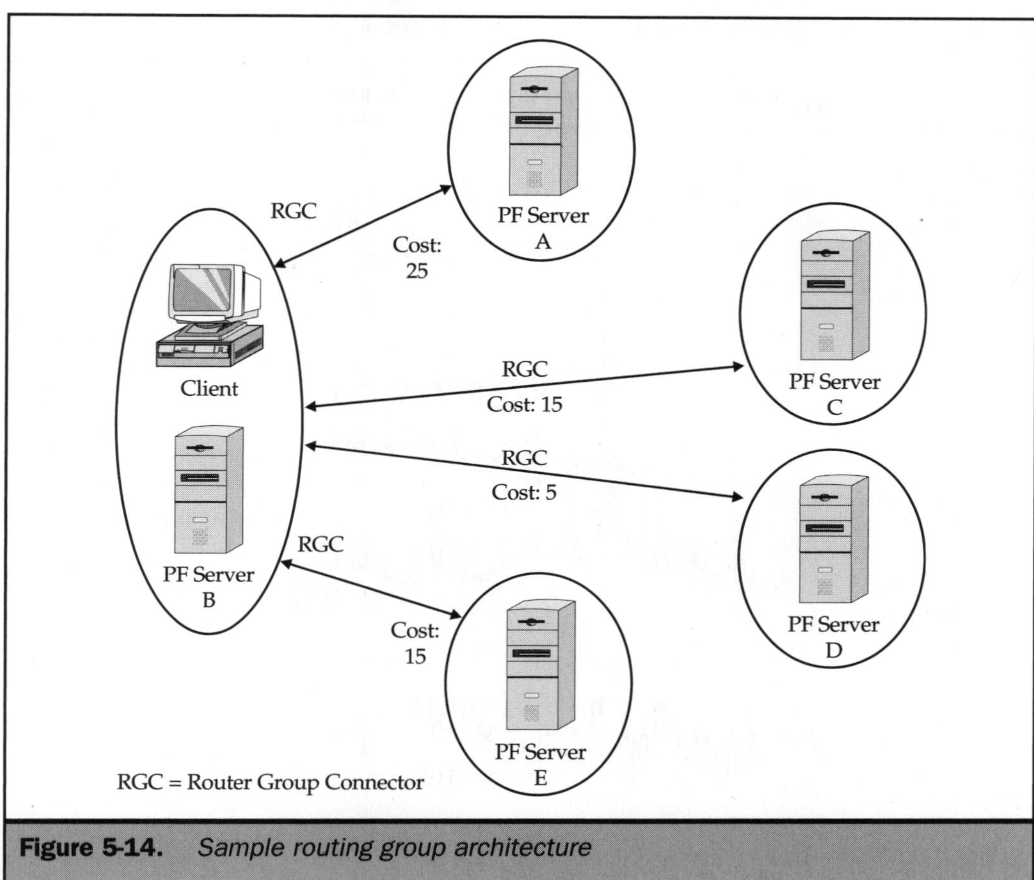

Figure 5-14. *Sample routing group architecture*

The client then attempts to connect to each server in its routing group. Routing group connectors determine the order for client connections for folders outside of the client's home site. If these connection attempts are unsuccessful, the information store directs the client to servers in other routing groups, in accordance with the cost values assigned to the routing group connectors. Connections with the lowest cost are attempted first; as each connection fails, the next highest cost is attempted, and so on, until a successful connection is established. Sites configured with the same cost are pooled together and chosen at random as if they comprised a single site.

In our example, the client attempts to connect to the server located in its site, Site B. If this attempt fails, it will try to connect to the server in Site D because it has the lowest cost value. Sites C and E both have a cost of 15, so they are pooled together as if they were a single site. The client tries to connect to a server in Site C or E, depending on which server is randomly selected. An attempt to connect to a server in Site A happens last because the routing group connector for that site has the highest cost.

Referrals are enabled by default on all routing group connectors. To disable a referral, use System Manager to navigate to the routing group connector's Properties. On the General tab, check the Do Not Allow Public Folder Referrals checkbox.

Public Folder Security

As with other aspects of Exchange 2000, the public folder infrastructure should be secured. Exchange 5.5 and earlier versions used Exchange directory objects and the concept of *roles* (predefined sets of permissions) to control access to public folder resources. As you can see from Figure 5-15, client permissions remain relatively unchanged in Exchange 2000. Exchange 2000 still uses the familiar concept of roles. For example, you can give someone full control over a public folder by assigning them the role of Owner. Or you can grant them read-only privileges by assigning them the role of Reviewer.

Like the private information store in Exchange 2000, security for the public information store is provided by Active Directory, which manages permissions on all Exchange objects. As a result, Exchange 2000 has a security model that is fairly granular. You can set folder-, item-, and property-level permissions using Windows 2000 security principals. Public folder security can be broken down into four categories:

- Client permissions
- Administrative rights
- Item- and property-level permissions
- Directory rights

Client Permissions

Public folders can be created in Exchange clients by users with the appropriate permissions. Permissions are used to specify what actions each user is allowed to perform in a public folder. Like its predecessors, Exchange 2000 assigns a set of permissions for each public folder that is created. By default, all users have read/write permissions. You can modify the default permissions or create new permissions. While prior versions of Exchange controlled permissions themselves, Exchange 2000 permissions are controlled and managed through the operating system. Instead of assigning folder permissions to a mailbox recipient in the Exchange directory, permissions are now granted to Active Directory security principals.

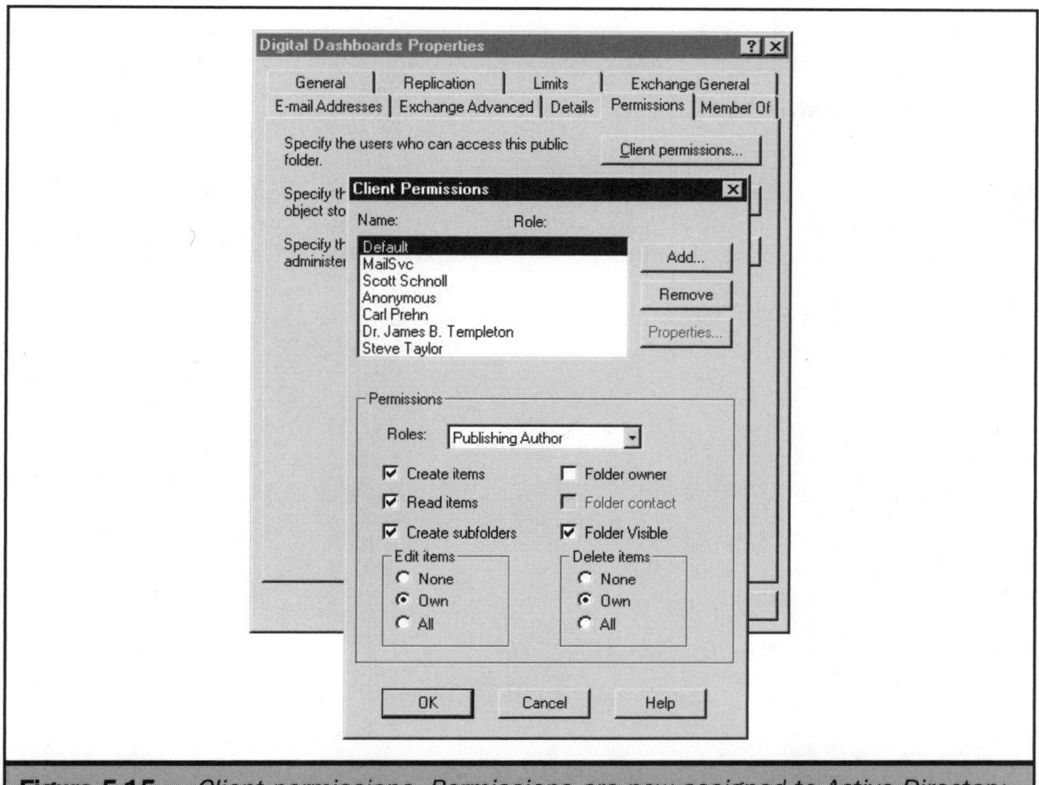

Figure 5-15. *Client permissions. Permissions are now assigned to Active Directory users and groups instead of MAPI address book entries.*

As a result of its integration with Windows 2000 and Active Directory, Exchange 2000 has a more granular security model. For example, prior versions of Exchange used per-folder access control. This enabled administrators to provide folder-level and item-level permissions. In the Exchange 2000 security model, permissions can be applied to folders, items, and item properties. Similarly, permissions in Exchange 5.5 and earlier were granted to recipients that were listed in the Global Address List. This meant that if you wanted to assign public folder permissions to a mailbox that was hidden, you had to (at least temporarily) unhide the entry to grant the permissions. Exchange 2000 assigns permissions Windows 2000 users and groups.

Administrative Rights

There are several administrative rights that can be assigned to public folders. You can assign these rights to administrators and nonadministrators. This enables administrative functions to be delegated without compromising security. For example, a departmental manager could be given the right to control who can access his or her department's folders. Figure 5-16 shows the interface used to configure administrative rights.

These rights can be granted to any Active Directory security principal. As with any delegation of administrative responsibility, it is important to understand what each right allows. You can explicitly allow or deny these permissions, and you should make sure you don't grant more permissions than are absolutely necessary. Table 5-5 lists the available permissions, their effect, the default assignments, and the locations in the hierarchy where they can be set.

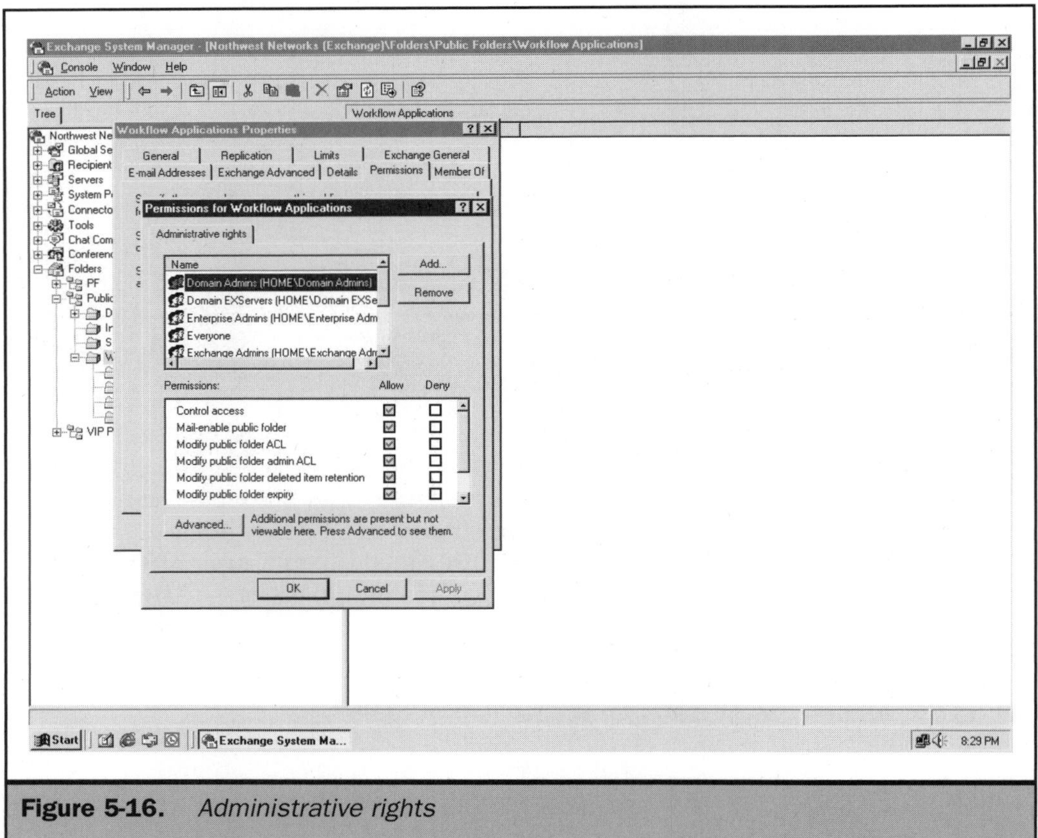

Figure 5-16. *Administrative rights*

Permission	Description	Assigned to by Default
Control Access	Enables a user to designate who can access a folder and what their access roles are	Administrators Authenticated users Enterprise administrators
Create Named Properties in the Information Store	Enables a user to add additional store attributes that can be accessed by name	Administrators Domain administrators Enterprise administrators
Create Public Folder	Enables a user to create a folder or subfolder	Administrators Domain administrators Enterprise administrators
Create Top-level Public Folder	Enables a user to create a folder at the top of the hierarchy	Administrators Domain administrators Enterprise administrators
Mail-Enable Public Folder	Enables a user to mail-enable (and mail-disable) a folder	Administrators Domain administrators Enterprise administrators
Modify Public Folder ACL	Enables a user to modify a folder's access control list	Administrators Domain administrators Enterprise administrators
Modify Public Folder Admin ACL	Enables a user to modify a folder's administrative access control list	Administrators Domain administrators Enterprise administrators
Modify Public Folder Deleted Item Retention	Enables a user to modify the length of time that items deleted from the folder are retained	Administrators Domain administrators Enterprise administrators
Modify Public Folder Expiry	Enables a user to modify the expiration date of content in the folder	Administrators Domain administrators Enterprise administrators

Table 5-5. *Administrative Rights that Can Be Assigned on Public Folders*

Permission	Description	Assigned to by Default
Modify Public Folder Quotas	Enables a user to modify the size limits for a folder	Administrators Domain administrators Enterprise administrators
Modify Public Folder Replica List	Enables a user to add or remove servers from a replica	Administrators Domain administrators Enterprise administrators
View Information Store Status	Enables a user to view information store data such as logons and resources	Administrators Domain administrators Enterprise administrators

Table 5-5. *Administrative Rights that Can Be Assigned on Public Folders* (continued)

Both administrators and users can control access to public folders at any point in the hierarchy. Folder permissions are grouped into predefined roles, which are sets of activities that can be performed. For example, users granted the Editor role can read, create, edit, and delete any items in the folder; however, this role does not allow the user to create subfolders. Users can set folder roles and permissions by selecting the Permissions tab on the public folder's Properties dialog box. Administrators can set public folder roles and permissions by clicking the Client Permissions button on the Permissions tab of the public folder's Properties dialog box.

Item- and Property-Level Permissions

Item- and property-level permissions are new to Exchange 2000. They enable administrators and developers to set ACLs on specific items and specific properties. This is very useful when you need to share only a portion of public folder data, or if you don't want any data to be modified. Item-level permissions are set through Windows Explorer using its native Windows 2000 security features.

Once the information store service is running, the ExIFS driver exposes the private and public information store as a file system to Windows Explorer. By default, the letter M is assigned as a logical drive letter to the root of the store. Security permissions are configured in the same way as NTFS file permissions:

1. Right-click on the folder or item you wish to secure and select Properties.
2. Select the Security tab.

3. Configure permissions as desired. Click the Advanced button to configure more granular permissions.
4. Click OK to save the changes.

Because Exchange 5.5 does not support item-level permissions, do not apply any item-level permissions to any folders that are replicated to Exchange 5.5 servers. Doing so will render the Exchange 5.5 replicas unusable.

Property-level permissions are very useful, but they cannot be configured as easily as client-, administrative-, or item-level permissions. Property-level permissions can only be set programmatically. This means you will need to obtain a third-party product or write your own custom application if you want to set permissions at the property level.

Directory Rights

Once a public folder has been mail-enabled, the System Attendant will create an Active Directory object for the public folder. There will then be a directory entry comprised of the public folder's name and GUID. Once the object and entry have been created, you can configure directory rights for the public folder. These permissions control what users can do to the directory object representing the public folder. As shown in Figure 5-17, directory rights can be allowed or denied using the directory rights button on the Permissions tab of the folder properties.

To configure directory rights for a particular public folder:

1. In System Manager, expand Folders, and then expand Public Folders.
2. Right-click on the desired folder and select Properties.
3. Click the Permissions tab.
4. Click the Directory Rights button.
5. Configure directory rights as desired.
6. Click OK twice to save your changes.

Public Folder Store Policies

Public folder stores can be managed through the use of system policies. These are sets of configuration settings that can be applied to one or more public folder stores. Policy-based administration reduces the amount of administrative time needed to manage public folders stores. Public store policies are created and managed using System Manager. You can set five different public store policies:

- **General** Configures a policy that specifies an associated public folder tree, client S/MIME signature support, and plain-text message display.

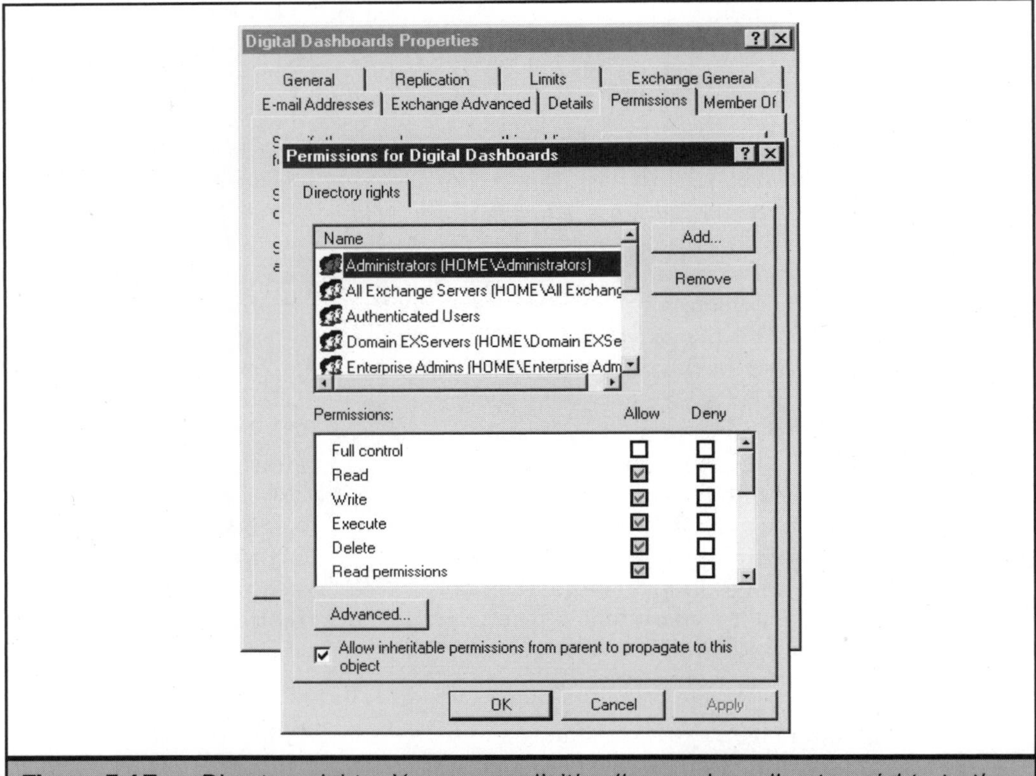

Figure 5-17. *Directory rights. You can explicitly allow or deny directory rights to the public folder object in Active Directory.*

- **Database** Configures a policy that specifies the MAPI and streaming databases, the maintenance interval, startup, and restore settings.
- **Replication** Configures a policy that sets the replication interval and replication limits.
- **Limits** Configures a policy that sets storage limits, storage limit warning messages, deleted item retention, and age limits.
- **Full-text indexing** Configures update and rebuild intervals for full-text indices.

To create a public store policy:

1. Launch System Manager.
2. Right-click the System Policies container. If you do not have a System Policies container, you will need to create one. To do this, you must first display Administrative Groups. To display Administrative Groups, right-click on the Organization name and select Properties. Check the Display Administrative Groups checkbox. Click OK to save the change. System Manager will display a message stating you need to restart System Manager for the changes to take effect. Acknowledge the message and restart System Manager.
3. Expand Administrative Groups.
4. Right-click on the administrative group in which you want to create the policy and select New | Server Policy Container.
5. Select the Property Pages that you want to appear. Select from General, Database, Replication, Limits, and Full-text indexing. A dialog box with a property sheet for each page you select will appear. Each selected property sheet will have (Policy) next to it. This dialog box will also have General and Details tabs that are used to provide a name and description of the policy.
6. Click OK to save the policy.

To apply a public store policy:

1. Launch System Manager.
2. Expand System Policies.
3. Right-click on the policy you want to apply and select Add Public Store.
4. Select one or more public stores and click OK.
5. Click Yes to confirm the action.

To remove an object from a public store policy:

1. Launch System Manager.
2. Expand System Policies.
3. Select the policy containing an object you want to remove.
4. In the right pane, right-click on the object you want to remove and select Remove From Policy.
5. Click Yes to confirm the action.

Internet Newsgroups

Newsgroups are a great way for people all over the world to exchange messages on any topic imaginable. Exchange 2000 enables knowledge workers to participate in online discussions using the Network News Transfer Protocol (NNTP). In addition, Exchange also enables NNTP clients to access public folders as newsgroups. NNTP, which is defined in RFC 977, is a TCP/IP-based application-layer protocol that defines the set of commands used to access newsgroups. By default, NNTP traffic occurs over TCP port 119 without SSL and TCP port 563 when SSL is used.

The Windows 2000 NNTP service replaces the Internet News Service in Exchange 5.x. By default, the NNTP service is designed to support a stand-alone newsgroup server. When Exchange 2000 is installed, the NNTP service is enhanced with the ability to communicate with other NNTP servers through the use of *newsfeeds*. Newsfeeds refer to the exchange of newsgroup article between NNTP servers.

NNTP virtual servers enable administrators to control authentication and manage client connections. A single server can host multiple NNTP virtual servers, each with unique configuration settings. NNTP virtual servers work in concert with the NNTP service. The NNTP service handles the actual transmission of NNTP messages, which are called *articles*. Articles can be posted to a newsgroup and read from a newsgroup using an NNTP client, such as Outlook Express, or they can be posted by a MAPI client to a public folder which has been mapped to an Internet newsgroup.

The first step in using newsgroups in your Exchange organization is creating a newsgroup topology. This involves configuring one or more virtual servers, creating newsgroups, and creating newsfeeds.

Configuring NNTP Virtual Servers

Exchange 2000 automatically creates a default NNTP virtual server during installation. NNTP virtual servers are configured using System Manager. To configure the default NNTP virtual server:

1. In System Manager, expand Servers, then the desired server, then Protocols, and then NNTP.
2. Right-click on Default NNTP Virtual Server and select Properties. The Properties dialog box for the default NNTP virtual server will be displayed (see Figure 5-18). The General tab is used to specify the IP address(es) and port(s) assigned to this virtual server.
3. Configure connection limits and timeout settings as desired.
4. You can enable protocol logging by checking the Enable Logging checkbox and configuring the log settings as desired.

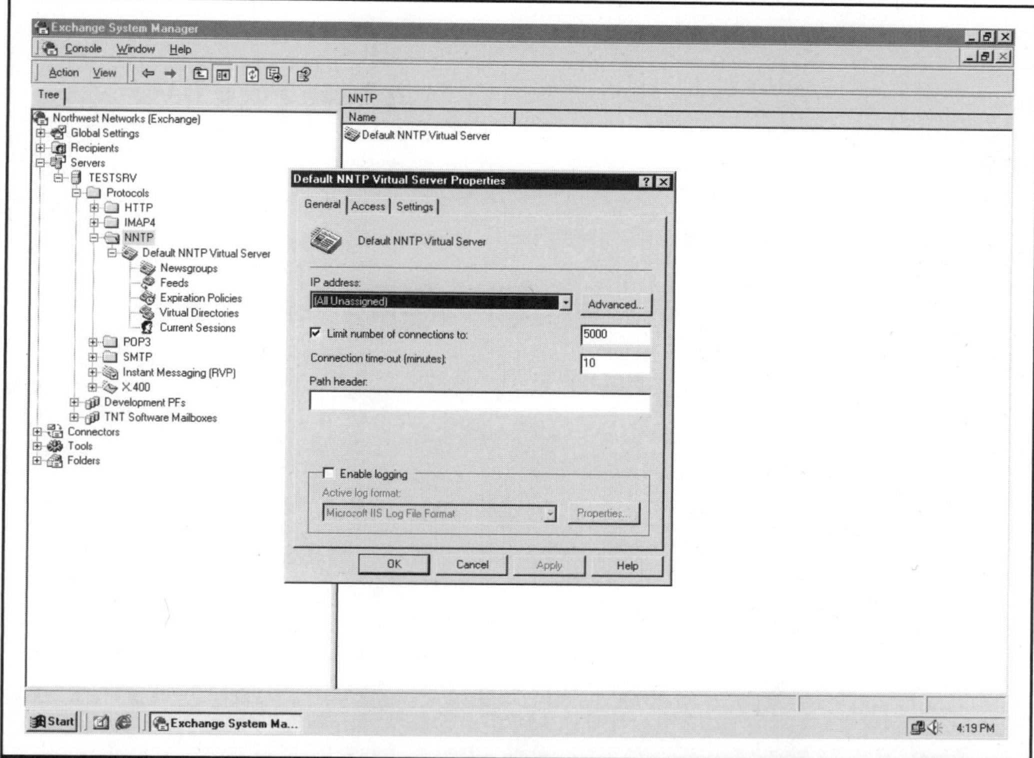

Figure 5-18. *Default NNTP Virtual Server Properties, General tab. Use this dialog box to configure connection settings, logging, security, and message size limits.*

5. The Access tab is used to specify authentication methods, configure certificates, and control access. On the Access tab, click the Authentication button (see Figure 5-19). Select from Anonymous, Basic, Integrated, or SSL. If you are using SSL with client certificate mapping, click the Client Mappings button to configure 1-to-1 or Many-to-1 certificate mappings. You can configure a variety of authentication methods:

    - The Certificate button launches the Web Server Certificate Wizard which enables you to add, remove, and modify server certificates.

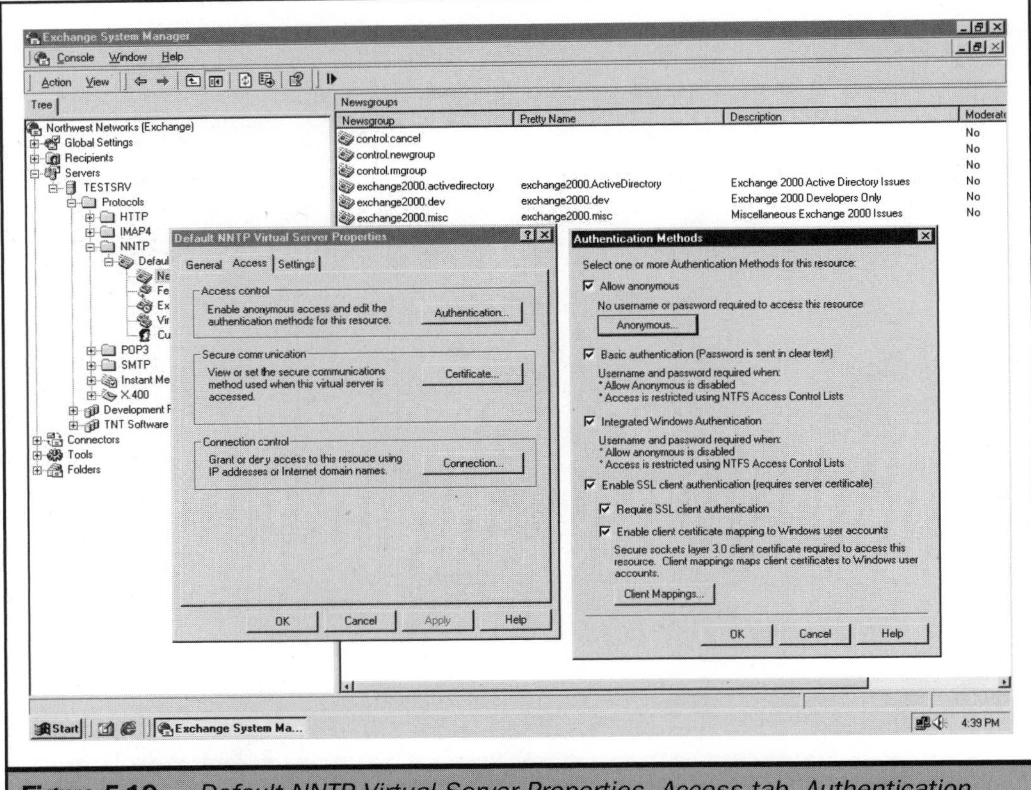

Figure 5-19. *Default NNTP Virtual Server Properties, Access tab, Authentication Methods*

- The Connection button is used to explicitly grant or deny access based on an IP address or a domain name.
- The Settings tab (see Figure 5-20) is used to configure post size limits, whether or not pull feeds are allowed, and moderator settings.

These settings configure moderation, pull feeds, and control message and post limits.

6. Click OK to save any configuration changes you made.

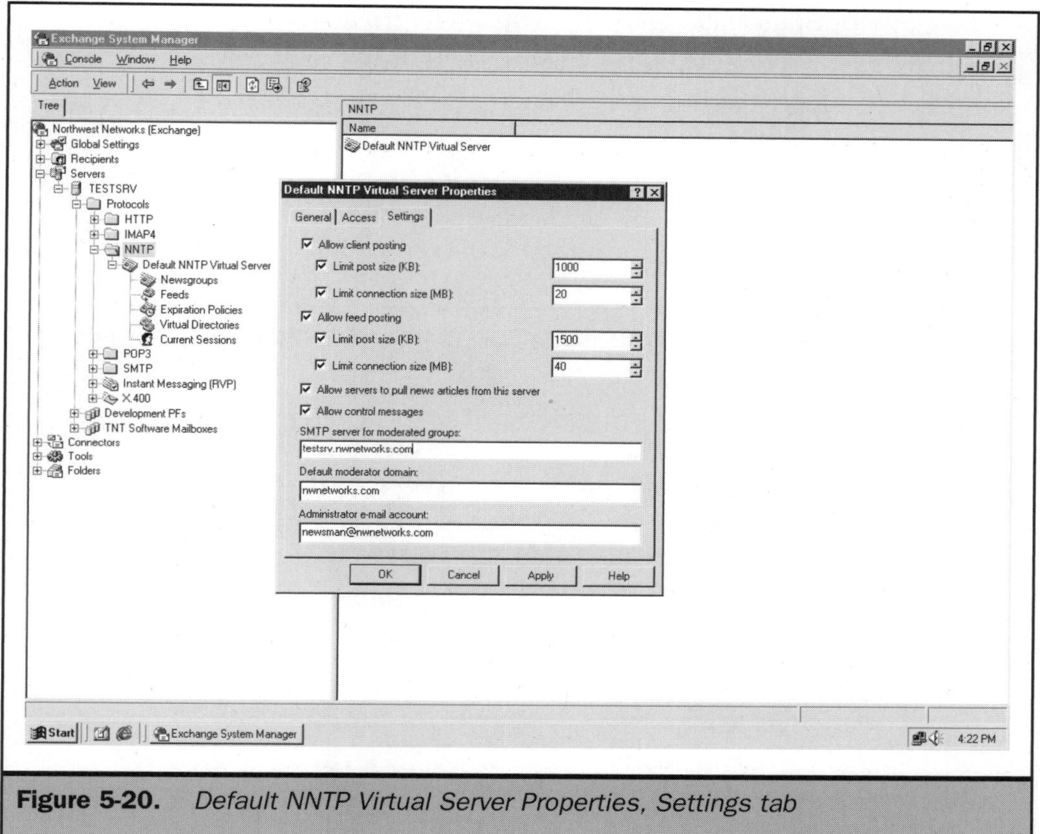

Figure 5-20. *Default NNTP Virtual Server Properties, Settings tab*

Creating Newsgroups

Newsgroups are also created using System Manager. A wizard guides you through the process of creating a newsgroup. To create a newsgroup:

1. In System Manager, expand Servers, then the desired server, then Protocols, then NNTP, and then the desired virtual server.
2. Right-click on Newsgroups and select New | Newsgroup. The New Newsgroup Wizard will launch.
3. In the Name field, provide a name for the newsgroup (for example, tntsoftware.beta.elm30.console). Click Next to continue.

4. In the Description field, enter a description for the newsgroup.
5. In the Pretty Name field, enter an alias for the newsgroup.
6. Click Finish to create the newsgroup.

As shown in Figure 5-21, once a newsgroup has been created, it can be configured. You can change the newsgroup description and alias, as well as mark the newsgroup read-only or specify a moderator. If a moderator is specified, all articles are sent to the moderator for approval before being posted to the newsgroup.

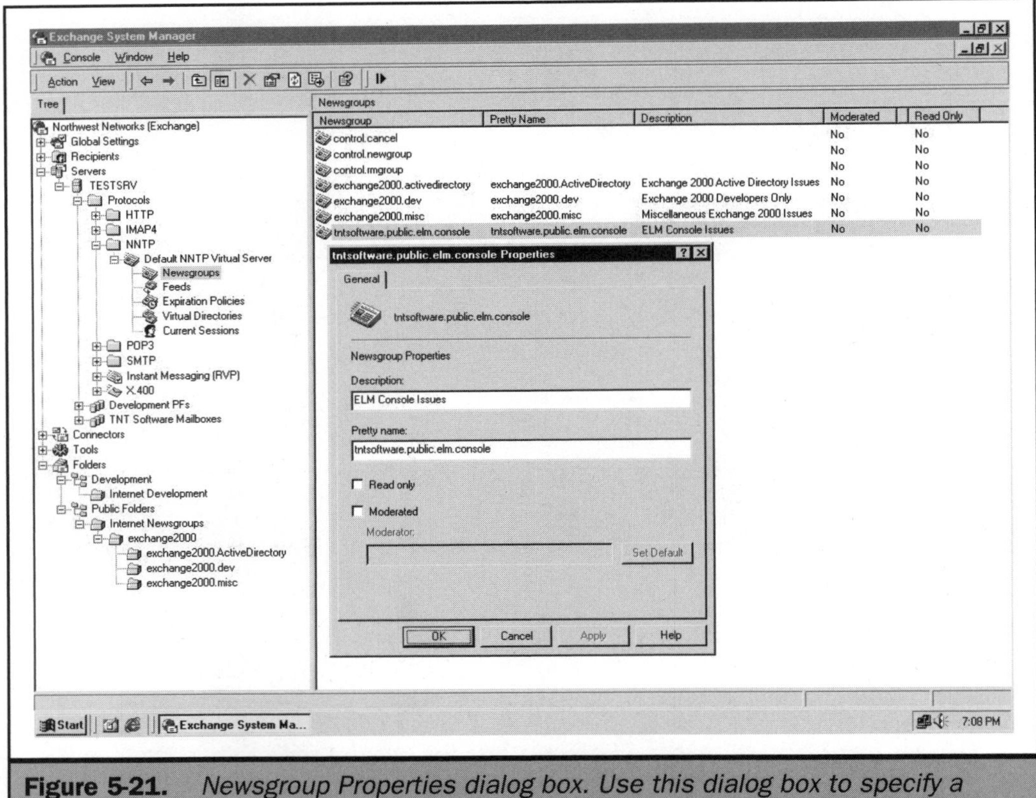

Figure 5-21. *Newsgroup Properties dialog box. Use this dialog box to specify a description and alias for a newsgroup or designate a newsgroup as read-only or moderated.*

Creating Newsfeeds

Newsfeeds are used to distribute newsgroups across multiple servers. Exchange 2000 supports three types of newsfeeds:

- Master feeds
- Slave feeds
- Peer feeds

There are two types of master newsfeeds: *push* feeds and *pull* feeds. In the push feed scenario, a remote NNTP server initiates a push of its newsgroups and articles to your Exchange server. In the pull feed scenario, your Exchange server initiates a pull of a remote NNTP server's newsgroups and newsfeeds. In either case, the master server is responsible for assigning a message ID number to all articles and for keeping slave servers synchronized.

A server hosting a slave feed receives articles and their message IDs from a master server. Multiple slave servers can be used to balance the load across NNTP servers, enabling Exchange to scale to tens of thousands of newsgroups containing millions of messages. In a peer feed, NNTP servers exchange articles between them, but this exchange does not include message IDs. As a result, each peer server is responsible for managing its own articles and message IDs. To create a new newsfeed:

1. In System Manager, expand Servers, then the desired server, then Protocols, then NNTP, and then the desired virtual server.
2. Right-click on Feeds and select New | Feed. The New NNTP Feed Wizard will launch.
3. Provide the name or IP address of the server with which you want to establish a newsfeed. Click Next to continue.
4. Select the Remote Server Role and click Next to continue.
5. Select Inbound and/or Outbound. If you select Inbound, select either Pull or Push. Click Next to continue.
6. If you selected a pull feed, select a starting date and time for articles you want to pull. Click Next to continue.
7. Select the newsgroups affected by this feed. The default is all newsgroups, as represented by the asterisk (*). Click Finish to create the newsfeed.

Summary

The public folder system in Exchange 2000 has been greatly improved over prior versions of Exchange. Exchange 2000 includes a number of enhancements to public folders, such as support for multiple information stores, integration with Active Directory, policy-based management, finer granularity of security, and integration with the Windows 2000 NNTP service.

Exchange public folders are comprised of a top-level hierarchy and public folder trees. Exchange 2000 supports multiple top-level hierarchies, although any additional top-level hierarchies you create are not accessible via a MAPI client. Nonetheless, you can create additional general purpose top-level hierarchies which can be accessed via a Web browser or the Exchange Installable File System.

Public folders can be replicated to multiple servers enabling administrators to locate relevant content in proximity of the knowledge workers who use it the most. The public folder referral process ensures that clients are directed to the public folder store closest to them that contains the content being sought.

Exchange public folders have always been able to store a wide variety of information, such as documents and files, project information, discussions, and custom forms, but Exchange 2000 takes public folders to a whole new level. By hosting collaborative applications, organizations can leverage their investment in Exchange by providing knowledge workers with information tools they can use in a familiar environment.

Part II

Administering Exchange 2000 Server

Chapter 6

Installing Exchange 2000 Server

Of all the factors that contribute to the success of your Exchange 2000 deployment, one of the most important is the integrity of your installations. Minor problems encountered during setup can end up as major problems and an interruption of services once your servers are placed into production. Even the smallest of installation anomalies can come back and haunt you after your users have been deployed.

The actual installation process is relatively straightforward: run setup.exe and step through the sequence of dialog boxes, providing some information along the way. However, the complexity of Exchange 2000 and Active Directory requires lengthy and careful planning. Depending on the size and needs of your organization, planning your Active Directory implementation alone could take months, and in some cases, more than a year. Because of the deep integration between Exchange 2000 and Active Directory, some additional planning will be required. Before installing Exchange 2000 into a production environment, you should consider the impact the installation will have on your network, your Active Directory, and any existing legacy Exchange servers in your company.

This chapter will take you through the installation process of Exchange 2000 Server from start to finish. This chapter does not cover upgrading an Exchange 5.5 server. For information on upgrading your Exchange 5.5 server to Exchange 2000, see Chapter 7. Refer to Chapter 15 for information on and instructions for installing Exchange 2000 Conferencing Server and to Chapter 20 for instructions on installing Exchange 2000 in a Windows 2000 cluster.

Installation Requirements

As with any software product, Exchange 2000 has specific hardware and software requirements that must be met prior to installing the product. In addition to these requirements, Exchange 2000 also has infrastructure requirements such as Windows 2000 Active Directory and healthy DNS services. In fact, properly installing Exchange 2000 into an existing Active Directory forest requires knowledge of Exchange 2000, Windows 2000, Active Directory, DNS, and general TCP/IP networking.

Hardware

In order to install any version of Exchange 2000, the computer must meet the following minimum hardware requirements:

- Intel Pentium 300MHz or faster processor
- 128MB RAM
- 500MB free disk space on the drive containing Exchange
- 200MB free disk space on system drive
- VGA or higher resolution
- CD-ROM drive

Keep in mind that the hardware requirements listed above are the *minimum* requirements. There is a major different between minimum requirements and necessary real-world production requirements. Your actual hardware requirements will depend on several factors, such as the services being provided and the number of users supported on each server.

Consider the following when sizing your servers:

- Don't skimp on RAM. In short, RAM is where the work gets done. The more RAM in your system, the more work it is able to do.
- Make sure your CPU(s) don't become a bottleneck as a result of having a lot of RAM. Quite often, beefing up one resource causes a bottleneck in another resource.
- If your server supports more than 100 users and your budget permits, use at least a dual processor machine. The performance gains are well worth the additional expense of the additional processor.
- If your budget is limited, prioritize your resources; you should buy RAM before buying additional CPUs.
- Faster disks are better. As a database application, Exchange is very I/O intensive. Exchange sequentially writes log files and randomly reads database files, so the faster your disk subsystem, the better your overall performance.
- Collect performance data regularly. You should start your performance data collection before your server is placed into production. This is known as a *baseline*. The baseline is the performance of the server without any users. Once your server is in production, continue collecting performance data at regular intervals throughout its production life cycle. This will provide you with a *trend*. A trend is simply the collected performance data viewed over time. Once you have established a baseline and trend, you can perform *capacity planning*. Capacity planning enables you to determine whether or not your hardware resources are sufficient to meet the needs of your users, and it is used to determine when additional hardware resources are needed.
- Do not install Exchange 2000 on an Active Directory domain controller unless absolutely necessary. This is one of those Microsoft "best practices" recommendations that, due to budget constraints and other factors, cannot be followed by all organizations. Undoubtedly there will be organizations that will install Exchange 2000 on an Active Directory domain controller. If yours is one of them, make sure you have more than sufficient hardware. The hardware resource requirements for an Active Directory domain controller are significantly higher than their Windows NT 4.0 predecessors.
- Use hardware RAID arrays, preferably RAID-5 arrays for all databases and RAID-1 arrays for all transaction logs, message tracking logs, connector directories, and the TEMP folder. This will provide fault tolerance for your server's most critical files and folders.

- Only use hardware on Microsoft's Hardware Compatibility List (HCL). This is especially important for clustered Exchange servers. Visit http://www.microsoft.com/hwtest/hcl for a complete listing of systems on the HCL.

Sizing Your Servers

The real-world hardware requirements also depend on what role the particular Exchange server plays in your organization. There are many types of Exchange servers:

- Mailbox servers
- Public folder servers
- Front-end servers
- Bridgehead or connector servers
- Conferencing servers
- Instant messaging servers
- Chat servers

The following tables contain processor and memory recommendations for each of the above type of servers.

Number of Users	Number of CPUs	Memory
500 or fewer	2	512MB
500–1,000	2 to 4	768MB to 1GB
1,000–2,000	4	1GB to 2GB
2,000–3,500	4 to 8	2GB to 4GB

Table 6-1. *Recommended Sizing for Mailbox Servers*

Number of Users	Number of CPUs	Memory
500 or fewer	2	512MB
500–1,000	2 to 4	768MB to 1GB
1,000–2,000	4	1GB to 2GB
2,000–3,500	4 to 8	2GB to 4GB

Table 6-2. *Recommended Sizing for Dedicated Public Folder Servers*

Number of Users	Number of CPUs	Memory
500 or fewer	1	128MB to 256MB
500–1,000	1 to 2	256MB
1,000–2,000	2	256MB to 512MB
2,000–3,500	2 to 4	512MB

Table 6-3. *Recommended Sizing for Front-end Servers*

Mail Traffic	Number of CPUs	Memory
Light	1	128MB to 256MB
Medium	1 to 2	256MB
Heavy	2 to 4	512MB

Table 6-4. *Recommended Sizing for Bridgehead and Connector Servers*

Number of Users	Number of CPUs	Memory
500 or fewer	1	256MB
500–1,000	2	256MB to 512MB
1,000–2,000	2 to 4	512MB to 1GB
2,000–3,500	4	1GB

Table 6-5. *Recommended Sizing for Conferencing Servers*

Number of Users	Number of CPUs	Memory
5,000 or fewer	1	256MB
5,000–10,000	2	512MB

Table 6-6. *Recommended Sizing for Dedicated Instant Messaging Servers*

Number of Users	Number of CPUs	Memory
5,000 or fewer	1	128MB to 256MB
5,000–10,000	2	256MB to 512MB
10,000–20,000	2 to 4	512MB to 1GB

Table 6-7. *Recommended Sizing for Dedicated Chat Servers*

Software

You must have the following software components installed prior to installing Exchange 2000 on a server:

- Windows 2000 Server family product with Service Pack 1 or higher
- Windows 2000 Post-SP1 rollup hotfix Q271976
- SMTP Service
- NNTP Service
- TCP/IP
- Windows paging file set to twice the amount of physical memory
- NTFS partition(s) for Exchange databases

Note *You can use NTFS or FAT partitions for the Exchange transaction logs. Some people prefer using FAT because it is slightly faster than NTFS. Others prefer NTFS because it allows for folder- and file-level security.*

In addition to the above software components, you should also install the latest available service pack for Exchange 2000. You should also regularly check Microsoft's download Web site (http://www.microsoft.com/downloads) for Exchange 2000 updates that have been released separately from service packs.

Windows 2000 and Active Directory Considerations

Exchange 5.5 and earlier versions could only be deployed in a Windows NT domain. Exchange did not need to be installed on a domain controller, but it did require a domain. Exchange 2000 will only install on a Windows 2000 Server family product. Since Exchange 2000 depends on Active Directory, it can only be deployed in an environment containing an Active Directory. It need not—and in most cases, should not—be installed on a domain controller, but Active Directory is a requirement. Only one Exchange organization can exist in one Active Directory forest, and an Exchange organization cannot span multiple forests. Therefore, the Exchange organization is the forest, and the forest is the Exchange organization.

When the first Exchange 2000 server is installed in your Active Directory, it will permanently extend the schema. These extensions can be disabled if Exchange 2000 is removed from Active Directory, but they cannot be reversed. Because the first server modifies the Active Directory schema, it can only be installed by using an account that is a member of the Enterprise Admins, Schema Admins and Administrators groups. The second and subsequent Exchange 2000 installation only requires Domains Admins group membership and local administrative privileges.

Installing Exchange 2000 into your Active Directory forest irrevocably modifies your Active Directory. Problems that occur during an Exchange installation could have catastrophic results later, including, possibly, the need to completely rebuild your Active Directory from scratch.

Installation Considerations

Before installing your organization's first Exchange server, it is important to validate your existing environment. As you know by now, Exchange depends heavily on the health and design of your Active Directory and your DNS name resolution services. We recommend preparing and validating your environment by performing some preinstallation tasks.

Install Windows 2000 Service Pack 1 and Q271976 Hotfix

Make sure Windows 2000 Service Pack 1 is installed on all domain controllers and Global Catalog servers throughout your Active Directory forest, not just your Exchange 2000 servers. Exchange 2000's setup process will check for the existence of Service Pack 1 on the intended Exchange server, but it will not check other important systems, such as domain controllers and Global Catalog servers for Service Pack 1. Microsoft has documented that intermittent delivery and performance problems can result if Service Pack 1 is not installed on domain controllers and Global Catalog servers.

The easiest way to determine if Service Pack 1 has been installed is to use winver.exe. This will produce a dialog box that displays which service pack has been installed. If you also need to know which hotfixes have been installed, you can use srvinfo.exe from the Windows 2000 Resource Kit to obtain this information.

The hotfix rollup described in Q271976 corrects two separate problems in Windows 2000. The first problem is poor performance due to memory heap fragmentation. When the Exchange 2000 store.exe process executes, it reserves a chunk—or heap—of memory. Exchange is a self-tuning application that will shrink its heap when another process needs memory and grow its heap when free memory is available. In the process of doing this, its heap becomes fragmented, much like a file system can become fragmented when file sizes increase and decrease frequently. Once memory heap fragmentation has occurred, the internal algorithm used to find free blocks of memory in the heap begins to perform poorly. This hotfix corrects the problem by implementing a new algorithm.

The second problem is a security error that occurs when the local Windows 2000 machine account on an Exchange 2000 system is reset. When the password for this account is reset, Exchange services no longer authenticate correctly. Instead, a cryptic error—0x8009030C (SEC_E_LOGON_DENIED)—occurs whenever authentication, such as SMTP authentication between servers, takes place.

While both fixes will be included in Windows 2000 Service Pack 2, don't wait for SP2 if you're deploying Exchange 2000. In fact, Microsoft recommends that all Exchange 2000 users apply this hotfix rollup to all Exchange 2000 servers and conferencing servers, all Active Directory Connector (ADC) servers, and all domain controller and Global Catalog servers.

If Windows 2000 Service Pack 2 or later is out and available by the time you read this, you can skip this hotfix and install Service Pack 2 or later.

Validate Name Resolution

If something goes wrong during setup, the first thing to check is DNS. You should verify that DNS is working properly and that you have good name resolution from the intended Exchange server to domain controllers and Global Catalog servers. A ping will verify basic IP connectivity and name resolution in most cases. You may also wish to use nslookup.exe to verify that the appropriate DNS entries exist and are correct.

Naming Standards

During installation, you will need to specify the names of various objects, including the organization name, a site name, and a server name.

Organization Name The organization name encompasses the Active Directory forest. All objects in an Exchange organization have the same organization name. This name will be visible to others outside your organization, and therefore it should be chosen carefully. It must be unique and, once specified, it cannot be changed. The organization name is used in generating foreign e-mail addresses and the distinguished names of all directory objects. Organization names can contain as many as 64 characters; however, it is generally recommended that you use names with fewer than 10 characters.

If you are upgrading an Exchange 5.5 environment, you should remove any invalid characters from your existing organization name. Exchange 2000 supports only the following characters in your organization name:

- A–Z
- a–z
- 0–9
- a hyphen (-) or a space

During an upgrade, Exchange 2000 will use the Exchange 5.5 display name as the organization name. If your existing organization name has any other characters in it, it will need to be changed or Setup will terminate prematurely with an error. Although you cannot modify Exchange 5.5's internal organization name, you can modify its display name. Thus, you have the opportunity to change your organization name.

Site Name Sites can be named a number of ways, including by location or by business units. Like organization names, site names must be unique and cannot be changed once specified. Site names also make up part of the foreign e-mail addresses and directory names. Like the organization name, site names can contain up to 64 characters, though it is recommended that site names use fewer than 10 characters.

The 10-character recommendation for your organization and site names is the result of both practicality and connectivity with legacy messaging systems.

Server Name Because Exchange uses the Windows 2000 Server name, you should decide on a name prior to installing Windows 2000 Server. Server names must also be unique and once Exchange 2000 has been installed, the name cannot be changed.

It's a good idea to plan out your Exchange infrastructure's naming conventions prior to deploying any servers.

Exchange 2000 Installation Types

Regardless of whether you are installing Exchange for the first time in your company or upgrading your existing Exchange infrastructure, there are four different types of installations that can be performed:

- **First installation** The installation of the first Exchange 2000 Server in your organization differs slightly from subsequent installations. This is when the Exchange organization is created and when the schema modifications are made.
- **Second and subsequent installations** These installations will detect the schema modifications made by the first installation. During the second and subsequent installation, Setup will look to Active Directory for some of the Exchange configuration information.

- **Unattended installations** Like many Microsoft applications, Exchange 2000 can be installed in an unattended manner. This involves creating and using a predefined initialization file. There are caveats to performing an unattended installation, which are discussed later in this chapter.
- **Preparatory installations** These types of installations are used to prepare an Active Directory forest and Active Directory domains for an Exchange 2000 infrastructure. In this scenario, the Active Directory schema is extended, the Exchange Organization object is created in Active Directory, and the domain security structure is put in place—all without actually installing any Exchange servers. In other words, this is a first installation without installing any of the Exchange components. Depending on the architecture of your Active Directory deployment and the administrative security model in place at your organization, you may find it preferable to perform preparatory installations prior to deploying any actual Exchange servers.

The Exchange setup application, setup.exe, has some command-line options—or switches—you can use to control how Setup behaves. The list of available switches can be viewed by executing **Setup /?**. The available options will be displayed, as shown in Figure 6-1.

Exchange Components

During the first, second, and subsequent installations, you select the Exchange components that will be installed on each server. You can use Setup to add or remove these components. Table 6-8 describes the available components.

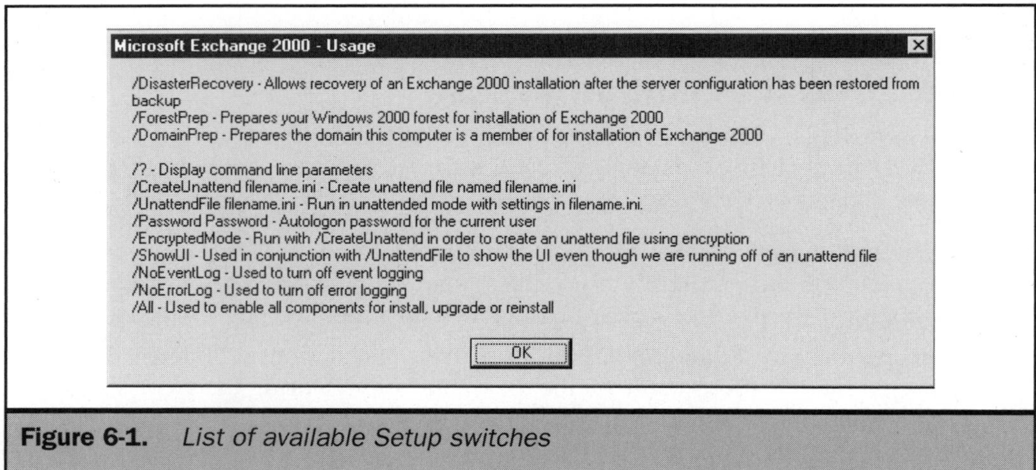

Figure 6-1. *List of available Setup switches*

Component	Description
Microsoft Exchange 2000	Core components of Exchange 2000, which are required for every server. This is part of a typical install.
Microsoft Exchange Messaging and Collaboration Services	Basic components of messaging and collaboration. These components are required for chat services and instant messaging. This is also part of a typical install.
Microsoft Exchange MS Mail Connector	This connector is only used to connect Exchange 2000 to a Microsoft Mail system. This component can be installed by performing a custom install.
Microsoft Exchange Connector for Lotus cc:Mail	This connector is only used to connect Exchange 2000 to a Lotus cc:Mail system. This component can be installed by performing a custom install.
Microsoft Exchange Connector for Lotus Notes	This connector can only be used to connect Exchange 2000 to a Lotus Notes system. This component can be installed by performing a custom install.
Microsoft Exchange Connector for Novell GroupWise	This connector can only be used to connect Exchange 2000 to a Novell GroupWise system. This component can be installed by performing a custom install.
Microsoft Exchange Key Management Service	Provides Exchange-specific security enhancements for Windows 2000 Server Certificate Services. This component can be installed by performing a custom install.
Microsoft Exchange System Management Tools	Installs System Manager and other tools used to manage Exchange. This is part of a typical install.
Microsoft Exchange 5.5 Administrator	Installs the Exchange 5.5 Administrator application, which can only be used to administer Exchange 5.5 servers. This component can be installed by performing a custom install.

Table 6-8. *List of Available Exchange Components*

Component	Description
Microsoft Exchange Chat Service	Installs components that enable Internet Relay Chat (IRC)-based communities. This component, which is only available in Exchange 2000 Enterprise Server, can be installed by performing a custom install.
Microsoft Exchange Instant Messaging Services	Installs components that enable Exchange instant messaging. This component can be installed by performing a custom install.

Table 6-8. *List of Available Exchange Components* (continued)

First Installation

Because the first installation modifies the Active Directory schema, it will take significantly longer than the second and subsequent installations. Once the schema modifications have been made, they will be replicated to every domain controller (in every domain) in your Active Directory forest. Depending on the number of domain controllers in your forest and the link speeds between them, replication of the schema modifications could have a serious impact on your network. It could take anywhere from a few minutes to several hours for replication to complete. For this reason, you may wish to perform the installation after hours or during a time when network activity is at a minimum. Alternatively, you may wish to perform a schema-only installation, which is discussed later in this chapter.

Note *You can use Replication Monitor (ReplMon) from the Windows 2000 Resource Kit to verify Active Directory replication. In addition, you can use the Windows 2000 LDP utility to query a domain controller for the following object: cn=ms-Exch-Schema-Version-Pt,cn=schema,cn=configuration,dc=<domain name> where <domain name> is the name of your domain (without the brackets). If the rangeUpper value is set to 4397, the Exchange schema extensions have been replicated to this domain controller.*

When performing the first installation, you must be logged on using an account that is a member of the Enterprise Admins, Schema Admins and Administrators groups. To perform your first Exchange 2000 installation, log on to a Windows 2000

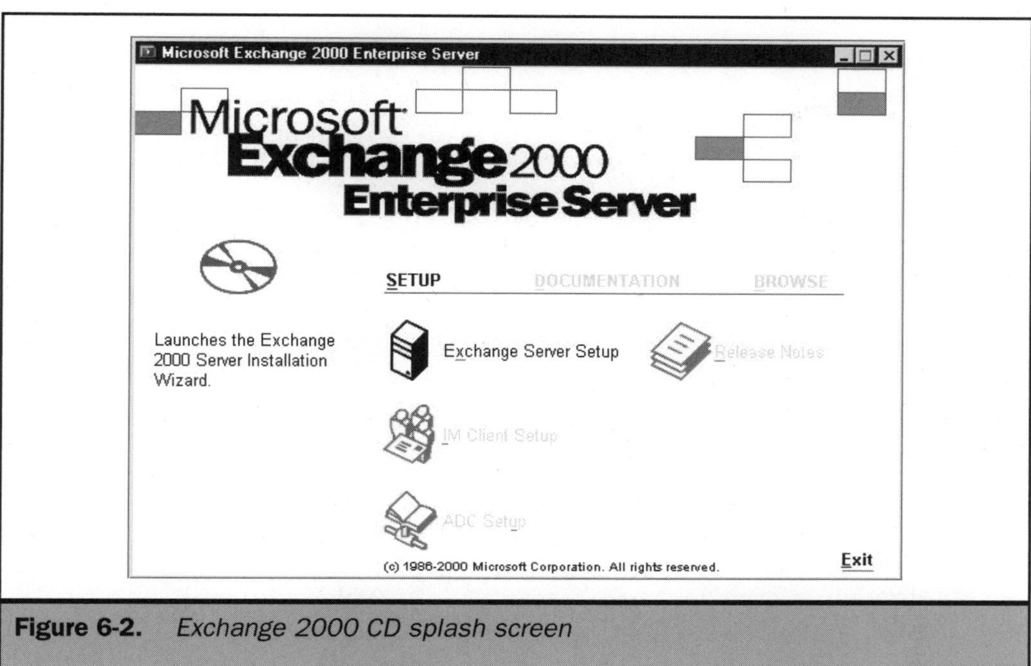

Figure 6-2. *Exchange 2000 CD splash screen*

server that is a member of a domain in your forest using an account that belongs to these groups. Then:

1. Insert your Exchange 2000 Server CD into your CD-ROM drive. The Exchange 2000 CD splash screen should automatically appear, as shown in Figure 6-2.

Tip *If the splash screen does not automatically appear, navigate to the root of the CD through the Windows Explorer or through My Computer, and then double-click launch.exe.*

2. Click Exchange Server Setup. This will launch the Administrator stage of the setup process. The Exchange Installation Wizard welcome screen will be displayed, as shown in Figure 6-3.
3. Click Next to continue. The End User License Agreement (EULA) screen will appear. Read the EULA carefully, and signify your agreement to its terms by

Figure 6-3. *Installation Wizard welcome screen*

selecting I Agree. If you do not accept the EULA, you will not be able to install Exchange 2000. Click Next to continue. The Product Identification screen will appear, as shown in Figure 6-4.

4. Enter your 25-digit CD key from the back of the Exchange 2000 Server CD. Click Next to continue. The Component Selection screen will appear, as shown in Figure 6-5.
5. You can use choose a minimal, typical, or custom installation. A minimal installation installs the required core components and the Microsoft Exchange Messaging and Collaboration Services. A typical installation includes these components and the Microsoft Exchange System Management Tools. A custom installation allows you to specify additional components for installation.

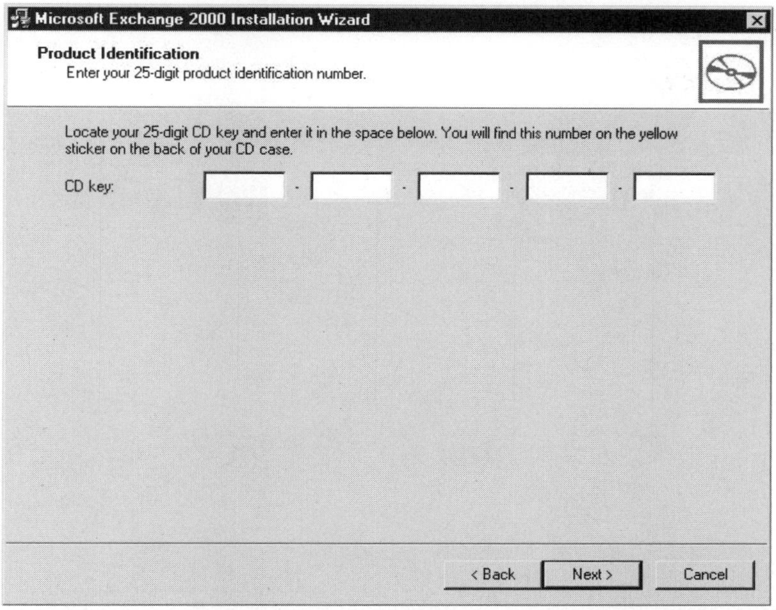

Figure 6-4. *Product Identification screen. You must enter your CD key to continue.*

> **Tip** *The type of installation you choose will depend on the components you wish to install. Very few installations will be minimal. Custom installations are recommended due to their flexibility in adding or removing components.*

Select one of these options to specify the components you want to install. The default destination path is C:\Program Files\Exchsrvr, which can be changed if desired. To change the destination drive for the installation, select Microsoft Exchange 2000, and then click the Change Folder button. Enter the path you wish to use (for example, D:\Exchsrvr). If the destination folder does not exist, Setup will ask you if you want to create it. When you have finished selecting the components and location for the installation, click Next to continue.

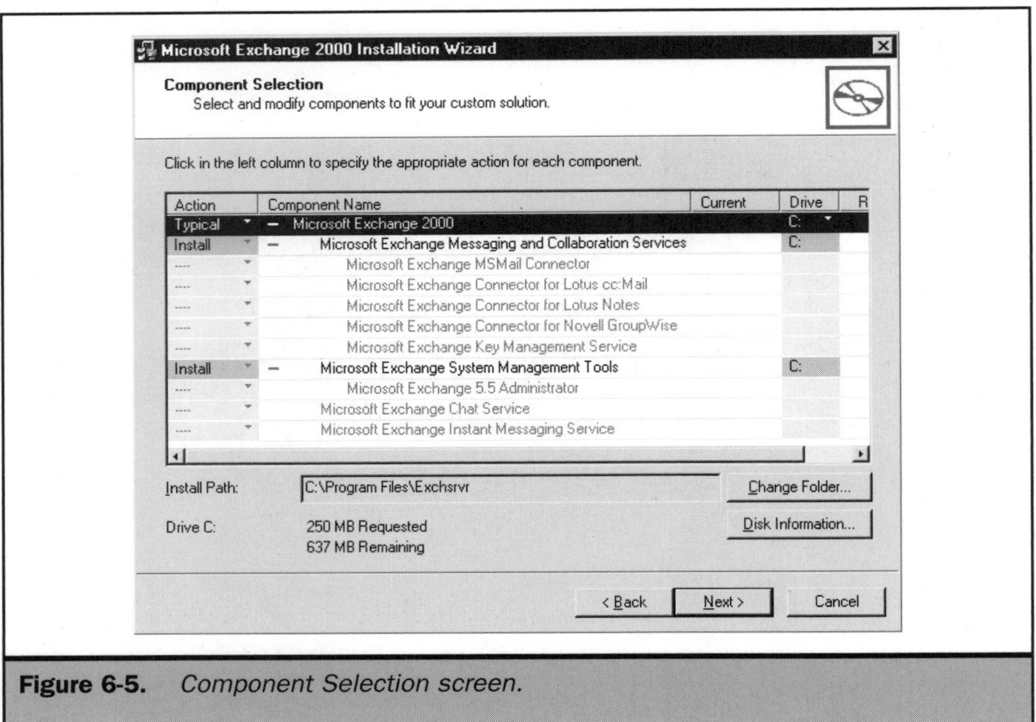

Figure 6-5. *Component Selection screen.*

Note *When deciding on an installation path, keep in mind that you can always use the System Manager to change the location of the Exchange databases and logs later on. So think of the install path as the installation destination for the Exchange binaries.*

The Installation Type screen will appear (shown in Figure 6-6).

6. You have two options: create a new organization or join an existing Exchange 5.5 organization. If you select Join or Upgrade an Existing Exchange 5.5 Organization, the Select a Server in an Exchange 5.5 Organization screen will appear, as shown in Figure 6-7.
7. You must select an online Exchange 5.5 server, and you will be prompted for the Exchange 5.5 service account and password. We'll get into upgrading and coexisting with an Exchange 5.5 organization in Chapter 7, so for now we'll proceed with the creation of a new Exchange organization. If you select Create A New Exchange Organization, the Organization Name screen will appear, as shown in Figure 6-8.
8. In almost all cases you will want to change the default organization name, which is First Organization.

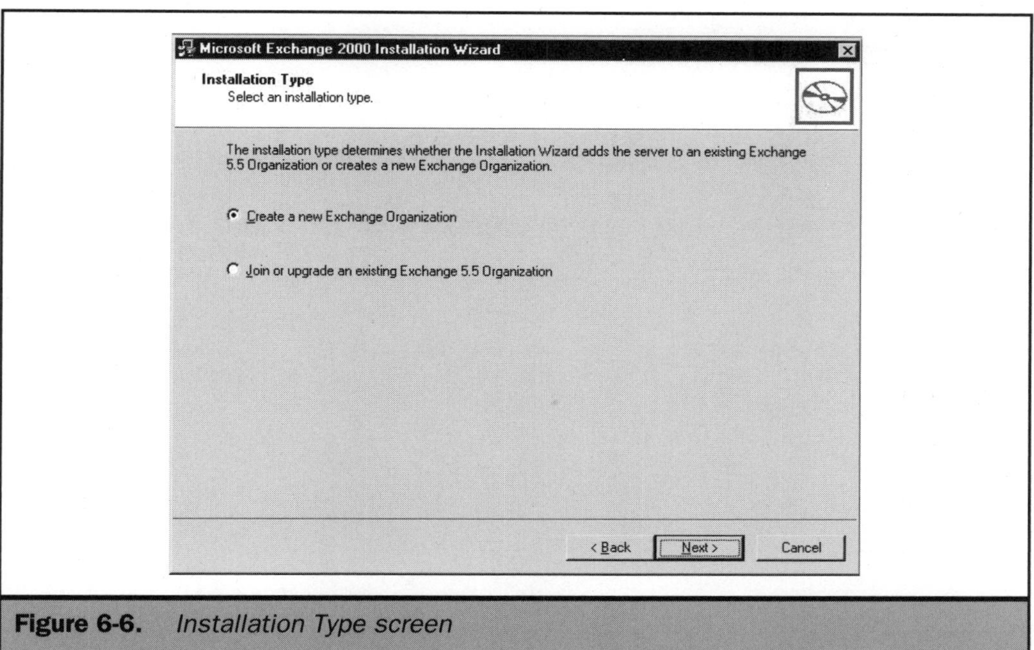

Figure 6-6. *Installation Type screen*

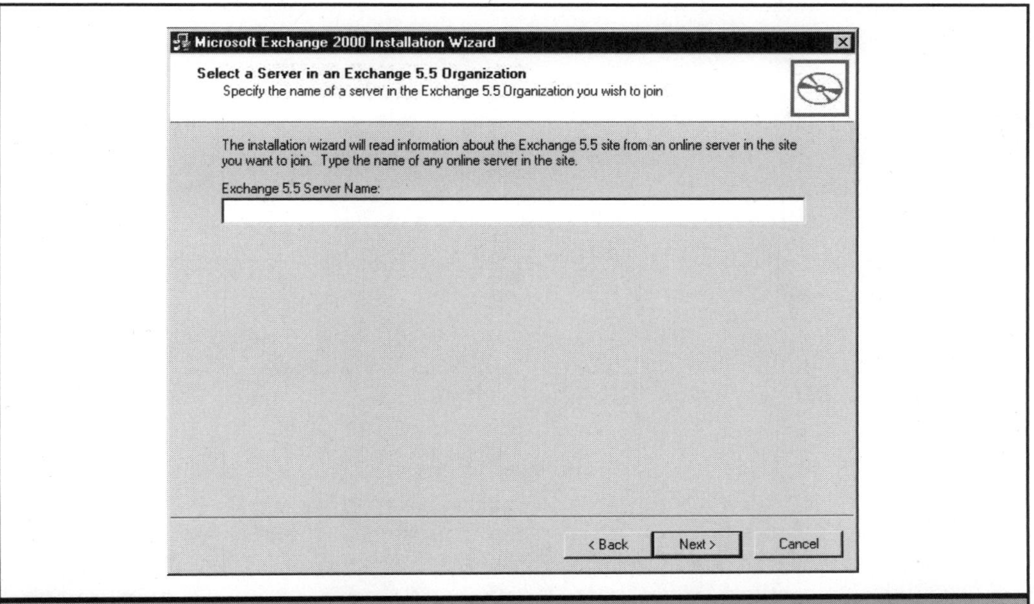

Figure 6-7. *Select a Server in an Exchange 5.5 Organization screen*

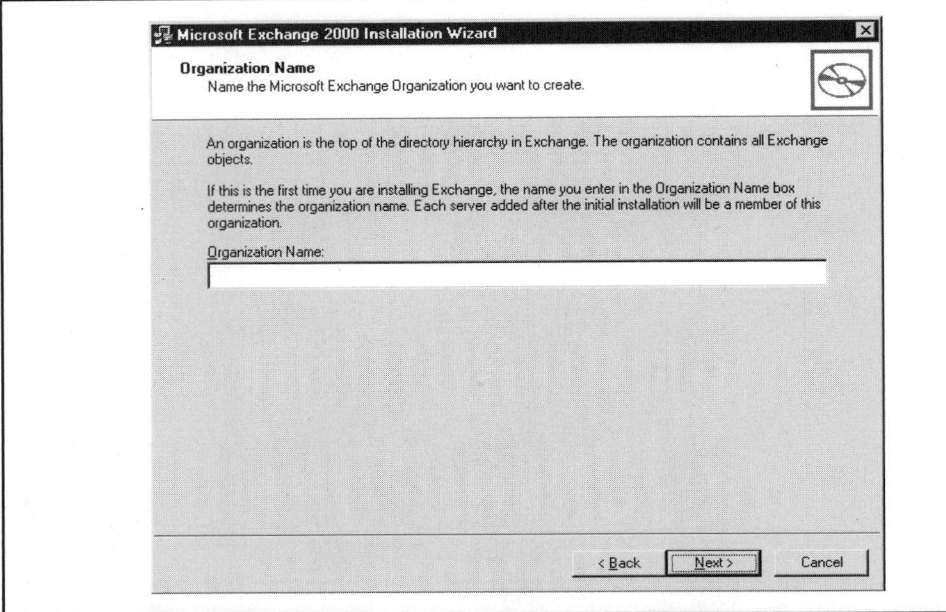

Figure 6-8. *Organization Name screen. The name you enter here cannot be changed.*

Caution *Be very careful when entering this name, as it cannot be changed once the installation process has completed.*

Enter the organization name you want to use and click Next to continue. The Licensing Agreement screen appears (shown in Figure 6-9).

9. Select "I agree that:…" and click Next to continue. The Component Summary screen will appear, as shown in Figure 6-10
10. Review the Component Summary screen. If you wish to make changes, click the Back button until you return to the Component Selection screen. Click Next to continue. The second and third stages of setup will begin, and the Component Progress screen will be displayed (shown in Figure 6-11).
11. When the file copy process is complete, Exchange 2000 will begin the Active Directory schema modifications. The installation process extends the Active Directory schema with Exchange-specific attributes. When the schema modifications are complete, the fourth and final stage of setup will begin. Setup will complete the file copy process and start the appropriate Exchange services. Finally, the Installation Wizard Completion screen will appear, as shown in Figure 6-12.

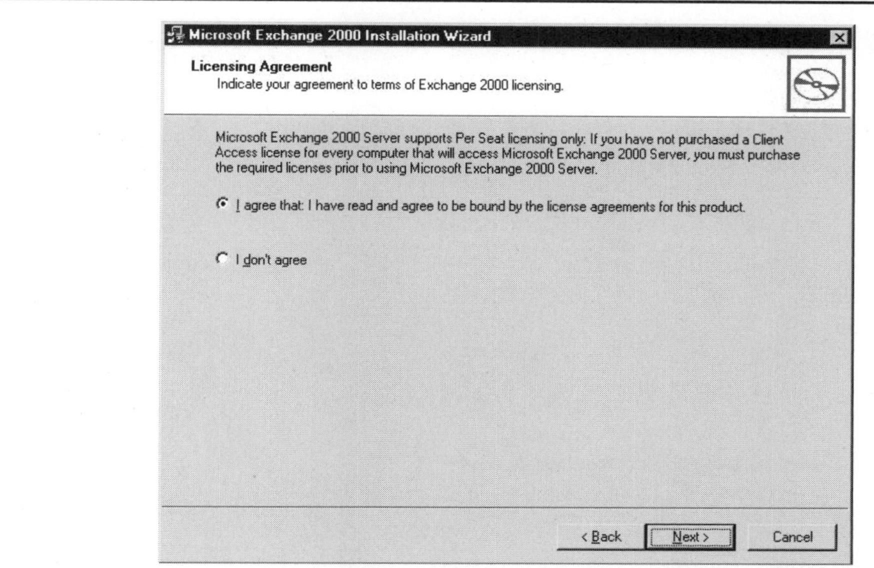

Figure 6-9. *Licensing Agreement screen. You must acknowledge that you have read and agree to be bound by the Exchange 2000 licensing agreement before you can continue.*

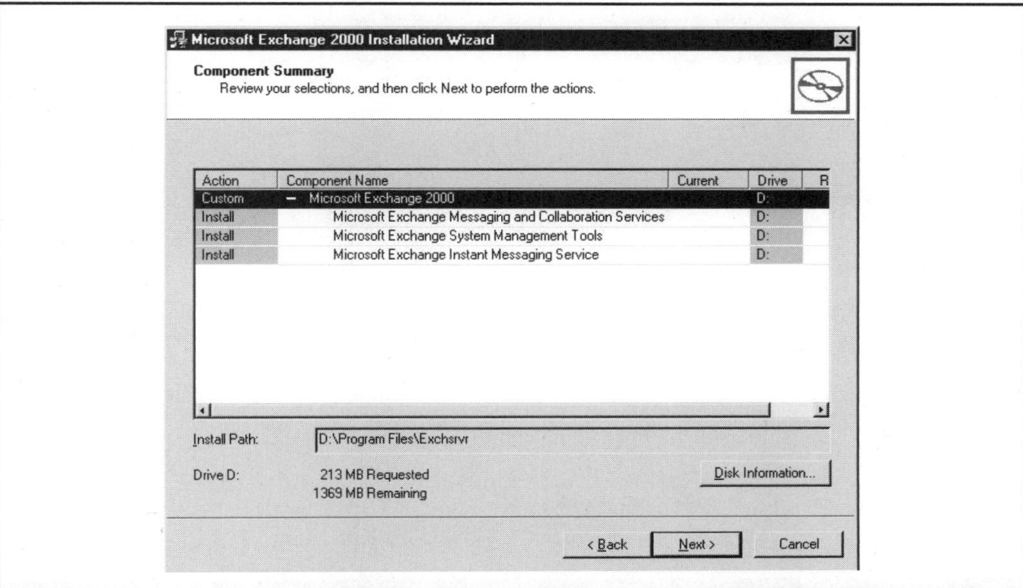

Figure 6-10. *Component Summary screen. This screen presents a summary of the components that will be installed and the destination path.*

ADMINISTERING EXCHANGE 2000 SERVER

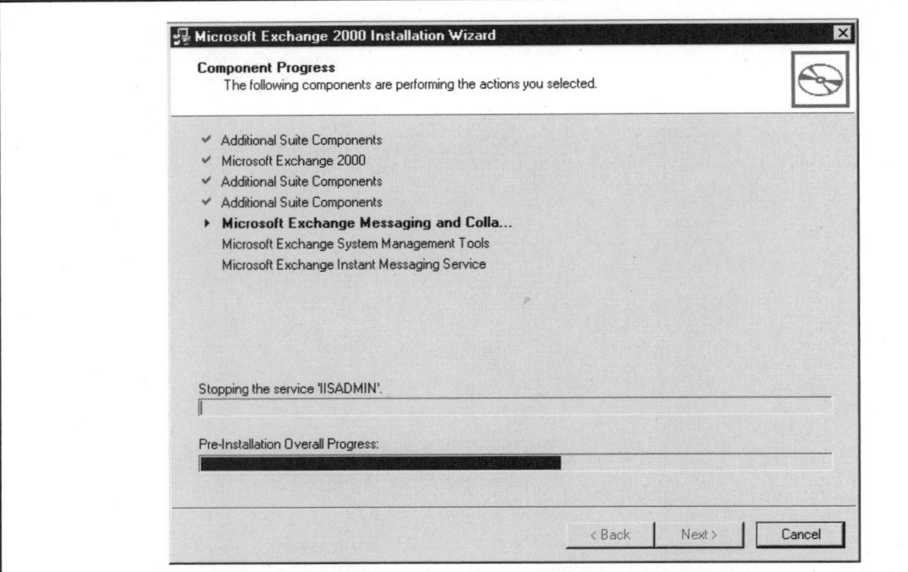

Figure 6-11. *Component Progress screen. This screen displays a status bar indicating the installation's progress.*

Figure 6-12. *Installation Wizard Completion screen*

Note *The schema modification process can take a considerable amount of time, and CPU utilization by the Local Security Authority process on the Active Directory domain controller will likely be very high while the modifications are being made. The Exchange 2000 Server and domain controller it is using may even appear hung during the schema modifications phase. At times, however, you should see its status get updated during the Active Directory schema modifications. This is normal behavior.*

12. Click Finish to complete the installation process. As with Exchange 5.5, you do not need to reboot the server after installing Exchange 2000. However, unlike Exchange 5.5, there is no Performance Optimizer for you to run.

Second and Subsequent Installations

Because only the first installation modifies the Active Directory schema, the second and subsequent installations take less time. Schema modifications aside, the second and subsequent installations are very similar to the first installation. However, unlike the first installation, you will be prompted to specify an administrative group and routing group for the second and subsequent servers in your forest.

When creating a new organization during the first installation, Setup automatically creates an administrative group called First Administrative Group and a routing group called First Routing Group. These groups can be displayed in System Manager, but you have to specifically enable them first. See Chapter 9 for instructions on how to do this. Once you configure System Manager to display administrative and routing groups, you can create new administrative and routing groups and select them during the second and subsequent installations. If you don't need multiple administrative or routing groups, select the default groups—First Administrative Group and First Routing Group—during the setup process.

Because no schema modifications need to be made during either the second or subsequent installs, the account used to install Exchange does not need to be a member of the Schema Admins group. It does, however, need to be a member of the Domain Admins group for the domain containing the intended server, and a local administrator on the intended Exchange 2000 server.

To install a second or subsequent Exchange server in your organization, the basic steps are identical to your first installation. The difference begins after the Licensing Agreement screen appears.

1. On the License Agreement Screen, click "I agree that…", then click Next. The Administrative Groups screen will appear.
2. Select the administrative group in which you want to install this server, then click Next. The Routing Groups screen will appear.
3. Select the routing group in which you want to install this server, then click Next. The Component Summary screen will appear.
4. Verify the installation options, and click Next to continue. The Component Progress screen will appear.

5. Setup will copy the necessary components to the server and start the appropriate Exchange services. When the installation process has finished, the Exchange Installation Wizard Completion screen will appear.
6. Click Finish to complete the installation process.

Unattended Installations

Exchange 2000 supports an unattended installation mode for the second and subsequent server installations. This process begins with the creation of unattended initialization file, which is later applied to other servers. Both the creation and usage of this file involve executing Setup with the appropriate command-line parameters. Table 6-9 describes the applicable command-line switches.

Switch	Description
/All	Used to enable all components for an install, reinstall, or upgrade.
/CreateUnattend *filename.ini*	Creates an initialization file called *filename*.INI, where *filename* can be any name you want. Microsoft does not support manual editing of this file. If you need to change a parameter, setting or option, you will need to rerun Setup and create a new .INI file.
/EncryptedMode	When used with the /CreateUnattend switch, the resulting initialization file is encrypted. It is also used when running Setup with an encrypted initialization file.
/NoErrorLog	Turns off error logging.
/NoEventLog	Turns off logging to the Windows 2000 event logs.
/Password	Sets an autologon password for the current user.
/ShowUI	Used with the /UnattendFile switch to display the user interface dialog boxes during setup. No changes can be made to these dialog boxes.
/UnattendFile *filename.ini*	Instructs Setup to use the predefined initialization file, *filename*.INI.

Table 6-9. *Unattended Installation Setup Switches*

Only basic installations can be performed in unattended mode. These include:

- Installation of messaging and collaboration services or system management tools
- New Exchange 2000 installs (mixed or native Exchange modes)
- Second and subsequent installs into a mixed environment

The following procedures cannot be performed in unattended mode:

- /forestprep or /domainprep
- Exchange 5.5 upgrade
- /disasterrecovery installations
- Cluster installations
- Maintenance mode (add/remove components)
- First Exchange 2000 install in an Exchange 5.5 organization
- Installing chat services or instant messaging services
- Uninstallation of Exchange 2000

Preparatory Installations

As mentioned previously, the first Exchange 2000 installation extends the Active Directory schema. Several factors combine to determine how long the modification process will take, including the size of your Active Directory, the proximity to an Active Directory controller, the available network bandwidth, and the speed of the Exchange server itself.

If you have a lot of Active Directory controllers in your forest, replication of the schema extensions could take considerable time. You can avoid replication issues altogether by performing a *preparatory* installation early on in your Active Directory deployment. A preparatory installation is similar to a first installation, except that the Exchange server components are not installed. The Exchange 2000 setup process is run and the Exchange organization is created. In addition, the Active Directory schema is modified, the Exchange organization name and object are created in Active Directory, and the domain security structure is put into place.

The first part of the preparatory installations—called "forestprep"— can only be performed using an account that is a member of the Schema Admins group. Thereafter, the remaining Exchange 2000 servers can be installed by others without having to add them to the Schema Admins group; however, membership in the Domain Admins group for the domain containing the Exchange server and local administrative privileges on the Windows 2000 server are required.

Note *Many organizations will likely keep the number of Schema Admins to a minimum. Exchange 2000 installations only require the use of an account with Schema Admin rights during the first installation or during the first part of a preparatory installation.*

To perform a preparatory installation, you must run setup.exe using two setup switches: /forestprep and /domainprep. The /forestprep switch behavior will differ depending on whether you plan on installing Exchange 2000 into an Exchange 5.5 site. You must be a member of the Enterprise Admins, Schema Admins and Administrators groups in order to use the /forestprep setup switch.

Using /forestprep in a New Exchange Organization When creating a new Exchange organization, the /forestprep switch will:

- Create the Exchange organization object with Active Directory using the name you provide. Like prior versions of Exchange, the organization name cannot be changed.
- Make Exchange-specific extensions to Active Directory. These changes affect the entire forest, and they will be replicated to all domain controllers in all domains.
- Create the Exchange organization name and object in Active Directory.
- Assign administrative permissions to the account you specify during setup. This account can then be used to install Exchange servers in the forest.

Using /forestprep in an Existing Exchange 5.5 Organization When installing Exchange 2000 into an existing Exchange 5.5 organization, the /forestprep switch will:

- Create the Exchange organization name and object in Active Directory based on your Exchange 5.5 organization. You cannot change the name of your organization during this process.
- Replicate the Exchange 5.5 site topology into the Active Directory configuration partition.
- Make Exchange-specific extensions to Active Directory. These changes affect the entire forest, and they will be replicated to all domain controllers in all domains.
- Assign administrative permissions to the account you specify during setup. This account can then be used to install Exchange servers in the forest.

Once you have run Setup using the /forestprep option, you must then run Setup with the /domainprep option in every domain in which you plan to install Exchange 2000. This process is the same regardless of whether you are creating a new organization or installing into an existing Exchange 5.5 organization.

Running Setup with the /domainprep option will:

- Create a domain global security group in the Users container called Exchange Domain Servers
- Create a domain local security group in the domain's Users container called Exchange Enterprise Servers

- Add the Exchange Domain Servers group to the Exchange Enterprise Servers group
- Grant various permissions on the domain object to the Exchange Enterprise Servers group
- Create a user account named EUSER_EXSTOREEVENTS, which was used for the script event host in the beta versions of Exchange 2000
- Grant permissions on the AdminSDHolder object to the Exchange Enterprise Servers group
- Create a Microsoft Exchange System Objects container under the domain node

Note *The original release of Exchange 2000 contained a security vulnerability involving the EUSER_EXSTOREEVENTS account. This account is a holdover from beta versions of Exchange 2000 and is not needed for the final product. You should therefore delete this account after Setup has completed. For more information on this issue, see Microsoft Security Bulletin MS00-088 at http://www.microsoft.com/security.*

Running Setup with /forestprep When performing a forestprep installation, you must be logged on using an account that is a member of the Enterprise Admins, Schema Admins and Administrators groups. To perform a forestprep installation, log on to a Windows 2000 server in your forest using such an account. Then:

1. Insert your Exchange 2000 Server CD into your CD-ROM drive. If you have copied the CD to a local or network drive, you can run Setup from that location.

Note *The CD should autoplay, but you can close the splash screen, as you'll be launching Setup from a command prompt.*

2. From a command prompt or from the Run dialog box, execute the following command: ***X*:\setup\i386\setup.exe /forestprep**, where *X* is the drive containing the installation bits. The Installation Wizard welcome screen will appear.
3. Click Next to continue. The End User License Agreement (EULA) screen will appear.
4. Read the EULA carefully, and signify your agreement to its terms by selecting I Agree. If you do not accept the EULA, you cannot install Exchange 2000. Click Next to continue. The Product Identification screen will appear.
5. Enter your 25-digit CD key from the back of the Exchange 2000 Server CD. Click Next to continue. The Component Selection screen will appear. You cannot select any components during a forestprep installation.
6. Verify that the action next to Microsoft Exchange 2000 is forestprep. If not, restart the process from scratch and verify you are using the correct syntax and spelling. If so, click Next to continue. The Installation Type screen will appear.

7. You have two options: create a new organization or join an existing Exchange 5.5 organization. If you select Join or Upgrade an Existing Exchange 5.5 Organization, the Select a Server in an Exchange 5.5 Organization screen will appear.
8. Once again, you'll proceed with creating a new Exchange Organization. If you select Create a New Exchange Organization, the Organization Name screen will appear.
9. In almost all cases, you will want to change the default organization name, which is First Organization. Be very careful when entering this name, as it cannot be changed once the installation process has completed. Enter the organization name you want to use and click Next to continue. The Exchange 2000 Administrator Account screen will appear.
10. Enter the account to which you want to grant full Exchange administrative privileges. This account is intended for use with the Exchange Delegation Wizard, which enables you to delegate some or all Exchange administrative rights to other users or groups. Click Next to continue.
11. The installation process then begins. When the installation process is complete, Exchange 2000 will make the Active Directory schema modifications. The installation process extends the Active Directory schema with Exchange-specific attributes. This process can take a considerable amount of time, and CPU utilization by the Local Security Authority process on the Active Directory server will likely be very high while the modifications are being made. The Exchange 2000 Server and domain controller may even appear hung. This is normal behavior. When the schema modifications are complete, the completion screen will appear.
12. Click Finish to complete the forestprep process.

Note *If you spell /forestprep incorrectly, the standard setup process will run. You will need to cancel out of the installation and rerun Setup with /forestprep spelled correctly.*

Running Setup with /domainprep Once the forestprep process has completed, you need to run Setup with the /domainprep option in every domain where Exchange will be installed, including the domain where the forestprep process was run. However, you do not need to run the domainprep process until you are ready to install Exchange on a server.

As mentioned previously, the domainprep process is the same whether you're creating a new Exchange organization or upgrading or integrating with an existing Exchange 5.5 organization. The account used to run the domainprep process must be a member of the Domain Admins group in the target domain. It must also be a local administrator on the server from which you are running domainprep.

If you spell /domainprep incorrectly, the standard setup process will run. You will need to cancel out of the installation and rerun Setup with /domainprep spelled correctly.

To run the domainprep process, log on to a Windows 2000 server that is a member of the domain in your forest using such an account. Then, from a command prompt or from the Run dialog box, execute the following command: **X:\setup\i386\setup.exe /domainprep**, where *X* is the drive containing the CD. Step through the Installation Wizard. Repeat the domainprep process in each domain that will contain an Exchange 2000 server.

When you run the domainprep process in the domain that was used for the forestprep process, the installation process is slightly shorter than it is for other domains. Specifically, you will not be prompted to accept the license agreement or enter your CD key. The Component Selection screen will eventually appear. As with a forestprep installation, you cannot select any components during a domainprep installation.

Changes Made by Setup

During the Exchange installation process, several changes are made to the target server. These include the creation of the directory structure, file shares, Exchange program group, and Exchange-specific services. In addition, a new local group is created and a domain group is made a member of the new local group.

Directory Structure

During setup, you specify the parent folder for the installation (for example, C:\Program Files\Exchsrvr). Table 6-10 describes the directory structure that is created below this parent folder.

Folder	Contents
ADDRESS	E-mail address generator and proxy DLLs. By default, DLLs for Microsoft Mail for PC and AppleTalk Networks, GroupWise, Lotus cc:Mail, SMTP, and X.400 are installed.
BIN	Exchange core components and System Manager tools.

Table 6-10. *Post-Installation Directory Structure*

Folder	Contents
CCMCDATA	Only present if Lotus cc:Mail connector is installed. Serves as temporary storage location for messages in transit between Exchange and cc:Mail.
CONNDATA	Supports the Microsoft Mail connector.
CONNECT	Contains the executables that comprise the MS Mail Interchange, the Schedule+ Free/Busy, AppleTalk, and cc:Mail components. It also includes language translator files.
DXADATA	Stores the directory synchronization database (xdir.edb), which is used by Microsoft Mail for PC Networks.
EXCHANGESERVER_ *SERVERNAME*	Full-text indices and server-specific configuration data. *Servername* is the name of the Exchange server.
EXCHWEB	Outlook Web Access files.
MAILROOT	Temporary storage location for incoming SMTP messages.
MDBDATA	Default location for public and private information stores (.ESE and .STM files) and their logs.
MTADATA	MTA configuration data and log files.
RES	String resource DLLs for the Windows 2000 Event subsystem.
SCHEMA	XML documents containing OLEBD schema data.
SERVERNAME.LOG	Message tracking and conferencing log files. *SERVERNAME* is the name of the Exchange server.
SRSDATA	Site Replication Service data.

Table 6-10. *Post-Installation Directory Structure* (continued)

Exchange-Specific Shares

The setup process also creates two shares: **address** and ***servername*.log**, where *servername* is the name of the server. Table 6-11 describes these shares.

Share Name	Path	Usage	Share Permissions
Address	\Exchsrvr\Address	Access to address objects	Administrators: Full control Servername (Exchange server itself): Full control Everyone: Read
Maildat$	\Exchsrvr\connect\msmcon\maildata	Hidden share for MS Mail messages	Administrators, Exchange server, Everyone group: Full control
Servername.log	\Exchsrvr\servname.log	Exchange message tracking logs	Administrators: Full control Servername (Exchange server itself): Full control Everyone: Read

Table 6-11. *Shares and Share Permissions Created by the Exchange Installation Program*

Exchange Program Group

Setup also creates a program group on the Start menu for Exchange. This group is called—appropriately—Microsoft Exchange, and it is located on the main Programs menu. This group contains five shortcuts:

- Active Directory Cleanup Wizard
- Active Directory Users and Computers
- Migration Wizard
- System Manager
- Exchange 5.5 Administrator (if installed)

This program group is created under the All Users profile, which means it will be on the Start menu for all users who log on locally at the Exchange server. If this is a concern to you, you can move or delete this program group without affecting Exchange.

Exchange-Specific Services

Several Exchange-specific services are added to the server during setup. Table 6-12 describes these services. Depending on the components you selected during installation, some of these services may not be present on your server.

Service	Description
Microsoft Exchange Chat	Provides support for chat communities and services Microsoft Chat and IRC clients.
Microsoft Exchange Connectivity Controller	Provides support for connectors, such as the GroupWise and Lotus Notes connectors.
Microsoft Exchange Connector for Lotus cc:Mail	Exchange uses this connector and the cc:Mail Import and Export programs to provide message transfer and directory synchronization with cc:Mail systems.
Microsoft Exchange Connector for Lotus Notes	Provides message transfer to/from and directory synchronization with Lotus Notes systems.
Microsoft Exchange Connector for Novell GroupWise	Provides message transfer to/from and directory synchronization with Novell GroupWise systems.
Microsoft Exchange Directory Synchronization	Synchronizes MS Mail Directory with Active Directory.
Microsoft Exchange Event	Provides event support for Exchange 5.5 applications.
Microsoft Exchange IMAP4	Provides access to Exchange information stores for IMAP4 clients.
Microsoft Exchange Information Store	Manages the public and private information stores.
Microsoft Exchange MTA Stacks	Provides X.400 services, including connectivity with foreign X.400 mail systems.
Microsoft Exchange POP3	Provides access to Exchange information stores for POP3 clients.

Table 6-12. *Exchange 2000 Services*

Service	Description
Microsoft Exchange Router for Novell GroupWise	Enables scheduling of collaboration with Novell GroupWise users
Microsoft Exchange Routing Engine	A COM component that acts as a simple state engine that executes and tracks processes in Exchange folders.
Microsoft Exchange Site Replication Service	Provides directory services to Exchange 5.5 servers using RPC and mail-based replication. This service works with the Active Directory connector to provide replication services between Active Directory and the Exchange 5.5 directory service.
Microsoft Exchange System Attendant	The primary administrative application used to perform miscellaneous system-related functions.
Microsoft Search	Provides full-text indexing of items in the information stores.
MS Mail Connector Interchange	Exchange uses the Connector Interchange to convert messages to MS Mail format and place them in the Microsoft Mail Connector Post Office for temporary storage.
MS SchedulePlus Free-Busy Connector	Enables sharing of Schedule+ Free/Busy information between Exchange and Microsoft Mail users. This enables users on both systems to schedule meetings and allocate resources with each other.

Table 6-12. *Exchange 2000 Services* (continued)

Security Group Changes

When the first Exchange server in a domain is installed, Setup creates a local security group in the domain called Exchange Enterprise Servers and a global security group called Exchange Domain Servers. The Exchange Domain Servers global security group is then added to the Exchange Enterprise Servers domain local security group.

Drive Letter Assignments

Once Exchange is installed and started, the contents of the information stores will be accessible via the file system and through network shares to those individuals and applications with the appropriate permissions. The Exchange Installable File System (IFS) assigns the letter M to the logical drive it creates for file system access to the information stores. You can also share this drive over the network, enabling users to access public folder and mailbox items through Windows Explorer, Network Neighborhood, Microsoft Office applications, and third-party applications.

If M is already assigned as a logical or physical drive on your server, Exchange will attempt to use the next letter and continue to do so until one is available. It is recommended, however, that you free up the M drive for use by Exchange.

Summary

Installing Exchange 2000 is a complex undertaking that requires a solid understanding of Exchange 2000, Windows 2000, and Active Directory. The first installation you perform will make permanent and extensive modifications to your Active Directory schema. Depending on your infrastructure, this could take anywhere from half an hour to an hour to complete, and it may have a serious impact on your network and your Active Directory controller. To minimize this impact, you may opt to perform preparatory installations instead.

After the first Exchange server has been installed, subsequent installations proceed more quickly. You can further optimize the installation process for additional servers by performing an unattended installation.

During the Exchange installation process, many changes are made to the server, such as the addition of directories, files and shares, and Exchange-specific services. Once the installation process has completed, Exchange can be further configured and managed using the System Manager application.

Chapter 7

Upgrading and Co-existing with Exchange 5.5

Although many companies will deploy Exchange 2000 as their first messaging system, or as a replacement for an existing messaging system, the majority of Exchange 2000 users will be existing Exchange users; that is, those upgrading to Exchange 2000 from Exchange 5.5. Generally speaking, upgrading from a Windows NT 4.0 domain and an Exchange 5.5 environment to a Windows 2000 Active Directory forest and Exchange 2000 is a relatively smooth and deliberate process. Certainly, the larger and more complicated your infrastructure, the more planning you'll need to do, and the more time you'll need to perform the migration.

The introduction of the first Exchange 2000 server into your existing Exchange 5.5 organization creates an Exchange 2000 organization in *mixed mode*. Your Exchange organization will remain in mixed mode until your last Exchange 5.5 server has been upgraded or decommissioned. Mixed mode refers to the co-existence of Exchange 2000 and pre-Exchange 2000 servers within the same organization. Once your last Exchange 5.5 server is upgraded or decommissioned, you can convert your Exchange organization from mixed mode to *native mode*. In native mode, all the servers in the Exchange organization are running Exchange 2000.

You may be familiar with the expression "the devil is in the details." When it comes to upgrading from Exchange 5.5 to Exchange 2000, the *angel* is in the details. In other words, pay attention to the details—Windows 2000 Active Directory design, Domain Name System (DNS) requirements, Global Catalog placement, effective communication with end users, and so on—and your upgrade should go well.

In this chapter, we'll discuss two important steps in your upgrade to Exchange 2000: upgrading from Exchange 5.5 and co-existing with Exchange 5.5. We are using the word "upgrade" and not "migration" because these are two different things. An upgrade is a process that advances your existing Exchange 5.5 servers and organization to the Exchange 2000 platform. This can be an in-place upgrade, where you install Exchange 2000 on top of an existing Exchange 5.5 server, or it can be a process that involves new Exchange 2000 servers and mailbox moves. Migration is a move from one mail system to a brand new Exchange 2000 organization. This move can be from any e-mail system, including Exchange 5.5. The key difference between an upgrade and migration is whether any existing Exchange 5.5 organization will be preserved and upgraded to Exchange 2000.

We are focusing solely on the upgrade process in this chapter. Obviously, you can't just flip a switch and upgrade everything overnight; you may need to co-exist with one or more Exchange 5.5 servers during the upgrade. So, this chapter also includes information on co-existing with Exchange 5.5. Each upgrade process differs, but generally speaking, the upgrade process occurs in three stages: *planning and design*, *development and testing*, and *deployment and production*. While each stage is an important factor in the success of your upgrade, the emphasis of this chapter will be on the Planning and Design stage. This is the most critical stage of the upgrade process, especially when upgrading from Exchange 5.5. Mistakes made here are not always correctable later on, and those that are correctable are often very expensive.

We will also step through the process for an in-place upgrade of an existing Exchange 5.5 server to Exchange 2000. Because the details for an upgrade from Windows NT Server 4.0 to Windows 2000 can consume entire chapters, we will begin our step-by-step upgrade with an Exchange 5.5 server that is already running Windows 2000.

This chapter is designed to be read in its entirety prior to planning or performing any upgrades. Although we cannot guarantee that every upgrade will be flawless, the information presented in this chapter should go a long way toward helping you achieve success with your upgrade.

Planning and Design

Let's face it—your upgrade can't go according to plan if you have no plan. Throughout your entire process there will be many important steps. However, none are as important as the initial planning and design steps that you perform prior to installing or upgrading anything. Depending on the size of your organization, you may be the only person performing the upgrade or you may be part of the team in charge of the upgrade process. In either case, a variety of disciplines are going to be needed in order to achieve a successful upgrade. These disciplines include knowledge of Active Directory, Domain Name System (DNS), Internet Information Services (IIS), and of course, Exchange 2000.

Fortunately, most Exchange 5.5 administrators already possess some or all of these skills. For example, Active Directory is based upon the Exchange 5.5 directory and directory service. In a way, Exchange 5.5 administrators have been managing Active Directory 0.9 for some time now. Moreover, many are also familiar with the intricacies of DNS, the use of virtual servers in IIS, and how to protect messaging systems from attacks, hacks, and viruses. So for most of you, the challenge will be in learning the new architecture, management tools, and functions of Exchange 2000.

Let's start the planning and design process by examining the requirements that will need to be met before you'll be able to upgrade. These requirements include a properly working Active Directory, healthy Dynamic DNS (DDNS) services, additional Windows 2000 components, and some legacy Exchange requirements. Much of this information was presented in Chapter 6, "Installing Exchange 2000," and we won't duplicate those efforts here. Instead, we will focus on what needs to be considered strictly from an upgrade point of view.

Network Considerations

Exchange 2000 will impact your network in several respects that merit some discussion.

Windows 2000 Site Design

Exchange 2000 relies on Windows 2000 sites to locate the closest Global Catalog servers and closest domain controllers. Windows 2000 *sites* should not be confused with the term *site* used in earlier versions of Exchange. Both concepts rely on reliable and fast connectivity, but that is where the similarities end. Sites in Windows 2000 have nothing to do with administering namespaces and domains as the term "Sites" did in legacy versions of Exchange.

Exchange 2000 requires constant access to domain controllers and Global Catalog servers. That isn't to say that it's in constant communication with these servers; however, you should treat the reliability and available bandwidth of the network connecting Exchange 2000 to these servers as if the servers were in constant communication. The same holds true for Exchange server to Exchange server communication, as well.

Note *Microsoft recommends that you have a minimum of one Global Catalog server for every four Exchange 2000 servers, and at least one Global Catalog server in each Windows 2000 site in your network. In addition, Microsoft recommends available bandwidth between an Exchange server and a Global Catalog server of 64K or higher.*

Replication

Because Active Directory is essentially the combination of your accounts database and your Exchange directory, you would think that the amount of traffic required to replicate this information around your network would be roughly the same. Unfortunately, that just isn't the case. We'll illustrate why by first examining the types of replication you should expect to see.

Active Directory Replication Active Directory replication is much more complex than Windows NT 4.0 SAM replication. In the strictest sense, Global Catalog servers are published endpoints—or target services—for replication. By default, all objects and selected attributes are replicated to all Global Catalog servers within the same domain. Exchange 2000 adds quite a few attributes for promotion and replication to the Global Catalog. In addition, some attributes are set for replication to Global Catalog servers in all of the domains in the forest.

Replication Between Exchange 5.5 and Active Directory All changes to objects in a directory need to be propagated out to all the directory service servers that store published information for the directory containing the changed object. Obviously, if you have a large directory and a large number of directory service servers, and you are making a great number of changes each day, a lot of replication data could traverse the network. To minimize the impact that changes (and therefore replication of those changes) have on your network, Active Directory implements a replication mechanism known as *per-property replication*. This means that when an Active Directory object is modified, only the modified properties are replicated.

Note *Per-property replication reduces the chances of conflict because two (or more) administrators can modify the same field at the same time. When this happens, the later of the two updates (based on a date and time stamp) prevails.*

Per-property replication is a wonderful mechanism; however, Exchange 5.5 does not support it. Exchange 5.5 only supports replication at the object level. This means that when an object in the Exchange 5.5 directory is modified and needs to be replicated to

Active Directory, the *entire* object is replicated. Once in Active Directory, however, per-property replication takes place.

Site Replication Service (SRS) The Site Replication Service (SRS) is installed on the first Exchange 2000 server installed in an Exchange 5.5 site. SRS works in conjunction with the Active Directory Connector (ADC) to provide intrasite remote procedure call-based replication and intersite mail-based replication between Active Directory and the Exchange 5.5 directory. The purpose of the SRS is to make an Exchange 2000 server appear as an Exchange 5.5 server to other Exchange 5.5 servers.

The SRS runs on an Exchange 2000 server and listens on TCP port 379. It is essentially a modified version of the Exchange 5.5 directory that uses Lightweight Directory Access Protocol (LDAP) to communicate with Active Directory and an Exchange 5.5 directory. SRS interacts with Exchange 5.5 servers as if it were a configuration and recipients replication partner.

Note *Once installed, you cannot move the SRS to a different server. This is because the SRS is server-specific, and is a hidden, enhanced version of the Exchange 5.5 directory. You can, however, create an additional SRS if needed by following the instructions in Microsoft Knowledge Base article Q255285.*

As previously mentioned, the Exchange 2000 version of the ADC replicates objects in both the site-naming context and the configuration-naming context. One of the results of this added functionality is that Exchange 2000 can read Connected Sites and Address Space information from legacy Exchange servers, and it can place this information into its link state table. This allows Exchange 2000 to utilize connectors on both Exchange 2000 and legacy Exchange servers. Likewise, Exchange 2000 connector information is replicated by the ADC and SRS to legacy Exchange servers, enabling legacy servers to use Exchange 2000 connectors. As you might have guessed, however, this means additional network traffic.

Note *The SRS works well in part because the code for it is based on the Exchange 5.5 directory service (DSAMAIN.EXE). As a result, legacy Exchange servers can send out normal directory replication notifications. In addition, the SRS requests changes in the same way as legacy versions of Exchange.*

Even though the SRS runs on an Exchange 2000 server, it is managed from the Exchange Administrator application and not from System Manager (although it can be viewed and deleted from System Manager). At first, this may seem confusing or disparate. However, when you consider that the SRS is really a modified version of the Exchange 5.5 directory, it makes sense. The SRS Properties dialog box, as shown in Figure 7-1, is very similar to the Directory Service Properties dialog box. There is an Update Now button for performing manual replication and a Check Now button for performing knowledge consistency checks of the directory.

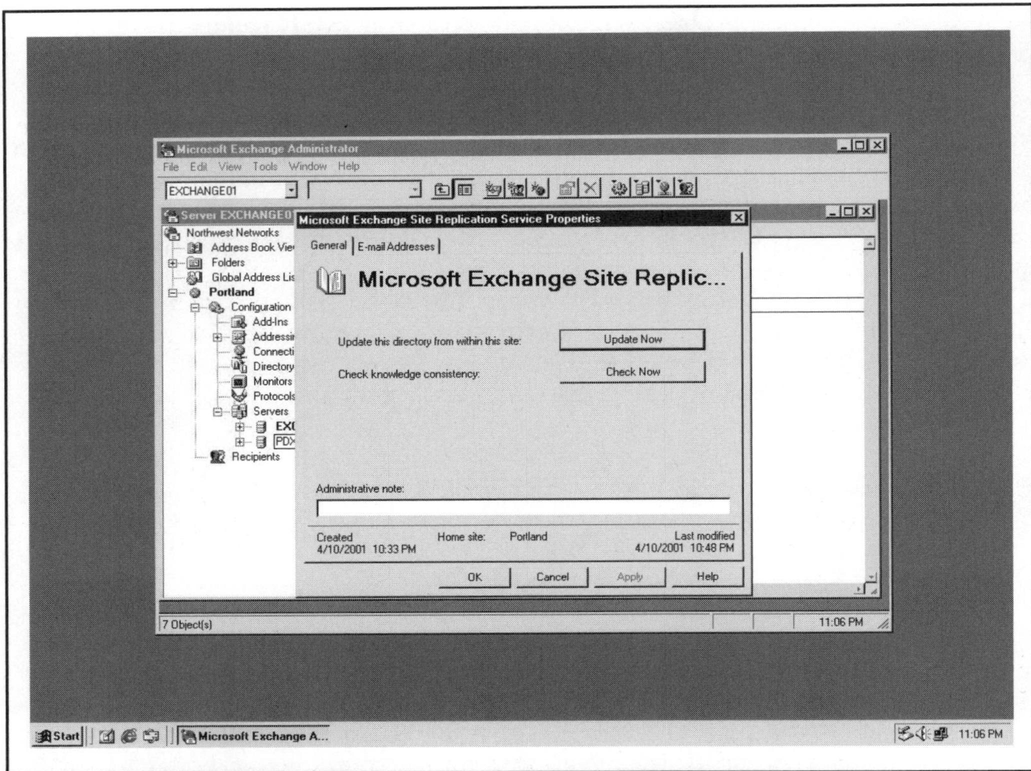

Figure 7-1. *Site Replication Service Properties dialog box as viewed from Exchange Administrator*

Dynamic DNS

As discussed in Chapter 2, "Active Directory," Dynamic DNS (DDNS) is a name server service that enables Windows 2000 computers to dynamically register several records for themselves in the DNS database. By default, every Windows 2000 computer attempts to register its own A record, its own PTR record, and Service Locator (SRV) records.

You're probably already using DNS in your environment. If you exchange SMTP e-mail with any other mail systems, then you definitely are. But you might not be using DDNS, nor might you be using a version of DNS that supports SRV records. Both Windows 2000 and Exchange 2000 require DDNS records that support SRV records as specified in RFC 2136.

Note *You're probably also using the Windows Internet Name Server (WINS) service in your environment. This service provides NetBIOS name resolution services to earlier versions of Windows. Although Exchange 2000 and Windows 2000 use DNS for name resolution, you may need to continue to have NetBIOS-dependent clients for some time. Until you're in a pure Windows 2000 environment that does not need NetBIOS in any form, keep your WINS services healthy and active.*

As the name implies, an SRV record maps the name of a network service to the IP address of the computer providing the service. Exchange 2000 doesn't register SRV records, but it needs SRV records to locate domain controllers, Global Catalog servers, and Windows 2000 sites. For example, as you now know, Global Catalog servers are very important to Exchange 2000 Servers. These special servers contain the naming contexts for the forest. Each one has a complete replica of the domain-naming context in which the server exists, and a partial replica of all other domains within the forest. Global Catalog servers register SRV records in DDNS so that users, applications, and services that need information from the Global Catalog can locate a Global Catalog server. Figure 7-2 illustrates a typical Global Catalog server SRV record.

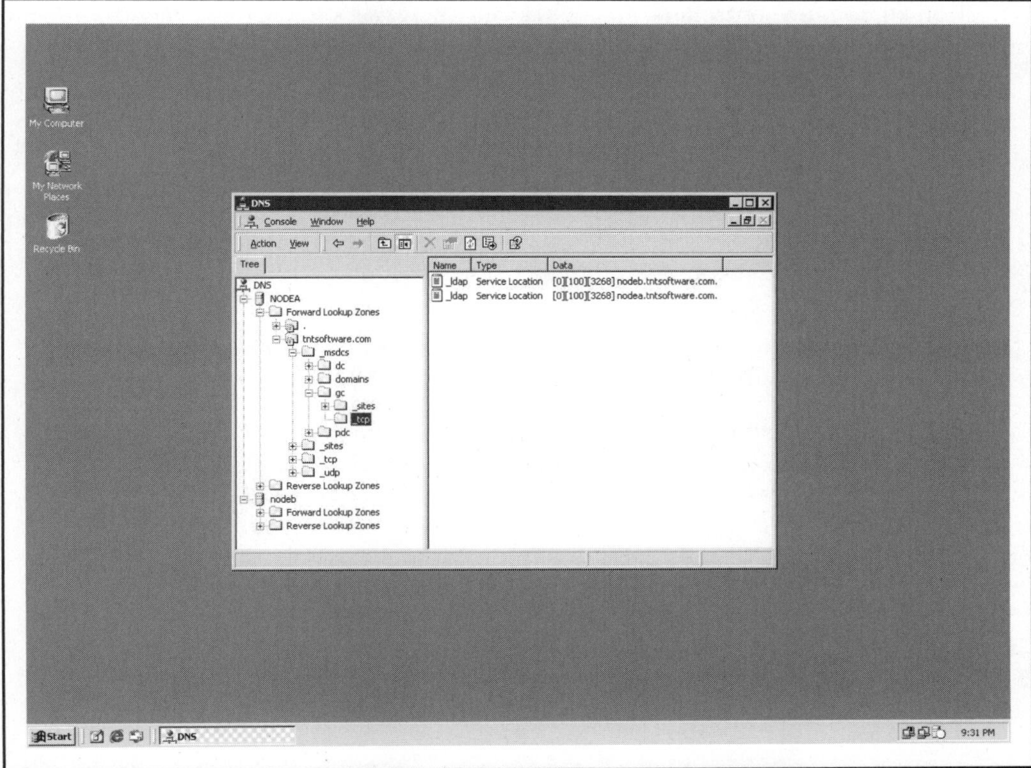

Figure 7-2. *Global Catalog server SRV record in Windows 2000 DNS*

Although DDNS is included for free with Windows 2000, you can use your existing servers if you already have DDNS in your environment. Whatever DDNS platform you use, it must support SRV records as defined in RFC 2052 and dynamic host updates as defined in RFC 2136.

Another option is to integrate your existing DNS services with the Windows 2000 DNS services. This means that if you are using DNS that does not support dynamic updates or SRV records, you can deploy Windows 2000 DNS services and integrate them with your existing DNS provider. For more information, refer to Microsoft Knowledge Base article Q255913.

Windows 2000 Considerations

In addition to the requirements set forth above, you're probably going to need to install some additional Windows 2000 components and updates. When getting ready to deploy Windows 2000 in anticipation of Exchange 2000, make sure that your deployment plans include the following software updates:

- **Windows 2000 Service Pack 1 or later** This service pack must be installed on all domain controllers, all Global Catalog servers, all Active Directory Connector servers, and all servers on which Exchange 2000 will be installed, including any Exchange 5.5 servers you plan to upgrade.
- **Post SP-1 Rollup Q271976 QFE Hotfix** This hotfix should be applied to the same servers described in the preceding entry. You can download the hotfix from http://www.microsoft.com/downloads/release.asp?ReleaseID=24075. If a more recent service pack or update is available, apply it instead of this update. You can visit http://www.microsoft.com/downloads and http://support.microsoft.com to find the most recent hotfixes for Windows 2000 and Exchange 2000.
- **Internet Information Services 5.0** This includes the World Wide Web Publishing service, the SMTP service, and the NNTP service.

You should also visit Microsoft's Windows Update Web site (http://www.windowsupdate.com) from each of these machines so that you can install the latest updates, fixes, and security patches. These types of updates, although optional, are important for the health and security of your servers. By installing all the software updates you can prior to putting the server into production, you'll save yourself at least one (if not more) maintenance routines.

Note

If Windows 2000 Service Pack 2 or later is applied to your servers, you do not and should not apply the Q271976 hotfix.

Active Directory Considerations

In case you skipped the first six chapters of this book, Exchange 2000 requires Active Directory. Exchange no longer has its own directory or directory service, opting instead to use Active Directory. If you haven't deployed any Active Directory domains in your organization, you should devise a comprehensive Active Directory design before contemplating an upgrade to Exchange 2000. This has several important ramifications for any organization that is upgrading from Exchange 5.5, and in particular, for the administrator(s) of those systems. Unless you're the sole administrator of all things IT in your organization, you're going to need to work with those who manage your accounts database, the network, name resolution services, and security.

Domain Administration

Whoever administers your existing Windows NT or Active Directory domains will need to be involved in the upgrade. You simply have no choice with Exchange 2000; you need Active Directory. This might mean upgrading an existing domain controller to Windows 2000, installing new Windows 2000 domain controllers, or installing a new Active Directory domain or forest. Until you have an Active Directory accounts database, Exchange 2000 will not even install.

User Administration

Once you've added your first Exchange 2000 server into your existing Exchange organization, you'll continue to manage the messaging components of each version using its own management applications. For example, to manage the Exchange 2000 side of a connector, you would use the System Manager snap-in; to manage the Exchange 5.5 side of that connector, you would use the Exchange Administrator application. The one exception to this practice is the administration of user objects.

Once your first Exchange 2000 server has been installed and properly configured, you should use the Active Directory Users and Computers snap-in to perform all user object administration, even for users who are using a legacy version of Exchange.

The entire messaging organization appears in the interface of both System Manager (Exchange 2000) and the Administrator program (earlier versions of Exchange). If you try to configure an Exchange 2000 object in the Administrator program, the changes you make appear to succeed; however, they are not carried out on Exchange 2000 objects. System Manager does not allow you to change objects that are managed only by earlier versions of Exchange.

Active Directory Schema Considerations

The decision to base Active Directory on the same Extensible Storage Engine (ESE) used in Exchange 5.5 was fairly obvious for Microsoft. To succeed, Active Directory needed directory service technology that was proven and scalable, capable of being extended (that is, extensible), and able to store rich data like the information in Exchange 5.5 directories. By design, the Active Directory schema—the set of object classes and attributes that describes all other objects stored in Active Directory—is *extensible.* The schema is designed to be extended in a way that allows applications to add to the list of available object classes and attribute definitions.

Exchange 2000 is one of the first applications from Microsoft—in fact *the* first application—to take advantage of this extensibility. As soon as you install your first Exchange 2000 server (or in the case of an upgrade, as soon as you install the Active Directory Connector, and again when you perform a /forestprep installation), your Active Directory schema will be permanently and irrevocably altered. Although you can uninstall Exchange 2000 and delete the newly created server from the domain, you cannot undo the schema modifications that Exchange 2000 makes. If you want to remove them, you will need to either rebuild your Active Directory, or restore it from a backup that was taken prior to installing Exchange 2000.

Note *There is another implication to consider, as well. As we discussed in Chapter 6, if you have a lot of domain controllers and Global Catalog servers in your forest, replication of the schema extensions could take considerable time. In the case of an upgrade, you'll be doing a preparatory installation prior to upgrading any of your Exchange servers. Therefore, if you have not yet deployed Active Directory, or if you're still in the early stages of deploying Active Directory, consider performing the preparatory—or /forestprep—installation early on in your Active Directory deployment.*

Active Directory Connector

As touched on in the chapter introduction, when upgrading from Exchange 5.5 to Exchange 2000 there will be a period of time during which your Exchange 2000 infrastructure will be in *mixed* mode. Mixed mode in the context of Exchange 2000 is different from Active Directory in mixed mode; however, the basic concept is the same—"mixed" refers to mixed vintages of servers, and "native" refers to all servers running the same version. For example, in a mixed-mode Active Directory, you have both Active Directory domain controllers and Windows NT 4.0 domain controllers. In a mixed-mode Exchange 2000 infrastructure, you have both Exchange 2000 servers and Exchange 5.5 servers. For our discussions, unless otherwise specified, *mixed mode* will refer to Exchange 2000 and not Active Directory.

One requirement for operating in mixed mode is the presence and use of an ADC in your Active Directory forest. The purpose of the ADC is to synchronize your Exchange 5.5 directory with your Active Directory. Although other directory synchronization tools that can perform a similar function, the ADC is a hard-coded requirement because it replicates legacy distinguished names and other important data that some tools don't. To ensure that this critical data is replicated properly, Microsoft requires the use of the ADC.

Before installing your first Exchange 2000 server in an Exchange 5.5 site, your Active Directory must be fully populated with a user object for every Exchange 5.5 mailbox in your organization. Remember, Exchange 2000 only knows about Active Directory. It does not—and cannot—access an Exchange 5.5 directory. This means that it is critical that your Active Directory accurately reflects the information in your Exchange 5.5 directory. The only way to do so is to make sure that the two directories remain synchronized at all times.

Note *The ADC synchronizes Active Directory objects with the same Security ID (SID) as objects in the Exchange directory. If the ADC finds a user object in the Exchange directory that does not have a matching SID in Active Directory, the ADC will create a user in Active Directory, and then write the SID to the SIDHistory attribute on the new object.*

The ADC will maintain synchronization between your Active Directory and your Exchange 5.5 infrastructure until the last Exchange 5.5 server in your organization is upgraded or decommissioned. As soon as you have completed the upgrade you can remove the ADC and convert your Exchange organization to *native* mode (that is, Exchange 2000 servers only).

There are two versions of the ADC: one that ships with Windows 2000 and one that ships with Exchange 2000. When upgrading from Exchange 5.5 to Exchange 2000, you must use the version of the ADC that is included on the Exchange 2000 CD. The Windows 2000 ADC only replicates objects in the site-naming context to Active Directory, whereas the Exchange 2000 ADC replicates data from both the site-naming and configuration-naming contexts. The Exchange 2000 version of the ADC can also perform the following tasks:

- Run on a continuous or scheduled basis
- Merge objects of similar properties and values
- Convert Exchange 5.5 mailboxes to mailbox-enabled users in Active Directory
- Convert Exchange 5.5 custom recipients to mail-disabled contacts in Active Directory
- Convert Exchange 5.5 distribution lists to universal distribution groups in Active Directory
- Replicate Exchange 5.5 site configuration information to administration and routing groups

Using the ADC, you configure *connection agreements* between servers that enable them to synchronize the Exchange directory with Active Directory. There are two types of connection agreements: *user connection agreements* and *configuration connection agreements*. User connection agreements—called simply, *connection agreements*—synchronize recipient information between the two directories, Active Directory and the legacy Exchange directory. Configuration connection agreements are used to replicate Exchange-specific configuration information between Active Directory and Exchange.

Active Directory Connector Requirements

Installing the ADC requires a Windows 2000 Server family product, Active Directory, and Exchange 5.5 with Service Pack 3 (SP3) or later. In fact, the best practices for this process is to have the same level of service pack—SP3 or later—on all of your Exchange servers prior to installing the ADC. Before you can install the ADC, you will need to gather the following information:

- The name and password used for the Exchange 5.5 service account
- A service account for the ADC service
- The name of the Exchange 5.5 organization
- The name and IP address of the Exchange 5.5 server to which you will connect with the ADC
- The name of the Active Directory organization unit (OU) that will be used to create the Exchange accounts in Active Directory

You will also need to perform the process using a logon account that has Enterprise Admin and Schema Admin rights in Active Directory, and local administrative rights on the server on which the ADC is installed.

Note *Although installing the ADC requires the Exchange 5.5 server to be at Service Pack 3 or later, installing Exchange 2000 into an Exchange 5.5 site only requires Service Pack 2 or later. Our recommendation is to run at least SP3. If you are affected by any of the issues described in the Microsoft Knowledge Base articles at http://support.microsoft.com/support/kb/articles/Q274/8/32.ASP and http://support.microsoft.com/support/kb/articles/Q274/8/33.ASP, then we recommend Service Pack 4. If you're already running SP4, you may want to look at the Microsoft Knowledge Base article at http://support.microsoft.com/support/kb/articles/Q282/5/33.ASP, which discusses some post-SP4 Quick Fix Engineering (QFE) files that have been released.*

During installation, the ADC will extend your Active Directory schema for use with Exchange, which is why you need Schema Admin rights. If the Schema Admin right is tightly controlled in your environment—as it should be—you can have someone with the Schema Admin right run Setup with a special switch that performs the schema modifications but does not install the ADC components. The /SchemaOnly setup switch is used for this purpose. Once the schema is extended, the person installing the ADC does not need Schema Admins rights.

ADC Account Mapping and NTDSNoMatch In Exchange 5.5, a single Windows NT domain account could be associated with more than one mailbox. For example, a user might have had his or her primary mailbox and one or more shared mailboxes where the user's account was also the *Primary Windows NT* account for those mailboxes. This type of account-to-mailbox mapping was possible because both the Windows NT account and the Exchange 5.5 mailboxes were directory objects stored in different directories. This made it possible to do mappings of a one-to-many relationship.

Exchange 2000 mailboxes are not directory objects. Instead, they are attributes of an Active Directory security principal object. As such, they cannot belong to more than one Active Directory object. This means that for each Exchange 2000 mailbox, a matching Active Directory object must exist. This doesn't mean you lose function, though. Permissions set directly on the mailbox object (for example, delegation and mailbox owner permissions) can be retained.

When the ADC encounters a situation where the same Windows NT account is the primary account on more than one mailbox, a problem arises. The ADC process moves in alphabetical order; the account closest to the start of the alphabet is processed first according to these three criteria:

- If the account exists in Active Directory and it is mailbox-enabled, the ADC will log an error and move onto the next mailbox.
- If the account exists in Active Directory but is not mailbox-enabled, the ADC will mailbox-enable the existing account.
- If an Active Directory account does not yet exist, the ADC will create a mailbox-enabled user account that is disabled from use.

The problem is that when the ADC encounters the second or subsequent mailbox that is associated with the same Windows NT account, it will find a pre-existing mailbox-enabled user account. When this happens, ADC creates a new user account using the name of the second mailbox, mailbox-enables it, and then sets it to disabled. The multiple Exchange 5.5 mailboxes become separate mailbox-enabled user objects in Active Directory that won't be accessible by the user whose Windows NT account was mapped to them.

Because accounts are processed by the ADC from A-Z, it's possible (and the larger your company the more probable) that a shared mailbox will be processed before a user's primary mailbox. If this happens, the user will have access to the shared mailbox that was matched to the user's Windows NT account, but not to his or her primary mailbox because that will be made an attribute of another Active Directory object.

Fortunately, you can control which mailboxes get matched to accounts and which don't. It involves setting Custom Attribute 10 on the Exchange 5.5 mailboxes (that is, the shared mailboxes) to NTDSNoMatch. When the mailbox's Custom Attribute 10—shown via an LDAP query as *Extension-Attribute-10*—is set to NTDSNoMatch the ADC does not try to match the mailbox to a user account and instead creates a new mailbox-enabled user account that is disabled. The upside is that this gives you control of the situation and prevents the problems we just described . However, there are two downsides:

- If you already have Custom Attribute 10 populated with data, you're going to either need to change the data or endure the problems we just described.
- The larger your Exchange directory, and the greater the number of shared mailboxes, the more difficult this task can be.

There is a solution for the second downside. Microsoft has a tool called NTDSNoMatch—also known as NTDSAtrb—which can be used to produce a report that specifies mailboxes that have the same primary Windows NT account. Microsoft has documentation on using this tool in its Knowledge Base at http://support.microsoft.com/support/kb/articles/Q274/1/73.ASP.

Tip *According to Microsoft Knowledge Base article Q274173, the NTDSNoMatch tool can only be obtained from Microsoft's Product Support Services. Despite what this article says, however, the tool can be downloaded from http://www.exinternals.com, an Exchange 2000 Web site run by a program manager at Microsoft. At this site, the tool is called NTDSAtrb. If you can't find it at this site, you can contact Microsoft PSS to obtain it.*

Installing the Active Directory Connector

Performing the actual installation process is relatively straightforward. As we mentioned previously, the ADC installation process will extend your Active Directory schema. The schema modification process and replication of the schema changes have an adverse effect on your domain controllers and Global Catalog servers. You may therefore choose to perform the installation during hours of low activity.

Before installing the ADC, make sure you have reviewed the installation requirements, which are documented in Microsoft Knowledge Base article Q253286. To install the ADC on an Active Directory domain controller:

1. Insert the Exchange 2000 Server CD into the CD drive and navigate to the ADC\i386 folder. Then, execute SETUP.EXE. The ADC Installation Wizard appears, as shown in Figure 7-3.

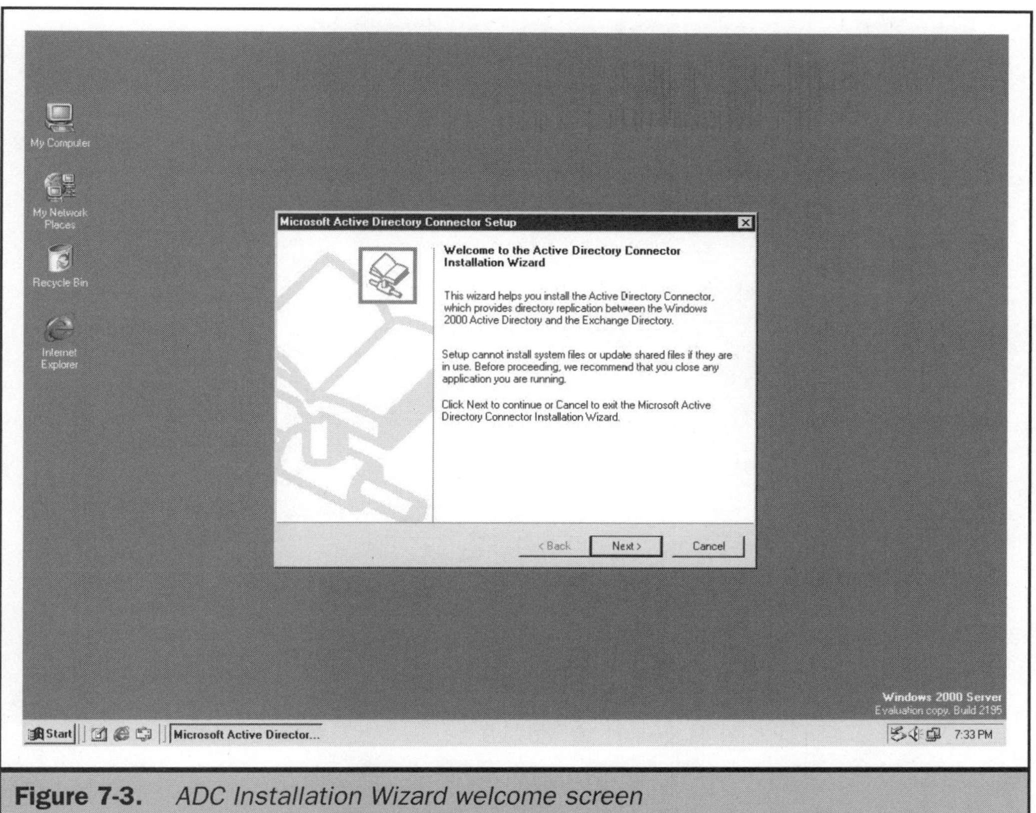

Figure 7-3. *ADC Installation Wizard welcome screen*

2. Click Next to continue.
3. On the Component Selection screen, which is shown in Figure 7-4, select both the ADC service component and the ADC management components, and click Next to continue.

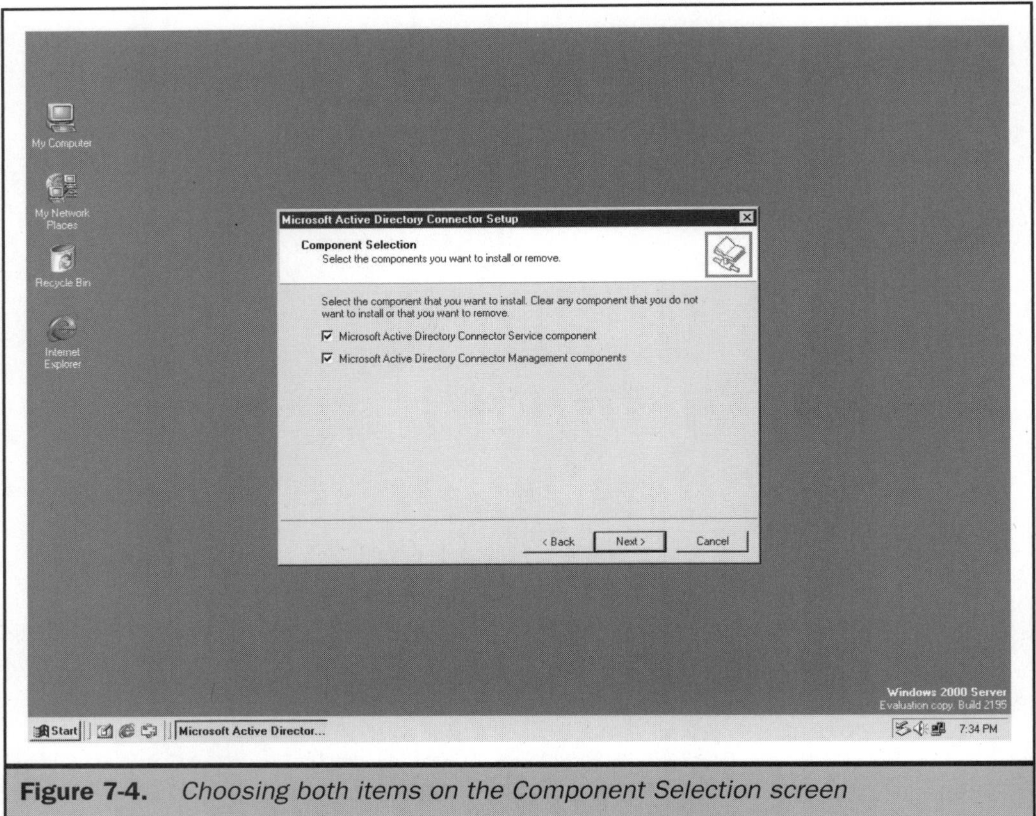

Figure 7-4. *Choosing both items on the Component Selection screen*

4. Specify where you want the ADC components to be installed. The default, as shown in Figure 7-5, is C:\Program Files\MSADC. Click Next to continue.

Note

You cannot manually enter anything in the Folder path. If you want to change the installation location, you must use the Browse button to browse to the desired location.

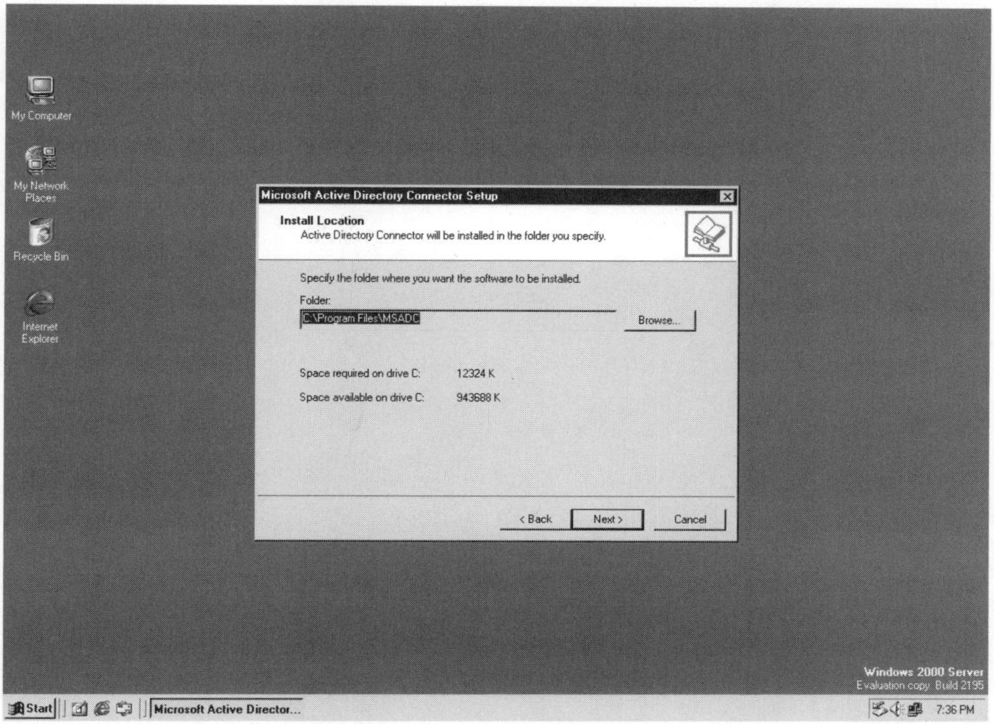

Figure 7-5. *Specifying the ADC's location on the Install Location screen*

5. Provide the account name and password for the service account you want to use for the ADC on the Service Account screen, which is shown in Figure 7-6. Click Next to continue.

You need to use a service account for the ADC because a subset of its components is included in Windows 2000. For additional information on the service account requirements for the ADC, see Microsoft Knowledge Base article Q249817.

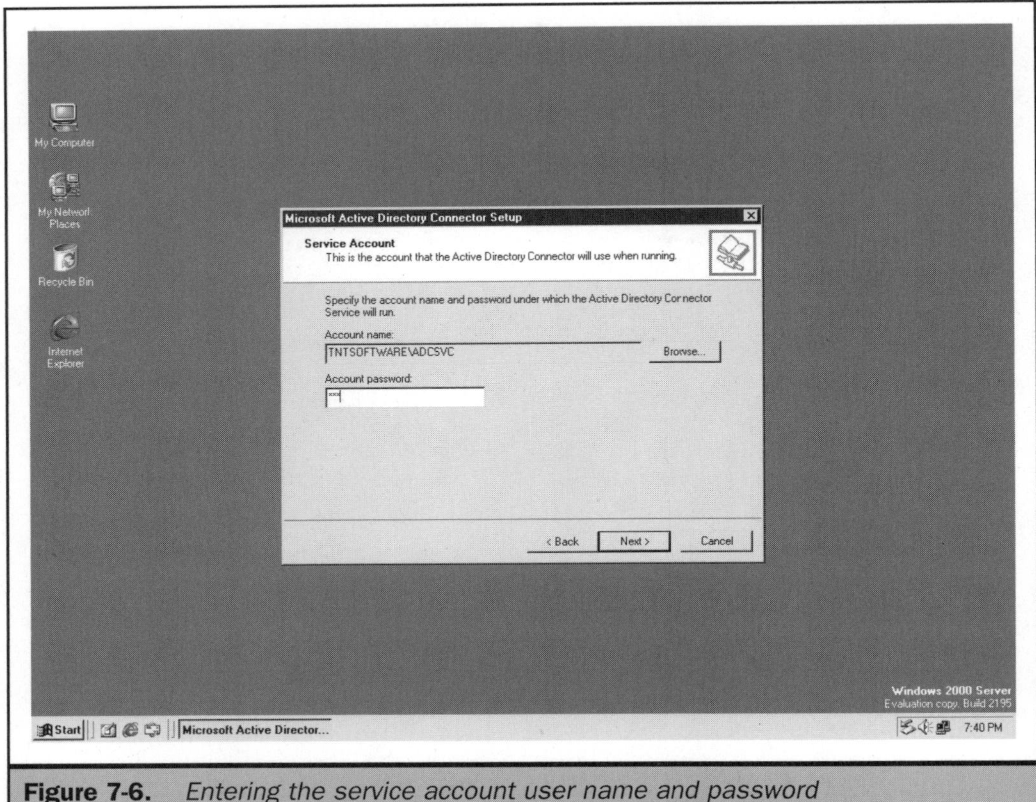

Figure 7-6. *Entering the service account user name and password*

Setup will copy the ADC files to the specified install location. Once the file copy process has completed, the Active Directory schema will be updated with new extensions that are required by the ADC, and ultimately by Exchange 2000. The schema update process may take a while to complete. In addition, CPU utilization by the Local Security Authority (LSASS.EXE) process on the domain controller on which the ADC is being installed may be very high while the modifications are being made. In fact, the domain controller may even appear to be hung during this phase. However, you should see its status being updated at times during the Active Directory schema modifications, as shown in Figure 7-7.

Once the schema modifications have completed, the setup process will configure the appropriate permissions and registry entries for the ADC and for ADC administration. At the end of the installation, a message indicating a successful installation should appear. Click the Finish button to close the ADC Installation Wizard. You'll find a shortcut for

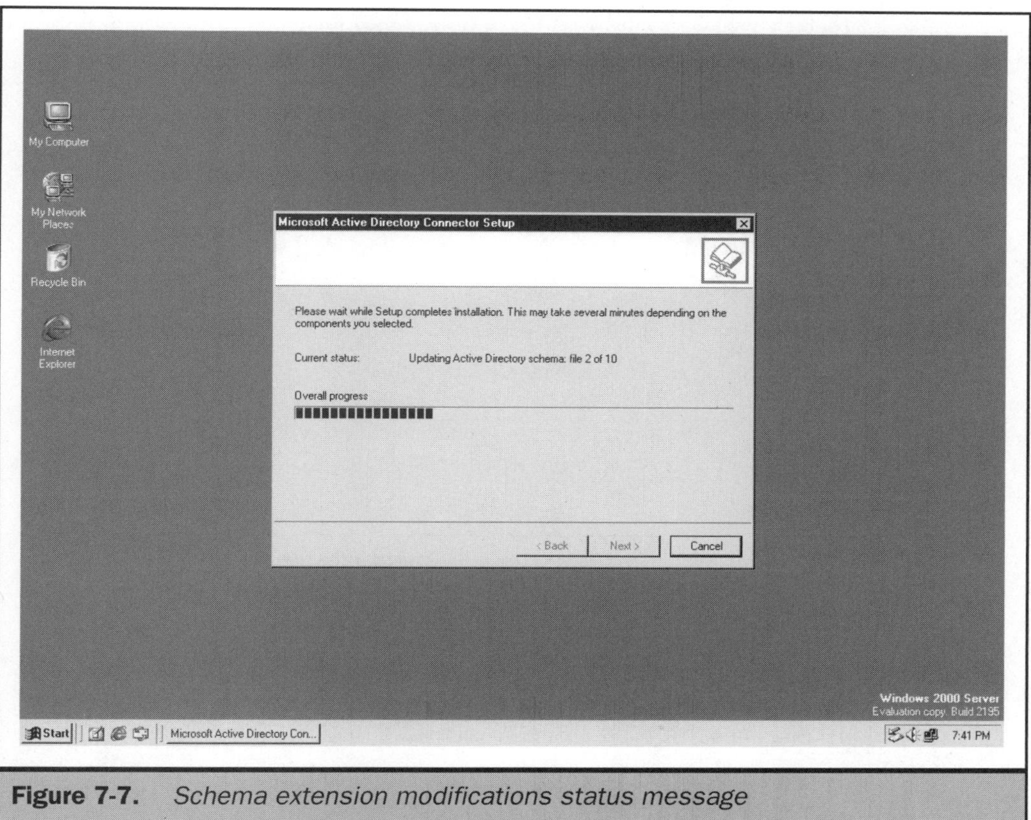

Figure 7-7. *Schema extension modifications status message*

launching the ADC Manager on the Start Menu, under Programs, and then Microsoft Exchange. A copy of that shortcut is also placed in the Administrative Tools menu.

Using the Active Directory Connector Manager

The ADC Manager is a Microsoft Management Console (MMC) snap-in that can be used to create, remove, and manage connection agreements. The Manager communicates with the ADC server process (ADC.EXE) when creating connection agreements and to get connection agreement status information.

Diagnostic Logging When troubleshooting replication issues, you can use the ADC Manager to turn on diagnostic logging. You can configure the ADC components to log events to the application event log on the ADC server. Diagnostic logging is available for replication, account management, attribute mapping, the ADC service, and LDAP operations. Seasoned Exchange administrators will recognize the familiar logging level settings of None, Minimum, Medium, and Maximum. By default, diagnostic logging is set to None.

To configure diagnostic logging for the ADC:

1. In ADC Manager, right-click on the Active Directory Connector (Server) object and click Properties.
2. Select the Diagnostic Logging tab, as shown in Figure 7-8.
3. Select the category for which you want to enable logging.
4. Select a logging level for that category.
5. Click Apply, and then click OK to enable logging.

If you want to set more than one category to the same level of logging, you can use CTRL*-click or* SHIFT*-click to select multiple categories.*

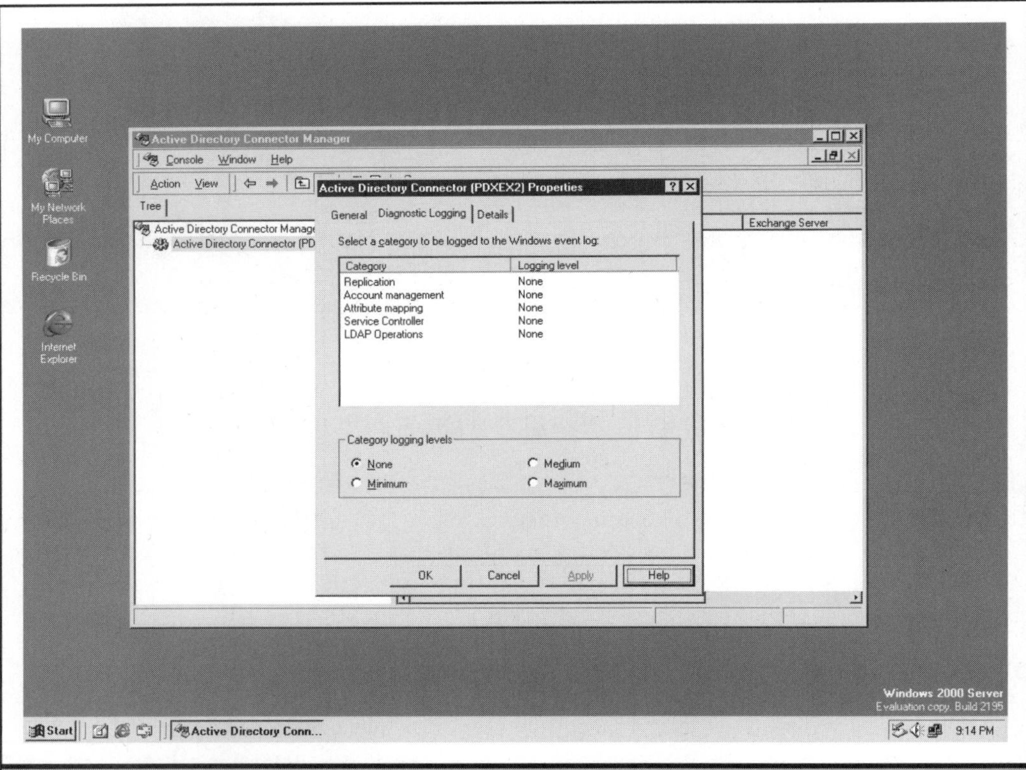

Figure 7-8. *Selecting the Diagnostic Logging tab on the Active Directory Connector Properties dialog box*

Creating Connection Agreements

Once the ADC is installed, the next step is to create a Recipient Connection Agreement (CA) between your Exchange 5.5 directory and your Active Directory. During this multistep process, you'll specify the replication direction, select one or more bridgehead servers, configure rules for item deletion, and specify a replication schedule.

To create a Recipient CA using ADC Manager:

1. Right-click on the Active Directory Connector (Server) object and select New | Recipient Connection Agreement. The new CA Properties dialog box appears, as shown in Figure 7-9.
2. In the Name field, enter a name for the CA.
3. In the Replication Direction field, select the type of replication you want to use. You can choose one-way replication in either direction or two-way replication (that is, replication in both directions). Depending on which selection you make here, some of the other tabs may be grayed out and unavailable.

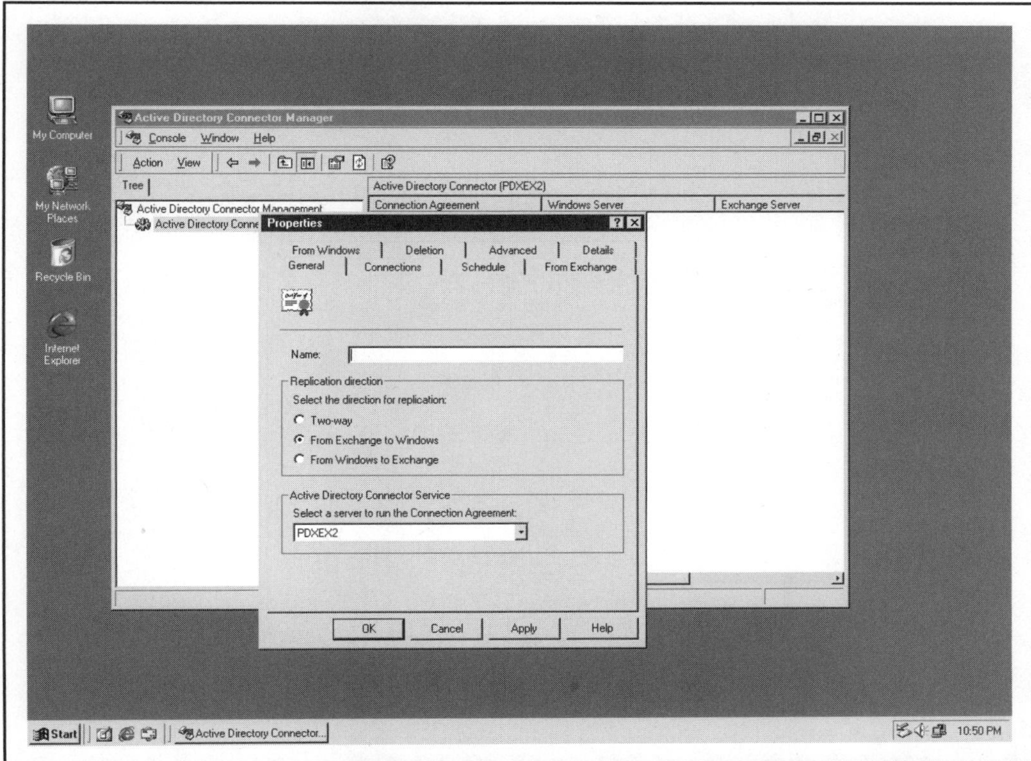

Figure 7-9. *Properties dialog box for New Recipient Connection Agreement*

Tip *If you want to manage objects from both Exchange Administrator and Active Directory Users and Computers, choose the Two-Way replication option. Otherwise, choose replication that moves from the platform used to manage the objects to the other platform. For example, if you are going to manage the objects using Exchange Administrator, choose the From Exchange To Windows option.*

4. Each ADC Server in your forest will be listed in the Active Directory Connector Service drop-down box. Select the server on which you wish to host the CA from this drop-down box.
5. Next, select the Connections tab, as shown in Figure 7-10.
6. In the Windows Server Information and Exchange Server Information sections, enter the server names, authentication settings, and credential information you want to use. You can choose from Basic With SSL, Windows Challenge/Response, and Windows Challenge/Response With SSL Authentication.

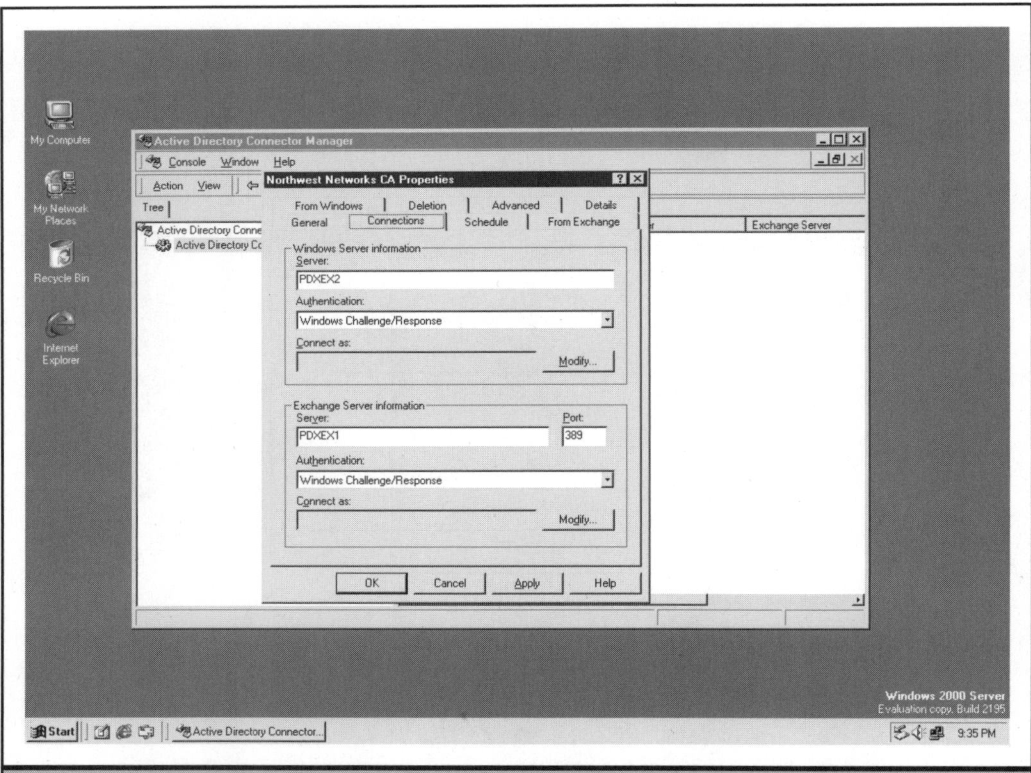

Figure 7-10. *Recipient Connection Agreement Connections tab*

Note

*If you chose Two-Way or From Windows To Exchange replication, the account you specify in the **Connect as** field for the Exchange Server information will need write permissions to your Exchange 5.5 directory. In addition, if the Exchange 5.5 server to which the connection is being made is running Windows 2000, you'll need to change the Port for the Exchange Server information to the port you specified for the LDAP service in Exchange Administrator when you upgraded to Windows 2000.*

7. After entering the connection information, select the Schedule tab, which is shown in Figure 7-11. Configure the schedule as your needs dictate. Increase the frequency of the schedule to correspond with your needs to have the changes made quickly. In some environments, it may be preferable to set the schedule to Always and replication to 15-minute intervals.

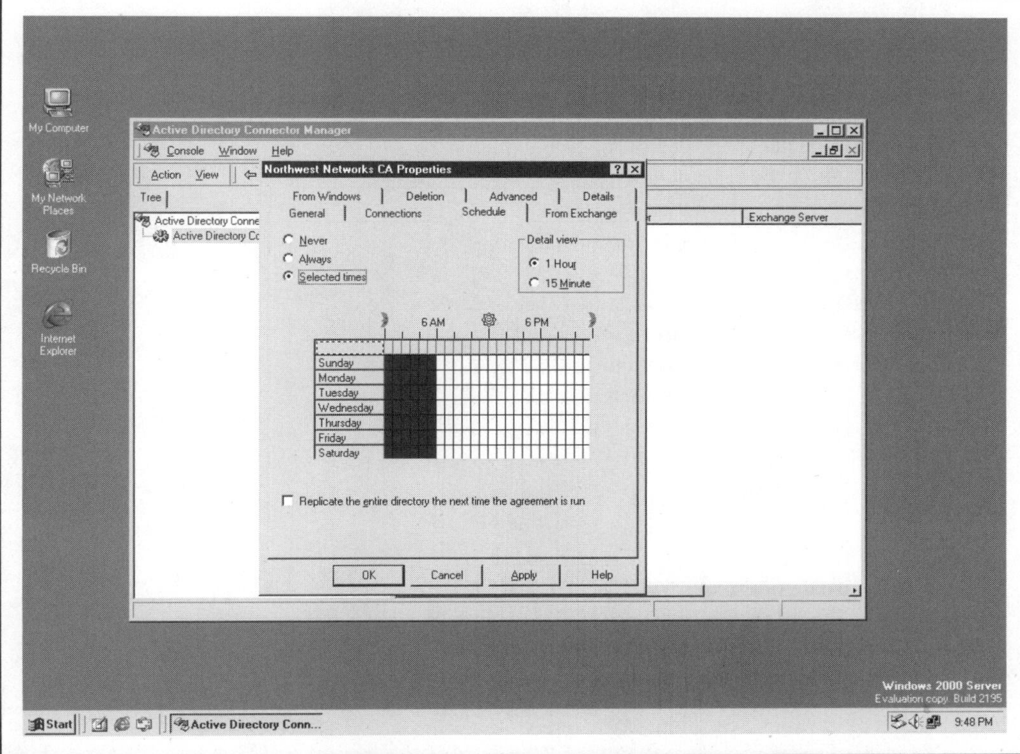

Figure 7-11. *Recipient Connection Agreement Schedule tab*

You can trigger full directory replication by checking the Replicate The Entire Directory The Next Time The Agreement Is Run checkbox.

8. Select the Deletion tab, as shown in Figure 7-12. Use the options on this tab to configure rules for deleting objects. We recommend using the Keep… options for both replication deletion settings. This will provide you with a fallback mechanism in case an object gets overwritten accidentally.
9. Select the Advanced tab, as shown in Figure 7-13. If you are replicating from Active Directory to Exchange 5.5, set the Windows Server Entries Per Page field to the desired level. If you are replicating from Exchange 5.5 to Active Directory, set the Exchange Server Entries Per Page field to the desired level. If you are using a two-way CA, set both options.

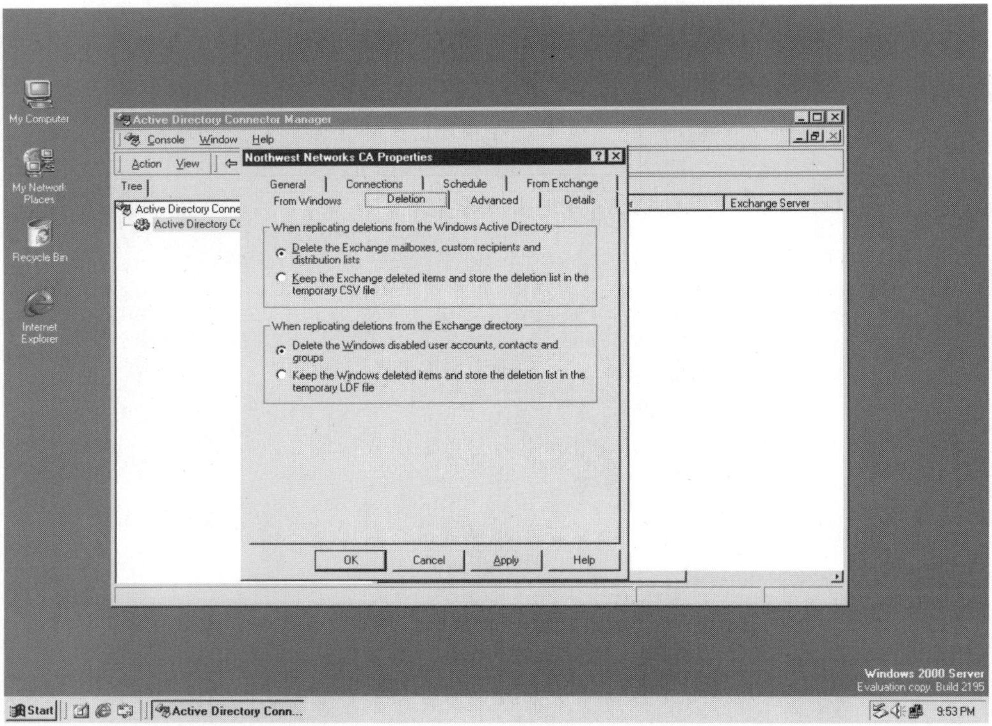

Figure 7-12. *Recipient Connection Agreement Deletion tab*

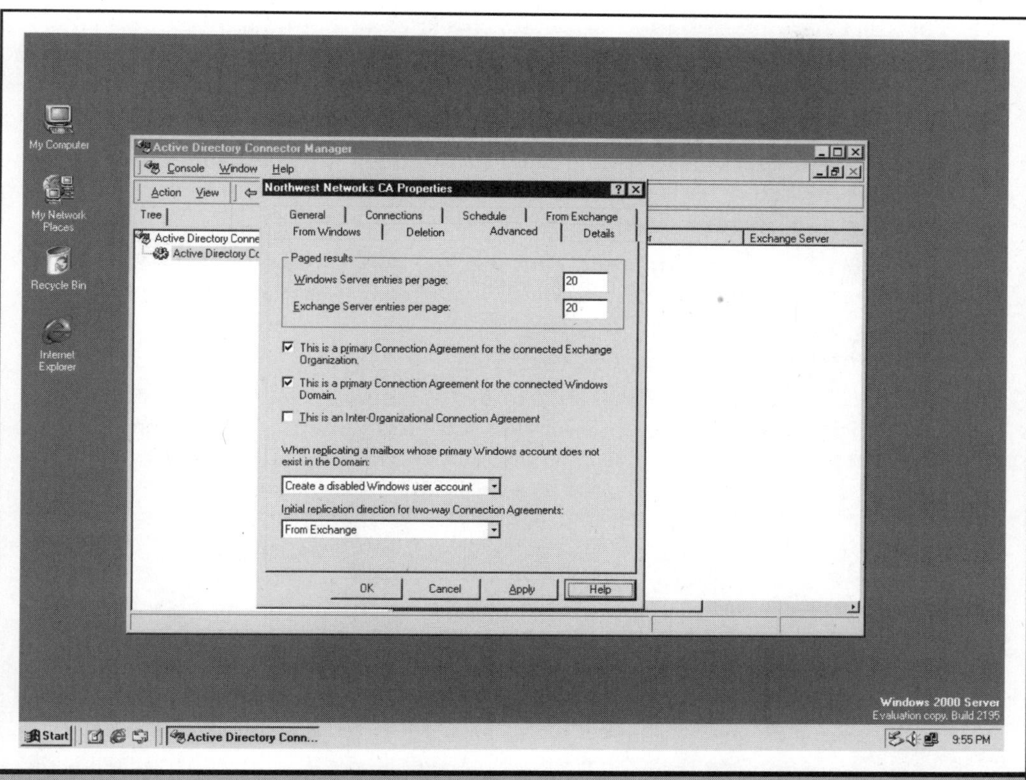

Figure 7-13. *Recipient Connection Agreement Advanced tab*

Note *For efficiency, the ADC uses a process called 'paging' to batch objects into groups for replication purposes. You can configure the number of objects (or entries) per page to control the number of replication requests. Larger page sizes that contain more than the default number of entries will cause fewer requests to occur. However, more memory will be required to accomplish this. Setting the entries per page to 0 turns off paging altogether. Be careful not to set the number of Exchange Server entries to a value higher than the value specified for the LDAP search results in Exchange.*

10. If this is the only Recipient CA for the Exchange organization, the This Is A Primary Connection Agreement For The Connected Exchange Organization checkbox will be checked by default. Likewise, if this is the only Recipient CA for the Windows 2000 domain, the This Is A Primary Connection Agreement

For The Connected Windows Domain checkbox will also be checked. If your Active Directory contains a different Exchange organization from the one you use in Exchange 5.5, enable the This Is An Inter-Organizational Connection Agreement checkbox.

11. Next, choose how you want to handle accounts for replicated mailboxes that do not have an Active Directory account. You can create a new user account, a new disabled user account, or an Active Directory contact.
12. The last Advanced tab option is choosing the initial replication direction for two-way CAs. If your CA is a one-way connection, you can ignore this drop-down box. If you are using two-way replication, select the direction in which you want the replication to occur first.
13. If you are replicating from Exchange to Active Directory, select the From Exchange tab, which is shown in Figure 7-14. Click the Add button to specify the recipients containers you want replicated. Then, click the Modify button to specify the

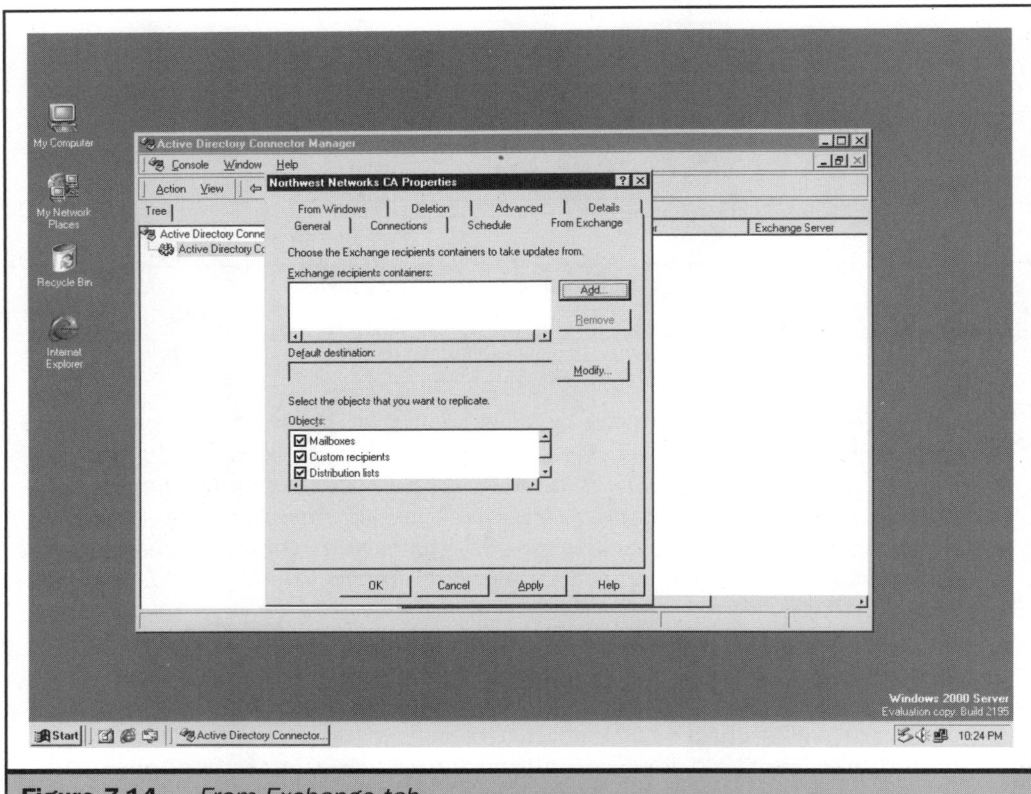

Figure 7-14. *From Exchange tab*

Active Directory OU to which you want the Exchange containers replicated. By default, mailboxes, custom recipients, and distribution lists are checked for replication. If desired, you can uncheck one or more of the objects.

14. If you are replicating from Active Directory to Exchange, select the From Windows tab, as shown in Figure 7-15. Use the Add button to add one or more OUs to be replicated to the Exchange 5.5 directory. Click the Modify button to specify the recipient container to which you want replication to occur. By default, user, contact, and group objects are replicated. If desired, you can uncheck one or more of these objects. If you want secured Active Directory objects—objects whose access control list (ACL) contains an explicit deny access control entries (ACE)—replicated to Exchange 5.5, put a check in the appropriate checkbox. If you want the Exchange 5.5 distinguished name to be referenced when creating the object, select the appropriate checkbox.

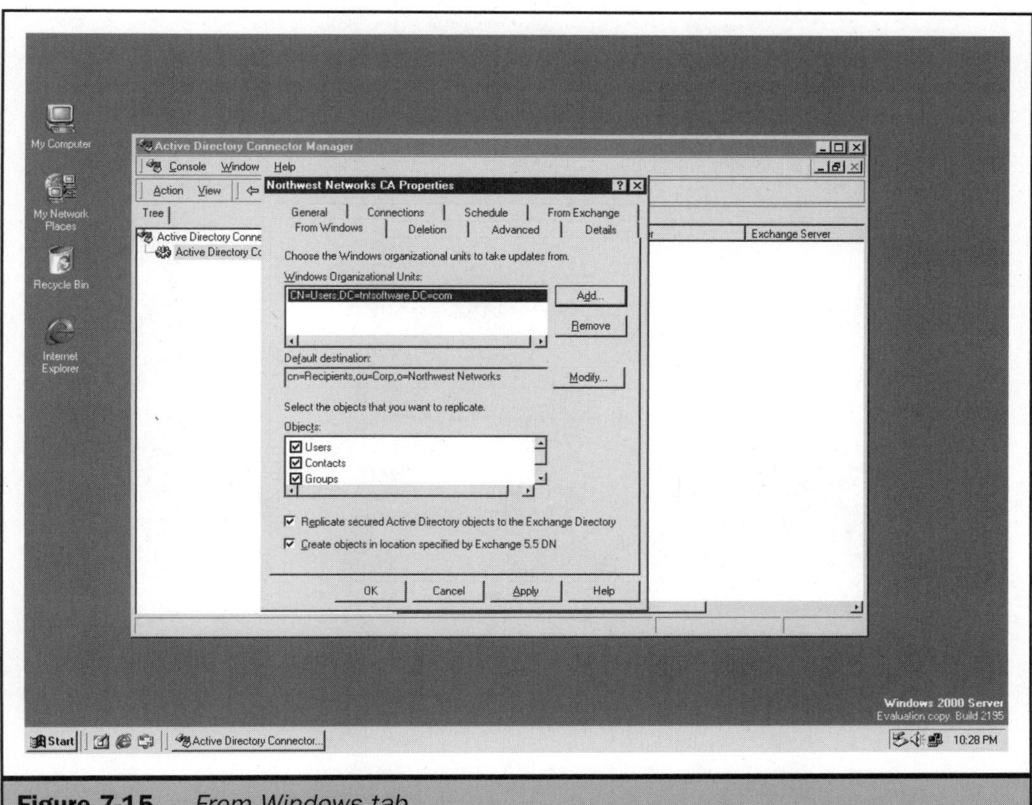

Figure 7-15. *From Windows tab*

15. Finally, click the Details tab, shown in Figure 7-16, and enter any administrative notes that you want.
16. Click OK to save the CA.

When creating your first connection agreement between Exchange 5.5 and Active Directory, you will receive a confirmation message after clicking OK. The message, which is shown in Figure 7-17, explains that the intra-organizational connections are used to synchronize Active Directory with Exchange 5.5 in preparation for the deployment of Exchange 2000 in the forest.

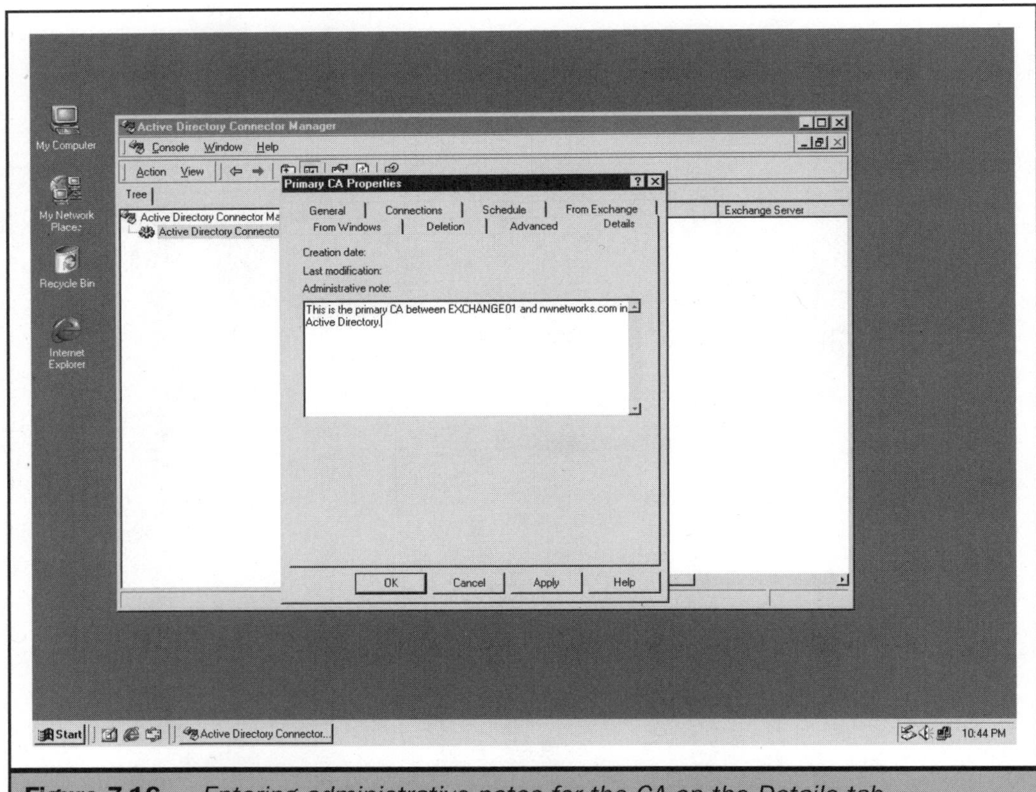

Figure 7-16. *Entering administrative notes for the CA on the Details tab*

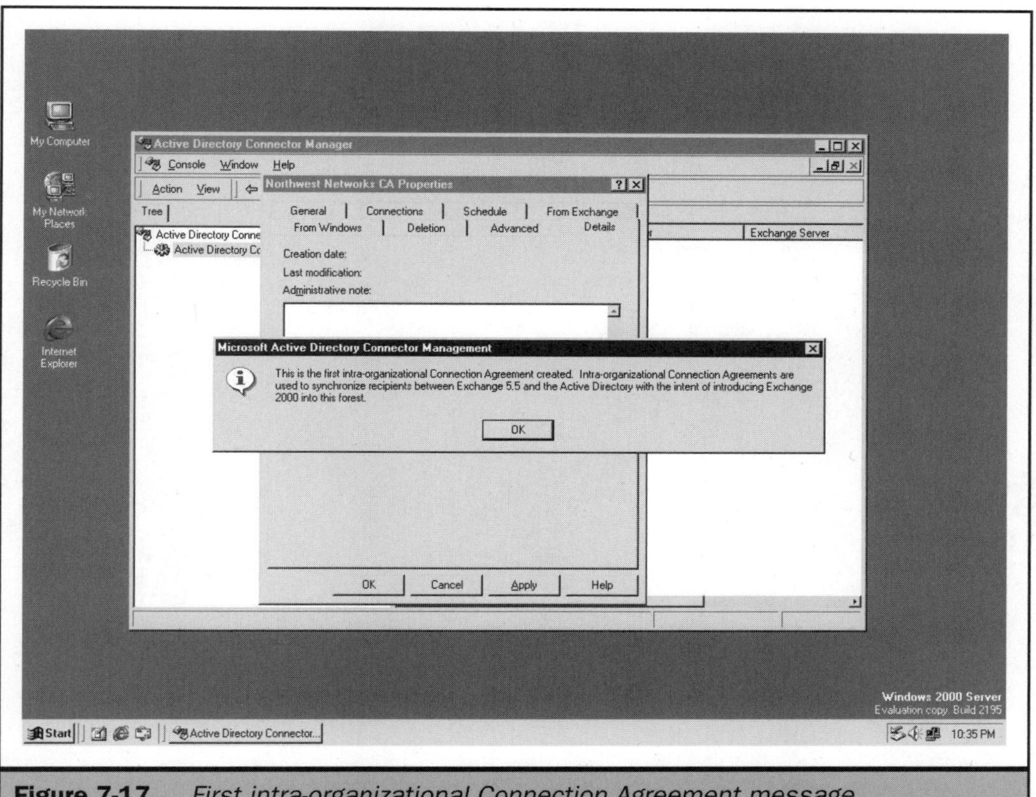

Figure 7-17. *First intra-organizational Connection Agreement message*

In addition, if the Windows 2000 domain in which the CA is being made is a mixed-mode domain, a second message dialog box will appear. This message, shown in Figure 7-18, recommends that you replicate your Exchange 5.5 distribution lists to a Windows 2000 domain that is running in native mode. If you do not heed this warning, your public folder permissions will be broken.

The ADC will also create two new Active Directory security groups: Exchange Enterprise Servers and Exchange Domain Servers. These groups, which will be created in the users container you specified on the From Windows tab, are used to hide distribution list membership for mail-enabled groups.

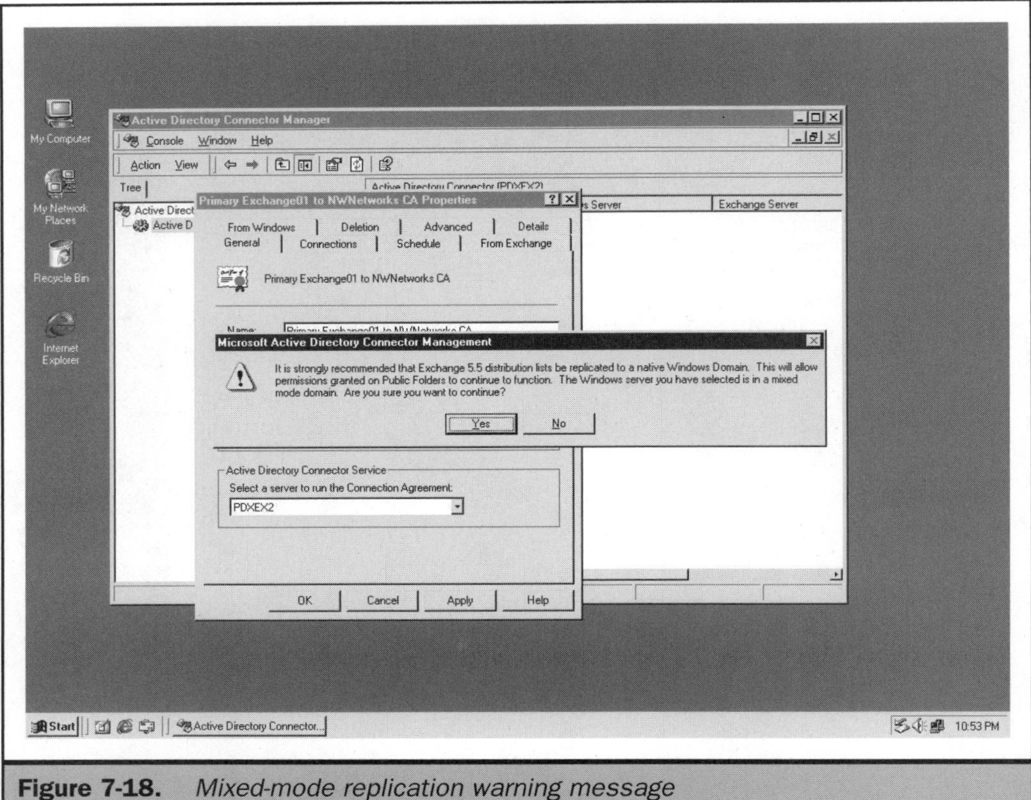

Figure 7-18. *Mixed-mode replication warning message*

Once the CA has been created, you can initiate replication immediately by right-clicking on the CA in ADC Manager, and then selecting Replicate Now.

Legacy Exchange Pre-Installation Requirements

Regardless of which upgrade path you choose, your legacy Exchange infrastructure must be running Exchange 5.5 with Service Pack 3 or later. For these machines to be upgraded directly, they will also need to be running a Windows 2000 Server family product with the additional software and components described earlier in the section,

"Windows 2000 Considerations." In addition, several pre-installation tasks need to be performed prior to upgrading an Exchange 5.5 server.

When describing these procedures, we assume you have already upgraded your Exchange 5.5 SP3 (or later) server to Windows 2000 and that you have met the Windows 2000 requirements set forth in the "Windows 2000 Considerations" section. For information on upgrading an Exchange 5.5 Server from Windows NT 4.0 to Windows 2000, see the Microsoft White Paper entitled "Upgrading Microsoft Exchange Server 5.5 to the Windows 2000 Platform," which can be downloaded from http://www.microsoft.com/exchange/techinfo/Upgrade2000.htm.

The pre-installation tasks are designed to verify and validate your existing environment before you upgrade, and to provide you with a fallback mechanism in case the upgrade fails or is unsuccessful. Specifically, you need to remove unsupported connectors, run the MTACheck utility, run the Knowledge Consistency Checker (KCC), run the DS/IS Consistency Adjuster, and take a full and complete backup of the system. Once these steps have been completed, you uninstall any software that is incompatible with Exchange 2000.

Removing and Rerouting Unsupported Connectors

If you're planning an in-place upgrade, remove any connectors that aren't supported by Exchange 2000. The following connectors are not supported by Exchange 2000 and need to be removed:

- IBM Professional Office System (PROFS)
- Vision/VM
- Systems Network Architecture Distribution System (SNADS)

If, after the upgrade, you will still need these connectors, install and configure them on another Exchange 5.5 server prior to upgrading. If you won't need these connectors after the upgrade, you can remove them completely.

Running MTACheck

As its name implies, the Message Transfer Agent Check (MTACheck) utility is used to ensure that the MTA database is in a consistent and healthy state. MTACheck scans the internal MTA database for objects that are damaged or that are interfering with normal queue processing. It can also remove directory replication, public folder replication, and link monitor messages that are interfering with normal operations. The utility is located in the \Bin folder on your Exchange 5.5 server, and it is run from a command line.

You should run this procedure on each Exchange 5.5 server you plan to upgrade. To run MTACheck as part of your pre-installation tasks:

1. Open a registry editor, navigate to HKLM\System\CurrentControlSet\Services\MSExchangeMTA\Parameters\MTA Database Path, and verify that this entry is pointing to the proper location. Close the registry editor when finished.
2. Stop the MTA service.
3. Back up all files with a .DAT extension in the MTA directory. Note: Do *not* delete anything.
4. Go to a command prompt and navigate to the \Exchsrvr\Bin folder.
5. Type the following command and press ENTER to execute it:

   mtacheck /f *mtacheck.log* /v /rp /rd /rl

   /f specifies the log file, which in this example is called mtacheck.log. You can use any file name you want.

   /v specifies verbose mode, which ensures that all the details (good and bad) get logged to the file.

   /rp specifies that public folder replication messages should be removed.

   /rd specifies that directory replication messages should be removed.

   /rl specifies that link monitor messages should be removed.

MTACheck is typically a fast procedure capable of processing about 1000 messages per minute. When the process has completed, the results will be displayed. If the returned results include any errors, delete all files from the \Exchsrvr\Mtadata\Mtadata.out folder and repeat steps 2-5 above. If no errors occur, MTACheck ends with the message "Database clean, no errors detected." Once this message is returned, you can restart the MTA service. Do not restart the MTA service until MTACheck returns this message.

Note *You may see a message that indicates that data was lost during this process. Items that were damaged or corrupted are typically one of two types: those that are disposable, such as replication and link monitor messages, and those that were unsalvageable to begin with. Replication and link monitor messages are regenerated, making them expendable. Continue to repeat steps 2-5 until the "Database clean, no errors detected" message is displayed.*

Running the Knowledge Consistency Checker

Once the MTACheck utility has completed without errors, the next step is to run the Knowledge Consistency Checker (KCC). Prior to Exchange 2000, each Exchange server had its own directory, which was synchronized with the directories on all other Exchange servers in the organization to ensure that each server had the same information about all the Exchange objects. Once each day, directory service knowledge consistency is automatically checked to verify synchronization.

When you upgrade an Exchange 5.5 server to Exchange 2000, the server's old Exchange directory will be removed because it is no longer needed. To make sure that the upgraded Exchange 2000 server inherits the most recent information about the Exchange 5.5 site it is joining, run the KCC. To run the KCC:

1. Open Exchange Administrator and navigate to the server you are upgrading.
2. Select the Directory Service object and click the Properties button.
3. On the General tab, click the Check Now button. Knowledge consistency will be checked and a success or failure message will be generated. In addition, an event similar to the following will be logged in the server's application log:

```
Event Type: Information
Event Source:     MSExchangeAdmin
Event Category:   Replication Configuration
Event ID:  2022
Date:      5/15/2001
Time:      2:44:09 PM
User:      N/A
Computer:  PDXEX1
Description:

Calling the knowledge consistency checker on server 'PDXEX1.'
```

4. Click OK to clear the message.

DS/IS Consistency Adjuster

The DS/IS Consistency Adjuster is used to recreate missing directory objects for mailboxes and public folders that exist in the information store but not in the directory. In addition, this process can remove invalid ACL entries from mailboxes and public folders, and reset the home database (Home-MDB) attribute for public folders that are homed on unknown servers or in unknown sites.

This process is used most often in restore and disaster recovery scenarios; however, it has a place in your upgrade procedure, as well. You'll want your Exchange 2000 server and Active Directory information as clean as possible. Many organizations, especially medium and large companies, have a lot of invalid data in their Windows NT 4.0 accounts databases and their Exchange directories. This leads to broken ACLs, invalid objects, ghosted objects, and so forth. During regular operations, these broken and invalid items don't present any real problems; they're just junk items on the ACL list.

Nonetheless, you need to remove this invalid data prior to upgrading because it represents a security problem that breaks public folders once they're in Active Directory. Active Directory translates Exchange 5.5 public folder ACLs into Windows 2000 ACLs. Active Directory locates the user associated with the Exchange 5.5 distinguished name, and stamps the user's new Windows 2000 Security ID (SID) on the public folder object. If Active Directory can't find a user because of invalid data (for example, the user account no longer exists), the distinguished name remains in the ACL. This makes the public folder inaccessible because Active Directory can't validate any credentials. If it can't validate credentials, Active Directory explicitly denies access to the object. Therefore, it is critical that you run the DS/IS Consistency Adjuster prior to upgrading. To run the DS/IS Consistency Adjuster:

1. Open Exchange Administrator and navigate to the server you are upgrading.
2. Select the server and click the Properties button.
3. Navigate to the Advanced tab.
4. Click the Consistency Adjuster button. The DS/IS Consistency Adjustment dialog box will appear, as shown in Figure 7-19.
5. Select all the checkboxes, and then check the radio button to filter all inconsistencies.
6. Click OK to start the adjuster.
7. A warning message appears. Click OK to proceed and perform synchronization.
8. Once this process has completed, click OK to close the server Properties dialog box.

System Backup

The last task before upgrading an Exchange 5.5 server to Exchange 2000 is to take a full and complete backup. This is a backup of everything on the server including the Exchange databases and log files, the Windows 2000 System State, and other critical information. This backup is necessary in case the upgrade fails and you need to revert back to Exchange 5.5.

Taking a full backup before upgrading isn't just common sense; it's a requirement if you need to be able to roll back a failed upgrade. Later in this chapter, we will discuss a process for rolling back from failed upgrades; having a full backup is the linchpin of that process.

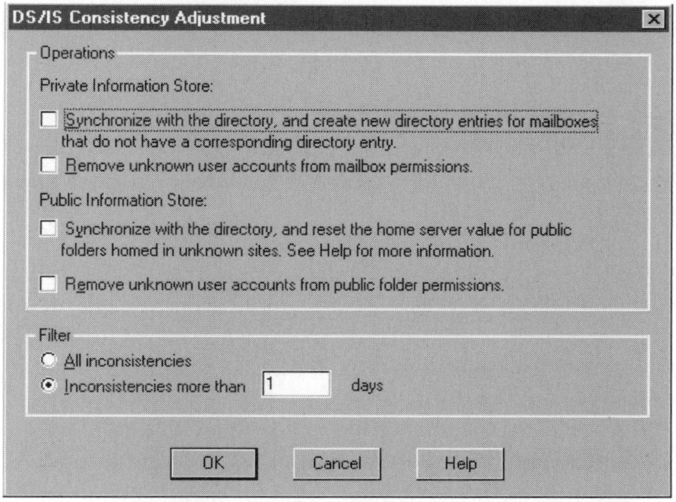

Figure 7-19. *Performing DS/IS Consistency Adjustment prior to upgrading*

To take this backup, you can use the Windows 2000 Backup utility or any other backup application that is Exchange-aware and supports backing up and restoring Windows 2000 System State data. Windows 2000 System State data includes critical system information such as the Windows registry, the IIS metabase, the COM+ class registration database, startup files, system files and files protected by Windows File Protection, and performance counter configuration information. System State data can also include other information, depending on the computer's role. For example, if the computer is an Active Directory domain controller, System State includes the Sysvol folder and the Active Directory database. On a certificate server, System State data includes the Certificate Service database. And for clustered servers, System State data includes the cluster database.

Once you have taken a full backup of the entire server, put the backup media in a safe place in case you need it later on.

Note *If you take offline backups, you do not need to use Exchange-aware backup software.*

Removing Incompatible Software

The last step before inserting the Exchange 2000 CD and running SETUP.EXE is to remove any software that is incompatible with or unsupported by Exchange 2000. This can include, but is not limited to, anti-virus software, workflow applications, event scripts, mailbox agents, and applications that monitor, back up, or report on Exchange server. This step is performed after taking the complete backup so that if you need to revert to your Exchange 5.5 server, you can do so with all your software intact.

Obviously, part of your planning will be to procure, test, and deploy upgrades to or replacements for any software you uninstall. Most anti-virus and backup application manufacturers have Exchange 2000-compatible software, so check with the developers to see if an upgrade is available.

Pay particular attention to all forms of backup and anti-virus software. The Exchange 2000 Installable File System (IFS) automatically exposes the information stores to the file system. When the information store service is running, Exchange dynamically maps the M drive (or if M is unavailable, the next available drive) to the root of the stores. Neither backup software nor anti-virus software should access this drive from the file system. Because the Exchange databases are exposed as a file system drive, some file-system virus scanners may start scanning the drive immediately. You'll want to prevent this from happening, so you should uninstall or neuter all anti-virus applications.

The IFS exposes a lot of the information within the database, but not all of it. Backup and anti-virus applications that read databases and the items within the databases do not see the entire picture. Whole sets of properties (not to mention critical files) are simply unavailable through the IFS. As a result, these types of applications are capable of damaging the databases and log files.

In case the point is being missed, never, under any circumstance, use a file-system based virus scanner against any of the Exchange data files. In addition, do not attempt a backup or restore of the M drive (or whatever drive the IFS exposes). Both of these actions are unsupported by Microsoft and are likely to corrupt the server.

Choosing an Upgrade Path

Once you have your Exchange 5.5 organization connected to your Active Directory, the next step is to select an upgrade path. There are three different upgrade paths from Exchange 5.5 to Exchange 2000: the *Move Mailbox* method, a variation of the Move Mailbox method called the *Swing Upgrade* method, and the *In-Place Upgrade* method. Each method has advantages and disadvantages, and ultimately, the needs of your organization will dictate which method—or which combination of methods—you use.

These are the Microsoft-specific upgrade paths. Another option is to use third-party tools to move from and co-exist with Exchange 5.5. A list of some companies that provide these tools can be found at http://www.microsoft.com/exchange/thirdparty/migratetools.htm.

The Move Mailbox Method

As you might guess from its name, the Move Mailbox method involves the movement of mailboxes from an Exchange 5.5 server to a newly built Exchange 2000 server. This method involves the following steps:

1. Take a full backup of the Exchange 5.5 server.
2. Verify that Active Directory accounts created by the ADC for the Exchange 2000 users are ready for use. If necessary, manually replicate information from Exchange 5.5 to Active Directory.
3. Install a new Exchange 2000 server on new hardware into an existing Exchange 5.5 site.
4. Use the Active Directory Users and Computers snap-in to move the mailboxes from the Exchange 5.5 servers in the site to the new Exchange 2000 server. Check for errors during the move mailbox process and verify that each mailbox has been moved correctly.
5. Have each user log on to the server. Provided that the user's original Exchange 5.5 server is online and the Exchange services are running, the client's MAPI profile (the mail profile in Control Panel | Mail) should be automatically updated with the new server information, and the user should be automatically redirected to that server. You may need to provide IMAP4, POP3, and HTTP clients with a new server name or with a new URL for accessing their mailbox.

Because a new Exchange 2000 server will eventually host the mailboxes, the Move Mailbox method has the advantage of causing the least amount of downtime. The only downtime users will experience is the time it takes to move their mailbox from the Exchange 5.5 server to Exchange 2000. This makes this method the easiest and most convenient.

If you are running a combination of Exchange 5.5 and earlier versions of Exchange, the Move Mailbox method can help you avoid upgrading all of your servers. You can't directly upgrade from Exchange 4.0 or 5.0 to Exchange 2000. And you can't introduce an Exchange 2000 server into an existing Exchange site, unless an Exchange 5.5 server running Service Pack 2 or later exists in that site. However, if you have one server in the site that is running Exchange 5.5 with SP3 or later, or if you can upgrade one of your existing servers to this level, then you have satisfied the requirements for installing Exchange 2000 into that site. Moreover, you'll be able to move the mailboxes from the Exchange 4.0 or 5.0 servers directly to Exchange 2000 without having to upgrade them or take them offline for the procedure.

You can also use this method to move Public Folders from a legacy Exchange system into Exchange 2000. Once you have finished moving mailboxes (or, if you are moving them leisurely, during the mailbox move), you can replicate public folders from

Exchange 5.5 to Exchange 2000, and then remove the replicas from Exchange 5.5 once replication has completed. This procedure is truly as easy as it sounds:

1. Using Exchange Administrator, replicate all public folders to the new Exchange 2000 server.
2. Wait for replication to complete.
3. Verify that replication completed successfully. You can do this by inspecting the public folders through System Manager, by comparing the number of items in the folders on the two servers, or by using a comparison method of your choice.
4. Remove the replicas from the Exchange 5.5 server. The public folders have now been moved.

You may wish to defer step 4 until all the mailboxes have been moved to Exchange 2000. This way, clients whose mailboxes are homed on the Exchange 5.5 server can still look to that server for public folder data.

The primary disadvantage of this method is obvious—you need to purchase additional hardware. The total cost will depend on the number of mailboxes, public folders, and applications each server supports, and on the number of servers you have. If you are planning on a one-for-one upgrade—that is, purchasing a replacement server for each existing server—this could be a substantial purchase. However, if your budget permits, this is a very viable upgrade path.

The Swing Upgrade Method

The Swing Upgrade method is a variation of the Move Mailbox method. Using this method, you can reclaim your Exchange 5.5 servers once all the data has been moved off of them; rebuild them as Exchange 2000 servers; and then move the users back to them once they are running Exchange 2000.

A Swing Upgrade—also known as a *leapfrog*—requires the purchase of additional hardware, but typically much less hardware than the Move Mailbox method. Specifically, this upgrade path requires the purchase of one or two new servers—called *swing servers*—and hardware upgrades for existing servers. The new servers are put into production, and store data from one or more Exchange 5.5 servers is moved to them. Then, the Exchange 5.5 servers are rebuilt as Exchange 2000 servers, and the users and public folders are moved back.

Once all the data has been moved off the Exchange 5.5 server, and once any connectors have been re-homed, the additional hardware is installed (for example, faster and/or additional processors, memory, and disk). Then, the server can be upgraded to Windows 2000 and Exchange 2000. Unless something prevents you from doing so, we recommend completely rebuilding your machines from scratch. After the fresh build of Exchange 2000 has completed, you move (or *swing*) the users back to their original server, which is now running Exchange 2000. You can then re-use the swing server to migrate the remaining Exchange 5.5 servers in the site by swinging the rest of the users and data from their Exchange 5.5 servers to the swing server and then back to their original server which is now running Exchange 2000.

Before choosing the Swing Upgrade method as your upgrade path, make sure that the hardware you're using for your Exchange 5.5 servers is on the Microsoft Hardware Compatibility List (HCL) for Windows 2000. You can check the HCL at http://www.microsoft.com/hcl to see if your hardware is listed. If your server, or one or more of its components, is not listed as compatible with or certified for Windows 2000, do not use it for a production Exchange 2000 server. If you believe your hardware is in fact certified, but it is not listed on the Microsoft HCL, contact your hardware manufacturer to determine why it isn't listed and to verify that it is supported hardware.

To perform a Swing Upgrade:

1. Perform the Move Mailbox procedures for the mailboxes and public folders, as described in the preceding section, moving them from the *original* server to the *swing* server.
2. Install the hardware upgrades, prepare the hardware, and then install Windows 2000 and other Exchange 2000 dependency software on the original server, as detailed in Chapter 6.
3. Install Exchange 2000 and any available service packs, security updates, and hotfixes on the original server, and then verify that Exchange 2000 is installed, configured, and working properly.
4. Perform the Move Mailbox procedures for the mailboxes and public folders in the reverse direction—from the swing server to the original server.
   - Use the Active Directory Users and Computers snap-in to move the mailboxes back to their original server.
   - Use System Manager to create public folder replicas on the original server, verify that replication has completed, and remove the replicas from the swing server.
5. Re-use the swing server to upgrade the remaining legacy Exchange servers to Exchange 2000 by repeating steps 1-4 as many times as necessary.

Note *Rebuilding an Exchange 2000 server from scratch is not a requirement of the Move Mailbox or Swing Upgrade methods. It is a recommendation. You can also perform an In-Place Upgrade of your Exchange 5.5 servers. It is simply our preference and professional recommendation that you build your new servers from scratch.*

A common disadvantage of both the Move Mailbox and Swing Upgrade methods is that there is no mechanism for moving Key Management Services (KMS) or any connectors you might have installed. This means it will take some additional administrative time to build new connections, and of course it results in the re-routing of some mail in your organization. KMS in particular is a bit of a headache. For example, you need to ensure that the domain controllers and Global Catalog servers used by your Exchange 2000 servers are in the same domain as the users who will update keys on them. Although KMS cannot be moved using the Move Mailbox or Swing Upgrade method, it does get automatically upgraded during an in-place upgrade.

The In-Place Upgrade Method

The In-Place Upgrade method involves performing an upgrade installation of Exchange 2000 on top of an existing Exchange 5.5 server running on Windows 2000. The downtime for users whose mailboxes are hosted on the server is greater than with one of the other methods; however, for larger environments that have a lot of small sites with one or two servers, an In-Place Upgrade is the most economical of the upgrade paths.

The key difference between an In-Place Upgrade and the other upgrade paths is that you don't move any mailboxes. Instead, the server is upgraded as is, *in place*. Because this is an as-is upgrade, you can't install any components that are not already installed on the Exchange 5.5 server you are upgrading. In addition, some or all of your connectors may be removed during the upgrade. Any unsupported connectors on your Exchange 5.5 server will be unavailable after you upgrade.

The In-Place Upgrade method upgrades the Exchange binaries and database to Exchange 2000. To do this, it requires at least 30 percent free disk space on the partition containing the information stores. In addition, the upgrade process itself may take some time, and could continue for several days or more. During this time, however, the server will be up and serving Exchange to users. Unlike upgrading to prior versions of Exchange (for example, from Exchange 4.0 to 5.0, or from 5.0 to 5.5), an upgrade to Exchange 2000 defers upgrading data until a user requests it. This deferred upgrade mechanism reduces the downtime needed for setup, and extends the conversion over time. As you might expect, the first time a user requests data, the retrieval time will be longer; however, the slowdown should go unnoticed by the user.

Before scheduling any downtime or putting the Exchange 2000 CD in the drive and running Setup, you should be aware of some caveats that apply to In-Place Upgrades.

Required Privileges You must have Exchange Full Administrator privileges in the forest in order to upgrade an Exchange 5.5 server. These privileges can only be assigned in one of two ways: by running the Exchange Administrative Delegation Wizard, or by delegating this right to an account during a preparatory installation, as shown in Figure 7-20.

This means that you must either perform a preparatory installation or install a new Exchange 2000 server into your organization before you can upgrade any Exchange 5.5 server. If you don't perform one of these tasks, you will not be able to delegate the Exchange Full Administrator privilege to any account, and therefore you will not be able to perform the upgrade.

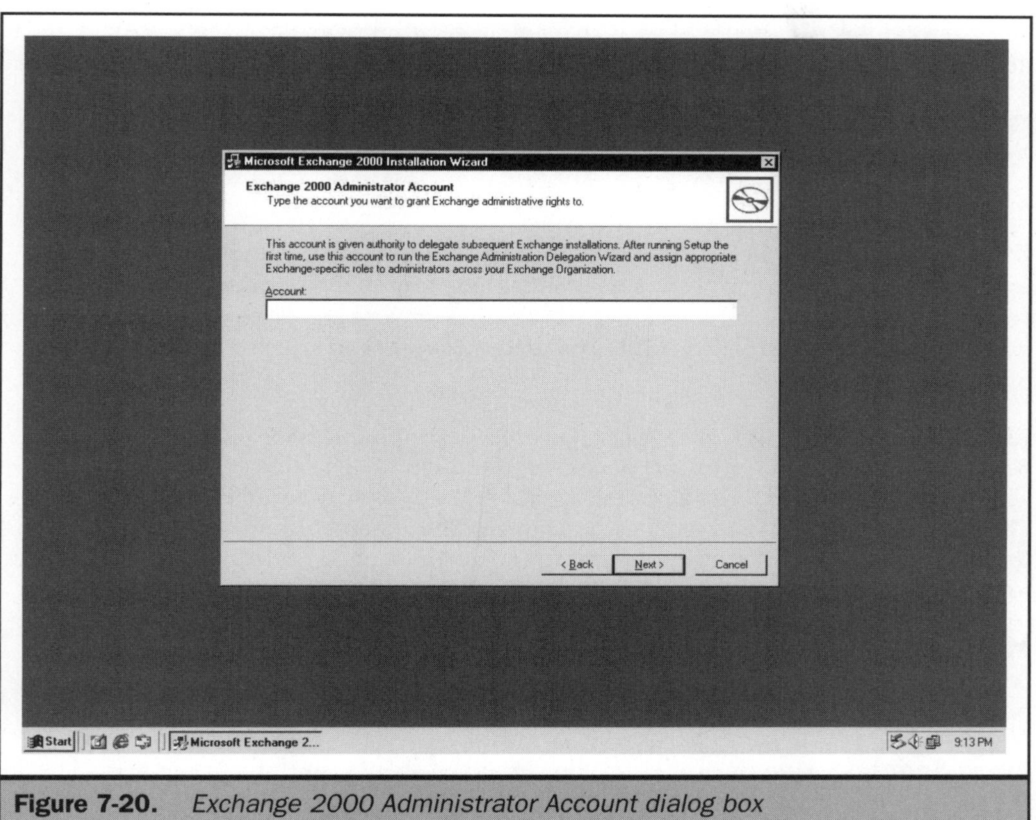

Figure 7-20. *Exchange 2000 Administrator Account dialog box*

Validated Accounts You should verify that each user whose data will be upgraded exists in Active Directory prior to upgrading. If Setup encounters an Exchange 5.5 mailbox that does not have an associated Active Directory user, it will place that mailbox object in the mailbox store's deleted items.

Existing Connectors Any supported connectors installed on your Exchange 5.5 server will be preserved. For example, the connection information for an X.400 connector will be preserved, and connection information for site connectors will be preserved in the equivalent routing group connectors. However, some connectors will need to be reconfigured. For example, the message format settings in your Internet Mail Connectors (IMC) will be converted to a global SMTP message format setting in Exchange 2000. However, any per-domain routing settings you had configured for the IMC will not be upgraded. Instead, you will need to manually configure an SMTP connector to each domain for which you had per-domain settings.

To ensure that you haven't lost any connectivity after upgrading, check the Exchange Server Setup log file, which will contain details about any connection information that was lost.

Existing Monitors Both server monitors and link monitors will be affected by the upgrade. During the upgrade process, existing server monitors are removed. Therefore, you should reconfigure your monitors on another server before upgrading. In addition, by design, link monitors do not get upgraded and will need to be reconfigured after the upgrade has completed.

KMS Servers An In-Place Upgrade of a server running KMS is only supported if both KMS Service and Certificate Service are running on the same operating system. This will be the case only if all of your Exchange servers are running Windows 2000. Therefore, you should not install the Exchange 2000 version of KMS into a mixed-mode Exchange organization. Instead, continue to use the Exchange 5.5 KMS until you are ready to move to a native-mode organization.

Message Tracking If message tracking is enabled for any of your Exchange 5.5 components during an In-Place Upgrade, it will be turned on for the entire server once the upgrade has completed.

Event Scripts After the upgrade, you should be able to continue to run any event scripts you were using in Exchange 5.5. Exchange 2000 includes a service that is compatible with Exchange 5.5 event scripts. Most scripts should run just fine without needing any modifications. However, because Exchange 2000 has tighter security, you may need to modify permissions for the script to run. Each script is different, so be on the lookout for event script related entries in your server's application or security event logs.

NNTP Feeds You'll need to reconfigure any NNTP feeds that you are hosting. The content itself will remain in the public store; however, the connector will not be upgraded. Therefore, you should document your configuration settings prior to upgrading, so that you can recreate the NNTP feed after the upgrade process has completed.

Third-Party Software You will need to remove any unsupported third-party software, including tools, connectors, and anti-virus applications. You can disable this software; however, to be safe, it is recommended that you remove third–party software prior to upgrading. Contact the vendor of any third-party application you are running to see if it has an Exchange 2000 version.

Outlook Web Access In-Place Upgrades Before performing an In-Place Upgrade, consider the impact it will have on Outlook Web Access. The Exchange 2000 plumbing of Outlook Web Access is very different from Exchange 5.5. Outlook Web Access 2000 has been completely rewritten. The interpreted code no longer exists, and MAPI is no longer used to communicate with the information store. Instead, the Web pages (HTML and active server pages scripts) are rendered directly in the STORE.EXE process. This provides enormous performance gains for Outlook Web Access over previous versions that suffered from ASP and MAPI bottlenecks.

Unfortunately, with this new architecture, customizations that you made to the ASP pages on your Outlook Web Access servers will no longer function (but they'll still be on the server in the Exchsrvr\Webdata folder). You will need to either customize Outlook Web Access 2000 from scratch—which is exceedingly more difficult than it was in earlier versions, and needs to be done programmatically—or you can point your users to a remaining Outlook Web Access 5.5 server that is running your customized version. Doing this will cause the Outlook Web Access 5.5 server to act as a front-end server for the client. But you'll still be running the legacy version of Outlook Web Access, which won't have any of the benefits, features, or performance aspects of the Exchange 2000 version and defeats the purpose of upgrading. Therefore, you'll want to carefully weigh the trade-off between your customizations and the new functionality and architecture of Exchange 2000.

Finally, if you are using a legacy Outlook Web Access front-end server (that is, a server running Exchange 5.5 Outlook Web Access without any mailboxes or public folders), you won't be able to upgrade it until the back-end server (the server containing the mailboxes) has been upgraded to Exchange 2000.

Connectivity Between Exchange 2000 and Exchange 5.5 In Exchange 5.5, servers communicated with one another over site connectors using encrypted remote procedure calls (RPCs). By default, Exchange 2000 servers in the same routing group communicate with one another using SMTP authenticated with Kerberos. One of the reasons SMTP was chosen over RPCs as the native routing protocol in Exchange 2000 was that it works well in low bandwidth environments.

However, when an Exchange 2000 server communicates via a site connector or routing group connector with an Exchange 5.5 server in the same site, it uses encrypted RPCs. For this reason, you will still need to have decent and reliable bandwidth between these servers.

Performing an In-Place Upgrade (Step-by-Step)

Once you've met all the requirements and performed all the procedures set forth in the preceding sections, you'll be ready to upgrade. In this example, we'll take an Exchange 5.5 server with SP4 running on Windows 2000 SP1+ and upgrade it to Exchange 2000. We'll assume that you have met all the requirements set forth in this chapter, that your forest and domain have been appropriately prepared, and that you are ready in all respects to upgrade an Exchange 5.5 server to Exchange 2000.

To upgrade from Exchange 5.5 to Exchange 2000:

1. Insert the Exchange 2000 Server CD into the CD-ROM drive. The Exchange 2000 CD splash screen will appear automatically.
2. Click Setup. This will launch the Administrator stage of the setup process. The Exchange Installation Wizard welcome screen will appear.
3. Click Next to continue. The End User License Agreement (EULA) screen will appear. Read the EULA carefully, and then indicate your agreement to its terms by selecting I Agree. If you do not accept the EULA, you will not be able to install Exchange 2000. Click Next to continue.
4. The CD Key installation screen will appear. Enter your 25-digit CD Key and click Next to continue.
5. The Component Selection screen will appear, and as shown in Figure 7-21, the word "Upgrade" should appear to the left of the components that will be upgraded. Click Next to continue.

Note *The default appearance of the Component Selection screen is a good indicator of the readiness of your Exchange infrastructure, Active Directory forest, DNS databases, and permissions. If the components do not have the word "Upgrade" to their left, the system cannot be upgraded. Typically, this is because something is configured incorrectly, replication has not finished, or permissions are not set correctly. If you change the Microsoft Exchange 2000 value on this screen by manually setting it to Upgrade, a dialog box should appear that indicates the problem(s) that are preventing the upgrade from completing. In this event, you'll need to spend some time troubleshooting the items that appear in this dialog box. For assistance in troubleshooting upgrade problems, see Microsoft Knowledge Base articles Q279218 and Q255869, review all event logs, and examine the Exchange Server Setup.log and Exchange Server Setup Progress.log files.*

6. The Service Account assignment screen will appear, and will be automatically populated with the account you are using for your Exchange 5.5 service account. Enter the password for that account in the Password field and click Next to continue.

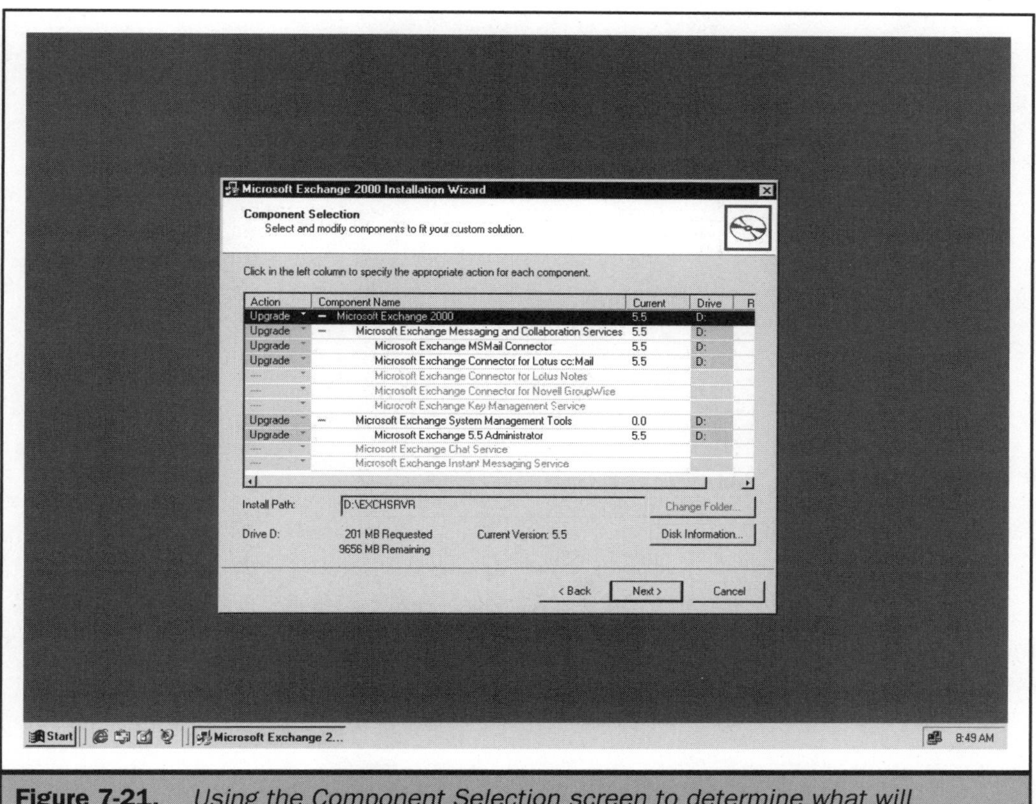

Figure 7-21. *Using the Component Selection screen to determine what will be upgraded*

7. The Component Summary screen, which displays a summary of the components that will be upgraded, will appear, as shown in Figure 7-22. Click Next to perform the upgrade.
8. The Component Progress screen will appear and display the status of the upgrade. During this time, you will see services stop, files copied, connectors installed, and services restarted.
9. At the end of the upgrade, the Wizard completion screen will appear. Click Finish to exit the Wizard.

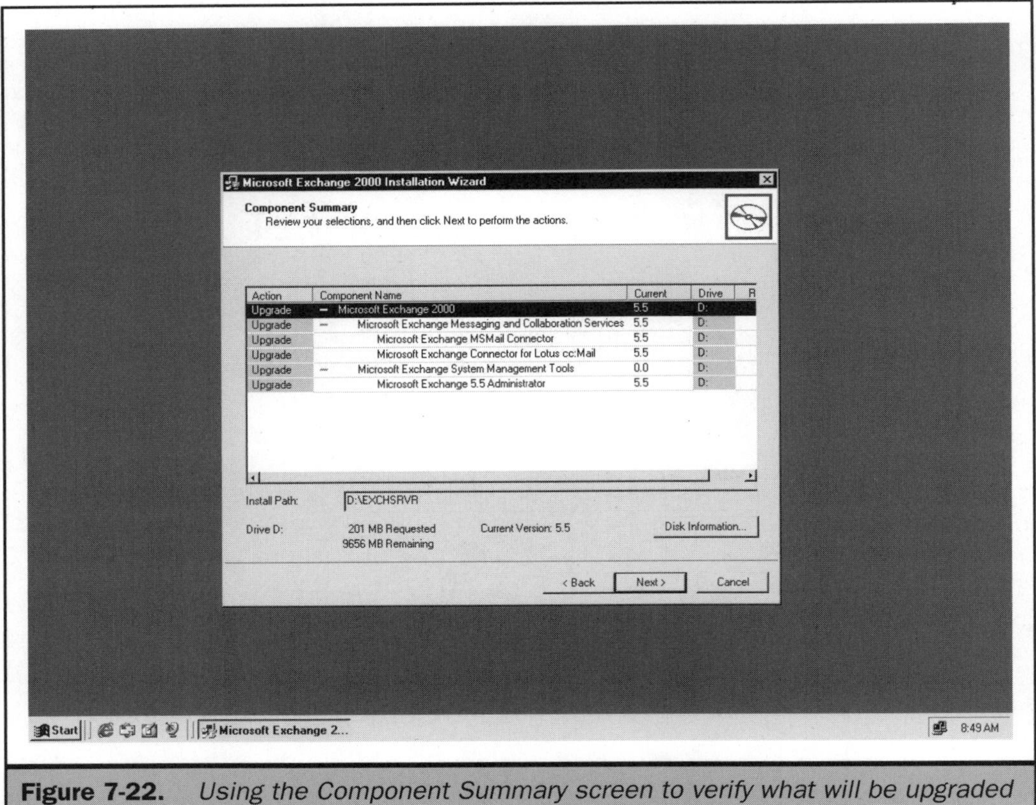

Figure 7-22. *Using the Component Summary screen to verify what will be upgraded*

At this point, you'll need to restart the server. A dialog box will appear asking you if you want to restart now. Click Yes to restart the system immediately. Do not try to configure settings or make other system changes (Exchange-related or otherwise) until the server has been restarted.

After the system has restarted, you'll want to ensure that the upgraded server is working properly. For example, you should

- Check all event logs for errors, warnings, audit failures, or other problems.

- Verify that the proper services, including Exchange and IIS services, have started successfully.
- Use System Manager to verify that the public and private stores have mounted successfully.
- Review the Setup log file (called Exchange Server Setup.log) for errors, failures, or problems. The last line of the log file should indicate an exit code of <0>, which means that Setup exited without errors.
- Verify that the mailboxes are accessible. It's probably impractical for you to manually check each mailbox, so a random sampling of a few mailboxes should be fine.
- Verify that the virtual directories for Exchange 2000 (for example, Exchange, Public, and ExAdmin) are started and accessible in Internet Services Manager.
- Verify connectivity with the remaining servers in your organization by sending a message from a new Exchange 2000 mailbox to an Exchange 5.5 mailbox in your organization. Once that message is received at the Exchange 5.5 mailbox, reply to it to verify mail routing and delivery in both directions.
- Install any Exchange 2000 service packs or hotfixes, as appropriate and, if necessary, reboot the server afterwards. Be sure to include any late-breaking Windows 2000, Exchange 2000, or IIS-related hotfixes and security updates.

Once you have done everything in the preceding list, take a complete backup of the system, including the System State data. Once the backup has completed, you can allow users to start accessing their mailboxes on this server.

Rolling Back from a Failed In-Place Upgrade

If the upgrade does not finish successfully and you cannot correct the problem(s) that remain, you'll need to completely roll back from the upgrade to the system's original state. A failed upgrade will leave the server in a partially upgraded state, making it inaccessible to both Exchange 5.5 and Exchange 2000 users. It is for this very reason that a complete backup is taken prior to upgrading. This tape is your only fallback; if you didn't take a good, complete backup prior to upgrading, you've got a serious problem on your hands, which may result in the loss of a substantial amount of data.

Rolling back from a failed upgrade involves a bit more than just wiping the server and restoring everything from tape. Specific configuration changes will need to be made because some or all of the information about this server will likely have changed in both the Exchange 5.5 directory and in Active Directory. Although the procedure is fairly straightforward, it's important to perform it precisely or you may not be able to recover this server.

To roll back to Exchange 5.5 from a failed or partial Exchange 2000 upgrade:

1. Start manually removing all traces of Exchange 2000 from the server by removing the following Exchange-related registry entries:
   - Open a registry editor and navigate to HKLM\System\CurrentControlSet\Services and delete the following subkeys:
     - DAVEX
     - ESE97
     - ESE98
     - EXIFS
     - ExIPC
     - EXOLEDB
     - IMAP4Svc
     - LME-* (that is, all LinkAge Message Exchange connectors)
     - MSExchange* (that is, anything that starts with MSExchange, such as MSExchangeAL and MSExchangeCCMC)
     - MSSEARCH
     - POP3Svc
     - RESvc
     - *SERVERNAME*-LME* (that is, any entry that begins with the name of the server, then a dash, and then LME).
   - Again in the registry, navigate to HKLM\Software\Microsoft\Exchange and delete the entire Setup key below Exchange.
2. Using Windows Explorer, rename all folders called Exchsrvr to Exchsrvr.old on all partitions. If you installed Exchange into a directory or subdirectory named something other than Exchsrvr, rename that directory.
3. Completely uninstall Internet Information Services (IIS).
4. Reboot the server.
5. After the reboot, reinstall IIS, and be sure to include the SMTP, NNTP, and Web Publishing services.
6. Reapply any post-SP1 Windows 2000 hotfixes, including the update described in Microsoft Knowledge Base article Q271976. If you are using a later Windows 2000 Service Pack, reapply that.

7. Delete the Exchsrvr folders you previously renamed. In other words, if you renamed Exchsrvr to Exchsrvr.old, delete Exchsrvr.old.
8. Insert the Exchange 5.5 CD and run setup /r. This setup switch installs Exchange 5.5 in *recovery mode*. During the setup process, make sure you use the same organization name and server as the existing server. If you do not, recovery will fail.
9. Once setup has completed, apply the same Exchange 5.5 service pack and hotfixes you had installed prior to attempting the upgrade.
10. Once the service pack and hotfixes have been installed, run the Exchange 5.5 performance optimizer and, if necessary, move the databases and/or log files to their original locations.
11. Restore your directory and information stores from the backup you took prior to attempting the upgrade.
12. Once the restore has completed, start the Microsoft Exchange Directory and Microsoft Exchange Information Store services.
13. Using Exchange Administrator, perform a manual intrasite replication.
14. Using the ADC Manager, manually replicate the Configuration Connection Agreement.
15. In Exchange Administrator, the admin display name and alias for the Site Replication Service to Directory Service, and edit the e-mail address to read "DSA" instead of "SRS."
16. Start Exchange Administrator in raw mode (using admin /r) and change the Serial-Number attribute to Version 5.5 (Build 2650.24: Service Pack 3), or whatever value it was set to prior to upgrading.
17. Remaining in raw mode, navigate to the server-level Protocols container for this server and recreate the LDAP object:
    - From the File menu, select New, and then Raw Object.
    - Double-click Protocol-Cfg-LDAP-Server.
    - Assign the object the following attributes and values:

Attribute	Value
Admin-Display-Name	LDAP (Directory) Settings
Anonymous-Access	1
Association-Lifetime	10
Directory-Name	LDAP

Attribute	Value
Enabled-Authorization-Packages	0 DPA 0 DPASSL 1 CLEARTEXT 1 CLEARTEXTSSL 1 NTLM 1 NTLMSSL
Enabled-Protocol-Cfg	1
LDAP-Search-Cfg	1
Object-Class	2A864886F71401034D 2A864886F71401034B 2A864886F714010344 550600
Outgoing-Msg-Size-Limit	100
Port-Number	389 (or the alternate port you specified if this is an Active Directory domain controller)
Use-Site-Values	1

- Stop and start the Microsoft Exchange directory service so that this new object will be added, recognized, and ready for use immediately.

18. Using ADSIEdit from the Windows 2000 Resource Kit, change the serialNumber attribute on the server to Version 5.5 (Build 2650.24: Service Pack 3), or whatever value it was set to prior to upgrading. Then, change the versionNumber to 2650, or whatever major revision this server had prior to upgrading.
19. Finally, perform manual intrasite replication within Exchange 5.5 once more, and then manually replicate the Configuration Connection Agreement using ADC Manager.

At this point, the rollback should be complete, and your Exchange 5.5 server should be functioning as it was prior to upgrading. You can proceed once more with upgrading this server, either by re-attempting an In-Place Upgrade, or by taking one of the other upgrade paths available to you.

Upgrading an Exchange 5.5 Cluster

The process for upgrading an Exchange 5.5 cluster isn't that different from upgrading a standalone (non-clustered) server. Because it's a clustered server, there are a couple of extra steps, but generally the process is the same. There are, however, a couple of caveats that need to be considered. For example, a clustered Exchange 2000 Server cannot be the first Exchange 2000 Server introduced into an Exchange 5.5 site. Remember, to provide directory replication between Active Directory and the Exchange 5.5 directory, the SRS is installed on the first Exchange 2000 Server installed into an Exchange 5.5 site. Because the SRS is not supported in a cluster, you must install a non-clustered Exchange 2000 Server in each site before you can upgrade your cluster. A clustered Exchange 2000 Server cannot act as a bridgehead server for an Exchange 5.5 site either.

Upgrading an Exchange 5.5 Cluster (Step-by-Step)

In this example, we'll take an Exchange 5.5 Server with SP4 running in a Windows 2000 Advanced Server SP1+ cluster and upgrade it to Exchange 2000. We'll assume that you have met all of the requirements set forth in this chapter, that your forest and domain have been appropriately prepared, and that you are ready in all respects to upgrade an Exchange 5.5 Server to Exchange 2000. This includes having a good and complete backup of your cluster before proceeding.

To upgrade an Exchange 5.5 cluster:

1. Using Cluster Administrator, take the Exchange resource group offline.
2. On the active node (the node that currently owns the Exchange resource group), navigate to the partition containing the information stores and rename the Mdbdata folder to **Mdbdata.old**.
3. Run the Exchange 5.5 Setup program and select Remove All. The Exchange 5.5 program files will be removed.
4. Install Exchange 2000 on each node in the cluster, as described in Chapter 20, "Clustering Exchange Server 2000."
   - Make sure that the cluster service account and the account being used for the installation have Exchange Full Administrator rights in Active Directory and local administrative rights on each node.
   - Install each node one at a time, and reboot the node prior to installing the next node.
   - Install the program files in the same location on the local storage system of each node.
   - Install the same components on each node.
5. Install any Exchange 2000 service packs, hotfixes, and security updates, as necessary on each node, rebooting each node before proceeding to the next node.
6. Using Cluster Administrator, create an IP Address and Network Name resource in the resource group that previously hosted your Exchange 5.5 virtual server. Bring the IP Address and Network Name resources online.
7. Create a Microsoft Exchange System Attendant resource in the same group, but leave it offline. See Chapter 20 for details on how to do this.

8. Navigate to the Mdbdata.old folder and copy the Priv.edb and Pub.edb files to the new Mdbdata folder that was created when you added the System Attendant resource to the resource group.
9. Rename the files to **Priv1.edb** and **Pub1.edb**, respectively.
10. Bring the Exchange resource group online using Cluster Administrator.

At this point, you should follow the same post-installation procedures that you would for a non-clustered Exchange 2000 server. This includes checking the event logs for problems, verifying that the stores are mounted and that mailboxes are accessible, and on a cluster, testing failover. You should perform several soft (manual) and hard (abrupt power-loss) failures and verify that the Exchange virtual server fails over and operates properly after these failures.

Mixed Mode vs. Native Mode

Mixed mode and native mode refer to the status of your Exchange organization. If your Exchange organization is running Exchange 2000 and any legacy version of Exchange, it is in mixed mode. If all of your servers have been upgraded to Exchange 2000, you are ready to convert to native mode. Mixed mode and native mode are also used to refer to the status of an Active Directory domain. An Active Directory domain running in mixed mode means that Windows NT 4.0 backup domain controllers (BDCs) are still members of and servicing that domain. A native mode Active Directory domain indicates that there are no Windows NT 4.0 BDCs, and that all domain controllers are running Windows 2000 with Active Directory. Although the terms used are the same, and although they have this apparent commonality regarding the co-existence of current versions with legacy versions, the similarities end here.

Although native mode and mixed mode in the contexts of Exchange 2000 and Active Directory apply to different things, a relationship exists between them. Specifically, the status of the Active Directory domain containing Exchange will have a direct impact on the types of groups—also known as "distribution lists"—that will be created in Active Directory for use with Exchange 2000. In almost all upgrade scenarios, you will want to have at least one Active Directory domain running in native mode.

Exchange 2000 requires Active Directory to be running, but you don't have to be finished with your Active Directory deployment before you can install Exchange 2000. If you aren't finished with your Windows 2000 deployment, consider using a *group management domain* to preserve the functionality of any existing distribution lists that you are using.

Using a Group Management Domain

Exchange 2000 only requires Active Directory; it does not require that the Active Directory domain be in mixed mode or native mode. Your business requirements—or more specifically, your distribution list requirements—will dictate whether you create one or more native-mode Active Directory domains. In Exchange 2000, universal security groups perform the same function as distribution lists did in Exchange 5.5. In Exchange 5.5 and earlier, distribution lists could be used for sending e-mail to groups and for setting permissions on Exchange objects. These distribution lists could include members from any Exchange site and could exist within (that is, be nested within) other distribution lists. Windows 2000 universal groups replace Exchange distribution groups.

To preserve the functionality used for controlling access to Exchange objects, you need to create a *group management domain*. This is a native-mode Active Directory domain that uses the ADC to replicate distribution lists from an Exchange 5.5 site. Any native-mode Active Directory domain in your organization can act as a group management domain. Your Exchange topology will determine whether you create additional group management domains. If you have multiple domains that manage distribution lists, you will need to configure an ADC connection agreement to these domains before upgrading.

If you don't want to use universal security groups, or if you don't want to (or can't) create a native-mode domain, you will have to use either domain-local or domain-global groups (or both) to control access to public folders. Managing distribution lists this way is strongly discouraged because it requires continuous maintenance and administration of these groups, as accounts, access rights, and so forth change.

Exchange 2000 Mixed Mode vs. Native Mode

As previously mentioned, a mixed-mode Exchange organization includes Exchange 2000 and pre-Exchange 2000 servers. Regardless of whether you are joining an existing Exchange 5.5 organization or creating a new Exchange organization from scratch, the default installation mode for Exchange 2000 is mixed mode. This is because the conversion from mixed mode to native mode is one-way, and once performed, it cannot be undone. You can confirm this by viewing the msExchMixedMode attribute on the Exchange organization object in Active Directory, which will be set to True when in mixed mode. You can also view the mode by right-clicking on the organization object in System Manager and selecting Properties. The status will appear in the Operation Mode field, as shown in Figure 7-23.

Mixed mode is used only for backward compatibility. If you created a new Exchange organization during the /forestprep setup, and if you will never add legacy Exchange servers to this organization, you can and should convert to native mode immediately. However, as long as you are co-existing with multiple versions of Exchange in the same Exchange organization, you will need to remain in mixed mode. Mixed mode imposes some restrictions on your Exchange infrastructure, and since you'll remain in mixed mode until your last legacy Exchange server has been upgraded or decommissioned, you should be aware of what those restrictions and limitations are.

Mixed-Mode Restrictions and Limitations The biggest restriction of mixed mode is that the rules that apply to legacy Exchange servers will apply to Exchange 2000, as well. For example, Exchange 2000 doesn't require the use of a user account for its services. Its services run under the LocalSystem account. However, the legacy Exchange components that communicate directly with Exchange 2000 won't understand—

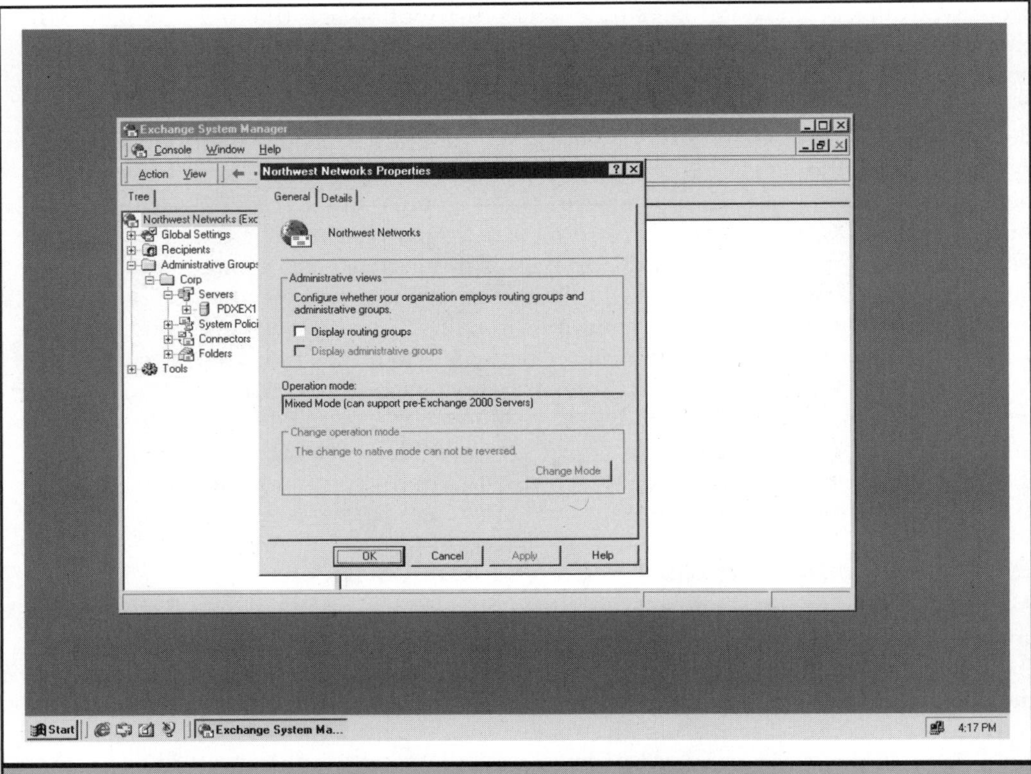

Figure 7-23. *Viewing the operation mode in the organization Properties dialog box*

and more importantly can't authenticate—the Exchange 2000 server's access token. To overcome this problem, components like the SRS and ADC should use the Exchange 5.5 service account, as should all Exchange servers in the same site.

Companies are likely to be upgrading to Exchange 2000, at least in part, because Exchange 2000 offers functionality that prior versions did not offer, such as the full flexibility provided by administrative groups and routing groups. When upgrading from Exchange 5.5, each Exchange 5.5 site is mapped to a single administrative group and a single routing group. Therefore, before you can add additional routing groups, you must define additional administrative groups. Once you have converted to native mode, routing groups can consist of servers that belong to different administrative groups, and you can move servers between routing groups.

Another major difference between a mixed-mode and a native-mode Exchange organization is the behavior of public folders. The default mail-enabled status of a public folder is different for mixed mode and native mode. In mixed mode, public folders in the MAPI TLH are automatically mail-enabled and not published (that is, hidden) in the global address list. In addition, you cannot mail-disable a MAPI public folder while in mixed mode. Public folders in the alternate TLH (also known as the Application TLH) are mail-disabled by default, although they can be manually mail-enabled if desired. Once they are mail-enabled, they will be published to the global address list.

As mentioned in Chapter 5, "Public Folders," MAPI public folders are always mail-enabled and cannot be mail-disabled in mixed mode because by default, Exchange 5.5 public folders are stored in the directory, but not displayed in the global address list.

Once you have converted to native mode, any new public folders in either hierarchy will need to be mail-enabled manually. Once you've done that, they will be published to the global address list.

Converting to Native Mode

As a general rule of thumb, you are ready to convert from mixed mode to native mode once you have upgraded or decommissioned your last Exchange 5.5 server, removed all ADC connection agreements and the SRS, and determined that you will never add Exchange 5.5 servers to your organization. If you never need to run gateway or connector software that requires Exchange 5.5, and if you have no need to co-exist with any pre-Exchange 2000 servers in the same organization, you should convert your Exchange organization from mixed mode to native mode. Once you have converted to native mode, you will not be subject to the limitations and restrictions described in the preceding section.

To convert to native mode:

1. Remove any Recipient or Public Folder connection agreements you made using the ADC Manager snap-in.
2. Remove all Configuration Connection Agreements using the Active Directory Sites and Services snap-in.
3. Stop the Microsoft Active Directory Connector service and set it to Manual startup.
4. Manually remove each instance of the Site Replication Service from any Exchange 2000 servers that have it installed.
    - Stop all instances of the Site Replication Service and set each to Manual startup.
    - In System Manager, expand Tools, and then Site Replication Service. Right-click each object in this container and select Delete.
    - Allow time for Active Directory replication of these changes to complete.
5. While you are waiting, uninstall any instances of the Exchange Administrator application that might be left on your Exchange 2000 servers.

6. Once Active Directory replication has completed, right-click on the organization object in System Manager and select Properties. The Exchange organization Properties dialog box will appear
7. Click the Change Mode button. A warning dialog box will appear, confirming that you want to make this change, and reminding you that this is a one-way permanent change. Click Yes on this message, which is shown in Figure 7-24.

Note *If the Change Mode button is grayed out and you have deleted all the Site Replication Service objects, replication may not have completed, or an SRS object still exists. Refer to Microsoft Knowledge Base article Q260781 for details on this issue.*

8. Click Apply to initiate the change. Click OK to close the Properties dialog box.
9. Allow time for Active Directory replication to occur before leveraging the added functionality of a native-mode Exchange organization.

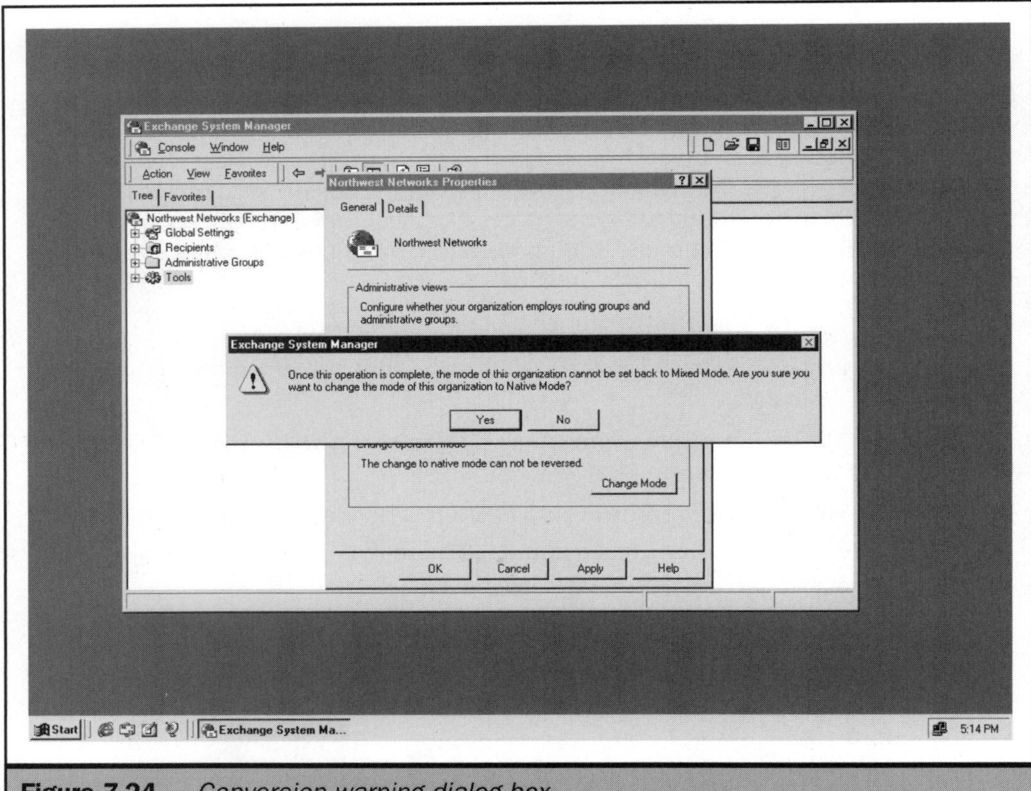

Figure 7-24. *Conversion warning dialog box*

Summary

This chapter focused on upgrading to Exchange 2000 from Exchange 5.5 and on co-existing with multiple versions of Exchange. The first Exchange 2000 server in your existing Exchange 5.5 organization creates a mixed-mode Exchange 2000 organization that will remain in place until your last Exchange 5.5 server has been upgraded or decommissioned. Once your last Exchange 5.5 server is upgraded or decommissioned, your Exchange organization can be converted to native mode, in which all the servers in the Exchange organization are running Exchange 2000.

The planning and design phase of the upgrade process is the most important phase. Mistakes made during this phase aren't always correctable later, and if they are correctable, they are often very expensive.

We discussed the various upgrade paths: the Move Mailbox method, the Swing Upgrade method, and the In-Place Upgrade method. And we stepped through an In-Place Upgrade. Then, we explained a method for rolling back from a failed upgrade, and how to upgrade an Exchange 5.5 cluster in place.

Finally, we discussed the differences between mixed mode and native mode, as it relates to Exchange 2000 and Active Directory. We also explained the limitations of and restrictions imposed by a mixed-mode Exchange 2000 organization, as well as the benefits of converting to native mode. Finally, we stepped through the mixed-to-native mode conversion process.

Upgrading to Windows 2000, Active Directory, and Exchange 2000 is a relatively straightforward process. Pay particular attention during your planning and design stages, and use the procedures in this chapter to make sure that your upgrade goes as smoothly as possible.

Chapter 8

Administering Recipients

Administering Exchange 2000 Server is a bit more complicated than what it might appear to be. In large organizations, it is often more than a one-person task. Many of the day-to-day administrative tasks involve the creation and manipulation of Active Directory objects. In this chapter, we'll discuss several important administrative actions that you'll conduct on a regular basis. First, we'll look at the administrative tools that are available to manage Exchange 2000. Then, we'll discuss the different types of recipients, when to create them, and how to create them. Finally, we'll discuss making bulk changes to the directory.

Preliminary Administration Steps

Exchange 2000 Server relies on Active Directory for recipients and distribution groups management. Active Directory can be modified by using the following pre-built set of tools:

- Exchange System Manager (ESM)
- ADSI Edit
- Active Directory Administration Tool (ldp.exe)
- Active Directory Schema

Exchange System Manager

The ESM is a Microsoft Management Console (MMC) snap-in, which is really a collection of Exchange 2000 tools that Microsoft has provided for our use. By adding the necessary snap-ins, you can manage an entire Exchange enterprise from a single console. Each tool in the ESM can be created into its own MMC so that persons responsible for specific administrative duties don't need to receive the entire default set of tools in the ESM. Instead, they can be given their specific tools in a separate MMC. So, in a nutshell, you can customize the MMC to give you single-seat administration or to parcel out individual administrative responsibilities to various administrators. Either way, the MMC is flexible enough to support your administrative model. To learn more about how to create a new MMC, please consult the Windows 2000 Resource Kit.

ADSI Edit

ADSI Edit, short for Active Directory Service Interface Editor (adsiedit.msc), is a low-level Active Directory editor that is used to view and modify objects in Active Directory, including attributes and properties of a specific object. You'll use ADSI edit to perform certain tasks that cannot be performed using the ESM or Active Directory Users and Computers. Figure 8-1 shows the exchange2000training organization object in the ADSI interface.

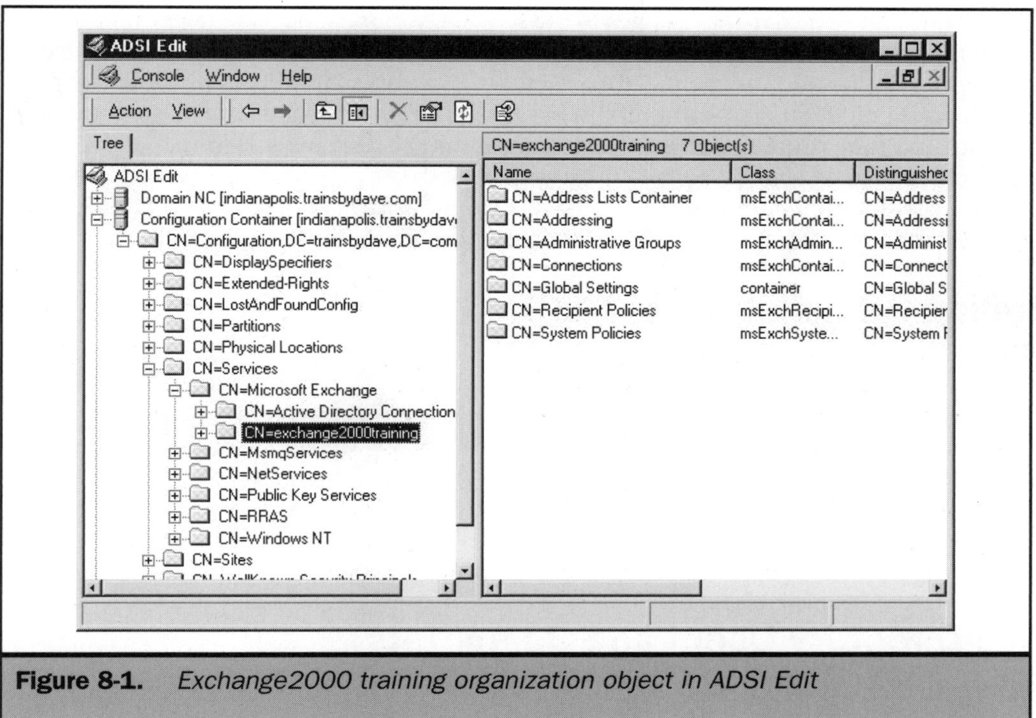

Figure 8-1. *Exchange2000 training organization object in ADSI Edit*

Referring to Figure 8-1, you'll also notice that the three Active Directory partitions are clearly seen, giving you a visual look at these partitions, which are discussed in the Windows 2000 literature. For more information about these three partitions (also called *naming contexts*), please refer to the Windows 2000 Resource Kit.

Active Directory Administration Tool

The Active Directory Administration Tool (ldp.exe) is a generic Lightweight Directory Access Protocol (LDAP) tool that is used to connect to an LDAP compliant directory. You can view and modify objects in Active Directory with this tool, though its interface is not as "friendly" as the interface of ADSI Edit. This tool is included in the Windows 2000 Server support tools.

Active Directory Schema

This tool is an MMC snap-in that allows you to view attribute and object class configuration information in the schema partition in Active Directory. You cannot view instances of an object from this tool, but rather, only its class and attribute definitions. In order to make changes to the schema, you must be a member of the Schema Admins security group and you must have direct IP connectivity to the schema master in your forest. And, before attempting to open this snap-in, you must first register its dynamic link library (schmmgmt.dll) by using the *regsvr32* command at the command prompt and then pressing ENTER. A message should be displayed stating that the registration was successful. So, to illustrate, given a default installation of Windows 2000, the complete command would be: *regsvr32 c:\winnt\system32\schmmgmt.dll*. Once registered, the MMC can be created and opened for your viewing pleasure.

Installing Administrative Tools

The ESM is installed by default during Exchange 2000 setup. By running setup, you can also install the ESM separately on a Windows 2000 computer. In the Components Selection screen, choose a Custom installation and then select the Exchange System Manager. Doing this will install only the ESM and not any of the databases or Exchange services. For more information about how to perform an installation of Exchange 2000 Server, please refer to Chapter 6.

The ldp.exe and ADSI Edit are installed when you install the Windows 2000 support tools from the Windows 2000 server CD-ROM.

Active Directory Users and Computers

When administering Exchange 2000 recipients, you'll use the Active Directory Users and Computers (ADUC) snap-in. In this section, we'll first cover the different types of recipients that are available in Exchange 2000 Server, and then in the next section we'll demonstrate how to create and administer those recipient accounts.

Types of Recipients

There are five types of recipients for Exchange 2000 Server. These recipients are Active Directory (AD) objects that are mail-enabled. Each of these recipients can receive e-mail through Exchange 2000, though not all can send e-mail through Exchange 2000. The various recipient types are:

- **Mailbox-enabled user**. This is a user account in AD that has been mail-enabled and associated with an Exchange 2000 mailbox. The user account is a security principle that can be used in an Access Control Lists (ACLs) for permission assignment. This is the most common type of recipient that you'll work with because this is the best recipient type for the users on your local area network (LAN).
- **Mail-enabled user**. This is a user account in AD that has been mail-enabled. However, this type of account does not have a mailbox associated with it. Instead the account's e-mail address is foreign, for example, benglish@ networknowledge.com, where networknowledge.com is not your domain

name. This account is a security principle that can be used to assign permissions in an ACL, and this account does authenticate with a Windows 2000 domain controller (DC), but its mail address is not a local address. This account is best for contractors hired to work at your company for a sustained period of time and who need to log on to your network but retain their e-mail address with their employer's mail system.

- **Mail-enabled contact**. A contact is an object that cannot authenticate in your domain or be used for permission assignment in an ACL. Contacts, when mail-enabled, always have an external e-mail address, so that messages sent to them flow out of your organization to another mail system. This is another very common recipient type that you will work with.
- **Mail-enabled group**. This recipient type replaces the distribution list in earlier versions of Exchange. A mail-enabled group can be set up solely as a distribution group, or it can be set up as a security principle that can be used for permission assignments in an ACL. E-mail sent to a mail-enabled group is automatically sent to the group's members. There are some "gotcha's" when using mail-enabled groups, which are discussed later in this chapter.
- **Mail-enabled public folder**. This recipient type becomes an object in the AD only when it is mail-enabled. As long as a public folder is not mail-enabled, it is not an object in the AD. Mail-enabled public folders cannot be used as security principles for permission assignments in an ACL.

Using the Exchange Tasks Wizard

In ADUC, you can use the Exchange Tasks Wizard to configure users, contacts, and groups. With this wizard, you can

- Add or remove mailboxes for users
- Establish or delete e-mail addresses
- Move a user's mailbox to another server
- Enable or disable Instant Messaging
- Hide or make known group memberships

Tip *If you want to hide the membership of a group, add the Everyone built-in security group to the Discretionary ACL (DACL) of the group, with Deny applied to the Read permission. You'll still be able to add members to the group, but the group's membership will not be available.*

Creating Mailbox-Enabled Users

To create a new mailbox for a user, right-click on the user's account in ADUC and select Exchange Tasks. The welcome screen for the Exchange Tasks Wizard should appear. At the bottom of the screen, there is a checkbox to select if you don't want to keep seeing this welcome screen. By all means, check that box because it's a waste of time to get welcomed to this wizard as often as you're going to be using it.

The next screen is the Available Tasks screen where you can add, delete, or move a mailbox; establish or modify an e-mail address; and enable or disable instant messaging. For purposes of this section, we'll choose to create a mailbox. All you need to do is highlight this option and click Next. The Create Mailbox screen will appear, as shown in Figure 8-2.

Select the desired server/storage group/mailbox store combination, modify the alias if needed and then click Next. The mailbox will be created and you'll be presented with the Finish screen. If you'd like to make any changes, before you click Next, click the Back button and you'll be able to make your changes.

After a mailbox is created, there may be times when you'll want to move the mailbox to another location, such as when there is a new server or when the user has changed locations in the company, to the home server closest to the user's new location. In these types of scenarios, you'll still use the Exchange Tasks Wizard to move a mailbox. Just start the wizard as described previously and select Move Mailbox. After making that selection, you'll be presented with the Move Mailbox screen (Figure 8-3), where in the current mailbox's location will be displayed along with the drop down boxes for you to select a new server/storage group/mailbox store combination. Make the desired

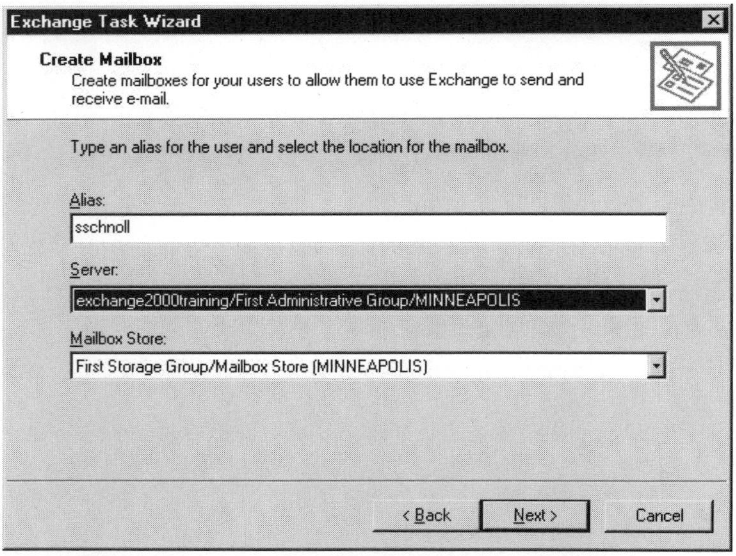

Figure 8-2. *Create Mailbox screen in Exchange Tasks Wizard*

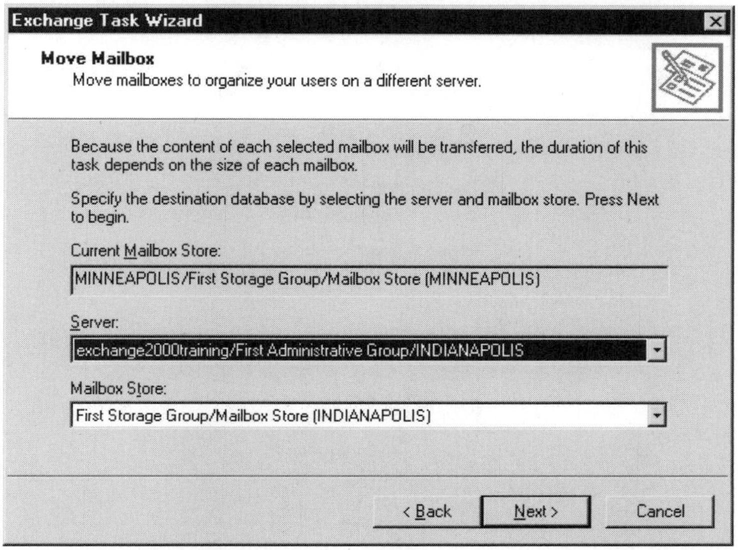

Exchange Task Wizard

Move Mailbox
Move mailboxes to organize your users on a different server.

Because the content of each selected mailbox will be transferred, the duration of this task depends on the size of each mailbox.

Specify the destination database by selecting the server and mailbox store. Press Next to begin.

Current Mailbox Store:
MINNEAPOLIS/First Storage Group/Mailbox Store (MINNEAPOLIS)

Server:
exchange2000training/First Administrative Group/INDIANAPOLIS

Mailbox Store:
First Storage Group/Mailbox Store (INDIANAPOLIS)

< Back | Next > | Cancel

Figure 8-3. *Move mailbox screen in Exchange Tasks Wizard*

selections and then click Next. The Task in Progress screen will appear and indicate how the move is progressing. After it is successful (or unsuccessful), you'll be presented with the Finish screen, where you can finish the wizard.

It is worth noting that if the mailbox move is unsuccessful, the Finish screen will indicate this too. If you look closely at Figure 8-4, you'll see that our efforts to move Sue Smith's mailbox failed because the MAPI provider failed. What is helpful is that some type of message is provided. In our example, the MAPI provider has failed, so we would start the troubleshooting process by verifying that the source and target mailbox stores are mounted. If either store is dismounted, this error message will be generated. So, if a task ends unsuccessfully, don't click on the Finish button until you've read through the screen to see what the error message is.

Creating Mail-Enabled Users

Creating mail-enabled users is very similar to creating a mailbox-enabled user, except that in the Exchange Tasks Wizard instead of choosing Create Mailbox on the Available Tasks screen, you'll select Establish e-mail addresses. Then, specify the type of e-mail address that should be created, input the address, associate the account with an administrative group, and then finish the wizard. It's really that simple.

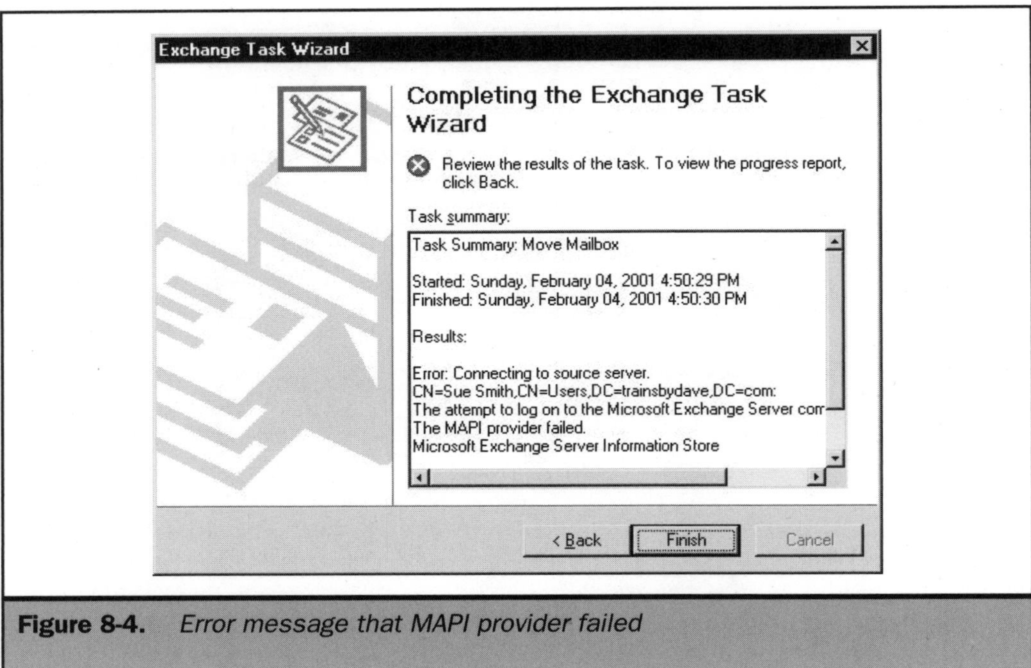

Figure 8-4. *Error message that MAPI provider failed*

Creating Mail-Enabled Contacts

Creating mail-enabled contacts can be done either when the contact is created or afterwards. When creating the contact, you can choose to mail-enable the object. After the contact is created, you can use the Exchange Tasks Wizard to mail-enable it.

If you choose to mail-enable a contact when creating it, select the "Create e-mail address" checkbox, choose the type of address you want to create, and enter the address information. All this is accomplished in the wizard you use to create the new contact. If the contact object already exists, use the Exchange Tasks Wizard to create a new e-mail address for it. When this wizard is run on a contact object in AD, the only available task is creating a new e-mail address. Other options will not appear since a contact object cannot have a mailbox or use instant messaging.

Creating Mail-Enabled Groups

Mail-enabling a group requires a bit of planning. There are two types of groups: distribution and security. Either can be mail-enabled, but only security groups can be used in ACLs for permission assignments, so that if you want to use the default

Domain users security group as a distribution group, you can mail-enable it. But doing so creates this situation: each user on that list must be a mailbox-enabled user on your LAN, and all the users on your LAN will have designated access to each resource to which you assign permissions for the default users group. The goal of allowing groups to be mail-enabled was to offset the need to create two identical lists of users, one for permission assignments and one as a mail distribution list. However, there is the possibility at some point in the future that you may not want these lists to be identical and would prefer the flexibility of two different lists. Therefore, thoroughly consider the ramifications when combining different functions into one type of group.

To create a new distribution group, right-click on the organizational unit (OU) in which you wish to create the group, point to New, and select Group. As shown in Figure 8-5, the procedure is to enter the Group name, select its scope and type, and click Next.

The screen shown in Figure 8-6 is where you specify that the group receives an e-mail address. You can input an alias that is different from the group's name and associate an administrative group with it. Click Next and then Finish, and both the group and its e-mail address will be created.

If the group already exists, use the Exchange Tasks Wizard to create a new e-mail address for the group.

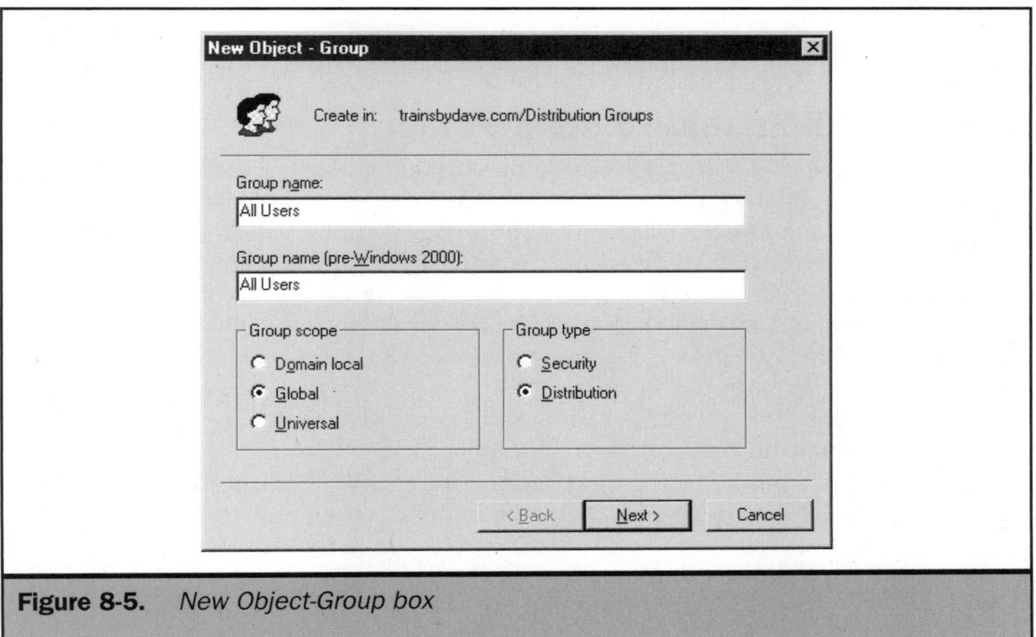

Figure 8-5. *New Object-Group box*

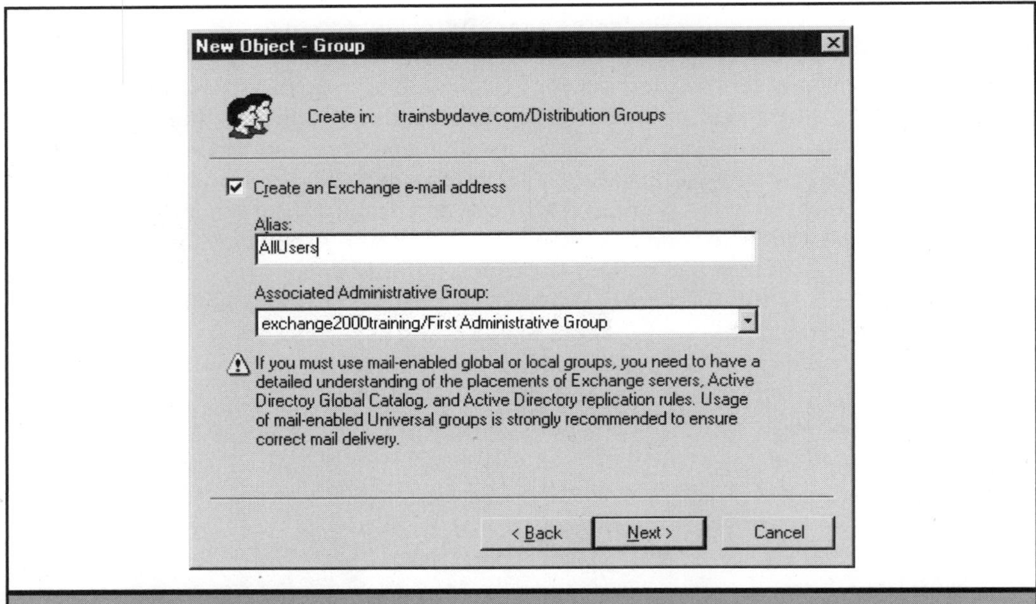

Figure 8-6. *Specifying an alias and administrative group for new mail-enabled group*

Creating a Mail-Enabled Public Folder

Working with public folders is different from working with users, contacts, or groups. Public folders are usually created using either the ESM snap-in or the Outlook client. However, the action of mail-enabling a public folder is accomplished using the ADUC snap-in. In some cases, public folders are automatically mail-enabled when they are created. For instance, in mixed mode, all public folders created in the default Public Folder Tree are mail-enabled. In native mode, they are not. New public folders in general purpose trees are not mail-enabled, whether Exchange is in mixed mode or native mode.

Except for public folders that are automatically mail-enabled in mixed mode, a public folder's e-mail address will be published to the Global Address List.

To mail-enable a public folder, right-click on the folder in System Manager, point to All Tasks, then select Mail-enable. After the folder has been mail-enabled, you can perform the same administrative routine to delete the folder's address by selecting Mail-disable from this menu.

Administering Mail-Enabled Accounts

Administration of mail-enabled accounts is accomplished in the ADUC snap-in. In this section, we'll take a look at how to administer mail-enabled accounts.

Mailbox-Enabled Users

This is the most complex account to administer. To administer a mailbox-enabled user, be sure to enable the advanced view in ADUC by navigating to the View menu then selecting Advanced. Unless you do this, you will not see the Advanced tab in a user's account properties.

There are four tabs that are used to manage a user's Exchange settings: General, E-mail address, Features, and Advanced.

The General tab, as shown in Figure 8-7, displays the user's current mailbox store and alias. In addition, delivery restrictions, delivery options, and storage limits can be configured. You can change the alias by typing in a new alias. The one that appears here is the default SMTP alias.

The delivery restrictions dialog box can be used to restrict messages based on message size as well as to specify particular accounts that can send mail to this account.

The delivery options dialog box allows you to configure "Send on behalf of" permissions, a forwarding address, and the maximum number of recipients for outgoing messages. The forwarding address section allows you to forward mail for this account to another account, which can be any mail-enabled object. It also allows you to deliver the message to both the forwarding address and the local mailbox. In this instance, Exchange is basically creating a blind-carbon copy (BCC) of a message and forwarding the message to the other specified e-mail account.

Under storage limits, you can configure the mailbox to hold a maximum-size limit of mail. Then you can configure limits for issuing a warning message or prohibiting a user from sending e-mail or from sending and receiving e-mail. In addition, deleted-item retention times can be configured so that if the user deletes an item from the deleted items folder in Outlook, it can be recovered within the retention period.

The E-mail Addresses tab is the location to specify multiple e-mail addresses for a user's account. By default, there is one SMTP and one X.400 address for each mail-enabled object in the AD. The SMTP address is necessary (and required) because Exchange 2000 is SMTP based. The X.400 address is no longer required but is there for connectivity to older systems that might use the X.400 protocol.

Multiple addresses can be associated with a single user account, and they do not need to have the same domain name. A typical example of when you would want to use this is if the user has a name that's difficult to spell name. For instance, the name "Gayle" can also be spelled "Gale" or "Gail." It might be a good idea to input the various misspellings of some user accounts so that the number of NDRs is reduced.

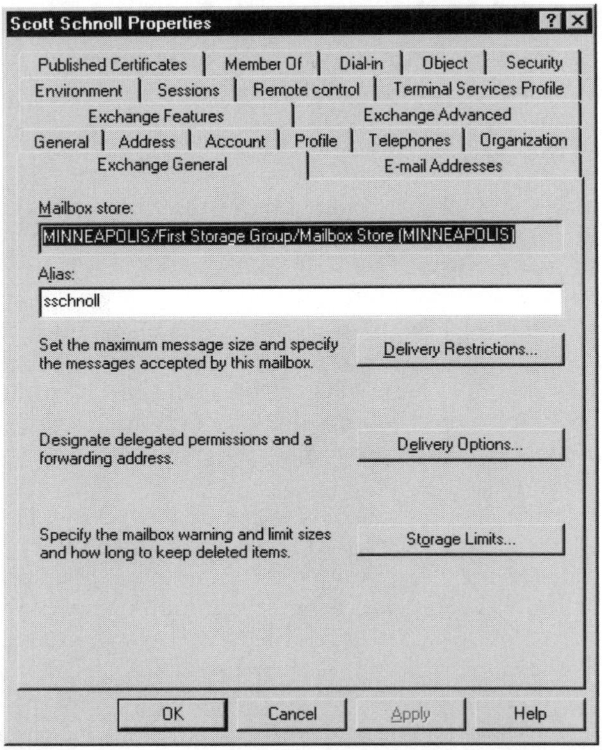

Figure 8-7. *Exchange General tab in user account properties*

The highlighted SMTP address is the one that is Set as Primary, which means that this will be the address that appears in the recipient's screen as the address for replying to e-mail.

The Exchange features tab is where you can enable or disable instant messaging for the user account. By default, it is disabled. Instant messaging is discussed further in Chapter 16.

The Advanced tab, as shown in Figure 8-9, is where several important configuration options appear, not all of them related to each other. First, you can enter a Simple display name—a name used by foreign e-mail systems that don't understand the display names in Exchange.

You can also hide this recipient from address lists, including the Global Address List, by selecting the "Hide from Exchange address lists" checkbox. In addition, if you have X.400 mail being sent from this box as high priority and you wish to downgrade

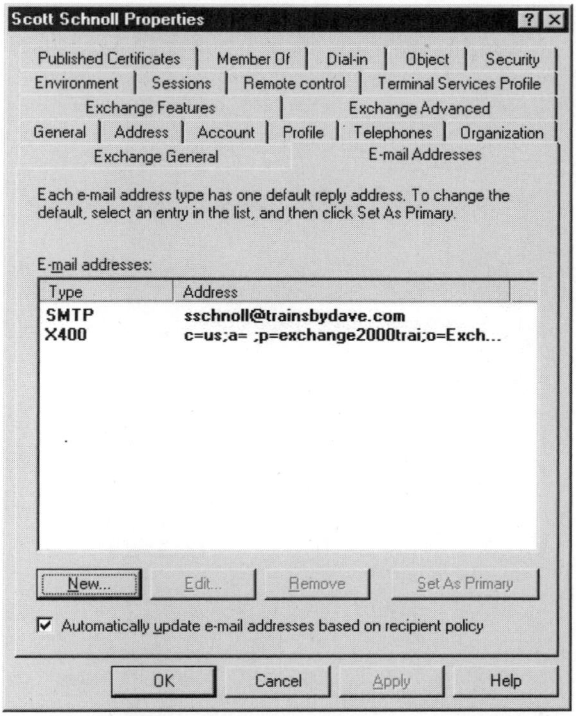

Figure 8-8. *E-mail Addresses tab in user account properties*

its priority to normal, then select the "Downgrade high priority mail bound for X.400" checkbox.

The Custom Attributes dialog box allows you to configure the data for a custom attribute for this user account. The Protocol Settings dialog box is used to enable or disable the HTTP, IMAP4, or POP3 protocol for this user account. Sometimes, it's nice to disable Outlook Web Access (OWA) for a particular mailbox, such as a journaling recipient, if you don't want the mailbox available over the internet. The ILS settings dialog box is where you input the Internet Locator Service server location, by name or IP address, for use with NetMeeting. Finally, you can configure mailbox rights using the Mailbox Rights dialog box, which is essentially configuring the DACL for the mailbox.

Tip *To learn more about the Discretionary Access Control List, please consult the Windows 2000 Resource Kit.*

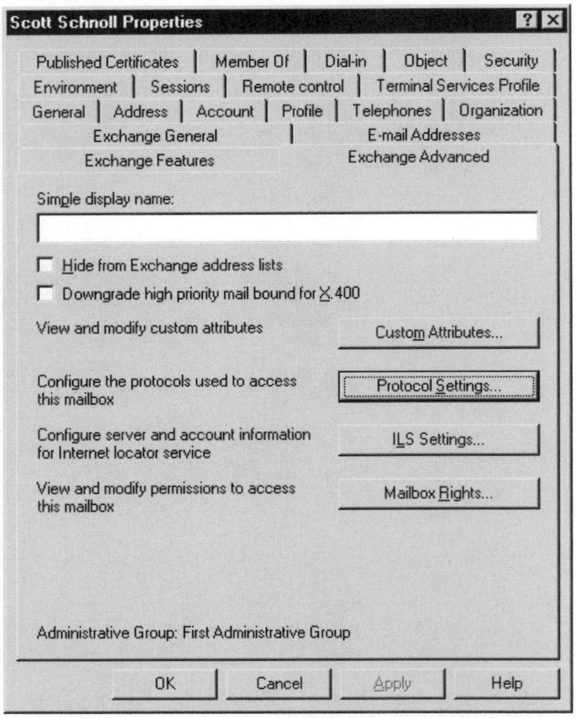

Figure 8-9. *Exchange Advanced tab in user account properties*

Mail-Enabled Users

Many of the configuration options for a mail-enabled user are the same as for a mailbox-enabled user. However, there are some differences that will be highlighted here.

First, on the General tab, shown in Figure 8-10, you can see that the account is associated with an SMTP address and that the alias for this account can be changed. In addition, there is only an incoming message size limit and no outgoing message size limit. On the Exchange Advanced tab, there are configuration options for only the Custom Attributes and the ILS Settings. The Mailbox Rights and the Protocols buttons are not needed for a mail-enabled user account.

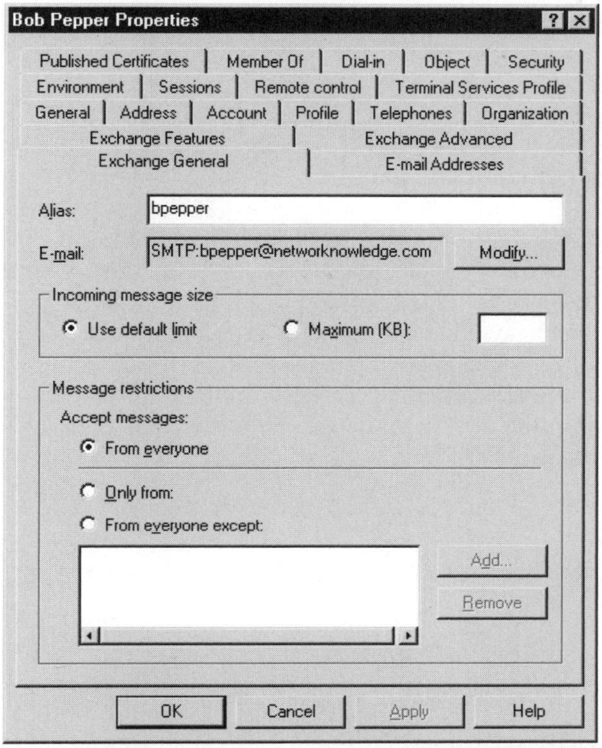

Figure 8-10. *Exchange General tab in mail-enabled user properties*

Mail-Enabled Contacts

The Exchange-specific properties of a mail-enabled contact are nearly identical to that of a mail-enabled user account. This type of account has three tabs: Exchange General, E-mail Addresses, and Advanced. The only difference between this account type and the mail-enabled user is that on the E-mail Addresses tab, you'll find only an SMTP address. There won't be an X.400 address because this object is strictly for holding foreign e-mail addresses and doesn't represent a unique object in the Exchange global address list. Otherwise, all the configuration options for this object type are the same as previously described for a mail-enabled user.

Mail-Enabled Groups

There are three Exchange-specific tabs for a mail-enabled group: Exchange General, E-mail Addresses, and Exchange Advanced. Each feature on each of these tabs has been described previously, with the exceptions described next.

On the Exchange Advanced tab, as shown in Figure 8-11, there are several options unique to managing a distribution list.

First, you can select to have out-of-office messages returned to the message originator instead of the distribution group itself. By default, this checkbox is cleared. Select it if you want the message originator to know that a recipient received, but did not read, the message because of being away from the office.

Second, you can choose to have delivery reports sent to the group owner or to the message originator or to not send back the delivery reports. If you think this one through, you'll realize that if a delivery report is requested for a distribution group of 500 recipients, then either the group owner or the message originator will receive up to 500 delivery reports in their inbox. In some circumstances, this might be desirable, such as when the

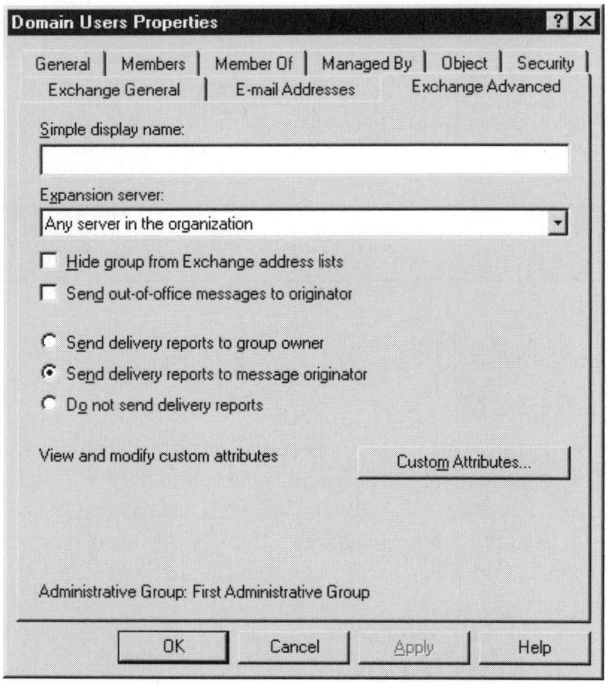

Figure 8-11. *Exchange Advanced tab for mail-enabled group*

message is of high importance or if there is a need to keep track of who has received the message. However, in most instances, there should be little need to have delivery reports generated. By default, delivery reports are sent to the message originator.

Mail-Enabled Public Folders

Public folders are their own beast. They are mail-enabled in System Manager and managed with the same utility. For our purposes, we created a MigrationProject public folder in the All Public Folders tree, which has been mail-enabled. When we right-click on this folder and open its properties, we find that there are three Exchange-specific tabs: Exchange General (shown in Figure 8-12), E-mail Addresses, and Exchange Advanced, which are shown in Figure 8-12.

You cannot change the tree in which the folder is created; however, you can change its alias. If you do, give it time to propagate to all the GCs, since that is where the DSProxy service refers client requests for address book lookups.

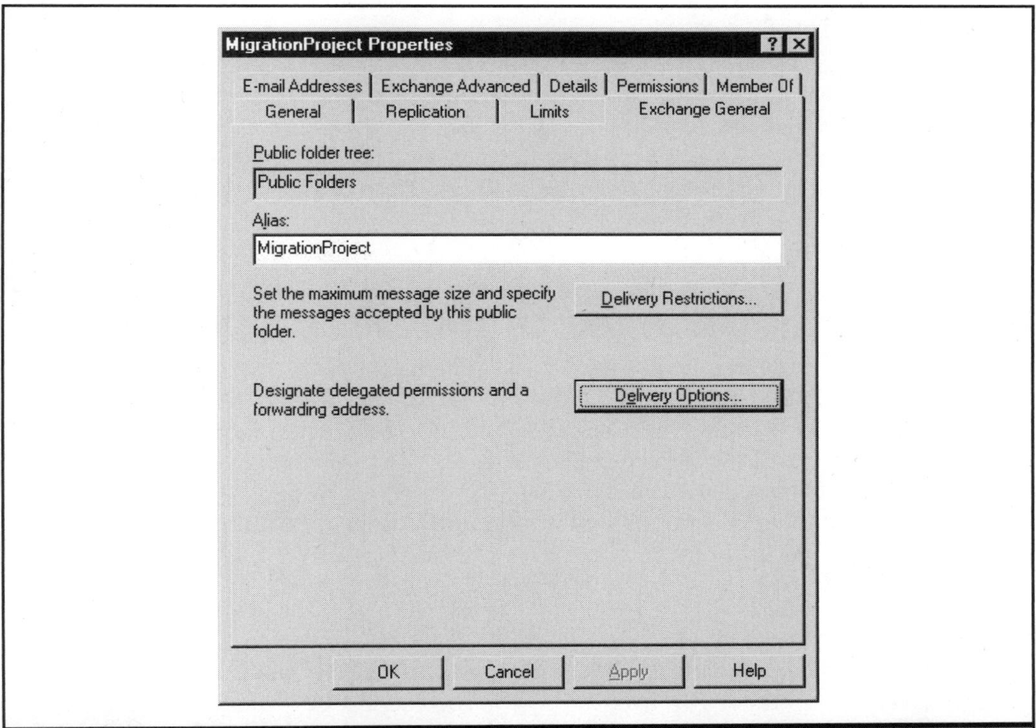

Figure 8-12. *Exchange General tab for mail-enabled public folder*

You can also set delivery restrictions and options. The restrictions available include outgoing and incoming message size as well as limitations on who can send messages to this public folder. The delivery options allow for configuring Send on Behalf of permissions and Forwarding addresses.

The features listed on the E-mail Addresses tab and the Exchange Advanced tab work the same as previously discussed under the Mailbox-Enabled Users section.

Note *Several things about Global Catalog servers (GC servers) are worth noting: 1) membership of global groups is not enumerated in GC servers, 2) membership of universal groups is enumerated in GC servers, and 3) all address book lookups are serviced by the GC in Exchange 2000. If you send a message to a mail-enabled global group in a remote domain, that group's membership will not be enumerated in the GC; in such cases, the GC will return a null response to your Exchange 2000 server, and the mail will not be sent. However, no error message or NDR will be generated. In order to send messages to mail-enabled groups whose membership is either partially or wholly housed in a remote domain, you'll need to use universal groups because their membership is enumerated in the GC, and distribution list expansion can occur. However, in order to have universal groups, you'll need at least one domain that is running in Windows 2000 native mode. Hence, during a migration from Exchange 5.5/Windows NT 4.0 to Exchange 2000/Windows 2000, it will be a good idea to create one empty, but native-mode domain for this purpose. Create universal groups inside this domain, then mail-enable these universal groups to send mail to users whose accounts have been created in different domains. Keep in mind that each time the membership of a universal group changes, it creates additional GC replication traffic. Therefore, use universal groups wisely.*

Making Bulk Changes to the Directory

From time to time, you may need to make bulk change to the Exchange recipients in the AD. There are two tools that can be used to make bulk changes to the AD: the Lightweight Directory Access Protocol Data Interchange Format Directory Exchange (LDIFDE) tool and the CSV Directory Exchange tool. Both can be used to extend the schema or add new objects into the schema.

By using these tools, it is possible to import and export large numbers of objects, such as users, groups, and computers, into or out of AD.

LDIFDE

LDIFDE is a command-line utility that works with the LDAP Data Interchange Format (LDIF) file format. It can be run from Windows 2000 Server or Professional. The LDIF format is based on the Lightweight Directory Access Protocol (LDAP) standard, an Internet standard for querying an X.500 directory. In most cases, an LDIF file will consist of a series of records divided by line separators. A *record* consists of one or more lines that either create a new object in the directory or apply a set of modifications to an existing object. At the time of this writing, the LDIF format itself is a draft Internet standard.

Using LDIFDE

To view the general parameters of the LDIFDE utility, open up a command prompt and type:

```
Ldifde /?
```

The built-in Help file will display the general parameters, the export and import parameters, and additional information about credentials. To export and then import a set of new user accounts and their organizational units from one directory to another, perform these steps:

1. Log on as an administrator in the Export domain
2. At the command prompt, type

```
Ldifde -f ou.ldf -s <servername> -d "dc=networknowledge; dc=com" -p subtree
```

As shown in Figure 8-13, running this command:

- creates an export ldif file called OU.LDF with the –f switch
- specifies the export server name with the –s switch

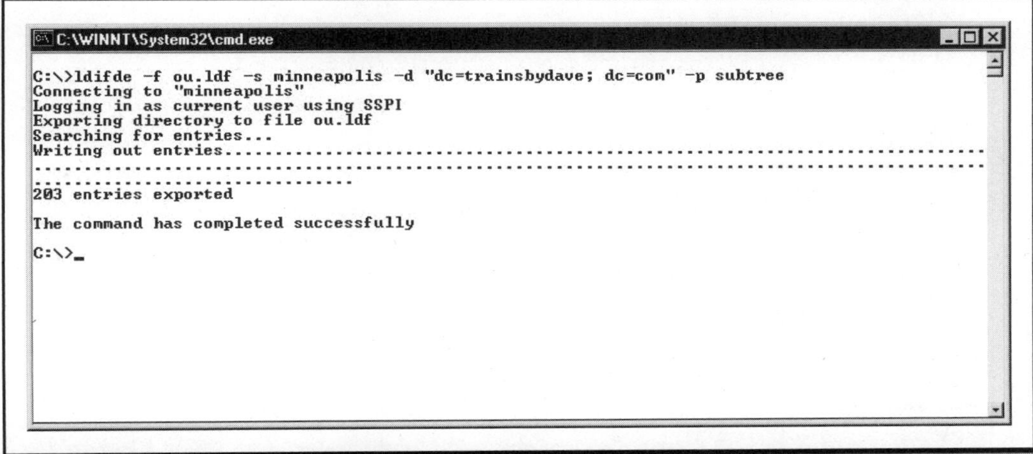

Figure 8-13. *LDIFDE command in the command prompt*

- specifies the root DN of networknowledge.com from which to conduct the search with the –d switch
- specifies that all subtrees should be searched and recorded in the OU.LDF file with the –p switch

Figure 8-14 shows the OU.LDF file in Microsoft Word 2000.

To export the user accounts in these OUs, type the following command at the command prompt:

```
Ldifde -f users.ldf -s <servername> -d "dc=networknowledge, dc=com" -p subtree
-r"(&(objectcatagory=person) (objectclass=user) (givename=*))" -l
"cn,giveName,objectclass,samAccountName"
```

The first part of the command is nearly identical to the OU export command previously discussed. Only two switches were added: the –r switch, which specifies the filter we want to use for exporting only certain object types, and the –l switch, which

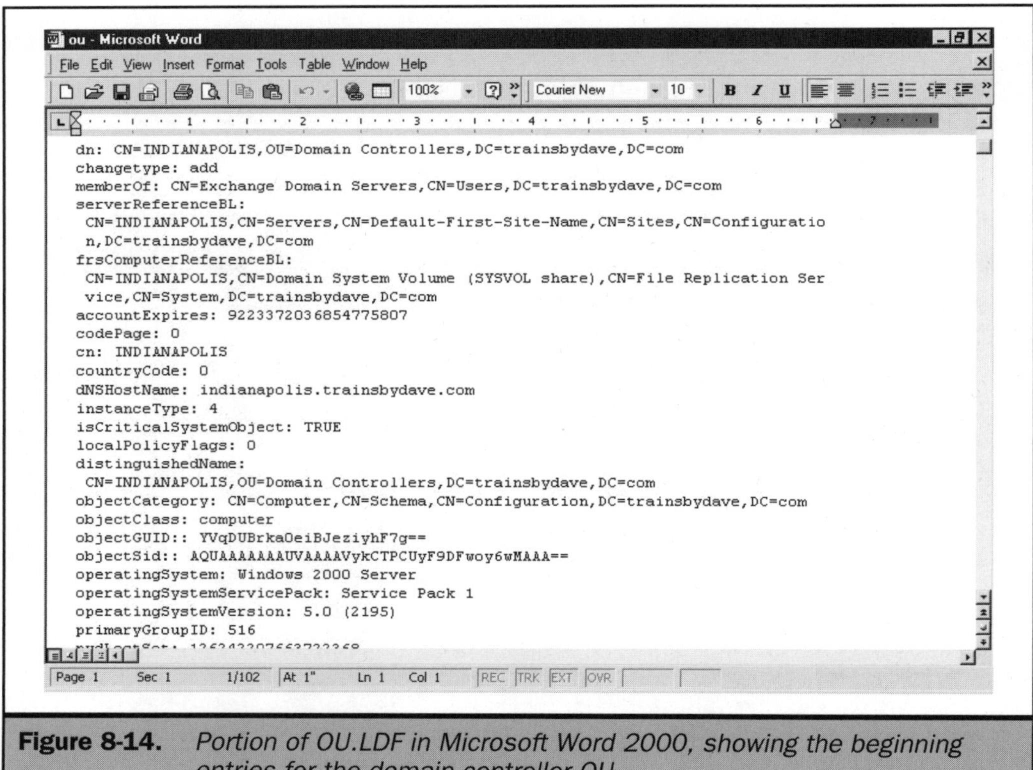

Figure 8-14. *Portion of OU.LDF in Microsoft Word 2000, showing the beginning entries for the domain controller OU*

specifies, in a comma separated format, the attributes of those object types we want exported to the USERS.LDF file.

If we had wanted to export the e-mail address attribute of the user objects for modification, we would have chosen the mail attribute.

Note *Passwords cannot be exported from AD using the LDIFDE utility. In addition, the default built-in user accounts do not have a given name; therefore, by default, LDIFDE does not export those accounts.*

After making the desired changes to the accounts in your spreadsheet, you're ready to import your information. First, to import OUs into AD, use the following command:

```
Ldifde -I -f ou.ldf -s <servername>
```

The –I switch is used to signify that this is an import operation. The –f switch specifies the file from which the information is being taken, and *servername* specifies the server that will receive the new information from the OU.LDF file.

Tip *In each file that you are modifying, be sure to replace all the "export" entries with "import" and change the domain name to reflect the target domain to which you are importing the information.*

After making changes to user accounts, you can import them into the new AD by using the following command:

```
Ldifde -I -f users.ldf -s <servername>
```

This is the same command used for importing the OUs. The file itself contains all of the necessary information to help the process know where to put the accounts during the import activity.

Note *If you are in a multidomain environment and you wish to export all of the user accounts in the forest, run the export command against a Global Catalog (GC) server. If there are certain attributes you need to export, you'll need to first ensure that those attributes have been selected to be included in the GC before performing the export operation. To run the export operation against the GC, use the –s switch to specify the server name of the GC and the –t switch to specify port 3268.*

Since you can't import user account passwords, when a user account is imported, the account is disabled and its password is set to null. In addition, the option to force the user to change their password at the next logon is selected. Therefore, after importing user accounts, you'll need to manually enable the accounts before they can be used.

Table 8-1 lists the switches that can be used with LDIFDE.

Switch	Specified Values	Meaning
-I	Mode	Specifies import mode. The default mode for LDIFDE is export.
-f	Name of file	Specifies the file name for the export or import operation.
-s	Server name	Specifies the name of the server for the export or import operation. If no server is specified, the server to which the user is currently logged on becomes the default server.
-c	Replaces the characters in string 1 with string 2	This is used when the import and export domain names are not the same. You'll replace the export domain name string of characters with the import domain name string of characters.
-t	Port number	Specifies the port number to be used during an export operation. To export from the AD, use port 389. To export from the GC, use port 3268.
-y	NA	Enables a lazy commit operation to the directory.
-u	Unicode	Enables Unicode support.
-g	Paged searches	This switch specifies that paged searches should not be performed. Paged searches are performed by default.

Table 8-1. *LDIFDE Switches*

Switch	Specified Values	Meaning
-j	Directory path	Sets the log file location. The default log file location is the current directory.
-n	Binary values	Specifies not to export binary values. This option is disabled by default.
-m	AD attributes	Omits AD attributes that apply only to AD objects. You'll use this option to export entries that will be modified and prepared for importation. Use of the –m switch also enables the linked attribute option so that if there is another object that is linked to the target object, the linked object's attributes will be appended to the end of the file. The –m option will not export read-only attributes.
-o	Attributes in results	Omits a specified list of attributes from the result set. If the –o switch is not used, then all attributes are included in the result set.
-l	Attribute list	Specifies the attributes of the object to be included in the result set.
-p	Scope	Specifies the search scope. Acceptable values are base, one level, and subtree.

Table 8-1. *LDIFDE Switches* (continued)

Switch	Specified Values	Meaning
-r	Attribute filter	Sets a filter on the selected attributes so that only those strings of characters in the specified attributes that meet the filter will be included in the result set.
-d	Base DN	Sets the base distinguished name of the search. If unspecified, the default is the root of the directory.
-k	Actions to be taken in case of errors	Specifies that errors should be skipped and processing should continue.
-a	User DN password or *	Specifies the user distinguished name and password context in which the command should be run. The "*" means that the password is hidden. The default is to run the command under the security context of the currently logged on user.
-b	User domain password or *	Specifies the user domain name and password context in which the command should be run. The "*" means that the password is hidden. The default is to run the command under the security domain context of the currently logged on user.
?	NA	Brings up the online help file.

Table 8-1. *LDIFDE Switches* (continued)

CSVDE

The CSV Directory Exchange (CSVDE) utility is meant to work with a text file where data is stored in comma-separated value (CSV) format. The CSV file format is supported by applications, such as Excel, that can read and save data in the CSV file format. CSVDE allows you *only* to add new objects. It cannot be used to modify objects that have been exported from a directory, though object attribute modification can be conducted in an Excel spreadsheet before the object is imported into the directory for the first time. CSVDE can be run on Windows 2000 Server or Professional.

Note *There are a number of considerations when using Exchange 5.5 Server as an import backbone. Let's assume that you have a high number of user accounts that you need to import into Active Directory and you're having a difficult time working with the CSVDE and LDIFDE utilities. Consider using an Exchange 5.5 Server as an intermediary platform from which to import your user accounts. If you are familiar with the Exchange 5.5 directory import tools, you know that as long as the accounts can be listed in CSV format, the import process is relatively easy. Plus, the Exchange 5.5 tools have a graphical interface, which is easier to work with than the command-line tools. So, install an Exchange 5.5 server into your Active Directory, import the new accounts into the Exchange 5.5 directory, then use the Active Directory Connector service to upload the accounts into Active Directory. This process gives you a graphical method of importing the user accounts. In addition, you don't need to work with the directory roots, such as dc=users, dc=networknowledge, dc=com, in your spreadsheets. The ADC will take care of this for you. This might also be a good alternative if you are migrating from messaging systems that have better tools for migrating to Exchange 5.5 than does Exchange 2000. The obvious downsides are that another server is required, and you need proficiency in working with the Active Directory Connector.*

It would be natural to think that this utility has its own set of switches that must be learned in order to use it proficiently; however, this isn't the case. CSVDE uses the same switches as LDIFDE.

When data is viewed in the csv file, the values for each object's attributes are listed left to right in the order in which the attribute names are listed in the initial entry. Every entry must account for each attribute listing in the initial entry. A missing or unsupported value will have an empty (",,") position in the string. In Figure 8-15, we exported the OU directory information to OU.CSV, and you can see that the information has been added to the Excel spreadsheet. We cannot use CSVDE to make changes and copy the information back into the trainsbydave directory to modify the OU structure or names. But if this spreadsheet contained *new* information, we could use it to import a new OU structure into the trainsbydave directory.

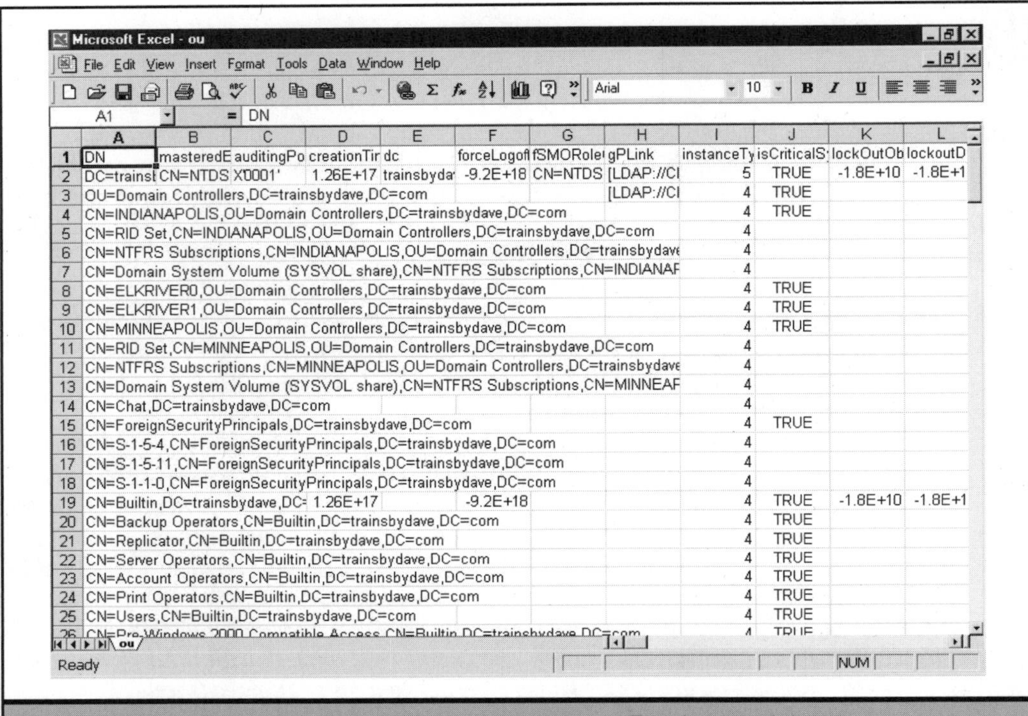

Figure 8-15. *OU information in a csv format in an Excel spreadsheet*

Windows Script Host

The Windows Script Host (WSH) is a language-independent host for running scripts in 32-bit Windows platforms using languages such as Perl, JScript, or Visual Basic. WSH enables scripts to be executed directly on the desktop or the command console without needing to embed the scripts in an HTML document. You must have Internet Explorer 3.0 or later installed before you can use WSH. WSH is also installed as part of Windows 98, Windows 2000, and Internet Explorer 5.0. WSH scripts can be run when a script file is invoked through a double-click event or when manually specified at the Windows run command or at a command prompt.

For example, here's a script that will create a new user account for Bill English in the users OU in the trainsbydave.com domain:

```
Dim oContainer 'Parent container of new user

Dim oUser 'Created user

Get
parentcontainerSetoContainer=GetObject("LDAP://OU=users,DC=trainsbydave,DC=com")

'Create user

Set oUser = oContainer.Create("User","CN=Bill English")

Assign properties values to user

User.Put "samAccountName","Bill"

User.Put "givenName","Bill"

User.Put "sn","English"

User.Put "userPrincipalName","benglish@trainsbydave.com"

User.SetInfo

'Clean up

Set oUser = Nothing

Set oContainer = Nothing

WScript.Echo "Finished"
```


After creating the script, you can save it in a file with a .vbs extension, then enter the correct information into the script for each new user and run it to create new users. In addition, controls can be embedded into a script like this to pull user specific information from an Excel spreadsheet or a SQL database. For more information on how to use these scripts and the Windows Script Host, please see the Microsoft Developer Network (MSDN) library online at http://msdn.microsoft.com/scripting/windowshost/default.htm.

Recovering a Mailbox

When users leave a company, you typically don't want to delete their mailbox right away, even though you may delete their user account. This is because when another person is hired to replace this user, they may need access to the departed user's e-mail in order to "get up to speed" more quickly. In addition, there are times when a mailbox might be accidentally deleted and need to be recovered.

Until Exchange 2000, the only way to recover an entire mailbox was to restore an entire database from tape backup. This was a poor way to recover a mailbox. In Exchange 2000, it's different. You can set a deleted-item retention time on a mailbox and give yourself an opportunity to recover the mailbox and, if necessary, associate it with another user.

Configuring Deleted Mailbox Retention Times

To configure the deleted mailbox retention times, navigate to the Limits tab of a mailbox store's properties and enter a value for the "Keep deleted mailboxes for (days)" input box. By default, this value is set to 30 days.

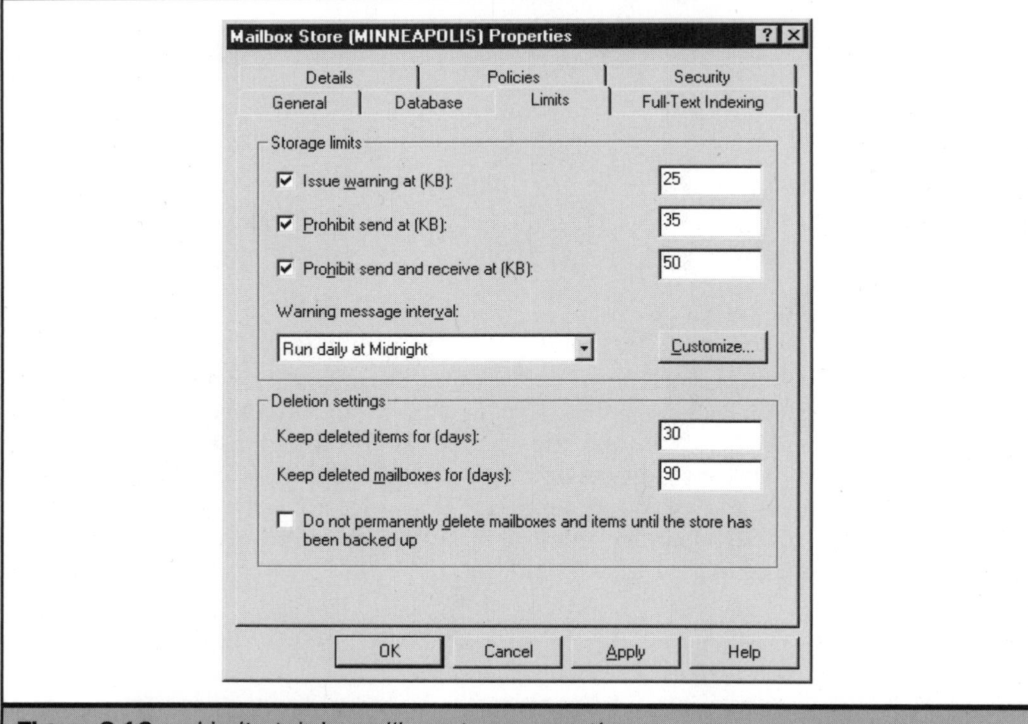

Figure 8-16. *Limits tab in mailbox store properties*

Once a user account that was mailbox-enabled is deleted, you'll find that the mailbox will appear in System Manager with a red X over the mailbox's icon. This mark indicates that the mailbox is in the Exchange information store but not associated with a user account.

If you want another user to use this mailbox, right-click on the mailbox and select Reconnect. Then, choose the user account to which you wish to connect this mailbox. The mailbox will then be available to the user to whom you just connected it.

Tip *The best practice is to have the "Keep deleted mailboxes for (days)" setting at least 30 days or longer. Doing this will save you (and your users) headaches when a single mailbox needs to be recovered.*

Summary

In this chapter, we described different recipient types, the properties for mail-enabled objects, and the use of LDIFDE and CSVDE utilities. We also discussed how to keep a deleted mailbox and how that mailbox can be assigned to a new user account. We also discussed the use of mail-enabled universal groups and some of the implications of using these types of groups. Finally, we looked at how Exchange 5.5 might act as an alternative method of importing objects into Active Directory as an alternative to using the LDIFDE utility.

Chapter 9

Managing Servers

Managing servers is an important part of administering Exchange 2000 Server. So, we'll cover four very important topics in this chapter: administrative groups, routing groups, the link state table, and addressing information. All four of these administrative areas are managed using the Exchange System Manager (ESM) snap-in.

This chapter also describes one of the major changes to Exchange administration. In Exchange 5.5, we have the concept of the *site*, which defined the administrative, routing, and namespace boundaries. These three boundaries have been broken apart and are now handled differently in Exchange 2000 Server.

Administrative boundaries are now managed by *Administrative Groups*, which is a collection of objects grouped together to which you can assign permissions and specific administrative functions. One nice feature of this arrangement is that the Administrative group is not geographically dependent: administrative functions can be applied to any Exchange 2000 server in the organization within an Administrative Group and assigned to any combination of users and groups.

Routing groups are now the way that we group servers in permanent, high-bandwidth environments. We recommend 256Kbps of available bandwidth for Exchange traffic for high-bandwidth environments. Unlike sites in Windows 2000, however, routing groups are not defined by the IP address subnet, but rather by creating the routing group and adding servers into the group. This means that you must know the physical location of each Exchange 2000 Server and the underlying physical topology in which it is situated in order to know if a server should be a member of one routing group or another. Bandwidth between routing groups is assumed to be low and unreliable, but does not need to be.

The last function served by an Exchange 5.5 site is *namespace function*. This is a rather technical detail, but if you've managed an Exchange 5.5 server, you might recall that when Exchange 5.5 is initially installed, the default Simple Mail Transport Protocol (SMTP) domain name is *sitename.organizationname.com*. This name was customizable in the Site Addressing properties so that you could make the default domain name for all recipients in the site whatever you wanted it to be. In Exchange 2000, namespace functions are managed by Active Directory (AD) and are not really a part of the Exchange 2000 platform.

We'll be taking a close look at two of these three changes: the administrative group and the routing group. But first, we need to describe how the Exchange System Manager snap-in works and familiarize you with its interface.

Using Exchange System Manager

The ESM snap-in has two panes, the left pane and the right pane. The left pane contains a console tree and the right pane contains the details for the object that has focus in the left pane. The hierarchy is compliant with the X.500 standard, which means, among other things, that it is composed of *containers* and *objects*. Figure 9-1 illustrates the ESM snap-in.

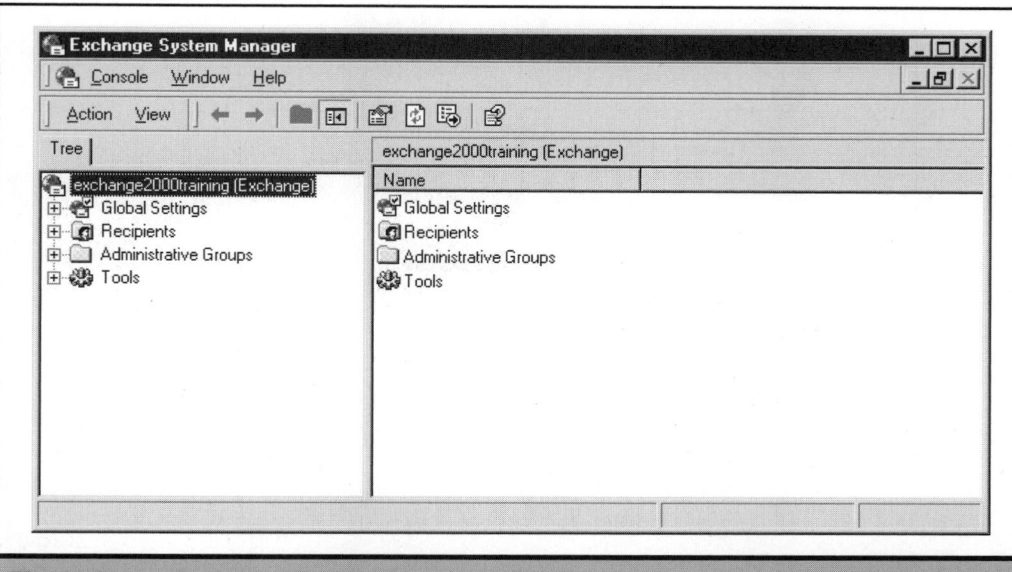

Figure 9-1. *Exchange System Manager snap-in*

A container is just that: a place to group objects in the directory. Usually, containers have little in the way of properties, other than a name, description, and an Access Control List (ACL). For instance, the visible properties of an administrative group container consist only of its name. The ACL is not visible in the ESM snap-in: you need to use the Active Directory Services Interface (ADSI) Edit utility to view the ACL of a container. Figure 9-2 shows the default ACL of the First Administrative Group.

Now, an object is different from a container in that an object represents an end point in the object hierarchy. An object may be defined as the basic element in Active Directory that is described and defined by attributes. Objects represent something on the network, such as a user, group, printer, computer, folder share, or an application.

An object may have numerous properties, such as the multitude of tabs and configuration options available on a user object, or a relatively few number of configuration options, such as for a mail-enabled public folder.

When navigating the ESM snap-in, a plus sign ("+") inside a square box usually indicates that there is another container or object nested inside the current container. However, one quirk of the ESM snap-in (and, for that matter, the Microsoft Management Console in general) is that when you read an end-point object, this sign will still appear next to the object even though there is nothing nested inside the object. Once the object is enumerated in the console, however, the plus sign will disappear if there are no subcontainers or child objects inside the object.

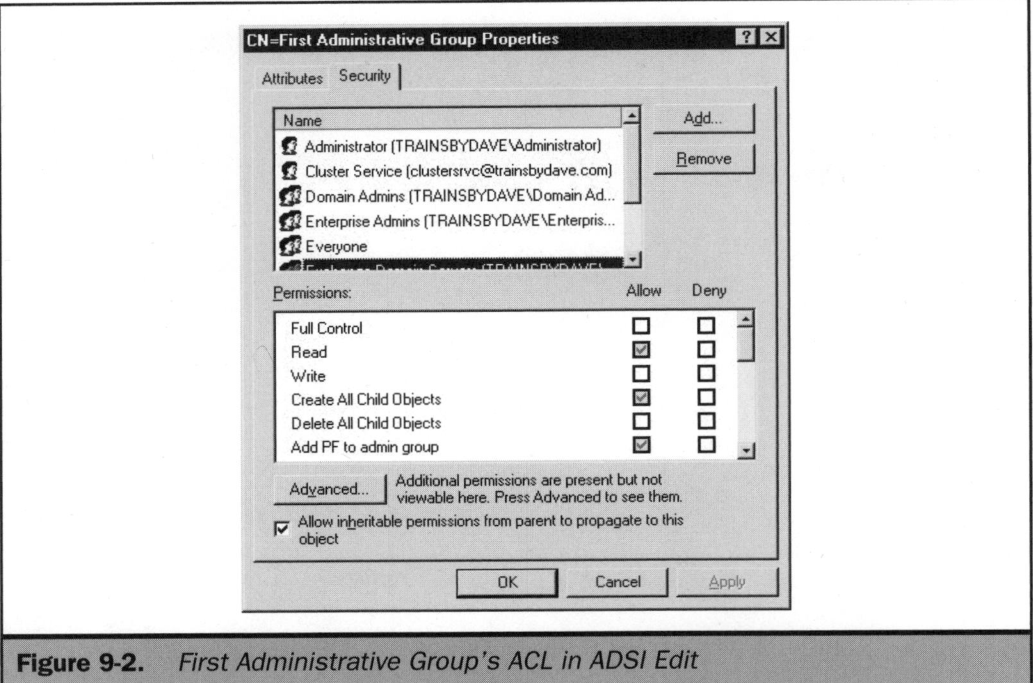

Figure 9-2. *First Administrative Group's ACL in ADSI Edit*

Working with Administrative Views

By default, Exchange 2000 is installed *not* displaying routing and administrative groups. It is installed in this way because most of the Exchange 2000 installations are made into environments where there are only one or two Exchange 2000 servers that require only one routing group and one administrative group. So, when Exchange 2000 is first installed, it will show seven containers in the containers pane in the ESM snap-in, as shown in Figure 9-3.

If you are going to work in a single routing group/single administrative group environment, then the default view should work for you. However, if you're going to be managing Exchange 2000 in a multi-routing group environment or a multi-administrative group environment, then you'll need to display the routing and administrative groups.

Even though administrative and routing groups are not displayed in the ESM snap-in, they are still displayed in the ADSI Edit utility.

To display either routing or administrative groups or both, right-click on the organization object and select either the Display administrative groups or Display

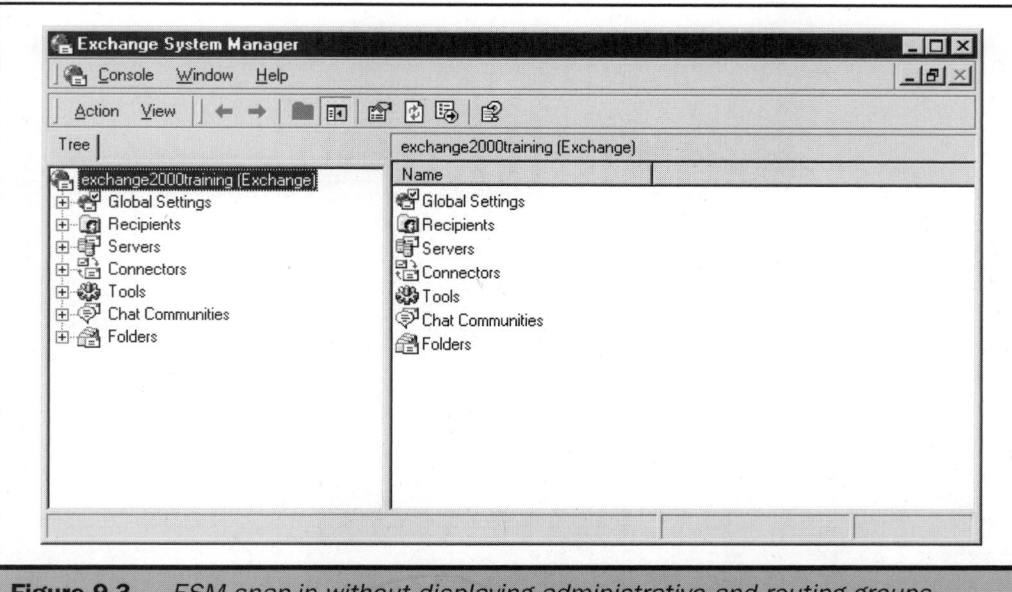

Figure 9-3. *ESM snap-in without displaying administrative and routing groups*

routing groups checkbox. If you choose to display just routing groups, you'll see the Connectors container replaced with a Routing Groups container. However, if you choose to display the administrative groups, you'll need to restart the ESM snap-in. Once it's restarted, you'll find that the number of containers initially displayed drops from seven to four, as shown in Figure 9-4, and that Administrative Groups is one of the top-level containers displayed.

If you choose to display both routing and administrative groups, the initial view does not change. However, under the administrative groups, you'll see the Connectors container replaced with the Routing Groups container.

Creating New Consoles from the ESM Snap-In

The ESM snap-in is actually comprised of multiple tools that can be opened inside of their own windows. Opening the snap-in is easily accomplished by navigating to the ESM snap-in menu option, right-clicking on the Exchange System Manager menu option, and selecting Author. The ESM snap-in will open up. Then, for each object that you right-click on and select New Window from Here, a new window focused on the selected object will be opened inside the same console. At this point, all you'll need to do is save that window as a new console and then it will be available for use as any other MMC console.

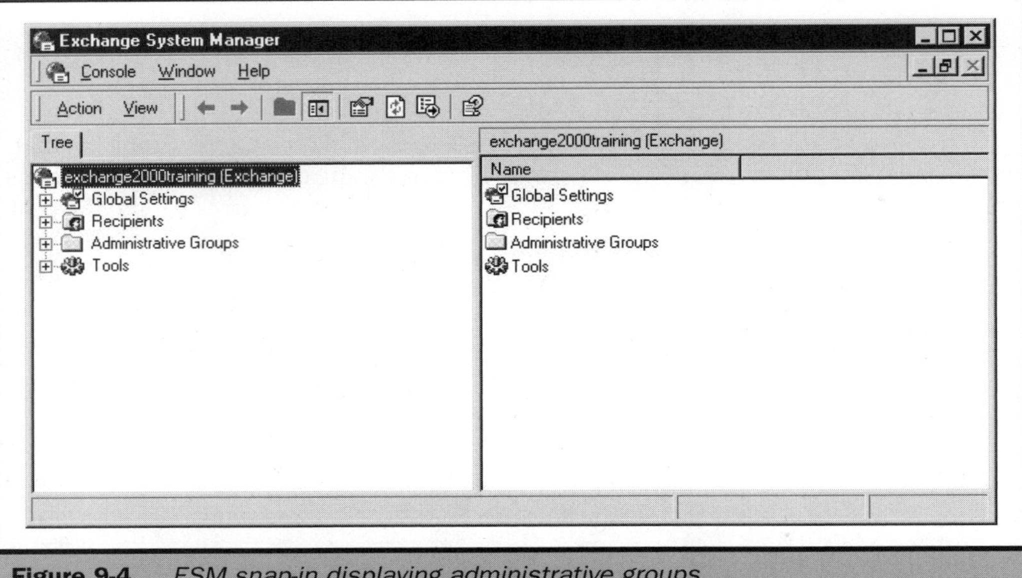

Figure 9-4. *ESM snap-in displaying administrative groups*

Administrative Groups

As we described earlier, administrative groups are containers in which administrative functions can be grouped and then assigned to individuals and groups. An administrative group is little more than a container to hold other administrative tools for administering Exchange 2000 servers. In this section, we'll take a look at planning for, pre-creating, and managing administrative groups.

Planning for Administrative Groups

When planning for administrative groups, you'll need to take some time and white-board how your administrative functions will be carried out and who will perform each one. In smaller environments with only one or two Exchange 2000 servers, doing this may not be a big deal. But in larger environments or those that include multiple servers placed in multiple locations, mapping out who will perform which duties is very important.

When planning for an administrative group topology, you'll have three basic choices: centralized, decentralized, or hybrid.

Centralized Administrative Model

In a centralized administrative model, all administrative functions are managed from a single location, regardless of how dispersed or centralized your user or server base is.

With a centralized model, you can achieve tight control over account management, server management, and policy management. A significant advantage is that you don't need to train other administrators to perform Exchange-specific administrative tasks in remote locations. The main disadvantage is that, in an environment where resources are dispersed, you may need to travel to remote locations in order to fix problems that might arise, especially if network problems inhibit your ability to manage remote servers. Of course, if the remote location is a beach in the Pacific, that may be considered a perk, not a problem.

In a centralized environment, all the administrative functions can be performed from within the default First Administrative Group, although this is not necessary to achieve a centralized approach. For instance, you may have a team of six Exchange administrators managing a worldwide network of 150 Exchange 2000 servers. You may decide to create an administrative group that will host all the routing groups. Then you create all the needed routing groups and assign permissions to that administrative group to three of your team members. Since the team members are all located in the same location, administration is centralized, though the administrative functions are divested between team members with the use of administrative groups.

Decentralized Administrative Model

In a decentralized administrative model, administrative functions are dispersed among the team members that, by geographical locations, require administrators in each location to administer the local Exchange 2000 servers or by divisional distinctions that require each division to pay for and manage its own set of servers.

The decentralized model allows for the same functions to be performed at multiple locations by different administrators. For instance, if you have five locations and decide to create an administrative group for each location, you could create a server policy for each location that is managed by an administrator at each location. In the aggregate, you'll have five different server policies, but each one will apply to servers in its own location and not to servers in other locations. This setup is helpful if each location has different policy needs.

Disadvantages of a decentralized model are possible loss of uniformity in configuration selections across the enterprise, increased administrative effort to create the correct permissions, and loss of centralized control.

Hybrid Administrative Model

In the hybrid administrative model, some administrative functions are dispersed and others are managed from a central location. A common scenario, for instance, is to centralize the administration of policies while allowing for the decentralization of other items, such as messaging connectors.

This model can also be used to combine one set of administrative functions and geographical considerations into one administrative model. For instance, you might create an administrative group to manage the routing groups, another to manage policies, and yet another group for a particular location. In other words, some administrative groups could be created for certain administrative functions while others reflect geographical needs.

Creating Administrative Groups

Creating an administrative group is relatively easy. Just right-click on the Administrative Groups container, point to New and select Administrative Group. As Figure 9-5 illustrates, you'll only need to input a new name for the group (we've chosen "Routing Group Admin Group") and then click OK. The administrative group will be created and can be seen in the ESM snap-in. The admin group name can contain a combination of letters and numbers only.

Once the new administrative group is created, it will appear empty inside the ESM snap-in, but this is not, in fact, the case. When we open up both the Active Directory Sites and Services snap-in as well as the ADSI Edit utility, we will see that there are two containers automatically created inside the new routing group: the Servers container and the Advanced Security container, as shown in Figure 9-6.

The Servers container is created to accept new servers into the new administrative group. The Advanced Security container is used to house a new Key Management Server service. The fact that these two containers are automatically created when a new administrative group is created brings up two points that we should consider.

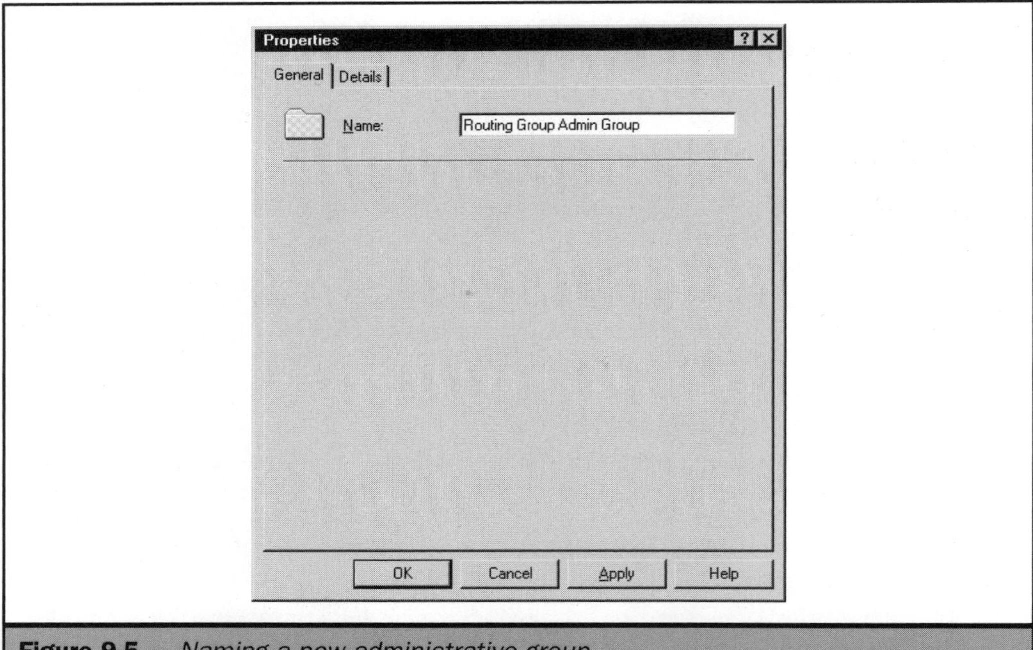

Figure 9-5. *Naming a new administrative group*

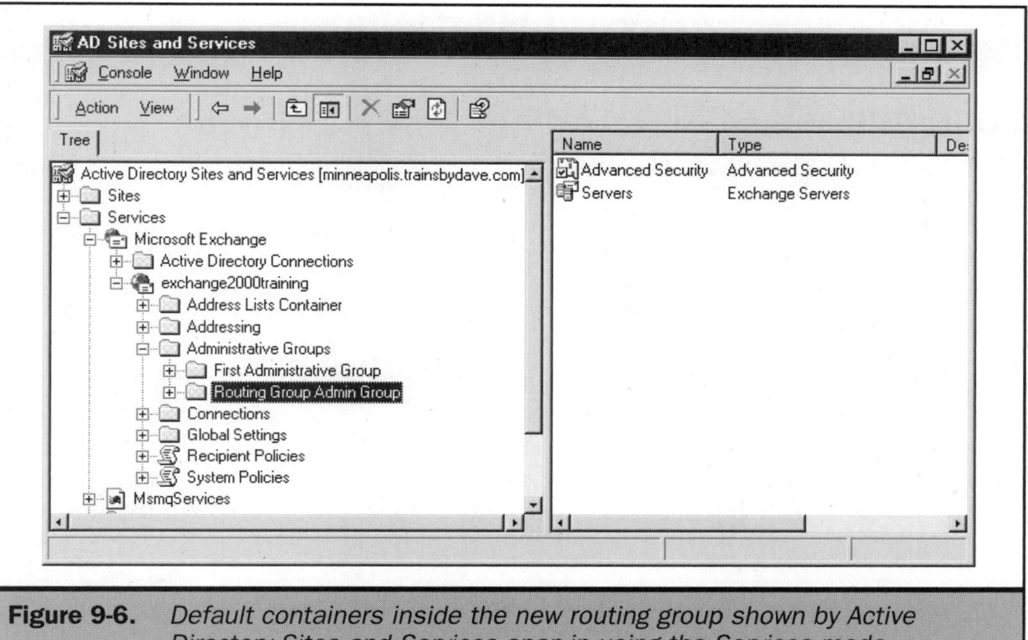

Figure 9-6. *Default containers inside the new routing group shown by Active Directory Sites and Services snap-in using the Services mode*

First, when you right-click on a new administrative group, you'll be given the option to create the following containers:

- Routing group container
- System policies container
- Chat communities container
- Public folders container

Notice that you are not given the option of creating a new Servers or Advanced Security container because these containers already exist inside of a new administrative group. Further, there can only exist one container of each kind inside an administrative group; therefore, if the container already exists inside the administrative group, it will not be available for creation from the context menu. Moreover, if the Servers or Advanced Security containers are deleted, they cannot be re-created in the ESM snap-in because they will not appear as a menu option in the administrative group's context menu.

Second, even though you cannot move servers between administrative groups using the ESM snap-in, you can do it using the Active Directory Sites and Services snap-in. Just right-click on the server you wish to move, navigate the directory hierarchy to the target server's container, and then click Move. The server will be moved and you can see the results of this action in the ESM snap-in.

Microsoft does not support the movement of servers between administrative groups using Active Directory Sites and Services.

Assigning Permissions to Administrative Groups

An administrative group is another object in the Active Directory (AD) in the configuration partition. As with any AD object, when it is created it will inherit its parent's permissions. Inheritance allows permissions to flow down the object hierarchy so that child objects do not need to have permissions assigned manually. This structure allows for the ability to set permissions for an entire range of objects by simply changing the permissions structure on the top-level object.

Assigning Permissions Using ADSI Edit

By default, the Enterprise Admins group has inherited full control permissions over your entire Exchange 2000 organization. This arrangement can be seen by opening up the organization object's properties in ADSI Edit and selecting the Security tab, as shown in Figure 9-7. If you need to change these permissions, you'll first need to clear

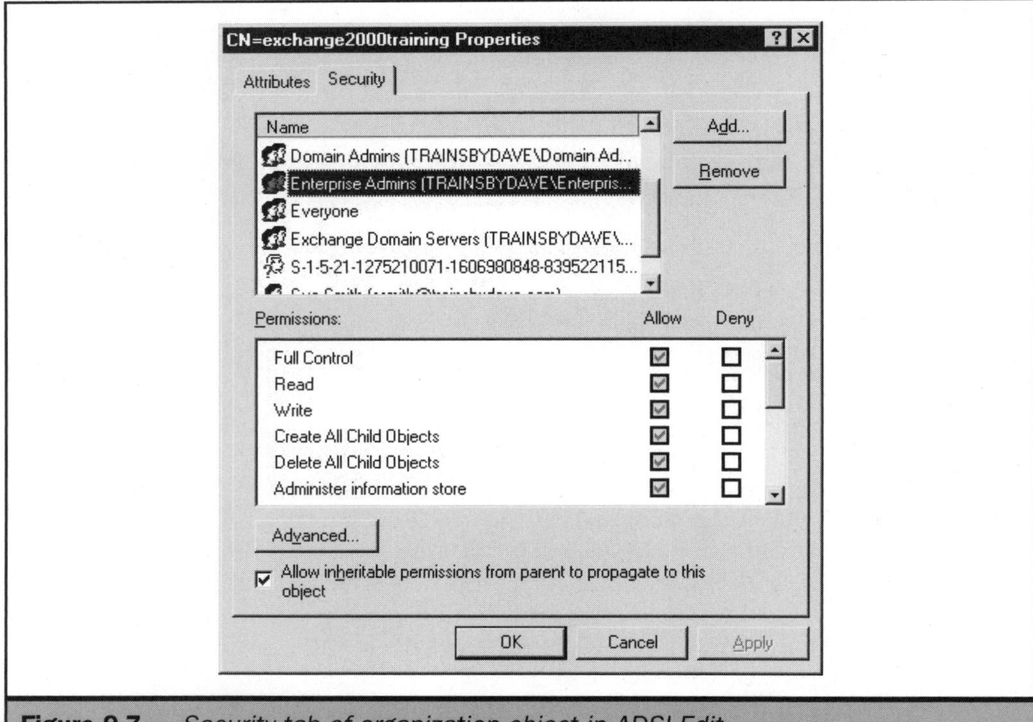

Figure 9-7. *Security tab of organization object in ADSI Edit*

the "Allow inheritable permissions from parent to propagate to this object" checkbox and then configure your permissions accordingly.

This checkbox should be cleared only when you have a full understanding of permissions inheritance and blocking permission inheritance. For more information on this topic, please consult Windows 2000 Administration, *George Spalding, Osborne/McGraw-Hill.*

When applying security to an administrative group using the ADSI Edit utility, you will need to access the Security page on the Permissions entry dialog box, as shown in Figure 9-8. You will need to select the desired propagation settings in the Apply To box. Doing this is necessary in order to specify exactly how you want your permission changes to propagate down the hierarchy of objects that exist inside the administrative group.

Note

The Security tab is not available by default on the organization and administrative group objects. To enable the security tab on these objects, create or edit the following registry key: HKEY_CURRENT_USER\Software\Microsoft\Exchange\EXAdmin\ShowSecurityPage=dword:00000001 (enable) or 00000000 (disable).

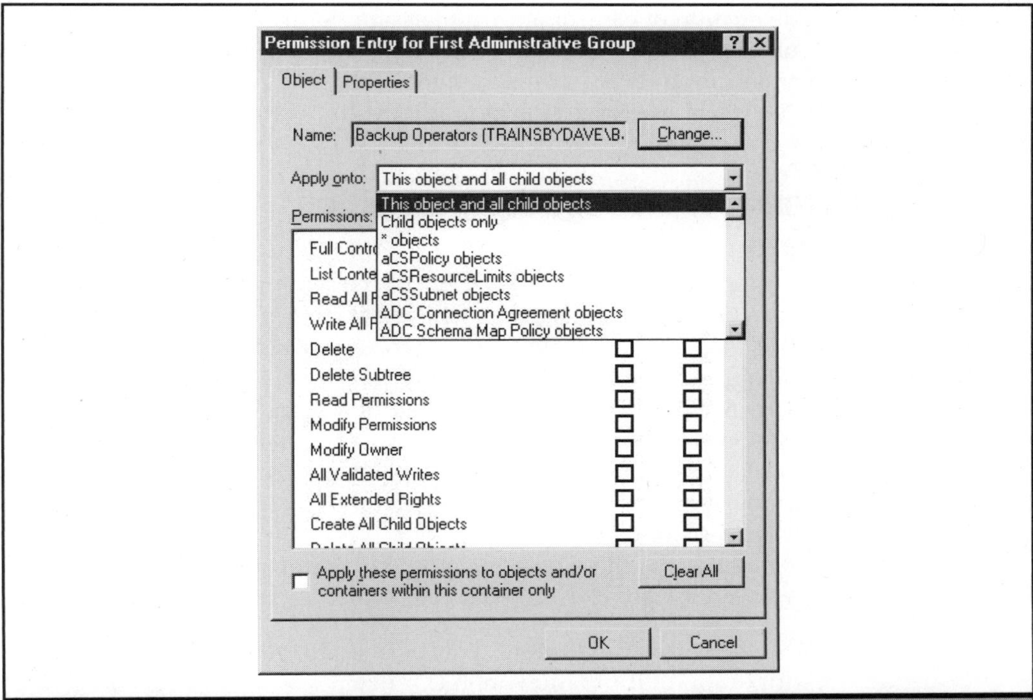

Figure 9-8. *The Permissions entry dialog box displaying the Apply To drop-down list*

When Exchange 2000 is installed, it extends the traditional NTFS permissions with Exchange specific permissions. The extended permissions include:

- Add PF to admin group
- Create public folder
- Open mail send queue
- Read metabase properties
- Administer information store
- View information store status
- Receive As
- Send As

The last two permissions—Receive As and Send As—are two that you should configure with caution. Any user who has Send As permissions on a mailbox can send mail impersonating that user. In the hands of the wrong person, this permission could spell disaster for innocent users on your network. The Receive As permission gives a user or group the ability to open another user's mailbox.

When using the delegation of control wizard to assign permissions, the Send As and Receive As permissions are automatically denied for all three administrative roles (see below). However, granting these permissions manually will result in full mailbox access and allow the assigned user or group the ability to impersonate the mailbox owner and read his or her e-mail.

Assigning Permissions Using the Delegation of Control Wizard

A second way to assign permissions is to use the Exchange Administration Delegation Wizard. This wizard can be run on the organization object or on an administrative group. To run the wizard, right-click on the object of focus and select Delegate control. A welcome screen will appear through which you will "Next" through to the Users or Groups selection screen, as shown in Figure 9-9. In this screen, you will choose to which users or groups you would like to delegate permissions, and the role you want to grant them. After making your selections, click on Next and then on Finish to end the wizard. These new permissions will propagate to all the child objects of the object the permissions were applied to.

In this wizard, you'll find that there are three possible permission assignments, known as *roles*, that you can assign. Here is what each one means:

- **Exchange View Only Administrator** This permission allows users to view Exchange configuration information only. Use this role to give the ability to Exchange administrators to view the configuration of objects for which they do not have direct administrative control.

- **Exchange Administrator** This permission allows users to fully administer Exchange system information. However, this permission does not allow the user to modify permissions. Use this role to delegate responsibility for day-to-day administration of Exchange objects.
- **Exchange Full Administrator** This permission allows users to fully administer Exchange system information and modify permissions on Exchange objects. Use this role to delegate who should be the big kahuna of your Exchange organization.

So, let's see how we might apply these permissions in the real world. Let's assume that you have two locations, one in Cleveland and the other in Orlando, and that you have decided on a decentralized administrative group strategy wherein each location has its own administrative group. Let's further assume that you have created two Exchange Admins security groups, one for each city. Now, let's assume that you want members of the two Exchange Admins security groups to be able to configure only their own object inside their own administrative groups. Finally, let's assume that you are a member of the Enterprise Admins security group and that you need to be able to

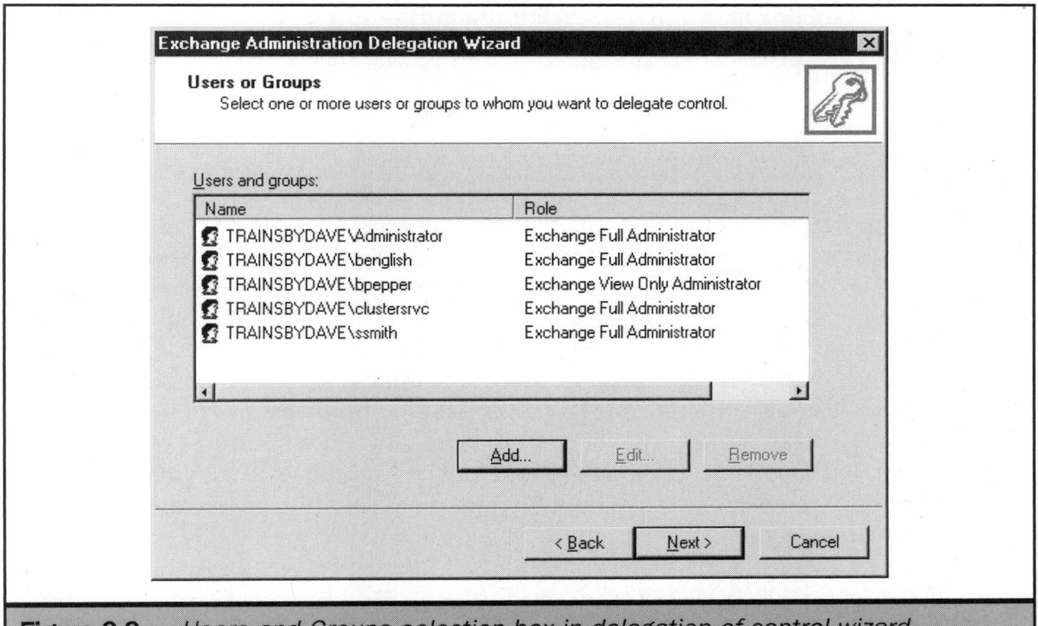

Figure 9-9. *Users and Groups selection box in delegation of control wizard*

configure objects in both administrative groups. (After all, you're the boss, right?) How would you accomplish this?

First, you would assign the Enterprise Admins security group the Exchange Full Administrator role at the organization object. This permission will be inherited by both administrative groups and all their child objects. This is a role-based security assignment that is in addition to the AD security inherited by the organization object in AD.

Second, assign the Cleveland and Orlando Exchange Admins security groups Exchange View Only Administrator role at the organization object. This, too, will be inherited by both administrative groups and their child objects. This permission will allow each group to view the configurations of objects in their peer groups without giving them permissions to make changes on those objects.

Third, override the permissions propagated from the organization object on each administrative group and assign each Exchange Admins security group Exchange Full Administrator role for their own administrative group. Doing this will override the Exchange View Only Administrator role that is being inherited from the organization object.

The net result is that each location's Exchange Admins security group will have full control over all the objects in its own administrative group, each Exchange Admins security group will be able to view but not modify the configuration options in the other administrative group, and the Enterprise Admins security group will have full control over all objects in both administrative groups.

Routing Groups

In many organizations, there will be multiple servers offering Exchange services to the network. Because of this, there will be a need to pass messages between these servers. You can group servers into routing groups to more efficiently route messages between servers. Servers grouped into the same routing will assume permanent, reliable, high-bandwidth connectivity. Now, Microsoft doesn't define what "permanent" or "high-bandwidth" is—that's your job as a system administrator. However, after accounting for all other traffic on the line, we recommend at least 256Kbps of available bandwidth for Exchange traffic for high-bandwidth environments. So, if you think that one of your WAN connections has enough permanence and available bandwidth to meet your idea of "permanent, high-bandwidth," then you can configure your Exchange 2000 servers accordingly by placing them in a routing group that encompasses that WAN link.

When Exchange 2000 Server is initially installed, a First Routing Group is created inside the First Administrative Group. Unless you create a new routing group, all subsequent servers installed into your Exchange organization will be installed into this routing group. By default, when you create a subsequent administrative group, a routing group is not created inside that administrative group. Hence, before you install additional Exchange 2000 servers in your organization, be sure to create all your planned routing groups so that you can install your Exchange servers in the proper routing groups.

Messages routed between servers in a routing group are sent point-to-point using Simple Mail Transfer Protocol (SMTP). This means that the *logical* topology between servers is a full-mesh topology inside the routing group. So even if your physical topology between servers is not a full-mesh topology, Exchange will send messages using the available physical paths in a logical full-mesh topology.

Messages routed between routing groups are driven over messaging connectors. Multiple connectors can be installed between the same routing groups, and bridgehead servers are used to host these connectors in each routing group.

In the next section, we'll take a look at how to plan for routing groups, how to connect the routing groups, and how the link state algorithm is used in message routing.

Planning for Routing Groups

As we stated earlier, routing groups are based on the concept of permanent, reliable, high-bandwidth connectivity. However, membership in a routing group is not based on the IP subnet that the Exchange server physically resides on, but rather is created by placing that Exchange server object inside the routing group container in the ESM snap-in.

Plan your routing groups primarily on the basis of your physical topology. If you have permanent, high-bandwidth connectivity between some of your Exchange 2000 servers, then you will place them in the same routing group. If such bandwidth is not

Planning for routing groups in mixed mode

One of the things that you may face is planning for multiple routing groups when running in a mixed environment of Exchange 5.5 and Exchange 2000 servers. If you're in this situation, keep in mind the following points. First, Exchange 5.5 servers do not recognize routing groups, so even though you might have multiple routing groups inside a single administrative group, all the servers in the routing groups will be seen as a list of servers in a site when viewed from the Exchange 5.5 Administrator utility. Secondly, Exchange 5.5 servers will communicate with all the Exchange 2000 servers in the administrative group as if they were in a single Exchange 5.5 site, which means using remote procedure calls in a full-mesh topology. RPCs need more bandwidth to operate correctly than does SMTP, so you'll need to ensure there is enough available bandwidth between your Exchange 5.5 and Exchange 2000 servers when managing coexistence between these two platforms. To be on the safe side, be sure to have at least 256Kbps of available bandwidth. Lastly, each administrative group will be seen as an Exchange 5.5 site, so Exchange 2000 servers housed in different routing groups that are in different administrative groups will be seen as residing in different Exchange 5.5 sites by the Exchange 5.5 servers. This will account for differences in how the list of servers appear in the Exchange Administrator versus the Exchange System Manager snap-in.

available, then you will create different routing groups and place those servers in their respective routing groups. Many administrators are finding that their routing group topology closely mirrors their Windows 2000 site topology, though this is not a requirement.

There is one other situation in which you might want to create a routing group even when you have wonderful bandwidth to work with: when you wish to isolate the use of an SMTP connector to one or more Exchange 2000 Servers in your environment. With the SMTP connector, you can restrict the connector's use to only those servers in the local routing group. For instance, if you have a group of users who send many messages with large attachments to a large customer, you may need to dedicate a T1 for this traffic and then use an SMTP connector to get them out to the Internet. In this scenario, if you don't want overall organization traffic to use that SMTP connector, then you can create a separate routing group that will host an Exchange server or servers that will service only those users, and you can restrict the connector's use to that routing group.

Creating a New Routing Group

To create a new routing group, just right-click on the Routing Groups container in the ESM snap-in, point to New, and select Routing Group. Input the name of the new routing group and then click OK. The new routing group will be created along with two folders inside the group: Connectors and Members. The server objects will be located inside the Members folder, and the connectors will be created inside the Connectors folder.

As long as the routing groups are within the same administrative group, servers can be dragged and dropped from one routing group to another. In addition, if you drag the routing group master (RGM) from one routing group into another, a new RGM in the source routing group will be automatically selected based on alphabetical order of the server name.

The Routing Group Master

One server in each routing group will be designated as the RGM. By default, it is the first server created or moved into a routing group. The RGM is responsible for updating the link state table information on each server in the routing group, including the bridgehead servers (see next section). We'll discuss the RGM's role and the link state table information more fully in the upcoming section "Link State."

Connecting Routing Groups

You'll connect routing groups using connectors. Servers that host routing group connectors are called *bridgehead servers*. There are three kinds of connectors:

- Routing group connector
- SMTP connector
- X.400 connector

Routing Group Connector

The routing group connector is the best connector to use in most situations. The routing group connector uses SMTP to transfer messages, so it is more tolerant of low bandwidth, high-latency environments than its predecessor, the site connector in Exchange 5.5 Server. You can configure multiple bridgehead servers at both ends of the connector to provide for fault tolerance in the event one of the bridgehead servers goes offline. In addition, it can be used to connect the Exchange 5.5 site connector and then use remote procedure calls to communicate with the site connector. However, between two Exchange 2000 bridgehead servers, SMTP is the protocol used to transfer messages.

When you configure multiple bridgehead servers for a routing group connector, Exchange will behave in the following manner:

- If one bridgehead server goes offline, the next server in the list of bridgehead servers will be used to transfer a message.
- During message transmissions, if all the target bridgehead servers are online, the message load will be balanced between all the bridgehead servers.
- If you configure a bridgehead server with multiple SMTP virtual servers, each virtual server can act as a separate bridgehead server.

To create a Routing Group Connector (RGC), navigate to the Connectors folder inside the routing group, right-click on the folder, point to New, and select Routing Group. Figure 9-10 illustrates the requirement for indicating on the General tab a name for the connector, the routing group with whom the connector is to connect, the cost of the connector, and whether you want to specify a local bridgehead server or allow all local servers to act as bridgehead servers for this RGC. In addition, you can stop public folder referrals from occurring over this connector. To learn more about public folder referrals, please refer to Chapter 5.

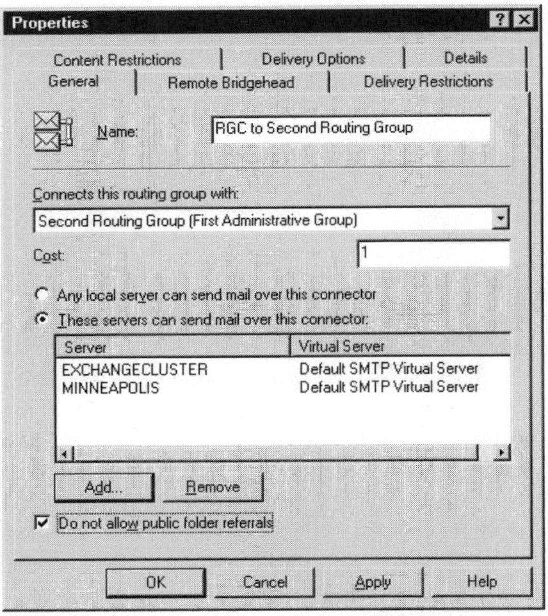

Figure 9-10. *General tab for new Routing Group Connector*

On the Remote Bridgehead tab, as shown in Figure 9-11, you'll need to add at least one server in the target routing group to act as the bridgehead server for the RGC in that routing group. If you are connecting to an Exchange 5.x server, you can input the override credentials on this tab so that the RGC can authenticate in the remote Exchange 5.5 site.

The Delivery Restrictions tab allows you to configure restrictions on who can send messages over an RGC. The Content Restrictions tab allows you to configure restrictions based on message type, message priority, and message size. The Delivery Options tab allows you to schedule timing of message transfer over this RGC. By default, the connector is available 24x7. However, as shown in Figure 9-12, the connector itself can be scheduled for message transfer and larger messages can be forced to adhere to a different schedule than smaller messages. For multinational companies, this is a welcome feature because in many parts of the world the best available bandwidth is a 56.6Kbps dial-up connection, and so the scheduling of message transfer is a premium consideration.

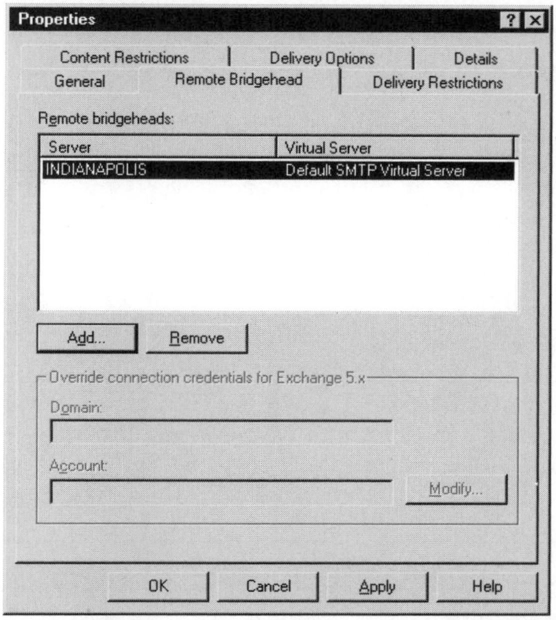

Figure 9-11. Remote Bridgeheads tab in new Routing Group Connector

Note *The ability to dial-on-demand when messages have been queued has been removed from the Exchange application and its connectors. You might have noticed that there is no Dynamic RAS connector in Exchange 2000 Server. If you need to connect to a remote region of the world that has only dial-up bandwidth, consider using Windows 2000 to schedule the dial-up of the phone line and then map the RGC schedule to allow for message transfer within the time configured in Windows 2000*

SMTP Connector

Since the RGC uses SMTP to transfer messages, you might be wondering when you would want to use the SMTP connector. Well, here are some instances when the SMTP connector would a better choice than using the RGC:

- If you want to connect to an Internet Mail Connector from an earlier version of Exchange
- If you need to set up a pull relationship from a remote SMTP server

- If you want to use Transport Layer Security on the connector rather than the virtual server
- If you want to use a connector for Internet mail

The SMTP connector obviously uses SMTP as its transport protocol. Multiple bridgehead servers can be configured for this connector, and all inbound and outbound messages are transferred through the bridgehead server. However, you do not configure remote bridgehead servers in the SMTP connector. Those must be created in their own SMTP connector.

The SMTP connector does not connect to another bridgehead server in the remote routing group because its primary use is to connect to another SMTP *service* rather than a designated bridgehead server.

It will use the DNS MX records to find a destination server to which it should pass a message. If there are multiple SMTP servers in a remote routing group or domain to which you need the SMTP connector to send messages, then you'll need to configure multiple MX records in DNS.

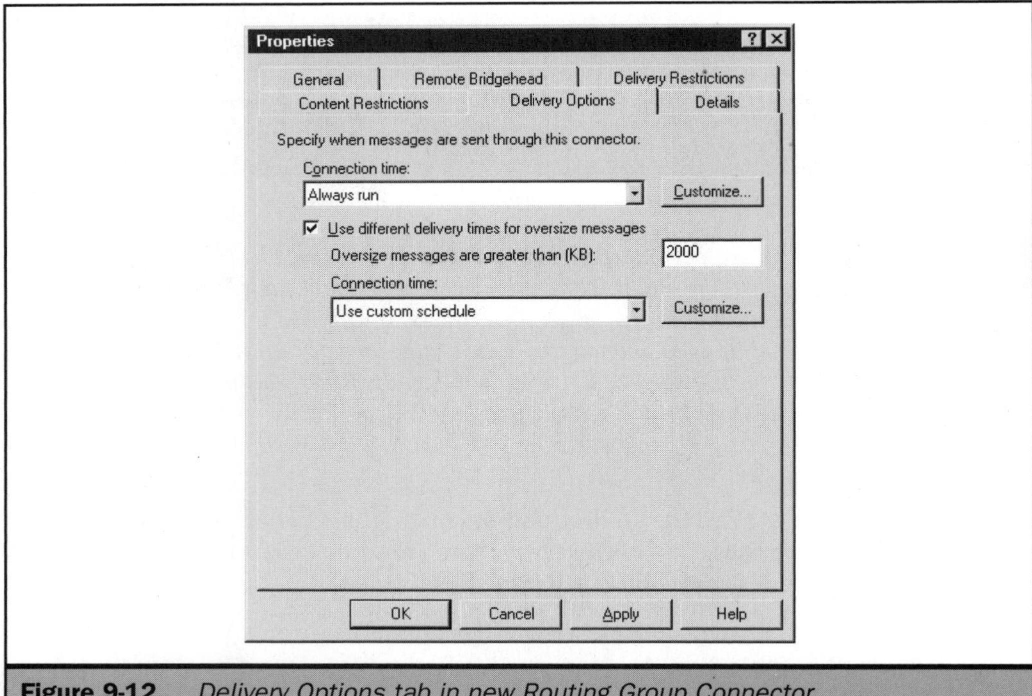

Figure 9-12. *Delivery Options tab in new Routing Group Connector*

If an MX record does not exist in the DNS tables for the target SMTP server, the SMTP connector will attempt to resolve the destination server by using the host name (A (Address) record), and if there is no such record in the DNS tables, the connection will fail.

The SMTP connector can also be configured to retrieve e-mail sitting in a queue for its domain name. So by using DNS MX records, you can configure mail to be held in a remote domain for your domain until the SMTP connector issues the ETRN or TURN SMTP command to de-queue your mail into your domain. To learn more about how the ETRN and TURN commands work in SMTP, please consult Chapter 10.

To create a new SMTP connector, right-click on the Connector folder, point to New, and select SMTP connector. On the General tab, as shown in Figure 9-13, you'll need to name the connector and then specify whether the connector should route mail based on the DNS MX records or if all mail should be forwarded to a smart host that will route the mail for you.

Tip *If the SMTP connector is going to be used to connect to the Internet, you should select the "Do not allow public folder referrals" checkbox to prevent Exchange 2000 from referring your users to alternative public folder stores over this connector.*

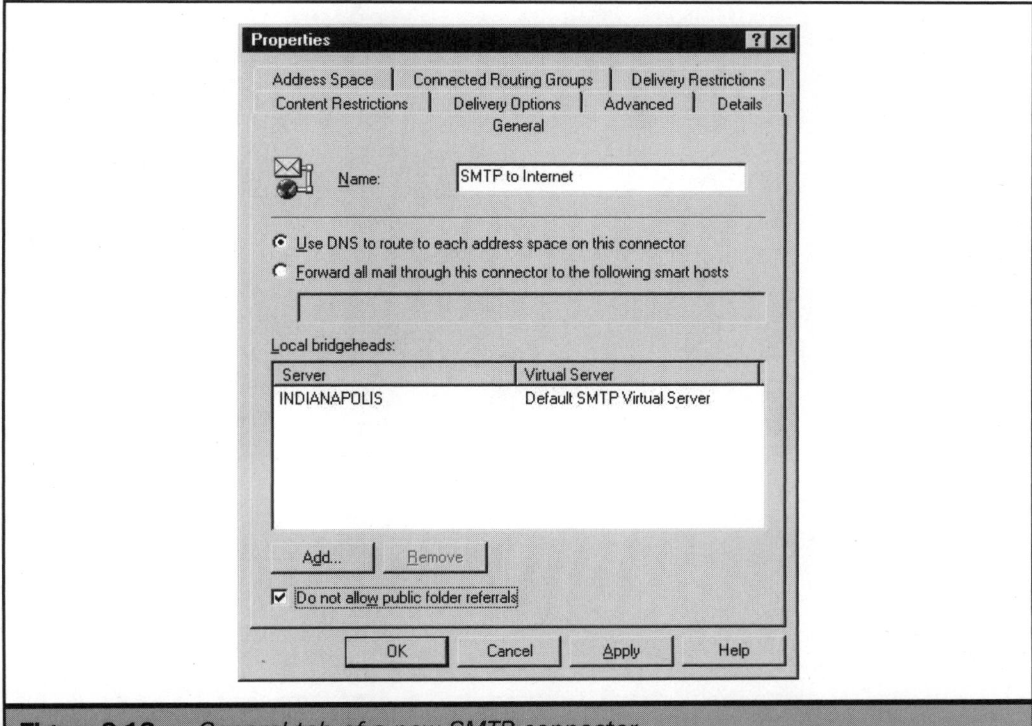

Figure 9-13. *General tab of a new SMTP connector*

On the Delivery Options tab, you'll be able to configure this connector to queue mail for remote, triggered delivery and to specify what account the remote SMTP server should use for authentication. Multiple accounts can be input for this connector, as shown in Figure 9-14. If this connector is going to be used for outbound mail, then you can use this tab to configure schedules, as we did with the RGC.

The Advanced tab, shown in Figure 9-15, is a plethora of configuration options. First, if you need to send the HELO instead of the EHLO command, select the first checkbox at the top of this tab. If you need to configure outbound security so that this connector can authenticate to a remote SMTP service before de-queuing e-mail, then click on the Outbound Security button and make the needed configurations. Incidentally, this is where you can enable TLS on the connector for outbound mail.

By default, the SMTP connector will not send an ETRN/TURN command, but it can be configured to do so in a variety of ways. First, by selecting the "Request ETRN/TURN when sending messages" radio button, you can set the SMTP connector to send the ETRN or TURN command from the SMTP server to which it is sending messages. This procedure would most often be used if you are forwarding all mail to a smart host that is

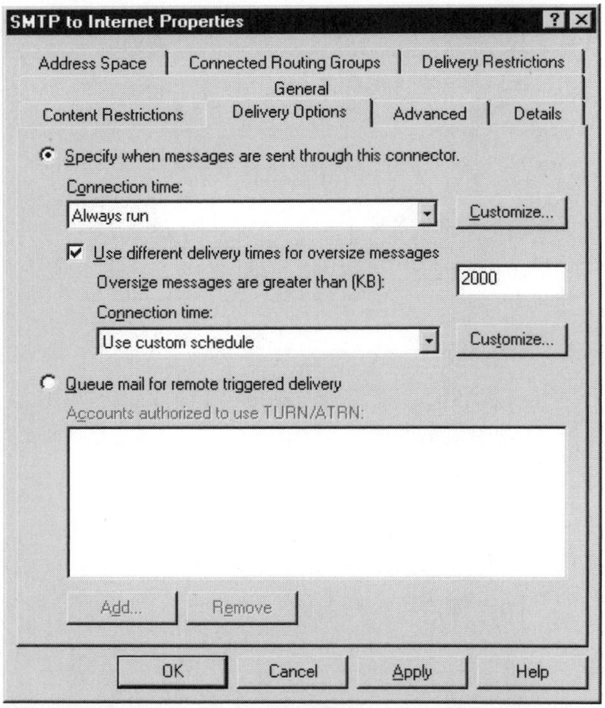

Figure 9-14. *Delivery Options tab for a new SMTP connector*

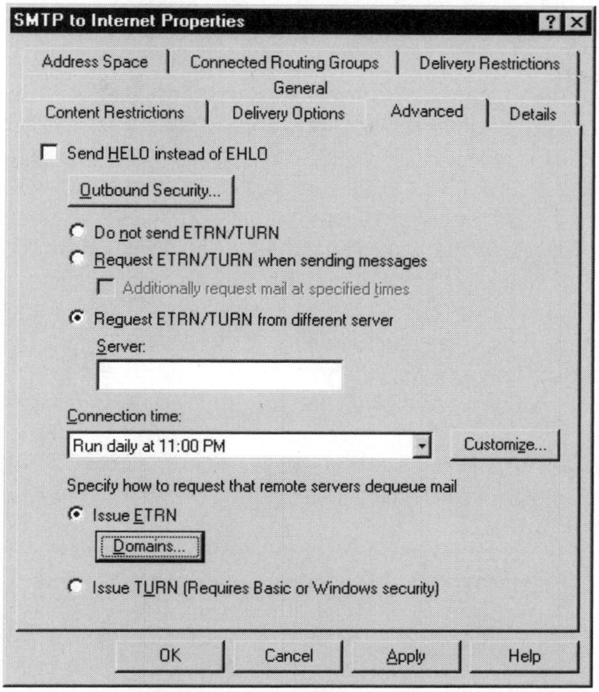

Figure 9-15. *Advanced tab in new SMTP connector*

also holding mail for de-queuing into your domain, such as would be the case for smaller companies working with an ISP. In addition, you can have the ETRN/TURN command sent at scheduled intervals for times when there was no outbound mail but you wanted to receive incoming mail.

Moreover, if you wanted to receive incoming mail from a different SMTP server than the smart host you are using for outbound mail, then you would select the Request ETRN/TURN from different server radio button and input either the server's Fully Qualified Domain Name (FQDN) or its IP address. In addition, you can schedule when the ETRN/TURN command should be sent when requesting from a different server by configuring the Connection Time beneath the Server input box.

Finally, by selecting the Issue ETRN radio button, you can specify which domains should be de-queued to this SMTP connector for routing. This is especially helpful if you have multiple domain names and need to issue the ETRN command for each one.

If the upstream SMTP server does not support the extended SMTP commands, you can have this connector issue the TURN command by selecting the Issue TURN radio button.

The Address Space (Figure 9-16) tab is the location to specify which domain names the SMTP connector will handle. An entry of "*" for the address space means that all domain names are managed. However, if you want to set up this connector to work with only certain domain names, you can enter that information here on the Address Space tab. This is also the location to enter the connector's scope, which can be restricted to the local routing group if necessary. Also, by selecting the "Allow messages to be relayed to these domains" checkbox, you'll be allowing incoming messages to be relayed through this connector to the domains listed on the Address Space tab. The default is to block relays. If you've configured the address space as "*" and then select this checkbox, you'll be effectively allowing relay of all messages through this connector.

Also, you can configure the connector to have a scope limited to the local routing group. The effect of making this selection is that the connector will be available for use only to those servers in the local routing group. The connector's existence will not be replicated to the link state tables of other Exchange 2000 servers outside the local routing group.

The Connected Routing Groups tab is the location to specify routing groups that are connected to this routing group via this SMTP connector. All routing groups must

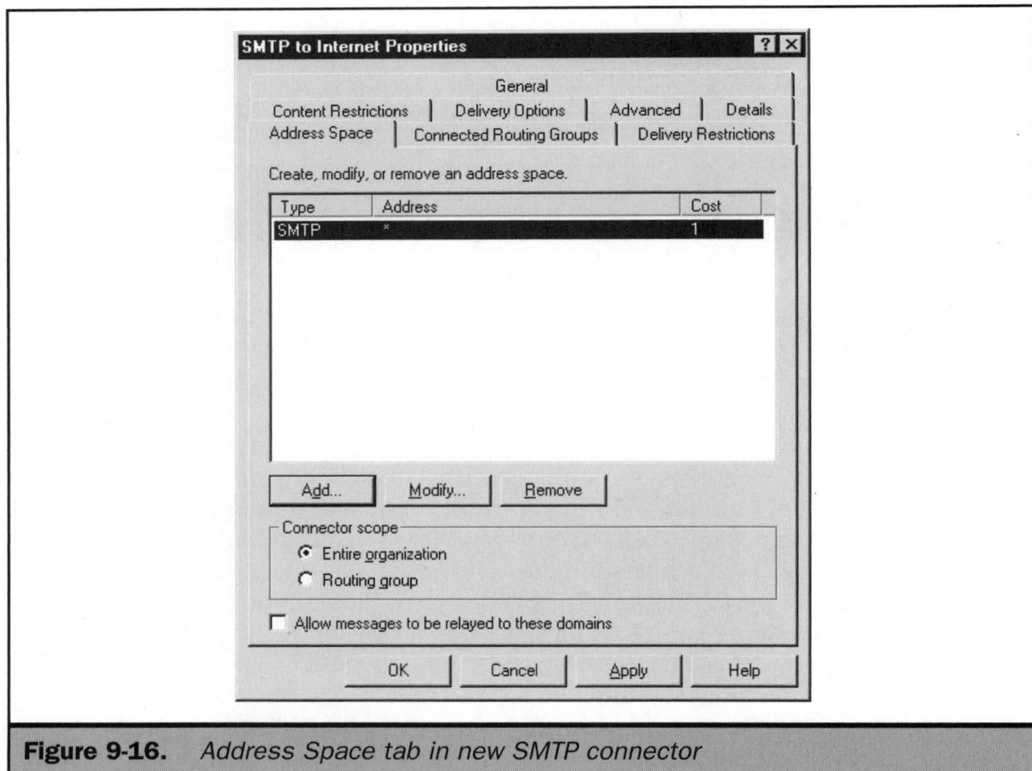

Figure 9-16. *Address Space tab in new SMTP connector*

be in the same Exchange organization. You'll choose the routing group based on its administrative group and routing group name, as shown in Figure 9-17. Notice also that you can select an Exchange 5.5 site, which would be correct if you're connecting to the IMC in Exchange 5.5.

X.400 Connector

If you've managed Exchange 5.5 X.400 connectors, doing this might be old hat for you. However, if you haven't worked with X.400 connectors, then read on and learn about how to create and configure an X.400 connector.

In many situations, you won't need the X.400 connector. However, if the bandwidth between two of your routing groups is such that it's too low or unreliable for SMTP, then the X.400 connector may be used for message transfer. The X.400 connector is good for very slow or unreliable connections. And you'll be forced to use the X.400 connector if you're using an X.25 packet switching backbone.

Before creating an X.400 connector, you'll need to install the TCP/IP X.400 Service Transport Stack, which can be accomplished by navigating to the X.400 protocol folder beneath the Server/Protocols folder, right-clicking on the folder, and selecting this transport stack. Accept the default name and then click OK. If you return later to this

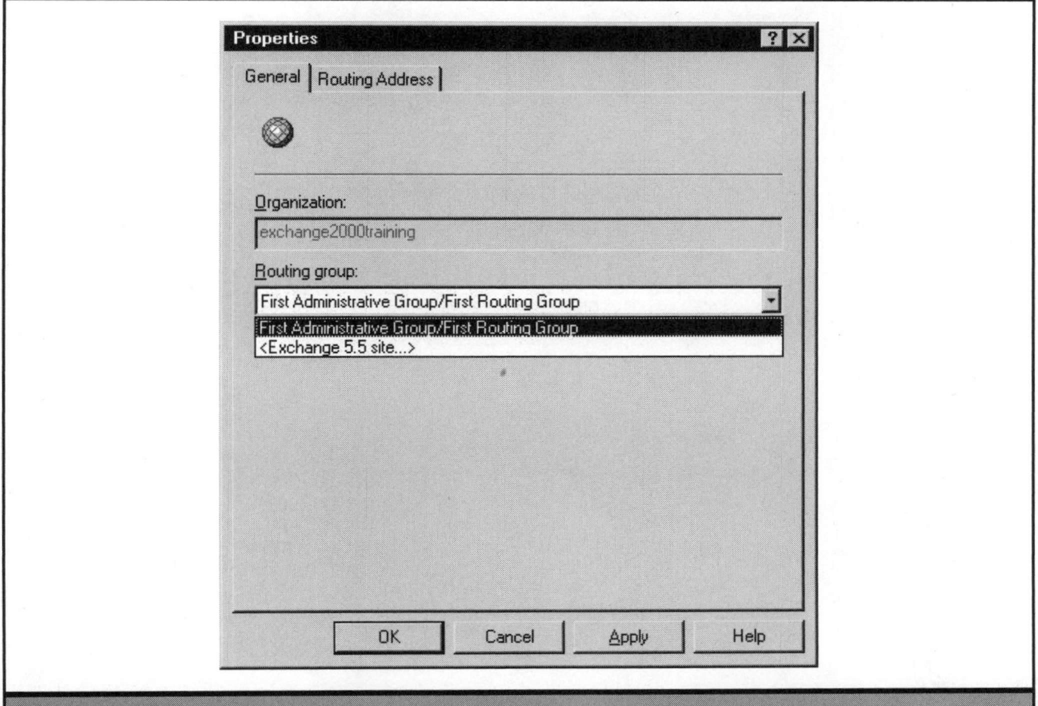

Figure 9-17. *Adding a connected routing group in new SMTP connector*

object and click on the Connectors tab, you'll find that all the X.400 connectors that are using this transport stack will be listed on that tab. You can't delete the stack until all the connectors are configured to use another transport stack.

To create a new X.400 connector, right-click on the Connectors folder and select X.400 Connector. On the General tab, shown in Figure 9-18, you'll need to name the connector and select a transport stack. If you want to configure message text word-wrap, select its checkbox and input the column at which you wish words to wrap. By default, there is no wrapping. You can also choose whether to allow public folder referrals and whether remote clients support MAPI (Message Application Programming Interface). Selecting the latter allows the connector to send rich-text characters, such as bold, italics, and color.

You'll also need to input the name of the remote X.400 server. When an X.400 connector needs to connect to another X.400 system, it will appear with its own name and a name with which to authenticate plus a password. All X.400 connections are secure, so authentication is a must. If the connector cannot authenticate, then the connection will be refused.

On the Schedule tab, you can select when you want the connector to be active for passing messages. Since you'll likely use this connector to pass messages over the

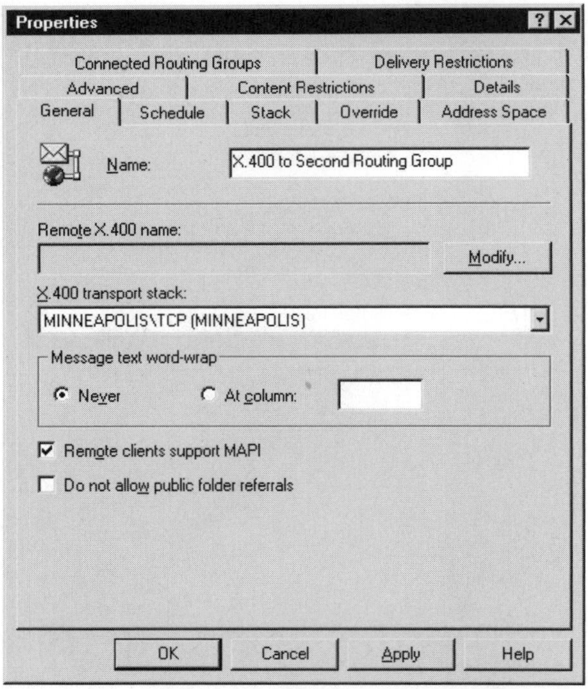

Figure 9-18. *General tab for new X.400 connector*

worst of WAN links, you may want to schedule the connector to run at off hours when use of the link is at its lowest. On the Stack tab, input the transport address information about the remote X.400 server to which this connector is connecting. This can be accomplished by either an IP address or an FQDN of the server. The Override tab, shown in Figure 9-19 is used to change the default X.400 transport stack attributes when connecting to a specific X.400 connector on a remote X.400 server.

Configuring the Connection Retry Values The Connection Retry values on the Override tab are there to tell the connector how to behave when the connector can make a connection but the connection keeps dropping off. The Maximum open retries specifies the number of times the connector will attempt to make a connection before returning NDRs on the messages. The Open interval value specifies the amount of time the connector should wait between connection attempts. The Maximum transfer retries specifies the number of times the connector should attempt transfer of a message over a connection that was established but that now might not be available. The default is two. And the Transfer interval is the configured time between transfer retries once a connection has been established.

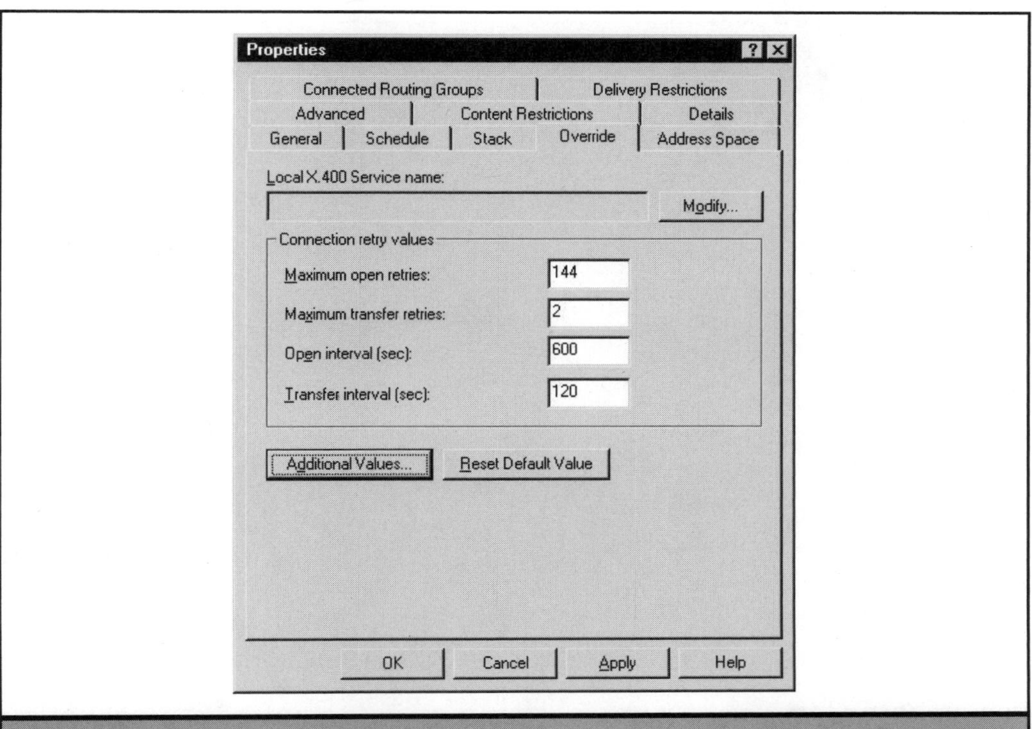

Figure 9-19. *Override tab in X.400 connector*

If you click on the Additional Values button, as shown in Figure 9-20, you'll be able to configure the Reliable Transfer Service (RTS) values, the Association parameters, and the Transfer timeouts values. Those who have managed the Message Transfer Agent (MTA) and/or the X.400 connector in Exchange 5.5 will readily recognize these values.

Configuring the RTS Values The checkpoint size in the RTS section indicates the amount of data, in kilobytes, to be transferred before the sending server expects to receive an acknowledgment from the receiving server. The window size is the number of checkpoints that can go unacknowledged while allowing the transfer of information to continue. In a slow or unreliable environment, consider increasing the number of checkpoints that can be unacknowledged but decreasing the size of the checkpoint. Because the X.400 connector will first attempt to commence retransmissions from the last acknowledged checkpoint after receiving an acknowledgement, altering these values will help lower the amount of data that is retransmitted should the physical line become temporarily unavailable. The recovery timeout value is the amount of time the connector will wait to receive an acknowledgment from the receiving server after all the unacknowledged data has been transferred. Again, increasing this value will make

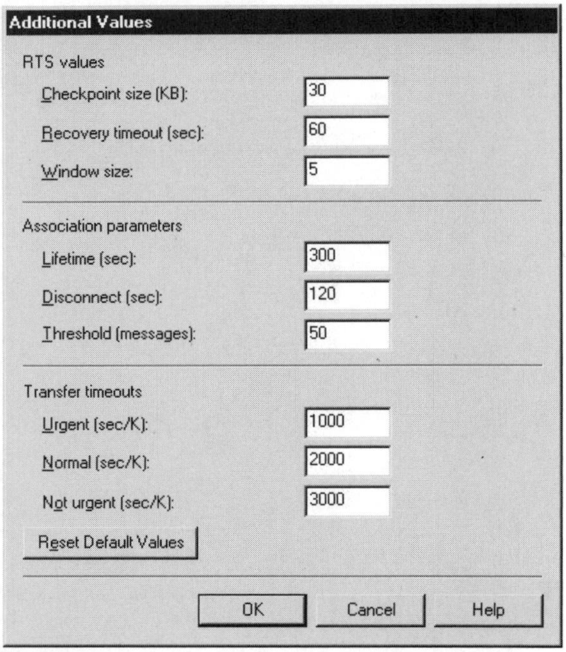

Additional Values

RTS values
Checkpoint size (KB): 30
Recovery timeout (sec): 60
Window size: 5

Association parameters
Lifetime (sec): 300
Disconnect (sec): 120
Threshold (messages): 50

Transfer timeouts
Urgent (sec/K): 1000
Normal (sec/K): 2000
Not urgent (sec/K): 3000

Reset Default Values

OK Cancel Help

Figure 9-20. *Additional Values in the X.400 connector*

the sending connector more forgiving of a physical line that is available only intermittently and will help reduce the amount of data that needs to be retransmitted. One thing to note here: if the recovery timeout value is reached and the sending server has not received an acknowledgment from the receiving server, it will assume that none of the data it transferred has been received, and, when it attempts to transfer information again to the receiving server, it will start at the beginning of the data stream, not at the last acknowledged checkpoint.

Multiplying the window size and the checkpoint size results in the Memory Size Allocation, which denotes the maximum amount of data that the MTA can transfer without an acknowledgment. Hence, a 30KB checkpoint size multiplied by a checkpoint number of 20 results in a maximum of 500KB being held in memory without an acknowledgement. The recommended maximum is dependent on the physical resources of the server, the number of X.400 connectors the server is hosting, and the available bandwidth. You'll need to monitor the X.400 connector in your environment to discern what is the best value at which to arrive for these options.

Configuring the Association Values An association is a virtual pipe through which messages between X.400 systems travel. When you use Windows sockets, the transport layer must create a TCP connection over port 102 before the connectors can create an association. This connection leaves the connector in a listening state, which can be seen using the Netstat utility.

Tip *Each association uses one control block. The default setting for the maximum number of control blocks is 20 per Exchange 2000 server. However, you can configure your Exchange 2000 server to accept up to 2000 control blocks simultaneously. Doing this might be necessary if the server experiences heavy messaging traffic over this X.400 connector. To increase the control block value, go to the HKEY_LOCAL_MACHINE\SYSTEM\CurrentControlSet\Services\MSExchangeMTA\Parameters registry key and configure the TCPIP control blocks value to what is needed. If you don't know how many control blocks you need, use this equation to arrive at a number: (Number of X.400 connectors x 10) + 1 = number of control blocks needed. As you can see, the default number of control blocks is configured for only one X.400 connector per Exchange 2000 server. If you need to host multiple X.400 connectors on a single Exchange 2000 server, you'll need to adjust the number of control blocks accordingly.*

The lifetime value indicates how long the port 102 connection should be maintained with no data transfer after all the data has been transferred. The default is 300 seconds or five minutes. If data is transferred over this connection during this five-minute interval, the clock will restart on this value after the data stream has been transferred. The disconnect value indicates how long this connector will wait to kill a connection for which a kill request has gone unacknowledged. For instance, assume that the sending server sends a data stream successfully and after five minutes, the sending server requests a termination with the receiving server and no acknowledgement is received. The connector will then wait, by default, an additional two minutes and, if no acknowledgment is received, it will kill the connection on its own. The threshold value is the maximum number of queued messages the system can send to the remote system without opening another association to the remote server. Because the establishment of a TCP connection involves a fair amount of overhead, it is usually best to raise the threshold if possible to avoid the need for multiple connections. On the other hand, if there are thousands of messages ready to be sent across this connection, it might be advantageous to allow a number of connections to be created so as to facilitate a higher throughput of messages to the receiving server.

Modifying the Transfer Timeout Values The transfer timeout values represent an amount of time, in seconds per kilobyte, the connector will wait before sending a non-delivery report (NDR) based on the urgency of the message. The default for a normal message is 2000 seconds. Hence, if the message is one kilobyte (1000 bytes), then the connector would wait two seconds (after it has decided it's time to generate an NDR) before sending the NDR (2000/1000=2). The default for an urgent message is 1000 seconds and the default for a not urgent message is 3000 seconds.

Advanced Settings for the X.400 Connector As shown in Figure 9-21, there are several advanced settings that you *might* need to think about if you're connecting to another X.400 system. Bear in mind that the connector installs with the most commonly used settings for each of these values, so your need to change them will probably not be very great. However, there might be some legacy systems with which you'll need to modify these settings.

If you need to send attachments in simple binary rather than having the attachments formatted as a body part, then clear the Allow BP-15 (in addition to BP-14) checkbox. This will force all attachments to be sent in BP-14 format. Remember, however, that much of your formatting for those attachments may be lost because of the downgrade of the attachment type.

If you want messages converted into the standard P2/P22 X.400 format, then clear the Allow Exchange contents checkbox. Doing this will force all messages to be converted out of the native format for Exchange into the standard X.400 format.

Tip *For more information on the specifics of the X.400 format, please download the X.400 specification, which is available at www.itu.org.*

If you would like your connector to be polite and take turns sending and receiving messages with the other X.400 connector, then make sure the Two-way alternate checkbox is selected. Otherwise, one connector will start sending out data and not stop until its queue has been emptied.

In nearly all cases, you'll want to leave the IA5 selection for the X.400 bodypart for message text drop-down box. However, if the X.400 system you are connecting to needs a different bodypart, then in all likelihood the other party that requires this body part

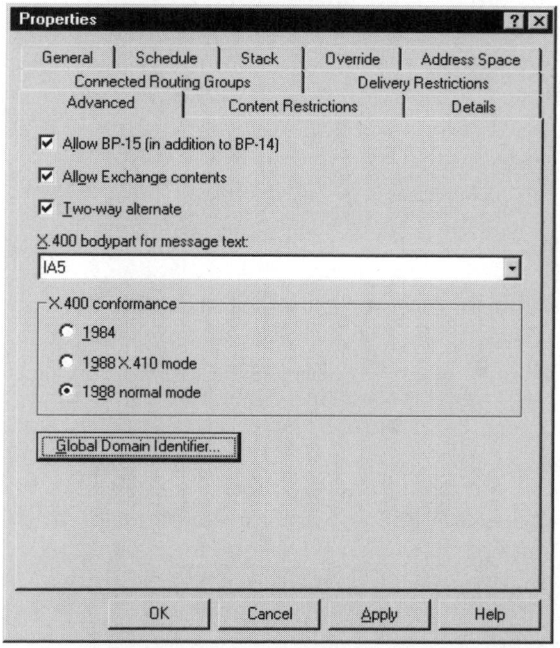

Figure 9-21. *Advanced tab in a new X.400 connector*

will tell you before you connect to them. For purposes of connecting Exchange routing groups, this will be a non-issue.

The X.400 conformance refers to the set of X.400 specifications the connector should adhere to. Again, most implementations of X.400 use the 1988 normal mode. When connecting routing groups, leave this at default.

And finally, the Global Domain Identifier will need to be configured if you selected the 1984 conformance radio button. In this identifier, you'll need to set the values for the country/region, private management domain, and administrative management domain. To learn more about what these domains are and what they mean, please consult the X.400 standard itself.

Link State

Microsoft has built on the link state family of protocols to create a fast and reliable method of ensuring that each Exchange 2000 server has up-to-date knowledge about the best routing path for a message destined for another Exchange 2000 server or the

Internet. For those who know Exchange 5.5, you'll recall that the Gateway Address Routing Table (GWART) was a site-level routing table that contained next hop information. The link state table (LST) is a major improvement to the GWART for reasons we will discuss in the next section.

Link State Architecture

All Exchange 2000 servers store link state information that is generated by the Link State Algorithm (LSA) protocol, which is based upon Dijkstra's algorithm. The end result is that each Exchange 2000 server knows the status of all other Exchange 2000 servers in the organization as well as the up or down status of the connectors in the organization.

Link state information identifies which servers are routing servers and which connectors are active and available. This information is held in memory in a link state table (LST). In addition to containing link state information, the in-memory link state table also includes routing group, connector, and bridgehead GUIDs; costs and address spaces; and the link state itself.

The size of the link state table—and therefore the amount of memory that will be consumed by each server maintaining the table—depends on the number of servers, connectors, and routing groups within your Exchange organization. Each of these objects will consume 32 bytes of memory. In larger organizations, such as those with over 1000 servers and 400 connectors, the LST grows to only 44.8KB.

Exchange 2000 servers obtain link state information in different ways:

- Each time two Exchange 2000 servers within the same organization exchange messages via SMTP, they compare link state information. During setup, Exchange 2000 extends the Windows 2000 SMTP transport stack to include additional SMTP command verbs to compare and update link state information.
- Exchange 2000 also extends the X.400 protocol, enabling X.400 connectors that are used as routing group connectors to update link state information across routing groups.

In both cases, the benefits are obvious. As messages flow throughout an Exchange 2000 organization, link state information is automatically updated. But, even if there are no messages moving between two routing groups, periodic polling keeps link state information updated.

Routing Group Master

Exchange 2000 servers within the same routing group receive link state updates from a *routing group master* (RGM). In each routing group, there is a server dedicated to being the RGM, which maintains the link state information for the routing group. When an Exchange 2000 server encounters a down link, it notifies the RGM in its routing group immediately. When the RGM receives this update, it immediately propagates it to all other Exchange 2000 servers in the routing group over TCP port 691. By default, the RGM is the first server moved into or installed into the routing group. Thereafter, other servers can become the RGM in one of two ways:

- If the RGM is moved to another routing group, a new server is automatically selected as the new RGM in alphabetical order.
- If the RGM goes offline, you must manually select another server in the routing group to become the RGM. When the original RGM comes back online, the current RGM remains the RGM unless you manually change this configuration.

If the RGM fails, link state information will be propagated only when:

- Messages are transferred between servers in the same routing group and the receiving server discovers as a result of this transmission that it does not have the same link state information as the other server. In this scenario, the server with the most recent information updates the other server.
- A bridgehead server in another routing group receives a link state table update, then updates its local link state table while trying to notify the RGM of the LST changes.

As long as there is no RGM in a routing group, other Exchange 2000 servers in the routing group will continue to use their LST, which may become very out of date as they are not updated to reflect changes to connectors and link status occur.

The status of the connectors can be viewed from the ESM snap-in under the monitors folder along with other servers in the organization. We'll discuss monitoring more fully in Chapter 21.

Viewing Link State Information

As mentioned in Chapter 4, the link state table of an Exchange 2000 server can be viewed using the WinRoute utility, which is found on the Exchange 2000 server CD-ROM under the support\utils\i386 folder. There is no installation of this program; just run the executable and then navigate the upper pane to the connectors folder. As shown in Figure 9-22, you'll be able to see the connectors in the organization and whether that connector is up or down.

Routing Messages in Exchange 2000

Exchange 2000 servers will use a selection and routing process to route messages within an Exchange 2000 organization. In this section, we'll look at how routing occurs in an Exchange 2000 organization.

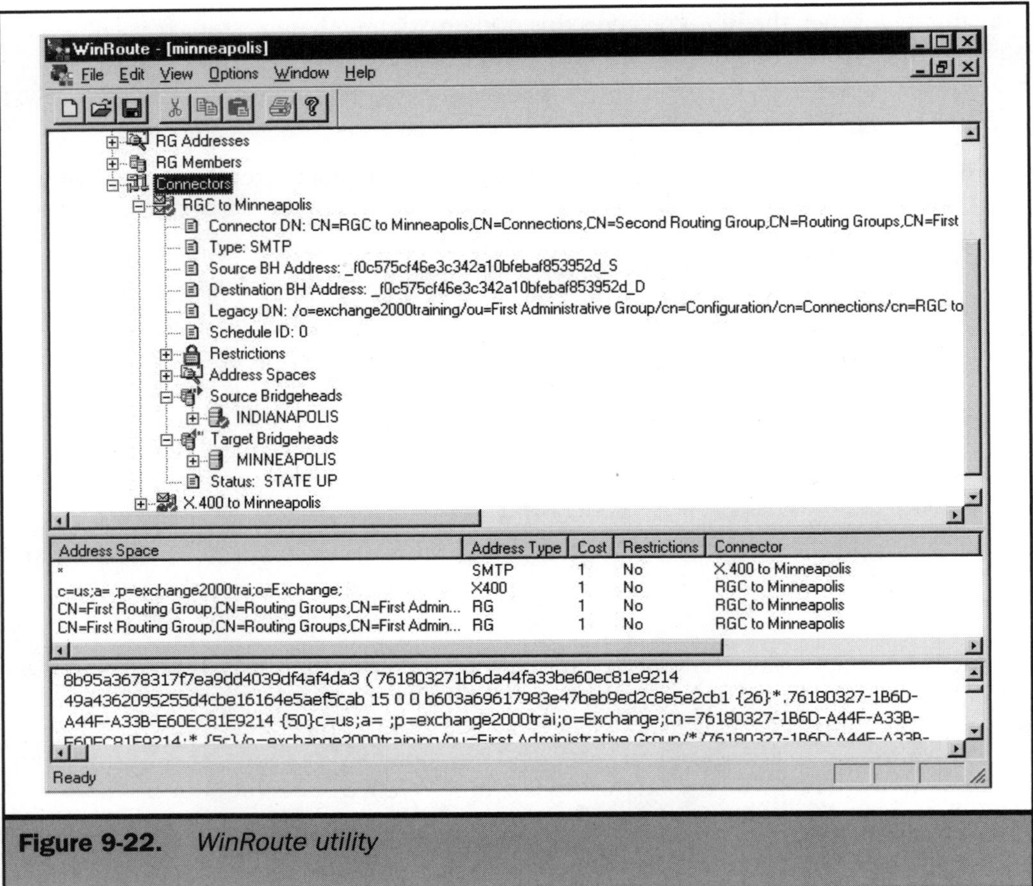

Figure 9-22. *WinRoute utility*

Routing and Selection Process

When the SMTP service receives a message sent to a user on a different server, it will make the following determinations:

- Which connectors are capable of delivering the message.
- What are the possible routes that can be used to route the message to its destination.

After all the available routes for the message have been identified, the SMTP service will remove all routes that meet the following thresholds:

- If the message exceeds any size limits on any of the connectors, that connector is removed from further consideration.
- Any connector that is not marked in the up state will be removed from further consideration.
- If there are two address spaces from two different connectors that can deliver the message, the closest match to the address space of the destination address is chosen.

So, let's see how this works. Figure 9-23 shows a fictitious topology for trainsbydave.com.

Let's assume that a 4MB message needs to be sent from the Nashville routing group to the New York routing group. You'll notice that there is no direct path between these two routing groups. So, the first thing that the SMTP service will do is look at all the possible connectors that can deliver the message. In our example, we'll assume that all the connectors could deliver the message.

Then the SMTP service will compile all the possible routes, which would be as follows:

1. Nashville/San Diego/Seattle/Chicago/New York
2. Nashville/Seattle/Chicago/New York
3. Nashville/Chicago/New York
4. Nashville/Seattle/New York
5. Nashville/Chicago/Seattle/New York

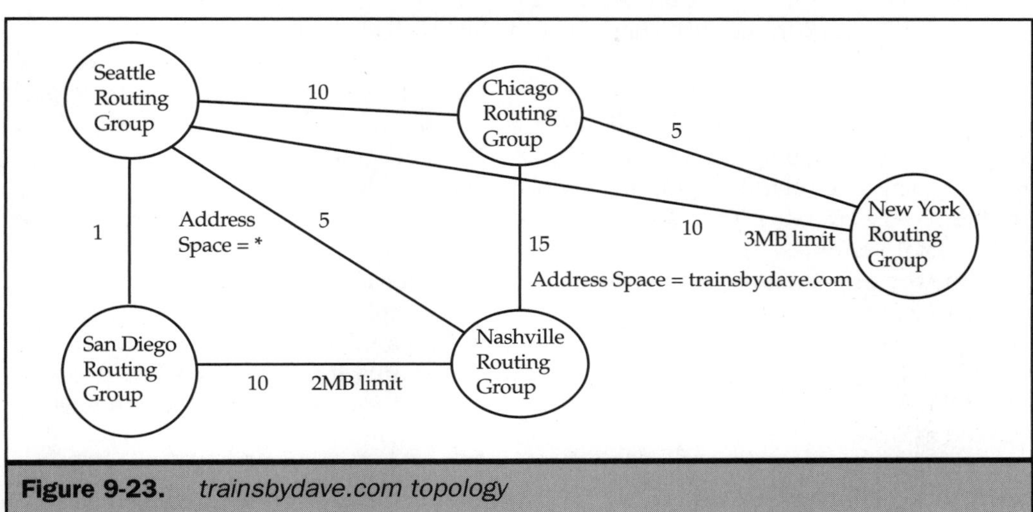

Figure 9-23. *trainsbydave.com topology*

Remember that at this stage all the SMTP service is doing is figuring out all the possible routes, regardless of how much sense it might make to us on paper. It is after all the possible routes are compiled that some limitations are applied. One limitation is the message size limit. If any of the connectors cannot handle the message because it is oversized, they are eliminated from the mix. Hence, in our illustration, the connectors between Nashville and San Diego, Seattle and New York are eliminated because our 4MB message exceeds the configured message size limit on these two connectors.

A second factor to consider will be the address space that most closely matches the destination address space. Since the connector between Nashville and Chicago is configured with the same destination address space as the message, the connector between Nashville and Chicago will be selected and the route for the message to travel will be Nashville/Chicago/New York.

Working with a Failed Link

The LSA can detect pretty quickly when a link has failed and then propagate that information to all the other servers in the organization. In this section, we'll discuss how the LSA works when a link has failed.

After Exchange 2000 determines that a link has failed, it will attempt to re-route the message and all future messages while the link is marked as down. It is the bridgehead server (BHS) that will initially detect that a link to a bridgehead server in another routing group has failed and start the process of updating all the LSTs in the organization.

When a BHS attempts to make a connection to another BHS in a remote RG, the BHS will first attempt to make a connection to each remote BHS specified in the connector. If it is unable to establish a TCP port 25 connection to any of these remote BHSs, it will enter the Glitch Retry state and will attempt to establish a session with each remote BHS three times at 60-second intervals. If unsuccessful, the link will be marked as down and the update of the LSTs commences. Thereafter, the BHS will attempt to establish a session with the remote BHS at the first, second, third, and subsequent retry interval values that you have configured on the SMTP virtual server that is attempting to send the message. These values, which are shown in Figure 9-24, can be found in the virtual server's properties on the Delivery tab. By default, after the three glitch retries, the server will wait for 10 minutes before attempting connection to the remote BHS on the first, second, and third retry intervals. Thereafter, it will attempt to establish a session with the remote BHS every 15 minutes.

If the server is unable to establish a connection after 12 hours and if there is no alternative message path to the destination recipients, all the message originators of messages in its queue will be sent a delay notification and an NDR will be sent after 48 hours. New messages will not arrive in this queue after it has been marked as down, so the timing applies only to messages that arrived in the queue before the link was marked as down.

Once the BHS marks the link as down, it will update its own LST and immediately notify the RGM over port 691. The RGM in turn immediately notifies all the other servers in the group over port 691 with the new LS information, and all the servers in

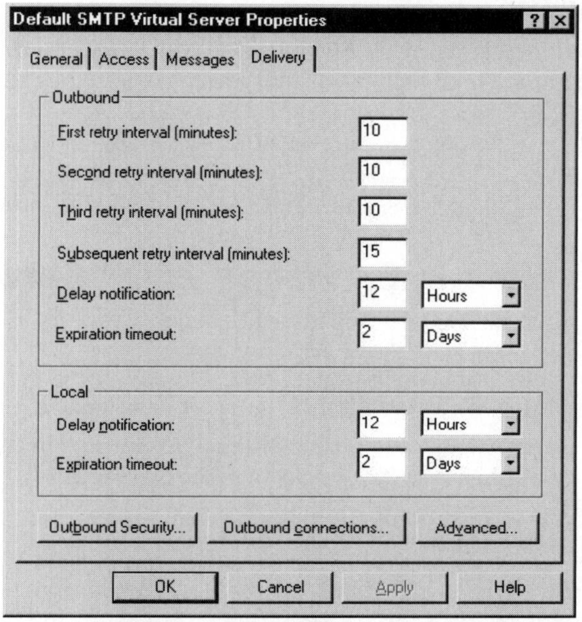

Figure 9-24. *Delivery tab in SMTP virtual server properties*

the RG update their own LST. If any of the other servers are also BHS for a different connector, they will pass the updated LST information to the remote BHS in the other routing groups over port 25, and the same process will repeat in each routing group that is either directly or indirectly connected to the originating routing group.

Now, if all available paths to the destination server are blocked because of downed links, then the server from which the message originates will hold the message in its outbound queue until an entire route becomes available. So, referring back to Figure 9-23, if a message sent from the San Diego routing group is destined for the New York routing group and both links between New York and Seattle and New York and Chicago are down, the BHS server in San Diego will hold the message until one of the links becomes available. It will not forward the message to a server in the Seattle or Nashville routing groups even though those links are up and running.

Once a link becomes available, at the next subsequent retry interval the BHS will be able to establish a connection to the remote BHS and the link will be marked as *up*. Then the RGM will be notified, and the same process will occur to update all the LSTs in the organization as occurred when the link was marked as *down*. In addition, any queued messages for which an NDR has not been generated will be transferred to the remote BHS for processing.

Address Lists

Because mail-enabled recipients are Active Directory (AD) objects, an address list is built by filtering the AD for mail-enabled objects that meet the defined criteria. Address lists are generated using LDAP search filter syntax against the Global Catalog (GC), which is a repository of all the domain objects from all the domains in the forest with a subset of each object's attributes.

There are three types of address lists: Default, Custom, and Offline.

Default Address Lists in Exchange 2000 Server

When you install Exchange 2000 Server, there are several default address lists that are automatically created for you. They are:

- **All contacts** This is a list of all the mail-enabled contacts in the forest.
- **All groups** This is a list of all the mail-enabled groups in the forest, regardless of whether their type is security or distribution.
- **All users** This is a list of all the mail-enabled users and mailbox-enabled users in the forest.
- **Public folders** This is a list of all the mail-enabled public folders in the forest that are not hidden from the address list.
- **Default global address list** This is a list of all mail-enabled objects in the forest, including contacts, groups, users, and public folders. Any mail-enabled object that is marked as hidden will not be displayed in this list.
- **All conferencing resources** This list is created when the conferencing server is installed and consists of all the mailbox resources associated with a Conferencing Management Site.

Custom Address Lists

Customized address lists that meet certain criteria can be created, either for online or offline use. However, because an online address cannot be copied to the offline folder, and vice versa, if you want to create a particular address list and make it available for both offline and online users, you'll need to create it twice. We'll show you how to create new address lists in the next section.

Offline Address Lists

Offline address lists are available for download by users to their local hard drive. In most situations, these hard drives will be in laptops and will be used by those who travel but who still need access to the address lists to perform messaging work when they are not connected to the local network. Offline address lists are held in an offline address book file with a .oab extension.

When a user composes a message while offline, the message is stored in the outgoing folder (for example, the Outbox) of the user's local messaging client. When the user connects to the network again, the message will be sent automatically.

In most cases, users will want to download the Global Address List (GAL) for offline use. The Outlook client can be set up to automatically download the offline GAL so that users don't forget to do this and end up with an out-of-date copy of the GAL when traveling. This is accomplished by first enabling offline folders in the Outlook client and then selecting the Download offline address book checkbox in the Offline Folder Settings dialog box, as shown in Figure 9-25, under the Tools/Options/Mail Services/Offline Folder Settings button. To learn more about configuring the Outlook client for offline folders, please refer to Chapter 13.

Creating Address Lists

To create a new address list, navigate to the Recipient folder, right-click on the All Address Lists, point to New, and select Address list. You'll need to name the address list and then click on the Filter Rules button. Remember, all we are really doing is filtering the GC for mail-enabled objects in the AD that meet a certain criteria. So, to create the new address list is little more than creating a new filter rule that will filter the AD.

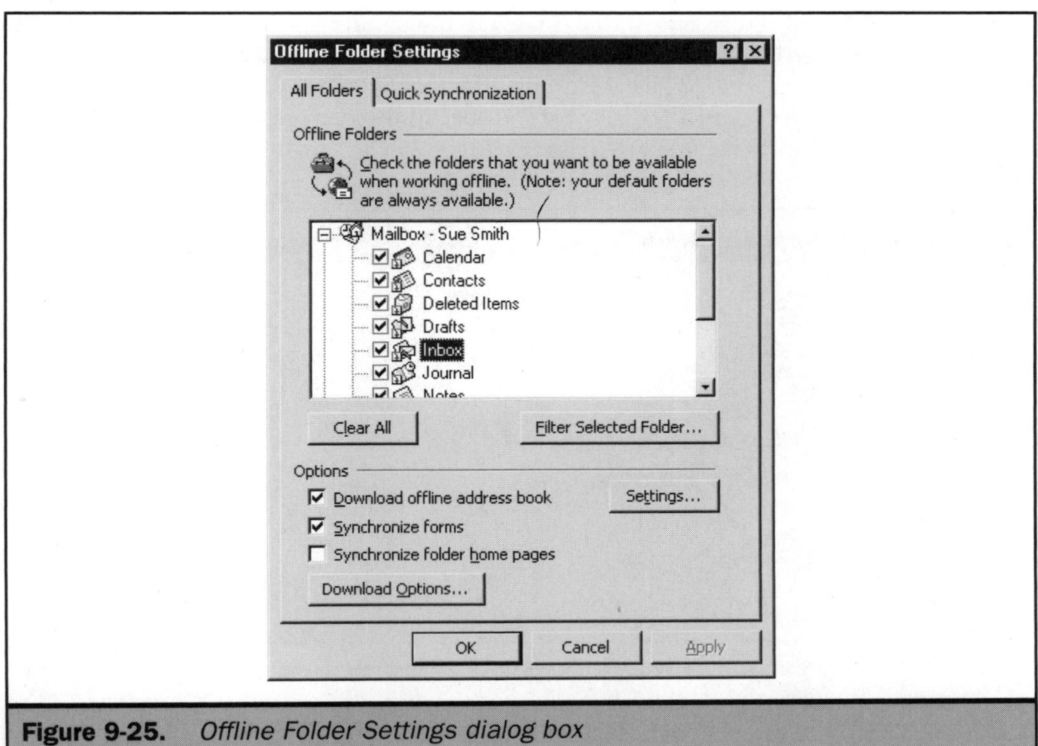

Figure 9-25. *Offline Folder Settings dialog box*

When you click on the Filter Rules button, the Advanced Find dialog box from the Active Directory Users and Computers snap-in appears. You'll use this dialog box to configure a set of search criteria that will be translated into a set of filter rules for this address list, as shown in Figure 9-26.

In our little scenario here, we need an address list for all the users in the Indianapolis location. So we'll create a filter rule that will search just for users with a mailbox and then define the search further by specifying that the City field must start with "Indiana," as shown in Figure 9-27. To accomplish this, we'll navigate to the Advanced tab of the Find utility, click on the Field drop down button, point to the User menu choice, and select City. Then we'll use the "starts with" condition and specify our value as "Indiana." The reason we do this is that it is possible to misspell "Indianapolis," so we shorten the word we are looking for to accommodate the possibility of a misspelled city name. Of course, it's possible to misspell "Indiana" too, but if the word is shortened too much, say to "Ind," then words like "India" would appear in the list and that would not be good. So, you'll need to make some choices about whether you want to attempt to accommodate misspellings when creating a new address list or not, and if so, what actions you'll take to accommodate those misspellings.

At this point, we'll test to see if the new rule gives us what we are after. We know that there are three users in the Indianapolis office, and this rule should return all three of them when the GC is filtered. So all we need to do is click on Find Now, and the rule will filter the GC and return its results. If we like the results, we can OK out of this box and the new address list and the new rule will be created and available for use by our LAN users. If, for some reason, we didn't like the results, we could tweak the rules to filter for the objects we were after. As you can see, all three users were returned by this rule, and so this address list is good to go (Figure 9-28).

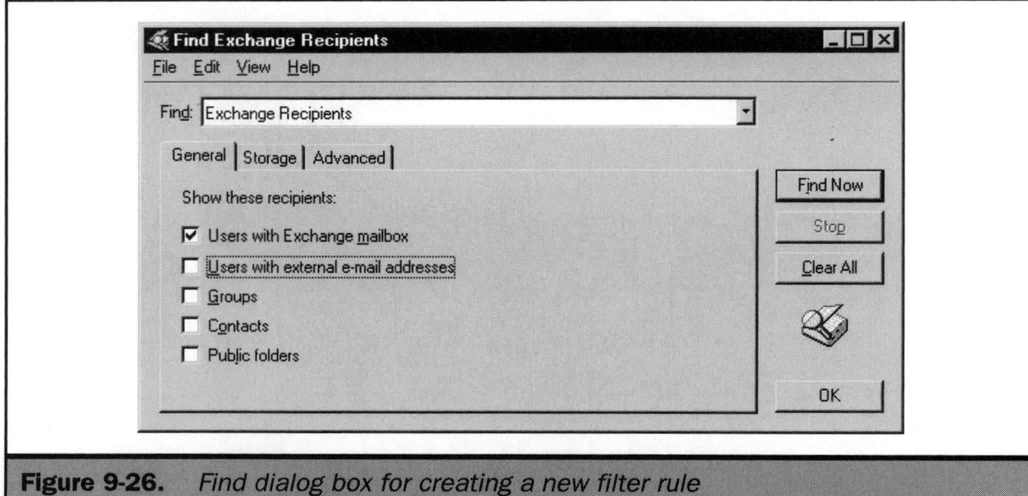

Figure 9-26. *Find dialog box for creating a new filter rule*

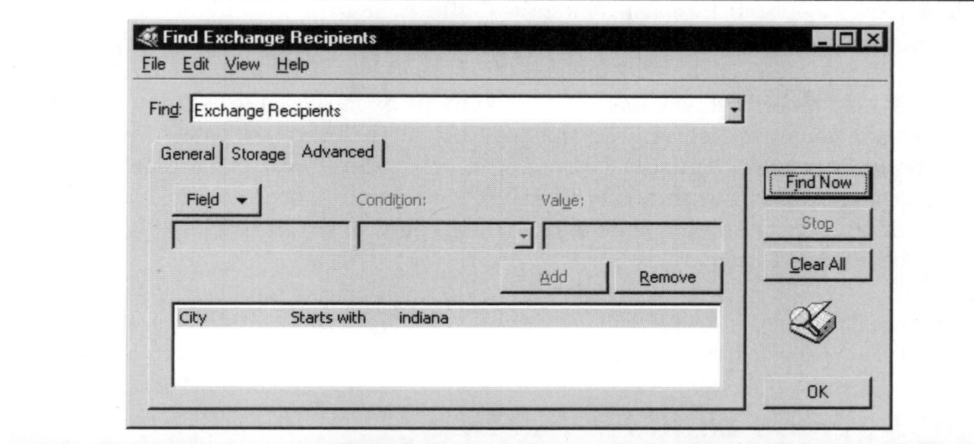

Figure 9-27. *Advanced tab showing the new rule created for the city Indianapolis*

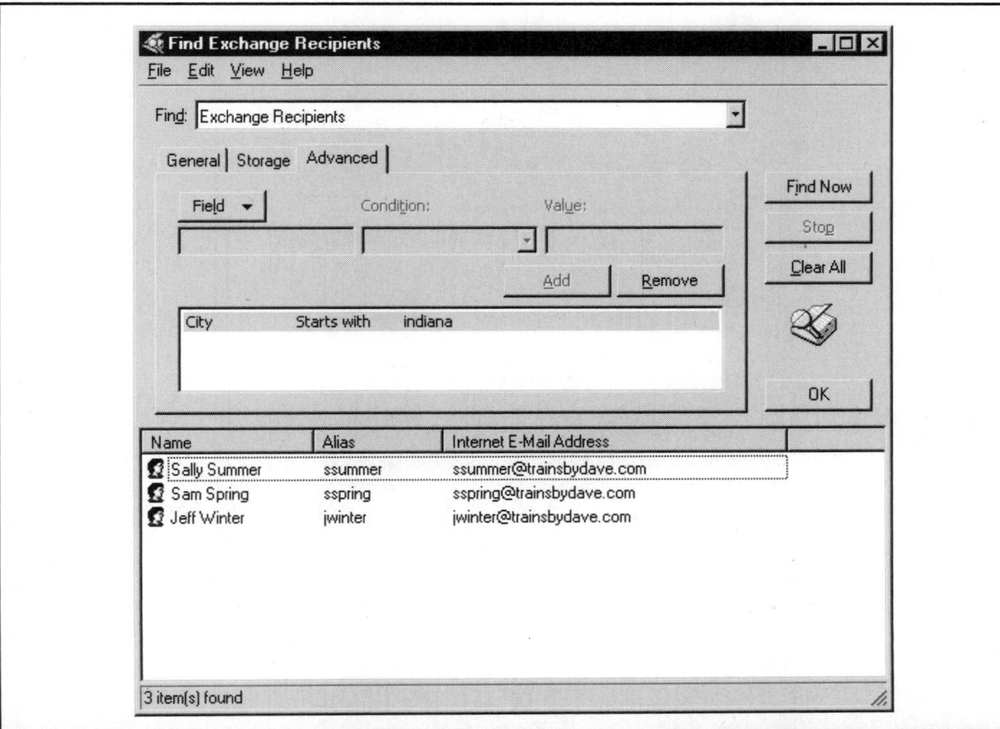

Figure 9-28. *Results of our new address list filter rule finding the Indianapolis users*

When a user views address lists using the Outlook client, the user will see the names on the basis of how the Full Name field appears in AD. The default for this field is *First Last*. If you want to change the way the Full Name field is generated, you can do so by using the ADSI Edit utility. Navigate the hierarchy by expanding the Configuration Container node, then the DisplaySpecifiers node, and then double-click 409 (or whichever number represents your language). Open the properties for CN=user-Display and find the createDialog property, as shown in Figure 9-29, and modify how the Full Name field is generated. If you want names to appear as *Last, First*, then enter "%<sn>, %<givenName>" (without the quotation marks).

The sn (surname) is the LDAP field name for Last Name, and givenName (yes, this is case sensitive and stands for given name) is the LDAP field name for First Name.

Securing Address Lists for Hosting

There may be times when you'll want to restrict who can see and use an address list that you've created. To secure an address list by using the Security tab of the address

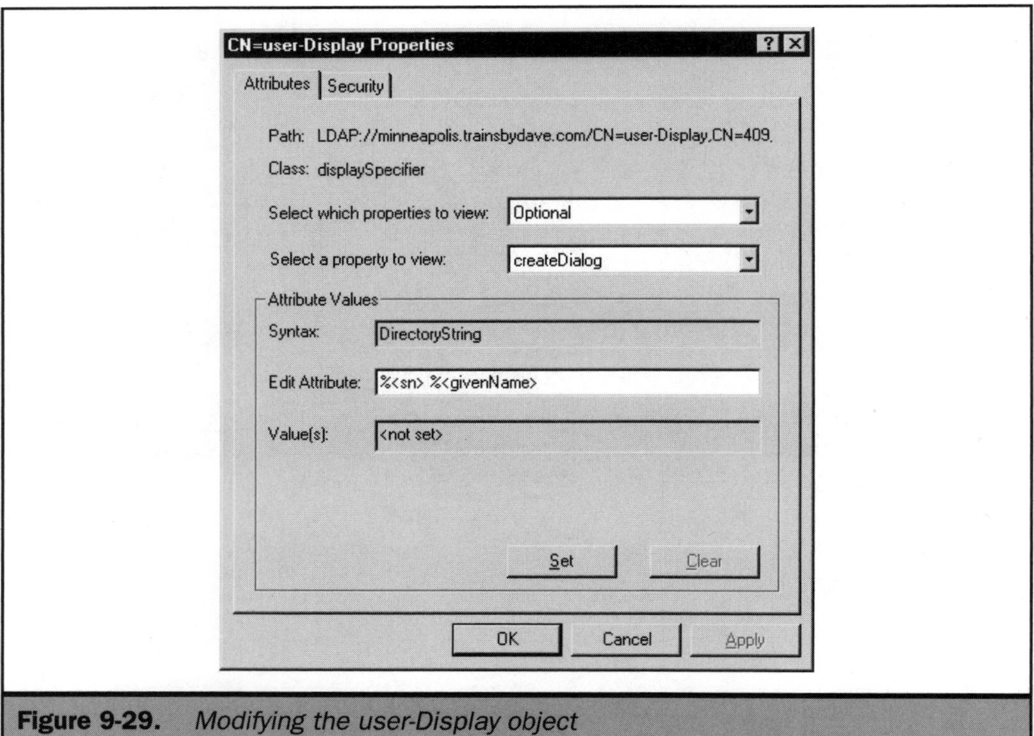

Figure 9-29. *Modifying the user-Display object*

list, you need to make your choices and secure the address list as needed by giving permissions to the desired users and groups.

Tip *When you open up the Security tab, you might find that the Authenticated Users security group appears to not have any permissions enabled. This really isn't true. Just click on the Advanced button and you'll find that the Authenticated Users security group has special permissions that can be viewed by opening up the Permissions Entry dialog box for this group. In it, you'll see that, by default, Authenticated Users has Read, Execute, List Contents and other permissions to an address list.*

If you want to restrict an address list from appearing to anyone but a certain group of users, then remove the Authenticated Users security group from the list's Security tab and add the security group from Active Directory that you wish to view the list. Assign that group at least Read permissions and that group should then have access to the list.

If you want to hide an address list altogether, create an empty address list that will act as a container for other address lists. Then deny the group or user the Open Address List permission on the parent address list; this will prevent the user from seeing any sub address lists that are created inside of the parent address list.

The Recipient Update Service

The Recipient Update Service (RUS) is responsible for building and maintaining the address lists that you have created along with all the default address lists. The RUS will poll AD for updated recipient information every 60 seconds and place new recipients in the proper address list(s).

Inside the RUS service, you'll find two objects: RUS (Enterprise Configuration) and RUS (installation Active Directory domain). The first object updates the e-mail addresses of objects in the configuration partition, and the second object updates the e-mail addresses for mail-enabled objects in the domain partition. You can right-click on either of these objects and select either Update Now or Rebuild. The Update Now will update the list with changes since the last update. The Rebuild will cause the filter rules of all the address lists to be re-run against the AD and, thus, to rebuild all the address lists.

If you have a Windows 2000 domain that has mail-enabled objects but does not have an Exchange 2000 server in the domain, you'll need to create an additional RUS on an Exchange 2000 server and point it to the specified domain. Remember that to add an RUS, you must have Full Administrator access on the organization object. To do this, right-click on the Recipient Update Service folder, point to New, and select Recipient Update Service. Then use the Browse button to navigate the domain structure of your forest and select the domain for which you wish to create the new RUS. Then finish the wizard, and the new RUS will be created and ready to go.

Creating and Managing Recipient Policies

A *policy* is designed to apply a set of configurations to a group of servers with one administrative act. In Exchange 2000, there are two types of policies, recipient and system. Recipient policies apply to recipient objects in the domain partition, and system policies apply to server objects in the configuration partition.

Exchange 2000 installs with a single built-in recipient policy used to generate e-mail addresses for mail-enabled recipients. You can create new policies at any time to configure how you want e-mail addresses to be generated. Recipient policies are applied in the background once the policy is associated with one or more recipient objects in the AD. The timing of policy application is based on the schedule of the Address List service running under the System Attendant.

System policies must be created manually. By default, they are turned off. You can create a public folder, mailbox, or server policy. Each policy takes common configuration values of these objects and allows them to be configured inside the policy, which is, in turn, applied to all the objects you specify.

In the next section we'll outline how both of the policies work and illustrate how to create and manage them.

Creating a Recipient Policy

You can create a new recipient policy using the ESM snap-in. Under the Recipients folder, highlight the Recipient Policies folder, right-click, point to New, and select Recipient Policy. The property sheets for a new recipient policy will appear. Enter the name of the new policy on the General tab and use the Modify button to create a filter rule to specify the AD objects to which this policy will be applied. This filter rule works exactly as described earlier under the Address List section of this chapter.

On the E-mail Addresses tab, you can configure rules for generating a variety of e-mail addresses. Address types that may be configured are:

- Custom
- X.400
- Microsoft Mail
- SMTP
- Lotus cc:Mail
- Lotus Notes
- Novell GroupWise

Select the address type you wish to implement, then configure it based on your needs. Since most places use SMTP, we'll illustrate how to create a couple of policies for different scenarios. If you'd like to create a recipient policy so that all your users have two types of e-mail address, this can be done. Let's assume you wish to have first.last@domain.com and firstinitiallast@domain.com.

Well, you would create a policy with two SMTP addresses with the following configurations:

- %g.%s@domain.com
- %1g%s@domain.com

If you create multiple recipient policies for the same address type, then the policy with the highest priority will be applied last and thus will override any conflicting configurations from other policies.

System Policies

As we stated previously, there are three types of system policies: mailbox, public folder, and server. We'll look at each one in this section.

Mailbox Policies

A mailbox policy will be applied to mailbox stores. You can use the policy to specify settings for multiple mailbox stores that appear on the store's General, Database, Limits, and Full-Text Indexing tabs.

On the General tab of a mailbox store, you'll be able to configure the default public store, the offline address list, the location to archive all messages sent or received, whether clients support Secure MIME (S/MIME) signatures, and whether messages should be displayed in a fixed size font (10 pt Courier).

To create a new mailbox store policy, you'll first need to create a new System Policies container in an administrative group. After creating this container, right-click on the container, point to New, and select Mailbox Store Policy. You'll be presented with a small box with checkboxes next to each of these four tabs. Select the tabs you wish to use for this policy, then click OK.

On the General tab of the policy itself, you'll need to input a name for the policy and then use the other tab(s) to make your configurations. For instance, if you want to enable Message Journaling on all the mailbox stores in your organization, you would first create a new mailbox store policy and select only the General tab, as shown in Figure 9-30.

After making this selection and clicking OK, the properties of the policy will appear and you'll need to name the policy before making your configurations in the policy. In our example, we named it "Message Journaling Policy," as shown in Figure 9-31.

Next, we move to the General (Policy) tab. Don't confuse the title of this tab with the General tab of the policy. The tab that we are configuring here are options that appear on the General tab of the mailbox store, not the policy itself. As you can see in

New Policy

Property pages:

- [x] General
- [ ] Database
- [ ] Limits
- [ ] Full-Text Indexing

OK Cancel

Figure 9-30. *Selecting the General tab for a new mailbox store policy*

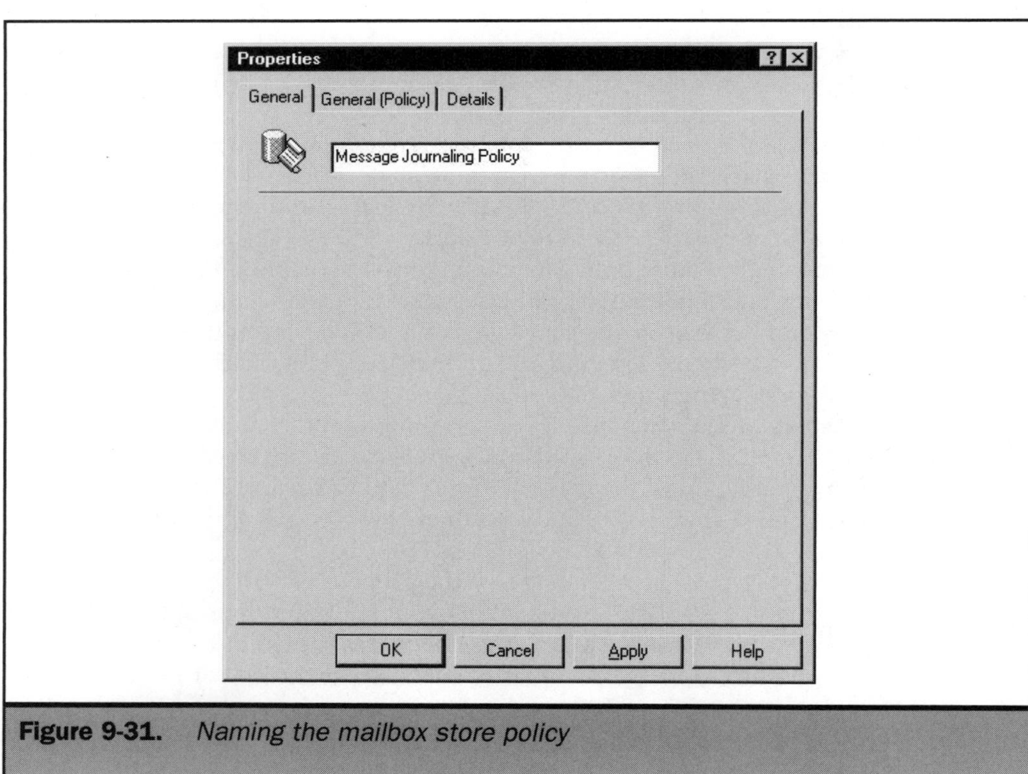

Figure 9-31. *Naming the mailbox store policy*

Figure 9-32, we could do a number of things on this tab, such as specifying a different default public store for a set of mailbox stores or a different default offline address list. In a very real sense, even though you might leave some of these options at default, they are still being applied to all the chosen mailbox stores. So, it's really impossible to create a policy for just one configuration option.

In our scenario, we'll click on the "Archive all messages sent or received by mailboxes on this store" and then browse to the Message Journal public folder. We plan to copy all user-initiated messages to this public folder. After specifying the Message Journal public folder, we'll click OK.

At this point, all we've done is create the policy. Now it needs to be applied to the mailboxes we select. To do this, we right-click on the Message Journal Policy and select Add Mailbox Store. In Figure 9-33, you can see that all the mailbox stores in our organization appear in the upper pane. All we need to do is highlight the desired stores to which we wish to apply this policy, click Add, and then OK. The policy is applied to all of the mailbox stores, and copies of user messages will be sent to the public folder.

You'll also find that once the stores are added to the policy, if you highlight the policy in the left pane of the ESM snap-in, all of the stores that are being managed by the policy will appear in the right pane.

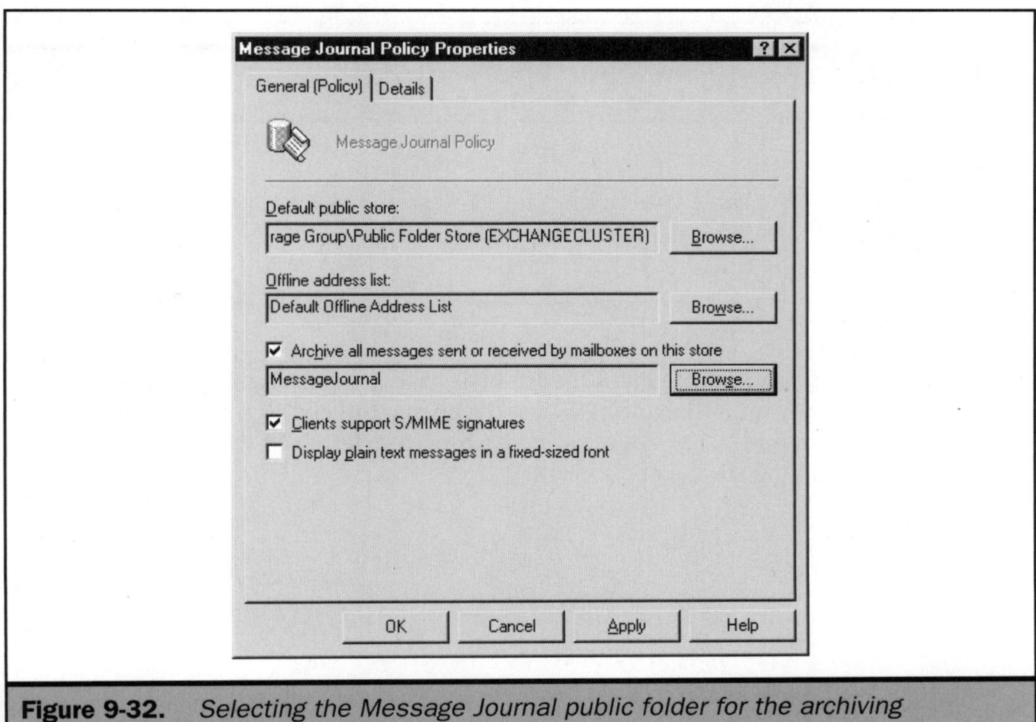

Figure 9-32. *Selecting the Message Journal public folder for the archiving of all messages*

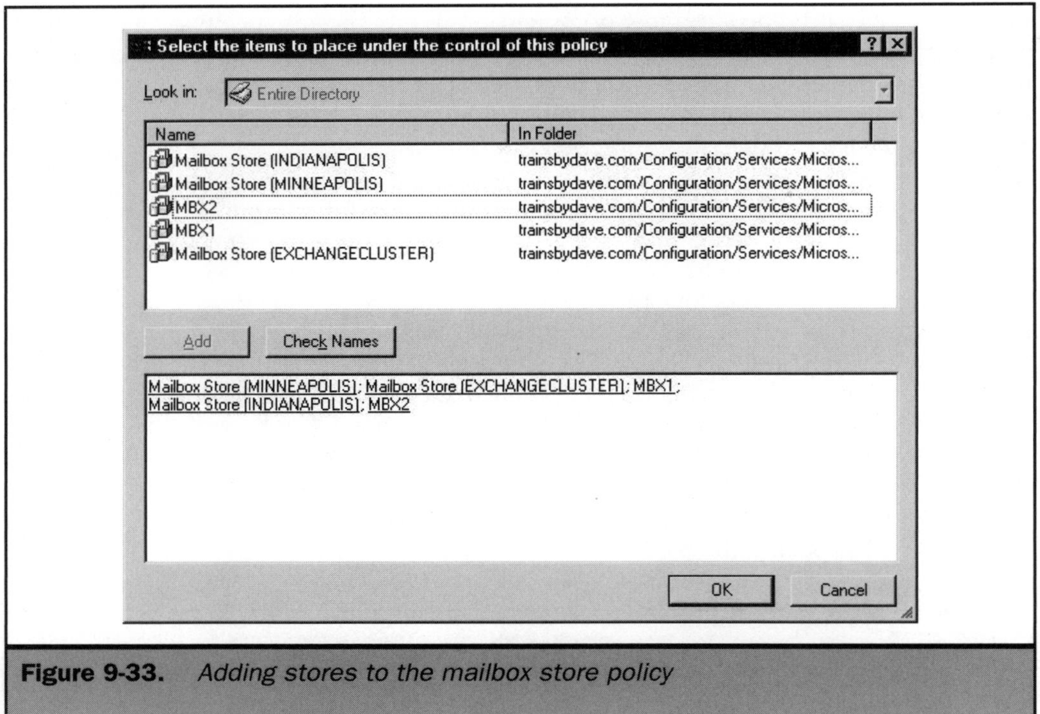

Figure 9-33. *Adding stores to the mailbox store policy*

Remember that you can create public store and server policies and that multiple policy types can be created if needed.

Summary

In this chapter, you have learned about administrative groups, routing groups, the link state architecture, address lists, and policies. It's been a full chapter, to say the least. In the next chapter, we'll turn our attention to learning the details of the protocols that make all this messaging stuff work so well.

The Complete Reference

Chapter 10

Managing Protocols

One of the key design goals of Exchange since its inception was to adhere to industry standards and provide a messaging platform that was not simply proprietary. Exchange 2000 is no exception. Exchange 2000 supports today's leading industry standard protocols in order to support the widest range of clients while still providing the highest level of compatibility with foreign messaging systems.

In this chapter, we will look at the five prominent messaging protocols supported by Exchange 2000: SMTP (Simple Mail Transfer Protocol), POP3 (Post Office Protocol version 3), IMAP4 (Internet Mail Access Protocol version 4), HTTP (Hypertext Transfer Protocol), and NNTP (Network News Transfer Protocol). We will first focus on general protocol management within Exchange 2000 and then dig a bit deeper into each protocol, focusing on management and security.

Note *For more information on these protocols, see Chapter 4.*

Exchange 2000 Protocol Management

Like Exchange 5.x, each Exchange 2000 server is responsible for the protocols it supports. That means that if you wish to perform any kind of protocol administration (configure, disable, enable, and so forth), with the exception of HTTP (which is managed within Internet Services Manager), you will need to do so within Exchange System Manager in the protocols container, which exists under the server object.

Management Permissions

In order to manage protocols, you will need to have either Exchange Administrator or Exchange Full Administrator permissions. These permissions are assigned at the Administrative Group level. You can use the Delegate Control Wizard to grant these permissions by right-clicking the administrative group and selecting Delegate Control.

Protocol Virtual Servers

In previous versions of Exchange, you could have an Exchange server support a protocol in only one particular configuration. For example, once you configured the POP3 protocol to require a secure sockets layer (SSL) connection for authentication, the protocol could be used only in that fashion. You had no means of supporting those clients that wished to connect within SSL. While this met the needs of a single company that only had a single e-mail namespace and used the same security or message restriction settings, it most likely will not meet the needs of today's e-mail users. For example, today's users within a single company may have multiple e-mail namespaces (as in the case of a worldwide company using appropriate country codes in their e-mail address for each company location). Another example would be the use of Exchange 2000 by an Internet Service Provider (ISP). An ISP may need to configure e-mail connectivity differently for each company it is hosting. Some companies may need security or message restrictions, while others are concerned only with basic connectivity.

Exchange 2000 uses protocol virtual servers, as shown in Figure 10-1, to allow you to configure each protocol on a single server to simultaneously support multiple namespaces and configurations for clients with varying needs. Exchange 2000 accomplishes this by supporting multiple virtual servers under each protocol.

Telling Virtual Servers Apart

Virtual servers generally differentiate themselves using unique IP addresses and/or TCP ports. By default, Exchange 2000 has one virtual server for each protocol, with that virtual server configured to be used over all unassigned IP addresses (meaning all IP addresses not currently in use by another virtual server for the same protocol) and the default TCP port for that protocol. Initially, therefore, the default virtual servers will work for any and all IP addresses you have configured on that server. Table 10-1 lists the protocols supported as virtual servers and the default TCP ports supported for both secure and unsecure communication.

Creating Virtual Servers

If you wish to create a virtual server for any of the five protocols, the process is the same. In Exchange System Manager, right-click the protocol in question within the protocols container, point to New and select the Virtual Server option for that protocol. Exchange 2000

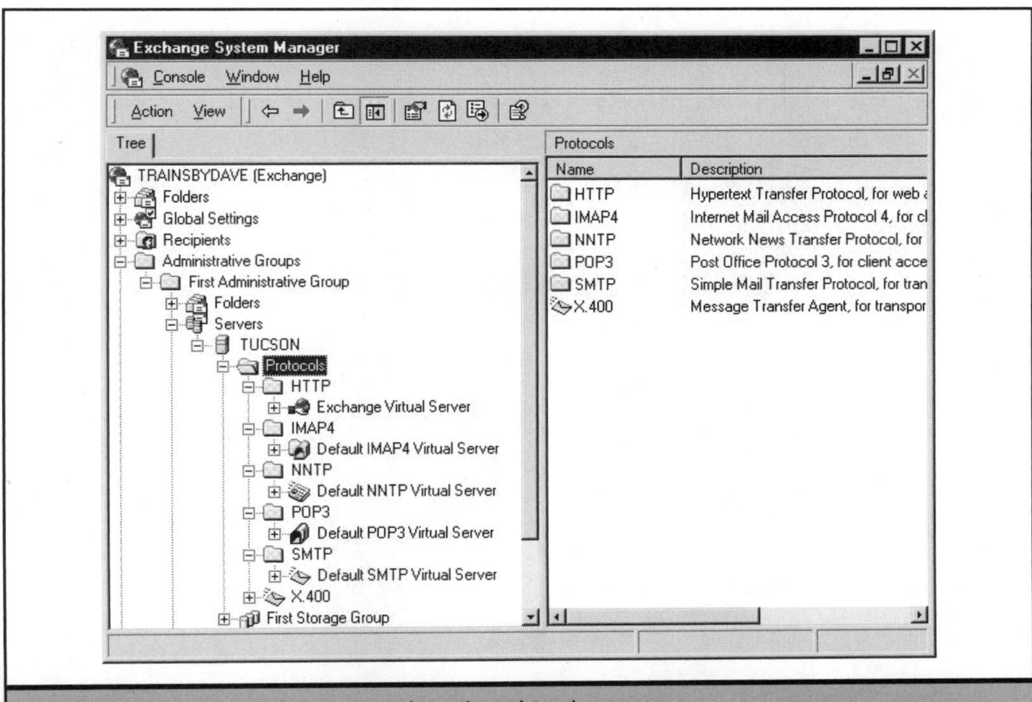

Figure 10-1. *Managing protocols using virtual servers*

Protocol	Unsecure TCP Port	Secure TCP Port
SMTP	25	465*
POP3	110	995
IMAP4	143	993
HTTP	80	443
NNTP	119	563

* While there is an industry standard port used for SMTP communications over SSL (TCP port 465), Exchange 2000 uses Transport Layer Security (TLS) to secure the channel over port 25.

Table 10-1. *Supported Protocols and their TCP ports*

starts the Virtual Server Wizard. You will be prompted to provide a name for the virtual server as well as the IP address associated with it. Figure 10-2 shows a portion of the Wizard that assists you with creating a new SMTP Virtual Server.

Managing Virtual Servers

To access the properties dialog box of a virtual server, you can do one of the following:

- Right-click the virtual server and choose Properties
- Select the virtual server and choose Properties from the Action menu
- Select the virtual server and click the Properties button in the toolbar

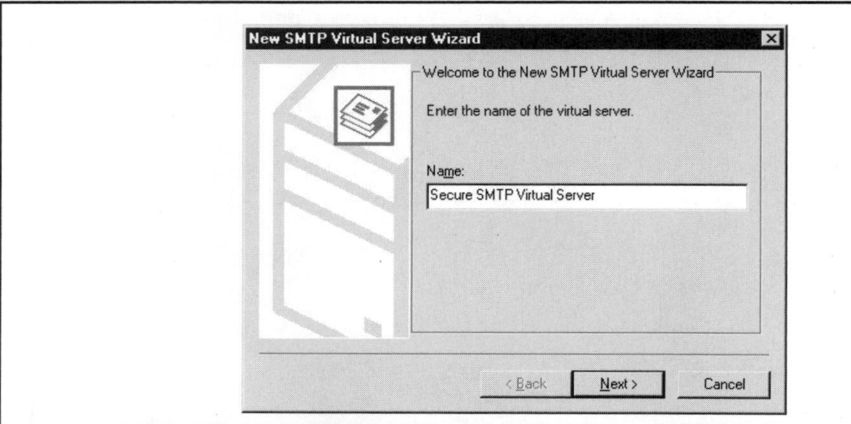

Figure 10-2. *Creating an SMTP Virtual Server using the Virtual Server Wizard*

You cannot manage an HTTP virtual server from within Exchange System Manager. You will need to manage it via the associated virtual directory in the Internet Services Manager tool. See "Managing HTTP" later in this chapter for more information.

Starting, Stopping, and Pausing

Each of the protocols can selectively be stopped, started, or paused at two levels: the service and the virtual server.

Services

Each service can be managed using the Services snap-in found in the Administrative Tools menu. Table 10-2 lists the protocol services used by Exchange 2000. You can also manage these services from the command line, from the Computer Management snap-in, and through a variety of other methods.

Stopping a service will stop all virtual servers for that protocol. Pausing a service allows all virtual servers for that protocol to continue running, but allows them to service only existing connections. No new connections are allowed. Starting a service will allow all virtual servers not in the paused or stopped state to support new connections.

Virtual Servers

The virtual servers can each be stopped, started, or paused, and doing so will only affect that individual virtual server. Using Exchange System Manager, navigate to the virtual server, right-click it, and select Stop, Start, or Pause, as appropriate. Stopping a virtual server will disconnect all connections to that virtual server. Pausing a virtual server will cause the virtual server to no longer service any new connections, while still servicing existing ones. Starting a virtual server will allow the virtual server to begin servicing new connections. If the protocol service is stopped and you start one of the virtual servers, the service will also be started.

Protocol	Service
SMTP	Simple Mail Transport Protocol (SMTP)
POP3	Microsoft Exchange POP3
IMAP4	Microsoft Exchange IMAP4
HTTP	World Wide Web Publishing
NNTP	Network News Transport Protocol (NNTP)

Table 10-2. *Service Names for Supported Protocols*

Managing SMTP

Because SMTP is the Internet standard for sending and receiving messages, everyone using Exchange 2000 will be using SMTP for Internet messaging connectivity. SMTP is implemented as the Microsoft SMTP Service in Windows 2000, which is a component of IIS. When Exchange 2000 is installed, it extends the SMTP stack in IIS to include additional command verbs and functionality. As a result, while SMTP remains part of IIS, you manage Exchange 2000's use of that protocol via the SMTP virtual servers defined in Exchange System Manager. Let's take a look at each of the property pages and then turn our focus to securing SMTP connectivity.

General

You can use the General page (Figure 10-3) to define basic connectivity to this virtual server. This tab is similar for the virtual servers of the other protocols. There may be a few additional options, but the overall purpose is the same.

IP Address

Specify a single IP address that should be associated with the virtual server in the IP address field. You can specify multiple IP addresses and custom TCP ports by clicking the Advanced button, as shown in Figure 10-4.

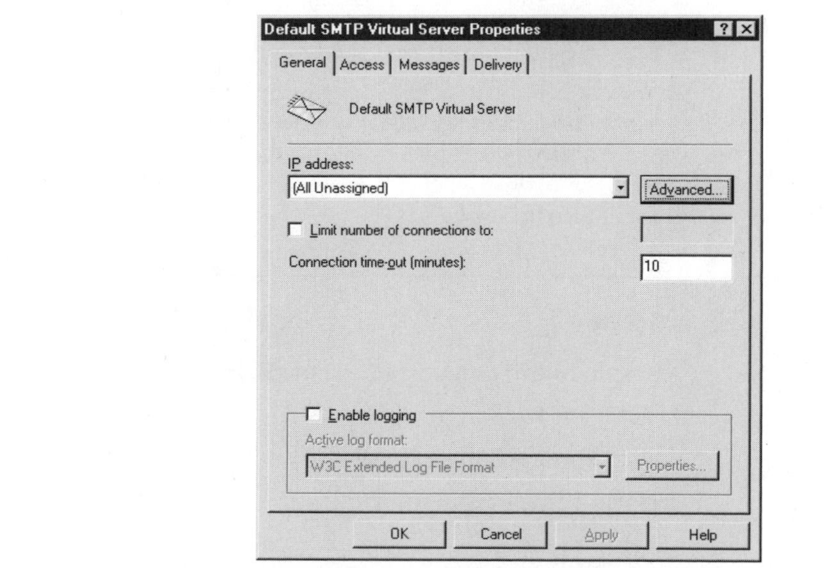

Figure 10-3. *General page of an SMTP Virtual Server*

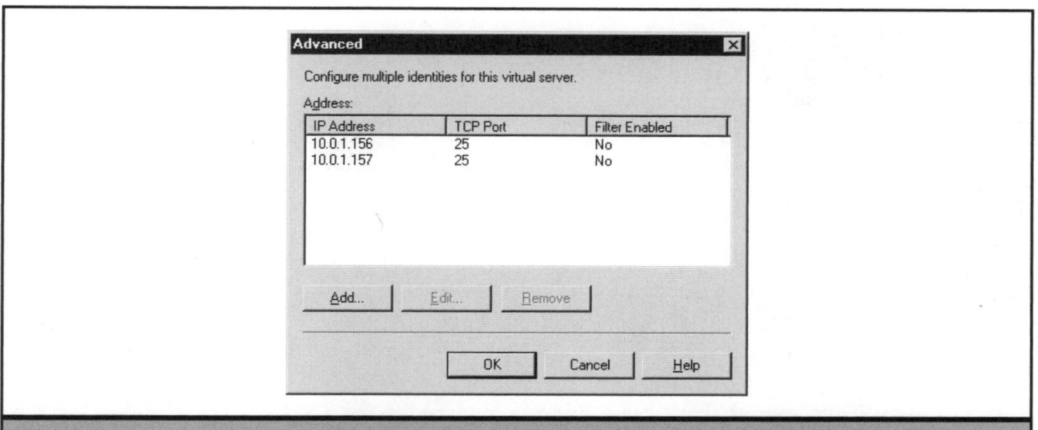

Figure 10-4. *Using the Advanced dialog box to specify multiple IP and port addresses for a virtual server*

Tip *You can filter messages from specific external addresses and have them apply to multiple SMTP virtual servers by selecting the Apply Filter checkbox in the Advanced dialog box. You can establish the filter on the Filtering page of the Message Delivery object under Global Settings (Figure 10-5).*

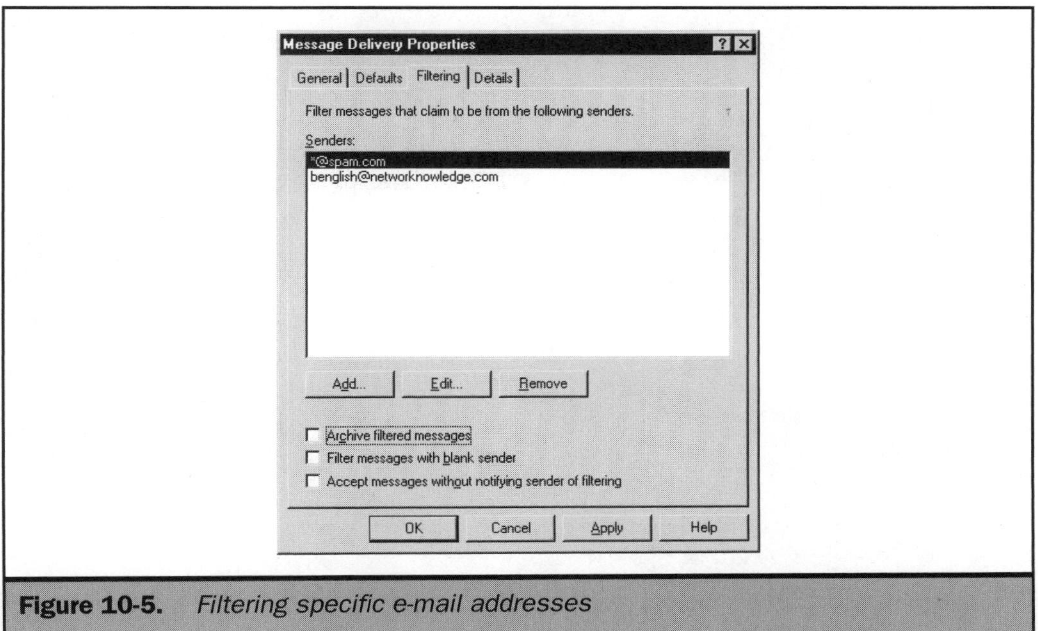

Figure 10-5. *Filtering specific e-mail addresses*

Connections

You have two methods of controlling inbound connections. You can limit the number of connections or establish a time-out for a prolonged connection to be disconnected. Acceptable values for this field are any number between 1 and 1,999,999,999.

Logging

If you want to monitor the transactions coming across this virtual server, you can choose to turn on logging. Exchange places an entry in the log for each message passing through the virtual server. You have the option of four message formats. Table 10-3 lists the four formats and describes each.

For text formats you can specify how often new log files should be created as well as the location for the files. The ODBC format requires that you provide the name of a database provider as well as a username and password for access.

Messages

This property page, shown in Figure 10-6, is used to establish message limits across this virtual server, and to designate what to do in the case of a non-delivery, among other things.

Limits

Specify the maximum message size and session size to maintain a balance between the actual needs of your users versus keeping someone from sending a 50MB video that they think is "Really cool. You've *got* to see this!" You also can specify the maximum number of messages per connection and the number of recipients.

Log File Format	Customizable?	Data Format	Log Location
W3C (World Wide Web Consortium) Extended	Yes	Text	File System
Microsoft IIS	No	Text	File System
NCSA Common	No	Text	File System
ODBC (Open Database Connectivity)	No	Data Fields	ODBC compliant database (such as Access or SQL)

Table 10-3. *SMTP Logging Formats*

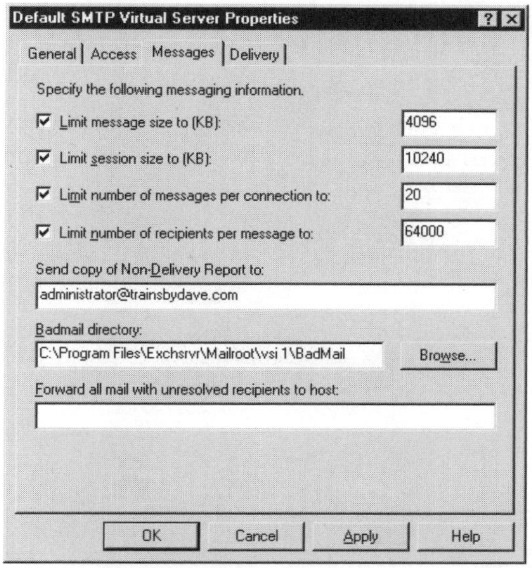

Figure 10-6. *The Messages page of an SMTP Virtual Server*

Non-Delivery Reports

You can specify who should receive a copy of Non-Delivery Reports (NDRs) in the event someone sends a message to a non-existent e-mail address within your company. Use the Badmail directory to specify where a copy of the undelivered message should be stored. Use the Forward All Mail With Unresolved Recipients To Host option to send all undelivered messages to another SMTP host that may be handling a different set of users.

Tip

You can use the forwarding feature during a migration from another e-mail platform. If the old system and Exchange 2000 are to coexist for some duration and both will need to support the same namespace (osborne.com, for example) for that duration, you can set up Exchange 2000 to receive all SMTP mail and use this forwarding field to specify the SMTP gateway for the old messaging system. The result is that all messages pass through Exchange. If your mailbox exists on Exchange, you'll receive your mail. If your mailbox exists on the old messaging system, the message is automatically forwarded to the old system for delivery. All users can maintain their e-mail address, despite the two messaging systems supporting it, and all valid users on either system will receive their e-mail.

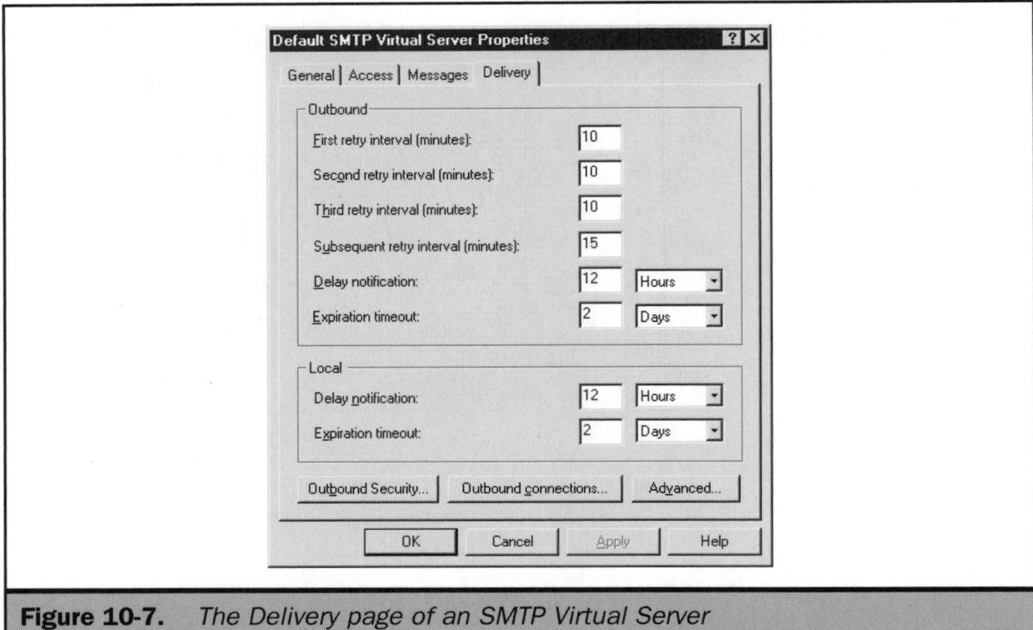

Figure 10-7. *The Delivery page of an SMTP Virtual Server*

Delivery

The Delivery property page, shown in Figure 10-7, is used to establish outbound message delivery intervals and timeouts. You can also configure options to implement outbound security, restrict outbound connections, as well as other advanced delivery options. The delivery options allow you to configure your SMTP virtual server to transmit (and potentially retry transmission) messages using the interval, security, connection, message transfer, and DNS settings you require.

Outbound Settings

Use this section to define how often Exchange should attempt to transmit a message to a foreign SMTP messaging system. You also can define how long Exchange should keep retrying to transmit a message before notifying the user that the message delivery has been delayed. Finally, you can set how long Exchange should continue to retransmit the message before returning the message to the sender as undelivered. The delay notification and expiration timeout can be set in intervals of minutes, hours, or days.

Local Settings

Use this section to define the delay notification and expiration timeout (same meanings as in the Outbound section), but only when the problem lies with the local mailbox store.

Outbound Security

The Outbound Security button yields a dialog box where you can establish what level of security is required by the SMTP hosts the virtual server will be connecting to. You will most likely use these settings only in a situation where the SMTP virtual server is connecting to another Exchange 2000 server; non-Exchange SMTP servers (such as a Unix server) support only Anonymous access.

Note *See the "Access Control" section under "Securing SMTP" later in this chapter for the "other half" of these security settings. The settings you establish here in Outbound Security will conform to the settings you establish when securing SMTP.*

Outbound Connections

The settings found here limit the number of connections made by this virtual server, the connection timeout for each, and the number of connections to each domain this virtual server can establish. You can also specify the TCP port (the default is 25) you want outbound connections to use. This setting would need to be changed only if the SMTP server you are connecting to uses a different TCP port.

Advanced Delivery

The options in this dialog box, shown in Figure 10-8, allow you to configure a number of message transfer and DNS options:

- **Maximum hop count** This establishes the maximum number of SMTP servers a message can travel through before reaching this virtual server. The default is 15. Every time an SMTP server handles a message, a line of text noting the SMTP server that handled the message (representing one hop) is added to the message header. If the number of hops exceeds the value set here, the virtual server will return the message undelivered.
- **Masquerade domain** If you do not want NDRs to be sent back to the domain in which your SMTP virtual server exists, but instead to an alternate domain, use the Masquerade Domain field to specify the domain name NDRs should be sent to.

Tip *When your company uses a number of FQDN's for correspondence, use the masquerade domain field to specify which one should be receiving NDRs.*

- **Fully qualified domain name** This establishes the name of the virtual server when it handles messages and communicates with other SMTP servers. The FQDN must have a valid DNS entry in an internal or external DNS server. You can use the Check DNS button to verify that the FQDN you enter resolves to the correct IP address.
- **Smart host** A smart host is an intermediary server used to process messages that are forwarded to it from other SMTP hosts. The smart host could be an

internal SMTP server that performs content or virus scanning or an SMTP host managed by your ISP. You can also choose to have Exchange try to send the message directly to the recipient's host before using a smart host. This procedure could be used when you want to send messages directly to another internal message system, but want to use a smart host for Internet e-mail.

Tip *Use the smart host setting to forward messages to a virus scanning or content filtering host before allowing messages to be sent to the recipient.*

- **Perform reverse DNS lookup on incoming messages** You can add the host name of the originating server to the message header using this option. Doing this will provide you a bit of history on any incoming messages.

Tip *Use reverse DNS lookups if your company is receiving a large amount of spam mail. This will allow you to find the originating domain (assuming it can be found in DNS). You can use this information to block messages from that domain. See "Securing SMTP" later in the chapter for information on how to block specific domains.*

- **Configure external DNS servers** You can use this option to specify which DNS servers this virtual server should use when sending messages. You may use this feature to utilize one set of DNS servers for intranet use, while using another set of DNS servers for Internet use.

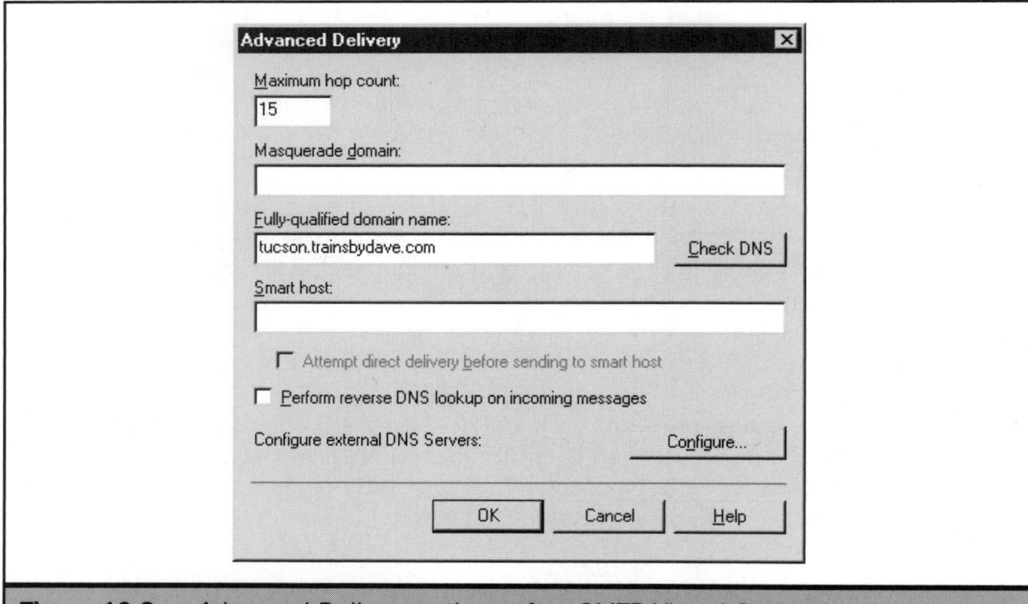

Figure 10-8. *Advanced Delivery options of an SMTP Virtual Server*

Managing SMTP Queues

Once you have configured how your SMTP clients and other SMTP hosts will interact with an SMTP virtual server, you may need to manage the use of that virtual server. You can accomplish the day-to-day management of an SMTP server by paying attention to the status of the SMTP queues belonging to that virtual server. Each SMTP virtual server will dynamically create and delete queues containing messages destined for various domains. The purpose underlying the dynamic creation of queues is the optimization of the connection to a foreign host by placing all messages for each host in an individual queue. In Exchange 5.x, all outbound messages were in the same queue and were processed on a first-in, first-out basis. Exchange 2000's use of dynamic queues optimizes this process. For example, if I were sending two messages, each destined for a different domain (for example, comsphere.com and networknowledge.com), Exchange 2000 would place each of these messages in a separate queue. That way, if more messages destined for either of those two domains are submitted, they will be placed in the queue associated with the target domain, and, once connected to the foreign SMTP host, the entire queue (or a subset, depending on the number of messages) can be transmitted at once.

You will manage the SMTP queues by navigating under the SMTP virtual server object, and expand Queues (Figure 10-9). Each basic queue entry gives you quite a lot of information about the queue:

- Connection Name
- Connection State (Ready, Retry, Scheduled, Active, or Remote)
- Time of Submission of Oldest Message
- Total Number of Messages
- Total Message Size (in KB)
- Time of Next Connection

While this information helps give you a bird's eye view of the queue health, managing a queue will involve drilling down a bit deeper into each queue. There are a few actions you can take to manage SMTP queues:

- **Enumerate** By default, Exchange 2000 does not show you the messages in the queue. You will have to enumerate the queue to see the first 100 messages. To do this, navigate to the specific queue, right-click it, and choose Enumerate 100 Messages. Then double-click on the queue to see the messages.
- **Freeze** You can freeze both messages and an entire queue. You may choose to freeze a message if it is large and holds up all subsequent messages in the queue from being transmitted. You can also freeze messages that you suspect are corrupt and holding up the queue. Freeze an entire queue to hold all messages in the queue. The queue will continue to accept messages, but no messages will be transmitted. You may choose to freeze an entire queue if there is a

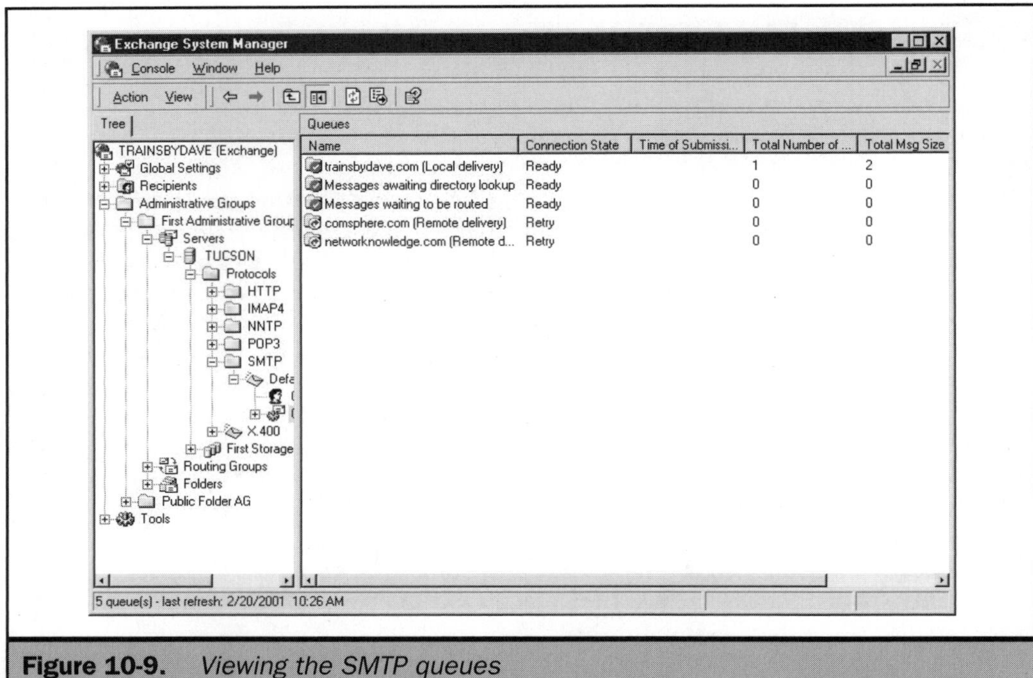

Figure 10-9. *Viewing the SMTP queues*

problem with the foreign SMTP host and you do not want Exchange 2000 to continue retrying the transmission of the message until reaching the maximum number of retries and returning the message to the sender. To freeze a message, right-click the message in question and select Freeze. To freeze an entire queue, right-click the queue and select Freeze All Messages.

- **Unfreeze** Any frozen messages or queues can be unfrozen to allow normal processing of that message or queue. To unfreeze a message, right-click it and choose Unfreeze. To Unfreeze a queue, right-click the queue and select Unfreeze All Messages.
- **Force Connection** Instead of waiting for the preset retry time to retransmit messages in the queue, you can force the queue to attempt a connection immediately. To force a connection, right-click the queue and select Force Connection.
- **Delete Messages** If needed, you can choose to delete all the messages in a queue and, optionally, provide the sender with an NDR. To do so, right-click the queue and select either Delete All Messages (no NDR) or Delete All Messages (send NDR).

- **Custom Filter** If you need to see messages matching specific criteria, you can create a filter through which to view the queue. You can filter on the basis of such criteria as message size, age, sender, and recipient.

Managing Current SMTP Sessions

In addition to managing the queues and their contents, you also can view information about users and other SMTP hosts that are connected to the virtual server including how long they have been connected. You also have the option of disconnecting all users and SMTP hosts by right-clicking the Current Sessions object under the SMTP virtual server and selecting Terminate All.

Securing SMTP

Most SMTP messaging systems do not require any form of security. In fact, in most cases communication between SMTP hosts is done with complete anonymity; no username or password is required, and no verification of the sender is required. However, in some cases it may be necessary to establish some level of security for your SMTP communication. Exchange 2000 provides you with a number of methods to secure your SMTP traffic.

Most of the settings involving the securing of SMTP will be found on the Access property page of the SMTP virtual server, shown in Figure 10-10. It is these settings

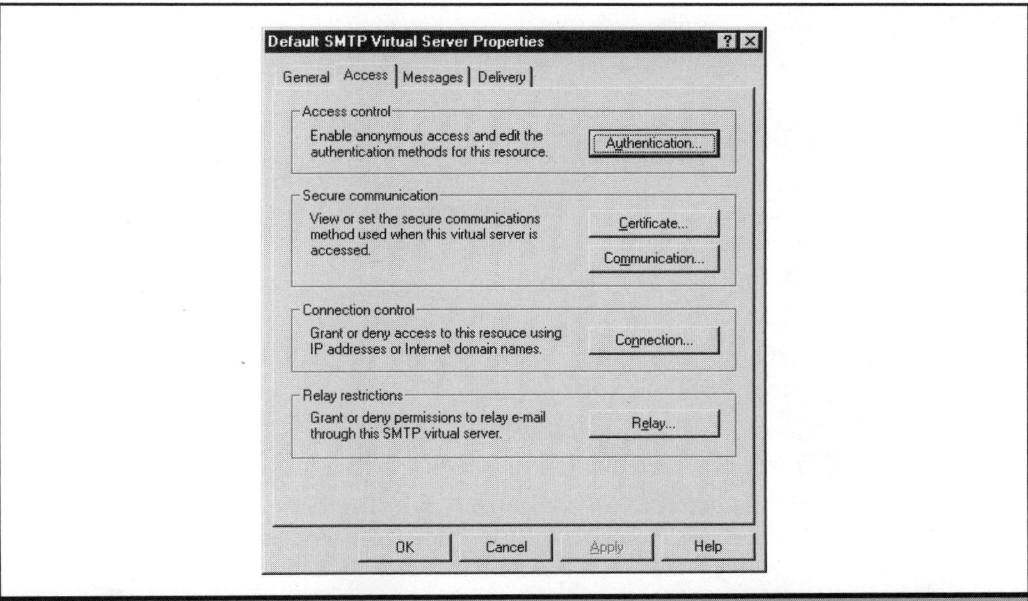

Figure 10-10. *Access property page of an SMTP Virtual Server*

that will determine who can connect, from where can they connect, how (secure or not) they connect, and where they can send messages.

Access Control

The Access Control section allows you to specify what authentication methods will be allowed. These authentication methods provide varying levels of security:

- **Anonymous access** This value, which is selected by default, requires no authentication whatsoever. Thus, the connection is made anonymously.
- **Basic Authentication** A username and password are sent over the network in clear text (that is, without any form of encryption). Because the passing of logon credentials goes hand-in-hand with the lack of security in this option, you do have the choice of requiring Transport Layer Security (TLS) or Internet Protocol Security (IPSec), which can encrypt account, password, and message information. If clients provide a username and password to authenticate, you can specify the default Windows 2000 domain name the user will authenticate against.

TLS, also known as Secure Sockets Layer (SSL), is supported by Outlook Express, Outlook 2000 and Exchange 2000.

- **Integrated Windows Authentication** User can provide a valid Windows 2000 account and password over an encrypted channel using Kerberos security or Microsoft Window NT LAN Manager (NTLM) security when Kerberos is not available. Message data is not encrypted using this option.

Secure Communications

The Secure Communications section establishes the secure channel used by SMTP clients. SMTP clients using TLS will utilize the security certificate chosen here to implement secure communications.

Certificate

This button will start the Web Server Certificate Wizard. You will create, assign, or import an existing X.509 security certificate to be used by SMTP for secure communications.

Communication

Once a certificate is installed, you can choose to require an SSL-based (Secure Sockets Layer) secure channel for SMTP communication. This means that all clients who are not using a secure channel to this SMTP virtual server will be denied access. You can also choose to require 128-bit encryption (the default level of encryption is 56-bit). This option was used only by clients within the United States and Canada; the U.S. government classified any encryption over 56 bits as dangerous, so this type of strong encryption (128-bit) was normally not used outside of the United States or Canada.

This restriction has been lifted by the U.S. government, and 128-bit encryption can be used worldwide, subject to local laws regarding encryption.

Check to see if the clients and other SMTP hosts support SSL before requiring encryption.

SSL can increase the load on the server and decrease server performance. You may chose to monitor the server's performance before and after the implementation of SSL to see the effect SSL is having on your server.

Connection Control

Use this option to specify which computers may access the SMTP virtual server. You can choose computers by specific IP address (which only would apply to one computer), by an IP subnet and subnet mask (which would apply to all computers on that IP subnet), or by a domain name (which would apply to all computers in that domain).

Relay Restrictions

Use this option to restrict who can relay off of this server. *Relaying* is the process of sending a message to an SMTP host destined for a recipient not on that host. The relay occurs when the SMTP host forwards the message to the appropriate SMTP host. For example, if you have a POP3 account with an ISP, you send your outbound SMTP messages to your ISP's SMTP host. Your ISP, in turn, relays your outbound messages to the destination SMTP host on the basis of the domain portion of the e-mail address(es) in the message headers.

By default, only authenticated users can relay off an SMTP virtual server. You do have the option of adding, like the Connection Control section, individual IP addresses, IP subnets, or domains of users. Additionally, you can choose to bypass any entries added to the relay list, by leaving selected the option to "allow all computers which successfully authenticate to relay, regardless of the list above."

Be very careful when relaxing your relay settings. Many "spammers" on the Internet (those who send unsolicited e-mail to massive amounts of recipients) try to find and use SMTP servers that will relay anonymously. This practice will put an additional, unsolicited load on your SMTP servers.

Managing POP3

POP3 is one of the early Internet standards for messaging clients to connect to their e-mail server and pull down their messages. Clients have access to their own Inbox on the server but not to any other folders, public or private, on the server. POP3 is responsible only for client retrieval of messages. The client transmission of messages is handled via SMTP. Although POP3, like SMTP, is an IIS component, its use by

Exchange 2000 is managed via POP3 virtual servers within Exchange System Manager. We'll first look at the property pages of a POP3 virtual server, then focus on securing it.

General

As with the SMTP virtual server, you will use the General page to assign the IP addresses and ports for this virtual server, as shown in Figure 10-11. You can also establish a limit to the number of inbound connections as well as a timeout that defines the period of inactivity for each connection before it is automatically disconnected.

For more information on assigning IP and port addresses to a virtual server, see "Managing SMTP" earlier in this chapter. The only difference in assigning IP and port addresses for a POP3 virtual server is that no filters can be applied to this virtual server.

Message Format

Use the Message Format page, shown in Figure 10-12, to specify how MAPI messages should be converted and presented to POP3 clients when retrieving their messages.

Message Encoding

You have the choice of converting messages to either MIME (Multipurpose Internet Mail Extensions) or UUEncode format. MIME format allows for the body of the

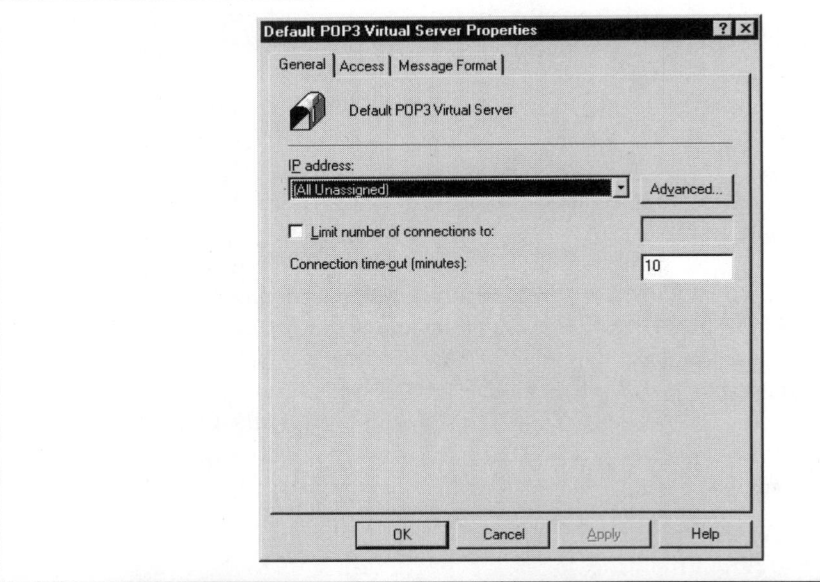

Figure 10-11. *The General page of a POP3 Virtual Server*

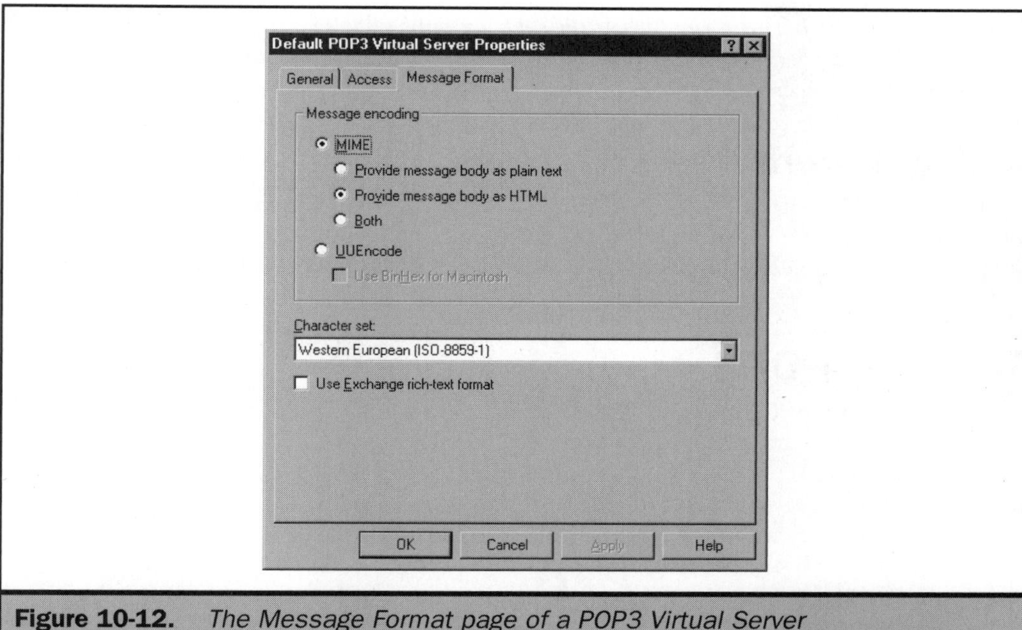

Figure 10-12. *The Message Format page of a POP3 Virtual Server*

message to be presented as text, HTML, or both, while UUEncode allows you to use the BinHex format for Macintosh clients. UUEncode is an older standard used for appending attached files to a message. MIME is a more current standard widely used by messaging systems today. Unless you specifically have clients who support only UUEncode, leave the value set to support MIME.

Character Set

MAPI messages sent by older MAPI clients, such as Outlook 97 or earlier, use Windows-based character sets rather than Internet standardized character sets. Use this option to specify the character set needed to support your Outlook 97 and earlier clients.

The character set option affects only Outlook 97 and earlier clients. Outlook 98 and 2000 already support the newer character sets.

Use Exchange Rich-Text Format

Selecting this option will send every message in Exchange Rich-Text format. Use this option only if *all* of the POP3 clients connecting to Exchange 2000 support Exchange Rich-Text format. POP3 and IMAP4 clients that don't support this format will receive garbled attachments named winmail.dat.

Exchange Rich-Text format is not the same format as the RTF (Rich Text Format) supported by Microsoft Word and other word processing applications. In fact, these formats are incompatible.

Managing Current POP3 Sessions

As with the SMTP virtual server, you can view the current user sessions to this virtual server. You also have the option of terminating all connections by right-clicking the Current Sessions object under the POP3 virtual server and selecting Terminate All.

Securing POP3

Unlike SMTP, POP3 requires that the client provide some form of identification in the form of a username and password to retrieve messages, which are usually the same username and password you use at your desk at work. However, as with SMTP, usually no effort goes into securing POP3 communications.

Because authentication is a normal part of accessing messages through POP3, you should think about securing both the POP3 authentication as well as the entire communications channel. We will look at establishing both of these areas of security by looking at the options found on the Access property page of the POP3 virtual server, shown in Figure 10-13.

Access Control

The Access Control section is used to configure authentication. Two options exist:

- **Basic Authentication** This setting, which is checked by default, allows clients to send their credentials as clear text (no encryption) across your intranet or the Internet. This means that the username and password are easily read by anyone with a packet capturing utility. Think of what could happen if you were to log on to your POP3 server using your administrator account! If multiple Windows 2000 domains exist in your company, you can provide a default domain name to be used when authenticating clients.
- **Integrated Windows Authentication** This setting, also checked by default, allows clients to secure their logon credentials using Kerberos or NTLM security.

Remember, these access control settings are for authentication only. Selecting either option (or both) does not secure the message data.

Secure Communications

You can choose to secure all traffic (authentication and message) between the POP3 client and server using an SSL-based connection. The Certificate button launches the

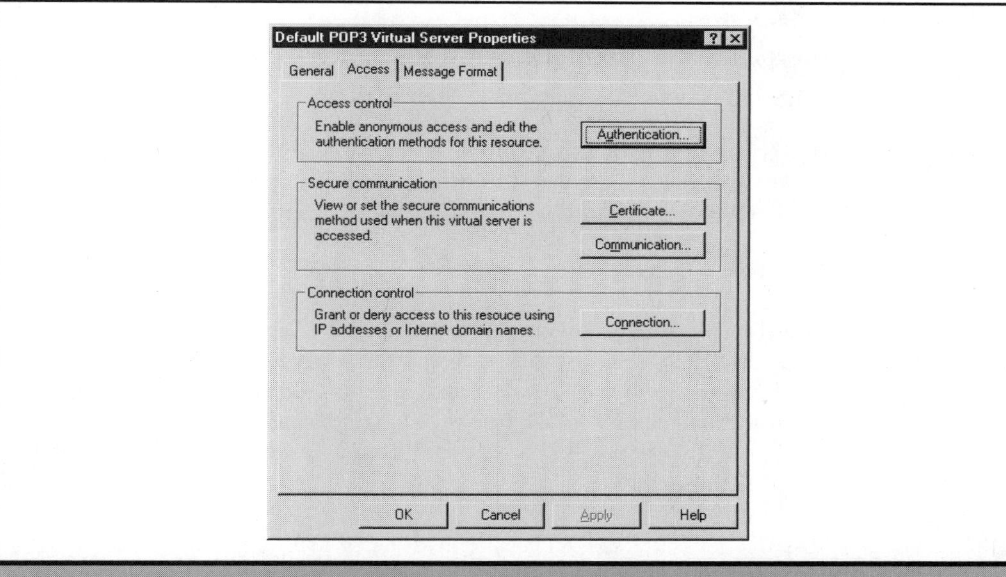

Figure 10-13. *The Access property page of a POP3 Virtual Server*

Web Server Certificate Wizard to install an SSL certificate. The Communication button yields the Security dialog box. In this box, you can choose to require a secure channel between the POP3 client and this virtual server as well as require a 128-bit encrypted channel (the default is only 56-bit encryption).

Connection Control

Use this option to restrict certain IP addresses, IP subnets, or entire FQDN domains from using this virtual server.

For more information on the security options for POP3, look at the equivalent settings in the "Securing SMTP" section, earlier in this chapter.

Managing IMAP4

IMAP4 is another popular messaging protocol. It not only provides message retrieval capabilities similar to POP3, but it also allows clients to do the following:

- Access multiple mailboxes
- Access public folders

- Retrieve certain messages
- Retrieve portions of a message, such as an attachment
- Mark messages to reflect that they have been read

Like POP3, IMAP4 is responsible only for retrieving messages. An IMAP4 client must use SMTP to transmit messages. We'll first look at the property pages used to manage an IMAP4 virtual server, and then focus on securing it.

General

As with the SMTP and POP3 virtual servers, you will use the General page, shown in Figure 10-14, to assign the IP addresses and ports for this virtual server as well as the maximum number of connections and connection timeouts. Additionally, you can choose to list public folders when IMAP4 clients request a list of folders from the virtual server and to have the virtual server approximate message sizes in order to speed up the retrieval of messages.

Some older IMAP clients will experience problems when using the fast message retrieval option. However, more recent IMAP clients (including all IMAP clients from Microsoft) will not.

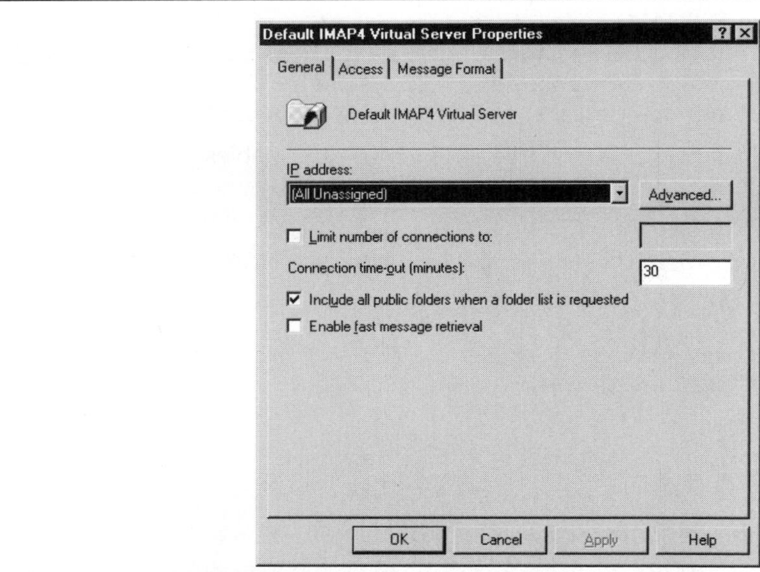

Figure 10-14. *The General page of an IMAP4 Virtual Server*

Message Format

Use this page to determine how MAPI messages are to be presented to IMAP4 clients as well as what character sets are supported and whether to use Exchange Rich-Text format. These settings are identical to those found under a POP3 virtual server.

For more information on IMAP4's message format settings, see "Message Format" in the "Managing POP3" section earlier in this chapter.

Managing Current IMAP4 Sessions

View the current IMAP4 users by selecting the Current Sessions object below the IMAP4 virtual server. You can also choose to disconnect all users by right-clicking Current Sessions and selecting Terminate All.

Securing IMAP4

You will find that the security concerns and default provisions taken to secure IMAP4 traffic is almost identical to that of POP3. By default, the authentication process is not secure, providing a clear text transmission of the credentials as well as no encryption during the retrieval of message data. You also have the identical set of options to that of a POP3 virtual server to secure your IMAP4 connections, and you will use the Access property page to establish your IMAP4 security settings.

Access

The Access property page, previously shown in Figure 10-10, enables you to define authentication and communication security as well as grant or deny access to the virtual server. These options are exactly the same as those found on the Access property page for a POP3 virtual server.

For more information on the security settings found on the Access property page, see "Securing POP3" earlier in this chapter.

Managing HTTP

HTTP access to Exchange mailboxes and public folders is accomplished by means of Outlook Web Access (for an Outlook-like interface) or via a standard URL using WebDAV (Web Distributed Authoring and Versioning).

All aspects of the Exchange Virtual Server will be managed using the Internet Services Manager snap-in found on the Administrative Tools menu. Instead of looking for a virtual server, you will be managing virtual directories underneath the Default Web Site. There are four virtual directories that pertain to Exchange 2000:

- **Exchweb** This virtual directory stores graphics and other files to be used by Outlook Web Access.
- **Public** This virtual directory provides access to public folders.
- **Exchange** This virtual directory provides access to mailboxes.
- **Exadmin** This virtual directory is used by Exchange administration tools to manage public folders.

Of these four, you will only need to manage and utilize *public* and *exchange*.

Securing HTTP

The Directory Security property page of the virtual directory, shown in Figure 10-15, provides you with all you need to properly secure access to the Exchange server via HTTP. As with the other protocols previously described in this chapter, you have the ability to manage the security of the authentication process and of the entire channel and to grant or deny access to the virtual directory based on IP address or domain.

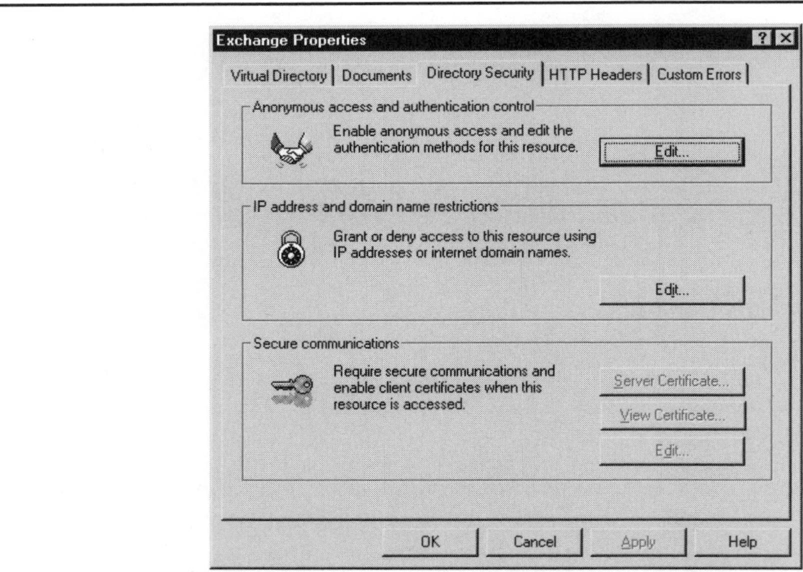

Figure 10-15. *The Directory Security property page of the Exchange virtual directory*

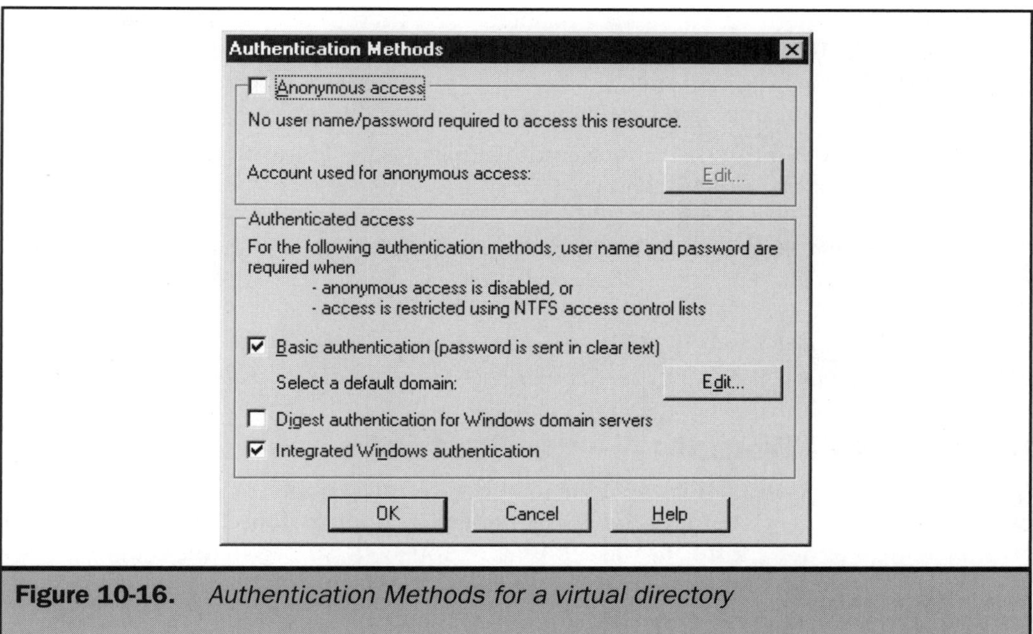

Figure 10-16. *Authentication Methods for a virtual directory*

Anonymous Access and Authentication Control

Use this section to specify the authentication method(s) you wish to use. Click the Edit button to access the Authentication Methods dialog box, shown in Figure 10-16, which gives you four methods of providing authentication security: anonymous and authenticated access.

Anonymous Access

Because IIS sees this virtual directory like all others, this option is a valid choice. However, in most cases, the only time you will utilize this option is when you wish to provide anonymous access to a specific public folder. Note that this option is deselected by default. Should you choose to provide anonymous access, you can click the Edit button to input the Anonymous User credentials that IIS will use in place of those a client would normally provide.

Authenticated Access

This section gives you three levels of authentication:

- **Basic Authentication** utilizes no encryption and sends the logon credentials as clear text.

- **Digest Authentication** sends a hash, rather than the credentials, across the network. The hash contains not only the username and password, but also other information provided by the server and client in this process. The result is a piece of unintelligible data being sent across the network.
- **Integrated Windows Authentication** allows clients to log on using NTLM or Kerberos v5 authentication.

For more information on authentication methods used by IIS 5.0, see "About Authentication" in the IIS 5.0 documentation.

No matter which level of authentication you choose, we recommend implementing an SSL connection. See "Secure Communications" later in this chapter.

IP Address and Domain Name Restrictions

Use this option to control which specific IP addresses, IP subnets, or entire domains can access this virtual directory. Management of this option is done in the same fashion as the identical option for the virtual servers previously discussed in this chapter.

Secure Communications

You can choose to implement and/or require a secure channel when accessing this virtual directory with this option. To enable secure communications, you will need to first install a certificate from a certification authority (CA). The CA can be an industry provider of certificates (such as VeriSign or RSA) or can be the Windows 2000 Certificate Services. In this chapter, we will assume you have Certificate Services running on your network and will utilize it as your CA.

To install a certificate, do the following:

1. Go to the Directory Security property page of the Default Web Site (the Exchange-related virtual directories all exist within this Website by default, and the certificate can be used by any virtual directory within the Website).
2. Click the Server Certificate button to begin the Web Server Certificate Wizard.
3. Choose to submit your certificate request to an online authority and complete the wizard (the process is explained in detail in Chapter 19).
4. Once the certificate is installed, you will need to configure your security settings for the specific virtual directory. Go to the Directory Security property page for the Exchange virtual directory, shown previously in Figure 10-14, and click the Edit button in the Secure Communications section.
5. The Secure Communications dialog box, shown in Figure 10-16, allows you to enable a secure channel either using the certificate you installed previously for the entire Website or using individual client certificates.

Require Secure Channel

Check this box to require that clients use an SSL-based connection to this virtual directory. The clients will be required to use "https://" at the beginning of the URL in their browser. You also have the option of using 128-bit encryption rather than the default of 56-bit encryption.

If your clients forget to specify a secure http session by typing "https://" at the start of the URL, they will simply get an error stating they will need to access this resource over a secure channel. They will be prompted to put "https://" at the start of the URL they are typing.

Client Certificates

In addition to establishing a secure channel over SSL, you can also require that clients present a certificate from a trusted CA to the server prior to allowing them to access the web page. By default, this option is not enabled. Enabling this option would provide an additional layer of verification over authentication only.

Enable Client Certificate Mapping

If enabling SSL and requiring a client certificate is not secure enough for you, you can map the individual client certificates to specific users. By doing so, merely the presence of a client certificate is not enough; the certificate must match up to a single Windows 2000 user or multiple Windows 2000 users.

For more information on certificates, see Chapters 18 and 19.

The advanced security methods, involving certificates, are more appropriate for the Exchange virtual directory than the Public virtual directory. In some cases, access to Public is done with anonymity since authenticated users can access both public folder and their mailbox through the Exchange virtual directory. Anonymous access to Public provides external users with access to various company resources in the form of messages, calendar, or contact information, or to Web Store applications.

Managing NNTP

NNTP is an application protocol that allows clients to participate in online discussions called *newsgroups*. Exchange 2000 supports NNTP to provide newsgroup access to native NNTP clients as well as to provide access to Outlook clients by representing a newsgroup on the Internet as a public folder within Exchange.

As with the other protocols described in this chapter, Exchange 2000's use of NNTP is managed via an NNTP virtual server. First we'll look at the property pages dealing with managing an NNTP virtual server; then we'll look at managing such other aspects of NNTP as newsgroups, feeds, and policies; and, finally, we'll focus on securing NNTP.

General

Use this property page, shown in Figure 10-17, much like the other protocols previously mentioned: to assign IP and port addresses, limit connections, specify connection timeouts, and enable the logging of NNTP sessions. In addition, you can specify a FQDN in the Path Header field to uniquely identify this NNTP virtual server.

The Path Header field is used to prevent looping, *a condition where NNTP servers with multiple feed providers pass the same messages back and forth in an endless loop.*

Settings

The Settings property page, shown in Figure 10-18, is the heart and soul of your NNTP services. A wide variety of settings affecting your NNTP services exist here:

- **Allow Client Posting** This option, which is selected by default, allows clients to post to newsgroups on this server. Without this option selected, all newsgroups would be read-only. You can also limit the size of individual messages as well as the combined total of all messages on this server.
- **Allow Feed Posting** This option, also selected by default, allows messages posted to this server to be pulled from other NNTP servers. Use this option if

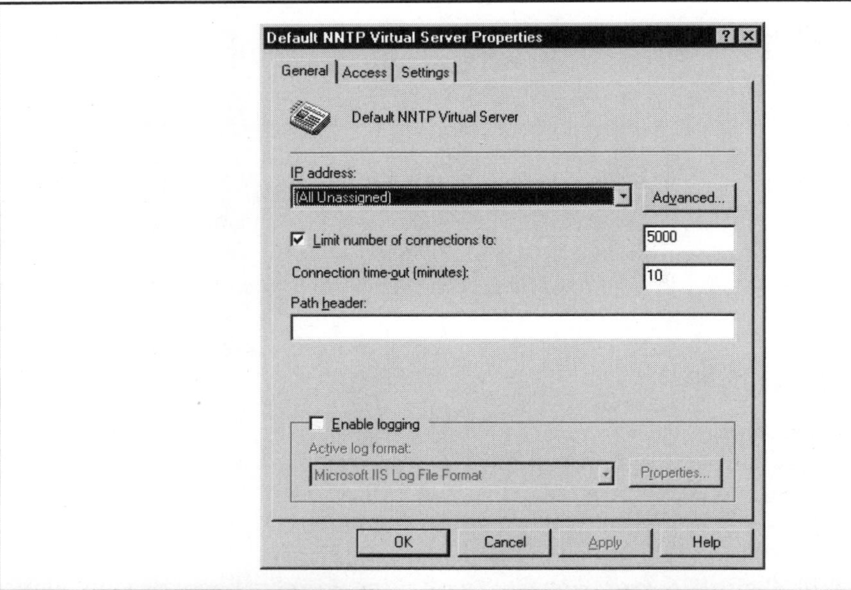

Figure 10-17. *The General page of an NNTP Virtual Server*

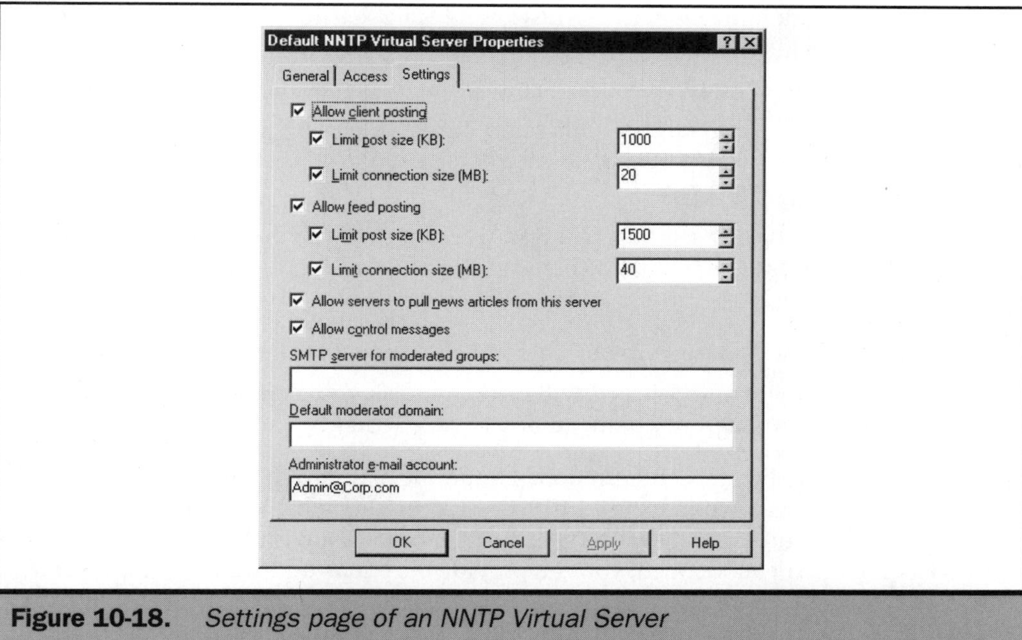

Figure 10-18. *Settings page of an NNTP Virtual Server*

the content of your newsgroups comes from other NNTP servers. You can also limit the size of messages that are retrieved from other NNTP servers as well as the maximum amount of data retrieved within a single session.

Note *Not all NNTP servers allow Pull feeds, so even if you set this option, you may not be able to pull the content down to your server.*

- **Allow Servers to Pull News Articles From This Server** This option allows the exact opposite of Feed Posting. In this case, your server's content is being pulled by another NNTP server.
- **Allow Control Messages** Control messages include the creation and deletion of newsgroups. This option, which is checked by default, tells the Exchange server whether to ignore control messages and allows for new newsgroups from another NNTP server to be automatically created. Control messages also enable users to cancel their own posts on the server.
- **SMTP Server for Moderated Groups** Since moderated newsgroups need to have each posting reviewed and approved by a moderator, you can specify the SMTP server that will be responsible for sending messages to the newsgroup moderator.

- **Default Moderator Domain** This setting specifies the domain responsible for moderating all postings.
- **Administrator E-mail Account** This setting specifies the e-mail address of the person who administers the virtual server.

Managing Newsgroups

Under an NNTP virtual server, you will find five objects. Each deals with a specific part of NNTP services. The first is the Newsgroup object. You can create a newsgroup by doing the following:

1. Right-click the Newsgroup object, point to New, and select Newsgroup.
2. The New Newsgroup Wizard will begin and ask you to provide a name, description, and a pretty name (a descriptive "friendly" name).

If you need to modify the configuration of a specific newsgroup, right-click it and choose Properties. As shown in Figure 10-19, you can modify what was entered under Description and Pretty Name as well as specify if the newsgroup is to be Read Only and/or Moderated. If it is to be moderated, you can provide the e-mail address of the moderator.

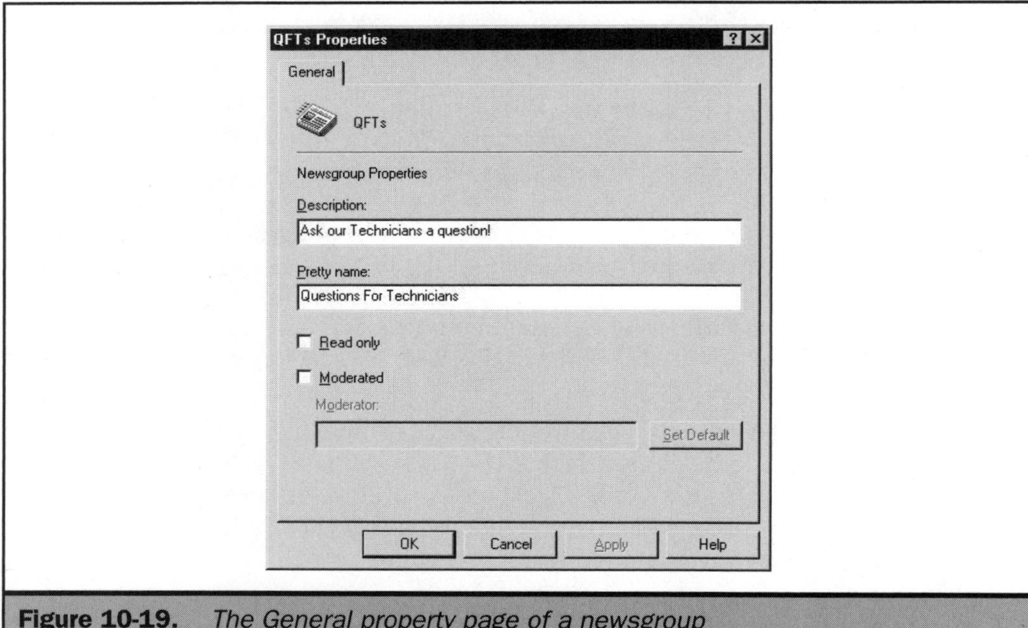

Figure 10-19. *The General property page of a newsgroup*

Even if you designate a newsgroup as read-only, you can still post messages to it using Outlook.

If you wish to rename or delete the newsgroup, simply right-click the newsgroup and choose either rename or delete, as appropriate.

Managing Feeds

A feed is a local copy of a remote newsgroup. For example, perhaps some of your employees frequent a particular USENET newsgroup. Instead of having them individually connect to the remote NNTP server and pull messages across the Internet, you can instead set up a feed that automatically pulls the entire newsgroup down into a public folder (providing that the NNTP server allows pull feeds) and have that local public folder be accessible to your employees.

Pulling a feed from a foreign NNTP server may be undesirable. When you pull down messages, you have no control over virus infection of those messages, spam messages in the feed, unwanted or inappropriate attachments, and so on.

To create a feed, perform the following steps:

1. Right-click the Feeds object under the NNTP virtual server, point to New, and select Feed.
2. The New NNTP Feed Wizard will start and prompt you for a remote server name or IP address.
3. Determine the remote server's role for the feed.
4. Specify the direction the exchange of posts will occur (inbound and outbound), the starting date and time of posts to be pulled (if inbound), the path header for this virtual server (if Outbound), and the local newsgroups that should be affected by this feed.

Once it's created, you can modify the Outbound IP Port (the default is TCP port 119 for NNTP) as well as what newsgroups should be pulled, the schedule at which they should be pulled, and any authentication required by the remote server.

If you wish to rename or delete the feed, simply right-click the feed and choose either rename or delete, as is appropriate.

Managing Expiration Policies

Most likely, you will not want every posted message to remain on your NNTP newsgroups forever. You will probably want to remove the older messages posted to leave room for newer posts. You also will probably not want to delete the messages by hand. An Expiration Policy will establish the amount of time (in hours) that messages will remain before being automatically removed. When creating a new expiration policy—by right-clicking the Expiration Policies object, pointing to New, and selecting Expiration Policy—you will run the New NNTP Expiration Policy Wizard. You will provide the wizard with the name of the policy, the newsgroups that should be affected by this policy, and the number of hours used to determine which messages should be removed.

Managing NNTP Virtual Directories

You may want to create more than one NNTP virtual directory. You may want to do this to provide different NNTP environments for different domains or to provide anonymous access to one, while requiring authentication to another. Although the default NNTP virtual directory exists as a public folder within Exchange, you can create additional virtual directories that exist within the file system.

To create an NNTP virtual directory, perform the following steps:

1. Right-click the Virtual Directories object under NNTP, point to New and select Virtual Directory. Doing this will start the New NNTP Virtual Directory Wizard.
2. The wizard will prompt you for the subtree name, which is the name for the particular subset of newsgroups.
3. Specify the location type (you can choose a public folder, file system, or network share). These three choices give you the flexibility to store your newsgroups within Exchange, on the local file system, or across the network on another server via a shared folder. Use public folders when you want native Outlook clients to access the same information. Use the file system or network share options when disk space or backups may be a concern.
4. Specify the path (to the public folder, file system location, or network share, as applicable) for the new virtual directory.

Once it's created, you can modify other parameters for the virtual directory, such as disallowing posting to this virtual directory, restricting access (you will need either the appropriate NTFS or Exchange public folder permissions), logging access to this virtual directory, and indexing the content of this virtual directory.

If you wish to log access to a virtual directory, you will need to ensure logging has been enabled for the associated NNTP virtual server.

Managing Current NNTP Sessions

View the current NNTP users by selecting the Current Sessions object below the NNTP virtual server. You can also choose to disconnect all users by right-clicking Current Sessions and selecting Terminate All.

Securing NNTP

Most public NNTP servers do not use any kind of authentication or encryption. However, there are cases where you will want to either provide NNTP to a select number of users, or provide encryption to ensure all reading and posting of messages are secure. Security can be implemented at a number of different areas within NNTP: virtual server, newsgroup, and virtual directory.

Securing an NNTP Virtual Server

You may decide to provide security at the front door of your NNTP services: the virtual server. All virtual server security is accomplished on the Access property page of the NNTP virtual server. Much like the previous protocols listed in this chapter, you can provide secure access using three methods:

- **Access Control** NNTP supports four levels of authentication: anonymous, basic authentication (clear text), Integrated Windows Authentication (using Kerberos or NTLM), and SSL client authentication.
- **Secure Communications** Secure the NNTP channel using SSL. Both the 56-bit and 128-bit implementation are supported.
- **Connection Control** You can grant or deny access to the NNTP virtual server by IP address, IP subnet, or domain name.

Note *For more information on these security methods, see "Securing HTTP" earlier in this chapter.*

Securing a Newsgroup

The use of a moderator for a newsgroup should be considered as a security measure. While it is not as automated and quick as an Access Control List on an NTFS file system, the use of a moderator does provide a security measure that ensures only appropriate content is posted to the newsgroup. A moderator can be specified at the bottom of the General property page for a given newsgroup.

Securing a Virtual Directory

A virtual directory can require a secure channel by clicking the Secure button on the General property page of the virtual directory. You can also use the Restrict Newsgroup Visibility option to allow only those users with correct permissions to access the virtual directory.

Summary

With Internet protocols being the standard methods of communication today, Exchange 2000 must be not only compliant and able to use the protocols but also truly able to allow you to take advantage of them. It's not enough that Exchange supports a particular protocol; it must additionally be able to utilize that protocol in a number of ways, including use over secure channels with SSL, requiring authentication, and restricting use. In this chapter, we have shown you how Exchange 2000 not only supports SMTP, POP3, IMAP4, HTTP, and NNTP, but can also utilize the security measures supported by each of those protocols. In the next chapter, we will take a look at the Exchange 2000 store architecture and its capabilities.

Chapter 11

The Exchange 2000 Store

Exchange 5.5 supported only two databases for storage of user data. The private information store, PRIV.EDB, held all the user mailboxes. The public information store, PUB.EDB, held all the contents of the public folders. Both databases stored data in the Microsoft Database Encoding Format (MDBEF). Based on this information alone, a few problems come into view.

First, having only two databases—one private and one public—means the size of each database will continue to increase as data is added. Backup-and-restore processes and offline maintenance will take increasingly longer to complete. A single database can only exist on a single physical volume, which can cause I/O bottlenecks. In addition, if one of the information stores (public or private) becomes corrupt and needs to be taken offline for maintenance, all users on that server are affected.

The second problem is the use of the Microsoft Database Encoding Format (MDBEF). Simple text messages can be saved in MDBEF just fine. But when you start trying to store messages that contain graphics, audio, and video attachments, the Internet Mail (IMAIL) process has to convert these messages to MDBEF before they can be written to the database. This process takes additional time and resources.

Resolution of these problems became two of the design goals for Exchange 2000. First, allow multiple databases to take care of database size issues and their repercussions; allow population of databases on multiple physical volumes for better I/O performance; and minimize the number of affected users should a database need to be taken offline. Second, provide a way for non-MDBEF data such as multimedia audio and video files and MIME content to be natively stored without conversion.

These two problems exemplify the need for a messaging system to have a scalable and robust storage architecture, capable of handling even the most demanding storage needs. In this chapter, we will look at the storage architecture used by Exchange 2000, as well as storage concepts like the Extensible Storage Engine (ESE) and the Exchange Installable File System (IFS). We will also discuss how Exchange 2000 can meet your storage needs.

Exchange 2000 Storage Architecture

The storage architecture of Exchange 2000 is based on a few important advances. The single information store from Exchange 5.5 has been replaced by the capability to maintain multiple stores on the same Exchange 2000 Server. Each of these multiple stores is maintained without affecting the other stores on the same server. The MDBEF database has been replaced with two databases: the rich-text store and the streaming (or native content) store. In addition, a new file system, the Exchange Installable File System (IFS), allows clients to access and utilize store contents as they would a shared folder, and the Microsoft Search service allows clients to more quickly query for items in a database.

Multiple Stores and Storage Groups

One of the biggest complaints administrators have about Exchange 5.x is the single instance of the public and private information stores. Given the size and management issues already raised, administrators of Exchange 5.x welcome multiple stores in Exchange 2000. Exchange 2000 supports the use of up to 20 stores per server. Multiple stores on a single server allows you to spread your users across the stores. Imagine, instead of having to manage a single 300GB store of 1,000 users, you can manage ten 30GB stores servicing 100 users each. The 30GB stores take far less time to restore or repair than the single 300GB store. Each store can be independently started or stopped (called *mounted* and *dismounted*). This allows you to manage a single store without affecting the others. If a store is stopped, the Store process and the other stores on the server continue to run and service client needs.

As shown in Figure 11-1, each store is located logically within a storage group. A storage group is the combination of an instance in memory of the Extensible Storage Engine (ESE) in memory and the set of database and log files associated with that instance. Each storage group can house up to five stores, and a server can have a total of four storage groups. A hidden sixth store is reserved for use by the information for recovery purposes. If a store needs to undergo offline maintenance, the server will create a copy of the store being fixed to work on. That means an additional store will be temporarily created in the storage group. If you wish to create one store per storage group in order to have all transactions in a set of transaction logs pertain to a single store, remember that this will also increase the load on your server, as it will have to manage the multiple sets of transaction logs.

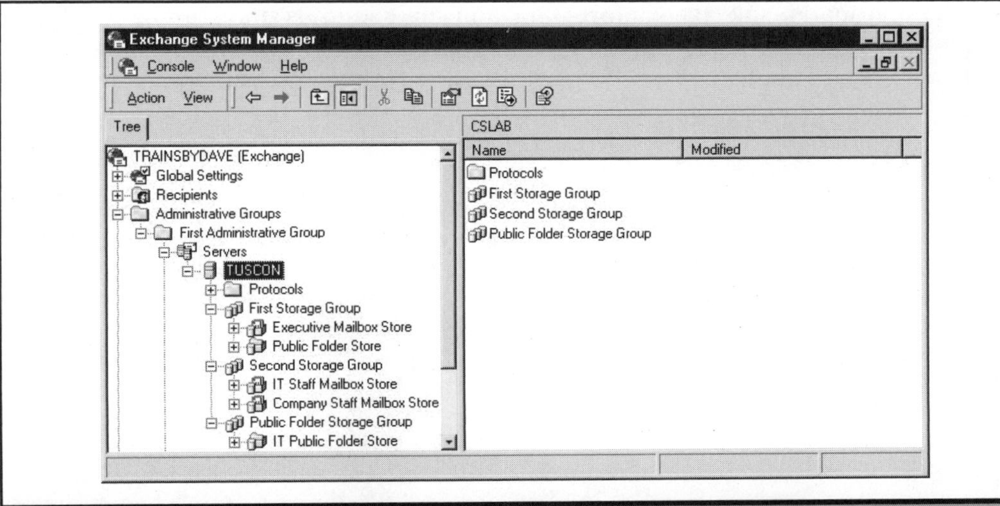

Figure 11-1. *Viewing multiple stores within multiple storage groups in Exchange System Manager*

Store Databases

Two types of stores are used in Exchange 2000: a mailbox store and a public folder store. A mailbox store replaces the private information store in Exchange 5.5, and it contains all the private mailboxes and messages of users. The public folder store replaces the public information store in Exchange 5.5. It contains all information located in public folders. Each store in Exchange 2000 is comprised of two separate files: the rich text file and the native content "streaming" file. It is important to emphasize that these two files *together* make up a store. When you back up or restore a particular store, both of these files are included in the process.

Rich Text File

The rich text file (ending in .EDB) is the equivalent to the database types we use in Exchange 5.5. Information stored in this database file uses MDBEF. Messaging Application Programming Interface (MAPI) clients, such as Outlook, use this database file to natively store their messages. No conversion is necessary to store or retrieve messages from this database to service MAPI client requests.

Native Content File

The native content file (ending in .STM) holds all non-MAPI data. This isn't as simple as Outlook users using the rich text file and everyone else, such as HTTP and IMAP4 users, using the native content store. Instead of converting all non-MAPI content (which is most of the information in today's messages — like audio, video, and other multimedia formats) and placing it in the rich text file, the raw data is stored in the native content store. Let us emphasize that point: Only the raw data is stored. All overhead information, like page information and checksums, is stored in the rich text file. This allows Exchange 2000 to be extensible to new data formats as they are established; because only the raw data is stored, any type of information can be placed in this file.

Streaming

The native content file is sometimes referred to as the "streaming" file. This is because when messages in the native content file are delivered to a user, they are streamed for faster access; that is, the data is sent in such a way that it can be immediately used by the client, without the client first receiving the entire data set. The faster access comes through the use of IFS, a Win32 kernel mode driver. IFS accesses the raw information in the native content file and streams that data to a client via the associated protocol stack in IIS.

What's So Important About Streaming?

Here's a simple example of why it benefits the user to have Exchange stream data. If you've ever downloaded an MPG and an AVI file from the Internet, you have already seen the benefit of streaming. When you download an MPG to be played in Windows Media Player, Media Player begins playing the sound or video as soon as enough information is present. In contrast, Media Player waits until the entire AVI file is downloaded before playing it. The MPG is streamed to the user and is played as it is downloaded. This allows you to enjoy the audio or video being downloaded before the download is complete.

The streaming process, shown in Figure 11-2, is as follows:

1. The Store process receives a client request for a message from the native content file. This could come from one of the Internet protocols via IIS or from a MAPI client, such as Outlook. If a MAPI client is used, the message will not be in a format that can be read, so on-demand content conversion occurs and the message is converted to a MAPI format.
2. A message handle is created by the store and used by IFS to reference and access the message. Because IFS will not have direct access to the message and needs to request it from the store, the message handle is used as the common reference to the set of data. This message handle contains the list of pages to be retrieved from the native content file.
3. IFS passes the retrieved message to the Windows 2000 Cache Manager, which holds the message in cache and gives control to the Auxiliary Function Driver (AFD).
4. AFD acts on behalf of WINSOCK and streams the file from the Windows NT Cache Manager to the user.

On-Demand Content Conversion

As mentioned earlier in the chapter, MAPI clients store their messages in the rich text file, and non-MAPI clients, such as HTTP and IMAP4 clients, store their messages in the native content store. So what happens when a client of one type wants to access a message originally stored by a client of the other type? For example, if an Outlook Web Access client (using HTTP) saves a message, it is posted to the native content file. If another HTTP client wants to retrieve the message, it can simply be retrieved from the

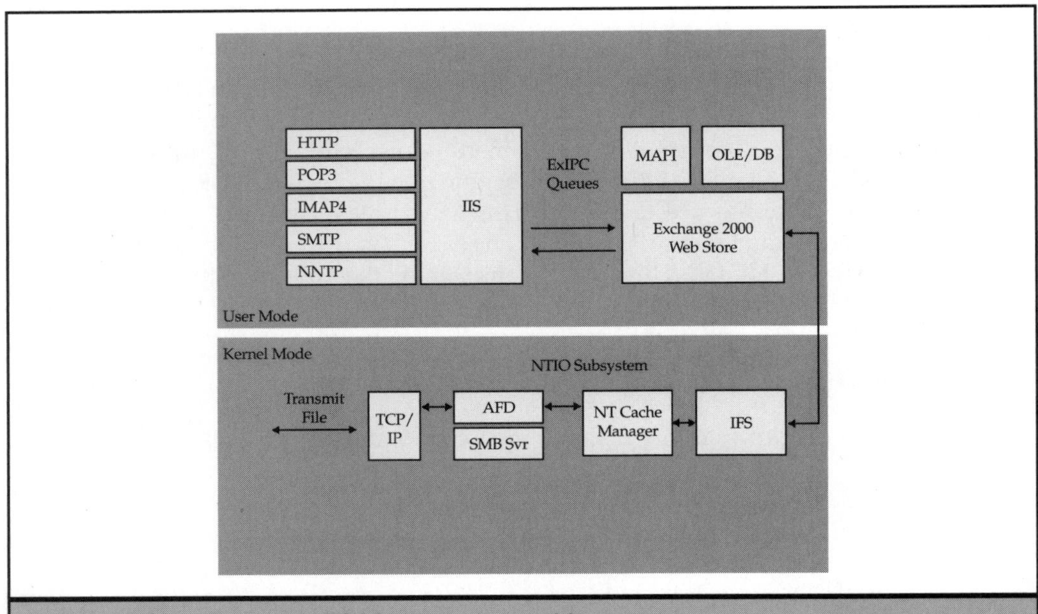

Figure 11-2. *Exchange 2000 streaming architecture*

native content file. When an Outlook client wants to access the same message, it needs to be retrieved from the native content file but the message is not in Outlook's native format. So, it must first be converted in Exchange Server's memory, and then presented to the client. This is known as *on-demand content conversion*. The actual data has not been converted; only an instance of it in memory has been converted to service the client request.

If the Outlook client makes a change to the message and saves it, the message will be copied from the native content file, converted, and written to the rich text file. If no other uses have pointers to the original message in the native content file, the message is also deleted from the native content file.

Single Instance Storage

Like Exchange 5.5, Exchange 2000 also supports single instance storage (SIS). This feature allows a message sent to multiple recipients to exist once within a store, instead of once for each recipient. The goal of SIS is to keep your databases as small as possible. The important thing to remember about SIS is that it works on a per-store basis. If you have multiple recipients on the same store, a single instance is maintained. However, if recipients exist in multiple stores, a copy of the message will exist once in each store.

Take the following example and look at Figure 11-3 to get a better understanding of SIS. Suppose Tom wants to send a 1MB message to 30 recipients. Without SIS, 32 copies of the message would exist, taking up 32MB of disk space: 1MB for each of the 30

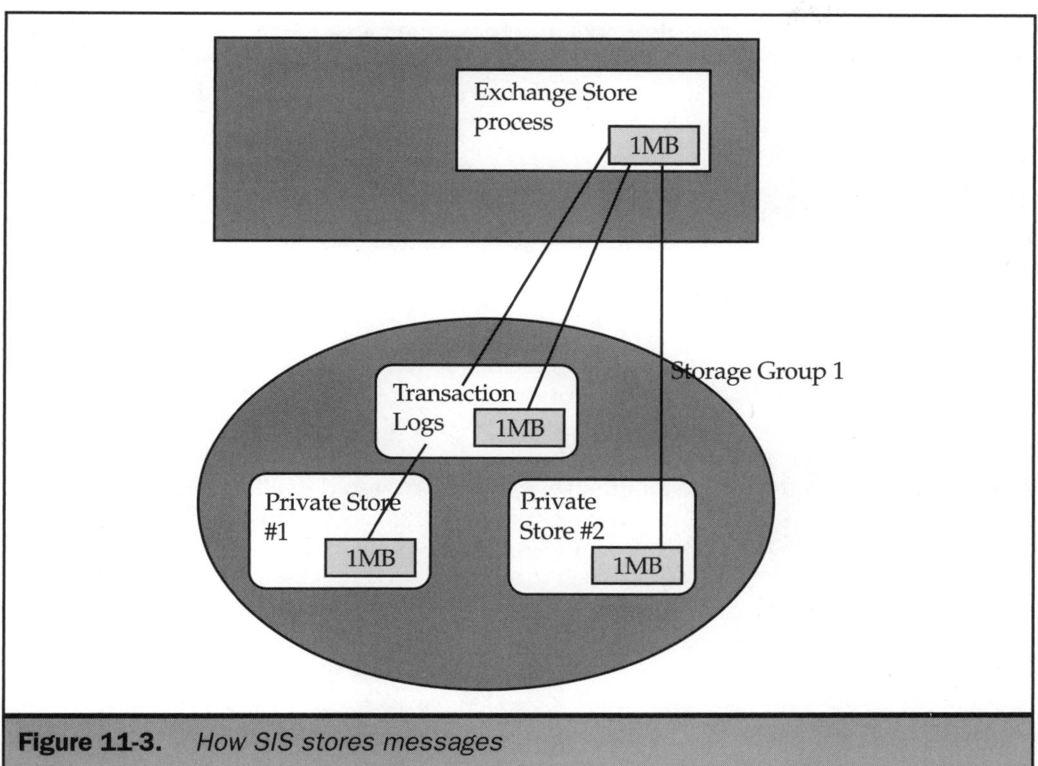

Figure 11-3. *How SIS stores messages*

recipients, 1 MB for the copy in Tom's Sent Items folder, and 1MB temporarily for the transaction logs. (Keep in mind that this would only be temporary, as users would possibly delete the message once they read it.) With SIS, only 2MB of disk space are taken up: 1MB in the transaction logs and 1MB in the mailbox store.

If the recipients were spread across two or more mailbox stores, a copy of the message would exist in each store, thus an additional 1MB of space would be used up by the message in each store. In addition, if the stores were in different storage groups, 1MB would be used up temporarily by the transaction logs for each storage group to log the message being created.

Let's summarize the SIS usage using the 1MB message example:

- 1MB for the Sender's Sent Items folder (if configured in Outlook)
- 1MB per store containing recipients, regardless of the number of recipients in that store
- 1MB for the transaction logs, per storage group containing recipients, regardless of the number of stores containing recipients

When any of the 30 recipients wants to retrieve the message, the same message on their store is opened. If one of the recipients modifies the message, a new version of the message is saved for that recipient only, and the other recipients will still interact with the original single instance of the message.

Transaction Logging

Transaction logging helps make Exchange 2000 a reliable messaging system. Before changes are written to the store databases, the changes are written to transaction logs, which keep a history of the changes made to the store databases. This history allows you to recover an Exchange database.

Transaction logs are divided into generations of transactions, which are stored in 5MB log files. If the transactions were not divided into multiple log files, you would have, in theory, a single ever-growing log file. Such a file would be neither manageable nor efficient. Each storage group maintains its own set of transaction logs. The most current transactions (on a per storage-group basis) are stored in a log file, E00.LOG. When this file reaches 5MB, it is renamed to E0000001.LOG, and a new E00.LOG file is created. As each E00.LOG fills up, it is renamed to the next numeric increment (E0000001.LOG, E0000002.LOG, E0000003.LOG, and so on) using numerical values.

If you view the size of a log file using Windows Explorer, it should read exactly 5,242,880 bytes. If the log file isn't this exact size, it is probably damaged.

Each transaction log contains two sets of information: the header and the data. The header contains references to the database it is associated with. This prevents a log file from being used with a mismatched database with the same name. The best way to see this information is by using the ESEUTIL utility, as shown in Figure 11-4, to dump the contents of a log header to the screen. Notice about halfway down the screen, the dump displays the log file signature, which names the stores affected by this log.

Using the ESEUTIL utility can cause serious damage to your databases if not used properly. Use the utility with caution and only if truly needed.

Each storage group also has two reserved log files, RES1.LOG and RES2.LOG. These two files are not used for normal transaction logging, but instead act as placeholders in case the transaction log drive runs out of space.

The Checkpoint File

If you have a number of transaction logs, each full of various changes to the store databases, how do you know which log entries have been written to the database and which have not? The checkpoint file, E00.CHK, records which transactions have been

```
C:\WINNT.SRV\System32\cmd.exe
C:\WINNT.SRV\Exchsrvr\MDBDATA\First Storage Group>eseutil /ml E0000002.log

Microsoft(R) Exchange Server(TM) Database Utilities
Version 6.0
Copyright (C) Microsoft Corporation 1991-2000.  All Rights Reserved.

Initiating FILE DUMP mode...

      Base name: E00
      Log file: E0000002.log
      lGeneration: 2 (0x2)
      Checkpoint NOT AVAILABLE
      creation time: 12/07/2000 03:05:49
      prev gen time: 12/07/2000 02:48:53
      Format LGVersion: (7.3704.2)
      Engine LGVersion: (7.3704.2)
      Signature: Create time:12/07/2000 02:48:53 Rand:5969393 Computer:
      Env SystemPath: C:\WINNT.SRV\Exchsrvr\mdbdata\
      Env LogFilePath: C:\WINNT.SRV\Exchsrvr\mdbdata\
      Env Log Sec size: 512
      Env (CircLog, Session, Opentbl, VerPage, Cursors, LogBufs, LogFile, Buffer
s)
          (    off,      202,    30300,     1365,    10100,       84,    10240,    4902
0)
      1 C:\WINNT.SRV\Exchsrvr\MDBDATA\pub1.edb
        streaming file: C:\WINNT.SRV\Exchsrvr\MDBDATA\pub1.stm
        dbtime: 15301 (0-15301)
        objidLast: 147
        Signature: Create time:12/07/2000 02:49:18 Rand:6008720 Computer:
        MaxDbSize: 0 pages
        Last Attach: (0x1,9,6C)
        Last Consistent: (0x0,0,0)
      2 C:\WINNT.SRV\Exchsrvr\MDBDATA\priv1.edb
        streaming file: C:\WINNT.SRV\Exchsrvr\MDBDATA\priv1.stm
        dbtime: 16864 (0-16864)
        objidLast: 115
        Signature: Create time:12/07/2000 02:49:29 Rand:5993641 Computer:
        MaxDbSize: 0 pages
        Last Attach: (0x1,8A,54)
        Last Consistent: (0x0,0,0)
      Last Lgpos: (0x2,27FF,0)

Integrity check passed for log file: E0000002.log

Operation completed successfully in 2.623 seconds.

C:\WINNT.SRV\Exchsrvr\MDBDATA\First Storage Group>
```

Figure 11-4. *Viewing a dump of a transaction log*

written to disk and which are pending. The checkpoint file helps speed up the recovery of your Exchange databases by telling ESE which transaction logs need to be replayed and which do not.

The Extensible Storage Engine

The Extensible Storage Engine (ESE) manages database storage and transaction logging for the stores. ESE, which is part of the Web Storage System process, manages the databases by organizing them into 4K chunks of data called *pages*. When data is read from the database, the page is considered *clean*. When changes are made to the data in the page, it is considered *dirty*, and needs to be written back to the database. A dirty page is not necessarily written immediately back to the database. Such actions would not be efficient and would only slow down the Exchange server. Instead, Exchange uses a write-ahead method of logging; that is, ESE writes the changes to the transaction log first, and then to the database later. Exchange optimizes its writes to the disk by using a form of lazy writes, where it writes a group of changes to the database once. This architecture makes Exchange's use of the store database much more efficient. Changes are written to the database when one of the following conditions is met:

- The Store process is shutting down, as in the case of a proper server shutdown.
- A full or incremental backup of Exchange occurs, using Exchange-aware backup software, such as Windows 2000 Backup, BackupExec, or ArcServe.
- ESE has too many dirty pages in memory and needs additional memory for new transactions.
- Another process on the Exchange server requests memory, causing ESE to flush the committed changes in order to release memory for use by that process.
- The checkpoint file falls too far behind, and the number of committed transactions reaches a predetermined threshold based on the number of buffers and the percentage of buffers in use.

As discussed in Chapter 4, ESE passes a well-known test called the ACID test (an acronym for Atomic, Consistent, Isolated, and Durable), to ensure the integrity of the Exchange databases. Before we discuss the ACID test, let's first cover a few terms:

- **Operation.** An operation is a single change, addition, or deletion to the database.
- **Transaction.** A group of related operations make up a single transaction.
- **Committed.** When a transaction has been written to the database, it is considered to be committed.

Let's use the following example and walk through the ACID test to see why it is so important to transactional databases. Suppose Tom wants to move a message in the public folder, *Projects,* that he and Shelly have been working on together to another public folder, *Completed Projects*. Although Tom sees this move as nothing more than a simple drag-and-drop activity, ESE must perform a number of operations:

- The message has to be deleted from the *Projects* folder.
- The message has to be added to the *Completed Projects* folder.
- The item numbers in each public folder have to be updated.
- Read and unread message flags must be processed.

Table 11-1 applies the ACID test to this scenario and describes a situation that might occur if the test was not applied.

ACID Test	Description	Without the Test
Atomic	Either all of the operations within a transaction complete, or the transaction is rolled back.	If the server crashed just after deleting the message from the Projects folder, the transaction would be considered committed and the message would disappear.
Consistent	Transactions are only performed on a database that is in a consistent state. Consistent means that the database is transformed from one valid and correct state to another. Consistent also means that transactions never leave the system in an unrecoverable state.	Suppose Shelly is in the middle of moving the same message to another folder (putting the database in an inconsistent state) when Tom tries to move it to *Completed Projects*. There would be a conflict because the message cannot be moved to two locations.
Isolated	Changes are made serially to the database and do not show up until the entire transaction has been completed. Once completed the transaction is considered to be *committed*.	If the message appeared prematurely in *Completed Projects*, and the server crashed, upon reboot, a phantom message would exist in *Completed Projects*.
Durable	Once a transaction has been completed, it is preserved even if the system or the database experiences a crash.	If the system crashed just after the message move, the message would be back in the *Projects* folder.

Table 11-1. *The ESE ACID Test*

When validating the ACID test, ESE's focus is not on the actual writes to the database, but on updating the transaction logs. Remember, the transactions are written to the database later. Even if the server were to crash and be rebooted before the transactions could be written to the database, when the Store process restarts, it will replay the logs, reload the changes from the logs, and write those changes onto the database.

Store Database and Transaction Log Placement

One of the key decisions that affects the recoverability of your Exchange server is the physical placement of the store databases and the transaction logs. First, the databases and the logs should be placed on separate volumes. If the volume containing your store databases were to crash, your transaction logs would still be alive and well on a separate volume. Assuming you are not using circular logging, you could recover by restoring the databases from the last full backup and allowing the logs to be replayed. This would bring your Exchange server back to the state it was in just prior to the crash.

The second concern is the use of RAID volumes for fault tolerance. A RAID 1 volume for the transaction logs and a separate RAID 5 volume for the store databases would give you a fault-tolerant storage environment. If you wanted better performance because the transaction logs were constantly being accessed, you could place them on a RAID 0+1 volume (that is, a mirrored stripe set without parity). The RAID 0 stripe set gives the performance, while the RAID 1 mirror provides the fault tolerance.

If you do not have a RAID solution (or do not have the funding for it), at least place the transaction logs and store databases on separate physical drives. This will give you some recoverability if the drive housing the store databases fails.

The Exchange Installable File System

In Exchange 5.5, the only way to access store content was via MAPI (e.g., by using Outlook), or through one of the standard Internet client protocols (for example, POP3, IMAP4, NNTP or HTTP). The Exchange Installable File System (IFS) exposes all store content as folders and files in a file system. This single enhancement allows client access to Exchange data from anywhere, using a multitude of clients. This is a major improvement to document management. Prior to IFS, documents were stored in a file system on a file server, or they were stored as attachments in Exchange public folders. IFS brings these concepts together with Exchange 2000 as the storage platform. Let's look at a few of the ways you can now access the Exchange store.

Native File System

Exchange creates a virtual M drive on the Exchange server for direct access to both mailboxes and public folders. Figure 11-5 shows the M drive on an Exchange server. You still must have the proper permissions to access a given folder or message. For example, only the owner of a mailbox has permissions to the folder representing his or her mailbox on the M drive.

Folder Shares

Because the virtual M drive exists as a file system drive, you can share a folder for access by Microsoft File and Printer Sharing clients. Folder and share permissions must be in place for you to access the folder or its data. Figure 11-6 shows the administrator's

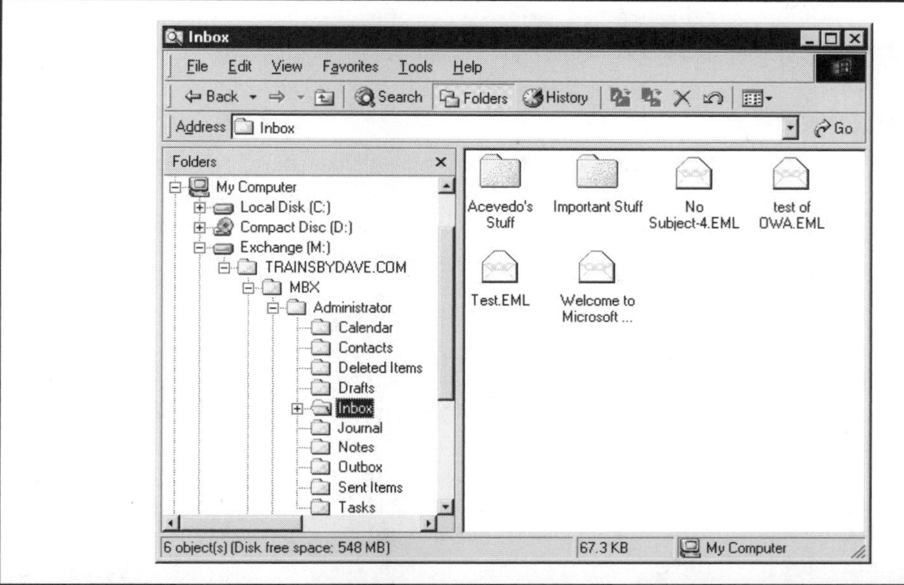

Figure 11-5. *Accessing the store locally through the file system*

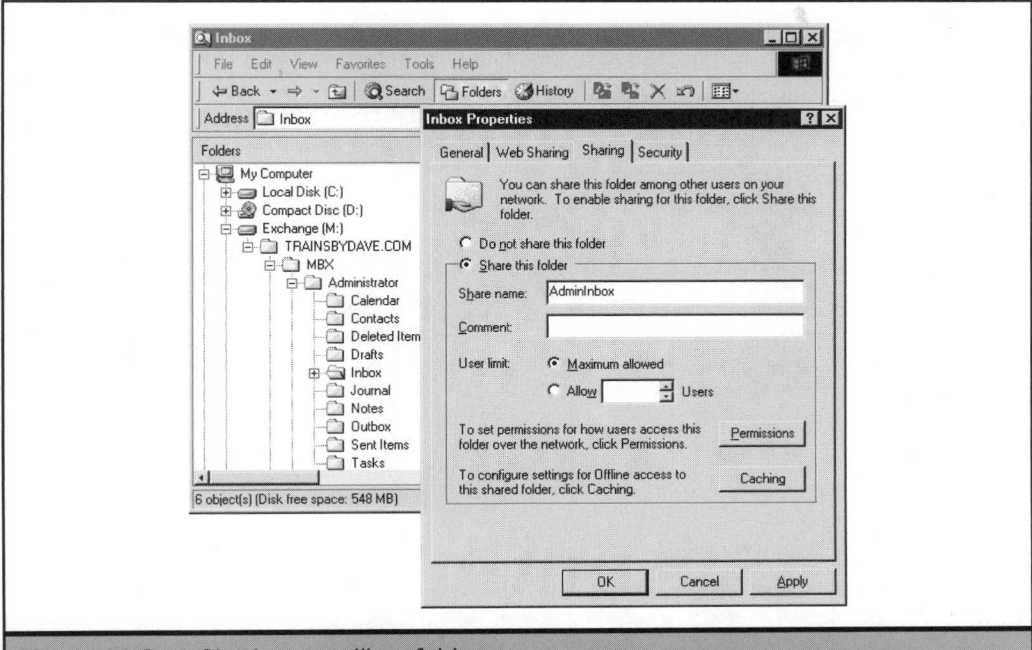

Figure 11-6. *Sharing a mailbox folder*

inbox shared as *AdminInbox*. Figure 11-7 shows a client accessing the share using a mapped drive.

Full-Text Indexing

Many of you have probably already used Outlook's Find command to search for a specific message. Perhaps you've noticed that the process can be a bit lengthy when searching in a single mailbox's folder with several thousand messages, such as Sent Items or Deleted Items. Now take that concept to a level where you are searching an entire set of public folders for one message with specific words in it. We would guess that a search of that magnitude would be quite lengthy.

In order to speed up searches of messages in mailboxes and public folders, Exchange utilizes the Microsoft Search service (MS Search). MS Search creates word-based indexes on a per-store basis of both message text and attachment content. Being word-based means that queries only return exact matches. For example, if you were to search for the word "excite", the word "excitement" would not be considered a match. In contrast, the other type of index (which is *not* used by Exchange) is character-based; queries return words containing the characters queried ("excitement" would be a match for a character-based query). MS Search also takes advantage of stemming, a process by which related words are considered matches. For example, when querying for the word "Work", stemming causes words like "works", "worked",

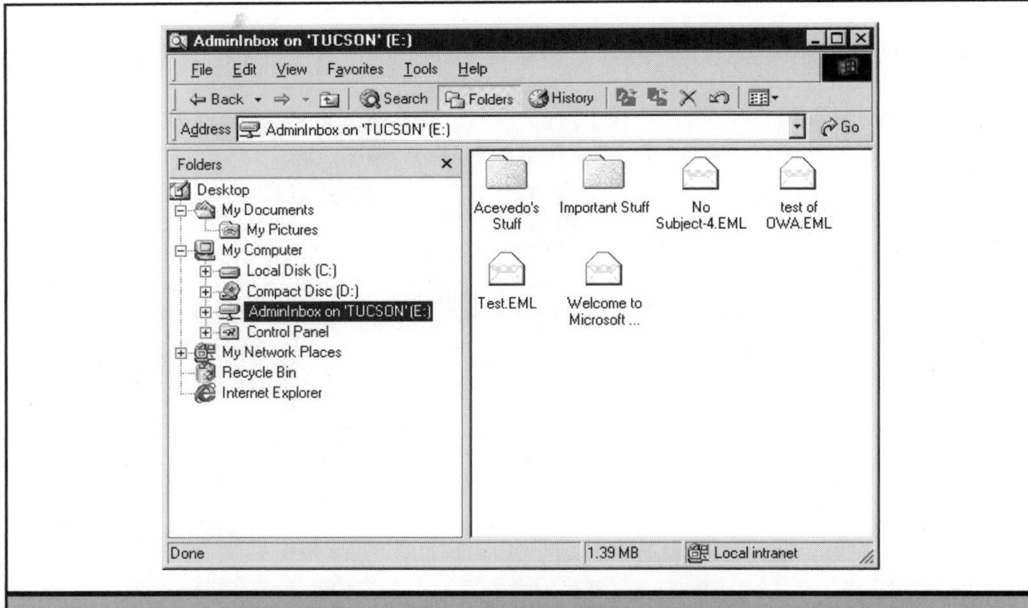

Figure 11-7. *Accessing the mailbox via a folder share*

and "working" to be matches. When an Exchange 2000 client performs a search against an indexed store, the query is performed against an index, instead of against the contents of every folder.

The MS Search service currently can index the content of the following attachment types:

- Microsoft Word files
- Microsoft Excel files
- The text portion of Microsoft PowerPoint files
- Office Templates (.DOT, .XLT, .OFT, .POT, and .OBT files)
- Text (.TXT files)
- HTML (.HTML, .HTM, and .ASP files)
- Embedded Multipurpose Internet Mail Extensions (MIME) messages (.EML files)

Indexing takes up anywhere from 10 to 30 percent of your database space and requires that both the Microsoft Exchange Information Store and the MS Search services are started on the Exchange server.

How Indexing Works

The MS Search service creates an index of every word in every message in every folder within a store, with the exception of noise words, like "the" and "a" . Because the initial index process needs to build an index from scratch, the initial process can take hours or days. It is recommended that you perform the initial index process while the server is least used (such as in the evening or over a weekend). Once the index is created, subsequent updates to the index only contain the changes to the database, which take far less time and resources. When a change to a folder is made, the Store process notifies the MS Search service via a synchronization event. Depending on how you have your indexing set up on the particular store, either the index will update at a particular time, or shortly after the change.

Tip *Microsoft's recommendation for the initial indexing is this: If the database is 6GB or less, perform the initial index overnight. Anything over 6GB and you should plan on performing the initial indexing over a weekend.*

If a document or message could not be indexed, a special file called a *gather* file is created, by default, in the \ExchangeServer_<*servername*>\Gatherlogs subfolder under the Exchange installation directory with an extension of .GTHR. A gather file lists all the messages and files that could not be indexed. A perfect example of a file that would be included here is a file type that is supported by indexing (such as a Word document) and is corrupt. MS Search would attempt to index the file, but due to its corrupt nature, would not be able to do so.

Configuring Full-Text Indexing

You begin a full-text index in Exchange System Manager by navigating to and right-clicking the store you wish to index, and then selecting Create Full-Text Index. A dialog box prompts you to provide the path to the catalog (you will have to manually type in this path and, regrettably, you will not be able to browse your file system to find the folder). Upon clicking OK, despite what you would expect, the initial indexing process does not begin. It will not begin until either the rebuild interval occurs (explained later in this section), or until you manually start the indexing (also explained later in this section).

Once the index has been created (although not populated, by default), the Full-Text Indexing property page for the store you've indexed becomes available for configuration, as shown in Figure 11-8.

The Update Interval field allows you to specify when the index should be updated with new references to data added to the store. Note that the updates do not remove references to items that have been deleted from the store. The Rebuild Interval field allows you to specify when the index should be completely rebuilt. Because the index is rebuilt from current information, rather than updates from the Store process, it requires the same time and resources as the initial index process.

You can make the index available to clients by selecting the This Index Is Currently Available For Searching By Clients checkbox. You can disable this option if the results of your client's queries contain too many references to deleted items (remember, the

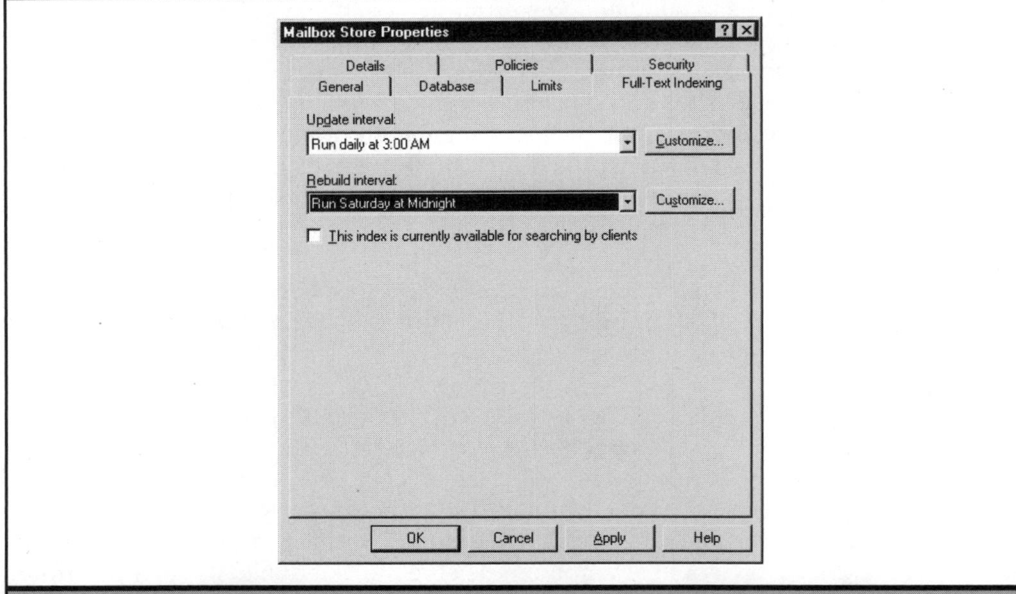

Figure 11-8. *The Full-Text Indexing property page of an index-enabled store*

update of the index only adds new references). Doing so will cause the clients to directly query against the contents of the store rather than the index. Even though it's a much slower process, the results of the query will contain current data only. You also can specify how important the indexing is via the Full-Text Indexing property page of the server's properties dialog box, as shown in Figure 11-9.

It is recommended that you run the updates of store indexes when any of the following conditions are met: noise words are changed, new document filters are added, the schema file changes, the store's SMTP address changes, during disaster recovery, or when a word-breaker is changed. Be sure to set the System Resource Usage field on the Full-Text Indexing properties page of the server object to Maximum prior to the rebuild, and then be sure to reset them to a lower setting afterwards.

Manually Populating the Index

If you need to update or rebuild the index immediately, you can do so in Exchange System Manager. By right-clicking the already indexed store, you have two options, shown in Figure 11-10: Start Incremental Population and Start Full Population. Choosing the incremental population will update the index with updates. Choosing the full population will rebuild the index. Use these options with the same considerations as when you select the intervals to update and rebuild the store indexes.

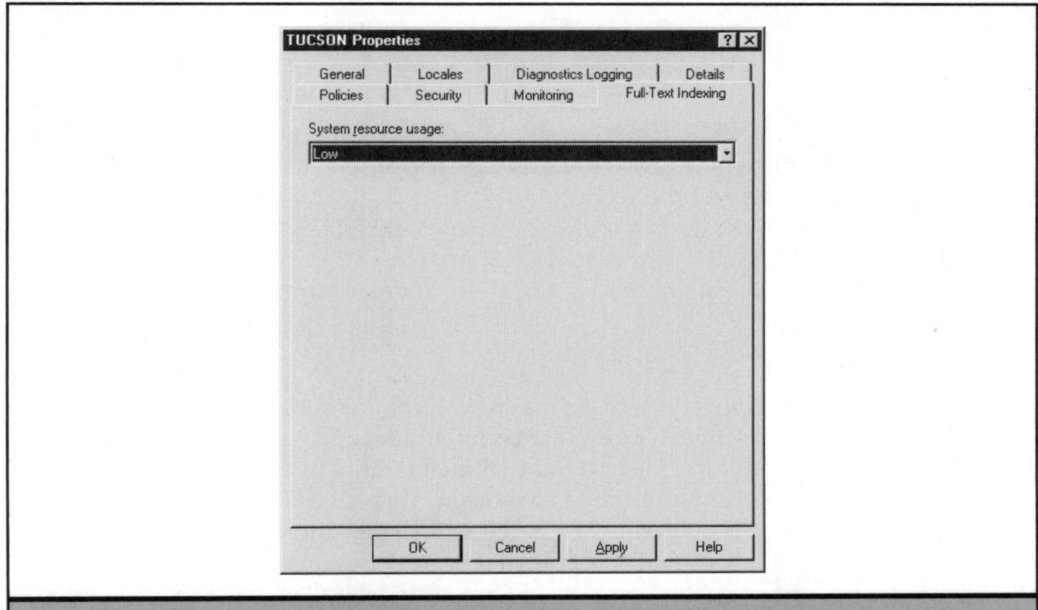

Figure 11-9. *Setting the indexing resource usage*

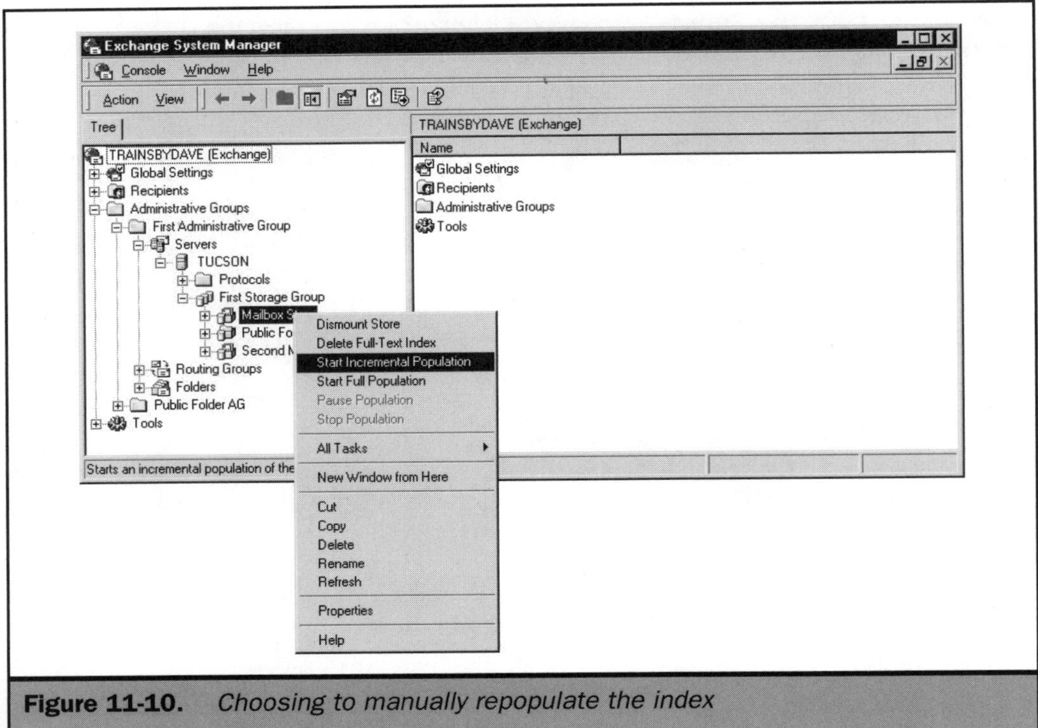

Figure 11-10. *Choosing to manually repopulate the index*

Client Usage of Indexing

Outlook clients can utilize index-based searches by performing an advanced find. A normal find will query against the actual store content. Figure 11-11 shows the query and results for all documents containing the word "excitement" using the M drive, which is the IFS driver-based file system access to Exchange stores. The word document that was found through the query contains the sentence "Exchange is pure excitement."

Web Store Events

Exchange 2000 allows applications to define custom actions based on a store event, such as a message being sent to a particular recipient or a document being placed in a folder. These actions customize and extend the functionality of the store. Applications can be created by using event-handling mechanisms through *event sinks*. Event sinks, which are pieces of code, are activated by a defined trigger, such as the reception of a new message. The code can be written in Visual Basic, Visual C++, VBScript, or any other language that supports the Component Object Model (COM). Two types of Web Store event sinks exist: synchronous and asynchronous. A synchronous event sink

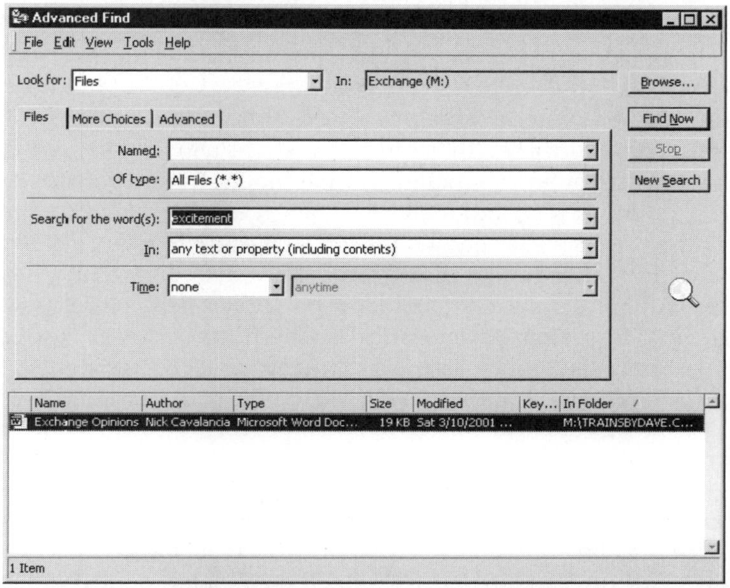

Figure 11-11. *Using the Advanced Find dialog box in Outlook to search the index*

triggers as the event that triggered them occurs. Asynchronous event sinks trigger after an event has occurred.

Web Store event sinks run on the server and can be written to handle events from specific client types, such as MAPI (Outlook), HTTP (Outlook Web Access) or Win32 (any Microsoft Office application).

Managing Exchange 2000 Storage

Let's put some tasks together with the information about Exchange 2000 storage that you've already learned in this chapter. We'll look at creating storage groups, modifying their configuration, and removing them.

Creating Storage Groups

Before you can create a mailbox or public folder store, you need to have a storage group to place it in. While a default storage group (named *First Storage Group*) already exists, you should carefully weigh whether you need an additional storage group. Remember, each storage group has its own set of transaction logs, which adds some overhead to the server, but will also provide you with a set of transaction logs specific to the stores in that storage group. For example, you could create one store per storage group (although we wouldn't necessarily recommend this due to the overhead it could place on the server). If you did, each store would have its own set of transaction logs. The benefit here is that the transaction logs are now specific to a single store and when replayed during a restore process, they only involve the single store.

To create a storage group in Exchange System Manager, navigate to and right-click the server object, point to New, and then select Storage Group. The Storage Group Properties dialog box appears, as shown in Figure 11-12. When you type in a name for the storage group, Exchange automatically provides a default path for the transaction logs and system path. The transaction log location applies to all stores you create in this new storage group. The system path location is where temporary or recovered files will exist should offline maintenance be necessary. You can also choose to either type in your own path or click the Browse button to navigate the file system to find the appropriate location for both the logs and the system path.

You may want to provide your own path for the transaction logs. For example, since the stores logically exist within a storage group, you may choose to create a folder on your server's D drive matching the name of the storage group. The transaction logs and system path could both be set to this. Then, when you create the various stores within the storage group (we'll show you how in "Creating Stores", later in the chapter), you could create subfolders within the storage group folder for each store. If you did this, the folder hierarchy would match the logical hierarchy found in Exchange System Manager.

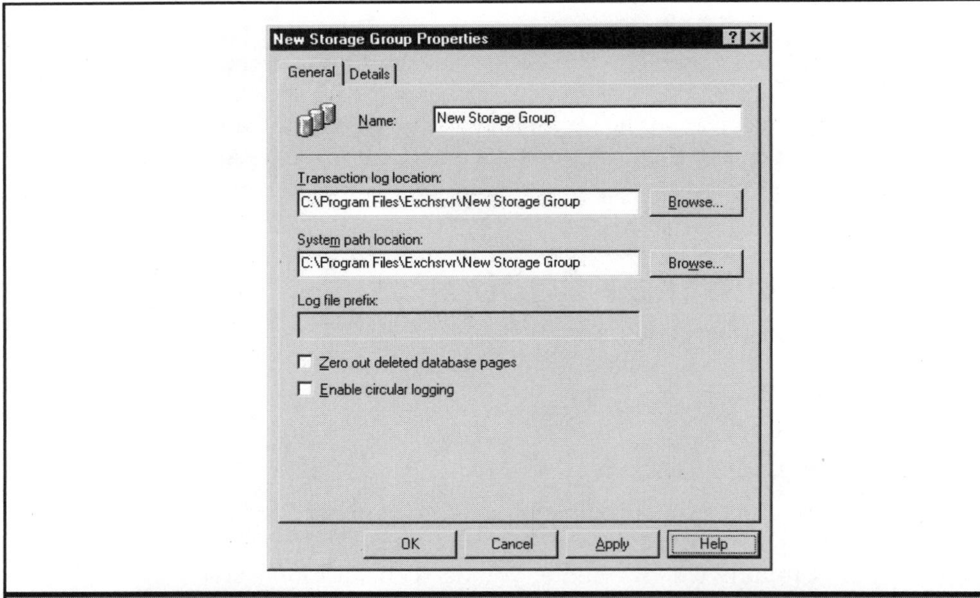

Figure 11-12. *Creating a new storage group*

You also have two checkboxes to deal with before you're done. The Zero Out Deleted Database Pages checkbox tells the Exchange server whether you wish to write zeros to the stores within the storage group when data is deleted from those stores. This is a security issue: Writing zeros over deleted data areas helps ensure that the data cannot be recovered. Keep in mind that with the added security of zeroing out the pages, you will take a performance hit, as this is an additional step in the deletion process.

The Enable Circular Logging checkbox tells the Exchange server whether you wish to reuse the same five log files over and over (thus the use of the term "circular") or allow Exchange to create as many log files as are needed. If you enable this checkbox, Exchange will fill the transaction logs and, when it fills the fifth log, it will overwrite the contents of the first log and begin the process again. This value affects three areas of Exchange.

The first effect is on what types of Exchange-level backups you can perform. Because the logs are overwritten as needed, they no longer represent all of the changes since the last backup, so you will no longer be able to perform incremental or differential backups. Only full backups are allowed. The second issue is recovery capability. Because you can only perform full backups with circular logging turned on, you will only be able to recover your server to the last full backup. The last issue is disk space implications. Because only five logs are used, you will save space on transaction logs.

Due to the recovery constraints that circular logging puts on your stores, we recommend that you do not use circular logging.

Creating Stores

The next step is to populate your storage group with a store. The process of creating a mailbox store is nearly the same as the process of creating a public folder store. The differences lie in the parameters you provide when creating each. Let's go over the creation process, and then look at each store's parameters. To create a store in Exchange System Manager, navigate to and right-click the storage group in which you wish to create the store, point to New, and then choose either Mailbox Store or Public Store.

Creating a Mailbox Store

When creating a mailbox store, you can simply give the store a name and click OK to accept all the default parameters. If you want to modify how the store is configured, you can either do so when creating it, or after it has been created. Let's look at each property page to see what parameters you can configure.

General The General property page, shown in Figure 11-13, is where you will provide the initial name for the mailbox store. Exchange already populates the Default Public Store and the Offline Address List fields for you. The Default Public Store field specifies the public store that the users of this mailbox store will use by default. The Offline Address List specifies the address list that will be downloaded to Outlook clients if they are configured for offline use of Exchange. You can change these options by clicking Browse and selecting an alternate public store or address list, as is applicable.

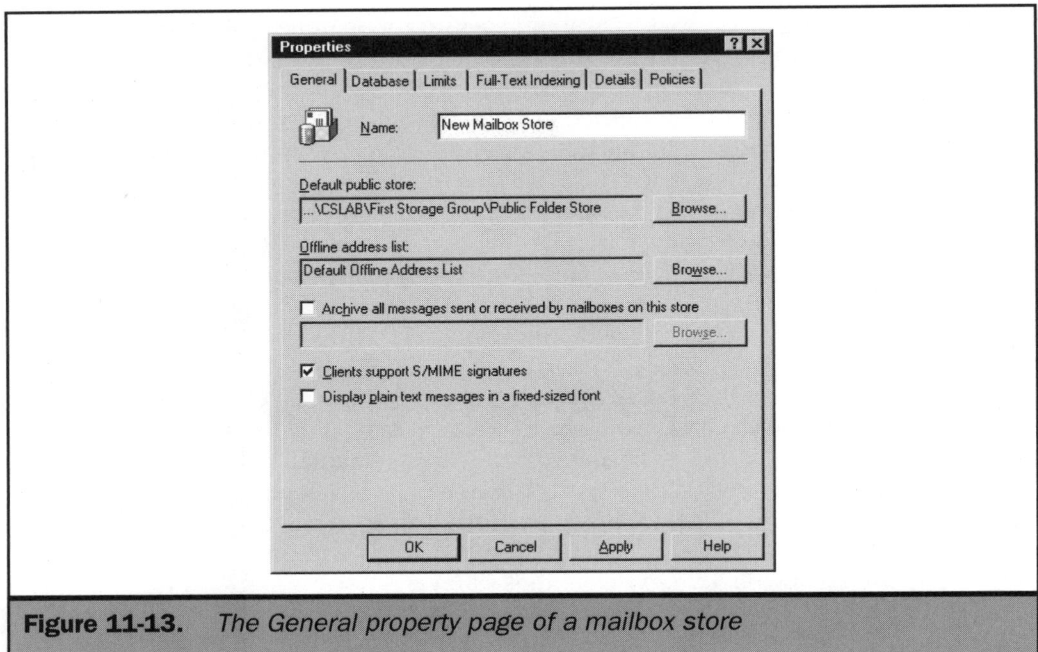

Figure 11-13. *The General property page of a mailbox store*

You also can choose to archive all messages sent from and received by the mailbox store. Enabling this option will cause Exchange to send a copy of every message sent and received to a specified mailbox or distribution list.

Tip *Normally you would only use the archiving feature as a temporary measure to view all messages involving the mailbox store. Enabling this feature adds overhead to the Exchange server and it is not recommended to leave this option enabled for a prolonged duration. Also, if you do not necessarily need to see the contents of messages, but only information showing what messages were sent or received, try using Message Tracking as an alternate solution. In industries that are more security conscious, this feature may be permanently enabled to provide a copy of every transaction (e-mail, calendar, tasks, and so on) for a number of years.*

The last two options on the General property page are client support options. If your Outlook clients are using Outlook 98 or later, leave the Clients Support S/MIME Signatures checkbox enabled. You can choose to have plain text messages displayed in a fixed-width font to allow text-based diagrams and the like to be displayed properly. For example, have you ever received a text message in which ASCII characters were used to draw a box, or a message in which the text forms a picture? If you have, and the font was not set to a fixed width, the picture or drawing was not displayed correctly. This option is not enabled by default.

Database The Database property page, shown in Figure 11-14, shows you the default locations and filenames for the rich text file (shown as the Exchange Database field) and the native content file (shown as the Exchange Streaming Database field), as well as the online maintenance interval. The database fields can be changed to maintain the folder hierarchy we spoke of in the "Creating Storage Groups" section of this chapter. You also will want the maintenance interval to work during off-peak hours of the day.

You can specify whether the mailbox store should be mounted at startup. You may want to check the Do Not Mount This Store At Start-up checkbox if you do not wish to have Exchange automatically mount the database when the information store is started. For example, if you are having problems mounting a database, or if the mounting causes Exchange to stop responding, you could select this option and restart the services or the server itself. That way, the next time the information store starts up, the database will not be mounted and you can perform the needed maintenance.

The This Database Can Be Overwritten By A Restore option gives you the ability to overwrite the database (the store) during a restore process. Because a restore process would normally overwrite the existing store, as a safety precaution, Exchange requires you to select this option prior to performing the restore. Because any information written to the store after the last backup will be lost, you will most likely only use this option in a situation where the store is corrupt beyond repair. In any event, you should be aware of the extent of the data loss should you choose to use this option and restore over a store.

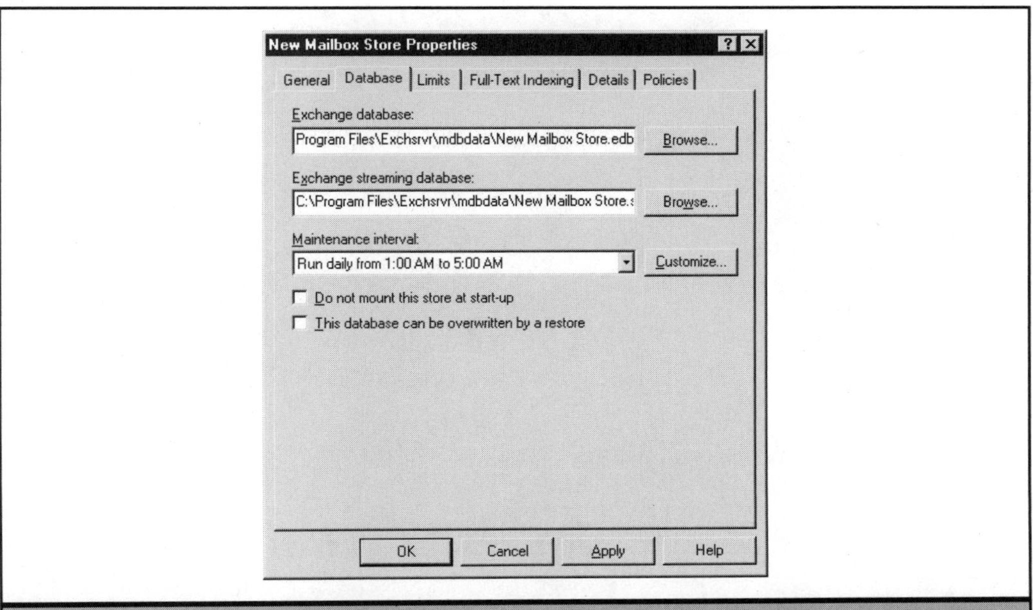

Figure 11-14. *The Database property page of a mailbox store*

Limits Use the Limits property page, shown in Figure 11-15, to specify the mailbox size limits you wish to place on mailboxes within this store. You also can establish deletion settings for mailbox items and mailboxes.

Use the Storage Limits section to establish the upper size limits for a mailbox. Instead of making the limit an absolute cutoff point, Exchange gives you three size levels that gradually take away a user's ability to use her mailbox as she gets closer to the mailbox size limit. You can use these three levels to lead up to the limit you actually wish to set, or you can simply enable a single level to specify the limit and the appropriate action that Exchange should take when a user has exceeded that limit. Table 11-2 lists the three levels and their effects when a user exceeds the specified limits.

A few notes about these limit levels. First, you don't have to use all three. You may find that the warning message is all you need to get folks to clean up their mailbox. Moreover, you may find that prohibiting the sending or receiving of email altogether is too restrictive, especially for VIPs within your organization. Second, to negate the effects of the storage limit options, all users have to do is decrease the size of their mailbox by deleting unwanted items or by exporting or copying them to a personal store (PST) file and then deleting them.

A common practice is to use all three levels to lead up to the desired limit. For example, suppose your size limit is 30MB per mailbox. You could enable all three options and set the levels to warn at 27MB, prohibit the sending of messages at 28MB,

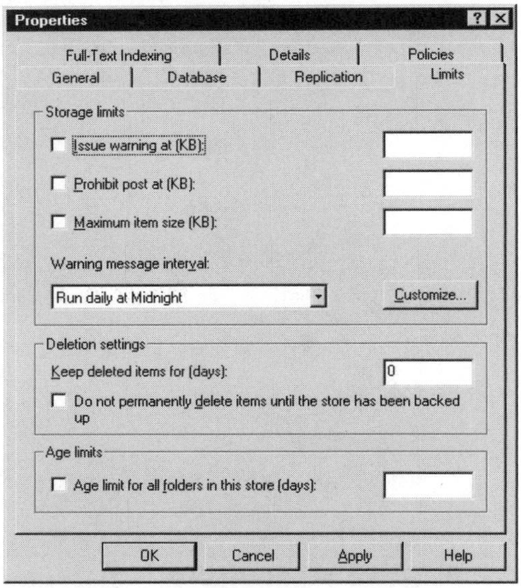

Figure 11-15. *The Limits property page of a mailbox store*

Storage Limit Level	What Happens When the User Exceeds the Specified Limit
Issue Warning at (KB)	When enabled, Exchange will send the user an e-mail warning that he is over the limit. This message is generated at the time specified in the Warning Message Interval field.
Prohibit Send at (KB)	When enabled, a user will not be able to send messages once the specified limit has been exceeded. However, the user will be able to continue receiving messages.
Prohibit Send and Receive at (KB)	When enabled, a user will not be able to send or receive messages until they delete some existing messages from their mailbox, or until this restriction is lifted.

Table 11-2. *Storage Limit Levels*

and prohibit all sending and receiving of messages at 30MB. That way, users have plenty of warning and can still remain functional as long as they don't wait until they reach the 30MB limit.

Tip *Although you can specify that the user is prohibited from sending and receiving messages, we recommend that you force compliance by only prohibiting the sending of messages. Prohibiting the sending* and *receiving of messages punishes the innocent correspondent who is sending a message to the offender that is not allowed to receive because they surpassed their limit. In addition, it looks bad when a company bounces your e-mail because of an internal behavioral problem. Prohibiting the sending of mail should be sufficient enough to cause users to pay attention to their mailbox storage usage.*

You can specify when Exchange should calculate who is above their limit and the appropriate action to take in the Warning Message Interval field.

Use the Deletion Settings section to specify how long Exchange should keep both deleted items and deleted mailboxes so that you will have the appropriate opportunity to recover those items. Also, as a precaution, you can choose to not allow permanent deletion of mailboxes until the store has been backed up.

How Big Is a Mailbox?

You may be thinking, "This mailbox limit thing is great. How do I tell how big a mailbox is? And how can my users tell?" You can tell in a variety of ways; we'll mention a couple. As the administrator, you can use Exchange System Manager and navigate to and expand the mailbox store housing the mailbox in question. Select the Mailboxes object beneath the store and in the right-hand pane you will see a listing of all the mailboxes in that store. Select the mailbox in question and look at the third column on the right pane. By default, the third column is the Size column (shown in KB). The value shown in this column is the size of the mailbox.

A user has it even easier. In Outlook, select Folder List from the View menu. Then right-click the Outlook Today container at the top of the folder list and select Properties. On the General property page, shown in Figure 11-16, click the Folder Size button to see the overall size of the mailbox, as well as the sizes of each folder and subfolder.

You can also use the Mailbox Statistics Tool (storstat.exe) from the Exchange 2000 Resource Kit to get the size of a mailbox, as well as other information. This is a MAPI-based tool that analyzes a user's mailbox and then develops statistics about it.

Finally, you can programmatically determine the size of a mailbox using ActiveX Data Objects (ADO). For details and code examples on this, see Microsoft Knowledge Base article Q255992.

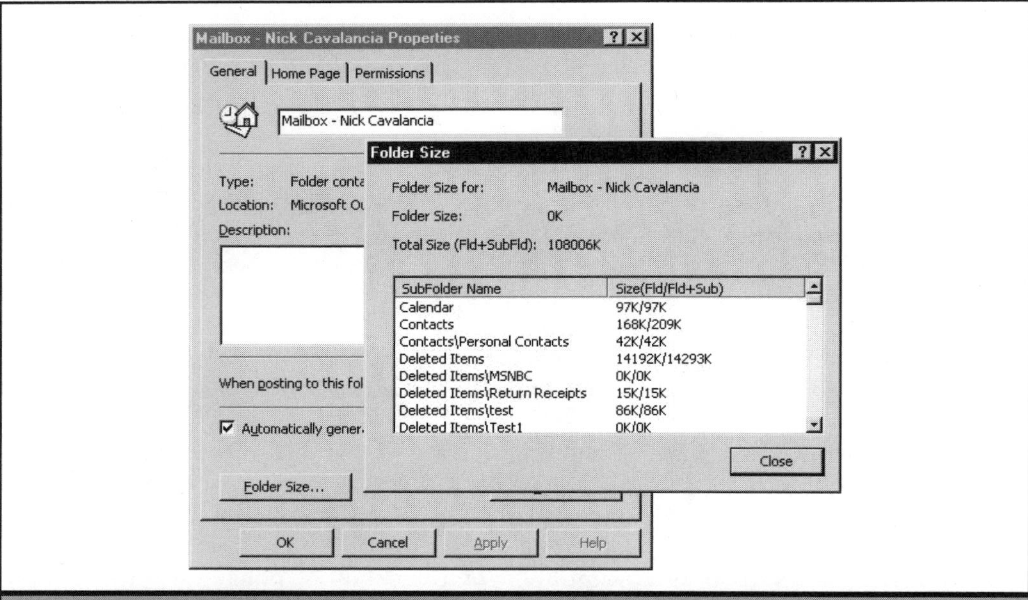

Figure 11-16. *Checking the mailbox size in Outlook*

Full-Text Indexing The Full-Text Indexing property page is disabled by default because full-text indexing is disabled by default. See the "Full-Text Indexing" section earlier in the chapter for the values of this property page and for more information on the topic.

Creating a Public Folder Tree

Before you can create a new public store, each store must be part of an associated public folder tree in order to establish a public folder hierarchy. Only one public store can be associated with any given public folder tree on a per-server basis. So a new tree must be created first. You would create an additional public folder tree if you wanted to keep the contents of one public folder store separate from another. By default, only one public folder tree exists with the default public store associated with it. If you attempt to create a public store without first having a public folder tree to associate it with, you will be prompted with a dialog box, shown in Figure 11-17, informing you that you should create the public folder tree first. It will appear that you will be allowed to continue creating the public store, but if you do not associate it with a public folder tree, you cannot finish creating the public store.

To create a public folder tree in Exchange System Manager, navigate to and right-click the Folders container, point to New, and then select Public Folder Tree. Give the tree a descriptive name and click OK. The associations between public folder trees and public stores are done when creating the public stores.

Any additional public folder trees you create aren't accessible by Outlook or other MAPI clients. The only public folder tree accessible to Outlook clients is the one associated with the client's mailbox store. This association can be found on the General property page of the mailbox store's properties under Default Public Store.

Creating a Public Store

Now that you have created the public folder tree, do the following to create a public store:

1. Navigate to and right-click the storage group in which you wish to create the public store.
2. Point to New, and then select Public Store.

Figure 11-17. *Warning message informing you that you must first create a public folder tree*

Because a public folder tree is available to associate with, no warning comes up and you can proceed with the creation of the public store. Although some of the property pages may look like the mailbox store property pages, let's walk through them and cover what options you can utilize.

General Specify the name of the public store on the General property page, shown in Figure 11-18. Click the Browse button to select the public folder tree to be associated with this public store. The same S/MIME and fixed-width font options as the mailbox stores are available here as well. (For more information on these two options, see "Creating a Mailbox Store" earlier in the chapter.)

Database and Full-Text Indexing These property pages have the same options as the mailbox store. See "Creating a Mailbox Store" earlier in the chapter for more information on these property pages.

Replication On the Replication property page, shown in Figure 11-19, specify the replication interval (which continually runs, by default), the maximum number of minutes between replication intervals (used if the replication interval is set to Always Run), and the size of the largest message that can be replicated. If bandwidth utilization between servers is a concern, you may want to change the replication interval to specific intervals. Values include every hour, every 2 hours, every 4 hours, and a customized

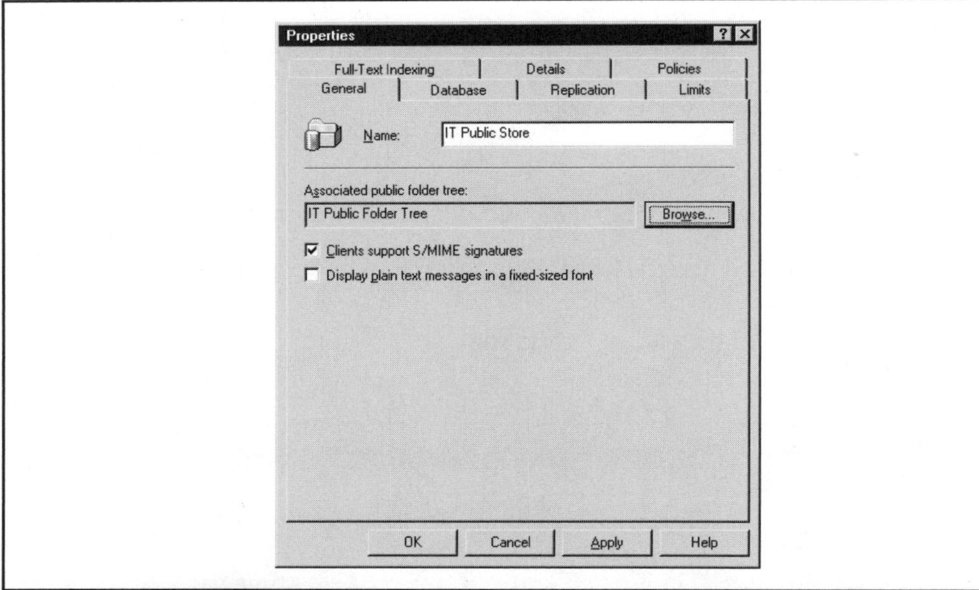

Figure 11-18. *The General property page of a public store*

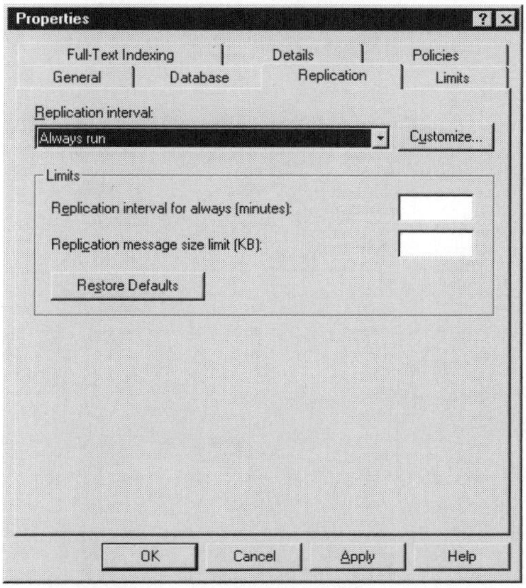

Figure 11-19. *The Replication property page of a public store*

schedule. Using a customized schedule is most beneficial, because you can move the replication to off-peak hours.

The Replication Message Size Limit field can help with bandwidth utilization. If you limit the size of messages being replicated, you can localize larger messages and not take up bandwidth replicating them to other servers.

Limits Although the options found on the Limits property page, shown in Figure 11-20, look identical to their counterparts for a mailbox store, a closer look shows them to be very different. The Storage Limits section has the same intent as the mailbox store: to limit the size of the public folders. When the Issue Warning option is enabled, a warning will be sent to users of the public store informing them of the reached limit. When the Prohibit Post option is enabled and the limit is reached, no user will be able to post new items in the public store. The Maximum Item Size value does not limit the overall public store; it limits the size of any given message being posted to the public store. Unless disk space is an issue, these options are usually not enabled.

You use the Deletion Settings section to specify how long Exchange should keep deleted items in the public store and whether the store should be backed up before permanently deleting the items. The default deletion retention time value of zero days means that Exchange does not retain items that are deleted by a client. If you wish to be able to recover deleted items, set the Keep Deleted Items For option to an appropriate

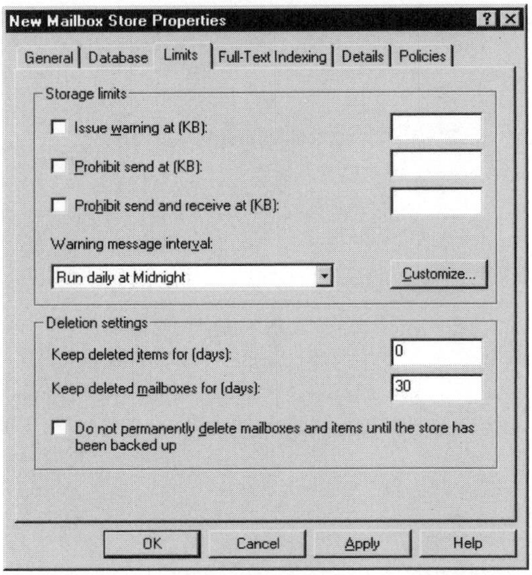

Figure 11-20. *The Limits property page of a public store*

number, and select the Do Not Permanently Delete Items checkbox. The benefit of retaining deleted items is, of course, the recoverability of those items. However, the cost of retention is disk space. When planning your deleted item retention time, think on a grand scale, in hundreds or thousands of messages, and not just about a single message being retained.

The Age Limits option specifies how old items in the public folders can be before they are automatically removed. If you enable this option and specify a number of days, all folders in the public store will adopt this value.

Moving Stores and Transaction Logs

Exchange 2000 sets the locations for the transaction logs and store databases when you create the storage groups and stores. The default location for store databases and transaction logs is the same drive Exchange was installed to (the C drive, by default). There may be a need somewhere down the road to move the logs or databases. For example, you may be running out of disk space on a particular drive on the server and wish to move the transaction logs to another drive. A more common example would be the following: A new Exchange server has been configured to have a hard drive configuration with separate locations for the operating system, pagefile, transaction logs, and store databases. The Exchange administrator is new to Exchange, so he or she sets up the various stores within the first storage group without concern for the location of the files. Now the administrator is left with an Exchange server that has all the transaction logs and databases on the C drive.

Moving Transaction Logs

Moving the transaction logs and databases should always be done through Exchange System Manager. To move transaction logs, navigate to and right-click the storage group using the transaction logs in question, and then select Properties. On the General property page, click the Browse button next to the Transaction Log Location field. In the Transaction Log Folders dialog box, navigate to the new location for the transaction logs and click OK. When you click either Apply or OK to accept the changes, a dialog box, shown in Figure 11-21, appears, verifying that you are about to move the transaction logs and informing you that the stores that use these transaction logs (e.g., all stores in the same storage group) will be temporarily dismounted during the move. This is because Exchange cannot log changes to the stores while the logs are being moved. So, the affected stores are dismounted, the logs are moved, and the stores are re-mounted.

Moving Store Databases

To move stores in Exchange System Manager, navigate to and right-click the store in question, and then select Properties. On the Databases property page, you can change the location of the rich text file (listed on the Databases property page as Exchange Database) and the native content file (listed as Exchange Streaming Database) separately. You can move either database by clicking the Browse button next to the file in question, navigating to the new folder location using a standard Save As dialog box, and then clicking Save. After clicking either Apply or OK to accept the changes, you are prompted with a dialog box, shown in Figure 11-22 and similar to the one seen when moving transaction logs. This dialog box prompts you to accept the changes being made and warns you that the store will be temporarily dismounted.

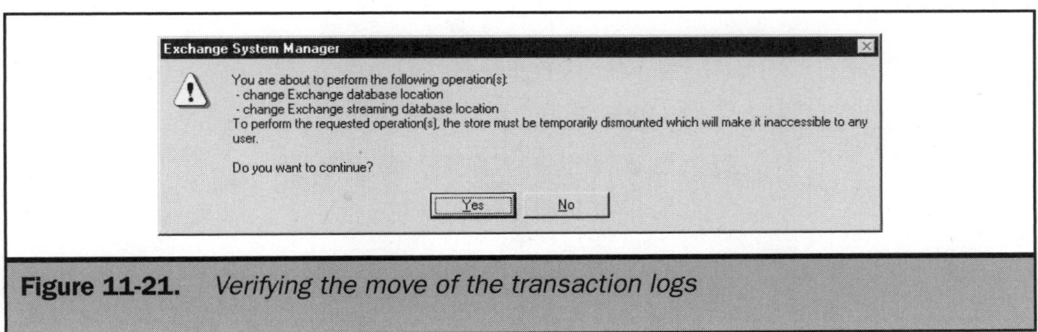

Figure 11-21. *Verifying the move of the transaction logs*

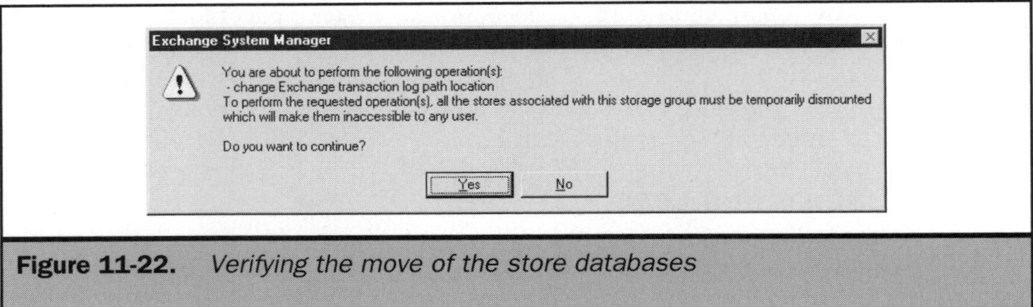

Figure 11-22. *Verifying the move of the store databases*

Deleting Stores and Storage Groups

You may find yourself in a situation where you need to delete a store or an entire storage group. Although the process is rather simple, it is important to understand the implications of deleting a store or storage group and the additional steps that are required.

Deleting a Store

You may ask yourself why would you ever want to delete a store. You may need to delete a store if you have a corrupt database with no backups to rely on. Or you may have created additional mailbox stores and decided to consolidate the mailboxes into one mailbox store. To delete a store in Exchange System Manager, navigate to and right-click the store you want to delete, and then select Delete. You will be prompted to verify that you want to delete the store, as shown in Figure 11-23.

After clicking Yes, you are notified, as shown in Figure 11-24, that the store has been removed and that you have to manually remove the database files yourself. This is because the store has only been logically removed from Exchange and Active Directory.

When you manually remove the database files, be certain you remove only *the rich text file (which end in .EDB) and the native content file (which end in .STM) and not the checkpoint or log files. By default, the storage group transaction logs and databases for the stores within that storage group reside in the same folder. If additional stores exist within the same storage group that you just deleted, the transaction logs are still in use!*

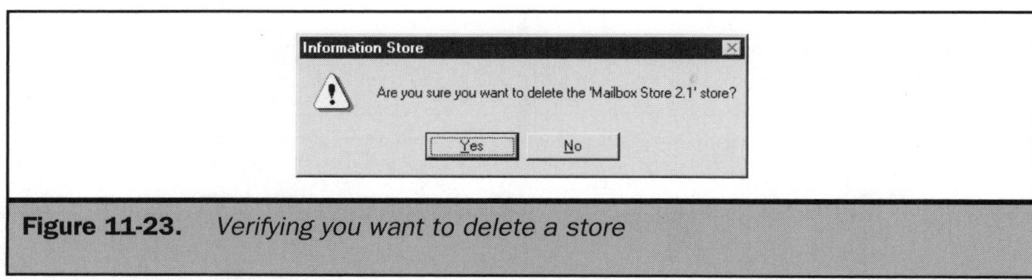

Figure 11-23. *Verifying you want to delete a store*

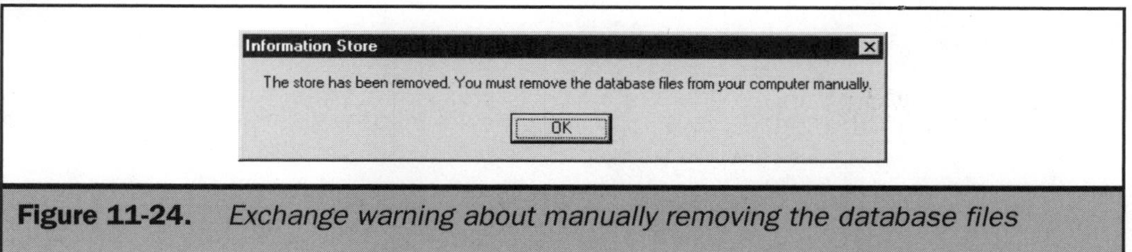

Figure 11-24. *Exchange warning about manually removing the database files*

Deleting a Storage Group

If no stores exist within a storage group, there is no reason to maintain the storage group. If you try to remove a storage group that still contains one or more stores, Exchange will warn you that the storage group contains stores, as shown in Figure 11-25. You will need to remove any stores within the storage group before you can delete the storage group.

To remove a storage group in Exchange System Manager, navigate to and right-click the storage group, and then select Delete. You will be asked if you want to remove the storage group. Click Yes to delete the storage group. Although no message appears when you delete the storage group, like the store databases when deleting a store, you will have to manually delete the log files.

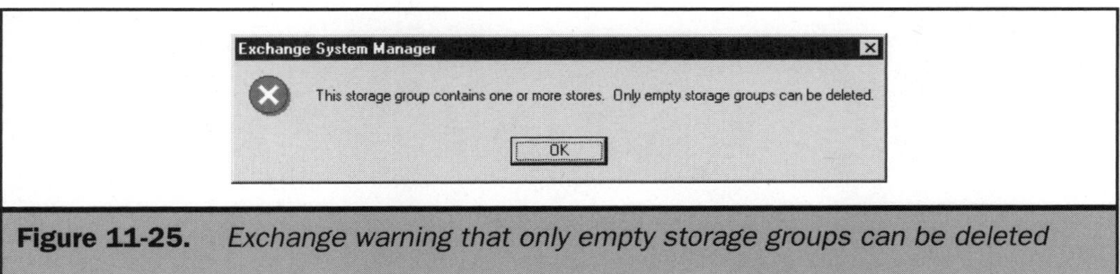

Figure 11-25. *Exchange warning that only empty storage groups can be deleted*

Summary

This chapter has covered quite a few concepts related to storage on Exchange. The fact that so many concepts related to storage exist shows you how very important storage is to the various functionalities of Exchange. In order for your storage to be as efficient as possible, you need to plan the location of your storage groups and stores, and you need to plan ahead for the possibility of a disaster that would require the use of your transaction logs to recover your databases. In the next chapter, we will cover backup-and-restore concepts and procedures that include disaster recovery.

Chapter 12

Backup, Restore, and Disaster Recovery

With messaging becoming (if it is not already) the most critical application that businesses use today, it is essential to not only have a backup and recovery plan, but also to be certain you back up the appropriate data. Although most administrators believe they have set up backups of Exchange correctly, you may find after reading this chapter that your backups are missing data that is important to Exchange's functionality. How, when, and how often you back up data is equally as important as what you back up. We'll address these issues when we cover the various backup types supported by Exchange.

Usually corporate management is not concerned with the backups as much as they are concerned that you have the capability to restore an Exchange server to full functionality. You should know not only what to restore, but also the order in which to restore it. We will cover the proper way to restore Exchange data in this chapter. Lastly, you should have a disaster recovery plan in place. This is different from a restore plan. We will cover what should be a part of your disaster recovery plan. Before we can back anything up, we need to know what should be backed up, so let's start by looking at the locations of important Exchange data.

Where Exchange 2000 Keeps Data

When most administrators think of the Exchange data they should back up, they think of the mailbox and public store databases. Some don't even realize that the transaction logs need to be backed up as well. Although the stores and their transaction logs are extremely important, Exchange 2000 is more than just databases and transaction logs. There is information stored in Active Directory, the IIS metabase, and on the file system on the Exchange server that all should be backed up. In addition, you may have data from one of the following services that should be backed up: Site Replication Service (SRS) and Key Management Server (KMS) database files, message tracking logs, workflow software, mailbox agents, scripts and sinks, and anti-virus software. Let's look at all the important locations and the data they hold to see what comprises a complete backup of an Exchange server.

Active Directory

In Exchange 5.5, the directory of information about the Exchange environment, as well as the mailboxes and other recipients, was saved in an Exchange-specific directory database (DIR.EDB) used only by Exchange. Exchange 2000 relies on Active Directory (AD) to maintain the same information. Almost all Exchange 2000 configuration information can be found in AD. You can move down the hierarchy in Exchange System Manager, and virtually all the information you find on any given property page comes from AD.

Data in AD, with respect to maintaining Exchange information, should be backed up whenever you make a major change. The next logical determination is exactly what constitutes a major change. It depends on what you consider important. Because everything except stores, transaction logs, and Internet Information Services (IIS) information is stored in AD, you should perform backups of AD daily to capture recipient changes. You may feel that backups are necessary only periodically, or only when a configuration change, such as the addition of an administrative group or another Exchange server, is made. Most likely, the frequency at which you back up Exchange data in AD will not depend merely on Exchange changes. Other factors, such as changes to AD sites, domain controllers, and operations masters, will also drive the backups. Exchange should simply be at an equal level of importance on the list of considerations when determining the frequency of your AD backups. For more information on Active Directory, see Chapter 2, "Active Directory."

You back up AD information by selecting the System State checkbox in the Windows 2000 backup utility. System State data includes the following:

- Startup and system files, as well as all files protected by Windows File Protection
- COM+ class registration database
- Registry
- Performance counter configuration information
- IIS metabase

System State may also include additional data, depending on the computer's role. If the computer is an Active Directory domain controller, System State data also includes the Sysvol folder and the Active Directory database (NTDS.DIT). If the computer is a certificate server, System State data includes the Certificate Services database. If the computer is a node in the cluster, the cluster database is also part of the System State data.

This information can also be backed up via third-party utilities, which we will discuss later in the chapter in the section titled "Backup Applications."

Databases and Transaction Logs

As we mentioned before, almost everyone is familiar with the need to back up the Exchange databases and transaction logs. Exchange-aware backup applications simplify the backup selection process by allowing you to select a server or storage group for backup with minimal user intervention. It is important that you know what files make up the databases and transaction logs for each store on your servers, so let's go over the specific files involved to ensure you have a good sense of what should be backed up.

Exchange Stores

Each mailbox and public folder store has two database files: a rich-text store file (which has an .EDB extension) and a native content file (which has an .STM extension). You can find out where these files are located for a particular store in Exchange System Manager by viewing the properties of each store. On the Database properties page, shown in Figure 12-1, the two databases that make up the store are listed in the Exchange Database and Exchange Streaming Database fields.

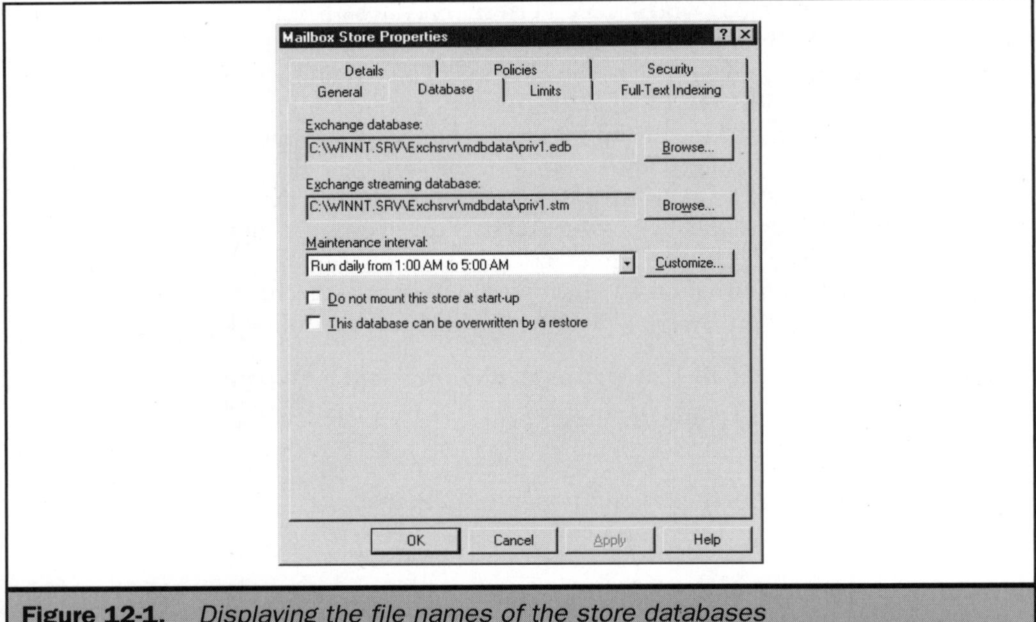

Figure 12-1. *Displaying the file names of the store databases*

Transaction Logs

Each storage group (which can contain multiple stores) has a single set of transaction logs for all the stores within the group. Each of these log files has a .LOG extension. You can find out where these files are located in Exchange System Manager by navigating to and right-clicking the storage group in question and selecting Properties. On the General properties page, shown in Figure 12-2, the folder storing the transaction logs is listed in the Transaction Log Location field. In addition, the Log File Prefix field lists the beginning of the name of each log file for this storage group. Should multiple storage groups utilize the same folder for transaction log storage, Exchange 2000 will use a different transaction log file prefix to distinguish one set of transaction logs from another.

For more information on Exchange 2000 databases and transaction logs, see Chapter 11, "The Exchange 2000 Store."

IIS Metabase

IIS plays an integral part in the functionality of Exchange 2000. Internet protocols like POP3, IMAP4, and SMTP, while used by Exchange 2000, are actually part of IIS. Because Exchange uses these protocols, you should back up the configuration of your IIS server. IIS stores its configuration information in the IIS metabase. The metabase is

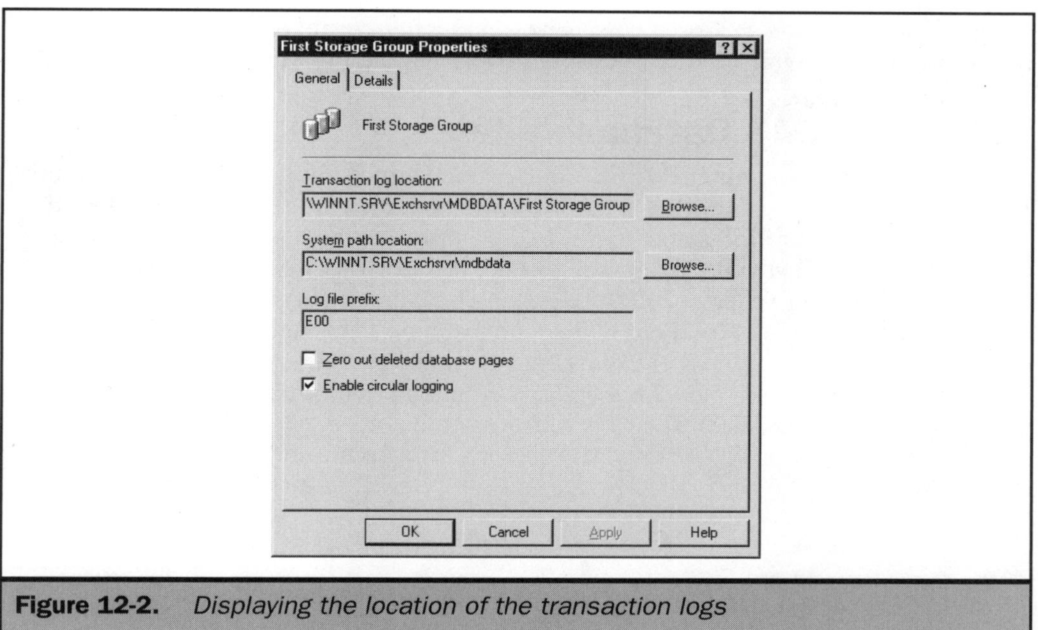

Figure 12-2. *Displaying the location of the transaction logs*

a hierarchical database, similar to the registry. A metabase, rather than the registry, is used to provide more granularity in respect to the level of detail needed for IIS configuration.

IIS stores this information in the *METABASE.BIN* file, which is located in the Inetsrv folder. This file is loaded when IIS starts and is saved when IIS shuts down. It is also periodically updated while IIS is in use. The metabase can be backed up within the Internet Services Manager tool by right-clicking the server you wish to back up and selecting Backup/Restore Configuration.

Although you can back up the metabase from within ISM, you should back up the metabase through the System State. See Microsoft Knowledge Base article Q269586 for more information.

Exchange Software

The most overlooked set of data that should be backed up is the files that make up the Exchange 2000 Server software. These files, by default, exist in the \Program Files\Exchsrvr folder on your server. They should be backed up in order to restore your server to the exact same state. (Keep in mind that service packs, post-SP fixes, patches from Microsoft, and the like that you apply after the initial installation of Exchange need to be put back in place to restore complete functionality.) You can choose to re-create your

Exchange server by reinstalling the Exchange 2000 software, but backing up this data would provide you with an easier recovery process should the Exchange server crash.

IM, SRS, and KMS Database Files

If you use Instant Messaging (IM), Site Replication Service (SRS), or Key Management Service (KMS) database files, you will need to include the databases associated with those services in your backup strategy. The database used by the Instant Messaging servers is called MSIMNODE.EDB and is in the IMData folder under the folder in which you installed Exchange 2000 by default. The database used by SRS is in the SRSData folder under the folder in which you installed Exchange 2000. SRS consists of the SRS database (SRS.EBD) and Extensible Storage Engine (ESE) transaction logs. KMS database files are located, by default, in the KMSData folder under the folder in which you installed Exchange 2000. The folder includes the KMS database (KMSMDB.EDB) and ESE transaction logs. With either service, backing up the entire service-related folder is best.

For more information on IM, see Chapter 16, "Exchange 2000 Instant Messaging." For more information on SRS, see Chapter 7, "Upgrading and Co-existing with Exchange 5.5." For more information on KMS, see Chapter 19, "Public Key Infrastructure Services."

Third-Party Applications

The last thing to remember to back up is any third-party software that extends your Exchange server's functionality. This would include the following software types:

- Anti-virus
- Backup
- Workflow
- Server monitoring
- Content scanning

Consult the documentation from the application vendor to see what needs to be backed up in order to regain full functionality in the event of a restore situation.

Types of Backups

In addition to knowing what you should back up, you should also know the various ways you can back up that data. When looking at each backup type, we'll discuss a few ramifications, such as what files are actually backed up and what state the files are left in after the backup. Also, we'll look at a few strategies you can use to back up your Exchange environment.

There are several different methods to back up Exchange. The first is an offline backup in which the backup is performed on a set of files manually selected by the backup operator while Exchange 2000 is offline. This method has nothing specifically to do with Exchange, but because Exchange is made up of a group of files, it can be backed up this way. When looking at offline backups, pay particular attention to the archive bit (also called the Archive attribute) of each file that is backed up. This bit is the center of attention during the backup process because it determines what is to be backed up. When a file is modified in the file system, Windows 2000 turns on the archive bit to signal to a backup application that the file needs to be backed up. When that file is backed up, the intent is to turn off (or clear) the archive bit, signaling that the file has been backed up. Keep in mind that even if a file has its archive bit turned on, only the files selected by the backup operator will be looked at to determine, based on the value of the archive bit, if they should be backed up.

The second method for backing up Exchange is an online backup done through an Exchange-aware backup application that communicates with Exchange during the backup process to retrieve the data to be backed up. In this method, the attention is given to the state of the transaction logs. In some cases, the logs will be flushed, that is, the history of transactions they contain can be wiped clean, as that data has been backed up and a history is no longer necessary. In other cases, only certain backup types can be performed due to the status of the transaction logs.

One last commonly used backup type exists: the mailbox-level backup. Many third-party backup utilities support backing up an individual mailbox in order to provide a more granular level of recovery.

Let's look at each backup method and see how it can be used to back up Exchange.

Offline Backups

The backup is called "offline" because it requires that Exchange be offline; that is, all of the Exchange services must be stopped. The first thing to know about offline backups is that the selection process is manual. This means that you are responsible for choosing what gets backed up. If you back up the store database files, but forget to back up the transaction logs, don't go blaming the backup utility! You will need at least Backup Operator privileges on the Exchange server to perform the backup. Depending on the backup application you use, there are up to five types of offline backups. Table 12-1 lists the backup types and describes what happens with each.

Backup Type	Backs Up Only Archived Files	Clears Archive Bit	Description
Normal (Full)	No	Yes	All selected files are backed up, regardless of the value of the archive bit. The archive bit is cleared after the file is backed up. The backup is sometimes called a Full backup.
Copy	No	No	This backup is intended to provide a copy of the files and backs up all selected files, regardless of their archive bit value. Because this is a copy and not a Full backup, the archive bit is not cleared.
Incremental	Yes	Yes	This backup is used to back up all selected files that have the archive bit turned on. Each Incremental backup you perform is intended to be the backup for the increment of time since the last either Full or Incremental backup.
Differential	Yes	No	All selected files with the archive bit turned on will be backed up. The difference between this backup and the Incremental backup is that the archive bit in a Differential backup is left on. The intent is to back up the changes since the last Full backup.

Table 12-1. *Offline Backup Types and Their Interaction with the Archive Bit*

Backup Type	Backs Up Only Archived Files	Clears Archive Bit	Description
Daily	No	No	The Daily backup checks the modified date, not the archive bit, of the file. This way, the files that have been modified on the current day will be backed up. Because the date is the focus of this backup, the archive bit is not modified in any way.

Table 12-1. *Offline Backup Types and Their Interaction with the Archive Bit* (continued)

No matter which backup type you choose, the offline backup process is the same. To perform an offline backup:

1. Dismount the store you wish to back up. If you wish to back up the transaction logs, all stores within the storage group must be dismounted. If you wish to also back up the Exchange server files, you will need to stop all Exchange-related services.
2. Start the backup of the Exchange data.
3. When the backup is completed, start the services, or mount the stores, as is applicable.

An offline backup is not recommended for two reasons. First, Exchange cannot continue to run and service other clients during the backup. Second, the database is not checked for errors during the backup and, therefore, a corrupt database can be backed up.

Online Backups

Online backups are much simpler, as the selection process is not focused on the specific files to be backed up, but instead on the logical groupings of servers, storage groups, stores, and in some third-party backup applications, individual mailboxes. Also, only three of the five backup types used for offline backups are commonly used in online backups. Daily and Copy backups, while supported by the Windows 2000 Backup utility, are not generally used because they back up the stores and logs, but they do not flush the logs. A Full backup provides the same level of backup as Daily and Copy, but it flushes the logs, which clears up disk space taken by the logs, and causes all transactions in the logs to be written to the store databases. Table 12-2 lists the different backup types and describes what they backup, as well as how they handle the transaction logs.

Backup Type	Backs Up Database	Backs Up Logs	Flushes Logs	Description
Normal (Full)	Yes	Yes	Yes	The transactions in the logs are written to the store databases, and then the databases are backed up. The transaction logs, which are no longer needed (as their changes have been written to the database), are flushed.
Incremental	No	Yes	Yes	The transaction logs are the focus of this backup, which backs up the log files prior to the checkpoint log file, and then deletes them. The changes stored in the logs are backed up, and because the intent is to back up the changes since the last Full or Incremental backup, the logs are flushed.
Differential	No	Yes	No	This type also backs up log files prior to the checkpoint log file, but unlike an Incremental backup, the logs are not deleted. The transaction logs are backed up and, since the intent of this backup (and subsequent Differential backups) is to backup all of the changes since the last Full backup, the logs are not flushed.

Table 12-2. *Exchange-Aware Backups and Their Interaction with Transaction Logs*

Flushing the Transaction Logs

The purpose of flushing or clearing the transaction logs is to keep the number of logs at a minimum and to store only recent transactions. Both Normal and Incremental backups clear the transaction logs. Once the logs are cleared, they will only represent the changes made since they were last cleared. This means subsequent backups can only go as far back as the transaction logs do. For example, if you perform a Normal backup at 11:00P.M. on Monday night and wish to perform an Incremental backup the next morning at 7:00A.M., the Incremental backup will only capture the changes made since 11:00P.M. the previous evening. Likewise, if you run a second Incremental backup on Tuesday at 3:00P.M., it will only represent the changes made since 7:00A.M.

Circular Logging

Although circular logging is covered in Chapter 11, it is important to recap this concept, as it has an effect on the types of online backups you can perform. Circular logging enables Exchange to use the same log file repeatedly, instead of creating a new log file when the log reaches 5MB in size. The upside to circular logging is that it conserves disk space; the downside is that it does not have the same recoverability as compared to leaving circular logging disabled. Circular logging is enabled on a per-storage group basis. It is enabled by navigating to and right-clicking the storage group in question, and then selecting Properties. At the bottom of the General tab, select the Enable Circular Logging checkbox, as shown in Figure 12-2.

If circular logging is enabled, you cannot perform Differential and Incremental backups. These backup types are designed to provide a complete set of changes since the last Full backup. Let's suppose you perform Full backups once a week on Sundays and either Incremental or Differential backups the other days of the week on an Exchange server with circular logging disabled. The Incremental or Differential backups that are run throughout the week are supposed to back up *all* changes since the previous Full or Incremental backup. If circular logging is enabled, there is a good chance that enough changes will be made to the databases that the logs will all be filled and the process of overwriting the first log will start. Once the overwriting of the logs begins, you no longer have a record of all the changes made since the last Full or Incremental backup. Therefore, when circular logging is enabled, only Full backups can be performed.

Patch File

During the backup process, Exchange still allows regular use by its clients. So, while you're trying to back up the store databases and the transaction logs, more changes are being made to the transaction logs. A step must be taken to ensure that you have a complete set of transaction logs while clients continue to use Exchange. This is accomplished through the use of a patch file. A patch file is a temporary log file used during the backup process. When a transaction occurring during the backup would normally affect a set of data that has already been backed up, it is called crossing the *backup boundary*, that is, the logical position in the database that designates what has already been backed up. Because the transaction should be written to an already backed up part of the database, the transaction is written to the patch file instead. There is one patch file for each database that is backed up. At the end of the backup process, the patch file is written to the backup along with the databases and logs, and the original patch files are deleted. Upon a restore, the patch files will be replayed just like the transaction logs to bring the store databases back to a consistent state.

Checksum

The Extensible Storage Engine (ESE) uses a checksum during the backup process to verify that each page of the database being backed up is valid. A checksum is a 4-byte hash string that is added to the header of each 4KB page in an ESE database. It is unique to each page. When the ESE reads the page from the database, should the data prove to be invalid by a failed comparison checksum calculated by the ESE, the backup process stops in order to keep from backing up a corrupt database. The same process of reading a page from an ESE database and comparing the checksum is performed by the ESE for each page read during normal operations. Should a checksum fail, the database is stopped, and an error is written to the event log.

Concurrent Backups

Exchange allows multiple stores to be concurrently backed up. The only caveat to this is that a patch file is created for each store being backed up.

Mailbox-Level Backups

A mailbox-level backup—also known as a *brick-level backup*—is just what it sounds like: a backup of Exchange at a mailbox level. The difference between this backup and an Exchange-aware backup is that the granularity of this backup is not at the store level (like the Exchange-aware backup), but at the individual mailbox level. Therefore, you can back up (and restore) a single mailbox, rather than an entire store. We've seen countless instances in which clients have one particular user complaining of losing something in his or her mailbox. Provided you have backed up that mailbox using a mailbox-level backup, you would be able to restore the mailbox for just that individual. The alternative is rather cumbersome: You would have to restore to a non-production server, export the mailbox to a personal store file (.PST), and then import that PST into the user's mailbox on the production server.

You must do a mailbox-level backup of the mailbox to be able to perform a mailbox-level restore of that same mailbox. You cannot perform an Exchange-aware backup at the store level and restore a single mailbox from that backup.

Note *Even when made Exchange-aware by the installation of Exchange, the Windows 2000 backup utility does not support or provide any mechanism for the backup or restoration of individual mailboxes. You will need to look to third-party applications if you want this functionality. In addition, performing mailbox-level backups is significantly slower than a regular backup of the entire store, and these types of backups can be unreliable, as well. Therefore, you should selectively implement mailbox-level backups, and only after all other alternatives have been fully explored.*

Backup Strategies

When you determine which type of backup is right for you, consider the amount of time it will take to back up and restore your Exchange server, what data you are backing up (AD, stores and logs, and Exchange software files), and the maximum amount of data that could be lost using your recovery method. Let's look at several common backup strategies and see what are the pros and cons of each.

- **Daily Full (Normal) Backups** A complete backup of Exchange is performed each business day. If you needed to restore using this method, you would have to perform a single restore session, and, depending on the type of failure, you could lose up to one business day's worth of information. On a daily basis, this method takes the longest amount of time to back up Exchange.
- **Weekly Full with Daily Incremental Backups** Once a week, a Normal backup of Exchange is performed. An Incremental backup (which backs up only the changes since the last backup) is performed on each of the remaining business days. To restore under this method, you would need to first restore the Full backup, and then restore each Incremental backup in the appropriate order. On a daily basis, this method takes the least amount of time to back up Exchange.
- **Weekly Full with Daily Differential Backups** Once a week, a Normal backup of Exchange is performed. A Differential backup (which backs up all the changes since the last Normal backup) is performed on each of the remaining business days. To restore, you would restore two sessions: the weekly Full and the last Differential. The Differential backup takes more time than an Incremental backup because it backs up all the data since the last Full backup, not just the last Differential backup.

Mission-Critical Backup Strategy

The three backup strategies listed in the preceding section only restore your Exchange server to the state it was in at the time of backup. For example, if you were to perform a backup at 11:00P.M., and the server crashed at 3:30P.M. the next day, the server would be restored to the state it was in at 11:00P.M., regardless of which of the three backup strategies you used. Many companies want to be up and running with their Exchange server in a state that it was in much closer to the time of a crash.

To accomplish this, many companies utilize a daily Full backup, with periodical Incremental or Differential backups. For example, you continue performing Full backups each night at 11:00P.M. In addition to those backups, you also perform a set of Differential backups every four hours throughout the day (8:00A.M., 12:00P.M., 4:00P.M., and 8:00P.M.). If the server crashed at 3:30P.M., two restores would be performed: the previous night's Full backup and the Differential backup at 12:00P.M. today. Once completed, your Exchange server would be running with data that is current as of 12:00P.M. today and not 11:00P.M. yesterday. That's a difference of 11 hours of messages.

You might say that you don't want to back up during operating hours because it may slow down the Exchange server. It's a valid concern. However, you will find that because your periodic Incremental or Differential backups are only backing up transaction logs, the amount of data (and, therefore, the amount of time) is minimal, usually several minutes. In some cases, it will probably take more time to rewind the tape for use than it will to actually back up the data.

Restoring Exchange 2000

If you took a survey of how many administrators regularly back up their Exchange servers, the percentage that do so would probably be pretty high. However, the percentage of those same administrators who have tested their backups with a restore would be much lower. Most administrators have some idea of what it takes to restore, but do not have a full understanding of the Exchange recovery process, which involves restores. Let's discuss what it takes to restore your Exchange 2000 server, as well as what happens during a restore.

Restore Strategies

The method that you will use to restore your Exchange 2000 Server depends on the backup method you use. Table 12-3 lists the tapes you will need to restore based on the backup method you used. It does not matter whether you performed offline or online backups of Exchange, the restore method is the same.

Backup Method	Restore Method
Daily Full	Restore the last Full backup only
Full with Daily Incrementals	Restore the Full backup and each Incremental backup since the Full backup
Full with Daily Differentials	Restore the Full backup and the last Differential backup

Table 12-3. *Restore Strategies*

Offline Restores

An offline restore requires more administrator intervention than an online restore. Just as in the backup process, you must make certain you restore all databases and transaction log files for a particular store or storage group. Also, you need to make certain that they are being restored to the appropriate folder on the Exchange server. The process of an offline restore is simple; let's look at the process of restoring a single store within a storage group:

1. The files are restored to their original locations.
2. The Exchange services are started.
3. The ESE parses the logs to replay any transactions that are not already committed. Assuming the Exchange services were shut down properly, all transactions should have been committed. Therefore, no additional transactions should have to be replayed.
4. The Exchange server is up and operational.

Online Restores

Online restores require less administrative work than their offline counterpart, but so much more happens during an online restore. All you do is select a store and click the Restore button in an application. Exchange does much more to ensure the integrity of not only the store you are concerned with, but also the other stores in the same storage group. The basic restore process is as follows:

1. The database must be dismounted and the This Database Can Be Overwritten By A Restore checkbox must be selected on the Database property page of the Store's properties.

2. The database engine and ESE enter restore mode.
3. The restore of the databases (both the .STM and .EDB files) occurs.
4. The log files and patch file are restored to a temporary location.
5. The restore database engine applies the log files and patch file to the databases.
6. The temporary log files and patch file are deleted.
7. The database engine and ESE return to normal operations.

Temporary Patch and Log Files

Step 4 of the online restore process deserves a bit more detail. Before a restore begins, the backup operator is prompted to specify a temporary location for the log and patch files. This is a critical step in the success of the restore process. If the logs and patch file are written to their original location, they will overwrite the existing set of logs. This will affect the other stores in the same storage group. For example, suppose you have four stores, named S1, S2, S3, and S4, within a single storage group, SG1. Because you back up S1 more frequently than the other three stores, you back up S1 separately. Remember, when you back up the store in an online backup, the databases, the logs from the *entire* storage group, and the temporary patch file are backed up.

Let's also suppose you have a problem with S1 that requires the store to be restored from tape. The logs on the tape for S1 also include transactions for S2, S3, and S4, because all four stores are in the same storage group, SG1. If you restored those logs to the original location, all existing transaction logs would be overwritten, the uncommitted transactions for S2, S3, and S4 contained within the existing logs would be lost, and data would be lost. So instead, the logs and patch file are restored to a temporary location and replayed from that location. Exchange knows that because you are only restoring S1, the logs are parsed only for transactions that apply to S1. Any transactions for the other three stores are ignored, as they have already been committed from the existing set of logs. Once the restore and log replay process is completed, the temporary files are deleted and the store is mounted and ready for use.

Restore.env

In addition to the logs and patch file, the RESTORE.ENV file is created in the temporary location. This file lists the log files to be replayed, as well as the databases that will be affected. To see the contents of the RESTORE.ENV file, use the following command:

Eseutil /cm <*restore.env location*>

For example, if your RESTORE.ENV file were located in the C:\Restore folder, the command would read:

Eseutil /cm C:\Restore

The output of this command can be seen in Figure 12-3. Notice values in the output of RESTORE.ENV to be replayed, such as the restore path, the storage group, the

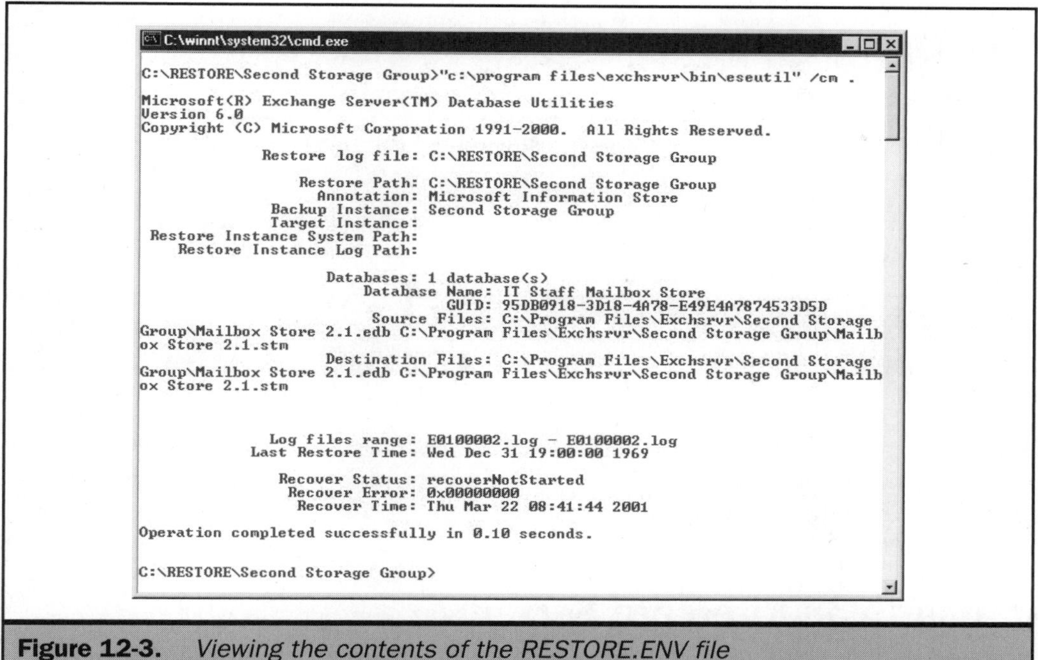

Figure 12-3. *Viewing the contents of the RESTORE.ENV file*

database name and GUID, and the log file range. Looking at these values makes it clear that RESTORE.ENV is in charge of the remainder of the recovery process.

For more information on the RESTORE.ENV file, see Microsoft Knowledge Base article Q253914.

Multiple Restores

If you perform Differential or Incremental backups of your Exchange server in addition to Full backups, you will need to perform more than one restore. Because Exchange wants to replay the logs once a restore is completed to bring the database to a consistent state, there needs to be a mechanism to tell Exchange that you will be performing multiple restores. In the case of Windows 2000 Backup, the mechanism is the Last Backup Set checkbox. Other third-party Exchange-aware backup applications have a similar checkbox. This box should only be selected when starting the last restore. Table 12-4 shows when you should select this option.

Concurrent Restores

Exchange allows you to restore to multiple databases concurrently within the same storage group—provided that they are part of the same restore job. You cannot launch

Backup Strategy	Select the Last Backup Set checkbox
Daily Fulls	When restoring the Full backup
Weekly Fulls with Daily Incrementals	When restoring the last Incremental backup
Weekly Fulls with Daily Differentials	When restoring the Differential backup

Table 12-4. *When to Specify the Last Backup Set*

multiple restore jobs against the same storage group, nor can you run simultaneous restores against a single store. When running concurrent restores, the most important step is to ensure that the temporary location for the log and patch files is different for each concurrent restore.

Restoring to an Alternate Server

You may need to restore your Exchange stores to an alternate, non-production server in the following situations: when you need to retrieve an individual mailbox (and use a backup solution that does not support mailbox backups), when you need to recover a deleted mailbox (after you have exceeded the mailbox retention time), or when you cannot overwrite the existing database with an older copy. To restore to an alternate server:

1. Establish a separate Active Directory (AD) environment.
2. Install Windows 2000 to a non-production server and apply Service Pack 1 (SP1), which is required to install Exchange 2000. Also, apply any post-Windows 2000 SP1 hotfixes, as well as any pre-Exchange 2000 SP1 hotfixes you already had on the original server.
3. Next run DCPROMO to promote the stand-alone server to a domain controller. Install the server into a new AD forest and tree. Name your AD tree something other than your production environment, for example, "recovery.mycompany.com."
4. Install Exchange 2000, making sure to use *the same organization name* as the original installation. Also, be certain the Administrative Group has the same initial name as the original installation. By default this name is "First Administrative Group." The reason for using the same initial name is that the LegacyExchangeDN (Distinguished Name) value of the new installation must match the original installation for a restore to work.

5. If needed, re-create the storage group and stores, using the *exact same names* and file system path as the original server.
6. Dismount the store to be restored and select the This Database Can Be Overwritten By A Restore checkbox in the store properties.
7. Restore the databases and logs and mount the store.
8. Run the Active Directory Account Cleanup Wizard (ADCLEAN.EXE). ADClean is a utility that searches AD to ensure that there is only one mailbox per account in AD.
9. Use Outlook to log on as the user who owns the mailbox, and then export the mailbox to a .PST file.
10. Import the needed data from the .PST file into the original mailbox on the original server.

You can also use the Exmerge utility to move the mailbox data from the alternate server to the original server. For more information on Exmerge, see the Microsoft Knowledge Base article Q174197.

Restoring a Single Mailbox

Without a third-party backup tool that supports mailbox-level backups, you cannot restore a single mailbox. You can go through the process listed previously in the "Restoring to an Alternate Server" section to get the data from a single mailbox, but that is not a very good solution. You can, however, take one proactive measure to protect against mailboxes that are accidentally deleted.

Each store has two settings that will preserve your mailboxes when they are deleted. On the Limits properties page of a given mailbox store, shown in Figure 12-4, you can specify how long Exchange should keep deleted mailboxes using the Keep Deleted Mailboxes For option. You can also specify that Exchange not permanently delete mailboxes until the store is backed up. This option is especially helpful: Because the deleted mailboxes are retained on the store until *after* the backup, a copy of the deleted stores is available on the backup media for later use, if needed.

If the account associated with a mailbox is deleted, or if the mailbox itself is deleted from within Active Directory Users and Computers, the mailbox object will still appear in Exchange System Manager and can be reconnected to a new user account. If you look at the contents of a mailbox store in System Manager by navigating to the Mailboxes container just under the mailbox store in question, you will see a list of the mailboxes on the right pane, as shown in Figure 12-5. The mailbox with the "X" is a deleted mailbox. Right-click on the mailbox and select Reconnect to associate the mailbox with a user account and recover it.

Tip

The account to which you re-associate the mailbox must not already have an Exchange mailbox.

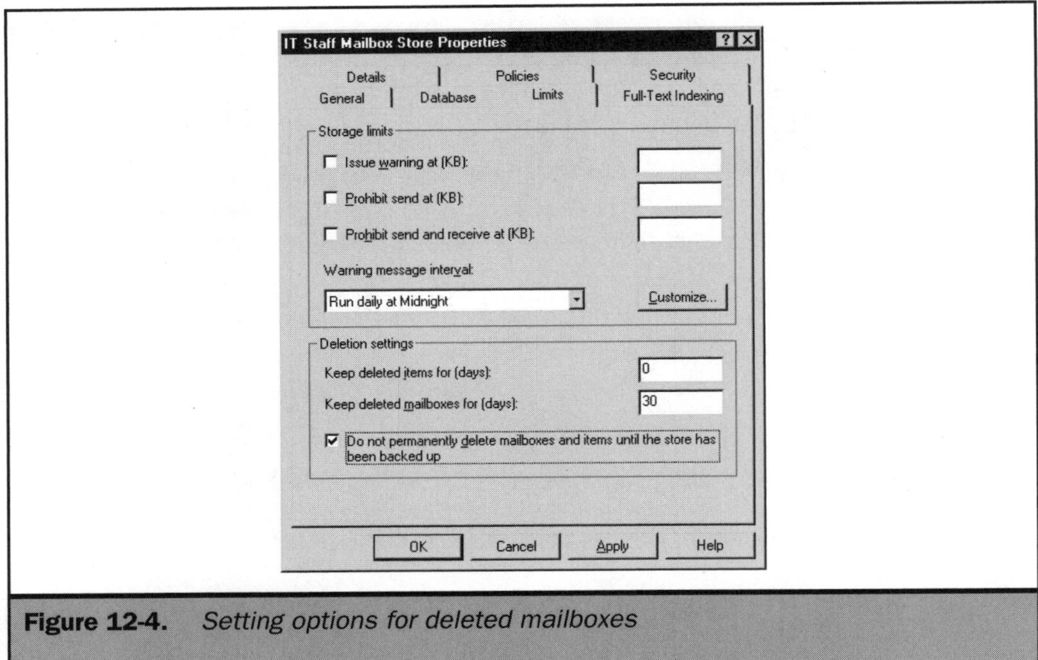

Figure 12-4. *Setting options for deleted mailboxes*

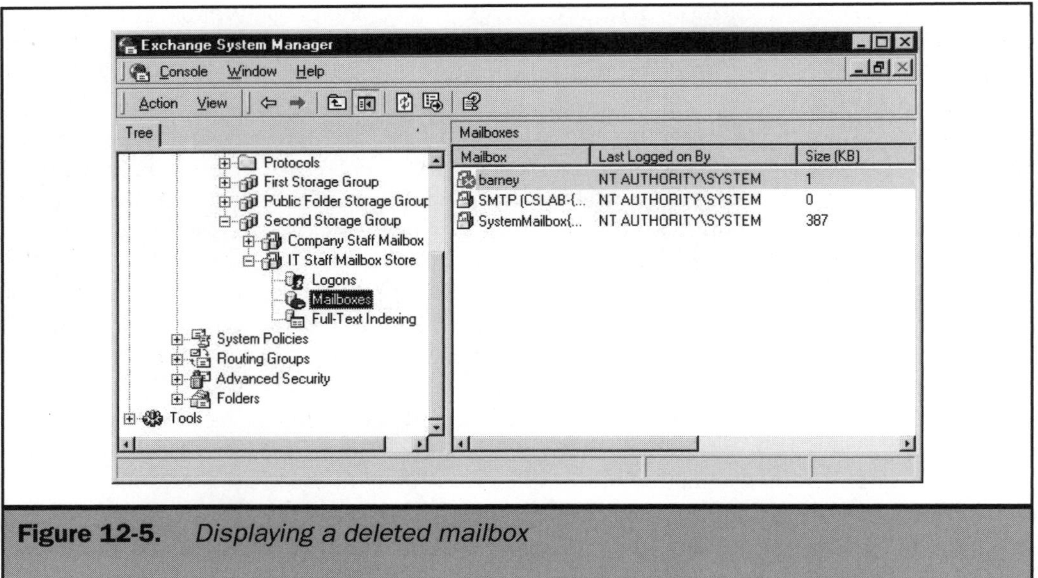

Figure 12-5. *Displaying a deleted mailbox*

Backup Applications

You have several choices when it comes to backing up Exchange 2000. Your first backup option is to use the Backup tool that comes with Windows 2000. Because it has some obvious shortcomings, such as not being able to perform mailbox-level backups, many administrators turn to third-party solutions. These solutions provide services that range from simple backup and restore, to complete disaster recovery backup and restore, to storage management. We'll look first at the native Windows 2000 Backup utility and show how to perform a simple backup and restore of Exchange 2000. Then we'll discuss some of the more commonly used third-party tools that back up Exchange 2000.

Windows 2000 Backup

The Windows 2000 Backup utility, shown in Figure 12-6, is shipped with Windows 2000 and allows you to back up your file system, as well as the System State (which includes Active Directory information) to a tape drive, or even to a file. When you install Exchange 2000, a DLL called ESEBCLI2.DLL is installed that makes the backup application Exchange-aware, enabling you to take online backups. In this section, we will cover how to perform an online backup of Exchange 2000.

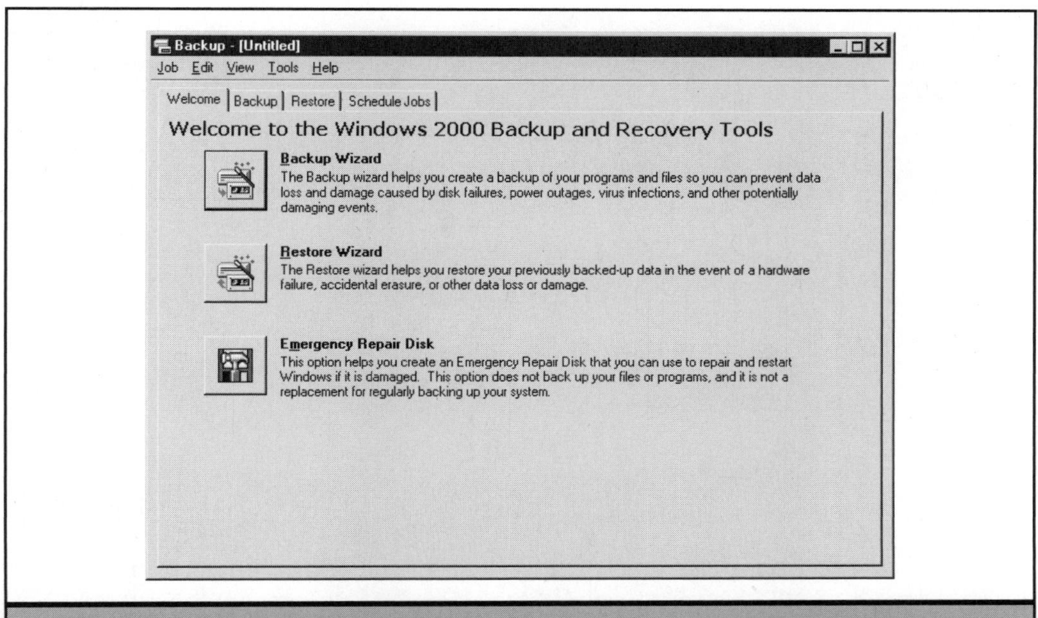

Figure 12-6. *The Windows 2000 Backup utility*

Backing Up Exchange

The first step in performing a backup is to select what you want backed up. When you select the Backup tab in the Backup utility, you can see all the file system drives, the System State, and Exchange-related selections, as shown in Figure 12-7. The two Exchange-related selections have different purposes. The Microsoft Exchange selection is for backing up stores on remote Exchange servers. You would most likely use this option to back up an Exchange server that is not part of the same organization as the backup server. If you double-click the Microsoft Exchange selection, you will be prompted for the name of the remote Exchange server, as shown in Figure 12-8, so that the remote server can be queried for a list of stores to back up.

The Microsoft Exchange Server selection, shown in Figure 12-9, is your starting point to navigate your Exchange environment's storage hierarchy. The hierarchy includes servers, storage groups, and stores. While you cannot make backup selections at the server level, you can select either individual stores or an entire storage group.

Don't forget to dismount the store(s) for an online backup, or stop the Exchange services for an offline backup.

After you have selected the data you want to back up, you need to specify a destination. The Backup Destination field, found at the bottom of the application

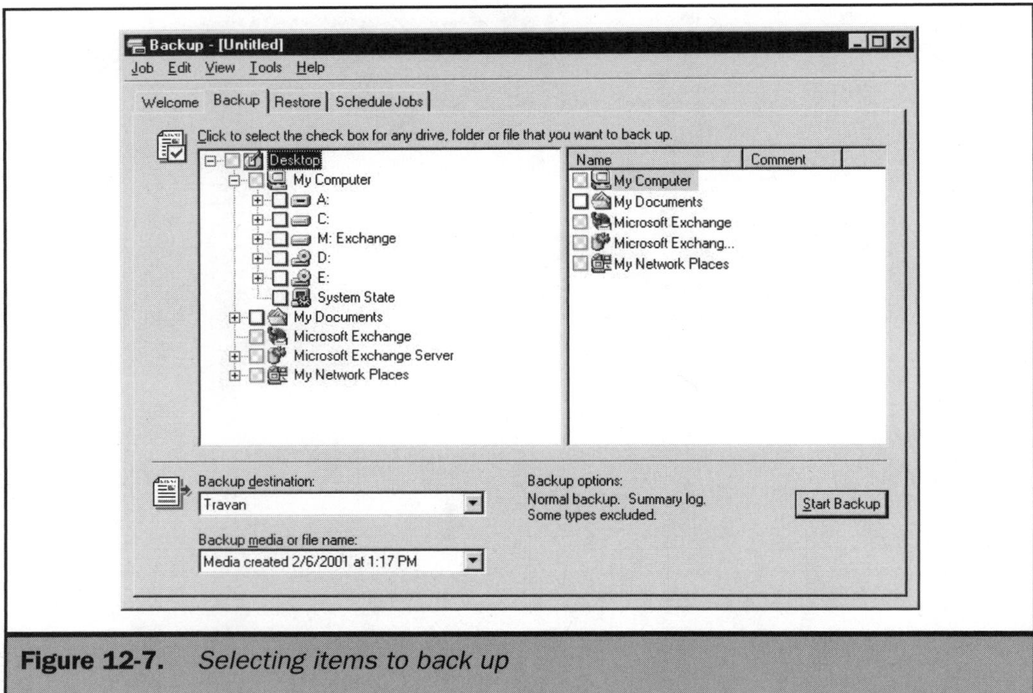

Figure 12-7. *Selecting items to back up*

Remote Store
Type the name of the server to query.
Server:
OK
Cancel
Browse...

Figure 12-8. *Connecting to a remote Exchange server*

window, allows you to back up to a file, tape, or any other supported medium. You also will need to select the type of backup. Make this choice by selecting Options from the Tools menu. The Backup Type properties page of the Options dialog box lists the five common backup types, as shown in Figure 12-10. When applying each of these types of online backups to Exchange, remember that Normal, Differential, and Incremental are the most commonly used.

Once you have completed your selections and are back on the Backup tab of the utility, clicking the Start Backup button at the bottom right will display the Backup Job Information dialog box, shown in Figure 12-11. In this dialog box, you will provide the description of the backup, for example, "Mailbox Store Full Backup 3/22/01." You also

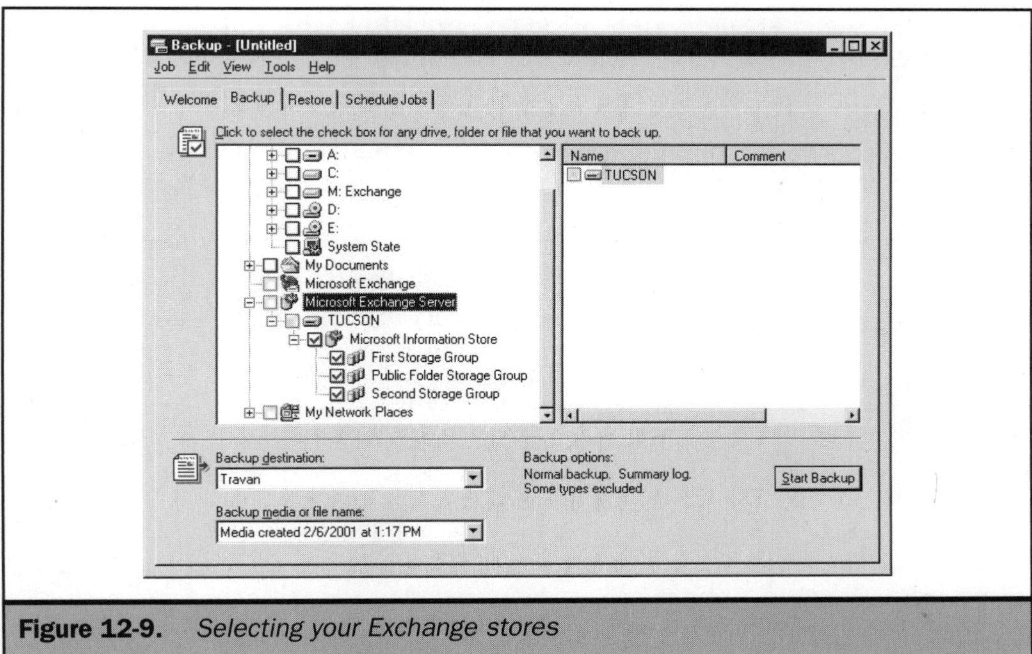

Figure 12-9. *Selecting your Exchange stores*

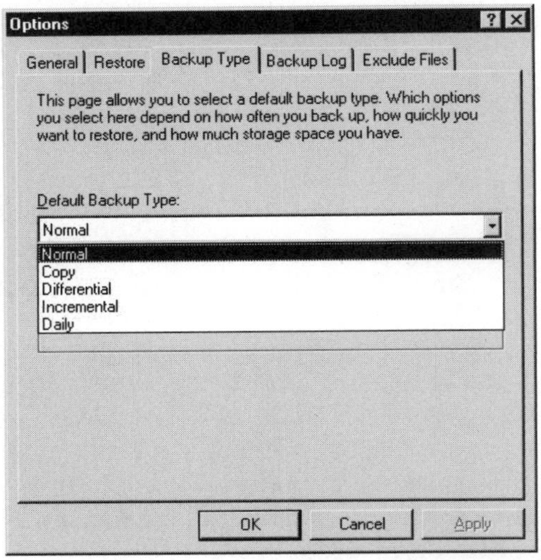

Figure 12-10. *Selecting the backup type*

can choose to have this backup job appended to previous jobs on the media, or to overwrite the media. Should you choose to overwrite the media, you can choose to restrict access to the media for restore use. This option protects against someone stealing a tape and restoring to an alternate server with the intent of reading the messages on the backed up store.

To set more advanced options, click the Advanced button. You can specify whether to verify the backed up data (ESE checks the data before it is written to tape, but the

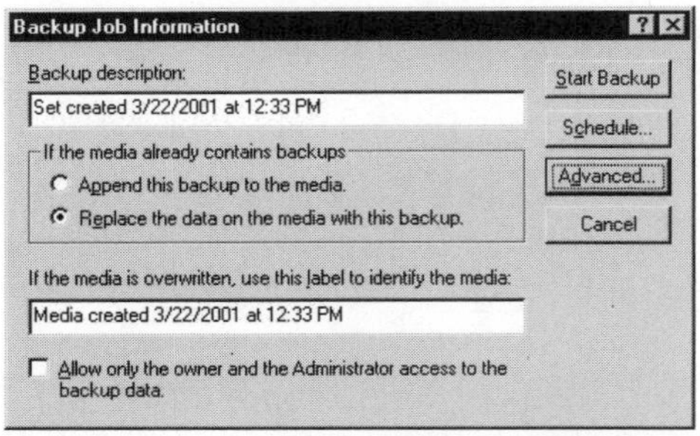

Figure 12-11. *Specifying the backup information*

tape itself could be bad). You can also override the default backup type (Normal, Differential, and so on) for this specific job.

Scheduling the Backup

Like the backup utility included with Windows NT 4.0, the version included with Windows 2000 (as well as the version included with Exchange 2000) supports scheduling the backups. However, unlike the Windows NT 4.0 backup utility, the Windows 2000 version has an interface into the Task Scheduler service. Click the Schedule button to specify the user account that should be used to run the backup, as shown in Figure 12-12, and be presented with the Scheduled Job Options dialog box, shown in Figure 12-13. Give the job a descriptive name and click the Properties button to specify a schedule.

The scheduler, shown in Figure 12-14, is quite flexible. You can select the backup to occur daily, weekly, monthly, and at other repeated intervals. You can also schedule multiple backups by checking the Show Multiple Schedules checkbox. This allows you to add multiple instances without each instance occurring at a particular time of a particular day repeating at a consistent interval (e.g., every Thursday at 11 P.M.). You can also click the Advanced button to specify that the task is repeated multiple times within a given timeframe. For example, you can specify start and ending dates, or a number of times to repeat the task.

Restoring Exchange

To begin a restore within the Windows 2000 Backup utility, choose the Restore tab. A catalog listing shows what backups have been performed, as shown in Figure 12-15. Choose the backup session you wish to restore, and then click the Start Restore button.

Be careful when selecting a session to restore. As shown in Figure 12-15, you can choose only the Logs or only the Databases. However, restoring an incomplete session by only selecting one or the other can have adverse consequences. You should always restore a complete session unless a specific need exists.

Figure 12-12. *Providing the account credentials for a scheduled backup*

Scheduled Job Options
Schedule data | Backup details
Job name: Full Backup of Mailbox Store | Delete
Start Date: Thursday, March 22, 2001 at 1:08 PM
Properties...
OK | Cancel

Figure 12-13. *Specifying the scheduled job options*

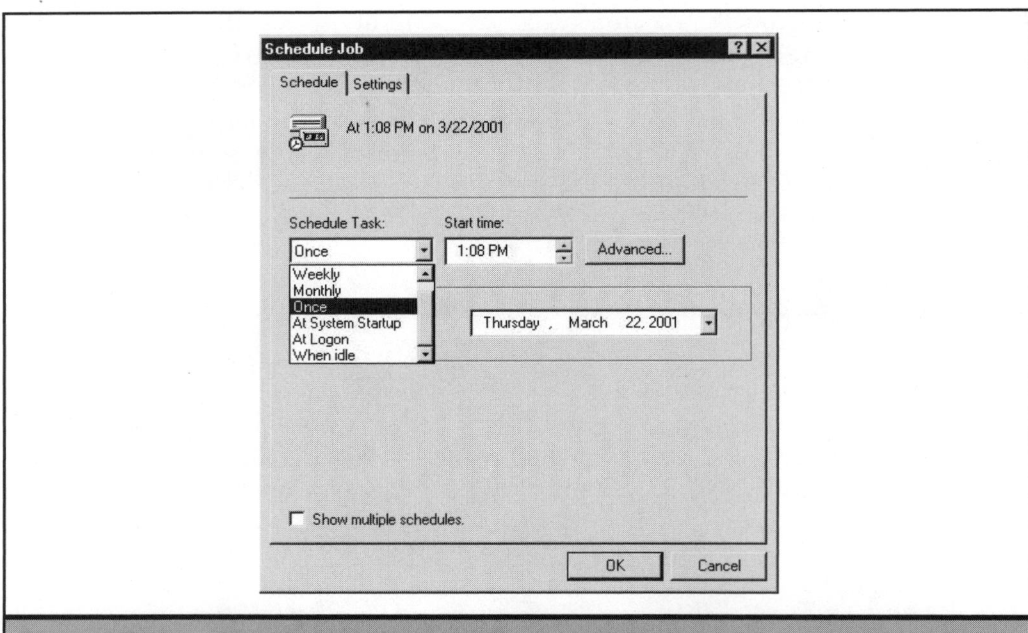

Figure 12-14. *Choosing the Schedule Task options*

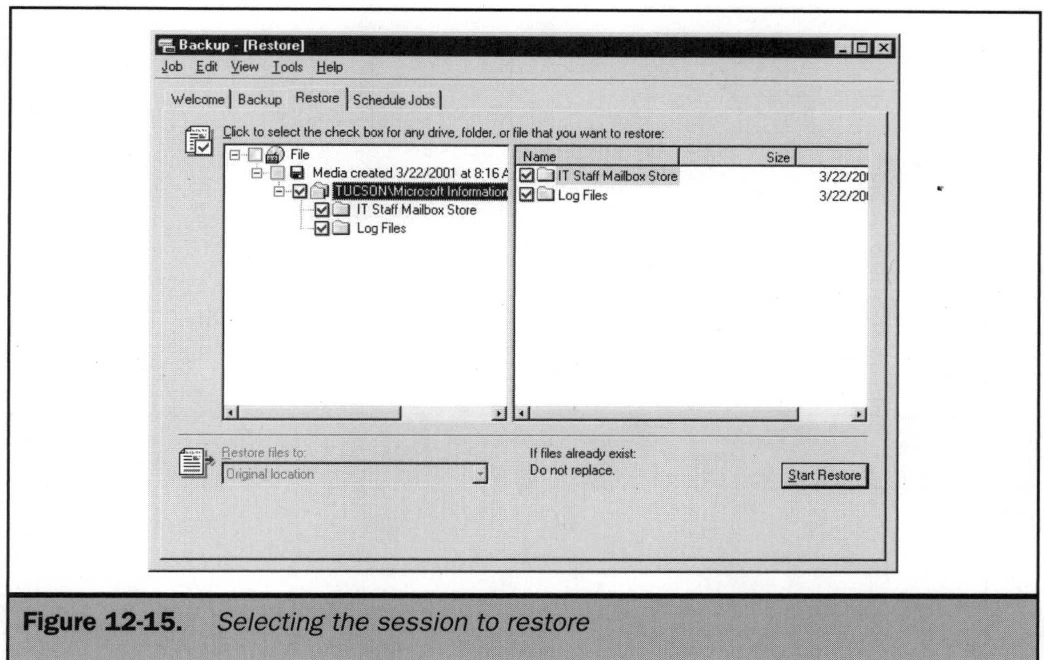

Figure 12-15. *Selecting the session to restore*

If you are restoring a store, the Restoring Database Store dialog box, shown in Figure 12-16, will appear. Here you can specify an alternate server to restore to (discussed later in the chapter), as well as the temporary location for your transaction logs and patch file. Check the Last Backup Set checkbox only if this is the last restore in the process and you plan to mount the database upon a successful restore. Once you click OK, the restore will begin.

For more information on the temporary location for logs and patch files, as well as the Last Backup Set checkbox, see "Online Restores," presented earlier in this chapter.

Third-Party Backup Applications

You may be impressed with the Backup utility that comes with Windows 2000. It gets the basic job done. But you may want to take advantage of a number of advanced features that many third-party backup applications offer. The most commonly used products include Vertias' BackupExec and Computer Associates' ArcServe. Each product has an Exchange agent specifically for online backups and restores. Third-party tools include the following features and benefits:

- Faster backups and restores
- Backup of storage group, store, or mailbox

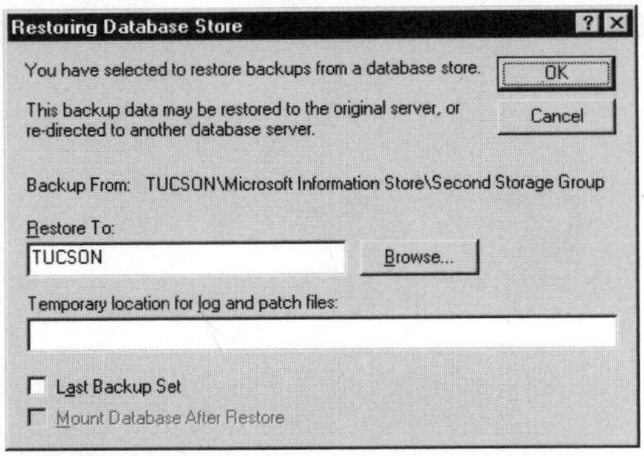

Figure 12-16. *Choosing database store restore options*

- Selective restore, down to the individual message level
- An "accelerator" agent to speed up backups of remote Exchange servers
- Disaster recovery wizard for complete recovery of Exchange servers
- Job notification via e-mail, broadcast, pager, and so on
- Backup of the Site Replication Service and Key Management Service
- Support for clustered Exchange environments
- Support for storage area networks (SANs)

Disaster Recovery

Disaster recovery of your Exchange server usually refers to a situation in which your Exchange server is no longer functional. We're talking about something more serious than corrupt stores or transaction logs; we mean a server that has experienced a hardware failure of some kind. In this section, we will assume that you have completely lost your Exchange server and need to restore your server to its original state. We'll also assume that your Exchange server is not a domain controller, but is only a member server running Exchange. Should you ever encounter a similar or less serious situation, you can use this example to implement the disaster recovery process as applicable.

Pre-Flight Checklist

Before you can begin a disaster recovery of Exchange, you must have the following files and backups for the recovery to be a success:

- **Windows 2000 and Exchange 2000 installation files** This includes the original CDs, service packs, patches, and QFE hotfixes.
- **System drive backups** A full backup of all logical drives containing vital information.
- **System State backups** A backup of the System State, which includes data that is not included in a file system backup. This information includes the registry, the IIS metabase, Active Directory (in the case of a domain controller), and other critical system data.
- **Exchange stores** Online backups of all store databases and transaction logs.
- **A server object in Active Directory** The recovery process will not work without the server object in AD that represents the dead Exchange server. If this is missing, a restore of a previous copy of AD is in order.

Installing Windows 2000

The key word to remember when installing Windows 2000 is "same." As you read through the installation requirements, notice the use of the word over and over again. The point to be driven home is that the recovery server needs to be an exact copy of the original server. The requirements are as follows:

- **Drive configuration** The same logical hard drive configuration needs to be maintained. For example, if the original server had the transaction logs on the D drive and the store databases on the E drive, but you install the recovery server with a single large C drive, the paths will not match when it comes time to restore the databases and logs. Configure RAID to have the same logical drives, or at least partition the disk on the recovery server to have the same logical drive structure. The amount of disk space on each logical drive does not have to match the original server, but it needs to be large enough to accommodate any data being restored to it.
- **OS version** Install Windows 2000 as a stand-alone server using the same version of Windows 2000 (Server, Advanced Server).
- **Server name** The server should be installed using the same name as the original server.
- **Server components** All the same components and subcomponents should be selected.
- **Domain membership** The server should not be made a part of the domain. The membership within the domain will be re-established with the restore of the System State data.
- **OS updates** You should reapply all the same service packs, patches, security updates, and hotfixes as the original server.

Restoring the System Drive

Application data should be restored to the original location. This could include user shares, service data (such as DHCP or WINS databases), or any other application data that may have existed on the Exchange server.

Restoring the System State

The System State contains, among other things, a copy of the registry. This is a vital piece of the recovery process. The registry contains information about the server's membership in the domain and returns the server's security ID (SID) to the one stored in AD. Upon reboot, the server will rejoin the domain.

Note *The registry also contains information about the services that run on the Exchange server. When you reboot after restoring the System State, you will see error messages stating that services failed to start. This is to be expected. The server thinks it has the Exchange services, and other related services, already installed. So when the server reboots, it will attempt to start those services and will, of course, fail to do so.*

Installing Exchange 2000 in Disaster Recovery Mode

It is important to note that when you install Exchange 2000 in disaster recovery mode, you are not going to perform a standard installation. If you were to do so, Exchange would attempt to create a new Exchange environment in AD. This is not necessary, as AD already contains configuration data for the Exchange organization. All that is missing is the server that uses this information. Installing Exchange 2000 in Disaster Recovery mode instructs Exchange 2000 to only install and copy all the necessary application files, leaving the AD configuration intact and unchanged.

Begin the installation by running Setup using the */DisasterRecovery* switch. All components to be installed are listed with the Disaster Recovery Action, as shown in Figure 12-17. If a component that should be installed, such as the Key Management Service, is not selected, select it manually with the Disaster Recovery Action chosen. Once the proper components are selected, click Next.

Once the Setup process completes the disaster recovery installation of Exchange 2000, you will be prompted to restore your databases and restart. Prior to restarting, restore your databases. Once the databases have been restored, if you do not have any other services that need to be restored, such as the Key Management Service, you can restart your server.

Restoring Service Databases

If you are running the KMS or SRS on the Exchange server being recovered, you will also need to restore their databases. The System State restore put back the registry

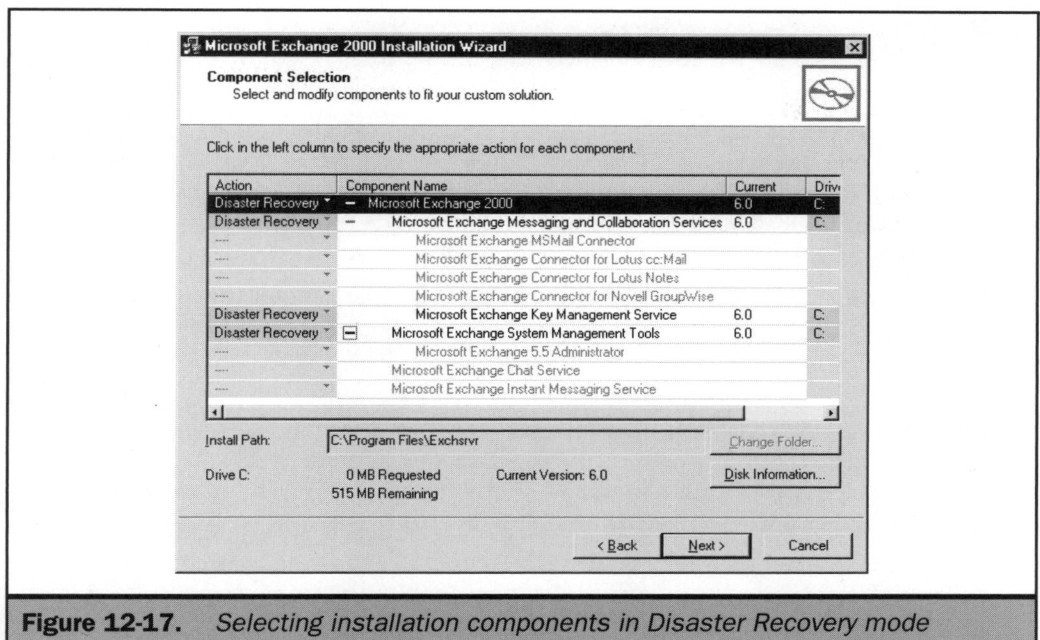

Figure 12-17. *Selecting installation components in Disaster Recovery mode*

entries, so Windows 2000 knows that the services exist. In the case of KMS, install the service files with the Disaster Recovery mode installation of Exchange 2000 (assuming you selected the service to be installed). Restore the KMS database files to their original location. In the case of SRS, install the Active Directory Connector and restore the SRS database files to their original location.

Note *If you are recovering one node of an Exchange 2000 cluster, see Chapter 20, "Clustering Exchange 2000 Server."*

Your disaster recovery of an Exchange 2000 Server is complete.

Best Practices

So much goes into understanding the backing up and restoring of Exchange that some best practices should be outlined to act as a guide for a successful backup and recovery environment. This section lists some of the more common practices.

- *Establish a comprehensive backup plan.* This plan should include the entire server and not only the store databases and logs.

- *Monitor backups.* If your backup solution supports notifications, use them to send you e-mails for both job successes and failures. If you do not receive a notification, you'll know immediately that something is wrong.
- *Verify backups.* Most backup solutions allow you to validate the backup by comparing a portion of the backup data to the original data on disk. Also use backup logs to verify job successes. For example, some third-party backup solutions indicate a backup job as failed if a single file was not backed up. Checking the backup logs can tell you whether a job was truly a failure or not.
- *Test backups.* More than one of our clients has a spare server that is used for regular Exchange 2000 restores. This helps verify the capability to recover from corrupt databases or server failures. If your budget permits a spare server, it is highly recommended.
- *Plan for disaster.* Devise a disaster recovery plan. It can include documentation on the installation process, copies of all needed software, information on database and application locations on the file system, and anything else you may need in order to have a successful recovery.
- *Use standardized hardware.* Your restore hardware must be compatible with production hardware. If you deploy new backup hardware in production, make sure that your recovery server has compatible equipment.
- *Rotate tapes frequently.* If you use magnetic tape, or any media with a limited life span, rotate the media so that they do not become overused. The last thing you want to encounter during any restore process is a bad tape or bad backup media. You should also use cleaning tapes regularly.

Summary

Hopefully, just from looking at what goes into a successful disaster recovery, you can see the need for being proactive and backing up a variety of data. In this chapter, we covered the various data sources that need to be backed up and the various types of backups you can perform with Exchange—offline as well as online. Restores got as much attention in this chapter as backups did. We explained how to restore everything from a single store, to alternate servers, to a complete disaster recovery.

In the next chapter, we'll look at the Exchange clients that are supported and how to configure them for use with Exchange 2000.

The Complete Reference

Part III

Exchange 2000 Server Collaboration

Chapter 13

Exchange 2000 Clients

Almost this entire book has focused on Exchange 2000 Server. However, it is important to discuss the various clients that are supported by Exchange 2000. This chapter will focus on four basic areas: legacy clients, existing clients, future clients, and Internet clients. You're probably thinking, "I didn't know there were so many." It is true: Quite a few clients are available for Exchange 2000. And that is a good thing. It means that you are not limited to just one or two client choices.

This chapter will cover the various clients you can use to connect to Exchange 2000. It will also go over the steps necessary to properly configure your Outlook 2000 clients to connect to Exchange 2000. However, because the focus of this book is Exchange 2000, we will not cover Outlook 2000 beyond its connectivity to and use with Exchange 2000.

Legacy Clients

The term *legacy client*, in our case, refers to viable Exchange clients that are no longer the most recent revision of a particular piece of software. Or perhaps they have been replaced with a newer, more feature-rich software product. This section will focus on three Exchange Messaging Application Programming Interface (MAPI) clients:

- Exchange 5.0 Client
- Outlook 97
- Outlook 98

These clients are considered to be legacy clients, as they have been replaced by Outlook 2000, which is soon to be replaced by Outlook 2002. All three clients are compatible with Exchange 2000; however, as you will see in Table 13-1, the functionality and compatibility with today's messaging standards dwindles as you use older clients.

The only reason you may want to install any of these clients or keep one that is already installed is for their lower minimum recommendations for memory and processor speed. You may also want to install a lower-level client like the original Exchange Client on the Exchange 2000 Server because of documented incompatibilities between versions of Outlook and Exchange 2000 Server running on the same computer. However, in order to take full advantage of any features Exchange 2000 has, we recommend that you use the latest version of Outlook.

Exchange Client

The Exchange Client was bundled with the first version of Exchange. It was the preferred client for Exchange until the release of Outlook 97. As a MAPI client, it has the capability to access Exchange mailboxes and public folders, but it does not have calendaring functionality. At the time of release, Microsoft's Schedule+ product was still in use for calendaring and was used in conjunction with the Exchange Client to provide messaging and calendaring functionality.

Client	Versions	Messaging	Calendaring	Internet Standards Supported
Exchange Client	32-bit Windows, 16-bit Windows, MS-DOS, and Macintosh	Yes	No (Schedule+ was used)	None
Outlook 97	32-bit Windows, 16-bit Windows, and Macintosh	Yes	Yes	POP3 and SMTP
Outlook 98	32-bit Windows, 16-bit Windows, and Macintosh	Yes	Yes	POP3, IMAP4, NNTP, LDAP, SMTP, S/MIME, vCalendar, vCard, and iCalendar

Table 13-1. *Legacy Client Comparison*

Outlook 97

With the release of Exchange 5.5 came a new exciting Exchange client: Outlook 97. It combined the functions of the previous Exchange client and Schedule+ into one application, supporting the use of Exchange's messaging and scheduling functions. In addition, it supported what is now considered a standard feature of Outlook: information services. These services act on an "add-in" basis in which you can add support for multiple messaging systems, directory services, and storage locations. In addition, Outlook 97 includes personal information manager (PIM) capabilities to store contacts, appointments, tasks, and notes.

Outlook 98

Outlook 98 represented Microsoft's dedication to the use of its Outlook product not only for Exchange and other mainstream messaging systems, but also to standardized Internet protocols. The number of Internet protocols increased dramatically from just the Simple Mail Transfer Protocol (SMTP) and Post Office Protocol v3 (POP3) that Outlook 97 had. Outlook 98 also included support for the Internet Message Access Protocol v4 (IMAP4), Secure Multipurpose Internet Mail Extensions (S/MIME), Network News Transfer Protocol (NNTP), and Lightweight Directory Access Protocol

(LDAP) standards, as well as vCards, vCalendar, and iCalendar standards for sending virtual business cards and meeting requests across the Internet.

Existing Client: Outlook 2000

The preferred client for Exchange 2000 is Outlook 2000. Very close to the print date of this book will be the release of Outlook 2002. This chapter will focus mainly on the functionality of Outlook 2000 and cover some of the features you should expect from Outlook 2002 as it pertains to Exchange.

Outlook 2000 was released in 1998 while Exchange 5.5 was still the premier messaging system from Microsoft. It enhanced the user experience with a myriad of new features and enhancements. Some of the more noticeable new features included:

- Personalized toolbars and menus
- Enhanced Outlook Setup Wizard
- Capability to save calendars as HTML
- Direct booking of mailboxes as resources
- Capability to schedule NetShow meetings
- Personal distribution lists stored in Contacts
- Auto-merge of duplicate contact information
- Capability to link folders to Web pages

Outlook 2000 Functionality

Outlook 2000, shown in Figure 13-1, has quite a number of its own functions, without Exchange 2000. Many of these functions are enhanced by the addition of Exchange 2000:

- **Messaging** Outlook supports a number of messaging systems, including Exchange, cc:Mail, MS Mail, and POP3/IMAP4 mail.
- **Calendaring** Besides basic scheduling of an appointment with a start and end time and date, personal scheduling capabilities in Outlook include re-occurring appointments, online meetings via NetMeeting and NetShow, and attendee invitation (via e-mail).
- **Contact Management** Outlook stores many different types of information about a contact, including basic address and phone information, spouse's name, birthdays, a journal of all activities with that client, and storage of digital IDs to send encrypted messages to that contact.
- **Journaling** Outlook can keep track of every phone call, fax, e-mail, and document that involves a particular contact.
- **Notes** Outlook gives you a place to store all the information that doesn't exactly fit in a contact record, calendar item, or e-mail message.

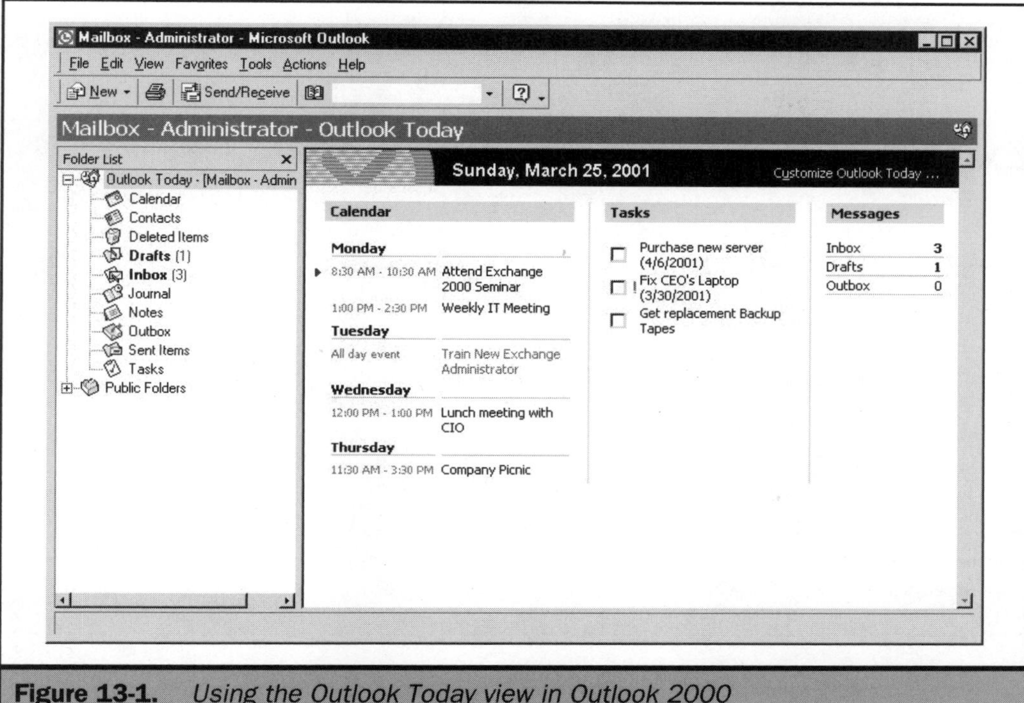

Figure 13-1. *Using the Outlook Today view in Outlook 2000*

- **Tasks** Tasks can be created and assigned along with a due date and the capability to provide status, billing, and hours worked information.
- **Outlook Today** Outlook gives you a summary of the pending items on your calendar, the tasks you have to accomplish, and the e-mail statistics, all of which is customizable in the Outlook Today view.

Configuring Outlook for Exchange 2000

When you first start Outlook 2000 after installation, the Outlook 2000 Startup application loads to finish the configuration of Outlook on your computer. You are prompted to import messages, address books, and settings from any previous e-mail applications, such as Outlook Express or the Microsoft Exchange client, as shown in Figure 13-2. If you are not migrating data from another application, choose None Of The Above and click Next.

Next, you are prompted to choose one of three e-mail services, as shown in Figure 13-3. These services will determine what functionality Outlook 2000 will have in addition to the standard messaging, calendaring, contacts, journaling, task, and note capabilities. The service you choose will depend on your messaging needs.

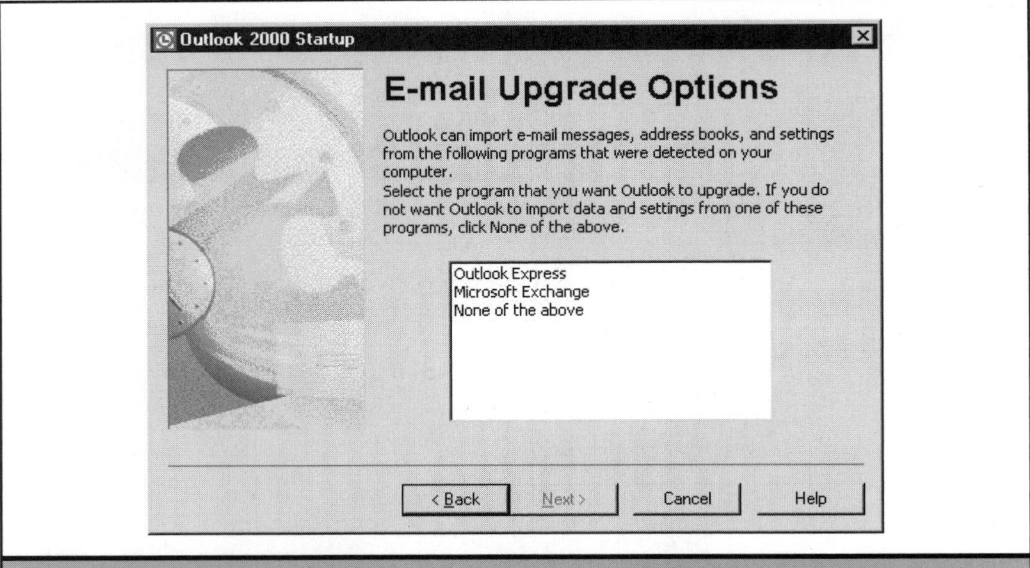

Figure 13-2. *Importing data and settings from another e-mail application*

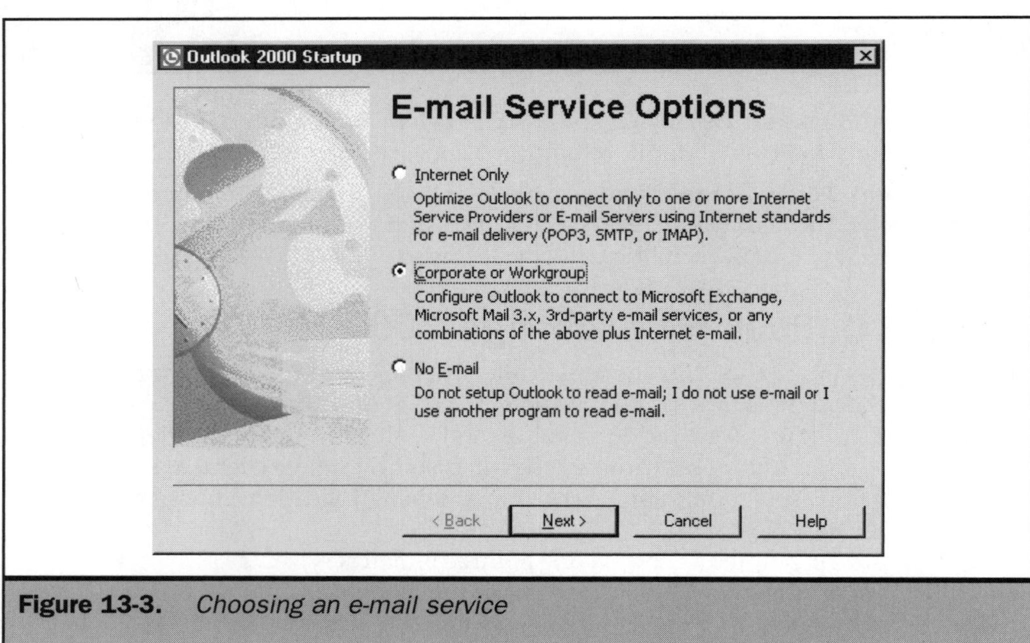

Figure 13-3. *Choosing an e-mail service*

No E-Mail

Choosing the No E-Mail service option denotes that you wish to use Outlook 2000 as a stand-alone personal information manager (PIM). Technically, the No E-Mail option supports POP3 and IMAP 4 messaging, but no messaging is configured by default. Because no messaging system is configured, there needs to be a place to store your PIM information. By default, a personal store file (.PST) is created for storage.

Internet Only

Choosing the Internet Only option means that you will use Outlook 2000 to act as a PIM, and at least one e-mail account will be set up using either POP3 or IMAP4 for message retrieval and SMTP for message transmission. Messages and other PIM information are stored in a .PST file. This option provides the same functionality as the No E-Mail option, with the exception that an e-mail account is initially set up.

Corporate or Workgroup

Choose this option if you are connecting to a messaging system, such as Exchange 2000, across a local area network (LAN). You may still need to use a .PST file for personal information storage if the messaging system you connect to does not have its own storage. For example, in the case of Outlook connecting to Exchange 2000, because your Exchange mailbox can store all of your data (messages, contacts, calendar, and so on), there is no initial need to have a local .PST file. You can add the use of a .PST file if you wish.

Selecting one of the three preceding service options will determine what happens next. Assuming you are going to use Exchange 2000, you would select the Corporate or Workgroup option and click Next. Outlook starts and the Outlook Setup Wizard starts, as shown in Figure 13-4, so you can add the information services you wish to use.

Although you can use this wizard to walk you through setting up Outlook to use Exchange 2000, we will use the Manually Configure Information Services option in order to show you all the options available to you. Selecting the manual option and clicking Next prompts you to provide a profile name. An Outlook profile is a collection of information services. Outlook allows you to utilize multiple profiles so that you can start Outlook using a variety of configurations. For example, you may have one configuration to use Exchange and another configuration that accesses mail from a POP3 account and stores it in a local .PST file. The profile name should be descriptive, such as "Corporate Exchange Settings" or "Personal Internet Mail."

The properties dialog box for the profile shows up next, as shown in Figure 13-5. On the Services properties page, click the Add button to add an information service, as shown in Figure 13-6. Table 13-2 lists the default information services and the functionality they provide.

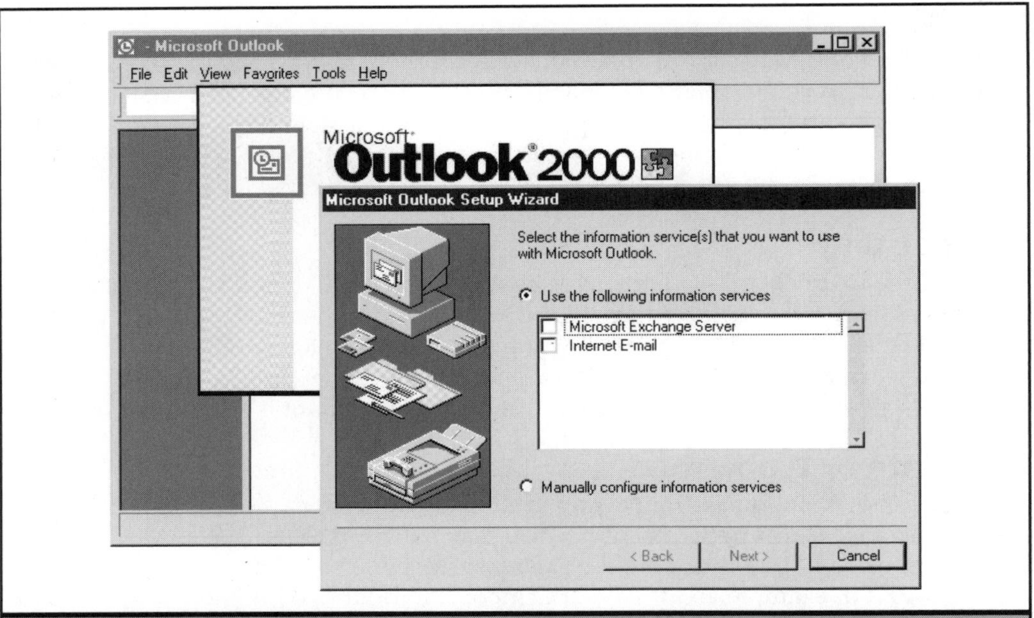

Figure 13-4. *Configuring the information services that Outlook 2000 will use*

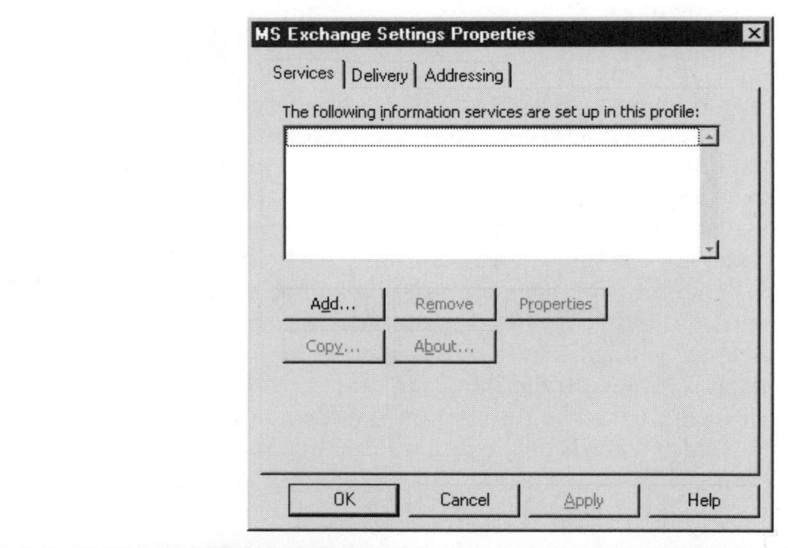

Figure 13-5. *Adding information services to your Outlook profile*

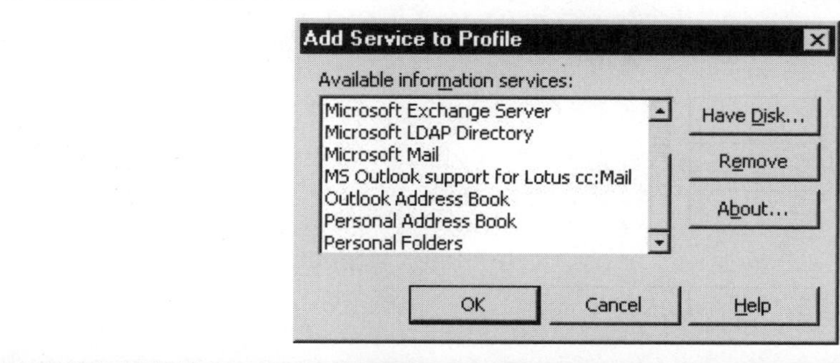

Figure 13-6. *Selecting an information service*

Information Service	Description
Fax Mail Transport	Use Microsoft Fax to send faxes from e-mail.
Internet E-Mail	Use a POP3 or IMAP4 account on the Internet. (IMAP4 is not available in Corporate/Workgroup mode.)
Microsoft Exchange Server	Allows Exchange messaging and collaboration with MAPI.
Microsoft LDAP Directory	Use an LDAP provider for directory lookups.
Microsoft Mail	Installs the MS Mail messaging client.
MS Outlook support for Lotus cc:Mail	Installs the cc:Mail messaging client.
Outlook Address Book	Uses Contacts folder within Outlook as an address book.
Personal Address Book	Uses a Personal address book (.PAB) file as an address book.
Personal Folders	Uses a Personal store (.PST) file for data storage of Outlook items.

Table 13-2. *Outlook 2000 Information Services*

In order to take advantage of all the messaging and collaboration features in Microsoft Exchange 2000, you only need to use the Microsoft Exchange Server information service.

Selecting Microsoft Exchange Server as your information service brings up the properties dialog box shown in Figure 13-7. Type in the name of the Exchange server and the name of the mailbox, and then click Check Name. This will cause the client machine to contact the Exchange server and verify that the mailbox exists on that server. Once the Exchange server and mailbox names have been matched with an actual mailbox, the names will be underlined and the Check Name button will be grayed out.

If you need to access a mailbox using an alternate set of user logon credentials, on the Advanced property page of the Microsoft Exchange Server properties, set the Logon Network Security to None. When you start Outlook, any existing credentials you have provided will be ignored and you will be prompted to log on to Active Directory. These credentials are only used to access a mailbox within Outlook.

Once the mailbox and Exchange server are configured, click OK twice. Your profile is now configured for Outlook to use Exchange 2000 Server.

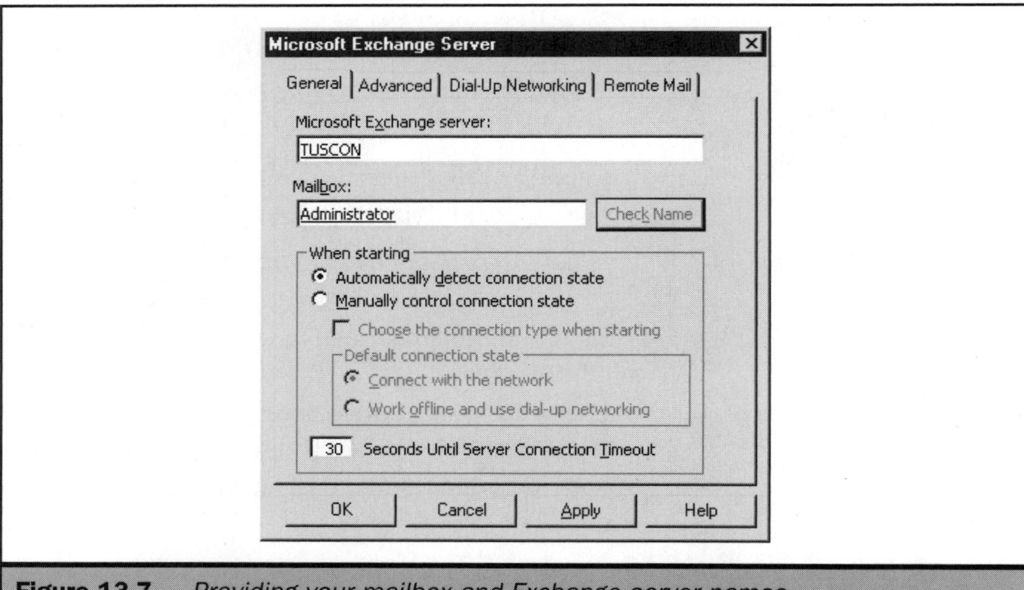

Figure 13-7. *Providing your mailbox and Exchange server names*

Future Clients: Outlook 2002

The newest client on the block is Outlook 2002, which is part of Office XP. Shown in Figure 13-8, Outlook 2002 still maintains the familiar Outlook interface, but noticeable differences begin to stand out as you look at and play with the interface. Enhancements in every aspect of Outlook can be found. We'll cover a few specific enhancement areas: messaging, calendaring and scheduling, and security, as well as one miscellaneous enhancement worth noting for Exchange users: the Mailbox Cleanup utility.

Messaging Enhancements

Outlook 2002 includes the following messaging enhancements: single e-mail account mode, the Profile Creation Wizard, friendly names, and autocorrect.

Single E-Mail Account Mode

With Outlook 2002, you no longer need to set up Outlook to run in Internet Only or Corporate and Workgroup modes. Although multiple profiles are still supported, you can now create multiple e-mail account types (Exchange, POP3, IMAP4, HTTP such as Hotmail, or other third-party types) in a single profile. If you set up a single profile with multiple e-mail accounts, you have the option of specifying which e-mail address a message should be sent from. Figure 13-9 shows the use of the Accounts button to select the account the message should be sent from.

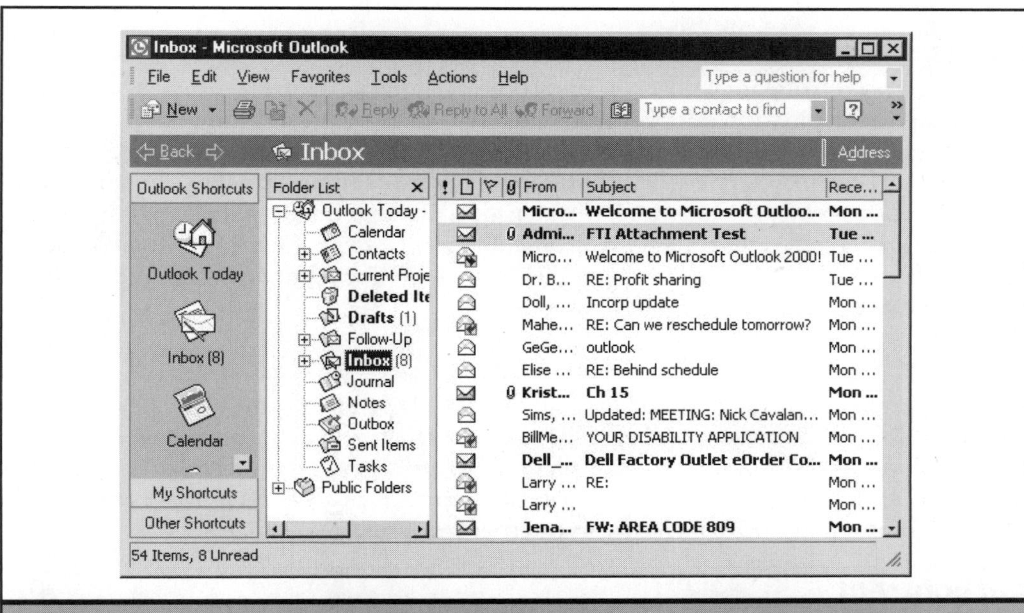

Figure 13-8. *Viewing the Inbox using Outlook XP*

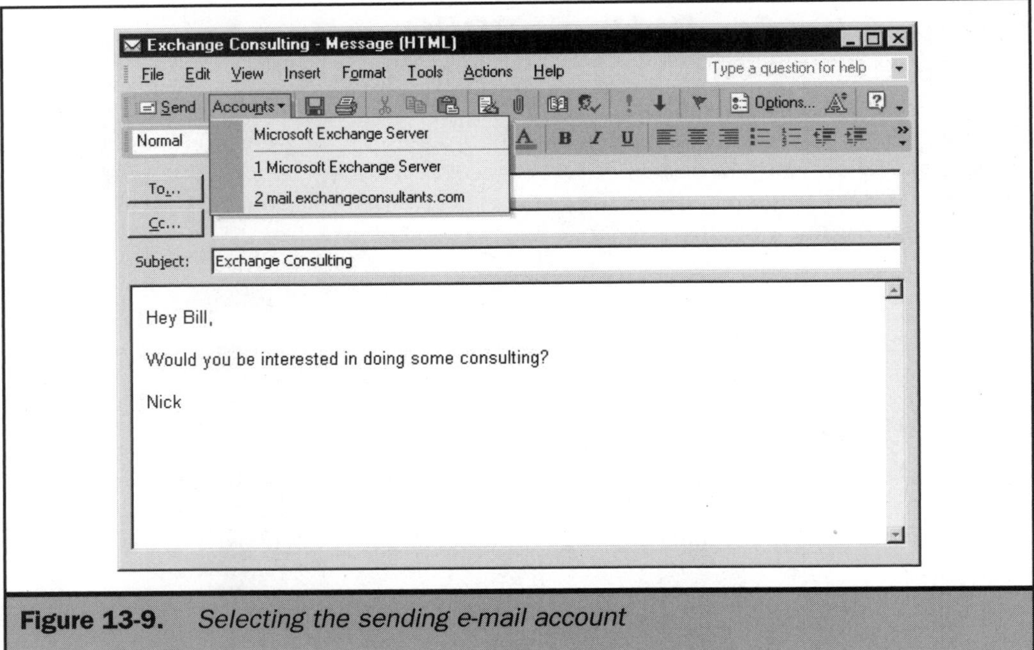

Figure 13-9. *Selecting the sending e-mail account*

Profile Creation Wizard

The wizard used to create your Outlook profiles, shown in Figure 13-10, has been redesigned to simplify the options needed to create a basic profile, while organizing the advanced options for easy access. The wizard breaks up the profile configuration into accounts and directory services. In addition, the wizard requires authentication in order to change your settings. In Figure 13-10, the user is prompted for logon credentials each time he or she accesses their Outlook profile. In previous versions, this authentication requirement was limited to accessing the Exchange mailbox, but now it includes making changes to the profile.

Friendly Names

The Contact page now includes a Display As field, shown in Figure 13-11. You can use this "friendly name" instead of the e-mail address when you compose a new message. Also, Outlook 2002 offers an auto-completion feature for typing in recipient names in the To, Cc, and Bcc fields of a message, as shown in Figure 13-12. This works much like the auto-completion of URLs feature in Internet Explorer.

Autocorrect

Even if Microsoft Word is not configured as your e-mail editor, Outlook 2002 automatically corrects typos, misspelled words, and incorrect capitalization.

E-mail Accounts

E-mail Accounts
You can select an account and change its settings or remove it.

Outlook processes e-mail for these accounts in the following order:

Name	Type
Microsoft Exchange Server	Exchange (Default)

Change...
Add...
Remove

Enter Password
User Name: sschnoll
Password:
Domain Name: comspherelab
OK Cancel Change Password...

Deliver new e-mail to the following location:

< Back Finish Cancel

Figure 13-10. *Setting up an e-mail account*

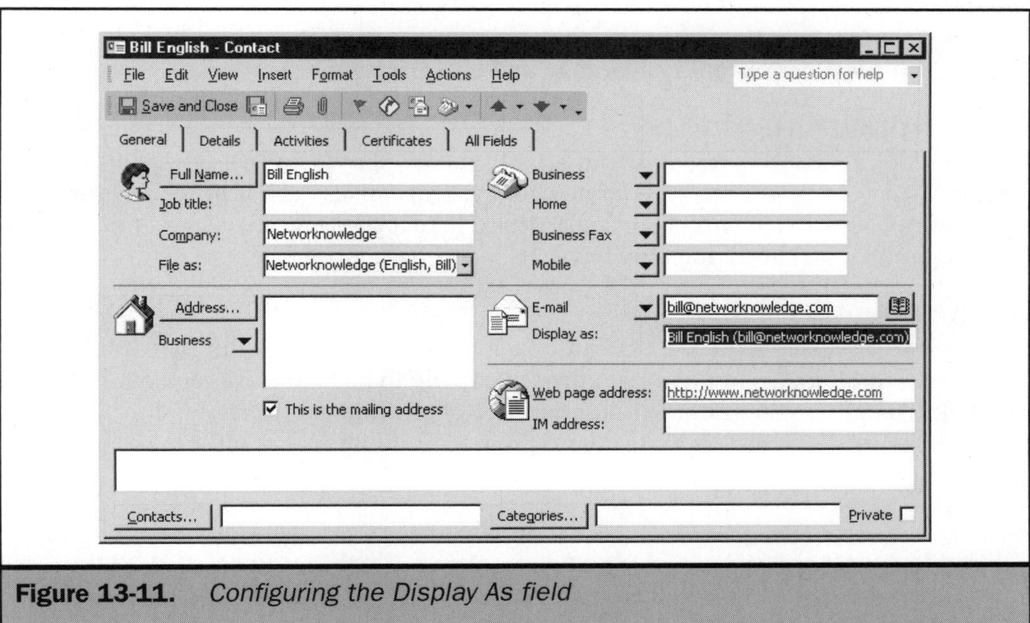

Figure 13-11. *Configuring the Display As field*

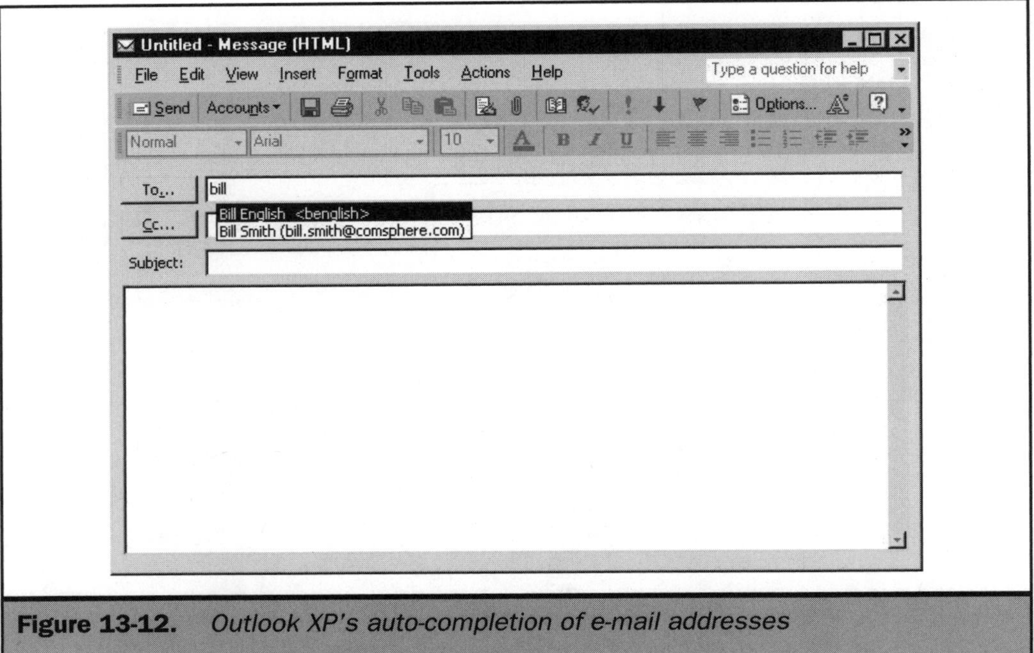

Figure 13-12. *Outlook XP's auto-completion of e-mail addresses*

Calendaring and Scheduling Enhancements

Outlook 2002 includes the following calendaring and scheduling enhancements: color appointments, a Dismiss All option, and group schedules.

Color Appointments

With Outlook 2002, you can color your appointments, shown on the right pane in Figure 13-13, using one of ten predefined colors. You can also change the label for each color to associate it with a particular task, client, importance level, or any other organizational need you may have.

Single Dismiss All

How many times have you opened Outlook and watched a number of schedule reminders simultaneously pop up on the screen only to have to close each one? Outlook 2002 gives you multiple reminders in a single dialog box, shown in Figure 13-14, and allows you to dismiss reminders individually or all at once.

Group Schedules

We have had so many requests from clients for the capability to see the calendar for a group of individuals working on a project together or in the same department. Outlook 2002 offers that solution. Figure 13-15 shows a group calendar created using the Schedules button on the toolbar. Multiple group schedules can be created and managed.

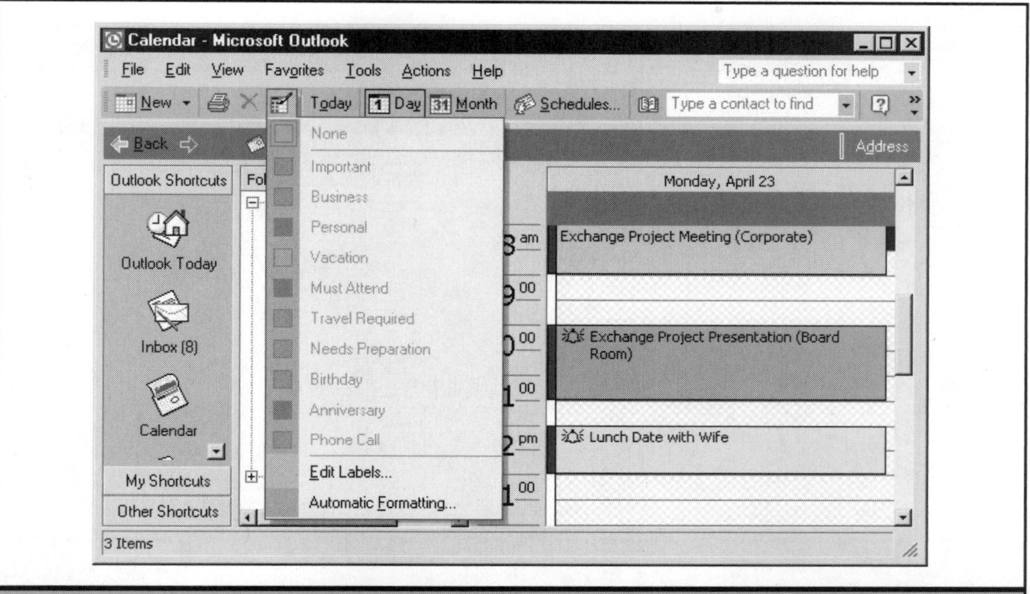

Figure 13-13. *Differentiating appointment types with customizable colors*

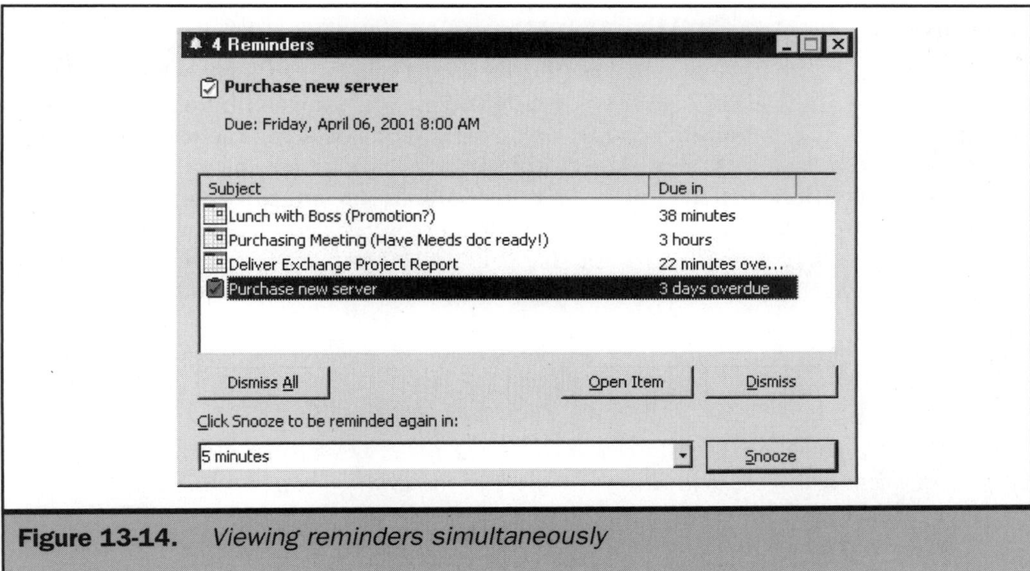

Figure 13-14. *Viewing reminders simultaneously*

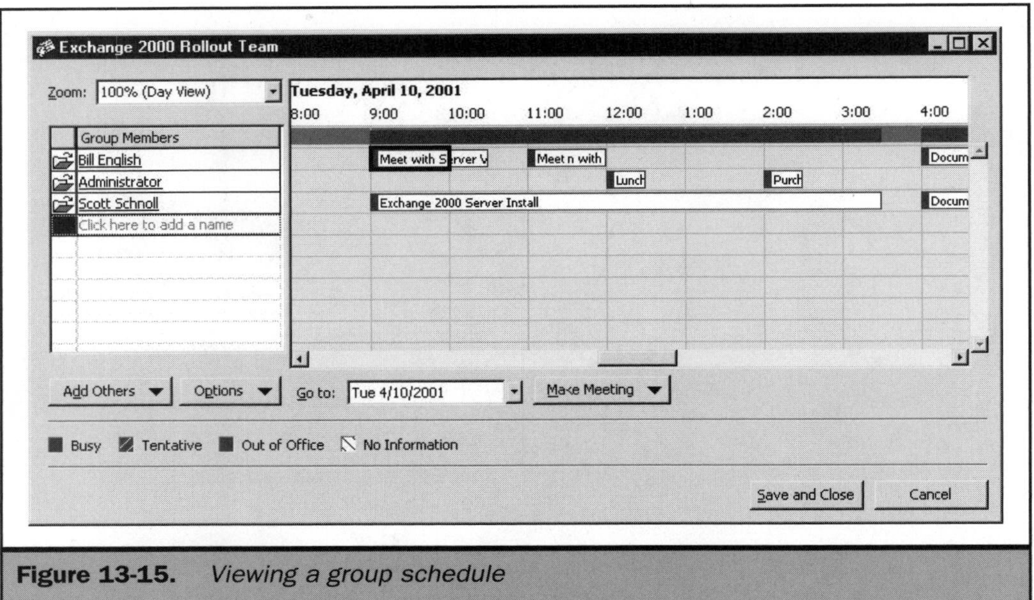

Figure 13-15. *Viewing a group schedule*

Security Enhancements

Outlook 2002 provides the following security enhancements: protection against potential viruses, attachment warnings, and protection against scripts and ActiveX controls.

Protection Against Potential Viruses

By default, Outlook 2002 does not allow the receiving of Level 1 file attachments (such as files with the .BAT, .EXE, .VBS, and .JS extensions). Messages with these attachments will have a paperclip icon indicating that an attachment exists, but the user will not be allowed to access the attachment. A note appears at the top of the message stating "Outlook blocked access to the following potentially unsafe attachments:" and then the names of blocked attachments are given. In addition, if you send an attachment type that is not allowed, Outlook warns you just prior to sending the message that other Outlook recipients may not be able to open the attachment, as shown in Figure 13-16.

For a list of the Level 1 file types, see the Microsoft Knowledge Base article Q262631.

Microsoft recommends that if you need to send another recipient a file with a Level 1 extension, send a shortcut to the needed file as the attachment instead. The recipient then can double-click on the shortcut to access the file. This method requires that the recipient have direct access to the file.

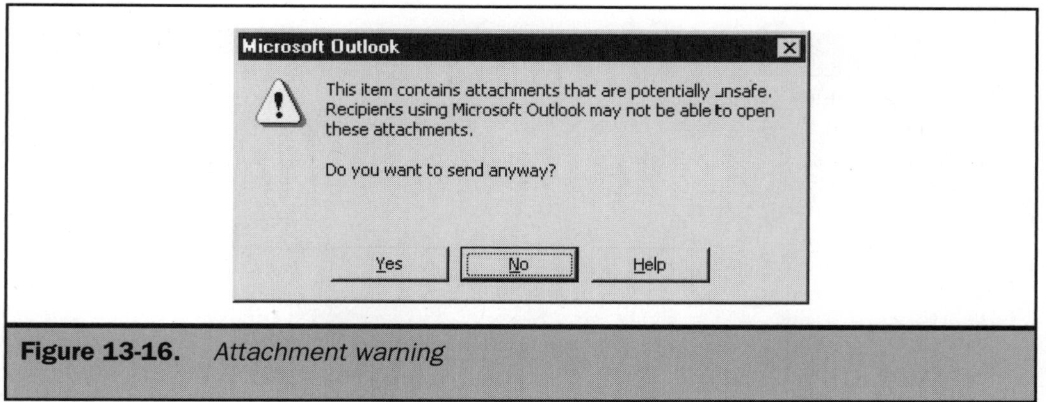

Figure 13-16. *Attachment warning*

Protection Against Scripts and ActiveX Controls

Outlook 2002 deactivates any scripts and/or ActiveX controls contained within HTML messages that you receive. This protects you against unwanted actions being taken on your computer. This deactivation takes place regardless of your Outlook security settings.

Mailbox Cleanup

We've heard the complaint too many times from users that when they see a mailbox size warning message generated by Exchange, they don't know what to clean up. Outlook 2002 gives them the tool to do a little much-needed housecleaning (and takes away the excuse!). The Mailbox Cleanup utility, shown in Figure 13-17, allows you to view the size of your mailbox, as well as the size of each folder within.

Once your users can see how large their mailbox is, they can run an Advanced Find against the mailbox using a provided set of search criteria: either by message size or by message age. What values your users put here should be based on corporate policy and the particular user's need to retain information. Because users may not want to delete any items from their mailbox (but they need to anyway to reduce the space taken up), they can use the AutoArchive button to immediately archive their messages. The settings that determine which messages get archived are found by selecting Options from the Tools menu, choosing the Other tab, and then clicking the AutoArchive button. In the dialog box that appears, you can specify what should be archived, when it should be archived, and where it should be archived. Lastly, the Mailbox Cleanup utility lets you empty the Deleted Items folder, as well as see the size of the folder.

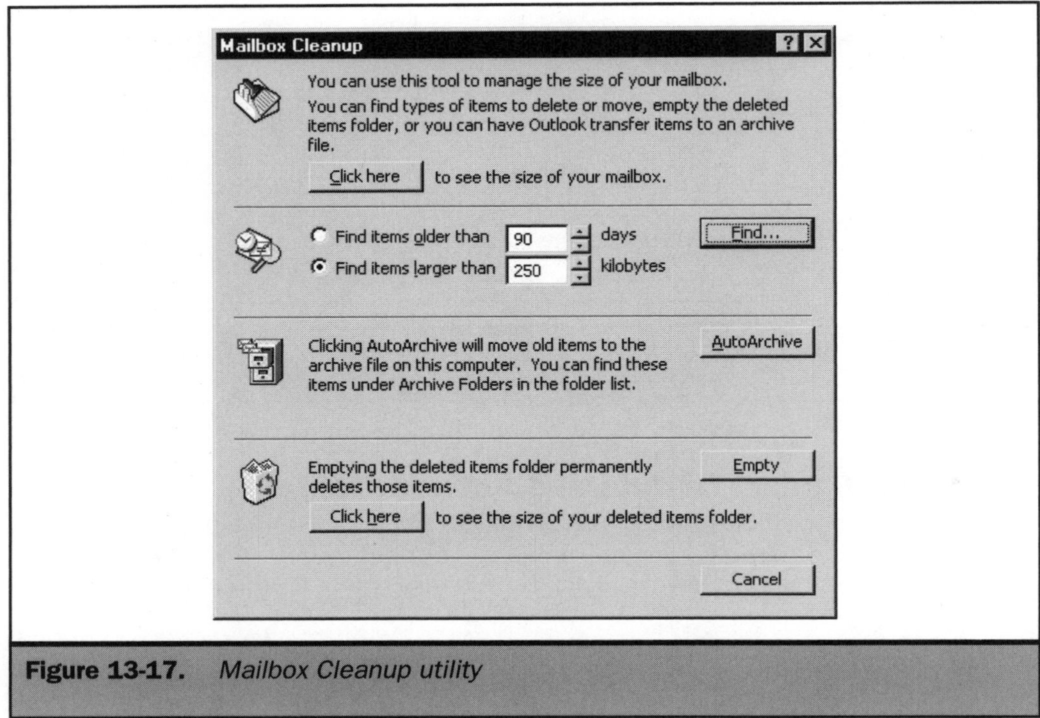

Figure 13-17. *Mailbox Cleanup utility*

Internet Clients

Access to Exchange 2000 is not limited by the use of Outlook in its variety of versions. You can access Exchange 2000 using five standardized Internet protocols: POP3, IMAP4, SMTP, NNTP, and HTTP. The beauty of these protocols being supported is that you are not limited to Microsoft client-side solutions. A third-party messaging client that complies with these protocols can utilize Exchange in the same fashion as the Microsoft client solution. Although we will use Microsoft products as our examples of client applications accessing Exchange from the Internet, we will also make general reference to the kinds of third-party products you can use for the same level of access.

Exchange 5.5 administrators would also tend to add LDAP to the list of protocols Exchange supports. However, when an Exchange 2000 client makes an LDAP query over TCP port 389, it is directed to Active Directory rather than Exchange 2000, as Exchange 2000 directory information is now stored in Active Directory.

Outlook Express

Outlook Express, shown in Figure 13-18, ships with Internet Explorer and has a similar look and feel as Outlook. It provides access to e-mail servers across the Internet via

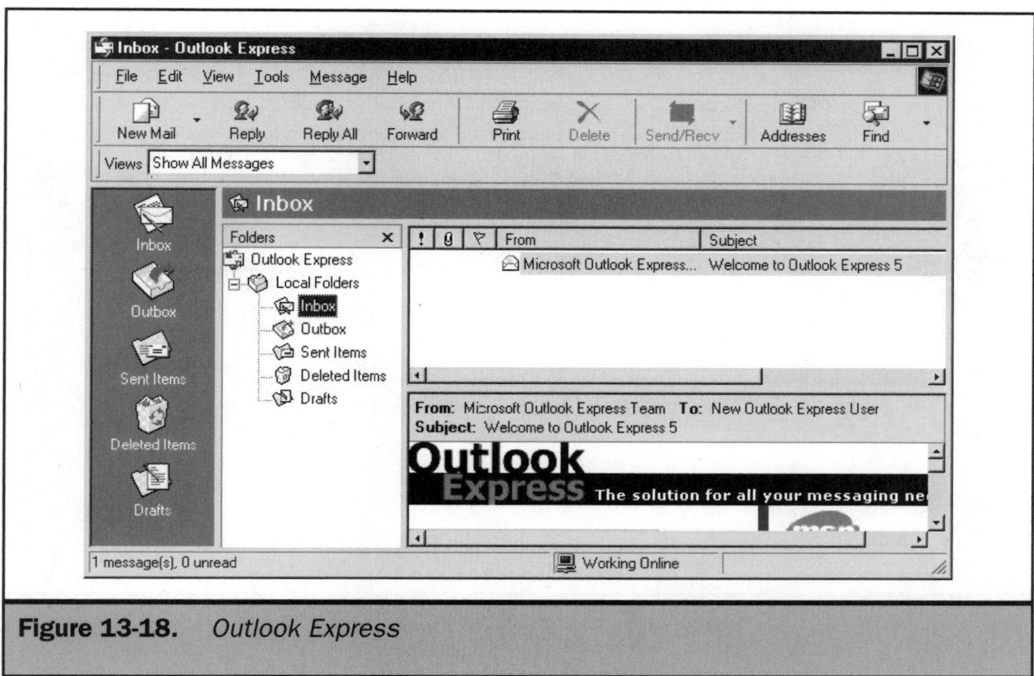

Figure 13-18. *Outlook Express*

POP3 and IMAP4. It also can transmit e-mail via SMTP. Although Outlook 2000 has the same POP3, IMAP4, and SMTP functionality, Outlook Express has the added capability to access Internet newsgroups via NNTP. This is the only real-world reason for using Outlook Express. All other Outlook Express services are available in Outlook 2000.

Because Exchange 2000 supports access to mailboxes via POP3 and IMAP 4, as well as public folder access via IMAP4, you can use Outlook Express as an Exchange 2000 client. In addition, any compliant POP3 or IMAP4 client can access Exchange in the same fashion.

Outlook Web Access

One of the most widely used clients, besides the various versions of Outlook, is Outlook Web Access, or OWA. OWA uses a standard browser, shown in Figure 13-19, to access your Exchange server via Internet Information Services (IIS). Because IIS is a prerequisite to installing Exchange 2000, OWA is installed by default as part of Exchange 2000.

OWA is most useful in three situations. First, it is widely used when users are out of the office and need access to their corporate e-mail from any PC with Internet access. As long as the IIS server running OWA is accessible from the Internet, users can retrieve messages from anywhere in the world. Second, OWA is useful if you have

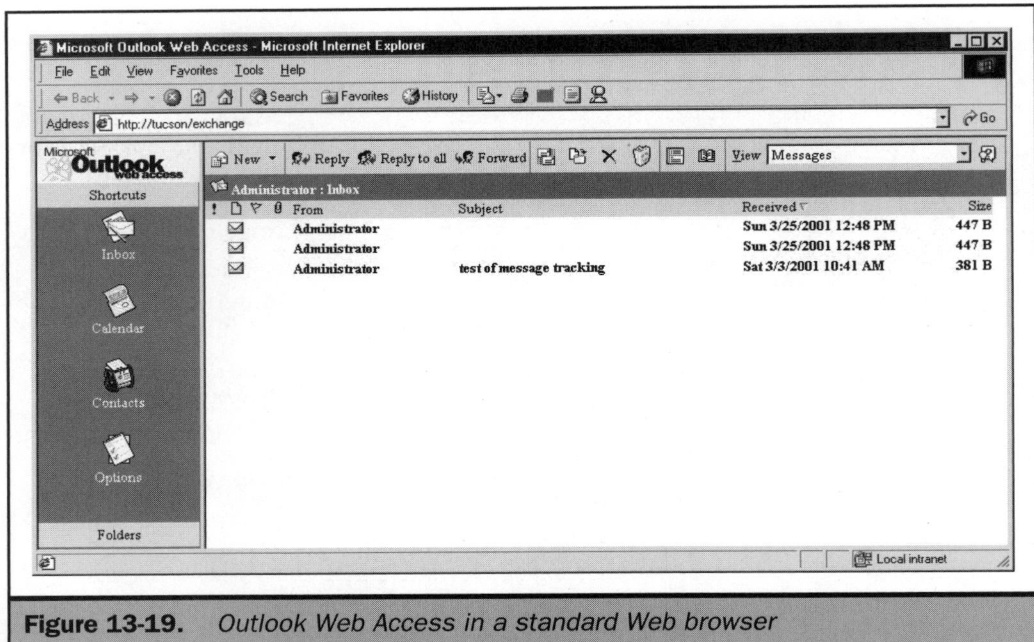

Figure 13-19. *Outlook Web Access in a standard Web browser*

minimal bandwidth across a wide area network (WAN) between offices, and users in the remote offices need to access their e-mail, calendar, contacts, tasks, and journal. Because OWA is browser based and messages are sent as HTML (which is text), your users can experience a rich messaging environment through OWA without the heavy network traffic that Outlook can take up. Third, your workstations may be older machines with slower processors, limited memory, and limited hard disk space. OWA is a great solution for the users of those machines to get their e-mail with greater speed than Outlook.

OWA is best experienced using Internet Explorer 5.0 or greater. See Chapter 14, "Outlook Web Access 2000," for more details on OWA and its architecture.

Unix-Based Clients

Although no Outlook product exists for Unix clients, you have a few solutions. Because a standard Web browser is usually part of a Unix implementation, you can access e-mail via OWA. Also, any POP3 or IMAP4 client software can be used to retrieve messages from Exchange 2000. If public folder access is necessary, an IMAP4 client is required. We recommend using OWA over a POP3 or IMAP4 solution, as OWA provides a messaging experience similar to that of Outlook.

Macintosh Clients

Macintosh clients are often left out of the discussion when talking about Exchange clients. However, there are still enough Macintosh clients in the industry for Microsoft to not only create an Outlook client for the Mac, but also to update it. Outlook 8.2.2 for the Macintosh exists to service Macintosh clients with Outlook 2001 for the Mac, currently in its Beta phase. The Macintosh versions of Outlook have nearly similar features to that of their Windows counterparts. In addition, Outlook Express 5.02 for the Macintosh is available for POP3 and IMAP4 access to Exchange 2000. And as always, Macintosh clients can use their browser (which includes Internet Explorer 5.0) to access Exchange via Outlook Web Access.

Note *For more information on Macintosh clients for Exchange, see Microsoft's Macintosh Web page at http://www.microsoft.com/mac.*

Choosing the Right Client

Several factors will play into your decision as to which Exchange 2000 client is right for you. Client hardware, available bandwidth, security needs, and desired functionality all help determine which client is appropriate. Table 13-3 lists the hardware requirements for each Exchange client.

Note *Also see the section titled "Introducing Outlook Web Access 2000" in Chapter 14, "Outlook Web Access 2000," for a comparison of features in Outlook 97/98, Outlook 2000 , and Outlook Web Access.*

Client	Processor	Disk Space (Typical Install)	Memory Win9X	Memory NT/2000
Outlook 97	486	31MB	8MB	16MB
Outlook 98	486/66MHz	34MB	8MB	16MB
Outlook 2000	Pentium 75MHz	153MB	24MB	40MB
Outlook 2002	Pentium 133MHz	85MB	32MB	72MB
Outlook Web Access (IE requirements)	486/66MHz	55MB	16MB	32MB

Table 13-3. *Exchange 2000 Client System Requirements*

Summary

Never before have you had so many choices of clients to connect to Exchange 2000 Server. While Outlook 2000 remains the premier client, oftentimes you cannot use this tool because of hardware limitations or as a MAPI client because of bandwidth issues. So, it is important to know what other clients are available to you. This chapter has covered all the clients available to access Exchange 2000.

Legacy clients are still viable tools with which to connect your older workstations to Exchange—with some feature limitations. The original Exchange Client, while extremely limited in functionality (compared to more recent clients), still allows basic messaging and public folder connectivity. With minimal hardware requirements, and still packed with features, Outlook 97 and 98 are even better choices.

Microsoft's current Exchange client, Outlook 2000, is a feature-rich client that takes full advantage of all the messaging and collaboration capabilities of Exchange 2000. Outlook 2002, with its enhanced, yet familiar interface and many new features, will be a welcome and appropriate replacement for Outlook 2000. With regards to feature sets, these two clients are your best choice.

Lastly, you can always use standardized Internet protocol-based access to Exchange 2000. You can use any standard POP3 or IMAP4 messaging client, such as Outlook or Outlook Express, to access messages. Also any browser can access Outlook Web Access (OWA) for fast mailbox access with limited workstation resources and limited bandwidth. While some features are either diminished or not available, OWA still provides you with the best possible access to Exchange outside of regular Outlook.

In the next chapter, we will look at the architecture of Outlook Web Access to see how it works "under the hood."

Chapter 14

Outlook Web Access

While most users will prefer the features and functionality of the Outlook 2000 client (and its successor), there are definite business cases and usage scenarios where a Web-based e-mail client is preferable. To accommodate these needs, Microsoft has included a Web-based e-mail client/server application in Exchange 2000 called Outlook Web Access. This chapter will introduce you to Outlook Web Access, providing you with details on its architecture, as well as step-by-step instructions for deploying Outlook Web Access in your organization. Finally, we'll discuss what it takes to secure and maintain Outlook Web Access.

Introducing Outlook Web Access 2000

A browser-based Exchange client has many advantages over its Office counterparts: it's free, it's easier to install, it requires less configuration, and end users feel comfortable with it. These days, you can find a Web browser on virtually every business desktop. Users have become comfortable with the Web-based information model, and the learning curve for mastering a Web browser is very short.

Outlook Web Access is a Web-based client for Exchange 2000 that provides secure access to mailboxes and public folders. Microsoft has stated that Outlook 2000 is the client of choice for Exchange 2000. With the release of Outlook 97 in January 1997, Microsoft provided consolidated e-mail, calendaring, and scheduling, and the beginnings of Internet standards-based protocol access in a single interface. Outlook 98 and Outlook 2000 further integrated standard Internet protocols, and the product matured in its ability to manage personal and corporate information. But there are many situations where a leaner, Web-based e-mail client is more appropriate. Microsoft's solution for that is Outlook Web Access.

Although not as functional as its Outlook counterpart, a browser-based e-mail client does have some advantages. For example, it makes it easier to use multiple computers in an office or to roam outside of the office with a portable computer. Instead of having to find and configure a computer with Outlook installed, a user can simply point his Web browser to an Outlook Web Access server located in the same site as his mailbox, log on, and access his e-mail.

Knowledge workers often work on their home computers, connecting to their office networks through dial-up, ISDN, or, more recently, DSL connections. Using a browser-based e-mail client means that someone from the IT department doesn't need to install and configure the Outlook client on users' home PCs. This translates into fewer support calls and helps keep the total cost of ownership to a minimum.

When it comes to deploying a Web-based e-mail client, managing user expectations is very important. The full Outlook client has many advanced features that Outlook Web Access doesn't have (and many that it never will). Table 14-1 provides a feature comparison (organized alphabetically) between Outlook 2000, Outlook Web Access 2000, and Outlook Web Access 5.5.

Feature	Outlook	OWA 2000	OWA 5.5
Access to additional public folders (general/alternate TLH)		X	
Access to default public folders (MAPI TLH)	X	X	X
Access to Global Address List	X	X	X
Advanced message security	X		
Browse Global Address List	X		
Calendaring and group scheduling	X		
Calendars	X	X	X
Contacts	X	X	
Create views	X		
Drag and drop	X	X	
Embedded items	X	X	
Integration with newsgroups	X	X	
Extended mail options	X		
Item copy between public and private folders	X		
Journals	X		
Mailbox rules	X		
Messaging (send/receive e-mails)	X	X	
Multimedia messages	X	X	
New message notification	X		
Offline access to e-mail	X		
Outlook folder bar	X	X	
Outlook shortcut bar	X	X	
Preview pane	X	X	
Reminders	X		

Table 14-1. *Outlook 2000, OWA 2000, and OWA 5.5*

Feature	Outlook	OWA 2000	OWA 5.5
Rich text	X	X	X
Search Global Address List	X	X	
Spell checker	X		
Stationery	X		
Tasks	X		
URL addressability of items	X		
Use views	X	X	
Voicemail/telephony	X		

Table 14-1. *Outlook 2000, OWA 2000, and OWA 5.5* (continued)

Note *Table 14-1 assumes that the Outlook Web Access client is Internet Explorer 5.0 or greater. If you use an earlier version of Internet Explorer or Netscape Navigator, your feature set will be reduced.*

While it has many of its features and functions, Outlook Web Access certainly isn't intended as a replacement for the Outlook client. Instead, it complements Outlook by providing quick and easy browser-based access to e-mail, calendar, and contact information.

Note *Outlook Web Access supports access to calendars in both private mailboxes and public folders. However, it does not support appointment list views, detailed views of free and busy times, tracking of meeting acceptance messages, or exporting to external devices.*

In addition, there are some differences in the user experience due to the browser model. The browser model is primarily a model of pointing and clicking to follow links. The experience tends not to be as rich and productive as what can be achieved by using a Windows application. For example, such things as appointment reminders or notifications of new mail aren't possible in Outlook Web Access.

Regardless of your business requirements, chances are you'll find a use for Outlook Web Access. Some usage scenarios include:

- **Web Store applications** Outlook Web Access can be combined with Web Store applications to create Windows DNA applications.

- **Support for roaming users and remote access** Users who travel away from their PCs (or users who share PCs) can access Exchange data using a Web browser.
- **Support for limited and non-Windows clients** Outlook Web Access can be accessed from Macintosh and UNIX workstations, as well as from PCs lacking the hardware resources necessary to run the full Outlook client.
- **Lowest-common denominator cross-platform system** Outlook Web Access can meet the needs of organizations that require only simple e-mail, scheduling, and collaborative applications, with identical clients on all platforms.
- **Extranet applications** Organizations that have connected their intranets to vendor, supplier, or customer intranets can use Outlook Web Access to secure, deploy, and share collaborative Web-based applications over these extranets.
- **Kiosks** A *kiosk* is typically a walk-up station that provides access to a single resource. For example, space is typically at a premium on factory floors. Instead of deploying PCs to all plant workers, companies can deploy browser-based kiosks in strategic locations that provide access to e-mail, calendars, and applications.
- **Light messaging requirements** Not everyone requires full messaging functionality. If the only requirements are simple e-mail and calendaring, Outlook Web Access is a preferred option over the full Outlook client.

New Architecture

Microsoft first introduced Outlook Web Access with Exchange Server 5.0. Their goal was to provide thin client access to Exchange. The first iteration of Outlook Web Access provided basic e-mail and public folder support. Because it lacked many of the popular features of Outlook, and because it wasn't very scalable in terms of the number of users who could simultaneously use it, Outlook Web Access didn't gain much respect as a viable Exchange client. Microsoft tried to address its limitations with the release of Service Pack 1 for Exchange 5.0, which added support for attachments and foreign languages, increased user capacity, and an interface that more closely resembled the Outlook client.

With the release of Exchange Server 5.5, Outlook Web Access was improved again. Microsoft continued to improve its scalability, and access to user calendars was added. Exchange 5.5 Service Pack 1 enhanced Outlook Web Access with the ability to create and manage contacts, change Windows NT passwords, and validate names against the Exchange Server Global Address List.

Exchange 2000 includes a completely redesigned version of Outlook Web Access that once again increases functionality, performance, and scalability. Figure 14-1 shows the new interface, which boasts new features, such as the message preview pane.

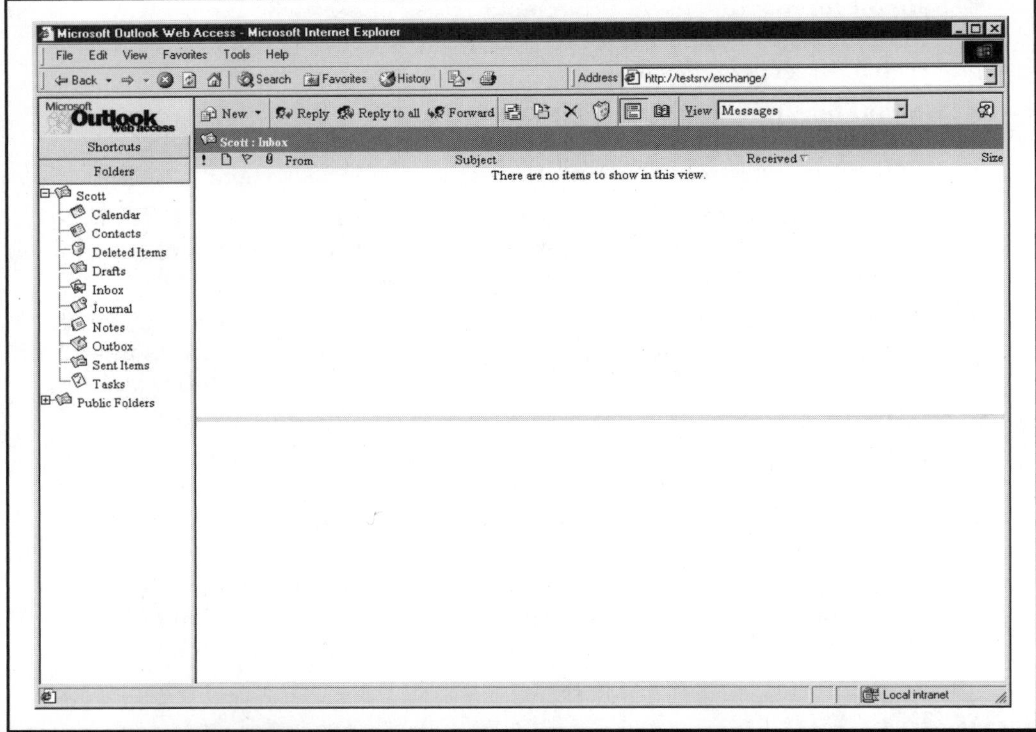

Figure 14-1. *Outlook Web Access 2000 more closely matches the look, feel, and functionality of Outlook 2000, the preferred Outlook client.*

New Capabilities

With Outlook Web Access 2000, Microsoft has provided a completely new architecture and added support for the latest technology, including ActiveX objects, multimedia, and dynamic HTML (DHTML). Outlook Web Access 2000 supports two classes of clients: browsers that support DHTML and browsers that don't. Browsers supporting DHTML, such as Internet Explorer 5.0, use DHTML to provide greater functionality and a richer user experience that more closely matches the experience with the Outlook client. For example, DHTML-enabled browsers can use drag and drop, rich text formatting (bold, underline, colors, and so on), and tree controls for opening new folders. Browsers that don't include support for DHTML must at least provide support for HTML 3.2 and JavaScript in order to use Outlook Web Access 2000.

Improved Scalability and Performance

Earlier versions of Outlook Web Access were implemented as a set of Active Server Pages (ASPs) that provided a limited subset of the functionality found in the full Outlook client. Outlook Web Access scripts in these ASPs used CDO and ADO to access e-mail and calendar information from the Exchange information store. This essentially made Outlook Web Access a part of Internet Information Server (IIS). The reliance on MAPI limited the number of people who could simultaneously use Outlook Web Access. In addition, each user kicks off an ASP session, which increases the load on the server, as each line of ASP code must be interpreted as it is executed. In addition, small amounts of JavaScript and Java were used to provide some of the UI controls used in the user's browser, which limited the class of browsers available to the end-user.

Outlook Web Access 2000 has been completely rewritten for Exchange 2000. The interpretive code no longer exists, and MAPI is no longer used to communicate with the information store. Users starting an Outlook Web Access session have the Web pages rendered directly from the information store, which increases performance and speed. Microsoft made a significant improvement to Outlook Web Access by uncoupling the Internet protocols from the Exchange information store. IIS now handles all client requests offloading this functionality from Exchange. Thus, Outlook Web Access can be considered a proxy for all message traffic between the Web browser and the Exchange server. When clients access an Outlook Web Access server with their browser, they are really using an Exchange application that has been implemented as an ISAPI filter. This application provides an interface that handles communication between IIS and Exchange.

Front-End/Back-End Configurations

Outlook Web Access makes good use of the front-end/back-end architecture of Exchange 2000. In this scenario, IIS services the requests on the front-end server and accesses client data on the back-end servers. Outlook Web Access 2000 uses a combination of HTTP and WebDAV (Web Distributed Authoring and Versioning—see Appendix A) to communicate with the Exchange information store through IIS. Clients continue to access data using HTTP; however, the IIS server hosting Outlook Web Access uses the new Exchange 2000 Web Store to provide access to the user's messaging functions. The IIS server passes the client request on to an Exchange ISAPI application, which communicates with the Exchange information store.

If the IIS server also happens to be the Exchange server containing the requested data, a high-speed channel is used to access the data. If the information being sought is on a different server, such as a back-end server, IIS uses HTTP to communicate with the Exchange information store that has the data. The information store then returns the requested data to the ISAPI application, which renders content appropriate to the client's browser (see Figure 14-2).

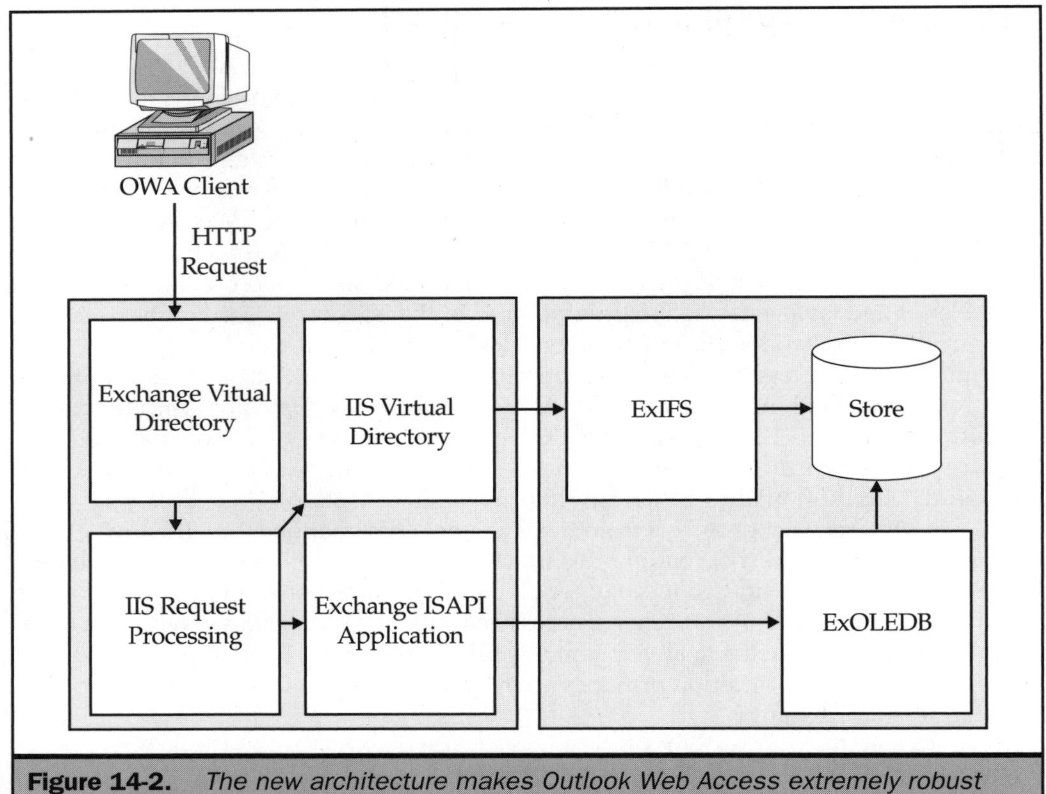

Figure 14-2. *The new architecture makes Outlook Web Access extremely robust and scalable.*

When it comes time to deliver the data back to the client, the Exchange ISAPI application returns data rendered in the best format for the requesting client. For example, users with Internet Explorer 5.0 or greater will have their content rendered with a combination of DHTML and Extensible Markup Language (XML).

Installing and Configuring Outlook Web Access

Every Windows 2000 server has IIS installed by default. In addition, every Exchange 2000 server has Outlook Web Access installed by default. This means that right out of the box, Outlook Web Access is ready for use. And as soon as you establish Internet connectivity and configure DNS, users can securely access Outlook Web Access over the Internet. Microsoft has also made setup easy for most international users. By default, versions of Outlook Web Access are installed using several different languages, including Chinese (simplified and traditional), French, German, Japanese, Korean, Spanish, and Italian.

Once installed, the components that make up Outlook Web Access are located in various subdirectories under \Program Files\Exchsrvr\Exchweb. Table 14-2 lists the components and their locations.

An Exchange installation also automatically creates four virtual directories in IIS that are used to serve Outlook Web Access. These virtual directories are located in the IIS default Web site. Table 14-3 lists the virtual directories, the resources they point to, and their functions.

Component	Description	Location
CAB files	Contains programs and controls for multimedia content	\Program files\exchsrvr\exchweb\cabs
Help files	User-oriented documentation	\Program files\\exchsrvr\exchweb\help
Images	Image files used by Outlook Web Access	\Program files\exchsrvr\exchweb\img
Language Files	Used for localized versions of help files	Located under various subfolders (e.g., \Program files\exchsrvr\exchweb\help for language-specific help files)
Program files	Executables, library, and companion files that make up Outlook Web Access	\Program files\exchsrvr\exchweb\bin
Scripts	JavaScript, cascading style sheet and HTML component files	\Program files\exchsrvr\exchweb\controls
Views	XSL style sheets used to render views	\Program files\exchsrvr\exchweb\views

Table 14-2. *Outlook Web Access Components*

Virtual Directory	Purpose	Points To
exadmin	Used to administer public folders	\\.\BackOfficeStorage
exchange	Serves as mailbox root	M:\<server dns name>\mbx
exchweb	Provides controls, scripts, images, and other files	\exchsrvr\exchweb
public	Root of public folder tree	M:\<server dns name>\public folders

Table 14-3. *Exchange-Created Virtual Directories*

User Access

Although Outlook Web Access is installed and available by default, you can control which users can access Outlook Web Access by enabling or disabling the HTTP protocol for them. To do this:

1. Open Active Directory Users and Computers.
2. If they are not already turned on, turn on viewing of the Advanced Features by selecting View | Advanced Features.
3. Double-click the user whose access rights you want to modify. This will display their Properties.
4. Select the Exchange Advanced tab.
5. Click the Protocol Settings button.
6. Select the HTTP protocol.
7. Check or uncheck the Enable For Mailbox checkbox as desired.
8. Click OK to save the changes, then OK two more times to exit the user's Properties.

Outlook Web Access URLs

Once installed, mailboxes can be accessed directly using human-readable URLs, such as http://*server*/exchange/*username* or, from the Internet, http://*fqdn*/exchange/*username*. The user's Inbox is the default folder. A user can also navigate to his mailbox using the format from earlier versions of Outlook Web Access: http://*fqdn*/exchange. This scheme also permits a user access to individual messages if he knows the message name.

Other folders can be addressed similarly by replacing "Inbox" with the other folder name (Calendar, Contacts, and so on). Public folders are accessible through individual mailboxes, but users can navigate to the Public Folder tree root directory by pointing their browsers to http://*server or fqdn*/public.

Parameters can also be passed in Outlook Web Access URLs to specify a particular action, such as opening or editing an item, accepting or declining meeting invitations, and displaying a custom view. The general format for an Outlook Web Access URL is

http://server/exchange_root/folder/?Option=option&Modifier=modifier

Table 14-4 lists the available options and their descriptions.

Table 14-5 lists the actions that can be used with the Cmd option.

Virtual Servers

Outlook Web Access services are accessed through HTTP *virtual servers* that run under IIS. In IIS, virtual servers are separate Web server instances, each of which can have its own configuration properties, such as security, IP address, and port number. They enable a single IIS server to host multiple Web sites. In a hosted environment, virtual servers are sometimes called "hosted organizations."

Note *You cannot manage the default virtual server with System Manager, because it is a component of IIS, not Exchange. As a result, you have to manage it with Internet Services Manager. If you try to use System Manager, you will get a message telling you to use ISM. Although they also exist in IIS, any additional virtual servers are created with System Manager, not with ISM. However, different aspects of them can be configured through each management tool.*

Option	Description
Date=*yyyymmdd*	Displays a specific date on the calendar
Page=*x*	Displays page *x*
Sort=*x*	Sorts by column *x*
View=*x*	Uses predefined Outlook view *x* to display page
Cmd=*action*	Performs a specific action

Table 14-4. *Valid Options for Use Within URLs*

Action	Description
Accept	Accepts specified meeting request
Contents	Displays the contents of a folder
Decline	Declines specified meeting request
Edit	Opens specified message or appointment for editing
Forward	Forwards specified message
Navbar	Displays the navigation bar
New	Creates a new item using the default item type for the specified folder
New&Type=	Creates a new item using the specified item type
Open	Opens specified item for viewing
Options	Displays Outlook Web Access options
Reply	Replies to the sender of the specified item
ReplyAll	Replies to sender of the specified item and all others in To and Cc fields
Tentative	Adds specified meeting request to calendar as tentative

Table 14-5. *Valid Action Variables for URLs*

Because the default virtual server for Outlook Web Access is located in the IIS default Web site, the only way to stop it is to either stop the default Web site or stop the World Wide Web Publishing Service. Thus, stopping the default Web site also stops Outlook Web Access.

Creating Virtual Servers

You can create virtual servers for users with different security requirements or access needs. A single Exchange server can host multiple virtual servers, or you can distribute virtual servers across multiple Exchange servers. Each virtual server you create must be unique, with its own IP address and port number. If you are hosting multiple virtual servers on the same Exchange server, you will need to have multiple IP addresses assigned to that server. In addition, you will also need to use unique host names, which need to be registered as a host record in DNS or listed in a client's *hosts* file. To create a virtual server:

1. Open System Manager.
2. Expand Servers, then expand the server on which you want to create the new virtual server.
3. Expand Protocols.
4. Right-click HTTP and select New | HTTP Virtual Server. A Properties dialog box for the new virtual server will be displayed, as shown in Figure 14-3. This tab is used to provide an identity and path for the virtual server.
5. Give the virtual server a descriptive name.

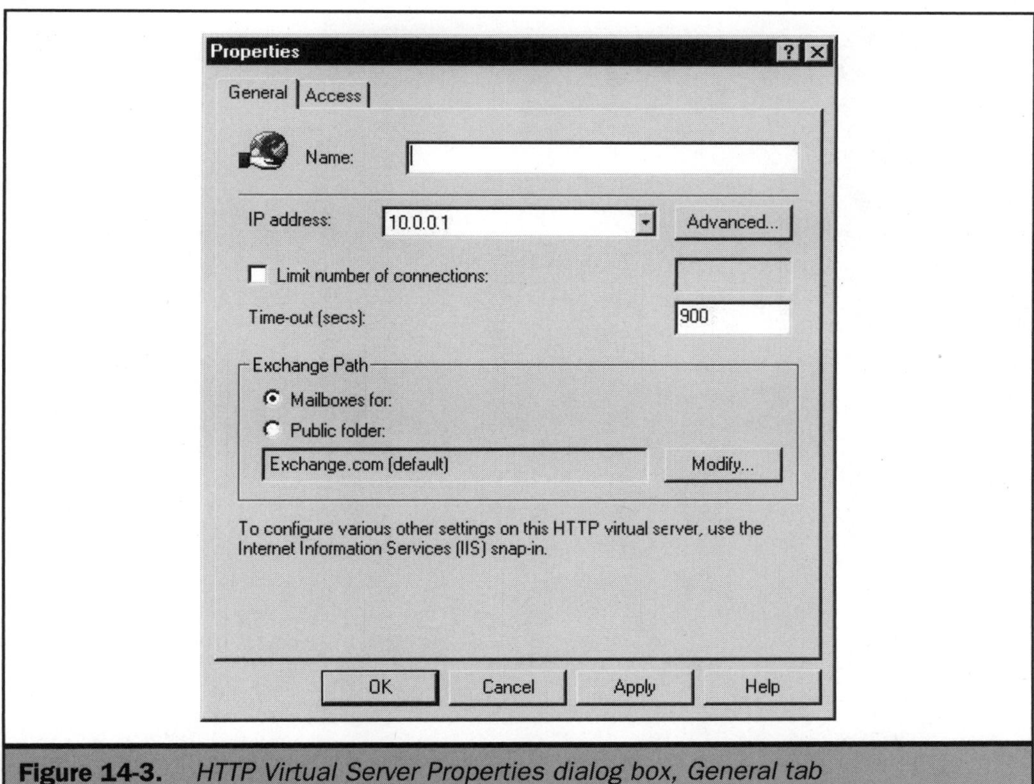

Figure 14-3. *HTTP Virtual Server Properties dialog box, General tab*

6. Select an IP address from the IP address drop-down list. Use the Advanced button to specify a unique IP address, port, and host name. A uniqueness confirmation message will be displayed. Click OK to acknowledge and clear the message.
7. If desired, set a connection limit or modify the timeout settings, which will be inherited from the IIS default timeout settings.
8. Select the Exchange path you want to use. If you select Mailboxes, the Modify button allows you to specify an SMTP domain. If you select Public Folders, the Modify button allows you to specify a public folder or public folder tree.
9. Select the Access tab, as shown in Figure 14-4. This tab is used to configure access rights and authentication settings.

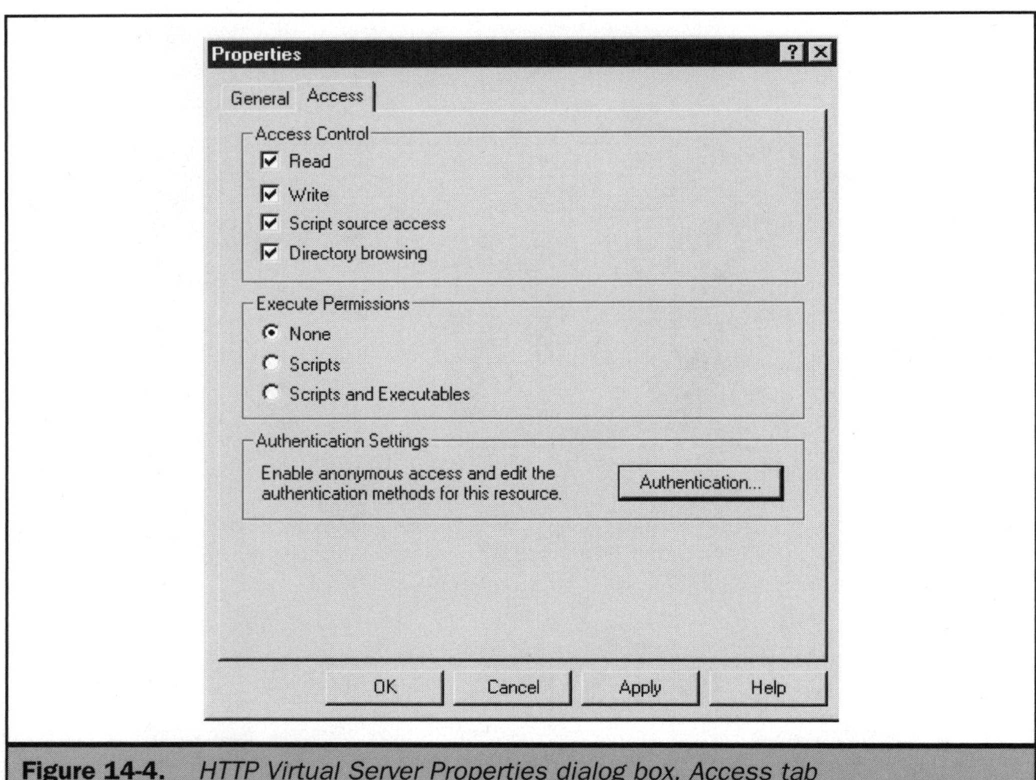

Figure 14-4. *HTTP Virtual Server Properties dialog box, Access tab*

10. Configure access permissions as desired. In most cases, you will not need to change the default access permissions.
11. Click the Authentication button.
12. Select the method(s) you wish to use for user authentication. Choose from Anonymous, Basic, and Integrated Windows Authentication, then click OK.
13. Click OK once more to create the new virtual server.

Once the new virtual server is created, it will be automatically started. If it does not automatically start, chances are its identity (its combination of IP address, port, and host name) is not unique. In this event, check the virtual server's configuration and make sure it is unique.

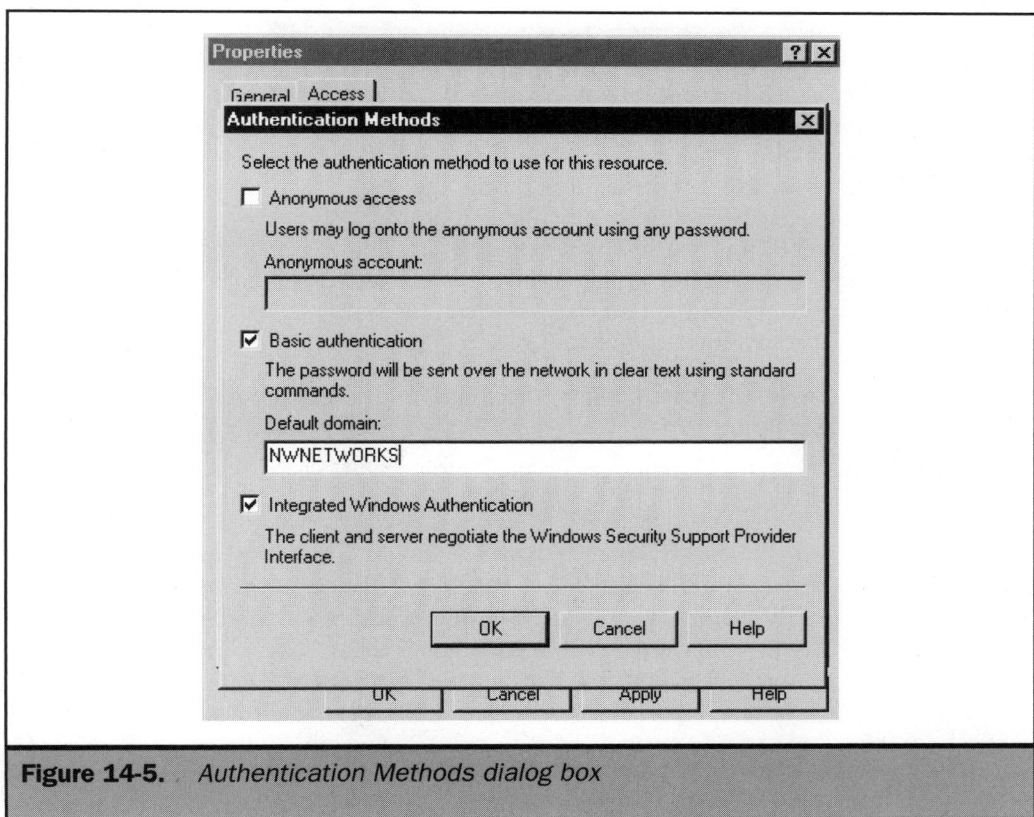

Figure 14-5. *Authentication Methods dialog box*

Deploying Outlook Web Access

Although Outlook Web Access is ready for use at install time, there are some deployment and configuration issues that need to be addressed, including:

- Server models
- Security
- Customization
- Ongoing maintenance

Server Models

Outlook Web Access can be deployed in one of two server models: a *single-server environment* or a *multiserver environment*. In a single-server environment, there are no other Exchange servers, so users are always accessing their data using the Outlook Web Access services on the Exchange server containing their data. In a multiserver organization, you have a choice of multiplying the single-server approach (all users use Outlook Web Access on the server containing their Exchange data), or you can use the front-end/back-end configuration approach, which is recommended for reliability and scalability. If you're upgrading from Exchange 5.5, the deployment model you choose will directly affect how you upgrade. In addition, the deployment model you select also dictates what security options are available to you.

The single-server model is obviously better for smaller organizations, but organizations of all sizes will benefit from taking the multiserver approach. This approach will vary from company to company, but the *best practices* approach is the front-end/back-end approach (as depicted in Figure 14-6):

- Dedicated, load-balanced IIS servers running Outlook Web Access (front-end servers)
- Dedicated, clustered Exchange servers running Outlook Web Access (back-end servers)

In this model, requests from a Web browser are sent via HTTP or HTTPs to the front-end server. The front-end server queries Active Directory to determine which back-end server should receive the request, and then proxies the request to that back-end server. There are several advantages to this model. First, it provides scalability. The resource load is balanced among several front-end servers, and the back-end servers do not have the overhead involved in serving clients directly.

Second, this allows you to define a user's mailbox in a single namespace. This eliminates the need to provide users with the name of the Exchange server containing their mailbox, as you do in the single-server model. If your Exchange infrastructure grows and you have a single namespace, servers can be added or removed and mailboxes can be moved around, but the URL used to access a user's mailbox remains the same. Without a single namespace, every time your organization grows or changes, requiring the moving of some or all mailboxes to another server, the users must be

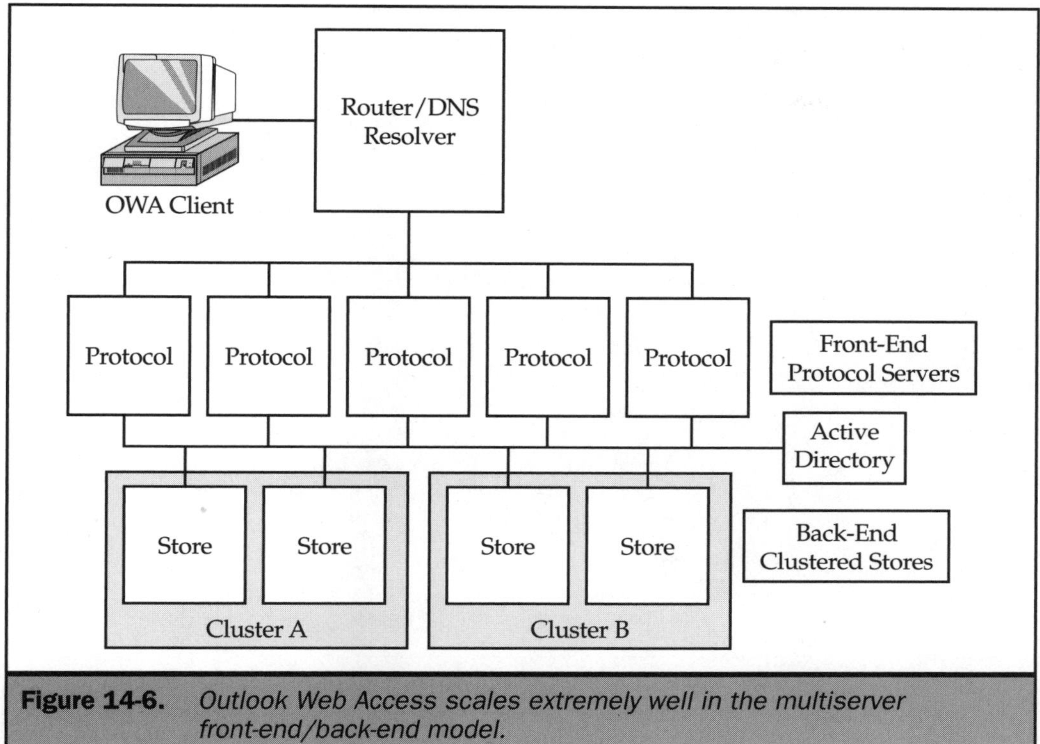

Figure 14-6. *Outlook Web Access scales extremely well in the multiserver front-end/back-end model.*

notified of the move and provided with a new URL. Using a single namespace also impacts scalability. With a single namespace, any changes you make to your Exchange infrastructure to accommodate growth will be transparent to end-users.

Configuring an Outlook Web Access server as a front-end or back-end server is as easy as checking a checkbox. In fact, that's the actual procedure. Servers are designated as front-end or back-end servers using System Manager. To configure a server as a front-end server, simply check the front-end server checkbox on the General sheet of the server's Property pages, as shown in Figure 14-7. Microsoft recommends no more than four back-end servers for each front-end server.

Load-Balancing Solutions When deploying multiple front-end servers, a single namespace is accomplished by using a *load-balancing solution*. This can be a software-based or hardware-based solution. Load-balancing solutions allow you to refer to a group of servers using a single name.

Windows 2000 Server provides a mechanism for *DNS round robin*. Round robin is a technique used by DNS servers as a form of load balancing. It works by rotating the order of resource record data (such as IP address) returned to a client in which multiple A records exist for the queried DNS name. Round robin is somewhat limited, as it cannot detect offline servers, calculate load-balancing needs across servers, or maintain

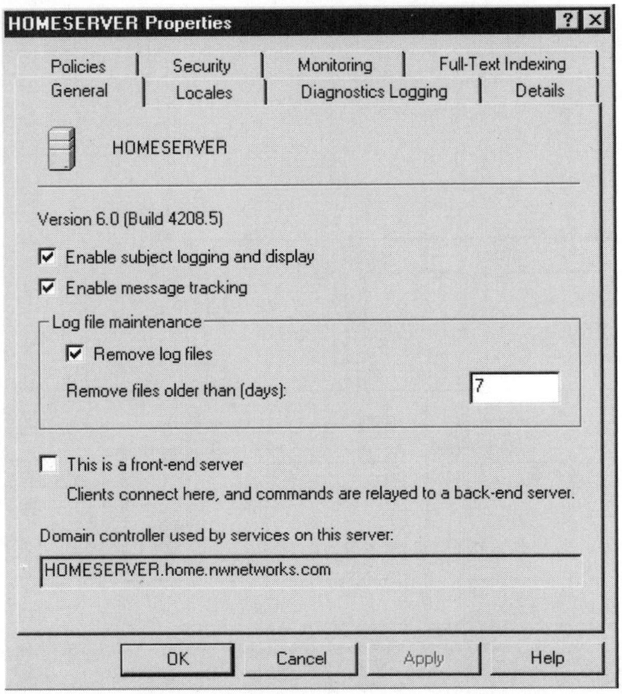

Figure 14-7. *General Properties for an Exchange server*

client sessions through the same front-end server. As a result, it is an available method, but not the preferred method. Moreover, it cannot be used in conjunction with SSL. SSL uses state information that is maintained on the IIS server. If the client is sent to a different server, the state is lost and must be rebuilt.

Windows 2000 Advanced Server and Datacenter Server include load-balancing software called network load balancing (formerly Windows Load Balancing Service). Network load balancing supports up to 32 servers in a load-balanced cluster. Load-balanced nodes in a cluster exchange heartbeats with each other to signal that they're up and available to handle requests. If a node fails to send or respond to heartbeat messages, the remaining nodes perform *convergence*, a process by which all nodes determine which nodes are active and current members of the cluster. After all nodes agree on the cluster membership, an algorithm is used to redistribute the client load, and convergence completes. Similarly, when new nodes join the cluster, they send heartbeat messages that trigger convergence. It is this dynamic convergence process that enables network load balancing to detect offline servers and distribute the load across all nodes. Network load balancing can redirect a client to multiple front-end servers without any problems; however, if you are using SSL in your environment, you can configure network load balancing to send the client to the same front-end server for the entire session.

Hardware load-balancing solutions typically use a technique called network address translation to provide virtual IP addresses to clients. This method involves the translating of an IP address (mapping it to its real IP address) and retransmitting the packets to the target server. This typically imposes added overhead and results in reduced bandwidth being available for the clients and applications. In addition, hardware solutions often represent a single point of failure for service and typically require upgrades in tandem with upgrades to the network infrastructure.

Clustered Back-End Servers The only currently available clustering solution for Windows 2000 is the built-in Microsoft Cluster Services in Windows 2000 Advanced Server and Windows 2000 Datacenter Server. Exchange 2000 Server supports active/active clustering in two-node clusters, which can run multiple instances of Exchange on one or all nodes in a cluster. Exchange uses the Microsoft Cluster Server concept of *virtual servers*, which are used to host individual instances of Exchange. In this context, a virtual server in a cluster is different from virtual servers for protocols.

Clustering provides high availability for Exchange for both planned and unplanned outages. Unplanned outages are typically the result of hardware or power failure. Unplanned outages result in the automatic failover of Exchange services from one node in the cluster to a remaining node in the cluster. For planned outages, you can manually failover a resource group and move it to another node. In either case, the client experiences only a minor interruption in service during the transition of services to the other node.

See Chapter 20 for more information on clustering Exchange 2000 and network load balancing.

Outlook Web Access Security

Once you've defined your server model, determining where to place and how to secure your servers is next. You can deploy Outlook Web Access servers in any location relative to your company network, including in a firewall or other secured environment. The decision on server placement directly impacts the security options available to you, as does the Web browser used for Outlook Web Access.

You should take the time to secure your Exchange infrastructure. This becomes especially important once you've started deploying Web Store applications that provide access to file system data, database services, and collaboration tools. Where Outlook Web Access is concerned, there are three paths of traffic that need to be considered: communication between the client and the front-end server, communication between the front-end server and an Active Directory controller, and communication between the front-end server and the back-end server.

Security in this context is divided into two distinct parts: client authentication, firewalls, and encryption. Additional information on securing Exchange 2000, above and beyond securing Outlook Web Access, can be found in Chapters 18 and 19.

Client Authentication

Before being allowed access to Exchange data, users must be authenticated. Authentication is the transmitting and validation of credentials used to verify the user's identity. The authentication methods available to you depend on the Web client being used and what security policies are in place. In Outlook Web Access, authentication is handled by IIS. IIS supports five authentication methods: *anonymous*, *basic*, *integrated Windows*, *digest*, and *certificate*. These authentication methods are configured using the Internet Service Manager MMC console, as shown in Figure 14-8.

By default, Outlook Web Access uses integrated Windows authentication, which, unlike earlier versions of Outlook Web Access, can provide secure, authenticated access to Exchange data without prompting the user for credentials. The IIS authentication methods are discussed below.

Anonymous Access Anonymous access should only be used for access to Exchange public folders or directory information because it grants access to resources without requiring the user to provide a user name or password. Because it works with all Web browsers, and because it doesn't require a user name or password, anonymous access is the easiest way to provide access to public folder data that is neither sensitive nor

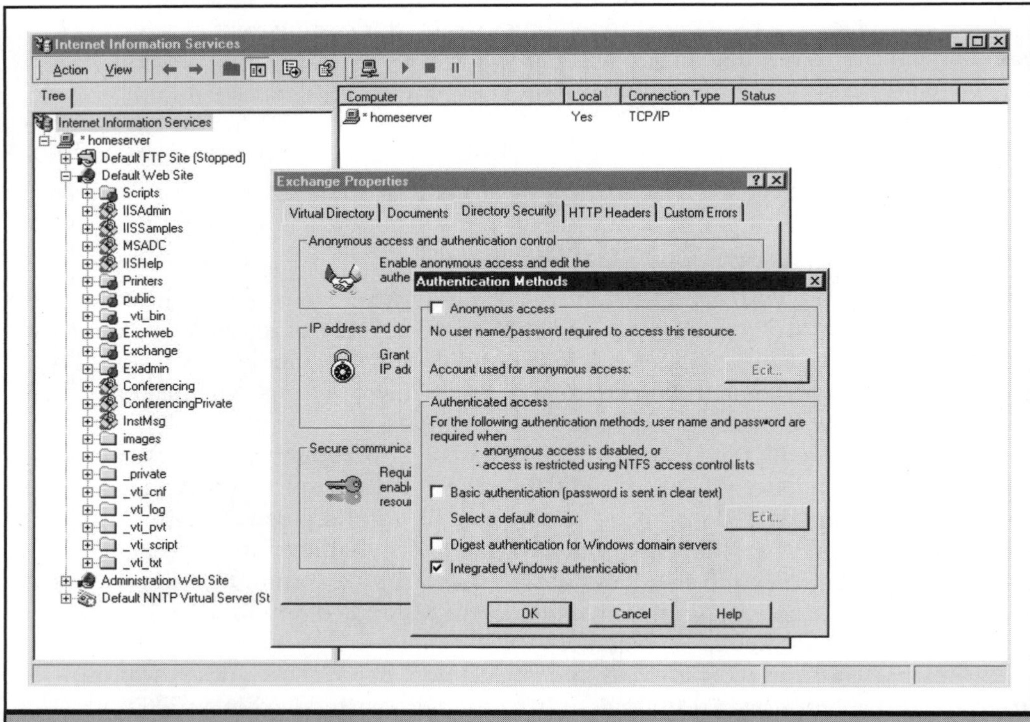

Figure 14-8. *Authentication settings are configured from the Directory Security sheet on the virtual directory property page.*

requires any special security measures. Before anonymous access can be used for public folder data, you must first publish the root anonymous public folder. If anonymous access is not explicitly set, users will be presented with a logon dialog box at each logon.

Basic Authentication Basic authentication is widely used in intranets. Basic authentication requires users to enter their user name, domain name, and password each time they log on. It works with most Web browsers and can also work through proxy servers and firewalls. The primary disadvantage to basic authentication is that the credentials are sent over the network in plain text. This means that a network trace application, or sniffer, could capture and collect user names and passwords, which represents an obvious security problem. For this reason, when using basic authentication, Microsoft recommends using Secure Sockets Layer (SSL) to encrypt the transaction and the credentials so they cannot be read by someone who has captured or intercepted the network traffic. The IIS documentation contains detailed, step-by-step instructions for using and configuring SSL.

Integrated Windows Authentication Integrated Windows authentication only works with Internet Explorer 2.x or later, and it cannot be used through proxy servers. There are two types of integrated Windows authentication: Kerberos V5 and NTLM (formerly known as Windows NT Challenge/Response). Regardless of which type is used, user names and passwords are not sent over the wire. Instead, the Web browser proves its knowledge of the password through a cryptographic exchange with the IIS server. When the client is running Windows 2000 and Internet Explorer 5.0 or later, the exchange of this information uses the Kerberos V5 authentication protocol. Support for Kerberos authentication is provided by the Windows 2000 Distributed Services architecture. Kerberos depends on both the client and the server having a trusted connection to a Kerberos Key Distribution Center (KDC) and being Directory Services–compatible. If the client is running Internet Explorer 4.x or Internet Explorer 5.0 on a 32-bit Windows platform other than Windows 2000, NTLM authentication is used instead.

Digest Authentication Digest authentication is new to Windows 2000. Digest authentication, which is defined in RFC 2617, encrypts passwords and provides a mechanism to aid in the prevention of some common server attacks. Digest authentication can be used with any HTTP 1.1–compliant Web browser, but only on back-end servers. Front-end servers cannot use digest authentication.

In digest authentication, the initial client request is rejected by a security challenge. The challenge instructs the client to use digest authentication and provides the client with a nonce value—a randomly generated value used to defeat replay attacks—that the client hashes along with the user name and password. The client then retransmits the original message along with the hashed data. The server recreates the string, hashes it, and checks the results. If everything matches, the server knows the request is authentic and grants the user access.

Certificate Authentication You can use SSL security features for two types of certificate authentication: *server certificates* and *client certificates*. Server certificates authenticate the Web server and client certificates authenticate users requesting information from the Web server. SSL authenticates by checking the contents of an encrypted digital identification submitted by the user's Web browser during the logon process. You probably won't need to use server certificates on your IIS server, but because they are very secure and supported by a wide variety of Web browsers, you might consider using client certificates for your users.

Client certificates, which can be obtained by a third-party certificate authority or generated with Microsoft Certificate Server, get mapped to Windows user accounts. Microsoft suggests that organizations can use certificates generated with Microsoft Certificate Server as long as they are used for access to Intranet resources. If there is a need to use a certificate to validate external resources, you should use a third-party certificate authority such as Verisign or Thawes.

Each time a user logs on with a client certificate, IIS automatically associates that user with the mapped user account. Clients can then be automatically authenticated without the use of basic, digest, or integrated Windows authentication.

Firewalls

Firewalls can be placed in front of and behind front-end servers. The protocols you use will determine what TCP ports will need to be opened on your firewalls. Table 14-6 lists the various protocols you may need in your environment and the default ports they use.

Protocol	Port
DNS	53 (TCP/UDP)
HTTP	80
HTTPS	443
Kerberos	88 (TCP/UDP)
LDAP	389
LDAP SSL	636
LDAP Global Catalog	3268
LDAP SSL Global Catalog	3269
NetBIOS	137-139
Netlogon	445
RPC Endpoint Mapper	135

Table 14-6. *Protocols and Ports You May Need in Your Environment*

Note *Kerberos authentication is encapsulated in the HTTP and SSL protocols, so no additional Kerberos ports need be opened; however, Kerberos clients need to contact an Active Directory controller to build their credentials, which they do through port 88.*

Back-end servers should reside in the corporate network. Front-end servers, however, can reside in the corporate network, on a perimeter network, or in a DMZ.

Front-end servers deployed in the corporate network can provide access for internal users, as well as for users who need to access to their Exchange data over the Internet. This allows you to use the same front-end servers for internal and external access (see Figure 14-9). Because the front-end servers are on the internal corporate network, they can be managed without any port or protocol restrictions.

Because the front-end servers in this configuration are dual-homed (that is, they have multiple network interface cards), they actually exist in two locations. To prevent direct routing to the corporate network, one interface is connected to an isolated network that doesn't route to the internal network. The other interface is connected to the corporate network for native access by internal users.

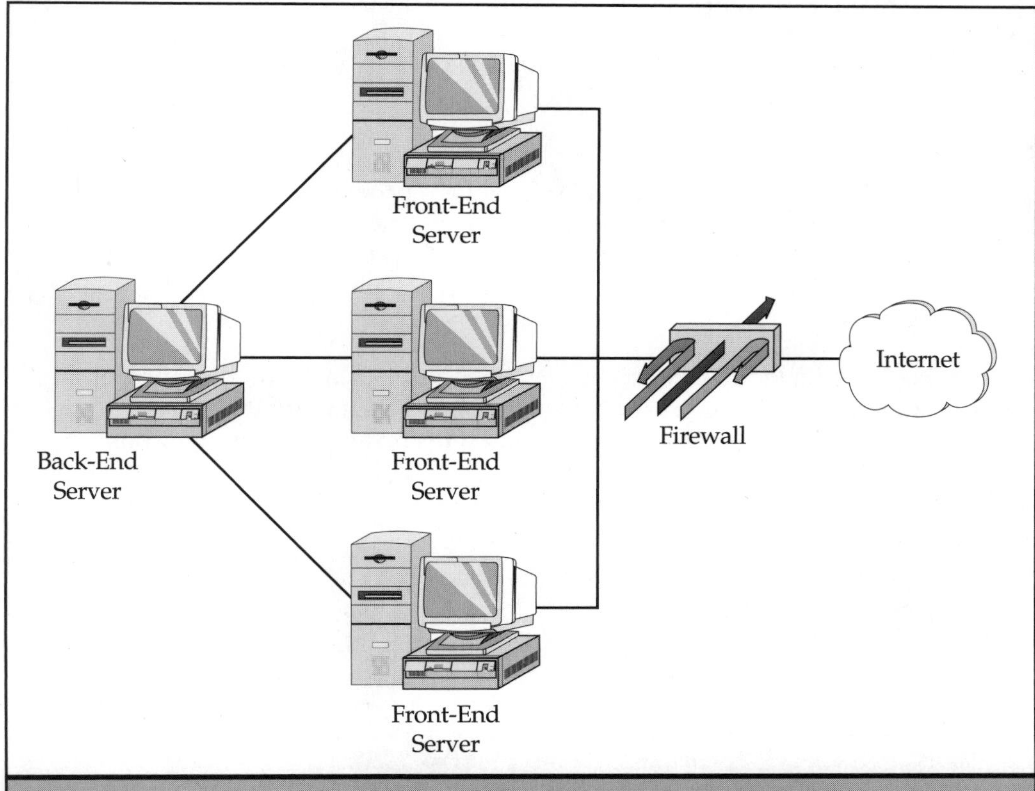

Figure 14-9. *You can provide secure access to internal and external users using the same front-end servers.*

A perimeter network is a network that exists outside a firewall or protected internal network. As shown in Figure 14-10, you can place front-end servers on a perimeter network. This is where there is a firewall between the front-end and back-end servers.

In this scenario, the front-end server is dual-homed and configured for port filtering. Static mappings can be used to ensure that the front-end server only attempts communications with the proper back-end servers. The front-end server is also hard-coded to use a specific global catalog server for lookups.

One disadvantage to this configuration is that it does not protect the front-end server from denial-of-service attacks. Another disadvantage is that SSL cannot be used to secure communication between the front-end server and the back-end server. Communication always takes place on TCP port 80, regardless of whether or not the Outlook Web Access client connected to TCP port 443 on the front-end server.

If you are using SSL on a front-end server, you must run the Windows 2000 License Logging Service. IIS does not allow more than 10 simultaneous SSL connections unless this service is running.

Placing front-end servers in a DMZ is another option, as illustrated in Figure 14-11. A DMZ—short for *demilitarized zone*—is an isolated network in the realm of firewall-based communications. All network communications to devices on the DMZ pass through the firewall.

Encryption

Using authentication and access control mechanisms provide only a minimum layer of protection. While they prevent the data from being directly accessed by an unauthorized user, they do nothing to protect the data while it is traveling over the network between servers or between server and clients. Where data encryption is concerned, you have two choices natively available to you: SSL and IPSec.

Secure Sockets Layer As previously mentioned, SSL can be used to encrypt the user name and password information when using basic authentication to access an Outlook Web Access server. SSL can also be used to encrypt all communications

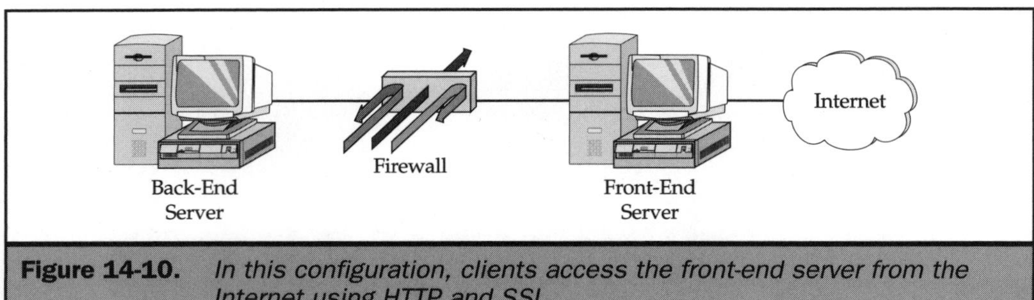

Figure 14-10. *In this configuration, clients access the front-end server from the Internet using HTTP and SSL.*

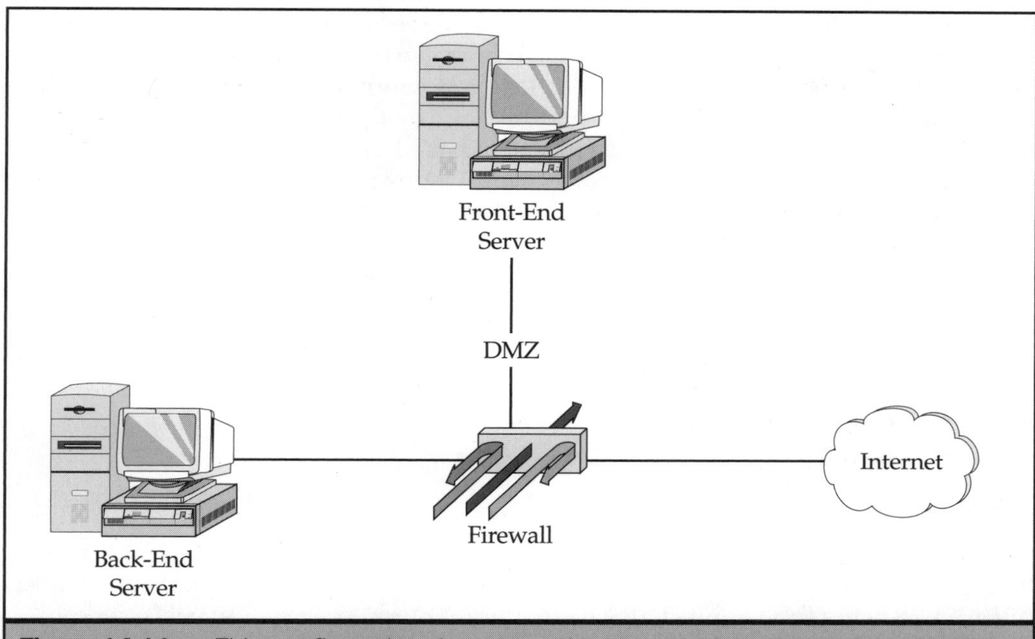

Figure 14-11. *This configuration decreases the network throughput of the front-end server, and it restricts the ability to manage the server.*

between the client and the server, regardless of the authentication method(s) being used. SSL protects communications by establishing a secure channel between the client and server and by encrypting communications between them. In order to use SSL for Outlook Web Access, you must first install the appropriate certificates and then configure the virtual server to use SSL.

Note *SSL consumes resources—and in particular, processor resources—due to the additional processing required for the encryption and decryption process. As a result, SSL communications will reduce performance on the authenticating server.*

SSL uses a combination of Rivest-Shamir-Adleman (RSA) public-key and symmetric-key encryption (also known as secret-key encryption). The session begins with an SSL handshake between the client and server. The server authenticates itself to the client using public-key encryption. If client-side certificates are being used, the client also authenticates itself to the server using public-key encryption. Once the authentication process has completed, the client and server cooperate to create symmetric keys that are used for encryption and decryption during their session.

One limitation of SSL is that it cannot be used between front-end and back-end servers. A front-end server can only access a back-end server on port 80. Therefore, if you want to secure communications between a front-end and back-end server, you should use IPSec.

IPSec While certificate services and KMS provide security on the application layer, IP Security (IPSec) provides security on the IP transportation layer—specifically the Network Layer (Layer 3) of the OSI mode. IPSec is a suite of protocols and cryptographic algorithms that have been defined through 12 RFCs by the IPSec Working Group of the IETF. It was designed to encrypt TCP/IP-based data traveling between two computers by protecting it from being viewed or modified. Windows 2000 adheres to the IPSec RFC suite (2401+), however, some aspects of the RFCs have not yet been implemented. IPSec provides several services:

- Authentication
- Data integrity
- Confidentiality
- Key management
- Nonrepudiation
- Antireplay

IPSec is managed as a set of security policies in Windows 2000. In this context, an *IPSec policy* is a set of IPSec-specific settings that can be delivered and applied to a host. When a policy has been applied, IPSec uses packet filters to scan all IP packets for addresses, ports, and transport protocols, and determines which traffic to secure, permit, or block.

Microsoft intends to change the policy storage formats in future releases of Windows 2000. Currently, the Windows 2000 IPSec directory policy and local registry storage formats are considered an unpublished data structure that is privately owned by Microsoft.

For more information on implementing SSL or IPSec in your Windows 2000 environment, see *Windows 2000: The Complete Reference*, by Kathy Ivens and Kenton Gardinier.

Customizing Outlook Web Access

Prior versions enabled administrators to modify the Active Server Pages comprising Outlook Web Access to provide a corporate look or to customize applications. Because this involved modifying the actual application code, it was problematic and potentially destructive to Outlook Web Access functionality. Because of its new architecture, there are no ASP files you can modify to customize the user interface. You can, however, reuse Outlook Web Access components in your applications, making it possible to provide a completely customizable version of Outlook Web Access.

Solutions for Knowledge Workers

Ultimately, your business requirements will determine the extent to which you customize Outlook Web Access. You may want to customize Outlook Web Access in some form or another.

Outlook Web Access can be customized in several respects. First, it can branded by placing corporate logos and other image files into the application's image folder (\exchsrvr\exchweb\img). Second, it can be extended using a variety of methods:

- **Using Web Store forms** Microsoft has provided an HTML forms authoring tool that allows you to use FrontPage 2000 to create Web Store forms that can be added to the Outlook Web Access Forms Registry. Web Store forms are browser-based forms that are stored in the Web Store and transmitted via HTTP directly to the browser by Exchange. Internet Explorer 5 provides additional user interface functionality, including drag and drop. This provides developers and designers with a powerful, integrated tool for building applications on the business logic, events, and metadata properties of the Web Store. These tools are freely downloadable from MSDN (http://msdn.microsoft.com/).
- **Exploiting Internet Explorer 5 behaviors** The Outlook Web Access user interface for Internet Explorer 5 and later is implemented as a set of *DHTML behaviors*. These are lightweight components that use cascading style sheets (CSS) to separate the script from the content and style of a document to bring the benefits of encapsulation and code reuse to DHTML. Behaviors are the components that define actions on a Web page. The \exchsrvr\exchweb\controls folder contains the behavior components (.htc files) that can be reused in custom pages that have been added to Outlook Web Access.
- **Using Active Server Pages** You can create ASP pages that contain scripted objects that access and display data from the information store. These pages can be saved in one or more public folders. Exchange 2000 renders HTML and executes ASP scripts directly in its core process—store.exe. This significantly increases the functionality and performance of Web-enabled applications that access data stored in Exchange 2000. Further, it enables developers to integrate Web Store content (contacts, documents, meetings, tasks, workflow processing, and so on) into their Web applications.
- **Third-party development resources** In addition to the development tools and code samples available through MSDN and MSDN Online, several third-party Web sites have information, instructions, applications, and code samples that will enable you to exploit the new customization features of Outlook Web Access. Sue Mosher's Slipstick Outlook & Exchange Solutions Center (http://www.slipstick.com/), Siegfried Weber's CDO Live Web site (http://www.cdolive.com/) and DevX's Exchange site (http://exchange.devx.com) are three excellent Exchange development resources.

Ongoing Maintenance

Maintenance of Outlook Web Access includes the application of service packs or other fixes, as well as the continuous monitoring and measuring of server performance. To monitor and measure the health, performance, and capacity of your Outlook Web Access servers, you should use System Monitor (formerly Performance Monitor)—or any other tool that collects performance counter data—on a regular basis.

Before you can properly analyze growth and its effect on performance, you must have a starting point for your analysis. This starting point is called a *baseline*. A baseline is the initial performance snapshot collected immediately prior to putting the server into production. Without a baseline, it is impossible to determine performance trends over time or perform any useful capacity planning.

Windows 2000 publishes an extensive and extensible list of collectable performance counter objects which can be monitored for bottlenecks and spikes and which can be collected for creating a baseline and for *trending*. Trending is the analysis of data collected over time. Analyzing trends is important for two reasons. First, it allows an administrator to assess usage patterns. Second, it provides a mechanism for capacity planning.

Usage of network resources always has highs and lows, especially in 24x7 environments. For this reason, it is important to collect performance data at regular intervals over a 24-hour period.

Each published object has one or more performance data counters that provide information on the object's utilization. Once installed, Exchange 2000 and Internet Information Services expand the list of available counters to include Exchange-specific and IIS-specific performance objects. While the list of available performance objects is long, you don't need to collect all of them to get an accurate picture of your Outlook Web Access server's health, isolate bottlenecks, or perform capacity planning.

In prior versions of Outlook Web Access, the most common areas that incurred bottlenecks were in the Active Server Pages and in the MAPI subsystem. Due to the scalability issues with ASP and MAPI sessions, Outlook Web Access for Exchange 5.5 typically only scaled to about 800 light users per server. Because Outlook Web Access for Exchange 2000 doesn't use ASP or MAPI, those bottlenecks are no longer present. When combined with the latest available hardware, including 8-, 16- and 32-way systems capable of supporting 64GB of RAM, Outlook Web Access scales considerably higher than prior versions.

What to Monitor

Despite the removal of the dependencies on ASP and MAPI, you still need to monitor your Outlook Web Access servers for the standard operating system bottlenecks, such as processor, memory, disk, and network, as well as Exchange- and IIS-specific bottlenecks. Table 14-7 lists some recommended objects and counters, along with their descriptions.

Object	Counter/Instance	Description
Logical disk	Current Disk Queue Length Disk Reads/sec Disk Writes/sec	Provides an overall picture of disk activity at the logical disk level
Memory	Available Bytes Page Faults/sec Page Reads/sec Page Writes/sec	Provides an overall picture of memory usage and paging activity
Physical disk	Current Disk Queue Length Disk Reads/sec Disk Writes/sec	Provides an overall picture of disk activity at the physical disk level
Process	% Processor Time—inetinfo, lsass, mad & store	Indicates application and security subsystem impact on processor(s)
Processor	% Processor Time	Provides an overall picture of processor activity
System	Context Switches/sec	Indicates the rate at which the processor(s) switch threads

Table 14-7. *Performance Counters That Should Be Monitored Regularly*

Summary

Outlook Web Access still doesn't match the power and feature set of Outlook 2000, but it is a robust and viable solution for a wide variety of messaging needs. Regardless of your business requirements, chances are you'll find a use for Outlook Web Access. Microsoft is positioning Outlook Web Access as a tool for remote, home, and occasional users. Certainly, that defines Outlook Web Access's core user base. But as more and more companies create virtual partnerships across the Internet, Outlook Web Access provides the unique ability to provide messaging services with equal fidelity inside and outside the corporate security perimeter.

Outlook Web Access can be deployed in any location relative to your company network. The decision on server placement directly impacts your available security options. Outlook Web Access can be secured using a variety of authentication mechanisms, access controls, and data encryption, enabling administrators to make it available internally and externally.

Finally, although Outlook Web Access does not have the scalability limitations found in prior versions, it should still be carefully monitored to ensure that it is performing at optimum levels. Native Windows 2000 tools go a long way toward providing the ability to monitor, collect, and analyze performance data, and a number of third-party tools are also available that provide monitoring above and beyond the native tools.

Because Outlook Web Access is installed automatically on every Exchange 2000 server, it is by far the easiest Exchange client you can deploy. Outlook Web Access provides a solid solution to many of the problems facing businesses that need to provide collaboration, knowledge management, and messaging throughout the entire organization. Although it isn't intended as a replacement for Outlook 2000, it can provide these services with greater ease and at a lower cost.

Chapter 15

Exchange 2000 Conferencing Server

Exchange 2000 Conferencing Server (ECS) is a technology that you're going to want to know how to implement and manage as the months pass because it will likely become a popular method of hosting long-distance face-to-face conferences. This capability could save your company significant dollars by having geographically dispersed knowledge workers meet online instead of flying from one city to another for a series of meetings. Corporations are not quite ready to implement conference services for the mere mortal on an as-needed basis. But as WAN bandwidth infrastructures are increased and as Exchange administrators gain more and better training on this service, the reasons to use this technology will be compelling.

In this chapter, we're going to cover a significant amount of ground. Since this is a new technology, this chapter is written from the perspective that you don't know anything about conferencing. Hence, we'll take some time to go over the basics of conferencing, then we'll discuss the architecture in depth, and finally, we'll illustrate how to install and configure both the conferencing server and the client.

Introduction to Exchange 2000 Conferencing Server

Microsoft Exchange 2000 Conferencing Server allows users to host virtual meetings and conferences through the use of audio, video, shared whiteboard, direct file transfer, and chat. This technology makes use of all the multimedia capabilities on the client.

Deploying or managing Exchange 2000 Conferencing Server requires you to learn a whole new set of terms. Here is a short list of the buzzwords in Conferencing Server:

- **Class D IP address** This is the range of IP addresses from 224.0.0.0 to 239.255.255.255. This range is reserved exclusively for IP multicasting.
- **Conference access pages** These are the Web pages used to join conferences. Each conference site has a Web site that hosts the conference access pages that users access to join the conference.
- **Conference calendar mailbox** This is the mailbox that stores all online conference information for a conferencing site.
- **Conference management service** This is the Exchange 2000 component responsible for the reservation and scheduling of conferences. It also manages resource mailboxes and conference profiles, and routes clients when they join conferences.
- **Conference resource mailbox** This mailbox is invited to the conference to reserve the virtual conference room.
- **Conference technology provider** The component providing the online conferencing service, such as a data conferencing technology provider or a video conferencing technology provider.

- **Conference window** The windows displayed in the browser when a user joins a conference. Its appearance is determined by the technology provider.
- **Conferencing manager** The Microsoft Management Console (MMC) snap-in used to administer conferencing services.
- **Conferencing site** Essentially a collection of conference resources and technology providers that work with the conference management service to provide a conference.

ECS has an easy deployment path. It utilizes Internet Information Services (IIS), Exchange services, and the Outlook client. The Conferencing Manager allows you to control both bandwidth utilization and security. Moreover, ECS has been designed to be scalable and offers fail-over capabilities to ensure that, as demand increases for the video conference, jitter or slow services are minimized by using the bandwidth as efficiently as possible.

Architecturally, conferencing is rather complicated. You must be familiar with several important concepts, including the International Telecommunications Union–Telecommunication Standardization Sector (ITU-T) T.120 Recommendation for Multimedia Conferencing (simply referred to as the *T.120 standard*) and the H.323 Recommendation for Packet-based Multimedia Communications Systems (referred to as the *H.323 standard*), IP multicasting (as defined in RFC 1112), and Windows 2000 Telephony API (TAPI) 3.0. In addition, there are several server-side components that you'll be working with, so let's take some time to learn about the architecture of ECS.

Conferencing Server Architecture

There are several key components that make up the conference server architecture. These components include the conference management service, data conferencing provider, and the video conferencing provider. Let's discuss each component individually.

Conference Management Service

The conference management service (CMS) is the heart of the conferencing system. The CMS manages the scheduling, startup, and breakdown of conference resources. There can be only one CMS active on the network at any given time, though you could have a backup CMS available, but offline.

When a conference is scheduled, the CMS creates a URL for the conference. Conference attendees use their browser and the URL to access the conference. The CMS stores the conference schedules in a specific mailbox created for this purpose. The CMS also controls the lifetime of the conference in cooperation with the conference technology provider so that the conference starts and ends on schedule.

Conferences can be either public or private. If public, they are included in a list of available meetings on the conference access page and any user may join the conference.

If private, they are not listed on the conference access page and a user must have the correct URL in order to join the conference.

The resources that CMS manages must be associated with a conference technology provider (CTP). Exchange 2000 Server ships with two CTPs: Data Conferencing Provider and Video Conferencing Provider. A CTP provides the conferencing service with the ability to publish free/busy information for resources associated with the CTP and defines what these resources are, such as virtual meeting rooms. A resource can be associated with more than one CTP. For instance, an integrated conference room could be associated with both a data conferencing and a video conferencing CTP to help a team of people collaborate on a document.

Third party Independent Software Vendors (ISVs) can write their own CTP to integrate with Exchange 2000 conference services.

Let's take a moment to discuss the data and video CTPs.

Data Conferencing Provider

The data CTP enables conference participants to share applications and whiteboards, to transfer documents, and to chat. This type of collaboration is accomplished using NetMeeting and the chat services that ship with NetMeeting.

Data CTP uses the T.120 standard, and it actively connects a conference participant to an MCU (Multipoint Control Unit) that is closest to his or her network location. This is done to minimize the use of bandwidth between the data CTP and the participant. If the client is running NetMeeting 3.01 or later, the data CTP places the controls for NetMeeting within the conference window.

For private conferences, client certificates will be necessary since the MCU will need to identify the client attempting connection to the private conference. This is done using a Windows 2000 Certificate Services. Without a valid certificate, the user will not be allowed into a private data conference.

Video Conferencing Provider

Video conferencing allows participants to exchange both voice and video. The video CTP can work with T.120 and H.323 clients. When a video CTP resource is scheduled, a multicast IP address is requested from the MADCAP (Multicast Address Dynamic Client Allocation Protocol) server and reserved for the conference. The expiration time of a MADCAP address is the scheduled conference time plus the maximum video conference extension time.The video CTP is managed by the CMS if you're using the T.120 multicast standard to stream the audio/video stream. However, if the video CTP is bridging to an H.323 environment, then it is managed by an MCU in the H.323 topology. To learn more about these standards, please refer to the Conferencing Standard section later in this chapter.

Conference Calendar Mailboxes

The conference calendar mailboxes are used to store the schedule for all online conferences. Each conference is stored as a single entry in the mailbox with the conference's properties, such as security and participants.

The conference resource mailbox is the mailbox defined for each conference room and it is the object that is invited to the conference as a resource. Each room used for a conference is virtual, meaning that there is no physical room to which users attach over the network to engage in a conference. Instead, the "room" is created when the resource is scheduled and at least one participant connects to the virtual room. In one sense (and don't press this analogy too far), it is like a conference call in that the conference "room" doesn't exist until at least one participant dials in to the conference call.

Conferencing Standards

There are a couple of standards that we should discuss as part of the overall look at the conferencing architecture. Those two standards are the T.120 International Telecommunications Union–Telecommunication Standardization Sector (ITU-T) Recommendation for Multimedia Conferencing and H.323, an ITU-T standard for packet-based multimedia communications systems. Since Exchange 2000 defaults to using the T.120 standard, we will start with this standard first.

Multipoint Control Unit

According to the T.120 standard, conferencing services must have multipoint communication. This means that if the conference participants are geographically separated, there is a requirement to join these locations together over a Multipoint Control Unit (MCU), which is more commonly known as a *bridge*.

MCU's can be deployed in such a way as to provide a backbone in which all users have low-cost, high-bandwidth connection to any conference on the network. If a user connects to a conference that is originating on another MCU, the data stream is passed through the MCU spanning tree and the user will receive the data stream from his or her local MCU. This tree is dynamically created based on user demand.

Multipoint connections can be as simple as a point-to-point connection between two users or as complex as needed, with multiple bridges forming a spanning tree of connected hosts. Figures 15-1, 15-2, and 15-3 illustrate the various forms of T.120 multipoint connection topologies.

Notice that in Figure 15-3, you don't need to have hosts connected to each MCU; instead an MCU can, in effect, bridge between two other MCUs without needing to offer services directly to a host.

The specifications for T.120, H.323, and related ITU Recommendations can be found at and purchased from http:// www.itu.int.

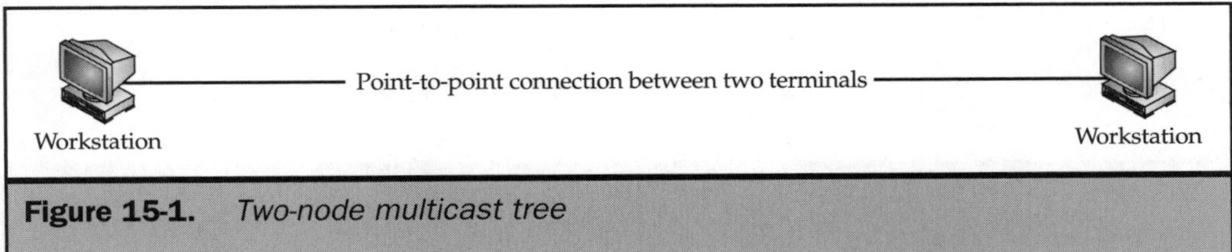

Figure 15-1. *Two-node multicast tree*

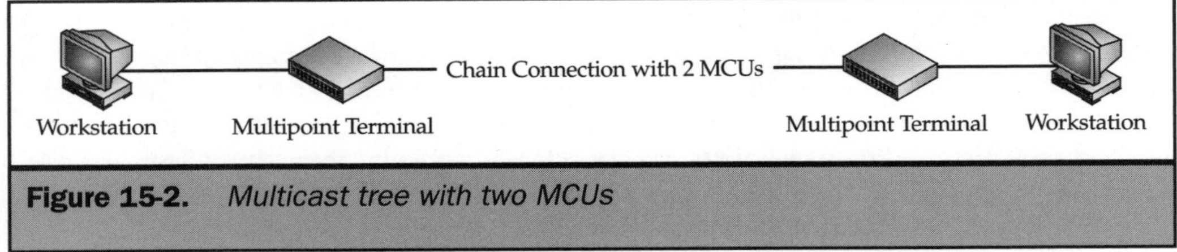

Figure 15-2. *Multicast tree with two MCUs*

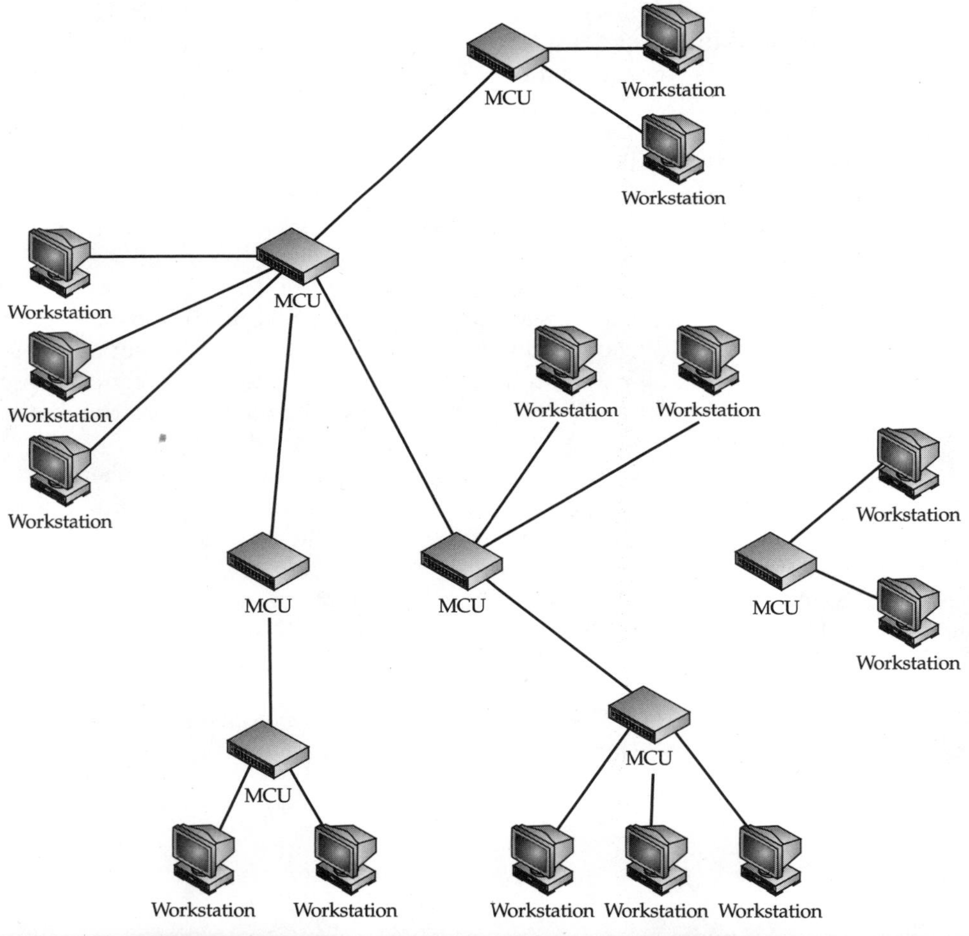

Figure 15-3. *Multicast spanning tree*

IP Multicasting

In most networking environments, packet delivery uses a one-to-one mechanism, employing a unicast address and routes to deliver the data stream. The problem with unicast is that the data stream is duplicated to each client and, with conferencing services, this one-to-one topology is not practical and is wasteful of bandwidth for conferencing services. Instead, we need a one-to-many delivery service and this service is provided by IP Multicast and IGMP (Internet Group Management Protocol).

Tip *IP Multicast is defined in the IETF's RFC 1112, which you can find at http://www.ietf.org.*

IP multicasting requires network hosts, such as a user's desktop, to inform the local routers of the user's interest in receiving multicast traffic so that the routers can forward this traffic to them.

The topology here is different from that of a regular broadcast, in which each node on the system sees the data broadcast and is processed by all nodes, including those to whom the packet is not addressed. In a multicast, a single datagram is sent and forwarded across routers to nodes that are interested in receiving the datagram. It is not forwarded to segments hosting disinterested nodes.

Hence, in a multicast environment, IP multicast traffic is sent to a single destination IP address but is received and processed by multiple hosts, which can be sitting on dissimilar IP networks. After a host registers with a router to receive the data stream, the host listens for traffic sent to that specific multicast IP address and processes the packets received at that address.

There are several elements of an IP multicast. First, all multicast traffic must be sent to a class D address, which is defined as the range of IP addresses between 224.0.0.0 and 239.255.255.255. This address range is reserved exclusively for IP multicast. All traffic addressed to the range 224.0.0.0/24 to 224.0.0.255/24 is for the local subnet and is not forwarded by the routers. All other class D addresses are generally processed and forwarded by routers.

Note *There are some multicast addresses that are reserved:*

- *224.0.0.1 all hosts on this subnet*
- *224.0.0.2 all routers on this subnet*
- *224.0.0.5 Open Shortest Path First (OSPF) version 2, designed to reach all OSPF routers on a network*
- *224.0.0.6 OSPF version 2, designed to reach all OSPF designated routers*
- *224.0.0.9 Routing Information Protocol (RIP) version 2*
- *224.0.1.1 Network Time Protocol*

Second, the set of hosts listening for traffic sent to a specific IP multicast address is called a *host group* (or *multicast group*), and the specific multicast address is called a *group address*. Third, group membership is dynamic, allowing hosts to join and leave the group at any time. Fourth, there are no limits on the size of the host group nor are there limits on the number of groups a host can join concurrently. Fifth, any host can send information to the host group without belonging to the group.

So how does a multicast server know which IP address to select for the multicast address? This is accomplished in Windows 2000 by using the Multicast Address Dynamic Client Allocation Protocol (MADCAP), which is an extension of DHCP (Dynamic Host Configuration Protocol), which is used to assign IP addresses and other IP settings to nodes on the network.

Note *In order for IP multicasting to work, there needs to be a range of multicast Media Access Control (MAC)-layer addresses reserved for multicasting as well. This range is 01-00-5E-00-00-00 to 01-00-5E-7F-FF-FF. So, when a node registers to receive a multicast, it informs the network layer to add the MAC-level multicast address that corresponds to the group address to the list of listening destination MAC addresses. To create this association, the low-order 23 bits of the IP multicast address are mapped directly to the low-order 23 bits in the MAC-layer multicast address. Let's illustrate this with the multicast IP address of 224.224.16.16. To use the 23 low-order bits, the first octet is not used and only the last seven bits of the second octet is used. Since a class D has the first four bits in cement, there are five bits in the first octet that will not map to the MAC-layer multicast address. So, with our address example, in the second octet, the last seven bits become 1100000, or 96. 96 in hex is 0x60. The third and fourth octets are 16 each, or 0x10, so that the MAC address for this multicast IP address is 01-00-5E-60-10-10.*

After the server determines the range of IP addresses for the multicast, it then sends the data stream to that IP address. In order for a host to receive the IP multicast, it must either join a group or create a new host group by performing two registrations: one with the router and the other with the network adapter. It informs the router that it is listening for a certain class D address, and then converts the address to a MAC address. The resulting MAC address is registered with the adapter as a secondary MAC address, and used to listen for IP multicast packets. The protocol used to register with the router is an an IGMP Host Membership Report message.

Routers and Multicasting

In order for multicasting to work, the routers must be multicast-enabled so that they can receive and forward multicast IP traffic, receive and process IGMP Host Membership Report messages, and communicate with other multicast-enabled routers.

Because the membership of a host group is subject to constant change, routers must exchange host membership information on a regular basis to maintain an accurate topology for the multicast. Group membership is communicated by exchanging group address and subnet information and by informing upstream routers about downstream group membership. This information is held in an IP multicast forwarding table on each router.

Periodically, the router will send a Host Membership Query message to all the hosts on a segment to see if there are any hosts listening for multicast traffic. Hosts on the segment that are listening for multicast addresses will respond with a Host Membership Report for all the host groups for which the host is a member. If there are no responses to the query or no response for a particular host group, the router will remove the group from its multicast forwarding table.

When a multicast is routed on the Internet, the data stream takes advantage of the Multicast Backbone, or *MBone*. The MBone is a series of MCU islands that pass multicast traffic between themselves to present conferences and other data streams to end users. It is estimated that, at the time of this writing, there are about 3,200 public networks on the Internet that help form the MBone. The MBone works with IGMP to run the multicast IP address. In addition, the MBone uses the Real-time Transport Protocol (RTP) to ensure packet delivery in environments that fluctuate frequently between being congested and being available. RTP is designed to work under these conditions. Control messages for RTP are handled by the Real-Time Control Protocol (RTCP), which is defined in RFC 1890. Each MBone-compliant application must be able to use both RTP and RTCP.

Windows 2000 itself is not RTP-compliant. However, Microsoft NetMeeting uses both RTP and RTCP.

Data conferencing requires the use of an MCU. When you install Exchange 2000 Conferencing Server, setup creates an AutoEnrollment object that attempts to retrieve a machine certificate from the root domain Certificate Authority. The Conference Management Service (through IIS) and/or the conference technology provider validate the credentials of each participant before allowing them to join the conference.The MCU also queries Certificate Services for a machine certificate, which it uses to authenticate participants. The Windows CryptoAPI (CAPI) is used to obtain a list of valid certificate authorities in the organization. The MCU compares this list against the certificate provided by the client for verification. Without a valid certificate, the MCU cannot host a private data conference.

In large environments, you should consider having multiple MCUs installed. Multiple MCUs will load-balance between each other and will fail over to another MCU should one go offline. In addition, the use of MCUs can reduce cross-subnet traffic. For instance, if ten users on subnet1 and ten users on subnet2 are both joined to the same conference, only the MCUs will pass information across the router to each other. The users will not, since each MCU is hosting the conference for the users closest to it.

Any T.120 client with ActiveX capabilities in their browser should be able to connect to an MCU and join a data conference. Microsoft's T.120 client is NetMeeting 3.01, which can be freely downloaded from http://www.microsoft.com/netmeeting.

Advantages and Limitations of IP Multicasting Multicasting has two advantages. First, network bandwidth is conserved because there is a single video/audio stream that doesn't require additional bandwidth as more users join the host group. In environments where conferencing is employed but bandwidth is limited, this feature is most appreciated. Second, every attendee can see video on all other attendees. For smaller meetings, this can be pretty helpful because much of our communication is nonverbal. Being able to see the other attendees aids in the overall communication between participants. In larger meetings where there are too many participants to view simultaneously on the same screen, this feature loses some of its impact, though the ability to see the another's nonverbal expressions and hear the voice tone enables better communication than a written word in an e-mail message or instant message.

Multicasting also has several limitations. First, the network routers between the host conferencing server and all the clients must be multicast enabled. If there is a router in the physical topology that needs to pass the data stream and it is not multicast-enabled, the stream will fail at that router and some users will not be able to register for the conference. Second, each client must be multicast capable. Clients who are not multicast capable will not be able to join the conference. Third, participating in a multicast can be processor intensive at the client because it is the client that performs the audio mixing along with receiving the video streams.

In spite of these limitations, IP multicast is the default method employed by conferencing services to push out a video conference. However, in some environments, IP multicast may not be available or its limitations may represent deployment issues. For these environments, the H.323 method can be employed to conduct a video conference.

H.323 H.323 is a point-to-point standard that provides audio and video streams to an H.323 client. Each client sends its audio and video stream to a multipoint control unit (MCU). The MCU mixes the audio from the clients and sends it back to them. The MCU is also responsible for switching the video feed between clients. Obviously, this standard usually requires more bandwidth to implement than does the T.120 standard. Moreover, because the video feed is switched between participants in the video conference, each individual participant cannot see the video of all the other participants simultaneously. Instead, they can only view one other participant at a time. Finally, it won't be readily apparent who the *active talker* is. Even in a conference with multiple participants, there is only one active talker at any given time. Whoever sent the last audio stream is considered to be the active talker. When someone starts speaking, their video won't appear immediately. The Active Talker algorithm in the Exchange 2000 H.323 Video Conference Bridge can take as long as seven seconds to start the active talker's video.

Microsoft implements the H.323 standard to ensure that all H.323 clients can connect to a video conference. Exchange 2000 Conferencing Server uses a customized model of the H.323 standard that only works with Microsoft NetMeeting. Instead of using an MCU, Exchange 2000 Server implements a bridge between the H.323 clients and the multicast stream. Thus, when a non-Windows 2000 client or a client that is not multicast-enabled attempts to join a conference, the client calls the H.323 bridge with enough information to identify the conference. The bridge verifies that it has connectivity to the multicast itself, obtains the data streams, and routes it back to the H.323 client. The bridge is also responsible for sending the client's participation to the multicast host group. Hence, the H.323 bridge connects non-multicast clients to a multicast conference. Bear in mind that these H.323 clients must be Microsoft NetMeeting. No other H.323 clients are supported.

The H.323 has four major components. The first are *terminals*, which are the client endpoints on the network. All terminals must support voice communication. Video and data support is optional in the H.323 standard.

The second component is a *gateway*, which is an optional element. Gateways bridge H.323 conferences to dissimilar networks, protocols, and formats. Gateways are not required if connections to other non-H.323 networks is not necessary.

The third component is a *gatekeeper*, which performs address translation and bandwidth management. Gatekeepers are not required in an H.323 network, but if one is available, it must be used.

The fourth component in an H.323 standard is the *Multipoint Control Unit* (MCU), which supports conferences between three or more endpoints.

MADCAP Multicast Address Dynamic Allocation Protocol is the method used by conferencing services to assign a Class D IP address to the conference. A MADCAP scope is created in the DHCP (Dynamic Host Configuration Protocol) Manager. To create a MADCAP scope, right-click on the server name in the DHCP Manager and select New Multicast Scope. Enter a class D IP address range, such as 229.0.0.1–229.0.1.0, enter any exclusions you might have, adjust the lease duration for what seems reasonable (30 days is the default), activate the scope and you're done.

Then, in order to get the resource to use this scope, you'll need to specify it in the Video CTP properties.

Multiple MADCAP servers can be installed to improve server reliability and efficiency. If one MADCAP server is down, then another one can be used from which to lease an address for the online conference. You'll need to configure each Video Conferencing Resource to use more than one MADCAP scope and you'll need to ensure that the scopes don't overlap between the DHCP servers.

Planning for Exchange 2000 Conferencing Services

Before you install Exchange 2000 Conferencing Services, you should take some time to plan for the installation and understand how ECS will impact your network.

Software Planning

In order to run ECS, you'll need to have these five server components running and available to ECS:

- Exchange 2000 Server ECS will require that Exchange 2000 Server is running in the same domain. It is not required that ECS be installed on the same server as Exchange 2000. In addition, ECS will need access to the Schedule+ Free Busy Information public folder, so this folder or a replica of this folder will need to be available in the domain in which you installed ECS.
- Windows 2000 Server ECS can be installed on either Windows 2000 Server or Windows 2000 Advanced Server. In addition, you'll need to create a separate Active Directory user account for each conference calendar mailbox and conference resource.
- Certificate Services ECS will need certificate services installed in the forest for issuing certificates to MCU servers and conference participants. These certificates are used to authenticate users to an online conference and by MCUs to authenticate between themselves.
- Multicast Address Dynamic Client Allocation Protocol (MADCAP) MADCAP services must be available on your network for serving out IP multicast address scopes for video conferences.
- Internet Information Services (IIS) ECS will need IIS installed to host the conference Web pages. IIS needs to be installed on the same site as the Conference Management Service.

On the client, we recommend the following software installed on the desktops of your users in order for them to take full advantage of ECS:

- Windows 2000 Professional or Server or later While most desktops will have professional installed, Windows 2000 Server will work here, too.
- Outlook 2000 or later The minimum e-mail application needed here is Outlook 97. Conferences can also be scheduled with Outlook Web Access.
- NetMeeting 3.01 or later This is automatically installed with the Windows 2000 operating system. Older versions of NetMeeting will work, but only users with 3.01 or later can participate in secure conferences.
- Internet Explorer 5.0 or later If you want to use a browser other than Internet Explorer, then be sure that it is frames-capable, that JavaScript is enabled, and that it is able to download Active X controls.

Hardware Planning

When looking at server hardware, the phrase "it all depends" is pretty accurate, meaning that it all depends on the amount of traffic the ECS server is going to experience. The minimum hardware requirements of a Pentium 133Mhz processor with 128 MB of RAM are too little for most environments. Microsoft's testing has determined that a Pentium 400MHz processor with 256 MB RAM will process around 500 simultaneous user connections. We recommend starting with a Pentium III 800MHz processor or higher with 512 MB of RAM as a starting point. Then, conduct performance monitoring on the ECS server to determine if or when additional hardware is required. Of course, if ECS is also installed with Exchange 2000 Services, you'll need to consider additional hardware requirements to satisfy both server platforms.

At the desktop, we recommend at least a Pentium 400 MHz processor with 128 MB of RAM, since most desktops will be running other applications along side NetMeeting. What is also important to consider at the desktop is the quality of the sound card, speakers and microphone, or headset that the users will be issued. Generally, it is better to have users working with headsets than a speaker and stand-alone microphone. Headsets prevent feedback, which if introduced into the data stream, can kill the audio stream for all confernce participants.

If users are going to be dialing up to your network to participate in the video conference, then make sure they have at least a 56.6 Kbps modem. It would be better if they had an ISDN (Integrated Services Digital Network) line, because the video over a 56.6 Kbps modem will probably have jitter and frozen images. An ISDN or DLS (Digital Subscriber Line) connection will help deliver a better flow of video frames to the end user. Obviously, the higher the bandwidth connection, the better the flow of the data stream.

Conferencing Server Placement

Since each network is different, it is impossible to spell out where you should place your Conferencing Sites. Each Conferencing Management Service (CMS) requires association with at least one Windows 2000 Site, and there can be only one CMS active and running in any given Windows 2000 site at any time. Multiple CMS servers can be installed in one Windows 2000 site, but only one can be active at any given time.

In environments with only one Windows 2000 site, you'll only be able to select one Conferencing Site. However, in networks with multiple Windows 2000 sites, you should consider several elements to develop your Conferencing Site strategy.

First, try to anticipate how conferencing will be used in your environment. Who are the users whom you think will most often utilize this technology? Will it be deployed organization-wide or just to a select group of users? If the latter, then try to deploy your ECS servers in the same Windows 2000 site in which the users are physically located. If the anticipated users are dispersed across multiple Windows 2000 sites and the Wide Area Network (WAN) connections are either unreliable or often saturated, consider installing an MCU in each Windows 2000 site and allow the MCUs to share the broadcast stream across the WAN connection.

If you are planning to deploy ECS to each user in your organization, then you might want to survey a sample of users across your organization to get an idea about how often they plan to use ECS and with whom would they be most likely to enter into a conference. Such data may help you map out conference traffic patterns, which will in turn influence your decisions about where to place ECS servers and how many Conferencing Sites you'll need. In multisite environments, installing multiple Conferencing Sites will allow for a balancing of network load among multiple MCUs, which in turn will result in improved performance. And remember that for each Conferencing Site you create, you'll need to create a Conference Calendar Mailbox and Conferencing Technology Providers.

If you plan to offer conferences over the Internet, consider creating a separate Conferencing Site just for public conferences. Users on the Internet can then access a list of public conferences, but they won't be able to see internal conferences in your organization. If you're in a single Windows 2000 site and you want to offer public conferences on the Internet while not allowing Internet users the ability to see internal conferences, then you'll need to create a second Windows 2000 site and either create a new IP subnet for this new site or move one of your IP subnets to this Windows 2000 site.

If you are running in a mixed environment of Exchange 5.5 and Exchange 2000 servers and you want users hosted on an Exchange 5.5 server to be able to schedule an online conference, you'll need to create a two-way Active Directory Connector (ADC) Connection Agreement (CA) to replicate conference resources from Active Directory (AD) to Exchange 5.5. However, if you're managing a mixed environment, chances are good that you have already installed the ADC service. In this case, you'll only need to create another two-way CA to get the conferencing objects replicated between the Exchange 5.5 directory and AD.

Each installation of ECS also installs a set of Conference Access Pages inside of IIS so that users can select conferences in which to participate. In a single Conferencing Site, usually a single IIS server hosting these pages will be sufficient. However, if the pages are heavily accessed, then you may need to host these pages on more than one IIS server. Doing so means that you'll need to communicate to your users the different Uniform Resource Locator (URL) of these pages so that users can connect to the pages that are closest to them or the pages that you direct them to use. Be sure to identify each conferencing server with the same virtual network name as the one configured in the Conference Management Service.

For Internet connections, you can secure Conference Access Pages by configuring Basic Authentication in the virtual root of the IIS directory so that users who do not have usernames and passwords in AD can still authenticate with a Guest-type account that you create specifically for this purpose.

In a multisite environment, consider directing users to the Conference Access Pages that has been installed in the local Conferencing Site. However, if they need to connect to a conference that is in a different Conferencing Site, the URL in the e-mail invitation will take them directly to the conference in the other site.

If you would like to have all the conferencing sites use the same access pages, then define a virtual host name in the Domain Naming System (DNS) and configure each Conferencing Management Service to use this virtual name for its access pages. This is configured on the Conference Settings tab in the Conferencing Site properties. Just type in the correct URL and all users in that conferencing site will be directed to the central access pages. In addition, all future scheduled conferences will use that URL as well as the access point for the conference.

Planning for the Multipoint Control Unit (MCU)

When users access a conference, they are directed to the closest MCU by the Data Conferencing Technology Provider. This provider knows where to send the client by finding the IP address in the client's browser, finding a conferencing site that has ownership for the client's IP address, and then connecting the client to an MCU in that conferencing site. Be sure to configure your users browsers to list the MCUs in its inclusion list for proxy server bypass.

If needed, you can secure an MCU by restricting user access to the MCU based on where the request is originating. An MCU can determine if the request is from a local Windows 2000 site, a remote Windows 2000 site, or from the Internet. You can configure restrictions from any of these three locations and by any combination of network addresses for each location.

For instance, if you have a group of users in one Windows 2000 site that should have conferencing services and these users reside on one set of subnets, you could configure an MCU to accept client requests only from the subnets on which the users reside by restricting access from all other subnets.

Planning for the Conference Calendar Mailbox

Since the Conference Calendar Mailbox contains a listing of all the conferences scheduled in the local Conferencing Site along with each conference's properties, this is a mailbox that would pose a significant loss of data if it become unavailable, not to mention that the Conferencing Management Service needs continuous access to this mailbox in order to perform properly. Therefore, you might want to consider isolating this mailbox in its own mailbox store or even its own storage group, though the latter would represent significant overhead for one mailbox. However, in the event of a failure, you would only need to restore one store and storage group in order to retrieve the information in this mailbox.

In addition, because this is a mailbox like any other mailbox, you should create an Outlook profile to access the mailbox and, as a matter of routine, purge old conference entries to keep the mailbox size from growing too large. Older scheduling information can be archived if this historic information is needed for some reason in the future.

Planning for Conferencing Resources

A Conference Resource is a resource that is associated with a Conferencing Technology Provider (CTP). It is the resource that is used by the users during an online conference. The CTP provides the resource. For instance, video conferencing resource will provide a stream of audio and video data to the conference attendees.

Conferencing resources are limited by the number of participants who can use the resource at any given time. For instance, the default number of participants who can use one data conferencing resource is 20. Going with this number, if a user schedules this resource to be used and specifies that there will be ten users joining the conference, then, *during the same scheduled time*, other online conferences can only be scheduled if their requested number of users does not exceed the participant limit of 20. Hence, a second conference could be scheduled that specified seven participants. But a third online conference could not be scheduled during the same time period as the other two if its specified number of participants was more than three.

The calculation of resource availability for each conferencing resource is performed by the CTP. If a user attempts to schedule a conference that exceeds the participant limit of the conference resource, the CPT will cause the resource to be shown as busy.

Planning for Multicasting and Routers

Before you deploy ECS on your network, you'll need to ensure that all your routers can pass multicast traffic and dynamically build the spanning tree. This is particularly a problem on the Internet right now because many routers are not configured to perform these functions. Hence, if you're planning on running conferences over the Internet, you should plan on installing sizable bandwidth into the MCU server that will host the Internet connections, because more than likely, you'll be running H.323 traffic to each Internet client. This means that for each client that connects to a conference over the Internet, the H.323 bridge will be sending out a separate data stream to that client. To be conservative, we'd suggest installing 256Kbps of bandwidth for each Internet client that will use data, audio, and video streams. Shave this in half to 128Kbps for each internet client that will use data and audio but not video.

Also, it is best to use routers that support the Resource Reservation Protocol (RSVP) so that you can configure a Quality of Service (QoS) policy to allocate network bandwidth for a given video/audio stream. QoS policies can be applied to the entire network or to each subnet or individual users.

The amount of time a multicast packet takes to travel from the source to the destination is called *latency*. Latency can be caused by any number of things, including delays in routers, network cards, software transport stacks, or saturated network lines. Minimizing delay improves the user's experience of the conference because the data and video streams arrive more quickly and are more smooth-flowing.

Both clients and servers running Windows 98 and Windows 2000 are automatically configured to use a QoS server to request bandwidth priority. Other devices can also be configured to use QoS, including NICs, switches, and routers. Look for hardware devices that are Subnet Bandwidth Manager (SBM) capable. Such devices will participate, along with Windows 2000 and Windows 98, to work together to elect a Designated SBM (DSBM) for each subnet which will act as the receiving point for all RSVP messages.

Hence, along with a QoS application, each device from the source to the destination can be configured by a QoS policy to reserve a certain amount of bandwidth for a conference data and video stream. This will minimize latency and improve performance.

For more information on configuring and managing QoS, please consult the Windows 2000 Server TCP/IP Core Networking Guide.

Naming Conventions

When it comes to naming conferencing resources, consider naming them with a number after the name so that users know which resource to use given the anticipated number of conference attendees. For instance, if you have a virtual conference room that provides data, audio, and video for ten participants, you might name this room *Conference Room 1 (10)*, where the "(10)" specifies the maximum number of conference participants that this conference room will accept.

In multiconference site environments, consider a naming scheme that will help users understand which site they should use. For instance, geographical names could be used to specify which conferencing site the conference resource is located in, such as *Conference Room 1 Phoenix (10)* or *Phoenix Conference Room 1 (10)*.

Conferencing across a firewall

If you need to run conferencing services across a firewall, there are a couple of ways to do this. First, you can associate a different Network Interface Card (NIC) with a different IP address and host name in DNS. Then, users on the Internet can resolve to the name (and subsequently connect to the NIC) that is configured for Internet access. Internal users can be given a different name to connect to so that Local Area Network (LAN)-based users connect to a different NIC on the server. On the firewall, you'll need to have port 80 open for Internet clients to access the Web pages, port 53 for DNS resolution, port 1503 for the T.120 NetMeeting client, 1731 for NetMeeting Audio Call Control, 1720 for the H.323 call setup, and some UDP (User Datagram Protocol) ports above 1024 open for the UDP dynamic port assignment for streaming H.323 RTP.

If Internet-based clients are going to perform Kerberos authentication on your network, then you'll need to open up the Kerberos port of 88.

Best Practices in planning for ECS

First, if you're planning to offer conferences on both the Internet and internally to your users, but you want to use the same Conference Access Pages, be sure that DNS will allow resolution to these pages from both your internal and external clients.

Second, place the conferencing resources and the Conference Calendar Mailbox the only mailboxes on the server, or at a minimum, the only mailboxes in a single mailbox store. This will increase performance of the Conference Management Service.

Third, use a naming strategy that will specify the conference resource's location and participant limit.

Fourth, configure an MCU for each set of subnets that enjoys permanent, high-bandwidth connectivity. This can be created by installing multiple Conference Management Sites or by installing multiple MCUs in the same Conference Management Site.

Fifth, consider a phased rollout of ECS so that problems can be detected and resolved before the services are deployed on an enterprise-wide basis. Also, consider restricting MCUs to accept calls from subnets that are participating in the rollout to ensure that only those users who should be in the rollout are using conferencing services.

Finally, ensure that all of your routers are T.120 compliant to prevent the need for H.323 bridging.

Installing and Configuring Exchange Conferencing Services

In this section, we'll cover how to install both the server and the client for Exchange 2000 Conferencing services. We'll also show you how to create an online conference and get others connected to the conference. So, let's start by installing the server side of conferencing server.

Installing Exchange 2000 Conferencing

To install Exchange 2000 Conferencing services, you'll need the Exchange 2000 Conferencing Server CD-ROM. This CD is different from the Exchange 2000 Server CD since Conferencing is considered a separate product from the Exchange 2000 platform. In order to set up conferencing services, you'll need

- Active Directory
- Windows 2000 Quality of Service (QoS) Admission Control components
- Multicast-enabled DHCP Server
- Internet Information Services
- Exchange 2000 Server
- Exchange 2000 Conferencing Server
- Outlook 2000 or later
- NetMeeting 3.01 or later
- Knowledge of your network topology

If your conferencing clients are running Windows 2000, chances are they already have NetMeeting installed. If your Windows 2000 clients do not have Windows 2000 Service Pack 1 or later installed, you will need to install it before they will be able to use ECS. Also, be sure to install the latest service pack for Windows 2000 and Exchange 2000, as there may be upgrades to the underlying services that support conferencing services. Finally, be sure to check Microsoft's Download Center Web site at http://www.microsoft.com/downloads to see if there are any hotfixes that have been published for Exchange 2000.

Exchange 2000 Conferencing Server gets installed on top of an existing Exchange 2000 Server or Exchange 2000 Enterprise Server computer. If you're running an environment of Windows 2000 Active Directory and Exchange 5.5 servers, you'll need to either upgrade one of the Exchange 5.5 Servers to Exchange 2000 or install a new Exchange 2000 Server in your AD forest in order to install Exchange 2000 Conferencing Server.

After running the setup program, you'll be presented with the generic welcome screen, after which some setup files will load. Thereafter, you'll need to agree to the license agreement and then enter the product key code. On the following screen, you can choose to perform a complete install, which installs all the components, or a custom install, which allows you to choose between installing four components (Figure 15-4):

- **Conference Management Service** Be sure to associate at least one CMS per Windows 2000 Site. Others can be installed but not started so that if the online CMS goes offline for some reason, another one can be quickly brought online to assume the CMS responsibilities for that site.
- **T.120 MCU/H.323 Conference Bridge** You'll need to install this component in order to install the T.120 multipoint services and the H.323 bridge.
- **Conference Access Web Pages** This selection installs the Web pages necessary for clients to connect to a video conference.
- **Conferencing Manager** This is the snap-in tool used to manage conferencing services. You can install this component on machines other than conference servers to perform remote administration of conferencing services.

After making your component selections, you'll be asked to choose which Exchange 2000 administrative group you would like to install the conference manager into, and then the installation will proceed.

If you install Exchange 2000 Server with Conference Management Service selected, you might find that the directory objects for conferencing are not added to the administrative group that you selected during the setup process. Instead, you'll find them under the administrative group of the initial conferencing server install. This behavior is by design. The setup process will determine if there is an existing conference zone that is already defined in the local Windows 2000 site. If there is one, then all the objects for conferencing will be placed in the administrative group of the first conference server installation.

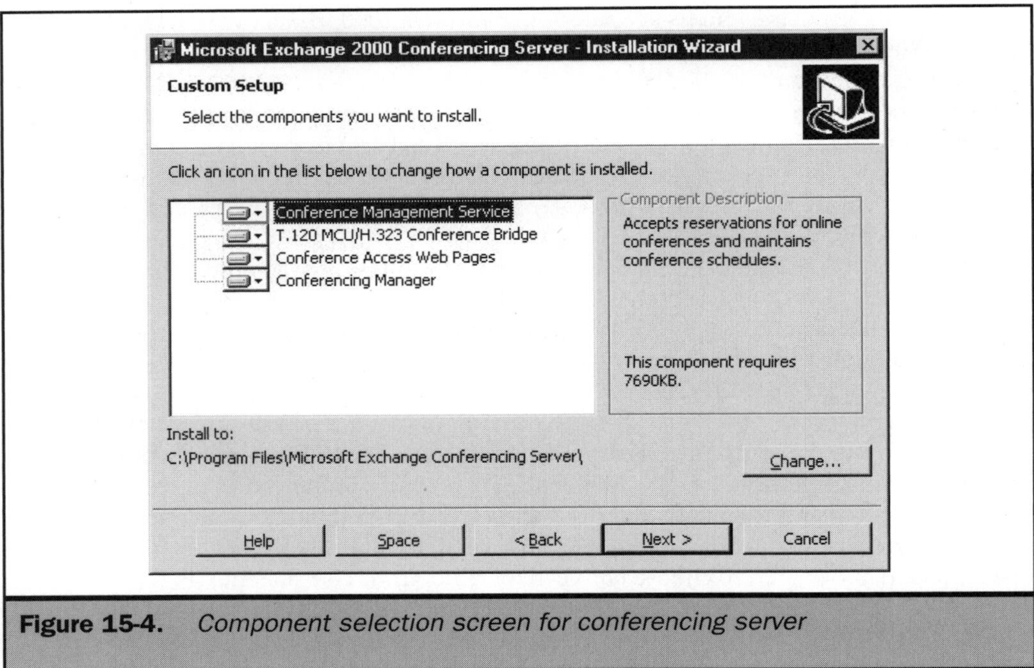

Figure 15-4. *Component selection screen for conferencing server*

After the installation process has finished, you're ready to configure conferencing services on the server itself.

Troubleshooting Failed Installations

In this section, we'll cover some of the problems with failed installations of Conferencing Server. Before you install conference server, it might be a good idea to enable verbose logging so that, if the installation fails, you'll be able to read the log and determine the point at which the installation failed. To enable verbose logging, add the following registry value:

HKEY_LOCAL_MACHINE\SOFTWARE\Policies\Microsoft\Windows\Installer
Value: Logging
Type: REG_DWORD
Data: impo!uwearcv

Tip *For details on deciphering the strange looking Data entry for the above value, see Microsoft Knowledge Base article Q223300.*

The log file will be named Msi#####.log and will be located in the Temp directory.

If you are using the Terminal Services client to install conferencing server and the source files are on a mapped drive that you created using the terminal services client, the installation will fail with an *Internal Error 2755.3* message. The resolution is to point to the source files using a Universal Naming Convention (UNC) path instead of a mapped drive. See the Microsoft Knowledge Base article Q286440 for details on this issue.

If the server in which you wish to install conferencing server has a different DNS (Domain Name System) suffix than the Windows 2000 domain of which the server is a member, the installation will fail. You'll need to either change the suffix of the local server or enter the following registry key:

HKEY_LOCAL_MACHINE\SOFTWARE\Microsoft\Exchange Conferencing\Parameters
Value Name: Setup Prerequisites
Type: REG_DWORD
Data: 000001a7 (hex)

Note *The hex value shown for the Data in the above registry entry is for the first installation of Exchange 2000 Conferencing Server with IIS. If this is not your situation (e.g., this is your second installation with IIS, or your first installation without IIS), the value you enter will be different. See the Microsoft Exchange 2000 Conferencing Server Release Notes (on the Exchange 2000 Conferencing Server CD) and Microsoft Knowledge Base article Q273655 for more information on this issue, including the list of valid entries.*

Configuring Exchange 2000 Conferencing Server

To configure Exchange 2000 Conferencing Server, navigate to the Conference Manager snap-in, which will be located in the Exchange 2000 menu options, and open the Exchange Conferencing Manager (ECM) snap-in.

At first, you'll be presented with only an Exchange Conferencing object in the console root. Your first action will be to right-click on this object and select Manage. Doing this will invoke a drop-down list in which you can select the Windows 2000 site that the current server is located in. Remember that you can have only one CMS running per Windows 2000 site, so be sure that there are no other CMS servers running in the site you select. Even though you're choosing from the list of Windows 2000 Sites, you're technically choosing a conference management site, and you'll see only the list of sites for which you have permission to either view or manage.

If this is your first time configuring the conferencing site, there will be a check to make sure there is a conference calendar mailbox available for scheduling in the site. In our example, this is the first time we've opened up the ECM snap-in, so we need to create a conference calendar mailbox. In the Conference Calendar Mailbox dialog box, we'll choose to create a new mailbox and input our information into the Create Conferencing Calendar dialog box, as illustrated in Figure 15-5.

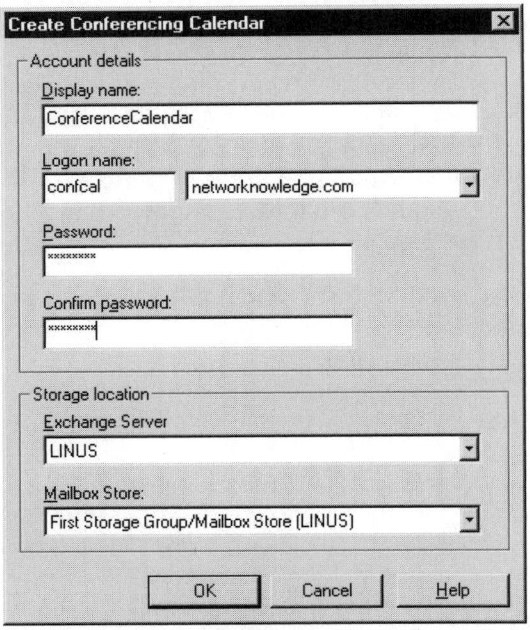

Figure 15-5. *The Create Conferencing Calendar dialog box*

After the mailbox is created, you'll see the results in the Conference Calendar Mailbox screen, as illustrated in Figure 15-6. The conference calendar mailbox is the central place where all conference schedules are stored for a conference site. A CMS must be associated with the conference calendar mailbox to work properly.

Multiple calendar mailboxes can be created in case the store that is hosting the active mailbox goes offline and you need to bring up another mailbox right away. Only one mailbox may be active at any given time in the CMS site.

The Logon Name is used to identify the SMTP address for the mailbox so that it can appear as a conference resource in the Outlook client. In addition, you can log in as the conference calendar mailbox and configure advanced security options using the mailbox profile (we'll illustrate this later in this chapter).

To set an offline mailbox as active, simply highlight the mailbox and click on the Set Active button. There won't be any visual change in the list of mailboxes, so you'll know the mailbox went active because the Set Active button dimmed when the action was applied.

In addition, when you set another box as active, the entire current conference schedule in the original mailbox will be invalidated and all existing conferences will

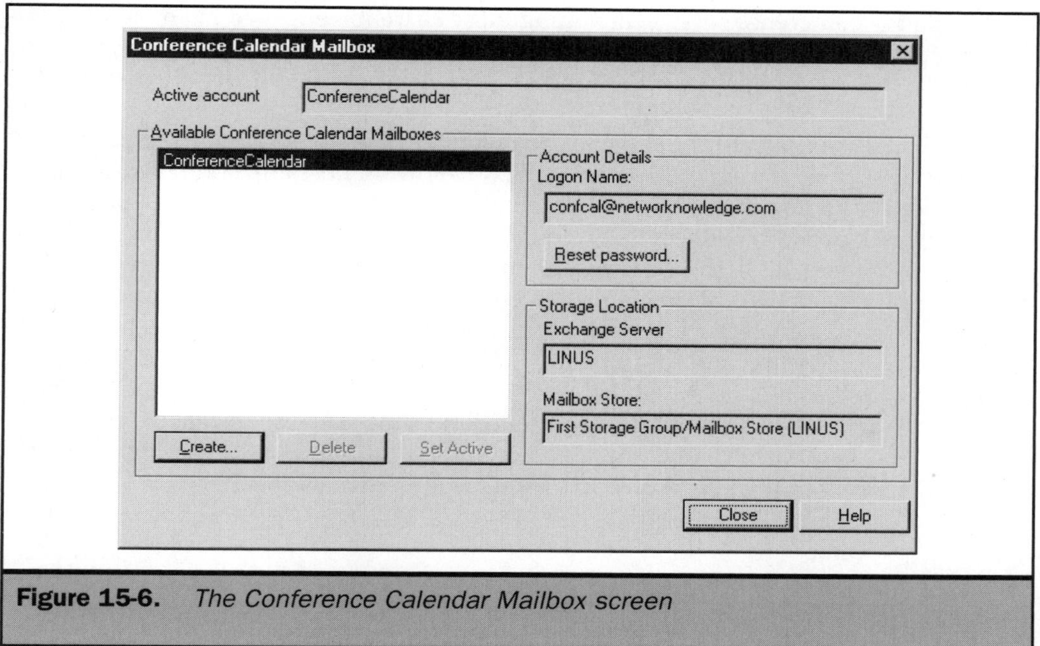

Figure 15-6. *The Conference Calendar Mailbox screen*

need to be rescheduled. Obviously, you won't want to change the active mailbox for a CMS site too many times. A warning screen reminding you of these points will appear and you'll need to "Yes" through the box in order to change the active mailbox.

If the mailbox you choose to set as the active mailbox is hosted on a different server than the server hosting the conferencing services, you'll receive a warning message indicating that performance may be degraded as a result of this configuration. You can then choose to continue with this configuration choice or choose No and go back to selecting a mailbox that is hosted on the same server as the conferencing service.

Now you're ready to configure the CMS service. If you open up the Conference Manager snap-in, you'll notice that under the CMS service are two CTPs, the Data Conferencing and Video Conferencing Providers. To configure the CMS service for the site, open the properties of the <sitename> Conferencing Site. To configure the CTP, open the properties of the desired provider. All these properties may be opened by right-clicking on the object and selecting Properties from the context menu.

Let's first configure the CMS service. When we open its properties, we'll see that there are four tabs: General, Conference Settings, Resources, and Logging. The General tab informs us as to the current host server for the conferencing services and the current active conference calendar mailbox. Selecting the Modify button for the host server allows you to select another server that has the CMS services installed to assume the role as the active conferencing host server. Doing so, however, will disconnect all users from the conference service, including those currently engaged in an online conference. Selecting the Modify button for the active site conference calendar mailbox will invoke the Conference Calendar Mailbox screen, which we previously discussed (Figure 15-7).

On the Conference Settings tab, you can enter a different URL than the default, which is http://<servername>/conferencing, to allow for customization in your environment. And you can configure the length of time before a conference starts during which a user can connect to the conference. The default is 20 minutes. It is best to leave this figure a bit high since it is difficult to get everyone in the conference to join it at the same time. However, ending a conference is different in that it is easier for everyone to leave a conference at nearly the same time. In some cases, it might be wise to extend the conference, and the maximum allowed time to extend the conference is configurable in the "Extend scheduled end time for conferences" input box. Only the conference organizer can extend the conference end time. You can also allow or disallow the organizer to change the conference end time and change the conference resource by selecting the appropriate checkboxes, shown in Figure 15-8.

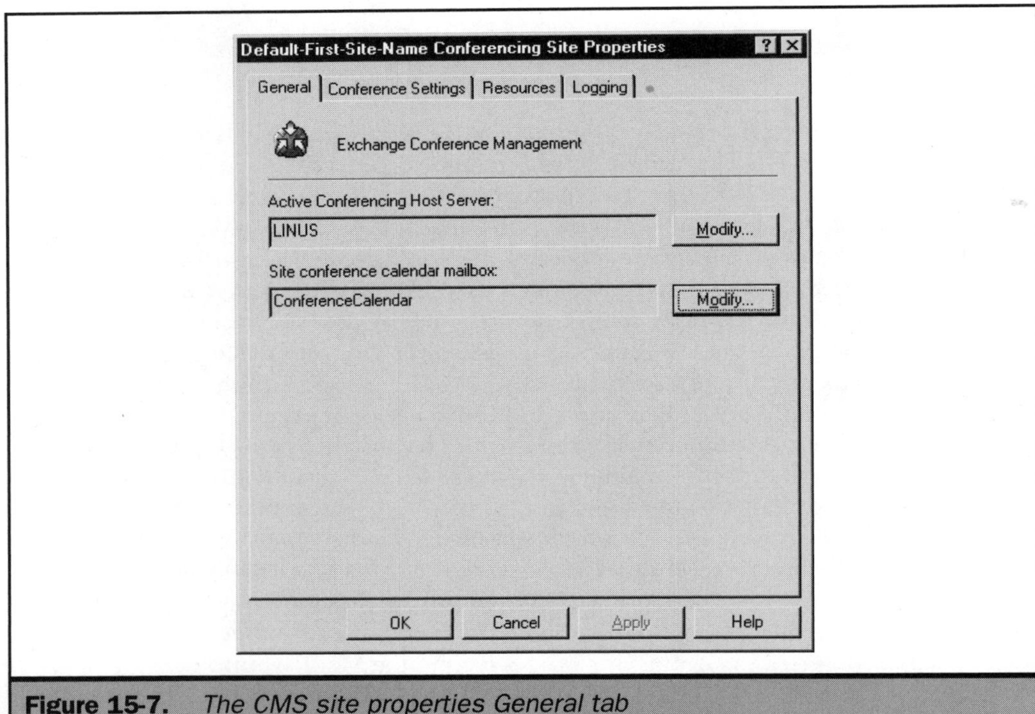

Figure 15-7. *The CMS site properties General tab*

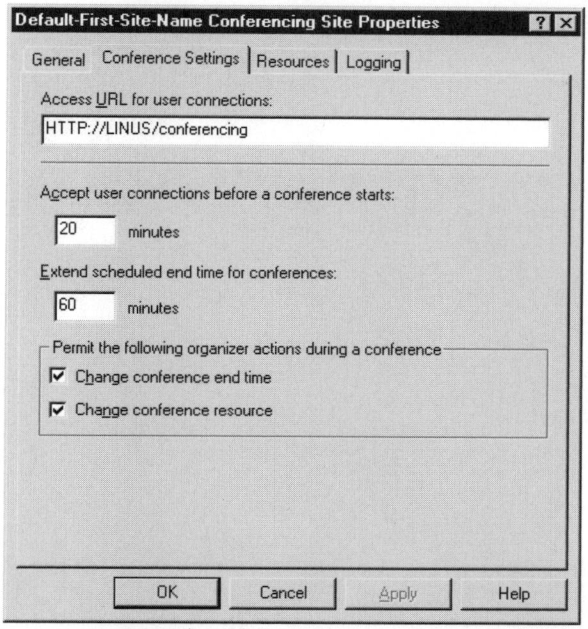

Figure 15-8. *Conference Settings tab in CMS properties*

The Resources tab will list the conferencing resources associated with the CMS site. You can add, modify, and delete resources from this location. The Logging tab allows you to select which type of event logging you need to appear in the application log of the Event Viewer.

Configuring Technology Providers

The CTP properties are not complex, but they are important to consider when managing a CMS site. First, let's look at the Data Conferencing Provider properties in Figure 15-9. You'll see that there are two input boxes and one checkbox.

The first option sets the total number of connections that can be made through the provider. This is the maximum number of simultaneous users that can make connections to all MCUs in the CMS site. If you want to limit the amount of bandwidth that is used by a CMS, then limit the number of users who can connect to all the technology providers concurrently.

So, let's illustrate this. Assume you have three resources scheduled for a CMS site, Room1, Room2, and Room3. Let's further assume that Room1 has a limit of

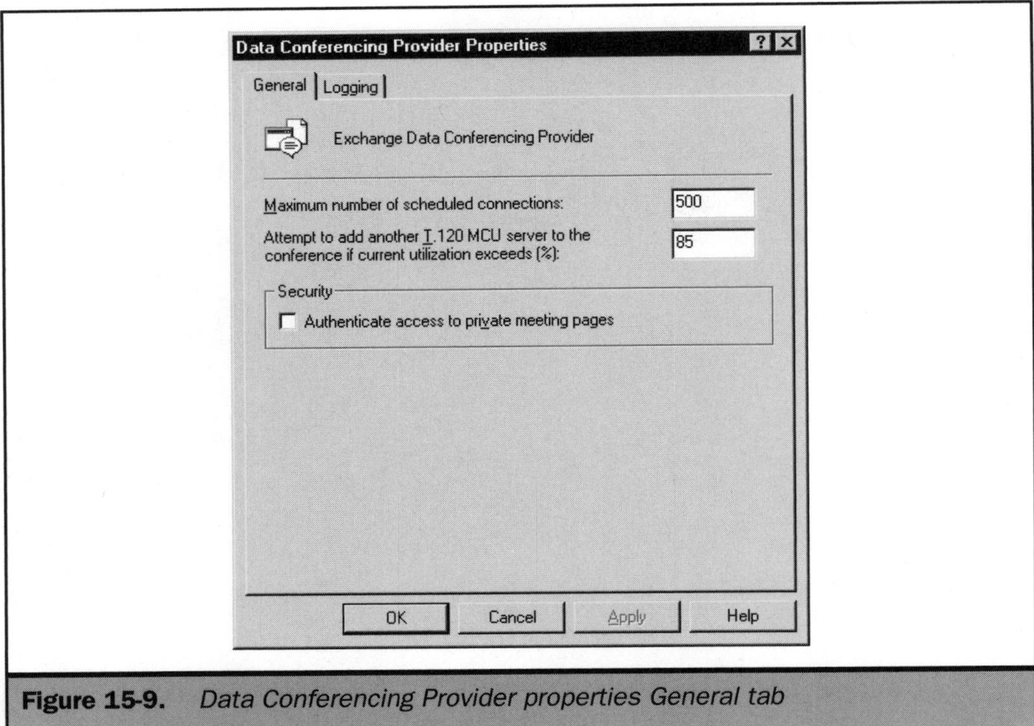

Figure 15-9. *Data Conferencing Provider properties General tab*

50 connections, Room 2 has a limit of 15 connections, and Room 3 has a limit of 20 connections, with a maximum of 65 total connections. If Joe reserves Room1 with 50 connections and then Sally reserves Room2, then the total connections is within the maximum limit of 65 and both conferences can be booked. However, if Dianne then tries to reserve Room3 during the same time period, the reservation will fail because the limit has been exceeded. In this scenario, the only option is to select a different time for the conference, unless the maximum limit can be increased to accommodate the additional user connections.

If you have more than one MCU configured in your environment, you can allow the CTP to add another MCU automatically by configuring a percentage of utilization on the working MCUs. The default is 85. This utilization percentage is a result of an algorithm that takes into account the MCU server's CPU, memory, and network utilization. Once the threshold is reached, client connections are not load-balanced between the MCUs. Instead, new client connections are sent to the new MCU.

Now, let's look at the Video Conferencing Technology Provider properties. Here, there is less to configure. You can set the maximum number of conference participants as well as the maximum amount of time the conference can be extended by the organizer. You can also require user authentication to access private conferences.

Configuring the T.120 MCU

The T.120 MCU can be found by highlighting the Data CTP in the left pane of the Conferencing Manager and seeing the MCU server in the right pane (Figure 15-10).

There isn't much to configuring the T.120 MCU. You can stop and start the MCU if needed, which is especially helpful if you need to bring another MCU online to help carry the load in a Windows 2000 site.

You can also restrict availability to the MCU by opening up its properties and selecting the Restrict Availability checkbox; the Visibility tab will be parsed for any administrator-defined IP ranges. What this means is that only participants with IP addresses that match the IP ranges defined by you will be allowed to join the MCU.

Putting MCUs in specific subnets and assigning visibility restrictions is ultimately a tradeoff between reliability and performance. If you do use restrictions, don't apply them to remote subnets. Instead, apply them to the entire site.

One thing to be aware of is that, by default, the name in the "Use network name" is the NetBIOS name of the server. Internet-based clients will need to resolve to the Fully Qualified Domain Name (FQDN) of the server. If you find that your Internet-based clients can get to the conference and that the left pane showing the conference information is the only pane available out of the three panes, then have the clients enter the FQDN of the server and its IP address in their hosts file. Doing this should help

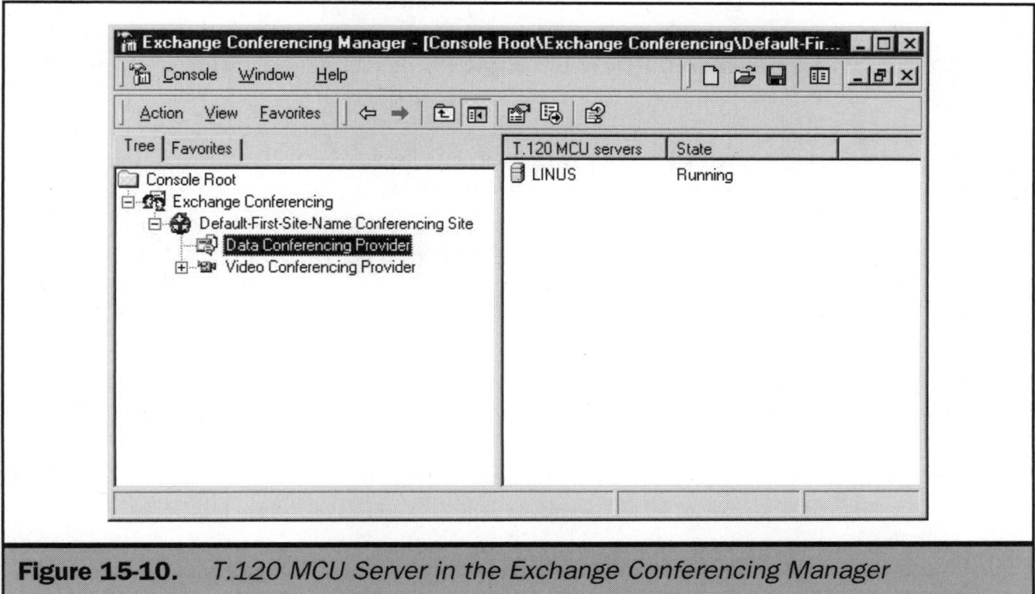

Figure 15-10. *T.120 MCU Server in the Exchange Conferencing Manager*

them resolve to all the URLs on the server. In addition, you should enter the server's FQDN under the "Accept client connections from the Internet" section as well.

Adding a Resource

Remember that a resource is just a virtual place to hold online meetings. You can create five different types of conference resources:

- Data only
- Audio only
- Audio and data
- Audio and video
- Audio, video, and data

If you've installed a third-party CTP, you can create other types of conference resources as well. To create a new conference resource, navigate to the Resources tab in the CMS properties and click Add. The first thing to do will be to set up a new resource mailbox that will handle scheduling for this resource. After setting up the resource mailbox, you'll then be asked to assign one or more technology conference providers. In our example, we'll add a Data Conferencing Technology Provider. When we select the CTP, we are presented with that provider's properties to configure before the CTP is associated with the resource. Once it's configured, we can click OK and the CTP is associated with the CTP (Figure 15-11).

The properties for a new video CTP are somewhat complex (Figure 15-12), so let's discuss each configuration option. First, as you can see, you can limit the number of participants even further than the default setting on the CTP by entering a lower value in the "Limit number of meeting participants to" input box.

By selecting the "Enable H.323 data provider fallback for audio/video conferences" checkbox, you'll enable the H.323 bridge, which has several implications. First, this allows non-multicast users access to the data stream via the bridge. Second, when this checkbox is selected, the compression type and video size options become unavailable, limiting your choices. Finally, just remember that when the H.323 bridge is enabled, you're increasing the system resource utilization because all the data for the conference for the H.323 clients must go through the bridge and then be sent back to the client in a unicast stream.

With the H.323 checkbox cleared, you'll have choices for audio and video playback to the client. Under the Audio section, you can select between the G.711 and GSM 6.10 codec type. The G.711 is the international standard for encoding telephone audio on a 64 Kbps channel. It is a pulse code modulation (PCM) scheme operating at an 8 KHz sample

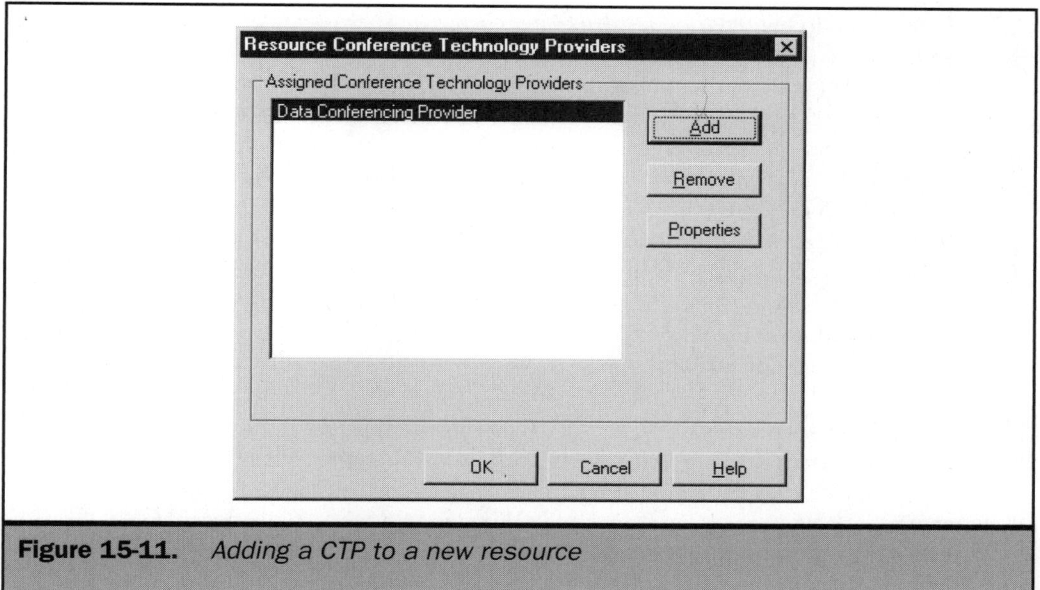

Figure 15-11. *Adding a CTP to a new resource*

rate using 8 bits per sample. The GSM 6.10 (Groupe Special Mobile) offers real-time compression, which makes this option a good one for recording a voice stream. The G.711 generally sounds better and has lower complexity, but it also has a larger data packet. Use the G.711 codec unless there are bandwidth considerations, such as low-connectivity with dial-in users. The G.711 codec generates about 70 Kbps of data compared to about 20 Kbps generated by the GSM 6.10 standard. About the only time you'll want to clear the checkbox to send audio automatically is when the conference attendees use the telephone to communicate instead of the data CTP.

Under the video section, you can choose the codec type of H.261 of H.263. A video codec encodes the video from the source (camera) for transmission and decodes the received video code, which is then displayed in the monitor. Part of the H.323 standard is the requirement that all H.323-compliant terminals be able to encode in H.261 QCIF (quarter common interchange format). Further, the standard allows a compliant terminal to encode using either H.261 or H.263 with CIF (common interchange format) or higher resolution. In neither case, however, is any error correction for framing allowed. Selecting the H.323 bridge defaults this selection to H.263. Generally speaking, if given the choice, we would recommend using the H.263 standard, since it has better overall performance than the H.261 standard.

Note *H.261 & H.263 Standards—A Brief Overview: The H.261 standard's bit rate is between 40 Kbps and 2 Mbps. The CIF format is 352 pels per line, with 288 lines per picture. The QCIF format has half the number of lines as the CIF format. Hence, image size is in pels by lines, so the CIF size of 352x288 is a larger screen size than the QCIF of 176x144. Obviously, the larger screen size will mean that it is easier to see the images in the screen, but it also means that more bandwidth will be consumed sending the video stream. If some of your clients are going to be connecting over an analog 56.6 Kbps connection, you may want to clear the "Automatically send client video at join time." Given that a QCIF video stream consumes between 80 and 130 Kbps of bandwidth, it's easy to understand why a dial-in client may be able to receive only the audio stream. The maximum number of bits created by coding any single CIF picture cannot exceed 256KB or 64KB for a QCIF picture.*

Note *The H.263 uses the same CIF and QCIF specifications as the H.26 standard. It also operates between 40 Kbps and 2 Mbps. However, this standard has better motion compensation than the H.261 standard, leading to a smoother flow of the picture. In addition, the picture rate is increased in this standard while not increasing the bit rate. Video data is supplied to the encoder modules every clock cycle and there is a better buffering architecture for this standard than the H.261 standard. Moreover, more options are available to the programmer on how to implement this standard, leading to an increase in the different picture formats than can be selected when writing components within this standard.*

Finally, you can select which multicast scope this resource should utilize. If you have more than one MADCAP scope created, one or all of the scopes can be selected for this resource to use.

Tip *Controlling Bandwidth and Conferencing Services Usage—As you might expect, video saps bandwidth more than most other technologies, so you might be wondering what kind of bandwidth does a video stream consume? Well, here are some averages. A QCIF (176x144) sized video stream will consume 80 to 130Kbps of bandwidth. A CIF (352x288) sized video stream will consume (approximately) from 210Kbps to 400Kbps of bandwidth. In addition, you must factor in the audio stream. The GSM 6.10 stream will consume about 20 Kbps of bandwidth, whereas other codecs can consume up to 70 Kbps of bandwidth. To limit the amount of bandwidth consumed by conferencing services, you can:*

- *Limit the number and size of available resources*
- *Limit the number of concurrent connections*
- *Use the smaller video size data stream*
- *Use the most compression for the audio stream*

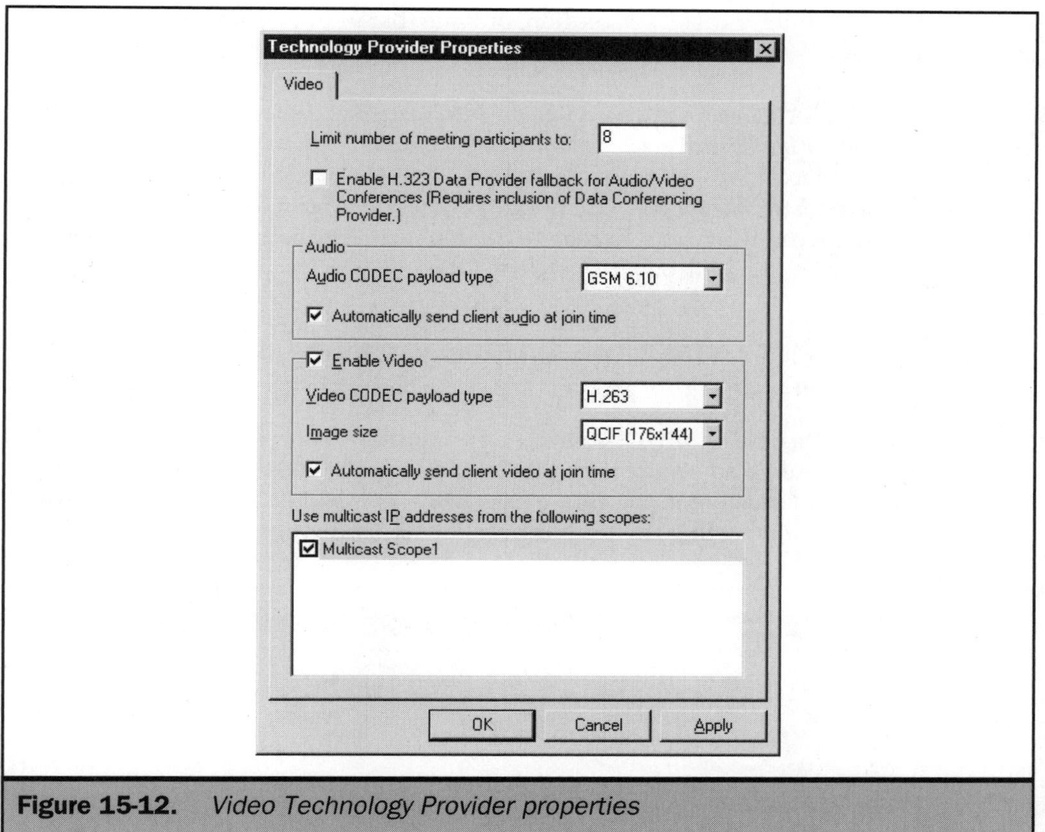

Figure 15-12. *Video Technology Provider properties*

Client Configuration

To configure the client, you'll need Outlook 2000 or later, a video camera, and a sound card with microphone and speakers. If you have Windows 2000 as the operating system, NetMeeting will be installed automatically. If you are using an operating system other than Windows 2000, you'll need to have NetMeeting installed on that client. In terms of a recommended sound and video card, we recommend a 32-bit sound card and a minimum display resolution of 800x600, which will allow for enough desktop space to run the whiteboard and share applications. We also recommend having a video card with 8MB of memory or greater. Headsets generally provide enough sound quality that other choices should be avoided, such as a stand-alone microphone with speakers. For most conferences, USB cameras should suffice. If you need better video than that provided by an off-the-shelf USB camera, then consider purchasing a video-capture card into which you'll plug any standard RCA or S-video camera, such as a camcorder.

This is definitely a more expensive solution, but one that might be warranted in environments that demand high resolution for the conference.

Video conferencing will not work with non-Intel platforms, because the ActiveX controls in the browser are written solely for Intel-based systems.

There is one registry addition to Outlook 2000 that you'll need to make before the Outlook 2000 client can work with Exchange Conferencing Services. Place the following information into a text file called O2KCONFSVC.REG:

REGEDIT4
[HKEY_CURRENT_USER\Software\Microsoft\Office\9.0\Outlook\ExchangeConferencing]

Users can run this file or have it distributed via group policies or a login script. This registry change should also be a part of all new Outlook 2000 installations if you plan to deploy video conferencing in the enterprise. When you add this registry key, several items are added to the meeting request form, as illustrated in Figure 15-13.

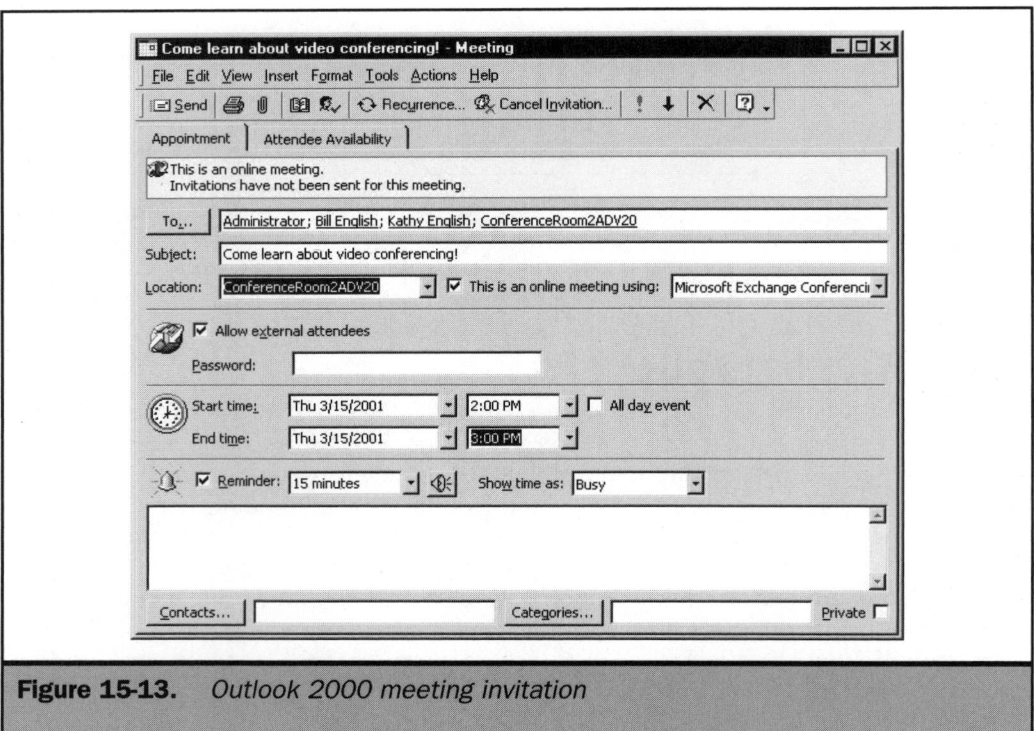

Figure 15-13. *Outlook 2000 meeting invitation*

You do not need to add this registry entry to Outlook 2002 clients. Outlook 2002 will automatically detect Exchange 2000 conferencing services.

First, you can select Microsoft Exchange Conferencing in the "This is an online meeting using" drop-down list. Second, you can allow external attendees to join the conference and protect it with a password. Finally, in the Address Book, there is a listing for All Conference Resources from which to select a virtual conference room in which to hold the conference. It can be displayed in the Location selection box.

At the receiving end of a meeting invitation, you can accept the request and then use the Join Conference menu choice from your calendar. Just right-click on the meeting in the calendar and select join conference. Doing this will invoke Internet Explorer and take you to the conference Web site.

Configuring Internet-Based Clients

There are two things that you'll need to do to allow Internet-based client access to a video conference. First, you'll need to configure the video CTP to use the H.323 bridge, since many Internet clients will not be running Windows 2000. Second, if you are in a single-site environment, you'll need to create a second site with a bogus IP address and a subnet mask of /32. Then you'll need to create a second bogus site and associate it with the IP address (not a range). Otherwise, the CMS cannot discern between client connections that are locally based and those that are Internet based.

Note

If a conference participant attempts to join a conference and receives a "Handled error #800704E1: Unable to locate the zone from the conference management configuration object," then you may need to look at your Windows 2000 site configuration. This error occurs because the "Default-First-Site-Name" site has been renamed and the World Wide Web Publishing service (W3SVC) has not been restarted since the name change. The solution is to restart W3SVC , and participants should be able to connect thereafter.

Scheduling a Conference

To schedule a conference, use the Outlook meeting request form and invite the participants as well as the conference room. Inviting a conference room really means to select a resource from the All Conference Resources in the address book. You can include a short description for the subject of the meeting, attach documents, input links, or type in expanded comments in the comments section (Figure 15-14). Note that you cannot book a conference more than one year in advance.

When you click to send the request, the CMS will attempt to reserve the resource. It is at this point that ECS checks for resource availability. It also will check for connection maximums to ensure this conference does not exceed the configured value. If everything is in order, the CMS will book the resource and you'll get a small box

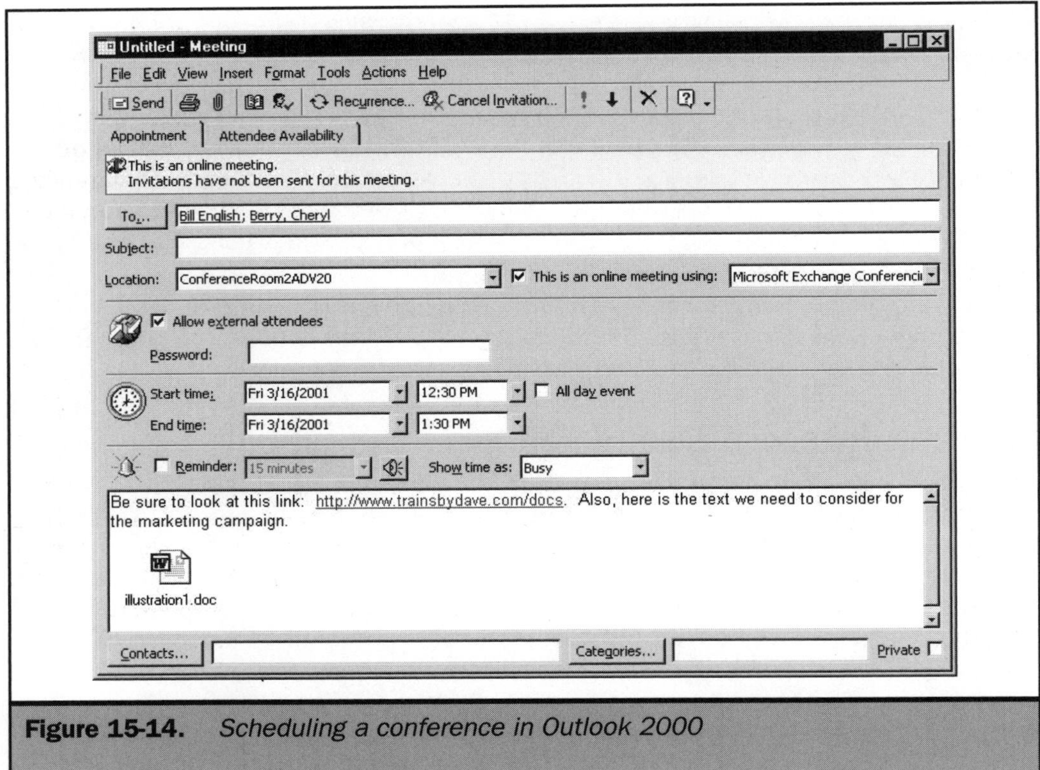

Figure 15-14. *Scheduling a conference in Outlook 2000*

indicating that the resources for the meeting were successfully booked. Those invited will receive the meeting request and they can accept or decline the meeting. The meeting request will also contain the URL to the conference, which can be copied and sent to any user whom you wish to participate in the conference.

If you need to secure a conference, there are two ways to do this. First, you can make the conference *private*, which means that you've cleared the Allow external attendees checkbox in the meeting request. With this box cleared, only those specifically invited are allowed into the conference. If the meeting is public, then it can be secured with a password, which can be entered into the Password field next to the Allow external attendees checkbox in the meeting request form.

Joining a Conference

There are several ways to join a conference. First, you can click on the link in the meeting request form and you will be taken directly to the conference. If you attempt to join a conference before it has started, you'll be told the conference is not available and there will be a clock counting down to the start time of the conference in the left pane of the browser. The second way to join a conference is to right-click on the meeting in the Outlook Calendar and select Join Conference. Finally, you can access the conference by opening any browser and entering the following: **http://<FQDN of Server>/conferencing**. Doing this will take you to the default Web site for conferencing services (Figure 15-15). Just click on the "Attend a conference now!" link and you'll be taken to a page (Figure 15-16) that lists the available conferences. Then, select the conference you need to attend, and you'll be joined to the conference.

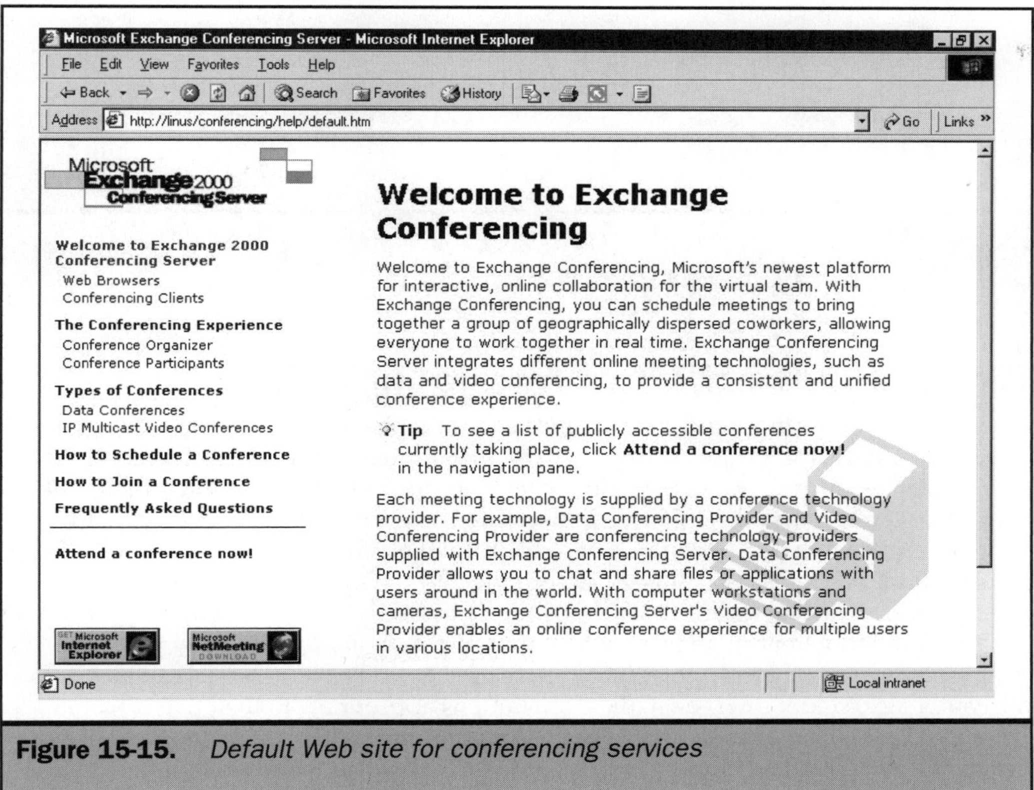

Figure 15-15. *Default Web site for conferencing services*

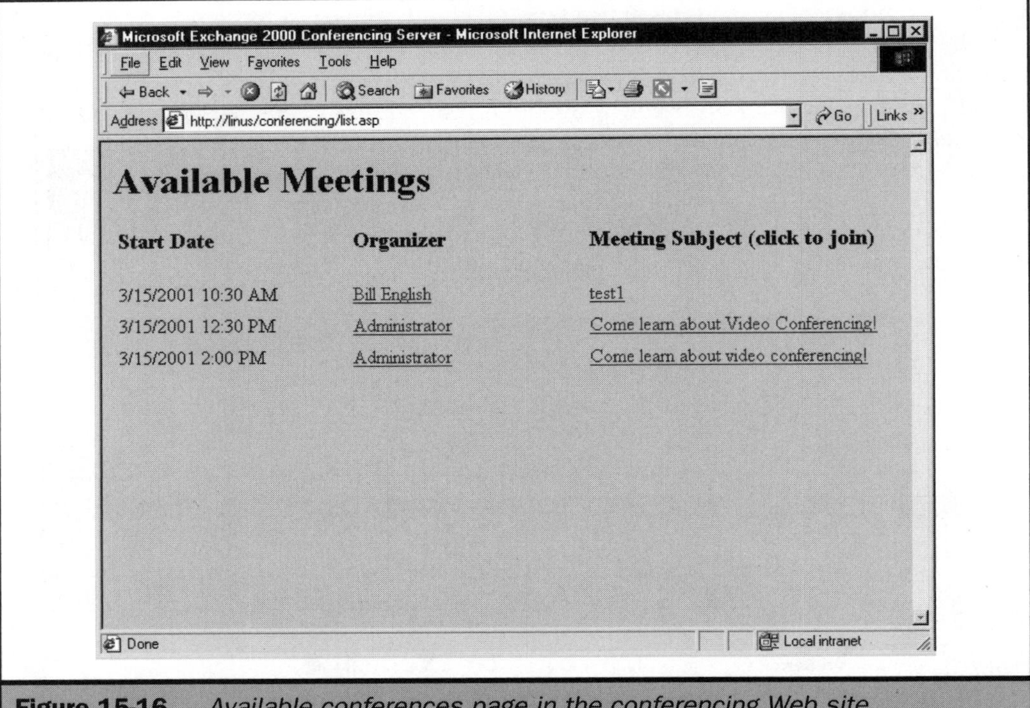

Figure 15-16. *Available conferences page in the conferencing Web site*

Working with the Conferencing Client

Figure 15-17 shows the default conference client that is built inside the Web browser. The client includes a number of tools and informational items. The left side of the client displays information about the conference, such as the countdown time, subject, organizer, and the resource in use. The conference organizer can extend the time and change the resource if needed. However, changing resources will mean that all participants will need to reconnect to the new resource—they are not transferred automatically.

The video conferencing area is in the top-right part of the screen. Here, you'll see yourself along with the video of all other participants who have video capabilities in the conference. Under each client, there are buttons appropriate to their participation. For audio clients, there is an audio button, for video clients there is a video button. By deselecting either of these buttons, you can disable that part of the overall conference feed.

Other participants in the conference (in our example, a white teddy bear) will appear in the right pane. This picture can be unlocked and moved if you want to place

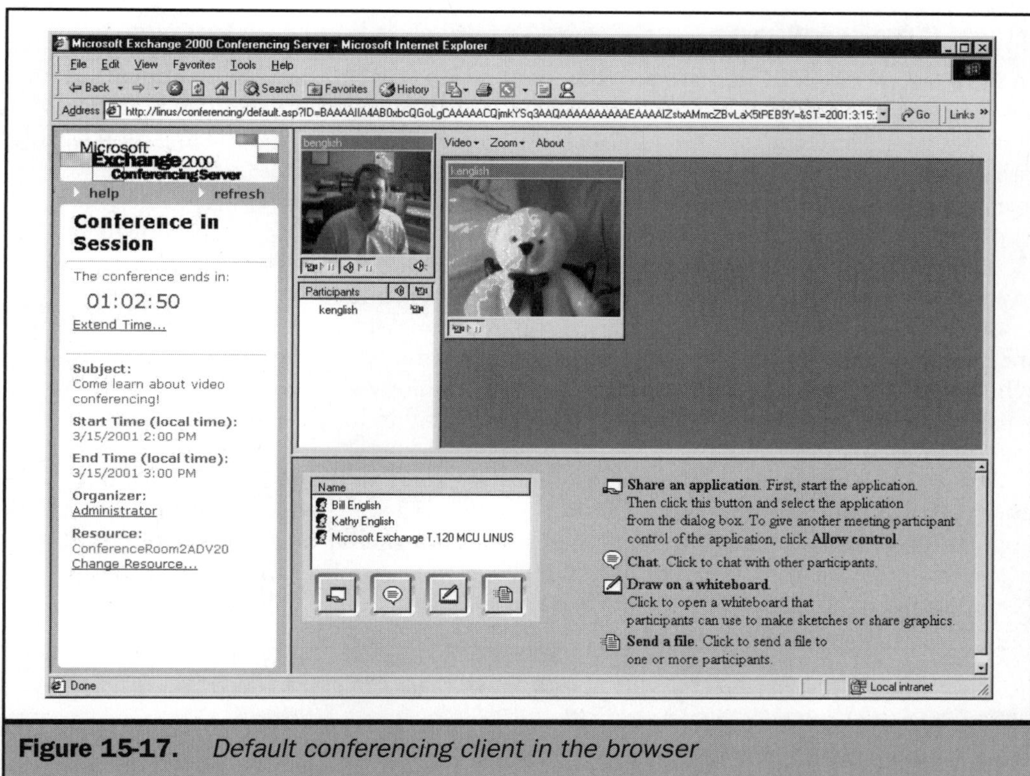

Figure 15-17. *Default conferencing client in the browser*

certain users in certain places inside the browser. In addition, their picture size can be enlarged or diminished by using the Zoom menu options. Anything over 100% will yield a picture of lower quality. When the video client first starts, it will attempt to use multicast protocols to join the conference. If doing this is unsuccessful, then the NetMeeting ActiveX controls in the browser will start and connect to the H.323 bridge. The resource must have the H.323 bridge enabled in order for this to work properly. Without a bridge configured, the client will not be able to connect and will receive a message saying the conference is not available. Even if the bridge is configured, if the client doesn't have NetMeeting installed, this same error message will appear.

Those using the H.323 bridge will be able to see only themselves and one other person in the conference. They will not have capabilities to view everyone in the conference simultaneously.

Under the self view is a play/pause button with a speaker icon. Use this button to open or close your microphone. When the mike is open, everyone in the conference can hear everything you say. Use this button to temporarily take your voice offline if you don't want to be heard.

Sharing Applications

In the conferencing client, there are four applications that automatically appear: Chat, Whiteboard, file transfer, and share program. These applications really make this conferencing client compelling as a business tool. With application sharing, you can collaborate in real time, combining a host of services. You can even use program sharing to show a colleague how a new software package would work. In fact, any application running on your PC can be shared with the meeting participants, including Control Panel applications and Internet Explorer. More often, however, sharing will involve an application such as Word, Excel, or PowerPoint.

Application sharing can save your company thousands of dollars by giving users the ability to meet and collaborate without needing to fly to other cities to meet. In fact, when combined with Instant Messaging, this technology will help users who wish to work out of the home to be more productive and stay in touch with users at the office in a fuller, richer experience.

To share an application running on your desktop, you'll first need to start the application. In our example, we'll use PowerPoint. All we need to do to share the application with other users in the conference is click on the Share application button in the lower right pane, then highlight the program we wish to share in the Sharing - Nothing dialog box, and click on Share (Figure 15-18).

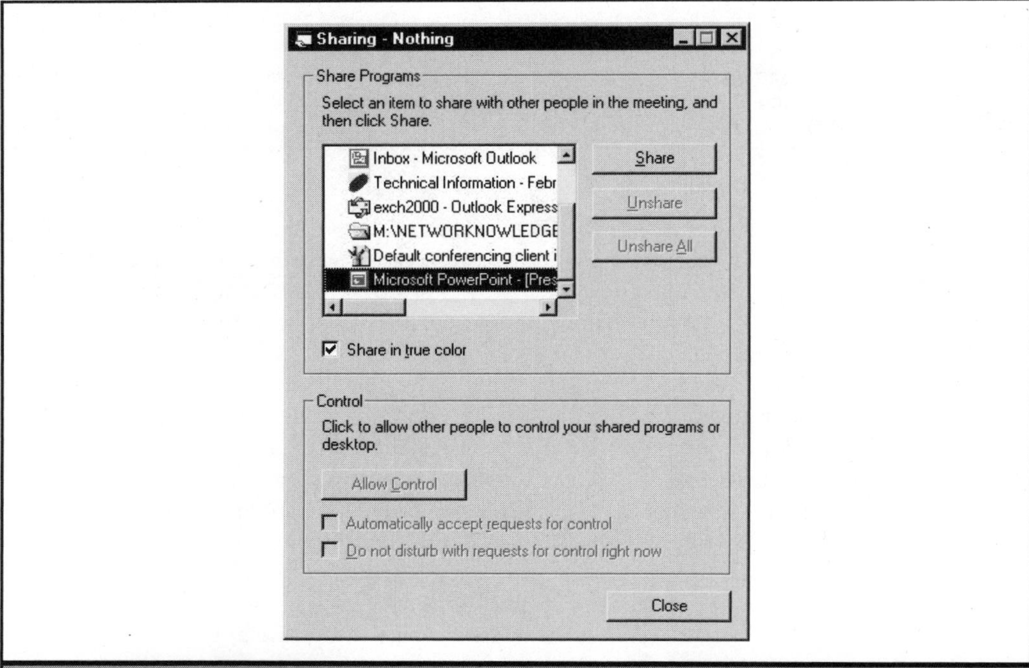

Figure 15-18. *Sharing a program in the conferencing client*

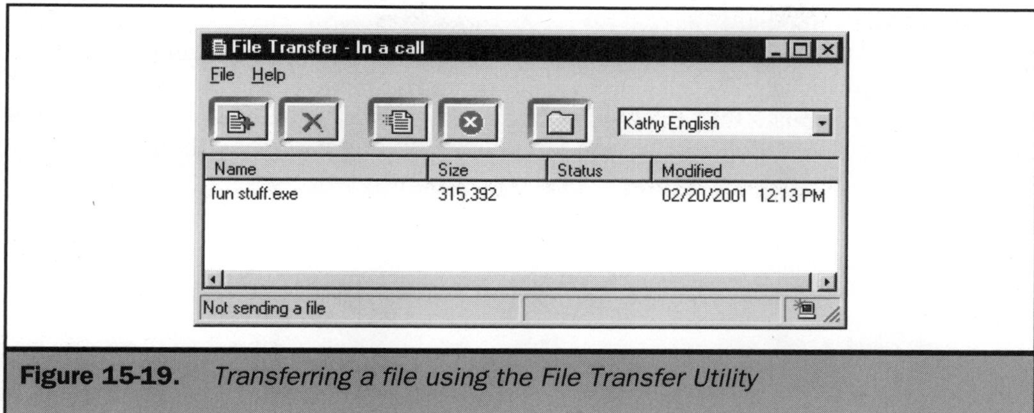

Figure 15-19. *Transferring a file using the File Transfer Utility*

Once the program is shared, you can set control options by clicking on the Allow Control button. Doing this will cause the two checkboxes beneath the button to activate so that you can automatically accept requests for control or decline control interruptions when you don't want to be disturbed.

Once the application is shared, it will appear inside a browser window on each participant's desktop. If another person wants to control the program, the request can be made via the Control menu. For all participants who don't have control over the program, their own mouse is disabled inside that browser window. However, they still have full functionality in all other programs. One "gotcha" is that for the other conference participants to see your shared application, it must have focus on your desktop. If any other program is covering your shared application, the other participants will see a dark, bland area inside the browser. So bear in mind that if you minimize the shared application for a minute, the other attendees will lose sight of the application, too. It's also best if all the attendees use the same color depth and screen resolution when sharing an application.

To transfer a file to one or more participants, add the file to the list (Figure 15-19 above), select the people who should receive the file, and click on Send. You will be shown the transmission's progress. The file will be placed, by default, in the c:\program files\netmeeting\received files folder.

Summary

Deploying Exchange Conferencing Server is not an easy task, but it is one that is worth effort and time to accomplish. Deploying Exchange Conferencing Server may require that you upgrade your network hardware infrastructure so that each device, a router, switch or network card, can take advantage of the QoS services of Windows 2000. In addition, you may need to install several Conference Management Servers or at least multiple Multipoint Control Units to account for low or unreliable WAN bandwidth.

And, if you are running clients older than Windows 2000, you'll likely need to install NetMeeting 3.01 or later for those users who expect to use the conferencing services.

We hope you've seen the great benefits of using Exchange Conferencing Server and the outstanding features that it provides. Once your users learn how to take advantage of this tool on a daily basis, they'll wonder how they ever got along without it.

Chapter 16

Exchange 2000 Instant Messaging

In an information-driven economy, there is only one thing worth more than information—time. The right information is useless if it's delivered too late. Companies of all sizes rely on face-to-face meetings, the telephone, and electronic mail for information exchange. Face-to-face meetings aren't always possible, especially in an urgent situation. While electronic mail is efficient, it isn't instantaneous. And although the telephone is instantaneous, it isn't always the most efficient. So what can a company do to provide its employees with fast, efficient, real-time communications? Deploy *instant messaging* services to its knowledge workers.

This chapter discusses instant messaging and the instant messaging services within Exchange 2000. You'll learn how to install and deploy Exchange 2000 instant messaging services throughout your organization, enabling your users to have ad hoc, real-time keyboard conversations with each other and others outside your organization.

What Is Instant Messaging?

Instant messaging enables users to have ad hoc, instantaneous keyboard conversations with each other in real-time. Instant messaging provides users with *presence information*, which refers to a user's instant messaging status. The status indicates whether or not the person is available for a conversation. Because the focus of this book is Exchange 2000, and because Exchange 2000 only works with the Exchange Messenger client, the scope of these discussions will only cover Exchange Messenger. Using the Exchange-aware MSN Messenger client (or a combination of the Exchange-aware client and the MSN Messenger services client, a person's status can be:

- Online
- Busy
- Be right back
- Away
- On the phone
- Out to lunch
- Offline
- Idle

Note *Non-Microsoft instant messaging clients may have different or additional status conditions. The preceding status conditions are for the Exchange/MSN Messenger client.*

Instant messaging also enables users to create subscriptions, also known as *buddy lists*, or, *contacts*. A subscription is a list of contacts whose presence information you want to track. By subscribing to a person's presence information, you can be notified of changes in his or her instant messaging status in real time. You can receive a message when a contact comes online, and then send the contact an instant message with the click of a mouse button. Subscription and status information is stored on and maintained by the instant messaging servers, allowing them to seamlessly roam with mobile and remote users.

Applications can also leverage presence information in the direction and redirection of information and information requests. For example, a company could deploy a workflow application that processes expense reimbursement forms. If more than one person has authority to approve expense reports, presence information can be used within this workflow application so that if Manager A is offline, the expense reimbursement request can be automatically re-routed to Manager B.

Instant messaging is similar to the telephone because it is instantaneous. However, unlike a telephone, you can see who is available to take your call prior to making it. Instant messaging is also similar to e-mail because it is electronic and the conversation occurs via a keyboard. The biggest difference between the two is that instant messaging is instantaneous. Instant messaging servers pass the messages immediately to the recipient, without any storing or forwarding. E-mail messages must be stored on one or more mail servers before they are sent to the recipient. This is a key distinction. E-mail is a recorded form of communication. Messages are stored within mail stores and are retrievable at a later date. Instant messaging communications are not stored as a matter of course. Once cleared from the instant messaging client user interface, they are gone permanently.

If you need to save the text from an instant messaging communication, you can copy the text of the message to the Windows clipboard, and then paste it into a text editor or word processor so that it can be saved.

Exchange 2000 Instant Messaging Services

Exchange 2000 instant messaging services provide instant messaging capabilities both within an organization and between organizations, enabling business-to-business instant messaging. It is comprised of client and server components. The client component is the Exchange instant messaging client, which is a modified version of the MSN Messenger client. Like MSN Messenger, the Exchange instant messaging client also works with the MSN Messenger Service and Hotmail.

Exchange 2000 instant messaging is made up of several components, as shown in Figure 16-1.

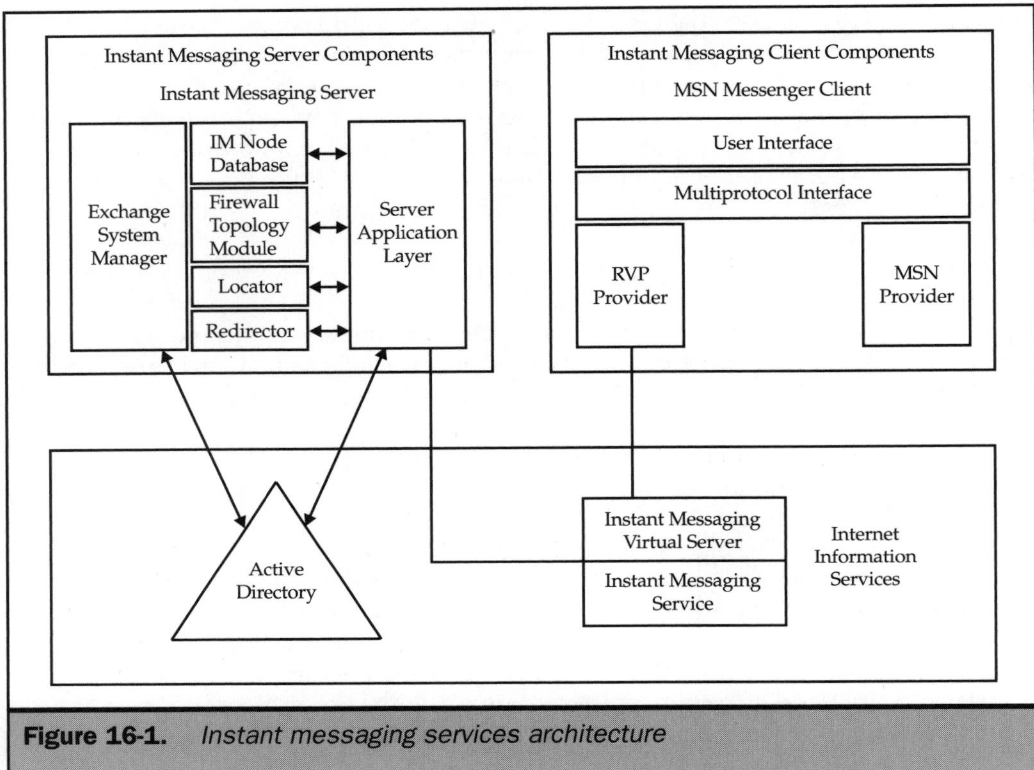

Figure 16-1. *Instant messaging services architecture*

Instant Messaging Server Architecture

At the server side, instant messaging services are provided by the following components:

- Server application layer, which performs the majority of processing by communicating directly with the Instant Messaging Node database, the Firewall Topology Module, the locator, redirectors, Active Directory, and IIS
- Instant Messaging Node database (**msimnode.edb**), which is an ESE database that contains subscription information—called the *subscription list*—for users who are on the same server
- Firewall Topology Module (FTM), which retains firewall information (for example, whether users are inside or outside the firewall and whether or not to use a proxy server)
- Locator, which is used to send notifications to a user's home server when they arrive via a bridgehead server

- Instant messaging routers—also known as *redirectors*—which unify the instant messaging communities and perform public-to-private instant messaging URL translations
- Instant messaging service, which is an ISAPI application (**msimsrv.dll**) that runs under Internet Information Services (inetinfo.exe)
- Exchange instant messaging virtual server, which is used by the Exchange Instant Messenger client to connect to the instant messaging service
- Exchange System Manager, which is used to configure and manage instant messaging virtual servers
- Multitiered instant messaging Active Directory security model, which authenticates users based on their logon credentials, enables users to control who can view their presence information, and enables administrators to specify who can use instant messaging services

All instant messaging traffic is client/server-based and consists of Extensible Markup Language (XML) data that is transmitted via HTTP/RVP. There is no peer-to-peer traffic in instant messaging. Figure 16-2 shows a basic instant messaging architecture.

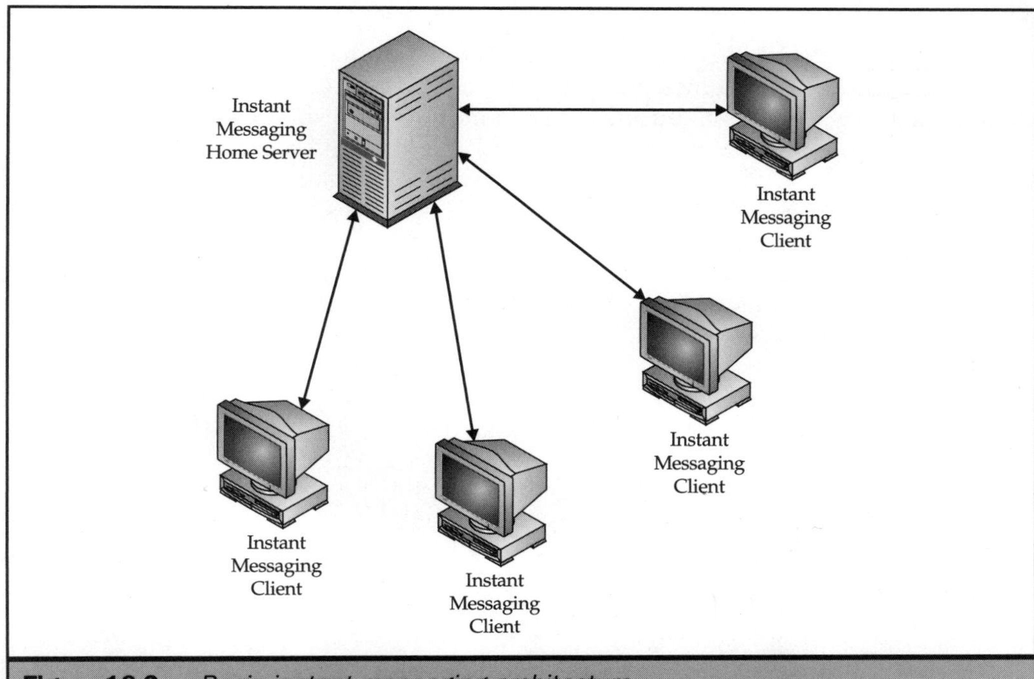

Figure 16-2. *Basic instant messaging architecture*

There are two types of Exchange 2000 instant messaging servers: home servers and instant messaging routers.

Instant Messaging Home Servers Home servers host user accounts, maintain subscription services and presence status, and communicate directly with the client when delivering presence information and instant messages. An instant messaging client uses Domain Name System (DNS) to locate a user's home server. Once the home server has been located, the instant messaging client updates the user's online status and receives the online status information for the user's subscriptions. Home servers also cache information from instant messaging routers, so the instant messaging client doesn't need to communicate with the router too often.

The number of home servers you need depends on the peak number of concurrent users. According to Microsoft, in a typical corporate environment, about 80 percent of all users who have instant messaging are online at any given time. Within an ISP or ASP environment, only about 5-10 percent of all users who are enabled for instant messaging are online at any given time. If you anticipate more than 10,000 concurrent users, you will need two or more home servers and at least one instant messaging router. If you have fewer than 10,000 concurrent users, you need only one home server.

Note *Instant Messaging home servers cannot be clustered or load-balanced.*

Instant Messaging Routers By using instant messaging routers, you can create a front-end/back-end instant messaging infrastructure that scales to virtually unlimited users and enables business-to-business instant messaging. Instant messaging routers perform two primary functions: redirection and gateway. Redirection—specifically an HTTP 302 redirect—is performed for internal requests and gateway is used for external requests. Instant messaging routers receive instant messages, locate the recipient's instant messaging home server, and then transmit instant messages to the home server for delivery to the recipient's instant messaging client. An instant messaging router cannot host user accounts; its only purpose is to route instant messages to instant messaging home servers.

Microsoft recommends one instant messaging router for every 20,000 online users. This recommendation assumes a dual PII-400MHz system with 256MB of RAM.

Instant messaging routers cannot be clustered, but they can be load-balanced using DNS round robin or Network Load Balancing.

Instant Messaging Client Architecture

At the client side, instant messaging functions are provided by an Exchange-aware version of the MSN Messenger client. This client is located on the Exchange 2000 Server CD; however, the most recent version of the client can be downloaded from http://www.microsoft.com/exchange/downloads/IMclient.htm. This client contains two instant messaging providers: an RVP provider for Exchange 2000 and an MSN provider for MSN Messenger.

The MSN Messenger client runs on Windows XP, Windows 2000, Windows NT 4.0, Windows 95 (with the Winsock 2.0 update), Windows 98, and Windows Me. Internet Explorer 5.0 is required for instant messaging services because it contains the XML parser needed to process instant messaging traffic.

Note *Down-level clients, such as Windows NT 4.0 and Windows 9x/Me require the installation of the Active Directory client in order to query DNS and Active Directory for instant messaging-related information. The Active Directory client components for Windows NT 4.0 can be downloaded from http://www.microsoft.com/windows2000/news/bulletins/adextension.asp.*

MSN Messenger provides both a user interface and multiprotocol interface. The user interface is the presentation layer of the application that users interact with. It enables them to log on, add or remove contacts, configure audio and video, set privacy restrictions, and configure proxy settings. The multiprotocol interface provides support for RVP and MSN.

Tip *Exchange 2000 ships with MSN Messenger 2.2. As of this writing, two more recent clients are available for download from Microsoft's Web sites: Exchange Messenger 3.5 is available from http://www.microsoft.com/exchange/downloads/IMclient.htm, and MSN Messenger 3.6 is available from http://messenger.msn.com. You cannot install a fresh installation of the MSN Messenger 3.6 client and communicate with Exchange. You must install a version of the Exchange Messenger client (either 2.2 or 3.5). Once this has been installed, you can upgrade to MSN Messenger 3.6 (or a later version if one is available) and retain the capability to communicate with Exchange 2000. Both clients are available in a variety of languages.*

Client System Requirements In order to install and run the instant messaging client, the system must meet or exceed the following specifications:

- Windows-based PC with a 486DX/66 or higher CPU
- Windows 95, Windows 98, Windows Me, Windows NT 4.0, Windows 2000, or Windows XP
- Windows 95 users require the Winsock 2.0 update, which can be downloaded from http://www.microsoft.com/windows95/downloads/contents/WUAdminTools/S_WUNetworkingTools/W95Sockets2/Default.asp. In addition, they'll need the Q266722 QFE Update for Windows 95, which can be downloaded from http://download.microsoft.com/download/win95/Update/9766/W95/EN-US/266772USA5.EXE.

- Windows 9x and Windows NT users require the Active Directory Services Client, which can be downloaded from http://www.microsoft.com/Windows2000/adclients/.
- Windows 98 users also need the Q266722 QFE Update, which can be downloaded from http://download.microsoft.com/download/win98/Update/9766/W98/EN-US/266772USA8.EXE
- 2MB free disk space
- 8MB RAM
- Internet Explorer 5.0 or later

Integration with DirectPlay Applications The DirectPlay application programming interface (API) is a component of Microsoft's DirectX set of technologies. This API enables developers to create shared multimedia applications such as multiplayer games, chat clients, and other network applications without having to write code for individual transports, protocols, or online services.

The MSN Messenger client references all DirectPlay applications that are listed in the registry, and exposes them for invitation to other contacts. For example, Microsoft NetMeeting is a DirectPlay application. This means that the MSN Messenger client allows you to invite a contact to start a NetMeeting session.

RVP

Instant messaging in Exchange 2000 is based upon a platform-independent protocol developed by Microsoft called RVP. RVP is oriented toward IMPP (Instant Messaging Presence Protocol), which is currently being drafted by the IETF. RVP enables developers to create interoperable solutions that can integrate instant messaging with different products that run on different platforms. You may have heard or read (even in some Microsoft literature) that RVP stands for the *Rendezvous Protocol*; this is not the case. Microsoft's original intent for RVP was to call it the Rendezvous Protocol; however, a protocol called the Rendezvous Protocol already existed. To avoid confusion, this name was dropped in favor of its shortened acronym—RVP. As a result, RVP is just *RVP*. It does not stand for anything.

Tip *Microsoft has a white paper on RVP at http://msdn.microsoft.com/library/default.asp?URL=/library/techart/Rvp.htm.*

An open protocol is key to interoperability between various instant messaging products, such as MSN Messenger, AOL Instant Messenger, ICQ, Odigo, and others. Both RVP and IMPP are extensions to the HTTP/1.1 protocol. All instant messaging communication takes place over an extended subset of WebDAV (see Appendix A, "Technology Primer—What Is WebDAV?"). WebDAV extends HTTP/1.1 by adding additional methods—or commands—that enable the functionality needed for collaboration on a Web server.

Until a standard instant messaging protocol is developed, the instant messaging client for Exchange 2000—MSN Messenger—can only be used with Exchange 2000, MSN, and Hotmail.

RVP uses XML and some of the WebDAV methods, as well as additional methods that are a part of the RVP protocol:

- **PROPPATCH**—This method is used to update a user's status property when his or her instant messaging status changes. For example, when a user's status is changed from Online to Offline, the Exchange messenger client uses PROPPATCH to change the user's status on the user's home server.
- **PROPFIND**—This method is used to query a user's status. When the Exchange Messenger client is started, it uses PROPFIND to query the status of a user's instant messaging contacts.
- **SUBSCRIBE**—Subscriptions are used to track the presence information of a given user. When the Exchange Messenger client starts up, it sends a subscription to the home servers of individuals on a user's buddy list or contact list. This ensures that the instant messaging client is kept up-to-date with presence information, regardless of what home server each user is located on.
- **UNSUBSCRIBE**—This method is used to instruct a home server to stop sending status updates.
- **SUBSCRIPTIONS**—This method retrieves the list of active subscriptions on an instant messaging server.
- **NOTIFY**—This method has two primary purposes:
  - Messages sent between instant messaging clients use the NOTIFY method.
  - Home servers use the NOTIFY method to provide instant messaging clients with status information.
- **ACL**—This method is used to determine who can view a user's presence information and whose presence information the user can view. ACL also specifies the authentication mechanism being used. Exchange 2000 instant messaging service supports NTLM and Digest authentication.

Note

Exchange 2000 Service Pack 1 includes a new method called POLL that reduces the network traffic generated by the exchange of presence information. In addition, the latest version of the Exchange Messenger and MSN Messenger clients enables the assignment of a static port for instant messaging clients. ISPs and ASPs will benefit greatly from this enhancement.

MSN The MSN provider enables the MSN Messenger client to connect to Microsoft Network-provided instant messaging services. This enables instant messaging users to conduct keyboard chats and voice conversations via PC-to-PC or PC-to-phone, and exchange files with other MSN Messenger users inside or outside of their organization. In order to use instant messaging services with MSN as the provider, the user must have a valid Hotmail, Passport, or MSN e-mail address. The server-side for this provider is The Microsoft Network, and therefore it is completely outside the control of Exchange administrators. However, as you will read later in this chapter, it can be controlled by your network or firewall administrator.

Microsoft has an instant messaging Frequently Asked Questions (FAQ) page that discusses the most common issues pertaining to Exchange 2000 instant messaging services. The FAQ can be found at http://www.microsoft.com/exchange/techinfo/IM_FAQ.htm.

Planning Your Instant Messaging Infrastructure

Before deploying an instant messaging infrastructure, it is a good idea to do some planning. Generally speaking, you'll want to consider the following issues:

- *How many users do you need to support?* An individual instant messaging home server is capable of supporting approximately 10,000 concurrent online users, and a single instant messaging router can support about 20,000 simultaneous users. As long as a user's instant messaging client is running with the user logged on, the user is considered online. Keep this in mind, especially when deploying 24x7 instant messaging services. Estimate your peak concurrent online activity and plan the number of instant messaging home servers and routers accordingly.
- *What naming convention will you use?* You should use an intuitive and consistent naming convention for your instant messaging servers, domains, and instant messaging addresses. This will help internal and external instant messaging users locate one another and subscribe to each other's presence information. You should also use DNS SRV records to unify your SMTP and instant messaging namespaces.
- *Will you be connected to the Internet?* If you need to connect your instant messaging infrastructure to the Internet or to another business, you should use instant messaging routers, firewalls, and reverse proxy servers. It is generally not a good idea to connect an instant messaging home server directly to the Internet. Doing so will expose server names to the Internet, and could allow the data on the server to be compromised by a hacker.
- *What kind of bandwidth is available?* According to Microsoft, a thousand simultaneous users consume about 56K worth of bandwidth. If you have users separated by expensive or low-bandwidth connections, you should deploy at least one home server in each location. However, because clients communicate with instant messaging routers less frequently, you can centralize your instant messaging routers.

Windows 2000 Considerations

Exchange 2000 Instant Messaging Services is an optional component you can install by using the Exchange Setup program. Chapter 6 has step-by-step instructions for installing Exchange 2000. As with other Exchange 2000 components, Active Directory, DNS, and Internet Information Services (IIS) play prominent roles in the deployment and usage of instant messaging.

Active Directory

During installation, the Active Directory schema is modified to include the classes and attributes necessary for the support of instant messaging. These are used for storing data, such as instant messaging addresses and URLs; security information and ACLs; firewall, proxy and topology information; database and log file locations; and user information and server information.

Active Directory stores all instant messaging URLs. All instant messaging users are identified by two unique URLs: an instant messaging URL and an instant messaging home server URL. You can use the Active Directory Users and Computers snap-in to view a user's instant messaging URLs. To do so:

1. Double-click the desired user to view its Properties.
2. Select the Exchange Features tab.
3. Select Instant Messaging, and then click the Properties button. The user's instant messaging user address, URL address, and home server URL address will be displayed, as shown in Figure 16-3.

An examination of the instant messaging client logon process illustrates the reliance on Active Directory by both client and server components:

1. A user logs on using his or her instant messaging user address and connects to an instant messaging router.
2. The router performs an Active Directory lookup for the user's home server.
3. The router then returns the user's instant messaging home server URL to the client.
4. The client uses this URL to connect to the home server.
5. The home server validates the user name and password against Active Directory.

Note *The MSN Messenger client caches the user's home server and will not go through a router to locate the user until the application has been restarted.*

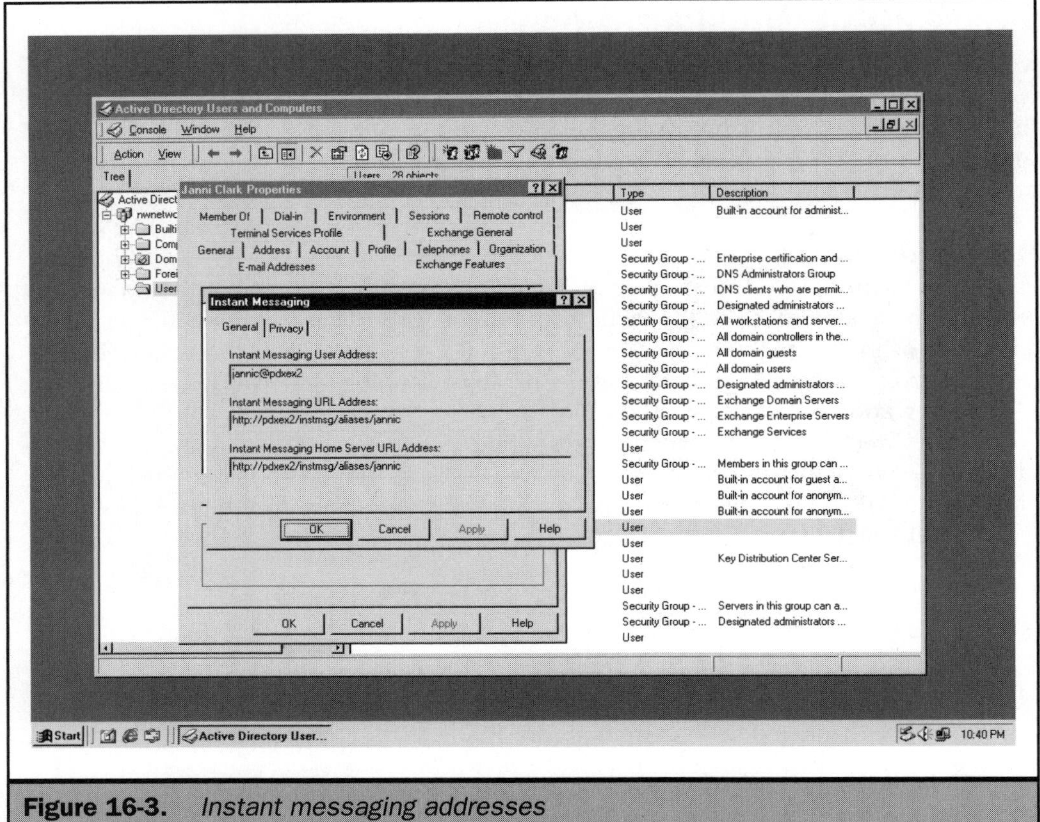

Figure 16-3. *Instant messaging addresses*

Instant Messaging Domains and DNS

An instant messaging domain is a DNS namespace that contains a logical group of virtual instant messaging servers and instant messaging users. Each instant messaging domain contains at least one home server. Home servers host names are not visible to external users. Within the instant messaging namespace, instant messaging routers receive instant messages and forward them to the instant messaging home server(s) of the intended recipient(s). To facilitate business-to-business and other external instant messaging services, instant messaging router DNS names are visible to external users.

Microsoft recommends a one-to-one relationship between e-mail domains and instant messaging domains, as well as the use of the prefix "im" in instant messaging domain names. For example, scott@tntsoftware.com should be in an instant messaging domain called im.tntsoftware.com. While many organizations may have only one instant messaging domain, large corporations, ASPs, and ISPs will likely have several instant messaging domains, such as im.portland.tntsoftware.com and im.vancouver.tntsoftware.com. The key here is that DNS SRV records are used to map instant messaging domain names to SMTP names. This creates a unified namespace that contains both SMTP addresses and instant messaging user addresses.

Instant Messaging SRV Records SRV records—also known as service records or service locator records—enable users and computers to locate published services, such as instant messaging. When an instant messaging client initiates the logon process, it performs a DNS query for the _rvp SRV record for the designated instant messaging domain. If the DNS lookup fails, the instant messaging client attempts to use the instant messaging domain listed in the user's instant messaging address.

Configuring DNS You must create at least one A record within each domain that hosts an instant messaging server. If you maintain separate DNS servers for internal and external addresses and you aren't using HTTP reverse proxy servers, you must use both internal and external records that refer to your instant messaging routers.

If you are using HTTP reverse proxy servers, external queries must pass through your reverse proxy servers. Reverse proxies accept connection requests and communications from outside a private network and relay the traffic to internal computers. These are just like regular Internet proxy servers, except that the behavior and flow of traffic is reversed. In this case, an HTTP reverse proxy receives instant messaging traffic and relays that traffic to one or more instant messaging routers. To facilitate this, external A records must refer to the reverse proxy server, and internal A records must point to your instant messaging routers.

If you use SRV records to allow users to use SMTP instant messaging addresses, each DNS zone containing an e-mail domain must have an SRV record that refers to that zone's instant messaging domain. This enables an instant messaging client to use an SRV record to construct a user's instant messaging address from the user's e-mail address. To create a DNS SRV record for an instant messaging server:

1. Open the DNS MMC.
2. Expand the DNS server you wish to use.
3. Expand the Forward Lookup Zone.
4. Right-click on the domain to which you want to add the SRV record and select Other New Records.
5. On the Resource Record Type tab, select Service Location, and then click Create Record.
6. Enter the following on the New Resource Record tab:

Service	_rvp
Protocol	_tcp

Priority	0
Weight	0
Port number	80
Host offering this service	FQDN of an instant messaging router

7. Click OK.

Internet Information Services

As mentioned previously, instant messaging is an ISAPI application (**msimsrv.dll**) that runs under Internet Information Services (**inetinfo.exe**). Instant messaging clients connect to an instant messaging virtual server that runs under a Web site within IIS. Instant messaging uses a one-to-one mapping of virtual servers to Web sites. The first instant messaging virtual server you create will be made under the default Web site. You must create an additional Web site before you can create additional virtual servers on the same IIS server.

Managing the Instant Messaging Database

As previously mentioned, all subscription information is held in the Instant Messaging Node database. This file—**msimnode.edb**—is an ESE database located by default in \Program Files\Exchsrvr\IMdata. Because it is an ESE database, you will also find transaction logs in this location.

Typically, this database requires little management beyond regular backups. However, there are a couple of administrative tasks worth mentioning: moving the database and log file location, and disaster recovery of the database.

Moving the Instant Messaging Database and Log Files You may wish to move the instant messaging database and log files for security and/or performance reasons. Moving these files is a relatively straightforward procedure; however, this procedure requires a restart of the instant messaging services. To move the instant messaging database and log files to another location:

1. In System Manager, right-click Instant Messaging (RVP), and then select Properties.
2. On the General tab, enter or browse to the new location for the database in the Database Location field.
3. Then, enter or browse to the new location for the log files in the Logfile Location field.
4. Save the changes, and then restart the World Wide Web Publishing service.

You cannot change the location of these files remotely. According to Microsoft Knowledge Base article Q252483, due to the complexity of setting file system paths remotely, Exchange 2000 only allows you to modify these settings from the Exchange server itself.

Instant Messaging Disaster Recovery If an instant messaging home server is lost, it can be recovered by means of a disaster recovery procedure. Like all disaster recovery procedures, the success of the recovery is contingent upon having good backups. Refer to Chapter 12 for details on backup, restore, and general disaster recovery.

The disaster recovery procedure for an instant messaging home server is documented in Microsoft Knowledge Base article Q270838, so we won't duplicate those efforts here. However, be aware that if you do not have an alternate home server to which you can move the affected users, your users will become IM-disabled when the server fails.

Configuring Firewalls

MSN Messenger uses different ports depending on what feature is being used. Table 16-1 describes the features and the default ports they use.

Feature	Outbound Port	Inbound Port
Text chatting	80 (TCP)	80 (TCP)
Voice communications – PC to PC	6901 (TCP/UDP)	6901 (TCP/UDP)
Voice communications – PC to Phone	6801 (UDP) 6901 (TCP/UDP) 2001-2120 (UDP – dynamically selected)	6801 (UDP) 6901 (TCP/UDP) 2001-2120 (UDP – dynamically selected) 7801-7825 (TCP – dynamically selected)
File Transfer	6891-6900 (TCP – dynamically selected)	6891-6900 (TCP – dynamically selected)
MSN Messenger Service	1863 (TCP) 80 (TCP)	80 (TCP)

Table 16-1. *TCP/UDP Ports Used by MSN Messenger*

Opening ports 6891 to 6900 enables up to 10 simultaneous file transfers per client. If you open one port (for example, port 6891), each client will be limited to one file transfer at a time. In addition, if you are only using the text chat services and do not wish to open any port besides TCP port 80, you can use a Winsock proxy client to proxy traffic destined for port 1863 to port 80. For more information on using the Winsock proxy client, refer to the documentation that ships with Microsoft Proxy Server or Microsoft Internet Security and Acceleration Server.

Managing Instant Messaging Services

Instant messaging services are created and managed using several MMC snap-ins, including Active Directory Users and Computers, Internet Services Manager, and System Manager. The following sections discuss the use of these snap-ins as they relate to instant messaging.

Creating Web Servers and Virtual Servers

As shown in Figure 16-4, the Exchange System Manager snap-in is used to create and manage the Instant Messaging virtual servers that are used for hosting instant messaging services.

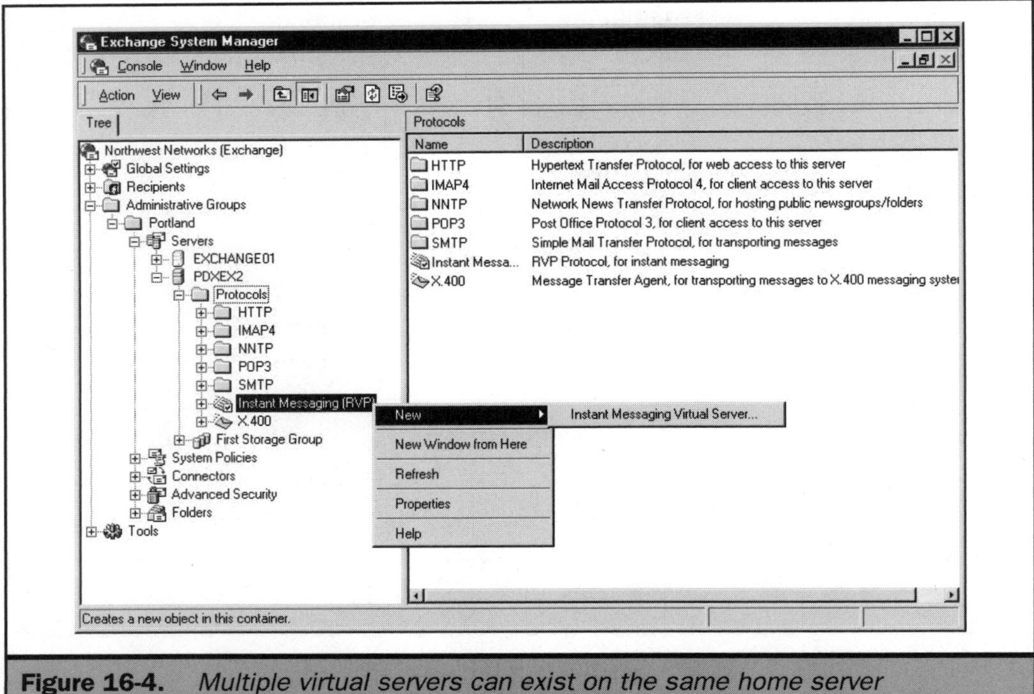

Figure 16-4. *Multiple virtual servers can exist on the same home server*

You must have one virtual server for each instant messaging home server. Before you can install additional instant messaging virtual servers in your organization, you must create a new IIS Web site for each instant messaging virtual server you want to create. To do this:

1. Launch an MMC console containing the Internet Services Manager snap-in.
2. Right-click on the IIS server that will contain the instant messaging virtual server and select New | Web Site. The Web Site Creation Wizard will begin. Click Next to continue.
3. Enter a description for the new site (for example, "Development instant messaging Web") and click Next.
4. Select the IP address you want to use for the new site. You must use port 80 for the instant messaging Web site. Click Next to continue.
5. Enter the path to the default home directory. You can use the same default home directory for your entire instant messaging Web site; however, it is not required. Click Next to continue.
6. Click Next to continue once more, and then click Finish to complete the wizard.

Creating Instant Messaging Virtual Servers

The Exchange 2000 System Manager is used to create and manage instant messaging virtual servers. Once you have created the desired number of IIS Web sites, you can create multiple instant messaging virtual servers. To create an instant messaging virtual server:

1. Launch an MMC console containing the System Manager snap-in.
2. Expand the Organization container. Then, expand servers, and then expand the Exchange server you want to contain the instant messaging virtual server.
3. Expand Protocols.
4. Right-click on instant messaging (RVP) and select New | Instant Messaging Virtual Server. The New Instant Messaging Virtual Server Wizard will begin. Click Next to continue.

Note *If you are trying to create a new virtual server under a new Web site you just created in IIS, and the Next button is unavailable, the most likely cause is a space within the Host header that was defined during creation of the new site. If this happens, see Microsoft Knowledge Base article Q270870.*

5. Enter a display name for the new virtual server. Click Next to continue.
6. Select the Web site you want to use for the virtual server. The first virtual server on an Exchange server will use the default Web site. Click Next to continue.

7. Enter the DNS name for the virtual server. Click Next to continue.
8. If you are creating an instant messaging home server, check the Allow This Server To Host User Accounts checkbox. If you are creating an instant messaging routing server, leave this box unchecked. Click Next to continue.
9. Click Finish to complete the wizard.

Once the wizard has completed, a new virtual directory called InstMsg will appear under the Web site within Internet Services Manager.

Enabling Instant Messaging for Users

The Active Directory Users and Computers snap-in is used to enable and disable instant messaging, and to control individual instant messaging privacy settings. By default, users are not enabled for instant messaging. To configure and manage instant messaging service, you must have the following permissions:

- To enable and disable instant messaging for your users, you must be a member of the Domain Admins security group in the domain containing the users.
- To manage all other instant messaging settings, such as firewall topology, proxy server configuration, home servers, and routers, you must be a member of the Exchange Admins security group.

To enable a user for instant messaging:

1. Launch an MMC console containing the Active Directory Users and Computers snap-in.
2. Right-click on the user you want to enable for instant messaging and select Properties.
3. Select the Exchange Features tab.
4. Select Instant Messaging from the Features list and click the Enable button. The Instant Messaging dialog box will appear.
5. Click the Browse button to select an instant messaging home server. A list of available instant messaging home servers will appear.
6. Select the instant messaging home server you want to use and click OK.
7. Select an instant messaging domain from the instant messaging Domain Name drop-down list.
8. Click OK to save the changes.
9. Click OK to complete the process and exit the user properties.

Note *When enabling your users for instant messaging, be on the lookout for instant messaging logon names that are longer than 20 characters. The logon field is designed to accept up to 129 characters (64 for the user name, 64 for the domain name, and 1 for the @ symbol); however, for backward compatibility with pre-Windows 2000 systems the user name is truncated to 20 characters when an account is created. The truncated name is used for generating the SMTP address and instant messaging logon. Therefore, if you truncate the user name and instant messaging address to 20 characters or less, you should be able to log on without any problems.*

The Active Directory Users and Computers snap-in is also used to configure instant messaging privacy settings. You can configure instant messaging to only accept messages from a specific individual or group of individuals, or to accept messages from everyone *except* a specific individual or group of individuals. To configure instant messaging privacy:

1. Launch an MMC console containing the Active Directory Users and Computers snap-in.
2. Right-click on the user you want to enable for instant messaging and select Properties.
3. Select the Exchange Features tab.
4. Select Instant Messaging from the Features list and click the Properties button.
5. Select the Privacy tab, shown in Figure 16-5.
6. By default, everyone is allowed to send users instant messages. If you want to modify the default settings, select one of the Allow Access options and use the Add button to specify servers and users.
7. Click OK when finished, and then click OK once more to exit the user's properties.

Using Instant Messaging Client Policies

By making registry modifications, administrators can control the behavior of the Messenger client. The client ships with some features (banner ads and software update messages) that administrators may wish to disable to save bandwidth and remove distractions. In addition, administrators can control which service providers are available to the client, specify a default domain for NTLM authentication, and display a custom message when a chat session is launched.

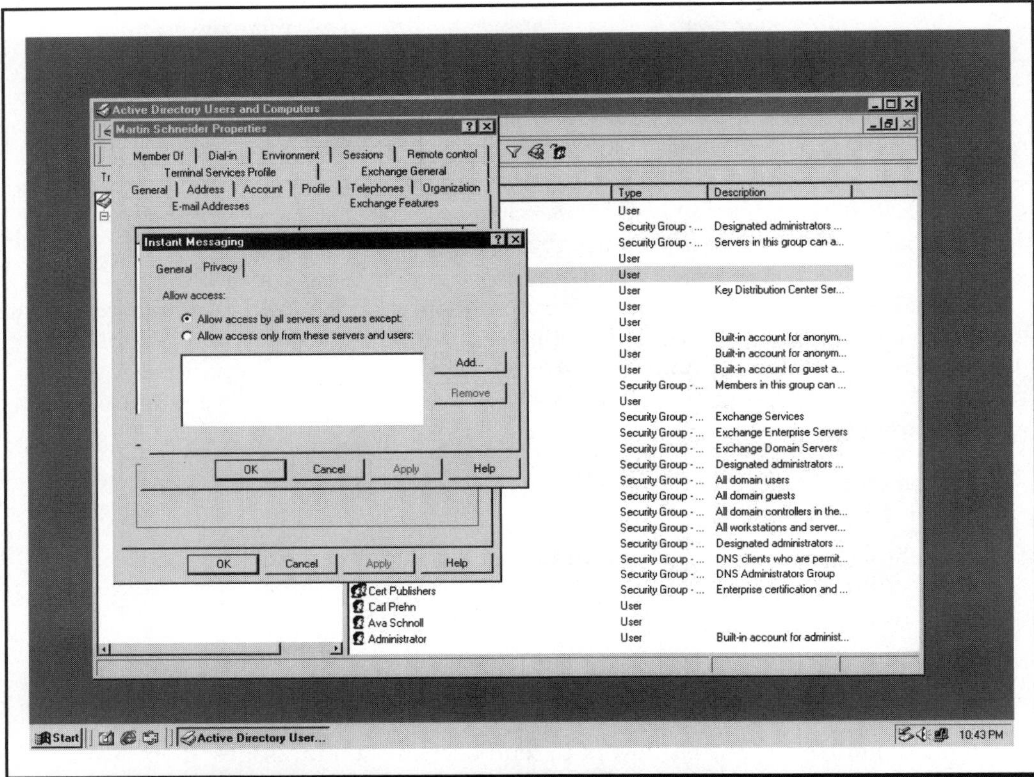

Figure 16-5. *Instant messaging user properties privacy tab*

Disabling Promotional Banner Ads By default, the MSN Messenger client receives a stream of data containing news, links, and Web banners. The DisableCrossPromo registry parameter disables the advertisements that are automatically displayed in the Messenger client. Once disabled, only the MSN logo will be displayed. To turn this service off:

1. Start RegEdt32.exe and navigate to: HKEY_LOCAL_MACHINE\SOFTWARE\Microsoft\MessengerService
2. If it does not exist, create a subkey called Policies.
3. Add a REG_BINARY value to this subkey called DisableCrossPromo.
4. Click the Binary radio button and enter any number other than 0 (for example, 10). Allow it to be padded with extra zeroes.
5. Add another REG_BINARY value called ExchangeConn.

6. Click the Binary radio button and enter **10**. Allow it to be padded with extra zeroes, as well.
7. Close the registry editor.

The changes will take effect when the client is started. If the client is running while these changes are made, it will need to be restarted.

Disabling Software Update Messages The MSN Messenger polls for software updates each time it is started. The DisableUpdates registry parameter controls whether the Messenger client processes the upgrade messages that the MSN Messenger service sends out when a client connects to it. To turn off this feature:

1. Start RegEdt32.exe and navigate to: HKEY_LOCAL_MACHINE\SOFTWARE\Microsoft\MessengerService
2. If it does not exist, create a subkey called Policies.
3. Add a REG_BINARY value called DisableUpdates.
4. Click the Binary radio button and enter any number other than 0 (for example, 10). Allow it to be padded with extra zeroes.
5. Close the registry editor.

Disabling Access to MSN Messenger Services The Exchange Messenger client includes both the RVP provider and MSN provider, enabling users with the appropriate Internet access to use MSN Messenger services. You can disable access to MSN Messenger using the ExchangeConn registry parameter, which controls which service providers are available, and which server is the primary default service provider. To restrict access to MSN Messenger services:

1. Start RegEdt32.exe and navigate to: HKEY_LOCAL_MACHINE\SOFTWARE\Microsoft\MessengerService
2. If it does not exist, create a subkey called Policies.
3. Add a REG_BINARY value called ExchangeConn.
4. Click the Binary radio button and enter one of the following values:
   - 0 – Used for normal operations
   - 1 – Both service providers available, and Exchange 2000 set to primary provider
   - 2 – Exchange 2000 instant messaging services only
5. Close the registry editor.

Adding a Custom Message The client can display a message when a chat session is started with a contact. The default message warns users not to divulge their passwords or credit card numbers in an instant message communication. Because instant messages are sent in clear text across the network by default, this is a warning that should be heeded. You can add your own custom message in place of this message by modifying the IMWarning registry parameter. To do this:

1. Start RegEdt32.exe and navigate to: HKEY_LOCAL_MACHINE\SOFTWARE\Microsoft\MessengerService
2. If it does not exist, create a subkey called Policies.
3. Add a REG_STRING value called IMWarning.
4. Enter the message you would like to display.
5. Close the registry editor.

If you don't want any message at all, enter a space in step 4.

Setting the Default Domain for NTLM Authentication If you are in a multidomain environment, you can specify which domain should be used for NTLM authentication (also known as Integrated Windows Authentication). The DefaultNTLMDomain registry parameter enables you to specify the domain to be used as the default for NTLM authentication. Once set, this string appears in the user's logon dialog box. To set this value:

1. Start RegEdt32.exe and navigate to: HKEY_LOCAL_MACHINE\SOFTWARE\Microsoft\MessengerService
2. If it does not exist, create a subkey called Policies.
3. Add a REG_STRING value called DefaultNTLMDomain.
4. Enter the name of the domain you wish to use.
5. Close the registry editor.

Instant Messaging Security

Exchange 2000 instant messaging uses a security model comprised of three tiers:

- User authentication
- Privacy of presence information
- Firewalls and proxy settings

User Authentication

Exchange 2000 instant messaging users require Active Directory accounts that are enabled for instant messaging. Each time an instant messaging user logs on, an Active Directory domain controller authenticates the user's account. In addition, logon authentication requires that users log on from within the internal network; therefore, placing an instant messaging router in a DMZ connected to the Internet does not provide remote users (or rogue users) with a way to log on to your instant messaging system.

Tip *Microsoft Knowledge Base article Q278974 discusses the most common causes of instant messaging authentication failures. These causes include stopped services, firewall and/or proxy server issues, and misconfigured virtual servers. The article also discusses possible resolutions for these issues.*

Although NTLM is the default method for instant messaging authentication, you can also use Digest authentication. Digest authentication, which is defined in RFC 2617, is new to Windows 2000 and IIS 5.0. This authentication method encrypts the user's password information and provides a mechanism to prevent a type of server attack known as a replay attack. The client makes an initial request that is rejected by a security challenge. The challenge specifies that the client is to use Digest and includes a nonce value (a randomly generated value used to defeat replay attacks) that the client hashes along with the user name and password. The client hashes the results using Message Digest 5, and then resends the original message with the hash data. The server recreates the string on its end, hashes it, and checks the results. If everything matches, the server grants the user access. In order to use Digest authentication, your IIS server must also be an Active Directory domain controller. In addition, you must enable the Instant Messaging Service to retrieve unencrypted user passwords from Active Directory. To do this, you must change the domain's password policy to store users' passwords in a reversible, encrypted format. Users whose accounts existed before the password policy is changed will need to reset their passwords.

Note *When a Windows 95 or Windows 98 user attempts to log on to an instant messaging server in a different domain using NTLM authentication, authentication problems may occur. For example, the user may be prompted to log on several times, or the user may be logged off as soon as he or she is logged on. If this happens, disable NTLM authentication on the instant messaging server and use Digest authentication instead. For details, see Microsoft Knowledge Base article Q267972.*

Privacy of Presence Information

As previously mentioned, the instant messaging administrator can use the Active Directory Users and Computers snap-in to specify who is allowed to send instant messages to each user. See the earlier section, entitled "Enabling Instant Messaging for a User," for instructions on how to do this. In addition, each user can control who can subscribe to his or her presence information by selecting Privacy on the Tools menu of the instant messaging client.

Firewalls and Proxy Settings

Firewall and proxy settings are configured using System Manager. These settings tell the instant messaging Firewall Topology Module (FTM) whether users are inside or outside a firewall and whether a proxy server is required for outbound communications. Once firewall and proxy settings have been configured, the FTM will take one of three actions in response to an instant messaging request:

- It can refer the sender of the request to another server.
- It can act as a gateway by connecting to another server on behalf of the requestor.
- It can reject the request altogether.

To configure firewall and proxy settings:

1. Launch an MMC console containing the System Manager snap-in.
2. Expand Global Settings.
3. Right-click Instant Messaging Settings and select Properties.
4. Select the Firewall Topology tab.
   - If you are configuring firewall settings, check the This Network Is Protected By A Firewall checkbox. Then, click the Add button to add the IP address range served by the firewall.
   - If you are configuring HTTP proxy settings, check the Use A Proxy Server For Outbound Requests checkbox. Then, specify the name of the proxy server and the port used for proxy traffic.
5. Click OK to save the settings.

Securing Internet Instant Messaging Traffic Microsoft recommends using the following strategies to secure instant messaging traffic between your organization and external networks such as the Internet. Standard practices include securing both inbound and outbound instant messaging traffic.

As shown in Figure 16-6, inbound Internet traffic can be secured by using reverse proxies and packet filters, and by placing an instant messaging router in a DMZ or perimeter network.

Using packet filters on inbound Internet traffic is a fairly common practice. Instant messaging traffic from the Internet is no exception. Packet filters can be used to filter out packets that meet your specific criteria, such as traffic destined for a specific IP address and port. Because all instant messaging traffic is HTTP, your packet filter should be configured to allow traffic to port 80 on your instant messaging router(s).

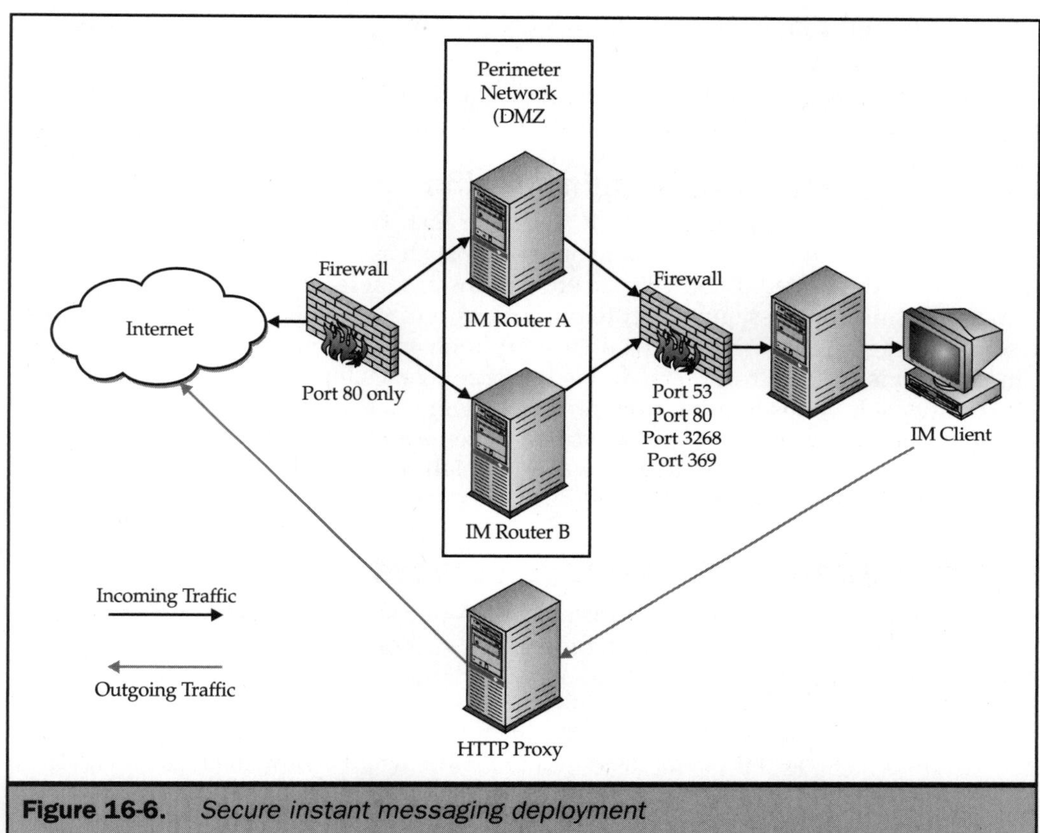

Figure 16-6. *Secure instant messaging deployment*

Note *Some filtering applications and devices do not recognize RVP and will therefore block it, even though port 80 might be open. In this event, check with the manufacturer to see if it has an update that correctly recognizes RVP. If not, you will need to turn off filtering in order for traffic to flow.*

The final task in securing inbound instant messaging traffic is to put an instant messaging router within a DMZ. A DMZ—or *demilitarized zone*—is an area of a network with limited external connectivity. The DMZ also needs to be configured to allow inbound traffic to flow to port 80 on your instant messaging router(s).

Outbound traffic can be secured through the use of HTTP proxy servers or Winsock proxy servers. The Exchange 2000 instant messaging client can be configured to use the same proxy settings as Internet Explorer. If you are already using one or more proxy servers to provide Web access to your organization, you do not need to do anything special. The Exchange 2000 instant messaging client can use the same proxy settings as Internet Explorer 5, or it can use a socks proxy (version 4 or 5).

Encrypting Instant Messaging Traffic

Native instant messaging traffic is XML and clear text. Therefore, it can be captured and interpreted with any general network sniffer such as Network Monitor. Currently, your choices are limited if you want to encrypt instant messaging traffic. One solution is to use the instant messaging SDK to build a customized version of an Exchange 2000 instant messaging client that has its own encryption and decryption mechanisms. You can obtain this kit from http://msdn.microsoft.com/exchange.

Another solution is to use virtual private network (VPN) technology to create secure tunnels between the instant messaging clients and their home servers. This type of solution can be cost-prohibitive; however, in high security environments that use instant messaging, it's an option that should be considered.

Monitoring Instant Messaging Servers

You should regularly monitor your instant messaging servers to ensure a consistent and enjoyable user experience. During the course of instant messaging server management, you should perform the following tasks:

- *Check the IIS log for the virtual server.* Instant messaging servers log inbound (client to server) protocol messages to the IIS logs. To view the logs, navigate to the instant messaging server's IIS log directory. The default directory is %SystemRoot%\System32\LogFiles\W3SVC1. Then, open one of the log files. Instant messaging entries will look something like this:

```
Software: Microsoft Internet Information Services 5.0
#Version: 1.0
#Date: 2000-05-18 17:18:33
#Fields: time c-ip cs-method cs-uri-stem sc-status
17:18:33 207.202.224.186 SUBSCRIBE /instmsg/aliases/jannic 401
17:18:33 207.202.224.186 SUBSCRIBE /instmsg/aliases/jannic 200
17:18:33 207.202.224.186 ACL /instmsg/aliases/jannic 401
17:18:33 207.202.224.186 SUBSCRIPTIONS /instmsg/aliases/jannic 401
17:18:33 207.202.224.186 ACL /instmsg/aliases/jannic 200
17:18:33 207.202.224.186 SUBSCRIPTIONS /instmsg/aliases/jannic 200
17:18:33 207.202.224.186 PROPPATCH /instmsg/aliases/jannic 401
17:18:33 207.202.224.186 PROPFIND /instmsg/aliases/jannic 207
```

When you view these logs, note that the time referenced for each event is different from your local time; the time in the log is the difference between your time zone and Greenwich mean time. For more information, see Microsoft Knowledge Base articles Q266754 and Q273718.

- *Monitor instant messaging server performance.* Exchange 2000 publishes the MSExchangeIM and MSExchangeIM Virtual Servers performance counter objects. You should regularly collect and trend the following performance counters:
  - **Current Inbound Requests**—The number of inbound requests currently being serviced
  - **Current Outbound Connections**—The number of currently open connections
  - **Current Outbound Requests**—The number of outbound requests currently being processed
  - **Current Subscriptions**—The number of currently active subscriptions
  - **Current Users Online**—The number of users currently online
  - **Failed Requests/sec**—The average number of requests that have failed (per second), including those rejected due to server load
  - **Failed Responses/sec**—The average number of responses that could not be sent (per second)
  - **Rejected Requests/sec**—The average number of requests rejected due to server load (per second)

Collecting this data through the MSExchangeIM Virtual Servers object enables you to have separate data for each virtual server installed. These are only recommended counters; depending on your environment, you may wish to collect additional MSExchangeIM counters, Exchange counters, IIS counters, and Windows 2000 counters.

Future of Instant Messaging

Instant messaging has a very promising future. Currently its growth is limited by the lack of standards and interoperability between the various instant messaging clients and servers. This has resulted in islands of instant messaging communities where members can only communicate if they use the same software. For example, Exchange 2000 instant messaging users can only communicate with other Exchange 2000 or MSN users.

Recently, instant messaging industry heavyweights such as Microsoft, AOL, and Yahoo have joined the IETF's Instant Messaging and Presence Protocol (IMPP) working group. According to its charter, the goal of the IMPP working group is "to define a standard protocol so that independently developed applications of instant messaging and/or presence can interoperate across the Internet." The IMPP submitted its original Internet draft of design goals in May 1999, and in July 1999, it submitted the draft to the Internet Engineering Steering Group for publication as an RFC.

More recently, RFCs 2778 and 2779 were published, which discuss A Model for Presence and Instant Messaging, and Instant Messaging/Presence Protocol Requirements, respectively. RFC 2778 defines an abstract model for a presence and instant messaging system. It defines instant messaging and presence terminology, identifies the various components, and outlines the services provided by an instant messaging system. Its goal is to provide a common vocabulary for future work on the requirements for protocols and markup for instant messaging and presence applications. RFC 2779 defines a minimal set of requirements that a standard instant messaging/presence protocol must meet.

In June 2000, AOL submitted its own proposal for Instant MessagingX—Instant Messaging Exchange—architecture. AOL's Internet draft, which can be read in its entirety at http://aim.aol.com/openim/draft-aol-imx-00.txt, is one of several drafts that have been submitted to the IETF for consideration.

Note *AOL's draft expired in December 2000; however, AOL maintains its commitment to instant messaging technology. AOL's statement on this issue can be read at http://aim.aol.com/openim/.*

Many of the same industry heavyweights have also formed a coalition of instant messaging providers called IMUnified (http://www.imunified.org). Its goal is to facilitate interoperability between the software and services provided by its members. As MSN is a founding member of IMUnified, eventually Exchange 2000's instant messaging services will be able to interoperate with instant messaging services other than Exchange 2000 and MSN.

Summary

Exchange 2000 instant messaging services enable users to see each other's presence information and communicate instantaneously with one another. These services can be provided both within an organization and between organizations. Moreover, they add a whole new dimension to applications by enabling them to leverage real-time presence information.

Instant messaging services are provided as an ISAPI application that runs under IIS. Instant messaging relies on Active Directory and DNS for proper operation. It is deployed within a client/server architecture where all traffic is XML data and clear text that is transmitted via HTTP and RVP.

The MSN Messenger client used by Exchange 2000 uses multiple providers—RVP and MSN—to communicate with internal Exchange 2000 users, external Exchange 2000 users, and MSN/Hotmail users. Currently, it cannot interoperate with other instant messaging systems such as AOL Instant Messenger and ICQ. Although it may take some time to accomplish and implement, eventually an open, interoperable instant messaging standard protocol will be approved by the IETF and integrated into instant messaging products from several vendors. Microsoft is actively involved in this process to ensure that the instant messaging services within Exchange 2000 and its successor products seamlessly integrate with any standard that is adopted.

Chapter 17

Chat Services

There is a cluster of three services that are considered *real-time collaboration (RTC)* services in Exchange 2000: instant messaging, conferencing, and chat. Chat services are best utilized when implemented in tandem with conferencing services. For example, chat services allow an audience member to ask questions via the chat channel while a speaker streams his or her video presentation to the audience.

Chat services are an open-forum mode of communication with the capability to regulate speech and membership in any chat room. Administrators have wide latitude to either let chat members regulate themselves or to implement significant control over the ebb and flow of a chat session. In this chapter, we'll cover the basics of Microsoft Exchange 2000 Chat Service, Chat Service architecture, the Microsoft Chat client, how to administer Chat Service, and how to troubleshoot it. This is a fun chapter, so we hope you'll enjoy it. And perhaps, you'll think of a time and reason to implement Chat Service in your organization.

Introduction to Chat Services

Microsoft Exchange 2000 Chat Service provides an environment for online group discussions. One chat room can handle up to 20,000 concurrent users. Each administrative group can have only one Chat Communities container in which multiple, virtual chat communities can be created. Each community can host multiple chat rooms, which are also called channels, and each room can be governed by its own set of administrative controls.

Chat services are based on the Internet Relay Chat (IRC) protocol. Internet Relay Chat Extension (IRCX) is a set of command extensions to IRC that enhance the functionality of the IRC protocol. These extensions, which were developed by Microsoft, are used to manage chat users and channels on a chat server.

Users connect to a chat server over TCP port 6667. Port 7000 is also available and, if needed, other port numbers can be used for client connectivity. Any IRC-based client that is RFC 1459-compliant will work with Microsoft's Chat Server, including mIRC (http://www.mirc.com) or PIRCH (http://www.pirch.com).

Chat Service Architecture

IRC was originally defined in RFC 1459. IRCX's RFC is currently in draft mode. Microsoft's implementation of chat services takes advantage of Active Directory (AD) to store configuration information on objects such as chat communities, channels, classes, bans, and chat servers. Each of these AD objects can be managed via the Exchange System Manager (ESM) snap-in.

The IRC protocol allows chat servers to form a spanning tree, so that messages can be sent from one chat server to another for distribution to a larger group of users. Because of this, each server in the chat network sees itself as the starting point for the other chat servers that it can see. Looping is not allowed in the spanning tree, so a request from one server to open a connection to another server that would form a loop will result in an error message.

IRC is intended to provide a method of communication in several different topologies, including one-to-one, one-to-many, and many-to-many. This communication is in real time, and security can be applied to ensure that messages are sent and received only by authorized personnel. In addition, the commands can be sent from a command prompt via a telnet session to both test and troubleshoot a chat server or client connection. Let's discuss each of these commands briefly.

Chat Commands

In this section, we'll outline the various chat commands in the IRC and illustrate how to use them. Then we'll show some screen shots that outline how to put these commands together to both troubleshoot and test your chat services.

PASS Command

The PASS command is used to send the password from the client to the server. This command should be sent before sending either the NICK or the USER command.

Example: PASS mypassword

The error messages generated for this command are:

ERR_NEEDMOREPARAMS

ERR_ALREADYREGISTRED

NICK Command

The NICK command is used in two situations: to give a new user a nickname and to enable a registered user to change his or her nickname. If a nickname is requested that is already in use, a nickname collision will occur and the user will be given an error message.

Example for a new user: NICK mynickname

Example for a registered user: :mynickname NICK newnickname

The error messages generated for this command are:

ERR_NONICKNAMEGIVEN

ERR_ERRONEUSNICKNAME

ERR_NICKNAMEINUSE

ERR_NICKCOLLISION

USER Command

Before a user can be registered with the chat server, the user must supply both a nickname and user name. The USER command is used for this purpose. In addition, this command is used to specify the host name of the user's workstation and the server name of the server to which the user wishes to connect. These two commands are used only in server-to-server communication.

The real name parameter must be the last parameter and must be prefixed with a colon ":".

Example: USER benglish workstation1snoopy :Bill English

In this example, the user Bill English is registering with a user name of "benglish" from the workstation "workstation1" to the server "snoopy", and his real name is "Bill English".

The error messages generated for this command are:

ERR_NEEDMOREPARAMS

ERR_ALREADYREGISTRED

SERVER Command

The SERVER command is used to tell a server at the receiving end of a connection that the connecting client is another chat server. A hopcount parameter can be input to tell the receiving server how far away the connection server is in the logical spanning tree. This command can only be accepted from a server that is not yet registered with the local server or from an existing server that is introducing a new server in its view of the spanning tree.

Example: SERVER chat.networknowledge.com 3 :[linus.networknowledge.com]

In this example, the server "linus" is introducing itself as "chat" and is attempting to register. Its real host name is inside the brackets. It is three hops away.

OPER Command

The OPER command is used to gain operating privileges in a chat room. Both the user name and password are required to gain this higher level of privilege.

Example: OPER benglish mypassword

A successful response from the chat server is RPL_YOUREOPER.

Error messages generated by this command are:

ERR_NEEDMOREPARAMS

ERR_NOOPERHOST

ERR_PASSWDMISMATCH

QUIT Command

The QUIT command ends the client's session with the chat server.

Example: QUIT I'm going home now

The message after the QUIT command is for personal use and is not required to successfully complete the command. There are no error messages for this command.

SQUIT Command

Servers use the SQUIT command to sever a connection to another server or to inform downstream servers about a dead server. A server that wishes to break a connection sends the SQUIT command along with the name of the other server. The result of this command is that the connection to the other server is severed. Chat administrators may also use this command to change the spanning tree topology. Both servers on either side of the command are required to send this command to all other servers in their spanning tree so that all servers can update their view of the chat network.

Example: : Snoopy SQUIT linus.networknowledge.com :Physical link has been separated

In this example, the SQUIT command is being issued to "Linus" from "Snoopy" because the physical link has been separated.

JOIN Command

A chat client uses the JOIN command to connect to a specific chat room. The server checks the client's request before letting the client into a chat room. After the first server has accepted the client, all other servers on the chat network accept the client's connection without re-checking the client against user bans that might be in place. When a user tries to connect to a chat room, the user's nickname, user name, and host name are checked against any active bans, and if there is a match, the client is rejected. If a password is required by the chat room, the proper password must also be entered.

Example: JOIN #chatroom1

A successful join to a chat room results in the RPL_TOPIC response from the server, which gives the topic of the chat room, and the RPL_NAMREPLY response, which lists the other members of the chat room.

Error messages generated by using this command are:

ERR_NEEDMOREPARAMS

ERR_INVITEONLYCHAN

ERR_CHANNELISFULL

ERR_NOSUCHCHANNEL

ERR_BANNEDFROMCHAN

ERR_BADCHANNELKEY

ERR_BADCHANMASK

ERR_TOOMANYCHANNELS

PART Command

The PART command severs a client from all the active lists of users for all channels listed in the command. The client runs this command.

Example: PART #chatroom1, #chatroom2

This command ends the client connection to two chat rooms: chatroom1 and chatroom2.

Error messages generated by this command are:

ERR_NEEDMOREPARAMS

ERR_NOTONCHANNEL

ERR_NOSUCHCHANNEL

MODE Command

The MODE command allows both user names and channels to have their modes changed. Channel operators may change the parameters of their chat room. Servers must be able to issue this command as well to change a channel's mode.

This command includes the following switches:

P	Private channel flag
S	Secret channel flag
I	Invite-only channel flag
t	Topic settable by channel operator only
n	No messages to channel from clients on the outside
m	Moderated channel
l	Set user limit to channel
o	Give/take channel operator privileges
b	Set a ban mask to keep out users

v	Give/take capability to speak on a moderated channel
k	Set a channel password
+	Add
-	Subtract

Some switches can be used after the nickname:

I	Makes a user invisible
S	Makes a user available to receive server notices
W	Sends a user a wallop

Example: MODE #chatroom1 +o benglish

This command gives the user "benglish" channel operator privileges in the "chatroom1" chat room.

Example: MODE #chatroom2 +im

This command makes the "chatroom2" chat room an invite-only, moderated chat room.

Example: #chatroom1 +l 25

This command sets a maximum limit of 25 users in the "chatroom1" chat room.

Example: benglish MODE benglish +I

The user "benglish" sends this command to make himself invisible in the chat room.

Error messages generated with this command are:

ERR_NEEDMOREPARAMS

ERR_CHANOPRIVSNEEDED

ERR_NOTONCHANNEL

ERR_UNKNOWNMODE

ERR_USERSDONTMATCH

ERR_UMODEUNKNOWNFLAG

ERR-NOSUCHNICK

ERR_KEYSET

ERR_NOSUCHCHANNEL

TOPIC Command

The TOPIC command is used to change the topic of a channel.

Example: TOPIC #chatroom1 :newtopic

This command makes the topic for "chatroom1" “newtopic”.

Example: :benglish #chatroom2 :Exchange 2000 Server

This command makes the topic for "chatroom2" “Exchange 2000 Server”.

Error messages generated by this command are:

ERR_NEEDMOREPARAMS

ERR_CHANOPRIVSNEEDED

ERR_NOTONCHANNEL

NAMES Command

The NAMES command allows a user to list all the nicknames that are not hidden in the chat room.

Example: NAMES #chatroom1

This command lists all the nicknames present in the chat room "chatroom1".

Example: NAMES

This command lists all the visible channels and users.

There are no error messages for this command.

LIST Command

The LIST command is used to list the channels and their topics. When used by itself, it lists all the channels. When a chat room is specified, it lists the topic for that chat room.

Example: LIST #chatroom2

The error message generated with this command is:

ERR_NOSUCHSERVER

INVITE Command

The INVITE command is used to invite users to a chat room. The target user's nickname and chat room name must be included in the command.

Example: :benglish INVITE kenglish #chatroom2

The user "benglish" issues this command to invite the user "kenglish" to chat room "chatroom2".

KICK Command

The PART command is issued by a client to leave a chat room. The KICK command is issued by a channel operator to forcibly remove a user from a channel.

Example: KICK #chatroom1 Sally :too many bad jokes

This command kick's "Sally" out of "chatroom1" for telling too many bad jokes. Error messages generated with this command are:

ERR_NEEDMOREPARAMS

ERR-BADCHANMASK

ERR_NOTONCHANNEL

ERR_NOSUCHCHANNEL

ERR_CHANOPRIVSNEEDED

PRIVMSG Command

The PRIVMSG command sends a message between two users. The receiver and the text of the message are part of the command. Automatic replies can be sent to a PRIVMSG command, but not to the NOTICE command. Otherwise, the NOTICE command is used similarly to the PRIVMSG command.

Example: :benglish PRIVMSG kenglish :I'll pick up bread and milk on the way home.

A successful generation of this command results in the RPL_AWAY response from the server.

Error messages generated with this command are:

ERR_NORECIPIENT

ERR_CANNOTSENDTOCHAN

ERR_WILDTOLEVEL

ERR_NOSUCHNICK

ERR_NOTEXTTOSEND

ER_NOTOPLEVEL

ERR_TOOMANYTARGETS

KILL Command

The server uses the KILL command to close a connection. This is most commonly used when a user attempts to register a duplicate nickname. It can also be used if a user is sending too much data to the chat room. Clients can automatically reconnect, which limits this command's usefulness in this situation.

Example: KILL benglish

Error messages generated with this command are:

ERR_NOPRIVILEDGES

ERR_NOSUCHNICK

ERR_NEEDMOREPARAMS

ERR_CANTKILLSERVER

PING Command

The PING command is used to verify the presence of an active client's connection. The PING message is sent at regular intervals if there is no activity from the client. If there is no response from the client, the connection is closed.

The PING command is responded to with a PONG command.

Example: PING benglish

Example: PING linus.networknowledge.com

In both examples, the PING message is being sent to see if the client connected to the local server is still there because there has not been any activity from that client for a predetermined period of time.

Error messages generated with this command are:

ERR_NOORIGIN

ERR_NOSUCHSERVER

Now, let's look at how these commands work, both from the command prompt and from the Comic Chat client. In our example, "kenglish" has joined the "chatroom1" channel as “guest1”. Then "benglish" leaves "chatroom1", rejoins, and then asks who is "guest1". You can see the reply from "kenglish" in both the Comic Chat client, shown in Figure 17-1, and the command prompt, shown in Figure 17-2.

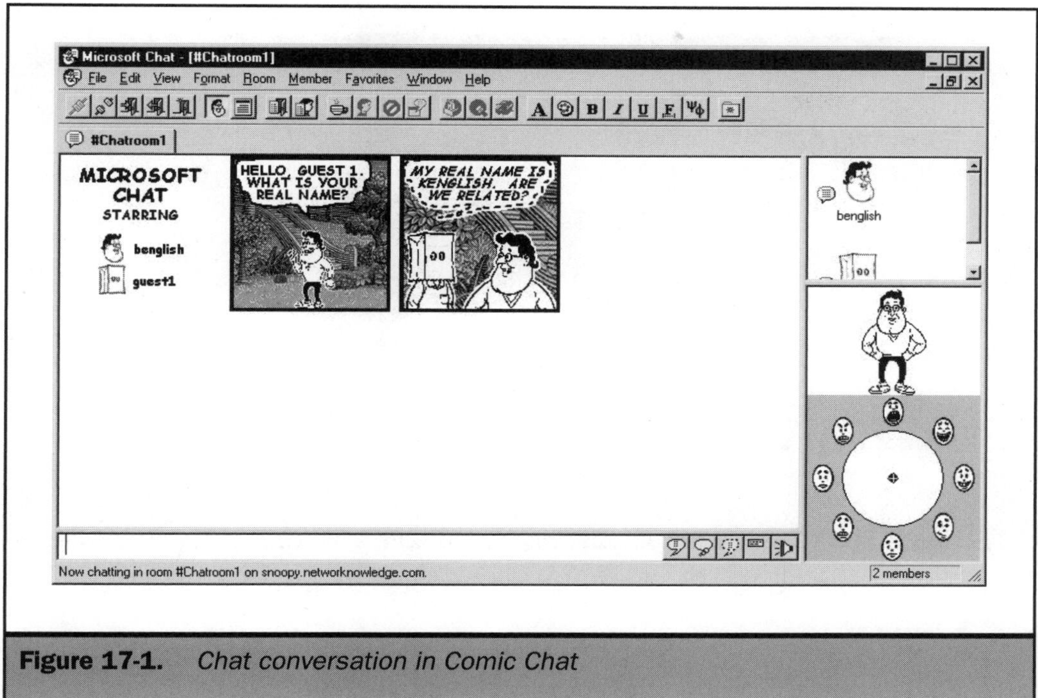

Figure 17-1. *Chat conversation in Comic Chat*

In Figure 17-2, notice that the USER command has a plethora of responses from the chat server, including the Message of the Day (MOTD) message. Notice also that the activities of the other person in the chat room leaving and joining was recorded in the command prompt interface for "kenglish". And if you refer back to Figure 17-1 for just a moment, you'll notice that "guest1" appears with a Comic Chat character, meaning that those who use chat services from the command prompt will appear in the graphical clients of chat services seamlessly.

One note on using the command prompt is warranted. If a command is mistyped in any way, even if you correct misspellings and the like, it will not be recognized and must be retyped in its entirety. Pressing the Backspace key does not delete a part of the command, and typing over a botched command does not erase earlier keystrokes. The only thing that clears out the keystroke cache is pressing the Enter key. In most cases where you've typed in a command incorrectly, you'll receive an error message, and then you can continue by typing in the properly-spelled command.

Let's take a brief look at the main concepts of chat services.

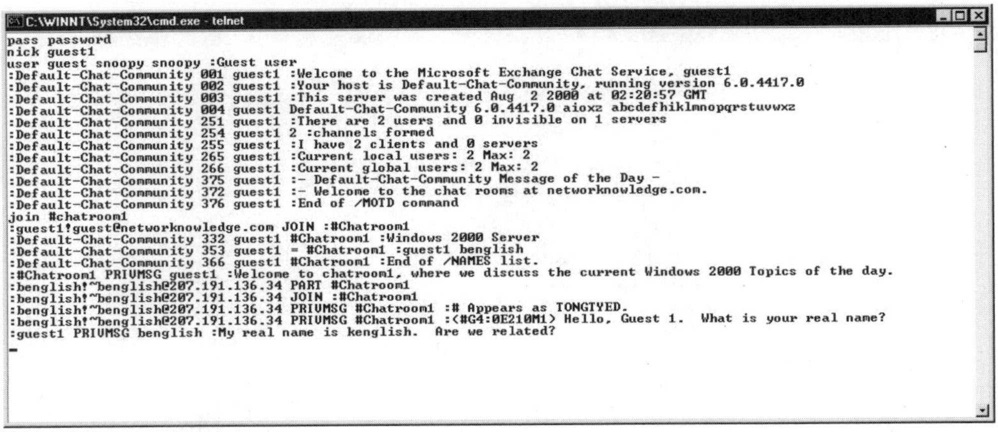

```
C:\WINNT\System32\cmd.exe - telnet
pass password
nick guest1
user guest snoopy snoopy :Guest user
:Default-Chat-Community 001 guest1 :Welcome to the Microsoft Exchange Chat Service, guest1
:Default-Chat-Community 002 guest1 :Your host is Default-Chat-Community, running version 6.0.4417.0
:Default-Chat-Community 003 guest1 :This server was created Aug  2 2000 at 02:20:57 GMT
:Default-Chat-Community 004 guest1 Default-Chat-Community 6.0.4417.0 aioxz abcdefhiklmnopqrstuvwxz
:Default-Chat-Community 251 guest1 :There are 2 users and 0 invisible on 1 servers
:Default-Chat-Community 254 guest1 2 :channels formed
:Default-Chat-Community 255 guest1 :I have 2 clients and 0 servers
:Default-Chat-Community 265 guest1 :Current local users: 2 Max: 2
:Default-Chat-Community 266 guest1 :Current global users: 2 Max: 2
:Default-Chat-Community 375 guest1 :- Default-Chat-Community Message of the Day -
:Default-Chat-Community 372 guest1 :- Welcome to the chat rooms at networknowledge.com.
:Default-Chat-Community 376 guest1 :End of /MOTD command
join #chatroom1
:guest1!guest@networknowledge.com JOIN :#Chatroom1
:Default-Chat-Community 332 guest1 #Chatroom1 :Windows 2000 Server
:Default-Chat-Community 353 guest1 = #Chatroom1 :guest1 benglish
:Default-Chat-Community 366 guest1 #Chatroom1 :End of /NAMES list.
:#Chatroom1 PRIVMSG guest1 :Welcome to chatroom1, where we discuss the current Windows 2000 Topics of the day.
:benglish!~benglish@207.191.136.34 PART #Chatroom1
:benglish!~benglish@207.191.136.34 JOIN :#Chatroom1
:benglish!~benglish@207.191.136.34 PRIVMSG #Chatroom1 :# Appears as TONGTYED.
:benglish!~benglish@207.191.136.34 PRIVMSG #Chatroom1 :<#G4:0E210M1> Hello, Guest 1.  What is your real name?
:guest1 PRIVMSG benglish :My real name is kenglish.  Are we related?
```

Figure 17-2. *Same chat conversation from the command prompt*

Chat Servers

Chat servers form the backbone of an IRC-compliant network, providing access points to which clients connect to converse with each other, as well as points to which other servers connect. The only network configuration allowed for an IRC-compliant network is that of a spanning tree in which each server acts as a central node for the rest of the network that it sees.

Chat Clients

According to the RFC, a client is anything connected to the server that is not another server. Each client must be distinguished by a unique *nickname,* which can be a maximum of nine characters. In addition to the nickname, all servers must have the following information about each client:

- Real name of the host upon which the client is running
- User name of the client on that host
- Server name to which the client is connected

Operators

Operators are a special class of clients that are allowed to perform basic administrative tasks on the network, such as disconnecting and reconnecting servers or removing a user from a chat room. Although this power can be abused, it is necessary to have it on the network for reasons we will discuss later. The key commands that can be issued only by an operator are:

KICK	Eject a client from the channel
MODE	Change the channels' mode
INVITE	Invite a client to an invite-only channel
TOPIC	Change the channel topic in a mode channel

A channel operator is also referred to as a "chop" or "chanop" and is considered to "own" that channel. Channel operator names are identified with an "@" symbol next to their nickname in the client's display.

Channels

A channel is a specific group in which one or more clients can send and receive messages. Channels can be created dynamically when the first client joins the room. It is the act of joining the room that also *creates* the room. By default, the first client to join (and create) the room also becomes the channel operator.

Channel names begin with either an "&" or an "#" and can be up to 200 characters in length. Channel names may not contain spaces, a control G "^G", or a comma ",".

Chat rooms can be created so that conversation flows in a one-to-one, one-to-many, or many-to-many topology. In addition, chat channels support a variety of channel modes. For example, *auditorium mode* is used to host a number of users who are listening to a few presenters. This mode prevents users in the room from seeing other users—only the presenters can be seen, and the presenters can see everyone else in the room. We'll discuss the various types of modes in more depth later in this chapter.

There are two types of channels: registered and dynamic. Registered channels are created by you, the chat administrator, and are permanent. Each registered channel can be configured to start when a client joins the room, or when the chat service is started. If the channels are not marked as secret or hidden, they will be visible to all chat clients. Dynamic channels are temporary channels that are created when a user joins the channel for the first time.

Channels can be configured to be secure, cloneable, or both. A secure channel is one to which access is restricted on some basis, such as to allow only authenticated users, invited users, or those who can enter the correct channel password. Active Directory groups can be used to restrict channel membership as well. Cloneable channels are those where, after a predefined client limit is reached, such as 25 simultaneous clients, another room is automatically created beginning with the 26th client. Any security settings that are configured for the initial channel are duplicated in the new channel.

Finally, channels can be moderated, meaning that only those who have been granted a "voice" to speak can actually send messages to them.

Installing Chat Service (Step-by-Step)

Before we demonstrate how to install Exchange 2000 Chat Service, here is a general overview of the Chat Service deployment process:

1. Plan out your server structure, including server location and the number and types of channels on each server. Also, in the planning stage, be sure to include the number and types of user bans, and which person(s) will administer this service.
2. Create a naming convention for your servers and rooms.
3. Install Chat Service on the appropriate Exchange 2000 Server(s).
4. Configure Chat Service.
5. Deploy the chat software to users.

Before you can install Chat Service, you must have the following:

- Microsoft Windows 2000 Server family product, installed either as a member server of a domain or as a domain controller
- Exchange 2000 Server with the Exchange Messaging and Collaboration Services installed on at least one Exchange 2000 Server in the same domain that Chat Service will be installed into
- Exchange System Manager snap-in for administering Chat Service

To begin the installation of Chat Service on an Exchange 2000 Server, you'll need to run the setup program from the Exchange 2000 Server CD-ROM. After clicking Next on the Welcome screen, the Component Selection screen appears, as shown in Figure 17-3. Because Exchange 2000 Server is already installed on the server upon which you will install Chat Service, you're not asked to agree to the license agreement or to enter the product key code.

Note *You'll need to have Exchange Full Administrator permissions on the organization object in Active Directory in order to add or remove a component.*

After selecting to install Chat Service, the Component Summary screen appears, and from there, the files are copied to the server and the service is installed.

Administering Chat Service

Chat Service administration is accomplished in the ESM snap-in, as shown in Figure 17-4. When Chat Service is initially installed, both the Chat Communities container and the Default-Chat-Community container are created. You can have only one Chat Communities container for each administrative group. Also, you'll notice that three folders— Channels, Bans, and Classes—are also created automatically with the service installation. This is where you'll administer each of these objects.

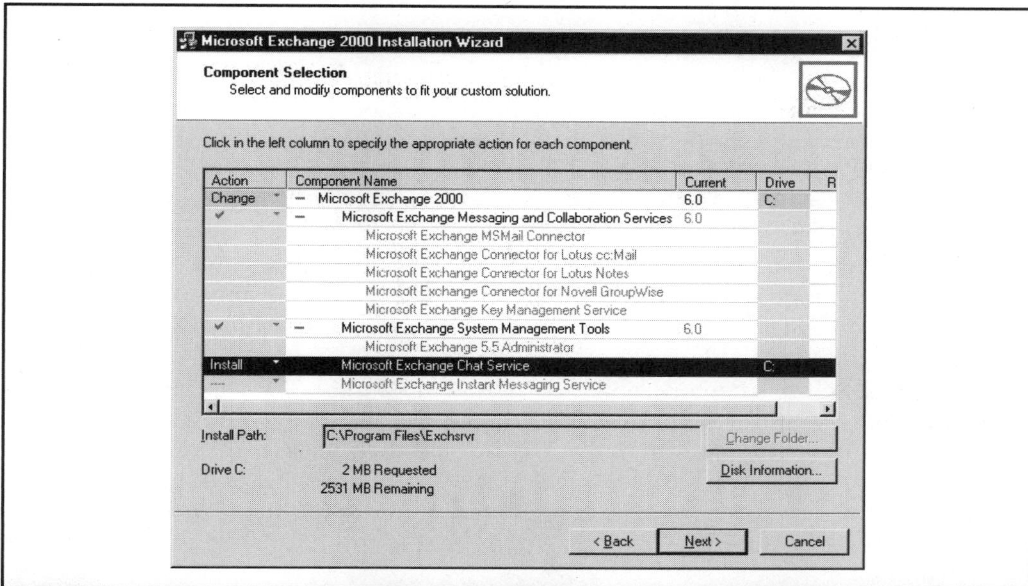

Figure 17-3. *Selecting to install Chat Service on the Component Selection screen*

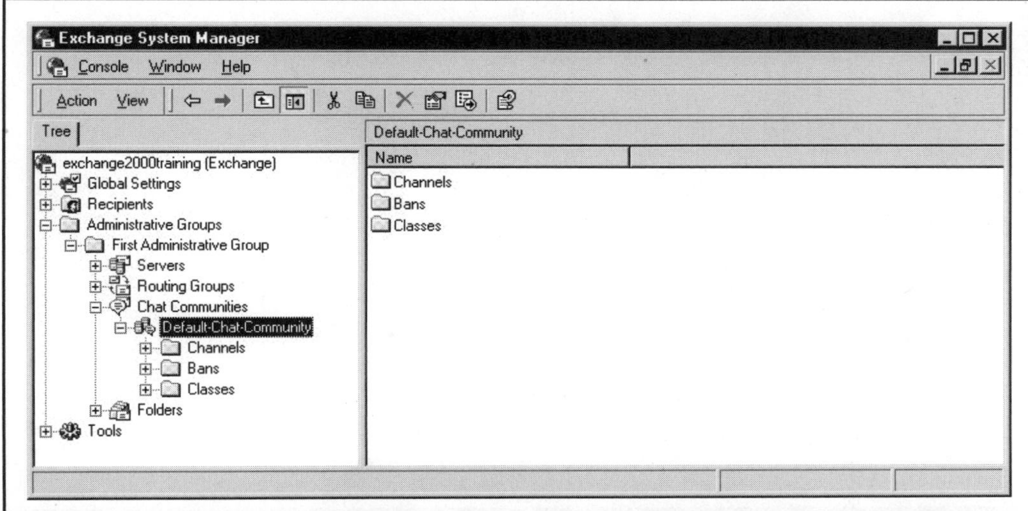

Figure 17-4. *Chat containers and folders in the ESM snap-in*

Managing Communities

When you create a new chat community, there is much to configure that impacts a user's experience in the channel(s) that are hosting inside that community. To create a new chat community, simply right-click on the Chat Communities container, point to New, and then select Chat Community. As shown in Figure 17-5, this invokes the New Properties dialog box containing five tabs: General, Channels, Messages, Security, and Authentication.

On the General tab, enter the new community's name in the Name field and configure client connection limits for both anonymous and total simultaneous connections. You can also specify whether the chat community should attempt to resolve the client's DNS name to an IP address before allowing that client to connect. There are three settings here: Disable, Attempt, and Require. The Disable setting means that no resolution attempt will be invoked. The Attempt setting means that the chat community will attempt to resolve the new client to a valid domain name, but if resolution is unsuccessful, the client will be able to connect to the community anyway. The most secure setting, Require, means that resolution will be attempted, and the client will be allowed to connect to the chat community only upon successful DNS resolution.

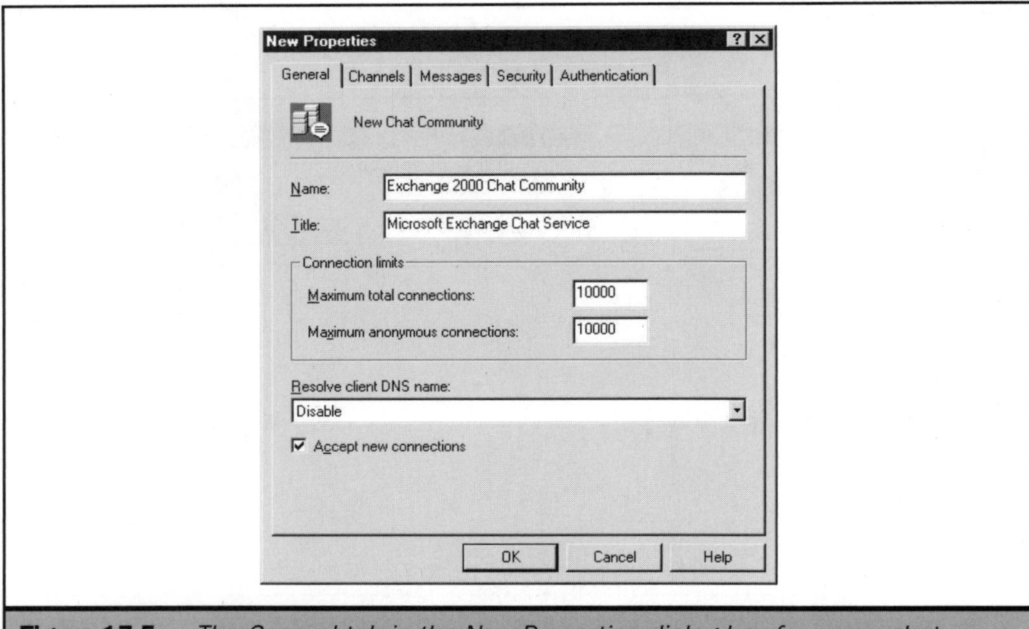

Figure 17-5. *The General tab in the New Properties dialog box for a new chat community*

Resolution of a client's IP address to a valid domain name helps ensure that if the connection is coming from the Internet, it is coming from a valid domain name on the Internet.

Finally, the chat community and all its channels can be configured to either accept new connections or reject new connections. Clearing the Accept New Connections checkbox does not sever existing connections. This is most useful when you need to bring down your chat server for regular maintenance but do not want to force everyone off at the last minute. This option allows a more graceful method of getting users off your server, although it does require some advanced planning as to when the checkbox should be cleared.

After creating the new chat community, you'll need to associate this community with the IRCX protocol folder in the ESM snap-in. To do this, right-click on the IRCX folder and open its properties. Click on the Add button and select the newly created community in the Chat Community drop-down list. When you make your selection and click OK, the Chat Communities properties dialog box appears. Select the Enable Server To Host This Chat Community checkbox, as shown in the following illustration.

Exchange2000 Properties

☑ Enable server to host this chat community

IP address: (All Unassigned) Advanced...

Maximum total connections: 10000

Extensions

Configure the chat server extensions for this chat community. Extensions...

OK Cancel Help

Click OK to exit this box and the IRCX properties box. Now the chat community is available for service on this server.

The Channels tab, shown in Figure 17-6, enables you to configure some channel defaults. For example, the default number of users allowed in a channel is 25. You can adjust this up or down as your needs and resources dictate. The Language field is where you specify, in International Standards Organization (ISO) terms, the language that this chat community is using.

Selecting the Allow An Owner Or Host For Channel checkbox allows a client who creates a new channel to also become the channel's owner or host. Clearing this checkbox means that the user will not become a channel's host or owner.

Notice that you can select a different maximum default number of clients for dynamic channels by configuring the Number Of Users Allowed In Channel field. You can also specify that users who are granted the chanop permission automatically become the owner of any channel that they join by selecting the Chat Sysop Joins As Owner checkbox.

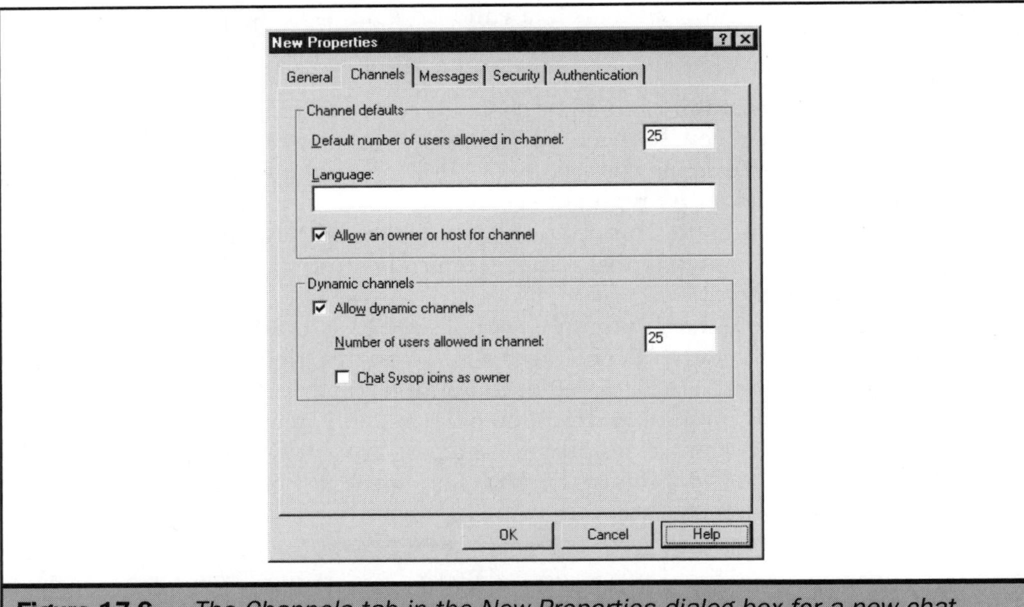

Figure 17-6. *The Channels tab in the New Properties dialog box for a new chat community*

The Messages tab is used to enter a message you want all users to see when they connect to the chat community. As soon as they connect, the message appears in their client. This can be useful for informing users if the channel is moderated or if their conversations are logged for future reference.

In the lower half of the tab, there is a place to enter messages for those who issue the ADMIN command. This should display information about the server, such as its IP address, the name and phone number of the person who is responsible for maintaining it, its hardware configuration, and similar types of data.

The Security tab is used to assign Active Directory security principles permissions to this container. The Authentication tab, as shown in Figure 17-7, allows you to set the level of authentication that you desire. Your choices here are Anonymous Access, Basic Authentication, and Windows Security Package. If you do not wish to authenticate users when they join a chat room in the chat community, leave the Anonymous Access checkbox selected.

You can use basic or integrated authentication to authenticate users when they connect to a chat room inside the chat community. Basic authentication means that the password will be sent in clear text using standard commands. If you'd like a server in a domain other than the one hosting the community to authenticate the user, enter the full name of the domain in the Domain field. Finally, use the Windows Security Package authentication process if you want users to authenticate using the Windows

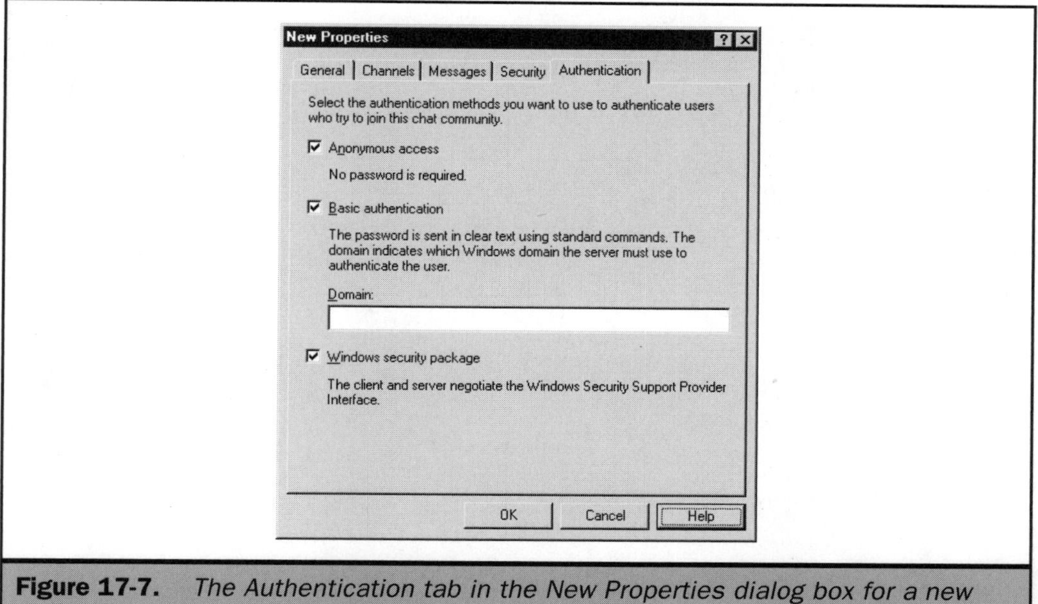

Figure 17-7. *The Authentication tab in the New Properties dialog box for a new chat community*

Integrated Authentication. Note that if you choose to use the Windows Security Package, you must clear the Basic Authentication checkbox.

Once the new chat community has been created, you can modify your selections by navigating to the chat community's properties and making your changes there.

Managing Channels

Now that you have a new chat community, we'll illustrate how to create a new chat channel with various configuration options. You'll recall that when a new chat community is created, three folders are automatically created inside the community: Channels, Bans, and Classes. In this section, we'll focus on the Channels folder.

To create a new chat channel, right-click on the Channels folder, point to New, and then select Channel. The New Properties dialog box appears for the new channel, as shown in Figure 17-8. On the General tab, enter the channel name, the topic of the channel, the subject (if needed), and the content rating. By selecting the Create This Channel When The Service Starts checkbox, you ensure that this channel is always available when Chat Service is running. Left unchecked, the channel only becomes visible when someone joins it.

Tip *For more information about content ratings and the Platform for Internet Content Selection (PICS), please go to http://www.w3.org.*

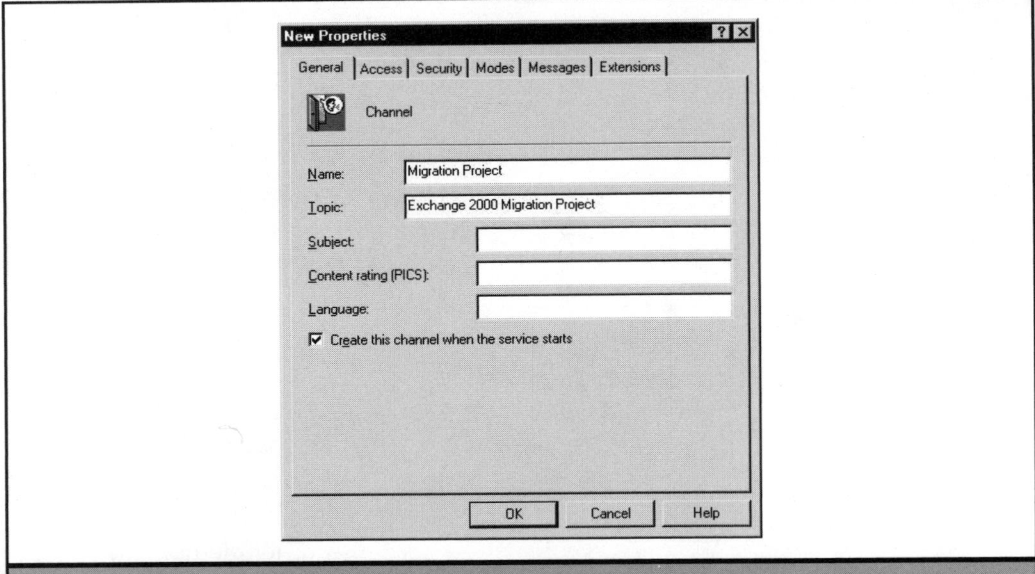

Figure 17-8. *The General tab in the New Properties dialog box for a new channel*

Channel Names

The channel name can have between 1 and 200 characters. Each channel must begin with a valid prefix (#, &, %#, or %&). The prefix denotes the type of channel. Table 17-1 outlines the prefixes and their associated types.

Channel Visibility

Channel visibility is configured on the Access tab, as shown in Figure 17-9. You can choose from four settings:

- **Public.** A public channel is not restricted in any way. All users can see the channel.
- **Private.** Only the channel name can be viewed in a private channel. In addition, channel membership can be determined and viewed by non-members.
- **Hidden.** Channel information can be viewed by users who are not invited to the channel.
- **Secret.** Channel information is not available through any type of query.

In most cases, you'll want to use the Public visibility setting for your channels. However, there may be times when you want to hide a channel from the public, and

Prefix	Type
#	IRC channel.
&	IRC channel.
%#	Extended channel. Extended channels have names that contain characters encoded in the Unicode Transformation Format 8 (UTF-8) and are visible only to clients that support the IRCX protocol, such as Microsoft Chat version 2.5.
%&	Extended channel. See preceding entry for notes on the meaning of an extended channel.

Table 17-1. *Summary of Prefixes and Their Associated Meanings When Creating a New Chat Channel*

then notify the invited members about the chat channel by another method. One example would be an online conference on your company's strategic plans that also includes a chat room for questions and sidebar conversations. The Private and Hidden settings give you some flexibility in how you want your channel to be restricted.

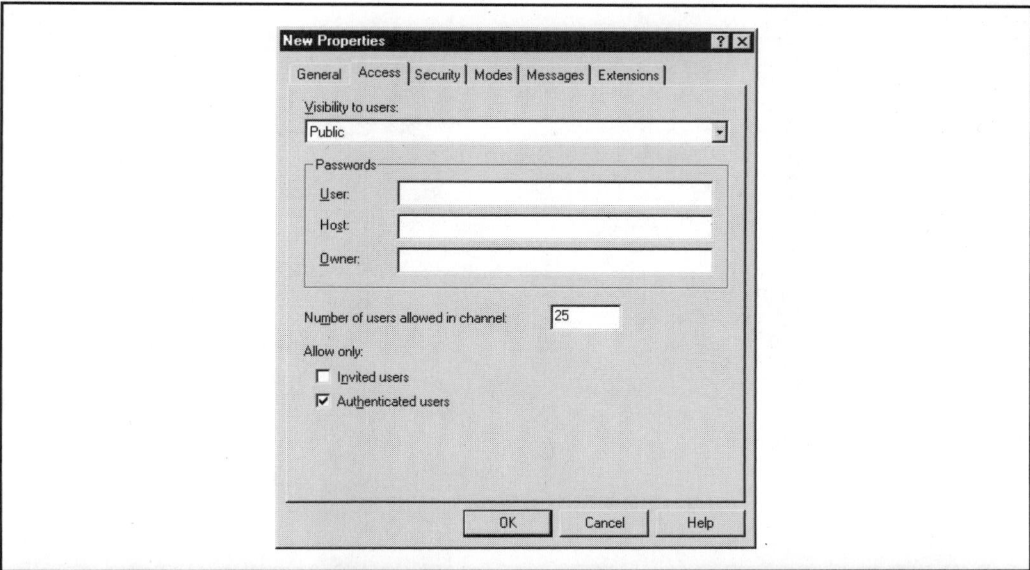

Figure 17-9. *The Access tab in the New Properties dialog box for a new channel*

The Passwords section allows you to enter different passwords for different roles in the channel. Obviously, the user password is disseminated to users who are invited to the channel, whereas the Host or Owner password might be entered on all channels for those designated as Host or Owner to join any channel with their advanced standing.

You can override the default setting for the maximum number of users allowed in the channel by entering a different number in the Number Of Users Allowed In Channel field. In addition, you can specify that this channel will allow only invited users and authenticated users.

Channel Modes

The Modes tab, shown in Figure 17-10, is where you configure channel modes. Starting at the top of the tab, three settings can be enabled or disabled for messages: The channel can be configured to accept messages only from channel members, to not format client messages, and to notify the host when users cannot join the channel.

The Do Not Format Client Messages checkbox is deceptive in its title, because when selected, it prevents the user from displaying the "from alias" prefix in channel conversations. This is not a security issue as much as it is an overhead-reducing issue. Selecting this checkbox improves server response by reducing server processing.

The Notify Host When Users Cannot Join option is useful if the channel is restricted and you want the host to know when an unauthorized person is attempting to connect to it.

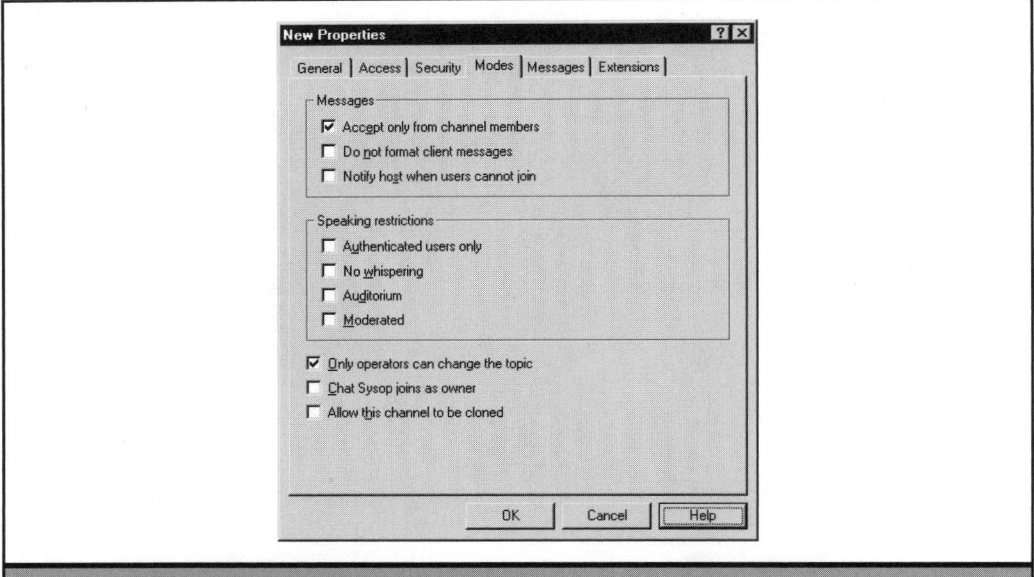

Figure 17-10. *The Modes tab in the New Properties dialog box for a new channel*

The Speaking Restrictions area can be used to restrict certain types of conversation and to define who can speak on this channel. There are four settings:

- **Authenticated Users Only.** When selected, only authenticated users can speak on this channel. This option is disabled if the Allow Only Authenticated Users checkbox is selected on the Access tab.
- **No Whispering.** A whisper is a private message that one member of the channel sends to another member in the same channel. Select this checkbox to prevent whispering.
- **Auditorium.** Auditorium channels are used for large chat events. A user joining this type of chat channel can only see the messages from the hosts in the channel. All other users are prevented from conversing with each other. In addition, only the hosts are notified when users join or leave the chat room.
- **Moderated.** These channels are used for small chat events. Users can post messages to the channel only when given permission by the host(s) in the channel.

The last three checkboxes are independent of each other. The Only Operators Can Change The Topic checkbox is selected by default. If you want to allow all users to change the topic of the channel, clear this checkbox. Chat sysops who join the channel as an owner or host can also change the topic, if needed. Select the Chat Sysop Joins As Owner checkbox if you want Chat sysops to join this channel as owners. The Allow This Channel To Be Cloned checkbox permits a new channel to be created when all the current channels with the same base name are full.

Tip

A cloneable channel must be properly named for this feature to work correctly. It is best to not end channel names with numbers because the naming convention for cloneable channels uses suffix numbers to uniquely identify new channels. For example, a channel named "migration" would clone as "migration01", and the next clone would be "migration02." This is why you don't name a channel "Exchange 2000": because the next clone would be "Exchange 200001". This would be slightly confusing, and might generate unnecessary help desk calls.

The Messages tab is where you enter messages that users will see when they join or leave the channel. This is useful for informing people when they join the channel that their conversations are being logged.

Note

Check with your company's legal counsel to ensure that any chat conversation logging, or any notification of such logging, complies with all relevant and applicable laws.

The last tab, Extensions, is used to list and configure extensions for this chat channel. Microsoft's implementation allows for two extensions: the profanity filter and channel transcription.

Profanity Filter A profanity filter detects and filters unwanted language in all messages, including whispers and invitations for both dynamic and registered channels. Individual filters can be applied to most types of messages as well as nicknames.

To create a profanity filter, you'll need to create a filter list containing the words you wish to prohibit from conversations. To create this list, right-click on the IRCX folder in the ESM snap-in and open its properties. From there, highlight the chat community in which you wish to configure the word list and click Properties; click the Extensions button, and then click Add. Choose the PFilter extension, and then click the Properties button. The dialog box shown in Figure 17-11 appears.

Be sure to stop and start Chat Service after you have added a filter but before you attempt to configure the filter.

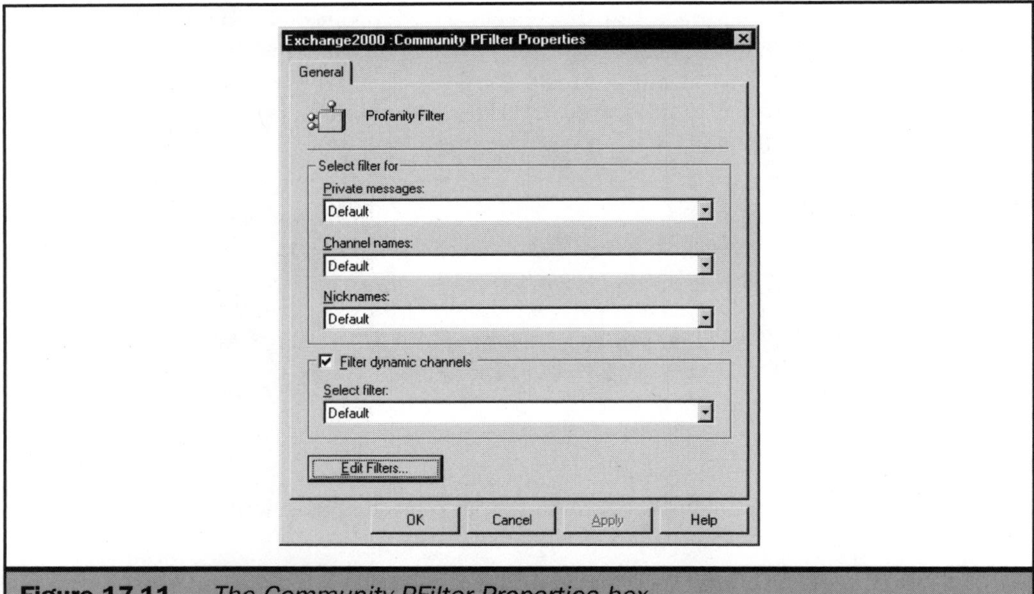

Figure 17-11. *The Community PFilter Properties box*

If you click the Edit Filters button, the Edit Filters dialog box appears, as illustrated here.

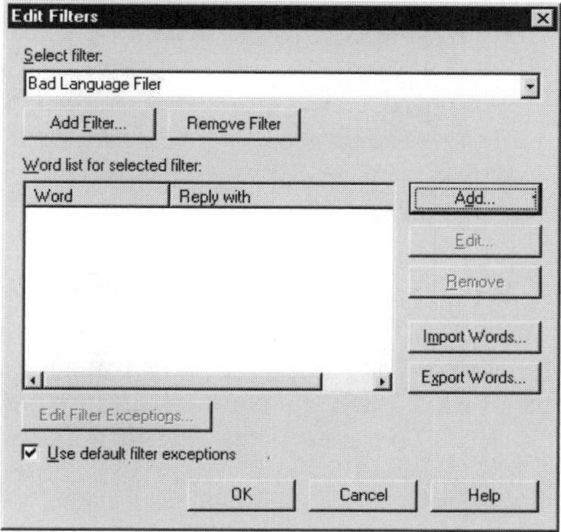

In the upper part of the screen, you can select which filter you want to configure, or you can add or remove a new filter by clicking the appropriate buttons. In the Word List For Selected Filter area, enter the words you wish to restrict. Note that you can import a group of words from a simple text file. You can also export the word list to a text file for use on another chat server in your organization.

When you add a word, you can enter a wildcard expression, as outlined in Table 17-2. And, in the Response To User Of Filtered Word field, you can enter a response that users will receive when they use restricted words.

To Match	Use This Wildcard	Examples
Any single character	?	As? matches ask and asp.
Any string of characters	*	S*t matches shot and slit.
A character inside specified brackets	[ ]	B[al]l matches ball and wall.
Any alphanumeric character in a range	[-]	Cl[e-e]r matches clever and lever.
Any single character except the characters inside the brackets	[^]	Th[^ou]ght matches though and dough.

Table 17-2. *Wildcard Filter Expressions for Chat Service*

Once the filter has been created, you can select it in the drop-down list for private messages, channel names, nicknames, and dynamic channels. After enforcing the filter against the message types you want, click OK until you have exited all of the dialog boxes, and then it should be ready to go.

Figure 17-12 illustrates what happens on the client end. We've restricted the words "rude" and "crude." When the word "crude" is typed in, the chat service responds to the user in question with the message that was configured for that word. In this case, we configured Chat Service to respond with the message "This word is not allowed in the chat room. Please do not use it again."

Channel Transcription With channel transcription, conversations in the chat rooms are saved to a file inside a directory named after the community. By default, this location is \exchsrvr\chatdata\transcript. The location of chat transcripts can be changed using the transcript extension properties. Each file contains all messages sent publicly to a channel within a 24-hour period. To install transcription for a chat community, add the Tscript extension to the community in the same manner as described for adding the profanity filter.

When a user first joins a channel that has transcription enabled, the user is informed of this fact immediately upon entering the room, as shown in Figure 17-13.

Messages between users are recorded in the transcription text file, as shown in Figure 17-14.

Figure 17-12. *Response to filtered word in the Chat client*

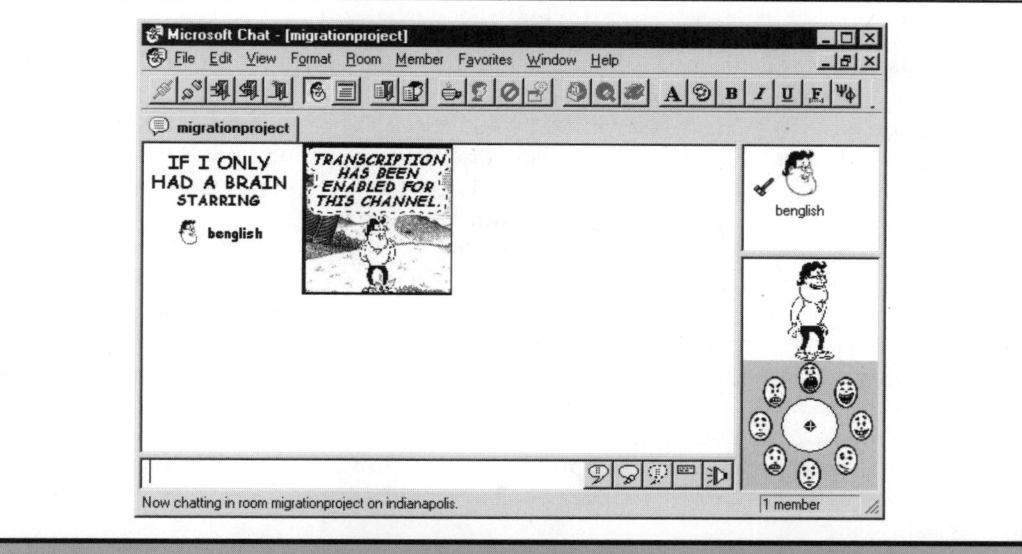

Figure 17-13. *Message indicating that transcription has been enabled*

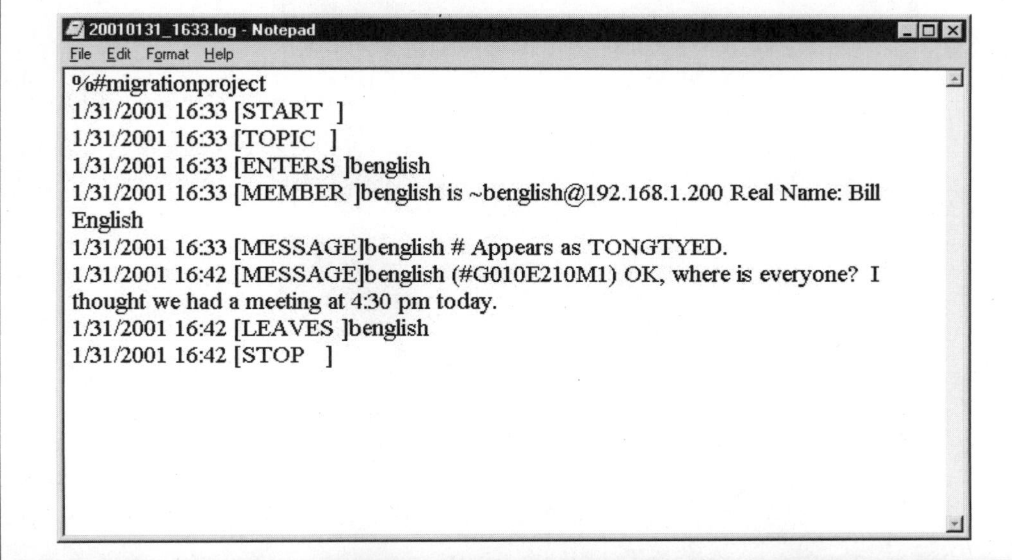
20010131_1633.log - Notepad
File Edit Format Help

%#migrationproject
1/31/2001 16:33 [START]
1/31/2001 16:33 [TOPIC]
1/31/2001 16:33 [ENTERS]benglish
1/31/2001 16:33 [MEMBER]benglish is ~benglish@192.168.1.200 Real Name: Bill English
1/31/2001 16:33 [MESSAGE]benglish # Appears as TONGTYED.
1/31/2001 16:42 [MESSAGE]benglish (#G010E210M1) OK, where is everyone? I thought we had a meeting at 4:30 pm today.
1/31/2001 16:42 [LEAVES]benglish
1/31/2001 16:42 [STOP]

Figure 17-14. *Sample transcription text file*

User Bans

The User Bans folder is the next folder beneath the Channels folder inside the chat community. User bans allow you to restrict access to a chat community for a specific user or group of users who are identified by their user name, nickname, domain name, or IP address. User bans can be in effect forever or for a specified period of time. One ban is defined for each community; therefore, a user banned in one community may be able to enter rooms created in another community.

To create a new user ban, right-click on the User Bans folder, point to New, and then select Bans. Only one tab needs to be configured: the General tab, shown in Figure 17-15. Enter the nickname, user name, domain name, or IP address of the user or group of users you wish to ban from the community. You can use wildcard characters (* and ?) if you'd like to encompass a range of names, such as hack*, for hacker, hacket, hacking, and so on.

To limit the ban to a particular time of day, configure the Time Active values as needed. The Reason For Ban field is optional but can provide other administrators valuable information as to why the ban was implemented.

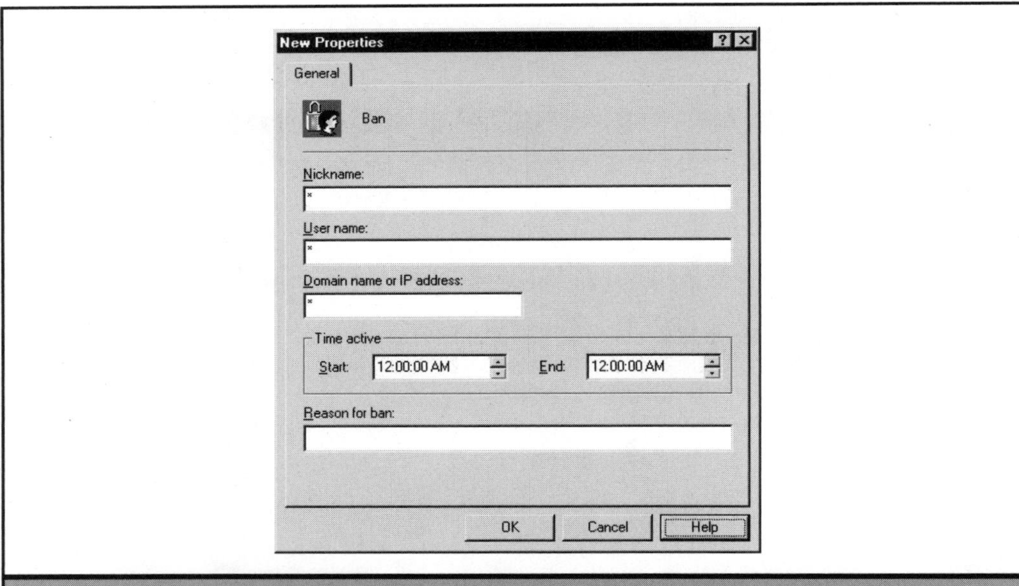

Figure 17-15. *The user ban configuration dialog box*

User Classes

User classes create membership for users based on one of several criteria: how the user is logged on, the user's identity mask, and the time of day. Classes are a more advanced method of placing restrictions on users than creating user bans. If a user matches any of the selection criteria that have been used to define a class, Chat Service adds that user to the user class and enforces that class's restrictions on the user.

When you create a new user class, configuration options appear on three different tabs: General, Access, and Settings.

The General tab, shown in Figure 17-16, is where you name the class, and then configure membership in the class based on nickname, user name, domain name, or IP address. Wildcards work here the same as they do in user bans. You can also add a network to the class by selecting the IP Address radio button, and then entering a network address. For example, if you entered 192.168.2.0 with a subnet mask of 255.255.255.0, any address in that range would be added as a member of this class. This section is useful for using one administrative act to set up restrictions for everyone in your company.

On the Access tab, shown in Figure 17-17, you can add users to a class based on their logon method to the chat community. This is helpful if you are running chat rooms for both LAN-based and Internet-based clients, and you would like to place restrictions on users coming in from the Internet but not on your internal users.

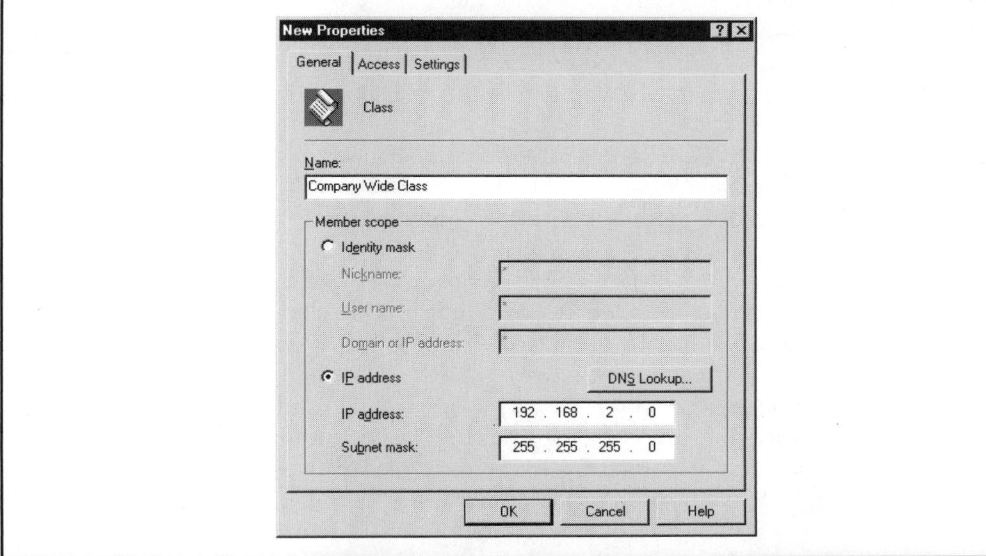

Figure 17-16. *The General tab used in creating a new user class*

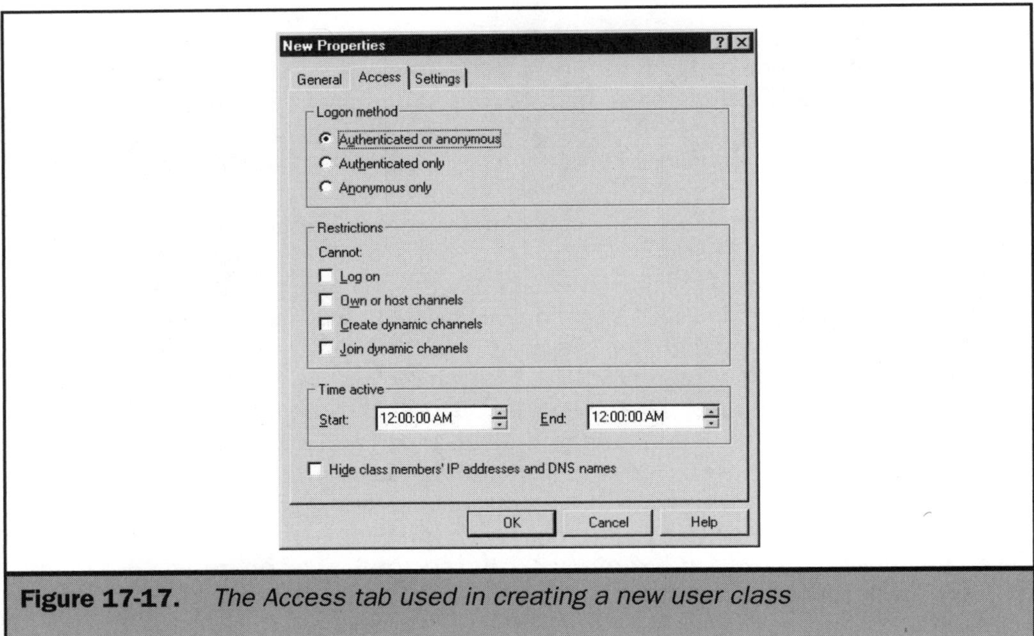

Figure 17-17. *The Access tab used in creating a new user class*

The restriction options prevent users from logging on, owning or hosting channels, creating dynamic channels, or joining dynamically created channels. Again, you can see that these options are useful if you only want registered, non-dynamic channels to be available to a group of users. To implement the restrictions, select the checkboxes that match your criteria.

Finally, the Time Active section applies these restrictions during the time you specify. By default, the restrictions are active for all 24 hours. Change the time values to meet your needs or leave them at default if you want the restrictions enforced at all times.

The Settings tab, shown in Figure 17-18, sets protection levels to prevent attacks from bringing down your server. One would not think that chat services present an opportunity to a would-be attacker to overwhelm your server and cause it to stop responding. However, there are three types of attacks that Microsoft security features can help you protect against: flooding attacks, clone attacks, and direct client attacks.

Flooding attacks are the result of a user sending large amounts of information to be processed that exceeds the server's capacity to manage. This type of attack can also cause another user's screen to scroll so fast that it is impossible to follow the chat session. As shown in Figure 17-18, flooding attacks can be controlled by lowering the output saturation limit for the class that is being configured. It is an excellent idea to create a class of all users, and then set an output saturation limit that applies to all users. This limit specifies the maximum amount of data that the server can buffer

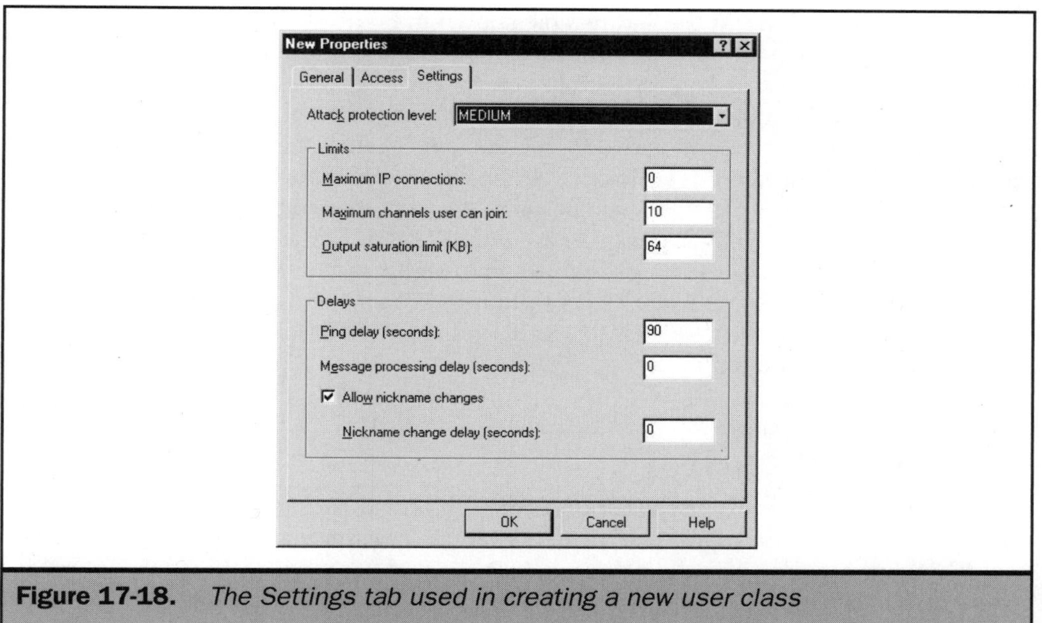

Figure 17-18. *The Settings tab used in creating a new user class*

before the server severs the client's connection to the server. Flooding attacks can also occur when a user sends a series of short, but very fast messages that may not ever invoke the output saturation limit, but still cause other users' screens to scroll too quickly. To prevent this, raise the Message Processing Delay value, which defines, in seconds, the amount of time the server waits before processing the next message from a client. Again, creating a class for all users with a value entered here can defend against a flooding attack.

Clone attacks occur when an attacker establishes several connections to a server from a single IP address and sends multiple, frequent messages to each connection. The effect of this type of attack is to create so much activity on the server that the server does not accept new connections from other users. This type of attack can be limited by configuring a low value for the Maximum IP connections value. Sysops and chat administrators are not affected by this limit.

Direct client attacks occur when a chat client launches an attack on another client by learning the other user's IP address and then sending large amounts of data to the user's modem while he or she is dialed in to the Internet. To stop this type of attack, enable IP/DNS masking, which masks a portion of each user's IP address or DNS host name, thus exposing only a portion of a user's identifying information. For example, if a user's DNS host name is "server1.networknowledge.com", the server masks the first portion of the name, or, "server1". And an IP address of 192.168.2.200 would be masked as 192.168.2.xxx.

Other configurations on the Settings tab shown in Figure 17-18 should be mentioned as well. Under the Delays section, you can configure the Ping Delay parameter. The server uses this PING message to test whether an active client is present. This is something like the heartbeat that passes between servers in a cluster except that the client responds with a PONG message. When the server receives this message, it knows the client is still active. If the client fails to respond, the server severs the connection. The timeout value can be set to anything between 15 and 3599 seconds. Both the PING and the PONG messages are only 83 bytes in size, which does not represent a huge bandwidth sapper in most environments.

Finally, the Nickname Change Delay option regulates how often a user can change his or her nickname. Best practice is to set this value at a high number; the highest number that can be entered is 9999.

Network Security

Exchange 2000 Chat Service uses TCP port 6667, a chat industry standard, as its default port for client communications. If all of your chat traffic is internal to your organization, you do not need to configure your external firewall(s) to pass 6667 traffic to the Internet. However, if you're in a geographically dispersed situation, with users using the Internet as their connection to get to your chat server, you should open up port 6667 for IRC traffic and port 53 for DNS resolution traffic. You may also need to open port 7000 because this is a second default port over which some chat communities operate.

All chat communications travel across the network as clear text. This obviously represents a security concern. IRC sessions currently lack encryption support, such as Secure Socket Layer (SSL) or Transport Layer Security (TLS) encryption. Hence, to secure chat traffic, you can use Point-to-Point Tunneling Protocol (PPTP), Layer 2 Tunneling Protocol (L2TP), or IPSec (Internet Protocol Security) tunnel to encapsulate a message stream. To learn more about how to implement PPTP, L2TP, or IPSec, please consult the Windows 2000 Server Resource Kit.

By default, there are no logon restrictions for chat users. However, you can provide security for chat communities by restricting unauthorized user access. You can require each participant to log on using either clear-text (unencrypted) passwords or Windows Integrated Authentication when connecting to a chat community, thereby preventing an unauthorized user from sending messages to the community.

Upgrading Exchange 5.5 Chat Service

If you are currently running Exchange 5.5 Chat Service and you wish to upgrade to the Exchange 2000 Chat Service, there is a chat migration utility, CHATMIG.EXE, in the exchsrvr\bin directory. However, before you run this utility, be aware of the following factors:

- The chat migration tool does not migrate extension data from Exchange 5.5 to Exchange 2000. Therefore, if you have configured a profanity filter or transcription extension, these must be migrated manually.
- If your Exchange 5.5 chat installation has one chat service that spans multiple Exchange 5.5 Servers, you must create a mirror image of these communities on each Exchange 2000 Server. Each chat community on the Exchange 2000 Server will operate separately, with separate user lists and channel lists.
- Before you run the chat migration tool, you'll need to install Chat Service on each Exchange 2000 Server that will host a chat community.
- The CHATMIG.EXE utility should be copied to the source server and run from that platform. When you run the utility, identify the older Chat Service as the source and Exchange 2000 Chat Service as the target. If the older Chat Service spans multiple servers, this utility only needs to be run from one source server.

There's not much to the CHATMIG.EXE utility. Just enter the requested information and click OK. The chat information will be migrated from your Exchange 5.5 Server to the target chat community in Exchange 2000 Server.

If you are installing Exchange 2000 Chat Service on a server that has the earlier version of Chat Service, you must modify the chat name by performing the following actions. First, use the Services snap-in to modify the display name of the earlier Chat Service. Then reconfigure the ports used by the earlier Chat Service to something other than 6667 or 7000. If you do not perform these functions, the migration utility will not work properly.

Managing Chat Clients

In this section, we'll look briefly at the Microsoft Chat client. This client can be found on the Exchange 5.5 Service Pack 3 CD. Interestingly enough, at the time of this writing, it is not available on the Exchange 5.5 Service Pack 4 CD.

Tip *The mIRC and PIRCH clients are more robust and offer more services than the Microsoft Chat client. However, due to space limitations, we were able to illustrate only one client and we chose to use the Microsoft Chat client. The other two clients are available for download over the Internet. See the web links earlier in this chapter for their web sites.*

Microsoft Chat can be launched by selecting the shortcut for it on the Programs menu. Click the Microsoft Chat shortcut. The Chat Connection dialog box appears, asking you to enter the name of the chat server and whether you want to go straight to a designated chat room or see all the available chat rooms hosted on that server. Figure 17-19 shows this dialog box with "indianapolis", the chat server on our test network. In most

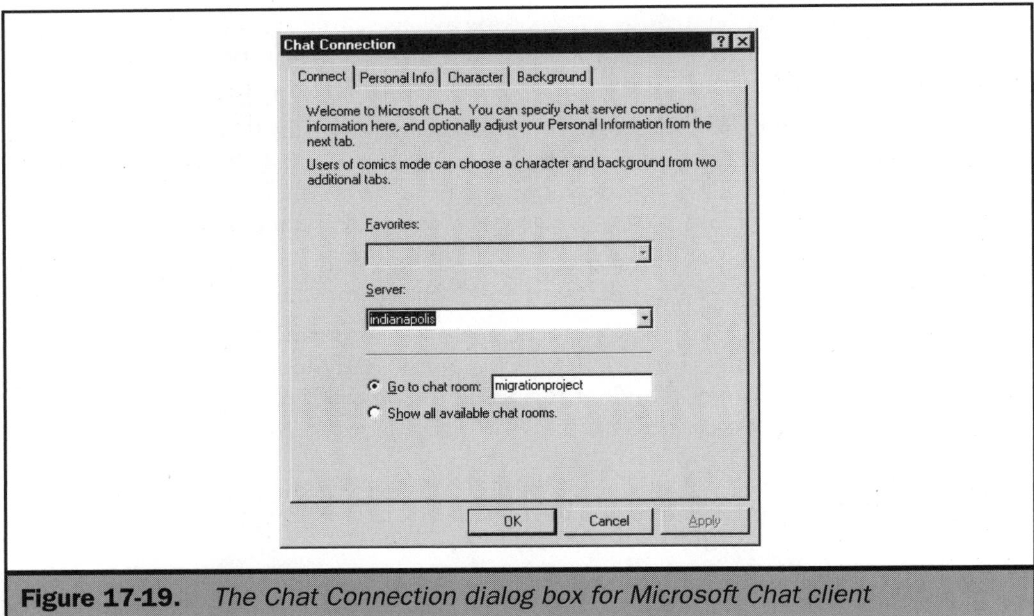

Figure 17-19. *The Chat Connection dialog box for Microsoft Chat client*

instances, you'll want to enter the FQDN of the server, especially when connecting to a chat server on the Internet.

In Figure 17-19, you'll notice four tabs on the Chat Connection dialog box. The Personal Info tab is where users can specify their real name, nickname, e-mail address, and home page URL, and enter a brief description of their person or work. The Character tab is where users can select a character to use in the comic strip format, and the Background tab provides the visual background for the character when communicating in a chat room. Once the desired selections have been made, click OK and the Chat client will connect to the chat room on the chat server.

Note *If a message of the day has been configured in the properties of the chat community, the message will appear before the user is connected to the chat channel. The client can choose to not see the message of the day by clearing the Show This Whenever Connecting checkbox on the popup screen.*

The comic strip view of a chat channel can be interesting. The characters interact with each other as if they were in a comic strip. Facial expressions can be customized when typing the message, and long entries are spread over multiple comic boxes with changing facial expressions. Figure 17-20 illustrates these two features well.

You can configure the Chat client to use a plain text view as well, but if the user goes back and forth between these views, not all of the previous conversations will

Figure 17-20. *Chat client with Sue and Bill typing in long entries to the chat room*

appear when the view is changed. In addition, other configuration options can be achieved in the View/Options menu area.

The Settings tab allows the client to have better interoperability with other IRC clients by selecting the Don't Send Microsoft Chat Specific Information To Other IRC Client option. In addition, users can individually set content ratings by making their configuration choices in the Content Advisor area. Also, a potpourri of choices can be made at the bottom of this tab, including whether or not to allow whispers, sounds, show arrivals/departures, get identity on arrivals and whether or not to receive chat invitations, file transfer requests, and NetMeeting calls.

The Comics View tab allows users to select the font they wish to use in the comic strip and to choose whether they want the strip to appear as two, three, or four panes wide on their screen.

The Character and Background tabs are the same as those in the Chat Connections box that first appears when the client connects to the chat community. But the Automation tab, as shown in Figure 17-21, is significant because it automates several tasks, including the following:

- If the user is the host of the room, allows user to send a custom greeting to all other users when they join the room

Figure 17-21. *The Automation Tab used to automate tasks*

- Allows user to determine whether the automatic greeting will be whispered or spoken out loud
- Allows user to ignore flooders by configuring a message count limit within a specified time limit
- Allows user to send specific messages by using specific keystroke combinations

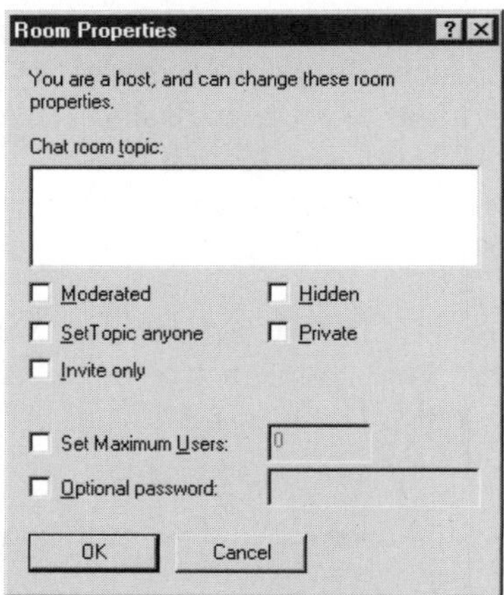

If the user right-clicks on another user's icon in the chat room, the context menu shown in Figure 17-22 appears with options about that user. For example, when Bill right-clicks on Sue's icon in his chat client, he can retrieve her profile and identity. He can also ignore her or open a whisper box to see if she is interested in a sidebar conversation. If she has configured her e-mail address, he can send her an e-mail or a file, visit her home page, invite her to a NetMeeting, find out the version of the chat client she is using, and determine her lag time and the local time on her computer.

This information will appear in the comic strip in Bill's view but will not appear in other strips of other users. The profile is entered in the Chat Connections dialog box when the user first connects to the chat community. The identity information is the username@IP address. As discussed earlier in the chapter, masking can be employed to mask a portion of the user's IP address or domain name.

If the user is also a host for the room, the room's properties can be changed on the fly by navigating to the room's properties in the Room/Room Properties menu. Here, the chat room topic can be entered and other selections made as well. All these options are dimmed for users who open the room properties but are not hosts of the room. The Room Properties dialog box is shown in Figure 17-23.

The Microsoft Chat client is a basic client that lacks some of the bells and whistles that some users may want. Since any IRC-compliant client will work, consider using either mIRC or PIRCH if you need a more robust chat client.

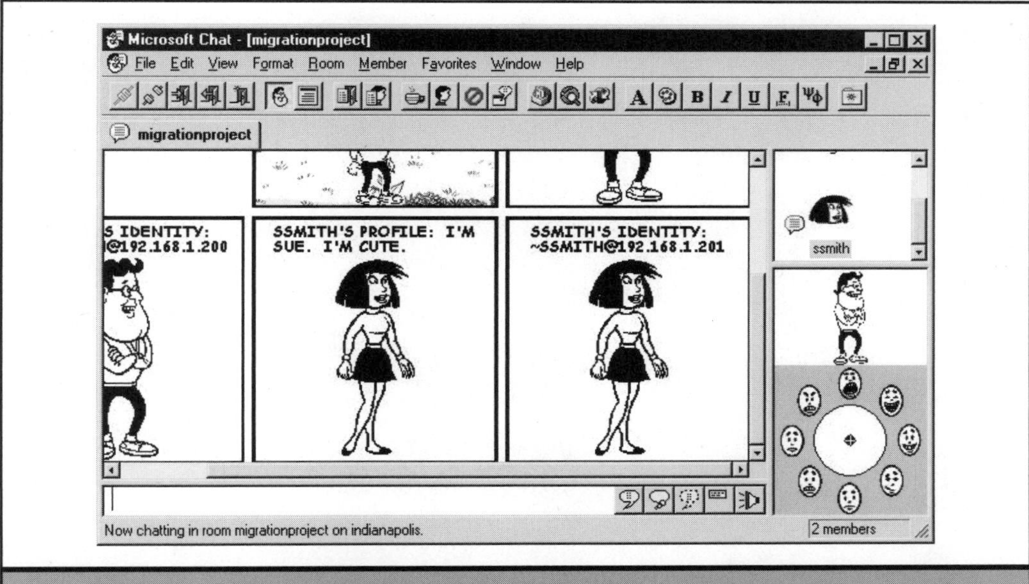

Figure 17-22. *Retrieving Sue's profile and identify information*

The Complete Reference

Part IV

Exchange 2000 Server Security

Chapter 18

Securing Exchange 2000 Server

The Internet isn't just the new digital marketplace, it's also the playground for those who would gladly shut down your e-mail, steal your company's credit card database, or hack into and modify your corporate Web site. Securing your Exchange 2000 environment is no longer just for the "big" companies; it is a necessity for anyone. That is why we felt is was important to dedicate a chapter to discussing the various methods of security you may want to implement to secure your Exchange 2000 environment. Let's begin by breaking up your security measures into two categories: internal and external.

Internal Security

Many companies have corporate firewalls, proxy servers, and non-routable IP addressing schemes—all to protect themselves from Internet-based attacks. Yet when you look at the permissions on a critical file share or the CEOs Calendar in Outlook, you find that they have given everyone full access. The point being made is that few companies actually focus on internal security.

Internal security with respect to Exchange 2000 ensures that only the appropriate users have access to Exchange resources as well as to the administration of Exchange. A malicious hacker doesn't necessarily have to exist outside your network—we have seen a few cases where an actual employee of the company was hacking from the inside! So let's focus on the security measures you can take to secure your Exchange environment from internal misuse.

Domain Security

The foundation for all internal (and even some external) security measures is to make every aspect of your network revolve around domain security. What we mean is that, as you implement other security measures, you will give (and deny) appropriate resource permissions to actual domain user and group accounts. In this way, every aspect of resource access can be tied back to a user's logon credentials.

Let's begin with these assumptions:

- Since Exchange 2000 requires Active Directory, you already have a domain environment in place.
- Any user who has an Exchange mailbox also has a unique user account in the domain.

The first step is to make sure you require that users log on using their unique account. Some of you may be thinking, "Of course I do!" But some networks we've seen use their unique accounts for authentication only when running Outlook Web Access. So, we'll say it again: make sure you require that users log on using their unique account before gaining access to any network resources. This requirement will determine the success and failure of the remaining internal security measures we'll cover in this chapter.

Exchange 2000 Shared Folders

By default, Exchange 2000 creates three shared folders. Table 18-1 lists the shares and indicates their location (which is listed using the default installation directory of C:\Program Files\Exchsrvr), whether they are hidden, and their contents.

Each of these shares has the same permissions assigned to it: Administrators have Full Control, the Exchange server has Full Control, and the Everyone group has Read. While you most likely won't need to change these, you should be at least aware that they do exist and that all users have at least read access to these shared folders. Of the three folders, we recommend paying closer attention to the message tracking share, which everyone has read access to. This share contains the logs listing all messages sent by an Exchange server. While no message data exists in the log, there is information about to whom and by whom mail is being sent. While it may seem harmless, in a company where security is a major concern, the permissions on this share would most likely be tightened, and use of this share outside of the administrative staff would be restricted.

IFS Shares

It is possible with Exchange 2000 for an administrator to share out the root or a subfolder of the M drive, which is the IFS-based access to the Exchange stores on the Exchange server. While access to a share on this drive doesn't necessarily mean you'll have access to a mailbox or public folder (we'll discuss access to those next), you should be aware of any shares on this drive so that improper access to mailboxes or public folders is not accidentally given to users.

Mailbox Access

In most companies, a common situation plays out: an administrative assistant needs access to the Calendar or Inbox (or both) of his or her boss. Yet, when you look at the

Share Name	Location	Hidden?	Contents
Address	C:\Program Files\Exchsrvr\address	N	Addressing DLLs
Resources$	C:\Program Files\Exchsrvr\res	Y	Event Logging Files
<svrname>.log	C:\Program Files\Exchsrvr\<svrname>.log	N	Message Tacking Logs

Table 18-1. *Exchange 2000 Shares*

access given to the boss' Calendar, you find that everyone has been given full access to read, write, and delete entries! Believe us, it is a common problem in smaller companies. Mailbox access should be taken as seriously as shared folder and NTFS permissions. You can set Mailbox access at three levels: at the mailbox itself, at the folder level within the mailbox, and through delegate access.

Mailbox Permissions

By default, only a user with domain administrator-level privileges can modify who has rights to a particular mailbox. You can view the rights that users and groups have to a particular mailbox within Active Directory Users & Computers. From the View menu, choose Advanced Features (you'll need to do this so you can see the Exchange Advanced property page). Navigate to and right-click the mail-enabled object and choose Properties. On the Exchange Advanced property page, click the Mailbox Rights button to see the Permissions dialog box, shown in Figure 18-1.

Table 18-2 describes the permissions you can allow and deny to a mailbox.

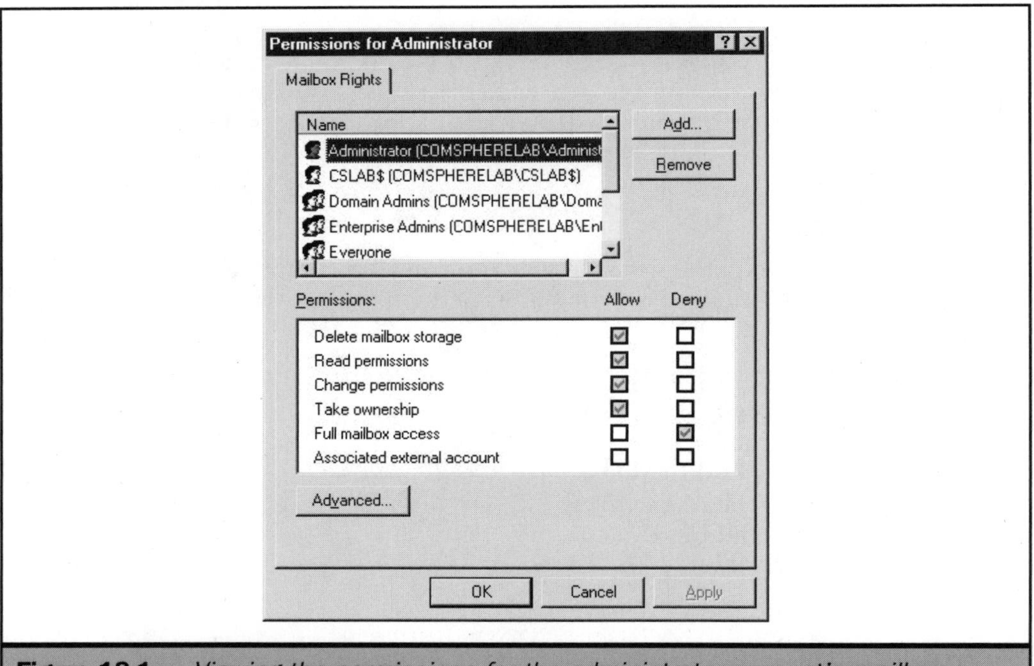

Figure 18-1. *Viewing the permissions for the administrator account's mailbox*

Permission	Description
Delete Mailbox Storage	Allows you to delete the mailbox
Read Permissions	Allows you to read the Mailbox Rights
Change Permissions	Allows you to modify the Mailbox Rights
Take Ownership	Allows you to take ownership of the mailbox, which, in turn, allows you to change permissions
Full Mailbox Access	Gives complete access to the mailbox
Associated External Account	Specifies that the account given rights is an account outside of AD (an NT 4.0 account, for example)

Table 18-2. *Mailbox Permissions*

Note here that the granularity of the permissions are down to the mailbox level and no deeper. This feature is extremely important when, for example, you want to give a user full rights to just the Inbox of a particular mailbox—this is not the correct place to do it.

The important permissions to watch out for are Delete Mailbox Storage, Change Permissions, Take Ownership, and Full Mailbox Access. The first three are assigned to specific administrative users and groups, and Full Mailbox Access is given only to the user who owns the mailbox. As a matter of fact, the administrative users and groups are actually *denied* Full Mailbox Access to ensure, by default, they cannot go into someone's mailbox.

Folder Permissions

By default, the only user that has access to a particular mailbox is the user associated with it. However, as stated before, additional users occasionally need permissions to a particular mailbox or, more specifically, one folder within the mailbox. This is accomplished in Outlook. Right-click the folder you wish to change permissions for and select Properties. Select the Permissions property page, shown in Figure 18-2. You can add any mail-enabled object by clicking Add and selecting it from the Add Users dialog box. Once the object is listed in the Name/Role box, you need to change its role to establish its permissions.

Table 18-3 describes the roles and their abilities.

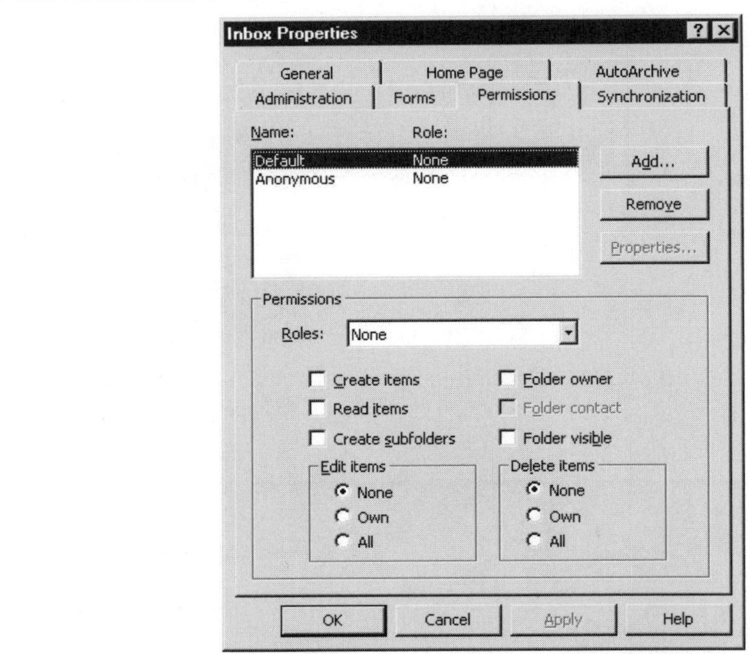

Figure 18-2. *Setting permissions for a mailbox folder*

Role	Abilities
Owner	Owners can create, read, modify, and delete all items and files. They can also create subfolders and change permissions for the folder. There can be more than one Owner.
Publishing Editor	Publishing Editors can create, read, modify, and delete all items and files, and create subfolders.
Editor	Editors can create, read, modify, and delete all items and files.
Publishing Author	Publishing Authors can create and read items and files, modify and delete items and files created by others, and create subfolders.

Table 18-3. *Permission Roles for Mailbox Folders*

Role	Abilities
Author	Authors can create and read items and files and modify and delete their own items and files.
Nonediting Author	Nonediting Authors can create and read items and files.
Reviewer	Reviewers can read items and files only.
Contributor	Contributors can create items and files only. Contributors cannot see the contents of the folder.
None	No permissions are granted for the folder.

Table 18-3. *Permission Roles for Mailbox Folders* (continued)

You can always grant your own combination of the tasks listed below the Roles drop-down list. If you do, the Roll list displays the roll as Custom. The default permissions are always set to the following:

- **Default— - None**. If you are an authenticated user and are not given permissions via your membership in a group or an assignment to your account, the Default will be your effective permissions.
- **Anonymous— - None**. If you are an anonymous user (such as someone accessing a folder from the Internet), the Anonymous permissions will take effect.

Consider using None as your default permission: that way you are assured that only the users listed in the Name/Role box will have permissions to the folder.

One of the most common permissions problems is giving too high a role to too many users. Rather than selecting the individual user (or having the Exchange administrator create a distribution group for a number of users) and assigning them the proper role, many users simply change the default to Owner or Editor. You should educate your users about the roles and the uses of Default and Anonymous as well as inform them of the dangers of "over-granting" permissions.

Delegate Access

A delegate is someone who has the ability to send a message on behalf of another user. A perfect example is an administrative assistant sending a meeting request for their boss. Sending the message as a delegate causes the message to appear to be sent from the assistant on behalf of the boss, rather than the assistant. There are two tools you can use to grant delegate access: Active Directory Users & Computers and Outlook 2000.

Active Directory Users & Computers You can specify users to have delegate access by looking at the properties of a mail-enabled user. Navigate to the Exchange General property page and click Delivery Options (Figure 18-3). If Bill adds Nick in the Send On Behalf section of the Delivery Options dialog box, Nick becomes a delegate of Bill, but grants Nick no permissions to the folders within Bill's mailbox. That means that all Nick can do is send a message and have it say it is from Nick on behalf of Bill.

Outlook You can also specify delegates from within Outlook. Select Options from the Tools menu and choose the Delegates property page (Figure 18-4). The difference between making delegates in Active Directory Users & Computers and within Outlook is that in Outlook, once you specify them as a delegate by clicking the Add button and choosing the object to be your delegate, you are presented with a Delegate Permissions

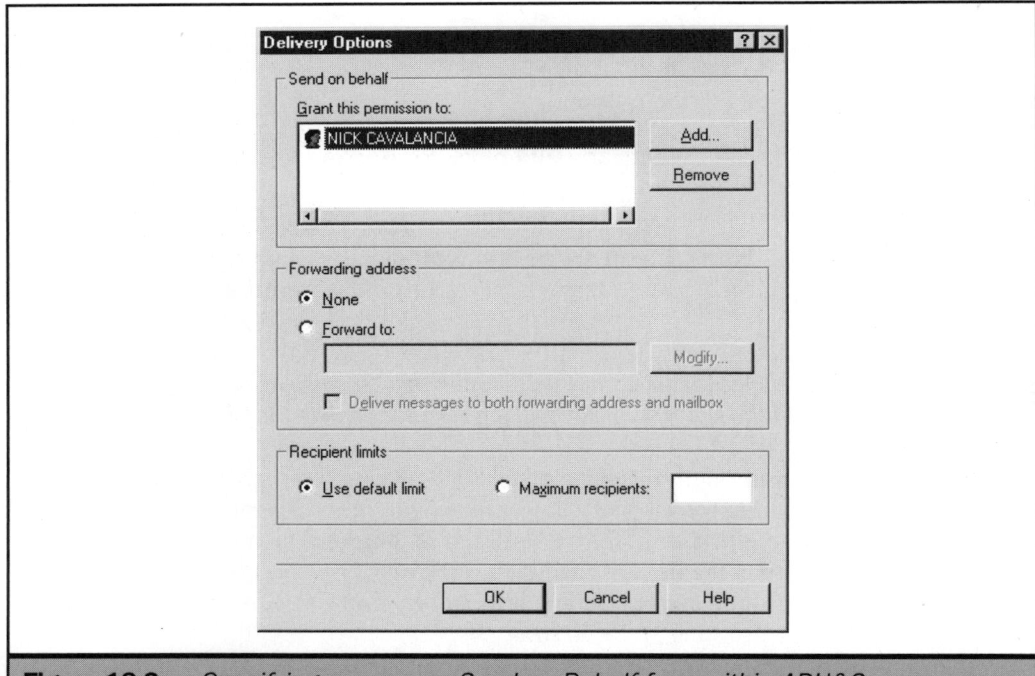

Figure 18-3. *Specifying a user can Send on Behalf from within ADU&C*

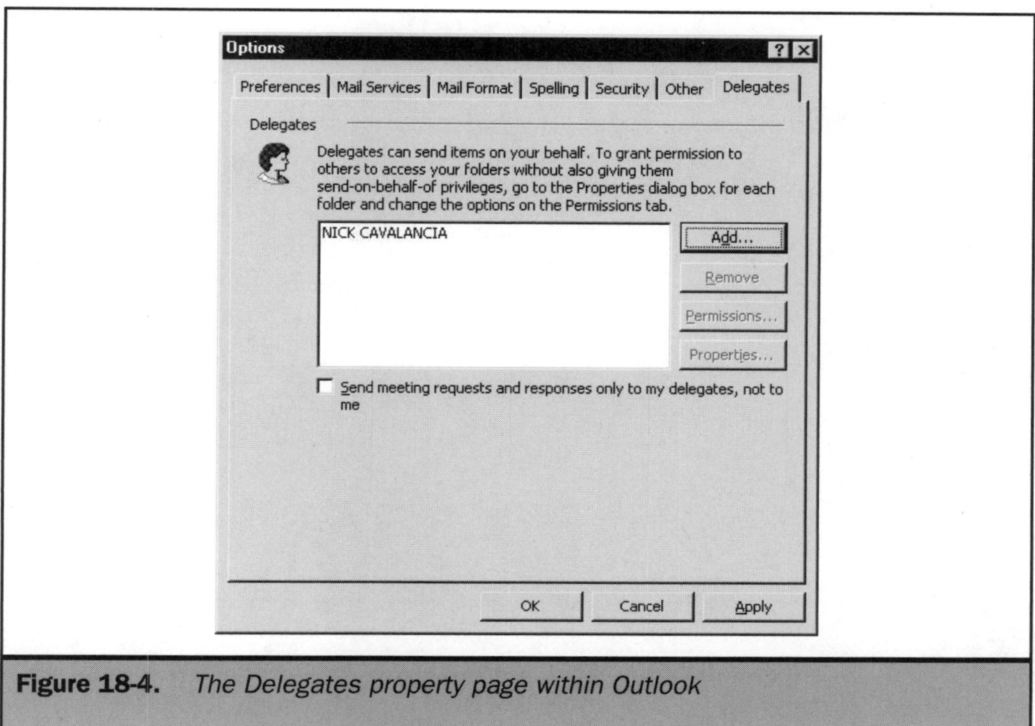

Figure 18-4. *The Delegates property page within Outlook*

dialog box, shown in Figure 18-5, to choose which folders they will have access to. Think of this method as a combination of the delegate access given in Active Directory Users & Computers and the individual folder permissions all wrapped into one administrative task. There is less granularity with the folder permissions granted here (four permission roles) than with assigning them at each folder (eight permission roles).

Tip *If you are a delegate, to send a message on someone's behalf, open a new mail message and select From Field from the View menu. Then put in the name of the person you are sending the message for. This works only within Outlook. Outlook Web Access does not support this feature.*

The concern here is twofold: you want to assign only the appropriate users delegate access and grant them permissions to only the folders they need and at the appropriate levels. Think of the chaos that could be caused with improper delegate assignments. Take this scenario: John inadvertently gets delegate access to the CEO's mailbox and is given Editor rights to the CEO's Calendar. John could delete appointments from the CEO's calendar and then send out messages, posing as the CEO and canceling the appointments—all without the knowledge of the CEO! So, the focus should be who gets to be a delegate and what permissions (if any) should they get to the other users' folders.

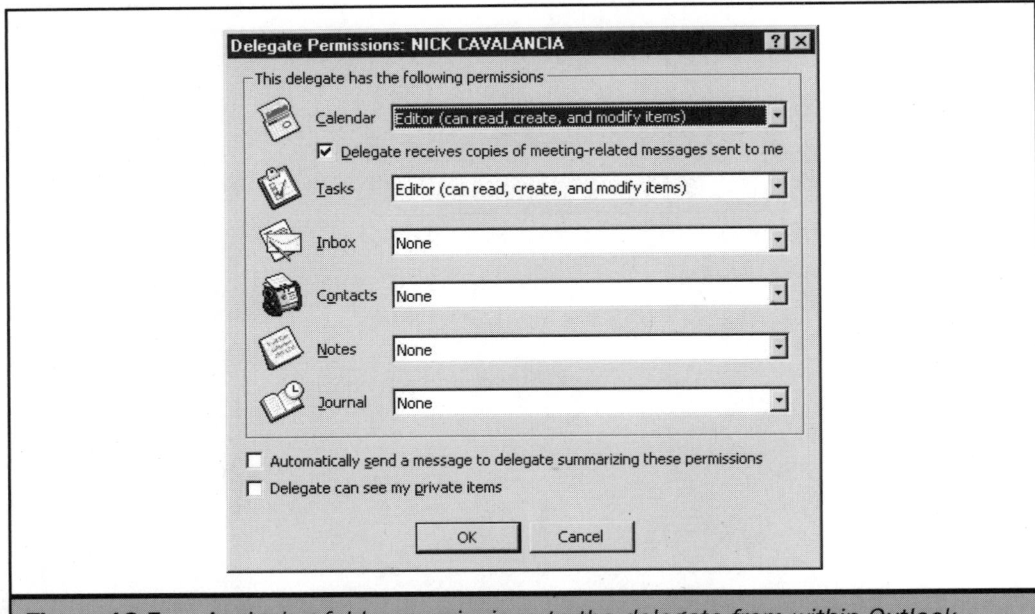

Figure 18-5. *Assigning folder permissions to the delegate from within Outlook*

Protocol Access

Unlike mailbox access, which deals mostly with unauthorized access to someone else's mail from within, protocol access deals with users trying to access their e-mail from the Internet. Exchange 2000 allows you to specify what Internet protocols a user can use. Inside the properties of a user account in Active Directory Users & Computers, choose the Exchange Advanced property page and click the Protocol Settings button. All supported protocols will be listed in the Protocols dialog Box, shown in Figure 18-6.

You can disable each protocol listed by selecting it and clicking the Settings button. A Protocol Details dialog box (shown in Figure 18-7) displays, allowing you to enable or disable the protocol.

Some of you may not like the idea of going to each user and disabling protocols because, rather than having an open protocol policy and restricting protocols for just a few (in which the preceding steps would be appropriate), you want to restrict protocol use on a much wider scale and open it for the few. The only way to accomplish this is much the way we did it in previous versions of Exchange: you will have to disable the protocols on certain Exchange servers and group those you wish to use the protocols in question on a server that still has the protocol enabled. In Exchange 2000, the method of "disabling" a protocol at the server level would be either to stop or delete the virtual server for that protocol or to enable access restriction for each protocol to only allow certain IP address or domain names to access the protocol. Taking this to an extreme,

Protocols

Select a protocol, and then click Settings to configure the protocols used to access this mailbox.

Protocol

HTTP
IMAP4
POP3

Settings...

OK Cancel Help

Figure 18-6. *Listing the protocols supported*

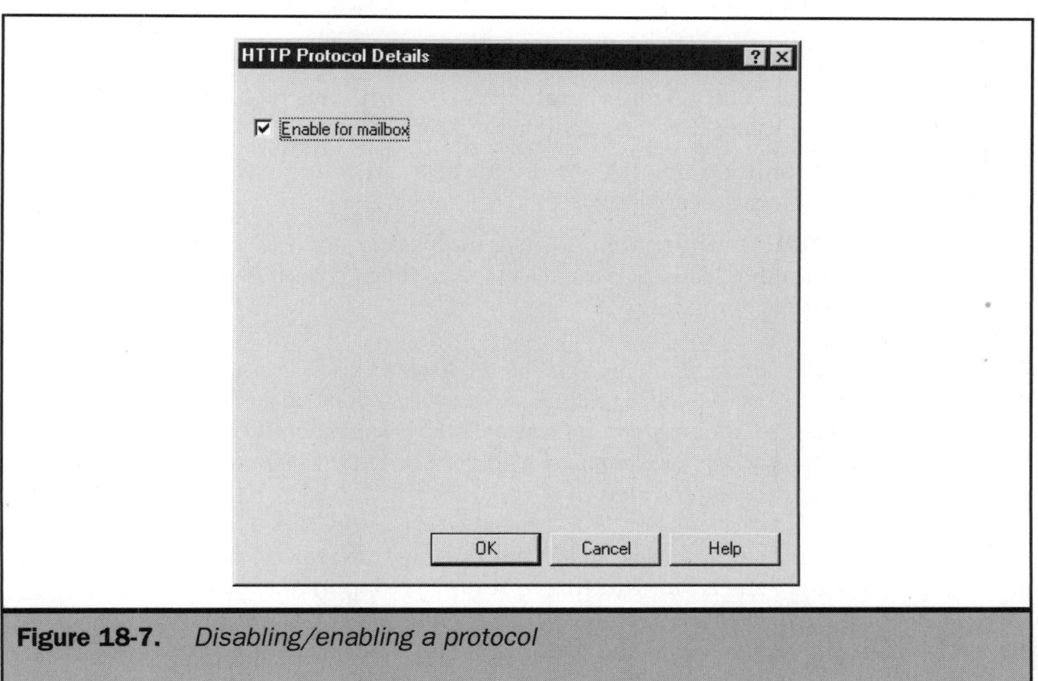

Figure 18-7. *Disabling/enabling a protocol*

if you do not want to support a particular Internet protocol, you can remove the virtual server entirely.

Note *For more information on managing virtual servers, see Chapter 10.*

The concern here is to make sure only those users who should have access to Exchange via Internet protocols do. You wouldn't want someone pulling down sensitive corporate e-mail to his or her home.

Administrative Access

Most of the chapter so far has dealt with improper access by users. Let's switch gears and focus on the administrative staff by making sure they have only the appropriate permissions to manage their assigned portions of the Exchange environment.

Exchange 2000 Delegation

Management of Exchange 2000 is broken down through delegation of control. At various levels within the Exchange organization, you have the option to delegate control to users or groups. Delegation can be accomplished at two levels: organization and administrative group. When you delegate control at one of these two levels, you are giving administrative access only to that portion of the Exchange organization. For example, if you delegate full administrative rights to a user at the administrative group level, that user only has full rights within that administrative group. There are three levels of permissions (called *roles*) you can grant at each level:

- **Exchange View Only Administrator** A user with this role can view the configuration of the delegation area.
- **Exchange Administrator** A user in this role can administer the objects within the delegation area.
- **Exchange Full Administrator** A user in this role can fully administer the objects within the delegation area, as well as modify permissions to objects within the delegation area.

Tip *In order for the Administrator or Full Administrator roles to be used, users must also be a local administrator of all Exchange servers they will manage. This is not done automatically (with the exception of Domain Admins automatically being a member of the local Administrators group) and can be done using the Computer Management snap-in on each Exchange server.*

To assign an administrative role to a user or group, navigate to and right-click the organization object, or the administrative or routing group in question, and select Delegate Control. The Exchange Administration Delegation Wizard will start. Click Next. The listing of current users and groups that have administrative access is listed on the Users or Groups screen of the wizard (Figure 18-8).

Exchange Administration Delegation Wizard

Users or Groups
Select one or more users or groups to whom you want to delegate control.

Users and groups:

Name	Role
TRAINSBYDAVE\Adm...	Exchange Full Administrator (Inherited)

Add... Edit... Remove

< Back Next > Cancel

Figure 18-8. *Listing the users and groups that have administrative access*

Click Add to select an additional user or group to administer Exchange, as shown in Figure 18-9. Choose the user or group by clicking the Browse button and then choose the administrative role that is appropriate. Click OK, Next, and then Finish to complete the wizard.

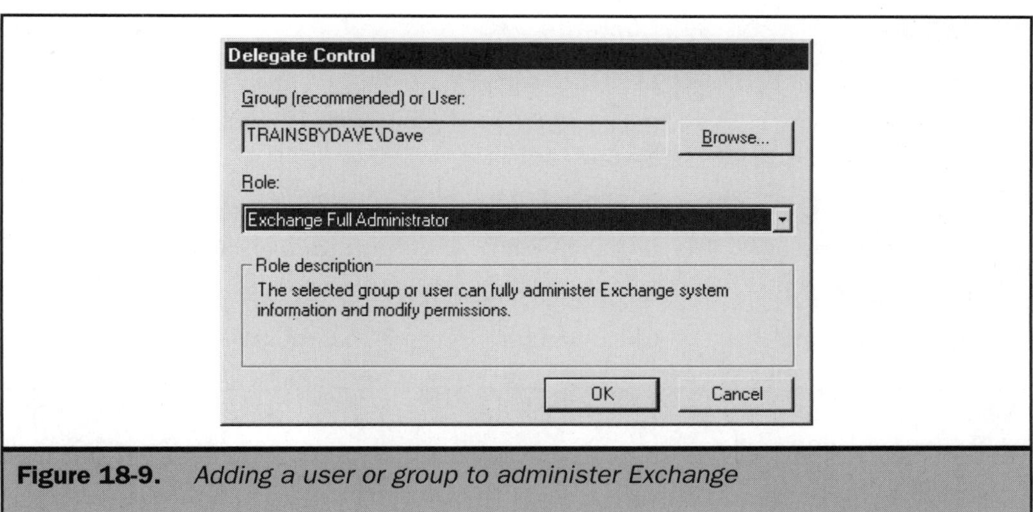

Figure 18-9. *Adding a user or group to administer Exchange*

Administrative Groups

Since a user that has been delegated control has control of only a certain area of the Exchange organization, you must plan ahead to ensure you have the correct level of granularity in your Exchange design to provide for an equal level of granularity in your administration. You have the ability to create multiple administrative groups within Exchange System Manager. An administrative group (AG) defines a boundary for administration. In other words, a single user or group can administer all objects that are in an AG. Each AG can be populated with a number of containers (Table 18-4 lists the container types and the contents of each), which, in turn, are populated with the associated objects. If you want to have individual administrative attention given to each area of Exchange (routing, servers, public folders, policies), then you would need to plan ahead and create an administrative group for each, populate it appropriately, and delegate control to each administrative group.

Exchange defaults to a single administrative group containing all objects. If your company needs to distribute administration among a number of administrators, remember to utilize several administrative groups, delegating the control of each only to those who need it.

External Security

Now that we've finished looking at all the ways you can secure your Exchange environment from unauthorized access originating within your company, let's spend some time focusing on the more common threat: unauthorized access from the Internet. Let's look at external security from a layered approach, beginning with nothing but an

Container	Contents
Servers	Exchange servers
System Policies	Policies that affect Servers, Public Folder stores, and Mailbox stores
Folders	Public Folders
Routing Groups	Routing Groups to define message routing
Advanced Security	Key Management Server configuration
Chat Community	Chat configuration and Chat rooms

Table 18-4. *Administrative Group Containers*

Exchange 2000 hosting a mailbox store that is directly connected to the Internet to see what can be done natively to secure Exchange 2000. Then we'll add on more and more layers using both hardware and software solutions and see how they will provide additional security.

Securing Protocol Access

Exchange 2000 supports a number of Internet-standard protocols out of the box: HTTP, POP3, IMAP4, NNTP, and SMTP. There are a few measures you can take to secure protocol access. The first is the most extreme: if you do not need a protocol to be in use by anyone, you can disable it. Alternatively, you can allow selective access to a protocol both from the outside and from the user. You can also require authentication for protocols that do not normally require it, or you can utilize certificates for encrypted access. Finally, you can change the port used by the protocol, a method providing the least amount of security. Let's look at each of these approaches.

Disabling Protocol Use

Disabling a protocol will keep everyone from using it. While doing this may affect your users (if they want to use the protocol), it also will definitely prevent hackers exploiting the protocol (and the service behind it) for their own benefit. You can disable protocol use at two levels: virtual server and service. Both of these actions are described in Chapter 10.

Selective Protocol Access

Selectively allowing access will keep unauthorized users out, while allowing others in. We've already shown in this chapter how to selectively disallow and allow users to use specific protocols. You also can selectively allow external use of protocols. You have the ability to restrict which IP addresses, IP subnets, or domain names can access all of the protocols Exchange 2000 supports (shown in Figure 18-10). POP3, IMAP4, NNTP, and SMTP all are managed via the virtual servers in Exchange System Manager. HTTP is partially managed within Exchange System Manager and via the virtual directories in Internet Services Manager. You can see more on how to restrict access to protocols in Chapter 10.

Requiring Authentication

Protocols like SMTP normally allow anonymous access to the server. In fact, the RFC requires anonymous access for SMTP transmissions. You can choose to require clients to authenticate before being allowed to utilize any protocol. This might be done in a case where two companies using SMTP to connect to each other want to ensure that they are the only two entities using their SMTP connection. It would also be done if you wanted clients to authenticate before using your SMTP server to relay their messages to other SMTP hosts.

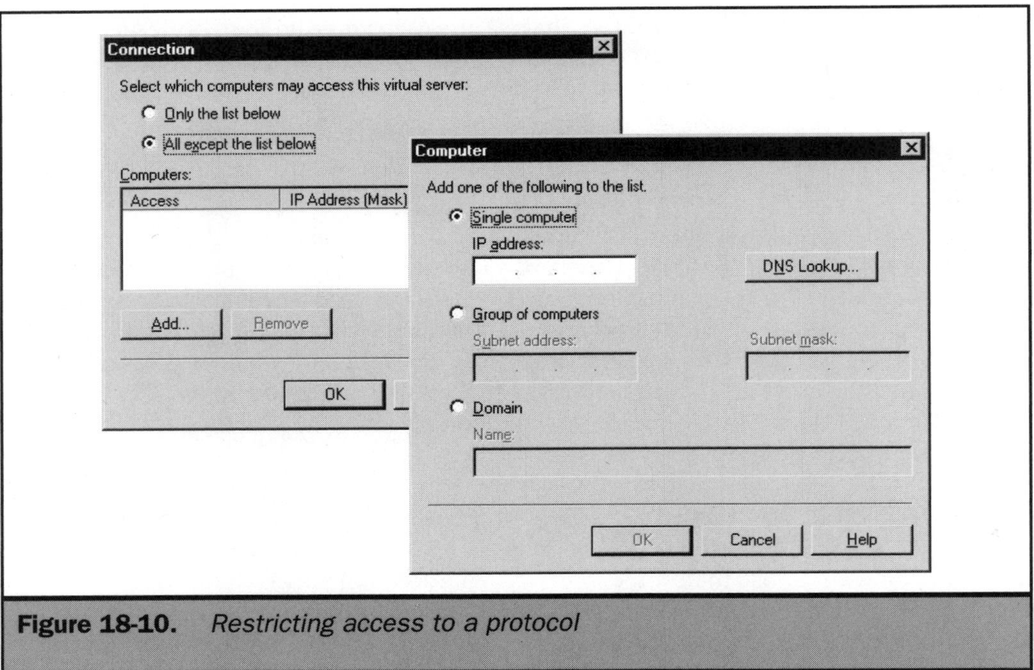

Figure 18-10. *Restricting access to a protocol*

On the Access property page of an SMTP virtual server, you can click the Authentication button to specify the authentication methods that are supported (shown in Figure 18-11). Leaving Anonymous Access unchecked requires that a client authenticate. More information on Virtual Servers and how to restrict access can be found in Chapter 10.

Using Certificates for Secure Access

Using certificates allows you to establish a Secure Sockets Layer (SSL) connection between the client and the Exchange server. While doing this will not prevent hackers attacks, it will encrypt the entire conversation between the client and server. That means that anyone trying to monitor the conversation with a packet sniffer (or the like) in the hopes of capturing your username and password will see only garbled information.

Note *For complete information on how to set up certificate use for each protocol, see Chapter 10.*

Changing the Port

Every industry standard protocol has a default port assigned to it. Changing this port from the default would prevent hackers from utilizing the protocol unless they knew the correct port address. For example, POP3 defaults to TCP port 110. If you were to change it to another value, only those clients configured for the new port could use

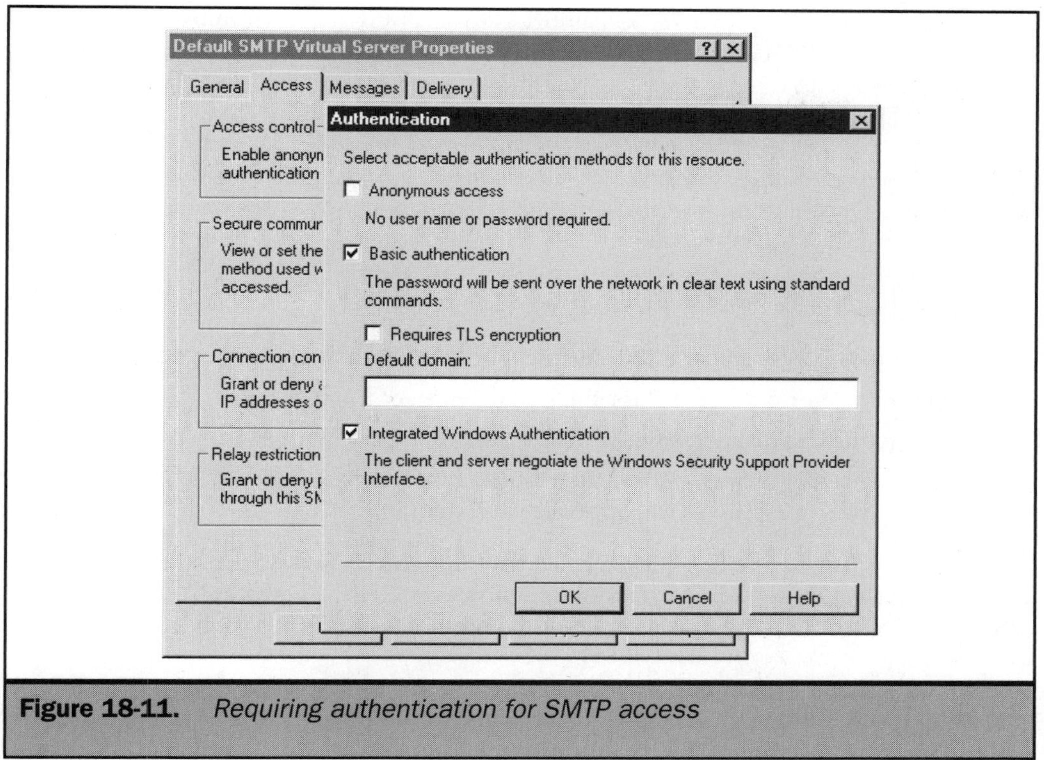

Figure 18-11. *Requiring authentication for SMTP access*

Exchange for POP3 access. We noted that this method provides the least amount of security—once hackers find out your new port—and this is extremely easy to do—they can attempt to break into your server.

For more information on TCP/IP port assignments, see the Microsoft Knowledge Base article Q278339 - TCP/UDP Ports Used By Exchange 2000 Server.

Securing protocols gives you only so much protection. A hacker can still access the enabled protocols and attempt to either access information on that server or shut down that server's services. Exchange 2000 supports the use of a Front-End (FE) Exchange server to proxy external requests for messages and data to the appropriate Back-End (BE) Exchange server within your company. While also facilitating access to all internal Exchange servers from a single access point, the use of a FE/BE configuration also provides an additional layer of services between the user on the Internet and the data on the server.

Here's how it works. An Exchange server is installed and is dedicated to acting as a FE server. This means that no users will have their mailboxes maintained on that server and that the FE server's entire responsibility is to accept requests from users on the Internet via POP3, IMAP4, and HTTP and to proxy those requests to the internal Exchange server that houses the users' mailboxes via the same protocol (POP3, IMAP4, HTTP) as the request made to the FE server.

Only servers running Exchange 2000 Enterprise Server can be Front-End servers. A Back-End server can run Exchange 2000 Server, or clustered servers running Exchange 2000 Enterprise Server.

The FE/BE process, shown in Figure 18-12, is as follows:

1. A request comes in from the Internet over one of the supported protocols.
2. The FE server queries AD for the home server of the user.
3. The request is proxied to the home server of the user.
4. The request is processed and the resulting information is sent to the user along the same path in the opposite direction.

The reason this can be considered a security measure is that no actual Exchange data exists on the FE server. If a hacker somehow causes the FE server to crash, no data would be lost and the FE server could be replaced simply by installing another Exchange server and configuring it to be a FE server.

To configure an Exchange server as a FE server, install Exchange 2000 as you normally would. The only configuration change you need to make is within Exchange System Manager. Navigate down to the server object you want to make the FE server. Right-click it and choose properties. On the General property page, shown in Figure 18-13, select the This Is A Front-End Server checkbox.

For more information on Front-End/Back-End configurations, see the Microsoft White Papers on Exchange 2000 at http://www.microsoft.com/exchange/techinfo/default.htm

Anti-Virus Software

Now that messages are coming in from the Internet, you definitely need to protect yourself from malicious viruses. Unless you've been hiding under a rock the last few years, you have heard about the string of e-mail viruses that replicate themselves by sending the virus file to everyone on your address lists. In addition to those types of viruses, there are still thousands of viruses floating around.

There are a number of third party vendors that make anti-virus solutions specifically for Exchange. The fact that the anti-virus solution is specifically for Exchange is the most important factor. A file-level anti-virus solution cannot read the data within the store databases, which makes that type of anti-virus solution useless. Actually, they can be considered a danger to Exchange 2000 because, when set to repair, they can corrupt a mailbox or public folder store, transaction logs, or queue

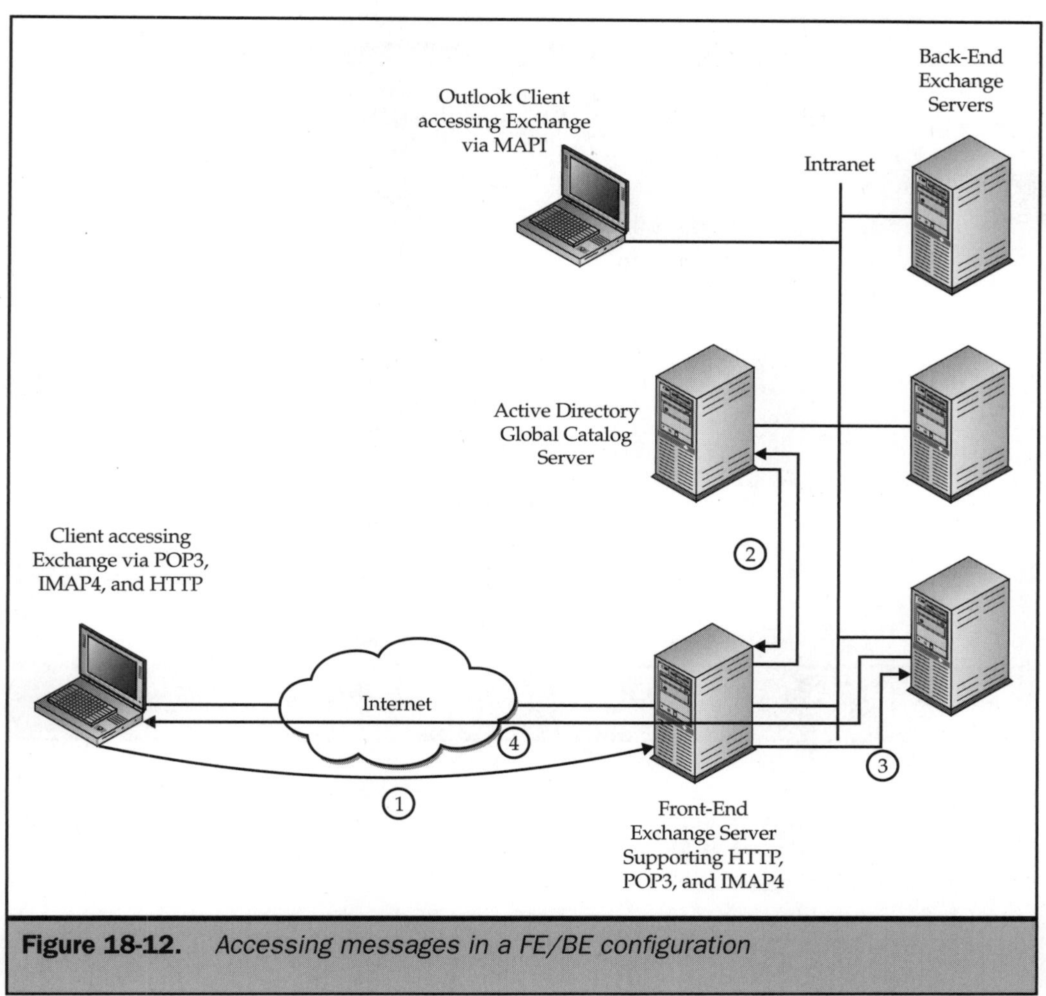

Figure 18-12. *Accessing messages in a FE/BE configuration*

files. A solution for Exchange will interface with Exchange to scan the contents of mailboxes as well as of messages either as they are sent or as they arrive in a mailbox.

Two application programming interfaces (APIs) can be used to scan for viruses. The messaging API (MAPI) allows an antivirus application to scan a message in much the same fashion as an Outlook user would access a message. The problem with MAPI-mode access is that it is possible for a user to receive a message in their Inbox and access before the antivirus application (running in MAPI-mode) can scan it. The second API is the Antivirus API (AVAPI) which runs more tightly integrated with the store process. When running in AVAPI mode, messages are not allowed to be sent to their intended recipient until they have first been scanned. The downside of this mode

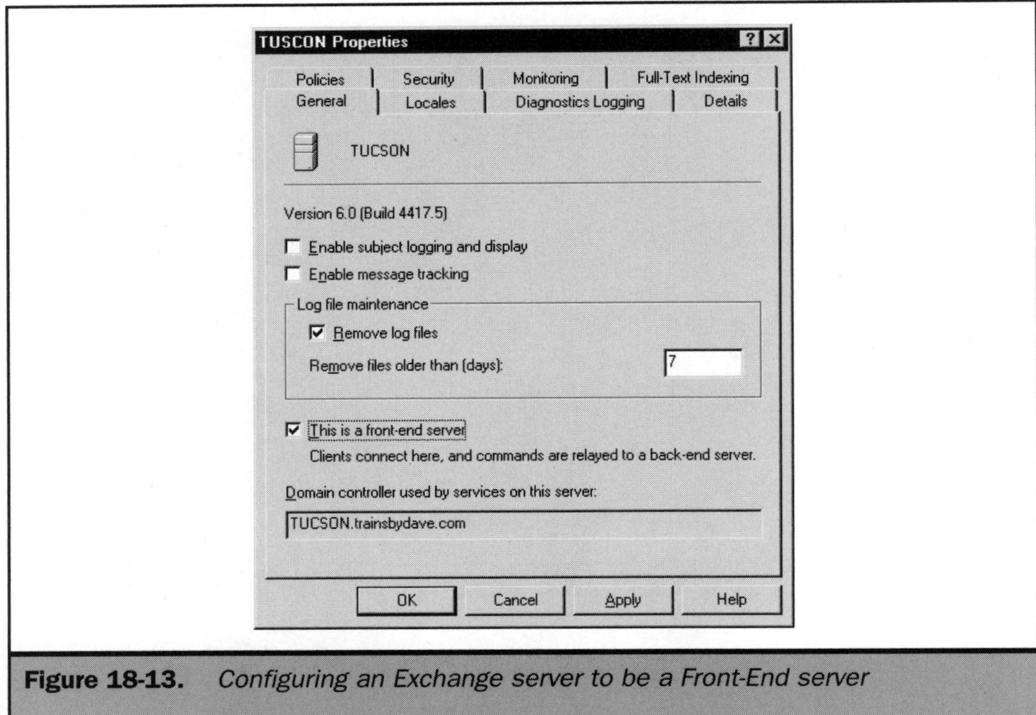

Figure 18-13. *Configuring an Exchange server to be a Front-End server*

is that message delivery time can slow down due to the mandatory antivirus scan. You could also write your own event sinks to scan messages in much the same way as both MAPI and AVAPI mode scanners do.

Internet Mail Scanner

Some companies also like to offload the burden of scanning Internet-based messages onto an Internet mail gateway. Putting in a third-party SMTP host that scans inbound and outbound mail for viruses is a smart idea. If you wish to utilize a virus scanner for inbound mail, two configuration changes are necessary. The first is configuring your MX records in DNS to have mail directed to the virus scanner instead of Exchange. The second is to configure the virus scanning SMTP gateway to forward messages to your Exchange organization. That way, messages coming in from the Internet will be directed to the virus scanning SMTP host, which scans the messages and, after eradicating any viruses, forwards them to Exchange. If you wish to utilize the virus scanner for outbound mail, one configuration change needs to be made within Exchange System Manager. On the General property page of the SMTP Connector you use to connect with the Internet, as shown in Figure 18-14, select Forward All Mail Through This

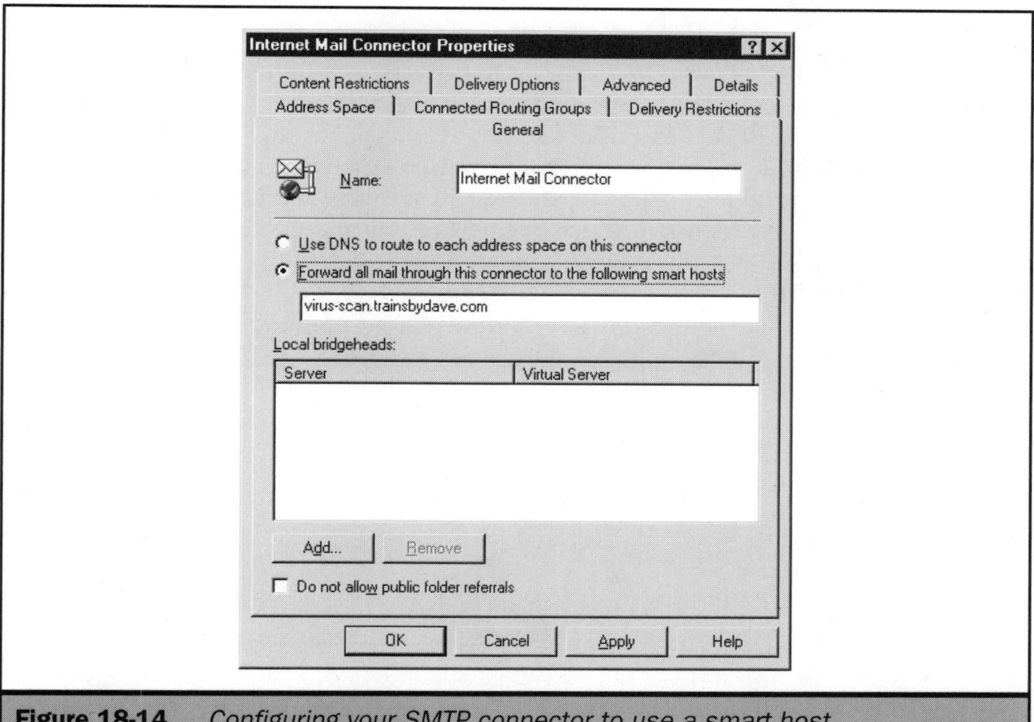

Figure 18-14. *Configuring your SMTP connector to use a smart host*

Connector To The Following Smart Hosts and then type in the fully qualified domain name of the virus scanner.

Additionally, some mail scanners look for content, rather than viruses. While this is normally used to look for "inappropriate" content, such as pornography, company secrets, résumés, and so forth, it can also be used as a first line of defense against unsolicited e-mail and viruses. In the case of unsolicited e-mail, you can block messages from specific accounts or entire domains. In the case of viruses, if an anti-virus pattern definition or signature file is not available from your anti-virus software vendor, you can configure the scanner to remove attachments by either name (if a consistent attachment name is used) or by file extension (such as .exe or .vbs). Additionally, your company may choose to make a corporate policy to not allow files with certain extensions (like the .exe and .vbs files) to take a proactive approach to protecting your network from viruses. This can be implemented using the security updates for Outlook 2000 or by using Outlook 2002. The upside to this approach is that no infected files of those file types are allowed in, regardless of the availability of an updated virus signature. The downside is that files of those same types that may actually be needed by members of your company will not be allowed in as well.

Firewalls

The most secure method of protecting your Exchange servers is the use of a firewall. A firewall acts as a filter between the Internet and your internal network. It will allow only the traffic you want to pass in and out of your network (Figure 18-15). In addition to filtering network traffic, many firewall products also do network address translation (NAT). There are several third-party hardware and software solutions as well as Microsoft's own new security product, the Internet Security and Acceleration (ISA) server.

Packet Filtering

A firewall can be configured to allow only certain packet types to enter or exit your network. This is accomplished through the use of IP addresses and port addresses.

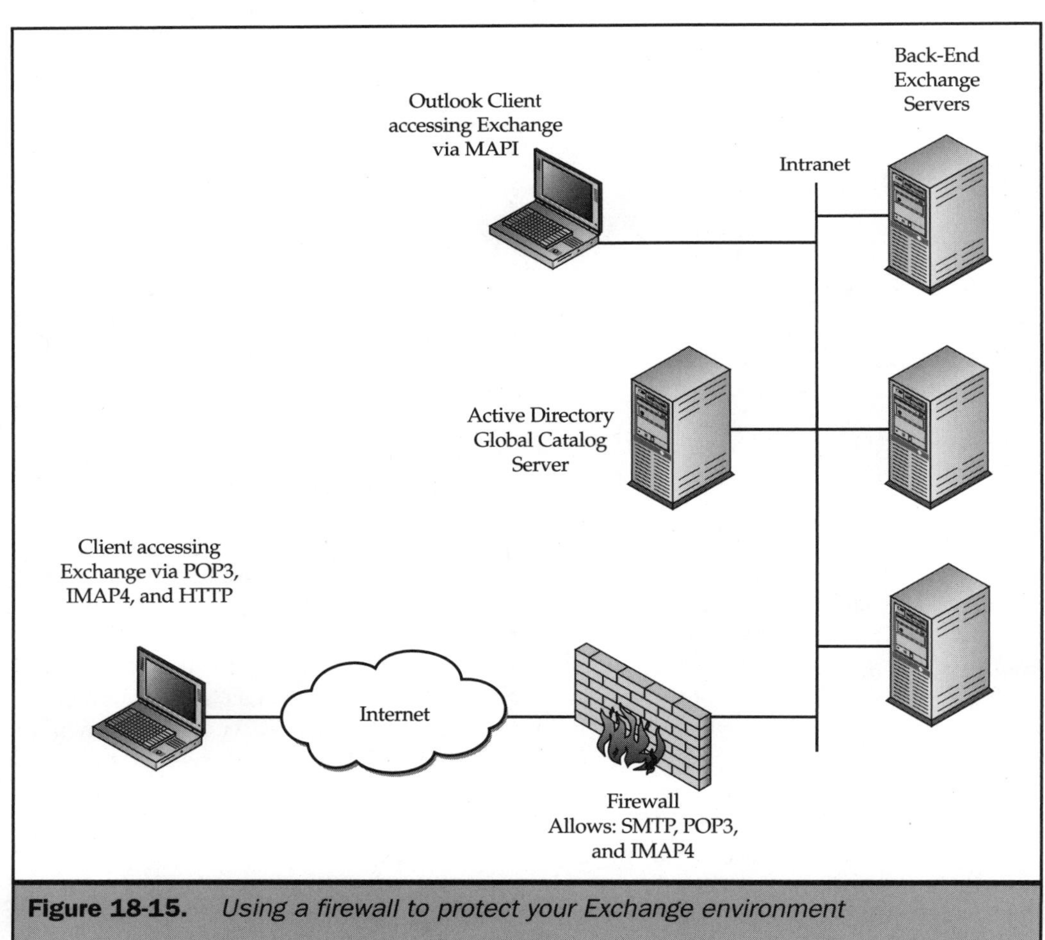

Figure 18-15. *Using a firewall to protect your Exchange environment*

While the IP address is usually unique to the computer, a port address provides a "sub-addressing" standard so that when a host receives a packet of information, the host knows which process to send the data to. Think of a port address much like the name of a person on an envelope. The envelope is routed to your home or office based on street address and delivered to you within that location by name. A packet is delivered by IP address and then to the appropriate service-based on port address. Table 5 lists the common port addresses used by Exchange for both secure and non-secure use of the standard Internet protocols.

When a packet destined for your Exchange server comes in from the Internet, the firewall can be configured to also act as an IP router (Figure 18-16). The packet is checked against a table of filters to determine if the packet should be allowed through to the server. When a packet is allowed through, it is passed along to the destination IP address of the server.

NAT

NAT allows you to maintain a legal external IP address outside of your network on the Internet while only having only an internal IP address on your Exchange server. All

Protocol	TCP Port	TCP Port over SSL
POP3	110	995
IMAP4	143	993
SMTP	25	n/a*
NNTP	119	563
HTTP	80	443
LDAP (Global Catalog server queries)	3268	3269
LDAP (Site Replication Service traffic)	379	n/a
LDAP (Active Directory queries)	389	636
DNS queries	53	n/a

*While there is an industry standard port used for SMTP communications over SSL (TCP port 465), Exchange 2000 uses Transport Layer Security (TLS) to secure the channel over port 25.

Table 18-5. *Common Port Addresses for Standard Internet Protocols*

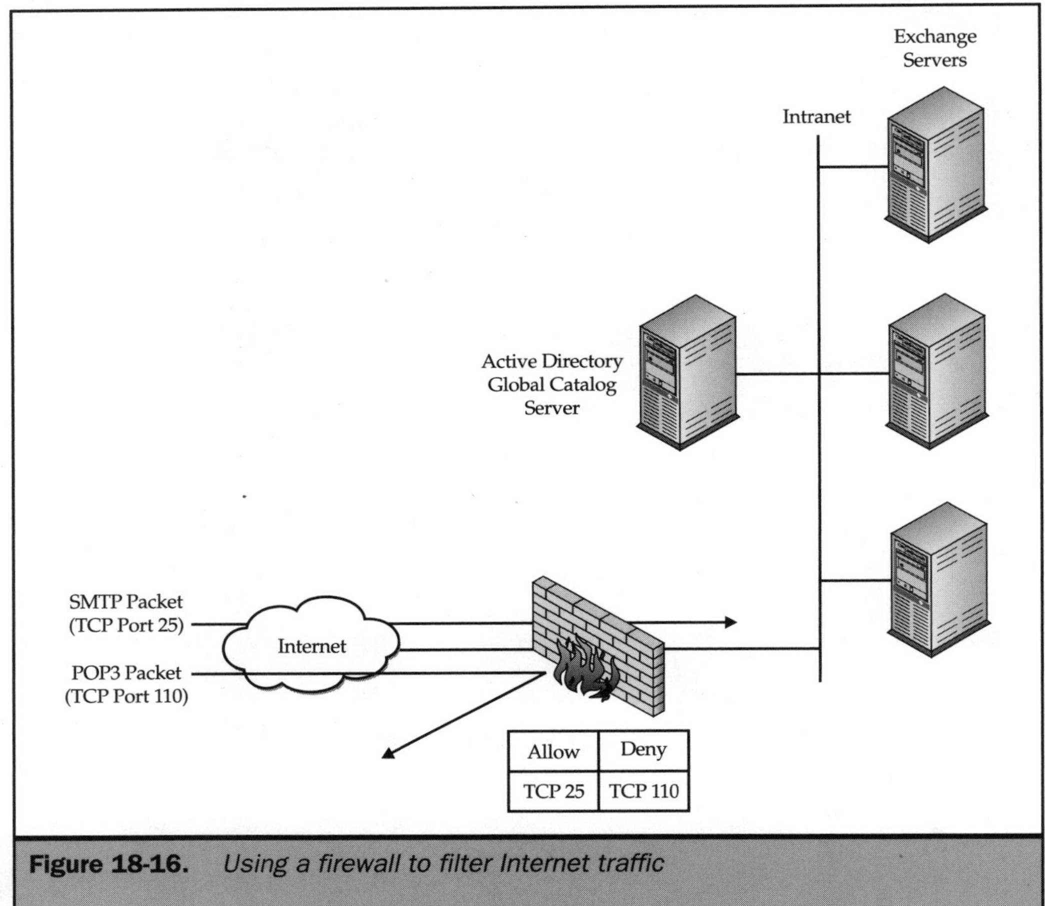

Figure 18-16. *Using a firewall to filter Internet traffic*

requests that come to the external address (Figure 18-17) are actually hitting the firewall. The firewall, in turn, checks its table of address translations and finds the matching internal address. The request is then sent on the internal network to your server's actual IP address.

One benefit of NAT is that you can establish separate address translations based on the port address. This means that you can use the same external IP address, shown

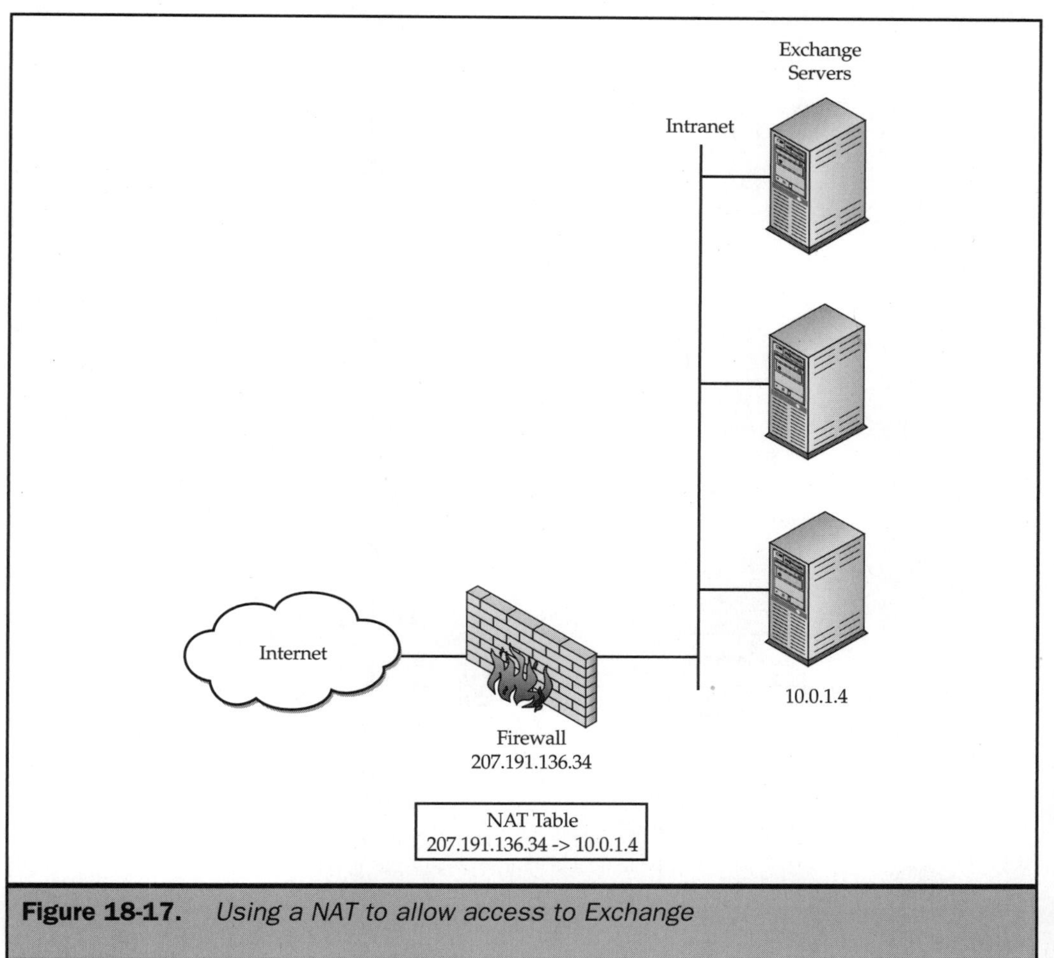

Figure 18-17. *Using a NAT to allow access to Exchange*

in Figure 18-18, for both SMTP and Outlook Web Access (via HTTP), but have SMTP (at port 25) translate to one internal server, and have HTTP (at port 80) translate to another server.

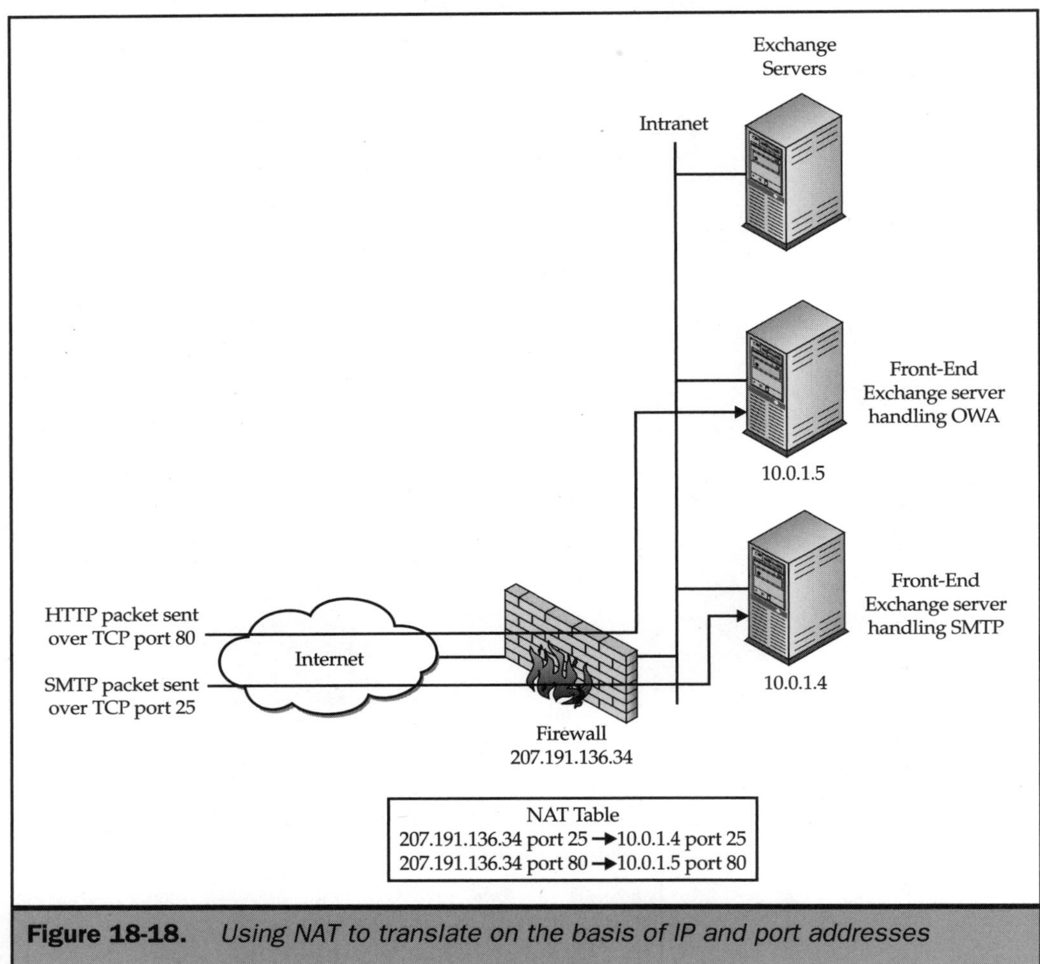

Figure 18-18. *Using NAT to translate on the basis of IP and port addresses*

Using a Firewall and a FE/BE Configuration

You can utilize a combination of a firewall and an Exchange server configured as a Front-End (FE) server to add another layer of security. In this scenario, the firewall, as shown in Figure 18-19, allows traffic to pass only to the FE server which, in turn, will send the requests to the correct Back-End server. The benefit of using a FE/BE configuration in conjunction with a firewall, is that you have to manage and allow traffic only to a single IP address, rather than the IP addresses of each and every Exchange server in your organization.

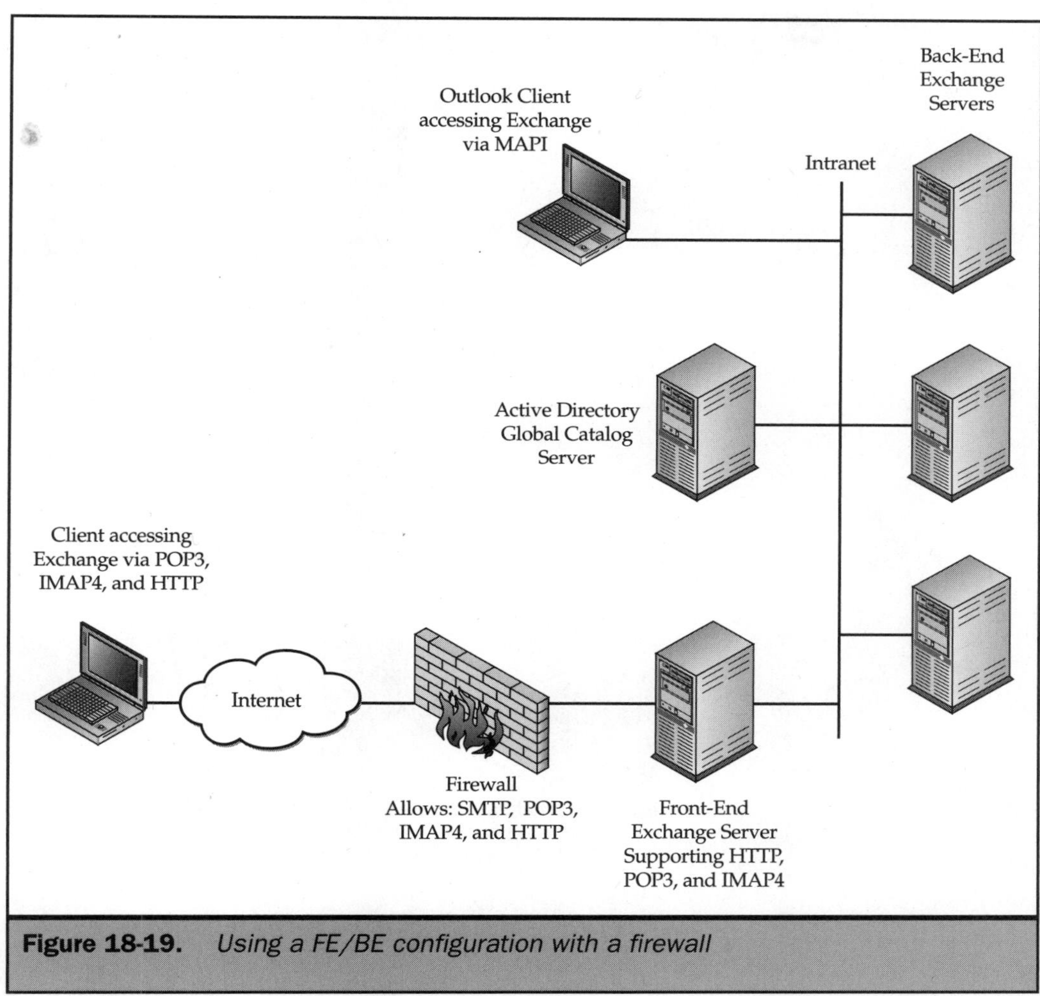

Figure 18-19. *Using a FE/BE configuration with a firewall*

You can take this one step further to completely protect your Exchange environment by creating a "De-Militarized Zone," or DMZ. The DMZ logically exists between two firewalls, one external and one internal. The FE server exists in the DMZ between the two firewalls. As shown in Figure 18-20, all of the major protocols (POP3, IMAP4, and HTTP) are allowed through the external firewall. The internal firewall is configured to allow traffic only from the IP address of the FE server, and over the ports of the appropriate Internet protocols (see Table 5, previously in the chapter), and on the LDAP ports needed to communicate with AD.

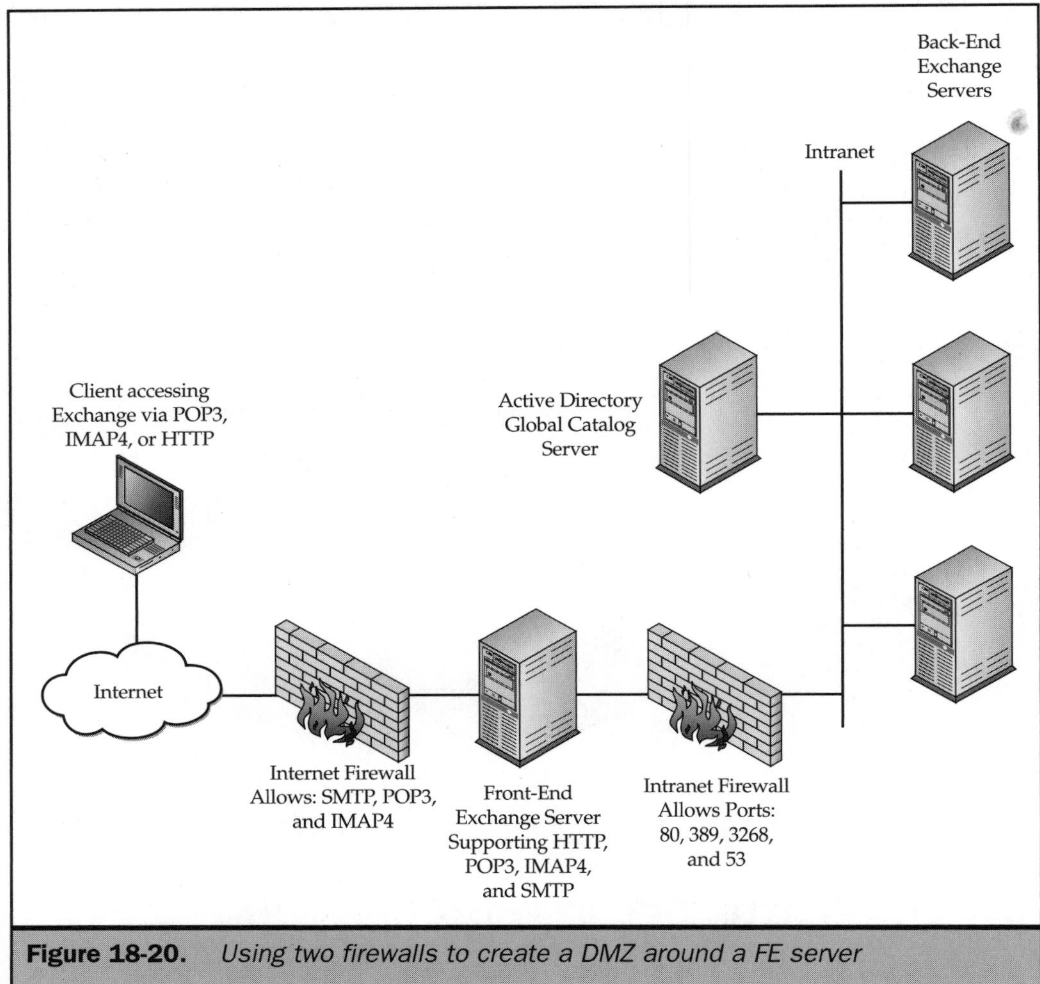

Figure 18-20. *Using two firewalls to create a DMZ around a FE server*

Putting It All Together

Now that you have seen each of the security measures available to you, let's put them together in one scenario. We'll paint the scenario, shown in Figure 18-21, by walking through the steps an SMTP request will take when entering trainsbydave.com.

1. The foreign SMTP host attempts to establish an SMTP session with a trainsbydave.com SMTP host at the legal IP address of 207.191.136.34. The SMTP message is passed through the external firewall (configured as a router

between the Internet and the DMZ), which allows access to 207.191.136.34 via TCP port 25.

2. The message is passed to 207.191.136.34, which is a virus/content-scanning SMTP host. The SMTP messages are scanned for viruses, and content filtering can be enabled here to deny messages with improper content.
3. Once scanning is finished, the virus/content-scanning SMTP host forwards the message to your FE Exchange server at 207.191.136.35.
4. After querying Active Directory for the home Exchange server of the message recipient, the FE Exchange server sends the message through the internal firewall to the appropriate home server. The internal firewall, also configured as a router, allows 207.191.136.35 access to the internal network over TCP port 25.

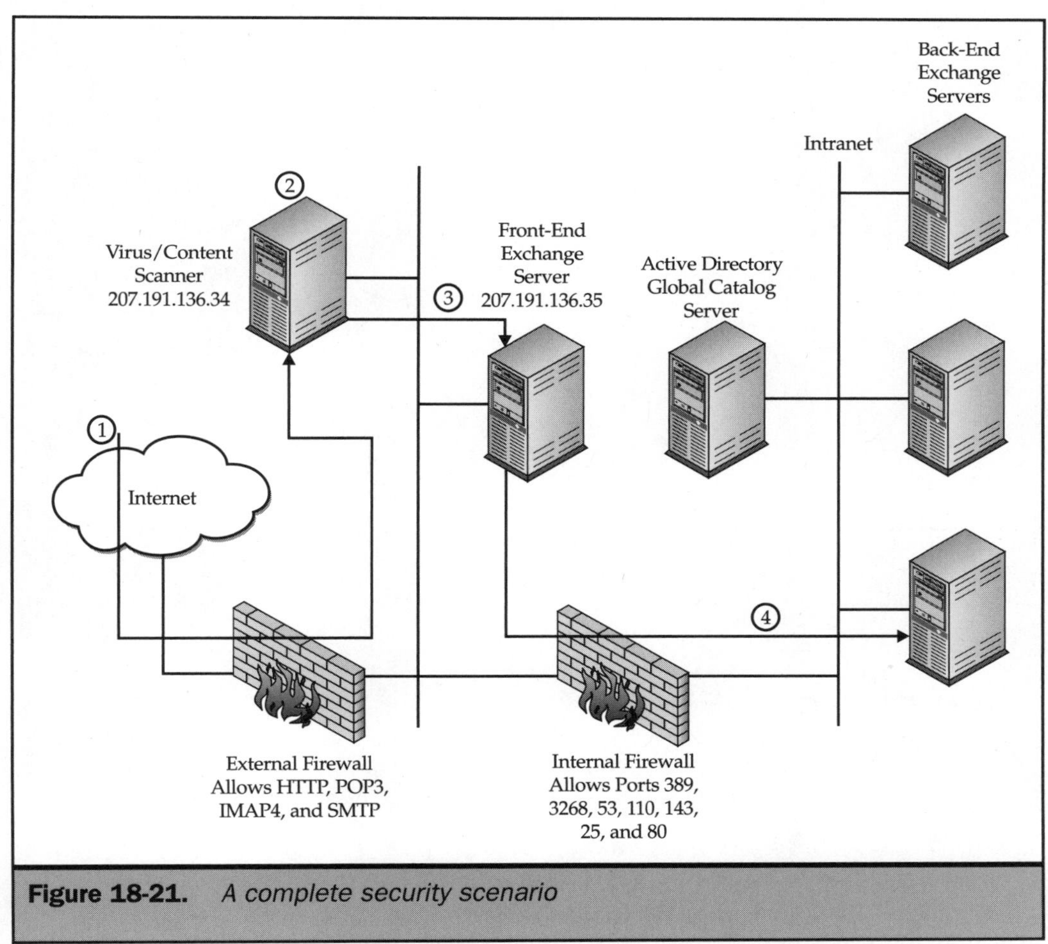

Figure 18-21. *A complete security scenario*

When a message is leaving your network, it will take the exact opposite path (assuming you have created your SMTP connector on the FE server) utilizing TCP port 25 on both firewalls.

Summary

The importance of providing security to your Exchange environment is so great that it has prompted the creation of all of the security measures described in this chapter. You have seen how to provide varying levels of security, to secure both your internal and your external access to Exchange as well as both client and administrative access. In the next chapter, we'll continue the focus on security by looking at public key infrastructure and how you can secure your messages within Exchange.

Chapter 19

Public Key Infrastructure Services

Today's e-mail is no longer confined within a single company; it has become an intercompany means of not only communication, but also of business. With business models including concepts like just-in-time inventory, business-to-business, distribution channels, and website storefronts all needing reliable, fast, and inexpensive intercompany communication, it is no wonder e-mail has become the communication medium of choice. In all this e-mailing back and forth, one element is as true today as ever: You must actively maintain the privacy and security of your company information. From simple e-mails to business plans, companies today want to ensure that their e-mail is read only by the intended recipient.

Exchange 2000 utilizes public key infrastructure (PKI) to facilitate two methods of messaging security: digital signatures and message encryption. Much of the implementation of these two methods involves Windows 2000 and has nothing specifically to do with Exchange 2000. However, because the end result (digital signatures and message encryption) involves Exchange 2000, we will cover the implementation process in detail in this chapter. Let's start with a focus on PKI, and then discuss its use by Exchange 2000.

PKI Security

PKI allows users to verify users' credentials (that is, make sure they are who they say they are) and encrypt data that is only accessible by the intended recipient. User credentials are verified through the use of a *digital certificate*. A digital certificate is a virtual ID badge that can be verified for its authenticity and validity and can also be used to replace easily guessed user IDs and passwords. In Exchange 2000, digital certificates are used with digital signatures and data encryption.

Both digital signatures and data encryption are performed using public-key cryptography. Public-key cryptography utilizes two "keys" (a public and a private key) to facilitate the encryption and decryption of data. One key is used during the encryption process; the other during the decryption process (these are called the public and private encryption keys, respectively). Likewise, one key is used to provide a digital signature and the other is used to validate that signature (these are called the public and private signing keys, respectively).

A few things about the key pairs are important. First, they are a corresponding pair; each key only works with the other. Second, they each can only facilitate one part of the encryption/decryption or digital signature process. That's what makes PKI so secure: the fact that two keys are used, both are necessary to complete the process, and one of the keys is always held by the owner, while the other can be made publicly available so anyone can participate in the process. Let's look at the two processes Exchange 2000 will utilize and how key pairs are used.

Message Encryption

When you send a message across the Internet, the message is sent in clear text, that is, with no encryption. If someone were to monitor your transmission, they could easily read the contents of your message. Message encryption encrypts the clear text message to make it unreadable while in transit. Once received by the intended recipient, the message is decrypted to make it readable.

During any PKI process, four keys can be involved:

- The sender's public key
- The sender's private key
- The recipient's public key
- The recipient's private key

Let's work through the logic to determine which keys should be used in the message encryption/decryption process and in what order. Suppose you wish to encrypt a message and send it to a specific recipient. Which key should you use to encrypt the message?

- **You would not use your public key.** Because only your private key can be used to decrypt the message and your private key is only accessible to you, only you could decrypt a message encrypted with your public key.
- **You would not use your private key.** If you did, your public key would be used to decrypt the message and potentially everyone could have a copy of that key. That means anyone could decrypt a message intended for only one user. Not a good idea.
- **You would not use the recipient's private key.** That key is only available to the recipient, so you can't gain access to that key anyway.
- **You would use the recipient's public key.** Anything encrypted with this key can only be decrypted with the matching private key, which is only accessible to the recipient.

The message encryption/decryption process, while involved, is completely seamless to the sender and recipient:

1. A one-time session key is generated to encrypt the body of the message.
2. The symmetric key is then encrypted by the recipient's public key and sent along with the encrypted message.
3. The message is received and the symmetric key is then decrypted with the recipient's private key.
4. With the symmetric key now decrypted, the message body can be decrypted using the symmetric key.

Digital Signatures

A digital signature is used to validate someone's credentials. In the case of Exchange 2000, you would use a digital signature to ensure that a message that states it came from a certain individual actually did. Let's look at the process:

1. The message is processed using a hash algorithm that produces a unique result. The hash is encrypted using the sender's private key.
2. The message and the hash are encrypted using the recipient's public key.
3. Once received, the recipient decrypts the message using his or her own private key and decrypts the hash using the sender's public key.
4. The "signature" on the message is the hash: the recipient will process the message using a hash algorithm. If the hash sent matches the hash just created, the recipient will know the message actually came from the claimed sender.

Certificates and Certification Authorities

Now that you have a basic understanding of PKI, it's important to know where the "keys" come from. Both public and private keys are stored in a Certification Authority (CA). The CA acts as a trusted third party during a PKI process and provides the public and private keys to requesting clients. A certificate is digitally signed by the CA when issued to a client and establishes what the public and private keys are. A CA is involved in the process because a single point of distribution for the keys is necessary. Think about it: If the sender generates his own keys and the recipient generates her own keys, the key pairs won't match, and the PKI processes won't work. Therefore, a CA used by both parties generates and distributes the key pairs.

CA Hierarchies

In a worldwide organization, you probably would not want every user to have to connect to a single CA. Likewise, when multiple companies are involved, they need a common trusted CA for intercompany security. They also need their own CA for intracompany security. These situations show the need for CA hierarchies.

CAs can be set up as root CAs, where they are the highest level of authority for a CA hierarchy. CAs can also be set up as subordinate CAs, that is, CAs that trust a higher-level CA as their authority. In the case of the worldwide company, it may choose to set up a root CA at the company's headquarters with subordinate CAs at strategic regional locations. In the case of multiple companies, each company may have its own CA, but it would be set up as a subordinate CA (Enterprise or Standalone) and utilize a trusted third-party root CA, such as VeriSign or RSA, to tie the CA hierarchies together, as shown in Figure 19-1.

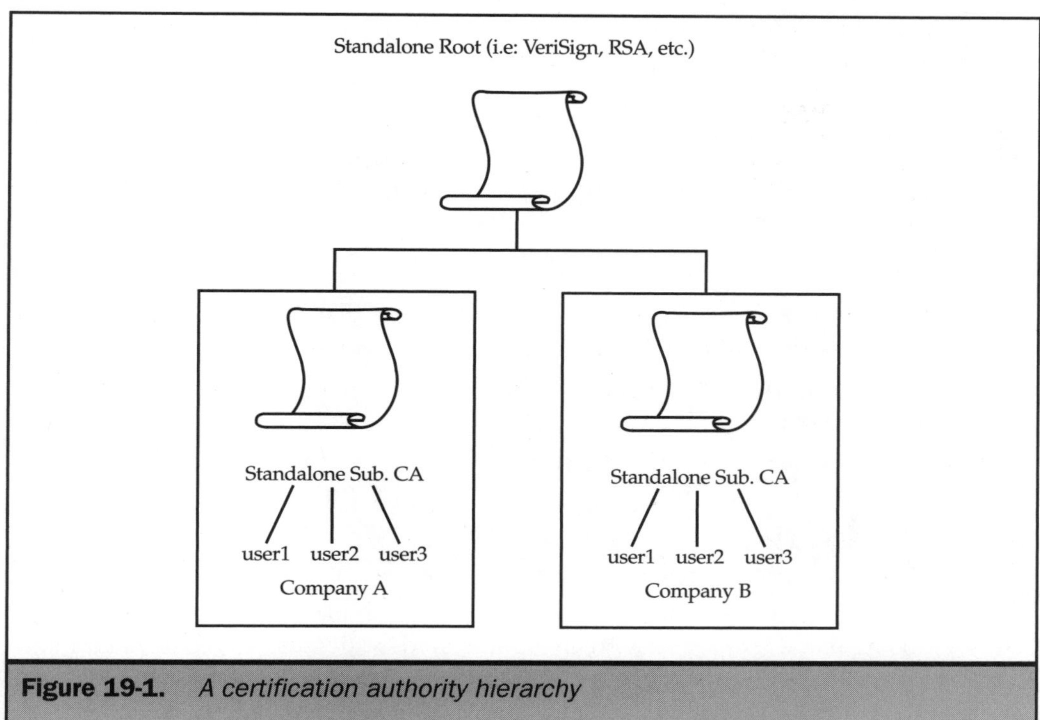

Figure 19-1. *A certification authority hierarchy*

Windows 2000 Certificate Services

Windows 2000 Certificate Services is a CA. Exchange 2000 can be configured to use Certificate Services to provide message encryption and digital signature capabilities. The most common certificates used today are based on the International Telecommunications Union (ITU-T) X.509v3 standard, which is implemented in Windows 2000, and supported by Exchange 2000, Outlook 2000, and Outlook 2002. Windows 2000 Certificate Services uses X.509 certificates to provide strong authentication, which uses PKI to verify the identity of the user. Most Secure/Multipurpose Internet Mail Extension (S/MIME) clients recognize X.509v3 user certificates, providing interoperability between different e-mail clients used by different businesses.

Note *Exchange 4.0 and 5.0, and Outlook 97, use X.509v1 certificates. If you have legacy clients in your organization, you can issue certificates using both versions. However, S/MIME clients only understand X.509v3 certificates, so you may need to upgrade to a later client if you need to use S/MIME.*

What Is an X.509 Certificate?

We've already discussed that a certificate, in general, provides information about a user or computer and validates the authenticity of their credentials. The X.509 standard was developed by the International Telecommunications Union (ITU). The standard defines what information should be included when a CA issues a certificate. Three versions of the X.509 standard exist. All versions include the following information in the certificate:

- **Version.** Defines X.509 certificate version being used.
- **Serial Number.** Used by the CA to distinguish one certificate from another.
- **Signature Algorithm ID.** Identifies the algorithm used by the CA to sign the certificate.
- **Issuer Name.** States who the certificate was issued to.
- **Validity Period.** Defines the period of time (using a starting and ending date and time) that the certificate is valid.
- **Subject Name.** Defines the entity identified on the public key.
- **Subject Public Key Information.** This is the public key of the entity being named, together with an algorithm identifier and any associated key parameters.

X.509 version 1 has been available since 1988; it is the most generic and the most widely used. X.509 version 2 introduced the concept of subject and issuer unique identifiers to handle the possibility of reuse of subject and/or issuer names over time. Version 2 certificates are not widely used. *X.509 Version 3* is the most recent version, introduced in 1996, and supports the use of extensions, whereby anyone can define an extension and include it in the certificate. Some common extensions in use today are: *KeyUsage* (limits the use of the keys to particular purposes such as signing-only) and *AlternativeNames* (allows other identities to be associated with this public key, for example, DNS names, e-mail addresses, and IP addresses). Extensions can be marked *critical* to indicate that they should be checked and enforced/used. For example, if a certificate has the KeyUsage extension marked critical and set to "keyCertSign", and if this certificate is presented during SSL communication, it should be rejected, because the certificate extension indicates that the associated private key should be used only for signing certificates and not for SSL use.

Certificate Services CA Types

When you install Certificate Services (or any other CA software), a CA can take a number of different roles. Windows 2000 Certificate Services supports four CA types:

- **Enterprise Root CA.** This is the root CA for the entire organization. This type of CA requires Active Directory. In addition to acting as the root CA, this CA can also issue certificates.
- **Enterprise Subordinate CA.** This CA exists below the Enterprise Root CA in the hierarchy. This type of CA also requires Active Directory and issues certificates.
- **Standalone Root CA.** This CA acts as the root CA for a CA hierarchy and issues certificates. Active Directory is not required.
- **Standalone Subordinate CA.** This CA exists below the Standalone Root CA. This CA also does not require Active Directory.

Installing Certificate Services

Before you begin the installation of Certificate Services, you should plan your CA needs. Once a certificate server is installed, the only way to change its CA type is to remove and reinstall it. Take a look at your company's security needs: Will security remain intracompany? Will a trusted third-party CA be necessary? Weigh these types of questions carefully prior to implementing Certificate Services.

To install Certificate Services, open the Control Panel and double-click the Add/Remove icon. Select the Add/Remove Windows Components icon to start the Windows Components Wizard. Navigate to and check the Certificate Services checkbox. A dialog box, shown in Figure 19-2, warns that the computer cannot be renamed or moved into or out of a domain once Certificate Services is installed. Click Yes (assuming no changes to the computer will be made and you want to proceed with the installation), and then click Next.

You will be prompted to choose a CA type, as shown in Figure 19-3. Choose the appropriate CA type, keeping in mind that you cannot change the CA type without reinstalling Certificate Services.

Choosing the Advanced Options checkbox will add the Public and Private Key Pair screen to the wizard , shown in Figure 19-4, where you can choose the encryption and hash algorithms that Certificate Services will use. Table 19-1 lists the options available on this screen.

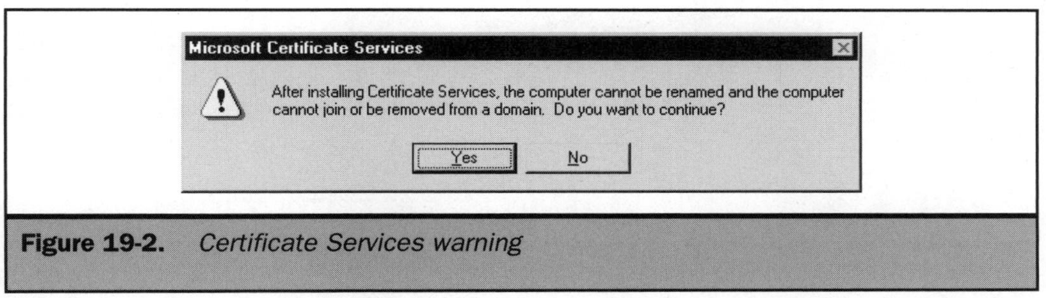

Figure 19-2. *Certificate Services warning*

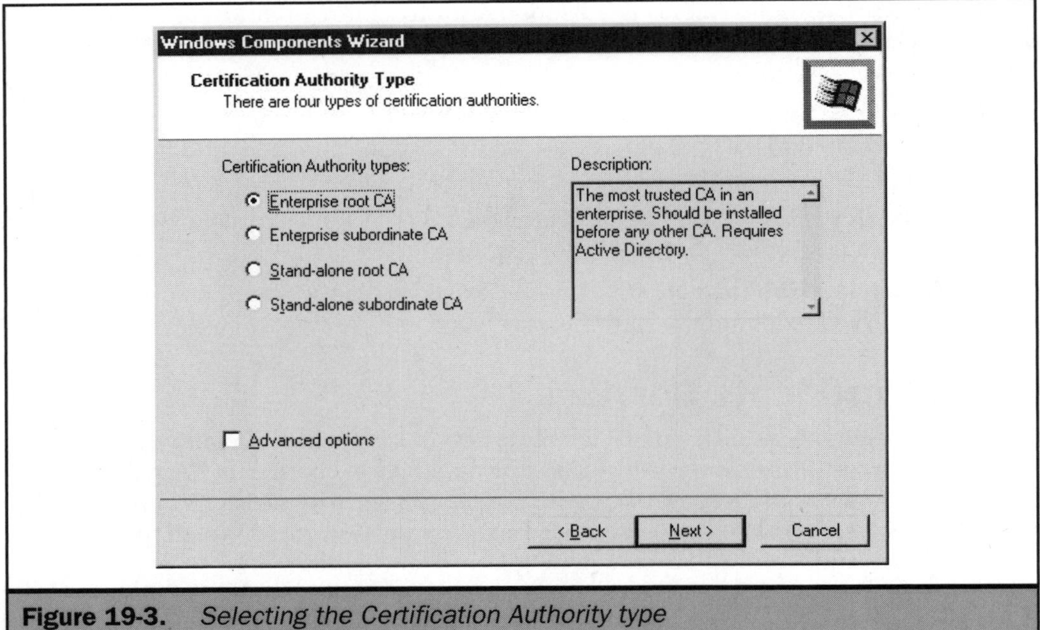

Figure 19-3. *Selecting the Certification Authority type*

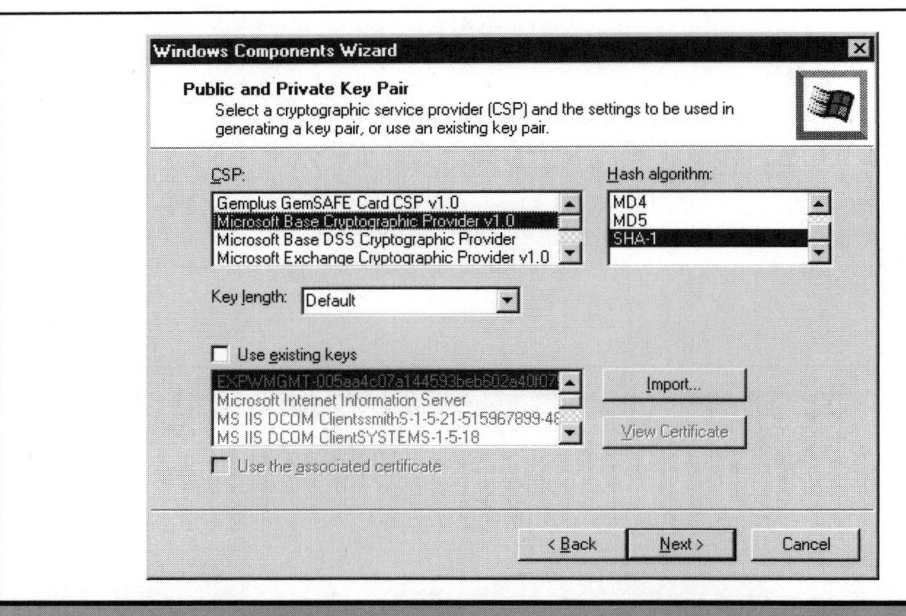

Figure 19-4. *Selecting advanced options on the Public and Private Key Pair screen*

Option	Description
CSP	The cryptographic service provider (CSP) is used to generate the key pair for the CA.
Hash Algorithm	The various hash algorithms encrypt data in different ways. For example, the default of SHA-1 (the Secure Hash Algorithm version 1) uses a 160-bit hash value, as opposed to a MD4 (Message Digest version 4) hash that uses a 128-bit hash value.
Key Length	The default key length for the Microsoft Base Cryptographic Provider is 512 bytes with the Enhanced Cryptographic Provider using 1024 bits. The longer keys provide more secure encryption.
Use Existing Keys	You can use a private key that already exists. This could be useful when rebuilding a failed CA.
Use the Associated Certificate	This selection tells the CA to use the certificate associated with the private key selected. Again, this is useful when rebuilding a failed CA.
Import	If the key is not in the list, you can import the private key from a file.
View Certificate	If you import a certificate, you can view the certificate to verify its issuer, valid dates, and other information in the certificate.

Table 19-1. *Advanced Options on the Public and Private Key Pairs Screen*

Next, you'll need to provide some information that identifies the CA, as shown in Figure 19-5. Some of this information is included in every certificate given out so clients can view details about a certificate, such as who is issuing it. Also note that you can set the period a certificate is valid for in this screen. The default is two years, but you can change that value based on your security needs.

The cryptographic keys are used for creating key pairs, and the next screen, shown in Figure 19-6, prompts you to provide a location for the certificate database to store this information. This location should be on an NTFS partition in a folder secured by permissions from unauthorized access. If you are not using Active Directory, you can store the configuration information in a shared folder for access by clients. If you are reinstalling a CA, select the Preserve Existing Certificate Database checkbox so the existing database is not overwritten with a new one.

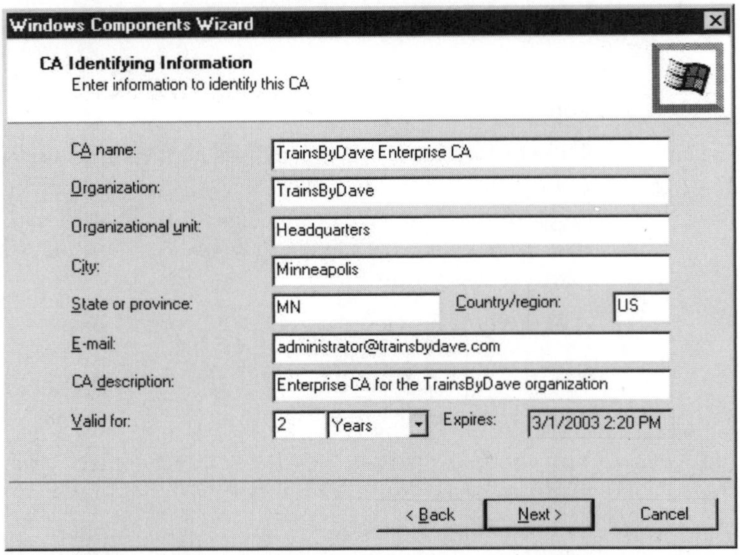

Figure 19-5. *Providing identification information for the CA*

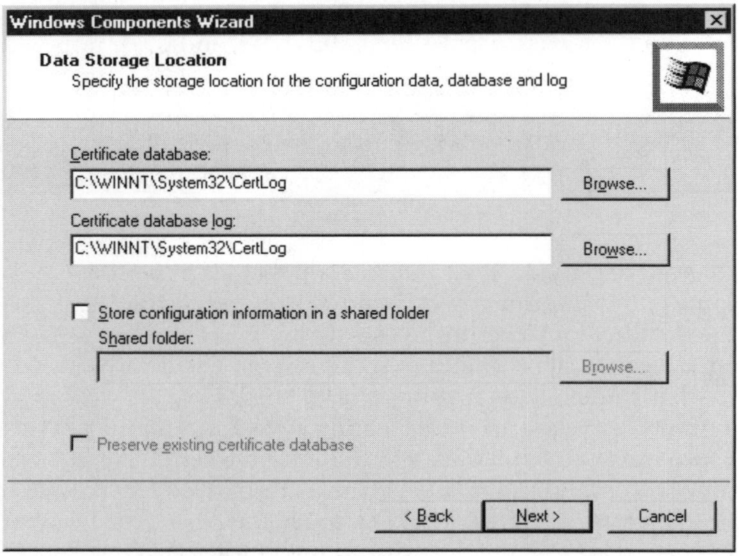

Figure 19-6. *Configuring the storage location for the CA database*

IIS will be automatically stopped and updated with information about the CA that it can now use to establish SSL connections. The files are copied from the Windows 2000 Server CD-ROM and the installation is completed.

Managing Certificates

After the installation of Certificate Services, a new tool, called *Certification Authority*, appears in Administrative Tools, as shown in Figure 19-7. You will use this tool to establish which certificate types this CA can issue, as well as to revoke issued certificates.

Note *For more information on Certificate Services, see "Windows 2000: The Complete Reference" (McGraw-Hill).*

Key Management Service

Although a CA is used to issue certificates, a second service is needed specifically to install the certificates on clients that wish to participate in message security. That service is the Key Management Service (KMS). KMS, a component of Exchange 2000, acts as a Cryptographic Service Provider (CSP) and is used by Exchange 2000 to act as a liaison between the messaging client and Certificate Services. Together, KMS and Certificate Services provide security at the application layer. Certificate Services issues the certificate and KMS installs that certificate on the messaging client to allow it to use encryption and digital signatures.

Note *Because Certificate Services and KMS encrypt the data at the application layer of the OSI model, virus-scanning and content-filtering software cannot function properly against encrypted messages. Because the messages are encrypted, they cannot be parsed by these types of software applications. As a result, you will need to devise alternative methods of protecting your infrastructure against trojans, viruses, and unacceptable content that may be contained within encrypted messages.*

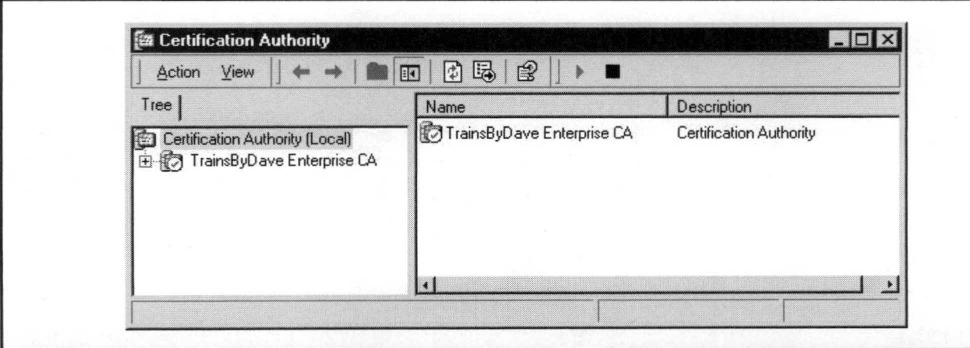

Figure 19-7. *The Certification Authority snap-in*

Pre-Installation Issues

Before you can install KMS, you need to ensure that Certificate Services can issue the needed certificate types (also called *certificate templates*). If you attempt to install KMS without configuring Certificate Services, you receive a message stating you need to add several certificate types to Certificate Server, as shown in Figure 19-8.

Whether or not you ran the Exchange 2000 setup prematurely, you will need to configure Certificate Services to support the following certificate types:

- Enrollment Agent (Computer)
- Exchange User
- Exchange Signature Only

These certificate types are needed for client authentication when sending secure mail. You make this configuration change in the Certification Authority snap-in, shown earlier in Figure 19-7.

To update the configuration, perform the following steps:

1. Navigate to and right-click the Policy Settings container.
2. Point to New and choose Certificate to Issue, as shown in Figure 19-9.
3. Select the three certificate templates and click OK.

Once this is done you can install KMS.

Installing KMS

Run the setup from the Exchange 2000 Server CD-ROM. At the Component Selection screen, shown in Figure 19-10, select Install next to Microsoft Exchange Key Management Service. Figure 19-10 shows an installation of KMS being added to an existing Exchange 2000 installation.

Figure 19-8. *KMS installation error stating Certificate Services must be configured with the correct certificates*

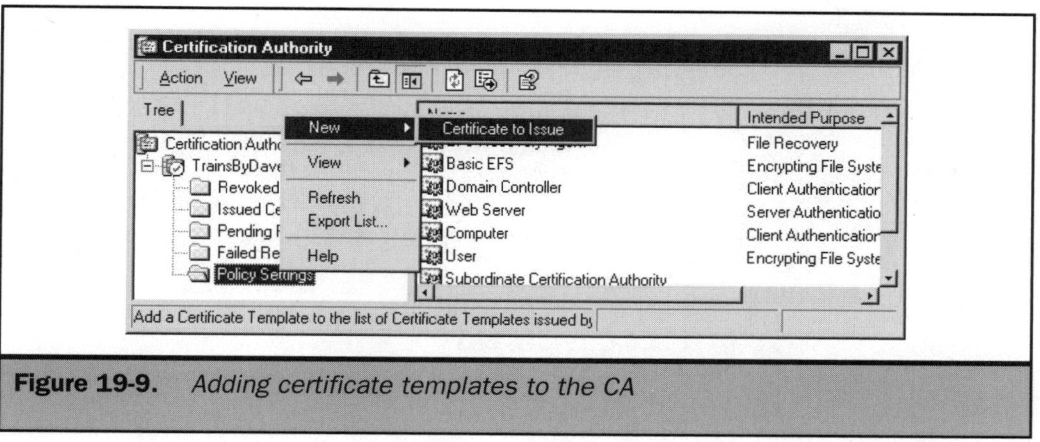

Figure 19-9. *Adding certificate templates to the CA*

Because KMS will manage keys to be used for encryption and digital signatures, a password is required, for security purposes, in order to start the service. The next screen in the installation wizard, shown in Figure 19-11, allows you to decide whether the password should be displayed on the screen (for you to write down and use later) or written to a file to be read at service startup.

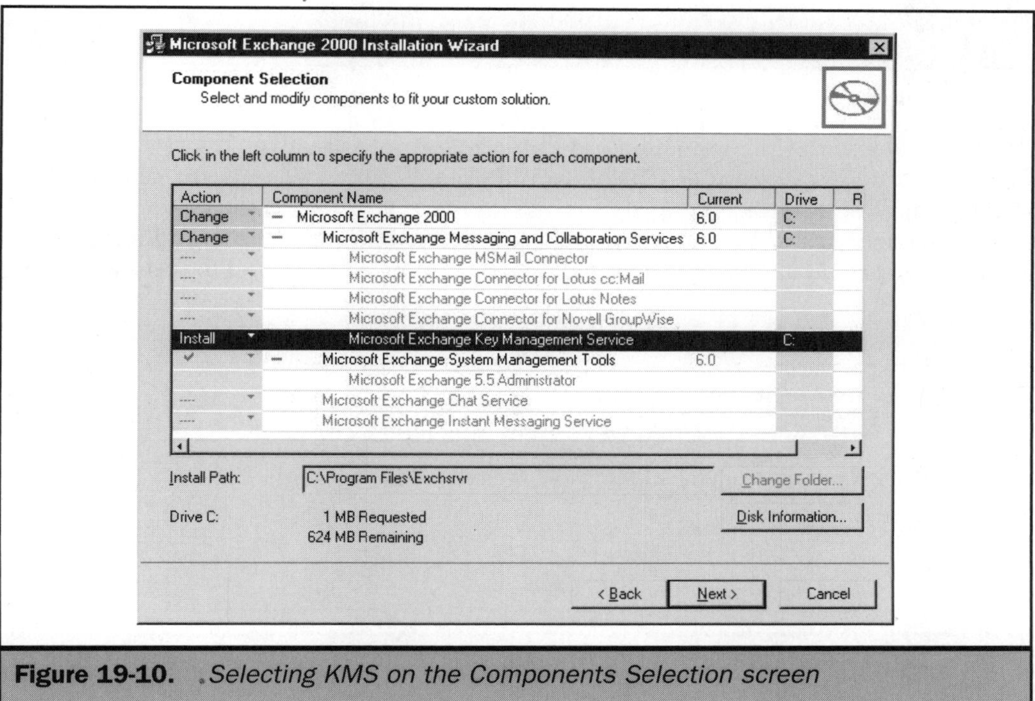

Figure 19-10. *Selecting KMS on the Components Selection screen*

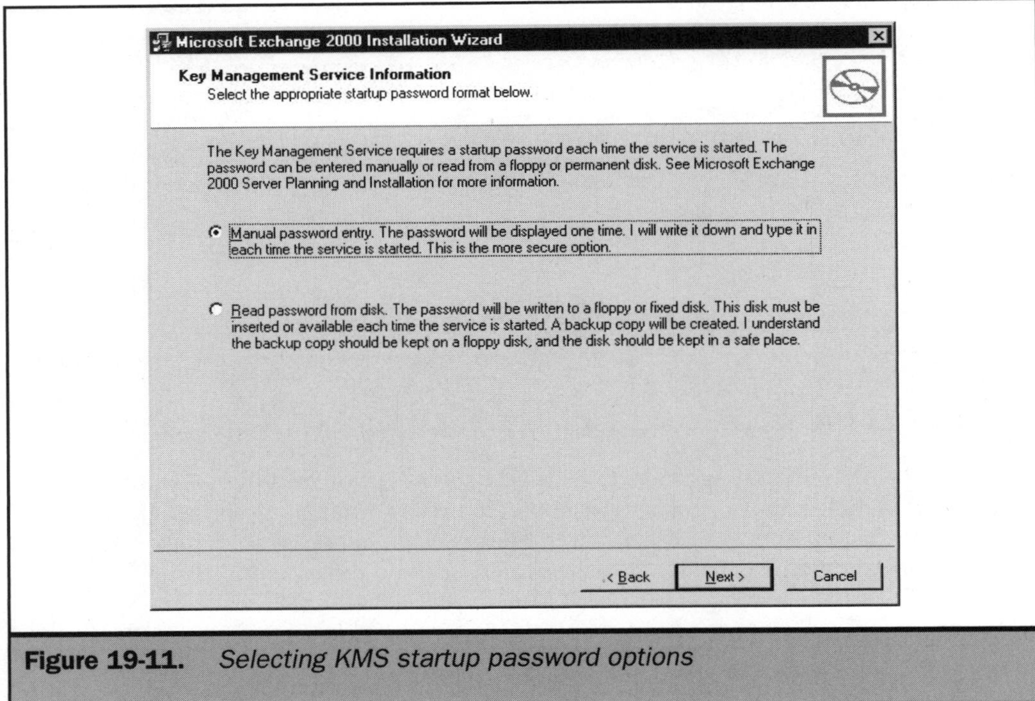

Figure 19-11. *Selecting KMS startup password options*

If you choose the Manual Password Entry option, you are given the KMS startup password, shown in Figure 19-12. You would use this password when manually starting the KMS service.

If you choose Read Password From Disk instead of Manual Password Entry, you are asked to provide a disk location for a master and backup copy of the password, as

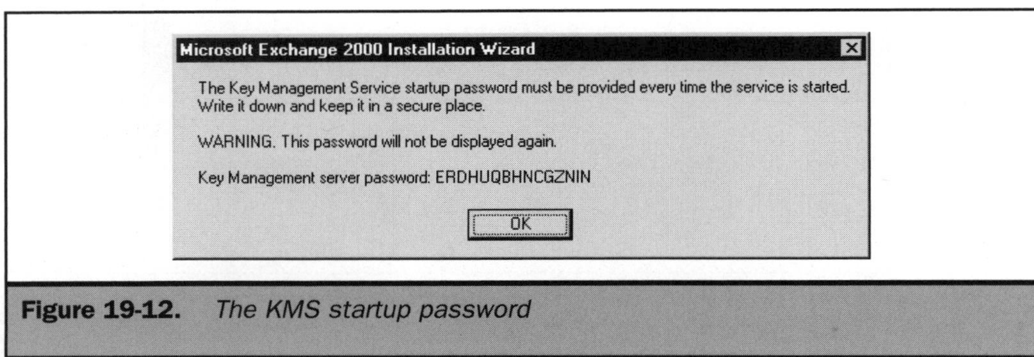

Figure 19-12. *The KMS startup password*

Starting the KMS Service Manually

If you choose to be given the startup password for manual entry, you will need to provide that password every time you start the Microsoft Key Management Service. You will do this in the Services tool in Administrative Tools. Navigate to the properties of the Microsoft Key Management Service. On the General tab, shown in Figure 19-13, enter the startup password in the Start Parameters field, and then click Start to start the service.

shown in Figure 19-14. When you start the service, the file (which is named kmserver.pwd) must be in the location you specify during the installation of KMS.

Tip *Use a location on Exchange server's disks that is secured with NTFS permissions instead of the floppy location provided by default.*

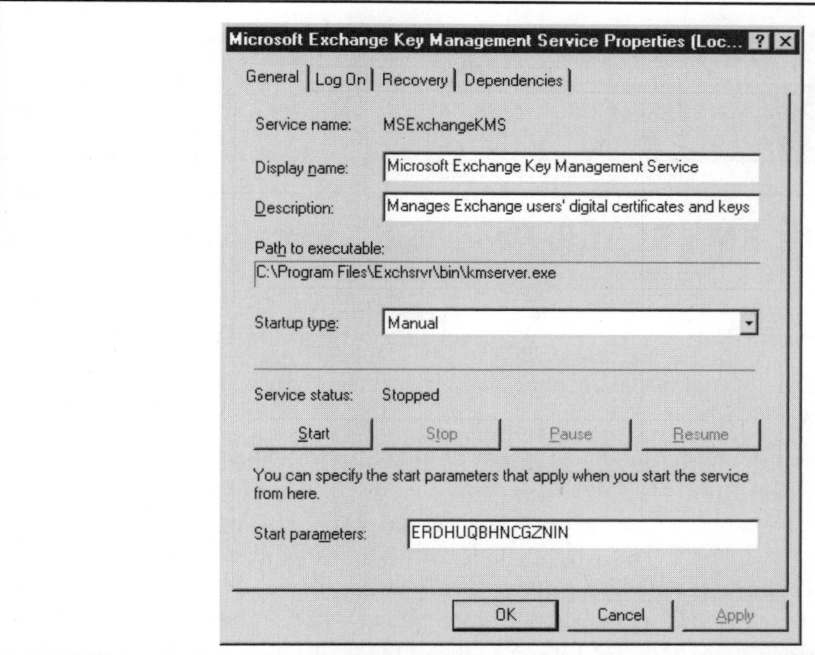

Figure 19-13. *Providing the KMS startup password to start the service*

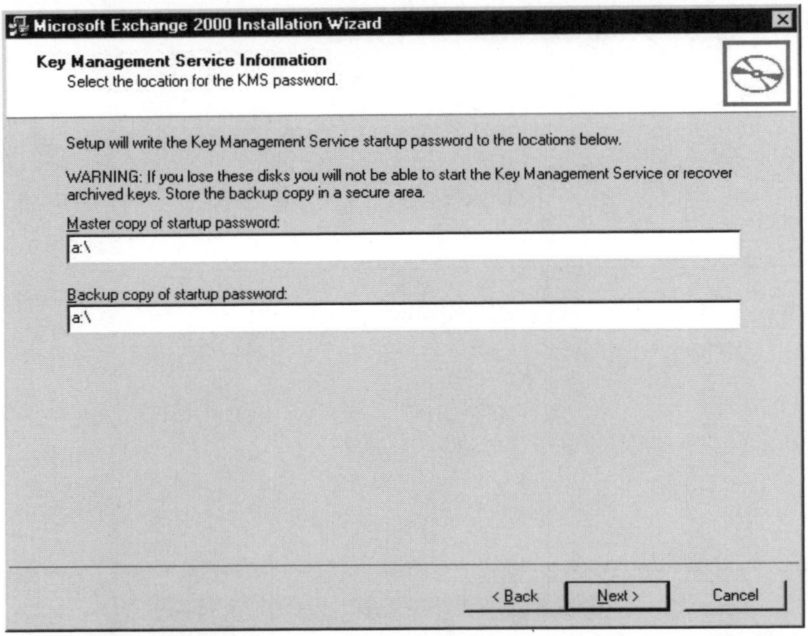

Figure 19-14. *Specifying the locations for the master and backup copies of the KMS startup password*

Changing the KMS Startup Password Location

If you accept the default password location of the floppy, or if you need to move the password location for some reason, there is a simple way to change where KMS looks for the password. In the registry, KMS looks for the following value:

HKEY_LOCAL_MACHINE\Software\Microsoft\Exchange\KMServer\MasterPasswordPath

Change this value to be the new location of the password file (and remember to move the file there, too!). The next time you start KMS, it will look in the new location for the password file, which is named *KMServer.pwd*. Also, you should use the Services snap-in to set the Startup Type for the Microsoft Key Management Service to Automatic so it will start automatically at bootup.

If you choose to manually provide the startup password, MasterPasswordPath will have a blank value. Changing this to a valid disk location causes KMS to look in that location for the password instead of expecting you to manually provide it at each startup. Also, you can set the BackupPasswordPath to specify an alternate location should the MasterPasswordPath not contain the password file. The password file should simply contain the password on the first line of the file.

KMS Management

Because KMS manages a user's ability to secure messages containing potentially sensitive data, it is imperative that you establish who can administer this service. By default, only the administrator account can manage KMS. You administer KMS within Exchange System Manager (ESM). To administer KMS, navigate to the Key Manager object, as shown in Figure 19-15.

Right-click the object and select Properties. A KMS Login dialog box will prompt you. Please note that the "password" field is listed as the KMS password. Although you may think you should enter the password associated with the user listed in the Domain Username field, you actually need to provide the password KMS has in its database for that user account. By default the password is "password". You can change the password once you have gained access to the Key Manager Properties dialog box. You will also notice, once you have gained access, that you have to provide this same user name/password combination each time you select a different tab. This is to assure you that even if you were to go to the properties of the Key Manager object and then walk away from your desk, the amount of changes another user could make in your absence is limited.

KMS Administrators

The first question to answer is "Who will be allowed to manage KMS?" You answer this question on the Administrators property page, shown in Figure 19-16. You can add

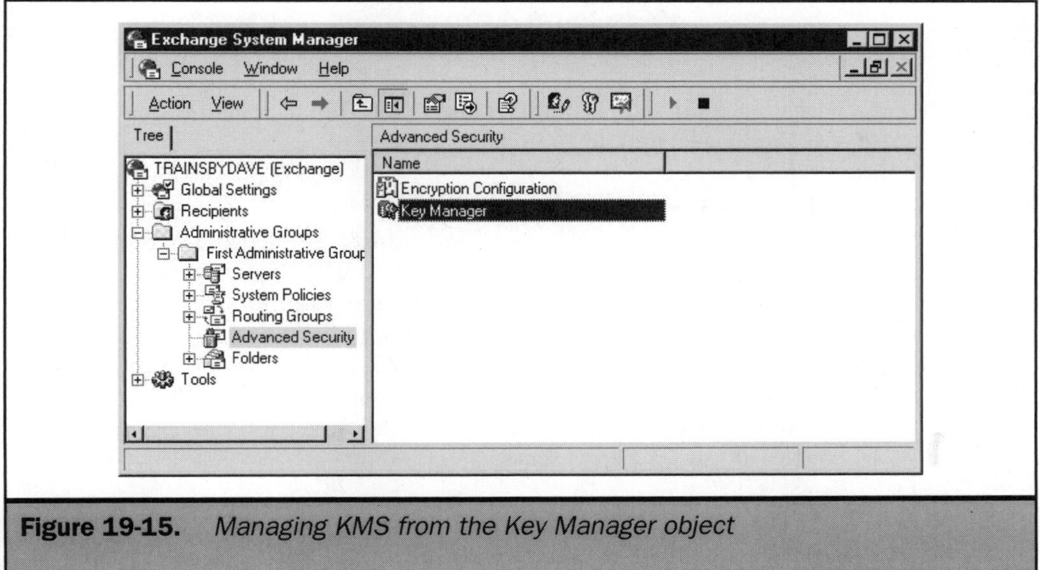

Figure 19-15. *Managing KMS from the Key Manager object*

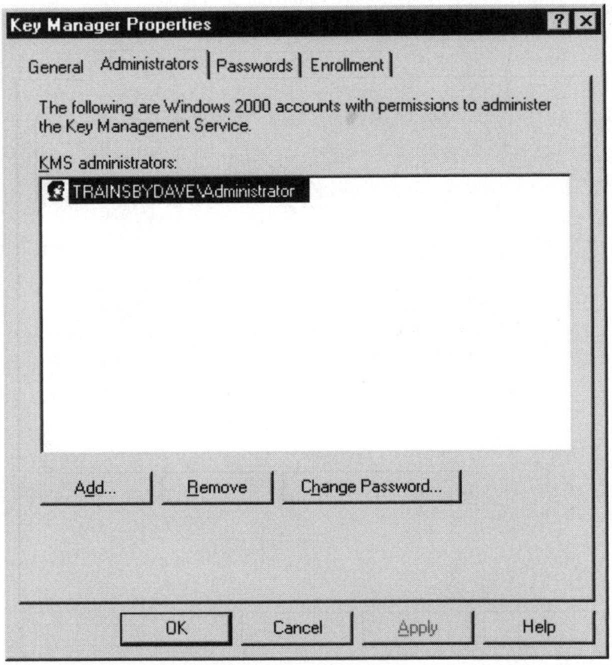

Figure 19-16. *KMS administrators list*

and remove the names of users who can administer KMS. You can also change the KMS passwords for each user you add to this list.

How Many Passwords?

Some companies may require more than a single administrator to perform some of the KMS management tasks. With the exception of small Exchange environments with one administrator where you have no choice, allowing a single administrator to manage KMS gives too much power to an individual. That is why you can specify how many administrator passwords are required for each KMS task, as shown in Figure 19-17. You can require as many passwords as you have administrators. Table 19-2 lists the tasks that you can require multiple passwords for and reasons for requiring more than one password.

Because the KMS parameters will not be changed all that often, we recommend that you require at least two administrators for each task. Be sure to assign KMS administrator privileges to users who will be available if a configuration change is necessary.

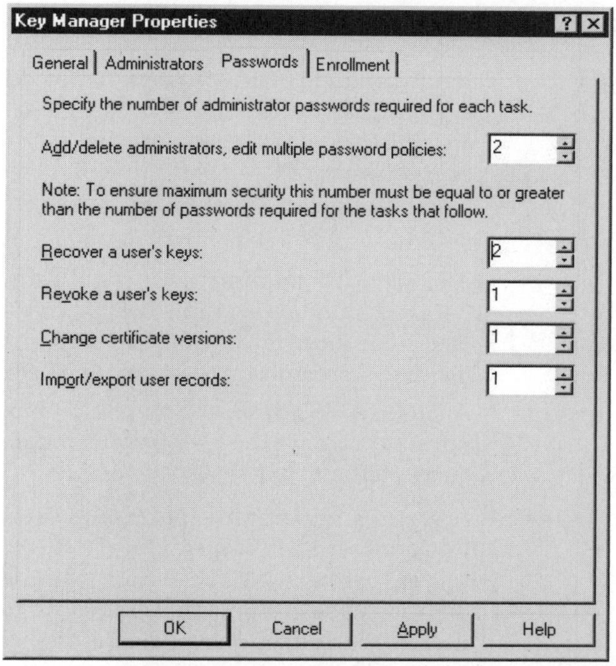

Figure 19-17. *Determining how many passwords are required for each KMS task*

Enrolling Users

The last administrative task is to enroll each user who will utilize KMS (you'll see this sometimes referred to as "e-mail security"). You have two methods of enrollment: mass enrollment or individual enrollment. As you choose which method to use, consider the security of each method. Let's look at the merits of each method.

Mass Enrollment

If all users in your organization (or some subset of all users) are to be enrolled, the easiest method is mass enrollment. Right-click the Key Manager object, point to All Tasks, and then select Enroll Users. A dialog box, shown in Figure 19-18, prompts you to choose whether to see an alphabetic address list or a list of mailbox stores, Exchange servers, and administrative groups.

Selecting an alphabetic list displays a dialog box where you select each user to be enrolled. Selecting the list of stores, servers, and administrative groups displays a list of those objects, as shown in Figure 19-19. Choosing one of these levels will enroll all

KMS Task	Why Require Multiple Passwords?
Add/Delete Administrators, Edit Multiple Password Policies	If only a single password is required, a KMS administrator could delete all the other listed administrators and change their password, locking everyone out of KMS. Additionally, the administrator could change the number of passwords required for each of the tasks listed here.
Recover a User's Keys	A single KMS administrator could use a recovered key, log on as another user in Outlook, re-establish that user's enrollment in e-mail security, and send messages pretending to be someone else.
Revoke a User's Keys	A single KMS administrator could revoke a user's keys, preventing the user from using message encryption or digital signatures.
Import/Export User Records	A single KMS administrator could export a user's keys into another KMS server. Once in the "other" KMS server (perhaps one of the KMS administrator's own devising), the administrator could pretend to be the user in much the same fashion as described under recovering a user's keys.

Table 19-2. *KMS Tasks and the Need for Multiple Passwords*

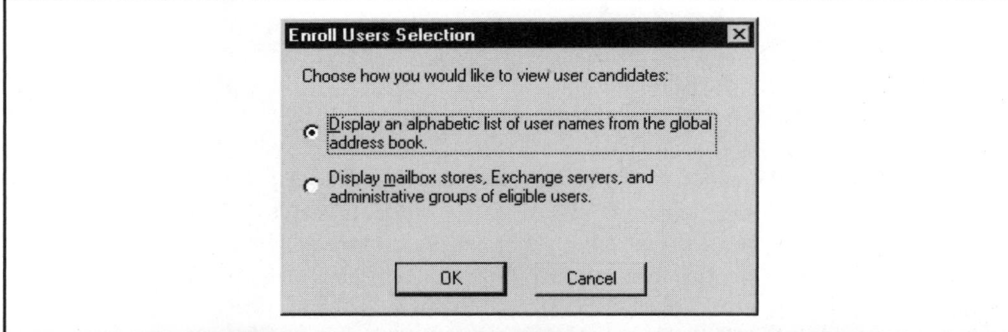

Figure 19-18. *Selecting how you want to mass enroll users*

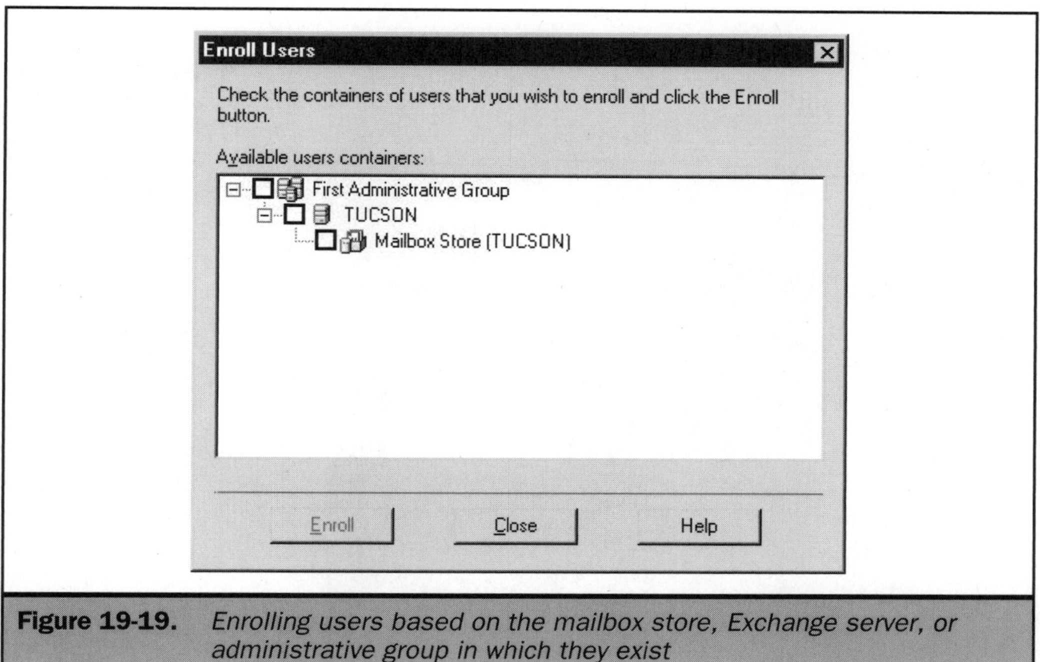

Figure 19-19. *Enrolling users based on the mailbox store, Exchange server, or administrative group in which they exist*

users who logically exist within the level. For example, if you were to select an administrative group, users existing in any mailbox store on any Exchange server within that administrative group would be enrolled.

Now that you have chosen who should be enrolled, you need to determine how to inform them of the enrollment. To do so, utilize the Enrollment property page, shown in Figure 19-20. You can select the Send Token In An E-Mail checkbox to have all enrolled Exchange users notified of their enrollment in e-mail security. The downside is the security aspect of this method. The token is a password unique to each user that will be used when the user completes the enrollment process from within Outlook. If this token is sent via e-mail (non-securely don't forget, as we haven't completed the setup of e-mail security to use encryption), it would be possible for someone to capture the data from the network or read the message at the user's desk while the user is away. While neither situation is very probable, token distribution by e-mail should be carefully considered if your company takes a serious stance on security.

Individual Enrollment

Because most companies (in our experience) only want to enroll a select few users who truly need the capability to either encrypt or digitally sign messages, the mass enrollment method is not viable. The more common method is to enroll one user at a

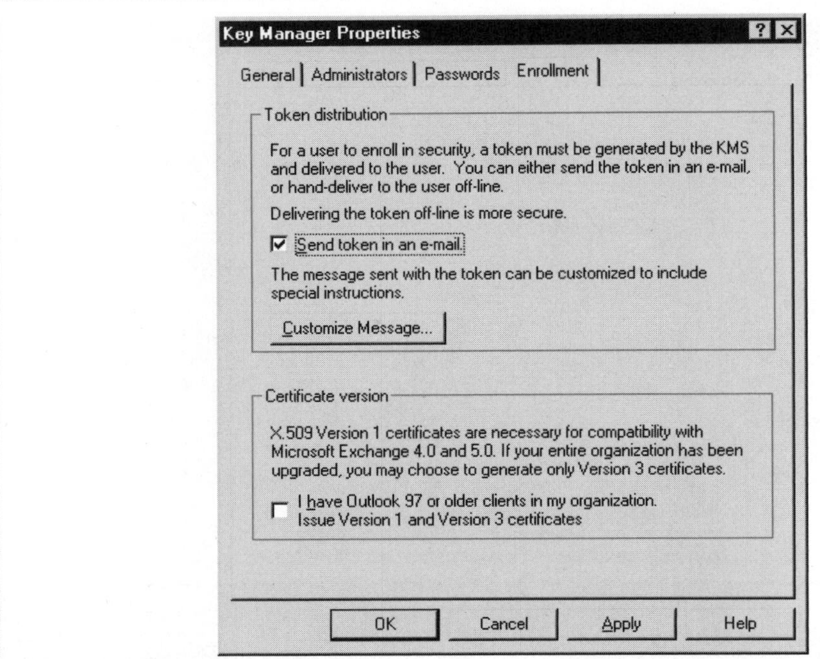

Figure 19-20. *Choosing to send the enrollment token via e-mail using the Enrollment property page*

Mass Enrollment: The Secure Way

The most secure way of enrolling a user into e-mail security is to enroll a single user, write down the user's token (see "Enrolling an Individual User," later in the chapter), and walk over to the user's desk to complete the enrollment. If you need to enroll all Exchange users, but don't want the token sent in a non-secure fashion, you can use the Enrollment property page to tell Exchange that you want to enroll all users, but not send the token to them.

The way to accomplish this is to customize the message sent to the user. As shown in Figure 19-21, the default message includes a variable, %TOKEN%. This value is replaced with the user's token. You can customize this message to not include the token, and instead inform the user that he or she has been enrolled, and that you will deliver the token by hand. You also can provide the steps in Outlook that the user needs to perform to complete the enrollment. If you choose not to include the token in the message, see "Recovering and Revoking Keys" later in the chapter to see how to view the token for each user.

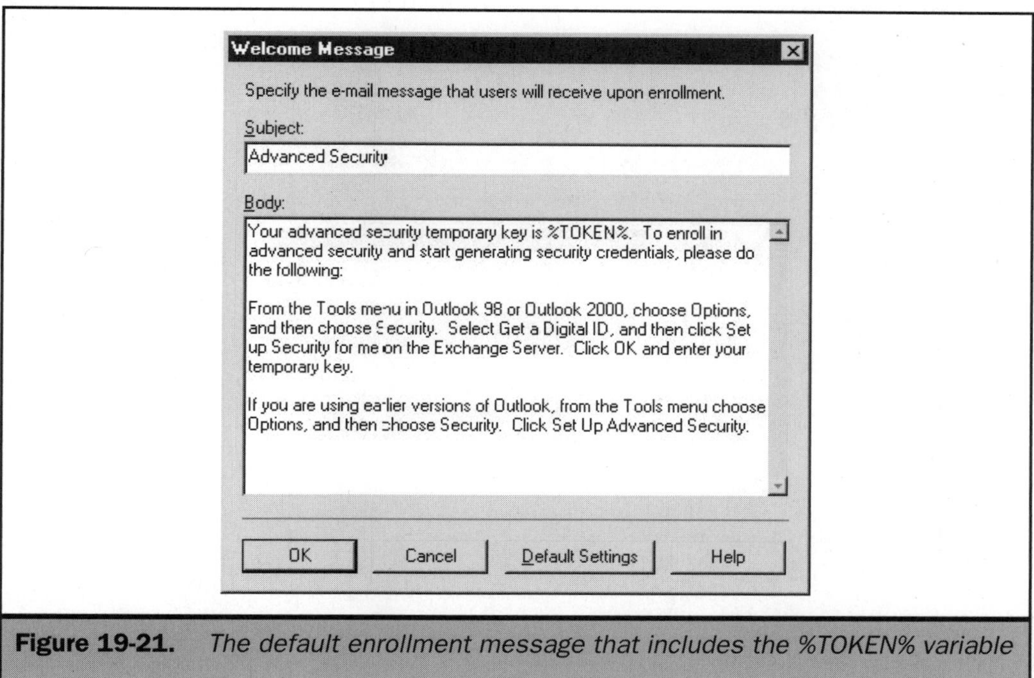

Figure 19-21. *The default enrollment message that includes the %TOKEN% variable*

time. Although this adds a step to the process (selecting the user to be enrolled), it really is not much more work. You enroll individual users in Active Directory Users and Computers.

To enroll a user in e-mail security, select the properties of the user in question, and then select the Exchange Features property page, as shown in Figure 19-22. Select E-Mail Security and click the Properties button.

You will be prompted to provide your KMS password (remember, it is your *KMS* password and not your user account password). Then you'll see the E-Mail Security dialog box. Click the Enroll button to be presented with the user's token, as shown in Figure 19-23. This password will be used in Outlook when completing the enrollment.

Completing the Enrollment

Enrolling a user, generating the token, and delivering it to the user (whether via e-mail message or by hand) is only the first half of the enrollment process. To complete the enrollment, Outlook needs to be configured to support e-mail security. We'll cover the enrollment completion using Outlook 2000 as our example. Outlook 97 and Outlook 98 are very similar in procedure, with minor tab, button, or dialog box name changes.

Figure 19-22. *Enabling e-mail security on the Exchange Features property page*

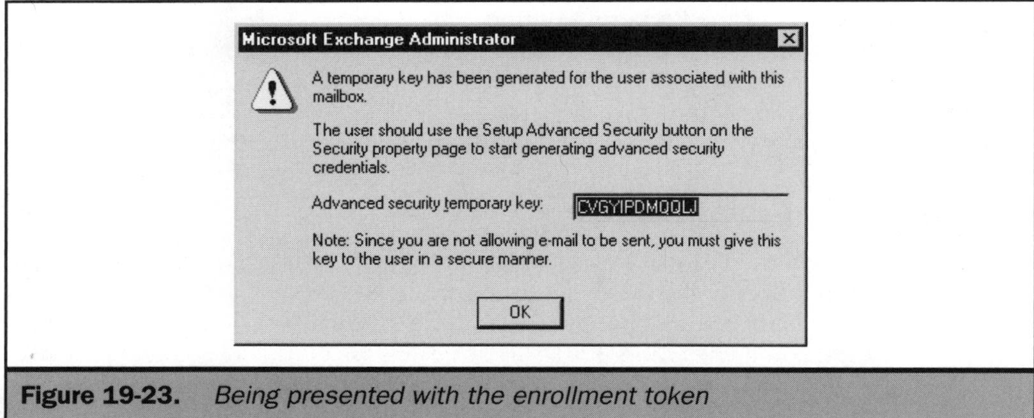

Figure 19-23. *Being presented with the enrollment token*

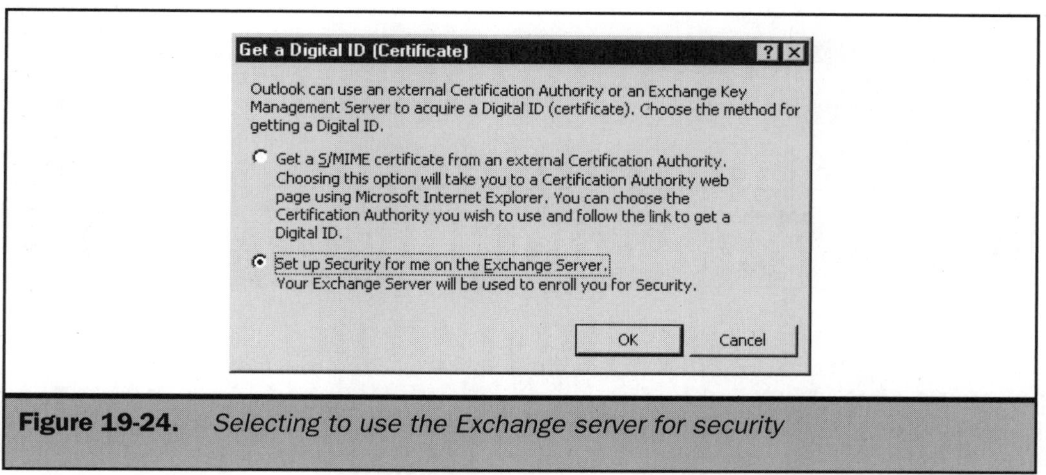

Figure 19-24. *Selecting to use the Exchange server for security*

To complete the enrollment process, perform the following steps:

1. Begin by opening Outlook.
2. Select the Tools menu and choose Options.
3. On the Security property page, click the Get A Digital ID button.
4. Choose the Set Up Security For Me On The Exchange Server option to utilize KMS for security, as shown in Figure 19-24.
5. Outlook prompts you to provide a digital ID name and token, as shown in Figure 19-25. The digital ID name is a friendly name for the digital ID (you could use something like "Exchange 2000 Digital ID" or whatever you like), and the token is the token you either sent via e-mail to the user or wrote down and delivered by hand.

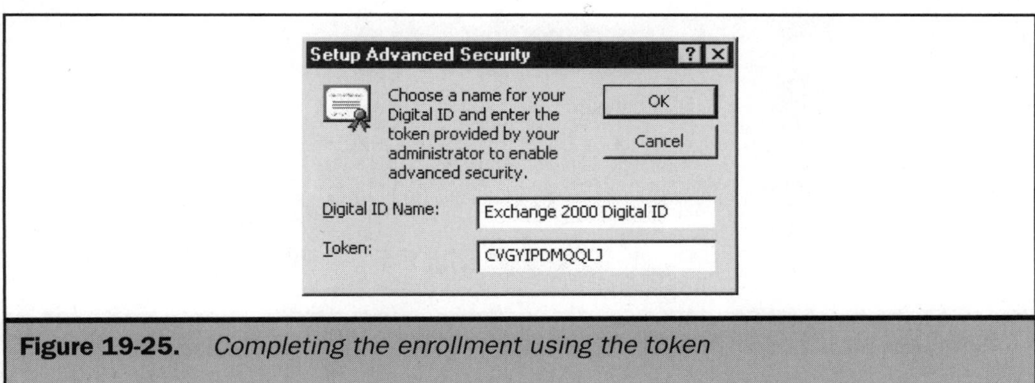

Figure 19-25. *Completing the enrollment using the token*

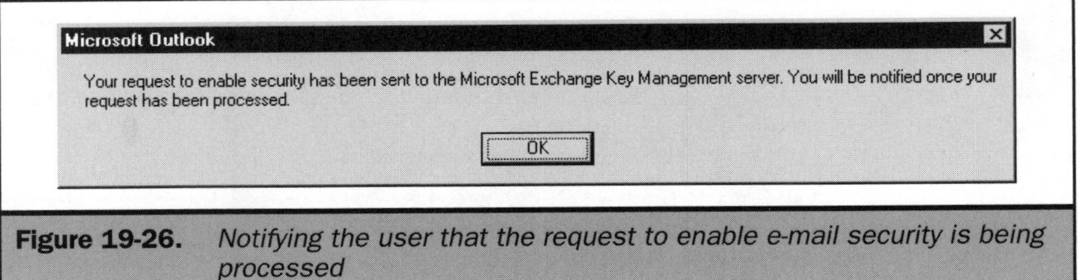

Figure 19-26. *Notifying the user that the request to enable e-mail security is being processed*

6. Because the user is not going to remember the token (nor does he or she need to), Outlook prompts you to provide a password to protect the digital ID. This password will be used whenever the user wants to either encrypt or digitally sign a message. The password need not be the same as the user's Windows 2000 account (nor do we recommend that it be the same). Outlook sends the user a message box stating that the request has been sent to KMS and is being processed, as shown in Figure 19-26.
7. Now you get to hurry up and wait. The user must wait until KMS processes the request, which, depending on the load on the KMS server, can take from minutes to hours.
8. Once processed, a message appears in the user's Inbox. You'll notice the message icon has a small blue lock next to it, meaning it is encrypted. When you open the message, you'll be prompted to enter the security password you created a few steps earlier.
9. A dialog box appears asking you to add a certificate to the root store, as shown in Figure 19-27. The root store, a part of the Security Support Provider Interface (SSPI) component of Internet Explorer's schannel.dll, lists all the CAs you trust.

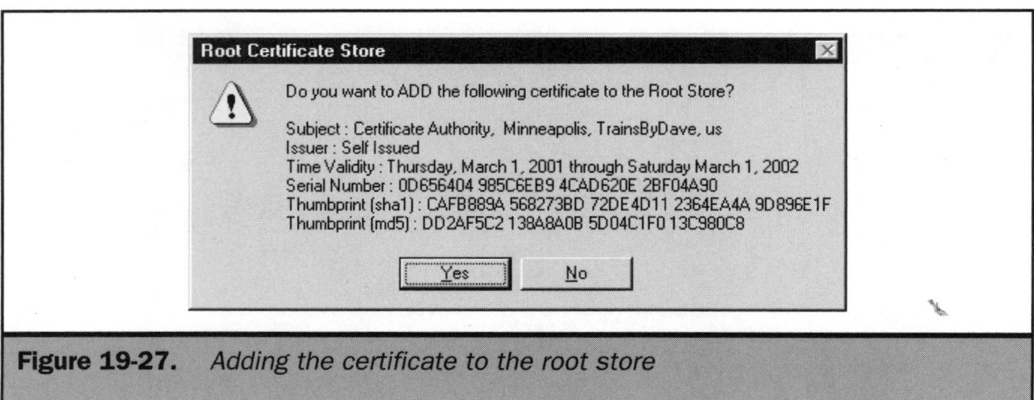

Figure 19-27. *Adding the certificate to the root store*

Adding the certificate received from KMS will allow future seamless interaction with KMS when the user needs to encrypt or digitally sign messages.

10. Once you have added the certificate to the root store, you will be informed that you can begin using e-mail security.

Using E-mail Security

Using e-mail security is rather simple. Before you send off that e-mail you just typed, click the Options button to see the Message Options dialog box, as shown in Figure 19-28. In the Security section, you have two options to utilize e-mail security on this message:

- **Encrypt Message Contents and Attachments.** Selecting this box encrypts the entire message. Note that you need the recipient's public key for this, which means that you will be able to encrypt a message only if the recipient's public key is available to you. In the case of another user in your Exchange organization who is set up via KMS for e-mail security, this is no problem and

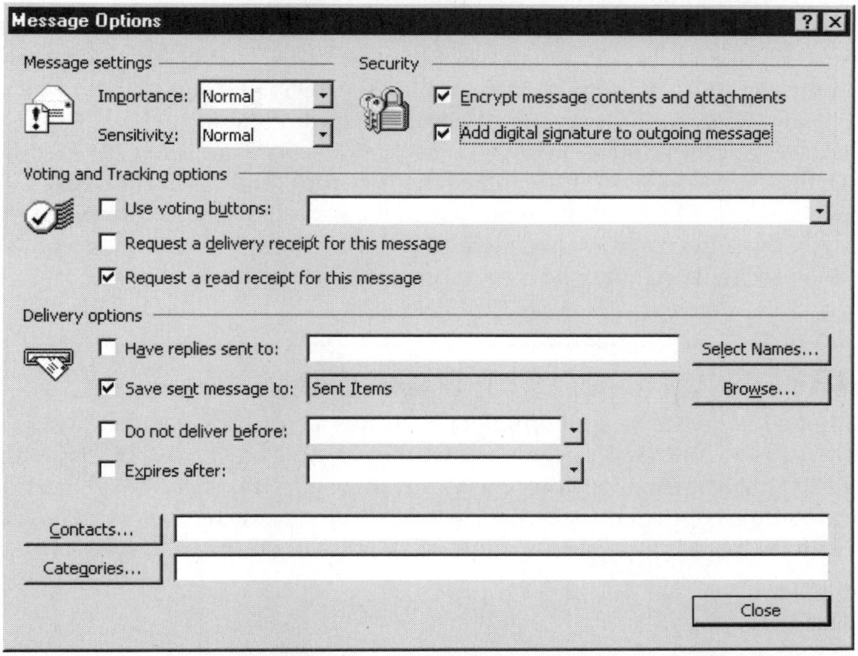

Figure 19-28. *Security options for a message*

will be seamless to the user sending the encrypted message. This is because the public key of each Exchange 2000 user who is enabled for secure e-mail is published as an attribute of the user's account in Active Directory. If the user is at another company, or is not using a third-party CA instead of KMS, you will need to manually obtain his or her public key.

- **Add Digital Signature To Outgoing Message.** Selecting this box adds a digital signature to the message.

When you receive an encrypted message, you will see the familiar blue lock next to the envelope icon for the message. A digitally signed message will have a quill next to it. In either case, after you open the message you can double-click either icon in the upper right-hand corner of the message to see the details about the certificate used to either encrypt or digitally sign the message.

Recovering and Revoking Keys

You should expect some users to lose their security settings, most likely through some problem dealing with recreating their Outlook profile, reinstalling Outlook, or perhaps receiving a new computer. In these situations you may need to recover a user key in order to re-enroll the user in e-mail security. In other cases, you may need, for security purposes, to revoke a user's ability to use e-mail security. That is why Exchange 2000 gives you the capability to both recover and revoke keys. You can do both on a per-user basis within Active Directory Users and Computers.

Open the Properties dialog box for the user in question and select the Exchange Features tab. Select E-mail Security and click Properties. The E-Mail Security dialog box, shown in Figure 19-29, allows you to recover and revoke a user's keys. If you click Recover, you'll be given a new token to enroll the user within Outlook. If you click Revoke, the user will no longer be able to use e-mail security.

Summary

This chapter covered the basics of public key infrastructure (PKI) and showed you how Certificate Services and the Key Management Service enable the use of PKI within Exchange 2000. It also showed you how to install, configure, and manage both services within the confines of providing e-mail security. In the next chapter, we'll look at how you can utilize clustering to provide high availability of your Exchange server.

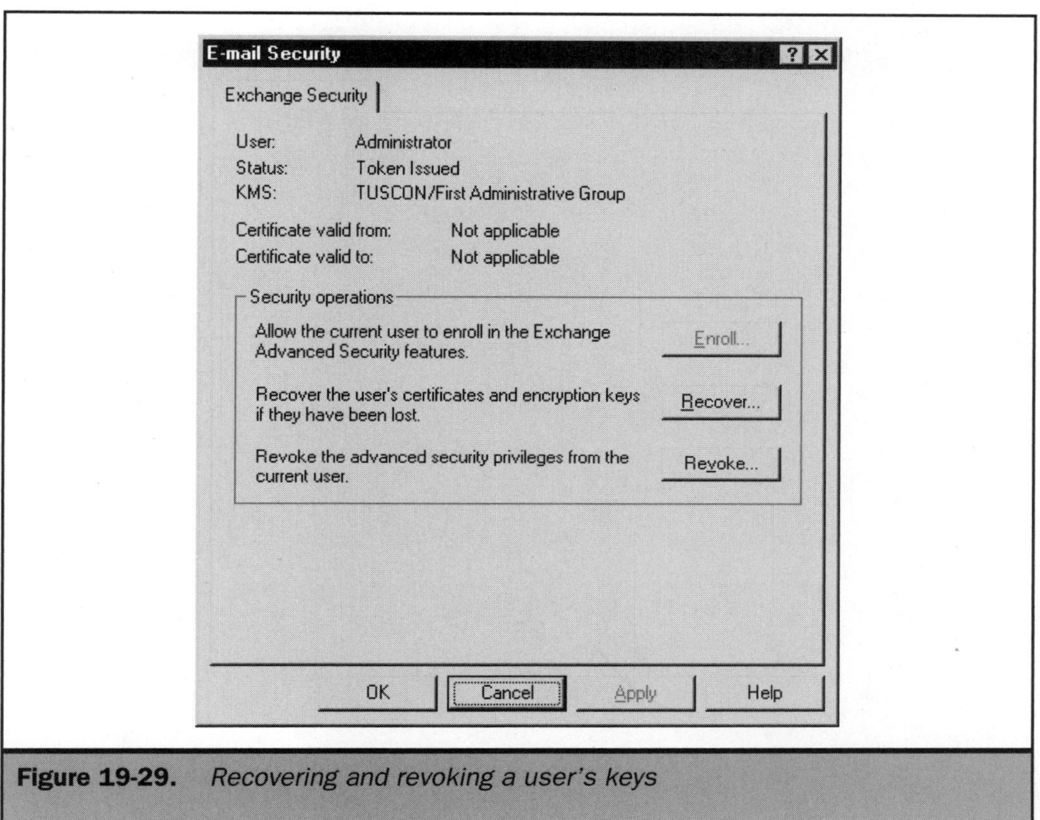

Figure 19-29. *Recovering and revoking a user's keys*

The Complete Reference

Part V

Exchange 2000 Server Scalability and Reliability

Chapter 20

Clustering Exchange 2000

In this chapter, we'll discuss clustering at several levels. First, we'll conduct a brief overview of what clustering is and why you might want to implement clustered Exchange servers. Next, we'll look at how Exchange 2000 works with the Windows 2000 Cluster Service. Then, we'll show you how to install Exchange 2000 Enterprise Server in a cluster environment. We'll also discuss Network Load Balancing and how to use a cluster in a front-end or back-end architecture. Finally, we'll provide an overview of the steps necessary to administer and perform recovery on a clustered Exchange server.

Because Windows 2000 Datacenter Servers can only be installed, configured, and maintained by certified Datacenter OEMs, this chapter focuses solely on Exchange 2000 Enterprise Servers running in a Windows 2000 Advanced Server cluster.

What Is a Cluster?

A cluster is a group of computers that work together as a single unit to ensure that mission-critical applications and resources are as available as possible. Windows 2000 Advanced Server and Windows 2000 Datacenter Server offer two types of clustering: the Windows 2000 Cluster Service and Network Load Balancing (NLB). Don't be confused by the use of the term "cluster" in the context of NLB. An NLB cluster is not the same as a cluster that's created using the Windows Cluster Service. However, the NLB service uses the term "cluster" to describe the group of servers over which it distributes client calls. Unless otherwise indicated, when we use the term cluster in this chapter, we are referring to the Windows 2000 Cluster Service.

Note *A server can not use the Windows Cluster Service and NLB simultaneously. In other words, a server can not be a member of a Windows 2000 cluster and an NLB cluster at the same time. This is true regardless of what applications the server is running. For more information, see Microsoft Knowledge Base article Q235305.*

Exchange 2000 Enterprise Server supports both clustering and load-balancing, and can be deployed in a manner known as the Front-End/Back-End configuration. This configuration uses back-end servers that are either non-clustered or clustered using the Windows 2000 Cluster Service, and front-end servers that are load-balanced using NLB. We'll talk more about this configuration later in this chapter.

There are two types of cluster models in the industry: the shared-device model and the shared-nothing model. In the shared-device model, applications running in a cluster can access any hardware resource connected to any node in the cluster. In this model, access to the data must be synchronized. In many implementations of this model, a component called a Distributed Lock Manager (DLM) is used for this purpose. A DLM manages access to cluster hardware resources. When multiple applications access the same resource, the DLM resolves any conflicts that might arise.

In the shared-nothing model, only one node can own and access a hardware resource at any given time. When failure on one node occurs, a surviving node can take ownership of the failed node's resources and make them available to users. By default, the Windows 2000 Cluster Service uses the shared-nothing model. It can, however, support the shared-device model if the clustered application provides its own DLM. Exchange 2000 does not include a DLM and therefore supports only the shared-nothing model when clustered with the Windows 2000 Cluster Service.

High Availability

By definition, the goal of a highly available system is to provide continuous access to critical data, applications, and services that keep businesses up and running, regardless of planned or unplanned interruption. High availability refers to a system uptime that approaches 100 percent. For example, an availability level of 99.999 percent (known in the industry as the *Five Nines*), works out to about five minutes of unscheduled downtime per year when calculated on an around-the-clock basis. By comparison, 99.99 percent translates to 52 minutes of downtime per year. A level of 99.9 percent translates to 8.7 hours of downtime, and a level of 99 percent equals about 3.7 days of downtime per year.

Certainly, Internet Service Providers (ISPs) and Application Service Providers (ASPs) hosting Exchange-based messaging and collaboration services will benefit from servers that are highly available. But the need for high availability is not limited to these 365x24x7 environments. Many organizations have services and applications that must be available during normal business hours or at critical times throughout the day. A system failure during these critical periods is unacceptable and often costly for these organizations.

Given the mission-critical nature of messaging in today's business environment, disaster recovery and high availability are at the top of most Exchange 2000 administrators' minds. Keeping Exchange 2000 services continuously available should be a key concern for many organizations.

Fault Tolerance

A fault-tolerant system is one that activates a backup solution when the primary solution fails. Fault tolerance is slightly different from high availability in that fault tolerance focuses on the capability to continue operation in the event of a component failure, power outage, or other similar occurrence. High availability focuses on offering services on a continuous basis. Whereas high availability is geared toward minimizing downtime, fault tolerance is intended to eliminate downtime altogether.

Fault tolerance comes in many forms. Error-correcting memory, symmetric multiprocessor systems, redundant power supplies (with separate power sources), uninterruptible power supplies, and redundant network interface cards are all examples of fault tolerance. The most common use of fault-tolerant technology is in disk subsystems. Disk subsystems that use RAID, which stands for Redundant Array of Inexpensive Disks (or Redundant Array of Independent Disks, or Redundant Array of Inexpensive Devices, depending on who you ask) are considered fault-tolerant. RAID refers to the grouping and usage of individual physical hard disks in a way that provides continued operation in the event of a single disk failure. There is hardware-based RAID (where a hardware RAID controller is used) and software-based RAID (where the functionality is provided by an operating system or application).

There are several forms (levels) of RAID. The most commonly used forms are:

- **RAID-0 - Stripe set without parity**. Stripe sets work well with databases due to the usually random I/O nature of database transactions. In RAID-0, data is divided into blocks and spread in a fixed order across all of the disks in an array. RAID-0 improves read/write performance by spreading operations across multiple disks, so that operations can be performed independently and simultaneously. While RAID-0 provides the highest performance, it does not provide any fault tolerance whatsoever. If a drive in a RAID-0 array fails, all of the data within the stripe set become inaccessible. For this reason, RAID-0 is used infrequently in Exchange deployments.
- **RAID-1 - Mirroring**. Disk mirroring provides a redundant, identical copy of a disk. Data written to the primary disk is also written to a mirror disk. RAID-1 provides fault tolerance and generally improves read performance, but it may also degrade write performance. Because dual-write operations can degrade system performance, many mirror-set implementations use duplexing, where each mirror drive has its own disk controller. While the mirror approach provides good fault tolerance, it is relatively expensive to implement because only half of the available disk space can be used for storage. The other half is needed for the overhead required for mirroring. Nonetheless, if your budget permits, RAID-1 is ideal for the operating system and the Exchange transaction logs because it provides redundancy and better write performance than RAID-5. In addition, RAID-1 works well for protecting the quorum resource in your cluster.
- **RAID-5 - Stripe set with parity**. RAID-5 provides redundancy of all data on the array, allowing a single failed disk to be replaced, in most cases without system downtime. RAID-5 offers lower performance than RAID-0 or RAID-1, but higher reliability and faster recovery. RAID-5 uses the equivalent of one disk for storing the parity data. The data and parity information are arranged on the disk array so that they are always on different disks. Because it offers superior fault tolerance, RAID-5 is best-suited for Exchange databases.

There are other implementations of RAID, such as RAID-0+1 (also referred to as RAID-10), RAID-2, RAID-3, and so on, but these are typically proprietary implementations that are unique to the hardware manufacturers that support them.

Check with your hardware manufacturer for details on what levels of RAID are supported in your disk subsystem.

While you can and should use fault-tolerant hardware components in your cluster implementation, Windows 2000 clusters are not completely fault-tolerant systems. Fault tolerance is a term that is more appropriate for systems with greater resilience than Windows 2000 clusters.

What Problems Does Clustering Solve?

Most researchers agree that the *least* likely component to fail in your environment is hardware. In fact, the leading causes of downtime—poorly-trained personnel, power outages, and third-party tools and drivers that interfere with the operating system—are related to events outside the server. Clustering will not help you solve those problems. For example, a cluster will not save you from software incompatibilities, corrupt databases, viruses, or other catastrophes.

Clustering is best implemented when a substantial proportion of your server downtime is caused by hardware failure. If your organization's leading cause of downtime is the result of failures in administration, software, or infrastructure, an investment in clustering technology may not reduce your downtime. First you need to assess the reasons for server downtime in your organization, look at the problems that clustering solves, and then make a business decision as to whether clustering is an appropriate solution.

The primary focus of clustering is solving problems that arise from hardware failure, such as a blown CPU, bad memory, or the loss of an entire server. In addition, clustering allows you to continue providing resources during planned outages that may cause downtime for users. A cluster system can allow resources to be manually moved—or *failed over*—to one server while the other is brought down to perform a *rolling upgrade*, a configuration change, or other maintenance.

A rolling upgrade is the process of applying a service pack or other hardware or software update to each node in the cluster while the other node continues providing service. Rolling upgrades are typically a series of stages:

- Move groups from the node to be upgraded to another node.
- Take the node that will be upgraded offline.
- Perform the installation on or upgrade to the offline node.
- Bring the upgraded node online.
- Move the groups back to the upgraded node.

Then repeat this process on each node in the cluster until the entire cluster is upgraded. Rolling upgrades are very attractive from a server management standpoint because services are only unavailable during the time it takes to move resources from one node to the other.

By design, clusters help increase uptime. Increased uptime really means reduced downtime. Clustering can help reduce both planned and unplanned downtime. When any mission-critical system fails, the consequences can include lost revenue, interruption of services to customers, and loss of productivity among knowledge workers. In organizations of all sizes, failures incur costs in many areas. Hidden costs often include damage to your reputation among customers, suppliers, and end-users, and the perception that your organization isn't able to satisfy customer needs.

Understanding the limitations of clustering is just as important as understanding the benefits. While clustering protects against the failure of a node in the cluster, it does not provide any protection against other problems, such as network failures, database corruption, loss of shared storage, or disasters. Therefore, before implementing a cluster in your environment, you should evaluate whether this solution really solves enough of your problems to justify its cost. Clustering adds complexity to your environment and administration. Therefore, it is important that you understand and evaluate this technology in relation to your overall goals and the needs of your network.

Cluster Terminology

Clustering introduces several new terms which should be thoroughly understood before clusters of any kind are implemented. Let's take a moment to review these key terms:

- **Node** The term used to refer to a server that is a member of a cluster.
- **Resource** A hardware or software component that exists in a cluster, such as a disk, an IP address, a network name, or an instance of an Exchange 2000 component.
- **Group** A combination of resources that are managed as a unit of failover. Groups are also known as *resource groups* or *failover groups*.
- **Dependency** An alliance between two or more resources in the cluster architecture. You'll need to understand cluster resource dependencies when installing a cluster.
- **Failover/failback** The process of moving resources from one server to another. Failover can occur when one server experiences a failure of some sort or when you, the administrator, initiate a proactive failover.
- **Quorum resource** This is a special type of cluster resource that provides persistent arbitration mechanisms by allowing one node to gain control of it and then defending that node's control. In addition, it provides physical storage that can be accessed by any node in the cluster (only one node can access the quorum at any given time). The quorum also maintains access to the most current version of the cluster database, and if a failure occurs, the quorum writes the changes to the cluster database.
- **Heartbeat** The network and Remote Procedure Call (RPC) traffic that flows between servers in a cluster. Windows 2000 clusters communicate by using RPC calls on IP sockets with User Datagram Protocol (UDP) packets. Heartbeats are

single UDP packets sent between each node every 1.2 seconds. These packets are used to confirm that the node's network interface is still active.

- **Membership** This term is used to describe the orderly addition and removal of active nodes to and from the cluster.
- **Global update** This term refers to the propagation of cluster configuration changes to all members. The cluster registry is maintained through this mechanism.
- **Cluster registry** Inside the Windows 2000 registry is the cluster registry—also known as the cluster database. This maintains configuration information on each member in the cluster, as well as on resources and parameters. This information is stored on the quorum resource.
- **Virtual server** A virtual server is a combination of configuration information and cluster resources, such as an IP address, network name, and application resource.
- **Active/Passive** This terms describes applications that run as a single instance in a cluster. Exchange 5.5 supported only Active/Passive clustering; only one instance of Exchange could exist in the cluster. This meant that one node typically sat idle until a failover occurred.
- **Active/Active** This describes applications that can exist as multiple instances in a cluster. Most Exchange 2000 components support Active/Active clustering, allowing you to create multiple virtual servers within the same cluster. This means that both nodes can actively service clients.
- **Shared storage** This refers to the external SCSI or fibre channel storage enclosures and the disks contained therein. Shared storage is a requirement for multi-node clusters. Although this storage is shared, only one node can access an external storage resource at any given time.

Failover and Clients

When an Exchange client such as Outlook connects to and communicates with an Exchange server, it creates a shared state for that session. One of the limitations of clustering is that this shared state is not preserved when a failover occurs. During failover, the Cluster service checkpoints the application, moves it to a surviving node, and then instantiates it according to its dependencies. This is analogous to stopping and starting the application; any in-progress transactions are aborted, and the shared state between the client and the server is lost.

In Exchange 5.5, failover of an average-sized information store could take anywhere from two to 10 minutes. Using fast technology like fibre channel storage and state-of-the-art disk controllers, failover could have been reduced; but even then, it still took approximately two to three minutes. Exchange 2000 reduces failover time by running the Information Store at all times, even in Active/Passive configurations that only contain a single EVS. As a result, when failover occurs, the surviving node takes ownership only of the resources, and then mounts the databases. Because the information store process is already running, the databases are mounted more quickly. Therefore, in some cluster implementations, you might see failover times of less than a minute.

No matter how quickly failover occurs, the shared state is still lost. Outlook includes the ability to reconnect to the Exchange server once it is available again, but any messages in progress could be lost. In addition, during failover, Outlook clients might not be able to view the contents of their mailbox. However, as soon as database is mounted, access to their mailbox should be restored dynamically without requiring a restart of the Outlook client.

Windows 2000 Clustering

Windows 2000 Advanced Server provides three clustering technologies that can be used independently or in concert: network load balancing (NLB), component load balancing (CLB, available with Application Center 2000), and the Windows 2000 Cluster Service.

NLB provides load balancing on incoming IP traffic for clusters of up to 32 nodes. It increases the availability and scalability of IP-based applications and services, such as a Web server. NLB is discussed in more detail later in this chapter. CLB is a feature of Application Center 2000. This service provides load balancing of different instances of the same COM+ components that are running on one or more servers. If a server or service fails, CLB re-routes client calls away from the failed server, ensuring continuous availability of the COM+ component to network requests.

Windows 2000 includes a service and software that exists as three components: the Cluster service, a Resource Monitor, and the Cluster Administrator application. The Cluster service runs on all nodes in a cluster and coordinates all cluster activities performed by each node. Working in concert, the Cluster service instances that are on each node communicate with one another regarding cluster events, such as resource or group failure or failover. The Cluster service also works closely with one or more Resource Monitors.

Resource Monitors are the Cluster service workhorses. The Resource Monitors isolate the Cluster service from individual resources, ensuring that no resource can directly affect the cluster. They monitor cluster resources, loading the various resource DLLs to provide the Cluster service with status and state information on each resource. Exchange 2000 includes its own resource DLL—ExRes.dll—making it a fully cluster-aware application. You'll typically need only one Resource Monitor to manage the entire Exchange 2000 cluster.

Windows 2000 clusters are managed using Cluster Administrator. Cluster Administrator (cluadmin.exe), which is shown in Figure 20-1, is a GUI tool installed

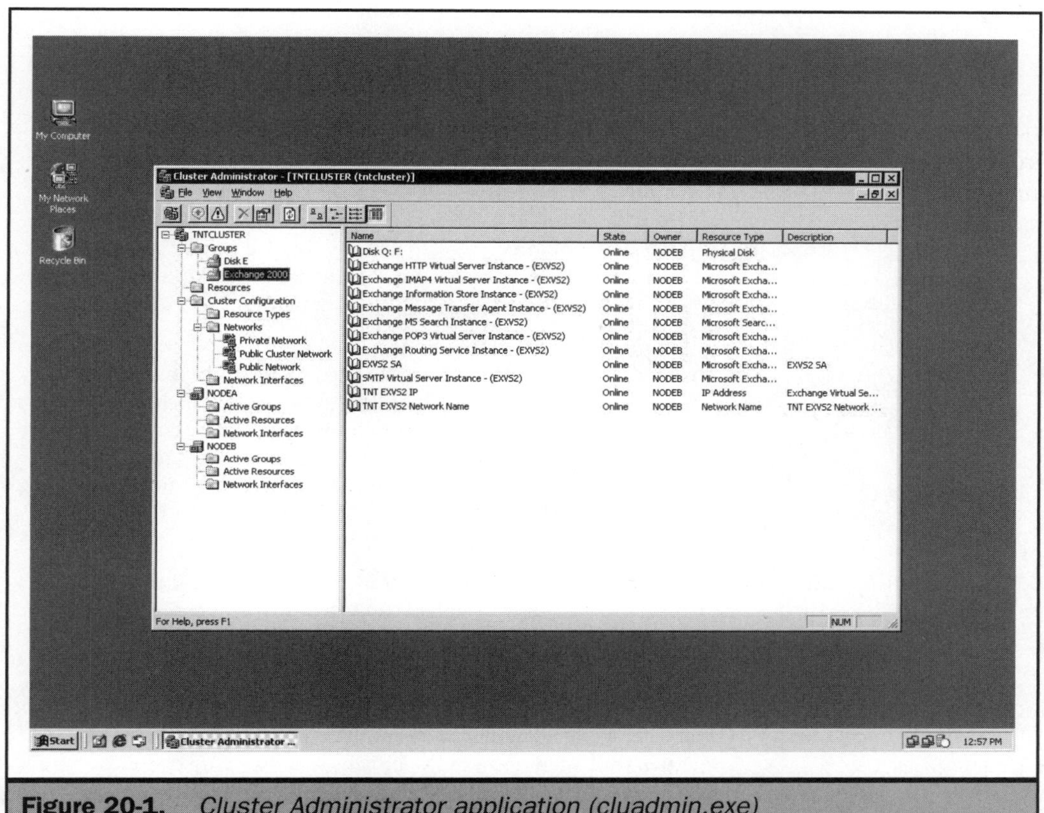

Figure 20-1. *Cluster Administrator application (cluadmin.exe)*

on each node when you install the Cluster service. Although Cluster Administrator resembles a Microsoft Management Console (MMC) snap-in, it is not an MMC snap-in, and therefore cannot be added to or integrated with any management consoles you may be using.

Microsoft's Cluster Service is implemented as a set of independent components that form a logical service. Several components work with the Windows 2000 operating system to provide cluster services. These components are listed in Table 20-1.

Component	Description/Function
Checkpoint Manager	This ensures that the Cluster service can successfully failover cluster-unaware applications by performing registry checkpointing. It monitors a registered resource's registry data and saves any changes—called checkpoint data—to the quorum recovery log. It also writes a checkpoint to the quorum disk when a resource is taken offline. In addition, when a node takes ownership of a resource, the Checkpoint Manager brings the resource's registry data up-to-date before the resource is brought online.
Communications Manager	This component—also known as the Cluster Network Driver—is responsible for delivering cluster heartbeat messages, responding to cluster connection requests, and notifying the entire cluster when resources are brought online or are taken offline. It also manages communication between the nodes in the cluster and maintains continual communication with the other nodes via RPCs.
Configuration Database Manager	The Configuration Database Manager manages and maintains information about the cluster configuration in the configuration database. The configuration database is stored in the registry of each node. It contains information about all of the entities of the cluster, such as resources, groups and the cluster itself.
Event Log Manager	The Event Log Manager is new to Windows 2000 clusters. It ensures that each node of the cluster has the same event log entries by performing event log replication between all nodes in the cluster.
Event Processor	This component is responsible for initializing the Cluster service and passing messages to and from the nodes in the cluster. It passes messages called *event signals* that are associated with such activities as status changes and requests to open or close applications. These event signals include critical information that must be disseminated to the other cluster components.
Failover Manager	This component is responsible for deciding which node in a cluster will take control of a resource in the event of a failover.
Global Update Manager	This component provides an interface for other components in the Cluster service to initiate and mange updates. It allows state changes (such as online to offline) to be propagated to the other nodes in the cluster. This component provides an atomic (all or none) update service to cluster members and cluster components.

Table 20-1. *Summary of Cluster Service Components*

Component	Description/Function
Log Manager	The Log Manager writes changes to recovery logs stored on the quorum resource. The recovery logs—also known as quorum logs—contain the transactions that have been made against the quorum.
Membership Manager	This component manages cluster membership and monitors the health of nodes in the cluster. When a node fails, the Node Manager will notify the Membership Manager, which triggers a regroup event. This event causes all nodes to update their membership information.
Node Manager	This component assigns resource group control to nodes based on group preference lists and node availability. The Node Manager detects failures using heartbeat messages that are delivered by the Communications Manager.
Object Manager	The Object Manager maintains an in-memory database of all cluster objects, such as nodes, groups, and resources. This database is used for managing Cluster service objects.
Resource Manager	This component is responsible for all resources and dependencies. It oversees and initiates such actions as starting or stopping resources and initiating resource group failover. This component receives resources and cluster state information from the Resource Monitor and Node Managers.
Resource Monitor	The Resource Monitor provides a communication mechanism between the Cluster Service and applications resources (also known as Resource DLLs). Resource Monitors each run in their own process and communicate with the Cluster service using RPCs. By default, there is a single Resource Monitor enabled per node; however, you can optionally employ additional Resource Monitors as needed.

Table 20-1. *Summary of Cluster Service Components* (continued)

These components, and their relationships to one another are illustrated in Figure 20-2.

Cluster-Aware vs. Cluster-Unaware

Applications that run in a cluster are separated into two categories: *cluster-aware* applications and *cluster-unaware* applications. Both types of applications can run in a cluster and provide highly available resources. The difference between cluster-aware and cluster-unaware applications is that cluster-aware applications include their own

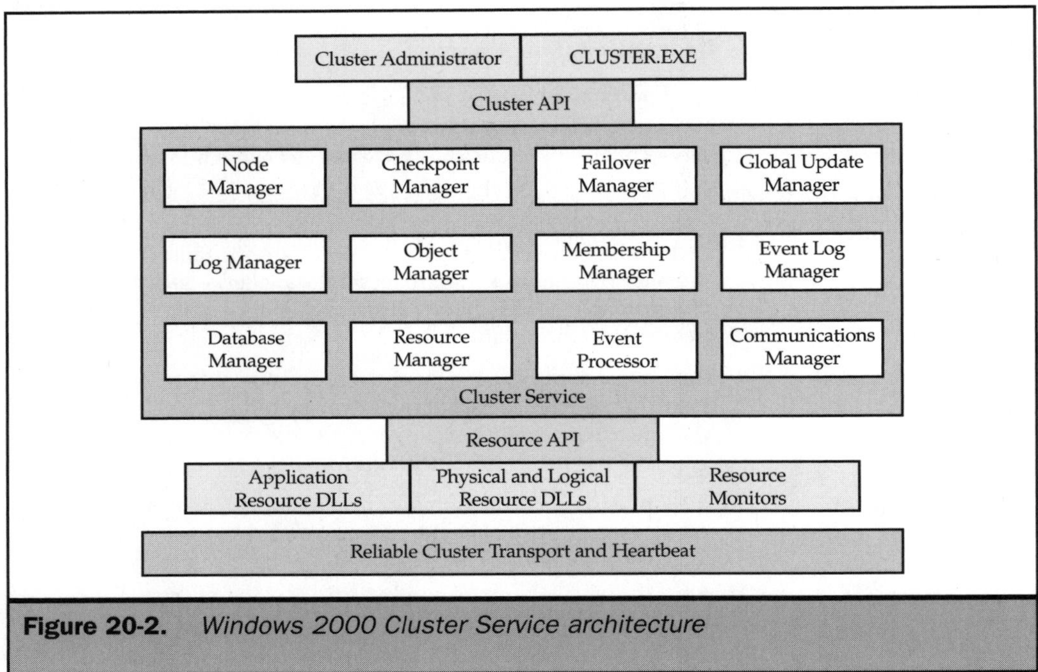

Figure 20-2. *Windows 2000 Cluster Service architecture*

Resource DLL which programmatically calls the Cluster Application Programming Interface (API) to determine whether or not resources are online and available. Resource Monitors track the status of cluster-aware resources by polling them through the application's resource DLL. This polling consists of a brief *LooksAlive* query and more thorough *IsAlive* query. If a LooksAlive or IsAlive call fails, the Resource Monitor initiates failover of the resource.

Cluster-unaware applications do not have any such resource DLL. Instead, they rely on the generic resource DLLs included with the Windows 2000 Cluster service. Exchange 5.5 Server–Enterprise Edition, which is not cluster-aware, was one of the first applications to take advantage of Windows clustering. The only component of Exchange 5.5 is the Setup process, which uses an Exchange-provided resource DLL to install Exchange into the cluster. Once installed, however, Exchange 5.5 used a general resource DLL that was included with Microsoft Cluster Server.

Exchange 2000's Resource DLL

The Exchange 2000 components that are supported in a Windows 2000 cluster are fully cluster-aware. As was previously mentioned, Exchange 2000 includes its own resource DLL, ExRes.dll, that handles such tasks as bringing resources online and taking them offline, checking resources with LooksAlive and IsAlive calls, and reporting failures. In addition, the Cluster service uses ExRes.dll to stop and start Exchange 2000 services.

ExRes.dll acts as a layer between the Exchange resources and the cluster's resource monitor. As you can see in Figure 20-3, the Cluster service communicates through a resource monitor to ExRes.dll, which in turn communicates with the Exchange resources.

Exchange 2000 Support for Windows 2000 Clustering

Exchange 2000 Enterprise Server supports two-node Active/Active clustering. This means that multiple instances of Exchange 2000 can exist in the cluster, which can only contain two nodes.

Note *With Service Pack 1, Exchange 2000 will support four-node Windows 2000 Datacenter Server clusters. Exchange 2000 was certified for Windows 2000 Datacenter in early 2001, and Exchange 2000 Service Pack 1 (SP1) will introduce support for four-node clusters. The released version of Exchange 2000 already contains the code needed to support four-node clusters, but this code was disabled because Datacenter server hadn't yet been released. SP1 activates the code and enables four-node Exchange 2000 clusters.*

Exchange 2000 exists as one or more virtual servers in a cluster. All of the components and resources required to run a virtual server are grouped into an Exchange virtual server (EVS). Multiple virtual servers that share the same physical disk resource must exist within

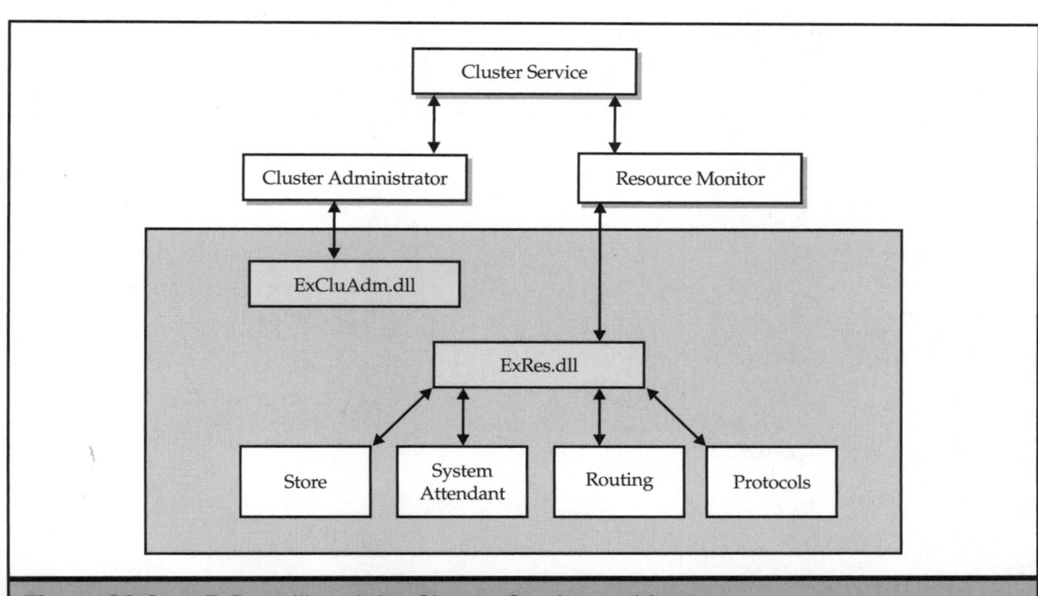

Figure 20-3. *ExRes.dll and the Cluster Service architecture*

the same resource group. This limitation is enforced to ensure that all resources and virtual servers all fail over as a single unit.

As you can see in Table 20-2, not all of Exchange 2000's components are supported in a cluster environment. While many components are supported in an Active/Active configuration, some only support Active/Passive, and others are not supported at all and therefore can not be clustered. Table 20-2 lists the components of Exchange 2000 according to their clustering capabilities.

There are several requirements that need to be met before you can install Exchange 2000 in a cluster:

- You must use SCSI or Fibre Channel storage for both internal and external cluster storage.
- Each node must have identical memory and processor configurations.
- All hardware must be listed on Microsoft's Hardware Compatibility List (HCL) in the cluster category.
- You must run Windows 2000 Advanced Server or Windows 2000 Datacenter Server on your clusters.
- You must run Exchange 2000 Enterprise Server on your clusters.

Active/Active	Active/Passive	Not Supported
System Attendant	Message Transfer Agent (MTA)	NNTP Virtual Server
Information Store	Chat Services	Instant Messaging
SMTP Virtual Server		Conferencing Services
HTTP Virtual Server		Key Management System
POP3 Virtual Server		Foreign System Connectors (e.g., PROFS, Lotus, etc.)
IMAP4 Virtual Server		
SMTP Connector		
Routing Group Connector		
X.400 Connector		
Microsoft Search		

Table 20-2. *Summary of Supported Exchange 2000 Components in a Cluster Environment*

Installing Exchange 2000 in a Cluster

To install Exchange 2000 into a cluster, the cluster service must already be installed and running on two Windows 2000 Advanced Servers. In this section, we'll show you how to install the Cluster service and Exchange 2000 Enterprise Server into a cluster environment.

The first step in installing the cluster service is to navigate to the Add/Remove Programs icon in the Control Panel, click on the Add/Remove Windows Components button, and then select the Cluster Service checkbox. You'll need the Windows 2000 Advanced Server CD-ROM in order to copy the required files to the hard drive.

During the installation of the cluster service, you'll be taken through the Cluster Service Configuration Wizard. After you click Next through the welcome screen, the Hardware Configuration screen appears. This screen reminds you that Microsoft will only support the cluster service that is running on Hardware Compatibility List (HCL) hardware. You must click on the I Understand button, shown in Figure 20-4, before the Next button will be available to take you to the rest of the wizard.

On the next screen, you'll be asked whether this is the first node in the cluster or whether you are joining an existing cluster. Make the appropriate selection, and then click Next to move to the Cluster Name screen.

Tip *If this is the first node in the cluster, when you click Next, the Wizard will look for an external set of disks upon which to place the quorum resource. The quorum disk must be formatted using NTFS and they must be Basic disks. Dynamic disks are not supported in a cluster. You won't need more than a 500 MB partition for your quorum drive.*

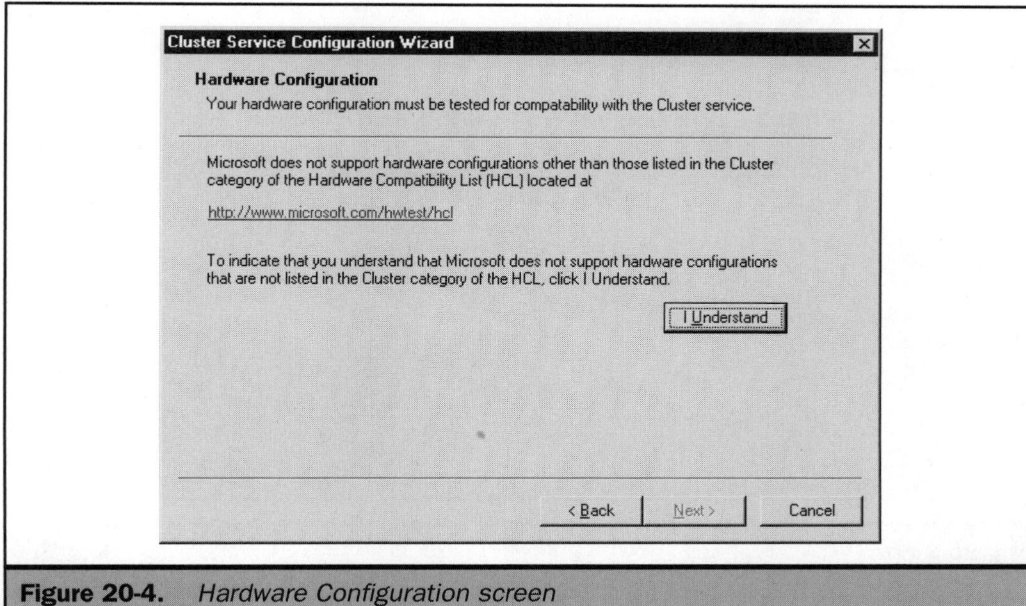

Figure 20-4. *Hardware Configuration screen*

On the Cluster Name screen, enter the name of the cluster. For our purposes, we named the cluster after the city of Duluth. On the next screen, enter the user name and password of the account that you want the cluster service to use for authentication. Be sure to give this account a difficult password; it will have pervasive rights to the cluster service and its resources. You must make the cluster service account a domain administrator or grant it Exchange Full Administrator rights. In addition, this account must have local administrative privileges on each node. If you forget to do this, the installation wizard will ask for your permission to add this account to the local Administrators group.

The next screen is the Add or Remove Managed Disks screen, shown in Figure 20-5. This is where you can specify which physical disks should be managed by the cluster service.

Even though we are using the term "disk" in a singular sense, most cluster implementations include hardware RAID controllers that present a set of disks to the operating system as a single disk.

The next screen is the Cluster File Storage screen, where you specify which physical disk will hold your quorum information, such as the cluster checkpoint and log files. Select the disk you wish to hold this information, and then click Next to the following set of screens, which will ask you to input network information.

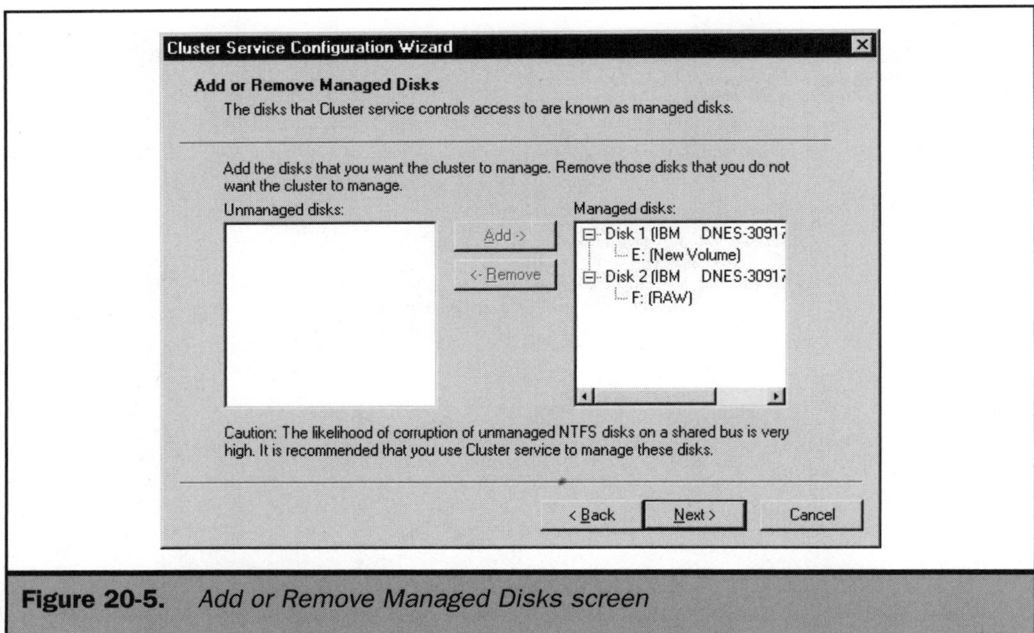

Figure 20-5. *Add or Remove Managed Disks screen*

Microsoft recommends a quorum log file size of 4,096 K. Once you've formed a cluster, use the Cluster Administrator application to modify its properties so the quorum log file resets itself at 4,096 K.

The next screen that requires your input is the Network Connections screen, shown in Figure 20-6. There are several items to configure here. First, you must specify a network name and whether the network is public, private, or mixed. Because we are not running a separate, private network for our heartbeat, we named our network connection the All Connections Network.

Note

Even though we use a mixed network in our illustration, we strongly recommend that you have a private network that is physically separate from your public network for the heartbeat. Also, remember that Microsoft will not support a cluster configuration that has a mixed network. It will only support the public/private network configuration.

The *private* network is a physically separate network that exists between the cluster servers only, as shown in Figure 20-7. It is intended only for the heartbeat, so that even if the public communications between the servers and the users becomes saturated, the heartbeat can pass between the servers without hindrance. The *public* network is the network used by clients and administrators to access the cluster. This means that you'll need two network cards in each server: one for the private network and the other for the public network.

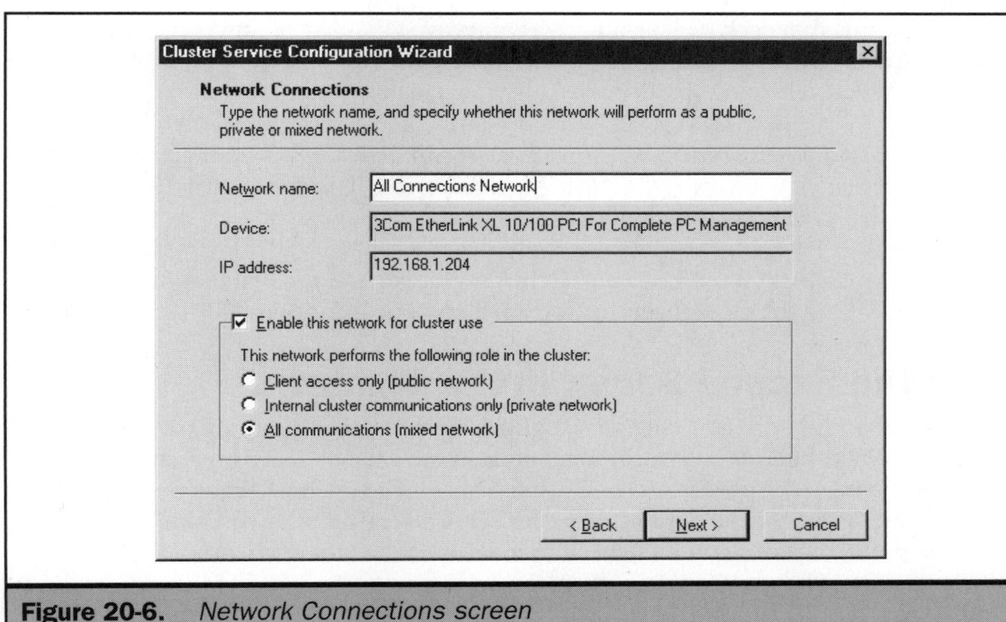

Figure 20-6. *Network Connections screen*

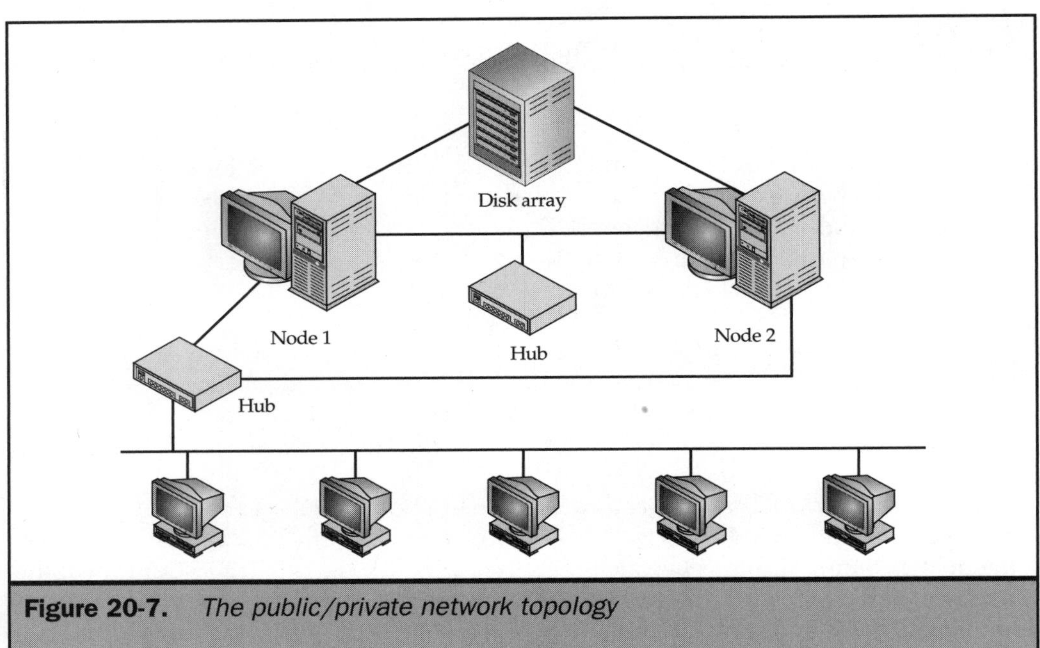

Figure 20-7. *The public/private network topology*

As you can see in Figure 20-8, you'll need to enter an IP address for the cluster itself. This means that each cluster will receive its own IP address, and each network card in each server in the cluster will receive a separate address. Be sure to plan accordingly when reserving IP addresses for your cluster.

The network cards connected to the private network should not be configured with valid Internet (public) addresses. You should use the private IP address blocks 10.0.0.0, 172.16.0.0, or 192.168.0.0.

After you click Next, you'll be able to click on Finish and the installation wizard will finish installing the cluster service software on your Windows 2000 Server.

Installing the Second Server in the Cluster

Installing the second node in a cluster is slightly different from installing the first node. When you specify that this is an additional node in the cluster, you'll be prompted to input the name of the cluster on the Cluster Name screen in the Cluster Service Configuration Wizard. Then, input the cluster service account password and click Next.

At this point, the software will check to make sure that there are no drive-letter conflicts. If any exist, you'll need to make the appropriate changes before moving on with the wizard.

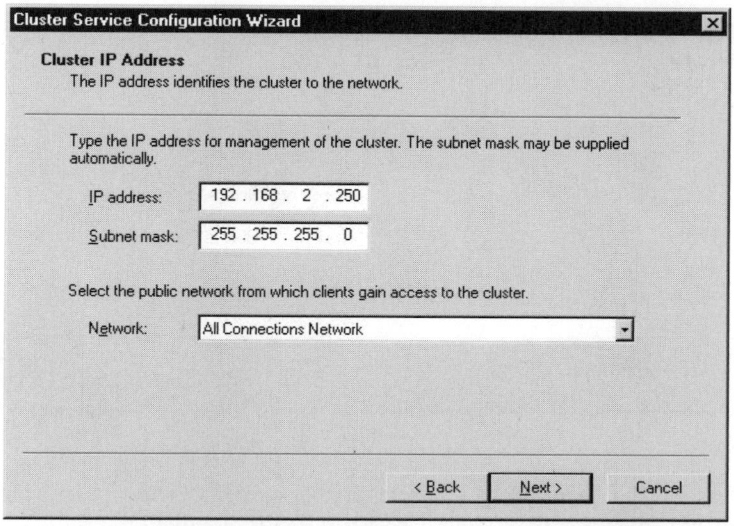

Cluster Service Configuration Wizard

Cluster IP Address
The IP address identifies the cluster to the network.

Type the IP address for management of the cluster. The subnet mask may be supplied automatically.

IP address: 192 . 168 . 2 . 250

Subnet mask: 255 . 255 . 255 . 0

Select the public network from which clients gain access to the cluster.

Network: All Connections Network

< Back | Next > | Cancel

Figure 20-8. *The Cluster IP Address screen*

Installing and Configuring Exchange 2000 in a Cluster

Before you install Exchange 2000 Enterprise Server in a cluster, you'll need to design your storage group architecture. With Exchange 2000's support for multiple virtual servers and multiple storage groups, the planning process can be rather complicated.

Note *Only Exchange 2000 Enterprise Server supports clustering. You can not install Exchange 2000 Server in a cluster.*

Exchange 2000 has a limit of four storage groups per server for both clustered and non-clustered servers. Each cluster node can not have more than four storage groups on it at any given time. When failover occurs and an Exchange virtual server is moved to another server, the total number of storage groups is still limited to four. Your failover rules must be configured to prevent any single server from exceeding the maximum four storage groups per server limitation. This means that your storage group distribution is limited to choices listed in Table 20-3.

Start the Exchange 2000 setup process as if you were installing it on a single server. If you don't know how to install Exchange 2000, please refer to Chapter 6.

Once setup starts, you'll be asked to agree to the licensing agreement and to input the 25-digit product key code. Then, the Component Selection screen will appear. It allows you to choose a minimal, typical, or custom installation. Choose the option that is appropriate for you, and then click Next.

No. Storage Groups on First Node	No. Storage Groups on Second Node
0	4
1	3
2	2
3	1
4	0

Table 20-3. *Distributing storage groups in a cluster*

Be sure to refer to Table 20-3 for a list of Exchange 2000 components that can be installed in a cluster environment. The setup program will allow you to select components that can not be installed in a cluster environment, but don't expect unsupported components to be installed.

The next screen reminds you that Exchange 2000 only supports per-seat licensing, and asks you once more to agree to the licensing agreement. The next screen is the Component Selection Summary screen, and when you click Next through it, the installation process starts.

During installation, Setup will detect the presence of the cluster and install the cluster-aware version of Exchange, as illustrated in Figure 20-9. Click OK to install the cluster version of Exchange 2000. You'll need to reboot each server after Exchange 2000 is installed, and then go to the Cluster Administrator to create the Exchange 2000 virtual server.

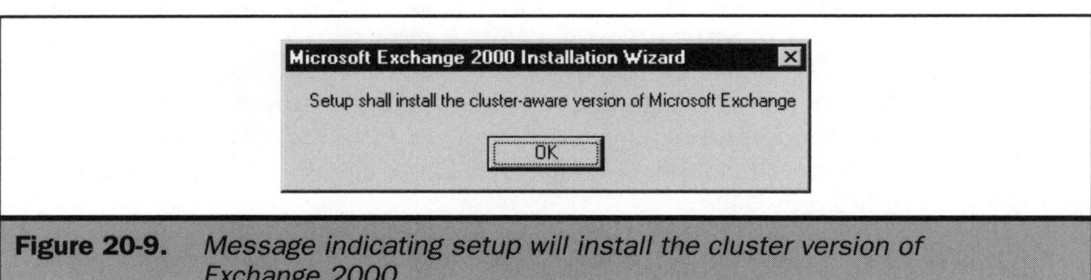

Figure 20-9. *Message indicating setup will install the cluster version of Exchange 2000*

To create an Exchange 2000 virtual server, you must use Cluster Administrator. To begin the installation of a new Exchange 2000 virtual server, create a new cluster group. To create a new group, right-click on the Groups container, point to New, and then select Group. The New Group Wizard starts. On the New Group screen, enter a name for the group and a description, as shown in Figure 20-10. The name you enter here is not the same name you will use for the network name of the Exchange virtual server.

Next, select the preferred owners of the group and list them in order of priority, from top to bottom. Be sure to make only one node the preferred owner, because if you designate both nodes as preferred owners and one node fails, the resource group will failover and failback repeatedly, effectively taking those resources offline. When you click Finish, the group will be created but will be offline. The small, yellow triangle and exclamation point over the icon indicates this.

Note *Remember that for each group you create in a cluster environment, you must have an at least one available disk, and a network name and IP address resources that are unique. Hence, the number of groups that can be created on a cluster is limited by the number of available resources.*

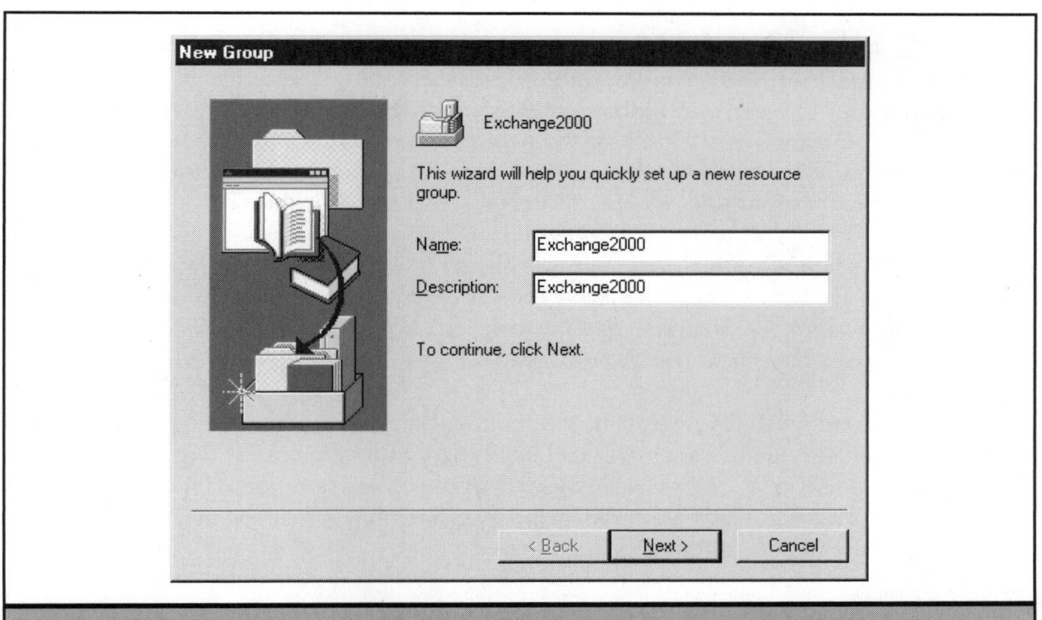

Figure 20-10. *Naming a new Exchange cluster group*

Creating an Exchange 2000 Virtual Server in a Cluster

Once you've created an empty resource group, you need to populate it with the required resources. Each Exchange resource group requires the following minimum resources to function:

- Unique IP address
- Unique network name
- One or more available disk resources
- Exchange System Attendant Resource

The first step is to add an available disk resource to the group. If you have not created resources for all of your available disks, you can do so using Cluster Administrator. Once you've created the resource group, add to it the shared disk resources you want to allocate to this EVS.

The next steps, which are described below, are to add an IP address and network name resource, and create an Exchange System Attendant resource. After adding the System Attendant resource, the additional Exchange 2000 resources (information store, MTA, routing, protocol virtual servers, and MS Search) will be automatically added.

Creating EVS Resources

To create a new IP address resource, right-click the Exchange resource group that you just created, point to New, and then select Resource. The New Resource Wizard starts. First, enter a name and description for the new resource, as shown in Figure 20-11. Then, click on the Resource type down-arrow and select IP address. If you want this resource to run in a separate Resource Monitor, select the checkbox.

Note *Resources typically don't need their own Resource Monitor. Separate Resource Monitors are used to isolate problematic or "buggy" resources from the rest of the cluster. You can safely assume that Exchange-related resources do not fall into this category and therefore do not require being run in a separate Resource Monitor.*

The next screen in the New Resource Wizard, shown in Figure 20-12, prompts you to specify which servers in the cluster can be owners of this resource. Only those servers selected will be available to be owners of the resource when a failover occurs. Specify at least two servers in your cluster to own each resource. The order of servers listed on this screen does not matter.

The next screen is the Dependencies screen, where you will specify which resources must be running in order for this resource to start properly.

New Resource

IP Address

Name: IP Address

Description: IP Address

Resource type: IP Address

Group: Exchange2000

Run this resource in a separate Resource Monitor

To continue, click Next.

< Back Next > Cancel

Figure 20-11. *Creating the IP address resource for the Exchange 2000 resource group*

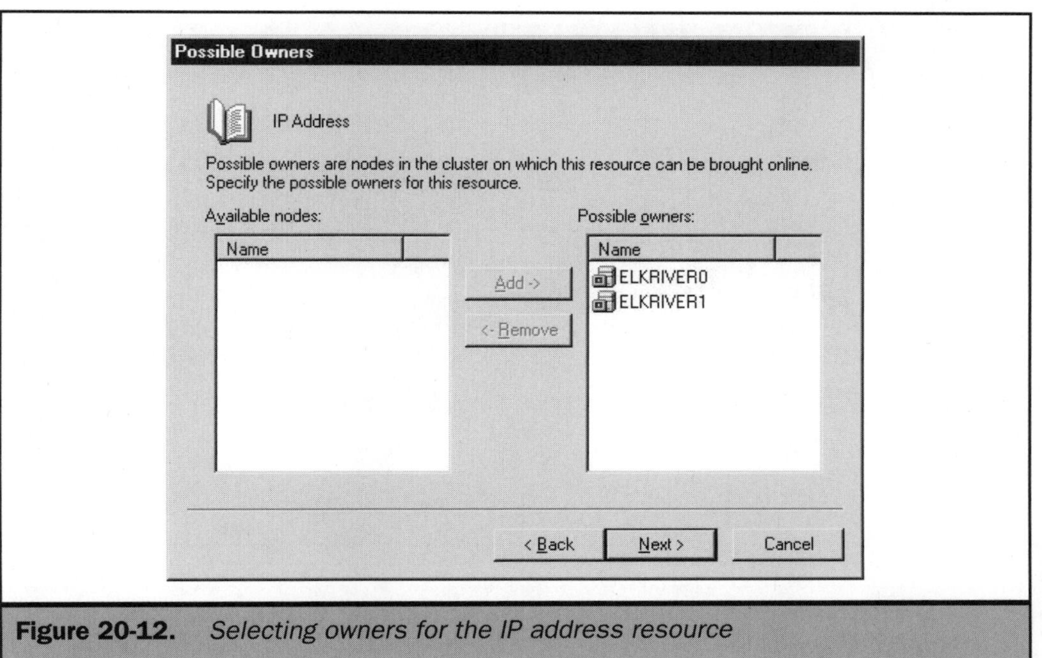

Figure 20-12. *Selecting owners for the IP address resource*

Although the IP address resource does not have any resource dependencies, it is generally a good idea to make it dependent on your disk resource. While the IP address resource is capable of coming online simultaneously with your disk resource(s),it won't do any good without the disk resource. Therefore, there's no point in bringing your IP address resource online unless your disk resources come online, too.

Click Next to bring up the IP address screen, and then enter the virtual server's IP address and subnet mask, as shown in Figure 20-13. Notice that there is no place to enter a default gateway. The cluster service will use the routing table entries to route packets outside the local subnet. Once you click Next, a message pop-up box should indicate that the IP address has been created successfully.

At this point, the IP address resource is created, but it is not online. You can bring it online in the Cluster Administrator by right-clicking on the IP address resource and selecting Bring Online. It should take a few seconds to start this resource.

Next, add a network name resource to the Exchange 2000 resource group. Start the process of creating a new resource as you did for the IP address resource. After selecting the possible owners, select the IP address resource as the dependency for this resource. Then, enter the network name, which will be the public name for this Exchange 2000 virtual server. Click Finish when you're done.

Finally, you need to create the System Attendant resource. To do this, right-click on the Exchange 2000 resource group, point to New, and then select Resource. This time,

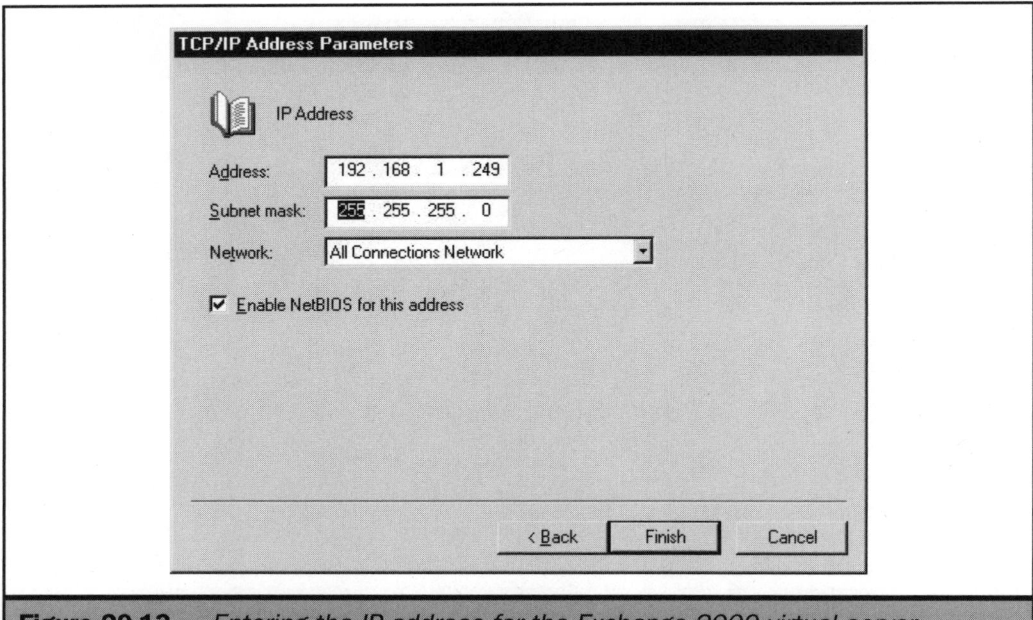

Figure 20-13. *Entering the IP address for the Exchange 2000 virtual server*

instead of selecting the IP address, select the Microsoft Exchange System Attendant resource, as shown in Figure 20-14.

Next, choose which servers in the cluster can be possible owners of this resource. Then click Next to go to the Dependencies screen, as shown in Figure 20-15, and specify which resources should be dependencies of this resource. Because the System Attendant resource depends on both the network name and the physical disk resource, add them both into the right pane.

Note *Each hardware manufacturer is required to provide a cluster resource DLL that enables their disks to act as cluster-aware resources. The Windows Cluster Service expects disk resource DLLs to identify the disks as a "Physical Disk." Some IBM and Compaq cluster configurations do not identify in this manner. If this happens, you will not be able to create the System Attendant resource until you obtain an updated driver. For more information on this issue, see Microsoft Knowledge Base article Q281450.*

On the next screen, you'll be asked for the directory in which you wish to store data. This is an important choice, because you're specifying the location for this virtual server's services, storage groups, and databases. Be sure that you've thought this through before you enter your selection. If the folder doesn't exist, the wizard will create it at this point. Click on Finish and the System Attendant resource will be created.

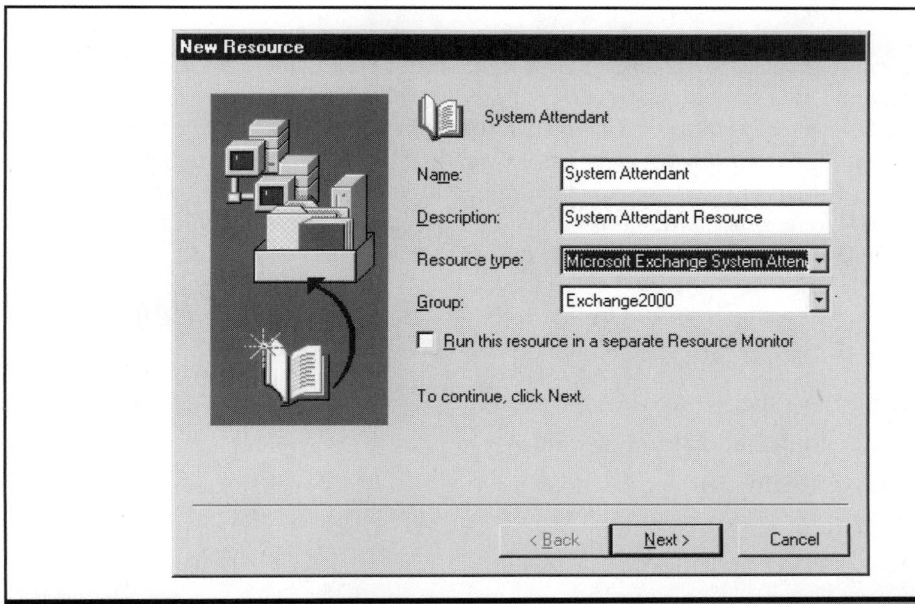

Figure 20-14. *Adding the Microsoft Exchange System Attendant resource*

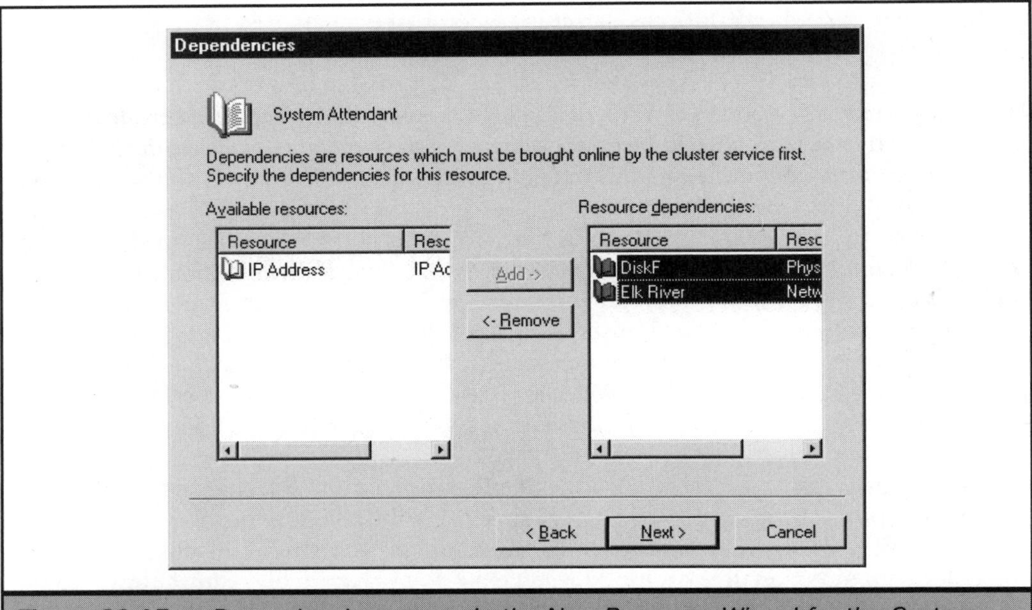

Figure 20-15. *Dependencies screen in the New Resource Wizard for the System Attendant resource*

Tip *If you failed to delegate Exchange Full Administrator permissions on the Exchange organization object to the cluster service user account, you'll encounter the following Win32 error message from the Microsoft Exchange Cluster Administrator Extension indicating that "an unknown error has occurred." Delegating control to the cluster service user account should resolve this error. Also, until you delegate control to the cluster service user account on the Exchange organization object, you'll be unable to create the System Attendant resource in the cluster.*

Creating a new system attendant resource will automatically create the following resources:

- Exchange Message Transfer Agent Instance
- Exchange Information Store Instance
- Exchange Routing Service Instance
- SMTP Virtual Server Instance
- Exchange IMAP4 Virtual Server Instance
- Exchange POP3 Virtual Server Instance
- Exchange HTTP Virtual Server Instance
- Exchange MS Search Instance

Each of these instances can be started individually or in concert by right-clicking on the Exchange 2000 resource group and selecting Bring Online.

Only one public folder store is permitted in the cluster. Therefore, if you create new Exchange resource groups after one exists in the cluster, you must delete the public folder store before bringing the new group online.

To create another Exchange 2000 virtual server in the cluster, you'll need a unique IP address, another network name, and an available disk resource. When creating multiple virtual servers in a cluster, remember to stay within the four storage-group limit in your failover scenarios.

The New Resource Wizard is context sensitive and will present you with the screens necessary to configure and install the type of resource that you've chosen.

Administering an Exchange 2000 Virtual Server

In this section, we'll provide an overview of administering an Exchange 2000 virtual server in a cluster. We won't discuss how to administer the Exchange services themselves, but rather how to administer the Exchange resources within the cluster. Cluster administrative actions are performed using the Cluster Administrator application or the Cluster.exe command line utility.

You can install Cluster Administrator on a non-clustered Windows 2000 server or on Windows 2000 Professional by executing Adminpak.msi from the i386 folder on the Windows 2000 Server CD.

Let's look first at how to manually initiate a failover and failback of your Exchange 2000 virtual server using Cluster Administrator. Manual failover is typically used when performing scheduled maintenance on one of the nodes in the cluster, or when you are performing a *rolling upgrade*. Rolling upgrades refer to upgrades made to hardware or software components within a cluster without impacting the availability of services or applications.

To initiate a manual failover of an Exchange 2000 virtual server from one node to another node, right-click on the resource group containing your EVS and select Move Group. This will take the group's resources offline, move the group to the other node, and instantiate them according to their dependencies. If all of the resources do not come online, failback can occur. If this happens, you will need to troubleshoot the cause of the failure.

We also recommend rigorously testing your cluster prior to putting it into production by simulating failures. For example, you can simply power off one of the nodes to simulate a power outage. You should also experiment with disconnecting network cables and simulating heavy stress. In some implementations, a disconnected network interface that affects clients may go undetected by the cluster service and its resource monitor. You definitely want to know how your cluster is going to react to a broken network connection before it begins servicing any clients.

Simulating the anticipated full load is necessary to ensure that your Exchange server remains able to respond to LooksAlive and IsAlive queries in time. If an EVS is under so much stress that it is unable to respond to these polls, failover can, and likely will, occur.

To initiate a manual failback of the Exchange resource group, perform the same actions you did to initiate the failover. This will take the group's resources offline, move the group back to the original node, and instantiate them according to their dependencies.

Configuring Resources

You can specify how a resource should behave when a failure occurs. To do this, navigate to the Advanced tab of the resource's properties, which is shown in Figure 20-16.

There are two restart options to choose from: **Do not restart** and **Restart**. These options determine what will happen if this resource fails. If an individual resource fails, that does not necessarily mean that a failover will occur. In fact, if you set this resource to **Do not restart**, the resource will remain in a failed state until administrative action is taken, but the resource group will not necessarily failover to the other node.

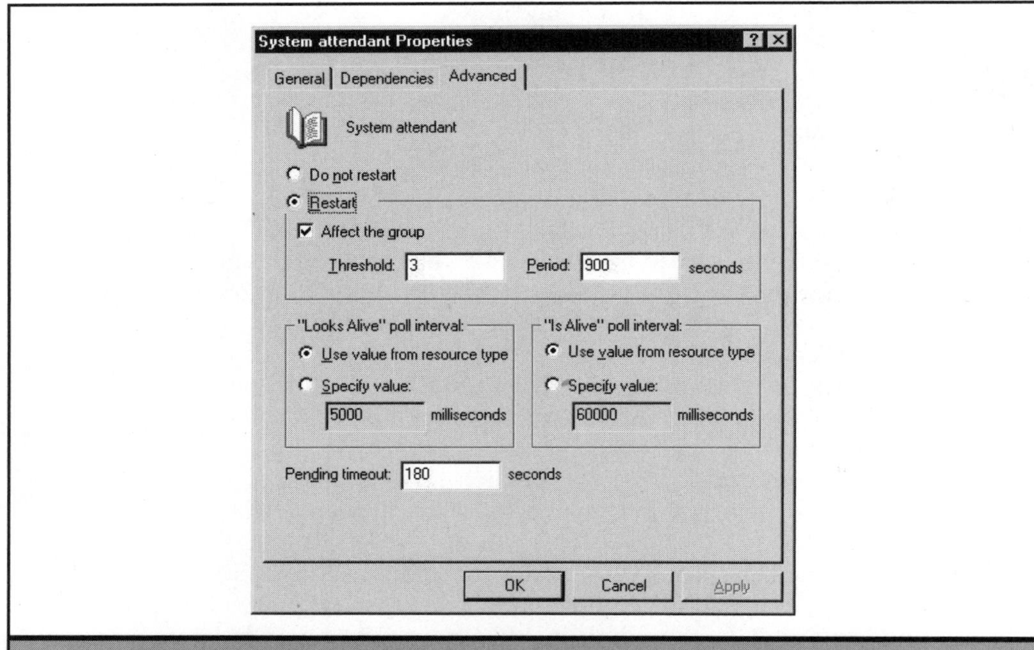

Figure 20-16. *Advanced tab for the System Attendant's resource properties*

If you configure a resource to **Restart**, and you check the **Affect the group** checkbox, you can specify the number of times it will restart, and a time limit (in seconds) for the restart attempts. These are the **Threshold** and **Period** fields, respectively. For example, if you set the **Threshold** to 3 and the **Period** to 900, failover will occur if the attempt to bring the resource online fails 3 times within 900 seconds.

Each application's resource DLL includes default polling intervals for both LooksAlive and IsAlive queries. If you want to override the defaults, you can also specify, in milliseconds, how often you want the to poll this resource.

Finally, the **Pending timeout** value, which is measured in seconds, is the amount of time a resource can remain in a pending state (for example, offline pending or online pending). We recommend using the default of 180 seconds (3 minutes).

Configuring Resource Groups

If you examine the properties of a resource group, you'll find three tabs: General, Failover, and Failback.

The General tab, shown in Figure 20-17, is used to modify the preferred owner is for the resource group. This tab also displays editable fields containing the resource group name and description.

As was previously mentioned, be sure to make only one node the preferred owner. If you designate both nodes as preferred owners and one node fails, the resource group will failover and failback repeatedly, effectively taking those resources offline.

On the Failover tab, shown in Figure 20-18, you can configure **Threshold** and **Period** settings. The threshold value specifies the number of times the resource group can failover during the failover period. If the number of failovers during the specified period exceeds the threshold, the resource group will remain offline, and therefore be unavailable until administrative action is taken.

On the Failback tab, shown in Figure 20-19, you can either **Prevent failback** of resources that have failed over to another node, or you can **Allow failback** immediately or within a specified time period. If you wish to specify a time period, enter a starting and ending time using any number between and including 0 and 23. These fields represent a 24-hour clock. Therefore, if you specify an ending time that is earlier than the beginning time, the interval will end on the following day.

Cluster.exe

Cluster.exe is a command-line utility that can be used to administer clusters. It is automatically installed when the Cluster Service or Cluster Administrator is installed. Cluster.exe supports the basic commands for:

- The cluster
- Nodes

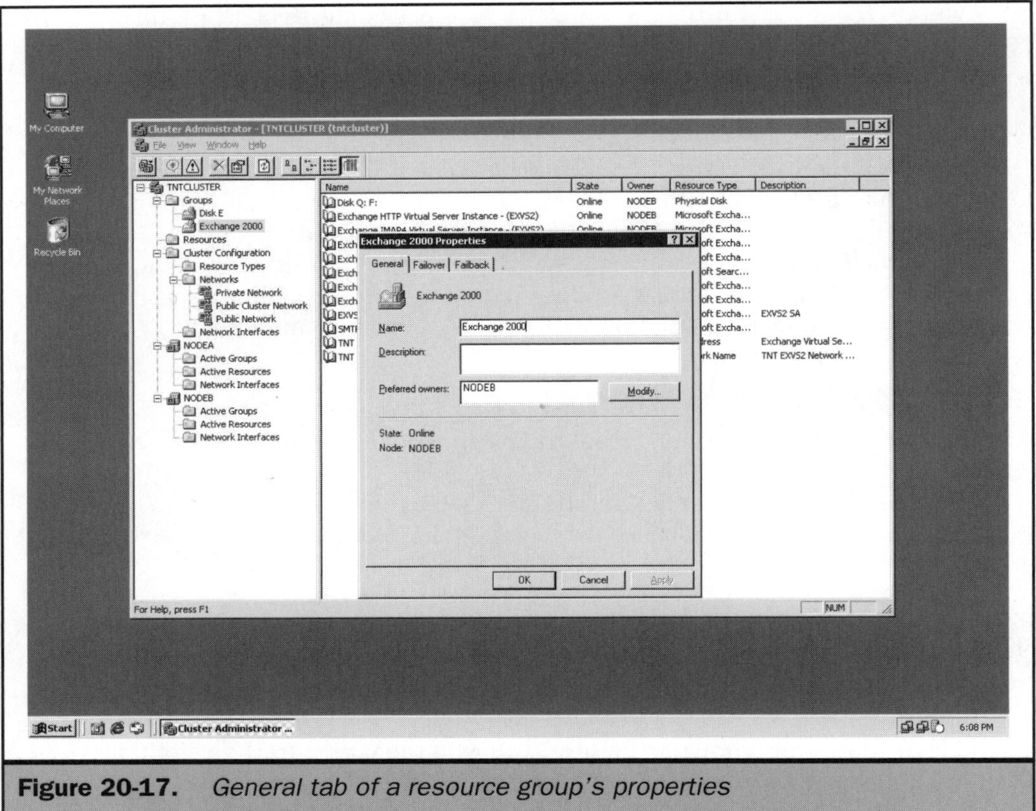

Figure 20-17. *General tab of a resource group's properties*

- Resources
- Resource Types
- Groups

Each of these commands includes syntax that is specific to the object being manipulated. Entering **cluster.exe /?** or **cluster.exe /help** at a command prompt will produce the following output, which details the available commands.

The syntax of this command is:

```
CLUSTER /LIST[:domain-name]
CLUSTER [[/CLUSTER:]cluster-name] <options>
<options> =
 /PROP[ERTIES] [<prop-list>]
 /PRIV[PROPERTIES] [<prop-list>]
 /PROP[ERTIES][:propname[,propname ...] /USEDEFAULT]
```

```
 /PRIV[PROPERTIES][:propname[,propname ...] /USEDEFAULT]
 /REN[AME]:cluster-name
 /VER[SION]
 /QUORUM[RESOURCE][:resource-name] [/PATH:path] [/MAXLOGSIZE:max-size-kbytes]
 /SETFAIL[UREACTIONS][:node-name[,node-name ...]]
 /REG[ADMIN]EXT:admin-extension-dll[,admin-extension-dll ...]
 /UNREG[ADMIN]EXT:admin-extension-dll[,admin-extension-dll ...]
 NODE [node-name] node-command
 GROUP [group-name] group-command
 RES[OURCE] [resource-name] resource-command
 {RESOURCETYPE|RESTYPE} [resourcetype-name] resourcetype-command
 NET[WORK] [network-name] network-command
 NETINT[ERFACE] [interface-name] interface-command
<prop-list> =
 name=value[,value ...][:<format>] [name=value[,value ...][:<format>] ...]
<format> =
 BINARY|DWORD|STR[ING]|EXPANDSTR[ING]|MULTISTR[ING]|SECURITY|ULARGE
CLUSTER /?
CLUSTER /HELP
```

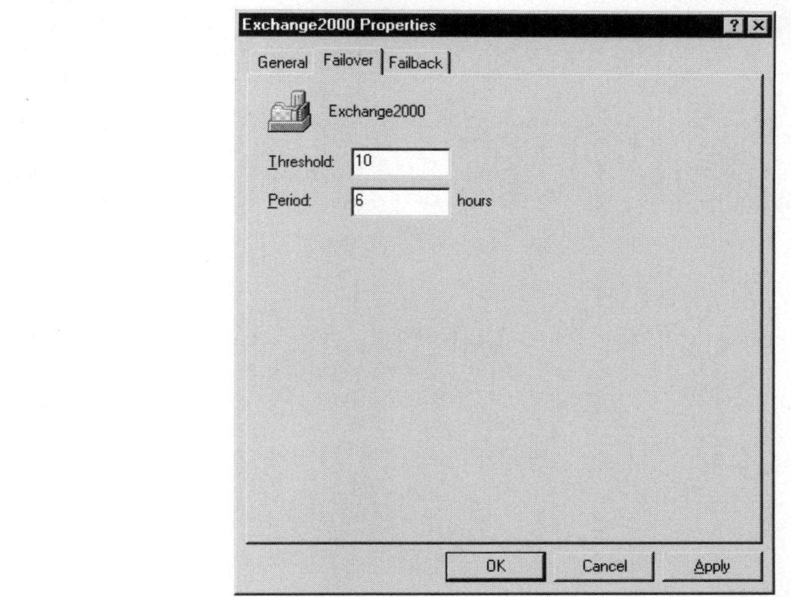

Figure 20-18. *Failover tab of a resource group's properties*

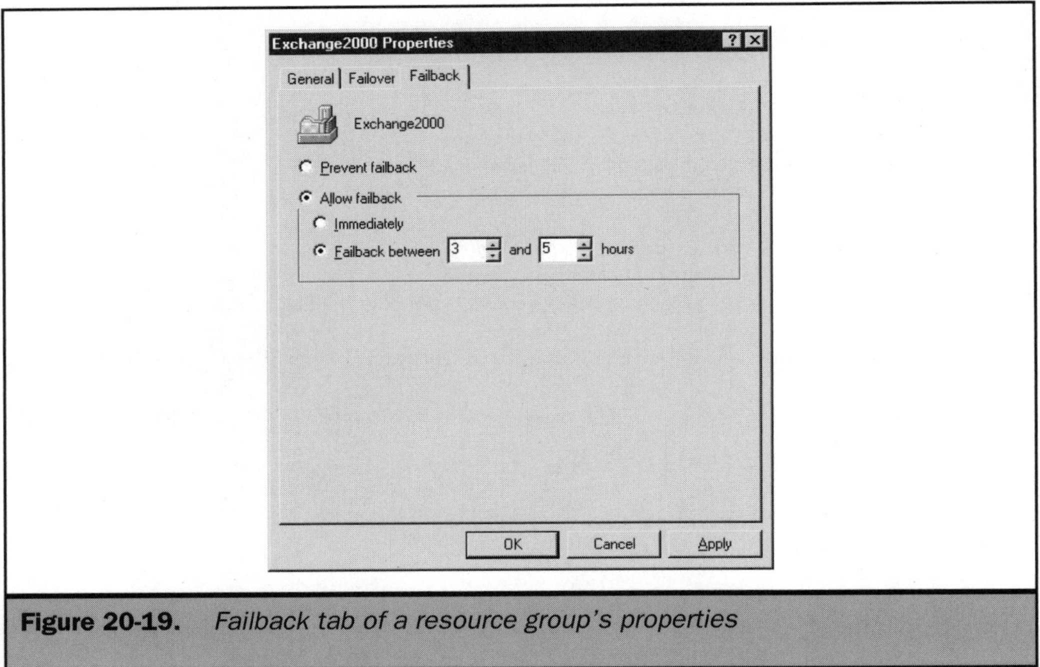

Figure 20-19. *Failback tab of a resource group's properties*

As you can see from the list of commands, a wide range of cluster functions can be accomplished via the command line. This enables administrators to manage their clusters using scripts or batch files. For example, the following command can be used to check the status of nodes in a cluster:

```
cluster /cluster:tntcluster node
```

In this example, the name of the cluster is **tntcluster**. The node command is used to display node status. The output of this command looks like this:

```
Listing status for all available nodes:
Node       Node ID Status
-------------- ------- ---------------------
NODEB         2 Up
NODEA         1 Up
```

The group command can be used to check on the status of groups:

```
cluster /cluster:tntcluster group
```

The output of the group command looks like this:

```
Listing status for all available resource groups:
Group          Node       Status
-------------------- --------------- ------
Exchange 2000    NODEB      Online
SQL Server 2000   NODEA      Online
```

For complete details on using Cluster.exe, see http://www.microsoft.com/TechNet/winnt/Winntas/manuals/ClustSvr/mscsadma.asp.

Network Load Balancing

Network Load Balancing (NLB) is a service that distributes client connections over multiple servers to provide scalability and high availability for TCP/IP-based applications. One of the most common uses for NLB is to distribute Web requests across a cluster of Internet-based applications such as Internet Information Services (IIS).

How NLB Works

The core of NLB is a driver named Wlbs.sys that operates between the network adapter driver and the TCP/IP protocol. This driver, which uses a statistical mapping algorithm, determines which server handles each incoming request. Client requests are actually sent to all servers in the NLB cluster. The statistical mapping algorithm maps client requests to an individual server in the cluster for processing, and the other servers drop the request.

Note *The name of the driver, Wlbs.sys, refers to NLB's predecessor, Windows Load Balancing Service (WLBS). WLBS was originally designed for Microsoft Windows NT 4.0 Server, Enterprise Edition. You will see WLBS referenced occasionally in NLB to preserve backward compatibility.*

The following items are included in the algorithm processing:

- Host priorities
- Multicast or unicast mode
- Port rules
- Affinity
- Load percentage distribution
- Client IP address
- Client port number

As in the case of Windows 2000 clusters, heartbeats are passed among the servers in an NLB cluster to inform peer servers about the presence of the other servers in the cluster. If a server fails to send or respond to a heartbeat within five seconds, it will be considered offline and the other servers in the cluster will perform a process called *convergence*. Convergence enables cluster members to determine which servers in the cluster are still active, elect a new default host, and then redistribute client load across the remaining servers. When a new server is configured to join the cluster, or when an offline server goes online again, it sends a heartbeat to the other servers in the cluster, triggering the same convergence process. The client load is re-distributed to include the new server and the process of convergence is completed. The process of convergence usually lasts less than 10 seconds, so client interruption is minimal. NLB distributes the load percentage based on the sum of the assigned load percentages for all the active servers in the cluster. So if one server fails, the remaining hosts will increase the number of client requests they handle in proportion to their original load percentage.

Affinity is the process of defining relationships among client requests from a single client address. The affinity setting determines which bits of the source IP and IP port number affect the choice of a host to handle that traffic. Affinity ensures that requests from a specific client are processed by the same host. This relationship is interrupted only when convergence is run or when you modify the affinity settings. This means that there is no time-out to the relationship.

There are three affinity settings:

- **None** This setting creates the most even client distribution across servers in the cluster. It also creates the fastest response time because a relationship between a server and a client is not maintained. The entire IP address and port number are used by the statistical mapping algorithm to determine which host should process a client request. Use this setting when you want to optimize response time to the client, achieve maximum load balancing across the servers, or if all the client requests are coming into the cluster from a single IP address, such as when the NLB cluster sits behind a reverse proxy.
- **Single** This setting forces client requests to be routed to the same host that processed the client's original request. This setting creates a slower environment and response time if too many clients place too much load on a single host in the cluster. With the single setting, the entire IP address of the client alone is used by the statistical mapping algorithm to decide which host should process the client request.
- **Class C** With this setting, client requests from any address within a network address are routed to a single host, because only the upper 24 bits of the client's IP address are used by the statistical mapping algorithm to influence which server should process a client's request. Setting affinity to Class C means that as long as all of the client's proxy servers are on the same class C subnet, state will be maintained.

Configuring NLB

With NLB, you can set port rules, cluster parameters, and host parameters. For instance, as we just discussed, you can route all requests of a single client to the host that processed the client's first request. This is called *single affinity*. In addition, you can specify that one host will process all client requests with the other server(s) in the cluster acting as failover servers only.

To install NLB, navigate to the network properties screen and select the Network Load Balancing checkbox, shown in Figure 20-20. Then click OK, and NLB will be installed. No menu option for this service will be configured in the Administrative Tools.

To configure NLB, navigate to the server's network properties screen, select the Network Load Balancing checkbox, and click on the Properties button. When you do, you'll be presented with a screen containing the Cluster Parameters, Host Parameters, and Port Rules tabs.

The Cluster Parameters tab, shown in Figure 20-21, is where you configure the IP address and subnet mask for the cluster and it's fully-qualified domain name, determine whether multicast is enabled, and determine whether remote control of this cluster is enabled and, if so, what the password is to remotely administer this cluster. Be sure to

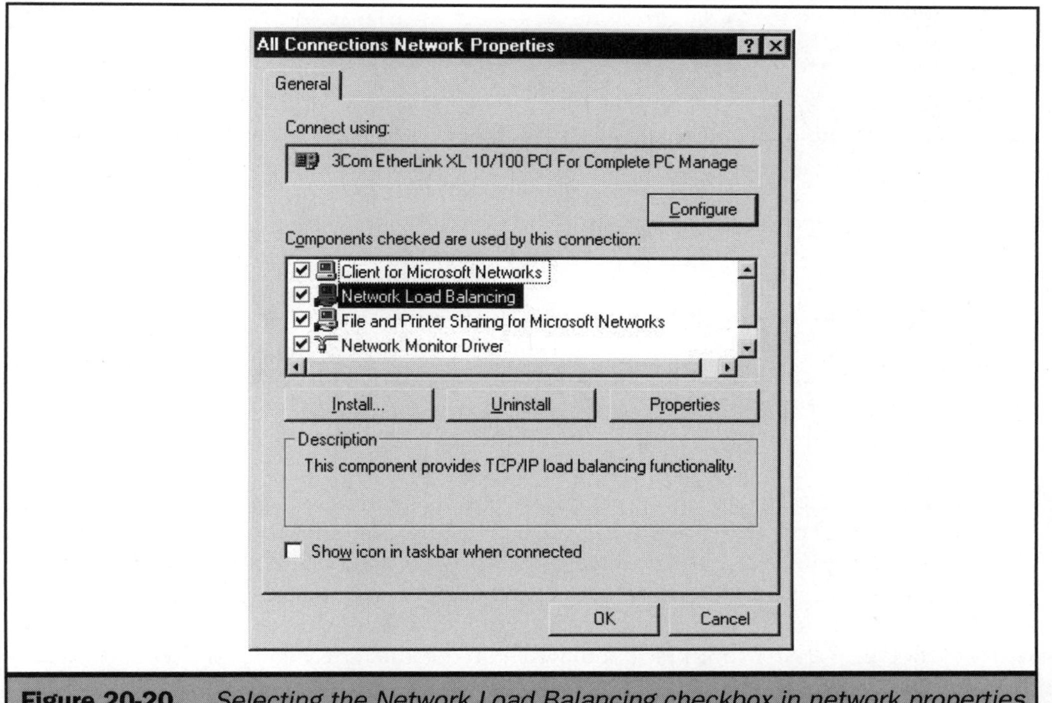

Figure 20-20. *Selecting the Network Load Balancing checkbox in network properties*

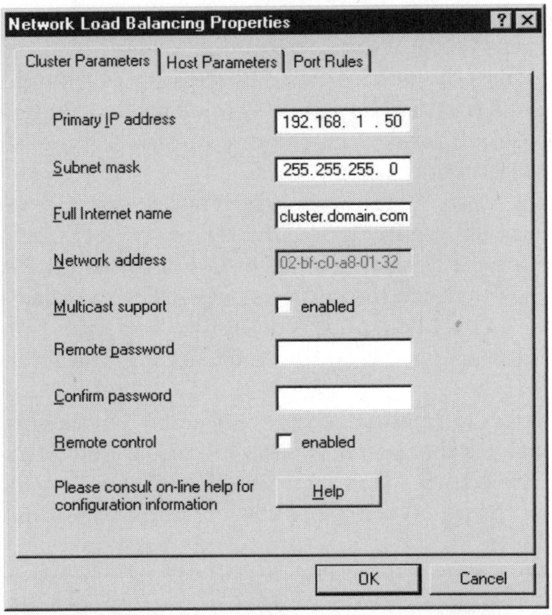

Figure 20-21. *Cluster Parameters tab in the Network Load Balancing Properties screen*

enter a difficult password here, because enabling remote control of your NLB cluster opens up some remarkable opportunities for those who might wish to bring down your network. Clearing both password fields *disables* the use of remote control passwords.

If multicast is enabled, NLB will convert the cluster MAC (Media Access Control) address into a multicast MAC address (FF-FF-FF-FF-FF-FF-FF-FF). If multicast is disabled, NLB overrides the hard-coded MAC address on each network card and substitutes a cluster MAC address to allow all the network cards to receive the packet simultaneously. Thereafter, it is up to the statistical mapping algorithm to determine which server in the cluster will respond to the client's request.

The Host Parameters tab, shown in Figure 20-22, is where you can configure the host's priority. This parameter specifies a host's priority for handling default network traffic that is not specified in the Port Rules section. It is used when a host within the cluster goes offline, and it determines which host within the cluster will handle the former host's traffic if needed. The lower the number, the higher the priority. You can also set whether the host should immediately join the cluster when Windows 2000 is

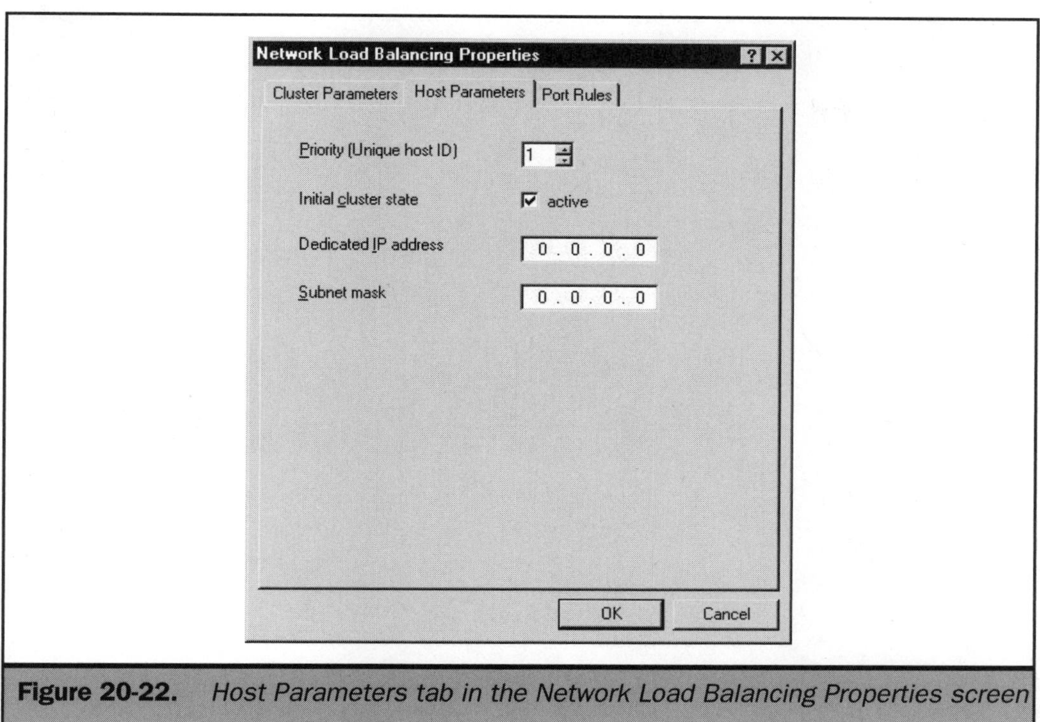

Figure 20-22. *Host Parameters tab in the Network Load Balancing Properties screen*

started by selecting the Initial Cluster State Active checkbox. Clearing this box means that you'll need to manually join the server to the cluster after Windows 2000 has started.

If you want to filter IP traffic based on port numbers within the cluster, you'll need to configure port rules on the Port Rules tab, shown in Figure 20-23. There are three possible filtering modes: multiple hosts, single host, and disabled.

Multiple hosts means that multiple servers in the cluster will handle traffic for the associated port rule. Single host means that only one server in the cluster will handle traffic for the associated port rule. Disabled means that all network traffic for the associated port rule is blocked on all servers.

There are several important things to remember when configuring a port rule. First, the number and type of rules must be the same for each server in the cluster. Second, if a server attempts to join the cluster with a different number of rules, it will be rejected and the servers in the cluster will continue to operate as usual. Third, the rules on each server in the cluster must having matching port ranges, protocol types, and filtering modes.

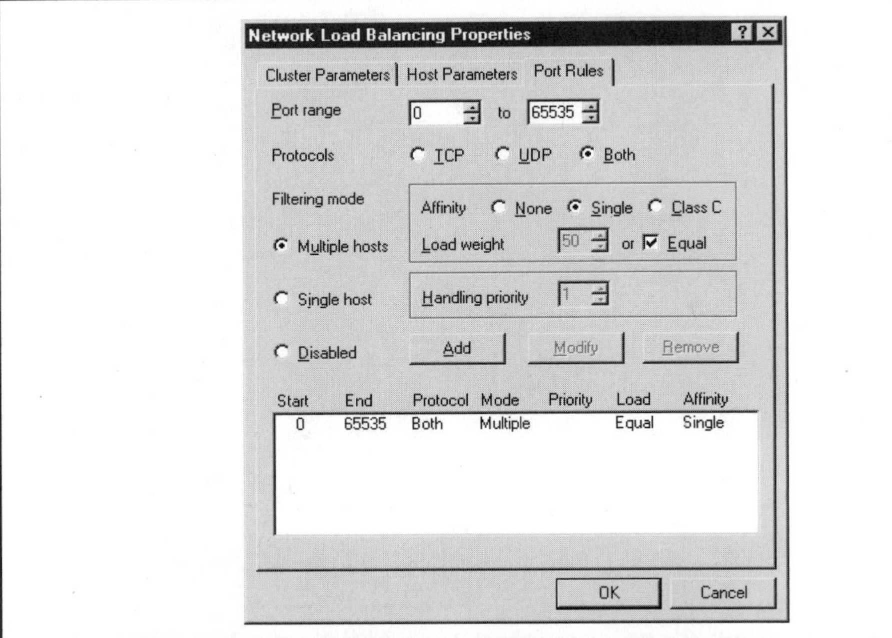

Figure 20-23. *Port Rules tab in the Network Load Balancing Properties screen*

Front-End/Back-End Configuration

In order for Exchange 2000 to scale to millions of users, its services must be able to be distributed. As previously mentioned, Exchange 2000 supports a new architecture called the Front-End/Back-End Configuration (FE/BE). A *front-end* server is a server that runs Exchange 2000 Enterprise Server and that does not host any information stores. A *back-end* server is a server that runs Exchange 2000 and that maintains at least one information store. Back-end servers are any servers that have not been configured as front-end servers. Back-end servers can be clustered or non-clustered. Figure 20-24 illustrates the FE/BE architecture.

The FE/BE configuration enables you to distribute protocol services and information store services across multiple servers. In earlier versions of Exchange, the information store process (store.exe) managed both the databases and the access protocols (for example, HTTP, IMAP4, and POP3). In Exchange 2000, the protocols are now managed by IIS. In an FE/BE configuration, clients connect to front-end servers, which in turn request information from back-end servers on behalf of the client. The front-end server proxies the client's request using the access protocol used by the client. For example, if an IMAP4 client

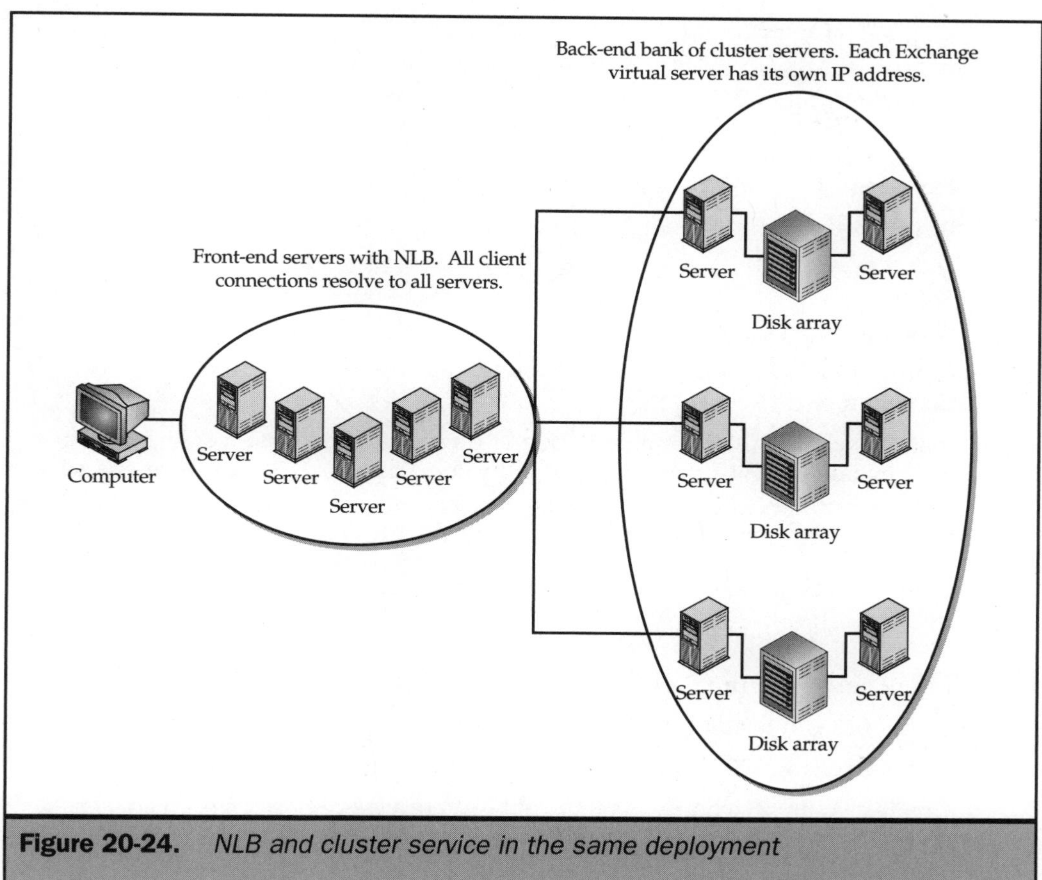

Figure 20-24. *NLB and cluster service in the same deployment*

connects to a front-end server, the front-end server uses IMAP4 when communicating with the back-end server. If a client connects via HTTP, the front-end server and back-end server communicate via HTTP.

The process typically flows as follows:

1. An Internet client sends logon request.
2. The FE server queries Active Directory using LDAP for the BE server containing user's mailbox.
3. The FE server redirects the logon request to the BE server.
4. The BE server authenticates the user and sends data to FE server.
5. The FE server sends the data to the Internet client.

Deploying the FE/BE architecture involves installing NLB on your front-end servers and clustering your back-end servers. A general overview of this process follows.

To set up the front-end servers using NLB, follow these steps:

1. Install Windows 2000 Advanced Server on each front-end server. Remember that each front-end server must reside on the same physical subnet.
2. Install the latest Service Packs, security updates and hotfixes on all servers.
3. Install the NLB service on each front-end server and configure the port rules as necessary. For details on installing NLB, refer to the Windows 2000 Advanced Server product documentation.
4. Configure DNS to resolve to the cluster IP address and fully qualified domain name.
5. Install Exchange 2000 Enterprise Server on each front-end server and configure each installation as a front-end server by checking the **This is a front end server** checkbox on the server's Properties dialog in System Manager. Be sure to remove the Exchange databases on each front-end server.

To set up a back-end bank of clusters, follow these steps:

1. Install Windows 2000 Advanced Server on each server that will be in a cluster.
2. Install and configure the Cluster service on each server.
3. Configure and test failover and failback.
4. Install Exchange 2000 Enterprise Server on each node in the cluster.
5. Create as many Exchange 2000 virtual servers as necessary on each cluster.
6. Be sure that DNS resolves to each IP address of each virtual cluster.

Note *The steps listed above are very general and not detailed enough to accomplish a successful installation of the FE/BE configuration. Refer to Chapter 6 for complete details on installing Exchange 2000. For more information on the FE/BE configuration, go to Microsoft's Front-End/Back-End Configuration white paper at http://www.microsoft.com/exchange. For more information on NLB, see http://www.microsoft.com/technet/win2000/nlbovw.asp and http://www.microsoft.com/windows2000/library/howitworks/cluster/nlb.asp.*

Microsoft recommends a ratio of one FE server for every four BE servers. In addition, you should make sure that you have enough domain controllers and Global Catalog servers available to manage the authentication and directory lookup traffic.

Clustering Caveats

Before you implement any clusters, it's a good idea to familiarize yourself with the cluster issues that are germane to Exchange 2000. In addition to the limitations of clustering described in this chapter, there are certain constraints that may impact the deployment of your Exchange 2000 clusters. Whether you are upgrading from Exchange 5.5 clusters, or starting fresh with brand new clusters, you should be aware of the following issues. The following sections cover both FE and BE servers.

Clustering in Mixed-Mode Environments

Many of the cluster caveats affect mixed-mode environments (environments that run Exchange 2000 and Exchange 5.5 in the same organization). For example, a clustered Exchange 2000 server may not be the first Exchange 2000 server in an Exchange 5.5 site, nor can it be a bridgehead server. Exchange 2000 requires the Site Replication Service (SRS) in a mixed environment, and SRS is not supported in a cluster.

When you are deploying FE servers, pay special attention to your routing group design, as well. If there are servers that runExchange 5.5 in the same routing group, you must configure the MTA to run on the FE server so that the MTAs can bind and transfer mail.

Configuration Issues

In many cases, the problems or limitations you encounter may be overcome by changing the configuration. Many of these issues are documented by Microsoft on Web sites that will provide you with additional information about these issues.

Using SSL with Exchange Virtual Servers

When you run Exchange 2000 in a cluster, make sure that your protocol virtual servers are not set to authenticate over Secure Sockets Layer (SSL) only. The Cluster service pings the IIS ports to determine if the service is still running. SSL-only connections will return data that the Cluster service can not understand. This causes the Cluster service to think that IIS is not working properly, which in turn causes the Cluster service to improperly failover Exchange 2000 services. For more information on this issue, see Microsoft Knowledge Base article Q241626.

Using SSL on Front-End Servers

SSL is recommended for all FE servers that are located directly on the Internet or in a DMZ. This will protect data communications between the Internet client and the FE server. You'll recall that the FE server will proxy the client's request to the BE server using the protocol used by the client to communicate with the FE server. However, this is not the case when SSL is used. SSL can not be used between an FE server and a BE server. Traffic between these two servers will take place on TCP port 80 regardless of the port the client uses to connect to the front-end server. If you need to secure communications between an FE server and a BE server, you will need to use an alternate method such as Transport Layer Security (TLS) or IP Security (IPSec).

If you do use SSL on an FE server, make sure the License Logging Service is running. IIS will not allow more than 10 simultaneous SSL connections if this service is not running.

Exchange 2000 Monitoring and the MTA

In an Exchange 2000 cluster, there can be only one instance of the MTA. Nonetheless, Exchange 2000's internal monitoring will report that the node without an MTA instance is in an error state. The default monitoring configuration on an Exchange 2000 server includes the Microsoft Exchange MTA Stacks service. This, in turn, can cause problems if Exchange 2000 is installed on a cluster computer. To work around this issue, go to the Properties of the server in ESM, navigate to the Monitoring tab, double-click Default Microsoft Exchange Services, and remove the MTA stack. Refer to Microsoft Knowledge Base article Q271449 for more information on this issue.

Using Multiple HTTP Virtual Servers in a Cluster

You should wait for Exchange 2000 Service Pack 1 before creating additional HTTP virtual servers in your cluster. If you create an additional HTTP virtual server in your cluster, it will be inaccessible because Exchange 2000 Setup doesn't create the correct HostName for WebDAV. This is a known issue that is slated for correction in Exchange 2000 SP1. In the meantime, the workaround is to refrain from creating additional HTTP virtual servers in a cluster. This issue is documented in Microsoft Knowledge Base article Q241627.

Using SMTP on Front-End Servers

By definition, a front-end server does not have any information stores present. The purpose of an FE server is to enable greater scalability by separating protocol services from information store services. However, if you have an FE server that accepts SMTP mail from the Internet, you must start the Information Store service and mount at least one private information store.

Using SMTP Protocol Logging

If you enable SMTP protocol logging for an SMTP virtual server in a cluster, you will need to manually change the path in ESM for the log files. By default, %systemroot%\System32\Logfiles is set as the path for the SMTP log files. In order for SMTP logging to operate properly in a cluster, the default path of the SMTP log files need to be on the shared disk, and not the local system drive. You can make this change in System Manager. To do this, right-click the default SMTP virtual server, and select Properties. Use the **Enable logging** check box to turn on logging, and then click Properties. Change the path to a directory on a disk resource in your Exchange resource group. You can find more information on this issue in Microsoft Knowledge Base article Q271407.

Using Static Domain Controller or Global Catalog Servers

In Chapter 3, we discussed how to hard-code a specific set of directory service servers for use by the DSAccess component in Exchange 2000. If you plan to hard-code the directory service servers used by your clustered Exchange servers, be sure to make the changes to the registry on both nodes. The DSAccess component is not cluster-aware. As a result, no checkpoints to the registry are made in case of failover. Therefore, if a static domain controller or global catalog server is being used, you must manually adjust the registry on both nodes.

Exchange Cluster Administration

Other than making regular backups, an Exchange 2000 cluster requires little day-to-day administration above and beyond the administration required for a non-clustered server. On any important server, you need to back up all mission-critical data. Exchange 2000 clusters are certainly no exception. In Exchange 2000, there are two types of data: *static data* and *dynamic data*. Static data typically includes the following types of data: Windows 2000 and its configurations; cluster software, and cluster administration software; Exchange binaries; third-party management software; and such applications as Web applications, mailbox agents, and workflow and management scripts. Dynamic data typically includes the Exchange databases and supporting files, and System State data, which includes the IIS metabase and the cluster quorum.

Note *During the backup of your cluster quorum, the NT Backup application may report the following error:* Completed with Skipped Files, examining the Windows 2000 Backup log, both CLUSDB and CLUSDB.LOG failed to be backed up. *If this happens, you can safely ignore this error; the backup was actually successful.*

Managing Services in a Cluster

The primary administrative difference between a clustered and non-clustered Exchange server is the manipulation of services. In a non-clustered environment, you can stop and start Exchange services a number of ways: using the **net stop** or **net start** commands at the command line; using the Services MMC snap-in; or by using certain Resource Kit utilities, to name a few.

In a clustered environment, however, only the Cluster Administrator application or the cluster.exe command line utility should be used to start and stop resources, or, to use the appropriate cluster terminology, for bringing resources online or taking resources offline. If you use any other method to stop or start services, the Cluster service may mistakenly interpret this as an error or failure and initiate failover procedures.

Exchange Cluster Recovery

There may be times when you'll need to either recover one or both nodes in your cluster. Let's look at these two situations and discuss what you'll need to consider when performing these tasks.

Recovering a Single Cluster Node

Performing recovery of a clustered Exchange server is similar to performing disaster recovery on a non-clustered Exchange server. There are a few additional steps that need to be performed, which are all cluster-related.

There are five basic steps to recovering a lost node:

1. Evict the old node from the cluster and verify eviction using Cluster Administrator.
2. Build a new cluster node and join the cluster. When doing this, use a new machine name for the replacement node. Do not use the name of the node that failed.
3. Restore the System State data on the new node only. Do not restore anything to the surviving node. Again, the System State data includes the registry, the class registration database, and the system boot files. If the node was a domain controller, System State data will also include Active Directory and the Sysvol directory.
4. Install Exchange 2000 Enterprise Server on the new node, and apply any relevant Service Packs and hotfixes.
5. Make the new node a Possible Owner of all of the resources in the cluster.

Recovering an Entire Exchange 2000 Cluster

Surprisingly, recovering an entire Exchange 2000 cluster isn't much different than recovering a single node. There are six basic steps to recovering an entire Exchange 2000 cluster:

1. Rebuild all nodes to the same specifications as before. In this case, you should use the same names as the original servers.
2. Install and configure the Cluster service, and recreate the original cluster group.
3. Restore the System State on each node.
4. Install Exchange 2000 Enterprise Server on each node.

5. Recreate all of your Exchange resources, again using the same names you had before.
6. Restore your databases from backup.

Performing Hard Recovery on a Clustered Database

Hard recovery is the process used to apply transaction logs and database patch files to a database that has been restored from online backup. Typically, these things happen automatically as part of the restore operation. For example, the Windows NT backup utility has a Last Backup Set checkbox that, when checked, causes hard recovery to occur automatically. If this checkbox is not checked for your restore operation, you must perform hard recovery manually. To do this, you can either simply restore the backup again (with the Last Backup Set checkbox checked), or run the **eseutil /cc** command.

If you elect to run the eseutil /cc command, you will need to first set the _CLUSTER_NETWORK_NAME_ environment variable. If you run eseutil /cc on a clustered database without setting this environment variable, you will likely receive the following error message: *Error returned from a callback function call (0x8004010F). Operation terminated with error -107 (JET_errInternalError, Fatal internal error).* This problem occurs because the eseutil utility uses the local computer name instead of the cluster name. Setting this environment variable corrects the problem. To set the variable, go to a command prompt and issue the following command:

```
SET _CLUSTER_NETWORK_NAME_=cluster_name
```

In the above example, *cluster_name* is the name of your cluster. When setting this environment variable, be sure to include the leading and trailing underscore characters. For more information on this issue, see Microsoft Knowledge Base article Q266689.

Summary

Clustering provides high availability, or increased uptime, for Exchange 2000 by reducing the downtime caused by planned and unplanned outages. This can be a very good solution if hardware failures are causing unacceptable levels of downtime for your organization. Exchange 2000 offers improved support for Windows 2000 clusters by supporting two-node Active/Active clusters on Windows 2000 Advanced Server and, with Service Pack 1 or later installed, four-node Active/Active clusters on Windows 2000 Datacenter Server.

Chapter 21

Performance Tuning and Monitoring

Exchange 2000 Server automatically installs with a standard set of values that are predetermined by Microsoft. In many environments, these default values will suffice for good performance of an Exchange 2000 Server. However, for some environments, especially high-traffic environments, some of these values will need to be tweaked.

In this chapter, we'll discuss how to tune Exchange 2000 Server to achieve maximum performance and efficiency. We'll also point out the limits of this program and provide some fairly detailed content. So, if you want to fine-tune your Exchange 2000 Server, read on!

Tuning Exchange 2000

Exchange 2000 is installed with a basic, one-size-fits-all set of configurations. Happily, in many environments, this generic size fits and works just fine. But for some environments, intermittent message transfer issues arise due to bottlenecks caused by limitations in the generic configuration.

Tuning Exchange 2000 involves getting into the registry and using ADSI Edit to make very detailed, but important, changes to the server. And it means understanding *why* you're making those changes. So, in this chapter, we'll cover not only the *what*, but also the *why*. We'll start by looking at the automatic tuning features of the online maintenance routine. Next we'll discuss, briefly, hardware selection. Then, we'll turn our attention to tuning the major components of Exchange 2000, and we'll finish up with a look at the proactive monitoring tools that are provided in the Exchange System Manager (ESM) snap-in.

Self-Tuning Enhancements

Each Extensible Storage Engine (ESE) instance within the information store process has a number of automatic maintenance routines that execute each night, by default, between 1:00A.M. and 5:00A.M. Some of the online maintenance activities include:

- Determining if there are any deleted mailboxes
- Cleaning out messages and mailboxes that are older than the configured retention period
- Performing online defragmentation of EDB databases

Let's look at each activity individually.

The streaming (STM) database does not get defragmented.

Finding Deleted Mailboxes in Active Directory

The first task is more costly on your domain controllers than on your Exchange 2000 Server. An LDAP lookup for each user in the mailbox store database is performed nightly to ensure that there is proper synchronization between the mailbox and the user account and to update the store with any changes to the mailboxes, such as a deletion activity. If you have multiple stores on multiple servers and haven't varied the online maintenance times, the load on the local domain controllers can be significant. In short, the effect that online maintenance has on Active Directory (AD) is proportional to the number of users in each store. Hence, if you have 7000 users hosted in a mailbox store, you will have 7000 LDAP lookups against AD at the beginning of that store's online maintenance schedule. If you have a large number of users, consider staggering the maintenance schedules for your mailbox stores.

Cleaning Out Messages and Mailboxes

The server that hosts the public folders and mailboxes that need to be cleaned is directly affected by this second maintenance activity. If you are in a situation where users are connecting 24x7 to your Exchange 2000 Servers, consider staggering the online maintenance times of the stores to improve server response to user requests.

Online Backups

You will probably implement online backups to be run automatically on a nightly schedule, so we include it in this discussion. It is critical to note that if an online backup starts against any store in a storage group in which any of the databases are performing nightly maintenance, all maintenance in the storage group will immediately stop until the online backup has been completed. You need to take pains to ensure that the timing of your online backups does not conflict with the timing of the maintenance schedule. Otherwise, you will lose not only the benefit of having older items cleaned out of the store, but also the assurance that the store is in sync with Active Directory due to the LDAP lookups each night.

The task of defragmenting the database is really 18 separate tasks that are grouped into one job. Not all 18 tasks need to be completed in order for the online maintenance to stop performing, but each individual task, once started, must complete. The process will exit when the maintenance window has passed, even if all the tasks are not complete. So, be sure to allow four hours for the online maintenance utilities to run. Staggering these times also means staggering your online backup times. With multiple servers and stores, it is best to work out a schedule that allows for both tasks to run and ensures that the backup processes do not overlap with the times when the maintenance activities are running.

Hardware Selection and Tuning

In this section, we focus on some of the hardware issues that you need to address as you consider building your Exchange 2000 Server. In all situations, however, it doesn't take a starburst of insight to see that better, faster, and larger capacity hardware will result, overall, in better, faster performance. Do keep in mind, however, that you should only use hardware that is listed on the Microsoft Hardware Compatibility List for Windows 2000, which can be found at http://www.microsoft.com/hwtest.

Processors

Several services in Exchange 2000 Server place a heavy load on the processor: search, conferencing, SSL (Secure Sockets Layer) traffic, and front-end server configurations.

When the Microsoft Search service is performing a crawl action, it places a heavy load on the processor, usually 60 percent or higher. And a full rebuild of an index will likely take the processor to 100 percent utilization. If you plan to update your indexes on an hourly basis, you'll probably need more processing power than if you plan to update them overnight when your users are not using the server. If you plan to implement an aggressive indexing schedule, consider faster and perhaps multiple processors. If you are going to index only public folders, consider using a dedicated server for this function.

Most of the components in Exchange 2000 Conferencing Server do not place much load on the server's processor. However, one component, the H.323 bridging service, can. In Conferencing Server, the heaviest use of the processor comes from two functions: the mixing of the audio feed and the reception of video streams. Conferencing Server supports two models that support these functions: IP Multicast and H.323. Microsoft uses a slightly modified version of the standard H.323 model. The Microsoft version connects IP Multicast with H.323 using bridges where connectivity breaks down or where multicast isn't available. This technique is used in the areas of your network that don't yet support IP multicasting, and for conferencing with any of the many H.323 clients in use today. If the processor is slow during a bridging operation, users will experience jitter and audio drops in the overall conferencing stream.

Note *Only H.323 clients that support interoperability with Microsoft NetMeeting are supported with Exchange 2000 H.323 services.*

When using pure IP Multicast, the heaviest CPU load will occur on the client because the client handles audio mixing and receives all the video streams. So jitters could mean that a client has a CPU bottleneck, as well.

Tip *When using H.323, keep the attendee size small. Audio and video performance and quality will degrade in large H.323 conferences. According to Microsoft, 40 H.323 attendees in a conference can exhaust CPU resources. Its statistics show that a 450MHz server with 256MB of RAM can support about 40 H.323 clients participating in different conferences on a single server. H.323 also uses more bandwidth than IP Multicast, so as you might expect, tuning of Conferencing Services goes beyond the server and client CPU resources to include the network.*

The front-end server configuration is written to handle thousands of client connections, and these connections are more processor intensive than memory or disk intensive.

Memory

The Extensible Storage Engine (ESE) is designed to allocate as much of the system memory to the STORE.EXE process as it can without injuring the other processes on the system. This pre-allocation of system memory is called *Dynamic Buffer Allocation* (DBA), and the amount allocated is based, in part, on the number and size of databases plus the number of transactions.

If your Exchange 2000 Server has more than 1GB of memory, you'll need to use the /3GB switch in the BOOT.INI file on the server. We'll discuss this in more depth later in this chapter. If the STORE.EXE process runs out of memory, even if there is available physical memory, memory allocations will fail and the only remedy is to restart the STORE.EXE process.

Network Interface

There isn't much to configure on the network cards, but if you plan to run IP Security (IPSec) on your Exchange 2000 Server, you should purchase special network cards that will offload the IPSec processing from the main processor. Both Intel and 3COM manufacture such cards, which can be found on their respective websites at http://www.intel.com/network/products/pro100ssrvr.htm and http://www.3com.com/products/nics/3cr990.html.

Disk Subsystem

The disk subsystem is probably one of the more frequently discussed topics in Exchange. As trainers and consultants, we are routinely asked questions about designing the optimal disk subsystem for Exchange 2000. Keep in mind the following ideas when designing a disk subsystem:

- Faster disks are better. As a database application, Exchange is very I/O intensive. It sequentially writes log files and randomly reads database files, so the faster your disk subsystem, the better your overall performance.
- Use hardware RAID arrays and separate the transaction logs from the databases. We find it best to place the transaction logs on a separate RAID array from the one containing the databases, especially when data recovery is important. Splitting the logs and databases on two different servers gives you a performance gain because of the sequential writes to the transaction logs. It also gives you better recoverability because the logs are quarantined for replay into the database during a recovery operation. Use RAID-5 arrays for all databases and RAID-1 arrays for all transaction logs, message tracking logs, connector directories, and the TEMP folder. This will provide fault tolerance for your server's most critical files and folders. If your budget allows it, consider using RAID0+1 (also known as RAID-10) for the databases, which is substantially faster than RAID-5.

- For less important servers: If the server is merely going to act as a bridgehead server, data recovery may not be very important. In this case, you can use one partition in a disk mirroring configuration, but you'll experience better performance using a disk striping configuration. Also, when tuning a bridgehead server, you'll want to span the mailroot directory over several disks to gain maximum performance for messages going into and out of the server.
- For more important servers: If the server is going to host mailboxes or public folders, you'll need to not only split out the transaction logs and databases on different spindles, but also you should ensure that you have not placed the pagefile or the Windows binary files on the same spindle as the transaction logs. Placing these files on the same spindle as the transaction logs will result in the loss of sequential writes to the disk and, therefore, a loss in performance.
- Consider the type of data that will be housed in the databases and consider splitting out the *.EDB and *.STM files to different physical disks. Remember that MAPI (Message Application Programming Interface) and OWA (Outlook Web Access) clients read and write data to and from the *.EDB file. (MAPI clients can request information from the streaming store, too.) All other clients use the *.STM file. If the majority of your clients will be using the *.EDB file, consider placing the *.STM file on a smaller disk. However, if there will be many large attachments to the messages, you may need a larger disk for the *.STM file to hold all the non-MAPI information, such as graphics, voice, and video.

If the server is going to be a front-end server, you can delete the Exchange databases from that server, which will free up memory and processor resources for incoming client calls. In this scenario, a mirrored pair of disks with a single partition will work just fine.

Tuning Exchange 2000 Components

In addition to tuning your hardware, you can tune Exchange 2000 to make it run more smoothly and efficiently. What follows in this section is a detailed look at how to tune the Exchange 2000 stores, the Simple Mail Transport Protocol (SMTP) service, the Message Transfer Agent (MTA), and Outlook Web Access (OWA).

Note

In the following sections, you'll be given counters to watch without any numerical benchmarks to follow. If we offered benchmarks for each counter, chances are that they would be wrong for your environment. You should monitor your Exchange 2000 Servers to gain a baseline of the counters you wish to track, and then make your own decisions about when certain values should be changed. Where available, we have provided suggested numbers from Microsoft.

Exchange 2000 ESE Stores and Transaction Logs

When working in a mixed environment of Exchange 2000 and Exchange 5.5 Servers, there will be an interplay between the Exchange 2000 information store and the MTA service. After messages are handed off to the store process from the inetinfo (Internet Information Services) process, they are handed to the Advanced Queuing Engine (AQE) for processing. You can monitor the queues of the MTA to make sure that there is no queue buildup. Here are a few of the parameters to tune if the message handoff between the MTA and the store process seems sluggish or if there is queue buildup. The parameters we discuss here are found in the following registry key:

HKEY_LOCAL_MACHINE\SYSTEM\CurrentControlSet\Services\
MSExchangeIS\\<<*server-name*> \ Private-<*database-guid*>

When to Change If there is message buildup in the MTA queues or if the passage of messages between the MTA service and the store process is slow.

- **Parameter to change:** *Gateway In Threads.* The gateway in threads parameter moves messages from the MTA into the information store's mts-out queue and out of the information store into the MTA's mts-in queue. Increasing this value increases the "pipe" between the MTA and the information store.
- **Actions to take:** The default value is 0x1. Consider increasing this to 0x3. Keep in mind that each thread will consume about 1MB of virtual memory and the actual number of threads created will be multiplied by the number of databases on the server. Hence, if you have five databases on this server, increase the value from 1 to 3 (for a total increase of four threads). This will increase the use of memory to 20MB (4x5=20) of virtual memory.

Note *You must add this registry value to all mailbox stores on the server. If there are two message databases (MDBs) on the server, there will be two Private-<MDBguid> values in the registry that need to be modified.*

- **Counters to watch:** MSExchangeIS Transport Driver\MSExchangeMTA Submits.

When to Change If the messages going out of the store to the MTA seem to be sluggish or slow, as determined by monitoring over time.

- **Parameter to change:** *Gateway Out Threads*. The gateway out threads parameter moves messages to the MTA from the information store's mts-out queue and to the information store from the MTA's mts-in queue. Increasing this value increases the "pipe" between the MTA and the information store.
- **Actions to take:** The default is 0x1. Consider increasing this value to 0x3. This action will have the same memory consequences as mentioned for the gateway in threads parameter.

You must add this registry value to all mailbox stores on the server.

- **Counters to watch:** MSExchangeIS Transport Driver\MSExchangeMTA Delivery.

Joint Engine Technology (JET) Heaps

Windows 2000 implements a process-wide heap manager to manage memory operations for each process. A default heap called *process-heap* is created for each process when the process is initiated. When Exchange 2000 Server is installed on a server that has more than four processors and also houses the maximum (or near maximum) number of allowed databases, you may need to adjust the number of heaps that JET creates by modifying a registry parameter. The parameter to adjust is located in HKE_LOCAL_MACHINE\SOFTWARE\Microsoft\ESE98\Global\OS\Memory. The REG_SZ parameter is MPHeap parallelism. Set the parallelism to 3 plus the number of processors. So, on a 16-processor server, set the registry key to 0x13 (19). After making this modification, you'll need to restart the information store service for the change to take effect.

ESE Database Cache Size

ESE is hard-coded with a maximum store database cache size of 900MB. On servers that have more than 2GB of memory, you may find benefit in increasing the size of this cache. However, it is recommended to not set this value higher than 1200MB due to limitations in virtual addressing.

Before increasing this cache, you should monitor it using the Process\virtual bytes counter; focus on the store instance. This will tell you how much virtual address space the store has allocated. If you decide to modify the cache size, be sure to limit the amount of cache depending on the BOOT.INI setting. For Exchange 2000 servers with over 1GB of memory, you should use the /3GB setting in the BOOT.INI file. In this scenario, the maximum cache size should be below 2.8GB. For systems not using the /3GB setting in the BOOT.INI file, the maximum cache size should be below 1.8GB.

Note

Servers with over 1GB of memory must use the /3GB switch in the BOOT.INI file because of the way Windows 2000 reserves memory. By default, Windows 2000 reserves 2GB of virtual memory for the kernel and allows applications running in user mode to have the other 2GB of virtual memory. The addresses in memory for a process are allocated when the process starts and the allocation of memory addresses often increases as the process runs and requires more memory. On an Exchange 2000 Server with over 1GB of memory, the /3GB switch tells Windows 2000 to allocate 3GB of virtual memory for user mode applications, including Exchange 2000 Server. A typical ARC (Advanced Risk Computing) path in the BOOT.INI file for the /3GB switch will look like this: multi(0) disk(0) rdisk(0) partition (1) \WINNT="Microsoft Windows 2000 Server" /fastdetect /3GB.

For more information on this topic, please see Microsoft Knowledge Base articles Q171793, Q189293, and Q266096.

To modify the store database cache size, use the ADSI Edit (Active Directory Services Interface) tool, which is located on your Windows 2000 Server CD-ROM in the Support Tools folder.

Inside of ADSI Edit, navigate to the CN=Configuration, CN=Services, CN=Microsoft Exchange, CN=<*organization*>, CN=Administrative Groups, CN=<*Admin Group*>, CN=Servers, CN=<*server*>, CN=InformationStore object and open its properties. Select Both from the Select Which Properties To View drop-down list. Then select the msExchESEParamCacheSizeMax attribute and adjust the value as needed. Interestingly enough, you won't see the default 900MB (230400) value in the interface, which is shown in Figure 21-1. You can adjust this size up to 307200, or, 1200MB.

After setting this value, allow enough time for it to be replicated throughout your forest. Once replication has completed, you can stop and re-start all your Exchange information store services, and the new cache size will be in effect.

ESE Log Buffers

There is an area in memory that is reserved for writing information to the transaction logs called the log buffers. In a front-end/back-end environment, the default value for log buffers is often set too low on the back-end servers, which can cause excessive disk I/O on the transaction log disk drive. The default number of log buffers is 84. On back-end servers, this value should be set to 9000. Each buffer holds one log sector.

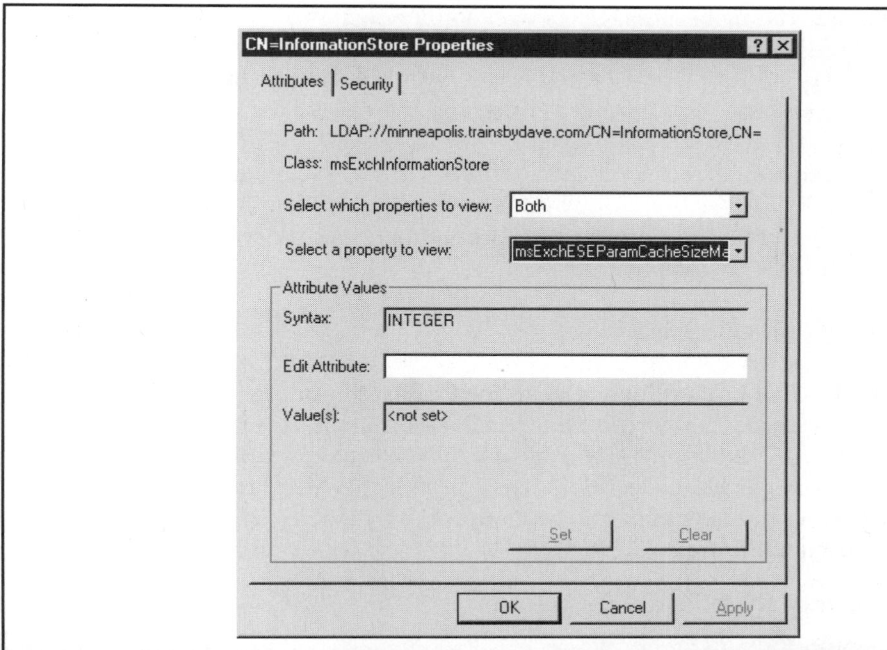

Figure 21-1. *msExchESEParamCacheSizeMax parameter in ADSI Edit*

Each log sector is equal to the sector size of your log disk, which is usually 512 bytes. Hence, 9000 x 512 bytes would be 4608000 bytes, or, 4.6MB of buffer space–a size nearly equal to one transaction log on your transaction log disk.

To modify this buffer size, navigate to the same information store object in ADSI Edit as outlined previously for the database cache size, and then configure the msExchESEParamLogBuffers attribute.

Simple Mail Transport Protocol (SMTP)

Given that the SMTP transport is the foundation of nearly all message movement in the Exchange 2000 platform, it makes sense that we spend some time covering how to tune this transport protocol.

When messages arrive at the SMTP transport stack inside of IIS (Internet Information Services), they are immediately written to the disk in the form of an NTFS file with an .EML extension. The default directory into which these messages are written is c:\program files\exchsrvr\mailroot. The default drive letter will be the same as the default partition that the Exchange 2000 binary files are installed on.

Mailroot Directory Location

In some instances, it is wise to change the location of the mailroot directory. One such instance would be when the partition that is currently hosting the mailroot is nearly full. Another case would be if this Exchange 2000 Server is acting as a hub server that passes a very large volume of messages between other Exchange 2000 and/or Exchange 5.5 Servers. This would also be the scenario for bridgehead servers in larger organizations that don't host any user mailboxes or public folders. In these situations, it may be wise to purchase very fast hard disks, and then move the mailroot directory to those disks.

To move the mailroot directory location, first stop the Exchange and IIS services on the Exchange 2000 server that you want to re-configure. Then manually move the VSI 1 directory and all its subfolders and contents under the mailroot directory to their new location.

Note *Do not move the mailroot folder itself.*

Next, open up ADSI Edit and navigate to the CN=Configuration, CN=Services, CN=Microsoft Exchange, CN=<*organization*>, CN=Administrative Groups, CN=<*Admin Group*>, CN=Servers, CN=<*server*>, CN=Protocols, CN=SMTP, CN=1 object and open its properties. Select Both from the Select Which Properties To View drop-down list. Enter the new path for the mailroot directory in the following attributes, as shown in Figure 21-2.

- msExchSmtpBadMailDirectory
- msExchSmtpPickupDirectory
- msExchSmtpQueueDirectory

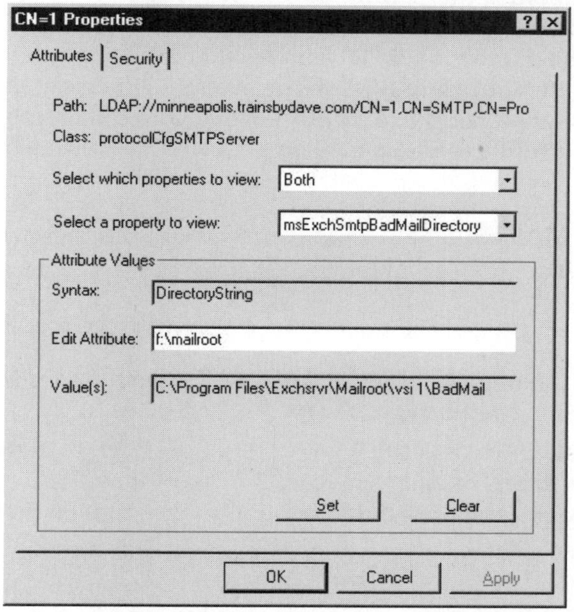

Figure 21-2. *Modifying the CN=1 properties to change the location of the mailroot directory*

After making these changes, you'll need to let them replicate throughout your forest. Then stop and start the System Attendant Service and the mailroot directory location will be changed. In addition, you should see three 1005 events in the Event Viewer indicating that the paths in the metabase for IIS were updated successfully.

SMTP File Handles

After a new message is received and written to the mailroot directory, a handle to that message is manifested and then sent through the Advanced Queuing Engine (AQE) before being sent on to another SMTP/Exchange 2000 Server, the information store process, or the MTA process. By default, the SMTP service is limited to 1000 simultaneous handles. In large environments, this will limit the SMTP server and could create a backlog of messages waiting to be processed. Microsoft implements the restriction to prevent out-of-memory, kernel-mode problems and to ensure that when asked, the SMTP service can flush all buffers, release all file handles, and shut down in a relatively short period of time.

On servers with over 1GB of RAM, you can raise the SMTP handle threshold. Each handle uses 5KB of kernel-mode memory and 10KB of memory inside the inetinfo (IIS) process. By increasing the number of file handles that can be opened at any given time, you enable more messages to be opened and processed simultaneously. Raising this value is going to result in better performance only if you have current SMTP queues that are above 1000 messages to begin with.

If you increase the number of SMTP handles that can be opened, you should decrease the maximum number of IFS handles, as outlined below, that can be opened to avoid running out of kernel-mode memory when your queues become large. What follows is a discussion of three parameters, two of which are located in the following registry key:

HEKY_LOCAL_MACHINE\SYSTEM\CurrentControlSet\Services\SMTPSVC\Queue

When to Change If your SMTP queues are consistently greater than 1000.

- **Parameter to change:** *MsgHandleThreshold*. This value specifies the number of simultaneous open handles for the SMTP service.
- **Actions to take:** Add this REG_DWORD value. Even though it's not displayed, the default is 0x3e8, or, 1000. Increase it to accommodate a value greater than the number of messages in the SMTP queue at any given time. Do not raise above 15,000 decimal.
- **Counters to watch:** SMTP NTFS Store Driver\Messages in the queue directory, Open message bodies, Open message streams.

When to Change If messages in the SMTP Queue are consistently above 1000.

- **Parameter to change:** *MsgHandleAsyncThreshold*. This value specifies the number of handles that can be opened asynchronously. The default value, though it is not shown in the registry, is 1000.
- **Actions to take:** Add this REG_DWORD value and configure it the same as MsgHandleThreshold.
- **Counters to watch:** Watch the same counters as MsgHandleThreshold.

In the HKEY_LOCAL_MACHINE\SYSTEM\CurrentControlSet\Services\Inetinfo\Parameters registry key, make the following changes:

When to Change If you increase the MsgHandleThreshold value, you need to decrease this value.

- **Parameter to change:** *FileCacheMaxHandles*. This value represents the number of simultaneous file handles that are cached for each 32MB of memory installed on the server.
- **Actions to take:** Add this REG_DWORD value. The default is 0x320, or, 800 handles for every 32MB of memory. Decrease this value to 0x258 (600).

After making these changes, stop and start all the Exchange and IIS services to apply these changes.

Note *Exchange 2000 ships with the file handle cache optimally set. Microsoft recommends that you only decrease these values from the default settings. If you increase the file handle cache value above 800, the server may become unstable. Also, when increasing this value, keep in mind that there is a maximum of 50,000 handles that cannot be exceeded, regardless of how much memory is in the server.*

SMTP Message Queue Sizes

Each message queued by the SMTP service consumes at least 4KB of memory. With very large queues, it is possible to run out of memory. This is especially true if the server is a bridgehead server in a large environment with thousands of users. If you want to limit the number of messages in the queue at any given time (and therefore the amount of memory used by the SMTP service for queued messages) you can modify the registry key given below.

Bear in mind that if you set the limit too low, some users may receive an out-of-memory (4xx (temporary)) error from the SMTP service. Once this limit is reached, the SMTP service will refuse any more inbound messages until some messages leave the queue.

Add the key "mailmsg" so that it forms this registry path: HKEY_LOCAL_MACHINE\Software\Microsoft\Exchange\Mailmsg. Then add the REG_DWORD *MaxMessageObjects* key. The default for this key is 0x186a0 (100,000). Reduce this value as needed based on your system's available memory. By default, the maximum amount of memory the SMTP service can consume is less than 40MB.

The registry value above represents the number of objects (messages) that can be in the SMTP queue at any given time. Remember, each message takes *at least* 4KB, not 4KB total.

Message Transfer Agent

If you have been working with Exchange 5.x, you may have noticed that the Performance Optimization wizard is missing in Exchange 2000 Server. This is because the majority of components that the Performance Optimizer tuned are now self-tuning in Exchange 2000 Server. However, the Message Transfer Agent (MTA) is not one of them. When it is installed, it retains the default values that existed in Exchange 5.5; hence, its use may need to be tuned for Exchange 2000 Server.

In a pure Exchange 2000 environment, the MTA is not involved in the transfer of messages and thus does not need to be tuned. However, in a mixed environment of Exchange 2000 and Exchange 5.x Servers, the MTA will be involved in message transfer between the two platforms. In the following paragraphs, we outline some of the registry keys and how they should be tuned given a specific situation. The parameters we discuss are found under the following registry key:

HKEY_LOCAL_MACHINE\SYSTEM\CurrentControlSet\Services\MSExchangeMTA\Parameters

When to Change If your MTA communicates with multiple Exchange 5.x Servers or if your Exchange 2000 Server was upgraded from an Exchange 5.x Server and it is hosting a messaging connector that was installed under the Exchange 5.x platform.

- **Parameter to change:** *DB data buffers per object*. The default is 0x3. This is the number of 4KB buffers configured for each cached MTA database file. Remember that the MTA saves a copy of each message that it sends until it knows that the message has been accepted by the information store or another MTA. More buffers require more memory, but more buffers also makes it less likely that some of the MTA cached information will be paged temporarily to disk.
- **Action to take:** Increase this value to 0x6, and then re-measure and tune as necessary.
- **Counters to watch:** MSExchangeMTA, Free Elements & Free Headers.

When to Change If this Exchange 2000 Server communicates with more than five Exchange 5.x Servers or if distribution lists are heavily used.

- **Parameter to change:** *Dispatcher threads*. The default is 0x1. The MTA requires at least six threads when the MTA process is started: two for the router, two for fanout, and two for results. As its name implies, router threads route messages. Fanout threads send messages to the proper destinations. For example, if a message has both local and remote recipients, the fanout thread sends a copy to the information store and another copy to another MTA. The results thread handles notifications, including delivery receipts and non-delivery reports. If this MTA is processing a large number of messages, consider adjusting this value upward.
- **Action to take:** Increase this value to 0x3, and then re-measure and tune as necessary. Note that a change in this number actually increases the thread count by three: one for each of the Dispatch functions.

When to Change If the Exchange 2000 Server is communicating with an Exchange 5.5 Server using RPCs over a slow WAN link where the Exchange 2000 Server is using the routing group connector to connect to a site connector on the Exchange 5.5 Server.

- **Parameter to change:** *Kernel threads*. This value represents the number of threads that are processed at the presentation and session layers of the OSI stack. Bottlenecks in low-bandwidth or high-latency environments can be alleviated by increasing this value. The better solution is to obtain greater bandwidth to support the RPCs of a site connector.

- **Actions to take:** Increase this value to 0x3 unless the Exchange 2000 Server belongs to a site containing more than 15 Exchange 5.5 Servers; in that case, increase the value to 0x8. If the Exchange 5.5 site has more than 30 Exchange 5.5 Servers, increase the value to 0xC, or, 12.
- **Counters to watch:** There are no counters to watch for this parameter.

When to Change If you increase the number of Gateway In/Out threads in the store process—which is recommended when Exchange 2000 co-exists with Exchange 5.5.

- **Parameter to change:** *Max RPC Calls Outstanding*. This value is the maximum number of RPC calls that can be processed simultaneously. Most RPC failures are not caused by setting this value too low, but by network and/or hardware saturation.
- **Actions to take:** Increase this value from the default of 0x32 to 0x80 (128 decimal).
- **Counters to watch:** There are no counters to watch for this parameter.

When to Change If you are experiencing slow performance on an Exchange 2000 Server that has multiple connectors to Exchange 5.5 Servers, or if your organization has more than 1500 users.

- **Parameter to change:** *MDB users*. This value specifies the number of domain names to cache in the directory. If this server does not host any user accounts, but instead, is acting as a hub server between multiple connectors, you may need to configure this parameter to reflect a higher number than the default setting of 500. This is because of the increased message traffic that will pass through this server.
- **Actions to take:** The default is 0x1f4. Set to 0x1388 (5000) or to 1/3 of the total number of users in your organization, whichever is less.
- **Counters to watch:** MSExchangeMTA\ExDS Read Calls/sec.

When to Change If the MTA on the Exchange 2000 Server needs to communicate with multiple Exchange 5.5 Servers, consider adjusting this value.

- **Parameter to change:** *RTS threads*. The Reliable Transfer Service (RTS) threads are considered platform threads that handle the RTS Element level of the OSI stack. The default setting is 0x1.
- **Actions to take:** Increase this value to 0x3, then re-measure and tune as necessary.
- **When to use:** If you are hosting more than one X.400 connector on an Exchange 2000 Server.

- **Parameter to change:** *TCP/IP control blocks*. Control blocks manage MTA associations. Each association over an MTA will consume a control block. As a result, this value corresponds to the maximum number of TCP/IP connections that can be made to this server's MTA. The default value is 0x14 (20), which is sufficient for Exchange 2000 Servers configured to host two X.400 connectors. Each connector needs 10 control blocks to make 10 associations: 9 associations for low- and normal-priority messages and 1 association for high-priority messages.
- **Actions to take:** Increase this number to 10 control blocks for each X.400 connector plus one control block for incoming connections.
- **When to use:** If the MTA communicates with multiple Exchange 5.5 Servers.
- **Parameter to change:** *Transfer threads*. A transfer thread is used to transfer messages in or out of the MTA. If the MTA is having difficulty clearing out its queues, consider increasing the number of threads available for message transfer.
- **Actions to take:** The default setting is 0x1. Increase to 0x3.

Remember, that for each registry entry you configure, the MTA service must be stopped and re-started for the changes to take effect.

Active Directory and Optimization

Tuning Exchange 2000 Server to work with Active Directory is necessary only if you are working with large, multiprocessor servers. Essentially, in a large environment where there are many Exchange 2000 Servers in a single Windows 2000 site, a heavy LDAP (Lightweight Directory Access Protocol) load could be placed on the domain controllers for that site. By default, a domain controller is configured to support a maximum of 20 pending LDAP requests. If this limit is reached, an LDAP_ADMIN_LIMIT_EXCEEDED error is returned. Anytime this error appears, you should consider increasing the maximum number of LDAP queries that your Windows 2000 domain controller can service.

Note *This change should be made only in very large, multiprocessor (six or eight CPUs) environments.*

To increase this value, you'll need to use the NTDSUTIL.EXE utility and perform the following steps:

1. Open a command prompt, type **NTDSUTIL**, and then press ENTER.
2. Type: **ldap policies**.
3. Type: **connections**.
4. Type: **connect to server** *<name of dc/gc server>*.
5. Type: **q**.

6. Type: **show values**.
7. Type: **set maxactivequeries to** <# *of queries desired*>.
8. Type: **commit changes**.
9. Type: **show values**.
10. Verify the new value is shown.
11. Type: **q**.
12. Type: **q**.

Active Directory picks up this change without requiring a restart. In addition, this setting is global throughout the forest. This change will take effect on each domain controller once it has been replicated to all the domain controllers in your forest. When you increase this value, the LSASS.EXE process on your domain controllers will use more memory; therefore, don't increase this value any higher than absolutely necessary. In its documentation, Microsoft uses a value of 40. We've illustrated this command sequence in Figure 21-3.

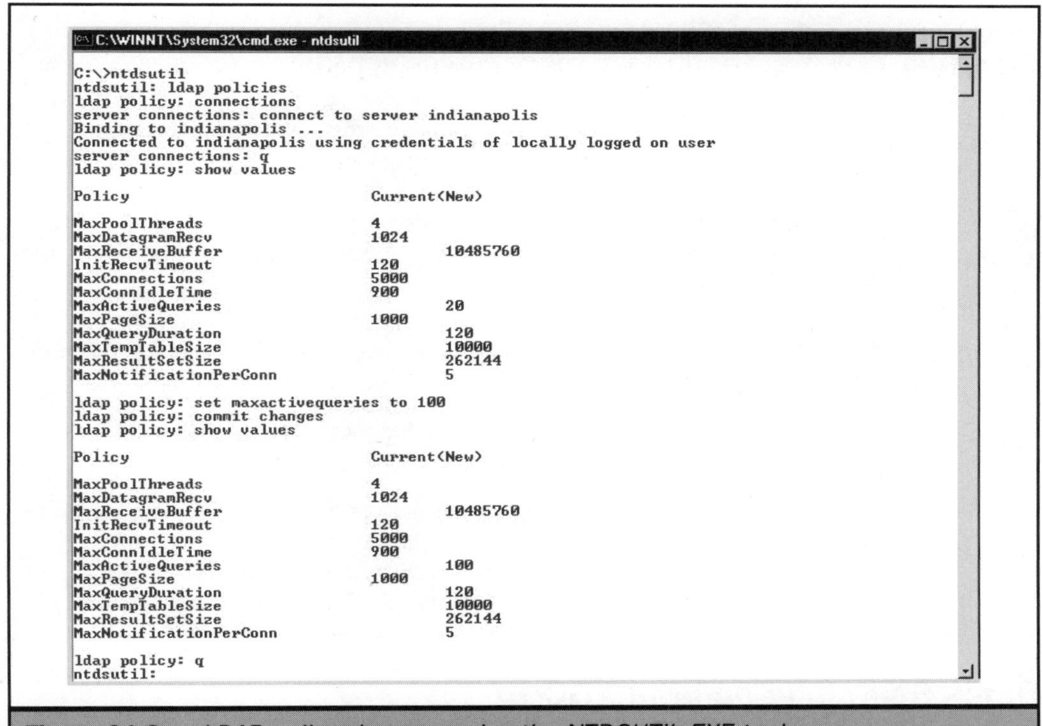

Figure 21-3. *LDAP policy changes using the NTDSUTIL.EXE tool*

Active Directory Connector

Tuning the Active Directory Connector (ADC) involves working with its default sleep time. By default, the ADC is permitted to work for 5 minutes and then sleep for 5 minutes to allow other applications processing time on the domain controller (DC) or Global Catalog (GC) server. In some situations, such as when the connector is first replicating changes to the AD or when large changes are being made to the source directory, it may be wise to have the ADC work without sleeping.

The way to attack this is to lengthen the "wake" time and minimize the "sleep" time. Remember that the registry changes you make will apply to all connection agreements (CA) running on the local server.

The registry location in which these two parameters are found is:

HKEY_LOCAL_MACHINE\SYSTEM\CurrentControlSet\Services\MSADC\Parameters.

When to Change If you want the ADC service to continue processing after the default 5 minutes.

- **Parameter to change:** *Max Continuous Sync (secs)*. Increasing this value dictates how long the ADC service will run continuously between sleep intervals.
- **Actions to take:** Add this REG_DWORD value. Its default is 0x12c (300). You can increase this as much as you want, but it's strongly recommended that you not increase this value to higher than 1200 seconds (20 min or 0x4B0). Setting the value too high may adversely affect other applications running on the server.

Modifying this value helps only if there is a fairly large amount of data to be replicated. If only a few entries need to be modified, the ADC will replicate and complete before the Max Continuous Sync value is reached.

When to Change If you want the ADC services to sleep less often than the default every 5 minutes.

- **Parameter to change:** *Sync Sleep Delay (secs)*. This value adjusts the default time for how long the ADC sleeps.
- **Actions to take:** Add this REG_DWORD value. Set the minimum to 60 seconds (0x3C) and be very careful about raising this value too high. If this value exceeds the CA's replication schedule, the ADC will never replicate. For example, if you set this value at 3600 seconds and the CA is scheduled to replicate every 15 minutes (Always), the ADC will never replicate.

Block Searching and the ADC

By default, the ADC replicates changes in blocks of 10,000 objects. If there are over 10,000 objects that need to be replicated, the ADC will process them in chunks or blocks of

10,000. If the bandwidth between your servers is even slightly irregular, it may be best to reduce the block size. If there is a loss of connectivity during the replication of a block, the ADC will re-replicate the entire block once connectivity is established.

When to Change If you need the ADC to write replicated objects to the AD more often, but in smaller blocks.

- **Parameter to change:** *Export Block Size*. This parameter sets the size of the block of objects that the ADC will replicate. After it has replicated the entire block, all the objects will be written to the AD.
- **Actions to take:** Add this REG_DWORD value. Its default is 0x2710 (10,000). Consider reducing this to 1,000 in a poorly connected environment. Doing so increases the overall time needed to replicate the objects, but decreases the number of times that re-replication of the same objects occurs.

To read more about this, please see Microsoft Knowledge Base articles Q253665 and Q253840.

Monitoring Exchange 2000 Health and Performance

In this section, we'll discuss how to discern the health of your Exchange 2000 Servers and outline ways in which you can be proactive in detecting problems before they become evident to users on your network.

We understand that in many environments, there is rarely time to think about performance monitoring and server health, let alone implement any proactive strategies. However, we encourage you to set aside some time each day to look at the health of your servers. In the long run, doing so will reduce the number of help desk calls and will result in better uptime of your servers.

Proactive Monitoring Techniques

In addition to tools for tweaking the registry, Microsoft provides tools to help with monitoring of Exchange 2000 Server. Let's discuss these tools.

Event Logs

The application event logs contain the messages that Exchange 2000 Server generates to inform or warn you as to events or problems that have occurred with one of its components, or a component upon which Exchange 2000 relies. This is one of the first places to go when trying to diagnose a problem. You can look up many of the events found in the event logs at http://www.microsoft.com/exchange/en/60/help/default.asp. TechNet and the Microsoft Knowledge Base also contain information on a number of Exchange 2000 event messages and errors, and some even recommend methods of resolution. In addition, if the source or event details of the event include an ESE error code, you can look up the code number in Microsoft Knowledge Base article Q266267.

Performance Data

When Exchange 2000 is installed, it also installs its own set of performance objects and counters that can track various parts of the Exchange 2000 application. Each object has at least one counter and can be used to monitor Exchange through the System Monitor snap-in in the Performance console.

With the Performance Logs and Alerts tool, you can log counter data information, which can be exported to spreadsheets or databases for analysis and report generation. Data can be exported in six formats: comma-separated text file, tab-separated text file, binary file, binary circular file, circular trace file, and sequential trace file. Performance logging runs as a service, so a user doesn't need to be logged on to the server for the logging sessions to run. You can also define the file size, start times, and stop times for logging, so that your log doesn't grow to be so large that it consumes all available disk space.

You can also create counter logs to collect data at a predefined interval. This is helpful for recording data about system services activities and hardware usage for the local or remote server, or both. Results can be viewed through the System Monitor snap-in and saved in a number of formats, including HTML.

Trace logs monitor data continuously and wait for specific events, such as page faults, to occur. When the specified event occurs, it is recorded into the trace log file. To read the file, you need a parsing tool, which is a specialized program that takes raw data and presents it in an understandable form. Developers can create parsing tools as needed using the APIs provided by Microsoft in the Platform SDK.

You can use a counter to trigger an alert that is sent to the specified recipients via the Messenger service. For example, if processor utilization exceeds 80 percent for 10 minutes, you can have an alert send a message or trigger a third-party application to contact you. You can also specify sample intervals so that the data is constantly, but not continuously, monitored. Use the alert feature of System Monitor when you want to be notified of an event that rarely or only intermittently occurs.

Performance Counters to Watch Because Exchange 2000 is tightly integrated with the Windows 2000 operating system, you'll need to watch both Windows 2000 and Exchange 2000 counters. What follows is a series of tables that outlines the various objects and counters with which you should concern yourself. Each table covers a different service of the Exchange 2000 application.

When you want to monitor the store process and its performance, use the counters in Table 21-1.

When you want to monitor the SMTP service and its performance, use the counters in Table 21-2.

To monitor the MTA, use the counters in Table 21-3.

Object	Counter	Comment
MSExchangeIS	User Count	This counter reports the number of users connected to the information store, not the number of TCP connections.
MSExchangeIS Mailbox and MSExchangeIS Public	Send Queue Size	This counter reports the number of outbound messages queued in the selected information store. This counter is further broken down into instances for each store.
MSExchangeIS Mailbox and MSExchangeIS Public	Receive Queue Size	This counter reports the number of inbound messages queued for the information store. A non-zero number is normal for this counter. A steadily rising number may indicate a problem with the information store. Like the Send Queue Size counter, this counter is further broken down into instances for each store.
MSExchangeIS Mailbox and MSExchangeIS Public	Messages Sent/Min	This counter shows the rate at which messages are sent to the transport. When monitored with the Send Queue Size counter, you can determine the speed at which messages are being processed for sending.
MSExchangeIS Mailbox and MSExchangeIS Public	Messages Delivered/Min	This counter shows the rate at which messages are delivered to its recipients. When monitored with the Receive Queue Size counter, you can determine the speed at which messages are being processed for delivery.

Table 21-1. *Information Store Performance Counters*

Object	Counter	Comment
SMTP Server	Local Queue Length	This counter displays the number of messages in the local queue. Normally, this should be zero. A number greater than zero may indicate that the server cannot process the messages as fast as they are arriving in the queue. This counter is further broken down into instances of SMTP virtual servers.
SMTP Server	Categorizer Queue Length	This counter displays the number of messages waiting to be run through the Message Categorizer before being placed in the local queue or routed out the SMTP service. A high number can indicate a number of things, including message flow problems or name resolution problems.
SMTP Server	Inbound Connections Current	This counter displays the number of current inbound connections. No connections for an extended period of time may indicate network connectivity problems.
SMTP Server	Message Bytes Received/Sec	This counter displays the rate at which inbound messages are arriving in average number of bytes per second. Trend this counter over time to determine a normal range for your environment.
SMTP Server	Message Bytes Sent/Sec	This counter displays the rate at which outbound messages are sent in average number of bytes per second. Also trend this counter over time to determine a normal range for your environment.

Table 21-2. *SMTP Performance Counters*

Object	Counter	Comment
MSExchangeMTA	Messages/Sec	This counter displays the number of messages sent and received each second by the MTA. Use this counter to determine real-time activity of the MTA.
MSExchangeMTA	Work Queue Length	This counter displays the number of messages in the MTA queue waiting for delivery to other servers and the number of messages in the receive queue. When this counter is divided by the Messages/Sec counter, you can get an idea as to how long messages are being delayed in the queue. An increasing number may indicate either a network connectivity or server performance issue.
MSExchangeMTA Connections	Queue Length	This counter displays the number of messages queued to another specified MTA. This is useful for determining which MTAs are involved in a message slow-down. This counter is broken down into instances for each SMTP virtual server and for the pending reroute queue.

Table 21-3. *MTA Counters to Watch*

If you want to monitor how the disk subsystem is performing, pay attention to the counters in Table 21-4.

Note *In Windows 2000, the LogicalDisk performance library object is turned off by default. To enable it, use the Diskperf command and reboot. For information on using Diskperf, see Microsoft Knowledge Base article Q253251.*

Object	Counter	Comment
LogicalDisk	% Free Space	This counter displays the percentage of free space available on a logical disk. You can set this up as an alert so that if the overall disk space falls below a predetermined percentage, such as 10 percent, you are automatically notified.
PhysicalDisk	% Disk Time	This counter displays the percentage of time that a hard drive is reading or writing. A constant value over 90 percent indicates that one or more disks might be bottlenecks in your system.
PhysicalDisk	Disk Reads/Sec; Disk Writes/Sec	These two counters give you the transfer rate of data to and from your hard disk.
PhysicalDisk	Current Disk Queue Length	This counter displays the number of disk I/O operations that are sitting in the queue waiting to be processed by the disk. A sustained number greater than 2 might indicate that your disk is a bottleneck in the system.
PhysicalDisk	Avg. Disk Read Queue Length	This counter displays the average number of read requests that were queued during the time the counter was being measured. An increasing number indicates your disk is a bottleneck.
PhysicalDisk	Avg. Disk Write Queue Length	This counter displays the average number of write requests that were queued during the time the counter was measured. An increasing number indicates your disk is a bottleneck.

Table 21-4. *Disk Counters to Watch*

If you want to measure the system for memory bottlenecks, watch the counters in Table 21-5.

If you need to monitor processor bottlenecks, use the counters listed in Table 21-6.

Object	Counter	Comment
Memory	Committed Bytes	This counter displays the amount of virtual memory space that has been committed to an application. If this value is higher than the size of the pagefile, the application has acquired too much virtual memory.
Memory	Pages/Sec	This counter displays the total amount of paging activity between physical memory and the PAGEFILE.SYS file. A sustained value over 20 may indicate the need for additional memory.
Memory	Page Faults/Sec	This counter displays the number of times that application data was not found in the application's working set in memory and the data had to be paged into memory from PAGEFILE.SYS. A sustained value over 10 may indicate the need for additional memory.
Process	Page Faults/Sec	This counter monitors individual processes, and then reports how many page faults each process is experiencing. This helps you understand which application is experiencing the most page faults when your value for Memory\Page Faults/Sec is high.

Table 21-5. *Memory and Processor Counters to Watch*

Object	Counter	Comment
Processor	Interrupts/Sec	This counter shows the average number of hardware interrupts the processor is servicing each second. If this value increases without a corresponding increase in other system counters, a hardware device may be interrupting the processor too often and may be malfunctioning.
Processor	% Processor Time	This counter displays the percentage of time that the processor is busy executing non-idle threads. An average value over 70 percent may indicate the need for an additional processor or a faster processor.
Processor	% Privileged Time	This measures the percentage of processor time spent in privileged mode. Privileged mode is used by operating system components and hardware-manipulating drivers. A high rate of privileged time could be attributable to a large number of interrupts generated by a failing device.

Table 21-6. *Processor Counters to Watch*

Baselining

One of the most difficult administrative duties is the regular monitoring of key performance counters for your servers. This is so difficult because most IS staffs are understaffed and there is little time to engage in this activity. And in larger environments, where there are 100 or more Exchange 2000 Servers, it just isn't practical to baseline each server.

But if you can, try to take some time each day to collect the counter data from your Exchange 2000 Servers, domain controllers, Global Catalog servers, and DNS servers. If you can develop a baseline of normal behavior for each Exchange 2000 Server, and then look at the trends of those results over time, you'll be able to predict how long the server will operate at peak performance before additional CPUs, memory, disks, or registry changes are needed.

This type of proactive administrative activity may help avoid server downtime in the long run.

Server Monitor Tools in Exchange 2000

You can use some tools in the ESM snap-in to help with your monitoring activities. We'll discuss those tools in this section.

The Exchange 2000 Server monitoring tools are found in the Monitoring and Status folder beneath the Tools icon in the ESM snap-in. This area lists the connectors and servers in the organization and what state they are in. We purposefully stopped the Exchange services on the cluster server to demonstrate how information about a downed server would appear, as shown in Figure 21-4.

A server can be in four different states:

- **Available** The server is functioning normally.
- **Unreachable** A main service is not running.
- **In maintenance mode** Monitoring has been disabled for maintenance or backup.
- **Unknown** The system attendant cannot communicate with the server.

Connectors can be in two different states:

- **Available** The connector is functioning normally.
- **Unavailable** A communication service is not running on the connector.

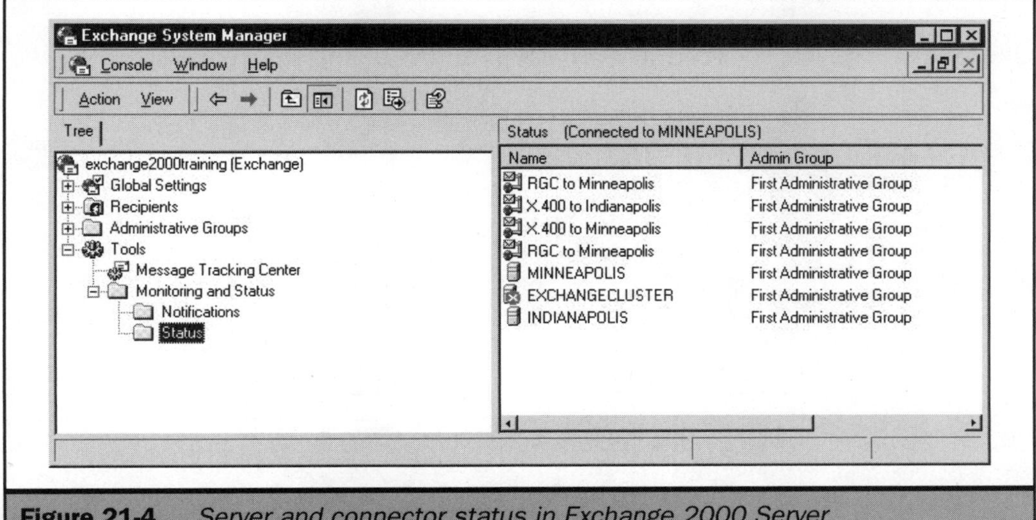

Figure 21-4. *Server and connector status in Exchange 2000 Server*

If a server is in a different routing group and the connector goes down, the server may appear as unreachable or unknown even though it is up and running. This is due to the connector being down. Hence, if a connector is down from your local routing group to another routing group, the servers in the group may also appear in a critical state with warning messages.

If you open one of the server's properties, you'll be presented with a single Monitoring tab that has to be the most confusing tab in all of Exchange 2000. It is shown in Figure 21-5. At first glance, it looks like the Minneapolis server is in a critical state because it is reported as being stopped. But what this screen is really saying is that if the Exchange services are stopped, the server will be listed in a critical state in the ESM snap-in status folder, which was shown in Figure 21-4. This screen is not saying that the services are stopped, only that stopped services will place this server in a critical state.

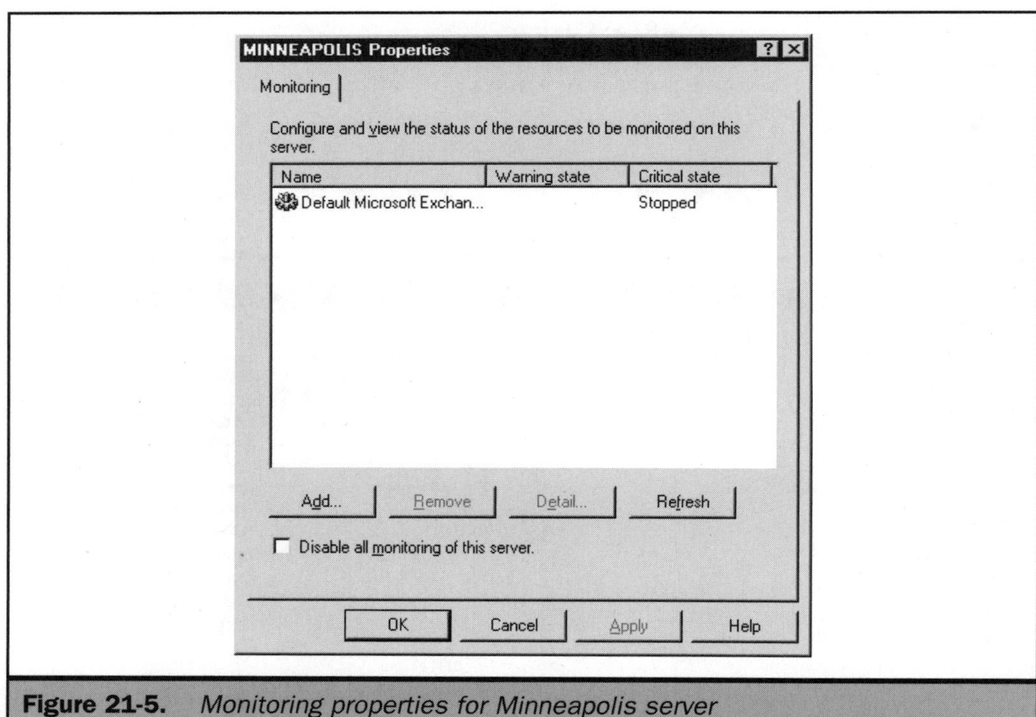

Figure 21-5. *Monitoring properties for Minneapolis server*

If you hover your mouse over the entry for the Default Microsoft Exchange Services, it becomes a link to another properties box which, when opened, displays the state of the monitored services, as shown in Figure 21-6.

If you click the Add button, you'll be able to use the Add Service dialog box to add any service currently installed on this server to the list of services that are monitored by the Exchange monitoring service. This is a nice feature if you wish to monitor non-Exchange 2000 services. The Exchange 2000 monitoring service monitors the following default set of services:

- Microsoft Exchange Information Store
- Microsoft Exchange MTA Stacks
- Microsoft Exchange Routing Engine
- Microsoft Exchange System Attendant
- Simple Mail Transport Protocol (SMTP)
- World Wide Web Publishing Service

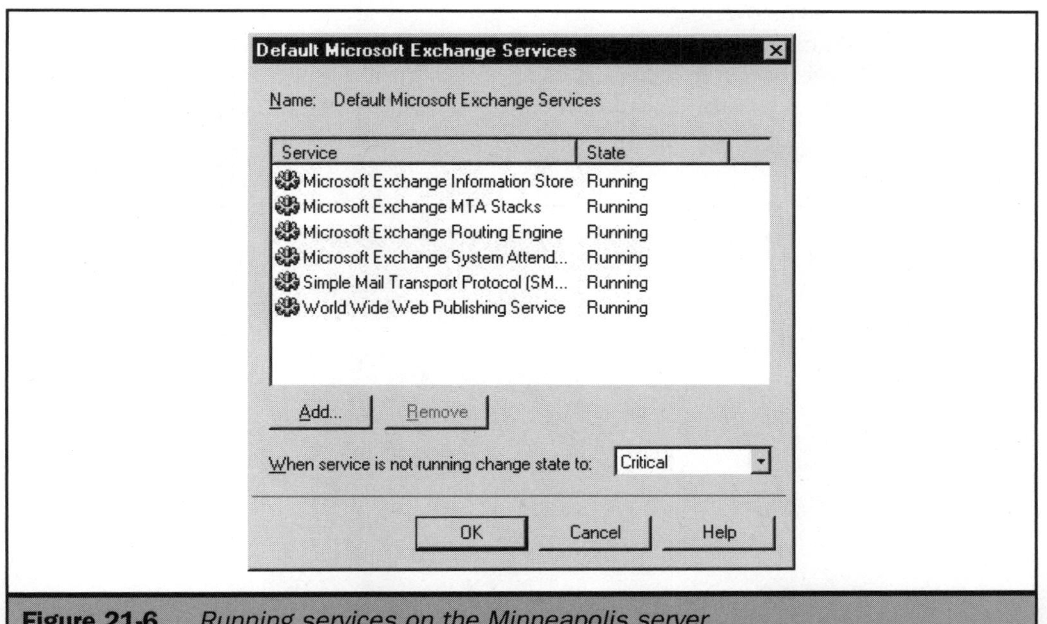

Figure 21-6. *Running services on the Minneapolis server*

If you want to monitor specific resources by using the Monitoring and Status tool, you can do so. To monitor a resource, click Add on the Monitoring tab, and then select the resource to monitor, as shown in Figure 21-7. You can monitor the following resources:

- Available virtual memory
- CPU utilization
- Free disk space
- SMTP queue growth
- Windows 2000 service
- X.400 queue growth

In our example, we'll choose the free disk space resource.

Once we click OK, the Disk Space Threshold dialog box appears, where we can choose which logical drive to monitor and set the minimum drive-space thresholds for a warning state and a critical state, both in megabytes. After we enter our configurations, we can see the results of this action in the Monitoring tab of the server's properties, as shown in Figure 21-8. Notice that we chose to put the resource in a warning state if the free drive space falls below 300MB on drive C and a critical state if it falls below 150MB.

In Figure 21-8, notice at the bottom of the tab is a checkbox to disable all monitoring of this server. This is useful if you need to have the server up and running, but you need to stop and start services for maintenance or testing purposes.

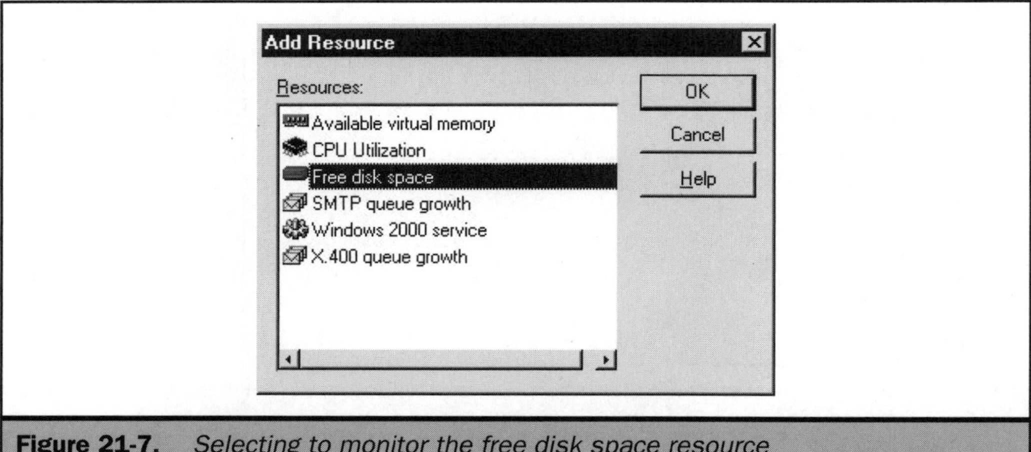

Figure 21-7. *Selecting to monitor the free disk space resource*

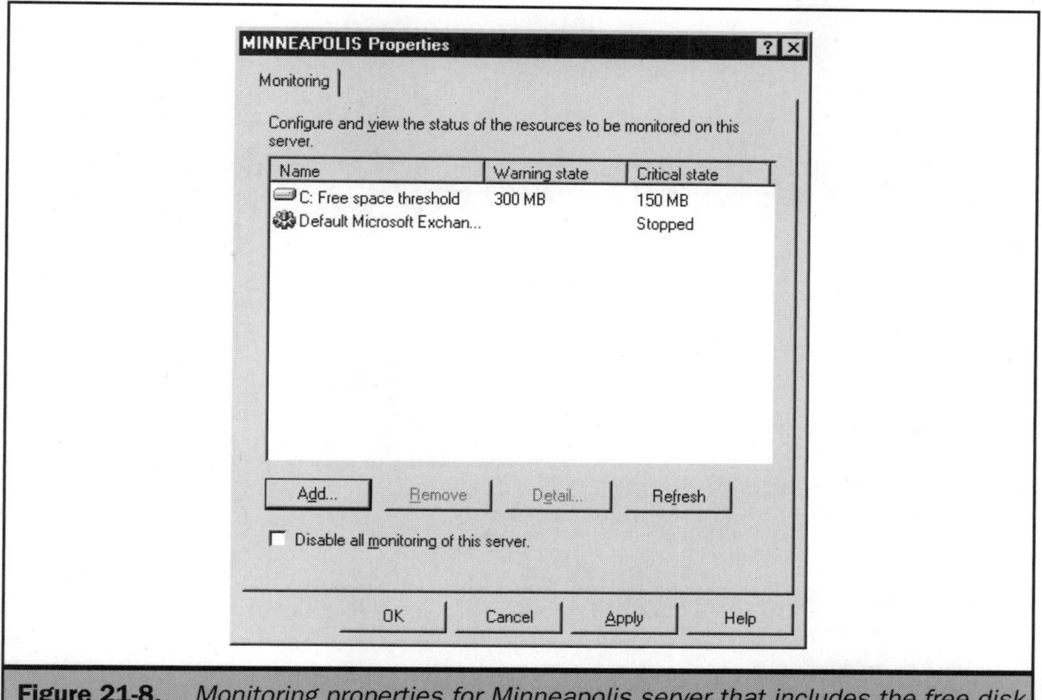

Figure 21-8. *Monitoring properties for Minneapolis server that includes the free disk space resource*

You can determine how you want to be notified when a server enters a warning or critical state by configuring a notification. Notifications can take the form of an e-mail or a customized script. To create a notification, right-click on the Notifications folder, point to New, and then select either the e-mail notification or the script notification. In our example, we have chosen an e-mail notification, as shown in Figure 21-9. This allows us to select which servers to monitor, when we want to be notified, who should receive the e-mail and the form of the message. It is a good idea to include the help desk people in such a notification so they know that there is a problem with one of the Exchange 2000 Servers when a user calls in complaining about a lack of services from that server.

The script notification is less complicated to create since all you'll really do is configure which servers and/or connectors you wish to have monitored, and then give the path and name of the script to run, such as D:\MYPAGER.EXE. If you want certain people to be notified with a script notification, they must be included in the script.

When choosing which objects you wish to be notified about, you don't have the option to select all servers and all connectors in the same notification configuration. If you want to be notified of problems with both servers and connectors, you'll need to

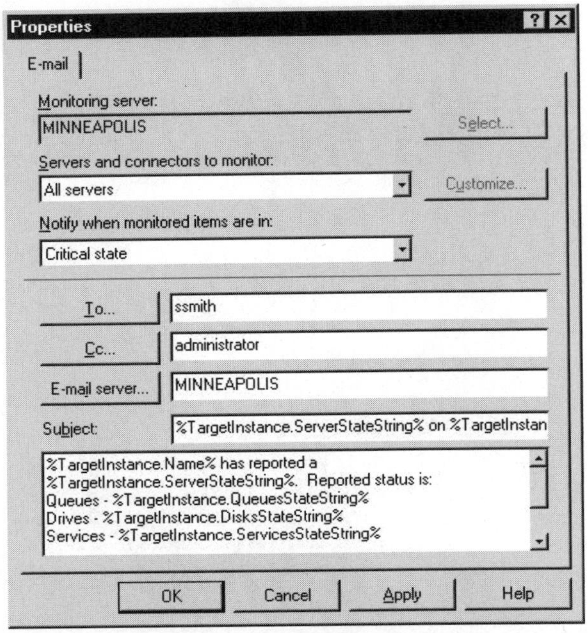

Figure 21-9. *Configuring an e-mail notification*

create two notifications: one for all servers and another for all connectors. It is done this way because the default e-mails are different, depending on whether a server or a connector is being monitored.

Logging Diagnostic Data

For many services in Exchange 2000 Server, you can enable the logging of diagnostic data, which is recorded in the application log. The following services can be logged for diagnostic purposes:

- IMAP4Svc
- MSExchangeAL
- MSExchangeIS
- MSExchangeMTA
- MSExchangeSA
- MSExchangeSRS

- MSExchangeTransport
- POP3Svc

Diagnostic logging gives you precise information about messages traveling in and out of the system and how the service is interacting with those messages. There are four logging levels from which you can select:

- **None** Log only error messages
- **Minimum** Log warning and error messages
- **Medium** Log informational, warning, and error messages
- **Maximum** Log troubleshooting, informational, warning, and error messages

Keep a few things in mind when selecting a logging level. First, the None level does not mean none; error messages are still logged to the application log. Don't think that just because the logging level is set to None, which is the default, that you won't see any messages from that service in the event logs. Second, if you want to select Maximum logging, be sure to *significantly* increase the size of the application log, or set the log files to overwrite events after a specific number of days, or as needed. The maximum logging level will fill up 512KB (the default size of each log file) very quickly. Failure to increase the size will result in important events not being logged because the log is full. Third, the Maximum setting significantly increases load on your system resources. Only choose this level when you are unable to diagnose a problem using other resources and strategies.

Tip *Once configured, the diagnostic logging settings are located in the registry under HKEY_LOCAL_MACHINE\System\CurrentControlSet\Services\<ServiceName>. Each <ServiceName> has a registry subkey named Diagnostics under which individual settings are stored. The registry settings are all DWORD values that translate as follows: None (0), Minimum (1), Medium (3), and Maximum (5). There is an undocumented value of 6, which translates to Advanced Diagnostic Logging. Microsoft PSS typically uses this value for the most difficult troubleshooting cases. As you might expect, a lot of the advanced diagnostic messages will be unintelligible to anyone outside the Exchange development team.*

Enabling Protocol Logging

Not only can you enable diagnostic logging for each service, but you can also enable protocol logging for each protocol. The SMTP, NNTP, and HTTP virtual servers provide this capability to enable you to track the commands the virtual servers and their clients pass back and forth.

In Chapter 10, "Managing Protocols", we cover the commands for each protocol and what those commands mean. It isn't just theory. If you enable protocol logging, you can open the log file and see the actual communications between the virtual servers and their clients. It's very useful for diagnostic purposes.

You can configure the SMTP and NNTP protocol logging using the ESM snap-in. Navigate to the General tab of the virtual server's properties and select Enable Logging, as shown in Figure 21-10. You can select among the following logging methods:

- **W3C Extended Log File Format.** This is the default file format for protocol logging in Windows 2000. Information is written to an ASCII text file. Unlike other formats, you can choose what is written into the log, and you can limit the size of the log file itself.
- **Microsoft IIS Log File Format.** This format has information written to a comma-delimited ASCII text file. Once it is written, it cannot be changed and the log format is not customizable.
- **NCSA Common Log File Format.** Information is written to an ASCII text file in the National Center for Supercomputing Applications (NCSA) format. Once written, data cannot be changed and the format is not customizable.
- **ODBC Logging.** Information is written to an open database connectivity (ODBC) compliant database.

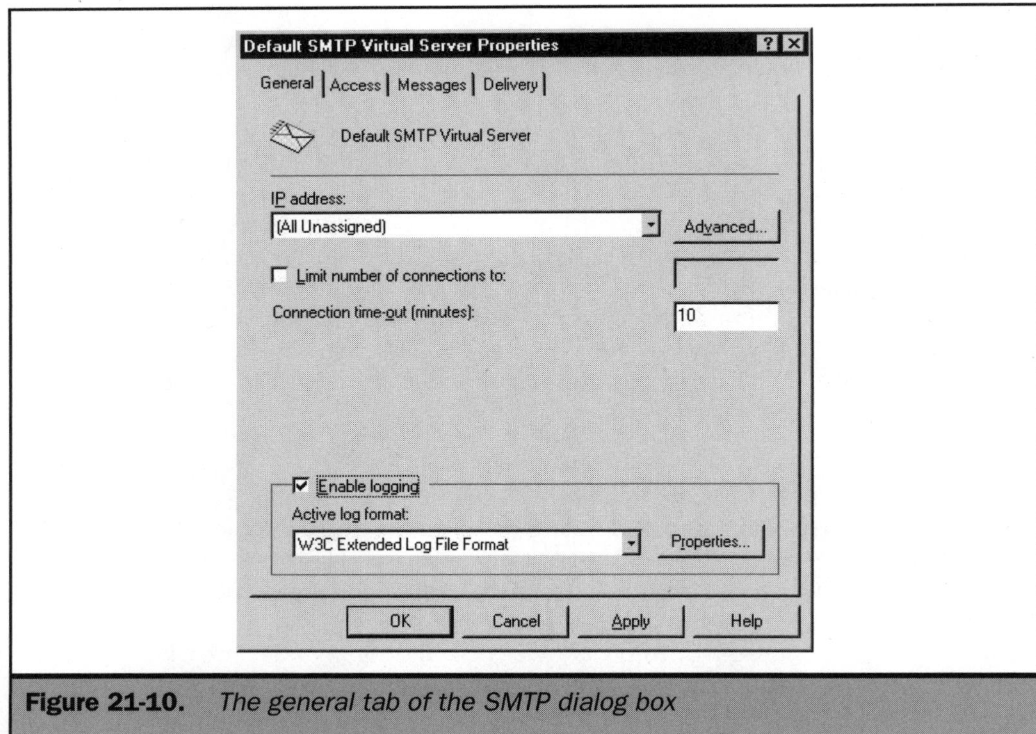

Figure 21-10. *The general tab of the SMTP dialog box*

Unless you have a particular reason for choosing otherwise, the default W3C Extended Log File Format should work for most environments and situations.

Summary

In this chapter, we covered how to tune and monitor Exchange 2000 Server. We presented fairly detailed information about some of the key registry values to manipulate in given situations, some of the more important counters to measure in System Monitor, and the built-in tools in the ESM snap-in that can be used on a daily basis.

Part VI

Appendixes

Appendix A

Technology Primer—What Is WebDAV?

Technology Primer: What Is WebDAV?

Every business needs its employees to collaborate with each other in order to survive. Business documents are not formed in a vacuum, nor does a single individual typically write them. Despite advances in computer technology, the document creation process remains relatively unchanged. Someone creates the first draft, which is in turn reviewed or edited by someone else and sent back for revisions. There may be several iterations before the document's final form is approved. With the advent of electronic mail, the process has gotten quicker. Users e-mail drafts back and forth until they arrive at a final version. Others use a common file store for their collaborative efforts, such as a file share or the public folder hierarchy in Exchange Server.

While these systems are ideal for sharing documents, they don't lend themselves well to the collaborative phase of the document. For example, there is no version control, making it difficult to track revision history, compare documents, or revert to previous edits. Likewise, there is no real method for file locking or edit-conflict resolution. To overcome these limitations, many businesses have implemented sophisticated document management systems which provide these features.

As document creation moves from the realm of traditional word processing applications to HTML and XML authoring tools, the need to collaborate remains intact. Unlike traditional tools, such as Microsoft Word, many HTML authoring tools do not provide direct access to the file system that contains the documents. Some, like Microsoft FrontPage, provide proprietary extensions that allow basic authoring and file system access. But because these tools are typically not cross-platform, their adoptability is limited in many environments.

Historically, the World Wide Web has been a read-only medium, even though the first Web browser ever invented had both read and write capabilities. Visitors to a Web site read content, click links, fill out forms, or order merchandise, but generally they don't change any of the content. Even as the Web gets more interactive with dynamic pages, multimedia, and personalization, there's something that's still missing—collaboration.

In December 1995, the World Wide Web Distributed Authoring and Versioning (WebDAV) working group began as an informative meeting of people at the World Wide Web Conference in Boston who were interested in remote authoring. In the spring of 1997, WebDAV was formally confirmed as a working group in the Internet Engineering Task Force (IETF). For the past several years, the WebDAV working group has been working on a set of extensions to the HTTP 1.1 protocol. These extensions provide additional functionality under the HTTP protocol, such as file locking, versioning, search, access control, and resource properties.

The WebDAV standard was approved by the IETF in December 1998, resulting in RFC 2518, "HTTP Extensions for Distributed Authoring—WEBDAV." According to its Abstract, RFC 2518 "specifies a set of methods, headers, and content-types ancillary to HTTP/1.1 for the management of resource properties, creation and management of resource collections, namespace manipulation, and resource locking (collision avoidance)."

At its most basic level, WebDAV lets users create and share server-based documents regardless of what platform they are on, what authoring tools they use, or what type of Web servers stores the documents. In essence, WebDAV turns the read-only Web into a collaborative, read/write medium, without requiring direct access to the storage device(s).

Current Web standards already include this functionality. Several existing HTML distributed authoring tools, such as Microsoft FrontPage, are already exploiting this ability and providing users with the ability to create and publish Web content. The problem, however, is that these solutions are platform-dependent. In order to use FrontPage, for example, you need to install FrontPage extensions on a supported Web server.

Overview of WebDAV Functions

The WebDAV Distributed Authoring Protocol includes three primary features: overwrite protection through file locking, property access through the creation of metadata, and namespace management, which brings file management functions to the HTTP protocol. WebDAV supports a variety of storage models by abstracting the data from the process using the concepts of *resources*, *collections*, and *properties*. Resources are anything that can be identified by a URL, such as a document. Collections are anything that contains a resource, such as a directory. Properties refer to data that describes the resource or collection. Under the WebDAV model, properties are expressed using Extensible Markup Language (XML), which provides a format for structured data. In fact, the WebDAV property model is based on XML.

Overwrite Protection

While it is perfectly fine for multiple users to simultaneously read the same document, it is problematic for multiple users to simultaneously edit the same document. If you and I are editing the same document and we both later save our edits, one of us is going to lose their changes. In this event, the last writer wins. As you might expect, this problem is magnified when there are more than two people who need to edit the same document.

Certainly, there are ways to overcome this problem:

- **Communication with fellow collaborators** You can call or e-mail other collaborators on the document and announce your intentions to edit the document. Once your edits are complete, you can contact them once more to let them know you've finished. This works, but only to a certain extent. For one thing, this is very inefficient. You might have to deal with geographic distances and different time zones, and you may not even be able to reach everyone on your team. Moreover, if each team member needs to make multiple changes, you might end up spending more time communicating the start and completion of changes than you would actually making the changes.

- **Exclusive locking** Exclusive locks guarantee conflict avoidance and therefore work best for collaborators who aren't fully aware of each other's activities or during periods of contention for the same document. Under the exclusive locking model, the computer controlling access to the document locks the document, thus preventing anyone other than the owner of the lock from modifying the document. Other authors who attempt to edit the document are denied access. This is certainly the most protective mechanism, but it is the least flexible. If the user neglects to update the document or release the lock, other users remain locked out of the document. When this happens, administrative intervention is usually required to manually unlock the document.
- **Shared locking** Shared locks work best when collaborators are aware of each other's activities. Under this model—also known as the reservation model—the computer controlling access to the document records the author's intent to edit the document. If another user attempts to edit the same document, the computer notifies him that the document is currently being edited. This is similar to exclusive locking, except that the second user can circumvent the lock and edit the document.

The WebDAV approach is a combination of shared and exclusive locking. By providing support for both models, WebDAV is able accommodate a wide variety of collaboration scenarios. Locks can have a scope or a hierarchy of resources, enabling collaborators to secure their documents and accompanying materials. A lock discovery mechanism—which is a WebDAV property—allows collaborators to determine if any locks exist on a resource. Locking mechanisms typically include notifications, so that collaborators can be informed by the computer when a lock is released. This lets collaborators become aware of each other's activities.

A WebDAV server need not provide any locking mechanism in order to comply with RFC 2518, but without such a mechanism, preventing one user from overwriting another user's changes becomes difficult. For this reason, most WebDAV servers include either a shared locking mechanism or an exclusive locking mechanism.

Property Access

All Web documents have elements called *properties* that describe it in one or more respects. Document properties include the title, the subject, the author, the creation date, and so forth. Sets of these properties are known as the document's *metadata*. Metadata is information that describes information. It's not the information you're looking for, but rather the information that helps you find the information you're looking for.

The actual metadata types vary according to the defined metadata schema. The metadata schema provides the structure for the metadata. It specifies what properties each document can have. WebDAV is metadata schema neutral; that is, it doesn't require any specific schema to be used. This means that each organization can create a document property schema that is tailored to their specifications.

WebDAV uses XML as the underlying language for expressing property values and for the storage of metadata. Since any number of XML tags can be introduced, the metadata schema can be extended easily, allowing you to add document properties as needed. In addition, XML supports multiple character sets, allowing people from different countries to access the metadata and collaborate with one another.

WebDAV properties are name-value pairs. The name of the property is the name of the XML element. The value of the property can be a well-formed XML element value or blank. For example, for this book, the name of one property is "Title" and its value is "Exchange 2000 Server: The Complete Reference." These names and values are indexed to provide fast and easy access to specific documents.

There are two types of properties: live and dead. A live property, which resides on the server, is always current and accurate. A dead property, which resides on the client, may not be current or accurate. The WebDAV model provides for a client-side property store that can be synchronized with server-side stores through replication of the most important information. Together, this provides efficient online access, as well as support for offline scenarios.

Namespace Management

WebDAV enables users to use Web documents and directories as if they were a file system. For example, users can copy, move, and delete files. This is extremely important if an intranet or the Web is to be used as a document repository. No matter where the documents are stored, users must be able to manage the namespace to which they are writing. WebDAV uses collections and resources to represent directories and document, respectively. A WebDAV server—such as Internet Information Server 5.0—maintains collections and resources. When a resource is added to the server (using the HTTP PUT command), it is automatically added to the appropriate collection.

Extending HTTP 1.1

WebDAV extends the HTTP 1.1 protocol by adding additional methods, or commands, that enable the functionality needed to collaborate on a Web server. The following paragraphs describe the HTTP methods added by WebDAV.

COPY The HTTP 1.1 protocol has existing methods—GET and PUT—that you can use to copy files from one location to another. As you might expect, the GET request is used to download the file from the Web server and the PUT request is used to upload it to the Web server. While this process works, it is slow and inefficient, especially over slow links. The COPY method overcomes the shortcomings of the GET/PUT combination by enabling users to copy a resource or a collection from one location to another.

The COPY method uses a request URL as the source and a destination header as the target. In the absence of a *depth* header, infinity is assumed. The depth header defines the scope of a given request. For example, a depth of zero indicates that the request applies only to the target URL. A depth of one indicates that the request applies to the target URL and all entities at its level. In file system terms, this is the equivalent of performing an operation on all files in a directory, but not in any subdirectories. A depth of "infinity" implies that the operation applies to the target URL, all entities at its level, and all subentities below it.

When a collection is copied, all of its properties are copied along with it. If desired, the request can also include an optional body containing a behavior element that supplies additional information. This lets you specify what properties must be copied in order for the operation to be successful. Once again, in file system terms, this would be similar to specifying what file properties (archive bit, ACLs, and so on) would transfer with the copied resources.

The COPY method can also use an *overwrite* header as part of the request. The overwrite header can be set to either T or F. If the destination exists prior to copying a resource and the overwrite header is set to T, the server will issue a DELETE on the target URL with a depth of "infinity." If overwrite is set to F, an error will be returned.

LOCK As previously mentioned, in a distributed authoring situation, file locks need to be invoked to prevent users from overwriting each other's changes. The LOCK method provides this functionality. It does so by sending XML in the body of the request. Locking lets you to serialize access to resources. This provides users with a reasonable guarantee that a fellow collaborator won't modify the resource currently being edited. A lock request looks similar to this:

```
LOCK /documents/mydoc.htm HTTP /1.0
Content-Type: text/xml
Host: nwnet01

<?xml version="1.0" ?>
<a:lockinfo xmlns:a="DAV:">
  <a:lockscope><a:exclusive /></a:lockscope>
  <a:locktype><a:write /></a:locktype>
  <a:owner>
    <a:href>http://managers</a:href>
  </a:owner>
</a:lockinfo>
```

The WebDAV specification provides for locks with two parameters that can be specified by the client: whether the lock is exclusive or shared and what type of access is to be granted. An exclusive lock grants access only to the user setting the lock. Like an exclusive lock, a shared lock prevents others from accessing the locked resource, but it also provides a mechanism for fellow collaborators to exercise their access rights. In other words, a shared lock allows multiple authors to set a lock.

According to RFC 2518, shared locks are included in the specification because exclusive locks don't work well in every situation. Exclusive locks work well for the general editing process. However, under certain conditions, locks aren't always released. For example, the authoring application could terminate improperly, or an author could fail to unlock the resource when he finishes editing it. In these events, the lock can be removed by an administrator, or it will release itself when the specified timeout is reached. However, it may be that the administrator is not available or that the timeout period is lengthy. As a result, shared locks have been provided to overcome these issues.

MKCOL The MKCOL method is used to create a new collection at the location specified in the request. The syntax for this method is simple:

```
MKCOL /somedir HTTP/1.1

or

MKCOL /somedir/somesubdir HTTP/1.1
```

If the resource identified in the request already exists, the request will fail. During processing of the request, unless the target URL is "/", a server will make the target URL a member of its parent collection. If the parent collection doesn't exist, the request will fail.

When using MKCOL to create a new collection, all ancestors must exist or the request will fail. For example, if a request to create collection /parent/child1/child2 is made, and neither /parent/ nor /parent/child1 exists, the request will fail.

There are several status codes that are returned by MKCOL:

- **201 (Created)** The collection or resource was successfully created.
- **403 (Forbidden)** This indicates one of two conditions: either the server doesn't allow for the creation of collections at the location specified in the request, or the parent collection of the target URL cannot accept members.
- **405 (Method Not Allowed)** The resource already exists.
- **409 (Conflict)** The required parent resource does not exist.
- **415 (Unsupported Media Type)** The server does not support the request type.
- **507 (Insufficient Storage)** The resource does not have storage space to execute the request.

MOVE The MOVE method performs similarly to the COPY method, with variations that perform a move by copying the target to the specified destination and then deleting the original resource. This operation employs a consistency maintenance routine which allows the server to perform updates caused by the move, such as updating references to the moved resource. In addition, the process is atomic—it is either completely successfully or completely rolled back.

While support for the MOVE method is required for compliance with RFC 2518, it does not guarantee the ability to move a resource to a particular destination. One of the goals of WebDAV is interoperability between different client authoring tools. This means that separate applications may control different resources on the same Web server. Therefore, it may not always be possible to move a resource in a namespace that appears to belong to the same server.

There are several status codes that can be returned by MOVE:

- **201 (Created)** The operation completed successfully.
- **204 (No Content)** The resource was successfully moved to a preexisting destination.
- **403 (Forbidden)** The source and destination are the same.
- **409 (Conflict)** The required parent resource does not exist.
- **412 (Precondition Failed)** The server failed to meet the conditions included in the request.
- **423 (Locked)** The source or the destination is locked.
- **502 (Bad Gateway)** The destination server refuses to accept the resource.

PROPFIND As its name implies, the PROPFIND method is used to discover properties and enumerate collections. It can be used to request a single property, all properties, or all property names. In addition, you can use the PROPFIND method to discover the properties of multiple resources. PROPFIND's usage is relatively straightforward:

```
PROPFIND /documents/mydoc.htm HTTP/1.1
Host: nwnet01
Depth: 0
Content-Type: text/xml
Content-Length: 420

<?xml version="1.0"?>
<a:propfind xmlns:a="DAV:">
  <a:prop>
    <a:creationdate />
    <a:resourcetype />
    <a:getlastmodified />
  </a:prop>
</a:propfind>
```

As you can see, the PROPFIND method also supports the use of a depth header to specify the scope of the request. The depth header can be set to a value of 0, 1, or infinity. In order to maintain compliance with RFC 2518, a WebDAV server must support depth headers.

A depth header of 0 indicates that only the properties of the target URL are sought. A depth header of 1 indicates a request for the properties of the resource and its children. Infinity returns the name of the properties on the collection and all its children. A PROPFIND method used without a depth header acts as if the depth header was set to infinity.

PROPPATCH The PROPPATCH method is used to set and/or remove properties defined for the target resource. The PROPPATCH method looks very similar to the PROPFIND method:

```
PROPPATCH /documents/mydoc.htm HTTP/1.1
Host: nwnet01
Content-Type: text/xml
Content-Length: 450

<?xml version="1.0" ?>
<a:propertyupdate xmlns:a="DAV:">
  <a:set>
    <a:prop>
      <a:owner>Karen Schulz</a:owner>
    </a:prop>
  </a:set>
</a:propertyupdate>
```

UNLOCK Any WebDAV server that supports the LOCK method must also support the UNLOCK method. As its name implies, the UNLOCK method is used to remove locks that were added by a LOCK request. The UNLOCK process is atomic. If all the resources under the existing lock token cannot be successfully unlocked, the UNLOCK request will fail.

An UNLOCK request looks relatively simple:

```
UNLOCK /documents/mydoc.htm HTTP/1.1
Host: nwnet01
Lock-Token: <opaquelocktoken:A4BE5221-CA1C-54A2-C2A1-

   111C4D1426612:125275949211>
```

In this example, the lock identified by the lock token (<opaquelocktoken:A4BE5221-CA1C-54A2-C2A1-111C4D1426612:125275949211>) is being removed from mydoc.htm.

The Future of WebDAV

RFC 2518 only describes the base specification of WebDAV, and the protocol is continuing to evolve. There are several issues currently under discussion:

- **Delta-V** It has been said that WebDAV should be called "WebDA" because the WebDAV working group didn't provide specifications for versioning. Versioning is a process that tracks and stores revisions of documents, much like existing document management systems. The IETF Web Versioning and Configuration Management—also known as Delta-V—has been charged with defining extensions to the HTTP and WebDAV protocols that allow distributed authoring tools to perform versioning and configuration management of resources.
- **Access control** A subgroup of the WebDAV working group has been charged with developing a remote access control protocol. This protocol will allow for permissions to be placed to resources, thereby controlling who can access a given resource and what rights they have.
- **DASL** The goal of the DAV Searching and Locating working group is to define and develop an extensible WebDAV Searching and Locating protocol. According to its charter, this group will "define the protocol elements that enable server-executed queries to locate resources based upon their property values and text content as expressed by the DAV data model."

WebDAV has some distance to go before it's finished, but with its strong industry support, it will no doubt evolve into a useful technology that enables collaborators around the world to coauthor documents directly at a URL.

Summary

WebDAV provides a wide variety of benefits to users who want to collaborate in a Web-based environment:

- WebDAV allows for interoperable publishing of all content to the Web.
- Teams can seamlessly collaborate on documents on the Web by using locking to prevent overwrite conflicts.
- WebDAV provides HTML and XML authoring support, as well as word processing, spreadsheet, text, graphics, and all other formats.
- WebDAV turns the Web into a network-accessible file system. Together, WebDAV and HTTP provide a common interface to a wide range of repositories,

such as document management, configuration management, file systems, databases, and so forth.

WebDAV has already been implemented in several Microsoft products, including Windows 2000, Internet Information Server 5.0, Exchange 2000 Server, Microsoft Office 2000, and Internet Explorer 5.0. For more information on WebDAV, including the latest WebDAV developments and links to the pertinent RFCs, visit http://www.ietf.org/ and http://www.webdav.org/.

Appendix B

Knowledge Management

In this appendix, we'll examine the practice of Knowledge Management and what it means to today's world of business. It addresses knowledge management, knowledge management systems, and customer relationship management. We'll start with an overview of knowledge management, and then discuss the differences between data, information, and knowledge. We'll delve into workflow and customer relationship management, and then discuss Microsoft's knowledge management offerings within Exchange 2000.

By the end of this chapter, you'll know the difference between data, information, and knowledge. More importantly, you'll learn how you can use Microsoft Exchange 2000 Server as a principal component of a knowledge management system for your organization, regardless of what industry you're in.

Overview of Knowledge Management

This is a cliché now, but the world is very different than it was. There is no doubt about it, we are in the Information Age: An age in which *information* has replaced capital and energy as the primary creator of wealth and the dominant means of employment. Managing, leveraging, and exploiting information is critical to the success of all organizations today. The need to leverage information in order to enhance organizational effectiveness and competitiveness is critical whether one is in manufacturing, advertising, insurance, software development, or any other industry. As a result, many organizations across all industries have implemented information management systems to give themselves significant competitive advantage. Yet because these tools are predominantly based on the Industrial Age, they fail to meet expectations in an Information Age world.

All companies, even non-profit ones, are ultimately evaluated in financial terms. The primary accounting system used to document a company's assets and liabilities dates back to 1494, when we lived in a world where everyone was either a farmer or shopkeeper. Aside from the addition of specialized reports such as cost accounting, balance sheets, and income statements, this process hasn't changed much in the last five hundred years. But it is about to change.

Information as an Asset

One problem with existing accounting methods is that they only recognize tangible assets. This method has no way to recognize a company's *intellectual* assets. The cost components in most products and services today are largely contained within research and development and intellectual assets. Our old accounting systems, which focus on the cost of material and labor, do not apply in this new paradigm. The effect of this is that companies are being sold for a value many times greater than the value of their physical assets (or "book value") based on the perceived value of their intangible assets. This amount is typically listed as "good will," but this is not an adequate representation. As a result, efforts in the form of knowledge management systems are being undertaken to enable companies to more accurately represent the value of their *corporate intellect*.

Think of it this way: If access to knowledge were enough, wouldn't there be long lines outside of libraries all over the world? Access is certainly important, but truly successful knowledge management also requires attention from others. In an age where information is the primary creator of wealth, one could argue that *attention* is the currency used within this age. Hence, the phrase, "pay attention!" As a result, the focus of current knowledge management efforts is the tracking of intellectual capital within organizations.

The increased interest surrounding knowledge management and intellectual capital has occurred simultaneously with the rise of digital technology and a flourishing service industry. As a result, two interesting aspects of knowledge management are evolving. First, there is the quest to develop better systems for creating, capturing, and disseminating knowledge within organizations. Second, there is growing sentiment that knowledge and know-how significantly add to the value of a business and, in some cases, represent nearly the entire value base.

Several implications of moving into the Information Age need to be understood. One is that the value of information is more difficult to measure than the value of capital assets. Moreover, you cannot readily insert "information" as a line item on a balance sheet or income statement. Clearly, information is an asset. Yet how can a value be placed on it? Information may be quantifiable, but to date, the measurement systems used to value information are at best underdeveloped, and in some cases, nonexistent.

Another implication of the Information Age is that information has economic properties that are different from traditional economic assets. The value of Industrial Age assets are typically highest when the asset is brand new. Over time, assets depreciate because they are consumed, or simply because they've been used. Eventually, as a result of this continued use over time, the asset will be deemed worthless. This process is accelerated when the asset is shared by others. Conversely, the value of information increases when it is shared; it does not follow the same decreasing value curve over time that a traditional asset does. For example, if two people share a physical asset, such as a computer, there is only one computer for the two of them to share. However, if they share an idea or information, it could easily result in the generation of multiple ideas, more information, or even knowledge.

If we consider *data*, most of us think that we have lots of it stored on computers, and that we have access to much of it. In fact, many organizations consider themselves to be "data rich" and "information poor." But what is the magical ingredient or transformation that converts data into information? And what turns this information into knowledge? To understand the answers to these questions, we must first start with some background.

What Is Information?

This can be a difficult question to answer. The word *information* is derived from the Latin word *informare*, which means "give form to." In the *Oxford* dictionary definition of information, it is connected both to knowledge and communication. In this context, the word "information" can refer to both the facts themselves and to the transmission of the facts. According to a 1994 article in *Wired* magazine, *"Information is an activity. Information is a life form. Information is a relationship. Information is a verb not a noun, it is something that happens in the field of interaction between minds or objects or other pieces of information. Information is an action which occupies time rather than a state of being which occupies physical space."*

It is very common to confuse data, information, and knowledge. Some say that information is data that has meaning or relevance. People agree that information is more valuable than data. We would rather have good information than good data, but often, good data is a prerequisite to good information.

To illustrate the differences between data and information, consider a typical *data-warehousing* project. Most data-warehousing projects begin with the collection and compilation of data derived from many sources. This process uses technology to bring the data from various places into a central repository. This central place might be a company mainframe, a database, a file system, or some other technological construct designed to contain data. When the data is presented in an organized fashion, it becomes *information*. Sales and inventory reports, payroll numbers, and customer support reports are all examples of data that, through organization, has been converted into information.

In 1990, Microsoft unveiled its "Information at your fingertips (IAYF)" campaign. According to Microsoft, IAYF means the right information at the right time for the right purpose. Microsoft's goal was to make finding, browsing, and retrieving information easy, as well as location-independent. IAYF embodies many things, such as database queries; compound documents with linking; rich authoring tools; and document-based macros. Microsoft's first effort afforded simple cut-and-paste, no application interoperability, and only basic connectivity. Next came WYSIWYG, cross-application integration, compound documents (in the form of OLE), and some distribution of application functionality. More recently, the concept of data warehousing arrived on the scene.

As Information Technology professionals, we typically assume that the most important knowledge is that which is captured in our relational databases. We readily build data warehouses in an attempt to put all the company's information at the fingertips of its employees. However, all of this information represents only one part of a company's knowledge. It is confined to information about products, competitors, activities, and so forth that is currently part of our environment. But this information only allows us to analyze the past. A data warehouse typically has little or no information about the future.

Companies use data and information all of the time. Yet, even those with robust data warehouses are still susceptible to data waste. Data waste is the amount of online data stored by a company minus the amount of data actually used by the company. Common examples of data waste include company intranets. Intranet home pages often feature news streams that race along a user's computer monitor. These streams might be used to relate the company's latest success in the market, or they might simply be reminders of scheduled system and network outages.

More often than not, these streams create no decision-producing intelligence; they are, in other words, data waste. Data waste turns into data overload when employees and managers aren't able to locate critical information amidst the sea of irrelevant data that floods corporate networks. Even worse, once workers start wading through useless information or hunting for lost data, productivity decreases.

Ironically, to best understand what information is, we need to look at it not from a technological point of view, but from a human point of view. Information is a vehicle by which we attempt to provoke—or evoke—a human response. By itself, information is static and lifeless. It simply exists—on computer screens, in books, in movies and TV, in reports, letters, e-mails, and so on—waiting for people to attach meaning to it.

Although information stands for meaning, it is never meaning itself. Meaning, after all, is a mental construct unique to the person who gives meaning to the information. Even identical information evokes different meanings in each of us. Rarely do two people attach the same meaning to the same experience, even when the experience appears to be identical—such as reading this chapter, watching a movie, or sitting on a jury. Identical information produces different meanings for each of us because our beliefs, interests, motivations, attitudes, and feelings are always personal, unique, and changing.

If even identical information is unique to each individual, why do we attach so much importance to it? Because information is a trigger that alerts us to the need to interpret events. Information provides us with an opportunity to make meaning of sensory input. Without information, there is nothing to provoke us to sit up and take notice. This, of course, is the primary value of information—the ability to provoke different people in different ways. Without information, our senses are devoid of stimulation. Indeed, it is information that defines our very existence: "I think, therefore, I am."

Our latest developments in technology challenge the interpretation of what information is. We tend to regard information as fixed. However, information contained on corporate networks and the Internet has no final cut. As with the tradition of relating information orally, digital information is added to in a continuous process. In fact, information that is unconstrained by packaging (unlike books or journals) reflects a process that is very similar to the telling of stories in the oral tradition, which change with every retelling.

What Is Knowledge?

If data is the raw bits that are stored on computer systems, and information is the meaning of the data, when does information become knowledge? According to the experts, information becomes knowledge at the moment of its interpretation. This makes perfect sense; after all, words don't have meaning. Although it seems otherwise, words don't have a direct relationship with the thing being talked about, or with the words used to talk about it. Only as a person relates words do they obtain meaning.

Knowledge is typically created through the reconstruction of older concepts, as well as the invention of new ones. Contrary to popular belief, knowledge is not discovered like a new planet or a new way to increase microprocessor speeds. Instead, it is constructed through the observation of objects and events. Something can't become knowledge until a person, a group, or society validates it as such.

If one thing can be said about the technology industry, it's that there is way too much to know. When I was new to this business, I would read computer books and magazines and not be bothered by the fact that most of it was a complete mystery to me. Most of the articles were on subjects that I was supposed to know something about. I could learn more about them if I only had the time to do so. You're probably the same; how many books do you own that you have meant to read, but haven't yet? You probably bought many books because they looked interesting, but you never got a chance to read them thoroughly because you didn't have the time. Using the "bandwidth" metaphor, we all have limited bandwidth. We can only absorb so many things.

Whether we're talking about people or computers, the attempt to absorb too many things at once leads to *information overload*. Since the early days of information theory, scientists have been studying information overload. Theorists say that information overload exists when a system receives more information than it can handle. Simple changes in some aspect of information, such as quantity or meaning, can create overload. The conclusion to be drawn from this is that, as the information input rate increases, output increases to its maximum, and then decreases as information overload occurs.

Despite these challenges, many companies are contemplating or deploying computer systems geared towards managing knowledge within the company. This knowledge is referred to as the *corporate intellect*. The purpose of this knowledge management is to build a symbiotic relationship between businesses, people, and technology. Externally, companies are finding the need to gain knowledge from their customers, as well as the need to offer customers additional knowledge. Internally, these same companies are discovering the need to build a culture of knowledge sharing, to measure the knowledge creation process, and to capture the tacit knowledge of employees so that it can be stored, shared, and, more importantly, re-used. Interestingly, this allows both the company, and the individuals that make up the company, to succeed in completely new ways. Individuals can create careers based on knowledge management, and companies can create new revenues from their knowledge base.

To accomplish this, many companies have begun to develop *knowledge management systems* with the goal of streamlining processes, leveraging corporate intellect, and providing an extra competitive edge. Boeing, for example, used a database shared by designers, subcontractors, and suppliers to create the Boeing 777, the first aircraft to be developed in a completely paperless environment. Chevron has streamlined its business practices by creating a "best practice" database that combines the experiences of drilling conditions with innovative solutions to problems. And Frito-Lay has provided its sales force with a mechanism to collect on-the-spot data about shelf space utilization for its products. This data is computed and combined with market information, and then re-fed to the sales force, which uses it to give retailers that carry Frito-Lay products information on the best way to utilize shelf space.

Knowledge Management Systems

The goal of the ideal information management system is not to present all the data to all the users, but instead to design mechanisms that enable users to receive only the information that they can absorb and use. The key here is to reduce the information that is presented, not increase it. For example, if we believe a reader can absorb only six items from a 200-page report, then we should augment the report with an excerpt or executive summary that presents the most important six items. This indicates that the effectiveness of information management systems is measured in terms of their capability to determine which information is important.

Most companies are less interested in defining knowledge, and more interested in determining what knowledge can do for them. The focus here is not so much on the discovery of truth, but what effective actions can be taken as a result of this truth. So knowing that information is the raw material used to produce knowledge, it makes sense that knowledge management is a circular process that continuously feeds itself to keep the process going.

The primary challenge is that knowledge cannot really be captured or managed, which makes the term *knowledge management* somewhat of a misnomer. Worse still, the language of knowledge management suggests that knowledge is a commodity that can be processed, delivered, or transmitted, when, in fact, it is not. What we know is only implicit; it can never be explicit, which is an inherent requirement that computers have in order to manage information.

Many have claimed for years that thinking computers are just around the corner. The problem with this is that only people can intelligently make sense of—and therefore provide an appropriate context for—information. Only people have the capacity to construct meaning from information and to sense meaning within themselves and from others. And only people can compare interpretations with views to achieve a shared purpose. So, no matter how elegantly it is processed or presented, information on its own is incapable of achieving anything. Ironically, this means that even this book contains no intrinsic meaning. Whatever meanings are ascribed to it are simply your interpretations and judgments.

Among knowledge management researchers and knowledge management users, two different tracks of activities have emerged. The first track is the management of people. This track is very old, and it isn't growing very fast. People in this field are typically educated in philosophy, psychology, sociology, or business/management. They are primarily involved in assessing, changing, or improving people's skills and behavior. To them, knowledge equals processes—a complex set of know-how and dynamic skills that is constantly changing. The second track is the management of information. This track is relatively new and, because it is assisted by the rapid development and improvement of technology, it is growing very fast. People in this track are typically educated in the fields of information science or computers. They are involved in the development of things like groupware, workflow, information management systems, business re-engineering, and, more recently, artificial intelligence. To them, knowledge equals objects that can be identified and handled within the confines of an information system. Clearly, there are differences in our understanding of what knowledge is.

Despite these differences, many companies are beginning to understand that their employees' knowledge is their most valuable asset. Still, few have actually begun to actively manage this asset on a broad scale. Thus far, these issues have been addressed at a technological or philosophical level, with little discussion about how knowledge can be used more effectively on a daily basis. Knowledge may be an asset, but to effectively manage it, companies need to invest other assets, namely labor and money. Employees need to be trained in the ways of capturing and categorizing knowledge. More importantly, they need the right hardware and software tools to do that.

Make no mistake, knowledge management can be expensive. But each company needs to ask itself, "What is the cost of ignorance?" How much will it cost an organization if it is unable to answer customer questions quickly or at all, or if poor decisions are made based on faulty knowledge? Just as companies are concerned about the value of quality, companies trying to assess the value of knowledge have begun to measure the cost of "not knowing." Of course, these assessments can and do lead to political problems within companies, but we won't discuss that here.

Humans are clearly preferred over computers when it comes to understanding, interpreting, and combining knowledge. Computers and communications systems, on the other hand, excel at capturing, transforming, and distributing highly structured knowledge that changes rapidly. While still a bit awkward to use, computers are becoming increasingly useful at performing similar tasks on less structured material. But even in today's digital society, most people don't turn to computers when seeking information within a particular domain of knowledge. As a result, organizations are finding the need to create hybrid environments that combine people and computers in complementary ways to perform knowledge management tasks. Just as many manufacturers have realized that "lights out" facilities aren't always the most effective or flexible solution, it is clear that knowledge factories need to offer not only the bits and bytes of a computer, but also a person or persons behind the technology.

The Sharing of Knowledge

All knowledge management systems are predicated on the basis of shared knowledge. And yet, despite our millions of years of evolution, the success of which is based on sharing information, sharing and using knowledge are often unnatural acts. We've all heard the statement that "knowledge is power," and many of us take this to heart in both personal and business-related matters. Some believe the withholding of knowledge is a key factor in job security. After all, if knowledge is valuable, it can be withheld in an attempt to increase the value of the person withholding it.

Have you ever been involved in a project where midway through the project, some key piece of information is shared that, had it been shared at the beginning of the project, would have fundamentally changed both the scope and the requirements of the project? This happens all the time, regardless of how well the project is managed or implemented. Many people are surprised when they find knowledge has not been used or shared, but this is due in part to the natural tendency of people to hoard knowledge and to look suspiciously upon knowledge that comes from others. This means that entering our knowledge into a system, as well as seeking out knowledge from others, is both time-consuming, resource intensive, and, to some, threatening; to undertake such work, therefore, requires a high level of motivation.

The sharing of knowledge is rooted in three primary areas, all of which must be carefully considered when developing a knowledge management system. Generally speaking, people tend to gain knowledge from their own personal experiences, from reviewing business information, and from the expertise of their peers. These are the starting points for the technology that will ultimately produce a knowledge management system that is capable of managing an organization's knowledge assets. In addition, they provide a focus for the process of contemplating the origin of knowledge assets, and how corporate information can be shared and reused through a knowledge management system.

Inherently, there are fundamental problems associated with identifying and managing knowledge assets, particularly in an efficient and cost-effective manner. Organizations of all sizes and in all industries need

- An enterprise-wide vocabulary to ensure that corporate knowledge is correctly understood
- A way to identify, model, and represent corporate knowledge
- A way to share and reuse corporate knowledge, especially among differing users who are using different applications (including existing and also users and applications)

In addition, organizations need to create a culture that encourages knowledge sharing.

Furthermore, activities underlying an organization's knowledge management strategies are made up of a combination of the construction, distribution, use, and maintenance of *corporate memory*. The challenge here is to manage disparate know-how and heterogeneous viewpoints, and to make it accessible to those who need it the most.

Knowledge Workers

The success of many companies depends on the productivity of their workers, measured as a function of information value, use, and effectiveness. Because of the shift from an emphasis on production to an emphasis on knowledge, the workplace and how each employee fits into the workplace has been redefined.

Out of the need to manage corporate intellect, new business concepts and phrases have developed. Most workers are now considered *knowledge workers*. Peter Drucker, a pioneer in the field of knowledge management, coined the term "knowledge worker." Drucker referred to the increasingly important role of knowledge work as early as 1959 in his book *Landmarks for Tomorrow*. Scientists, engineers, managers, trainers, and researchers are all knowledge workers of one kind or another. You're reading this book because you either need to learn about, manage, or implement Microsoft Exchange 2000 Server, which in all likelihood, makes you a knowledge worker, as well.

According to Microsoft, knowledge workers comprise roughly 90 percent of PC users today. These are typically people whose job functions require them to perform some sort of analysis, reporting, or presentation. Often these workers require the capability to be mobile, and are therefore seeking ways to work with corporate data offline. This means that, in addition to the large repository of data stored at a company's headquarters, knowledge workers also require data that is stored locally; for example, on a laptop, a home computer, a personal digital assistant (PDA), or a handheld PC (HPC). Without local data, it would be impossible to do meaningful work while away from the office.

Microsoft further says that *task workers* comprise the remaining 10 percent of the PC market. These individuals generally use a single application to carry out some process-oriented task. As task workers increasingly adopt technology, their management is seeking to improve their productivity through empowerment.

It is clear that IT systems intended to support knowledge management efforts need to also support the capturing of undocumented information, the sharing of ideas and documents, and the finding of this information in a fast and accurate manner. These premises need to be the foundation of a knowledge management system, if it is to be able to manage information, and more importantly, transform information into corporate knowledge.

Designing a knowledge management system that meets the needs of knowledge workers can be challenging, primarily because the term "knowledge management" is vague and not nearly understood as well as related terms, such as *collaboration* or *workflow*. Moreover, vendors in the business of knowledge management system development have their own idea of what such a system should contain. With the exception of electronic communication (for example, e-mail), collaboration features, and the capability to add workflow logic to the system, there is no commonly accepted functionality related to knowledge management. On the one hand, this is a good thing; it allows organizations to select, design, or implement a knowledge management system that most closely matches their internal requirements. On the other hand, it can be a bad thing. The absence of commonly accepted knowledge management system functions can make it difficult for organizations to develop internal requirements in the first place.

Workflow

Workflow enables businesses to streamline their processes for greater efficiency. Workflow means different things to different people. For some, the terms *groupware* and *workflow* are interchangeable. Traditionally, workflow has been defined as the sequence of actions in a business process. Each organization varies in terms of its business processes, but one example of workflow is the purchase order process. Generally speaking, a purchase order starts with an individual requesting the allocation of corporate funds in order to purchase something. The purchase order is typically routed through an organization from the originator to the originator's manager, from the manager to a purchasing department, and from the purchasing department back to the originator.

Workflow and workflow technologies are evolving in a number of areas. Workflow vendors have created products that focus on particular needs and functional capabilities. This specialization can lead to isolation and incompatibility between many automation processes. There are many different types of workflow systems available and new ones are constantly being introduced. These systems cross many areas of business needs, such as image processing, document management, groupware applications, project-based and transaction-based software, and electronic mail.

Workflow can be broken down into four specific elements: the tasks to be carried out; the roles used to carry out tasks; the data to be used in each task; and the timetable or schedule for each task. There are no official workflow standards; however, there is substantial cross-industry interest in establishing workflow standards. In 1993, companies such as SAP AG, IBM, Microsoft, Hewlett Packard, Oracle, Baan, Documentum, Inc., FileNet, and over 200 others from a wide range of industries formed the *Workflow Management Coalition* (WfMC). The WfMC has created a framework for the establishment of workflow standards called the *Workflow Reference Model.*

As you can see from the WfMC Reference Model, workflow systems have multiple components:

- **Workflow API and enactment services**—Enactment services provide a run-time execution environment in which business process instances are created, managed, controlled, and executed. Applications interface with enactment services via workflow APIs (WAPIs) and interchange formats. WAPIs enable interoperability between applications and the other components of a workflow management system.
- **Process definition tools**—These tools are used to define business process specifications. In addition, they often define the data interchange requirements between workflow activities or steps, relevant sequencing instructions, and routing instructions. The completed process specifications are used as a template for creating specific instances of a business process.
- **Administration and monitoring tools**—These tools are used in the configuration, management, and control of the overall workflow environment. Examples of workflow administration and monitoring functions include the establishment of users (user names, passwords, and role specifications); assignment of work items; exception and error processing; auditing, event generation, and notification; tracking and reporting of workflow processing results; reporting of aggregate statistics; business process versioning and change management; and monitoring of workflow execution results.

- **Workflow client applications**—These applications utilize workflow services. A queue of work items is called the worklist. Interaction between the workflow client application and the workflow engine occurs through the use of the worklist.
- **Invoked applications**—These applications are invoked by the workflow engine in order to perform the processing of work items. This can occur in a synchronous or asynchronous manner.
- **Workflow engines**—Workflow engines provide a run-time execution environment that manages the overall processing and execution of workflow process instances. Processing functions provided by workflow engines include interpretation of business process specifications; creation of new business process instances; execution of business process instances and management of that execution; management and control of workflow control information; request routing; and communication of data interchange between workflow process instance activities.

Workflow management has existed for quite some time. Before the advent of *workflow automation*, all workflow was done manually. The production of an automobile, the processing of customer orders, the creation of information products and services, and the purchasing of raw materials in a manufacturing environment are all examples of manual workflow processes that require a complex set of coordinated activities. Manual workflow has several deficiencies. It is labor-intensive, with no easy method to track status, measure performance, or gather cost statistics. More importantly, it allows tasks to fall through the cracks. To track the status of a particular task an individual typically has to ask someone for a status report.

When technology is applied to workflow, it enables the creation of *automated workflow*. Workflow technology encompasses the methodologies and software needed to support (i) the capture of business processes as workflow specifications through business process modeling, (ii) the optimization of specific processes through business process re-engineering, and (iii) the automation of workflow automation through the generation of workflow specifications.

The explosion of digital technology has made it possible to automate workflow. Computer software is continuously being improved in the ongoing effort to replace paper forms with intelligent electronic forms. Relational databases with huge disk subsystems provide a means of storing vast amounts of information that used to reside in file cabinets. And electronic mail provides a popular and near-instantaneous means of routing information to one or more people.

Designing an Effective Knowledge Management System

The most effective knowledge management systems don't begin with technology. Instead, they begin with the defining of what knowledge an organization has, what knowledge is needed for the organization to be extremely competitive, and what knowledge is needed for critical decision-making processes. Clearly, knowledge cannot be managed by an organization until one or more individuals within the organization has been given responsibility for the job. Among the tasks that such a person or group might perform are collecting and categorizing knowledge, establishing a knowledge-oriented infrastructure, and monitoring the use of knowledge. Those charged with these responsibilities are known as *knowledge managers*. This, of course, doesn't mean that a knowledge manager is more knowledgeable than any other individual within the organization. Knowledge managers facilitate the creation, distribution, and use of knowledge by knowledge workers.

When designing a knowledge management system, it is often tempting to begin with a model that is aligned with the organization's hierarchy. This is roughly analogous to creating a corporate "yellow pages" where information resides within one category, and where the categories (and not the information) are indexed. This can make locating information difficult, particularly if the information applies to more than one category. Consider a large supermarket that has a small cafeteria and a flower shop. If only one category is available, do you list the supermarket under "groceries," "restaurants," or "florists?" Obviously, the overriding inclination is to categorize it under "groceries." After all, that's its primary function. But if the consumer is looking for flowers or a place to get a quick bite to eat, he or she will search other categories to find a business that meets these needs. This is unfortunate for the consumer, because this supermarket might be the closest business that has the products or services being sought. It might have better pricing, or higher-quality merchandise, or some other aspect that makes it a better value for the consumer than businesses that might be listed in another category.

It is also important for a knowledge management system to provide an atmosphere of sharing and cooperation. An individual's contribution to an organization often involves the creation of new corporate knowledge through the infusion of his or her personal experiences into the corporate intellect. If the culture of an organization does not provide an atmosphere that promotes the sharing of ideas, information, and know-how, the corporate intellect will suffer. Only through the direct interaction of people and the blending of their combined personal experiences will the corporate intellect grow.

A well-designed knowledge management system will undoubtedly draw from a multitude of technologies. Among these will be Internet-related technologies, document management, groupware, relational databases, and workflow. But more importantly, it will also include other disciplines, such as library and information science, semantic networks, artificial intelligence, and the cognitive sciences. And as each of these areas grows and evolves, so does the domain of knowledge management.

Finally, the most effective knowledge management systems stick to the eight primary functions of the knowledge management process:

- Capturing
- Collecting
- Organizing
- Storing

- Distributing
- Sharing
- Applying
- Leveraging

By their nature, these functions will be implemented in a distributed manner with different parts of a knowledge management system performing different functions. In order to allow this, a knowledge management system must be *cross-platform*. Because no single manufacturer offers a product or combination of products that meets all the requirements and capabilities of a complete knowledge management system, we can assume that all knowledge management systems will be *multivendor*.

Customer Relationship Management

As mentioned at the beginning of this chapter, companies need to leverage information in order to enhance organizational effectiveness and competitiveness. Certainly the quality and value of a company's products and services is important. But equally important is the company's *customer relationship management* activities. While each industry has different customer relationship management objectives, tools, and techniques, all industries share the common need to continuously improve their customer relationship management systems.

Customer relationship management (CRM) is a vertical implementation of knowledge management. It is a business strategy that shifts an organization's business model from one that is product- or service-focused to one that is customer-centric. CRM is an IT term for the methodologies and tools that help companies manage their customer relationships in an organized way.

Organizations have different kinds of customers. They have external customers; these people and businesses buy the organization's products or services. They also have internal customers; these people make up the organization and rely on services from other departments within the organization. For example, corporate employees are also customers of the company's IT department. Finally, organizations also have a special kind of customer called a *partner*. Depending on an organization's relationship with its partners, a partner customer may be internal, external, or a subtle combination of both. An outsourced IT department, or businesses that combine their intranets to form an *extranet*, are two examples of these partnerships.

The Components of Customer Relationship Management

According to an article published by the CRM Forum (http://www.crm-forum.com) there are four elements of customer relationship management: *know*, *target*, *sell*, and *service*. Various techniques are employed to facilitate the incorporation of these elements into a CRM system. Knowing customers means gathering and analyzing detailed data from them. This allows companies to determine which customers are the most profitable and most satisfied. Data warehousing tools, and more recently, data mining applications are usually called into play to provide this data. A data warehouse is an electronic system that brings together corporate information from various sources. Data mining is used within CRM systems to enable organizations to manage their customers on a one-to-one basis.

The same tools are used to target customers. Targeting can involve new or existing customers. It can be the result of knowledge obtained by analyzing market segment data, consumer satisfaction, or emerging trends. Sales and sales force automation tools are used to sell to the customer. These tools range from contact management and personal information management software, to sophisticated journaling systems and custom applications. Finally, CRM systems help in serving the customer. This involves meeting or exceeding customer expectations, achieving customer loyalty, and providing customer assistance.

Microsoft Knowledge Management Offerings

As previously mentioned, the methods and technologies used to manage information help determine an organization's success or failure. Successful companies in an information-based economy have the tools and processes needed to process information quickly, learn from experience, and as a result, develop new strategies.

Microsoft's vision for these tools and processes is embodied in what it calls a *digital nervous system*. A digital nervous system is a combination of Microsoft BackOffice, Microsoft Site Server, Microsoft Office, other Microsoft products such as Visual Basic for Applications and Visual Basic Scripting, and third-party products. Exchange 2000 plays a central role in Microsoft's knowledge management offerings.

Microsoft has several key initiatives within Exchange 2000 Server for enabling and empowering knowledge workers: the Digital Dashboard; Web Storage System Forms, Team Centers; mobile computing devices such as laptops, home PCs, wireless devices, and handheld PCs running Windows CE; and intelligent interfaces. Microsoft has augmented these initiatives with software development kits aimed at empowering ordinary users to create their own collaborative solutions within Exchange 2000 Server.

Digital Dashboard

Today, knowledge workers are getting more information than they can assimilate. Moreover, the data is often delivered without regard to its importance or format. This results in lost information, missed trends, and a repetition of work that has already been completed elsewhere. To solve the combined problems of information overload and anytime, anywhere information access, Microsoft has created the *Digital Dashboard* initiative, which is currently in version 2.2.

Microsoft developed the Digital Dashboard after its research revealed that most people preferred to work within Office applications such as Word or Excel, but at the same time, needed information from other corporate repositories, and from the Internet.

A digital dashboard is a knowledge management solution for delivering corporate knowledge to knowledge worker desktops. It can deliver a wide variety of information such as database, contact, sales, and Internet. By delivering the most important content directly to the desktop of knowledge workers, businesses can enable better and faster decision-making processes. If you've ever used the *Outlook Today* feature within Outlook 98 or Outlook 2000, you've used a basic digital dashboard.

Note *Although Outlook 2002 is the preferred viewer for digital dashboards, Web browsers such as Internet Explorer can also be used to view digital dashboards. This makes digital dashboards valuable tools for Outlook and Outlook Web Access users.*

The design of a digital dashboard should include the following elements:

- *A focus on critical information.* This is key to preventing information overload. It is highly unproductive for knowledge workers to sort through a raft of information in order to find one piece. By delivering focused, vital business information companies can prevent information overload and provide knowledge workers with the information they need when they need it.
- *Information from multiple sources.* Corporate knowledge is almost always contained in multiple repositories. This includes mainframe data, database tables, e-mail containers, and documents stored in the file system. It can also include data from the Internet or a company intranet.
- *Knowledge from other knowledge workers.* The larger a company gets, the more difficult it can be for knowledge workers to collaborate with one another. A digital dashboard addresses this problem by enabling knowledge workers to communicate and collaborate, regardless of their physical location.
- *Offline access to key information.* The Internet has allowed many companies to globalize. As a result, more and more knowledge workers are required to travel to meet with clients, suppliers, and partners. Because a digital dashboard is contained within Outlook 2000, all the information presented in the digital dashboard can be viewed with or without a connection to the Internet or corporate network.

The foundation of the digital dashboard is the Microsoft Outlook 2000 client, but other software, namely Office XP, Office 2000, Microsoft NetMeeting, Exchange 2000 Server, SQL Server, and Windows Media Services often come into play. At the most basic level, a digital dashboard is simply a dynamic Web page—referred to as a *portal*—that is displayed within Microsoft Outlook. Dashboards can include information from virtually any source, which means that companies that deploy digital dashboards do not need to go through lengthy data extraction or data conversion processes. Digital dashboards allow mailbox folders and public folders to point to Web pages instead of traditional Exchange 2000 server content. This allows the creation of customized views by organizational units, workgroups, departments, teams, and so forth. Every level of your organization can have a customized information portal at its disposal.

Implementing a digital dashboard begins with the installation of the Digital Dashboard Resource Kit. This kit, which is freely downloadable from Microsoft's Digital Dashboard Web site, enables developers to create sophisticated digital dashboards using tools such as Visual Interdev or any other XML editor.

The information displayed within a digital dashboard is referred to as a *Web part*. Web parts are a conceptual way of looking at data. The technical method to render Web parts can be in the form of an ActiveX control, Active Server Pages, or an XML data feed. Every Web part needs a unique identifier, but any naming convention is acceptable. An HTML class called "content" identifies the body of a Web part. Web parts are reusable and can be copied among multiple digital dashboards.

Digital dashboards are easy to create, deploy, and manage, yet they enable knowledge workers with the powerful capability to instantly view the corporate knowledge that is most critical to their particular area of responsibility. Moreover, they enable knowledge workers to remain within the comfortable and familiar environment of Office 2000 or Office XP.

More importantly, third-party value-added resellers and software developers can leverage the digital dashboard architecture to create customized dashboards that leverage their products and services. In addition, some software developers, such as Decision Support Panel (http://www.dspanel.com), are offering Web parts that are completely integrated with Outlook. Indeed, it may be that one day soon, digital dashboards will replace traditional intranets. You can get the latest information on digital dashboards from Microsoft's business knowledge management Web site, found at http://www.microsoft.com/business/DigitalDashboard/.

Team Centers

Closely related to digital dashboards is a concept called *Team Centers*. Unlike digital dashboards, which can be integrated into any level within an organization, Team Centers, as the name implies, are built around teams. This could be either a department team or a project team; in other words, any group of people that need to collaborate with one another.

In many organizations that have deployed Outlook and Exchange, the public folder features and capabilities remain largely untapped. Typically, this is because the groups of people within the organization that need to share information don't have the skills needed to develop solutions that enable them to do so. Even though these skills may be present in an organization's IT department, the cost of leveraging the skills for small groups is, more often than not, too high to be practical. Team Centers address this issue by providing tools for Outlook users that enable them to create collaborative solutions without having to be software developers.

Team Centers are Web applications that teams can use to collaborate and share information. They leverage the Web Storage System within Exchange 2000 as well as the security model. Team Centers are protected by permissions that control folder access, so only team members and designated administrators can access the information. The user who uses the Team Center Wizard to create Team Centers is granted Owner rights, making him or her the Team Center administrator. The Team Center Wizard allows the administrator to select team members from the Exchange Server Global Address List (GAL). By default, users who are selected from the GAL are granted Author rights, which enable them to create items within any of the Team Centers.

To download the Exchange 2000 Web Storage System SDK and learn more about Team Centers in general, visit the MSDN Web site at http://msdn.microsoft.com/exchange.

Workflow

In addition to these initiatives, Microsoft has enhanced the *workflow* platform capabilities of Exchange 2000 Server. Exchange 2000 Server lends itself quite well to creating automated workflow processes. A workflow process consists of a series of tasks and actions, and the order in which they must occur. Within Exchange 2000 Server, scripts can be executed for each action, allowing a wide variety of actions to occur within or outside of the Exchange server environment.

Microsoft had positioned prior versions of the Exchange server as reliable workflow systems, but it has gone to even greater lengths to make Exchange 2000 Server the workflow platform of choice. For example, the Exchange 2000 Software Development Kit includes a new Workflow Designer for Exchange 2000 Server.

The Workflow Designer uses Collaboration Data Objects (CDO) Workflow Objects for Exchange, a set of COM components that integrate seamlessly with the ActiveX Data Objects (ADO) 2.5 component. The Workflow Designer allows users to perform basic tasks, such as creating an action table and adding actions and scripts. However, developing an enterprise-class application requires an understanding of CDO Workflow Objects and ADO 2.5.

When a user creates a workflow process, the Workflow Designer creates rules for the designated folder and its association with an event sink. The set of rules is called a *process definition*; the association is called an *event registration*; and the event sink is called a *CDO workflow event sink*. The workflow event sink is the interface between the Exchange 2000 Web Store process and the workflow engine. The association between the folder and the event sink makes it possible for the Web Store to notify the event sink when an event occurs in the folder, such as the creation of a new item in the folder.

But, don't be mislead by these statements. Although the Workflow Designer makes designing workflow easier, it does nothing to simplify the process of creating the workflow applications themselves. Solid programming skills and knowledge of CDO, ADO, COM, and other technologies are needed if a company plans to build custom workflow solutions on Exchange.

Tip *In addition to MSDN, there are some great Exchange development-oriented sites with a lot of information, technical literature, and sample code, such as http://www.slipstick.com, and http://exchange.devx.com.*

SharePoint Portal Server

SharePoint Portal Server (SPS) is a new offering in Microsoft's .NET server family of products. As its name implies, it is a portal-based solution for locating shared information and documents. SPS, formerly codenamed "Tahoe" offers a slew of new features aimed at simplifying document management, indexing, and ultimately the publishing and locating of information.

Each time an organization creates or collects information, its knowledge workers must spend time searching, organizing, and managing that information. The goal of SPS is to reduce the amount of time spent on these tasks by integrating document management and search functions with tools used by knowledge workers every day: Windows Explorer, Microsoft Office, and Internet Explorer, to name a few.

SPS has four main components or services:

- Document publishing and document management
- Indexing and search services
- A digital dashboard site
- SPS server workspaces

Even with the advances made by Microsoft with its Windows and Office product lines, knowledge workers still have difficulty locating information in large or complex networks. Compounding this problem is the fact that company information is typically stored in a variety of data stores: file servers, e-mail servers, databases, and so forth. Likewise, knowledge workers are challenged to collaborate with one another on documents where more than four authors are involved. Documents get lost, changes are overwritten, or the information cannot be located.

Even though there are a number of document management applications, many companies are still reluctant to deploy these systems, or worse, some companies deploy them only to let them languish. With its SPS offering, Microsoft aims to streamline document development and avoid these problems. SPS addresses these issues by providing the following key features within its document management component:

- Version tracking, which tracks revisions and document history
- Searchable descriptions for documents
- Controls for document publishing
- Document routing
- Web-based discussion forums
- Access control

SPS also includes full-text indexing from a variety of content sources, including file servers, Exchange servers, and databases. Items can be categorized through the use of a Category Assistant, which automatically selects the best category matches.

For more information on Microsoft's SharePoint Portal Server, visit http://www.microsoft.com/servers/sharepoint/default.htm.

Summary

Adopting knowledge management strategies and techniques is essential to retaining a competitive advantage. In a knowledge-based economy, organizations need to re-think their business strategies, reassess costs, and organize themselves in a way that allows them to leverage their corporate intellect. They must investigate and employ knowledge-based products that complement the emerging electronic marketplace, and develop the corporate agility to take quick, effective action on informed decisions. Both these efforts require a conscious decision by senior management to develop a corporate strategy for knowledge management.

In order to leverage the collective knowledge of highly-skilled employees and to create process efficiencies, companies need to sequence their major processes according to what needs to be known at each step.

Knowledge requirements have to be identified. From outside an organization, firms need instant access to and analysis of market trends, regulations, competitors' activities, and journals. They also need immediate access to subject matter experts for instant consultation. From within an organization, performance information, lessons learned, and sources of internal skills and expertise need to be identified. Even with the best taxonomies and delivery systems, it is often necessary for a subject-matter expert to place information in context in order to make it relevant and meaningful. Accordingly, the need for customized business research and analysis will grow with the complexities of the global marketplace and the ever-increasing capacity of systems to inundate users with information.

Index

A

access
    anonymous, 355, 474–476, 601
    delegating mailbox, 601–603
    enabling and disabling protocol, 604–606
    for POP3 virtual servers, 350, 351
    selectively allowing protocol, 609
    setting administrative, 294–295, 606–608
    setting mailbox permissions, 597–604
    setting user, 602
    See also permissions
access control entries (ACEs), 51
access control lists (ACLs)
    discretionary, 51, 88
    viewing, 285, 286
    See also permissions
Access Control section (Default SMTP Virtual Server Properties dialog box), 346
Access tab
    for Default NNTP Virtual Server Properties dialog box, 156
    for Default POP3 Virtual Server Properties dialog box, 350–351
    for Default SMTP Virtual Server Properties dialog box, 345–347
    for HTTP Virtual Server Properties dialog box, 468
    for New Properties dialog box, 572–573
    for User Class Properties dialog box, 581–582
ACEs (access control entries), 51
ACID (atomic, consistent, isolated, and durable) test, 98–99, 375
ACLs (access control lists)
    discretionary, 51, 88
    viewing, 285, 286
Active Directory, 28–53
    architecture of, 30–32
    backing up, 400–401
    considerations before installing Exchange 2000, 170–171
    DNS and, 32–36
    DSProxy lookups in, 74–76
    Exchange 2000 directory services vs., 31
    Exchange 2000 integration with, 7–8
    Exchange directory data stored in, 67
    forest changes with Exchange 2000 installations, 171
    handling namespace function in Exchange 2000, 284
    increasing LDAP queries processed by domain controller, 716–717
    instant messaging services and, 535–536
    integrated with DNS, 34, 35–36
    LDAP, 36–37
    logical structure of, 37–44
    making bulk changes to, 270–278
    monitoring replication during Exchange installations, 176
    overview of, 28–30, 53
    physical structure of, 44–50
    preparatory installations to extend schema, 187–191
    replication between Exchange 5.5 and, 198–199
    schema modifications during Exchange installation, 182, 185

security of, 50–52
structure of, 31
tools for modifying recipients, 254–256
upgrading from Exchange 5.5, 203–204
See also Active Directory schema
Active Directory Administration Tool (ldp.exe), 255
Active Directory Connector. *See* ADC
Active Directory Connector Manager, 213–214
Active Directory schema
modifications to during Exchange installation, 182, 185
preparatory installations to extend, 187–191
upgrading from Exchange 5.5 and, 203–204
Active Directory Schema snap-in, 42, 43, 57, 255–256
Active Directory Service Interface Editor. *See* ADSI Edit
Active Directory Sites and Services snap-in, 42, 43, 290, 291
Active Directory tools, 254–256
Active Directory Administration Tool, 255
Active Directory Schema, 42, 43, 57, 255–256
Active Directory Users and Computers, 61, 256, 602
ADSI Edit, 254–255, 285, 286, 292–294
Exchange System Manager, 254
installing, 256
Active Directory Users and Computers (ADUC), 61, 256, 602
Active/Active clustering, 663, 670
Active/Passive clustering, 663, 670
ActiveX controls, 451
ActiveX Data Objects (ADO), 10
ADC (Active Directory Connector), 204–224
account mapping and NTDSNoMatch, 207–208
adjusting default sleep time for, 718
creating connection agreements for, 215–224
improving block searching performance, 718–719
installing, 208–213
paging process in, 219
requirements for installing, 206–208
service account requirements for, 211
upgrading from Exchange 5.5 and, 204–206
using Active Directory Connector Manager, 213–214
ADC Installation Wizard, 209, 210, 211, 212, 213
Add or Remove Managed Disks screen (Cluster Service Configuration Wizard), 672
Add Resource dialog box, 730
Add Service to Profile dialog box, 443
Additional Values button (X.400 Connector Properties dialog box), 309, 310
Additional Values dialog box, 310
address lists, 80–83, 320–325
about, 22–23, 320
building and maintaining with RUS, 325
creating, 321–324
custom, 320
default, 82–83, 320
finding filter rules for, 322–323
GAL, 82
offline, 84–86, 320–321
securing for hosting, 324–325
unreplicated to Exchange 5.5 directory, 81
See also GAL
address share, 192–193
Address Space tab (SMTP Connector Properties dialog box), 306
addresses
Class D IP, 495
reserved multicast, 491
administering
clustered virtual servers, 683–684
Exchange clusters, 699–700
administering chat services, 566–584
applying profanity filter, 576–578
authenticating chat room users, 570–571
channel modes, 574–579
channel transcription, 578–579
channels, 565, 571–584
creating new channels, 571
creating user classes, 581–584
in ESM, 566, 567
managing communities, 568–571
naming channels, 572, 573
setting channel visibility, 572–574
user bans, 580
administering mail-enabled accounts
mailbox-enabled users, 263–266
mail-enabled contacts, 267
mail-enabled groups, 268–269
mail-enabled public folders, 269–270
mail-enabled users, 266–267
administration and routing models, 114–119
administrative groups, 114–117
centralized administration model, 115–116
distributed administration model, 116
link state table, 118–119
mixed administration model, 116, 117
redefining, 114
routing groups, 117–118
server and recipient administration, 114
administrative groups, 288–291
administering, 114–117
assigning permissions to, 292–296
centralized administrative model for, 115–116, 288–289
containers for, 608
creating, 290–292
decentralized administrative model for, 289
defined, 16–17, 18, 288
designating KMS administrators, 639–640
displaying, 286–287, 288
hybrid administrative model for, 289–290
managing administrative boundaries with, 284
moving servers between, 291–292
roles for, 18, 294–295, 606–607
administrative rights for public folders, 148–150
ADO (ActiveX Data Objects), 10
ADSI Edit (Active Directory Service Interface Editor)
about, 254–255
assigning administrative group permissions with, 292–294
viewing container ACLs with, 285, 286
ADUC (Active Directory Users and Computers), 61, 256, 602
Advanced button (Default SMTP Virtual Server Properties dialog box), 336
Advanced Delivery dialog box, 341–342
Advanced dialog box, 337
Advanced Find dialog box (Outlook), 382, 383
Advanced Queuing Engine, 104
Advanced tab
for CA Properties dialog box, 219
for Find Exchange Recipients dialog box, 323
for SMTP Connector Properties dialog box, 304–305
System Attendant Properties dialog box, 684
for X.400 Connector Properties dialog box, 313
affinity settings, 690
algorithms
NLB statistical mapping, 689
for routing engine, 105
aliases for mail-enabled group, 261, 262
anonymous access
to HTTP servers, 355
for mailbox folders, 601
for Outlook Web Access 2000, 474–476

anti-virus software
configuring third-party SMTP host to scan mail, 614–615
encrypted messages and, 633
enhanced protection in Outlook XP clients, 450
as security measure, 612–614
warnings about file-system based scanners, 230
applications. *See* software
Apply onto checkbox (Permissions Entry dialog box), 293
architecture, 92–120
of Active Directory, 30–32
for administration and routing models, 114–119
of Conferencing Server, 486–495
event sinks, 113–114
Exchange 5.5, 96
Exchange 2000, 92–96, 120
for IM servers, 528–530
of link state, 314
message flow and, 97–109
of multiple stores and storage groups, 367
on-demand content conversion, 369–370
of Outlook Web Access 2000, 459–462, 470–471, 472
of public folders, 124–129
single instance storage, 370–372
of storage, 366–383
for storage group of clustered server, 675, 676
of store databases, 368–372
streaming, 368–369, 370
of Web storage system, 110–113
of Windows 2000 Cluster Service, 668
archive bit for offline backups, 406–407
archiving messages, 386
associations for X.400 connectors, 311
attributes
Active Directory, 37
Global Catalog, 77
msExchESEPParamCacheSizeMax, 709
NTDSNoMatch, 207–208
auditorium mode, 565
Authenticated Users security group, 325
authentication
certificate, 476
for chat room users, 570–571
digest, 475
for HTTP virtual server access, 355–356
for instant messaging users, 546–547
integrated Windows, 475
integrating Exchange 2000 and Windows 2000, 86–87
Kerberos and NTLM, 52
for Outlook Web Access 2000 client, 474–476
for POP3 servers, 350
protecting domains with user, 596
requiring for protocol access, 609–610
setting default domain for NTLM, 546
for SMTP messaging systems, 345, 346
Authentication Methods dialog box, 156, 469
Authentication tab (New Properties dialog box), 570, 571
Author, 601
autocorrect feature for Outlook XP clients, 446
automating tasks in Microsoft Chat client, 587–588

B

back-end servers
clustered, 473
defined, 694
See also front-end/back-end servers
backfill request timeouts, 142
backfilling, 142
backing up, 400–412
Active Directory, 400–401
before updating legacy systems, 228–229
cluster quorum, 699
Exchange 2000 Server software, 403–404
IIS metabase, 402–403
IM, SRS, and KMS database files, 404
location of Exchange 2000 data, 400–404
M drive, 230
offline backups, 405–407
online backups, 407–410, 703
overview, 404–405
recommended practices for, 429–430
software applications, 404
storage groups and multiple databases, 103
stores, 401, 402
strategies for, 411, 412
third-party backup applications, 425–426
transaction logs, 402
with Windows 2000 Backup, 419–425
See also disaster recovery, online backups, restoring
backup boundary, 410
Backup Job Information dialog box, 422
Backup Type tab (Options dialog box), 422
bandwidth
planning for routing groups, 297–298
required for instant messaging, 534
setting for conferencing services, 514
baselining performance, 726
BHS. *See* bridgehead server
bifurcation, 105
binding information, 42
bridgehead server (BHS)
configuring for routing group connector, 299
function of, 299
sizing for, 169
SMTP connectors and, 302
transferring routing groups through, 18
working with failed links, 318–319
browser, conferencing client inside, 520, 521
bulk changes to Active Directory, 270–278
with CSVDE, 277–278
with LDIFDE, 270–276

C

CA (Certificate Authorities)
about certificates and, 626–627
adding certificate templates to, 634, 635
hierarchy for, 626–627
types of, 628–629, 630
See also certificates, KMS
CA Identifying Information screen (Windows Components Wizard), 631, 632
CA Properties dialog box, 215
caching
increasing size of ESE database cache, 708–709
manually adjusting DSAccess cache parameters, 70–74
viewing cache lists of domain controllers and Global Catalog servers, 69
Calendar (Outlook XP), 449
calendaring
for Outlook 2000, 438
for Outlook XP clients, 448–450
capacity planning, 167
CDO (Collaboration Data Objects) support, 10
CD-ROM installations of Exchange 2000 Server, 176–185
centralized administrative model for administrative groups, 115–116, 288–289
Certificate Authorities. *See* CA
Certificate button (Default SMTP Virtual Server Properties dialog box), 346
certificate templates, 634, 635
certificates
about CAs and, 626–627
adding certificate templates to CA, 634, 635
adding to root store, 648
authenticating, 476

installing SLL, 351
KMS and, 633
managing with Windows 2000 Certificate Services, 633
for POP3 messaging, 350–351
providing Certificate Services with correct, 634
for secure HTTP communications, 356, 357
for secure protocol access, 610
for SMTP messages, 346
X.509, 627, 628
See also CA (Certificate Authorities)
Certification Authority snap-in, 633, 635
Certification Authority Type screen (Windows Components Wizard), 629–630
Change Schema Master dialog box, 47
channel modes, 574–579
channel operators, 564–565
channel transcription, 578–579
channels, 571–584
channel modes, 574–579
channel transcription, 578–579
cloneable, 565, 575
defined, 565
naming, 572, 573
profanity filter, 576–578
setting speaking restrictions for, 575
setting visibility of, 572–574
user bans, 580
Channels tab (New Properties dialog box), 569, 570
character sets for POP3 protocol, 348, 349
Chat Connection dialog box, 586
chat servers, 170, 564
chat services, 13, 554–589
about, 554
applying profanity filter, 576–578
channel modes, 574–579
channel operators for, 564–565
channel transcription, 578–579
channels, 565, 571–584
clients for, 564
commands for, 555–564
installing, 566, 567
IRC protocol and architecture for, 554–555
managing chat clients, 585–589
managing communities, 568–571
naming channels, 572, 573
protecting from attacks, 582–583
security and, 584
servers for, 170, 564
setting channel visibility, 572–574
upgrading Exchange 5.5, 584–585
user bans, 580
See also channels, Microsoft Chat
CHATMIG.EXE utility, 584–585
checkpoint file, 372–373
checksumming
during online backups, 410
for information store files, 98, 99
circular logging
backups and, 409
recommendations against, 100, 385
Class D IP addresses, 495
classes
Active Directory, 37
user, 581–584
cleaning out mailboxes automatically, 703
client certificate mapping, 357
Client Permissions dialog box, 147
client policies for instant messaging, 543–546
adding custom messages, 545
disabling access to MSN Messenger, 545
disabling promotional banner ads, 544–545
disabling software update messages, 545
setting default domain for NTLM authentication, 546
clients, 436–456
architecture for IM, 530–532
chat, 564
choosing, 455
configuring Internet-based Conferencing Server, 517–518
existing Outlook 2000, 438–444
failover and, 663–664
features of IMAP4 messaging protocol for, 351–352
future Outlook XP, 445–452
hardware required for Conferencing Server, 515–516
instant messaging policies for, 543–546
Internet, 452–455
legacy, 436–438
managing chat, 585–589
name resolution in Exchange 2000 Server, 8
permissions for public folders, 146–147
protocol support for Microsoft and non-Microsoft, 23–26
system requirements for Exchange 2000, 455
using indexing, 382
working with conferencing, 520–521
clone attacks, 583
cloneable channels, 565, 575
Cluster Administrator, 664–665, 693–684
Cluster.exe utility, 685–689
cluster groups, 677
cluster installation, 670, 671–683
adding or removing managed disks, 672
configuring hardware, 671
creating virtual server in cluster, 678–683
designing storage group architecture, 675, 676
entering network connections, 673
including cluster IP address, 674, 675
installing Exchange 2000 in cluster, 675–677
installing second server, 674
Cluster IP screen (Cluster Service Configuration Wizard), 675
Cluster Parameters tab (Network Load Balancing Properties dialog box), 691, 692
cluster registry, 663
Cluster Service
architecture of, 668
implementing components of, 664, 665–667
See also Windows 2000 clustering technologies
Cluster Service Configuration Wizard, 671
cluster-aware vs. cluster-unaware applications, 667–668
clustering, 658–701
administering Exchange clusters, 699–700
back-end servers for Outlook Web Access 2000, 473
Cluster.exe utility, 685–689
configuring resource groups, 685, 686, 687
configuring resources, 684–685
considerations about, 697–699
defined, 658–659
failover and clients, 663–664
fault tolerance and, 659–661
four-node active/active, 11–12, 669
front-end/back-end configuration, 694–696
highly available systems, 659
installing Exchange 2000 in cluster, 670, 671–683
instant messaging servers and routers and, 530
managing virtual servers, 683–684
NLB, 689–694
recovering Exchange cluster, 700–701
as solution to hardware failure, 661–662
support for Windows 2000, 669–670
terminology for, 662–663
two-node active/active, 11–12
upgrading Exchange 5.5 clustered servers, 244–246
Windows 2000 clustering technologies, 664–669
See also cluster installation
collaboration
by Web Storage System, 110
collaborative environments, 12–13
Collaboration Data Objects (CDO), 10
comic chat characters, 563, 586–587
commands, 555–564
INVITE, 561
JOIN, 557–558

KICK, 561
KILL, 562
LDIFDE, 271
LIST, 560
messaging via IFS and DOS, 111
MODE, 558–560
NAMES, 560
NICK, 555
OPER, 556
PART, 558
PASS, 555
PING, 562
PRIVMSG, 561–562
QUIT, 557
SERVER, 556
SQUIT, 557
USER, 556, 563
Communication button (Default SMTP Virtual Server Properties dialog box), 346–347
communities, 568–571
Community PFilter Properties dialog box, 577
Completion screen (Microsoft Exchange 2000 Installation Wizard), 184
component performance, 706–716
changing location of mailroot directory, 710–711
ESE database cache size, 708–709
for ESE stores and transaction logs, 707–713
increasing size of ESE log buffers, 709–710
for JET heaps, 708
of MTA, 713–716
raising threshold of SMTP file handles, 711–713
SMTP message queue size, 713
for SMTP protocol, 710
Component Progress screen (Microsoft Exchange 2000 Installation Wizard), 184
Component Selection screen (Microsoft Exchange 2000 Installation Wizard), 180, 239, 240, 635
Component Summary screen (Microsoft Exchange 2000 Installation Wizard), 183, 240
components
adding during In Place Upgrade, 238, 239
of DNS, 31–32
for Exchange 2000 installation, 174–176
of IM server architecture, 528–529
load balancing, 664
of Outlook Web Access 2000, 463
selecting and installing, 178–180, 209, 210
tuning performance of, 706–716
See also component performance
concurrent restores, 415–416
Conference Calendar Mailbox Properties dialog box, 508
Conference Calendar Mailbox screen, 507
conference calendar mailboxes, 488–489, 499
Conference Management Service, 13–14, 487–488, 503
conference planning, 495–502
Conference Calendar Mailbox, 499
Conference Resource, 499–500
conferencing across firewall, 501
hardware, 496–497
MCU, 499
multicasting and routers, 500–501
naming conventions, 501
planning placement of conferencing server, 497–499
recommended practices, 501–502
software, 496
Conference Settings tab (Conference Calendar Mailbox Properties dialog box), 508–509
conference technology providers. *See* CTPs
conferencing
across firewall, 501
adding resources, 512–515
advantages and limitations of IP multicasting, 493–494
changes in support for data, 95
data, 14
Intel platforms required for video, 516
joining, 518–520
naming resources, 501
performance issues for processors during, 704
planning resources, 499–500
scheduling conferences, 517–518
setting bandwidth for, 514
sizing servers for, 169
technological standards for, 489–495
Web sites for, 519, 520
See also Exchange 2000 Conferencing Server
conferencing clients
sharing applications, 522–523
transferring files among, 523
working with, 520–521
Conferencing Manager snap-in tool, 487, 503
conferencing resources
adding, 512–515
naming, 501
planning, 499–500
Conferencing Server, *See also* Exchange 2000 Conferencing Server
conferencing standards, 489–495
H.323, 494–495
IP multicasting, 491–494
MADCAP, 495
Multipoint Control Units, 489–490
configuration domain controller, 68–69
configuring
deleted mailbox retention times, 280–281
Exchange 2000 Conferencing Server, 505–509
firewall and proxy settings for instant messaging, 548–550
full-text indexing, 380–381
Internet-based Conferencing Server clients, 517–518
NLB, 691–694, 695
NNTP virtual servers, 154–157
Outlook 2000 client for Exchange 2000, 439–444
Outlook Web Access 2000, 462–465
public folder replication, 142–143
public stores, 391–394
recipients, 257–262
resource groups, 685, 686, 687
resources, 684–685
security permissions, 150–151
SMTP outbound message delivery, 340–342
user bans, 580
values for Reliable Transfer Service, 310–311
X.400 connectors, 312–313
conflicts in public folder replication, 143–144
Connected Routing Group tab (SMTP Connector Properties dialog box), 306, 307
connecting routing groups, 299–313
about connectors, 299
with routing group connectors, 299–300
with SMTP connectors, 301–307
with X.400 connectors, 307–313
connection agreements
creating ADC recipient, 215–224
message confirming first intra-organizational, 223
user and configuration, 205–207
Connection Control section (Default SMTP Virtual Server Properties dialog box), 345, 347
connection retry values for X.400 connectors, 309–310
connections
configuring SMTP outbound, 341
controlling inbound SMTP, 338
between Exchange 2000 and Exchange 5.5, 237
for instant messaging, 534
maintaining with In-Place Upgrade, 235–236
restricting access to SMTP virtual server, 347
restricting POP3, 351
See also connection agreements
Connections tab (CA Properties dialog box), 216
connector servers, 169
connectors
maintaining connectivity with In-Place Upgrade, 235–236
removing and rerouting Exchange 5.5, 225

routing group, 117, 299–302
SMTP, 301–307
types of, 299
X.400, 307–313
See also routing group connectors, SMTP connectors, X.400 connectors
consoles, creating, 287
Contact screen (Outlook XP), 447
contacts
in instant messaging, 527
mail-enabled, 65–66
containers
administrative group, 608
chat, 567
creating for administrative groups, 290–291
function of, 285
public store, 128–129
Contributor, 601
convergence, NLB and, 690
COPY method for HTTP, 745
corporate option for Outlook 2000 client, 441
counters. *See* component performance
CPUs (central processing units)
performance counters for, 725
performance with front-end servers, 704
recommended for Exchange servers, 168–170
system requirements for, 166, 167
tuning LDAP queries for large multiprocessor environments, 716–717
Create Conferencing Calendar dialog box, 506
Create Mailbox screen (Exchange Tasks Wizard), 258
Create New Folder dialog box (Outlook), 131
creating
ADC recipient, 215–224
address lists, 321–324
administrative groups, 290–292
cluster groups, 677
connection agreements for ADC, 215–224
DNS SRV record for instant messaging server, 537–538
group management domain, 246–247
instant messaging servers, 540–542
Internet newsgroups, 157–158
IP addresses for resource group, 679–680
mailbox stores, 385–391
mailbox-enabled users, 257–259
mail-enabled contacts, 260
mail-enabled groups, 260–262
mail-enabled public folders, 138, 139, 140, 262
new channels, 571
newsfeeds, 159, 361
newsgroup objects, 360
Outlook XP client profiles, 446, 447
protocol virtual servers, 333–334
public folder tree, 391
public folders, 129–131
public store policies for objects, 153
recipient connection agreements, 215–224
recipient policies, 326–327
RGCs, 299–300, 302
routing groups, 300
SMTP connectors, 303–307
storage groups, 383–385
stores, 385–394
top-level folders, 129–140
user classes, 581–584
virtual M drive, 376, 377
virtual server in cluster, 678–683
X.400 connectors, 308
CSVDE (CSV Directory Exchange) utility, 277–278
CTPs (conference technology providers)
about, 488
adding to new resource, 512–515
configuring, 509–510
current session management
IMAP4, 353
NNTP, 363
POP3, 350
SMTP, 345
custom address lists, 320
custom recipients, 20
customer relations and knowledge management, 764–765

D

DACLs (discretionary access control lists), 51, 88
daily full backups, 411, 412
damaged logs, 372
data
backing up Active Directory, 400–401
encrypting with SSL, 478–479
location of Exchange 2000, 400–404
lost during MTACheck, 226
monitoring performance, 720–726
System State, 401
See also databases, directory data
Data Conferencing Provider Properties dialog box, 509–510
data conferencing providers, 488, 509–510
Data Storage Location screen (Windows Components Wizard), 631, 632
Database tab (Mailbox Properties dialog box), 387
databases
assigning locations and filenames for mailbox, 387
backing up IM, SRS, and KMS, 404
changing location of after installation, 180
data lost during MTACheck, 226
deleting store, 396–397
information store, 101–102
MAPI store, 101
moving instant messaging, 538–539
moving store, 394–396
online backups of, 408
performing hard recovery on clustered, 701
public folder database and its subtrees, 126
restoring service, 428–429
storage groups and multiple, 102–103
store, 368–372
storing different types of information to single, 110
support of multiple, 11, 102–103
system limits on, 102
See also ESE databases
decentralized administrative model for administrative groups, 289
default address lists, 82–83, 320
Default IMAP4 Virtual Server Properties dialog box, 352–353
Default NNTP Virtual Server Properties dialog box, 155
Default POP3 Virtual Server Properties dialog box, 348–351
Default SMTP Virtual Server Properties dialog box, 318, 319, 336
Access Control section, 346
Access tab, 345–347
Advanced button, 336
Certificate button, 346
Communication button, 346–347
Connection Control section, 345, 347
Delivery tab, 340
General tab, 336, 734
Messages tab, 338–339
Relay Restrictions section, 345, 347
Secure Communications section, 346
Delegate Control dialog box, 607
Delegate Permissions dialog box, 604
Delegates tab (Options dialog box), 603
delegating access to mailboxes, 601–603
from ADUC, 602
assigning folder permissions, 602–604
from Outlook, 602–603
sending messages as delegate, 603
deleting stores and storage groups, 396–397
Deletion tab-CA Properties dialog box, 218
delivering NDRs, 339, 340
Delivery Options dialog box, 602
Delivery Options tab
Routing Group Connector Properties dialog box, 302
SMTP Connector Properties dialog box, 304
Delivery Restrictions tab (Routing Group Connector properties dialog box), 300

Delivery tab (Default SMTP Virtual Server Properties dialog box), 340
demilitarized zone (DMZ), 621–622
dependencies of IP address resources, 680
Dependencies screen (New Resource Wizard), 682
deploying Outlook Web Access 2000, 470–473
Details tab
CA Properties dialog box, 222
Properties dialog box, 135
development platform, 9–11
Diagnostic Logging tab (Active Directory Connector Properties dialog box), 214
differential backups, 411
digest authentication, 475
Digital Dashboard
about, 765–767
public folders and, 123
digital signatures, 626, 650
direct client attacks, 583–584
directory data, 67–76
DSAccess, 67–69
dsadiag.exe utility, 69–70
DSProxy, 74–76
manually adjusting DSAccess cache parameters, 70–74
stored in Active Directory, 67
directory rights for public folders, 151, 152
Directory Security tab (Exchange Properties dialog box), 354–357
directory services, 56–89
address list services, 80–83
directory data, 67–76
Exchange directory objects, 58–67
Global Address List (GAL), 67
improvements in Exchange 2000, 56–58
integration with Windows 2000, 7–8, 56–58
new features of Exchange 2000, 92, 93
offline address lists, 84–86
replicating additional Global Catalog attributes, 76–80
security for Active Directory and Exchange 2000, 86–89
structural changes made during Exchange installation, 191–192
See also Active Directory, Exchange directory objects, virtual directories
directory system agent (DSA), 37–38
DirectPlay applications, 532
disabling
access to MSN Messenger, 545
promotional banner ads, 544–545
protocol access, 604–606
referrals, 146
software update messages, 545
software update messages for MSN Messenger, 545
disaster recovery, 426–429
backup strategies and, 411, 412
Exchange 2000 installation in disaster recovery mode, 428, 429
installing Windows 2000, 427
for instant messaging, 539
location of Exchange 2000 data, 400–404
materials needed for, 426–427
restoring Exchange 2000, 412–419
restoring service databases, 428–429
restoring system drive, 428
restoring System State, 428
third-party backup applications, 425–426
types of backups, 404–412
Windows 2000 Backup, 419–425
disaster recovery mode, 428, 429
discretionary access control lists (DACLs), 51, 88
disk drives
adding or removing clustered, 672
disk subsystem performance, 705–706, 723–724
disk mirroring, 660
disk resource DLL, 681
disk space requirements
minimum system, 166, 167
sizing servers, 168–170
disk subsystem performance, 705–706, 723–724
displaying
administrative groups, 286–287, 288
names of store database files, 402
routing groups, 286–287, 288
state of monitored services, 729
distinguished names, 59
distributed administration model, 116
Distributed Lock Manager (DLM), 658
distributed services, 12
distribution groups, 21, 62
DLLs
for ExIPC protocols, 106, 107
ExRes.dll, 668–669
SMTP protocol engine (smtpsvc.dll), 105
DLM (Distributed Lock Manager), 658
DMZ (demilitarized zone), 621–622
DNS (Domain Name Service), 32–36
about, 32
Active Directory integration with, 34, 35–36
components of, 31–32
creating DNS SRV record for instant messaging server, 537–538
Dynamic, 34–35, 200–202
Internet DNS namespace, 33–34
as namespace, 32
documents, property promotion of, 112
domain controllers
Active Directory physical structure and, 37
avoiding installation of Exchange 2000 on Active Directory, 167
clustering with static, 699
configuration, 68–69
increasing LDAP queries processed by, 716–717
in physical structure of Active Directory, 44–48
viewing cache lists of, 69
domain local groups, 61
Domain Name Service. *See* DNS
domain names and HTTP access, 354, 356
domain queues, 104
Domain Users Properties dialog box, 268
domainprep switch, 190–191
domains
DNS and instant messaging, 536–538
domain directory partitions, 43
in hierarchical structure of objects, 38–39
setting default for NTLM authentication, 546
upgrading from Exchange 5.5 and Active Directory, 203
drivers
SMTP store, 105
Wlbs.sys, 689
drives
M, 196, 230, 376, 377
restoring system, 428
DS/IS Consistency Adjuster, 227–228, 229
DSA (directory system agent), 37–38
DSAccess API
hard coding DSAccess cache, 73–74
manually adjusting cache parameters for, 70–73
role of, 67–69
dsadiag.exe utility, 69–70
DSProxy, 74–76
Dynamic DNS, 34–35, 200–202

E

Edit Filters dialog box, 576
editions and features of Exchange 2000 Server, 7
Editor, 600
e-mail
adding digital signature to outgoing, 650
enabling KMS security for user's, 645, 646, 648
encrypting message contents and attachments, 649–650
filtering addresses with SMTP protocol, 337
instant messaging vs., 527
See also messaging
E-Mail Accounts screen (Outlook XP), 447
E-Mail Addresses tab for user account properties, 265
E-mail Security dialog box, 651
enabling
anonymous access to HTTP servers, 355

client certificate mapping in HTTP, 357
instant messaging, 542–543
protocols, 604–606
encryption
effects of on scanning and filtering, 633
with instant messaging, 550
for Outlook Web Access 2000 security, 477–480
PKI process for, 625
encryption keys
issued by certificate authorities, 626–627
options for public and private key pairs, 630, 631
recovering and revoking, 650, 651
types of PKI, 625
See also KMS
Enroll Users dialog box, 643
Enroll Users Selection dialog box, 642
enrollment, 640–645, 646
completing, 645, 646–649
individual KMS, 643, 645
mass, 641, 642, 643, 644, 645
enrollment token, 644, 646, 647
errors
for Internet-based clients joining conferences, 517
messages for ESE98 database, 99
moving mailboxes with MAPI, 259, 260
ESE (Extensible Storage Engine) databases, 11, 30, 31
ACID test, 98–99, 375
cache size, 708–709
checksumming during backups, 410
error messages for ESE98, 99
function of ESE98 in information store, 98
log buffers, 709–710
maintenance routines for enhanced performance, 702–703
stores and transaction logs, 707–713
transaction logging for, 100, 373–375, 707–713
Esefile, 98
ESEUTIL utility, 372
ESM (Exchange System Manager)
about, 254
administering chat services in, 566, 567
creating consoles from, 287
displaying administrative groups in, 286–287, 288
managing protocol virtual servers in, 333
managing servers with, 284–288
monitoring tools in, 727
viewing SMTP queues with, 343, 344
event logs, 719–720
event scripts, 236
event sinks, 113–114
functions of, 113
types of, 113–114
Web Store, 114, 382–383
Exchange 4.0, X.509v1 certificates for, 627
Exchange 4.0 and 5.0 compatibility checkbox (Offline Address Lists dialog box), 85
Exchange 5.0, X.509v1 certificates for, 627
Exchange 5.0 Client, 436, 437
Exchange 5.5
architecture of, 96
concept of site in, 284
GWART replaced by link state tables, 314
as intermediary platform in importing user accounts, 277
item-level permissions unsupported in, 150–151
namespace function in Exchange 2000 and, 284
problems of scalability and message format in, 366
requirements before upgrading, 224–230
routing groups in Exchange 2000 and, 284
upgrading chat services from, 584–585
See also upgrading from Exchange 5.5
Exchange 2000 Chat Service. *See* chat services
Exchange 2000 Conferencing Server, 13–14, 486–524
adding resource for, 512–515
client configuration, 515–520
conference calendar mailboxes, 488–489, 499
Conference Management Service, 13–14, 487–488
conference resource planning, 499–500
configuring, 505–509
data conferencing, 14
data conferencing providers, 488, 509–510
firewalls, 501
hardware planning for, 496–497
installing, 502–504
joining conference, 518–520
MCU planning, 499
multicasting and routers, 500–501
naming conventions, 501
planning placement of conferencing server, 497–499
recommended practices, 501–502
scheduling conferences, 517–518
setting up Internet-based clients, 517–518
software planning for, 496
standards for conferencing, 489–495
T.120 MCU server configuration, 511–512
terminology for, 486–487
troubleshooting failed installations for, 504–505
video conferencing, 14
video conferencing provider, 488
Web sites for, 519, 520
working with conferencing client, 520–523
See also planning for conferencing
Exchange 2000 Server, 6–27
adjusting default sleep time for ADC, 718
administering clusters, 699–700
backing up, 403–404, 420–423
clients and client support, 23–26
clustering, 11–12, 669–670
collaborative environments, 12–13
Conferencing Server, 13–14
configuring Outlook 2000 to work with, 441, 442
development of, 6, 27
as development platform, 9–11
distributed services, 12
editions and features of, 7
Enterprise Server, 11
Exchange 5.5 vs., 94–96, 284
Exchange server directory services vs. Active Directory, 31
fault-tolerant SMTP routing, 9
front-end/back-end architecture, 461–462
improving ADC block searching performance, 718–719
indexing and searching for, 9
as information service for Outlook 2000, 444
installing in cluster, 671–689
installing in disaster recovery mode, 428, 429
integrated directory services, 56–58
integration with Windows 2000 and Active Directory, 7–8
Internet clients for, 452
location of data in, 400–404
managing, 14–20
multiple database support of, 11
optimizing to work with Active Directory, 716–719
Outlook 2000 client as preferred client, 438
recovering server cluster, 700–701
replicating folders between organizations, 141
restoring, 412–419, 423, 425
routing messages in, 315–319
selecting components to install, 174–176
starting and stopping clustered resources, 699–700
user management concepts, 20–23
Exchange 2000 Server CD splash screen, 177
Exchange 2000 Server Enterprise Server, 11

Exchange Administration Delegation Wizard
assigning permissions with, 294–296
delegating control of Active Directory objects with, 17, 18
granting administrative roles in, 18, 607
listing users and groups with administrative access, 606, 607
Exchange Administrator permission, 295, 606
Exchange Advanced tab
for domain user properties, 268
for user account properties, 266
Exchange directory objects, 58–67
groups, 61–63
mailbox-enabled users, 65
mailboxes, 66
mail-enabled contacts, 65–66
mail-enabled objects, 63–65
revised terminology for, 58–59
users, 59–61
Exchange Features tab (Administrator Properties dialog box), 646
Exchange Full Administrator permission, 295, 606, 682
Exchange General tab
for mail-enabled public folder, 269
for user account properties, 264
Exchange Interprocess Communication (ExIPC) layer, 105–106
Exchange Rich-Text format, 349–350
Exchange Server, 6
Exchange System Manager (ESM)
about, 254
administration tasks with, 15–16
Exchange Tasks Wizard, 257–261
creating mailbox-enabled users, 257–259
creating mail-enabled contacts, 260
functions of, 20, 21, 257
setting up mail-enabled users, 259
Exchange View Only Administrator permission, 294, 606
exchange virtual directory, 354
ExIPC (Exchange Interprocess Communication) layer, 105–106, 107
Exmerge utility, 417
exporting user accounts with LDIFDE, 271–273
ExRes.dll, 668–669
Extensible Markup Language (XML) support, 9–10
Extensible Storage Engine databases. *See* ESE databases
Extensions tab (New Properties dialog box), 576
external security, 608–624
anti-virus software, 612–615
complete scenario for, 622–624
firewalls, 616–622
securing protocol access, 609–612
See also security

F

Failback tab (Resource Group Properties dialog box), 685, 688
failover, 662, 663–664
failover groups, 662
Failover tab (Resource Group Properties dialog box), 685, 687
fast message retrieval for IMAP4 virtual servers, 352
fault tolerance
clustering and, 659–661
clustering as solution to hardware failure, 661–662
fault-tolerant SMTP routing, 9
FE/BE configuration. *See* front-end/back-end servers
file systems
IFS, 110
using NTFS or FAT partitions for Exchange transaction logs, 170
warnings about file-system based virus scanners, 230
See also IFS
File Transfer Utility, 523
files
assigning names for mailbox, 387
backing up IM, SRS, and KMS database files, 404
checkpoint, 372–373
checksumming for information store, 98, 99
displaying names of store database, 402
.EDB (rich text), 349–350, 368, 369, 401, 402
Level 1 file types, 450
METABASE.BIN, 403
moving instant messaging log, 538–539
native content, 368–369, 370
Outlook XP protection against attachments, 451
personal store, 410
recognizing damaged logs, 372
RESTORE.ENV, 414–415
restoring patch and log, 414
.STM, 401, 402
streaming, 368–369, 370
transferring among conferencing clients, 523
filtering
address lists, 322–323
chat channels, 576–577
e-mail addresses with SMTP protocol, 337
encryption's effects on, 633
packets with firewalls, 616–617, 618
recognizing RVP protocol during, 549
with wildcard expressions for restricted words, 577
Filtering tab (Message Delivery Properties dialog box), 337
Find Exchange Recipients dialog box, 83, 322, 323
firewalls, 616–622
about, 616
combining with front-end/back-end server, 620–622
conferencing across, 501
and default ports used by MSN Messenger, 539–540
illustrated, 478
NAT, 617–620
packet filtering, 616–617, 618
and proxy settings for instant messaging users, 548–550
first installations
about, 173
performing with Installation Wizard, 176–185
First Routing Group, 296
Five Nine's, 659
flexible single-master operation (FSMO) roles, 45–46
flooding attacks, 582–583
flushing transaction logs, 409
Folder Size dialog box, 390
folders
creating top-level, 129–140
edit conflicts for replicated public, 143–144
locating documents by properties, 112
permissions for mailbox, 599–601
propagating properties of parents to subfolders, 135–138
shared, 597
sharing mailbox, 376–378
sharing with IFS file system, 110–111
User Bans, 580
See also public folders
forestprep switch
with existing Exchange 5.5 organizations, 188–189
with new Exchange organizations, 188
running setup with, 189–190
forests
configuration and schema directory partitions, 43
Exchange 2000 installations and changes to Active Directory, 171
in hierarchical structure of objects, 39–41
using ADC for synchronizing upgraded, 204–205
forwarding messages with unresolved recipients, 339
four-node active/active clustering, 11–12, 669
friendly names, 446, 447
From Exchange tab (CA Properties dialog box), 220
From Windows tab (CA Properties dialog box), 221

front-end servers
- configuring, 614
- defined, 694
- performance issues for processors with, 704
- running SSL with, 478
- setting up Outlook Web Access 2000, 477–478
- sizing for, 169
- SMTP on, 698
- SSL recommended for, 697–698
- *See also* front-end/back-end servers

front-end/back-end servers
- changing ports for, 610–612, 613
- clustering and, 658, 694–696
- firewalls with, 620–622
- load balancing for, 658
- used by Outlook Web Access 2000, 461–462

FSMO (flexible single-master operation) roles, 45–46

full-text indexing, 378–382, 383
- about, 378–379
- client use of indexing, 382
- configuring, 380–381
- how indexing works, 379
- for mailbox stores, 391
- manually populating index, 381–382

Full-Text-Indexing tab (Mailbox Store Properties dialog box), 380

future
- of instant messaging, 551–552
- of WebDAV, 750

G

GAL (Global Address List), 22–23, 67

gatekeepers, 495

gateways for H.323 clients, 495

General tab
- for Conference Calendar Mailbox Properties dialog box, 508
- for Default IMAP4 Virtual Server Properties dialog box, 352
- for Default NNTP Virtual Server Properties dialog box, 155, 358
- for Default POP3 Virtual Server Properties dialog box, 348–349
- for Default SMTP Virtual Server Properties dialog box, 336, 734
- for Find Exchange Recipients dialog box, 322, 323
- for HTTP Virtual Server Properties dialog box, 467
- for Mailbox Properties dialog box, 385–386
- for New Properties dialog box, 568, 571–572
- for Public Store Properties dialog box, 392
- for Resource Group Properties dialog box, 685, 686
- for Routing Group Connector properties dialog box, 300
- for SMTP Connector Properties dialog box, 303
- for System Manager Properties dialog box, 132
- for User Class Properties dialog box, 581
- for X.400 Connector Properties dialog box, 308

Get a Digital (D (Certificate) dialog box, 647

Global Address List (GAL), 22–23, 67

Global Catalog servers
- about, 270
- clustering with, 699
- DSAccess detection of, 68
- in hierarchical structure of objects, 41–43
- ratio of Exchange 2000 Servers to, 198
- replicating additional attributes, 76–80
- SRV record, 201
- viewing cache lists of, 69

global groups, 61

goals of systems for knowledge management, 757–758

group management domain, 246–247

Group Schedule screen (Outlook XP), 450

groups, 61–63
- about, 61
- administrative, 114–117
- creating cluster, 677
- domain local, 61
- functions as distribution and security, 62–63
- global, 61
- hiding membership in, 257
- membership limitations for, 64
- storage, 102–103
- universal, 62

GUID (globally unique identifier), 66

GWART (Gateway Address Routing Table), 314

H

H.261 technology standards, 514

H.263 technology standards, 514

H.323 technology standards, 489, 704

hardware
- adding or removing managed disks in cluster, 672
- clustering as solution to hardware failure, 661–662
- configuring for cluster, 671
- list of compatible, 168
- needed for MSN Messenger client, 531–532
- planning for Conferencing Server, 496–497
- required for Conferencing Server clients, 515–516
- requirements for Exchange 2000, 166–168
- selection and tuning of, 703–706
- sizing servers, 168–170

Hardware Configuration screen (Cluster Service Configuration Wizard), 671

heartbeat
- defined, 662–663
- for NLB, 690
- using private network for, 673

hierarchical structure
- for certificate authorities, 626–627
- domains, 38–39
- forests and trees, 39–41
- Global Catalog server, 41–43
- of objects, 38–44
- organization units (OUs), 39
- partitioning, 43–44
- of public folders, 124–129

highly available systems, 659

history
- of Exchange 2000 Server, 6, 27
- of WebDAV, 742–743

Host Parameters tab (Network Load Balancing Properties dialog box), 692–693

hotfixes, 171–172, 202

HTTP protocol, 353–357
- COPY method, 745
- determining access by IP address and domain names, 354, 356
- enabling anonymous access to servers, 355
- enabling client certificate mapping, 357
- installing certificate for secure communications, 356
- LOCK method, 746–747
- managing virtual server for, 335
- MKCOL method, 747
- MOVE method, 747–748
- PROPFIND method, 748–749
- PROPPATCH method, 749
- requiring client certificates, 357
- requiring secure channel, 357
- selecting authentication for virtual servers, 355–356
- starting, stopping, and pushing, 335
- UNLOCK method, 749
- using multiple virtual servers in cluster, 698
- WebDAV methods for, 112–113, 745–749

HTTP Virtual Server Properties dialog box, 467

hybrid administrative model for administrative groups, 289–290

I

ICANN (Internet Corporation for Assigned Names and Numbers), 33, 34

IFS (Installable File System), 376–378
- advantages of, 376

creating virtual M drive, 376, 377
defined, 110
folder sharing, 110–111, 376–378
implications of sharing on M drive, 597
sharing objects, 110–111
IIS (Internet Information Services)
backing up metabase, 402–403
instant messaging and, 538
integration with, 8, 93
messaging scenarios via, 107–109
protocol support for Exchange 2000 by, 103–109
queuing with ExIPC layer, 105–106
IM. *See* instant messaging
IM home servers, 530
IM routers, 530
IMAIL message conversion, 101
IMAP4 protocol
fast message retrieval option, 352
managing current sessions, 353
messaging options for, 353
as messaging protocol for clients, 109, 351–352
security for, 353
setting properties for, 351–353
starting, stopping, and pushing, 335
importing user accounts with CSVDE utility, 277–278
inbound messages from Internet to Outlook user, 108–109
Inbox for Outlook XP clients, 445
Inbox Properties dialog box, 377, 600
incremental backups, 411
indexing, 378–382, 383
about full-text, 378–379
client use of, 382
configuring full-text, 380–381
how it works, 379
manually populating index, 381–382
searching and, 9
information
as asset, 752–753
nature of, 753–755
information stores, 97–101
changes in Exchange 2000, 92–93, 94
checksumming on files in, 98, 99
databases, 101–102
ESE databases and ACID test, 98–99, 375
Exchange 5.5 architecture, 96
Exchange 2000 architecture, 97
functions and evolution of, 97–98
IMAIL message conversion, 101
MAPI store database, 101
monitoring performance counters for, 721
native content store of, 101–102
single-instance message storage, 99–100
transaction logs for ESE databases, 100
See also ESE databases, Web Storage System
In-Place Upgrade method, 237–244
impact of, 234–237
performing, 237–241
rolling back from failed upgrade, 241–244
Installable File System. *See* IFS
installation of Exchange 2000 Server, 166–196
changes made by setup, 191–196
in cluster, 670, 671–683
in disaster recovery mode, 428, 429
Exchange components to select from, 174–176
first installations, 173, 176–185
hardware requirements, 166–168
installing service packs and hotfixes before, 171–172
preparatory installations, 174, 187–191
second and subsequent installations, 173, 185–186
selecting KMS component, 634–637
sizing servers, 168–170
software components required for, 170
types of installations, 173–174
unattended, 174, 186–187
validating name resolution before, 172–173
Windows 2000 and Active Directory considerations before, 170–171
See also Setup switches
Installation Type screen (Microsoft Exchange 2000 Installation Wizard), 181
installing
Active Directory administrative tools, 256
ADC, 208–213
certificate for secure HTTP communications, 356
Certificate Services, 629–633
chat services, 566, 567
Cluster Administrator, 693–684
components, 178–180, 209, 210
Exchange 2000 Conferencing Server, 502–504
Exchange servers in cluster, 670, 671–683
Key Management Service, 634–638
Outlook Web Access 2000, 462–465
quorum disk, 671
service packs and hotfixes before, 171–172
SLL certificates, 351
Windows 2000 after disaster, 427
Windows 2000 Certificate Services, 629–633
See also installation of Exchange 2000 Server
instant messaging (IM), 526–552
about, 12–13, 526–527
architectural components of, 528
authentication of users, 546–547
backing up database files for, 404
client architecture for, 530–532
client policies for, 543–546
database management for, 538–539
disaster recovery for, 539
as DNS namespace, 536
e-mail vs., 527
enabling, 542–543
FAQs about, 534
firewalls and default ports used by MSN Messenger, 539–540
future of, 551–552
IIS and, 538
IM home servers, 530
IM routers, 530
managing, 540–546
message status for, 526
monitoring IM servers, 550–551
MSN providers and, 533–534
planning infrastructure for, 534
RVP protocol, 532–533
security for, 546–550
server architecture for, 528–530
sizing servers for, 169
SRV records, 537
warnings about clear text communications in, 545–546
Windows 2000 and, 535–540
integrated directory services, 56–89
address list services, 80–83
directory data, 67–76
Exchange directory objects, 58–67
Global Address List (GAL), 67
improvements in Exchange 2000, 56–58
integration with Windows 2000, 7–8
offline address lists, 84–86
replicating additional Global Catalog attributes, 76–80
security for Active Directory and Exchange 2000, 86–89
integrated Windows authentication, 475
internal security, 596–608
about IFS shares, 597
administrative access and, 606–608
delegate access to mailboxes, 601–603
designing administrative groups for security, 608
mailbox folder permissions, 599–601
permissions for shared folders, 597
protecting domains with user authentication, 596
protocol access, 604–606
setting permissions for mailbox access, 597–604
See also security

Internet
  configuring third-party SMTP host to scan mail, 614–615
  instant messaging and connectivity, 534
  ports for protocols, 334, 476–477, 617
  securing instant messaging traffic on, 548–550
Internet clients, 452–455
  about, 452
  Internet only option for Outlook 2000 client, 441
  Macintosh, 455
  Outlook Express, 452–453
  Outlook Web Access, 453–454
  Unix-based, 454
Internet Corporation for Assigned Names and Numbers (ICANN), 33, 34
Internet DNS namespace, 9–10, 33–34
Internet Information Services. *See* IIS
Internet Mail Connector Properties dialog box, 615
Internet newsgroups, 154–159
  advantages of public folders for, 123–124
  configuring NNTP virtual servers, 154–157
  creating, 157–158
  creating newsfeeds, 159
  NNTP service and, 154
Internet-based Conferencing Server clients, 517–518
intra-organizational connection agreement message, 223
INVITE command, 561
IP addresses
  adding for cluster, 674–675
  creating for resource group, 679–680
  determining HTTP access by, 354, 356
  for network cards connected to private network, 674
  resources dependencies of, 680
  specifying for SMTP virtual server, 336–337
IPSec (IP Security)
  performance of with network cards, 705
  securing Outlook Web Access 2000 with, 480
IRC (Internet Relay Chat) protocol, 554–555
item-and property-level permissions for public folders, 150–151

J

JET (Joint Engine Technology) heaps, 708
JOIN command, 557–558
joining conferences, 518–520

K

KCC (Knowledge Consistency Checker), 227
Kerberos
  defined, 52
  integrating Exchange 2000 and Windows 2000 service, 87–88
  ports for, 476, 477
key distribution center (KDC), 87
Key Management Service. *See* KMS
Key Management Service Information screen (Microsoft Exchange 2000 Installation Wizard), 636, 638
Key Manager, 639
KICK command, 561
KILL command, 562
KMS (Key Management Service), 633–649
  about, 89
  backing up database files for, 404
  changing startup password location, 638
  completing enrollment, 645, 646–649
  designating KMS administrators, 639–640
  effects of In-Place Upgrade on, 236
  enabling for e-mail, 645, 646, 648
  enrolling users, 640–645, 646
  individual enrollment for, 643, 645
  installing, 634–638
  Key Manager function in, 639
  mass enrollment for, 641, 642, 643, 644, 645
  overview of, 644
  providing Certificate Services with correct certificates, 634
  setting multiple passwords for KMS tasks, 640–641, 642
  starting manually, 636, 637
  startup password for, 636–638
knowledge
  nature of, 755–756
  sharing, 758–759
Knowledge Consistency Checker (KCC), 227
knowledge management, 752–770
  about, 752
  customer relationship management and, 764–765
  designing systems of, 762–764
  Digital Dashboard, 765–767
  goals of systems for, 757–758
  information as asset, 752–753
  knowledge workers, 759–760
  Microsoft technology for, 765–770
  nature of information, 753–755
  nature of knowledge, 755–756
  SharePoint Portal Server (SPS), 769–770
  sharing knowledge, 758–759
  Team Centers, 767–768
  workflow and, 760–762
  workflow capabilities of Exchange 2000, 768
knowledge workers
  advantages of instant messaging for, 526
  defined, 759–760
  Outlook Web Access 2000 custom solutions for, 480–481

L

last backup set, 415, 416
latency, 500
LDAP (Lightweight Directory Access Protocol)
  about, 36–37
  fields for first and last names, 324
  increasing queries processed by Windows 2000 domain controller, 716–717
  search filters creating default address lists, 82–83
LDIF records, 270
LDIFDE utility, 270–276
  about, 270–271
  switches for, 274–276
  unable to export passwords with, 273
  using, 271–273
legacy clients, 436–438
  about, 436, 437
  Exchange 5.0 Client, 436, 437
  Outlook 97, 437
  Outlook 98, 437–438
legacy DN (distinguished name), 66
legacy systems. *See* Exchange 5.5, preparing legacy systems for updates, upgrading from Exchange 5.5
Level 1 file types, 450
License Logging Service, 698
Licensing Agreement screen (Microsoft Exchange 2000 Installation Wizard), 183
Lightweight Directory Access Protocol (LDAP), 36–37
Limits tab (Properties dialog box), 134, 280, 388–389, 393–394
link queues, 104
link state algorithm (LSA), 9, 318
link state tables, 313–315
  architecture of link state, 314
  collecting link status via routing group master, 118–119
  as improvement to Exchange 5.5 GWART, 314
  routing group master and, 314–315
  viewing information with WinRoute utility, 315, 316
  viewing link state information, 315
LIST command, 560
load-balancing solutions
  for IM routers, 530
  for multiple front-end servers, 471–473

Local Security Authority (LSA), 50–51
locating documents in folders by properties, 112
LOCK method for HTTP, 746–747
logging, 372–376
  with Active Directory Connector Manager, 213–214
  backing up logs, 402
  of chat conversations, 575
  checkpoint file and, 372–373
  circular, 100, 385, 409
  diagnostic data, 732–733
  enabling Conferencing Server verbose, 504–505
  enabling protocol, 733–735
  enabling SMTP, 338
  for ESE databases, 100
  ESE management of, 373–375
  flushing transaction logs, 409
  importance, 372
  moving instant messaging log files, 538–539
  moving logs, 395
  public folder messages, 142
  restoring log files to temporary location, 414
  SMTP formats for, 338
  SMTP protocol, 698–699
  store database and placement of log, 376
  using NTFS or FAT partitions with Exchange, 170
  viewing log dump, 373
logical structure of Active Directory, 37–44
  hierarchical structure of objects, 38–44
  objects, 37
  schema, 37–38
LogicalDisk performance library object, 723
Logons container, 128
logs
  backing up, 402
  changing location of after installation, 180
  flushing transaction, 409
  hard recovery of clustered, 701
  increasing values for ESE log buffers, 709–710
  monitoring event, 719–720
  online backups of, 408
  online backups of logs, 408
  recognizing damaged, 372
  size of quorum, 673
LSA (link state algorithm), 9, 318
LSA (Local Security Authority), 50–51

M

M drive
  created during installation, 196, 376, 377
  implications of sharing on, 597
  warnings against backing up and restoring, 230
Macintosh Internet clients, 455
MADCAP (Multicast Address Dynamic Allocation Protocol), 495
mailbox folder permissions, 599–601
mailbox policies, 327–330
Mailbox Properties dialog box, 385–386
mailbox servers, 168
mailbox stores
  about, 367
  adding to mailbox policies, 329–330
  assigning locations and filenames for databases, 387
  creating, 385–391
  full-text indexing and, 391
  setting limit levels for, 388–389, 390
mailbox-enabled users, 65
  administering, 263–266
  defined, 20, 256
  property pages for, 22
mailboxes, 66
  accessing with alternate set of user credentials, 444
  ADC account mapping and NTDSNoMatch attribute, 207–208
  backing up and restoring, 405, 410–411
  checking size of in Outlook, 390
  cleaning out automatically, 703
  cleanup utility in Outlook XP for, 451–452
  conference calendar, 488–489
  creating in Exchange Tasks Wizard, 257–258
  delegate access to, 601–603
  finding deleted, 702–703
  folder permissions for, 599–601
  Move Mailbox upgrade method, 231–232
  moving data to original server with Exmerge utility, 417
  permissions for, 598–599
  policies for, 327–330
  recovering, 280–281
  recreating missing directory objects, 227–228
  restoring single, 417–418
  unable to backup with Windows 2000 Backup, 411
  URLs for Outlook Web Access 2000, 464–465, 466
mail-enabled contacts
  about, 65–66
  administering, 267
  creating, 260
  defined, 257
mail-enabled groups
  administering, 268–269
  creating, 260–262
  defined, 257
mail-enabled objects, 63–65
mail-enabled public folders
  additional property sheets for, 140
  administering, 269–270
  creating, 138, 139, 140, 262
  defined, 257
mail-enabled users
  administering, 266–267
  defined, 20, 256–257
  property page for, 22
  setting up, 259
mailroot directory, 710–711
maintaining
  Outlook Web Access 2000, 482–483
  storage groups and multiple databases, 103
managing Exchange 2000 Server, 14–20
  administering policies, 19–20
  administration tasks with Exchange Server Manager, 15–16
  with administrative groups, 16–17, 18
  merging tools in MMC, 14–15
  with routing groups, 17–18
manually populating index, 381–382
MAPI
  default public folder tree for, 125
  errors moving mailboxes with, 259, 260
  storing client messages in rich text file (.EDB), 369
MAPI store database, 101
masquerade domain, 341, 342
materials needed for disaster recovery, 426–427
MBX folders, about, 110–111
MCUs (Multipoint Control Units)
  conferencing standards for, 489–490
  configuring T.120 MCU server, 511–512
  planning for, 499
MDBEF (Microsoft Database Encapsulated Format), 366
memory
  implications of increasing ESE database cache size, 708–709
  performance counters for, 725
  performance issues for, 705
  system requirements for, 166, 168
message categorization, 104–105
message edit conflicts for public folder replication, 144
message encoding, 348–349
message encryption
  with instant messaging, 550
  PKI process for, 625
  scanning and filtering with, 633
Message Format tab (Default IMAP4 Virtual Server Properties dialog box), 353
Message Journal Policy Properties dialog box, 328, 329
Message Options dialog box, 649–650
message routing and routing groups, 297
message tracking, 236

Messages tab
- Default SMTP Virtual Server Properties dialog box, 338–339
- New Properties dialog box, 575

messaging, 97–109
- by Internet protocols, 103–107
- configuring SMTP outbound message delivery, 340–342
- configuring third-party SMTP host to scan mail, 614–615
- delivering NDRs, 339, 340
- enabling archiving for mailbox, 386
- encrypting message contents and attachments, 649–650
- expiration policies for posted newsgroup messages, 361–362
- forwarding messages with unresolved recipients, 339
- inbound messages from Internet to Outlook user, 108–109
- information store and, 97–101
- information store databases, 101–102
- limiting message size and number on SMTP virtual server, 338
- message status for instant, 526
- NNTP support for, 109
- options for IMAP4, 109, 353
- from Outlook user to Internet recipient, 107–108
- between Outlook users on same server, 107
- POP3 client support for, 109
- problems in Exchange 5.5, 366
- prohibiting sending and receiving messages, 389
- scheduling for X.400 connectors, 308–309
- schematic of, 97
- sending messages as delegate, 603
- SMTP routing and selection process for, 316–318
- storage groups and multiple databases, 102–103
- via IFS and DOS commands, 111
- *See also* instant messaging

METABASE.BIN file, 403
metadata, 744
Microsoft Active Directory Connector Installation Wizard, 209–213
Microsoft Chat
- automating tasks, 587–588
- comic strip view of chat channel, 586–587
- configuring, 585–589
- retrieving user profile and identity information, 589
- setting up daily message on, 586
- *See also* chat services

Microsoft Cluster Server, 11–12
Microsoft Database Encapsulated Format (MDBEF), 366
Microsoft Exchange 2000 Chat Service. *See* chat services
Microsoft Exchange 2000 Conferencing Server Installation Wizard, 504
Microsoft Exchange 2000 Installation Wizard
- Completion screen, 184
- Component Progress screen, 184
- Component Selection screen, 180, 239, 240, 635
- Component Summary screen, 183, 240
- Installation Type screen, 181
- Key Management Service Information screen, 636, 638
- Licensing Agreement screen, 183
- Organization Name screen, 182
- Product Identification screen, 179
- Select a Server in an Exchange 5.5 Organization screen, 181
- Welcome screen, 178

Microsoft Exchange 2000 Server. *See* Exchange 2000 Server
Microsoft Exchange program group, 193
Microsoft Exchange Site Replication Service Properties dialog box, 200
Microsoft Internet Information Services. *See* IIS
Microsoft knowledge technology, 765–770
- Digital Dashboard, 765–767
- SharePoint Portal Server (SPS), 769–770
- Team Centers, 767–768
- workflow capabilities, 768

Microsoft Mail, 6
Microsoft Management Console (MMC)
- about, 14–15
- console for, 17
- Exchange Administrator application and, 96
- Exchange System Manager as part of, 16
- illustrated, 15
- single-seat administration and, 56

Microsoft Office, 112
Microsoft Outlook 2000. *See* Outlook 2000 client
Microsoft Outlook 2002. *See* Outlook XP clients
Microsoft Outlook Setup Wizard, 442
Microsoft Outlook Web Access. *See* Outlook Web Access
Microsoft Outlook XP. *See* Outlook XP clients
Microsoft Search, 9
Microsoft Windows 2000. *See* Windows 2000
migration
- forwarding messages with unresolved recipients, 339
- running chat migration utility, 584–585

MIME (Multipurpose Internet Mail Extensions), 348–349
mIRC clients, 585
mixed administration model, 116, 117, 118
mixed mode, 246–250
- about native and, 246
- clustering in, 697
- converting to native mode, 249–250
- creating group management domain, 246–247
- operating upgraded systems in, 204–205
- planning for routing groups in, 297
- replication warning message for, 224
- restrictions and limitations of, 247–249

MKCOL method for HTTP, 747
MMC (Microsoft Management Console), 14–15
MODE command, 558–560
moderators and newsgroup security, 363
Modes tab (New Properties dialog box), 574–575
Modify Columns dialog box, 128
monitoring, 719–726
- Active Directory replication during Exchange installations, 176
- baselining performance, 726
- default service monitors, 729
- effects of In-Place Upgrade on server and link, 236
- event logs, 719–720
- IM servers, 550–551
- performance data, 720–726
- *See also* performance counters

Monitoring and Status tool, 727–732
Move Mailbox method, 231–232
Move Mailbox screen (Exchange Tasks Wizard), 259
MOVE method for HTTP, 747–748
moving
- instant messaging database and log files, 538–539
- mailboxes, 258–259
- servers between administrative groups, 291–292
- stores and transaction logs, 394–396

msExchESEPParamCacheSizeMax attribute, 709
MSN Messenger
- disabling access to, 545
- disabling software update messages, 545
- firewalls and default ports used by, 539–540

MSN Messenger client
- DirectPlay applications and, 532
- features offered with, 530–531
- MSN providers and, 528, 533–534
- versions of, 531

MSN providers, 528, 533–534
MTA (Message Transfer Agent)
- clustering and, 698

optimizing performance of, 713–716
performance counters for, 723
MTACheck utility, 225–226
Multicast Address Dynamic Allocation Protocol (MADCAP), 495
multicast trees, 490
multicasting, 491–494
advantages and limitations of, 493–494
conferencing standards for, 491–494
latency in, 500
MAC-layer addresses reserved for, 492
overview of, 491–492
planning for routers and, 500–501
reserved multicast addresses, 491
routers and, 492–493
multiple databases
considerations for deploying storage groups and, 103
function of, 102–103
support for, 11
multiple public folder trees, 126–129
multiple restores, 415, 416
Multipoint Control Units. *See* MCUs
multiserver environment for Outlook Web Access 2000, 470–471, 472

N

name resolution
about, 8
validating before installing Exchange 2000, 172–173
NAMES command, 560
namespaces
Active Directory as, 30–32
DNS as, 32
Exchange 5.5 vs. Exchange 2000, 284
instant messaging, 536
Internet DNS, 9–10, 33–34
WebDAV management of, 745
naming
administrative groups, 290
channels, 572, 573
conventions for Conferencing Server, 501
for instant messaging, 534
mailbox store policy, 327, 328
organizations, 172–173
servers, 173
sites, 173
using friendly names, 446, 447
NAT, 617–620
native content files (.STM)
about, 368
backing up, 401, 402
streaming, 368–369, 370
used by non-MAPI clients, 369
native content store, 101–102
native mode
about mixed and, 246
converting from mixed mode to, 249–250
creating group management domain, 246–247
mixed mode vs., 246–250
restrictions and limitations of mixed mode, 247–249
nature
of information, 753–755
of knowledge, 755–756
NDRs (Non-Delivery Reports)
directing to masquerade domain, 341, 342
specifying delivery of, 339, 340
network cards
IP addresses for connections to private network, 674
performance of IPSec with, 705
Network Connections screen (Cluster Service Configuration Wizard), 673
Network Load Balancing. *See* NLB
Network Load Balancing Properties dialog box, 691, 692, 693, 694
Network Properties dialog box, 691
networks
configuring for clustered servers, 673
design of Windows 2000 and Exchange upgrades, 197–198
Dynamic DNS service and Exchange upgrades, 200–202
public/private topology for, 673–674
replication issues for Exchange upgrades, 198–200
New Group dialog box, 677
New Object-Group dialog box, 261, 262
New Policy dialog box, 328
New Resource Wizard, 678–683
New SMTP Virtual Server Wizard, 334
newsfeeds
about, 154
creating, 159, 361
newsgroup object, 360
Newsgroup Properties dialog box, 158, 360
newsgroups
expiration policies for posted messages, 361–362
managing, 360–361
moderators as security for, 363
NNTP and, 357
setting up newsfeeds, 159, 361
NICK command, 555
nicknames, 564
NLB (Network Load Balancing), 689–694
about, 664
configuring, 691–694, 695
defined, 658, 689
process of, 689–690
NNTP protocol, 357–364
about, 357
configuring settings for, 358–360
configuring virtual server for, 154–157
current sessions, 363
effects of In-Place Upgrade on NNTP feeds, 236
expiration policies for posted messages, 361–362
general properties for, 358
Internet newsgroups and, 154–159
managing newsgroups, 360–361
managing virtual directories, 362
moderators and newsgroup security, 363
securing virtual server, 363
security, 363–364
setting up newsfeeds, 361
starting, stopping, and pushing, 335
supporting messaging, 109
virtual directory security, 364
Non-Delivery Reports. *See* NDRs
None default permission setting, 601
Nonediting Author, 601
NTLM authentication, 52, 546
NTSDUTIL.EXE utility, 716–717

O

objects
Active Directory, 37
containers vs., 285
creating, applying, and removing public store policies for, 153
creating newsgroup, 360
defined, 37
enabling Security tab for organization and administrative group, 293
Exchange directory, 58–67
groups, 61–63
hierarchical structure of, 38–44
mailbox enabled users, 65
mailboxes, 66
mail-enabled, 63–65
mail-enabled contacts, 65–66
revised terminology for Exchange directory objects, 58–59
See also forests
Office, 112
offline address books, 23
offline address lists, 84–86, 320–321
offline backups, 405–407
Offline Folder Settings dialog box, 321
offline restores, 413
OLE DB support, 10
online backups, 407–410
about, 405
checksumming during, 410
circular logging and, 409
concurrent backups for stores, 410
of databases and transaction logs, 408
dismounting stores for, 420
flushing transaction logs, 409

patch files and, 409–410
performance tuning, 703
online restores, 413–416
basic process for, 413–414
concurrent, 415–416
multiple, 415, 416
RESTORE.ENV file, 414–415
specifying last backup set, 415, 416
temporary patch and log files, 414
OPER command, 556
Organization Name screen (Microsoft Exchange 2000 Installation Wizard), 182
organization objects, 294
organization units (OUs), 39
organizations
naming, 172–173
replicating folders between, 141
outbound messages
configuring SMTP delivery of, 340–342
security for SMTP outbound connections, 341
Outlook 97
legacy clients, 437
X.509v1 certificates for, 627
Outlook 98 legacy clients, 437–438
Outlook 2000
comparison of Outlook Web Access versions and, 457–458
creating public folders in, 129–131
delegating user access from, 602–603
updating registry for Conferencing Server, 516
Outlook 2000 client, 438–444
adding services to, 441, 443
Advanced Find dialog box, 382, 383
checking mailbox size in, 390
choosing Exchange 2000 as information service, 444
configuring for Exchange 2000, 439–444
corporate or workgroup option for, 441
functionality of, 438–439
inbound messages from Internet to user, 108–109
Internet only option for, 441
messages from user to Internet recipient, 107–108
messaging between users on same server, 107
as preferred client for Exchange 2000, 438
public forms in, 123
using as personal information manager, 441
viewing domain local and global group membership, 62
Outlook 2000 Startup screens, 440
Outlook 2002. *See* Outlook XP clients
Outlook Express clients, 452–453
Outlook Web Access 5.5, feature comparison of Outlook family, 457–458
Outlook Web Access 2000, 456–484
architecture of, 459–462
client authentication for, 474–476
controlling user access to, 464
customizing, 480–481
deploying, 470–473
effects of In-Place Upgrade on, 237
feature comparison for Outlook and, 457–458
firewalls for, 476–478
front-end/back-end configurations for, 461–462
installing and configuring, 462–465
as Internet client, 453–454
maintaining, 482–483
new features of, 438
overview of, 456–459, 483–484
security for, 473–480
server models for, 470–473
support for new technologies in, 460
URLs for mailboxes, 464–465, 466
user interface of, 460
virtual servers for, 465–469
Outlook XP clients, 445–452
autocorrect for text, 446
calendaring and scheduling with, 448–450
creating profiles with wizard, 446, 447
Inbox for, 445
mailbox cleanup utility, 451–452
protection against scripts and ActiveX controls, 451
single e-mail account mode for, 445–446
using friendly names, 446, 447
virus protection enhancements in, 450
Override tab (X.400 Connector Properties dialog box), 309
overwrite protection by WebDAV, 743–744
Owner, 600

P

packet filtering by firewalls, 616–617, 618
PART command, 558
partitioning Active Directory, 43–44
PASS command, 555
passwords
changing location of KMS startup, 638
KMS startup, 636–638
LDIFDE utility unable to export, 273
setting multiple passwords for KMS tasks, 640–641, 642
patch files
hard recovery of clustered, 701
online backups and, 409–410
restoring to temporary location, 414
performance, 702–735
adjusting default sleep time for ADC, 718
archiving and, 386
baselining, 726
clustering and fault tolerance, 659–662
of components, 706–716
ESE maintenance activities for enhanced, 702–703
hardware requirements and, 166–168
hardware selection and tuning, 703–706
highly available systems, 659
improving ADC block searching, 718–719
membership limitations for groups and, 64
monitoring SSL for server, 347
of Outlook Web Access 2000, 461
reducing network traffic generated by presence information, 533
restricting availability of MCUs and, 511
server monitor tools, 727–735
SSL reductions of, 479
techniques for monitoring, 719–726
tuning LDAP queries for multiprocessor environments, 716–717
performance counters
for disk subsystems, 723–724
for memory and processors, 725
MTA, 723
for Outlook Web Access 2000 servers, 482–483
SMTP, 722
for store performance, 721
Performance Monitor, 69
permissions
assigning administrative group, 292–296
assigning administrative roles, 294–295, 606–607
assigning with Exchange Administration Delegation Wizard, 294–296
for Authenticated Users security group, 325
client permissions for public folders, 146–147
configuring client, 136
configuring Receive As and Send As, 294
controlling user access to Outlook Web Access 2000, 464
for enabling instant messaging, 542–543
In-Place Upgrade method and required, 234
for mailbox access, 597–604

mailbox folder, 599–601
public folder item-and property-level, 150–151
for public folders, 122
setting cluster's administrative, 682
for shared folders, 597
types of mailbox, 598–599
Permissions Entry dialog box, 293
Permissions for Administrator dialog box, 598
Permissions for dialog box, 148
Permissions tab (Properties dialog box), 136
per-property replication, 198–199
personal information manager, 441
personal store file (.PST), 410
PFRA (public folder replication agent), 141
physical structure of Active Directory, 44–50
domain controllers, 44–48
domain modes, 49
sites, 49–50
PING command, 562
PIRCH clients, 585
PKI (public key infrastructure), 624–651
certificates and certificate authorities, 626–627
digital signatures, 626, 650
Key Management Service, 633–649
message encryption, 625
overview of, 624
recovering and revoking keys, 650, 651
using e-mail security, 649–650
Windows 2000 Certificate Services, 627–633
See also certificates, KMS, Windows 2000 Certificate Services
planning
for conferencing, 495–502
infrastructure for instant messaging, 534
routing groups, 297–298
system capacity, 167
policies
administering, 19–20
defined, 326
disabling software update messages, 545
for instant messaging, 543–546
mailbox, 327–330
for public folder stores, 151–153
for recipients, 326–330
system, 326–330
POLL method, 533
POP3 protocol, 347–350
about, 347–348
choosing character sets in, 348, 349
enabling Exchange Rich-Text format in, 349–350
managing current sessions, 350
POP3 client support for messaging, 109
restricting connections for, 351
securing communications for, 350–351
selecting message encoding in, 348–349
setting access for, 350, 351
starting, stopping, and pushing, 335
Port Rules tab (Network Load Balancing Properties dialog box, 693, 694
ports
changing for security, 610–612, 613
for chat services, 554, 584
enabling instant messaging simultaneous file transfers with, 540
MSN Messenger TCP/UDP, 539
for protocols, 334, 476–477, 617
separating address translations based on, 618–619, 620
TCP 691, 119
Possible Owners screen (New Resource Wizard), 679
preparatory installations
about, 174
performing, 187–191
preparing legacy systems for updates, 224–230
DS/IS Consistency Adjuster, 227–228, 229
removing and rerouting Exchange 5.5 connectors, 225
removing incompatible software, 229–230
running Knowledge Consistency Checker, 227
running MTACheck, 225–226
with system backup, 228–229
presence information
about, 526
defined, 13
privacy of, 547
reducing network traffic generated by, 533
privacy
of presence information, 547
unprotected in instant messaging, 545–546
Privacy tab (Instant Messaging dialog box), 544
private networks, 673
PRIVMSG command, 561–562
processors. *See* CPUs
Product Identification screen (Microsoft Exchange 2000 Installation Wizard), 179
profanity filter, 576–578
profiles for Outlook XP clients, 446, 447
prohibiting sending and receiving messages, 389
promotional banner ads, 544–545
Propagate Folder Settings dialog box (System Manager), 137
properties
for NNTP, 358
promotion of document, 112
propagating from parent folder to subfolders, 135–138
Properties dialog box (System Manager), 132
property access by WebDAV, 744–745
PROPFIND method for HTTP, 748–749
PROPPATCH method for HTTP, 749
Protocol Details dialog box, 604, 605
Protocol dialog box, 604, 605
protocol events, 114
protocol logging, 733–735
protocol virtual servers, 332–335
creating, 333–334
distinguishing between, 333, 334
function of, 332–333
managing, 334–335
starting, stopping, and pushing protocols, 335
protocols, 332–364
benefits of WebDAV, 750–751
certificates for secure access, 610
changing ports for security, 610–612, 613
corresponding DLLs for ExIPC, 106, 107
distributing across multiple servers with front-end/back-end configuration, 694–696
enabling and disabling, 604–606
in Exchange 5.5, 96
HTTP, 353–357
IMAP4, 351–353
managing permissions for, 332
NNTP, 357–364
for Outlook Web Access 2000 environments, 476
POP3, 347–351
ports associated with, 334, 476–477, 617
protocol virtual servers, 332–335
requiring authentication for access, 609–610
RVP, 532–533
selectively allowing access to, 609
service names for supported, 335
SMTP, 336–347
starting, stopping, and pushing, 335
support for Microsoft and non-Microsoft clients, 24–26
support provided in IIS, 103–109
See also specific protocols
proxy settings for instant messaging users, 548–550
.PST files, 410
Public and Private Key Pair screen (Windows Components Wizard), 629–630
public and private keys
encrypting messages with, 625
options for pairing, 630, 631
public folder replication agent (PFRA), 141
public folder servers, 168
public folder stores, 683

public folder trees, 124, 125, 126–129
  about, 124–125
  creating, 391
  default MAPI, 125
  multiple, 126–129
public folders, 122–160
  about, 110–111
  administrative rights for, 148–150
  backfilling of, 142
  client permissions for, 146–147
  creating mail-enabled, 262
  creating top-level, 129–140
  directory rights for, 151, 152
  function of, 122–124
  hierarchical structure of, 124–129
  Internet newsgroup access to, 123–124, 154–159
  item-and property-level permissions for, 150–151
  logging messages for, 142
  mail-disabled, 139
  mail-enabling in System Manager, 138, 139, 140
  managing public folder stores, 151–153
  preventing referrals over SMTP connectors, 303
  propagating properties to subfolders, 135–138
  public folder database and its subtrees, 126
  public folder trees, 124, 125, 126–129, 391
  recreating missing directory objects, 227–228
  referrals by, 144–146
  replicating, 140–144
  security for, 146–151
Public Folders objects, 124
Public Folders Properties dialog box (Outlook), 130
public key infrastructure. *See* PKI
public stores
  about, 368
  configuring, 391–394
  containers for, 128–129
  managing hierarchy of, 127–129
  policies for, 151–153
  replication of, 392–393
  setting storage limits for, 393–394
public virtual directory, 354
public/private topology for networks, 673–674
Publishing Author, 600
Publishing Editor, 600
pull feeds, NNTP servers and, 359

Q

Q271976 hotfix, 171–172, 202
queuing
  domain and link, 104
  with ExIPC layer, 105–106
  managing SMTP, 343–345
  setting size of SMTP message queue, 713
QUIT command, 557
quorum, backing up cluster, 699
quorum disk, 671
quorum log file, 673
quorum resource, 662

R

RAID (Redundant Array of Inexpensive Disks)
  clusters implementations as, 672
  defined, 660
  suggestions for fault tolerance, 167
recipient connection agreements, 215–224
recipient policies, 326–330
  creating, 326–327
  defined, 20, 326
Recipient Update Service (RUS), 325
recipients
  administration of, 114
  configuring, 257–262
  creating and managing policies for, 326–330
  forwarding messages with unresolved, 339
  friendly names for, 446, 447
  mailbox-enabled users, 257–259, 263–266
  mail-enabled contacts, 260, 267
  mail-enabled groups, 260–262, 268–269
  mail-enabled public folders, 262, 269–270
  mail-enabled users, 259, 266–267
  making bulk changes to Active Directory, 270–278
  recovering mailboxes, 280–281
  scripts creating user accounts, 278–279
  tools for modifying Active Directory recipients, 254–256
  types of, 256–257
  types of Exchange 2000, 256–257
recommended practices
  for back up and restoring, 429–430
  for Conferencing Server, 501–502
records, LDIF, 270
recovering
  Exchange cluster, 700–701
  mailboxes, 280–281
  and revoking keys, 650, 651
  rolling back from failed In-Place Upgrade, 241–244
  with storage groups and multiple databases, 103
referrals by public folders, 144–146
registry
  enabling verbose logging for Conferencing Server, 504–505
  location of diagnostic logging settings in, 733
  updating Outlook 2000 for Exchange 2000 Conferencing Server, 516
Relay Restrictions section (Default SMTP Virtual Server Properties dialog box), 345, 347
relaying, 347
Reliable Transfer Service (RTS), 310–311
Reminder screen (Outlook XP), 449
Remote Bridgeheads tab (Routing Group Connector properties dialog box), 300, 301
Remote Site dialog box, 421
replication
  of Active Directory during Exchange installations, 176
  of additional Global Catalog attributes, 76–80
  backfilling of public folders, 142
  configuring public folders for, 142–143
  conflicts in public folder, 143–144
  between Exchange 5.5 and Active Directory, 198–199
  of public folders, 140–144
  of public stores, 392–393
  setting up for connection agreements, 215–216
  SRS for, 199–200
replication messages, 141–142
Replication tab (Properties dialog box), 133, 392–393
Resource Conference Technology Providers dialog box, 512, 513
resource DLL (ExRes.dll), 668–669
resource groups
  configuring, 685, 686, 687
  creating IP addresses for, 679
  creating virtual server resources, 678–683
  defined, 662
  resources required for, 678
Resource Monitors, 664, 667, 678
resources
  adding system attendant, 681–682
  configuring, 684–685
  defined, 662
  dependencies of IP address, 680
  disk resource DLL, 681
  starting and stopping clustered, 699–700
RESTORE.ENV file, 414–415
restoring, 412–419
  to alternate server, 416–417
  Exchange 2000, 412–419
  Exchange with Windows 2000 Backup, 423, 425
  location of Exchange 2000 data, 400–404
  M drive, 230
  offline, 413
  online, 413–416
  recommended practices for, 429–430
  service databases, 428–429

single mailbox, 417–418
strategies for, 412–413
system drive, 428
System State, 428
See also backing up, disaster recovery
Restoring Database Store dialog box, 426
restricting language in chat rooms, 576–578
reverse DNS lookups, 342
Reviewer, 601
RGCs. *See* routing group connectors
rich text file (.EDB)
backing up, 401, 402
like Exchange 5.5 MDBEF files, 368
MAPI client message storage in, 369
vs. RTF format, 349–350
Role Seizure Confirmation dialog box, 49
Role Transfer Confirmation dialog box, 48
roles
granting administrative, 18, 294–295, 606–607
for mailbox folders, 600–601
rolling back from failed In-Place Upgrade, 241–244
rolling upgrades, 661
Room Properties dialog box, 588
Root Certificate Store dialog box, 648, 649
root domain, 34
root store, 648
routers
instant messaging, 530
multicasting and, 492–493, 500–501
routing engine algorithm in SMTP, 105
routing group connectors (RGCs), 117
configuring bridgehead servers for, 299
creating, 299–300, 302
dial-on-demand message option removed for, 301
SMTP connectors vs., 301–302
routing group master
collecting link status via, 118–119
designating, 298
link state tables and, 314–315
routing groups, 117–118, 296–313
about, 284, 296–297
collecting link status via routing group master, 118–119
connecting, 299–313
creating, 300
defined, 17–18
designating routing group master, 298
displaying, 286–287, 288
First Routing Group, 296
message routing and, 297
for mixed administration model, 118
in mixed mode, 297
planning, 297–298
referrals and, 145, 146
referrals between, 144–146
servers communicating as, 117–118
See also connecting routing groups
routing messages in Exchange 2000, 315–319
routing and selection process for messages, 316–318
working with failed links, 318–319
RTF vs. Exchange Rich-Text format, 349–350
RTS (Reliable Transfer Service) values for X.400 connectors, 310–311
rules address list filters, 322–323
RUS (Recipient Update Service), 325
RVP protocol
functions of, 532–533
unrecognized by some filtering applications, 549

S

S/MIME (Secure/Multipurpose Internet Mail Extension), 627
scalability
front-end/back-end configuration and clustering for, 694–696
of Outlook Web Access 2000, 461
problems in Exchange 5.5 with, 366
See also clustering
Schedule Job dialog box, 424
Schedule tab (CA Properties dialog box), 217
Scheduled Job Options dialog box, 424
scheduling
backups for Windows 2000 Backup, 423, 424
conferences, 517–518
messaging by X.400 connectors, 308–309
with Outlook XP clients, 448–450
schema
about, 37–38
Active Directory, 57
modifications to during Exchange installation, 182, 185
preparatory installations to extend Active Directory, 187–191
upgrading from Exchange 5.5 and Active Directory, 203–204
schema master, 46–48
scripts
creating user accounts, 278–279
event, 236
protection against, 451
second and subsequent installations
about, 173
performing, 185–186
secure channels, 357, 565
Secure Communications section (Default SMTP Virtual Server Properties dialog box), 346
Secure Sockets Layer. *See* SSL
security, 86–89, 596–624
of Active Directory, 50–52
address lists, 324–325
administrative access and, 606–608
administrative group design for, 608
anti-virus software, 230, 450, 612–615, 633
certificates and certificate authorities, 626–627
for chat services, 584
delegate access to mailboxes, 601–603
digital signatures, 626, 650
enabling KMS for e-mail, 645, 646, 648
encrypting message contents and attachments, 649–650
fault tolerance and clustering, 659–662
firewalls, 616–622
for HTTP, 356–357
IMAP4 options for, 353
implications of sharing on M drive, 597
for instant messaging, 545–550
integrating Exchange 2000 and Windows 2000, 56, 86–89
KMS, 89, 236, 404, 633–649
mailbox folder permissions, 599–601
for NNTP, 363
for Outlook Web Access 2000, 473–480
permissions for shared folders, 597
PKI, 624–651
for POP3, 350–351
protecting chat services from attacks, 582–583
protecting domains with user authentication, 596
protocol access, 604–606
for public folders, 146–151
scenario for external, 622–624
setting outbound security for SMTP hosts, 341
setting permissions for mailbox access, 597–604
for SMTP messaging systems, 345–347
See also authentication, certificates, encryption, firewalls, permissions
security certificates. *See* certificates
security groups
changes made during installation to, 195
permissions for Authenticated Users, 325
universal, 63
Security tab (Properties dialog box), 292, 293
Select a Server in an Exchange 5.5 Organization screen (Microsoft Exchange 2000 Installation Wizard), 181
SERVER command, 556
server monitor tools, 727–735
enabling protocol logging, 733–735

logging diagnostic data, 732–733
Monitoring and Status tool, 727–732
server states, 727
servername.log share, 192–193
servers, 284–330
address lists, 320–325
administration models for, 115–117
administration of, 114
architectural components for IM, 528–530
changes made by Exchange setup on target, 191–196
chat, 564
communicating via routing group connectors, 117
configuring NNTP virtual, 154–157
configuring third-party SMTP host to scan mail, 614–615
creating and managing recipient policies, 326–330
creating instant messaging Web and virtual, 540–542
distinguishing between protocol virtual, 333, 334
enabling to host chat community, 569
fault tolerance and clustering, 659–661
function of bridgehead, 299
function of protocol virtual, 332–333
handling administrative groups, 288–291
highly available systems, 659
IM home, 530
installing second server in cluster, 674
LDAP queries in multiprocessor environments, 716–717
link state protocols and, 313–315
managing with ESM, 284–288
as member of either Windows 2000 or NLB cluster, 658
message routing and routing groups, 297
monitoring IM, 550–551
moving between administrative groups, 291–292
name resolution in Exchange 2000, 8
naming, 173
planning placement of conferencing, 497–499
protocol virtual, 332–335
ratio of Exchange 2000 servers to Global Catalog servers, 198
rebuilding with Move Mailbox and Swing Upgrade methods, 233
restoring to alternate, 416–417
routing groups for, 296–313
routing messages in Exchange 2000, 315–319
sizing Exchange, 168–170
types of events for, 10–11
unable to move SRS to different, 199
upgrading clustered server from Exchange 5.5, 244–246
See also bridgehead server, virtual servers
Servers container, 290
service account requirements for ADC, 211
service packs, 171–172
installing before upgrading from Exchange 5.5, 202
services
added during setup, 194–195
adding to Outlook 2000 client, 441, 443
Set Account Information dialog box, 423
Settings tab
Default NNTP Virtual Server Properties dialog box, 157, 358–360
User Class Properties dialog box, 582–583
Setup Advanced Security dialog box, 647
setup changes on target server, 191–196
to directory structure, 191–192
drive letter assignments, 196
Exchange-specific services added during, 194–195
Microsoft Exchange program group, 193
to security group, 195
shares created during, 192–193
Setup switches
domainprep, 190–191
forestprep, 188–190
options for, 174
for unattended installations, 186
shared device model, 658
shared nothing model, 659
shared storage, 663
SharePoint Portal Server (SPS), 769–770
shares created during Exchange installation, 192–193
sharing
applications with conferencing clients, 522–523
files among conferencing clients, 523
knowledge, 758–759
mailbox folders, 376–378
single cluster node, 700
single e-mail account mode for Outlook XP clients, 445–446
single instance storage (SIS), 99–100, 370–372
single-seat administration
with Microsoft Management Console snap-ins, 56
user object and, 59
SIS (single instance storage), 99–100, 370–372
Site Replication Service (SRS), 199–200, 404
sites
naming, 173
in physical structure of Active Directory, 44
sizing servers, 168–170
smart hosts, 341, 614–615
SMTP connectors, 301–307
creating, 303–307
preventing public folder referrals for, 303
RGC connectors vs., 301–302
using MX records, 302–303
SMTP protocol, 336–347
Advanced Queuing Engine, 104
changing location of mailroot directory, 710–711
component performance for, 710
configuring message transfer and DNS for, 342
configuring outbound message delivery, 340–342
controlling inbound connections, 338
directing NDRs to masquerade domain, 341, 342
enabling transaction logging, 338
engine for, 105
fault-tolerant routing, 9
on front-end servers, 698
handling queues, 343–345
IIS protocol support for, 104
limiting size and number of messages, 338
logging on virtual servers, 698–699
managing current sessions, 345
Message Categorizer in, 104–105
message queue size, 713
monitoring performance counters for, 722
raising threshold of SMTP file handles, 711–713
routing and selection process for messaging, 316–318
routing engine algorithm in, 105
security for messaging systems, 345–347
security for outbound connections, 341
specifying delivery of NDRs, 339, 340
specifying IP addresses and custom TCP ports for virtual server, 336–337
starting, stopping, and pushing, 335
store drivers, 105
using certificates, 346
using with Exchange 2000, 336
SMTP protocol engine (smtpsvc.dll), 105
sn (surname) field, 324
software
anti-virus, 230, 450, 612–615, 633

backing up third-party applications, 404
cluster-aware vs. cluster-unaware, 667–668
comparison of Outlook and Outlook Web Access versions, 457–458
designing knowledge management systems, 762–764
knowledge management systems, 757–758
planning for Exchange 2000 Conferencing Server components, 496
removing unsupported programs from legacy systems before updating, 229–230
required for Exchange 2000 installations, 170
requirements for installing ADC, 206–208
server monitor tools, 727–735
sharing with conferencing clients, 522–523
system requirements for MSN Messenger client, 531–532
third-party backup, 425–426
Windows 2000 Backup, 419–425
spamming, 347
speaking restrictions for channels, 575
SQUIT command, 557
SRS (Site Replication Service), 199–200, 404
SRV records, 537–538
SSL (Secure Sockets Layer)
clustering and, 697
data encryption with, 478–479
installing certificates, 351
Kerberos authentication encapsulated in, 477
performance issues for processors using, 704
recommended for front-end servers, 697–698
require for SMTP communications, 346–347
running with front-end server, 478
Start menu, Microsoft Exchange program group created for, 193
starting
KMS manually, 636, 637
and stopping clustered resources, 699–700
static domain controllers, 699
storage, 366–397
accessibility and IFS, 376–378
characteristics of store databases, 368–372
creating storage groups, 383–385
creating stores, 385–394
deleting stores and storage groups, 396–397
full-text indexing, 378–382, 383
limiting size of mailbox stores, 388–389, 390
mailbox stores, 385–391
moving stores and transaction logs, 394–396
multiple stores and storage groups, 367
problems addressed by Exchange 2000 design, 366
public stores, 391–394
setting limits for public stores, 393–394
setting up public folder tree, 391
shared, 663
transaction logging, 372–376
Web Store events, 114, 382–383
See also storage architecture
storage architecture, 366–383
about, 366
multiple stores and storage groups, 367
on-demand content conversion, 369–370
single instance storage, 370–372
store databases, 368–372
streaming, 368–369, 370
transaction logging, 372–376
Storage Group Properties dialog box, 384
storage groups
creating, 383–385
deleting, 396–397
distributing in cluster, 675, 676
multiple, 367
multiple databases and, 102–103, 367
store databases, 368–372
on-demand content conversion, 369–370
single instance storage, 370–372
streaming, 368–369, 370
transaction log placement and, 376
store drivers, 105
STORE.EXE process, memory allocation and, 705
stores, 385–394
backing up, 401, 402
deleting, 396–397
dismounting for online backups, 420
mailbox, 385–391
mounting and dismounting, 367
public, 368, 391–394
rich text file and native content streaming file in, 368–369
updating indexes for, 381
See also mailbox stores, public stores
strategies for restoring, 412–413
streaming file
characteristics of, 368–369, 370
importance of streaming data, 369
stripe sets, 660
subfolders, propagating properties of parents to, 135–138
Swing Upgrade method, 232–234
switches
domainprep, 190–191
forestprep, 188–190
for LDIFDE utility, 274–276
for unattended installations, 186
syntax, 38
system attendant, 681–682
System Attendant Properties dialog box, 684
System Attendant screen (New Resource Wizard), 681
system drive, restoring, 428
System Manager
address lists in, 22–23
administering KMS from, 639
administering policies with, 19
creating Internet newsgroups in, 157–158
creating public folders in, 131–139
illustrated, 19
mail-enabling public folders in, 138, 139, 140
managing hierarchy of public stores, 127–129
viewing multiple stores in, 367
System Monitor
monitoring Outlook Web Access 2000 with, 482–483
viewing DSAccess cache performance, 69
system policies
defined, 326
mailbox policies, 327–330
system requirements
for cluster installation, 670
for Exchange 2000 clients, 455
for installing ADC, 206–208
for MSN Messenger client, 531–532
System State data
about, 401
restoring, 428

T

T.120 MCU server, 511–512
T.120 MCU/H.323 conference bridge, 503, 521
T.120 standard, 489
TCP ports
port 691, 119
for protocols supported as virtual servers, 334
specifying for SMTP virtual server, 336–337
TCP/IP Address Parameters screen (New Resource Wizard), 680
Team Centers, 123, 767–768
Technology Provider Properties dialog box, 515
technology standards
for conferencing, 487, 489–495
for H.261 and H.263, 514
for H.323, 489, 494–495, 704
for instant messaging, 551–552
for IP multicasting, 491–494
for MADCAP, 495

for Multipoint Control Units, 489–490
for X.500, 30–32, 36
for X.509 certificate, 627, 628
terminals for H.323 clients, 495
terminology
for clustering, 662–663
for Conferencing Server, 486–487
for directory objects, 58–59
text from instant messaging, 527
TGT (ticket-granting ticket), 87, 88
third-party backup applications, 425–426
third-party software
backing up, 404
effects of In-Place Upgrade on, 236
tools for Exchange 5.5 upgrades, 230
ticket-granting ticket (TGT), 87, 88
TLHs (top-level hierarchies), 124, 125, 126
TLS (Transport Layer Security), 346
top-level folders, 129–140
creating in Outlook 2000, 129–131
creating in System Manager, 131–139
transaction logging. *See* logging, logs
transfer timeout values for X.400 connectors, 312
transport events, 10, 114
Transport Layer Security (TLS), 346
transport stacks, 8
trees
in hierarchical structure of objects, 39–41
multicast, 490
public folder, 124, 125, 126–129, 391
subtrees of public folder database, 126
troubleshooting
errors for Internet-based clients joining conferences, 517
failed installations for Conferencing Server, 504–505
trusts, non-transitive and transitive, 41
two-node active/active clustering, 11–12
two-node multicast tree, 489
Two-way alternate checkbox (X.400 Connector Properties dialog box), 312, 313

U

unattended installations, 186–187
about, 174
performing, 186–187
setup switches for, 186
universal security group, 63
Unix-based Internet clients, 454
UNLOCK method for HTTP, 749
updating store indexes, 381
upgrading from Exchange 5.5, 196–251
Active Directory Connector, 204–224
chat services, 584–585
choosing upgrade path, 230–237
for clustered server, 244–246
considerations with Active Directory, 203–204
In-Place Upgrade method, 234–237
mixed mode vs. native mode, 246–250
Move Mailbox method, 231–232
network considerations for, 197–202
overview, 196–197
performing in-place, 237–244
pre-installation requirements for legacy systems, 224–230
Swing Upgrade method, 232–234
third-party tools and upgrades, 230
Windows 2000 considerations for, 202
URLs
for Outlook Web Access 2000 mailboxes, 464–465, 466
store for instant messaging, 535
user accounts
exporting all, 273
importing with CSVDE utility, 277–278
scripts creating, 278–279
validating before In-Place Upgrade, 235
user bans, 580
USER command, 556, 563
user interface of Outlook Web Access 2000, 460
user management concepts, 20–23
address list services, 22–23
distribution groups, 21–22
types of users, 20
user principal name, 59
User Properties dialog box, 60
users, 59–61
administering after upgrading from Exchange 5.5, 203
authenticating, 86, 596
controlling access to Outlook Web Access 2000, 464
delegating administrative roles to, 294–295, 606–607
enabling instant messaging for, 542–543
enrolling in KMS, 640–645, 646
management concepts regarding, 20–23
retrieving chat profile and identity information, 589
types of, 20
See also mailbox-enabled users
UUEncode format, 348–349

V

validating name resolution, 172–173
verifying movement of stores and transaction logs, 395–396
video conferencing
about, 14
changes in support for, 95
hardware required for, 515–516
video conferencing provider, 488
Video tab (Technology Provider Properties dialog box), 515
viewing
ACLs with ADSI Edit, 285, 286
cache lists of domain controllers and Global Catalog servers, 69
configuration domain controller, 68–69
instant messaging URLs, 535, 536
link state information, 315, 316
VIP mailboxes, 103
virtual directories
created by Exchange in Outlook Web Access 2000, 464
managing NNTP, 362
security for, 364
virtual servers
administering clustered, 683–684
clustering multiple HTTP, 698
creating, 467–469
creating IIS Web site for instant messaging, 541
creating in cluster, 678–683
creating instant messaging, 541–542
defined, 663
managing for HTTP, 335
monitoring IM, 550–551
for Outlook Web Access 2000, 465–469
problem authenticating SSL for clustered, 697
protocol, 332–335
securing NNTP, 363
using SMTP protocol logging on, 698–699
virus protection
configuring third-party SMTP host to scan mail, 614–615
encrypted messages and virus-scanning software, 633
enhancements in Outlook XP clients, 450
as security measure, 612–614
warnings about file-system based scanners for, 230

W

Web Distributed Authoring and Versioning protocol. *See* WebDAV protocol
Web Server Certificate Wizard, 346
Web sites
for conferencing, 519, 520
creating for instant messaging virtual servers, 541
FAQs page about instant messaging, 534
Web Storage System, 110–113
functions of, 110

HTTP support by WebDAV protocol, 112–113
public folders and, 123
Web Store events
about, 382–383
defined, 114
WebDAV (Web Distributed Authoring and Versioning) protocol, 742–751
benefits of, 750–751
extending HTTP 1.1 methods, 112–113, 745–749
features of, 112–113
future of, 750
namespace management, 745
origins of, 742–743
overwrite protection, 743–744
property access, 744–745
RVP and, 533
support for, 10
Welcome Message screen, 645
welcome screen for Installation Wizard, 178
wildcard expressions for restricted words, 577
Windows 9X
authentication problems logging on to instant messaging server, 547
system requirements for MSN Messenger client, 531–532
[Win]dows 2000
considerations before installing Exchange 2000, 170–171
Exchange 2000 Server integration with, 7–8
Exchange 2000 Server support for clustering, 669–670
improvements in Active Directory, 29
installing after disaster, 427
instant messaging and, 535–540
network considerations for Exchange upgrades, 197–198
pre-installation requirements before upgrading Exchange 5.5, 225
upgrading from Exchange 5.5 and, 202
Windows 2000 Backup, 419–425
about, 419
backing up Exchange with, 420–423
restoring Exchange, 423, 425
scheduling backups, 423, 424
unable to backup mailboxes with, 411
Windows 2000 Certificate Services, 627–633
installing, 629–633
managing certificates, 633
types of CAs, 628–629, 630
X.509 certificate and, 627, 628
Windows 2000 Cluster Service, 664, 665–667, 668
architecture of, 668
See also Windows 2000 clustering technologies
Windows 2000 clustering technologies, 664–669
Cluster Service components, 665–667, 668
cluster-aware vs. cluster-unaware applications, 667–668
Exchange 2000 resource DLL support for clustering, 668–669
overview of, 664–667
supported in Exchange 2000, 669–670
Windows 2000 Datacenter Servers, 658
Windows 2000 Service Pack 1 installation, 171
Windows Components Wizard, 629–630
Windows Internet Name Server (WINS), 201
Windows Load Balancing Service. *See* NLB
Windows Script Host (WSH), 278–279
WinRoute utility, 315, 316
WINS (Windows Internet Name Server), 201
Wlbs.sys driver, 689
workflow
Exchange 2000 capabilities for, 768
knowledge management and, 760–762
workflow applications, 123
workgroup option for Outlook 2000 client, 441
WSH (Windows Script Host), 278–279

X

X.400 connectors, 307–313
advanced settings for, 312–313
configuring association values for, 311–312
configuring connection retry values, 309–310
creating, 308
modifying transfer timeout values, 312
scheduling messaging by, 308–309
setting up RTS values, 310–311
X.500 standards
Active Directory and, 30–32
LDAP and, 36
X.509 certificate, 627, 628
XML (Extensible Markup Language) support, 9–10

Z

zone transfers, 34
zones, 34

INTERNATIONAL CONTACT INFORMATION

AUSTRALIA
McGraw-Hill Book Company Australia Pty. Ltd.
TEL +61-2-9417-9899
FAX +61-2-9417-5687
http://www.mcgraw-hill.com.au
books-it_sydney@mcgraw-hill.com

CANADA
McGraw-Hill Ryerson Ltd.
TEL +905-430-5000
FAX +905-430-5020
http://www.mcgrawhill.ca

GREECE, MIDDLE EAST, NORTHERN AFRICA
McGraw-Hill Hellas
TEL +30-1-656-0990-3-4
FAX +30-1-654-5525

MEXICO (Also serving Latin America)
McGraw-Hill Interamericana Editores S.A. de C.V.
TEL +525-117-1583
FAX +525-117-1589
http://www.mcgraw-hill.com.mx
fernando_castellanos@mcgraw-hill.com

SINGAPORE (Serving Asia)
McGraw-Hill Book Company
TEL +65-863-1580
FAX +65-862-3354
http://www.mcgraw-hill.com.sg
mghasia@mcgraw-hill.com

SOUTH AFRICA
McGraw-Hill South Africa
TEL +27-11-622-7512
FAX +27-11-622-9045
robyn_swanepoel@mcgraw-hill.com

UNITED KINGDOM & EUROPE (Excluding Southern Europe)
McGraw-Hill Education Europe
TEL +44-1-628-502500
FAX +44-1-628-770224
http://www.mcgraw-hill.co.uk
computing_neurope@mcgraw-hill.com

ALL OTHER INQUIRIES Contact:
Osborne/McGraw-Hill
TEL +1-510-549-6600
FAX +1-510-883-7600
http://www.osborne.com
omg_international@mcgraw-hill.com